Routledge Handbook of International Human Rights Law

The *Routledge Handbook of International Human Rights Law* provides a definitive global survey of the discipline of international human rights law. Each chapter is written by a leading expert and provides a contemporary overview of a significant area within the field.

As well as covering topics integral to the theory and practice of international human rights law, the volume offers a broader perspective through examinations of the ways human rights law interacts with other legal regimes and international institutions, and by addressing the current and future challenges facing human rights.

This highly topical collection of specially commissioned papers is split into five parts:

- **Part I:** Introduction and overview.
- **Part II:** The nature and evolution of international human rights law, discussing the origins, theory and practice of the discipline.
- **Part III:** Interaction of human rights with other key regimes and bodies, including the interaction of the discipline with international economic law, international humanitarian law and development, as well as other legal regimes.
- **Part IV:** Evolution and prospects of regional approaches to human rights, discussing the systems of Europe, the Americas, Africa and South East Asia, and their relationship to the United Nations treaty bodies.
- **Part V:** Key contemporary issues and the challenges for the future, including non-state actors, religion and human rights, counter-terrorism, and enforcement and remedies.

Providing up-to-date and authoritative articles covering key aspects of international human rights law, this book is an essential work of reference for scholars, practitioners and students alike.

Scott Sheeran is a Senior Lecturer, School of Law and Human Rights Centre, at the University of Essex, and Director of the LLM in International Human Rights Law.

Sir Nigel Rodley is Professor of Law and Chair of the Human Rights Centre at the University of Essex. He is currently the chair of the UN Human Rights Committee, established under the International Covenant on Civil and Political Rights.

Routledge Handbook of International Human Rights Law

Edited by Scott Sheeran and Sir Nigel Rodley

LONDON AND NEW YORK

First published 2013 by Routledge

2 Park Square, Milton Park, Abingdon, Oxon OX14 4RN
711 Third Avenue, New York, NY 10017, USA

Routledge is an imprint of the Taylor & Francis Group, an informa business

First issued in paperback 2016

British Library Cataloguing in Publication Data
A catalogue record for this book is available from the British Library

Library of Congress Cataloging-in-Publication Data
Routledge handbook of international human rights law / [edited by] Scott Sheeran, Nigel Rodley.
    p. cm.
  Includes bibliographical references and index.
    ISBN 978–0–415–62073–4 (hardback) — ISBN 978–0–203–48141–7 (ebk)   1. Human rights.
    I. Sheeran, Scott (Law teacher), editor of compilation.   II. Rodley, Nigel S., editor of compilation.
    III. Title: Handbook of international human rights law.
    K3240.R699 2014
    341.4'8—dc23

                                                                                    2013026256

ISBN: 978–0–415–62073–4 (hbk)
ISBN: 978-1-138-20397-6 (pbk)

Typeset in Bembo
by RefineCatch Limited, Bungay, Suffolk

Contents

Contents

Contents

Contributors

Sir Nigel Rodley KBE is a Professor of Law and Chair of the Human Rights Centre at the University of Essex. From 1993–2001 he served as Special Rapporteur on Torture. Since 2001 he has been a Member of the UN Human Rights Committee, and since 2013 the Chair of that Committee. He has published extensively on international human rights law and public international law, and is author with Matt Pollard of *The Treatment of Prisoners under International Law* (Oxford University Press, 2009).

Scott Sheeran is Senior Lecturer in the School of Law and Human Rights Centre at the University of Essex, and Director of the LLM in International Human Rights Law and provides legal support to the mandate of the UN Special Rapporteur for Iran. He worked previously as a New Zealand diplomat and legal adviser, including in New York and Geneva, and is on the advisory council of several human rights NGOs. He has published on international human rights law, public international law and law of the United Nations.

Wiktor Osiatyński is Professor of Law at the Central European University in Budapest. He also teaches human rights to the postgraduate students at the University of Siena, Italy. Since 1989, Osiatynski has been an advisor to constitutional committees in Poland and other countries, and is associated with the Open Society Institute. He is the author of the comparative study of individual rights and constitutionalism *Human Rights and Their Limits* (Cambridge University Press, 2009).

Guglielmo Verdirame is Professor of International Law at the Department of War Studies and School of Law at King's College London. Before taking on this position, he was a Lecturer at the University of Cambridge and Fellow of the Lauterpacht Centre for International Law. His main areas of research and teaching are public international law, and legal and political philosophy. He is a barrister at 20 Essex Street Chambers, London.

Michael Freeman is a Research Professor in the Department of Government, University of Essex, where he teaches political theory and human rights. He is the author of *Human Rights: an Interdisciplinary Approach* (Polity Press, 2011) and many other works on the theory and practice of human rights. He is a former Chairperson of the British Section of Amnesty International. He is currently working on world poverty as a human rights issue.

Micheline Ishay is Professor and Director of the Human Rights Program at the Josef Korbel School of International Studies at the University of Denver, the largest interdisciplinary human rights programme in the USA. She is the author or editor of numerous books and articles. Her *History of Human Rights: from Ancient Times to the Era of Globalization* (University of California Press, 2004) has been translated into several languages.

Antony Anghie is the Samuel D. Thurman Professor of Law at the S.J. Quinney School of Law at the University of Utah. He has written on a range of issues including the history and theory of international law, human rights, the use of force, international economic law and globalisation. He is the author of *Imperialism, Sovereignty and the Making of International Law* (Cambridge University Press, 2005).

Radhika Coomaraswamy was appointed as the Under-Secretary-General, Special Representative for Children and Armed Conflict from 2006–12. She was also the Special Rapporteur on Violence against Women from 1994–2003. She has served as a member of the Global Faculty of the New York University School of Law, and has published widely, including two books on constitutional law and numerous articles on ethnic studies and the status of women.

Bruno Stagno Ugarte is Executive Director at Security Council Report in New York. He recently concluded a sixteen-year career in the Costa Rican Foreign Service, which included serving as Ambassador and Permanent Representative to the United Nations (2002–06), as Foreign Minister (2006–10) and as President of the Assembly of States Parties of the International Criminal Court (2005–08). He is a graduate of Georgetown University, Université de la Sorbonne and Princeton University.

Andrew Clapham is Director of the Geneva Academy of International Humanitarian Law and Human Rights. He is Professor of Public International Law at the Graduate Institute of International and Development Studies, which he joined in 1997. He has published numerous books and articles including *Human Rights Obligations of Non-State Actors* (Oxford University Press, 2006) and *International Human Rights Lexicon* with Susan Marks (Oxford University Press, 2005).

Michael O'Flaherty is Chief Commissioner of the Northern Ireland Human Rights Commission. He is Professor and holds the Chair in Applied Human Rights at the University of Nottingham and is Co-Chair of its Human Rights Law Centre. He has been Vice-Chairperson of the UN Human Rights Committee and served in a number of senior positions with the UN. He has published extensively including *Human Rights Field Operations, Law, Theory and Practice* (Ashgate, 2007).

Daria Davitti is a Lecturer in Law at Keele University and a doctoral candidate at the University of Nottingham. She has worked with various NGOs on human rights as well as with OHCHR. From 2006–08 she was a human rights officer for the UN Assistance Mission in Afghanistan. She has published on human rights fieldwork, forced migration, investment and human rights, and the recently launched UN Framework and Guiding Principles on business and human rights.

Françoise J. Hampson OBE is a Professor of Law at the Human Rights Centre of the University of Essex. She was a member of the steering group and group of experts for the Red Cross study on customary international humanitarian law, and a member of the UN Sub-Commission on the Promotion and Protection of Human Rights from 1998 to 2007. She has been legal representative before the European Court of Human Rights. She has published in the fields of law of armed conflicts and human rights law.

William Schabas is Professor of International Law at Middlesex University in London. He is also professor and chairman of the Irish Centre for Human Rights at the National University of Ireland Galway. He is the author of more than twenty books and 300 journal articles, on such subjects as the abolition of capital punishment, genocide and the international criminal tribunals, such as *The International Criminal Court: A Commentary on the Rome Statute* (Oxford University Press, 2010).

Cornelis Wouters is the Senior Refugee Law Advisor within the Division of International Protection of UNHCR in Geneva. He is responsible for doctrinal guidance in international refugee law and judicial engagement work. He has worked at Leiden and Mahidol Universities, various human rights and refugee NGOs, and was a member of the Sub-Committee on Asylum and Refugee Law of the Permanent Committee of Experts on International Immigration, Refugee and Criminal Law.

Sheldon Leader is a Professor of Law at the Human Rights Centre at the University of Essex. He is Director of the Essex Business and Human Rights Project (EBHR) and a member of the Advisory Group to the Human Rights Committee of the Law Society of England and Wales. He teaches at the University of Essex, University of Paris-Ouest and a number of US universities. His work with the EBHR involves advice and training on issues involving business and human rights in various parts of the world.

Peter T. Muchlinski FRSA is Professor in International Commercial Law at the School of Oriental and African Studies (SOAS), University of London. He is the author of *Multinational Enterprises and the Law* (Oxford University Press, 2007) and is co-editor of the *Oxford Handbook of International Investment Law* (Oxford University Press, 2008). He acts as an adviser to the United Nations Conference on Trade and Development (UNCTAD) on investment law issues.

Karen Hulme is a Professor in the School of Law at the University of Essex. She has written on environmental security, environmental damage in wartime, climate change and warfare and teaches in environment and human rights. Her book entitled *War Torn Environment: Interpreting the Legal Threshold* won the American Society of International Law's Francis Lieber Prize for 2004 for 'outstanding scholarship in the field of the law of armed conflict'.

Evadné Grant is Associate Head of Department and Director of Postgraduate Programmes in the Department of Law, University of the West of England, Bristol. She has taught at the Universities of Cape Town and of the Witwatersrand, as well as City University London and Oxford Brookes University. Her research covers a variety of issues in international human rights law, including human dignity and social, economic and cultural rights, and human rights and the environment.

Alain Pellet is a Professor of Public International Law at the University Paris Ouest, Nanterre/ La Défense where he was Director of the Centre de Droit International (CEDIN) from 1991 to 2001. He is a former Member and Chairperson of the UN International Law Commission (ILC), and Special Rapporteur for the ILC's work on reservations to treaties. He has been counsel before international tribunals including the ICJ, and is author of numerous books and articles on public international law.

Lee Swepston is Former Senior Advisor on Human Rights at the International Labour Organization (ILO) and is now a teacher (including at University of Lund and Raoul Wallenberg Institute) and consultant. He joined the ILO in 1973, after a year with the International Commission of Jurists. He has written numerous books and articles on human rights and international labour law, child labour, freedom of association, discrimination, HIV/AIDS, migrant workers and indigenous/tribal peoples.

Awn Shawkat Al-Khasawneh was a Judge of the International Court of Justice from 2000 to 2011 and also held the position of Vice-President. He was appointed Prime Minister of Jordan in 2011 and decided to resign in 2012. He is a Jordanian international lawyer, statesman and diplomat, and has written and lectured extensively on international law. He has served on many inter-national bodies, including the UN International Law Commission and the Sub-Commission on the Prevention of Discrimination and Protection of Minorities.

Catherine Bevilacqua is Deputy Director of the Human Rights in Iran Unit, which provides support to the mandate of the UN Special Rapporteur on Iran. She has worked for Amnesty International's office to the UN in Geneva and its Asia-Pacific Programme, and with grassroots organizations in Europe, South Asia and Brazil. She holds degrees from Harvard University and the University of Essex, where she researched the relationship between UN Security Council powers and international human rights law.

Philip Leach is Professor of Human Rights, a solicitor, and Director of the European Human Rights Advocacy Centre (EHRAC), based at Middlesex University. He has extensive experience of representing applicants before the European Court of Human Rights, and is the author of *Taking a Case to the European Court of Human Rights* (Oxford University Press, 3rd ed., 2011). He has researched and written widely on a variety of human rights issues especially in the European and UK contexts.

Clara Sandoval is a Senior Lecturer in the School of Law and Human Rights Centre at Essex University and Director of the Essex Transitional Justice Network. She teaches and researches on the Inter-American System of Human Rights, legal theory, business and human rights and transitional justice. Most of her recent scholarship has been focused on reparations for gross human rights violations. Clara also engages in human rights litigation, training and capacity-building with various organisations.

Frans Viljoen is Professor and Director of the Centre for Human Rights, University of Pretoria. He is acknowledged as an internationally recognised researcher (National Research Foundation, SA) and has won the Exceptional Achiever award at the University of Pretoria. He is the editor of the African Human Rights Law Reports and African Human Rights Law Journal. He has numerous publications including *International Human Rights Law in Africa* (Oxford University Press, 2007).

Vitit Muntarbhorn is a Professor of Law at Chulalongkorn University in Bangkok. He teaches international law, human rights, humanitarian law and a variety of other subjects. He has served in various capacities in the United Nations system, including as the Special Rapporteur on the sale of children, child prostitution and child pornography from 1990 to 1994, and since 2005 has been the Special Rapporteur on the Situation of Human Rights in the Democratic People's Republic of Korea. In 2004 he was awarded the UNESCO Prize for Human Rights Education. His recent publications include *A Commentary on the United Nations Convention on the Rights of the Child: Article 34: Sexual Exploitation and Sexual Abuse of Children* (Martinus Nijhof, 2007).

Mervat Rishmawi is a Palestinian human rights activist and human rights consultant. She is a Fellow of the Human Rights Centre, University of Essex, and the Human Rights Law Centre, University of Nottingham. She previously worked with Amnesty International for approximately twelve years, most of which as Legal Advisor to the Middle East and North Africa

Region. She has been a consultant to UN agencies and OHCHR, as well as a number of regional and international organisations.

Lorna McGregor is a Reader in the School of Law and Director of the Human Rights Centre, University of Essex. She was the International Legal Adviser at REDRESS where she was involved extensively in international and national human rights litigation. Her expertise is public international law with a focus on international human rights law, including core violations, systems of access to justice, international law in national courts and procedural rules under international law.

Paul Hunt is a Professor in Law at the Human Rights Centre, University of Essex and Adjunct Professor, University of Waikato. He was a member of the UN Committee on Economic, Social and Cultural Rights (1999–2002) and the first UN Special Rapporteur on the right to the highest attainable standard of health (2002–08). He has published extensively in the field of economic, social and cultural rights, and has significant experience in human rights NGOs in the UK and Gambia.

Judith Bueno de Mesquita is a Lecturer in the School of Law and a Member of the Human Rights Centre at the University of Essex, UK. Her teaching, research and publications focus on economic, social and cultural rights, and sexual and reproductive health and human rights. From 2009-2011 she worked as a consultant with the Department of Reproductive Health and Research, World Health Organisation. From 2001-2008 she worked a Senior Research Officer in the Human Rights Centre, University of Essex, in support of the mandate of the UN Special Rapporteur on the right to the highest attainable standard of health.

Joo-Young Lee is a Lecturer of Human Rights and associate of the Human Rights Centre at Seoul National University in South Korea. She is the author of *A Human Rights Framework for Intellectual Property and Access to Medicines* (Ashgate Publishing, 2014, forthcoming). She teaches and researches on international human rights law, human rights and development, and business and human rights, with particular focus on economic, social and cultural rights.

Sally-Anne Way is currently Human Rights Officer at the UN OHCHR, and was previously Co-Director of the LLM in International Human Rights Law and Lecturer in the School of Law at the University of Essex. Her interests focus on the history, theory and practice of economic, social and cultural rights and on rights-based approaches to development. From 2001–2007, she worked at the Graduate Institute of International and Development Studies in Geneva, serving as Senior Adviser to the UN Special Rapporteur on the Right to Food. Her publications include '*The Fight for the Right to Food*' (Palgrave Macmillan, 2011).

Malcolm Evans OBE is Professor of Public International Law at the University of Bristol, where he was Head of School (2003–05) and Dean of the Faculty of Social Sciences and Law (2005–09). He has researched and published extensively on the international protection of human rights, with particular focus on freedom of religion and the prevention of torture, and also the law of the sea. He has various other roles, including Chair of the UN Sub-Committee for the Prevention of Torture.

Martin Scheinin is Professor of Public International Law at the European University Institute, Florence, and served ten years (1998–2008) as Professor of Constitutional and International Law and Director of the Institute for Human Rights at Åbo Akademi University. He was a member of the UN Human Rights Committee (1997–2004) and Special Rapporteur on human rights and counter-terrorism (2005–11). Since 2010 he has been the President of the International Association of Constitutional Law.

Upendra Baxi, an Emeritus Professor of Law at the Universities of Warwick and Delhi, has previously served as the Vice-Chancellor of the Universities of South Gujarat and Delhi and as the Honorary Director of the Indian Law Institute and President of the Indian Society of International Law. His recent works include *The Future of Human Rights* (Oxford University Press, 2008) and *Human Rights in a Posthuman World: Critical Essays* (Oxford University Press, 2011).

Andrew Byrnes is Professor of Law at the University of New South Wales and Chair of the Australian Human Rights Centre. He teaches and publishes in international law, in particular human rights, and has published on the Convention on Elimination of Discrimination Against Women (CEDAW) and the human rights of women. He has acted as a consultant on gender and other human rights issues to various organisations including OHCHR and the UN Division for the Advancement of Women.

Ralph Wilde is a member of the Faculty of Laws at University College London, and has taught at Cambridge, LSE, Texas and Georgetown Universities. His research focuses on many areas of international law including extraterritorial application of human rights. His book *International Territorial Administration: How Trusteeship and the Civilizing Mission Never Went Away* (Oxford University Press, 2008) was awarded a Certificate of Merit by the American Society of International Law.

Dinah Shelton is the Manatt/Ahn Professor of Law at the George Washington University Law School. She has written and published extensively on international law, human rights law, and international environmental law, including *Remedies in International Human Rights Law* (awarded the 2000 Certificate of Merit, American Society of International Law). She was a member of the Inter-American Human Rights Commission and in 2010 she served as President of the Commission.

Megan Hirst is Legal Officer in the Victims' Participation Unit at the Special Tribunal for Lebanon. Previously she worked in the Victims Participation and Reparations Section at the International Criminal Court. She has also worked in Timor-Leste for the International Center for Transitional Justice (ICTJ) and the Commission for Truth, Reception and Reconciliation, and has worked in legal system monitoring in both Timor-Leste and Kosovo.

Nadia Bernaz is Senior Lecturer in law and programme leader of the MA Human Rights and Business at Middlesex University in London, and adjunct lecturer of the Irish Centre for Human Rights (NUI Galway, Republic of Ireland). She is the co-editor of the *Routledge Handbook of International Criminal Law* (2011) and has written and presented papers on a wide range of subjects in international law and human rights law.

Ted Piccone is a Senior Fellow and Deputy Director for Foreign Policy at the Brookings Institution. He was Executive Director and Co-Founder of the Democracy Coalition Project (2001–08) and served in the Clinton Administration in various roles. He has written on US–Latin American relations, democracy and human rights, and multilateral diplomacy, including

Catalysts for Rights: The Unique Contribution of the UN's Independent Experts on Human Rights (Brookings, 2010).

Allehone M. Abebe is a former Ethiopian diplomat with an extensive background in the UN Human Rights Council. He has served as a co-chair of the Technical Advisory Group of the Global Commission on HIV/AIDS and Law. His research examines the role of regional normative standards in the protection of the human rights of internally displaced persons in Africa. He now works at UNHCR and is currently a doctoral candidate under the supervision of Professor Walter Kalin.

Juan E. Méndez is a Visiting Professor of Law at the American University-Washington College of Law and UN Special Rapporteur on torture since 2010. He has held numerous roles in universities and society, including President of the International Center for Transnational Justice, and Special Advisor on the Prevention of Genocide (2004–07). He was a member of the Inter-American Commission on Human Rights of the OAS (2000–03) and served as its President in 2002.

Catherine Cone is Law Clerk to the Honorable Anna Blackburne-Rigsby, District of Columbia Court of Appeals, and a JD graduate of the American University's Washington College of Law. She was formerly research assistant to Juan E. Méndez, UN Special Rapporteur on torture. Catherine has worked at the Center for Family Representation, a legal and social assistance provider to families in crisis. She also provided programmatic support to technical legal assistance programmes of the American Bar Association's Rule of Law Initiative.

Acknowledgements

We would like to thank the authors who have given their scarce time to this project. It has been a large volume to bring to fruition, and without their strong contributions it simply would not have been possible. We thank the international human rights law students at the University of Essex who assisted significantly with the large task of preparing and editing this volume. This included Alex Moorehead, Alice Lixi, Ronnate Asirwatham, Christina Beninger, Francesca Tronco García, Shannon Gough, Lucy Graham, Ota Hlinomaz, Adeyinka Ige, Douglas Kerr, Charlotte Pier, Leah Mansfield, Marina Themistocleous, Isaline Wittorski, and Ashirbani Dutta. The team at Routledge, including Mark Sapwell, were very patient and helpful along the way, as was RefineCatch the copyeditors. Scott would also like to thank Haidi for her constant love and support, along with my mother, and Valentino and Leo. Nigel, as always, is deeply indebted for the unstinting contribution of Dr Lyn Rodley, his sternest critic and acutest editor.

Scott Sheeran
Sir Nigel Rodley

Part I
Introduction and overview

The broad review of international human rights law

Scott Sheeran and Sir Nigel Rodley

The genesis of this collaborative scholarly project was the recognition of a timely point to pause and undertake a broad and thorough review of the architecture of international human rights law. This is after a period that seems, at least with the benefit of hindsight, to have been one of almost constant, even meteoric development. While this volume examines the origins, nature and practice of international human rights law, the main thrust is an exploration of transverse themes, and the evolution, interaction with other bodies of law, and future of the discipline. The contributions draw on perspectives from different regions, by both emerging and established scholars and practitioners from diverse backgrounds and with varied expertise. As such, this volume provides one of the most comprehensive surveys of the discipline to date. The editing of contributions has confirmed many of our own intuitions, but has also challenged our thinking and provided new insights. It is from this privileged and overarching position, informed by the contents of this volume, that we venture a few key reflections on the *corpus* of international human rights law as a whole.

The human rights project, a great societal endeavour, has been a work in progress for two to three centuries nourished by foundational precepts of philosophy, political theory, and ecclesiastical thought of more than two millennia. A pivotal element of the project has been the establishment and significant influence of the discipline of international human rights law, characterised by impressive growth over the last sixty years and increasing specialisation. From the 1948 Universal Declaration of Human Rights, and the concepts and trends that preceded and underpinned that instrument, the body of international human rights law is now both vast and complex. The discipline's influence has extended into broader public international law and became integral in national and international life in respect of a wide range of issues. International human rights law is dynamic and its evolution is not linear; there is no static end point. As societies continuously evolve, so too does the way in which human rights are internalised and manifested, and the role they play in the social compact. In safeguarding human conscience and dignity, human rights concepts and law will continue to be a central pillar of the evolution of the societies that we have created.

Due to the impressive breadth and complexity of the body of international human rights law, a few important subjects could not be fully covered in this volume. Yet, despite its breadth, the human rights project is not without its potential gaps, whether substantive (e.g. no explicit right of freedom from corruption), in conflicting interpretation and views on the scope of rights (e.g. the freedom of religion), or a simple lethargy of significant development (e.g. right to political participation, cultural rights).

International human rights law is now more encompassing than was expected or even conceived in the Charter and Universal Declaration. Its growth has largely obviated for example the distinction between nationals and non-nationals within the jurisdiction of the state, thereby somewhat eclipsing other areas of law (e.g. diplomatic protection, international refugee law). With the development of extraterritorial obligations, which are accepted by most States, the scope and reach of human rights has enlarged into challenging areas such as overseas military operations and economic sanctions. A significant exception to this growing reach of human rights obligations has been the accountability of international organisations, such as the UN and international financial institutions, for the impact of their direct actions and exercise of public power on the enjoyment of human rights.

The international community has affirmed the approach, articulated in the 1993 UN Vienna Declaration and Programme of Action, that '[a]ll human rights are universal, indivisible and interdependent and interrelated'. However, the attractive simplicity of such a statement masks many issues that are not yet fully explored or resolved. For example, in light of the *jus cogens* status of such rights as the prohibition against torture, and the associated consequences under the law of responsibility, questions arise on aspects of hierarchy within international human rights law. In reality there is also a continuing challenge in respect of the judicialisation and legal enforceability of economic, social and cultural rights, evidenced *inter alia* by a fundamental lack of political will. The growing economic development and political strength of the Global South, a long-time supporter of such rights, may provide influences that both promote and undermine those rights.

While the topics in this volume are underpinned by the common pursuit of realising human rights through international law, a challenge of fragmentation and consistency exists *within* international human rights law (i.e not just vis-à-vis general international law, as identified in the work of the UN International Law Commission on fragmentation). For example, it is still contested whether the 'respect, protect and fulfil' framework applies within international human rights law as a whole (*cf.* economic, social and cultural rights). The degree of growing specialisation and professionalisation has bred highly expert communities on subtopics of human rights (e.g. business and human rights), and consequently, a knowledge divide and sometimes scepticism on the part of some engaged with issues at the practical and day-to-day level. The fragmentation tension also has an institutional dimension, for example, presenting itself in the varied interpretations of human rights concepts and law across different fora and bodies, both specialist and general, in multilateral, regional and national contexts.

The changing nature of conflict globally – towards civil conflicts, insurgency and terrorism, and away from inter-state war – has engaged human rights in areas traditionally perceived as the reserve of other bodies of law, such as international humanitarian law. This has also contributed to fragmentation tensions, as the overlap and complex relationship of human rights with other regimes of law has needed to be tackled. Nevertheless, the real challenge to the apparent *acquis* of international human rights law that the first responses to the atrocities of 11 September 2001 seemed to represent, have in the end been in large measure successfully resisted.

Human rights have also had to coevolve with changes in social concepts and values. The development and differentiation of sex and gender identity in the social sciences and everyday life has challenged international human rights law. There have been normative and institutional advances to meet the changes, which have been controversial with some states, especially in the area of non-discrimination and rights of lesbian, gay, bisexual and trans-gender (LGBT) people.

In the contemporary context, human rights are primarily conceived and understood as *legal* rights. This dominant perspective is partly attributable to a continuing deficit in a theory of human rights beyond legal positivism, that is, the intellectual explanation and basis of 'the inherent dignity of the human being' and universal norms. While a basis *beyond* law is unresolved, there is a growing appreciation of the broader meaning of human rights *within* the international legal order. The protection of human rights under international law extends beyond international human rights law *stricto sensu*. Human rights concepts inform and shape other areas of international law, for example, international humanitarian, criminal and refugee law, which in turn contribute to the legal framework for the protection and promotion of human rights. At a deeper level, the human rights project has also 'humanised' international law impacting on its general content and probably its very foundations. This has occurred at both the doctrinal and structural levels (e.g. through obligations *jus cogens* and *erga omnes*) and in the nature of international law and its interpretation. It reflects a move towards a 'living' and constitutional approach to international law, particularly as based on the UN Charter as a constitutive instrument. The Charter may now be considered to reflect a positvisation of human rights within the international legal order.

The human rights project faces subterranean challenges that are interwoven into the fabric of international law. These center on international and domestic politics, history, religion and belief, culture and tradition, and have made it difficult for some globally, especially in developing countries, to fully embrace the project. International human rights law does not operate in a vacuum, but in the full context of national and international society. To date, important debates and challenges to universalism, including from cultural relativism (and sometimes even regionalism), have not been fully resolved. Democracy, in its most basic sense, is not a guarantee of respect for human rights: there remains the potential tyranny of the majority. For some, international human rights and religion are mutually exclusive and hermeneutically sealed. Human rights have been successfully manipulated and the subject of *realpolitik* by political elites and decision-makers. Regional human rights systems may provide a counterweight to some of these problems, as evident with the Inter-American system and that region's lack of overt rejectionism or relativism. However, such regional systems are absent in most areas of the world, and some of those that exist are substandard or underdeveloped.

The existing gap between international human rights law and practice will only continue to undermine the progress of the project. Despite the establishment and impressive develop-ment of an international system to protect human rights, the state-centric fundamentals of the international system's architecture are largely unchanged since the adoption of the UN Charter and the Universal Declaration. While legal doctrine has developed to impressive levels of sophistication in some areas, the means of implementation and enforcement have generally lagged behind and maintained recommendatory in nature. The growing role of the UN Human Rights Council, building after a shaky start on the achievements of its prede-cessor the Commission on Human Rights, while not transformative has been important and progressive despite the strong political headwinds. However, human rights are still not fully mainstreamed in the UN system. This is evident in the UN Security Council's practice, which largely treats human rights as a second tier issue, useful for 'mopping up' after violence, even though today's serious human rights violations often develop into tomorrow's conflicts. At the day-to-day level, the political will for full implementation of human rights is often lacking, conditional or circumspect.

There are also challenges that loom ahead for international human rights law to effectively respond to fundamental global trends. While a number of such international issues have been identified, their full impact on human rights is yet to be realised and understood. These global trends include, for example, population growth and the need for environmental protection (e.g. the right to food, water and sanitation) and proliferation in technology and new media (e.g. the right to privacy).

In summary, as the human rights paradigm has moved – after unquantifiable sacrifice – from the political and legal fringes to the (still contested) national and international mainstream, there has been a tendency to look for new areas in which the concept can take hold. The tendency has been met with varying degrees of success. What emerges from the present volume, which explores many of the new territories, is the continuing relevance and centrality of the core human rights paradigm that aims to protect the autonomy and dignity of the individual human being from the potentially oppressive power of the organised community.

Part II

Nature and evolution of international human rights law

2

The historical development of human rights*

Wiktor Osiatyński

1 Introduction

The concept of human rights consists of at least six fundamental ideas:

1. That the power of a ruler (a monarch or the state) is not unlimited.
2. That the subjects have a sphere of autonomy that no power can invade and some rights and freedoms that need to be respected by a ruler.[1]
3. That there exist procedural mechanisms to limit the arbitrariness of a ruler and protect the rights and freedoms of the ruled (points 1 and 2, above, have already transformed subjects into the ruled) who can make valid claims upon the state for such protection.
4. That the ruled have rights that enable them to participate in decision-making (with this, the ruled have changed into the citizens).
5. That the authority has not only powers but also some obligations, which may be claimed by the citizens.
6. That all these rights and freedoms are granted equally to all persons (this transforms individual rights/privileges into human rights).

The ideas on this list have been emerging, disappearing, re-emerging and evolving throughout history, reflecting changing social conditions and serving various needs.[2] Before the concept of human rights could be formulated and adopted, a number of specific customs, legal provisions, institutions and ideas had to emerge. Eventually, it found its quasi-legal incorporation in the Universal Declaration of Human Rights (UDHR) adopted by the UN

---

* This chapter is a shortened and adapted version of the first chapter of my book *Human Rights and Their Limits* (Cambridge, CUP, 2009). I express gratitude to Cambridge University Press for its kind permission to include it in this volume.
1 This is not the same as the preceding point. The power of a ruler can be limited, for example, by God's commandments, with the subjects still having no rights.
2 This list can be also used as a yardstick to help gauge precisely where a given culture, state or nation stands in relation to rights.

General Assembly on 10 December 1948. The idea of human rights was first announced in the Atlantic Charter, an eight-point declaration issued on 14 August 1941 by United States President Franklin D. Roosevelt and British Prime Minister Winston Churchill, who reasserted the basic ideas of democracy and individual freedom as a shared goal among the Allies. It was upheld in the Charter of the United Nations, signed on 26 June 1945 in San Francisco. Along with the Convention on genocide, human rights were to codify natural law, which had been used with some reluctance in the Nuremburg trials of Nazi leaders. Although most post-WWII constitutions provided for institutional arrangements that could refine and balance the passions of a majority, human rights could limit the risk that formally legitimate governments might commit crimes and cruelties in the name of a majority, or a nation, as was the case in Nazi Germany. The work of the Economic and Social Council focused on enshrining within human rights documents at least some of the progressive labour legislation that had been developed by welfare state reformers and accepted by the International Labour Organization (ILO) between the two World Wars.

2 Universal origins of human rights

Undoubtedly, all these rights had Western origins, but now they were to be treated as truly human, that is, extended to all of the world's people. In some sense, human rights could be seen as a self-limitation of dominant powers, just as a constitution can be perceived as the self-limitation of those who wield the power within a state. A closer look at the origins of human rights, however, reveals a more complex picture. While the idea of human rights was attractive to Western intellectuals and many non-governmental organisations (NGOs), preparatory work on human rights did not have strong support from Western governments, particularly the Great Powers.[3] Each of these had a record that was incompatible with the standards proclaimed: Russia had domestic terror and the Gulag; Great Britain and France had colonies; and the United States had racism and segregation.[4] The Great Powers also wanted to protect their supremacy in the post-WWII world, and used the concepts of domestic jurisdiction and state sovereignty to exclude possible interventions in their affairs by less powerful nations. Therefore, to these powerful states, 'the human rights project was peripheral, launched as a concession to small countries and in response to demands of numerous religious and humanitarian associations that the Allies live up to their war rhetoric.'[5]

---

3 See P.G. Lauren, *The Evolution of International Human Rights: Visions Seen* (University of Pennsylvania Press, 1998) 165–71; M.A. Glendon, *A World Made New. Eleanor Roosevelt and the Universal Declaration of Human Rights* (Random House, 2001) 4–20; and M. Freeman, *Human Rights. An Interdisciplinary Approach* (Polity Press, 2002) 32–40.

4 The position of the United States was more ambivalent than was the case with Great Britain or the Soviet Union. Initially, President Roosevelt was committed to his Four Freedoms policy (see G.T. Mitoma, 'Civil Society and International Human Rights: The Commission to Study the Organization of Peace and the Origins of the UN Human Rights Regime' 30(3) *Human Rights Quarterly* 607–30 at 616). It seems that Roosevelt's enthusiasm for the international bill of rights significantly waned after his meeting with Churchill and Stalin in Teheran from 28 November to 1 December 1943. After that, Secretary of State Cordell Hull 'effectively ended participation by outside groups in . . . the development of specific human rights policy' (Mitoma, 621).

5 Glendon (n. 4) xv.

In April 1945, at the beginning of the San Francisco conference of the United Nations (UN), it was obvious that the Great Powers would not foster the idea of human rights.[6] During the conference, however, they realised that:

> [C]rusades once unleashed are not easily reined in or halted. Expectations had been raised, promises made, and proposals issued during the 'people's war' that were not about to be denied. Countless men and women, including those among minority groups, smaller nations, and colonial peoples, had been led to believe that their personal sacrifices in war and their witness to genocide would bring certain results to the world.[7]

Such sentiments were voiced by representatives of the smaller nations that had managed to subvert the plans of the Great Powers. The organisers of the San Francisco conference invited all those states that had declared war on Germany and Japan by 1 March 1945.[8] The largest group of participants was made up of the independent states of Latin America. The non-Western countries represented were China, the Philippine Commonwealth, India, Iraq, Iran, Syria, Lebanon, Saudi Arabia, Turkey, Egypt, Ethiopia, Liberia and South Africa. Most of these countries found a spokesman in Carlos Romulo of the Philippines, a journalist who had received the Pulitzer Prize for a series of articles about the coming end of colonialism. Romulo succeeded in inserting the formulation on the 'self-determination of peoples' as one of the purposes of the UN in the Charter's Preamble. He also pressed anti-discrimination provisions, for which he gained support from representatives from Brazil, Egypt, India, Panama, Uruguay, Mexico, the Dominican Republic, Cuba and Venezuela.

On the insistence of the coalition of NGOs and smaller countries, the Charter of the United Nations included a reference to human rights among the UN's purposes in the Preamble and in an additional six articles.[9] Article 68 assigned to the Economic and Social Council the task of establishing a commission for the promotion of human rights. This commission was created in February 1946.[10] The commission's work was dominated by a small number of leading participants, including Chinese philosopher, playwright and diplomat Dr Peng-chun Chang; French Nobel Peace Prize laureate Rene Cassin; existentialist philosopher Charles Malik, who became the main spokesman for the Arab League after his homeland, Lebanon, had received independence; and Eleanor Roosevelt, who brought the commitment of her late husband and her own dedication to humanitarian causes. Other active participants included Canadian director of the United Nations Human Rights Division John P. Humphrey, who prepared the Declaration's preliminary draft; Carlos Romulo; Hansa Mehta of India, who helped to bring the issue of women's rights into the Declaration; and

---

6 Ibid. 10.
7 Lauren (n. 4) 171. Similarly, M. Mazower, 'The Strange Triumph of Human Rights, 1933—1950' 47(2) *The Historical Journal* 379–98 at 392 notes that the British and the Russians 'had failed to foresee the force of public opinion within the US, as well as the storm of criticism from governments across the world—from India and New Zealand to South America—which greeted the Dumbarton Oaks attempt to backtrack on the many wartime declarations promising human rights in the future.'
8 As well as Argentina, which declared war in March 1945.
9 Articles 1, 13, 55, 62, 68 and 76.
10 The first item on the Commission's agenda was the discussion of a draft international bill of rights prepared in 1943 by British jurist Hersch Lauterpacht.

Chilean leftist Hernan Santa Cruz, who brought to the work a Latin American dedication to social and economic rights.

From among the official representatives of the participating states, Latin American governments were the most dedicated advocates of the adoption of the Declaration. Toward the end of 1948, as the final draft was under discussion by the Third Committee, the Latin American states were joined by representatives of a number of Islamic and Buddhist states, as well as those of some independent African countries. It was this coalition of states and individuals that pressed for the adoption of the UDHR and influenced its content. The character of this coalition suggests that, at the time, 'the mightiest nations on earth bowed to the demands of smaller countries for recognition of common standards by which the rights and wrongs of every nation's behavior could be measured.'[11] Many colonial nations of Asia, and particularly of sub-Saharan Africa, were not represented in the UN in 1948. Subsequently, the newly independent states adopted the Declaration, confirming their dedication to the idea of human rights, and signed the human rights covenants after they were adopted in 1966.[12] Before this, at a conference of non-aligned states held in April 1955 in Bandung, Indonesia, six independent African states and all independent Asian states declared their 'full support of the fundamental principles of human rights'.[13] One hundred and seventy-one states sent their delegates to the 1993 Vienna conference on human rights. The UDHR served as a model for some 90 constitutions and in 19 constitutions of new post-colonial states, mainly in Africa, specific references to the Declaration were made.[14] However, the support for the UDHR by the developing world did not automatically translate into dedication for the entire body of human rights-related values or individual freedoms. Since the nineteenth century, progressive philosophers and political leaders in colonial countries were convinced that the concept of freedom applied to nations rather than to individuals and that such freedom should be perceived in the context of nationalism and progress. Such progress should be achieved through a strong state.[15] After World War I in Central Europe, and after World War II in the Third World, rights and freedoms of individuals were subordinated to the right to self-determination and, later, to the nation-building process.[16] Self-determination and the promise of national independence were the elements of

---

11 Glendon (n. 4) xv.
12 As of 15 May 2000, 144 states signed had the International Covenant on Civil and Political Rights (ICCPR) and 142 had signed the International Covenant on Economic, Social and Cultural Rights (ICESCR).
13 R. Burke, 'The Compelling Dialogue of Freedom: Human Rights at the Bandung Conference' (2006) 28(4) *Human Rights Quarterly* 947–65 at 956. In Egypt's closing address, President Nasser endorsed the conference as a success because of the 'deep concern and full support which all the Asiatic and African countries have shown with regards to the question of human rights' (ibid., 952).
14 For a full list see Glendon (n. 4) 228, which is the source of all data in this paragraph.
15 R. Afshari, 'On Historiography of Human Rights. Reflections on Paul Gordon Lauren's The Evolution of International Human Rights: Visions Seen' (2007) 29(1) *Human Rights Quarterly* 1–67 at 36–39 demonstrated this for Sun-Yat-sen in China, Ataturk and the Young Turks and Reza Shah of Iran.
16 Afshari argues that anti-colonial struggles 'heroic as they were, remained in essence a single-issue struggle, lacking the necessary human rights conscience' (ibid. 44).

the drafting process within the UN that attracted the elites of colonial or post-colonial nations.[17] 'Their minds engaged the rhetoric of rights as the most potent weapon in their anti-colonial arsenal.'[18] Their human rights demands were directed against the imperial West and were not concerned with their own future states. At home, human rights were subordinated to self-determination, nation-building, statism and progress via the unlimited state. In the course of this process, many rights of indigenous populations were violated, both during national liberation struggles and later, when local communities were forcibly subordinated to centralised independent states.[19] Reza Afshari claims that indications of an instrumental attitude to human rights were already visible at the 1955 Bandung Conference. The primary goal of the conference was to consolidate the non-aligned movement around the developmental needs of African and Asian states, as well as around a common struggle against racism, colonialism and neo-imperialism.[20] The second summit of the non-aligned states in Belgrade in 1961 adopted 27 demands and postulates, primarily addressed to the West, without even mentioning the obligation of the states to protect the rights of citizens internally. By then, most post-colonial leaders had become dictators and were violating human rights and basic principles of rule of law.[21] 'National liberation movements of the post-Declaration entrapped the individuals it liberated into vicious circles of authoritarian rules, military coups, and blatant disregard for the equal dignity of all citizens.'[22]

3 International human rights

It took 20 years to adopt two enforceable human rights covenants within the UN framework. Kenneth Roth and Joanna Weschler suggest that the purpose of the exclusive focus of the UN Commission on Human Rights on drafting human rights treaties and standards was 'to avoid even the discussion of human rights violations in specific countries'.[23] Although the drafting was almost complete by 1953, the covenants were shelved for more than 10 years because of ideological rivalry and the Cold War. In the Soviet bloc, Stalin's terror reigned and the very mention of human rights could land one in prison. China had fallen into

---

17 It should be noted that while the UDHR provided arguments in favour of self-determination and for claims by newly independent states for international aid, human rights were not a driving force of the decolonisation itself. More important were nationalist sentiments of the elites of colonised people as well as economic and military assistance provided by the Soviet Union (and later by China). National liberation movements were perceived by Communist powers as an important arena of the Cold War. This factor, along with the re-creation of the colonial power structure by post-colonial elites, was an important factor in the rapid emergence of oppressive regimes and dictatorships in post-colonial states.

18 Afshari (n. 16) 44.

19 Afshari (ibid. 49–50) writes: 'Human rights, properly understood as such, became the victims of success of the right to self-determination . . . national independence became an albatross hanging around the necks of the citizens of the new nations . . . Anti-colonialism had became a consequential ideology, not much different than Communism, in the sense that as it liberated nations it also paralyzed the human rights discourse and left the individual citizen unprotected in the hands of the indigenous elites.'

20 See Afshari (n. 16) 55–58.

21 '[I]t is curious to see how much post-colonial despots often resemble their old colonial masters', writes Buruma (2005).

22 Afshari (n. 16) 66.

23 K. Roth and J. Weschler, 'Das Versprechen muss gehalten werden', in G. Köhne (ed.), *Die Zukunft der Menschenrechte* (Rowohlt, 1998) 1.

Communism. Indeed, Western European states had assured human rights for their citizens in the European Convention of 1950, but they were suddenly even further away from universal human rights than during World War II. European colonial powers sought to stop national liberation movements unleashed before 1948. France went to war to perpetuate its colonial rule in Indochina and Algeria; Great Britain used force to suppress the Mau Mau uprising in Kenya. Western representatives in the UN Third Committee argued for a special clause that would exempt their colonies from the application of human rights covenants. Rene Cassin, one of the main drafters of the UDHR, now argued in favour of relativism, asserting that 'human rights might "endanger public order" among backward colonial populations, and "subject different people to uniform obligations"'.[24]

The United States emphasised its sovereignty, rather than international human rights. It had a well-developed system of constitutional and statutory rights that were enforceable in domestic courts. It did not include the rights of African-Americans or other vulnerable groups not covered by the US system of rights. In the atmosphere of the Cold War, the US government did not support individual human rights.[25]

During the thaw that followed Stalin's death and the twentieth Congress of Soviet Communists, the international situation improved enough for the adoption of human rights covenants by the UN General Assembly in 1966. The division of human rights into two documents, originally proposed by India, was not a result of the Cold War conflict. Instead it reflected the consciousness of the different means for implementation of the two categories of rights,[26] rather than a perception of their importance or hierarchy. Wheelan and Donelly write:

> The covenants simply recognized that most states in the 1950s and 1960s had considerable capability to create subjective civil and political rights in national law for all individuals, whereas most states lacked the combination of will and resources needed to provide comparable legal guarantees for most economic and social rights.[27]

It took another ten years for the covenants to be ratified and enter into force. By then, however, the first steps toward the international enforcement of human rights had been taken.

---

24 Burke (n. 14) 962. Burke summarises the arguments of a Belgian representative as follows: 'Human rights were for advanced, civilized people, not those in African and Asian colonies'.

25 The human rights scene in the United States at this time was vividly described by Michael Ignatieff: 'McCarthy was persecuting the liberal internationalists of the previous era; Republican Senator John Bricker fulminated against UN human rights documents as "completely foreign to American law and tradition". One of John Foster Dulles's first acts as the incoming secretary of state was to pull Mrs. Roosevelt off the Commission on Human Rights at the UN . . . America effectively withdrew all efforts to turn the Declaration into a binding covenant. Successive secretaries of state, from Dulles to Kissinger, regarded human rights as a tedious obstacle to the pursuit of great power politics.' M. Ignatieff, 'Human Rights: The Midlife Crisis' (1999) 46(9) *The New York Review of Books* 58–62 at 59.

26 The United States did not ratify the ICESCR primarily because it could make many aspirational rights enforceable in US courts. The scepticism toward the ICESCR was also a result of the so-called market revival and general departure from New Deal ideas. In the 1970s, the US Supreme Court moved further away from the recognition of social rights: 'Nixon appointees stopped an unmistakable trend in the direction of recognizing social and economic rights', writes Cass Sunstein. C.R. Sunstein, *The Second Bill of Rights: FDR's Unfinished Revolution and Why We Need It More than Ever* (Basic Books, 2004) 168–69.

27 (2007, 933).

The UDHR did not provide for monitoring or reporting on the implementation of human rights standards. Already by 1947, the Commission decided that it had no power to take any action related to individual complaints.[28] This situation changed when numerous African states in the UN attempted to put an end to apartheid in South Africa. From 1963 on, the Security Council passed a number of resolutions that made reference to the UDHR and called upon the government of South Africa to take specific measures to deal with detentions, fair trial procedures, amnesty for political prisoners, suspension of the death penalty, return of exiles and other human rights issues.[29] As part of the UN's anti-apartheid policy, the Economic and Social Council (ECOSOC) adopted Resolution 1235 in June 1967 authorising the Commission on Human Rights 'to make a thorough study of situations which reveal a consistent pattern of violations of human rights'.[30] In 1970, ECOSOC Resolution 1503 created a procedure toward this end by authorising the UN Sub-Commission on the Prevention of Discrimination and Protection of Minorities 'to develop a mechanism for dealing with communications from individuals and groups revealing "a consistent pattern of gross and reliably attested violations of human rights"'.[31] Being originally meant for South Africa, these measures were supported both by the Soviet bloc and by Western states. Their potential, however, was universal. Initially, complaints were accepted from state governments only. With time, the Commission on Human Rights developed a set of so-called special procedures that included working groups, special rapporteurs, independent experts and special representatives that could monitor a given human rights situation in a particular country or specific types of violations globally. In March 1976, the First Optional Protocol to the International Covenant on Civil and Political Rights (ICCPR) entered into force. It introduced a mechanism for complaints of violations of rights under the Covenant to be submitted by individuals and groups after having exhausted domestic remedies. The UN Human Rights Committee was empowered to consider such complaints, to bring it to the attention of the relevant party[32] and to forward its conclusions to the complainant and to the state involved.

This development of instruments for the international protection of human rights would not have been possible without the revolutionary change in the attitude toward rights by governments and societies that took place in the 1960s and 1970s. It was then that human rights began to play an important role in international politics.

---

28 See Roth and Weschler (n. 24); and Mazower (n. 8) 395. The Commission did not investigate the observance of human rights on its own initiative.
29 This was a departure from the Security Council's principle of strict separation between peace and security (that belonged to the Council competencies) on the one hand and human rights (which, as the Security Council maintained, were beyond its mandate and interests) on the other. (See J. Weschler, 'Human Rights', in D.P. Malone (ed.), *The UN Security Council: From the Cold War to the 21st Century* (Lynne Rienner Publishers, 2004) 55.)
30 Economic and Social Council, Resolution No. 1235 (XLII) (6 June 1967), para. 3.
31 T. Buergenthal, 'The Normative and Institutional Evolution of International Human Rights' 19(4) *Human Rights Quarterly* 703–23 at 710.
32 By the end of 2008, 111 states had become parties to the First Optional Protocol. Similar mechanisms were introduced by optional protocols to the UN Convention on the Elimination of All Forms of Discrimination against Women (in 2000) and to the UN Convention on the Rights of Persons with Disabilities (in 2008).

4 The restoration of rights

The politicisation of human rights was a relatively late event in the Cold War. Earlier on, in the late 1940s and early 1950s, the Cold War had been fought not with ideas but with the increasing militarisation of Europe by American and Soviet troops. The main instruments of this war were NATO and the Warsaw Pact, nuclear tests, the American money helping to rebuild Western Europe under the Marshall Plan, and the US and British military aircraft carrying food to Berlin during the Soviet blockade of 1948–49.

The weapons of the Communists consisted of money, arms and ideology. Slogans of equality, social justice and the end of neo–colonial exploitation constituted great-sounding justification for a worldwide Communist mission, accompanied of course by criticism of Western colonialism and American racism, as well as by reports of the apparent economic successes of Communist countries. In 1957, such a success story manifested in the form of the Soviet satellite, Sputnik.

By the mid-1960s, however, the picture of the Soviet empire was no longer so idyllic. In fact, Soviet leader Nikita Khrushchev, at the twentieth party congress in 1956, had already revealed the horrendous crimes committed under Stalinism. This secret speech soon leaked its way out into the world. After a short thaw period, during which some victims were rehabilitated,[33] the repressions against critics of the regime and dissents increased again. Controlled by politburos and armies, the economies of Communist countries were unable to adapt to the demands of the intensive phase of industrialisation. They fell into stagnation, instead. Attempts at reform from within ended in 1968, with purges of revisionists from the Communist Party in Poland and the invasion of a reforming Czechoslovakia by Warsaw Pact troops. Dissidents and oppositionists began to appear in Soviet bloc countries, seeking legitimacy for their calls for freedom and expressing their reliance on Western support. As it happened, they too found in the idea of human rights.

In the other camp of the Cold War, developments took a different course. The Western European states, however reluctantly and not without bloodshed, had let go of their colonies. In the United States, the Supreme Court initiated the rights revolution, directed against racism and discrimination. African-Americans and white Americans participated hand-in-hand to form the civil rights movement, which initially gained support from the Supreme Court and eventually also from Presidents John F. Kennedy and Lyndon B. Johnson. The latter persuaded Congress to adopt civil rights legislation that made legal equality one of the principles of American domestic policy. The American Civil Liberties Union solidified human rights legislation and, through deliberate strategic litigation, dismantled the legacy of Senator Joseph McCarthy.[34]

With their newly clean hands, Western leaders discovered in human rights a new weapon in their battle with Communism. After the forced resignation of President Richard Nixon that followed the Watergate affair, sensitivity to rights heightened in the United States. In 1974, Nixon's successor, President Gerald Ford, was forced by Congress to create the post of Undersecretary for Human Rights at the State Department. Consequently, human rights

---

33 Interestingly, the party was much more interested in the persecuted Communists (who comprised a minor fraction of all victims) than in the plight of ordinary Soviet citizens; only a handful of the latter were rehabilitated. (See V. Chalidze, *To Defend these Rights: Human Rights and the Soviet Union*, (Random House, 1974) 51.) This is one of a number of reasons why Khrushchev's policies can be best understood as a bill of rights for the party apparatchiks.

34 See A. Neier, *Taking Liberties: Four Decades in the Struggle for Rights* (Public Affairs, 2003) 1–145.

were added on as a third basket, augmenting the agreements on cooperation and security in Europe.[35] In 1977, President Jimmy Carter and his national security adviser Zbigniew Brzezinski adopted human rights as a major principle of American foreign policy.

After the 1 August 1975 signing of the Final Act of the Helsinki Conference on Security and Cooperation in Europe, human rights became an accepted standard of international conduct. The signatory states could monitor the observance of human rights and appeal for ending violations of rights by other governments that were party to the Agreement.[36]

The Covenant on Civil and Political Rights and the Helsinki Agreement provided international recognition and support for human rights groups emerging in the Soviet bloc. They found legal basis in the right to know one's rights inserted into the Helsinki Agreement.[37] In May 1976, a group of Soviet dissidents founded the Moscow Helsinki Group, the first human rights organisation to attempt to work openly in the Communist world.[38] Similar organisations and movements were soon formed in Poland and Czechoslovakia. In June 1976, with dissenting intellectuals in Poland rushing to defend the rights of workers, human rights became an effective instrument for mobilising mass support for the opposition. These developments gave new impetus to the emerging international human rights movement.

The movement was a reaction to a number of often unrelated events in many countries.[39] Perhaps the first was the public exposure of the atrocities committed by General Augusto Pinochet after the 1973 *coup d'état* in Chile.[40] In India, massive reprisals against the opposition, following the introduction of military rule by Indira Gandhi in 1975, led to the relaunch of the India Civil Liberties Union. The human rights movement was further fuelled by support for victims of dictatorships in Latin America and elsewhere, as well as by anti-apartheid campaigns. The 1976 Soweto Riots and the murder of Steve Biko brought about worldwide awareness of gross violations of human rights in South Africa. The Nobel Peace Prize awarded in 1977 to Amnesty International (established in 1961 in connection with an international

---

35 See W. Korey, *NGOs and the Universal Declaration of Human Rights 'A Curious Grapevine'* (St Martin's Press, 1998) 229–48.

36 The CSCE was institutionalised, first by establishing follow-up meetings in Belgrade (1977–78), Madrid (1980–83), Vienna (1986–89), Copenhagen (1990), Helsinki (1992), Budapest (1994), Vienna and Lisbon (1996) and Vienna and Istanbul (1999). Then, in 1995, it was turned into the Organization for Security and Cooperation in Europe. Despite initial setbacks (the 1977–78 meeting in Belgrade did not produce consensus), with time the CSCE made progress in upgrading standards and seeking precision in the original formulations of the Helsinki Document. The conference held in Vienna in 1986–89 was very successful. Korey (n. 36) demonstrates that a turning point was the adoption by the US delegation of a policy to link Western concessions in the field of security (demanded by Moscow) with increased respect for human rights in the Soviet bloc. Another important factor was Mikhail Gorbachev's cooperation during the 1986–89 meetings in Vienna.

37 In Chapter VII of the Helsinki Agreement, entitled 'Respect for Human Rights and Fundamental Freedoms', the signatory states agreed to monitor the observance of human rights and confirmed 'the right of the individual to know and act upon his rights and duties in this field'.

38 Human rights organisations existed in the Soviet Union before 1976. The first one was the Committee on Human Rights founded in 1966 by Valerii Chalidze. An unprecedented fact was that the Moscow Helsinki Group publicly announced its formation, as well as the names and addresses of its founders.

39 For more on the events in the late 1970s that prompted the growth of human rights movements, see Neier (n. 35) 149–52.

40 There had been many violent *coups d'état* before Pinochet. But his was the first in the television age. TV reporters were able to bring immediate footage from the scene to audiences all over the world.

campaign to pardon prisoners of conscience in Portugal) was a sign of recognition and a boost of confidence for human rights activists worldwide. In 1978, a number of other human rights organisations were created, including Human Rights Watch (renamed from Helsinki Watch), the Lawyers Committee for Human Rights and the International Human Rights Law Group.[41] Human rights had become, at last, a truly powerful idea.

However, the concept of human rights that became popular in the 1970s was different from the one that had been formulated in the UDHR some thirty years earlier. The Soviets and the Pinochets of the world were violating civil liberties and political rights, not social ones. In fact, the Soviets took great (and otherwise false) pride in their protection of social and economic rights. The West, in turn, accused the Soviets of violations of civil liberties and political rights. Meanwhile, United States foreign policy could not promote, or even condone, social and economic rights that the US itself did not recognise. Thus, civil and political rights became what Western governments concentrated their attentions upon. Similarly, the emerging non-governmental human rights movement was forming itself around monitoring and protesting the violations of civil liberties and political rights taking place in Chile, India, South Africa and the Soviet Union. Social and economic rights dropped out of the picture and would long remain neglected by Amnesty International, Human Rights Watch and other international human rights organisations and by private and governmental international donors.

One aspect of this process was the juridification of the concept of human rights. The ability to claim rights in courts, known as justiciability, was elevated to a constitutive element; if something was not justiciable it could not be considered as belonging to human rights.[42] While justiciablity is an indispensable element of civil rights, in 1948 human rights were defined much more broadly, including also aspirations that were to be achieved gradually through political process. The positive obligations of states, constitutional directives, state tasks and other instruments were to serve human rights as well. The narrowing of rights to what is merely justiciable weakened these political aspects of rights, as well as the moral dimension of human rights as a kind of yardstick for the assessment of existing laws (or a sort of higher law). Justiciability is not the only measure of a given institution's moral value, nor is it even the highest.

5 New challenges

Over time, human rights have become a recognised code of conduct, making their way into a majority of contemporary constitutions and providing a standard for relations between the state and the citizen. In the 1990s, human rights were advancing to the centre of international relations. Paragraph 4 of the 1993 Vienna Declaration on Human Rights stated that 'the promotion and protection of *all* human rights is a legitimate concern of the international community'.[43] Thus, one obstacle to the implementation and protection of rights was rejected, namely 'the artificial distinction between domestic and international human rights concerns'.[44]

---

41 See Korey (n. 36); and J. Weschler, 'Non-Governmental Human Rights Organizations' (Summer 1998) *The Polish Quarterly of International Affairs* 137–54.
42 A textbook example of this reasoning is provided by M.W. Cranston, *What Are Human Rights?* (Bodley Head, 1973).
43 UN General Assembly, 'Vienna Declaration and Programme of Action' (1993) UN Doc A/CONF.157/23 para. 4 (emphasis added).
44 Buergenthal (n. 32) 713.

Also refuted were the most radical arguments against human rights based on cultural relativism. Paragraph 5 announced that 'all human rights are universal, indivisible and interdependent and interrelated'.[45] Considered similarly interdependent and mutually reinforcing were democracy, development and respect for human rights and fundamental freedoms. The Vienna Declaration also increased the catalogue of human rights by adding rights that had turned out to be inadequately protected, such as the rights of refugees and internally displaced persons, the rights of minorities and indigenous people, the rights of women and of children, the rights of the disabled and rights emphasising humanitarian law issues.

In the 1990s, in the context of immense minority problems accompanying the dissolution of the Soviet empire and the brutal wars that included ethnic cleansing in the former Yugoslavia, the international community undertook new efforts to protect minorities.[46] Around the same time, the system of special procedures within the UN came to fruition.

> With just a few such mechanisms in the early 1980s, some thirty had been authorized by mid-1990s to address problems such as extrajudicial executions, disappearances, torture, arbitrary detention, racism, violations of freedom of expression, religious intolerance, and human rights violations in more than a dozen countries.[47]

The UN Security Council also became involved in human rights. With rare exceptions, the Council had for a long time narrowly understood its mandate to mean protection of international peace and security as distinct from human rights and humanitarian considerations.[48] After 1997, a new UN Secretary General, Kofi Annan, 'particularly during his first years, emphasized that human rights were integral to all UN activities, including security and development'.[49]

Simultaneously, the principle of responsibility for perpetrators of international crimes and human rights violations began to outweigh the importance of state sovereignty and impunity of top officials.[50] Moreover, responsibility was moved from the states to individual perpetrators and leaders who condoned crimes and abuses.[51] In the General Pinochet case of

---

45 Vienna Declaration para. 5.
46 See Buergenthal (n. 32) 721; and A. Vijapur, 'International Protection of Minority Rights' (2006) 43(4) *International Studies* 367–94.
47 Roth and Weschler (n. 24) 2.
48 The Council accepted human rights as its legitimate concern in Resolution 688 on Iraq, issued in 1991, in which it explicitly stated that 'repressions led to threats against international peace and security'. Later, however, this resolution was not quoted as the basis for subsequent ones as is usual practice within the United Nations. See Weschler (n. 30) 57.
49 See Weschler (n. 30) 64. The author gives specific examples of Annan's commitment to human rights.
50 'Potential violators will obviously not be deterred from engaging in massive human rights abuses . . . if they know that they will enjoy domestic impunity and that, at most, only the state will be held internationally responsible for their acts', writes Buergenthal (n. 32) 717.
51 For details of the enforcement of international human rights by international criminal tribunals see T. Meron, 'Human Rights Law Marches into New Territory: The Enforcement of International Human Rights in International Criminal Tribunals' (Marek Nowicki Memorial Lecture, Warsaw University, 29 November 2008). In conclusion, he writes: 'By criminalizing . . . human rights norms, the Tribunals have also enhanced the bite of human rights law. Although victims of human rights violations were once confined to seeking redress from States through civil remedies, by importing human rights norms into the courtroom, the tribunals are providing additional enforcement mechanisms for human rights against individual actions.' Ibid. 36.

1998, the English Law Lords declared that the duties of a head of state do not include ordering or accepting torture or sanctioning killings and treacherous political assassinations; therefore such acts by a head of state should not be protected by immunity.[52] At the same time, human rights, along with humanitarian law and the laws of armed conflict, provided standards for the International Criminal Court and for ad hoc tribunals. International criminal justice enlarged the instruments of human rights enforcement and changed the balance between the principle of sovereignty and the principle of individual responsibility for crimes. It is expected that bringing tyrants to justice can stop ongoing violations and deter others.[53]

In the 1990s, with the collapse of Communism, the end of the Cold War, the end of apartheid, and the democratisation of many authoritarian states in Latin America and Asia, it seemed that human rights would prevail all over the world. Francis Fukuyama wrote about the 'end of history' and the coming triumph of liberal ideas and institutions. But his hope, shared by many intellectuals, constitution-makers and political leaders, did not materialise. New problems have emerged, and the very idea of rights has once again been challenged. These new challenges are of a practical rather than ideological nature. Paradoxically, they pose more serious threats to human rights than any ideology ever has or could.

Some threats are related to globalisation. This process is driven by private companies rather than by states. Private entrepreneurs are acting on a global scale, benefiting from unequal labour costs and other factors of production. Technological innovations permit the transfer of capital in a fraction of a second to anywhere on earth. The essential problem of globalisation is the disproportion between the economy and the political principle of the sovereignty of national states. No international political mechanism exists capable of regulating the global economy and imposing rules of conduct on multinational corporations outside their home countries. Often, those of their activities that violate human rights evade the coercive power of any given state. As a result, traditional mechanisms for the protection of rights from abuse by private actors via instruments of national laws are inadequate.[54]

Recently, the UN has been trying to address this issue. In July 2005, the Secretary-General appointed John Ruggie as a special representative on the issue of human rights and transnational corporations and other business enterprises. His final report to the UN Human

---

52 *R v Bow Street Metropolitan Stipendiary Magistrate, ex p Pinochet Ugarte (No. 3)* [2000] 1 AC 147.
53 The first step toward criminal responsibility for war crimes was the Nuremberg trials at which the leaders of Nazi Germany were held responsible. Their trials exposed the magnitude of the crimes in a way consistent with the principles of the rule of law. (It is worth noting that Winston Churchill had opposed the trials, preferring summary execution of captured Nazi leaders. See R. Goldstone, 'The Tension Between Combating Terrorism and Protecting Civil Liberties', in R.A. Wilson (ed.), *Human Rights in the 'War on Terror'* (Cambridge, CUP, 2005) 178.) However, while in Nuremberg, Nazi criminals were tried on the basis of natural law, today there exist recognised international standards for bringing criminals to justice, as well as an availability of institutions through which said justice can be administered. Since 1994, the United Nations has created or participated in the establishment of international courts and tribunals to deal with crimes committed in Rwanda, Sierra Leone, East Timor, the former Yugoslavia, Cambodia and Lebanon.
54 See J. Ruggie, 'Protect, Respect and Remedy: A Framework for Business and Human Rights'. Report of the Special Representative of the Secretary-General on the issue of human rights and transnational corporations and other business enterprises (2008) UN Doc A/HRC/8/5, para. 3.

Rights Council presented a conceptual and policy framework to deal with the issue of human rights in business. It comprises three core principles: 'the State duty to protect against human rights abuses by third parties, including business; the corporate responsibility to respect human rights; and the need for more effective access to remedies'.[55]

Human rights are also threatened by a number of developments in international and national politics. The supremacy of trade interests over human rights concerns was, perhaps, the first element that eroded human rights principles as part of international politics. Established democracies were inconsistent in their relations with dictatorial and atrocious regimes, often giving priority to business and profit over principles. Some US diplomats have, in turn, insisted that free trade is one of the basic human rights. Such practices have eroded the appeal of human rights among many people in developing countries for whom free trade was equivalent to the economic supremacy of the West.

Double standards have also been applied for political reasons. During the Cold War, the Great Powers expressed criticism of the violations of rights by their enemies while turning a blind eye on the abuses by friendly regimes, as with Panama, Guatemala and other US allies, as well as a number of African regimes befriended by France. This was paralleled by Soviet criticism of neo-colonialism and racism, coupled with the USSR's simultaneous support for the Castro regime in Cuba and other oppressive regimes in Africa and Asia. Soon after the end of the Cold War, double standards reappeared with the introduction of the 'war on terror'.

In the United States, the war on terror has dominated the internal political agenda, pushing away civil liberties and being used to justify the undue increase of unaccountable presidential power. In Western Europe, the need to deal with growing immigration and the fear of Muslim minorities has taken priority over the protection of human rights. In post-Communist countries, many former human rights defenders who today hold positions of power are preoccupied with economic problems, the frustrated expectations of the masses and the deterioration of law and order. Fear of crime breeds repressive attitudes, rather than sensitivity to human rights. At times, leaders of transition countries have discounted their former human rights activities in exchange for popularity and votes. They have come to believe that a strong, centralised government would be more suitable for dealing with problems of transition. Some of them end up turning to traditional conservative and right-wing ideas that are sceptical, if not hostile, to the ideas of rights, separation of powers and checks and balances. In many post-Soviet countries, former elites have tried to find new sources of legitimacy. Often, it has been nationalism that has posed the greatest threats to minorities. In multi-ethnic Yugoslavia, nationalism led to the disruption of a state, to war and to mass atrocities. In Central Asia, Belarus and, recently, Russia, post-Communist regimes have become clearly authoritarian, oppressive and opposed to human rights.

In the face of populism, nationalism and various fundamentalisms, human rights must be defended as strongly as ever. The difference is that both the role played by defenders of rights and the public attitude toward them have recently changed. Under an oppressive regime, when any person can become a victim, the human rights movement tends to speak for all of society. When regimes collapse, however, this changes, and human rights movements begin

---

55 Ibid. 1. As a part of the duty to protect, 'governments need actively to encourage a corporate culture that is respectful of human rights at home and abroad', noted Ruggie introducing his report to the Human Rights Council on 3 June 2008, available at http://www.business-humanrights.org/Documents/Ruggie-Human-Rights-Council-3-Jun-2008.pdf, accessed on 7 March 2012.

to defend specific vulnerable groups, which are perceived as interest groups by all of society. In such an environment, defenders of rights count on support from foreign foundations far more than on their own governmental institutions or civil society. Despite the great wave of democratisation that swept through the developing world in the 1990s, many modern-day elections held in Asia, Africa and South America do not offer the citizens any real choice, leading to what Fareed Zakaria has called illiberal democracies.[56]

An informal coalition of such illiberal democracies and authoritarian countries has been acting to slow down the process of inclusion of human rights into the main purposes of the UN.[57] As a result, the UN Security Council, which during the late 1990s and early 2000s had come to accept and appreciate the importance of including human rights at all levels of its activity, has recently been retreating from such a proactive position. After the 2006 replacement of the Commission on Human Rights with the newly established Human Rights Council, some governments have argued that all human rights issues should be considered by the new body, and that even by considering such issues the Security Council would be encroaching upon the competencies of the Human Rights Council. Other international organisations have been similarly guided by the dominance of security considerations over human rights. With the reversal from democratisation and liberalisation in the former Soviet Union, the Organization for Security and Cooperation in Europe (OSCE) and its Office for Democratic Institutions and Human Rights (ODIHR) have become less effective than they used to be. In the new international atmosphere, the US and Russia speak against attaching much weight to human rights in ODIHR activities. The OSCE itself has also become an overly centralised bureaucratic organisation.[58]

Even in established liberal democracies, human rights appear to be in a state of retreat. One example is the changing attitude toward personal liberty, perhaps the most fundamental of all rights and freedoms, increasingly violated as an ever-greater number of people are kept in detention before receiving a legitimate court sentence. Globally, on a randomly chosen single day, three million people are held in pre-trial detention; in the course of a year that number is of course much higher.[59] Pre-trial detainees constitute 48 per cent of all persons incarcerated in Asia, 35 per cent of all those incarcerated in Africa and 20 per cent of those in Europe. But when we examine the ratio of pre-trial detainees to the total population, in 2006 only North America (137 imprisoned per 100,000) and Europe (46.2) were above the world average (43.6).[60] What this could show is that Western countries are not as seriously committed to principles of personal liberty and the presumption of innocence as one might expect. With rare exceptions, politicians, journalists and the public in general seem to be insensitive to this

---

56 F. Zakaria, *The Future of Freedom: Illiberal Democracy at Home and Abroad* (Norton, 2003) 89–118.
57 For the strategies adopted for that purpose, see Roth and Weschler (n. 24).
58 Human rights NGOs with whom ODIHR used to cooperate complain that the latter has become increasingly self-sustaining and less cooperative than before. Moreover, the short tenures and fast rotation of international officials makes cooperation based on durable personal links difficult.
59 'If the world's three million pre-trial detainees were to stand in a straight line with arms outstretched and touching, they could form a continuous line stretching from London to New York City, with enough people to spare to continue to reach Washington, DC'. M. Schönteich, 'The Scale and Consequences of Pretrial Detention around the World', in Open Society Justice Initiative, *Justice Initiatives: Pretrial Detention* (Open Society Justice Initiative, 2008) 4. The actual number may be much higher, for nobody knows the true number of detainees in China.
60 All figures are from ibid.

huge abuse of pre-trial detention. Security, law and order and simple fear seem to trump human rights.

New emphasis on duties, priority of community over individuals and issues such as social cohesion have been growing in popularity. US neoconservatives and right-wing parties in Europe have long blamed human rights for an excessive sense of entitlement, neglect of normal people, rampant permissiveness and the breakdown of law and order. Such were the criticisms voiced by George W. Bush and his neoconservative advisors during the 2000 presidential campaign. After 11 September 2001, President Bush's administration was able to implement these ideas within the framework of the war on terror.[61] Their decisions have since led to an unprecedented increase of the power of the executive branch, a high level of abuse and the creation of additional threats to human rights.

The newest challenge is the rise of China as the new great economic power, paralleled by Russia's recovery as a major exporter of natural gas. In fact, a new coalition of rich authoritarian regimes is emerging. It includes Russia, China, Iran and Venezuela. This coalition expresses openly its reservations toward human rights, as well as its weariness of NGOs that sustain and protect rights. In this new international order, the ability of the West to influence other states has been steadily declining.[62] The West cannot impose its standards unilaterally on others, even if it were to decide to use force. The only potential instrument for influencing China or Russia is the UN. Both countries, however, have veto powers in the Security Council that limit this potential influence; Russia and China can always veto international measures that threaten their and their clients' interests.[63]

Perhaps the more effective way to influence China would be by pressure from regions other than the West, preferably those countries where China buys its resources. More generally, there continues to be a growing role for the global South in the protection of rights worldwide. India is still committed to democracy and human rights. And while the governments of Brazil and the Republic of South Africa do not care much about human rights, in both countries there exist vital human rights NGOs that could pressure their governments to take a stronger stand globally. Therefore, future development in North Africa and the Arab peninsula undoubtedly will influence the global fate of human rights.

Select bibliography

R. Afshari 'On Historiography of Human Rights. Reflections on Paul Gordon Lauren's The Evolution of International Human Rights: Visions Seen' (2007) 29(1) *Human Rights Quarterly* 1–67.

61 For analysis of the war on terror from the perspective of various ideologies, see S. Holmes, *The Matador's Cape: America's Reckless Response to Terror* (Cambridge, CUP, 2007) 131–213. Holmes refers to the war in Iraq as the conservative intifada (ibid. 197).

62 R. Gowan and F. Brantner, 'A Global Force for Human Rights? An Audit of European Power at the UN' (European Council on Foreign Relations, September 2008) 2: 'In the 1990s, the EU enjoyed up to 72% support on human rights issues in the UN General Assembly. In the last two Assembly sessions, the comparable percentages have been 48 and 55%. This decline is overshadowed by a leap in support for Chinese positions in the same votes from under 50% in the later 1990s to 74% in 2007–8. Russia's support was 76%, while the support or the US position dropped from 77% in the 1977–8 session to 30% in 2007–8.' Ibid., 4.

63 China and Russia are leading the axis of sovereignty in the UN. Chinese and Russian vetos blocked the US and UK resolution on Burma in 2007 and a resolution on Zimbabwe in 2008. The UN Security Council's failure to condemn Zimbabwe was hailed by Russia's ambassador to UN as a victory of traditional sovereignty (ibid. 6.)

M. Freeman *Human Rights. An Interdisciplinary Approach* (Polity Press, 2002).

M.A. Glendon *A World Made New. Eleanor Roosevelt and the Universal Declaration of Human Rights* (Random House, 2001).

M. Ignatieff 'Human Rights: The Midlife Crisis' (1999) 46(9) *The New York Review of Books* 58–62.

P.G. Lauren *The Evolution of International Human Rights: Visions Seen* (University of Pennsylvania Press, 1998).

R.A. Wilson *Human Rights in the 'War on Terror'* (Cambridge, CUP, 2005).

F. Zakaria *The Future of Freedom: Illiberal Democracy at Home and Abroad* (Norton, 2003).

3

Human rights in political and legal theory

*Guglielmo Verdirame**

1 Introduction

Contemporary academia generates vast amounts of human rights theory. Lawyers and anthropologists, philosophers and political scientists, historians and even natural scientists have contributed, and are contributing, to it. This chapter focuses on debates about human rights in legal and political theory. Providing a comprehensive exposition of theoretical argument in these two fields is still no easy task, particularly if one aims to offer an account that is not confined to the province of the present and includes a broader temporal dimension.

To navigate these challenges I have chosen four avenues of inquiry. The first one concerns the relationship between the idea of human rights and the natural rights tradition: are human rights a restatement or an evolution of natural rights? Or do they represent a genuine novelty? Secondly, the debate on foundations is examined, distinguishing between those who argue that foundational inquiries should be at the centre of theorising about human rights and those who consider argument about foundations to be inconclusive and even counterproductive. The last two avenues of inquiry focus on the two terms that shape any dialectics on human rights: the individual and power. Every theory of human rights will rest on, and in some cases openly advance, a conception of the individual and a phenomenology of power.

These four avenues do not purport to be exhaustive of the debates in legal and political theory about human rights. The goal is to offer an analytical discussion that conveys a range of philosophical arguments about human rights in some depth.

2 The relationship with the natural rights tradition

Inquiry into the intellectual origins of the idea of human rights is laden with a political anxiety. This anxiety is prompted by the frequent criticism that human rights are a 'Western'

* I am grateful to the Templeton Foundation for its support, via the Freedom Rights Project, for my research on the philosophy of human rights. I am also indebted to the comments I received from the editors of the *Handbook*, and from Vidya Kumar, Ned Lebow, Larry Siedentop, John Tasioulas and Leif Wenar.

idea.[1] Insofar as theoretical argument takes the idea of human rights back to one or more of the Western philosophical traditions whence it might have sprung – medieval scholastics, natural law, the Enlightenment, or liberalism – it is viewed with suspicion and apprehension by those keen to defuse this political attack and avoid the association of human rights with the West.

Were it not for its political significance, the criticism of human rights based on their intellectual origins would deserve no attention. It is just an *ad hominem* fallacy on a civilisational scale which, curiously, is often advanced by individuals who are themselves part of the West. Its dubious logic notwithstanding, this argument recurs in discussions about international human rights. One explanation for its success is that the international arena in which the human rights project is situated is defined by peculiar forms of legitimation and de-legitimation. In that universe the geopolitical labelling of a project and an idea matters a great deal.

Among the contemporary thinkers who see clear continuity between the natural rights tradition and the modern idea of human rights is James Griffin.[2] He has developed a theory of human rights, centred on the notion of personhood combined and on certain practical considerations, which purports to build on what he calls the 'Enlightenment Project on Human Rights'. 'There has been no theoretical development of the idea itself since then', he maintains, but the term human rights is 'nearly criterionless' and suffers from an indeterminateness which must be remedied: here lies, in his view, the challenge for present-day theorists.[3] John Tasioulas has similarly argued that there is 'a vital commonality between the discourses of human rights and natural rights'.[4]

Others argue that the origins of the idea of human rights go back to the time before the Enlightenment, in particular – as explained by Larry Siedentop – 'to innovations in canon law of the twelfth and thirteenth century' with Christian moral intuitions playing such 'a pivotal role in shaping the discourse that gave rise to modern liberalism and secularism' that 'the pattern by which liberalism and secularism developed from the sixteenth to the nineteenth century resembles nothing so much as the stages through which canon law developed from the twelfth to the fifteenth century'.[5] 'Rather than entering 'Western political thought with a clatter of drums and trumpets in some resounding pronouncement like the American Declaration of Independence or the French Declaration of the Rights of Man', this account of the origins of human rights sees them first coming into existence 'almost imperceptibly in the obscure glosses of the medieval jurists'.[6]

---

1 Although this criticism has been almost a cliché, it has also been articulated in an intellectually more refined way. See, for example, Makau Mutua, *Human Rights: A Political and Cultural Critique* (Philadelphia, Pennsylvania University Press, 2002). For a response to these criticisms, see Michael Freeman's chapter on universalism and cultural relativism in this collection.

2 J. Griffin, *On Human Rights* (Oxford, OUP, 2008).

3 Ibid. at 13, 14 and ff. On the natural law tradition see B. Tierney, *The Idea of Natural Rights* (Michigan, Eerdmans Publishing, 1997) and, for a more Thomistic account, H. Rommen, *Die Ewige Wiederkehr des Naturrechts* (Vienna, Verlag Jakob Hegner, 1936), translated as *The Natural Law: A Study in Legal and Social History of Philosophy* (Indianapolis, Liberty Fund, 1998).

4 J. Tasioulas, 'Towards a Philosophy of Human Rights', 65 *Current Legal Problems* (2012) 26.

5 L. Siedentop, *Inventing the Individual* (London, Allen Lane, forthcoming 2013) 212 (manuscript with the author).

6 Tierney (n. 3) at 344. In contrast with Tierney's account, the great French intellectual historian, Michel Villey, saw William of Ockham as the critical figure in the development of the modern idea of natural rights. For Villey this idea rests on a nominalist philosophy and should be abandoned in favour of a return to an Aristotelian idea of natural law. See M. Villey, *La formation de la pensée juridique moderne* (Paris, PUF, 2003) 220–76.

Whether the Enlightenment repackaged these earlier intuitions and ideas for modern consumption, or whether it made an original contribution, is open to debate. Griffin is certainly not the only thinker to situate the modern human rights project principally in the later natural rights tradition of the Enlightenment.[7] Also firmly of this view was Ernst Cassirer, whose book on the Enlightenment has had great influence.[8] Even so, an important question remains: *which* Enlightenment? For the German jurist Georg Jellinek, who inaugurated the twentieth century's interest in bills of rights with a famous book published in 1901, the French Declaration shared the same intellectual matrix as the American bill of rights.[9] For others, the French Declaration owes 'something to the American example but most to radical *philosophique* literature'.[10] Differently put, the issue is the extent of Jean-Jacques Rousseau's influence on the development of the two main bills of rights bequeathed to us by the eighteenth century.[11]

Crediting the Enlightenment, rather than the medieval natural law tradition, with the invention of human rights may assuage political anxiety in one crucial respect: the secular credentials of the Enlightenment reassure that wide spectrum of modern opinion which tends to think of the Middle Ages as a dark time when people in the West were oppressed by religious beliefs and institutions. But anxiety often diverts from the truth. The Whiggish idea of the Enlightenment as the time when progress and liberty triumphed over superstition and bigotry is problematic for at least three reasons: it underestimates the importance that the idea of liberty had already acquired in the Middle Ages;[12] it downplays the role still played by

---

7 Griffin does recognise the importance of the pre-Enlightenment natural law tradition for the emergence of the idea of right emphasising the importance of William of Ockham (Griffin (n. 2) at 30ff.). An important role in the development of the idea of human rights was also played by the Spanish Scholastics in the sixteenth century. See A. Pagden, *Spanish Imperialism and the Political Imagination* (New Haven, Yale University Press, 1990).

8 E. Cassirer, *The Philosophy of the Enlightenment* (Princeton, Princeton University Press, 1951) 248–53.

9 G. Jellinek, *The Declaration of the Rights of Man and the Citizen* (New York, Henry Holt, 1901). See also: D. Kelly, 'Revisiting the Rights of Man: Georg Jellinek on Rights and the State', 22 *Law and History Review* (2004) 493.

10 J. Israel, *Democratic Enlightenment: Philosophy, Revolution, and Human Rights 1750–1790* (Oxford, OUP, 2011) 908.

11 Rousseau's influence on the revolutionary generation in America was very marginal. Gertrude Himmelfarb writes: 'Rousseau became known in America only after the Revolution, and even then it was *Emile*, not the *Social Contract*, that was generally read (and not always in approval).' *The Roads to Modernity: The British, French and American Enlightenments* (New York, Knopf, 2004) 217).

12 See for example the 1315 ordinance on serfdom issued by King Louis X which is, in many ways, as good as any of the eighteenth-century proclamations. It reads: 'As, according to the law of nature each must be born free, and that by some usages or customs . . . many of our common people have fallen *into servitude and divers conditions* which very much displease us; *we*, considering that our kingdom is called and named *the kingdom of the Franks* (free men) and wishing that the thing should truly be accordant with the name, and that the condition of the people *should improve on the advent of our new government*, upon deliberation with our great council, *have ordered, and order*, that, generally throughout our kingdom, so far as may belong to us and our successors, *such servitudes be brought back to freedom*, and that all those who from *origin or antiquity* or recently from *marriage* or from *residence in places of servile condition*, are fallen, or may fall, into bonds of servitude, *freedom be given upon good and fitting conditions*. . . . we . . . command you . . . that . . . with all such our men treat and grant them . . . general and perpetual liberty' (original emphasis). F. Guizot, *The History of Civilisation* (London, Bohn, 1856, trans. by W. Hazlitt) Vol. III at 149–150. On this, see Siedentop (n. 5) at Ch. XII. As Guizot observes, '[i]n our days [i.e. the nineteenth century] emperor Alexander would not have dared to publish in Russian such an ukase' (ibid.).

religious belief in the eighteenth century;[13] and it rests on a mistaken assumption about the origins of secularism – an idea for which Christianity itself deserves at least some credit, if not more than the Enlightenment.[14]

It is however true that changes in the nature of religious belief would, with time, have an impact on the idea of natural rights. In its earlier version the concept of natural rights had been of the order of natural law. It was also integrated into a system of belief centred on the doctrine of sin and the idea of salvation. Natural rights protected man from certain external constraints, while the doctrine of sin focused on self-restraint. A liberated man was one whose natural rights were upheld but also one who, as far as humanly possible, held sin at bay. With the repudiation of religious doctrines of self-restraint, the concept of emancipation changed fundamentally. Much conservative thought of the nineteenth century, beginning with Burke, is a response to these developments: it does not object to the idea of natural rights per se, but rather to a broader political doctrine that affirms natural rights on the one hand, but entirely rejects traditional authority.[15] For Burke, rights, abstracted from any tradition and juxtaposed to all authority, become mere desires. The liberal-conservative Burke would have agreed with the radical Marx on this: the human rights that had emerged from the French revolution represented the freedom of 'egotistic man', of 'man as a monad isolated and withdrawn into himself'.[16]

An eighteenth-century concept which has received considerable attention in contemporary human rights literature is dignity.[17] All dignity-based accounts of human rights are inspired in one way or another by Immanuel Kant. Kant introduced the idea of dignity in his discussion of the implications of the categorical imperative. In one of the principal formulations of the categorical imperative found in the *Grundlegung*, Kant writes that we must always 'act in such a way as to treat humanity, both in one's own person and in the person of others, never as a means but always as an end'.[18] Kant calls the unique moral sphere that emerges from

---

13 On religion and the Enlightenment see: C. Becker, *The Heavenly City of Eighteenth Century Philosophers* (New Haven, Yale University Press, 1932) and Cassirer (n. 8) at 134ff.

14 Siedentop (n. 5).

15 On this see Russell Kirk, *The Conservative Mind: From Burke to Eliot*, 7th edn (Washington, Regnery Publishing, 1985) 47ff. (on Burke).

16 K. Marx, 'On the Jewish Question' in J. O'Malley (ed. and transl.) *Early Political Writings* (Cambridge, CUP, 1994) 44 and 45.

17 R. Dworkin, *Justice for Hedgehogs* (Cambridge MA, Belknap, 2011) 191ff.; M. Rosen, *Dignity*, (Cambridge MA, Harvard University Press, 2012); J. Waldron, 'Is Dignity the Foundation of Human Rights?', NYU School of Law, Public Law and Legal Theory Research Paper Series, Working Paper No. 12–73 (January 2013). Modern interest in the idea of dignity goes back at least a generation, prompted by the prominence of this term in such fundamental documents as the Universal Declaration of Human Rights and the German Constitution (see for example: O. Schachter, 'Human Dignity as a Normative Concept', 77 *American Journal of International Law* (1983) 848; C. McCrudden, 'Human Dignity and Judicial Interpretation of Human Rights', 19 *European Journal of International Law* (2008) 655).

18 The translation above is my own. The *Cambridge Edition* translates the German *brauchen* in the sentence above with the verb *to use* ('So act that you *use* humanity . . .'), which obviously indicates instrumentality. While this might be correct in relation to the negative part of the precept (i.e. do not treat people as a means), it is clearly wrong in relation to the positive one (i.e. treat them as ends). Kant, 'Groundwork of the Metaphysics of Morals' (hereinafter *Groundwork*) in P. Guyer and A.W. Wood (eds) *The Cambridge Edition of the Works of Immanuel Kant: Practical Philosophy* (Cambridge, CUP, 1996) 80 (German standard edition: *Kant: Gesammelte Schriften – Akademieausgabe* (Berlin, Georg Reimer, 1900-) Vol. IV at 429, available at: http://www.korpora.org/kant/verzeichnisse-gesamt.html (hereinafter *KGS-AA*)). On the idea of dignity before Kant, see Rosen (n. 17) at 11–19.

this obligation as 'the kingdom of ends'.[19] A fundamental distinction must be drawn in the kingdom of ends between what has price and what has dignity. Anything that has price can be replaced with something else, while 'what on the other hand is raised above all price and therefore admits of no equivalent has a dignity'.[20] Nearly everything has a price according to Kant, including important and distinctively human traits like 'wit, lively imagination and humour'.[21] What however can have no price, and must therefore have dignity, is morality, understood by Kant as 'the condition under which alone a rational being can be an end in itself, since only through this is it possible to be a lawgiving member in the kingdom of ends'.[22] Unlike everything else, morality is irreplaceable and incommensurable. In a Kantian sense, therefore, human dignity pertains to human beings because they are the only creatures capable of moral self-legislation *in accordance with* universal reason.[23] Humanity has dignity only 'insofar as it is capable of morality' in this universal sense.[24]

If one follows Kant's argument closely, it is not clear, therefore, whether dignity, as he understood it, can really provide a foundation for human rights.[25] Modern theories of human rights centred on dignity tend to neglect the link between the self-legislating moment and universal reason that is analytically central to Kant's argument. Dignity is instead derived from conceptions of normative agency as process[26] or as potentiality,[27] which, on close analysis, may not be as Kantian as they sound.

Some contemporary writers on human rights have proposed an account that differs from all of the above in that it rejects any meaningful link between the idea of human rights and any of the philosophical traditions of the past. Among them is Samuel Moyn. He argues that the idea of human rights emerged as a result of events that 'occurred only a generation ago'. The key to its emergence was 'the move from the politics of the state to the morality of the globe',[28] after the failure of other ideologies, from nationalism to communism, had created an

---

19 *Groundwork* at 83; *KGS-AA* Vol. IV at 433.

20 *Groundwork* at 84; *KGS-AA* Vol. IV at 434.

21 *Groundwork* at 84; *KGS-AA* Vol. IV at 435.

22 Ibid.

23 This explains the sentence on the following page: 'Autonomy is therefore the ground of the dignity of human nature and of every rational nature' (*Groundwork* at 85; *KGS-AA* Vol. IV at 436), although the purpose of the addition of 'every rational nature' (*jeder vernünftigen Natur*) in that sentence is unclear. See also: *Groundwork* at 88–89; *KGS-AA* Vol. IV at 439–440. On these passages, see Rosen (n. 17) at 20–31). Elizabeth Anscombe famously dismissed the whole of idea of morally legislating for oneself as 'absurd' (in 'Modern Moral Philosophy', 33 *Philosophy* (1958) 2).

24 Above n. 21. Michael Rosen rightly emphasises the importance of this passage (Rosen (n. 17) at 144).

25 An author who would agree with my assessment is B. Ladwig, 'Menschenwürde als Grund der Menschenrechte? Eine Kritik an Kant und über Kant hinaus', *Zeitschrift für Politische Theorie* 1 (2010) 51.

26 This is the case of Dworkin, although he maintains his account of moral responsibility (Dworkin (n. 17) at 266). Dworkin's moral responsibility is, however, defined mainly as process (ibid. at 113ff.).

27 Griffin, for example, defines autonomy as 'a capacity to recognise good-making features of human life, both prudential and moral, which can lead to the appropriate motivation and action' (n. 2 at 156). This idea of autonomy as a capacity to recognise captures only one aspect of Kant's idea of autonomy. For Kant, autonomy is not defined exclusively by capacity, but also by will. The concept of the will (*Wille*), which Kant developed in the *Metaphysics of Morals (Cambridge Edition* (n. 18) at 375; *KGS-AA*, Vol. VI at 213), encompassed the idea of reason, in contrast with what Kant calls choice (*Willkür*). On this point, see Rosen's criticism of certain voluntarist readings of Kant (n. 17) at 145ff.

28 S. Moyn, *The Last Utopia: Human Rights in History* (Cambridge MA, Harvard University Press, 2010) 41 and 43.

opportunity for alternatives. It was Hannah Arendt, according to Moyn, who saw the novelty of human rights 'most clearly', as is evidenced from her discussion of human rights in *Origins of Totalitarianism*.[29] But Moyn misreads Arendt. It is true that Arendt sees an unsettling novelty in the idea that a person deprived of citizenship and severed from any political community could still bear rights, in what with a powerful image she calls the 'abstract nakedness' of being nothing else but man.[30] But Arendt was examining the concept of human rights in the Enlightenment declarations of human rights: whatever novelty she may have ascribed to the idea of human rights originated in the eighteenth century and not the twentieth. Although Arendt does not elaborate on the connection between human rights and natural rights, it is clear from various passages that she sees the two concepts as almost interchangeable.[31] Crucially, the conclusion of her reflection is the 'ironical, bitter and belated confirmation' that Burke's criticism of the French Declaration had been right.[32] Arendt is defending an organic conception of liberty. For her, the individual and the political community are so deeply interconnected that there cannot be a theory of individual liberty that is abstracted from the political community. This is the sense of her 'abstract nakedness' comment.

It would be wrong to dismiss these disputes on the origins of the idea of human rights, and on its relationship with political theories of the past, as relevant to no one other than intellectual historians. As discussed, the issue of intellectual origins has political relevance. Even more importantly, it is intertwined with the philosophical debates surrounding the foundations of the idea of human rights. It is now time to turn to them.

3 Foundationalism and non-foundationalism

3.1 Foundations and beginnings

The international human rights regime began with an argument about foundations. In 1947, the year which preceded the adoption of the Universal Declaration of Human Rights, UNESCO invited the French philosopher Jacques Maritain 'to consult philosophers and assemble their replies' on the question of the philosophical foundations of human rights.[33] Various thinkers took part, including E.H. Carr, Benedetto Croce, Mahatma Gandhi, Aldous Huxley, Harold Laski and Quincy Wright.

By far the most thoughtful contribution came from Jacques Maritain himself. He offered a clear and succinct account of his natural law theory, but preceded it with a series of observations which are worth reproducing in full:

> The effects of the historic evolution of humanity and of the ever more universal crises of the modern world, coupled with the advance – be it never too precarious – of moral consciousness and reflection, have resulted in men apprehending today more clearly than heretofore, though still very imperfectly, a certain number of practical truths about their

---

29 Ibid. at 12; H. Arendt, *The Origins of Totalitarianism* (Harcourt, New York, 1966).
30 Arendt (n. 29) at 300.
31 H. Arendt, *Origins of Totalitarianism* (San Diego, Harcourt, 1973) 297–98.
32 Ibid. at 299.
33 UNESCO, 'Human Rights: Comments and Interpretations', UNESCO/PHS/3 (Paris, 25 July 1948) i. The story is also told in Mary Ann Glendon's book on the UDHR: *A World Made New* (New York, Random House, 2002) 73ff.

life together, on which they can reach agreement, but which, in the thought of the different groups, derive, according to types of mind, philosophic and religious traditions, areas of civilisation and historical experience, from widely different, and even absolutely opposed, theoretical concepts. Though it would probably not be easy, it would be possible to arrive at a joint statement of these practical conclusions, or in other words, of the various rights recognised as pertaining to the individual as an individual and a social animal. But it would be quite useless to seek for a common *rational justification* of those practical conclusions and rights. That way lies the danger either of seeking to impose an arbitrary dogmatism, or of finding the way barred at once by irreconcilable divisions. While it seems eminently desirable to formulate a universal Declaration of Human Rights which might be, as it were, the preface to a moral Charter of the civilised world, it appears obvious that, for the purposes of the Declaration, *practical* agreement is possible, but *theoretical* agreement impossible.[34]

These difficulties were summarised in the comment of one of the delegates relayed by Maritain: 'Yes we agree about the rights but on condition that no one asks us why.'[35] Maritain did not dismiss the philosophical importance of arguments about foundations. On the contrary, this kind of argument – he wrote – 'matters essentially'.[36] But he had doubts about the usefulness of engaging in it as part of an attempt to reach international consensus on a universal instrument on human rights.

The subsequent adoption of the many treaties and resolutions which make up the inter-national human rights regime was not accompanied by philosophical consultations similar to the one organised by UNESCO in the run-up to the Universal Declaration. If it is not so surprising that diplomats chose to avoid a speculative approach, it is more surprising that, in the decades that followed the Universal Declaration, human rights were the object of at best scant theoretical attention from scholars. Until well into the 1980s it was mainly international lawyers who showed interest in the phenomenon of international human rights. However, with the exception of the first generation of international lawyers who wrote about human rights and, in some cases, helped develop them,[37] international lawyers generally disposed of foundational issues with the question-begging line that human rights are rights held by human beings simply by virtue of being human beings.[38] For at least a generation, therefore, human rights expanded as political and legal praxis with very little theory behind it – whether with a view to establishing foundations or to examining the phenomenon.

This is not to say that the question of individual liberty and, more generally, that of the relationship between the individual and the state was ignored. On the contrary, those ques-tions received sustained attention in philosophy departments with the revival in political theory which is generally believed to have been triggered by the publication in 1971 of

---

34 J. Maritain, 'Philosophical Examination of Human Rights' in UNESCO (n. 33) at 59 (emphasis in the text).
35 Ibid. at i.
36 Ibid. at iii. Maritain goes on to explain that the 'irreducible ideological contrast' on foundations is between supporters of natural law and their opponents (at v).
37 See especially H. Lauterpacht, *An International Bill of the Rights of Man* (New York, Columbia, 1945).
38 On this point I agree with Charles Beitz, *The Idea of Human Rights* (Oxford, OUP, 2009).

Rawls's *A Theory of Justice*. But, initially at least, this revival of political thought took little notice of the development of international human rights.[39]

By the time, philosophers, as well as the more philosophically informed among the jurists and the political scientists, turned their attention to international human rights, they came across a phenomenon which had by then reached a certain level of complexity. As James Nickel put it, the international system of human rights was 'not part of a political philosophy with an accompanying epistemology',[40] but was instead 'an international political movement with aspirations to create international law' and, as such, 'did not place great emphasis on identifying the normative foundations of human rights'.[41]

3.2 'Human rights without foundations'[42]

Should it matter to our philosophical enquiry that the phenomenon of international human rights seems to have grown regardless of agreement on its foundations? Isn't it still essential to the idea of human rights that it should rest on solid philosophical foundations? In Richard Bernstein's suggestive analysis, our attraction to foundational argument is motivated by 'Cartesian anxiety'. This is an intellectual numbing malaise which he explains as follows: 'The spectre that hovers in the background of this journey [i.e. the journey of the soul undertaken by Descartes in the *Meditations*] is not just radical epistemological skepticism but the dread of madness and chaos where nothing is fixed, where we can neither touch bottom nor support ourselves on the surface.'[43] According to Bernstein, Descartes put us in front of a 'grand and seductive *Either/Or*[:] [e]ither there is some support for our being, a fixed foundation for our knowledge, or we cannot escape the forces of darkness that envelop us with madness, with intellectual and moral chaos'.[44]

Bernstein's analysis is part of a broader revolt, championed mainly by pragmatist philosophers, against foundational argument. Pragmatists think we should rise above Cartesian anxiety and 'simply give up the philosophical search for commonality'.[45] We should instead 'think of moral progress as more like sewing together a very large, elaborate, polychrome quilt, than like getting a clearer vision of something true and deep'.[46] To investigate the foundations of human rights 'presupposes that moral progress is at least in part a matter of increasing moral knowledge, knowledge about something independent of our social practices: something like the will of God or the nature of humanity'.[47] All of that – say pragmatists – is metaphysical nonsense.[48]

---

39 An exception was Allan Gewirth, who openly put human rights at the centre of his moral and political theory. See A. Gewirth, *Reason and Morality* (Chicago, University of Chicago Press, 1978) 64–104 (where he refers to them as 'generic rights'). Gewirth's theory of human rights was expounded in *Human Rights* (Chicago, University of Chicago Press, 1982) and in *The Community of Rights* (Chicago, University of Chicago Press, 1996).

40 J. Nickel, *Making Sense of Human Rights* (Oxford, Blackwell, 2007) 7.

41 Ibid.

42 This is the title of an essay by Joseph Raz, discussed below (see Raz n. 54).

43 R. Bernstein, *Objectivism and Relativism: Science, Hermeneutics and Praxis* (Philadelphia, University of Pennsylvania Press, 1983) 17.

44 Ibid.

45 R. Rorty, *Philosophy and Social Hope* (London, Penguin, 1999) 86.

46 Ibid.

47 Ibid. at 84.

48 Alasdair MacIntyre famously described belief in human rights as 'one with belief in witches and unicorns' – see *After Virtue*, 3rd edn (London) 90. His criticism has however nothing in common with Rorty's. MacIntyre rejects human rights on an Aristotelian basis that the key to morality is not to be found in notions of autonomy or moral agency, but in the concept of virtue.

Pragmatism is particularly important in this context because of its dominance – both directly through legal pragmatism and indirectly as a result of its role in shaping academic fields like political science and economics – over American legal academia. The two main schools of legal thought to emerge from the US over the last 30–40 years – law and economics, and critical legal studies (CLS) – rest on pragmatic assumptions.[49] They follow pragmatism in either neglecting or dismissing foundational argument. Applied to the human rights field, this approach has led to outcome-focused critiques of the international human rights system, attempting to show for example that it does not influence state behaviour.[50] Others, especially among CLS scholars, have sought to expose the political bias or inconclusiveness of human rights theory and practice, but generally avoided engaging in any reconstructive theory. Duncan Kennedy, for example, dismisses 'the project of reconstructing outside rights through political philosophy', with what he calls 'fancy theories', as 'another context for loss of faith' in rights.[51]

A recent non-foundationalist contribution to human rights theory has come from Charles Beitz. Charles Beitz proposes an account of human rights as a 'global practice' which is 'both discursive and political' and 'consists of a set of norms for the regulation of the behaviour of states together with a set of modes or strategies of action for which violations of the norms may count as reason'.[52]

Joseph Raz has also advanced a theory of international human rights based on political practice. Human rights – he argues – are 'rights which are assertible in the international arena' and 'need not be universal or foundational'.[53] Their main characteristic is that they 'disable a certain argument against interference by outsiders in the affairs of a state'.[54] Raz's account of international human rights law is explanatory. His previous work, in particular the *Morality of Freedom*, places him in the camp of those who believe that there are specific liberal human rights (as opposed to international human rights as legal rights) which are founded on morality.[55]

As Rawls did in *The Law of Peoples*,[56] Beitz and Raz also situate their respective theories of international human rights firmly in *international* political theory rather than general political theory. Human rights are conceived mainly as limits to the sovereignty of states which can be

---

49 G. Verdirame, 'The "Divided West": International Lawyers in Europe and America' 18 *European Journal of International Law* (2007) 558ff.
50 See, for example, J. Goldsmith and E. Posner, *The Limits of International Law* (Oxford, OUP, 2005) 108ff.
51 D. Kennedy, *A Critique of Adjudication* (Cambridge MA, Harvard University Press, 1997) 333. Kennedy rejects the argument that such openly unconstructive criticism might be dangerous with some curious remarks: 'My own experience has been that some people who lose faith in rights become more politically committed, some become less, and some stay the same . . . But there is an aspect of the sense of danger that I want to acknowledge as rationally grounded. Undermining faith in rights threatens to undermine the unity of the left' (at 337–38).
52 Beitz (n. 38) at 8.
53 Ibid.
54 J. Raz, 'Human Rights Without Foundations' in S. Besson and J. Tasioulas (eds) *The Philosophy of International Law* (Oxford, OUP, 2010) 332.
55 J. Raz, *The Morality of Freedom* (Oxford, Clarendon, 1986) esp. 245ff.
56 Both Raz and Beitz claim at least some affinity with Rawls's theory. See Raz (n. 54) at 328ff.; Beitz (n. 38) at 96ff.

enforced by other states. Their violation is a matter of 'international concern'[57] and a potential basis for interference.[58]

Non-foundationalists like Beitz firmly reject the criticism that their views lead to scepticism. On the contrary, they maintain, it is 'theoretical defence [which] invites philosophical scepticism',[59] whereas a practical conception of human rights can provide an effective answer to the sceptical challenge. In this vein, Beitz argues that 'once we have on hand a practical conception, what began as a temptation to generalised scepticism resolves into one or another more specific concern about matters such as the importance of the interests protected by a right, the nature of the historical and contemporary relationship of the victims and the potential agents, and the propriety of protecting the threatened interest by the means likely to be within it.'[60] In this way, '[w]hat began as a problem about the practice becomes a problem within it.'[61] This is because the practical conception leaves no room for grand scepticism; it dissects it into discrete and narrower sceptical claims each of which can be addressed on its own merits.[62]

If we can even rout the sceptics with non-foundationalism, should we continue to concern ourselves about the foundations of the idea of human rights? There are two reasons why the answer to this question should be affirmative.

First, foundational argument may matter regardless of its practical applications. As Jeremy Waldron has explained, theorists pursue foundational inquiries not 'in order to equip their more practical-minded colleagues with impressive sounding arguments that will work in the courtroom', but because 'it is intrinsically important to have a deep and abstract as well as surface-level and practical understanding of these rights we claim to take so seriously'.[63]

Secondly, and more importantly, it is fair to ask whether non-foundationalist accounts of human rights add very much to what we already know about human rights from law or political science without the aid of philosophical enquiry. In most cases, these practical conceptions provide analytical accounts of the features of the human rights system as it is, which, while perhaps conceptually quite sophisticated, do not essentially depart from the approach of doctrinal jurists. In other words, they may have some explanatory power, but do they have any evaluative power?[64] Moreover, if it is true, as some have argued, that participation in human rights treaties seldom reveals genuine commitment,[65] a practical conception of human rights may commit the further error of taking a rather narrow view of what practice

---

57 Beitz (n. 38) at 137.

58 Raz (n. 54) at 328 and 332; J. Rawls, *The Law of Peoples* (Cambridge MA, Harvard University Press, 1999) 80.

59 G. Kateb, *Human Dignity* (Cambridge MA, Belknap Press, 2011) at 2. Kateb summarises this position in the quotation above, but does not agree with it.

60 Beitz (n. 38) at 201.

61 Ibid.

62 In Jürgen Habermas, one finds an attempt to develop a philosophy which is significantly influenced by pragmatism, rejects any charge of scepticism and even proposes a reconstruction of a discursive idea of reason that can survive the demise of metaphysics. Habermas applied his theory of communicative action to the law in *Between Facts and Norms* (London, Policy Press, 1996, trans. by William Rehg) and deals with human rights in Chapter 3 of that work.

63 Waldron (n. 17) at 10.

64 Griffin denies they even have sufficient explanatory power. See J Griffin, 'Human Rights and the Autonomy of International Law' in Besson and Tasioulas (n. 54) at 351.

65 Oona Hathaway, 'Do Human Rights Treaties Make a Difference?' 111 *Yale Law Journal* (2002) 1935.

is.[66] Its explanatory power may be skewed in favour of extrapolating ideas from a practice that, if comprehensively examined, does not yet quite support them.

If human rights practice had already crystallised into a global tradition, then one might rely on it to justify human rights with a Burkean argument. In the same way as the idea of 'ancient liberties' has traditionally been understood in England to require no further justification, one could say that international human rights, once they are supported by the weight of substantial common historical experience, will in practice need no other grounding than what that tradition accords. However, quite aside from the problem that the question of justification or foundation might exist independently of its practical convenience, international human rights are nowhere near this heightened stage of acceptance.

Practical theories are no better at providing guidance for assessing claims to human rights. Beitz suggests 'a schema for justifying claims about the content of human rights doctrine',[67] which is centred on the notion of sufficiently important interests, without however identifying either 'a single master value' (in which he does not in any event believe) or even a 'list of relatively specific interests or values to serve' as grounds.[68] Beitz's proposed schema can work as a 'framework or outline of the reasoning that would be necessary to arrive at judgments about the protections that should make up a public doctrine of human rights', but 'the details of this reasoning will vary with the nature of the protection in question'.[69] As Beitz himself admits, in other words, '[b]y itself a schema does not settle anything'.[70] In particular, it does not tell us why some interests, but not others, should be singled out as sufficiently important to generate human rights.

It may be that the best a philosophy of human rights can do is to provide such analytical frameworks to help us understand a certain praxis, or guide us through the process of making normative claims. But it is difficult to escape the sense that crucial questions are missing from a philosophical investigation thus conceived. To put it somewhat ungenerously perhaps, one is left with the impression that the accomplishments of this type of philosophical inquiry into human rights are rather modest.

This impression is rendered more vivid by the observation that, in spite of the undeniable success represented by the emergence of a global system of human rights, disagreement on fundamentals persists. The answer to the very basic question 'Should we have human rights?' may seem incontrovertible to the point that it deserves no theoretical engagement in Boston or New Haven. But it is not so elsewhere.

To illustrate this point one example, an arena where foundational argument still clearly matters, is the Egyptian Parliament, which has been discussing a new constitution and new bill of rights. The female member of parliament who wishes to see strong constitutional protection for human rights will need arguments to contrast the belief-based refutations of human rights which her Salafist or Muslim Brotherhood colleagues will deploy. Like a novel Grotius, she will need to persuade her contemporaries that a set of fundamental rights must

---

66 On the meaning of 'human rights practice' in the practical conceptions of human rights, see also Griffin in Besson and Tasioulas (n. 54) at 344.

67 Beitz (n. 38) at 137. Beitz's theory is thus in the camp of interest-based theories of rights. On the distinction between will and interest theories of rights, which I have not explored in this chapter, see: L. Wenar, 'The Nature of Rights', 33 *Philosophy and Public Affairs* (2005) 223.

68 Ibid. at 138–39.

69 Ibid.

70 Ibid. at 141.

be recognised by people with different beliefs, as well as by believers and non-believers alike. This is not just any foundational claim: it is a foundational claim that must be strong enough to allow her to prevail in public argument against opponents armed with belief. Of course, even assuming that we can equip her with the best of all foundational arguments, it is not certain that she will prevail. She will need to articulate that foundational argument in terms that are attuned to her society. She will, in other words, need a strategy of persuasion. Such a strategy may involve, for example, advancing foundational claims which evoke one of the 'visions of freedom' found in classical Islamic political thought.[71]

When a number of liberal democracies are undermined by populism and apathy; when the promises of liberty of the Arab Spring are being disavowed; when for the first time in at least half a century liberal democracies appear to be economically less successful than their competitors (in particular autocratic state capitalism, e.g. China, and rentier state capitalism, e.g. the Gulf states, both associated with a poor record on human rights) – to think that we have reached the stage where we can put foundational argument on human rights behind us and simply explain the practice seems, to say the least, wishful. The sense of urgency about strong justifications for human rights is, in other terms, a very real and practical need which a self-avowed practical conception should not ignore. There is no Cartesian anxiety here, rather an attempt to draw attention to the fact that postmodern anxiety about foundational inquiry may also have its numbing effect on the intellect. Perhaps, borrowing from T.S. Eliot, it is time we faced up to our illusion of being disillusioned.[72]

3.3 Types of foundationalism

What are exactly foundations? Waldron has identified 'four possible accounts of what it might mean to say that one concept, α, is the foundation of another concept, β': origins and genealogy; source and legitimacy; a genuine basis for derivation; and a key to interpretative understanding.[73] It is the third account – the basis for derivation – that offers the greatest theoretical promise. There are, in turn, different ways of theorising foundations as bases for deriving human rights. An important distinction – it has been suggested – is between naturalistic foundationalism and agreement foundationalism.[74] An example of the former is Griffin's theory of human rights:[75] from the ideas of personhood and dignity, combined with a set of practical considerations, he derives a catalogue of fundamental rights. An example of the latter would be the attempt to derive a catalogue of human rights from the Rawlsian idea of overlapping consensus.[76]

---

71 On this see Patricia Crone's work on Islamic Political thought: *God's Rule, Government and Islam: Six Centuries of Medieval Islamic Political Thought* (New York, Columbia University Press, 2004) 315ff.

72 To the critic who wrote that with *The Waste Land* he had expressed the 'disillusionment of a generation', Eliot responded that this was 'nonsense'. He wrote: 'I may have expressed for them their own illusion of being disillusioned, but that did not form part of my intention' (T.S. Eliot, *Thoughts After Lambeth* (London, Faber & Faber, 1931) 10).

73 Ibid. at 12 and ff.

74 Beitz (n. 38) at 49ff. and 74ff. respectively.

75 Griffin (n. 2).

76 As Beitz explains (n. 38) at 76, Rawls did not use overlapping consensus to derive human rights, but others have done so. An example of a human rights theory based on overlapping consensus which is cited by Beitz is M. Nussbaum, 'Human, Rights Theory: Capabilities and Human Rights', 66 *Fordham Law Review* (1997) 286. However, Amartya Sen's account of the theory of capabilities does not deal with overlapping consensus (*The Idea of Justice* (London, Allen Lane, 2010)).

The distinction between naturalistic foundationalism and agreement foundationalism in contemporary thought mirrors that between rationalistic accounts of natural rights and contractarian ones in classical political thought. The main example of rationalistic accounts is Kant's universal principle of right: 'Any action is *right* if it can coexist with everyone's freedom in accordance with a universal law, or if on its maxim the freedom of choice of each can coexist with everyone's freedom in accordance with a universal law', with the corollary that, if an individual action or situation can coexist with the freedom of everyone, 'whoever hinders me in it does me *wrong*.'[77] In John Locke's version of the social contract, human beings quit the perfect freedom of the state of nature because that condition 'is full of fears and continual dangers' and they become 'willing to join in Society with others who are already united, or have in mind to unite for the mutual *Preservation* of their Lives, Liberties and Estates'.[78] On the Lockean account the triad – Life, Liberty and Property – comprises the fundamental ends of political society and the inalienable rights of its individual members.

Utilitarianism is another traditional type of foundationalist argument which might be seen as a sub-species of rationalist theory or as a third genus. Classification aside, the main feature of utilitarian theories of human rights is that rights exist as means for advancing utility. The classical account of a utilitarian theory of fundamental liberty is found in John Stuart Mill. His harm principle states that 'the sole end for which mankind are warranted, individually or collectively, in interfering with the liberty of action of any of their number, is self-protection' and 'the only purpose for which power can be rightfully exercised over any member of a civilised community, against his will, is to prevent harm to others'.[79] While still avowedly utilitarian, Mill's theory of liberty is at the less instrumental end of utilitarian theories of rights.[80] A modern utilitarian theory of human rights has been advanced by William Talbott who argues that universal rights are justified by the good consequences they produce, in particular their being a necessary condition for a political system to be 'self-improving and self-regulating'.[81]

Another strand of foundationalist argument has sought to ground human rights in basic human needs.[82] The trigger for this approach has been the work of developmental psychologists, such as Abraham Maslow,[83] on the physical and psychological needs of human beings. The appeal of basic needs theories is that they seem to solve the problem of universality by grounding human rights in a scientifically based theory of human nature. In reality, however, science is still a long way away from providing uncontested accounts of the fundamentals of human nature. Moreover, the problem with basic needs theory is not just insufficient

---

77 Kant, Metaphysics of Morals in *Cambridge Edition* (n. 18) at 387 and *KGS-AA* Vol. VI at 231. On the relationship between Kant's moral thought and the natural rights tradition see: T.J. Hochstrasser, *Natural Law Theories in the Early Enlightenment* (Cambridge, CUP, 2000) 197ff.; J.B. Schneewind, 'Kant and Natural Law Ethics', 104 *Ethics* (1993) 53.

78 J. Locke, *Second Treatise of Government*, Ch. IX para. 123.

79 J.S. Mill, *On Liberty* (Oxford, OUP, 1991) 14.

80 On one reading of *On Liberty*, Mill pre-empts a purely instrumental reading of liberty when he explains that, although he regards utility 'as the ultimate appeal on all ethical questions', 'it must be utility in the largest sense, grounded on the permanent interests of man as a progressive being' (ibid. at 15).

81 W. Talbott, *Which Rights Should Be Universal?* (Oxford, OUP, 2005) 37.

82 E.g.: P. Streeten, 'Human Rights and Basic Needs: Theory and Practice', 8 *World Development* (1980) 107.

83 See A.H. Maslow, 'A Theory of Human Motivation', 50 *Psychological Review* (1943) 370.

information. In *Brave New World*, Aldous Huxley imagined a society that kept everyone happy through both genetic manipulation and a pervasive system of nudging. As no one has unsatisfied needs and everyone is happy, this society could on the surface appear to be ideal. But in reality it would be the worst of all dystopias – one where human beings have satisfied all their needs but they have 'no imagination and hence no aspirations', and where 'the immemorial pathologies of tyranny and despotism have been transmuted into a dreadful kindness'.[84]

Some contemporary theorists argue that a foundationalist position can coexist with a pluralist outlook.[85] They contend that human rights need *some* foundations, but not necessarily one foundation. A plurality of justificatory arguments may ground human rights in a way that is more effective and also takes into account individual, cultural and legal differences.[86] This is not tantamount to relativism, for the simple reason that the proposition 'ω may be founded on α and/or β and/or γ' is analytically different from the propositions 'ω is founded on nothing at all' or 'all talk of ω being founded on anything is meaningless'.

One general problem with foundations as bases for deriving rights is that at some point in this reverse process of justification we may have to introduce postulates, i.e. principles which are not derivable from another principle. As one theorist put it, the foundationalist is faced with a dilemma: 'whether to disappear down a road of infinite regress or to stand firm on a dogma'.[87] If it is so, the non-foundationalist (sceptics and non-sceptics alike) will object that the whole foundationalist exercise becomes futile.

In response, it must be emphasised that not all foundationalism rests on a series of non-demonstrable postulates. A purely Kantian foundationalist account, for example, does not: indeed, for Kant, liberty and fundamental rights are derived entirely by reason. But it is true that contemporary foundationalist theories do not normally make such a comprehensive claim to theoretical justification and are comfortable with making some minimal assumptions. For example, in James Nickel's approach, the unifying idea is 'a life that is decent or minimally good'.[88] From this idea he then derives four core claims which make up his proposed framework for human rights. Even if these theories do not have an answer to all first principles questions, they have a good claim to be preferable to those that answer none.

---

84 Kateb (n. 59) at 41. In the final pages of *Democracy in America*, de Tocqueville imagines a similar dystopia (A. de Tocqueville, *Democracy in America* (University of Chicago Press, 2000, ed. and transl. by H. Mansfield and D. Winthrop) 662–63, Part IV Ch. 6).

85 See for example: Nickel (n. 40) at (inter alia) 53 and J. Tasioulas, 'Human Rights, Universality and the Values of Personhood: Retracing Griffin's Steps', 10 *European Journal of Philosophy* (2002) 79 at 88ff. Tasioulas, however, rejects foundationalism on the grounds that it constrains the 'the values that ground human rights' (Tasioulas (n. 4) at 25), but his rejection is based on normative reasons. He objects to the kind of foundationalism that precludes the recognition that 'a plurality of values plays a role in grounding human rights' (ibid. at 26).

86 Foundationalism pluralism is theoretically linked to ethical pluralism. An example of this position is K.A. Appiah, *The Ethics of Identity* (Princeton, Princeton University Press, 2005) 73–83. In international legal and political theory, the term pluralism also denotes the existence of multiple legal orders which are not structured hierarchically. See J. Cohen, *Globalisation and Sovereignty: Rethinking Legality, Legitimacy, and Constitutionalism* (Cambridge, CUP, 2012); N. Krisch, *Beyond Constitutionalism: The Pluralist Structure of Postnational Law* (Oxford, OUP, 2010); N. Walker, 'The Idea of Constitutional Pluralism', 65 *Modern Law Review* 317 (2002). See also my 'A Normative Theory of Sovereignty Transfers', 49 *Stanford Journal of International Law* (forthcoming 2013).

87 M. Freeman, 'The Philosophical Foundations of Human Rights', 16 *Human Rights Quarterly* (1994) 491 at 496.

88 Nickel (n. 40) at 62.

3.4 The 'international' factor

Should a theory about *international* human rights differ from a general theory of human rights? For most of the classical political theorists, the key frame of reference was the individual and the state, and the political space in which this relationship was defined was entirely domestic. The international nature of human rights was the main reason for John Rawls's minimalist conception in the *Law of Peoples*.[89] A further consequence, on which both Rawls and Raz agree, is that international human rights norms should be viewed essentially as standards for interference by one state in the affairs of another or even for the use of force.[90] Among the critics of this idea is John Tasioulas who observes that the discourse of human rights is 'difficult and contested enough' and wonders what there is to be gained by taking 'the further step of linking the very idea of human rights to the existence of a state system and to the *pro tanto* justifiability of international intervention against states that commit rights violations'.[91]

At this point it may be helpful to leave political and legal theory, and consider how the question of intervention would be dealt with under a doctrinal account of international law. The international law of state responsibility authorises states, in certain circumstances, to take countermeasures against a state which is responsible for an internationally wrongful act. Countermeasures are defined as 'measures which would otherwise be contrary to the international obligations of the injured state vis-à-vis the responsible state if they were not taken by the former in response to an internationally wrongful act by the latter in order to procure cessation and reparation'.[92] The breach of any rule of international law can thus potentially create an entitlement on an injured state to adopt countermeasures, including non-forcible interventions such as diplomatic protest or trade sanctions.[93] The key point is that international law treats the countermeasure, which might follow from the breach of a rule, as analytically distinct from the rule itself.

It is a distinction that seems entirely appropriate and defensible even beyond the positive law. The breach of positive rules generally has consequences. Yet, we would not normally explain the basis or content of a rule on the basis of the consequences that follow from its breach. We would not, for example, think of the prohibition on murder as a standard for the deprivation of liberty. True, upon a conviction for murder, imprisonment is almost certain to follow. But, if we want to understand the criminal law of murder even if in a purely functionalist or descriptive sense, we would have to look beyond the consequences that follow from the violation of that law. The point can also be illustrated with an example closer to human rights: it is a feature of the constitutional law of most countries that a statutory provision found to be inconsistent with the bill of rights will be invalidated. Yet, a conception of constitutional rights which sees them as standards of invalidation would strike us as narrowly and perhaps mistakenly focused. The principles (or the rules) and the consequences that follow from their violation pertain to separate categories: not much is gained, descriptively or prescriptively, by defining the ones on the basis of the others.

---

89 Rawls (n. 58) at 78ff. Nickel speaks of 'Rawlsian ultra-minimalism' (n. 40 at 98).
90 See discussion of Raz and Beitz in the main text, and Rawls (n. 58) at 79.
91 J. Tasioulas, 'Are Human Rights Essentially Triggers for Intervention', 4/6 *Philosophy Compass* (2009) 938 at 947.
92 J. Crawford, *The International Law Commission's Article on State Responsibility* (Cambridge, CUP, 2002) 281. See Articles 49–54, International Law Commission Articles on the Law of State Responsibility.
93 The law of countermeasures expressly excludes the obligation to refrain from the threat or use of force. See Article 50(a), International Law Commission Articles on the Law of State Responsibility.

Conceptualising international human rights as standards for intervention does not therefore take us very far. Other reasons, which have nothing to do with intervention, may however justify distinguishing a conception of international human rights from a conception of non-international human rights (for example, constitutional rights). Rawls maintained that there should be such a distinction: human rights are different 'from constitutional rights, or from the rights of liberal democratic citizenship, or from other rights that belong to certain kinds of political institutions, both individualist and associationist'.[94]

Would such a differential approach be irreconcilable with a foundationalist account of human rights? Or, at least, does it not lead us away from the kind of foundationalist account that grounds human rights in some genuinely universal principle? It may be, of course, that what that universal principle can justify is only a minimum of rights on the international plane, and that states and societies will then bear additional obligations which have arisen in a different way – through, for example, a Burkean idea of 'ancient liberties' which is contingent on a particular history and tradition, or a Rawlsian overlapping consensus. It is entirely plausible, in other words, to come up with a foundational theory that justifies a core minimum on a universal basis, but also admits of the possibility of constitutional supererogation: international minimalism but constitutional maximalism. Interestingly, however, the current legal position is the exact reverse: international human rights law in its current form is far from minimalist and tends to protect a wider range of human rights than the constitutions of most liberal democratic states.[95]

3.5 Beliefs and assumptions

A radical criticism of all non-theistic attempts to ground human rights has been advanced by Nicholas Wolterstorff. In a series of compelling and elegant essays on human rights, he has sought to show that all secular foundational theories of human rights fail, and that the only solid foundation for human rights is theistic.[96] In particular, Wolterstorff argues that both the capacity for rational agency and the idea of personhood fail to provide a strong enough grounding for human rights, since they exclude those human beings who lack these attributes, for example, because of severe impairment.[97]

By contrast, if, to cite Wolterstorff's conclusion in one of his essays, one really believes that through incarnation God gave human beings 'the extraordinary honor' of assuming human nature, the dignity that derives from that belief is unassailable: '[t]o torture a human being is to torture a creature whose nature has been assumed by the second person of the Trinity.'[98] This justification has the psychological motivating force of beliefs, as well as the epistemic force of a proposition which derives directly from an *a priori*.

But the epistemic value of beliefs is not always so straightforward. It depends on what it is that we believe. In principle, we could devise a set of clearly formulated beliefs which would

---

94 Rawls (n. 58) at 79–80.

95 A normative conception of human rights that differentiates between international and non-international human rights may also be consistent with a pluralist approach of the kind advanced by John Tasioulas (n. 4).

96 The two most important of these essays are now collected in N. Wolterstorff, *Understanding Liberal Democracy* (Oxford, OUP, 2012) Chs 7 and 8. Similar arguments have been made by Michael Perry in *The Idea of Human Rights: Four Enquiries* (Oxford, OUP, 1998).

97 See Wolterstorff (n. 96 at 186–93.

98 Ibid. at 200.

allow us to derive human rights through a series of cogent inferences. But real beliefs are more complicated than that. For example, someone may believe at the same time that all humans were made in the image of God, and that God made men and women different. One of those beliefs may form the epistemic foundation for gender equality, the other for gender inequality.

The other problem with theistic justifications is that they only succeed insofar as we share belief, whereas it is clearly the case that we do not. Even if we look at the history of humanity as a whole, we obviously never really did. Outside religion, there is no comprehensive theory that tells us what we *must* believe. There is, however, a tradition of political thought, principally represented by Alexis de Tocqueville, which has explained the importance of belief in the development of social and political institutions. This tradition can help us address a series of important questions for our era: what happens once belief is replaced by disbelief? Will the *good* assumptions (for instance, in the case of Christian belief, about human equality, about the inviolability of the person and the sacredness of life) that are generated by religious belief survive its demise?[99]

Articulating the case for human rights in religious terms may still have an important practical advantage in some situations. In the contest with the belief-based opposition to rights – such as in the situation discussed above of a pro human rights member of parliament in Egypt having to make the case for human rights to colleagues holding fundamentalist beliefs – a series of belief-based arguments for human rights may prove an effective rejoinder.

The other, and to some extent alternative, route we should explore builds on Jacques Maritain's remarks during the UNESCO consultation. It might help, for example, to speak of assumptions rather than foundations. The difference between the two is this: foundations entail a claim to truth (and invite counterclaims to a different truth or, simply, to the falsification of the proposed truth); the term assumption does not come laden with the baggage of 'truth'.

Naturally, even if we agreed that we need common assumptions, we may continue to disagree on what those assumptions should be. A fundamentalist might, for example, argue that a proper assumption is inequality of men and women. The assumptions themselves will be contingent on some other principle on which, since we posited fundamental disagreement, we cannot agree, e.g. do we need to share assumptions in order to guarantee minimal social interactions? Or in order to thrive as human beings? Or to pursue the good life?

Nevertheless, speaking of assumptions rather than foundations offers, at the very least, the presentational advantage of avoiding a truth-based claim. This may just be enough to persuade some to set aside strongly held beliefs not with a view to replacing them (which a believer will not be prepared to do) but as part of a dialogue on how best to coexist with others and to organise society. If human rights are presented as a mutually convenient way of organising society rather than as a set of legal principles derived from a common moral truth, they will not be measured against the standard of religious belief (where they may fail or succeed, depending on the belief). And it is not inconceivable that a person who has accepted to agree on the need to agree on *something* might then be prepared to accept a further step: that the process of generating certain assumptions necessary even for minimal social interactions is best approached as a normative exercise. I do not for a second foresee fundamentalists jumping on a Kantian bandwagon, but we may at least spark a disposition to question in a precious few,

99 The most comprehensive philosophical investigation of this question by a contemporary theorist is C. Taylor, *A Secular Age* (Cambridge MA, Belknap Press, 2007).

particularly if we bear in mind that beliefs, powerful though they are, also have a certain malleability and do not provide clear and coherent answers to all social and political questions.

4 The conception of the individual

A theory of human rights is as much a theory of the *human* as it is a theory of *rights*. Not every human rights theory will openly advance a theory of the self or – to borrow from the title of a complex and elegant book by the Italian Catholic existentialist Luigi Pareyson – an ontology of liberty.[100] But every theory of human rights will rest on a set of assumptions, whether stated or not, about the individual. The political anxiety, discussed in the first section of this chapter, plays a role in contemporary inquiries into the ontological dimension of human rights. The fear is that a Western conception of the individual, or even more so a whole philosophy of individualism, will be transposed onto the idea of human rights.

An analysis of the ontological dimension of human rights theory would require a very extensive investigation, which cannot be undertaken here.[101] But one general observation should be made. Rather than determining whether there is a conception of the self which we must adopt in full in order to justify human rights, we may instead try to identify conceptions of the self that are irreconcilable with the idea of human rights. I can think of at least four.

First, human rights cannot exist without a conception of the individual. This may seem obvious but, as Larry Siedentop has explained, the Western idea of the individual is an invention that has taken centuries to develop.[102] This idea of the individual, which we are now inclined to take entirely for granted, would have been almost incomprehensible to the Greeks and the Romans. For that reason, the idea of human rights would have also been incomprehensible to them.

It seems incontrovertible that individuality, rather than individualism, is a necessary condition for human rights *as we generally understand them*. Individuality need not entail the idea of a unitary and consistent self, and can accommodate a vision of the self as 'multiple, inconsistent, labile and evolutionary', such as the one advanced by Lebow.[103] The qualification

---

100 L. Pareyson, *L' Ontologia della Libertà* (Turin, Einaudi, 1995).

101 In the vast literature on these issues, there are three recent works which, albeit not specifically on human rights, in my view stand out and also offer great potential for application to the theory of human rights: R.N. Lebow, *Politics and Ethics of Identity* (Cambridge, CUP, 2012); J. Seigel, *The Idea of the Self* (Cambridge, CUP, 2005); Siedentop (n. 5).

102 Siedentop (n. 5).

103 Lebow (n. 101) at 321. Lebow discusses four strategies for constructing identity. The first one 'seeks to recreate a world dominated by a religious-based cosmic order in which there was little tension between individuals and their society' (4–5). It is typical of millennial movements like Dispensationalism. The second one 'attempts to do away with interiority and reflexivity as far as possible' as its proponents 'want to create a largely secular society that removes all distinctions of wealth and honour and deprives people of privacy, free time and all forms of individual differentiation' (5). The third one understands 'interiority and reflexivity as compatible with the social order' and considers 'society a source of diverse role models that people can emulate, even mix and match and transform in the process of working out identities of their own' (ibid.). The fourth one condemns 'society as oppressive, and encourages people to turn inwards, or to nature, to discover and develop authentic, autonomous identities' (ibid.).

Of these four strategies, the first two seem to me to be clearly incompatible with any meaningful concept of human rights, while the last two can sustain, and perhaps to a significant extent even require, human rights.

'as we generally understand them' is meant to address the objection that even non-human beings may have some rights. Wolterstorff mentions, for example, the right not to be mutilated for no reason other than the pleasure of the person inflicting the mutilation.[104] This is an example of a right which many of us (myself included) are prepared to accord to animals and cannot, therefore, be predicated on individuality. But human rights as we generally understand them include claims, such as to the right to bodily integrity or freedom of conscience, that are predicated on individuality.

Secondly, human rights are incompatible with theories that see the individual as entirely subordinate to communal interests. Conceivably even a strong form of communitarianism can accommodate some fundamental individual rights.[105] But, for any meaningful idea of human rights to exist, we must accept some area where individual claims will defeat communal ones.

Thirdly, although a reductionist conception of the individual may accommodate some human rights, the human rights that will attach to individuals thus conceived will be, at best, very sparse. The main example of the kind of human rights that a reductionist account of human nature produces is found in Hobbes. In *De Cive* Hobbes had accepted the view, which was prevalent in his time, that power over a person, even when not exercised, is a constraint on liberty.[106] At that point he therefore accepted a conception of liberty capable of accommodating even potential interference. In *Leviathan*, however, Hobbes abandons that view for a much narrower and materialistic conception of liberty as absence of physical impediments ('externall Impediments of motion') reflecting the mechanistic conception of human nature which he had by then fully embraced.[107] Accordingly, the natural liberty which Hobbes recognises in *Leviathan* is only deceptively generous; in practice, it stands ready to be sacrificed to the higher cause which the sovereign embodies. A reductionist ontology leads to an idea of liberty that is so shorn of meaningful content or of purposive protection as to be devoid of any real quality. After all, if man is no more than a complicated machine, why should he deserve to be free?[108]

Ontological reductionism has far from lost its appeal. It survives, and thrives, for example, in behaviouralist accounts of human nature. It is certainly no coincidence that the founder of behaviouralist psychology, when he applied his theory to the concepts of freedom and dignity, argued that these should be set aside.[109] A theory that sees fundamental similarities between human beings and Pavlov's dog, that speaks of behaviour rather than action, that thinks of the will as completely susceptible to manipulation, will not be able to sustain a meaningful idea of human rights. If there is one threat to human rights coming from Western academia

---

104 Wolterstorff (n. 96) at 188.

105 On liberalism and communitarianism, see S. Mulhall and A. Swift, *Liberals and Communitarians* (London, Blackwell, 1992).

106 See Q. Skinner, *Hobbes and Republic Liberty* (Cambridge, CUP, 2008) esp. 124ff.

107 Hobbes, *Leviathan*, esp. Ch. XXI.

108 Humean reductionism, while not as mechanicistic as Hobbesian reductionism, is also problematic. The reductionist tendency of much empiricism is the reason why I am more hesitant to link British empiricism with liberalism (Lebow (n. 101) at 5). With De Ruggiero (*Storia del Liberalismo Europeo* (Bari, Laterza, 1925) 15–24) I also tend to think of liberalism as influenced by, and in many ways dependent on, certain 'spiritual forces' (at 15) more than an empirical disposition. When empiricism leads to reductionism and utilitarianism, as was often the case in British political thought, the liberal tradition may have maintained itself in that country in spite of, rather than thanks to, empiricism.

109 B.F. Skinner, *Beyond Freedom and Dignity* (Indianapolis, Hackett, 1971).

nowadays, it is the firm grip of neo-positivism in the political and social sciences.[110] When neo-positivism joins forces with utilitarianism (as it almost inevitably tends to do), then the battle for human rights is all but lost.

Fourthly, a conception of human beings that refuses to accept any universal commonality also makes human rights impossible. There are two versions of this denial of a universal commonality: one derives from an extreme form of epistemological subjectivism; the other from what, with an ugly word, we might call hard 'identitarianism' – the view that certain collective identities (gender, sexual orientation, race, class etc.) define us so fundamentally that we can dispense with even a minimal sense of human commonality.[111] By contrast, soft 'identitarianism', while emphasising the role of collective identities, does not dispense with the idea of minimal human commonality.

Soft identitarianism has gained considerable force in public argument in recent decades. It has yielded an ever expanding catalogue of rights which vests exclusively in individuals defined by their possession of certain collective traits. Although soft identitarianism is not prima facie incompatible with human rights, it does risk undermining them to the extent that it grounds them ever more in the particular rather than the general. The particular should feed and enrich our concept of the general. The fact that we accept, recognise and protect human conditions which were previously ignored or neglected should lead us to deepen our appreciation of the human, *and to expand our imagination* – for, ultimately, one of our most formidable traits as a species is that we can imagine to be what we are not. But if we are not careful, this particularistic drive could push us all into 'little platoons' without any sense of connection to the general condition of being human,[112] with the consequence that an identitarian 'rights tribalism' would replace human rights as a general category.

5 The phenomenology of power

In liberal accounts of human rights, the individual is the main bearer of rights.[113] But on whom should the corresponding obligations fall? In terms of positive international law, the answer is straightforward: the state is the main duty holder. The apparent reason for treating the state differently from other entities is that it wields a unique power, in both a qualitative and quantitative sense. But does that justify making the state the sole duty holder?

---

110 See Verdirame (n. 49).
111 This would not be the position of the greatest representative of radical feminism, Catherine MacKinnon. In one of her essays on human rights, she attacks postmodernism precisely because of the postmodernist attempt to dismantle any of universality (*Are Women Human?* (Cambridge MA, Belknap, 2006) 53).
112 'Little platoon' is an expression used by Edmund Burke which I am here citing out of context. The citation of the passage where Burke introduces this expression reads: '[t]o be attached to the subdivision, to love the little platoon we belong to in society, is the first principle (the germ as it were) of public affections. It is the first link of the series by which we proceed towards a love for our country and to mankind.' (*Reflections on the Revolution in France* (London, Penguin, 1982, C. Cruise O' Brien ed.) 135). Unlike my use of 'little platoons' in the text above, therefore, for Burke the 'little platoons', albeit particular rather than universal, are not defined by a particular collective identity but essentially by proximity.
113 This is not to say that human rights may not be born by collective entities, or that human rights which have traditionally vested in individuals are not also susceptible of vesting in collective entities. See, for example, Leif Wenar's work on the extension of the right to property to natural resources ('Property Rights and the Resource Curse', 36 *Philosophy and Public Affairs* (2008) 2).

At the outset it should be noted that the idea of the state as sole duty holder is not a requisite of the main classical theories of human rights. Locke, for example, did not seem to have any doubt about the fact that natural rights created juridical relationships between individuals (rather than just between the individual and the state). Natural rights originate in the state of nature, where there is no political society and where the only duty holders are other human beings. As Locke explains, the right to life, liberty and property is held 'against the Injuries and Attempts of other Men'.[114] Similarly, Kant's universal principle of freedom generates moral and legal relationships between private individuals.[115] The particular obligations of the state vis-à-vis the natural rights or the human rights of individuals derive from the state's ability not only to respect these rights but also to ensure that others under its control do so. The state is thus singled out as a key duty holder (but, analytically, not the sole one), not so much because of its unique capacity to commit fundamental wrongs (although this might also be a consideration) but because it alone has the power to enforce rights and punish wrongs.[116]

The idea of the state as sole duty holder has been the object of severe criticism from feminist legal theorists. The starting point in the argument is the criticism of the public/private distinction, which Nicola Lacey summarises as follows:

> Typically, liberal political thought assumes the world to be divided into public and private spaces and issues: governmental action, and hence liberal principles, apply primarily to the public world, while private lives and private spheres are properly subject to the regime of individual autonomy and negative freedom. This distinction is, of course, reflected in many codes of human rights such as the US Bill of Rights or the European Convention on Human Rights, which concern themselves exclusively with state or public actions.[117]

The principle of the state as sole duty holder is seen by these feminist thinkers as a way of shielding power in the private sphere from scrutiny and sanction. Yet, as mentioned before, on at least two of the traditional liberal accounts, natural rights were considered perfectly capable of generating obligations incumbent upon private individuals. To paraphrase Rawls, if the so-called private sphere is alleged to be a space exempt from the application of the law of the state, then there is no such thing in liberal thought.[118]

---

114 Locke (n. 78) at Ch. VII para. 87.

115 See for example this statement of that principle of freedom found in Kant's essay 'On the Common Saying': 'No one can coerce me to be happy in his way . . .; instead, each may seek his happiness in the way that seems good to him, provided he does not infringe upon that freedom of others' (Kant, 'On the Common Saying: This May Be Correct In Theory, But It Is of No Use In Practice', in Gruyer and Wood (eds) (n. 18) at 291).

116 As I have argued elsewhere, from a liberal perspective, the role of the state as protector of human rights imposes limits on the transfer of sovereign powers to international organisations. See G. Verdirame, 'A Normative Theory of Sovereignty Transfers', 49(2) *Stanford Journal of International Law* (2013).

117 N. Lacey, 'Feminist Legal Theory and the Rights of Women', in K. Knop, *Gender and Human Rights* (Oxford, OUP, 2004) 21–22.

118 Rawls's comment was on justice, but it was also in response to the public/private critique. It reads: 'The spheres of the political and the public, of the non-public and the private, fall out from the content and application of the conception of justice and its principles. If the so-called private sphere is alleged to be a space exempt from justice, then there is no such thing.' (J. Rawls, *Justice as Fairness: A Restatement* (Cambridge MA, Belknap Press, 2001) 166).

Yet, modern legal systems do differentiate between the individual–state relationship and individual–individual relationships, with human rights being generally reserved to the former. An example where the public or private nature of the conduct changes the legal characterisation is the infliction of severe pain on an individual for the purposes of extracting a confession. If this conduct is imputable to a public official, it will be considered torture or, at the very least, cruel or inhuman treatment. If a treatment of the same severity is inflicted on a woman by a partner who is seeking to extort a confession of an imagined or real 'betrayal', the law does not regard that as torture. It will still, of course, be regarded as an offence, but it will not carry the stigma of torture because, in law, torture can only be committed 'by a public official or a person acting in a public capacity' (Article 1, Convention Against Torture).[119] Some theorists see in this, and in other examples that could be offered, a demonstration of the enduring force of the public–private divide.[120] Yet, in a Kantian or Lockean perspective, it is difficult to find a basis for distinguishing the two moral wrongs in the examples above.

So why did the eighteenth-century bills of rights legislate in individual–state terms? The reason has nothing to do with the intention to allow powers, the exercise of which by the state was now being subject to limitations, to continue to be exercised without any limitations in the private sphere. More likely explanations have to do with the fact that these were revolutionary enactments adopted at the end of a prolonged struggle with public power. This is not of course to detract from the fact that, until very recently, the power of the male head of the family was far from adequately constrained and that the law had systemic gendered 'blind spots'. But this was neither the cause nor the consequence of the framing of those bills of rights in individual–state terms.

The feminist attack on the public/private distinction is not the only critique of human rights which begins with a claim to uncover the true face of power. All radical criticism of human rights follows a similar pattern. The blueprint was set out by Marx in his essay *On the Jewish Question*.[121] As mentioned before, Marx argued that the human rights guaranteed in the eighteenth-century bills of rights were premised on an egotistic conception of man. Not only do they pay no regard to the social nature of man, they actually estrange man from any such inclination. Marx is generally more positive about political rights, and concentrates his criticism on freedom of religion and on the right to property. Both of these rights – Marx argues – end up protecting traditional and social practices which hinder human emancipation, or facilitate exploitation.[122]

How one should react to the flaws of the idea and practice of human rights remains contested among neo-Marxist scholars – a dispute which has taken place against the background of a broader argument on the relevance of international law. One reading of Marx's criticism of human rights would suggest disengagement as the appropriate strategy. Insofar as human rights perform a function of legitimation for forms of social and economic

---

119 UN General Assembly, Convention Against Torture and Other Cruel, Inhuman or Degrading Treatment or Punishment, 10 December 1984, United Nations, Treaty Series, vol. 1465, p. 85.

120 The fact that 'private torture' is not characterised as 'torture' under human rights law does not mean that states are at liberty to tolerate it. If, for example, the domestic legislation of a state permitted the infliction of physical pain by men on women as a form of private punishment, that state would still find itself in breach of a number of human rights obligations.

121 See n. 16.

122 On exploitation see: S. Marks, 'Exploitation as an International Legal Concept' in S. Marks (ed.) *International Law on the Left* (Cambridge, CUP, 2008) 281.

exploitation, they will be inimical to a Marxist project of emancipation. On a different reading – and one that many neo-Marxist scholars of international law seem to favour – human rights have an emancipatory potential, and their limits and disadvantages can be addressed, if not completely rectified, by a practice that takes Marx's criticisms into account and refocuses the project accordingly.[123]

Other radical theorists, for whom Marx has been an influence, take the main lesson of the Marxist critique to be an invitation to be constantly alert to the way in which power manifests itself and reinvents itself in each society and in the world. Human rights theory thus ends up overlapping almost perfectly with a theory of power. This is the case, for example, with Catherine MacKinnnon's approach to human rights. For MacKinnon, with all their limits and biases, international human rights can still fulfil an emancipatory role as long as the practice of human rights is embedded in a truthful narrative of power (particularly its gendered dimension).[124]

6 Conclusion

Contemporary theoretical argument tends to take place within distinct disciplinary boundaries. There may sometimes be good reasons for this. If the assumptions and the questions differ completely, dialogue is difficult or even frustrating. But the point and the beauty of philosophical investigation is that it should invite us to challenge the assumptions and to rethink the questions.

With the proliferation of human rights, the growth in the number of human rights institutions and expansion of human rights jurisprudence, the attraction of 'current developments' scholarship and of specialisation has also increased. It is probably fair to say that most human rights scholarship these days is informed by one or both of these trends. Yet, the importance of questions about the first principles of human rights cannot be escaped. If human rights, as a legal and institutional phenomenon, become too far removed from a discernible moral and political idea, they will in the long run become indefensible . . .

Select bibliography

C. Beitz, *The Idea of Human Rights* (OUP, Oxford, 2009).

M. Freeman, 'The Philosophical Foundations of Human Rights', 16 *Human Rights Quarterly* (1994) 491.

J Griffin, *On Human Rights* (OUP, Oxford, 2008).

H. Lauterpacht, *An International Bill of the Rights of Man* (Columbia, New York, 1945).

J Nickel, *Making Sense of Human Rights* (Blackwell, Oxford, 2007)

M. Mutua, *Human Rights: A Political and Cultural Critique* (Pennsylvania University Press, Philadelphia, 2002).

J. Tasioulas, 'Towards a Philosophy of Human Rights', *Current Legal Problems* (2012) 26.

J. Waldron, 'Is Dignity the Foundation of Human Rights?', NYU School of Law, Public Law and Legal Theory Research Paper Series, Working Paper No. 12–73 (January 2013).

---

123 Among the international law and human rights sceptics is China Mieville, *Between Equal Rights: A Marxist Theory of International Law* (Leiden, Brill, 2005). Among those who think that Marxism does not entail rejection of human rights (and of the international law project) see: B. Roth, 'Retrieving Marx for the Human Rights Project', 17 *Leiden Journal of International Law* (2004) 31; R. Knox, 'Marxism, International Law and Political Strategy', 22 *Leiden Journal of International Law* (2009) 413; and Marks (n. 122).

124 See MacKinnon (n. 111).

4

Universalism of human rights and cultural relativism

Michael Freeman

1 Introduction

The universality of human rights is a fundamental principle of international human rights law (IHRL). The main source of IHRL is the Universal Declaration of Human Rights (UDHR). Article 2 of the UDHR says that everyone is entitled to all the rights set forth in the Declaration. The Vienna Declaration (1993) affirmed that the universality of human rights was 'beyond question'.[1]

Yet the universality of human rights has been questioned. In 1947 the Executive Board of the American Anthropological Association (AAA) published a 'Statement on Human Rights', in which they asserted that values and standards 'are relative to the culture from which they derive'.[2] This cultural relativism was motivated by a fear that the promotion of human rights as universal values would lead to the hegemony of the dominant global powers. The AAA now supports human rights, but 'extends' them to the collective rights of cultural groups.[3]

In the 1990s the dominant conception of universality was challenged on the basis of 'Asian values' by certain Asian governments and intellectuals, who insisted that there was a distinctively Asian conception of human rights.[4] Similar challenges have been made by some African scholars,[5] and on the basis of Islam.[6]

These challenges are often interpreted as manifesting a contest between the West and the rest, but Western culture does not always support human rights. Conservatives and leftists have reservations about IHRL. Communitarian philosophers have argued that the

---

1 Vienna Declaration and Programme of Action (1993) UN Doc A/CONF.157/23, para. 1.
2 The Executive Board, American Anthropological Association, 'Statement on Human Rights' (1947) 49(4) *American Anthropologist* 539–43 at 542.
3 K. Engle, 'From Skepticism to Embrace: Human Rights and the American Anthropological Association from 1947–1999' (2001) 23(3) *Human Rights Quarterly* 536–59.
4 J. Bauer and D. Bell (eds), *The East Asian Challenge for Human Rights* (Cambridge, CUP, 1999).
5 M. Mutua, *Human Rights: A Political and Cultural Critique* (University of Pennsylvania Press, 2008).
6 A. Mayer, *Islam and Human Rights: Tradition and Politics*, 4th edn (Westview Press, 2007).

individualism of human rights is not a cultural universal.[7] The liberal philosopher, John Rawls, regarded only Articles 3 to 18 of the UDHR as 'human rights proper', on the basis of a distinction between liberal and 'decent', non-liberal societies, and thus a form of cultural relativism.[8] Some philosophers hold that liberty rights are universal but welfare rights are not, because the former entail universal obligations whereas the latter do not. Some supposed 'rights' are thought too expensive and therefore not genuine rights.[9] Some have argued for universality on the ground that there is an 'overlapping consensus' on human rights. However, this claim is disputed; in particular, there is no consensus on the rights of women. Some anthropologists doubt whether the concept of human dignity that underlies human rights is universal.[10] One sense in which human rights are not universal is that they are unfamiliar to most people, even in the West.[11]

Human rights advocates argue that cultural relativism is used as ideological cover by authoritarian governments that have little respect for traditional cultures in their search for development. Many human rights violations have no basis in traditional culture.[12] Nevertheless, some universalists believe that human rights should take cultural diversity seriously.[13]

To assess the challenge of cultural relativism, it is necessary to clarify why human rights are thought to be 'universal', what 'cultural relativism' argues, and what force, if any, the challenge of cultural relativism may have.

2 Universalism

IHRL formulates universalism in several ways. The UDHR says it is 'a common standard of achievement' for all peoples. It affirms that everyone is entitled to all human rights. The International Covenant on Civil and Political Rights (ICCPR) and the International Covenant on Economic, Social and Cultural Rights (ICESCR) maintain that human rights 'derive from the inherent dignity of the human person'.

IHRL nevertheless places limits on human rights. Article 29(2) of the UDHR provides that everyone's rights may be limited by law to protect others' rights, and to meet 'the just requirements of morality, public order and the general welfare in a democratic society'. Article 4 of the ICCPR permits state parties to derogate from their obligations in a public emergency, subject to certain conditions. Some rights are protected from derogation.

There is a human right to culture. Article 27 of the UDHR says that everyone has the right freely to participate in 'the cultural life of the community'. The common Article 1 of

---

7 C. Brown, 'Universal Human Rights: A Critique', in T. Dunne and N. Wheeler (eds), *Human Rights in Global Politics* (Cambridge, CUP, 1999) 103–27.

8 J. Rawls, *The Law of Peoples* (Harvard University Press, 1999) 80.

9 O. O'Neill, *Towards Justice and Virtue: A Constructive Account of Practical Reasoning* (Cambridge, CUP, 1996) 130.

10 J. Donnelly, 'The Relative Universality of Human Rights', (2007) 29(2) *Human Rights Quarterly* 281–306 at 290; M. Goodale, *Surrendering to Utopia: An Anthropology of Human Rights* (Stanford University Press, 2009) 43, 131.

11 D. Chong, *Freedom from Poverty: NGOs and Human Rights Praxis* (University of Pennsylvania Press, 2010) 99.

12 J. Donnelly, *Universal Human Rights in Theory and Practice* (Cornell University Press, 1989) 59–60, 64–65.

13 J. Donnelly, *Universal Human Rights in Theory and Practice,* 2nd edn (Cornell University Press, 2003) Part II.

the ICCPR and ICESCR recognises the right of all peoples to self-determination, by virtue of which they may freely pursue their cultural development. The Vienna Declaration says that 'the significance of national and regional particularities and various historical, cultural and religious backgrounds must be borne in mind'.

IHRL is reticent about its philosophical foundations. This is necessary to secure widespread agreement on its norms. The price that it must pay, however, is that the philosophical basis of its claim to universality remains unclear and controversial.

3 Cultural relativism

Cultural relativism holds that some or all beliefs, values, norms and practices are not universally valid, but valid only for some cultures. It was introduced into anthropology by Franz Boas in opposition to the prevailing evolutionary theories, which held that Western cultures were the most evolved, and 'primitive' cultures the least evolved. Cultural relativism entailed a respect for all cultures. It became orthodox in anthropology and influenced popular moral relativism. Cultural relativism is part of Western culture.[14]

Cultural relativism is popular, even among those who support human rights, because it appears to express two attractive ideas: (1) everyone is equally entitled to respect; (2) to respect a person entails respect for that person's culture, because culture constitutes, at least in part, a person's identity.

Some believe that cultural relativism is required by the value of toleration. Universalism is thought to be intolerant of all cultural elements that do not conform to universal principles. Toleration is said to be intrinsically virtuous and valuable as a means to such ends as peaceful relations among cultures.

Some argue that different cultures hold different beliefs and values and there is no culture-independent way to distinguish between valid and invalid beliefs and values. IHRL makes cultural assumptions that are not in fact universal. Different cultures value individualism and the common good differently and each should be free to do so according to its history and culture, as there is no universally correct way to do this. Practices considered wrong in some contexts are justified in others. Human rights are expressed in general terms. It is appropriate to interpret them differently in different cultural contexts. This is supported by the right of peoples to determine their own social and cultural development as recognised by IHRL.

Cultural relativists believe that all values are the product of socialisation and power. Universalists mistake their own culture for universal principles; they are ethnocentric and cultural imperialists. IHRL is a cultural product that is modern, secular, cosmopolitan and, of course, legalistic. It derives from a Western cultural tradition that considers rights prior to culture. Relativists argue that culture determines rights. IHRL permits 'experts' in *its* culture to apply its standards to cultures they do not have the time, skills or, sometimes, the will to understand, and to which the culture of IHRL is alien. This may disrupt valuable local practices.

A neglected problem of universalism is that there is no universal language in which to express the meaning of human rights. IHRL is expressed in a limited number of official languages. If human rights are to be understood universally, they must be translated into

---

14 M. Baghramian, 'A Brief History of Relativism', in M. Krausz (ed.), *Relativism: A Contemporary Anthology* (Columbia University Press, 2010) 44.

other languages. Since each language reflects its culture, this translation involves a degree of cultural relativism. Thus linguistic relativism is a necessary condition of human rights universalism.[15]

4 Problems of cultural relativism

Some arguments for cultural relativism undermine it. The toleration principle is a universal principle that is inconsistent with cultural relativism, which says that intolerant cultures are valid. Cultural relativism is also morally implausible because it requires us to tolerate cultures that are cruel, unjust, dysfunctional, imposed by alien powers and/or imperialistic.[16] Cultural relativism provides little protection for cultures, because some cultures seek to destroy others. Universalism can endorse the value of toleration and culture-friendly principles.[17] Human rights universalism cannot value toleration without qualification, because it cannot tolerate human rights violations.[18] Cultural diversity does not refute universalism because human rights universalism encourages diversity; it assumes that free individuals will choose diverse ways of life. The 'Asian values' challenge to human rights universalism was defective because it understated the cultural diversity of Asia.

The lack of agreement on the philosophical foundations of human rights does not justify cultural relativism, because there is similarly no agreement on the validity of cultural relativism. IHRL does not seek uncontroversial philosophical foundations, for these do not exist, but relies on good moral arguments that can be endorsed by the various religions and philosophies of the world.[19] There is no absolute 'proof' of human rights, but this is probably true of any belief, including belief in cultural relativism.[20]

The argument that the uniqueness of each society's history and its right to self-determination justify cultural relativism is also implausible, because history and self-determination can produce atrocities; Nazism was a product of German history and the *right* to self-determination is limited by other human rights. It is right and prudent for universalist policies to take account of a particular society's history and culture, but wrong to do so uncritically. The point of human rights is to improve the quality of people's lives, and it cannot do that if it ignores the social context in which they live.[21]

Human rights are not ethnocentric, in that they ascribe equal rights to everyone, irrespective of ethnicity. Cultural relativism cannot consistently condemn ethnocentrism, for many cultures favour ethnocentrism, whereas universalism can condemn ethnocentrism.[22] Human rights may have Western origins, but the validity of an idea depends not on its origins but on its merits. Western governments may misuse human rights in their foreign policies, but taking human rights seriously would improve the lives of more non-Westerners than Westerners. The West may be 'hegemonic', but local hegemonies – for example, of male

---

15 M. Garre, *Human Rights in Translation: Legal Concepts in Different Languages* (Copenhagen Business School Press, 1999).
16 J. Nickel, *Making Sense of Human Rights,* 2nd edn (Blackwell, 2007) 172.
17 J. Tilley, 'Cultural Relativism' (2000) 22(2) *Human Rights Quarterly* 501–47 at 545–46.
18 Ibid. 542–43.
19 Ibid. 539.
20 Ibid. 545, fn. 76.
21 Ibid. 520, 531–32.
22 Ibid. 527.

religious elites – may be more significant for millions.[23] The idea of human rights, precisely because it is egalitarian and universalistic, far from being imperialistic, provides a basis for criticising imperialism. Cultural relativism is not necessarily anti-imperialistic, because it cannot criticise imperialistic cultures. The argument that human rights do not apply to non-Westerners has been used by Westerners to justify the worst atrocities of imperialism.

The appeal to cultural relativism by non-Westerners is sometimes less an objection to human rights than to Western hegemony. Cultural assertiveness may be an expression of dignity. The legacy of Western colonial oppression may explain some of the resistance to the universality of human rights, but resistance to Western domination should not obstruct careful consideration of the advantages of human rights for non-Westerners.[24]

Human rights norms are expressed in general terms. However, this is no argument for cultural relativism; it means only that these norms require interpretation, and that interpretations may be subject to controversy. It does not mean that any norm can be justified by culture; dictators who kill people who annoy them are immoral, universally.[25]

Universalism is not necessarily dogmatic. It makes claims about the *scope* of human rights, not their *certainty*. Universalist claims can be challenged, debated, refined or rejected if sufficiently good reasons are forthcoming. That universalist human rights claims can be controversial provides no support for cultural relativism, which is, of course, also controversial. Although human rights are sometimes expressed in absolute terms, universalism does not entail absolutism. There may be reasonable disagreement among universalists about which human rights, if any, are 'absolute' in the sense that nothing can ever override them.[26]

Cultural relativism may claim to be true absolutely or relatively. If it claims to be absolutely true, it contradicts its relativism. If it claims to be relatively true, it is not true for those cultures that reject it (including the culture of human rights universalism). Cultural relativism also suffers from the fact that cultures may contain false beliefs, e.g., that killing witches protects groups from harm. Cultural relativism invalidates challenges to existing cultures; if cultural relativism were true, then Martin Luther King would have been acting *immorally* in challenging racial discrimination in the southern states of the USA. Indeed, the leading cultures of the contemporary world – for example, Christianity and Islam – originated in challenges to existing cultures. A cultural relativist would have to say that Christians were right to follow Jesus, but that Jesus had been wrong to challenge the Jewish orthodoxy of his time.[27] Cultures can allow self-criticism; if so, the criticism may appeal to universal values.

Culture is complex, horizontally and vertically. Horizontally, culture covers a range of social practices from religious observance to fashions in dress. Vertically, it ranges from the core political culture of a country to the culture of street gangs. Cultures are often contested: even when we can identify a culture fairly confidently – say, British Muslim culture – those who uncontroversially 'belong' to the culture may disagree on at least some of its values and norms. Cultures are also nowadays typically *interactive* – they influence each other and create hybrids; thus, British Muslim culture is different from British Jewish culture, but each has a British component. Cultures are dynamic; they are constantly changing. Finally, cultures are

---

23 B. Simmons, *Mobilizing for Human Rights: International Law in Domestic Politics* (Cambridge, CUP, 2009) 369–71.
24 Donnelly (n. 13) 99, 103.
25 Tilley (n. 17) 529.
26 Ibid. 526.
27 Ibid. 511–12, 543–44.

structured by inequalities. Cultural relativism is ideologically conservative; it benefits the rich and powerful more than the poor, and men more than women. Since human rights address abuses of power, they must approach cultures critically as well as respectfully. This task is helped by the fact that cultural interaction, hybridisation and contestation increasingly include a human rights component.

The most difficult case for human rights universalism, however, is that in which those who are victims of human rights violations support the culture that legitimates those violations. Women who are malnourished, for example, sometimes support the cultures that cause this condition. Martha Nussbaum argues that the victims' views are not morally decisive, because the injustice that denies them food and education denies them the ability to imagine alternatives.[28] In these situations intercultural dialogue may be inadequate because the victims may be excluded. External intervention may be problematic because it may have undesirable consequences; local traditions that are not fully compliant with human rights may support ways of life that are satisfying and that may be adversely affected by the insensitive application of human rights standards.[29] There is no general solution to this problem because it involves judgement rather than theory, but the best strategy requires the kind of cultural critique proposed by Nussbaum and a contextually sensitive understanding of the likely consequences of intervention.

5 Qualified universalism

The principles used to defend cultural relativism are often *universal* principles; for example, the principle of toleration. These universal principles, however, suggest a qualified universalism. For example, the universalist disapproval of ethnocentrism should lead Western human rights advocates to make strenuous efforts to see human rights problems from non-Western perspectives. James Griffin has suggested that Westerners and non-Westerners have exaggerated the homogeneity both of the West and of the Rest, and the differences between them.[30] The consensus on the universality of human rights expressed by the Vienna Declaration may contain some hypocrisy and conceal important disagreements, but it suggests that the problem of cultural relativism for the universality of human rights may have been overstated. The standard, universalist conception of human rights includes limits and flexibilities of interpretation, and, although this does not mean that cultural differences can be ignored, it may mean that tensions between the 'West and the Rest' may be at least as much caused by political and economic differences as by cultural diversity.

Article 27 of the Universal Declaration recognises that everyone has the right freely to participate in the cultural life of the community. Article 22 recognises the right of everyone to the realisation of the economic, social and cultural rights 'indispensable for his dignity and the free development of his personality'. Article 27 of the ICCPR prohibits the denial to persons belonging to ethnic, religious or linguistic minorities the right, in community with the other members of their group, to enjoy their own culture. Article 15 of the ICESCR affirms the right of everyone to take part in cultural life. The UN Committee on Economic, Social and Cultural Rights has emphasised that cultural rights are 'an integral

---

28 M. Nussbaum, 'Commentary on Onora O'Neill: Justice, Gender, and International Boundaries', in M. Nussbaum and A. Sen (eds), *The Quality of Life* (Oxford, Clarendon Press, 1993) 324–35.
29 S. Scheffler, *Boundaries and Allegiances: Problems of Justice and Responsibility in Liberal Thought* (Oxford, OUP, 2001) 125.
30 J. Griffin, *On Human Rights* (Oxford, OUP, 2008) 138.

part of human rights', universal, and 'essential for the maintenance of human dignity'. The human right to culture is an individual right; individuals have the right to participate or not to participate in particular cultural practices. Although the right to culture is an individual right, culture is a collective phenomenon, and therefore the right to culture implies some form of group rights. According to the Committee on Economic, Social and Cultural Rights, States have an obligation to respect the cultural diversity of individuals and communities. They must implement the right to culture in a way that is compatible with their obligations to respect all other human rights. No one may invoke cultural diversity to violate human rights. The right to culture may be limited to protect other human rights, but such limitations must be the least restrictive measures necessary for the general welfare in a democratic society.[31]

International human rights institutions accept that universal human rights standards should be interpreted differently in different cultural contexts. The composition of bodies to draft new human rights treaties, and of treaty-monitoring bodies, are required to represent 'the different forms of civilisation' and different legal systems. The acceptance of regional human rights regimes and of special divisions of international human rights law for particular categories of persons (e.g., women, children, disabled persons, indigenous peoples) is a legal means to reconcile universality and diversity.[32]

It is generally accepted that human rights should be implemented in a culturally sensitive and appropriate manner. The Human Rights Committee has allowed that the right to family life may vary according to socio-economic conditions and cultural traditions.[33] It has also said that 'a certain margin of discretion' must be accorded to national authorities when freedom of expression comes into conflict with public morals.[34] The Committee on Economic, Social and Cultural Rights says that health facilities, goods and services must respect the culture of individuals, minorities, peoples and communities.[35] The UN Special Rapporteur on the Right to Health has affirmed that a health system 'must be respectful of cultural difference'. Health workers should be sensitive to issues of ethnicity and culture. Cultural respect was 'of course' right as a matter of principle. It also made sense as a matter of practice: cultural sensitivity led to higher levels of ownership by the community, programme acceptance and programme sustainability.[36] The Special Rapporteur on the Right to Education has emphasised the right of parents to have their children educated in conformity with their religious, moral or philosophical convictions.[37] The Office of the UN High Commissioner for Human Rights has specified that the right to food implies the availability of sufficient

---

31 UN Committee on Economic, Social and Cultural Rights, General Comment No. 21, 'Right of Everyone to Take Part in Cultural Life' (43rd session) (2009) UN Doc. E/C.12/GC/21, paras 1, 7, 15–19, 40.

32 E. Brems, *Human Rights: Universality and Diversity* (Martinus Nijhoff, 2001) 343.

33 UN Human Rights Committee, *Aumeeruddy-Cziffra and 19 Other Mauritian Women v Mauritius* (1981) UN Doc. CCPR/C/OP/1 at 67 (1984).

34 UN Human Rights Committee, *Hertzberg and Others v Finland* (1982) UN Doc. CCPR/C/15/D/61/1979.

35 UN Committee on Economic, Social and Cultural Rights, General Comment No. 14, 'The Right to the Highest Attainable Standard of Health' (22nd session) (2000) UN Doc. E/C.12/2000/4, para. 12.

36 Report of the Special Rapporteur on the Right of Everyone to the Enjoyment of the Highest Attainable Standard of Physical and Mental Health (2008) UN Doc. A/HRC/7/3, 12.

37 Preliminary Report of the Special Rapporteur on the Right to Education (1999) UN Doc. E/CN.4/1999/49, 22.

food 'in a form that is culturally acceptable'; that the right to housing includes the right to housing that is 'culturally acceptable' to the inhabitants; that the right to health includes the right to health facilities, goods and services that are 'culturally appropriate' and to services that are 'are respectful of the culture of all individuals, groups, minorities and peoples'.[38] In contrast to these concessions to cultural diversity, Article 5 of the Convention on the Elimination of Discrimination Against Women requires states parties to modify cultural patterns of conduct with a view to achieving the elimination of prejudices and any practices based on the idea of the inequality of the sexes or on stereotyped gender roles.

Universal standards are modified legally by reservations that states make in ratifying human rights treaties. Some reservations take the form of understandings that a state agrees to be bound by a particular provision only with a specified interpretation. Reservations that are incompatible with the objects of the treaty are prohibited, although the meaning of this rule for human rights treaties is a subject of controversy.[39] Some reservations protect national constitutional provisions that reflect the national culture; Ireland, for example, accepted a paragraph of the ICCPR on the understanding that it did not imply a right to divorce, which was prohibited by the Irish constitution. The USA has made a reservation to the prohibition of cruel, inhuman or degrading treatment or punishment, limiting its acceptance to the protection provided by the US Constitution. Some reservations reject some human rights, but others are based on differences between treaty language and reasonable conceptions of rights in particular countries.[40]

It is common for states, both Western and non-Western, to limit human rights for the sake of security, economic conditions and cultural values.[41] Different societies set these limits differently, thus creating important differences in the interpretation of human rights. For example, the decision whether or not to criminalise hate speech varies from one society to another within the framework of universal human rights.[42] IHRL cannot specify its own best interpretation. The interpretation and application of human rights must be informed by local cultures if they are to realise their aims and to be accepted as legitimate.

The argument against human rights universalism on the basis of cultural relativism is often confused with arguments based on state sovereignty, because both are used to keep outsiders from interfering with the internal affairs of a society. The logics of these two arguments are, however, quite different, and, to some extent, mutually inconsistent. The appeal to state sovereignty is not an appeal to cultural relativism, because the principle of state sovereignty is as universal as that of human rights. The principle of state sovereignty is fundamental to international law, but its relations with human rights are notoriously problematic. Sovereign states may crush cultures. It is important, therefore, to distinguish arguments about sovereignty from arguments about culture.

---

38 Office of the United Nations High Commissioner for Human Rights, 'Principles and Guidelines for a Human Rights Approach to Poverty Reduction Strategies' (2006) HR/PUB/06/12, 28, 30–31, 35, 37.

39 L. Henkin, G. Neuman, D. Orentlicher and D. Leebron, *Human Rights* (Foundation Press, 1999) 788–93. See also the Guide to Practice on Reservations to Treaties and commentaries adopted by the ILC in 2011, Report of the International Law Commission (2011), GAOR 66th Session Supp 10 (UN Doc. A/66/10/Add.1).

40 G. Neuman, 'Human Rights and Constitutional Rights: Harmony and Dissonance' (2002–2003) 55(5) *Stanford Law Review* 1863–1901 at 1888–90.

41 Brems (n. 32) 381.

42 Donnelly (n. 13) 95.

Eleanor Roosevelt said that human rights begin 'in small places, close to home'.[43] The distance from the places where IHRL is made to these small places, close to home, is considerable, and IHRL is not the only means of transmission of human rights from the former to the latter. Human rights are interpreted and applied at local level by a variety of agents, legal and non-legal, and the 'translation' of IHRL into local discourses is bound to be strongly influenced by local cultures. This translation carries dangers of distortion and weakening of rights, but also opportunities of strengthening the fulfilment of rights by making sense of them in local contexts.

6 The margin of appreciation

Article 1 of the European Convention on Human Rights (ECHR) establishes that States parties are the primary guarantors of human rights. The European Court of Human Rights is therefore subsidiary to State institutions. The Court has employed the doctrine of the margin of appreciation (DMA) to allow states some discretion in determining how to implement the Convention. The DMA assumes a common commitment to human rights and cultural diversity in Europe. It does not, therefore, apply to gross human rights violations or to other clear violations of Convention rights. The DMA accommodates not only cultural diversity, but also national security concerns, socio-economic policy, and political and legal differences.[44]

The DMA can be used to balance individual rights with the common good, resolve conflicts of rights and interpret general concepts. The ECHR allows states to restrict rights for the sake of collective goals under certain conditions. The Court applies the DMA to determine whether the conditions justifying the restriction are present.[45] It is likely to apply the doctrine to what it considers to be matters of fact, such as whether the action of the state was 'proportional' or 'necessary in a democratic society'.[46] All countries prohibit some forms of expression, but different countries have different policies in such areas as blasphemy, pornography and hate speech. The DMA allows some variation in such policies provided that they do not violate the 'core' of the right to freedom of expression. The Court affords stronger protection to political than to cultural expression on the ground that the former is more fundamental to democracy.[47] This has been criticised on the ground that cultural freedom is as necessary as freedom of political expression to democracy.[48]

The Court has applied the DMA for the protection of morals on the ground that morals are diverse in Europe and states should be allowed to determine difficult cases.[49] The Court has been criticised for inconsistency in the way it balances human rights with public morals.

---

43 E. Roosevelt, 'In Your Hands', speech made at the presentation of *In Your Hands: A Guide for Community Action for the Tenth Anniversary of the Universal Declaration of Human Rights*, United Nations, New York, 27 March 1958, available at: http://www.udhr.org/history/inyour.htm, accessed on 27 November 2011.

44 Brems (n. 32) 361–63.

45 G. Letsas, 'Two Concepts of the Margin of Appreciation' (2006) 26(4) *Oxford Journal of Legal Studies* 705–32 at 709–10.

46 J. Kratochvíl, 'The Inflation of the Margin of Appreciation by the European Court of Human Rights' (2011) 29(3) *Netherlands Quarterly of Human Rights* 324–57 at 330–31.

47 Brems (n. 32) 372–419.

48 Lord Lester of Herne Hill, 'Universality Versus Subsidiarity: A Reply' (1998) 1 *European Human Rights Law Review* 73–81.

49 *Handyside v The United Kingdom* Application No. 5493/72 (ECtHR, 7 December 1976).

In *Müller and others v Switzerland* public morality was allowed to trump freedom of expression, whereas in *Dudgeon v The United Kingdom* the right to privacy was given priority over public morality.[50] The Court tends to allow a relatively wide margin of appreciation for cases involving sovereignty, such as those concerning national security, immigration and socio-economic policy, where national authorities are thought to be 'better placed' than European judges to achieve the best balance between rights and the public interest, and family matters, where cultural diversity may be reasonable. Where an individual right conflicts with the interest of society, the Court will require the latter to be very weighty before it can override the former, and will consider whether the degree of restriction of the individual right is proportional to the public interest to be protected.

The Court will allow a wider margin of appreciation when it thinks there is no European consensus on the issue, and a narrow margin when it believes there to be a consensus. It has, however, been criticised both for failing to develop a rigorous method to determine whether such a consensus exists and for not applying this principle consistently. Some critics have argued that the uncertainty of the 'consensus' principle has allowed the Court to implement its own moral judgements.[51] Reliance on consensus has also been criticised for giving state practice and majority opinion priority over the rights of dissidents and minorities.[52] Two arguments for the 'consensus' principle are that judges should not make policy on issues about which reasonable people disagree – here democratic processes rather than judicial decisions should predominate – and the Court should not stray too far from the policies of the states that have consented to its authority – the subsidiarity principle.[53]

Some have criticised the Court's failure to develop clear criteria for the application of the DMA on the ground that citizens cannot know their rights, and states cannot know their obligations, with the degree of certainty that the rule of law requires.[54] Others hold that a combination of vague terms, such as 'reasonable', 'necessary' and 'proportionate' in the Convention and the particularities of individual cases make such a development difficult.[55] The DMA is partly political in that the Court must retain its legitimacy with the states and their peoples, and partly respectful of the legal sovereignty of states.[56] It has been criticised for subordinating the universality of human rights to state sovereignty and cultural relativism.[57] It has been defended on the ground that liberal democracy requires a balance between the will of the majority and the rights of the individual, and the DMA is necessary to secure this balance.[58]

---

50 *Müller and others v Switzerland*, Application No. 10737/84 (ECtHR, 24 May 1988); *Dudgeon v The United Kingdom*, Application No. 7527/76 (ECtHR, 22 October 1981); J. Brauch, 'The Margin of Appreciation and the Jurisprudence of the European Court of Human Rights: Threat to the Rule of Law' (2004–5) 11(1) *Columbia Journal of European Law* 113–50 at 133.

51 Brauch (n. 50) 138–39, 146.

52 Ibid. 146.

53 Letsas (n. 45) 730.

54 Kratochvíl (n. 46) 330, 341, 351–52.

55 N. Lavender, 'The Problem of the Margin of Appreciation' (1997) 2(4) *European Human Rights Law Review* 380–90.

56 R. Macdonald, 'The Margin of Appreciation', in R. Macdonald, F. Matscher and H. Petzold (eds), *The European System for the Protection of Human Rights* (Martinus Nijhoff, 1993) 83–124.

57 E. Benvenisti, 'Margin of Appreciation, Consensus, and Universal Standards' (1999) 31(4) *New York University Journal of International Law and Politics* 843–54 at 844.

58 P. Mahoney, 'Marvellous Richness of Diversity or Invidious Cultural Relativism?' (1998) 19(1) *Human Rights Law Journal* 1–6.

Political philosophers generally agree that individual rights should be balanced with the common good, but they do not agree about how this should be done. It is, therefore, not surprising that the Court, in using the DMA to help it to decide cases that raise the question of this balance, should struggle to develop a clear, coherent and consistent doctrine. Critics maintain that it should either improve the clarity and consistency of the DMA or abandon it and concentrate on interpreting the text of the Convention in accordance with established international legal principles of treaty interpretation.[59]

7 Subsidiarity

The principle of subsidiarity underlies the Court's application of the DMA, although it does not always make this explicit, nor has it given a clear interpretation of the principle. The concept of subsidiarity is part of the law of the European Union, and is intended to secure an acceptable balance between the sovereignty of the member states and the powers of the Union. It has, however, been suggested as a principle of IHRL. It affirms the idea that large associations exist to help small associations, and small associations exist to help individuals. In large associations power should be located as close to the individual as is consistent with efficiency. Large associations should act only when lower associations or individuals cannot or will not act for the common good. The principle of subsidiarity is therefore thought to support democracy and human rights. Critics say that the principle is indeterminate because, on complex and controversial questions, plausible arguments could be made either for the Court to defer to, or overrule, national authorities. This indeterminacy in the principle of subsidiarity is reflected in the uncertainty in the DMA. The indeterminacy of the principle of subsidiarity supports the conclusion that one person's 'cultural relativism' may be another person's respect for democracy.[60] The principle of subsidiarity manifests the tension between the universality of human rights and the pluralism of forms of social life that a respect for human freedom entails.[61]

The application of the principle of subsidiarity to IHRL has three main implications: (1) a degree of local discretion over the interpretation and implementation of rights; (2) integration of local and international interpretation and implementation; and (3) the international community should assist national communities in implementing human rights without usurping their autonomy. Subsidiarity would not change the existing structure of IHRL, but would, so it is claimed, limit excessive activism by international institutions and legitimate their intervention when it was necessary for the common international good, including the protection of human rights. Although international institutions such as the treaty-monitoring committees have made progress in proposing specific interpretations of general human rights norms, they cannot impose their interpretations on states parties, which retain considerable interpretive latitude. Limitations on rights within treaties and treaty reservations increase the interpretive freedom of states. This permits a degree of 'cultural relativism' in IHRL. The concept of subsidiarity is said to be superior to that of sovereignty because it values decentralisation not as a right against the international community but as a means to balance universal and local values.

59 Letsas (n. 45), 714–15.
60 P. Carozza, 'Subsidiarity as a Structural Principle of International Human Rights Law' (2003) 97(1) *American Journal of International Law* 38–79 at 51, 56–57.
61 Ibid. 45–47.

Subsidiarity is also friendlier to the values of sub-state entities. Human rights lawyers may suspect that, by its emphasis on the local, subsidiarity risks weakening the universality of human rights. It may also be doubted whether the concept adds anything to the existing theory or practice of human rights, or solves any of its problems. Against these objections, subsidiarity argues for the virtues of interpreting the general principles of IHRL in the light of local facts and values, both as a matter of principle and, pragmatically, to legitimate universal standards locally. Subsidiarity assumes that the implementation of human rights involves some balancing of values, and that local knowledge and judgement may be better placed to do this than more remote institutions. Subsidiarity affirms the universality of human rights but not the uniformity of their interpretation. Subsidiarity does not provide a mechanical rule for deciding difficult cases, but a guiding principle to balance universal and local values. It does not allow clear violations of human rights simply because they are locally approved, and it does allow intervention by higher authorities when local institutions are unwilling or unable to protect human rights.[62]

8 Conclusions

Human rights can be implemented 'close to home' only if local cultures are understood and taken into account. Human rights advocates must, however, take a critical attitude to these cultures if they are to remain true to their own values. Because cultures are contested, inter-active and dynamic, there is space for the progressive realisation of human rights within the diverse cultures of the world. Conservative religions may provide some of the most difficult cultural obstacles to human rights advances, but the history of human rights shows that human rights can overcome religious opposition and become reconciled to diverse religious and philosophical views. It is likely that the conditions that facilitate this progress are at least as much political and economic as they are cultural.

Human rights advocates facing problematic cultures have the disadvantage of being outsiders. Some cultures may be irrationally xenophobic, but many have suffered from outside interventions, and thus have reason to distrust outsiders. International law respects the sovereignty of states and the self-determination of peoples while seeking to combine them with universal rights. Cultural relativism manipulates the real value of culture to create a smoke-screen for the injustices and cruelties that human rights are intended to oppose. The abuse of cultural relativism should not, however, divert attention from the need for universalists to take culture seriously, on principle and for pragmatic reasons.

'Culture' is not the only obstacle to the implementation of human rights, although non-cultural obstacles can appear as culture. For example, child prostitution in Thailand has some support in the culture, but the culture itself is a response to dire poverty. Problems attributed to cultural beliefs and practices may be caused by poverty and ignorance. Thus, human rights reform may not require direct confrontation with local cultures, but, rather, interventions that address the underlying social causes of those cultural commitments. UN treaty-monitoring committees are less tolerant of cultural obstacles to human rights implementation than of political or economic difficulties.[63] However, culture is in part the product of political and economic power, and the solution to the problem of cultural resistance to human rights may be political and economic change.

62 Ibid.
63 Brems (n. 32) 351–52.

IHRL has to reconcile the right to culture with a critique of cultural practices that are incompatible with human rights. It must also recognise that culture can be a resource motivating human rights advances; for example, kinship networks may deliver the right to food when governments fail to fulfil this obligation. Sometimes local people are more favourable to human rights than their governments are (and thus bad government, not cultural relativism, is the problem), but at other times governments with good-faith human rights policies may face resistance from local cultures, which may be defending the power of local elites but may have popular support. IHRL, national legislation and independent judiciaries are important protectors of human rights, but they are not sufficient. Human rights are most secure when they are embedded in cultures, and this may be achieved by political mobilisations. To secure human rights, it is important to know the limits of law.

Some human rights violations are so gross that they require little cultural understanding; others may be embedded in culture so that human rights reform requires cultural knowledge that is not easy for outsiders to acquire. Governments and other elites may claim to represent the culture of the people, but there are good reasons for outsiders to distrust such claims. We can know what the people think about culture and human rights only if they have a secure set of rights. Paradoxically, to advance human rights against culture, we have first to understand the culture, but we cannot understand the culture unless certain human rights are guaranteed.

There is no simple, general formula to relate the universality of human rights to cultural diversity. There is no universally agreed philosophical foundation of human rights, and therefore there is no universally agreed method for settling disagreements about the interpretation and implementation of human rights. This does not mean that 'anything goes' or that 'it is all relative'. There are important moral reasons that support, and widespread agreement about, much of the content of IHRL. Where disagreement remains, simple appeals to universalism or relativism are likely to be neither convincing nor effective. Careful analysis of the disagreement is necessary, and this is likely to involve not only cultural but also political and economic factors. Human rights can conflict with culture, and the conflict can be difficult to resolve, but we should remember that IHRL imposes limited obligations on states; beyond that, it leaves culture alone.

Eleanor Roosevelt said that human rights begin 'close to home'. Close to home we find local cultures that may be expressed in languages very different from that of IHRL. IHRL aims to protect the basic interests of everyone, but everyone does not speak the language of human rights. If those most vulnerable to human rights violations are to participate effectively in their own emancipation, IHRL must be interpreted in the light of local cultures. The spirit of IHRL is democratic and popular; its practice can be elitist and arcane. The challenge is to reconcile the culture of IHRL and the cultures of the diverse peoples it seeks to protect.

Select bibliography

M. Baghramian, 'A Brief History of Relativism', in M. Krausz (ed.), *Relativism: A Contemporary Anthology* (Columbia University Press, 2010).

J. Bauer and D. Bell (eds), *The East Asian Challenge for Human Rights* (Cambridge, CUP, 1999).

E. Brems, *Human Rights: Universality and Diversity* (Martinus Nijhoff, 2001).

J. Donnelly, 'The Relative Universality of Human Rights', (2007) 29(2) *Human Rights Quarterly* 281–306.

J. Tilley, 'Cultural Relativism' (2000) 22(2) *Human Rights Quarterly* 501–47.

5

The evolving study of human rights: interdisciplinarity and new directions*

Micheline Ishay

Human rights can be rooted in the Enlightenment period, and arguably earlier. Yet as a focus of academic inquiry, human rights gained legitimacy only after World War II. As the world underwent significant changes after 1945, the preoccupations of human rights scholarship experienced corresponding shifts. While the subject received consistent attention within the field of international law, greater attention from other disciplines became more significant starting in the mid-1960s. Yet it was only after the Cold War, in the era of globalisation, that human rights research became a well-entrenched interdisciplinary field. If the human rights discourse was greatly enriched by new infusions of interdisciplinary knowledge, at times it has succumbed to fragmented disciplinary relativism. In an effort to promote the integration of various disciplinary approaches within a consistent methodological and normative framework, this chapter will argue for Kantian and critical theory guidelines to inform the study and practice of human rights.

Toward that end, this chapter begins by considering the reasons for changing perspectives on human rights since World War II. It then addresses the more recent efforts to incorporate history and political theory within the field of human rights, and a final section will offer a methodological toolkit aimed at strengthening the interdisciplinary study of human rights.

1 Changing perspectives of human rights since World War II

1.1 Post-World War II

In the shadow of World War II, the goals of preserving inter-state peace and preventing genocide seemed immediate and inseparable, as unprecedented carnage had included both international aggression and the Holocaust. The International Convention against Genocide (1948) and the United Nations Universal Declaration of Human Rights (1948) became early

---

* This is a revised version of an article drawn from Micheline Ishay, 'Human Rights and History,' in Robert Denemark (ed.), *The International Studies Encyclopedia* (Blackwell, 2010).

focal points for legal scholars and politicians, who debated what constituted genocide, the level of responsibility attributed to those who committed crimes against humanity, and the responsibility of the international community. The Universal Declaration, a landmark document growing out of long debate within the first UN Human Rights Commission, was announced to the world in a new creed of human rights. That document stipulated five central families of rights: security, civil, political, socio-economic and cultural rights – all seen as indivisible and inalienable. With a new international architecture with the United Nations, the United Nations Charter (1945) and the UN Universal Declaration of Human Rights (1948) as its foundations, tensions between the rights of states and their obligations to international human rights treaties would absorb the attention of leading international legal scholars for decades to come.[1]

1.2 The early Cold War

From the time of the Declaration of Human Rights until the late 1960s, the Cold War revealed its ugly geopolitical face. Russian tanks crushed the Hungarian uprising of 1956 and the Prague Spring of 1968, and the United States supported repressive regimes in Latin America, the Middle East and Africa. In this cynical climate of bipolar rivalry, social science and international relations scholarship suffered from the marginalising of moral preferences (let alone human rights), in favour of a perceived necessity to depict 'impartially' the structural and functional dynamics of the domestic and international order. The social sciences gravitated around positivist, structuralist or realpolitik approaches as standards for evaluating political decisions in a world that seemed stultified by the nuclear balance of terror.

What accounts for the apparent lack of interest in human rights outside the legal world during the peak of the Cold War? There are many overlapping reasons: the appeal of realpolitik in the conflict between two superpowers; the context of heightened ideological tension between capitalism and communism; the sense, born of the Cold War and the nuclear arms race, that human rights was an intangible utopian vision incapable of addressing imminent dangers; and the growing regard for positivism and behaviourism as safeguards against utopian or irrational political impulses that could lead to a nuclear holocaust. In one form or another, these sentiments were reflected in the words of the American historian and diplomat, George F. Kennan, who saw human rights as antithetical to the national interest: 'National sovereignty', he flatly asserted, '[does] not represent the moral impulses that individuals in society may experience.'[2]

1.3 Circa 1968

By the late 1960s, the world was gradually changing in ways that had a growing impact on international institutions and legal human rights documents. The composition of the UN membership began to change, with the admission of newly independent states as a result of decolonisation. The United Nations adoption in 1966 of two major International Covenants

---

1 M. McDougal, H. Lasswell and L. Chen, *Human Rights and World Public Order: The Basic Policies of an International Law of Human Dignity* (Yale University Press, 1980): D. Weissbrodt and F. Newman, *International Human Rights: Law, Policy, Process* (Anderson Publishing, 1990): H. Steiner and P. Alston, *International Human Rights in Context: Law, Politics, Morals* (OUP, 1996).
2 G. Kennan, 'Morality and Foreign Policy', Winter (1985–86) *Foreign Affairs* at 206.

on Human Rights – the International Covenant of Civil and Political Rights (ICCPR) and International Covenant of Economic, Social and Cultural Rights (ICESCR) – had seen each covenant stipulate the right to self-determination in its first article. Debating these covenants, legal scholarship was split between defenders of the concept of civil and political rights, on the one hand, and advocates of socio-economic rights, on the other hand. Western countries and their allies privileged the ICCPR for reasons of justiciability, or as central to the struggle between capitalist democracies and state communist regimes. The post-colonial world and communist states emphasised the ICESCR, arguing that this approach addressed a more fundamental obstacle to human rights: the level of poverty within the developing world.[3] Armed with civil, political and economic advantages, it was the West, animated by anti-communism, that largely shaped the legal discourse of rights during the Cold War.

Notwithstanding occasional efforts to consider the role of human rights in foreign policy by scholars on the left such as Richard Barnet and Marcus G. Raskin,[4] Philip Green,[5] Noam Chomsky,[6] Joyce and Gabriel Kolko,[7] Richard Falk[8] and by leading realist scholar Hans Morgenthau,[9] the field of international studies was still lagging behind with respect to human rights. It focused instead on the nuclear arms race, geopolitics and the bipolar structure of the international system. Nevertheless, many scholars in the social sciences and humanities grew disillusioned with the hegemonic claims of Cold War contending superpowers, each invoking human rights to serve its interests. Political upheaval in the 1960s intensified that disenchantment and opened the doors of academia to new disciplinary inquiries, which illuminated the grievances of politically or economically disenfranchised peoples.

While the language of rights was emerging thanks to non-governmental organisations (NGOs) such as Amnesty International, from the early 1960s the quest for social justice for marginalised groups moved to the forefront of the progressive agenda in academic settings. The scholarship on social movements, including women's rights,[10] gay rights,[11] the demands of the national liberation movements in former colonies[12] and ecological groups,[13] made slow yet steady inroads in academia. In the American Political Science Association (APSA), the Caucus for a New Political Science was established in 1968, providing a progressive alternative to allegedly 'value-free' research. Drawing on mounting opposition to the Vietnam War, the Caucus emerged as a formidable alternative forum to the political

3 D. Meyers, 'Human Rights in Pre-Affluent Societies' (1981) 31(123) *Philosophical Quarterly* at 139: R. Thakur, 'Liberalism, Democracy, and Development: Philosophical Dilemmas in Third Word Politics' (1982) 30(3) *Political Studies* at 333.

4 R. Barnet and M. Raskin, *After 20 Years: Alternatives to the Cold War in Europe* (Random House, 1965).

5 P. Green, *Deadly Logic: The Theory of Nuclear Deterrence* (Ohio University Press, 1966).

6 N. Chomsky, *American Power and the New Mandarins* (Pantheon Books, 1969).

7 J. Kolko and G. Kolko, *The Limits of Power: The World and United States Foreign Policy* 1945–1954 (Harper & Row, 1972).

8 R. Falk, *The End of World Order: Essays on Normative International Relations* (Holmes & Meier, 1983).

9 H. Morgenthau, 'A Political Theory of Foreign Aid' (1962) 56(2) *American Political Science Review* at 302.

10 B. Friedan, *The Feminine Mystique* (W.W. Norton, 1963).

11 B. Adam, *The Rise of a Gay and Lesbian Movement* (Twayne Publisher, 1997).

12 F. Fanon, *Wretched of the Earth* (Grove Press, 1963).

13 H. Marcuse, 'Liberation from Affluent Society', in D. Cooper (ed.), *The Dialectics of Liberation* (Penguin, 1968).

science mainstream. During this period, demands for group rights began to impact the UN General Assembly, which adopted the International Covenant on the Elimination of all forms of Racial Discrimination in 1963, and the Convention on the Elimination of all forms of Discrimination against Women in 1979.

1.4 Globalisation

With the fall of the Berlin Wall and the progress of globalisation, a forth milestone in the journey of the field, human rights gained new international currency. Human rights spread further beyond legal scholarship and journalism, and towards broader fields of academic research. While legal standards continued to be an important anchor for human rights scholarship, human rights-oriented research on subjects ranging from transitions to democracy, nation-building, poverty, humanitarian intervention and war prevention began to draw attention from different academic disciplines. Many scholars in the social sciences and the humanities were now seeking a new vision of multiracial social justice, a universalist ideology which would unapologetically espouse neither the free market nor the alleged universal socialism championed by the defunct Soviet Empire. In a post-Cold War ideological vacuum, human rights were a largely untapped wellspring from which new internationalist world-views could be drawn.

The end of the Cold War, coupled with the mushrooming of non-governmental human rights organisations, stimulated a dramatic expansion of human rights scholarship. These developments led to the birth of a new international human rights regime, which found manifold grass-roots expressions within civil societies, beyond the corridors of institutional power.[14] These social trends also carved new academic multidisciplinary spaces for human rights discourse. One result of these changes was the 2001 inauguration of the Human Rights Section of the APSA, soon to be followed by the establishment of similar sections in the International Studies Association, the American Sociological Association and other professional academic organisations.

As post-colonial, gender, political identity, environmental and development discourses were taking root within academic curricula, human rights concerns became more fragmented, even as the field became more interdisciplinary. The end of the Cold War, and the new focus on globalisation, only intensified that fragmentation, highlighting the need for a more comprehensive approach. Clearly, efforts to integrate disparate struggles for human rights across time and space required greater attention to historical research and interpretation. As human rights campaigns were expanding from West to East, and now to the 'Global South', more historical narratives began to appear to respond to this need. The following section examines this growing role of history and theory in the literature of human rights, before presenting a toolkit that can illuminate efforts to integrate interdisciplinary thinking.

2 The emergence of history

Since the 1960s, there have been a number of important historical studies of human rights. The first encompassing histories of human rights were published only after 2000; by then,

---

14 M. Keck and K. Sikkink, *Activists Beyond Borders: Advocacy Networks in International Politics* (Cornell University Press, 1998): J. Smith, *Social Movements for Global Democracy* (Johns Hopkins University Press, 2008).

however, many important historical human rights studies had already appeared, focusing on particular epochs, regions or themes.

Epoch-specific accounts, mostly covering various periods between the eighteenth and twentieth centuries, generally emphasised the language of emancipation or social justice and seldom that of rights. Thus, Robert R. Palmer[15] described with great eloquence the various achievements of struggles for justice during the democratic revolutions of the Enlightenment; Lynn Hunt[16] explored in depth the human rights impact of the French Revolution; Eric Hobsbawm[17] authored masterful accounts of pivotal battles for justice in 1830, 1848 and 1875. Other scholarship described and analysed the campaigns by organised labour for political and economic justice. One nineteenth-century account, which was cast in human rights terms, was T.H. Marshall's book of collected essays, *Class, Citizenship and Social Development*.[18] Marshall's work charted the historical evolution of human rights themes, tracing the right to human security to the adoption of the principle of habeas corpus during the Enlightenment, the struggle for voting rights to the first British Reform Act of 1832 in the nineteenth century, and depicting the institutionalisation of welfare rights in Europe during the second half of the twentieth century. With an introductory overview of earlier periods, Paul Gordon Lauren offered an unprecedented account of the evolution of the human rights struggle during the twentieth century.[19]

In 2004, my *History of Human Rights* represented another step toward a comprehensive historical treatment, synthesising developments from the Mesopotamian Codes of Hammurabi to the era of globalisation, and chronicling the clash of social movements, ideas and armies that have played a part in this struggle. The book was structured around six core questions that have shaped human rights debate and scholarship: What are the origins of human rights? Why did the European vision of human rights triumph over those of other civilisations? Has socialism made a lasting contribution to the legacy of human rights? Are human rights universal or culturally bound? Must human rights be sacrificed to the demands of national security? Is globalisation eroding or advancing human rights? Since the publication of *The History of Human Rights*, there has been a growing stream of new contributions adding to the historical records and to the effort to draw the most useful lessons.

Regional or country-specific accounts of the history of human rights violations usually recount suffering under colonialism, the fight for independence, or efforts to govern following independence. For example, Adam Hochschild offered a gripping historical depiction of the human rights violations committed under King Leopold during the 1870s in the Congo.[20] Other works, include Katerina Dalacoura's exploration of the twentieth century's tension between Islam, liberalism and human rights,[21] Edward Cleary's history of the emergence of human rights campaigns in response to military repression throughout Latin America in the

15 R. Palmer, *The Age of the Democratic Revolution: A Political History of Europe and America 1760–1800* (Princeton University Press, 1959–64).
16 L. Hunt, *Inventing Human Rights: A History* (W.W. Norton & Company, 2007).
17 E. Hobsbawm, *The Age of Revolution 1789–1848* (New American Library, 1962): E. Hobsbawm, *The Age of Capital 1848–1875* (Wiedenfeld & Nicolson, 1975): E. Hobsbawm, *The Age of Empire 1875–1914* (Phoenix Press, 1987).
18 T. Marshall, *Class, Citizenship and Social Development* (Anchor Books, 1965).
19 P. Lauren, *The Evolution of International Human Rights: Vision Seen,* 2nd edn (University of Pennsylvania Press, 2003).
20 A. Hochschild, *King Leopold's Ghost* (Houghton Mifflin, 1998).
21 K. Dalacoura, *Islam, Liberalism and Human Rights,* revised edn (I B Tauris, 2003).

1970s,[22] and Marina Svensson's history of twentieth-century China, which emphasises the slow, yet persistent, penetration of human rights into Chinese political discourse.[23]

Theme-specific histories of human rights or stories of social emancipation began to appear in growing numbers after 1968. Sheila Rowbotham illuminated the story of women's roles in popular movements from the seventeenth to the twentieth centuries, investigating their struggles for universal suffrage, birth control, abortion and equality in the work force.[24] Beginning with the history of homosexuality from ancient times, Vern L. Bullough explored the contemporary criminalisation of homosexuality, the birth of the gay liberation movement and the battle for same-sex rights in the twentieth century.[25] David Brion Davis provided a compelling history of slavery, including the various slave revolts and abolitionist movements in the US and Great Britain.[26] A more recent contribution is from Kevin Bales, who depicts the new incarnation of this ancient scourge by linking African slavery to human trafficking and modern-day slavery.[27] In his thorough account of the practice of torture throughout European history, Brian Innes concluded with a study of then current practices and views.[28] Narrating the history of genocide during the twentieth century, Samantha Powers sought to explain US leaders' unwillingness to intervene and halt horrors committed against Armenians, Jews, Cambodians, Iraqi Kurds, Rwandan Tutsis and Bosnians.[29] Eric Weitz connected the phenomenon of genocide to racist and nationalist ideologies that compel such brutality.[30] Finally, William Rubinstein provided an excellent survey depicting genocides across historical epochs, beginning in pre-modern times.[31]

Overall, despite a significant body of enriching historical scholarship, it remains the case that both history and historiography have been widely overlooked, not only in the burgeoning human rights academic field, but also in most disciplines within the social sciences. What accounts for that neglect? How can we reclaim the study of human rights and engage it in interdisciplinary way? The following section addresses these questions, highlighting the contribution of critical theory as a useful method of inquiry for the field of human rights.

3 New theoretical infusions

Until the Cold War, the study of international relations had been grounded in efforts to integrate political theory and history. As ideological confrontation heightened during the Cold War, history became more descriptive, formalistic, and divorced from political theory, or from any normative or political purpose, prompting leading intellectual and historian

---

22 E. Cleary, *The Struggle for Human Rights in Latin America* (Praeger, 1997).

23 M. Svensson, *Debating Human Rights in China: A Conceptual and Political History* (Rowman & Littlefield, 2002).

24 S. Rowbotham, *Hidden from History: Rediscovering Women in History from the 17th Century to the Present* (Pantheon Books, 1973).

25 V. Bullough, *Homosexuality, a History: From Ancient Greece to Gay Liberation* (New American Library, 1979).

26 D. Davis, *Inhuman Bondage: The Rise and Fall of Slavery in the New World* (OUP, 2006).

27 K. Bales, *Disposable People: New Slavery in the Global Economy*, revised edn (University of California Press, 2004).

28 B. Innes, *The History of Torture* (Brown, 1998).

29 S. Powers, *A Problem from Hell: America and the Age of Genocide* (Basic Books, 2002).

30 E. Weitz, *A Century of Genocides: Utopias of Race and Nation* (Princeton University Press, 2003).

31 W. Rubinstein, *Genocide: A History* (Pearson Longman, 2004).

E.H. Carr[32] to denounce his British colleagues' historical work as politically irrelevant. Had Carr made the same accusation about social or political scientists, it would have had an equally powerful element of truth.

With the end of the Cold War, the advance of globalisation, the war on terror, and the 2008 meltdown of the global economy, the past 20 years have sent a succession of shocks through the nervous system of the international order. The sense of being buffeted by unpredictable events stimulated new efforts to comprehend the direction of history, or, alternatively, to assert its timeless truths. If history and theory were back, how should we approach it in the field of human rights?

At one end of the spectrum, international relations, in its empirical expression, is seen as a narrative of chronological facts. In the world of realists, power, drawn from the realm of experience, is privileged over morality as the ultimate driving force of history. At the other end of the spectrum, in its ideational iteration, history is viewed as a sequence of juxtaposed normative world views. In the Kantian world, the actualisations of the moral categorical imperative represents, in different time and space, signs of progress, and indicators that history is moving toward greater freedom. Other historical approaches lie somewhere in the middle, including historical materialism, Frankfurt School critical theory, post-structuralism (or post-positivism) and social constructivism. Let us begin with the latter, which has gained a prominent position within the mainstream study of world politics, including the study of human rights.

With the spread of informational technologies, NGOs, and inter-governmental organisations (IGOs), the realm of communication has expedited the development of international human rights. In the field of international studies, social constructivism explains how social values, history, practices and institutions shape human behaviour and identity. Social constructivists hold that all institutions, including the state, are socially constructed in terms of shared beliefs about political practice, acceptable social behaviour and values. In much the same way, the individual members of the state or other units are socially constructed; they reflect an 'intersubjective consensus' of shared beliefs about political practice, acceptable social behaviour and values. In that context, social constructivism has been seen as a congenial framework for capturing the institutionalisation of human rights norms, and has been widely adopted in human rights studies.[33] Social constructivism is an offshoot of, and arguably an improvement over structural realism, which has focused on changes within the international system. This approach does not, however, shed sufficient light on what qualitative changes, institutional or otherwise, may be salutary for human rights.

By focusing on the reification of norms within institutions, social constructivism tends to be trapped in a static limbo within the closed walls of institutional networks. When norms are instrumentalised, materialised and self-generated, it is unclear what makes history move forward or even backward. While institutional dynamics are an important aspect of social relations, they may also be inbred and sclerotic, failing to recognise the plight of those who fall below the radar of recognised institutions.

---

32 E.Carr, *What Is History?* (Knopf, 1961).
33 J. Donnelly, 'The Social Construction of International Human Rights', in N. Wheeler and T. Dunne (eds), *Human Rights in Global Politics* (Cambridge University Press, 1999): N. Stammers, 'Social Movements and the Social Construction of Human Rights' (1999) 12(4) *Human Rights Quarterly* at 980.

Other theoretical perspectives oscillate sharply back and forth between these two ideational and empirical poles characterising the field of international studies. Searching for ways to unveil the discrepancy between norms (e.g., the rhetoric of rights) and actions (e.g., power politics) may offer more dynamic narratives of historical change. It is worth noting that post-structuralism, along with social constructivism, has been favoured in human rights disciplines over the more economic approaches associated with historical materialism, or even the less economic orthodox adaptation of historical dialectic as understood by the Frankfurt School. In general, the relative neglect of more leftist historical approaches was no doubt connected to the overall marginalisation of the left in the context of the Cold War.

In brief, historical materialism based the analysis of society on how humans produce collectively basic necessity for their livelihood (the infrastructure); social classes, political structure and ideology are seen as shaped by the materialist conditions of economic life (the superstructure). Historical materialism explains the intersection between economic condition and superstructure in a dialectic movement, which shapes the main trends of historical development. In this tradition, politically conscious agents of history are seen as instruments of change, and the contradictions of a given economic system as opportunities for social transformation. Within that tradition, some scholars have focused on the systemic nature of the international economy, others on competing institutional dynamics that lead to economic crises[34] and others on the vibrancy (or lethargy) of civil society as a barometer of social change.[35] Drawing on the Marxist conception of historical materialism, scholars loyal to the Frankfurt School tradition have focused on a dialectic approach, in which individual ideas and actions represent the main engines of social transformation.[36] They propose to revive critical thinking by unveiling the discrepancy that exists between theory and practice – a task which is a launching pad for change and the understanding of human rights.

Post-structuralism tends to elevate local narratives, as they confront the prevailing structure of ideology and power; such clashes are viewed as significant moments for social change.[37] Yet that approach to history is rightly seen, from a critical theory approach *à la* Frankfurt School, as random, genealogic or cyclical, and relativistic as all forms of local struggle (just or unjust) are ultimately corrupted when they are institutionalised as power. If all future human rights endeavours inexorably yield to the outcome of political corruption, then why should one challenge any particular exclusionary ideology or corrupted power structure? Post-structuralists may have opened the disciplinary doors by elevating particular narratives of oppression, and they may have contributed in opening up interdisciplinary approaches in order to understand of grievances, but they have failed to provide practical judgments with respect to legal standards and policies concerning human rights. While human rights have benefited from interdisciplinarity, the field needs to carve a space that situates inquiry somewhere between overly static consideration of rights and the relativism associated with post-structuralism. The following is an effort in this direction.

---

34 I. Wallerstein, *The Modern World-System*, vols I–III (Academic Press, 1974–1989); J. Galtung, 'Violence, Peace, and Peace Research' (1969) 6(3) *Journal of Peace Research* at 167.
35 E. Thompson, *The Making of the English Working Class* (Vintage, 1966).
36 S. Bronner, *Reclaiming The Enlightenment: Towards a Politics of Radical Engagement* (Columbia University Press, 2004).
37 C. Douzinas, *The End of Human Rights: Critical Legal Thought at the Turn of the Century* (Hart Publishing, 2000).

4 Human rights interdisciplinary toolkit

Just as the Earth orbits the Sun, history is driven by rules of its own, in the sense that it has a life beyond people's dreams and actions, beyond people's comprehension and awareness. History is a realm, *sui generis,* in which institutional dynamics, wars and economic forces interact in the absence of autonomous human beings. Many historical accounts, perhaps most famously Tolstoy's *War and Peace*, reflect that position.[38] Yet history is surely more than that. It is a realm in which conscious agents pursue visions of human progress, attempt to draw lessons from past failures, and strategically engage prevailing rules, norms and institutions in order to make them better. If utterly beyond human intervention, history would be merely the work of an invisible hand, the whims of the gods of war, or the will of Providence. The intellectual, the legal scholar and the activist, each has a responsibility to intervene, first by understanding geopolitical, institutional or economic interests; then by unearthing contradictions between facts and norms; next, by identifying the possibilities for narrowing these gaps, and finally by applying knowledge of legal and other skills toward the realisation of a vision of the common good.

Envisioning the future realisation of universal rights may be another utopian project in a dystopian age, and yet it is perhaps especially relevant in difficult times to learn from past lessons, in pursuit of effective ways to develop new human rights opportunities. The task of the intellectual is incomplete if she or he remains a mere narrator of actions or changes. For those who seek to escape the theoretical confines of realism, constructivism or post-structuralism, and to base scholarship on the search for human progress, the following sketches out a few guidelines – a toolkit of questions that would hopefully prove useful for the student or the scholar seeking to reconcile the 'is' and the 'ought' toward the end of advancing human rights. The questions are as follows.

First, why must we understand the nature of exclusion or oppression? Second, for whom should we change history? Third, why should we assign a moral and universal purpose to history? Fourth, how can we avoid making tragic mistakes in the name of progressive change? Fifth, why is a dialectic approach relevant to historical human rights? Sixth, what are the roles of interdisciplinary and multilevel analyses?

4.1 Why must we understand the nature of exclusion or oppression?

'There is no document of civilization', the critical theorist Walter Benjamin reminds us, 'which is not at the same time a document of barbarism.'[39] Oppression and emancipation are closely intertwined, requiring scholars of human rights to understand how the nature and extent of power politics or corporate economic interests, hiding behind the veneer of civilisation, shape different forms of struggles for human rights. As such, the civil, religious and economic oppression of most people during the age of Absolutism galvanised revolutionary forces for civil rights, religious freedom and property rights during the Enlightenment. At the same time, economic disenfranchisement and political discrimination during the Enlightenment invited struggle for political rights and economic equality during the Industrial age. Finally, the repression of minorities by states or colonial forces during the nineteenth and twentieth centuries fomented yearnings for self-determination.

---

38 L. Tolstoy, *War and Peace* (1869; Modern Library, 1931).
39 W. Benjamin, *Illuminations* (Harcourt, Brace and World, 1968).

The presence of barbarism does not imply that people always react by struggling against it. Social and economic conditions have to be ripe. When they are, the victims of one generation can become the agents of change (or the vengeful oppressors) of the next generation. In all circumstances, however, the human rights scholar needs to ask if a given nation or people has reached a level of political consciousness sufficient for pursuing their own emancipation, or whether fear of a tyrannical regime precludes all forms of human rights dissent, as in George Orwell's masterly dystopia *1984*,[40] or whether political consciousness has been subsumed by the illusion of a commodified notion of freedom, so powerfully analysed in Herbert Marcuse's *One-Dimensional Man*.[41]

But regardless of whether the root of the problem is manipulated or repressed political consciousness, or alternatively, paralysing fear of vicious police states, the five families of rights (security, civil, political, socio-economic, cultural rights), understood as indivisible and inalienable, stand as an enduring set of standards for assessing the level and scale of oppression. Further, these standards of human rights and human development have formed the basis for indices, which has been designed (and progressively refined) for the purpose of empirically assessing where and by how much states fall short. While there is a valuable ongoing debate among empirical social scientists about the relative utility and validity of particular measures of rights compliance, it is fair to say that it is no longer realistic for governments to disguise blatant failures to protect human rights. (That does not prevent regimes, as in the recent cases of Ahmadinejad, Qaddafi or Assad, from trying.) In short, the compliance of states with the spectrum of human rights can be studied, through a combination of theoretically informed standards based on the five families of rights, investigation by human rights NGOs and IGOs of the facts on the ground, and the use of standardised empirical indices of the forms and scale of government-sanctioned suffering.

4.2 For whom should we change history?

That human rights activists seek to improve the lot of the oppressed, the less fortunate and the marginalised has consequences for how we engage history. If we do not keep in mind what we wish to see changed, we lack guidance in choosing what to search for in history. In *The Second Sex*,[42] Simone de Beauvoir asked scholars to unearth women's participation in history as a way to reclaim women as active agents of politics. In *Bury the Chains*,[43] Adam Hochschild recounts the history of abolition to show how past strategies can inform future campaigns of emancipation. Human rights history, in short, is history from the vantage point not of the victors but of the oppressed and those who join their struggle for emancipation. Yet advancing the rights of victims is not always such an easy proposition, as one may inadvertently promote the rights of some at the expense of others. As such, history needs to be entrusted with a moral and universal purpose.

4.3 Why should we assign a moral and universal purpose to social investigation?

In his book, *Their Morals and Ours*, Leon Trotsky wrote:

---

40 G. Orwell *1984* (Harcourt & Brace, 1949).
41 H. Marcuse, *One-Dimensional Man* (Beacon Press, 1964).
42 S. de Beauvoir, *The Second Sex* (Knopf, 1953).
43 A. Hoschild, *Bury the Chains: Prophets and Rebels in the Fight to Free an Empire's Slaves* (Houghton Mifflin, 2005).

> History has different yardsticks for the cruelty of the Northerners and the cruelty of the Southerners in the [American] civil war. A slave-owner who through cunning and violence shackles a slave in chains, and a slave who through cunning and violence breaks the chains . . . are not equal before a court or morality.[44]

Assuming for a moment that there are different criteria for judging the violence of the oppressors and the oppressed, surely the oppressed cannot be justified in moving from victory to revenge, thereby continuing the vicious cycle of oppression? In his *Wretched of the Earth*, Frantz Fanon[45] reminded us that oppressed people during the decolonisation process had internalised the forces of domination and brutality, and reproduced them when they achieved positions of power. While Fanon does not provide us with a solution for transcending this pernicious cycle, he correctly warned his readers that nationalism, as empowering as it may well be, is not a political programme, or a historical end.

This implies that not all purposes assigned to history are supportive of human rights. Realists contend that the desire for power and self-aggrandisement is the driving engine of history. 'The record of truth revealed by experience', wrote Lord Acton, 'is eminently practical, as an instrument of action and power that goes to making the future.'[46] Yet Acton, with other realists, warned that great powers tend to plant the seeds of their own demise; his adage contending that 'absolute power corrupts absolutely' is an unforgettable formulation of that danger. In this respect, the regimes of Louis XVI, Napoleon Bonaparte and Hitler followed Acton's prophecies. From this realist (and also in an odd way, post-structuralist) perspective, history is cyclical, making all achievements – progressive or otherwise – ephemeral, soon to be defeated by the reinstitution of the struggle of power and order.

If nationalism or power politics are to be rejected as historical ends, if we are to avoid circularity, or even regression, what ends need to be embraced as the purpose of history? Here, one powerful indication of historical progress is the fact that visions of which humans deserve rights have progressively widened toward the inclusion of all humanity. Moreover, despite continuing controversy over the substance of human rights, the UN Universal Declaration provides a powerful set of standards. To summarise the central implications: it is an unacceptable assault upon a person's dignity to be prevented from speaking one's mind, to be barred from participating in political life, to be forced by hunger to beg for food, or to be subjected to torture or the threat of death. While the Declaration is not a blueprint for political action, it does provide a vision of the future and a basis for measuring our progress. It also provides a clear set of foundational principles for international human rights law. If understanding the complexities of past and future human rights struggle remains an interdisciplinary social science and historical project, the strength of relevant international law, and the status of its transnational reach across the borders of sovereign states give us the clearest possible picture of how the key dimensions of human dignity are faring during a given moment in history.

44 L. Trotsky, *Their Morals and Ours* (Pathfinder Press [1938], 1973).
45 Fanon (n. 13).
46 J. Acton, *Essays on Freedom and Power* (World Publishing, 1964).

4.4 What mistakes should we avoid in the name of progressive change?

Many liberals have argued, with great optimism, that the progress of history was linear. Immanuel Kant and Thomas Paine, among others, saw the Enlightenment's ideals in terms of progress from tyranny to cosmopolitan rights. With the spread of social evolutionary theory in the nineteenth century, Auguste Comte's conception of history was divided into the theological, metaphysical and the positivist stage brought about by modern science. With Comte, Herbert Spencer and other social Darwinists, linear views of progress have shaped the underlying idea that history was moving from savagery and ignorance toward prosperity and peace. In the 1960s, these ideas resurfaced in the form of democratisation theory,[47] and more recently gained popularity in the work of Francis Fukuyama.[48] The problem with these perspectives on change is that they adopt a one-sequence strategy for social transformation superficially modelled after the Western world, while overlooking the fact that transitions from feudalism to capitalism and democracy in the West were accompanied by expansion, colonialism and neocolonialism, and included the destruction, enslavement or exploitation of masses of humans.

Ironically, we can find some overlap between some modernisation theories and orthodox Marxism, insofar as the latter approach privileges economic advancement and industrialisation as a necessary precondition for political emancipation. While some Orthodox Marxists[49] highlighted the importance of political reform during the historical stage preceding socialist freedom, the actual process of modernising and industrialising economically backward societies in the avowedly socialist states of Stalin's Soviet Union and Mao's China was accompanied by severe repression, purges and mass executions. The cost of progress toward achieving democracy under capitalism or justice under communism was far too high, suggesting that the notion of a linear sequence of events (e.g., security, then industrialisation, then political freedom) may be undermining the very goal of sustained progress.

Unfortunately, the Universal Declaration of Human Rights and other international human rights covenants do not provide clear guidelines for reconciling means and ends. Yet, human rights ideals have to be used as a normative framework for assessing both the acceptability and long-term viability of any proposed solution for advancing human rights. One can imagine forging a human rights agenda which synthesises the different solutions for achieving human rights and peace, based on combined efforts to integrate different families of rights – security, political, civil, economic, social and cultural rights, in ways that are tailored to different stages of social transition. Amartya Sen understood the importance of integrating the spectrum of rights at every stage of development;[50] that aspiration is equally applicable to war-torn societies aspiring to peace and human rights.

---

47 S. Lipset, *Political Man: The Social Bases of Politics* (Doubleday, 1960): W. Rostow, *The Stages of Economic Growth: A Non-Communist Manifesto* (Cambridge University Press, 1960): M. Friedman, *Capitalism and Freedom* (Chicago University Press, 1962).
48 F. Fukuyama, *The End of History and the Last Man* (Free Press, 1992).
49 K. Kautsky, 'Dictatorship and Democracy' and 'Transition to Capitalism', in P. Goode (ed. and transl.), *Karl Kautsky: Selected Writings* (St Martin's Press, 1983): E. Bernstein, *Evolutionary Socialism* (transl. E. Harvey) (Schocken Books, 1961).
50 A. Sen, *Democracy as Freedom* (Knopf, 1999).

4.5 Why is a historical dialectical relevant for a historical understanding of human rights?

A dialectic approach permeated by a comprehensive embrace to human rights is the most illuminating path to address dilemmas over transitions from poverty or tyranny. Envisioning a moral purpose to history does not imply the absence of setbacks. Indeed, history shows that major strides in human rights were followed by severe defeats. This does not mean that one step forward is inexorably neutralised by one step backward, as in the myth of Sisyphus. Despite long histories of barbarism and ruthless power, the human rights struggle survived the tests and contradictions of history, learning from setbacks, and providing an evolving corpus of shared conceptions of universal human rights that transcend class, ethnic and gender distinctions. Indeed, despite various episodes of regression, the history of human rights shows a clear dimension of progress: slavery has been abolished (even if intolerably it persists), democracy has spread, women in most of the world have been granted the right to vote, and living standards have risen for most of the world's inhabitants.

Many have criticised the historical dialectic for its allegedly predetermined narrative and its foregone political conclusions (e.g., Hegel's triumph of the Prussian state, or Marx's class-less society). What is often misunderstood is that a dialectic approach is not a meandering process driven by contradictions, articulated by a thesis–antithesis–synthesis (*aufhebung*) process, sacrificing people as lambs at the altars of the gods of history, in order to reach the awaited apex of morality at the end of time. On the contrary, while assigning a purpose to the dialectic is critical for avoiding the curse of historical circularity, the dialectic, as the Frankfurt School understands it, keeps readjusting the narrative of freedom to new hopes, or to different times and circumstances. Thus understood, history is a dialectic process of many progressive ends. It permits people to pause, reflect on their situation and reorient history toward different goals.

Insofar as self-conscious people shape history, history is not deterministic. It is unpredictable, as conscious actors can transcend pathological historical repetitions of conflicts and envision progress not just as an instrumental notion of freedom, but as the substantive actualisation of human rights. While history is transformed through a collision between matter and ideas, it remains formalistic unless it promotes universal progress. Sketching ways to move forward enables us to actualise a higher form of freedom, beyond the physical realm, so as not to fall victim to the clockwork mechanism of time or the greed for power. The Frankfurt School[51] insisted on inserting a Kantian, categorical imperative barometer into the heart of the unfolding dialectic mechanism – to assess whether moral intentions had been met in the process of actualisation, to gauge the price of liberty both in terms of means and ends. While Kant's a priori formulation of universal ethics does not provide a fully satisfying way to understand history, the ethical standards he proposed to serve us as a powerful antidote to excesses of power and historical backlashes.

4.6 What are the roles of interdisciplinary and multilevel analyses?

Human rights should be approached through multiple levels and disciplines. Looking down from a higher altitude, we can understand the broad trajectories of human rights across

---

51 M. Horkheimer, *Eclipse of Reason* (Continuum International, 1946): J. Habermas, *Theory of Communicative Action* (Beacon Press, 1984).

centuries, trajectories in which barbarism and human rights have been interspersed as if in a deadly cosmic contest.[52] From a terrestrial plane, we can focus our social inquiry into the fate of state and/or civil societies in which violations and struggles occurred;[53] from a psychological outlook, we can apprehend the psychological life of the collective in its political behaviour, its desires for revenge, or its hopes for a better future.[54] Because one may overlook changes that occur on one plane but not another, there is a need to approach human rights inquiries on more than one level of analysis. As such, international systemic analysis should be checked against historical local narratives, and vice versa. In other words, one must link subterranean seismic forces to social, economic, legal and institutional shifts, to lessons drawn from broad social history, if one seeks to gain a richer understanding of the direction of human rights progress. Reclaiming a historical approach of that sort, one committed to theoretical rigour and creativity, is a challenge from which the intellectual 'engagé' should not shy away.

While critical theory has originally fought against 'economism', which had been treated in isolation from other political spheres, it prefers combined interdisciplinary perspectives, drawn from political economy, sociology, cultural theory, art, philosophy, anthropology and history.[55] At the same time, it overcomes the endemic fragmentation that exists in many academic disciplines, as it argues for a holistic approach in its search for the manifold aspiration of emancipation. The task for the critical theorist is to connect these various trends, and to develop a comprehensive approach committed to human rights. How human rights can be enforced both in the legal and political dimension remains in this respect a critical issue in multilevel and interdisciplinary analysis.

4.7 How should we study the enforcement of human rights?

Multilevel efforts in the legal, political and civil society spheres remain more conducive to a comprehensive approach about ways to enforce human rights. As mentioned earlier, the UN Charter relies on the rights of sovereign states, which are the highest authority in the international order. Yet the UN also accepts and has moved closer to acting upon the approved principle that the international community can intervene when states harm their own citizens (e.g., the Genocide Convention, and the Responsibility to Protect (R2P) principles). Here critics can rightly point out that it is the leaders of weak or failed states who are always on trial, whereas those of great powers are left immune from indictment as international criminals. If power politics is a hindrance to universal justice, citizens of powerful states can still hold leaders accountable for their international crimes, and should certainly not turn a blind eye to the Pol Pots and Qadaffis of the world. Human rights advocates need to insist that all perpetrators of major human rights violations are held accountable.

There are also legal and political tensions within states which have never achieved any meaningful form of democracy and the rule of law, as there are states (whether impoverished or not) which have failed to deliver basic economic rights to their people. The violations of civil and political rights are deemed more urgent in international human rights law (see the

---

52 Benjamin (n. 40).
53 A. Gramsci, in G. Hoare and G. Smith (eds and transls), *Selections from the Prison Notebooks by Antonio Gramsci* (International Publishers, 1971).
54 E. Fromm, *Man for Himself* (Holt, Rinehart & Winston, 1947).
55 Bronner (n. 37).

ICCPR). Yet it is surely the case that civil and political rights have little meaning when detached from economic ones. In the words of the nineteenth-century socialist Louis Blanc: 'What does the right to be cured matter to a sick man whom no one is curing? Right considered abstractly is the mirage that has kept the people in abused condition since 1789.'[56] In this respect, international political will is important for mobilising assistance to the most impoverished, and for condemning those who have a surplus of resources but do not distribute them equitably.

Broadly speaking, a republican government (as Kant used the term), with its separation of powers and constitution (or fundamental laws), coupled with a fair modicum of popular representation, has proven to be the best form of government over time for implementing rights and limiting wars of aggression against similarly governed countries. Yet arriving at this goal is an enormous challenge for countries which have never experienced democracy. While legal scholarship has addressed questions of transition (e.g., the literatures on transitional justice and on constitutional design), social scientists have not fully taken up the challenge of incorporating the full spectrum of human rights principles into political transitions. For instance, for those who are undergoing a revolution from below, the destination may seem clear, but the path is hard to navigate: it requires ripe revolutionary conditions, a vibrant civil society with a leading hegemonic group capable of uniting disparate social factions in civil society under a common worldview, hopefully inspired by universal human rights principles. The process of consolidation demands a balancing act between the need for significant rights-based changes and the simultaneous need to prevent social collapse – a challenge that is particularly daunting if there is no hegemonic group with the capacity to rule effectively. Whether revolutions are from above or from below, the consolidation process has to avoid entirely uprooting old institutions; it is more analogous to pruning diseased branches without killing the tree in the process. This challenge is faced after every successful revolution: keeping the old bureaucracy (civil and economic) and military intact will likely cripple needed change, while removing it wholesale would likely lead to social collapse. Human rights scholarship should envision steps toward a practical synthesis between human rights progress and social order.

In sum, building on the achievements of international legal rights scholarship, this toolkit, drawn from reflections on Kant and the Frankfurt school, offers a preliminary way to approach the critical questions posed in human rights scholarship. It calls for theoretically informed historical inquiry into how specific forms of oppression have generated human rights struggle at different stages, why human rights rebellions have lagged or why the oppressed remained silent. It defends scholarship that takes the side of the unfortunate and the marginalised, and supports changes guided by a universal purpose. It rejects the cost of progress made under the conditions of unfettered capitalism, totalitarianism or communism – and as such abides by Kantian ethics and related international legal rights – to adjudicate whether normative intent and practical actions are synchronised. It recognises the importance of a historical dialectic, not merely because institutional contradictions create the conditions for social change (and vice versa), but also because progressive social movements have to be readjusted to alleviate the painful cost of progress. It engages various disciplines in order to understand the complexity of oppression and opportunities under its emancipatory guidelines. It is a multi-disciplinary dialectical approach committed to social progress, and avoids the pitfalls of

---

56 M. Ishay, *History of Human Rights: From Ancient Times to the Era of Globalization* (University of California Press, 2008) 140.

relativism, or a predetermined *telos*. It proposes a multilevel effort to enforce human rights, which integrates scholarship on law, political change and institution-building committed to human rights principles as both means and ends. Human rights scholarship is well positioned to explore new frontiers for societies suffering from the impasses of war, economic malaise and political repression. That is progress enough to inspire future scholarly efforts to advance a more enriched, programmatic vision, in the indomitable spirit rekindled by the 1948 Universal Declaration of Human Rights.

Select bibliography

S. Bronner, 'Introduction' of *Critical Theory and Its Theorists* (Routledge, 2002).

E. Carr, *What Is History?* (Knopf, 1961).

J. Donnelly, *Universal Human Rights in Theory and Practice* (Cornell University Press, 2003).

H. Grotius, *The Law of War and Peace* (transl. F. Keisley) (Bobs-Merill, 1925).

M. Ishay, *History of Human Rights: From Ancient Times to the Era of Globalization* (University of California Press, 2008).

I. Kant, *Perpetual Peace*, at: http://www.gutenberg.org/etext/26585.

P. Lauren, *The Evolution of International Human Rights: Vision Seen*, 2nd edn (University of Pennsylvania Press, 2003).

T. Marshall, *Class, Citizenship and Social Development* (Anchor Books, 1965).

H. Shue, *Basic Rights: Subsistence, Affluence, and US Foreign Policy* (Princeton University Press, 1996).

6

The relationship of international human rights law and general international law: hermeneutic constraint, or pushing the boundaries?

Scott Sheeran

1 Introduction

The relationship between general international law (GIL) and international human rights law (IHRL) is a complex narrative of tension, evolution and juxtaposition. IHRL and its strong proponents the 'human rightists' have been criticised for separatist tendencies and single-mindedness, 'human rights triumphalism', and a lack of understanding that it is a 'sub-branch' of international law subject to the latter's rules and methodology.[1] By contrast, human rights lawyers have argued that IHRL is a separate regime and the significant influence of IHRL on GIL 'is highly desirable in order to *soften* the international legal order's predominantly state-centred nature and to accommodate the special, non-reciprocal nature of . . . human rights' obligations.[2]

A typical consideration of this broad topic centres on the influence of one *corpus juris* on the other.[3] As such, the analysis has primarily considered the doctrinal impacts and their

---

1 A. Pellet, ' "Human Rightism" and International Law', Gilbert Amado Lecture (18 July 2000) 6, available at: http://www.alainpellet.eu/Documents/PELLET%20-%202000%20-%20Human%20 rightism%20and%20international%20law%20(G.%20Amado).pdf (accessed 10 February 2013); M. Kamminga/ILA, 'Final Report on the Impact of International Human Rights Law on General International Law', in M. Kamminga and M. Scheinin (eds), *The Impact of International Human Rights Law on General International Law* (OUP, 2009) 4; I. Brownlie, *Principles of Public International Law,* 6th edn (OUP, 2003) 529–30.
2 ILA Final Report (n. 1) 4, 21 (Conclusion 1).
3 E.g. see ILA Final Report and the various subject-specific chapters (e.g. law of treaties, treaty inter-pretation, reservations, state succession, formation of customary international law, structure of international obligations, immunity, consular notification, diplomatic protection, state responsi-bility) in Kamminga and Scheinin (n. 1); A. Bianchi, 'Immunity versus Human Rights: The Pinochet Case' 10(2) *European Journal of International Law* (1999) 237; Kamminga, 'State Succession in Respect of Human Rights Treaties', 7 *European Journal of International Law* (1996) 469.

direction of travel, and missed an opportunity to consider the relationship at a deeper, holistic level, including in interpretation and hermeneutics. The opportunity is thus not seized to uncover and understand the structural as well as substantive effects of the growing role of human rights in the international legal order. In recent times, a key manifestation of this topic has been the debate on fragmentation of international law, including the UN International Law Commission (ILC)'s reports on this topic.[4] The contours of the general debate are well summed up by Lindroos:

> International law has become more specialised and multi-levelled as special regimes, systems, and sub-regimes have emerged. Each such system or regime, such as the law of the sea, environmental law, human rights law, or trade law, functions in its own normative environment, with distinct particularities and often on the basis of differing institutional and legal rationales. . . . [T]hese legal orders appear to exist in a normative jungle, where each system may create solutions entirely opposite to the solutions of another system, and where general international law may be interpreted and applied in different ways. . . . Although these systems are part of the wider framework of international law, their relationship to it and to each other is far from clear.[5]

The tensions in the fragmentation debate are particularly acute in the context of the relationship between IHRL and GIL, and concern systemic issues such as normative hierarchy, basis of obligation, and doctrinal issues such as jurisdiction and immunity, and rules of interpretation. The ILC and the International Law Association (ILA) have both sought to resolve the tension, broadly speaking, through affirming the unity of international law and a 'reconciliation' or 'harmonisation' approach.[6] They have concluded that there are no self-contained and hermeneutically sealed regimes in international law.[7] This approach has the effect of re-entrenching, albeit with some caveats, the state–centric paradigm of international law based on positivism, state sovereignty and subjecthood.

This traditional perspective also does not fully recognise the legal evolution achieved through the normative growth of human rights, which has undoubtedly challenged the mainstream paradigm of international law. While the *corpus juris* of human rights is embedded in and constrained by the superstructure of international law, it has been successful in pushing and enlarging the discipline's boundaries. As Reiter notes, the conclusions on the relationship

---

4 ILC, 'Conclusions of the Work of the Study Group on the Fragmentation of International Law: Difficulties Arising from the Diversification and Expansion of International Law' (2006) (adopted by the ILC and appearing in the *Yearbook of the International Law Commission, 2006,* vol. II, Part Two); ILC, 'Fragmentation of International Law: Difficulties Arising from the Diversification and Expansion of International Law: Report of the Study Group of the International Law Commission Finalised by Martti Koskenniemi' (2006) UN Doc. A/CN.4/L.682; G. Hafner, 'Risks Ensuing from Fragmentation of International Law', Official Records of the General Assembly, Fifty-fifth session, Supplement No. 10 (2000) UN Doc. A/55/10, Annex at 321.
5 Anja Lindroos, 'Addressing Norm Conflicts in a Fragmented Legal System: The Doctrine of Lex Specialis', 74 *Nordic J. Int'l L.* (2005) 27–66 at 31.
6 ILC Conclusions (n. 4) para. 10; ILC Report (n. 4) paras. 37–43; ILA Final Report (n. 1) 1.
7 E.g. see ILC Report (n. 4) para. 148 (quoting Arangio-Ruiz that 'none of the supposedly self-contained regimes seems to materialize *in concreto*').

'are often too modest; falling short of accounting for the actual impact of human rights *sensu largo* and community interests on general international law'.[8]

It is challenging to address so large a subject in a short chapter. In addition to the two-way influence, there are a range of other important questions to consider. Is IHRL simply a sub-regime of international law? Where norm conflict exists what are the optimal techniques for interpretive resolution? What is the relationship of IHRL and GIL at the level of the theory of international law? This chapter will explore these key issues for the relationship in three main sections: (a) the foundation principles of the relationship; (b) the constraints upon human rights by GIL; and (c) the pushing and enlarging of the disciplinary boundaries of international law by human rights. The chapter will finish with a few key conclusions.

2 The foundation principles (real or perceived) of the relationship

This section examines the real or perceived foundations of the relationship between GIL and IHRL, and helps to orient the analysis of the following sections. The points made are of course general, and will be considered critically further on. It is necessary at the outset to note the general meaning of the two bodies of law in focus. The ILA Committee's Final Report on the Impact of International Human Rights Law on General International Law (the ILA Report) described its mandate as 'not merely human rights law *stricto sensu,* but any international norm capable of conferring rights and duties directly on individuals regardless of nationality, including under international humanitarian law and international criminal law'.[9] This is a broad perspective on 'human rights' law although one which is appropriate. It covers the various international human rights treaties and instruments such as the Universal Declaration of Human Rights (UDHR), as well as aspects of cognate fields such as international humanitarian law (IHL), international criminal law and international refugee law. The central focus is international law, which provides rights, duties and protections for people, and is concerned with respecting and promoting the 'inherent dignity' of the human being.

General international law, on the other hand, is a concept that is not usually defined. It has been characterised as endowed with a 'certain degree of imprecision' even though it has featured in international instruments.[10] The ILC does not try to precisely define GIL and indicates that it is best to consider what is 'general' by reference to its logical opposite, namely what is 'special'.[11] The key examples of GIL include the law of responsibility, as codified in

---

8 A. Reiter, 'Much Ado About Nothing? (Publication Review: M. T. Kamminga and M. Scheinin, The Impact of Human Rights Law on General International Law)' 4(1) *Euro. J. of Legal St.* (2011) 214–24 at 222.

9 ILA Final Report (n. 1) 2; ILC Report (n. 4) para. 56; see also A. Cassimatis, 'International Humanitarian Law, International Human Rights Law, and Fragmentation of International Law' 56(3) ICLQ (2007) 623–39 at 628, 633 (he refers to the 'common humanitarian foundations of IHL and IHRL' and that '[b]oth regimes have a protective purpose').

10 A. Gourgourinis, 'General/Particular International Law and Primary/Secondary Rules: Unitary Terminology of a Fragmented System' 22(4) *European Journal of International Law* (2011) 993–1026 at 1011–12; M. Wood, 'The International Tribunal for the Law of the Sea and General International Law', 22 *Int'l J. Marine & Coastal L.* (2007) 351 at 354; G. Buzzini, 'La «généralité» du droit international général: réflexions sur la polysémie d'un concept', 108 *Revue Générale de Droit International Public* (2004) 381 at 391.

11 ILC Conclusions (n. 4) para. 10, fn. 6; ILC Report (n. 4) 254–56.

the ILC's two sets of draft articles,[12] or the law of treaties as codified in the Vienna Convention on the Law of Treaties (VCLT). In practice, lawyers usually deal with the basic definition of GIL in a 'contextual' way.[13] While GIL is commonly associated with 'secondary' rules and customary international law that applies to all states, as the ILA notes and elaborated further below, it possibly includes other forms of unwritten law such as 'fundamental' or 'constitutional' principles of international law.[14] In this sense, GIL is closely related to, but not synonymous with, the broader term of international law or public international law that describes the whole discipline. For some purposes in this chapter, such as considering conceptual origins, the term GIL will be used somewhat interchangeably with international law.

2.1 A unitary relationship not fragmentation

At a broad level, GIL and 'special regimes' such as IHRL are cast in a unitary relationship and not one characterised by fragmentation.[15] IHRL is seen as a sub-branch of the discipline of international law. The tension, therefore, is whether to emphasise 'the special, distinctive nature of international human rights law and assume . . . that the rules and principles of [GIL], or at least some of them, are not applicable to it'.[16] This question is identified with the general issue of 'self-contained regimes' within international law, which is a key focus of the fragmentation debate. The ILC, for example, focused its fragmentation work on the substantive issue of 'the splitting up of the law into highly specialized "boxes" that claim relative autonomy from each other and from the general law'.[17] In this regard, the ILC recognised, as many others have, that international human rights law is a special regime.[18]

The recognition of special regimes does not lead to an acceptance of completely self-contained regimes in international law. As the ILC notes, such regimes are not fully isolated from GIL ('formed closed legal circuits') nor do they exclude future recourse to remedies under the law of responsibility.[19] In his ILC report, Special Rapporteur Arangio-Ruiz defined self-contained regimes as sets of rules that were hermetically isolated from international law, and found 'none of the supposedly self-contained regimes seems to materialize *in concreto*'.[20] It is clear when reviewing the decisions and views of human rights courts

---

12 See James Crawford, *The International Law Commission's Articles on State Responsibility: Introduction, Text and Commentaries* (Cambridge University Press, 2002); ILC, Draft Articles on the Responsibility of International Organizations, UN Doc. A/66/10 (2011).

13 ILC Conclusions (n. 4) para. 10, fn. 6.

14 ILA, 'Final Report of the Committee on the Formation of Customary (General) International Law, Statement of Principles Applicable to the Formation of General Customary International Law, Report of the Sixty-Ninth Conference, London' (2000) at 716–17; cf. ILC, 'Fourth Report on the Law of Treaties by Mr. G. G. Fitzmaurice, Special Rapporteur' [1959] vol II Yearbook *of the ILC* 42, para. 1.

15 ILC Conclusions (n. 4) para. 10; ILC Report (n. 4) paras. 37–43; ILA Final Report (n. 1) 1; Reiter (n. 8) 215.

16 ILA Final Report (n. 1) 1–2.

17 ILC Report (n. 4) paras. 13, 129. The ILC referred to sub-disciplines or 'special' fields such as: international human rights law, WTO law, European law/EU law, humanitarian law and space law.

18 ILC Conclusions (n. 4) para. 14.

19 ILC Report (n. 4) 123; B. Simma and D. Pulkowski, 'Of Planets and the Universe: Self-contained Regimes in International Law', 17 *European Journal of International Law* (2006) 483 492–93.

20 G. Arangio-Ruiz, Fourth Report, Yearbook of the ILC, vol. II, Part One (1992) 40, para. 112.

and treaty bodies that they make constant use of GIL, and it is not excluded in the application and interpretation of their special regimes.[21] The ILC notes that 'such exclusion may not be even conceptually possible'.[22]

The basic relationship of GIL and IHRL is therefore conceived as one of unity. As IHRL is a 'special regime', and not general or complete, it relies on the foundations of international law (as manifest in GIL) for its implementation and very existence. This unity does not resolve inherent tensions between GIL and IHRL, which are also not unique to these two bodies of law. Norm conflict is a fact of life for international law, and indeed all law.[23]

The ILC and ILA both conclude that special regimes like IHRL are a part of international law – i.e. general regime and special regime – and therefore they should be reconciled or harmonised with GIL. Indeed, the fragmentation debate presupposes there is a priori a unified legal system.[24] The ILC uses the 'principle of harmonisation' to confirm that it 'is a generally accepted principle that when several norms bear on a single issue they should, to the extent possible, be interpreted so as to give rise to a single set of compatible obligations'.[25] The ILA Report also states that it 'unanimously considers that the *reconciliation* approach is preferable to the fragmentation approach, if only because it is overwhelmingly in conformity with international practice'.[26] The unity of international law is thus a foundation stone of the relationship.

2.2 Basis and purpose of GIL and IHRL

It is clear that PIL and IHRL have distinct origins and *raisons d'être*. The discipline of international law is traditionally considered as the rules and processes created by sovereign states to govern their interactions with each other.[27] Since the development of modern international law from the time of the Treaties of Westphalia in 1648, the discipline has developed a remarkable commonality of structure and method based in legal positivism as well as obligations deriving from state consent. The rationale was a dispute settlement-focused model of law, based on reciprocity and bundles of bilateral obligations, which promoted the peaceful interaction of autonomous, sovereign (and self-interested) states. In simple terms, the sovereign states were bound by international law to which they consented as, in the Austinian sense, there was no higher authority than the sovereign.

The classical positivism of international law and its emphasis on state consent stands in stark contrast to the general foundations of IHRL, that is, the 'inherent dignity' of the human being and constraint of state or public power.[28] The motivating force and origins of human

---

21 ILC Report (n. 4) para. 172.
22 Ibid., para. 152(5).
23 ILC Conclusions (n. 4) para. 1.
24 S. Singh, 'The Potential of International Law: Fragmentation and Ethics', 24 *Leiden J. of Int'l L.* (2011) 23–43, at 31; Simma and Pulkowski (n. 19) 495–96.
25 ILC Conclusions (n. 4) para. 4.
26 ILA Final Report (n. 1) 1–2.
27 E.g. see Rosalyn Higgins, *Problems and Processes: International Law and How We Use It* (OUP, 1994) 1–2.
28 See ILC Report (n. 1) para. 15 (' "Human rights law" aims to protect the interests of individuals'); G. Verdirame, 'Human Rights in Political and Legal Theory' and N. Rodley, 'Non State Actors and Human Rights', in this volume.

rights are found in liberal philosophy and political theory, as evident in the constitutions of France and the United States; the international labour movement's experiences during the inter-war period; the Holocaust; and the UN Charter, which led to the adoption of the UDHR in 1948; and even ecclesiastical thought.[29] While the origins of international law are inter-state, the main focus of human rights is intra-state (which also makes it somewhat different in character to many other special regimes of international law). As Rodley indicates, 'the original idea of human rights was one which was understood to mean those rights that the individual could assert against the organized power of the State.'[30] The focus is thus on the individual, their rights and social compact with the state, and at the international level these obligations are essentially non-reciprocal in nature. As the UN Human Rights Committee has recognised, international treaties are normally 'exchanges of obligations between States', but 'it is otherwise in human rights treaties, which are for the benefit of persons within [the state's] jurisdiction.'[31]

In the fragmentation context, the ILC has recognised that special regimes such as IHRL have their own unified object and purpose: 'The significance of a special regime often lies in the way its norms express a unified *object and purpose* . . . Each rule-complex or "regime" comes with its own principles, its own form of expertise and its own "ethos".'[32] Accordingly, while GIL and IHRL are part of a unified system of law, they have distinct conceptual bases and origins, and a different 'object and purpose'.[33] That said, the mainstream source of obligation of both bodies of law is still considered to be ultimately established, justified and explained via the traditional positivist methodology of state consent.[34]

2.3 Relationship of primary and secondary rules

A central connection between GIL on the one hand, and IHRL and other special regimes on the other, is through the so-called 'secondary rules' of international law.[35] The concept of primary and secondary rules of law, generally attributed to Hart, essentially concerns the distinction between substantive and adjectival (or procedural) rules.[36] The ILC refers to primary rules as 'rules laying down particular rights and obligations' and secondary rules as

---

29 For further discussion, see W. Osianytski, 'The Historical Development of Human Rights' in this volume and Verdirame ibid.

30 Rodley (n. 28).

31 UNHRC, General Comment No. 24: Issues relating to reservations made upon ratification or accession to the Covenant or the Optional Protocols thereto, or in relation to declarations under Article 41 of the Covenant (1994) UN Doc. CCPR/C/21/Rev.1/Add.6, paras 8, 17. Non-reciprocity is also recognised in various cases such as: *Reservations to the Convention on the Prevention and Punishment of the Crime of Genocide*, Advisory Opinion, ICJ Rep (1951) 21, at 23; *Loizidou v Turkey (preliminary objections)*, Application No. 15318/89, ECtHR, Series A no. 310 (1995) para. 70, quoting *Ireland v United Kingdom* (App no. 5310/71) Series A no. 25 (1978) para. 239; Inter-American Court of Human Rights (IACtHR), Advisory Opinion OC-2/82, *The Effect of Reservations on the Entry into Force of the American Convention on Human Rights (Arts 74 and 75)*, IACtHR Series A No. 2 (1982).

32 ILC Conclusions (n. 4) para. 13; ILC Report (n. 4) para. 15 (emphasis added).

33 The 'object and purpose' is a concept generally associated with law of treaties and reservations, see Vienna Convention on the Law of Treaties 8 ILM 679 (1969) Art. 19(c).

34 Pellet (n. 1) 5.

35 Simma and Pulkowski (n. 19) 492–93.

36 H.L.A. Hart, *The Concept of Law* (OUP, 1961) 90–92.

'rules about rule-creation and change, responsibility and dispute settlement'.[37] The latter include rules of GIL such as state responsibility, jurisdiction and immunity. While this distinction has been criticised as an unclear one in theory, others consider that it 'in fact plays a crucial normative role in the international legal argument'.[38] The ILC relied on the distinction in its work on the law of responsibility, as it proved useful as an analytical device even if in practice there was a degree of interdependence.

Most multilateral human rights treaties go beyond primary rules, and establish a 'system' of sorts to address the monitoring, implementation and interpretation of the substantive obligations, which by definition will include secondary rules. The ILC's early work on state responsibility thus noted the competence of states to establish special treaty regimes was both central and also problematic for its codification work. This was because, as Riphagen indicated:

> International law as it stands today is not modelled on one system only, but on a variety of international sub-systems within each of which the so-called 'primary rules' and the so-called 'secondary rules' are *closely intertwined – indeed, inseparable.*[39]

This intersection is a significant cause of tension between GIL and IHRL – that is, between the rules of human rights and secondary rules of international law. In IHRL, the UN Human Rights Committee established by the International Covenant on Civil and Political Rights (ICCPR) determines the scope and application of the treaty obligations, and may consider complaints under the Optional Protocol and make recommendations for remedies. This adjudicative and interpretive role may operate in tension with the customary international law on jurisdiction and immunity, the VCLT rules of interpretation, and the law of responsibility reflected in the ILC Articles on State Responsibility. The secondary rules of GIL are thus part of the 'normative environment' of a special regime such as IHRL, which itself is embedded more broadly in international law.

2.4 Interpretation and priority: the VCLT and lex specialis

In the context of a unitary relationship of GIL and IHRL, there is a need for tools of interpretation and prioritisation to assist with resolving the inevitable conflict of norms. As elaborated below, there are many areas in which human rights may appear to conflict with GIL. The tools of legal reasoning either harmonise these apparent conflicts through interpretation or, if that is not possible, establish relationships of priority between the norms.[40]

---

37 ILC, Study Group on Fragmentation, Fragmentation of International Law Topic (a): The function and scope of the lex specialis rule and the question of 'self-contained regimes': An outline, available at: http://untreaty.un.org/ilc/sessions/55/fragmentation_outline.pdf (accessed on 12 March 2013). See also A. Marschik, 'Too Much Order? The Impact of Special Secondary Norms on the Unity and Efficacy of the International Legal System' 9 *European Journal of International Law* 9 (1998) 212–39 at 212; U. Lindefalk, 'State Responsibility and the Primary–Secondary Rules Terminology – The Role of Language for an Understanding of the International Legal System', 78 *Nordic J. Int'l L.* (2009) 53; Gourgourinis (n. 10).
38 Gourgourinis (n. 10) 1025.
39 W. Riphagen, 'Third Report on State Responsibility', *Yearbook of the ILC* vol. II, Part 1 (1982) 28, para. 35.
40 C. McLachlan, 'The Principle of Systemic Integration and Article 31(3)(c) of the Vienna Convention', 54 ICLQ (2005) 279–320 at 286, though it is not a neat distinction between the two.

The ILC Report of the Study Group on fragmentation (the ILC Report), for example, refers to four ways to helpfully understand or deal with normative conflict: (i) special and general law; (ii) prior and subsequent law; (iii) law at different hierarchical levels; and (iv) the 'relations of law to its "normative environment" more generally'.[41] These approaches are tools that attempt to clarify the relationship between two or more norms in conflict, and may thus help justify a particular normative choice or conclusion. As the ILC notes, they 'do not do this mechanically, however, but rather as "guidelines"'.[42]

The VCLT provides general rules of interpretation for all treaties including human rights treaties.[43] It codifies the law of treaties and is now considered customary international law. The ILC Report states that 'one can draw from practice and literature . . . that articles 31 and 32 of the VCLT are always applicable unless specifically set aside by other principles of interpretation',[44] and also suggests this has been affirmed by practically all international law-applying bodies.[45] Article 31 sets out the 'general rules of interpretation' (e.g. good faith, ordinary meaning, object and purpose, and context) while Article 32 provides the 'supplementary means of interpretation' (e.g. the preparatory work of a treaty or *travaux préparatoires*).

A further important rule of interpretation, which is not mentioned in the VCLT, is *lex specialis derogat legi generali* (*lex specialis*).[46] This maxim suggests that whenever two or more norms deal with the same subject matter, priority should be given to the norm that is more specific.[47] It is a generally accepted technique of interpretation and conflict resolution, which has a long pedigree in international law.[48] The role of *lex specialis* is important for the unitary relationship of GIL with special regimes such as IHRL. It is relevant in respect of competing substantive or primary rules within IHRL, between GIL and IHRL, and for IHRL's relationship with other special regimes such as IHL.[49]

While not explicit in the VCLT, it is generally understood that treaties displace or super-sede customary international law.[50] In this regard, *lex specialis* is reflective of the informal hierarchy between treaties and custom in international law. As the ILC Report notes, 'treaties generally enjoy priority over custom and particular treaties over general treaties . . . This

---

41 ILC Report (n. 4) para. 18.
42 Ibid., paras 34–36.
43 VCLT (n. 33).
44 ILC Report (n. 4) para. 174.
45 Ibid., fn. 231. The ILC Report lists cases and decisions from the ICJ, the WTO dispute settlement system, the IAmCtHRs, NAFTA, Iran–US Claims Tribunal, and the ECtHR. See also Lindroos (n. 5) 48–64.
46 For examples on the application of *lex specialis* in international law, see Lindroos (n. 5) 48–64; J. Pauwelyn, *Conflict of Norms in Public International Law: How WTO Law Relates to Other Rules of International Law* (Cambridge University Press, 2003); Nancie Prud'homme, 'Lex Specialis: Oversimplifying a More Complex and Multifaceted. Relationship?', 40 *Isr. L. Rev.* (2007) 355–95.
47 ILC Conclusions (n. 4) para. 5.
48 ILC Report (n. 4) para. 56. See also A. McNair, *The Law of Treaties*, 2nd edn (Clarendon Press, 1961) 393–99; Articles on State Responsibilty (n. 12) Art. 55; Simma and Pulkowski (n. 19) 487.
49 E.g. For discussion of IHRL, IHL and *lex specialis*, see *Legality of the Threat or Use of Nuclear Weapons, Advisory Opinion*, ICJ Rep 1996, para. 25 and *Legal Consequences of the Construction of a Wall in the Occupied Palestinian Territory, Advisory Opinion*, ICJ Rep 2004, para. 106; Prud'homme (n. 46) 372.
50 ILC Report (n. 4) para. 79 ('That treaty rules enjoy priority over custom is merely an incident of the fact that most of general international law is *jus dispositivum* so that parties are entitled to dero-gate from it by establishing specific rights or obligations to govern their behaviour').

informal hierarchy follows from no legislative enactment but, emerges as a "forensic" or a "natural" aspect of legal reasoning.'[51] It is important to note that an underlying rationale for *lex specialis* is grounded in state *consent* and *intent*.[52]

IHRL is a form of *lex specialis* to GIL, not only by providing detailed substantive primary rules, but also by displacing some secondary rules of GIL (e.g. right to a remedy, as in law of responsibility). The ILC Report indicates that IHRL is a special regime which is not self-contained, and suggests that *lex specialis* and the VCLT's rules of interpretation are a central tool for organising the relationship of GIL with special regimes.[53] There are obviously limits to the *lex specialis* concept's utility, however, as the relationship and resolution of conflicting norms is both complex and debateable.[54] The ILC notes that, in terms of codifying and applying *lex specialis*, '[n]o general, context-independent answers can be given.'[55] Importantly, the ILC also states that the concept 'may be *offset* by normative hierarchies or informal views about "relevance" or "importance"', which suggests that general rules (e.g. of GIL) may trump specific rules (e.g. of IHRL) due to their overriding character.[56]

3 The situation of IHRL within GIL: the hermeneutic constraint

IHRL is applied and interpreted within a powerful hermeneutic constraint of the rules and structure of GIL. This interaction is shaped by a dialectic of harmony and conflict. The ILC's fragmentation work adopted a wide notion of norm conflict – stating that it is almost everywhere and 'that most forms of international behaviour also have some bearing on human rights'.[57] The norm conflict concerns not just the rules or obligations, but also the objectives of different bodies of law or treaties.[58] The human rights treaty bodies (e.g. UN Human Rights Committee, European and Inter-American Courts of Human Rights) and national courts regularly refer to rules and principles of GIL, which concern not only treaty interpretation but also matters such as statehood, jurisdiction and immunity.[59] In doing so there may be a conflict with IHRL, as will be demonstrated below, which is often resolved in favour of GIL. This section will briefly address four areas that demonstrate this general point: (i) secondary rules as systemic constraints on human rights; (ii) subjects/objects and limitations on non-state actors' obligations; (iii) jurisdiction and immunities precluding access to courts and remedies; and (iv) the dominant role of the VCLT and *lex specialis*.

---

51 Ibid., para. 85.
52 Paulwelyn (n. 46) 385–439 (the 'most closest [*sic*], detailed, precise or strongest expression of state consent, as it relates to a particular circumstance, ought to prevail').
53 ILC Conclusions (n. 4) para. 14 ('[a] special regime may prevail over general law under the same conditions as *lex specialis* generally').
54 Simma and Pulkowski (n. 19) 486 ('While the wording of Article 55 is short and straightforward, it is both one of the most important and most debatable provisions of the ILC's Articles'); Prud'homme (n. 46); ILC Report (n. 4) para. 112.
55 ILC Report (n. 4) para. 119.
56 Ibid. para. 58 (emphasis added) and references in fn. 62. See also I. Sinclair, *The Vienna Convention on the Law of Treaties,* 2nd edn (Manchester University Press, 1984) 95–98.
57 ILC Report (n. 4) paras 25, 117. See also Singh (n. 24) 28; Cassimatis (n. 9) 627.
58 Cassimatis (n. 9) 627; ILC Report (n. 4) paras 21, 43.
59 See L. Caflisch and Antonio C. Trindade, 'Les conventions americaine et européenne des droits de l'homme et le droit international général', 108 *Revue Générale de Droit International Public* (2004); ILC Report (n. 4) para. 161.

3.1 Secondary rules as systemic constraints

At the systemic level, the foundation concepts and rules of GIL, including secondary rules of international law, may dominate, constrain and even overrule aspects of IHRL. The doctrine and practice alike suggests that GIL, including general customary law and general principles of law, is always applicable.[60] In terms of GIL and the variety of sub-regimes of international law, there is a close linkage between the special regime (e.g. IHRL) and secondary rules of GIL.[61] In this regard, Simma and Pulkowski state that 'general international law provides a *systemic fabric* from which no special legal regime is completely decoupled'.[62] Gourgourinis goes further and suggests that 'it becomes apparent that a primary norm cannot prevail as "special" to a secondary norm'.[63] This latter argument appears accurate, for example, in cases in which there is a tension between an individual's right to access to courts or a remedy and state immunity. For these reasons, many rules of GIL – e.g. on immunity, jurisdiction and subjects – are seen as 'justifiable limitations' on the subsystem of IHRL rules and obligations.

The ILC's work on fragmentation recognised that strong or more 'exclusive' forms of special regimes may have their own secondary rules which claim 'priority over the secondary rules in the general law of state responsibility'.[64] The two main examples provided by the ILC include: (i) the *Tehran Hostages* case, in which the ICJ identified diplomatic law as a self-contained regime as it set up its own 'internal' system for reacting to breaches;[65] and (ii) the WTO dispute settlement system, as the Dispute Settlement Understanding (DSU) excludes unilateral determinations of breach or countermeasures outside the 'specific subsystem' of the WTO regime.[66]

The ILC's work both on fragmentation and state responsibility suggests that human rights treaties are a weaker form of a special regime, which generally does not exclude rules of GIL.[67] The ILC Report on fragmentation, for example, indicates in relation to the European Convention of Human Rights, it 'has not been conceived as a self-contained regime in the sense that recourse to general law would have been prevented'.[68] The ILC Report adds that on 'the contrary, the Court makes constant use of general international law with the presumption that the Convention rights should be *read in harmony* with that general law and without an a priori assumption that Convention rights would be overriding'.[69] This contrasts somewhat with the view of Simma and others that GIL as *lex generalis* is the 'fall back' from IHRL.[70] Further, as addressed below under the discussion of interpretation, it suggests that secondary rules and 'harmony' also engage elements of priority and hierarchy.

---

60 See Arangio-Ruiz (n. 20) 36–38, paras 99–106; ILC Report (n. 4) para. 174.
61 Riphagen (n. 39) paras 35, 54; ILC Report (n. 4) paras 179, 182.
62 Simma and Pulkowski (n. 19) 492–93, 529.
63 Gourgourinis (n. 10) 1025–26.
64 ILC Report (n. 4) paras 124, 134, 150.
65 *Case Concerning the United States Diplomatic and Consular Staff in Tehran (United States of America v Iran)* ICJ Rep 1980, para. 86; ILC Report (n. 4) para. 124. Cf. Simma and Pulkowski (n. 19) 485.
66 Dispute Settlement Understanding (DSU), Art. 23, Annex 2 to the WTO Agreement (1994) 33 ILM 1226; G. Marceau, 'WTO Dispute Settlement and Human Rights', 13 *European Journal of International Law* (2002) 757–79; ILC Report (n. 4) para. 134.
67 J. Crawford, 'Third Report on State Responsibility', UN Doc. A/CN.4/507/Add.4 (2001) para. 420; ILC Report (n. 4) para. 150.
68 ILC Report (n. 4) para. 164.
69 Ibid. (emphasis added).
70 Simma and Pulkowski (n. 19) 507–10.

3.2 Subjects, objects and non-state actors' obligations

The non-state actors (NSAs) and 'subjects' debate in international law is sometimes seen as a manifestation of unfulfilled claims and aspirations of human rights lawyers. The more ambitious claims concerning NSAs are one element of the 'human rightism' criticisms. The traditional positivist approach focuses on 'subjects' of international law, of which states are the primary manifestation. Individuals are seen as 'objects' and not 'subjects', and only the latter are endowed in international law with sovereignty and a full range of rights and obligations. In the *Danzig* case (1925), the Permanent Court of International Justice (PCIJ) recognised that nothing prevents individuals from acquiring rights directly under a treaty if that was the intent of the state parties.[71] This traditional position has been challenged by the growing role on the global plane of the individual and other NSAs, such as armed opposition groups, non-governmental organisations (NGOs) and multinational enterprises.[72] This has led to two main claims closely connected to human rights: first, that IHRL obligations apply to NSAs, as well as to states; and second, that individuals have a direct role and status within the international legal system.

The ILA Report recognises, as various scholars do, that the growing importance of NSAs has led to only a 'partial alteration of the *status quo* in international law'.[73] Despite the innovative and expansive arguments of Clapham and others on this issue,[74] it still not accepted in mainstream law and practice that IHRL obligations attach directly to NSAs.[75] This is pointed out by Rodley, who also notes the expansive view would also in some respects even undercut the promotion of human rights.[76] As a result of these problems, the terminology of 'participants' and 'legal personality' has become more popular in international law scholarship, as espoused by Higgins and others.[77] However, this too has not translated to legal status and IHRL obligations beyond that which is closely linked to state consent and intentions, as originally reflected in the *Danzig* case.

The ILC's codification of the law of diplomatic protection, for example, engaged a conflict between the human rights and *Danzig* case approaches on a number of key issues.[78] The ILC's draft articles essentially affirmed the traditional state-centric approach – that a state

---

71 *The Jurisdiction of the Courts of Danzig*, Advisory Opinion, PCIJ Series B No. 15 (1928) at 17.

72 ILA Final Report (n. 4) 2; Rodley (n. 28).

73 Reiter (n. 8) 218; Rodley (n. 28).

74 A. Clapham, *Human Rights Obligations of Non-State Actors* (OUP, 2006) 43–56; cf. P. Alston, 'The "Not-a-Cat" Syndrome: Can the International Human Rights Regime Accommodate Non-State Actors?', in P. Alston (ed.), *Non-State Actors and Human Rights* (OUP, 2005), 3; Rodley (n. 28).

75 Rodley (n. 28); Alston (n. 74) 3–5; John Ruggie, Special Representative of the UN Secretary-General for Business and Human Rights, Guiding Principles on Business and Human Rights: Implementing the United Nations 'Protect, Respect and Remedy' Framework, endorsed in Human Rights Council res. 17/4 (2011) principle A.1 and commentary (' "States" . . . obligations require that they respect, protect and fulfil the human rights of individuals . . . This includes the duty to protect against human rights abuse by third parties, including business enterprises').

76 Rodley (n. 28).

77 E.g. see Higgins (n. 27) 41–55; Jean d'Aspremont (ed.), *Participants in the International Legal System – Multiple Perspectives on Non-State Actors in International Law* (Routledge, 2011).

78 ILC, Draft Articles on Diplomatic Protection with Commentaries, UN Doc. A/61/10 (2006) appears also in *Yearbook of the ILC*, 2006, vol. II, Part Two, Arts 1, 2 (foundation principles) and 19 ('Recommended practice'). See also C. Cerna, 'Impact on the Right to Consular Notification', in Kamminga and Scheinin (n. 1); Reiter (n. 8) 217.

has no requirement to exercise diplomatic protection on behalf of its injured national, and there is no requirement for the state to provide an individual with compensation it obtains for the individual's injury.[79] Reiter notes thus that 'human rights law has only impacted marginally, if at all, on the development of general international norms regarding diplomatic protection' and also more broadly 'the right to consular notification, and the attribution of state responsibility'.[80] States are thus still the main repositories of sovereign authority over territories and people, and subjecthood has not been significantly extended to other NSA 'participants' in the international legal system. In broad terms, under IHRL individuals still only have the substantive and procedural rights bestowed by states through treaty or customary international law.

3.3 Jurisdiction and immunity as constraints

The rules of jurisdiction and state immunity are central to the competence of international courts and treaty bodies to implement and enforce the obligations of IHRL. The GIL on jurisdiction and state immunity continues to operate as a constraint on the enjoyment of various human rights (e.g. right to a remedy, access to courts, implementing the prohibition against torture). The ICJ and other tribunals generally take the position that serious violations of IHRL or IHL do not override state immunity.[81] The immunity of sovereign states and international organisations continues to be pre-eminent vis-à-vis IHRL, and the position is relatively settled in a number of cases in different fora including the ICJ's recent *Jurisdictional Immunities (Germany v Italy)* case.[82] As Reiter notes, state immunity has been 'assailed from a human rights perspective; yet, without much success'.[83]

In the European Court of Human Rights context, a series of cases have made clear that rules of human rights will be subservient to principles of GIL such as immunity and jurisdiction. In the *Bankovic* case, for example, which dealt with the question of extraterritorial jurisdiction and obligations in the conflict in the former Yugoslavia, the Court stated: 'The Convention should be interpreted as far as possible in harmony with other principles of international law of which it forms part.'[84] The European Court takes a similar position

---

79 Draft Articles (n. 78), Art. 19 and commentary.
80 Reiter (n. 8) 217; Cerna (n. 78).
81 E.g. in In *Jurisdictional Immunities of the State (Germany v Italy: Greece intervening)* ICJ Rep 2012, the Court concludes (at para. 91) that 'under customary international law as it presently stands, a State is not deprived of immunity by reason of the fact that it is accused of serious violations of international human rights law or the international law of armed conflict'; T. Rensmann, 'Impact on the Immunity of States and their Officials', in Kamminga and Scheinin (n. 1); L. McGregor, 'Torture and State Immunity: Deflecting Impunity, Distorting Sovereignty', 18(5) *European Journal of International Law* (2007) 903–19; ILC Report (n. 4) para. 91.
82 *Jurisdictional Immunities* (n. 81); see also *Case Concerning the Arrest Warrant of 11 April 2000 (Democratic Republic of the Congo v Belgium)* ICJ Reports 2002; *Al-Adsani v the United Kingdom,* Judgment of 21 November 2001, ECHR 2001-XI, 79. For other European cases, see ILC Report (n. 4) para. 437, fn. 603; *Jones v Ministry of Interior Al-Mamlaka Al-Arabyia AS Saudiya (the Kingdom of Saudi Arabia)* [2006] UKHL 16. For a critique, see A. Orakhelashvili, 'Restrictive Interpretation of Human Rights Treaties in the Recent Jurisprudence of the European Court of Human Rights', 14(3) *European Journal of International Law* (2003) 529; 'Immunities of State Officials, International Crimes, and Foreign Domestic Courts: A Reply to Dapo Akande and Sangeeta Shah', 22(3) *European Journal of International Law* (2011), 849–55.
83 Reiter (n. 8) 217.
84 *Bankovic v Belgium and others,* Decision of 12 December 2001, Admissibility, ECHR 2001-XII, 351, para. 57; discussed in ILC Report (n. 4) para. 217.

in cases concerning conflict between state immunity and human rights, for example, the right to fair and public hearing.[85] In the *Al-Adsani v UK*, *Fogarty v UK* and *McElhinney v Ireland* cases, the Court held that the right of access to the courts was not absolute, and could be subject to the restriction of state immunity.[86] In *Fogarty*, which concerned a claim against the UK for access to courts against the US Embassy in London, the Court stated that 'recognized rules of public international law on state immunity cannot in principle be regarded as imposing a disproportionate restriction on the right of access to a court . . . being those *limitations generally accepted by the community of nations* as part of the doctrine of state immunity'.[87] There are various other ways in which such decisions are rationalised. Several judgments have asserted that immunity, as a procedural rule, does not affect substantive norms but merely diverts the claim to an alternative forum.[88]

An implicit hierarchy of norms applies even in cases of violations of *jus cogens* – e.g. torture, crimes against humanity, self-determination[89] – or the non-derogable component of right to a remedy.[90] In the *Jurisdictional Immunities* case, the ICJ determined that the violations against the Italian population by German armed forces in WWII, to the extent they were norms *jus cogens*, did not conflict with Germany's assertion of state immunity. The ICJ held that the 'two sets of rules address different matters' and 'rules of State immunity are procedural in character'.[91] This approach contrasts with a broad notion of norm conflict and the 'inter-twined' nature of primary and secondary rules (i.e. substantive and procedural) generally supported by the ILC and others in the fragmentation discourse. It thus seems possible, using legal hermeneutics or latent legal reasoning, not to find a norm conflict with human rights where there clearly appears to be one. The ILC Report can be criticised for taking this approach in its analysis:

> The law of State immunity and the law of human rights, for example, illustrate two sets of rules that have very different objectives. . . . . While such 'policy-conflicts' *do not lead into logical incompatibilities between obligations upon a single party*, they may nevertheless also be relevant for fragmentation.[92]

In light of this, it is not surprising the ILC Report did not focus to any significant extent on the contentious human rights cases on torture and immunity. These cases and others that concern jurisdiction, may serve to illustrate an implicit normative hierarchy – that is,

---

85 European Convention on Human Rights (1952) 213 UNTS 222, Art. 6(1). E.g. see *Al-Adsani* (n. 82) paras 55–56; *McElhinney v Ireland,* Judgment of 21 November 2001, ECHR 2001-XI, paras 36, 85.

86 McLachlan (n. 40) 305.

87 *Fogarty v the United Kingdom,* Judgment of 21 November 2001, ECHR 2001-XI, para. 36 (emphasis added).

88 See McGregor (n. 81) 905–907.

89 E.g. see *Al-Adsani* (n. 82) for torture; *Jurisdictional Immunities* (n. 81) for crimes against humanity; *Case Concerning East Timor (Portugal v Australia)* ICJ Rep. 1995 for self-determination.

90 E.g. see *Jurisdictional Immunities* (n. 81).; *Jones v Saudi Arabia* (n. 82); UN Human Rights Committee, General Comment No. 29: States of Emergency, UN Doc. CCPR/C/21/Rev.1/Add.11 (2001) para. 14 (where the HRC essentially equates the core of the right to a remedy under Art. 2(3) ICCPR with a non-derogable and peremptory norm).

91 *Jurisdictional Immunities* (n. 81) para. 93.

92 ILC Report (n. 4) para. 24.

individual rights give way to state sovereignty and interests, and a normative preference is given to GIL over IHRL.

3.4 The central roles of the VCLT and lex specialis

The VCLT is dominant in treaty interpretation for IHRL, notwithstanding the underlying differences of human rights treaties compared to most other treaties. Despite debates on this issue in the ILC's development of the VCLT,[93] that treaty set out a uniform approach and theory of interpretation for all treaties. Christoffersen, a contributor on this topic to the ILA Report, concludes that while some suggest the interpretation of human rights treaties is governed by specific rules, human rights supervisory bodies rely on general principles of treaty interpretation.[94] Focusing on the relevant case law of the European Court of Human Rights, he considers that human rights law has not impacted substantially on GIL law at the methodological level.[95] In a fairly typical statement, the European Court in *Al-Adsani* indicated that 'the Convention has to be interpreted in the light of the rules set out in the Vienna Convention'.[96]

The ILC Report on fragmentation endorses the perspective that the VCLT is central to managing interpretation, as it provides a *comprehensive* approach for both treaties *and* custom. The ILC concludes that '[w]hen seeking to determine the relationship of two or more norms to each other, the norms should be interpreted in accordance with or analogously to the VCLT and especially the provisions in its Articles 31–33 having to do with the interpretation of treaties'.[97] Article 31 sets out the 'general rule of interpretation' that is determined by the ordinary meaning, light of the context, object and purpose of the treaty language, general context of the treaty, as well as subsequent agreements and practice, and '*any relevant rules of international law applicable in relations between the parties*'. This last concept, which is contained in Article 31(3)(c), and also known as the principle of systemic integration, has only been the subject of significant attention since the ICJ's *Oil Platforms* case (2003).[98]

The ILC's formulation of 'harmonisation' through the 'principle of systemic integration', which it bases in Article 31(3)(c) of the VCLT, introduces aspects of hierarchy for GIL over IHRL. The ILC's Conclusions on the work of the Study Group on fragmentation (the ILC Conclusions) include a principle of harmonisation, which by itself is relatively

---

93 E.g. see G. Fitzmaurice, 'Third Report on the Law of Treaties', *Yearbook of the ILC*, vol. II (1958) paras 74–79.

94 J. Christoffersen, 'Impact on General Principles of Treaty Interpretation', in Kamminga and Scheinin (n. 1) 37, at 60–61.

95 Ibid.

96 *Al-Adsani* (n. 82) paras 55, 56. See also Nineteenth meeting of chairpersons of the human rights treaty bodies Geneva, 21–22 June 2007, Sixth Inter-Committee Meeting of the human rights treaty bodies Geneva, 18–20 June 2007, Report of the Meeting of the Working Group on Reservations, UN Doc. HRI/MC/2007/5 (2007) para. 16.3 ('general treaty law remains applicable to human rights instruments').

97 ILC Conclusions (n. 4) para. 3.

98 *Case Concerning Oil Platforms (Iran v United States of America)* 42 ILM 1334 (2003) para. 41; McLachlan (n. 40); G. Zabalza, *The Principle of Systemic Integration: Towards a Coherent International Legal Order* (Cologne Studies in International and European Law 2012); J. d'Aspremont, 'The Systemic Integration of International Law by Domestic Courts: Domestic Judges as Architects of the Consistency of the International Legal Order', in O. Fauchald and A. Nollkaemper (eds), *The Practice of International and National Courts and the (De) Fragmentation of International Law* (Hart, 2012).

uncontroversial – that is that competing or conflicting norms 'should, to the extent possible, be interpreted so as to give rise to a single set of compatible obligations'.[99] The ILC also concludes, importantly, that Article 31(3)(c) 'gives expression to the objective of '*systemic integration*' according to which, whatever their subject matter, treaties are a creation of the international legal system and their operation is predicated upon that fact'.[100] This principle of systemic integration is considered by some to be a customary rule and is generally supported in both theory and practice.[101] For example, Jennings and Watts in *Oppenheim's International Law* referred to a 'presumption that the parties [to a treaty] intend something not inconsistent with generally recognized principles of international law'.[102] In *Al-Adsani* the European Court made express reference to Article 31(3)(c) in interpreting the human rights obligations of the Convention.[103]

The ILC's approach to systemic integration, however, supports a hierarchical interpretive approach that applying human rights treaties is predicated on full and unaltered application of GIL rules (e.g. state responsibility, jurisdiction and immunities). McLachlan's work on systemic integration, which was influential on the ILC's thinking, refers to GIL rules such as state immunity and suggests 'the significance of such rules is that they perform a systemic or *constitutional function* in describing the operation of the international legal order.'[104] This view is evident in practice, as the ICJ and other bodies have shown 'a marked reluctance to vindicate individual rights in cases of clashes with traditional state interests or prerogatives, leading to a rather patchy reception of the integration process'.[105]

In further support of systemic integration, the ILC also proposes a structural exception to the *lex specialis* principle in situations where 'the application of the special law [e.g. IHRL] might frustrate the purpose of the general law', and notes that this 'involves an inherent ranking of norms'.[106] This ILC exception is tautological in some respects, as *lex specialis* is relevant usually only where there are competing norms or norm conflict in the special and general law, and therefore the special law's application would inevitably lead to a 'frustration' of the general law's purpose. As Gourgourinis suggests, 'the qualification of international law as "general" *vis-à-vis* "special" treaty regimes has been resorted to as means of concealing the true character of general international law as "residual" . . . unless explicitly derogated from'.[107]

---

99 ILC Conclusions (n. 4) para. 4; McLachlan (n. 40) 280.
100 ILC Conclusions (n. 4) para. 17.
101 d'Aspremont (n. 98) 151; McLachlan (n. 40) 281; see summary of state practice, jurisprudence and doctrinal writings in M. Villiger, *Customary International Law and Treaties* (Nijhoff, 1985) 334–43.
102 R. Jennings and A. Watts (eds), *Oppenheim's International Law,* 9th edn (Longman, 1992) 1275. See also Pauwelyn (n. 46) 240–44.
103 *Al-Adsani* (n. 82) paras 55–56; see also *Fogarty* (n. 87) paras 35–36; *McElhinney* (n. 85) 36–37.
104 McLachlan (n. 40) 313 (emphasis added); Gourgourinis (n. 10) 1004 ('For, notwithstanding their specificities', all specialised regimes 'are founded on, and connected with, general international law, and many disputes arising in their context can be settled only by reverting to rules of that law'); L. Caflisch, 'International Courts and Tribunals – The Challenges Ahead: The Law – Substantive and Procedural Questions', 7 *The Law and Practice of Int'l Courts and Tribunals* (2008) 289 at 297.
105 Reiter (n. 8) 218.
106 ILC Conclusions (n. 4) paras 10, 62.
107 Gourgourinis (n. 10) 1004.

In summary, the interpretive principles of harmony and systemic integration – as reflected in the VCLT and elaborated by scholars and courts – are a legal fiction that, despite international lawmaking being fragmented and decentralised, any new rule is made taking into account other existing rules.[108] In that sense, the principle of systemic integration is based on the formal unity of the legal system, and a hierarchical relationship of rules of GIL over IHRL obligations. While authors such as Pellet criticise human rights 'separatism', these interpretive principles detailed above reflect, as Simma and Paulowski suggest, that a 'presumption in favour of general international law is widely shared among public international lawyers'.[109]

4 IHRL and GIL: pushing the disciplinary boundaries

While being constrained by the foundational structure and principles of international law, IHRL has challenged and succeeded in pushing the boundaries of the discipline of international law. There is significant literature that demonstrates the impact of IHRL on GIL in specific areas of law and on the structure of international legal obligations.[110] However, the impact goes beyond this traditional dialectic of GIL versus human rights, to the powerful hermeneutic constraints and even the very foundations of international law. The influence of human rights on GIL cannot be divorced from the broader debate on unity or fragmentation,[111] as otherwise it fails to grapple sufficiently with the systemic and integral nature of the relationship. The ILC Report recognises this point, albeit mostly through a negative lens: 'Very often new rules or regimes develop precisely in order to deviate from what was earlier provided by the general law. When such deviations are or become general and frequent, the unity of the law suffers.'[112] The ILC overlooks that many of the notable developments in international law are reactions to GIL's shortcomings in achieving the 'object and purpose' of human rights, and are not deviations but rather are part of the changing structure of international law.

4.1 Jus cogens *and* erga omnes: *structure and hierarchy*

The influence of human rights has been central to the development of the concepts of *erga omnes* and *jus cogens*, which have introduced a hierarchy of norms and altered the structural fabric of international law.[113] It is important to note that the concept of *jus cogens* came from *within* GIL (i.e. the VCLT) and not from the human rights treaties or instruments; while

---

108 E.g. see d'Aspremont (n. 98) 148.
109 Simma and Pulkowski (n. 19) 505.
110 E.g. ILA Final Report and various chapters in Kamminga and Scheinin (n. 1); R. Higgins, 'Human Rights: Some Questions of Integrity' 15 *Commonwealth Law Bulletin* (1989) 598; M. Reisman, 'Sovereignty and Human Rights in Contemporary International Law', 84 *American Journal of International Law* (1990) 866; P. Wachsmann, 'Les méthodes de l'intérpretation des conventions à la protection des droits de l'homme', in: SFDI, *La protection des droits de l'homme et l'évolution du droit international, Coll. 1998* (Pedone, 1998) 188–199; see also n. 3 for other relevant literature.
111 Cf. Reiter (n. 8) 218 (who says it should be divorced).
112 ILC Report (n. 4) para. 15.
113 Reiter (n. 8) 216–17; see also S. Sivakumaran, 'Impact on the Structure of International Obligations', 133–50, in Kamminga and Scheinin (n. 1); P. Weil, 'Towards Relative Normativity in International Law?' 77 *American Journal of International Law* (1983) 413; A. Orakhelashvili, *Peremptory Norms in International Law* (OUP, 2009).

erga omnes came from the ICJ's *Barcelona Traction* decision.[114] Both concepts are reflected in the law of state responsibility, as codified by the ILC, and are associated with GIL and secondary rules.[115]

Yet, the two concepts of *jus cogens* and *erga omnes* have a significant heritage in human rights. Almost all the commonly cited *jus cogens* norms have a close connection to human dignity – that is genocide, slavery and slave trade, racial discrimination and apartheid, torture, crimes against humanity, right to self-determination, prohibition of aggression, as well as fundamental rules of international humanitarian law.[116] As Sivakumaran notes, '[p]eremptory norms are thus by and large human rights norms.'[117] In the 1970 *Barcelona Traction* case, where the ICJ referred to obligations *erga omnes* for the first time, it stated they derive from acts of aggression, genocide and 'principles and rules concerning the basic rights of the human person'.[118] Subsequently, self-determination, torture, and certain obligations of IHL have also been identified as obligations *erga omnes*, including by the ILC and ICJ.[119]

There is justified scepticism, however, as to the degree of real impact of *jus cogens* and *erga omnes* on international law and practice. Paulus, for example, suggests that 'the indeterminacy of the content and the precise legal effect of *jus cogens* has largely condemned it to practical irrelevance'.[120] The ILA Report addressed this issue and stated that:

> [A]lthough the two concepts have had an important symbolic effect and have generated much interest among scholars and human rights activists they have not yet had much effect in practice. While the existence of the concepts is beyond doubt, the floodgates have not opened; states have remained reluctant to rely on them in their legal arguments.[121]

As noted above, in the state immunity context the ICJ and other tribunals have been reluctant to rely on or even mention the notion of *jus cogens*.[122] In the *Arrest Warrant (DRC v Belgium)* case the ICJ declined to discuss the Belgian argument that *jus cogens* overrides

---

114 VCLT (n. 33) Art. 53; *Case Concerning the Barcelona Traction, Light and Power Company, Limited (Belgium v Spain) (Second Phase)* ICJ Rep 32; ILA Final Report (n. 1) 4, 21 (Conclusion 2).

115 Articles on State Responsibility (n. 12) Art. 40 (serious breach of a peremptory norm), Art. 41(2) (non-recognition), Art. 41(1) (cooperation to bring it to an end) and Art. 48 (invocation of responsibility by other than an injured state).

116 E.g. see *Case Concerning Armed Activities on the Territory of the Congo (Democratic Republic of the Congo v Rwanda)* ICJ Rep 2006, para. 64; Sivakumaran (n. 113) 145; for norms *jus cogens*, see Articles on State Responsibility (n. 12) commentaries to Arts 26 and 40.

117 Sivakumaran (n. 113 146.

118 *Barcelona Traction* (n. 114) para. 34.

119 Articles on State Responsibility (n. 12) Art. 48(1)(b) and commentary; see also *East Timor* case (n. 89) para. 29; *Wall* advisory opinion (n. 49) paras. 155 and 159 (*erga omnes* obligations include 'certain . . . obligations under international humanitarian law' and the right of self-determination); *Case Concerning Application of the Convention on the Prevention and Punishment of the Crime of Genocide (Bosnia and Herzegovina v Yugoslavia)*, Preliminary Objections, Judgment, ICJ Rep 1996, para. 31; *Case Concerning Armed Activities on the Territory of the Congo (Democratic Republic of the Congo/Rwanda)* ICJ Rep 2006, para. 64; *Prosecutor v Anto Furundzija*, Judgment of 10 December 1998, Case No. IT-95–17/1, Trial Chamber II, ILR, vol. 121 (2002) para. 151.

120 A. Paulus, '*Jus cogens* Between Hegemony and Fragmentation: An Attempt at a Re-appraisal', 74 *Nordic J. Int'l L.* (2005) 297 at 330.

121 ILA Final Report (n. 1) 5.

122 Ibid. 6–7.

immunity.[123] In the *Armed Activities (DRC v Rwanda)* case it referred to the concept only in a narrow context and did not accept that genocide could override consent to jurisdiction.[124] In *Jurisdictional Immunities*, however, the ICJ dealt more substantially with the concept but its conclusion was in effect the same. The existence of *jus cogens* and *erga omnes* is clear, therefore, but application with legal consequences in international cases is still relatively rare

While *jus cogens* and *erga omnes* have not opened the 'floodgates', this overlooks a broader understanding of their legal and practical impact, and also how they have changed the structure and fabric of international law to promote and protect human rights. As indicated above, a significant focus on *jus cogens*' impotency has been the direct clash with state immunity. But there have been advances, for example, as reflected in the *Pinochet* case with a former head of state not being accorded immunity for allegations of torture while in office.[125] Despite the various legal rationalisations of this precedent, there is no doubt that the lack of immunity was an infringement on state sovereignty. Further, as Reiter notes in the context of *jus cogens*, 'the ongoing debate and some contrary decisions and dissenting opinions foretell that the overall balance might lean in the opposite direction in the future.'[126] The *Al-Adsani v UK* case, for example, was decided by the European Court by a slender margin of 9–8 for the key issue of state immunity of Kuwait in UK courts for the alleged violation of torture.

In relation to *erga omnes*, states have not heavily utilised the standing provided by *erga omnes* to pursue human rights-related cases against other states. This, however, is perhaps also a narrow doctrinal perspective, for as Judge Cancado Trindade has stated, 'there could hardly be better examples of mechanism[s] for application of the obligations *erga omnes* of protection (at least in the relations of the State Parties *inter se*) than the methods of supervision seen in the human rights treaties themselves, for the exercise of the collective guarantee of the protected rights.'[127] Human rights treaties, such as the ICCPR and European Convention, provide states parties with standing to bring complaints against any other state party for violation of the obligations.[128] This does not fit well the traditional bilateral conception of treaty obligations and duties. The Human Rights Committee has conceived that every state party has a legal interest in other states' obligations following from 'the fact that the "rules concerning the basic rights of the human person" are *erga omnes*'.[129]

---

123 *Arrest Warrant* case (n. 82) para. 58.
124 *Armed Activities* case (n. 116) para. 64.
125 *R. v Bow Street Metropolitan Stipendiary Magistrate, ex parte Pinochet Ugarte (No. 3)*, 24 March 1999, House of Lords, 119 ILR, 113, 136, 166 (Lords Browne-Wilkinson and Hutton); *R. v Bow Street Stipendiary Magistrate and others, ex parte Pinochet (No. 1)* [1998] 4 All ER 897, 939–40, 945–46 (Lords Nicholls and Steyn); Bianchi (n. 3) 245 (though noting, for example, that Lord Browne-Wilkinson's reasoning on torture and *jus cogens* 'is not deprived of ambiguities').
126 Reiter (n. 8) 217.
127 *Las Palmeras v Colombia (Preliminary Objections)*, IACtHR, Judgment of 4 February 2000, Series C No. 67, sep. op. of Judge Cancado Trindade, para. 14.
128 For provisions on interstate complaints, see ICCPR (n. 2), Art. 41; ECHR (n. 875), Art. 33; and cases such as *Ireland v United Kingdom*, 23 Eur. Ct. H.R. (ser. B) (1976), *Greece v UK (First Cyprus)*, App. No. 176/56, 1958–1959 Y.B. Eur. Conv. on H.R. 174, and *The Greek Case*, App. Nos. 3321/67, 3322/67, 3323/67, 3344/67, 1969 Y.B. Eur. Conv. on H.R. 1. See also Human Rights Committee, General Comment No. 31, 'Nature of the General Legal Obligation on States Parties to the Covenant', UN Doc. CCPR/C/21/Rev.1/Add.13 (2004) para. 2.
129 General Comment 31 (n. 128).

The significant theoretical development within international law arising from *jus cogens* and *erga omnes* was highlighted (although more as a warning) in 1983 in Prosper Weil's influential article 'Towards Relative Normativity in International Law?'[130] This article reflected that the concept of *jus cogens* introduced a special place for entrenched values, mostly connected to human rights, which trump other norms such as is often the case in a domestic constitutional system.[131] This was at odds with the traditional conception of international law based on state consent and a lack of formal hierarchy of norms. Further, despite *jus cogens* being external to the UN Charter, it provides one of the only agreed limits to the the pre-eminence of Charter obligations under Article 103.[132] A statement from the ICJ's *Legal Consequences of the Construction of a Wall in the Occupied Palestinian Territory* opinion provides a good example of the way in which the two concepts, intertwined with human rights, have altered the traditional fabric of responsibility and obligations in international law:

> Given *the character and the importance of the rights and obligations involved*, the Court is of the view that *all states* are under an *obligation* not to recognize the illegal situation resulting from the construction of the wall . . . They are also under an *obligation not to render aid or assistance* in maintaining the situation created by such construction. It is also for *all States*, while respecting the United Nations Charter and international law, *to see to it* that any impediment, resulting from the construction of the wall, to the exercise by the Palestinian people of its right to self-determination *is brought to an end*.[133]

This conception of legal obligations upon all states for 'important' rights and obligations is a far cry from the traditional international law, and would have been difficult to imagine in an ICJ decision even twenty years ago. It demonstrates the growing impact that human rights have *within* the content and structure of international law.

4.2 Human rights reshaping GIL and state responsibility

The general principles of state responsibility, including as codified by the ILC, have been shaped by progressive development associated with human rights. As mentioned above, the special regime of IHRL comes into contact and tension with GIL and its secondary rules of state responsibility. The ILC considered that IHRL was relevant to the development of general provisions in the Articles on State Responsibility, not least as the commentaries are replete with human rights cases and examples.[134] Despite this obvious influence, perspectives are either reticent or not well informed on the full extent of influence of human rights on

---

130 Weil (n. 113).
131 Simma and Pulkowski (n. 19) 498 ('[t]he canon of *jus cogens* rules can certainly be said to embody 'fundamental value judgments'); ILA Final Report (n. 1) 6.
132 See P. Sands and P. Klein, *Bowett's Law of International Institutions,* 6th edn (Sweet & Maxwell, 2009) 458–59; Michael Wood, *The UN Security Council and International Law*, Hersch Lauterpacht Memorial Lectures, University of Cambridge, 8 November 2006, paras. 36–37; Sivakumaran (n. 113) 148. While not dealing with *jus cogens*, but rather various human rights including the core of a right to a remedy, see European Court of Justice, Joined Cases C-402/05 P and C-415/05 P, *Kadi and Al Barakaat v Council of the European Union*, 3 CMLR 41 (2008).
133 *Wall* advisory opinion (n. 49) para. 159.
134 R. McCorquodale, 'Impact on State Responsibility', in Kamminga and Scheinin (n. 1) 235–54 at 237.

GIL. As indicated above, the ILC has largely treated human rights as a 'special regime'. McCorquodale in his review of the issue concludes that IHRL:

> [H]as interpreted the nature of a state's obligations and extended the scope and depth of those obligations. As a consequence, *there could be some impact* by international human rights law on the general international law of state responsibility.[135]

In this author's view, this underestimates the true influence, as there are three key areas in which human rights have impacted on GIL and its rules of state responsibility: development of positive obligations; the law of attribution; and reparations and remedies. In addition, one must recognise as the ILC and ICJ do that the legal understanding of responsibility is different to its implementation: for example, immunity does not absolve responsibility.[136]

The development of positive obligations and state 'due diligence' has been central to human rights.[137] A foundation stone of IHRL is the obligation to 'ensure' the respect of the rights for all people within a state's territory and subject to its jurisdiction.[138] The UN Human Rights Committee has stated that the general obligation to respect and ensure respect under Article 2(1) of the ICCPR includes that 'States Parties must ensure that individuals also have accessible and effective remedies to vindicate those rights', and a failure to investigate or to 'ensure that those responsible are brought to justice' (which includes NSAs) may constitute a violation by the state.[139] McCorquodale in his research suggests that the acceptance of positive obligations 'arises primarily from the practices and principles developed within international human rights law', which have had 'a significant, and potentially longlasting, impact on the general law of state responsibility'.[140] This influence of positive obligations is central in GIL including the way in which *jus cogens* and *erga omnes* have shaped state responsibility. The statement above from the ICJ's *Wall* opinion is predicated on these concepts which are now codified in the Articles on State Responsibility.[141]

The development of positive obligations is also intertwined with attribution in the law of state responsibility. While Reiter and others suggest that 'the impact of human rights on general international law concerning the issue of attribution remains minimal',[142] a broader and more nuanced perspective may suggest otherwise. There is a growing acceptance of secondary forms of responsibility – such as non-recognition, failure of cooperation, and aid or assistance – as recognised in the Articles on State Responsibility and ICJ cases such as the *Wall* opinion

---

135 Ibid. 249.
136 E.g. see *Difference Relating to Immunity from Legal Process of a Special Rapporteur of the Commission on Human Rights* (Advisory Opinion), ICJ Rep. 1999, 62, at 87.
137 E.g. see *Velasquez Rodriguez v Honduras, Preliminary Objections*, Judgment of June 26, 1989, Inter-Am. Ct.H.R. (Ser. C) No. 1 (1994) para. 172 (referring to 'the lack of due diligence to prevent the violation or to respond to it as required by the Convention'); McCorquodale (n. 134) 246–51.
138 ICCPR, Art. 2(1); General Comment 31 (n. 128) paras. 3 and 10.
139 Ibid. para. 15.
140 McCorquodale (n. 134) 246–51; S. Ghandi, 'Review of Books: The Impact of Human Rights Law on General International Law By Menno T Kamminga and Martin Scheinin', 80(1) BYBIL (2009) 434–39 at 438.
141 Articles on State Responsibility (n. 12) Art. 40 (serious breach of a peremptory norm), Art. 41(2) (non-recognition), Art. 41(1) (cooperation to bring it to an end), and perhaps to a lesser extent Art. 16 (prohibition of aid and assistance).
142 McCorquodale (n. 134) 245 ('overall international human rights law has had minimal impact on the general international law of state responsibility in regard to attribution to the state'); Reiter (n. 8) 211l; Ghandi (n. 140) 438.

and *Bosnian Genocide*.[143] There can now be violations of human rights-related norms where the attribution connection is less direct, and responsibility can extend beyond the primary violator to a larger number of states with a lesser role. The evolution of positive obligations and secondary forms of responsibility have helped to combat the shortcomings of the state-centric international legal order.

While a more comprehensive examination is beyond the scope of this chapter, the issue of 'effective control', attribution and jurisdiction also demonstrates a human rights approach to a core issue of GIL and state responsibility. The 'effective control' test is central for attribution of a state's extraterritorial conduct and internationally wrongful acts, as well as for establishing jurisdiction and states' extraterritorial responsibility for human rights violations.[144] As covered elsewhere in this volume,[145] the development of extraterritorial IHRL has challenged traditional notions of territory and sovereignty. While operating as a 'special regime', human rights has reshaped what is at heart a GIL concept reflected in the Articles on State Responsibility, that is, how conduct and violations are attributed to the state.

It is helpful to illustrate the divergent approach to the 'effective control' test with a few examples from human rights cases. In the *Loizidou v Turkey* case, the European Court suggested that when a state exercises 'effective *overall* control' with respect to a territory, it leads to a generalised obligation to secure the 'entire range of substantive rights' in the area in question.[146] In a further departure in *Ilascu and others v Moldova and Russia*, the Court held that Transdniestria 'remains under the effective authority, or at the very least under the decisive influence, of the Russian Federation, and in any event that it survives by virtue of the military, economic, financial and political support given to it by the Russian Federation'.[147] While the ICJ has upheld the traditional notion of 'effective control' in *Nicaragua v USA and Armed Activities* (DRC v Uganda), it has arguably taken a different approach in substance in cases such as the *Wall* opinion.[148]

In relation to the concept of remedies or reparations in international law, the PCIJ's *Chorzow Factory* case (1927) recognised that 'any breach of an engagement involves an obligation to make reparation'.[149] This classical statement of principle concerned a state's responsibility to make reparation to another state. Of more recent origin is the extension to encompass an individual's entitlement to reparations from a state for human rights violations or violations of international humanitarian law.[150] The nature of the right to a remedy in state

---

143 *Wall* advisory opinion (n. 49) and *Bosnian Genocide* case (n. 119).

144 E.g. see *Military and Paramilitary Activities in and against Nicaragua (Nicaragua v United States of America) (Merits)* ICJ Rep 1986, paras 109, 115; *Armed Activities* case (n. 116) 116; *Bosnian Genocide* case (n. 119) paras 398–407; General Comment 31 (n. 129) para. 10.

145 R. Wilde, 'The Extraterritorial Application of International Human Rights Law on Civil and Political Rights' in this volume.

146 *Loizidou* (n. 31) para. 77.

147 *Ilascu and Others v Moldova and Russia*, Application No. 48787/99, ECtHR [Grand Chamber], Reports 2004-VII (2004) para. 392.

148 *Nicaragua* and *Armed Activities* (n. 144); *Wall* advisory opinion (n. 49) paras. 138–40 (where the ICJ does not appear to apply the 'effective control' test, which may not be satisfied on the facts); McCorquodale (n. 134) 240–46.

149 *Case Concerning the Factory at Chorzow (Germany v Poland) (Claim for Indemnity) (Merits)*, PCIJ Rep Series A No. 17, 28, para. 73.

150 E.g. see *Wall* advisory opinion (n. 49) paras 152–53. This entitlement to reparation has been developed through the jurisprudence of human rights courts, and codified as part of the Basic Principles and Guidelines on the Right to a Remedy and Reparation for Victims of Gross Violations of International Human Rights Law and Serious Violations of International Humanitarian Law, GA Res 60/147 (2005) Arts 15–23.

responsibility has been influenced by human rights, and includes potential basis of compensation such as suffering and pain.[151] Articles 31 and 36 of the Articles on State Responsibility introduce the idea of personal suffering as damage. Further, the relevant commentaries define 'moral' damage as including 'individual pain and suffering, loss of loved ones', which arguably may be compensatable by damages.[152] In *Diallo (Guinea v DRC)*, a diplomatic protection case, the ICJ decided that compensation was due to an injured state in respect of damages suffered by that state's national (Mr Diallo) as a result of human rights violations concerning wrongful arrest, detention and expulsion.[153] In its judgment, the Court determined that the DRC was under an obligation to pay Guinea US$85,000 for non-material injury (pleaded by Guinea as 'mental and moral damage') suffered by Mr Diallo and US$10,000 for material injury.[154] This sort of claim and remedy demonstrates a change of approach in the ICJ in respect of human rights-related claims in public international law.

4.3 Positivism and formation of international obligations

The dominant positivist paradigm of international law is based on the consent and will of states. As Oppenheim stated in 1908: '[I]nternational law is not a law above but only between the states. A rule of international law cannot, without their special consent, be imposed upon the states.'[155] Human rights have been a key factor in recent developments that demonstrate, at a deeper level, international law is no longer explained in purely positivist terms. Higgins goes so far as to state that human rights treaties 'are not just an exchange of obligations between states where they can agree at will' since they 'reflect rights *inherent* in human beings, not dependent upon grant by the state.'[156]

The traditional approach to formation of customary international law relies on *opinio juris* to confirm that state practice reflects an obligation, or to even infer *opinio juris* from state practice (the 'traditional mode').[157] In matters connected to human rights, for example torture and self-determination, the ICJ and other tribunals and bodies have put more emphasis on *opinio juris* than actual state practice, at times even glossing over inconsistent practice (the 'modern mode').[158] The ICTY in *Tadic* took a position that 'battlefield practice' was inherently

---

151 E.g. see *Velasquez Rodriguez v Honduras* Compensatory Damages (Art. 63(1) American Convention on Human Rights), Judgment of July 21, 1989 Inter-Am.Ct.H.R. (Ser. C) No. 7 (1990) paras 51–52 (for discussion of 'moral damages').

152 Ibid.; see Articles on State Responsibility (n. 12) Arts 31 and 36 and commentaries, which, read contextually, suggest possible space for financial claims between states for serious personal suffering.

153 *Ahmadou Sadio Diallo (Republic of Guinea v Democratic Republic of the Congo) Compensation Owed by the Democratic Republic of the Congo to the Republic of Guinea* (Judgment) ICJ Rep 2012.

154 Ibid., paras 29–55, 61(1).

155 L. Oppenheim, 'The Science of International Law: Its Task and Method', 2 *American Journal of International Law* (1908) 313–56 at 332–33.

156 Higgins (n. 110) 607.

157 ILA Final Report (n. 1) 7; J. Wouters and C. Ryngaert, 'Impact on the Process of Formulation of Customary International Law', in Kamminga and Scheinin (n. 1) 112–15, 118–19; A. Roberts 'Traditional and Modern Approaches to Customary International Law: A Reconciliation', 95 *American Journal of International Law* (2001) 757–91.

158 Roberts, ibid.; e.g. see *Prosecutor v Anto Furundzija*, Judgement ICTY Case No. IT-95–17/1-A (21 July 2000) paras 155–57, which held that torture was a norm *jus cogens* despite its widespread use in state practice.

159 *Prosecutor v Tadić*, Decision on the defence motion for interlocutory appeal on jurisdiction, ICTY Appeals Chamber, Case IT-94–1-AR72, 2 October 1995, para. 99.

untrustworthy,[159] and the International Committee of the Red Cross (ICRC')s study on customary international humanitarian law attached more importance to *opinio juris* and the ICRC's own official statements, than to actual operational practice.[160] Reiter sums up this trend as 'the progressive reliance on *deduction from fundamental principles* in lieu and place of induction from state practice, as well as the emphasis on states declarations and professed intentions or the pronouncements of international bodies rather than their actual deeds.'[161] This has led to a significant evolution in formulation of customary international law in the fields of IHRL, IHL and international criminal law, based on normativity rather than strict positivism.

There is another, more narrow, manifestation of the human rights impact on positivism and formation of obligations. This is the doctrine of 'automatic succession' which has been applied by human rights treaty bodies to *successor* states, for example, in the contexts of the former Yugoslavia and USSR (cf. the *continuator* state, i.e. Russia). Generally speaking, in contrast with the traditionally accepted 'clean slate' doctrine, successor states have been bound immediately by the former state's obligations under human rights treaties (e.g. of USSR), and this is not dependent on any confirmation made by them.[162] Kamminga and others focus on this development as a major exception to GIL on state succession, but it is noteworthy also from a positivist perspective. As a new entity, it is very difficult to infer consent from a successor state (e.g. Ukraine) as by contrast it may be for a continuator state (e.g. Russia).

It seems clear that state practice and consent are not essential for formation of obligations concerning human rights. In relation to *jus cogens* norms, there is a challenging assumption of 'universal acceptance', or as the VCLT puts it, such norms are 'accepted and recognised by the international community of states as a whole'.[163] The UN Human Rights Committee takes this general point further in its General Comment 26, in which it concludes 'the drafters of the Covenant deliberately intended to exclude the possibility of denunciation [i.e. withdrawal]' and 'once the people are accorded the protection of the rights under the Covenant, such protection devolves with territory and continues to belong to them'.[164] The Committee justifies this departure from strict positivism on the basis that the ICCPR codifies in treaty form the universal human rights enshrined in the UDHR and guaranteed under the Charter.

4.4 The VCLT and interpretation: human rights exceptionalism and incorporation

The VCLT's general regime of interpretation has been challenged by human rights exceptionalism. It has been also influenced by human rights-related developments in relation to teleological interpretation, treaty reservations and treaty bodies' interpretative roles. The ILA Report, for example, underlines the general inadequacy of the VCLT in providing

---

160 J. Henckaerts and L. Doswald-Beck, ICRC, *Customary International Humanitarian Law. Volume I: Rules* (Cambridge University Press, 2005) xxxviii; Wouters and Ryngaert (n. 166) 112.

161 Reiter (n. 8) 216.

162 E.g. see discussion of cases, treaty body statements, and practice in Kamminga (n. 3); M. Kamminga, 'Impact on State Succession in Respect of Treaties', in Kamminga and Scheinin (n. 1) 99–110; cf. A. Rasulov, 'Revisiting State Succession to Humanitarian Treaties: Is There a Case for Automaticity?', 14 *European Journal of International Law* (2003) 141.

163 VCLT (n. 33) Art. 53.

164 HRC, General Comment No. 26: Continuity of Obligations, UN Doc. CCPR/C/21/Rev.1/ Add.8/Rev.1 (1997) paras 2, 4; Kamminga (n. 162) 105–106 (discussing the example of the UN Office of Legal Affairs and its contrary practice vis-à-vis Kazakhstan).

the answer to all difficulties arising from fragmentation and human rights.[165] While some commentators argue that human rights treaty bodies 'have not shaped the [interpretive] field in any significant manner' as they have mostly applied the VCLT,[166] a broader perspective demonstrates some influence and shaping of GIL. This issue is also connected to the ILC's application of the 'principle of systemic integration', which has significant potential for human rights and is discussed below.

The *corpus juris* of human rights features a dominant dynamic or teleological method of interpretation,[167] which considers treaties as 'living' instruments, rather than tied to the original intent of state parties.[168] As the European Court has observed, for a 'normative treaty' the interpreters should look for the 'object and purpose', and not to the most limited understanding of the obligations of states parties.[169] The human rights treaty bodies have focused on points such as this to distinguish their interpretive methodology from the ICJ and other general adjudicative bodies.[170] This links also to the point made above that customary international law formation is increasingly based on deduction from fundamental principles in place of state practice. This more dynamic approach to interpretation has now featured in various ICJ cases, such as *Armed Activities* and the *Wall* opinion, and in interpretation of GIL, such as in the *Western Sahara* opinion and *Nicaragua v USA*.[171]

The creation of international treaty bodies and experts to monitor and promote compliance with human rights obligations, enhance enforcement, and provide remedies for violations, has impacted on the autonomy of state interpretation in international law. It is noteworthy the ILC Report and ILA Report did not attempt a thorough analysis of institutional competence and the interpretation of treaties.[172] The human rights treaty bodies have taken on a position as authoritative interpreters of state obligations under the treaties (e.g. for reservations) which is sometimes at odds with the VCLT's state-centric position on interpretation. The ILC in its work culminating in the Guide to Practice on Reservations to Treaties (2011), while initially resistant eventually adopted a general rule that recognised the competence of a 'treaty monitoring body' to interpret the treaty,[173] a departure from the

---

165 ILA Final Report (n. 1) 22, para. (6).
166 ibid. 10; Reiter (n. 8) 216; Christoffersen (n. 94) 60–61.
167 ILC Report (n. 4) paras 130, 157; Simma and Pulkowski (n. 19) 500–50; Wachsmann (n. 110).
168 E.g. see *Consular Assistance,* Advisory Opinion of 1 October 1999, Int-Am CHR Series A, No. 16, pp. 256–57, paras 114–15.
169 *Wemhoff v FRG,* Judgment of 27 June 1968, ECHR (1968) Series A, No. 7, p. 23, para. 8.
170 *Loizidou* (n. 31) paras 70–72, 84–85 ('such a fundamental difference in the role and purpose of the separate tribunals [which] provides a compelling basis for distinguishing Convention practice from that of the International Court'). *Consular Assistance* (n. 168) paras. 114–15 (a part of the 'corpus juris of human rights law' is the principle that 'human rights treaties are living instruments whose interpreters must consider changes over time and present-day conditions'); General Comment 24 (n. 31) para. 17 (on reservations); ILC report (n. 4) paras 69–70. See also Working Group on Reservations (n. 96) (which concludes that general treaty law 'can only be applied taking fully into account [human rights treaties'] specific nature, including their content and monitoring mechanisms').
171 *Western Sahara, Advisory Opinion,* 12 ICJ Rep 1975, paras 54–59; *Wall* (n. 49); *Armed Activities* (n. 116); *Nicaragua* (n. 144).
172 ILC Report (n. 4) para. 13; ILA Final Report (n. 1) 9–10; Reiter (n. 8) 221.
173 ILC, Guide to Practice on Reservations to Treaties, UN Doc. A/66/10 (2011), rule 3.2.4. More generally, there was also significant and constructive dialogue between the ILC Special Rapporteur, Alain Pellet and the UN human rights treaty bodies, e.g. see Working Group on Reservations (n. 96) paras 16.6 and 16.10.

general rules of the VCLT. The treaty bodies have also engaged directly at times in interpretation of GIL. The Inter-American Court, for example, has used its advisory jurisdiction to interpret not only other human rights instruments (such as the European Convention or the two Covenants), but also treaties such as the Vienna Convention on Consular Relations.[174]

The ILC's separate work on reservations to treaties illustrates the exceptionalism of human rights and, in particular, the generalist's reaction to resist a specific (valid) approach for human rights and rather mainstream that approach into GIL. The 'objects and purposes' compatibility test for reservations, which is enshrined in Article 19(c) of the VLCT, derives from the ICJ's *Genocide Reservations* case.[175] That case identified the difference of human rights or humanitarian-related treaties to traditional international law, and developed the 'object and purpose' test for a non-reciprocal and normative treaty such as the Genocide Convention.[176] Yet, the UN Human Rights Committee has stated that the VCLT's provisions are 'inappropriate to address the problem of reservations to human rights treaties'.[177] The European Court in *Belios v Switzerland* in particular developed the doctrine of severability – i.e. that the consequence of an invalid reservation is the presumption that the state becomes party to the treaty without the benefit of the reservation.[178] The doctrine of severability also challenges the idea of state consent.

The ILC's Special Rapporteur, Alain Pellet, did not at first embrace the doctrine of severability (e.g. the USA, UK and France do not endorse the doctrine), and considered that the reserving state must decide whether an invalid reservation constitutes an essential element of its consent to be bound. Pellet as Special Rapporteur stated that 'no organ can take the place of the reserving state in determining the latter's intentions regarding the scope of the treaty obligations it is prepared to assume'.[179] However, the final Guide to Practice of the ILC took on and adopted the human rights approach – the doctrine of severability – as the general rule and presumption.[180] There were various other such tensions encountered in the ILC's work, including on treaty bodies' roles, and the GIL and IHRL perspectives on the 'object and purpose' of a treaty.[181]

As described above, the 'principle of systemic integration' is a central tool in the GIL hierarchy and constraint of human rights law and principles. In McLachlan and the ILC's pioneering work on the principle, the most notable omission is any reference to its intellectual heritage and origins. It appears most related to an idea developed by Dworkin in *Law's Empire* in his theory of 'law as integrity'. Dworkin suggests that adjudicators have

---

174 See *'Other Treaties' Subject to the Consultative Jurisdiction of the Court*, Judgment of 24 September 1982, OC-1/82, Int-Am CHR Series A, No. 1.

175 *Reservations to the Genocide Convention, Advisory Opinion* ICJ Rep 1951, 15, at 23–34.

176 Ibid.

177 General Comment 24 (n. 31) para. 17; see also conclusions of the Working Group on Reservations (n. 96) para. 16.

178 See *Belilos v Switzerland*, Judgment of 29 April 1988, ECHR Series A, No. 132 (1988) para. 60.

179 ILC, Second Report of the Special Rapporteur (reservations to treaties), Report of the International Law Commission on the work of its forty-ninth session, UN Doc. A/52/10 (1998) para. 157.

180 Guide to Practice (n. 173) rule 4.5.3.2.

181 Initially, ILC draft guideline 3.1.12 on 'Reservations to general human rights treaties' referred to 'the gravity of the impact the reservation has' (see draft Guide to Practice (2010) UN Doc. A/65/10) whereas the HRC's General Comment 24 (n. 31) does not distinguish between reservations which have a grave or minor impact on a right. Cf. the final rule approved, rule 3.1.5.1, which does not replicate this and is general and not specific human rights.

a duty to decide cases so that the law becomes more coherent and is the product of a single vision:

> Judges who accept the interpretative ideal of *integrity* decide hard cases by trying to find, in some coherent set of principles about people's rights and duties, the best constructive interpretation of the political structure and legal doctrine of their community. They try to make that complex structure the best it can be.[182]

This quote demonstrates a broader philosophical vision than what appears in Article 31(3)(c) of the VCLT (i.e. taking into account 'any relevant rules of international law applicable in the relations between the parties'). Dworkin's principle has a broader heritage than just a rule of interpretation; it is a dynamic constitutional principle, with the capability to inject normative content and values into the law. McLachlan recognises the principle of systemic integration 'has the status of a constitutional norm within the international legal system'[183] and it is 'a larger process of fitting the treaty obligation into its proper place within the larger normative order'.[184] The ILC also recognises this:

> But law is also about protecting rights and enforcing obligations, above all rights and obligations that have a backing in something like a general, public interest. Without the principle of 'systemic integration' it would be impossible to give expression to and to keep alive, any sense of the common good of humankind, not reducible to the good of any particular institution or 'regime'.[185]

These sentiments from the ILC and McLachlan, regrettably, are not reflected in their conclusions. While both cite European Court cases in support of their argument that the special regime yields to the general, it is easy to read these cases in a different manner. Firstly, the European Court's typical formulation that the Convention 'should be interpreted *as far as possible* in harmony with other principles of international law of which it forms part' is a principle of constructive interpretation, rather than a 'constitutional norm'.[186] Second, the principle may also be used to expand, and not just contract, the scope of human rights obligations. McLachlan suggests that in *Golder v UK* the European Court used Article 31(3)(c) to refer to the ICJ Statute and 'general principles of law recognised by civilised nations' in order to find that a right of access to civil courts was such a general principle of law.[187] Third, if one elevates the principle of systemic integration to a constitutional level, as the ILC and McLachlan ostensibly do, one must also recognise and engage at the constitutional level, and in a broader intellectual and balanced way. To borrow from Dworkin, one would need to seek the 'best constructive interpretation' for the international legal order.

---

182 R. Dworkin, *Law's Empire* (Belknap Press, 1986) 280.
183 Ibid. 280.
184 McLachlan (n. 40) 312; see also McNair (n. 48) 466.
185 ILC Report (n. 4) para. 480.
186 *Bankovic* case (n. 84).
187 McLachlan (n. 40) 294; *Golder v UK*, Judgment, 21 Feb 1975, ECHR Ser. A no. 18; 57 ILR 200, at 213.

4.5 State sovereignty, human rights, and constitution of the international legal system

The growing influence of the inherent dignity of the human being has successfully eroded state sovereignty. It has developed human rights both as a constitutive principle within the UN Charter and arguably as a secondary foundation of the international legal order. This perspective builds upon and brings together conclusions from prior sections above, and deals with challenging themes beyond the modest scope of this chapter. The tensions of GIL and human rights can be dealt with at the doctrinal level, but this is only half the picture. We should also step back, not into pure theory or philosophy, but enough to reassess the overarching interactions and principles of international law including its hermeneutics and constitutional foundations. The impact of IHRL, while only a relatively recent phenomenon in international law – sixty or so years within a history of more than 250 years since de Vattel's conception of state sovereignty – has been transcendental. As Simma and Pulkowski suggest:

> Human rights can no longer be fenced in an exclusive *domaine reservé*; once their genie was out of the bottle, human rights necessarily transcended to the realm of general international law. As Reisman put it, human rights are 'more than a piecemeal addition to the traditional corpus of international law'. They bring about 'changes in virtually every component'.[188]

State sovereignty is too servile normatively and practically to be the sole contemporary foundation of the international legal order. It is relatively recent that scholars and courts have begun to engage more with international law as values and developing the normative basis of the international legal order.[189] This approach is reflected for example in Simma's influential theory 'from bilateralism to community interest'.[190] The constant interaction of state sovereignty and human rights is also represented well in the dialectic in international law between soft rhetoric (values, justice) and hard rhetoric (state consent) as described by Koskennimi and others.[191]

A debate on foundational ideals and human rights within the international legal order may be too ephemeral for many practitioners, but it also has a doctrinal or even positivist expression in UN law and practice. The Charter has been understood to positivise the Kantian ideal in the international legal order and strengthen the power of the cosmopolitan over the sovereign state.[192] The 'constitutional character of the Charter' is recognised even by the ILC, which concludes 'that the United Nations Charter itself enjoys *special character* owing to the

---

188 Simma and Pulkowski (n. 19) 225, quoting Reisman (n. 110) 872.
189 E.g. see B. Simma, 'From Bilateralism to Community Interest', 250 *Recueil des Cours de l'Académie de Droit International* (1994) 217; T. Franck, *The Power of Legitimacy among Nations* (OUP, 1990); B. Kingsbury, N. Krisch and R. Stewart, 'The Emergence of Global Administrative Law', 68 *L. and Contemp. Probs.* (2006) 15–61; M. McDougal and M. Reisman, 'International Law in Policy-Oriented Perspective', in Macdonald and Johnston, *The Structure and Process of International Law: Essays in Legal Philosophy, Doctrine and Theory* (Martinus Nijhoff, 1983) 103; A. Verdross and B. Simma *Universelles Völkerrecht: Theorie und Praxis,* 3rd edn (Duncker and Humblot, 1984).
190 Simma (n. 189).
191 This is a central thesis of M. Koskenniemi's *From Apology to Utopia: The Structure of International Legal Argument* (CUP, 2006).
192 Verdross and Simma (n. 189) 328–34.

fundamental nature of some of its norms, particularly its *principles and purposes* and its *universal acceptance*.[193]

The 'Purposes' and 'Principles' of the United Nations are set out in Articles 1 and 2 of the Charter respectively and include: the sovereign equality of states; the prohibition of use of force against states' territorial integrity or political independence; non-intervention in states' internal matters, and promoting respect for human rights and fundamental freedoms.[194] The Universal Declaration is often seen as an expression of human rights as mentioned in Articles 1(3) and 55, and the UN Human Rights Committee has stated that the ICCPR is the codification of the Declaration. As indicated by the Committee, and generally recognised by the UN Secretariat, 'there is a United Nations Charter obligation to promote universal respect for, and observance of, human rights and fundamental freedoms.'[195] Human rights are thus a legitimate counterweight to state sovereignty and the principle of non-intervention in domestic affairs.

There are various examples of the operation of human rights as a counterweight to state sovereignty within the UN legal order based on the Charter. The trend is broadly positive and progressive, though with continuing constraints and resistance. States have objected to encroachment on the non-intervention principle reflected in Article 2(7). As Shelton notes, '[s]uch objections have become less frequent with general recognition that human rights is a legitimate matter of international concern under the United Nations Charter, but they have not entirely disappeared.'[196] Briefly, examples of the areas of progression include: (i) the enlargement of the 'threat to international peace and security' concept grounded in Article 39 of the Charter, to include internal human rights violations, and a correlative reduction in the scope of the non-intervention norm; (ii) the development of 'sovereignty as responsibility' and subsequently 'responsibility to protect' as a basis for intervention by the Security Council for peace and security; (iii) the establishment of 'protection of civilians' as an organising concept for the permissible extent of the use of force under a Chapter VII mandate of the Security Council; and (iv) the growth of human rights as a normative constraint on the organisation itself.

It is better for GIL and human rights interaction in difficult cases to engage in balancing of fundamental and underlying principles in the international legal order, than to always doctrinally find in Judges Fitzmaurice and Spender's words 'the correct legal view'.[197] Some of the irreconcilable scholarly debates following the *Jurisdictional Immunities* case illustrate this point well. This balancing is distinct from harmonisation, which the ILC Report recognises has a definite limit. The ILC recognizes that while harmonisation 'may resolve apparent conflicts; it cannot resolve genuine conflicts'.[198] This is a perspective arguably at odds with the ILC's actual conclusions and guidance on fragmentation. Human rights must be seen as a central part of the international legal order. It is a false dialectic to speak, as the ILC largely does, in terms only of unity or fragmentation and separate legal systems. A balancing of fundamental principles to help resolve significant norm conflict involves a less tidy but more open process for considering competing normative considerations,

---

193 ILC Conclusions (n. 4) paras 35, 36.
194 Charter of the United Nations (1946), Arts 2(1), 2(4), 2(7), 1(3) respectively.
195 General Comment 31 (n. 128) para. 2.
196 D. Shelton, 'Enforcement and Remedies' in this volume.
197 *South West Africa (Ethiopia and Liberia v South Africa)*, Joint Dissenting Opinion of Judges Sir Gerald Fitzmaurice and Sir Percy Spender, ICJ Rep 1950, 128 at 466.
198 C. Borgen, 'Resolving Treaty Conflicts', 37 *George Washington International Law Review* (2005) 605–06; also cited in ILC Report (n. 4) para. 42.

a perspective which is promoted by Higgins and others.[199] While human rights is more recent and definitely a weaker and secondary foundation of international law – as Simma implicitly recognises with his 'community interests' vis-à-vis state sovereignty – the inroads made are significant. There is little doubt that trend will continue, and the balance between the foundational principles of state sovereignty and human rights will continue to shift over time.

This balancing of fundamental principles of sovereignty and human rights is reflected in international cases. In *Al-Adsani*, the strong dissent by judges was based on state immunity ceding precedence to a peremptory rule of international law (i.e. prohibition of torture), rather than GIL being excluded from the interpretation of Article 6 of the Convention (right to a fair trial).[200] In the ICJ's *Arrest Warrant* case, Judges Higgins, Buergenthal and Kooijmans, in considering the balance to be struck between conflicting state immunity and liability for international crimes, stated in their joint opinion that: 'International law seeks the *accommodation* of this value [the preservation of unwarranted outside interference in the domestic affairs of states] with the fight against impunity, and not the triumph of one norm over another.'[201] In the ICJ's majority decision in the recent *Jurisdictional Immunities* case, the Court, while not finding in favour of the Italian claimants, saw sufficient merits in their cases to recommend that Germany and Italy negotiate a solution.[202]

It may be questioned why human rights are special in this foundational way for international law. Why not international environmental or trade law, also identified as important special regimes by the ILC and others? A short answer is that human rights, and the inherent dignity of the human being, are a fundamental unit of modern law and state as reflected in the views of legal theorists.[203] As such, developments have made human rights inherent in the notion of law, state and society. As Rodley explains:

> [F]rom Locke to Rousseau and Tom Paine, from Magna Carta and the English Bill of Rights to the Virginia Bill of Rights and the *Déclaration des droits de l'homme et du citoyen*, the idea of an individual human *domaine réservé* was born and consecrated. [It] was now not only of equal worth and respect as the duty to obey the sovereign, it was now, in some limited but basic respect, superior to that duty . . .[204]

In short, the development of the UN Charter, IHRL and human rights more broadly in international law has essentiality extrapolated the constitutive role of human rights in the legal order, from the national to international context.

5 Conclusions

Human rights are a part of both the lexicon and grammar of international law. While embedded within the superstructure of international law – including the foundation

---

199 E.g. see Higgins (n. 27); McDougal and Reisman (n. 189).
200 *Al-Adsani* (n. 82) Dissenting Opinion of Judges Rozakis and Caflisch, joined by Judges Wildhaber, Costa, Cabral Barreto, and Vajic, 49–51.
201 *Arrest Warrant* case (n. 82) Joint Separate Opinion, para. 79.
202 *Jurisdictional Immunities* (n. 81).
203 E.g. on social contract or social compact theory, see J. Rawls, *A Theory of Justice* (Belknap Press, 1971); J. Rousseau, *Du contrat social ou Principes du droit politique* ('Of The Social Contract, Or Principles of Political Right') (1762); J. Locke, 'Second Treatise of Civil Government'(1690).
204 Rodley (n. 28).

principles and secondary rules – human rights have pushed, challenged and enlarged the boundaries of the discipline. The ILC conclusions on fragmentation, with some caveats, retrench and insulate the state-centric paradigm of international law from the transcendental impact of human rights. That is partly a problem of the ILC having treated a complex theoretical subject as one of codification and doctrinal development. This hides from view the possibility of a more humanised international legal order. It also contributes to creating legal polemics and dialectics that entrench difficult debates, which cannot be resolved with the 'correct legal view'.

We need to fully recognise the legal evolution achieved through the normative growth of human rights, which has challenged the mainstream paradigm of international law. It has been 'a quiet resolution which invariably targets international law's most "statist" features'.[205] In this process, values and communitarian goals have been injected into the state-centric, bilateral and consent-based international legal order. Human rights has 'softened' and 'humanised' general international law, and thankfully this is a trend that is likely to continue. While the effect of human rights on intentional law is more than commonly acknowledged, where there is conflict with fundamental principles of state sovereignty, the influence is usually modest, in keeping with maintaining sufficient political support for the whole system. But the important point is that at a deeper and holistic level, including of epistemology and hermeneutics, there is understanding of the structural effects and change from the growing role of human rights in the international legal order. In conclusion, Pellet implies that human rights is not more than a branch of the tree,[206] this author considers that it is now a modest but growing part of the roots.

---

205 ILA Final Report (n. 1) 22.
206 Pellet (n. 1) 13–14 (in respect of human rights and other special regimes, he suggests jurists 'should be careful to avoid cutting the branch from the tree').

7

International human rights law and a developing world perspective

Antony Anghie

1 Introduction

Since the beginnings of modern international human rights law, most powerfully and comprehensively embodied by the Universal Declaration of Human Rights (UDHR), a number of controversies have emerged regarding what might be termed the 'Developing World Perspectives on International Human Rights Law'. These debates are various, intense, and ongoing, and include debates on the 'Western' character of human rights law, the contribution of the developing countries to human rights law, the emphasis by developing countries on 'collective' rather than individually based human rights, and the relationship between human rights and imperialism. Several of the other chapters in this book deal in detail with some of these debates which are central to the very character and operation of contemporary international human rights law. In this chapter, however, I provide an overview of these debates, this in an attempt to sketch the larger patterns that may connect them in various ways, and to see them within a broader framework of the evolution of human rights law.

My general argument is that attitudes and approaches of the developing countries to international human rights law may be usefully explored as an aspect of a broader thematic, the attitudes of new states to international law itself. That is, many of the approaches of developing countries towards human rights law can be seen as an aspect of their approaches to the broader context of public international law itself. Second, inevitably, international human rights law has profoundly altered its character and its scope as a result of the many developments that have occurred since the drafting of the Universal Declaration. Decolonisation, the Cold War, the emergence of authoritarian regimes in the third world, the fall of the Berlin Wall and the collapse of Communism, the intensification of globalisation and neo-liberal economic policies, massive civil wars in Africa and the Balkans, and the ongoing war on terror, are some of the major and overlapping events that have generated changes both in the international systems and to the approaches of third world countries themselves.[1] My

---

1 I use the terms 'developing countries', 'third world' and 'South' interchangeably here.

argument here is that while certain preoccupations, such as the universality of human rights, and the relationship between rights and duties have been a relatively consistent aspect of developing country approaches to human rights, these issues have taken on a different character and significance, depending on the local and global political and social circumstances of the time. Throughout all this, developing countries have been consistently preoccupied by the projects of decolonisation, sovereignty and development, and they have viewed human rights law principally in terms of its effects on these projects.

A further important change has been a profound transformation in the developing countries themselves. While initially united by their opposition to colonialism and their aspiration to create a New International Economic Order, the broad rubric of 'Developing Countries' obscures a number of significant differences that have now emerged among countries that originally constituted the Non-Aligned Movement, and which are manifested not only in their distinctive approach to human rights law, but in their relative economic status. It would have been difficult to foresee in the year 2000 that the global economic system would become so reliant on developing countries, particularly the BRIC countries – Brazil, Russia, India and China.

There is another sense in which we might approach the question of developing countries and human rights; that is, by focusing not so much on the human rights policies of the governments of developing countries, but on the experiences of developing countries as an epistemology, as a means of understanding the character of international human rights law. Several prominent scholars, such as Upendra Baxi, Francis Deng and Yash Ghai have used the experiences of developing countries and, perhaps even more particularly, the peoples of these developing countries as a prism to explore and elaborate on the project of human rights, and have produced as a result a rich and suggestive literature. Having sketched some of these developments and changes, this chapter will conclude with some necessarily tentative suggestions about the future of human rights in developing countries.

2 Developing countries and the historical and philosophical origins of international human rights law

A major theme that has preoccupied many scholars and states from the Global South is the question 'Are Human Rights Western?'[2] – and the many issues and implications arising from the answer to this question. The critical argument, here, is that the international human rights law presents, as universal and as binding on all states, a very specific model of society whose origins can be traced back to localised, particular, Western experiences. It is this Western experience masquerading as a universal law, that as such excludes the experiences of other peoples and alternative visions of a just society. Further, to the extent that it embodies the standards or principles that all societies are to comply with, it is inappropriate and even imperial.[3]

---

2 See e.g., A. Sharma, *Are Human Rights Western? A Contribution to the Dialogue of Civilizations* (New Delhi, OUP, 2006); C.G. Weeramantry, *Justice Without Frontiers*, Vol. I (Kluwer Law Publishers, 1997).

3 M. Mutua, 'The Ideology of Human Rights' (1995–1996) 36 *Virginia Journal of International Law* 589–657 at 592–93; M. Mutua, 'Savages Victims and Saviors: The Metaphor of Human Rights' (2001) 42(1) *Harvard International Law Journal* 201–45 at 204–206.

While this debate is a very old one, it has recently been revived in various ways as a consequence of a number of important books written on the history of international human rights law.[4] These works trace the origins of human rights from the natural law tradition, focusing on the elaborations of that tradition which occurred at key moments such as the French Revolution and the American Revolution. These accounts tend to confirm the view that to the extent that modern international human rights law owes its existence to these natural law origins, it is a natural law that is very much a product and reflection of the Western societies that authored it. The issue of how we identify 'universal natural rights' has always been problematic. And historical accounts of natural law have tended to suggest that particular societies characterise them in different ways depending upon the challenges that confront them; thus, the Haitian, French and American Revolutions – all of which may be seen as a product of the Enlightenment, and all of which, having occurred within a relatively short space of time, offered very different ideas of the state, the individual, society and the citizen.[5]

Developing countries, or, to avoid an anachronism, the non-European societies and their cultures and values, feature unevenly in these works. However, other scholars who have focused on the role of non-European peoples in this prehistory of international law have suggested, for instance, that the great religious and philosophical traditions of Confucianism, Buddhism, Islam and Hinduism have many ideas that correspond with international human rights law in that they attempt to protect human dignity and impose duties on the ruler.[6] Further, the campaign to abolish the slave trade was a major precursor of international human rights law.[7] Looking back even further within the natural law tradition, the writings of sixteenth-century Spanish thinkers such as Francisco Vitoria and Bartoleme Las Casas can be viewed as early attempts to extend natural rights to the non-European peoples, and thus, to give real effect to the argument that natural rights, like contemporary international human rights law, are truly universal and are enjoyed by everyone, no matter how alien. Vitoria and Las Casas might be seen as early champions of the principles of natural law, as they argued that the peoples of the New World possessed certain fundamental rights that the conquering Spanish had to respect. In a time of massive, unprecedented violence against the native peoples, Vitoria and Las Casas were brave champions who spoke for them at considerable personal risk. More recent scholarship, however, has suggested that the works of scholars such as Vitoria may be reinterpreted as justifying imperialism. In extending universal natural rights to the Indians, Vitoria's jurisprudence is said to have also demanded that the Indians comply with these universal principles. Because these universal principles were largely reflections of the Western views of society and economy, the native peoples inevitably violated such principles. As a consequence, it was then open for the Spanish to wage war on the Indians for their violations of natural law and natural rights.[8] In short, the effect of the

---

4 L. Hunt, *Inventing Human Rights: A History* (W.W. Norton & Company, 2007); P.G. Lauren, *The Evolution of International Human Rights: Visions Seen,* 2nd edn (University of Pennsylvania Press, 2011); M.A. Glendon, *A World Made New: Eleanor Roosevelt and the Universal Declaration of Human Rights* (Random House, 2001).

5 See S.N. Grovogui, 'To the Orphaned, Dispossessed, and Illegitimate Children: Human Rights Beyond Republican and Liberal Traditions' (2011) 18(1) *Indiana Journal of Global Legal Studies* 41–63, at 44.

6 See for instance, Lauren (n. 4); Weeramantry (n. 2).

7 See J. Martinez, *The Slave Trade and the Origins of International Human Rights Law* (OUP, 2012).

8 See A. Anghie, 'Francisco De Vitoria and the Colonial Origins of International Law' (1996) 5(4) *Social and Legal Studies* 321–36.

extension of a Western-based natural law and right to the Indians was to justify the sanctioning and transformation of the native to enforce their conformity with natural law. These critical arguments, which have been largely inspired by post-colonial theory, have generated a considerable controversy by interrogating notions of the Kantian 'cosmopolitan right', which have remained somewhat impervious to the colonial dimensions of these traditions. Intellectual historians have now elaborated on the ambiguous legacies of the natural law tradition.

Richard Tuck argues, for instance, that natural rights included the right to self-preservation, and if necessary the taking of lands from people who do not utilise them in a manner compliant with the Western ideas of political economy.[9] Similarly, the idea of the 'cosmopolitan right' developed by Kant, that was long posited as one of the philosophical foundations of international human rights law, has been subject to new scrutiny, and intellectual historians have pointed to the imperial dimensions of Kantian thought.[10] In all these different ways, the natural rights legacy of human rights law, conventionally understood to be anti-imperial and progressive, is being rethought and reassessed.[11] One of the key questions here, is whether what we might provisionally term the 'progressive' aspects of the natural rights tradition can be separated from the other, more imperial principles which also stem from the same origins. This is a crucial issue as it is becoming increasingly clear that many of the most enduring, even if not explicit, natural law principles relate not so much to the protection of human rights, but to systems of political economy, of trade and property. These principles were a crucial aspect of the justification for imperialism, whether in terms of opening up non-European societies to Western trade, or dispossessing indigenous peoples of their land.

It is this history that has led many scholars from the developing world to be ambivalent about international human rights law even while recognising the enormous appeal and promise of the project. If nothing else, it is a history that informs the vision of many developing countries, human rights being an aspect of the 'civilising mission' that sought to legitimise the West's intrusion into the non-European world. Such an account of the past, therefore, provides a lens by which to view subsequent developments in international human rights law that could replicate these patterns, of which some endure.

3 Developing countries and the making of contemporary human rights law

3.1 The drafting of the Universal Declaration

After their decolonisation, 'new states', as they were termed in the language of the time, the 1950s and 1960s, were enthusiastic champions of international law. Those states believed that they could use international law to transform the international system into a just world order, one that would properly serve their legitimate interests. Developing states were particularly intent on changing various doctrines of international law, such as the law of

---

9 R. Tuck, *The Rights of War and Peace: Political Thought and the International Order: From Grotius to Kant* (OUP, 1999) at 195–96.

10 See for instance, J. Tully, *Public Philosophy in a New Key: Volume II: Imperialism and Civil Freedom* (Ideas in Context 94, CUP, 2008) 143.

11 See for instance, ibid.; S. Muthu, *Enlightenment Against Empire* (Princeton University Press, 2003); Emmanuel Chukwudi Eze, 'The Color of Reason: The Idea of "Race" in Kant's Anthropology', in *Postcolonial African Philosophy: A Critical Reader* (Blackwell Publishers, 1997) 103.

foreign investment, in which they had played no part in making and that were used to further colonial rule and exploitation.[12] The Western states, however, were opposed to such attempts, and argued that if the developing countries wanted to be accepted as members of the international community as sovereign states, they were required to observe the relevant rules. Complex legal and diplomatic disputes resulted. With respect to human rights, however, this major area of contestation did not arise quite so immediately. The emergence of the new states was simultaneous with the emergence of international human rights law. Indeed, decolonisation and the construction of an international human rights system were two of the most radical and unprecedented projects undertaken by the United Nations. Each of them sought to challenge, in different ways, long-established ideas of sovereignty and international order. In short, developing countries could participate, as equal and sovereign member states of the United Nations system, in the making of this new body of law, international human rights law.

Despite this, arguments have persisted, indeed increased, as to the Western character of human rights law and the degree to which developing countries contributed to the international human rights regime. Many of these debates focus on the founding document of international human rights law, the UDHR, and the personalities involved in its drafting. Importantly and interestingly, the division between civil and political rights, on the one hand, and economic and social rights on the other, which in time became seen as emblematic of the division between developed and developing countries,[13] was not a major reason for the claim that the UDHR was essentially Western. The UDHR, after all, outlined both sets of rights; indeed, the economic and social rights were far-reaching and extensive, and no suggestion appeared in the UDHR that one set of rights took priority over the other.[14] The argument, rather, was that the Declaration, whatever its attempts to universalise rights, was firmly based on principles of individual rights and a particular relationship between the state and the individual.

The UDHR was drafted by a complex process involving a number of different Committees and personnel. Officially, the task of drafting the UDHR was assigned to the Commission on Human Rights, created by the Economic and Social Council of the United Nations.[15] The importance of drafting a document that was acceptable to all the nations of the world and the different cultural and political traditions they represented, was reflected in the composition of the Commission, which included Chile, China, Egypt, India, Iran, Lebanon, Uruguay and Yugoslavia, in addition to the major Western powers and the Soviet Union.[16] Eleanor Roosevelt chaired the Commission. The Commission in turn created a Committee entrusted with the task of providing a working draft of the Declaration. Prominent members of that Committee included John P. Humphrey of Canada, Rene Cassin of France (debate exists as

---

12 For an account of the views of the new states at this time see R.P. Anand, *New States and International Law,* 2nd edn (Hope India Publications, 2008); S.K.B. Asante, 'Stability of Contractual Relations in the Transnational Investment Process', in F.E. Snyder and S. Sathirathai (eds), *Third World Attitudes Towards International Law: An Introduction* (Martinus Nijhoff Publishers, 1987).

13 V.T. Thamilmaran, *Human Rights in Third World Perspective* (Har-Anand Publications, 1992) 266.

14 See generally, J.M. Woods and H. Lewis (eds), *Human Rights and the Global Marketplace: Economic, Social and Cultural Dimensions* (Transnational Publishers, 2005).

15 For a detailed account of the different stages involved in the drafting of the Declaration, see J. Morsink, *The Universal Declaration of Human Rights: Origins, Drafting and Intent* (University of Pennsylvania Press, 1999) 1–35.

16 Ibid., 4.

to the roles played by each of these major figures), Peng-chun Chang of China and Charles Malik of Lebanon[17] (the latter two had studied for their doctorates in US Ivy League schools).[18] Malik's approach was powerfully shaped by his Thomist natural law philosophy. Chang was diplomatically insistent on the inclusion of the Chinese and Confucian perspectives in the drafting of the document.[19] It is notable that not a single sub-Saharan African country or representative was involved in the drafting process. The Latin American countries and their diplomats, especially Hernan Santa Cruz of Chile, played an important role. It is arguable that the very presence of developing countries in the Commission that drafted the Universal Declaration demonstrated that they were closely involved in the making of human rights from the very outset of the entire project. However, it is difficult to escape the conclusion that the document which finally emerged was largely reflective of Western traditions and concepts of the individual, society and state.[20]

This situation was perhaps affected by related political factors. On the whole, the developing country representatives argued powerfully for the universality of international human rights law, in part because several developed country representatives, being concerned about the implications of human rights in their colonial territories, had wanted to include a 'colonial clause' – the basic argument here was that 'Western-based' human rights norms were inappropriate for the 'backward' indigenous inhabitants.[21] This approach, of insisting on the universal applicability of international human rights law and international law, more broadly, was part of the general approach of the developing countries to international law. Thus, for instance, the first generation of scholars from the new states argued that their own cultural traditions and histories embodied their own versions of principles regarding, for example, diplomatic immunities, treaties, laws of war and so on). While the broad ideas of human dignity and the imposition of limits to sovereign rule were to be found in all the great religious and cultural traditions of developing countries, international human rights law represented a particular version of how these general concerns and issues were to be addressed. In many developing countries the emphasis was less on the individual and more on the collectivity, on society; and social order involved not only rights, but duties. Article 29(1) of the UDHR, which deals with the issue of human duties, is thought to represent the concern of the developing countries about duties rather than rights, and, further, it includes the concept of the community, whereas much of the UDHR focuses on the individual and the state.[22] Here again, easy assumptions based on the nationality of the participants prove to be unfounded. It was the French jurist, Rene Cassin who had drafted a more elaborate set of principles regarding the duties; and it was the Chinese jurist, Chang, who minimised these principles, and indeed proposed that the Article dealing with duties should be at the end rather than at the beginning of the UDHR.[23] Chang had attempted to infuse the UDHR

---

17 Ibid., 5.
18 Ibid., 30.
19 Ibid., 5. Some tension seems to have existed between Chang and Malik.
20 This possible anomaly may be explained by the concern of the developing countries, at this time, to demonstrate that they too were adherents to the civilised Western principles of international law.
21 R. Burke, *Decolonization and the Evolution of International Human Rights* (University of Pennsylvania Press, 2010) 40–41.
22 Article 29(1) reads: 'Everyone has duties to the community in which alone the free and full development of his personality is possible.' Universal Declaration of Human Rights (adopted 10 December 1948) UNGA Res. 217A(III), UN Doc. A/810 at 71 (1948) Art. 29(1).
23 Morsink, (n. 15) 245.

with the Confucian concept that suggested 'sympathy' or 'two-man mindedness', to add to the communitarian dimension of the UDHR through the inclusion of the word 'conscience' in its opening article: 'All human beings are born free and equal in dignity and rights. They are endowed with reason and conscience and should act towards one another in a spirit of brotherhood.' It is doubtful, however, that the term conscience adequately conveys the complexity of the concept it was supposed to represent.

There are two distinct aspects of the intermediate ideas of 'community' and 'duty' which are espoused by developing country states and scholars. First, there is the idea that the individual cannot be conceived of independently of the community to which he or she belongs. Correspondingly, there exists the idea the individual owes duties to other members of that community.[24] Article 29(1) of the Declaration, which is supposed to embody this concept, has not generated a major jurisprudence, and this is understandable given that the enforcement of human rights is structured to deal with the state violations of individual rights. Arguably, however, recent jurisprudence, particularly in relation to the protection of the rights of women, seek to protect rights in the private sphere, that is, in effect, enforcing rights as between individuals. This is achieved by asserting that the failure of the state to protect an individual against another individual through adequate policing and a proper legal system is a violation by the state of its duties (the 'due diligence' principle). In this way, the traditional enforcement structure is extended to address violations by individuals of the rights of other individuals. Second, the focus on community as an intermediate entity between the individual and the state suggests that it is the community, a collectivity, that should also be the bearer of rights. These conceptualisations of rights, together with the emphasis by developing countries on the importance of economic and social rights, have been heatedly debated on the basis that they contravene the classical ideas of rights which focus on the negative rights of individuals in relation to the state, and that dangerous political consequences could follow with the supposed rights of the community – itself a vague term – being used to suppress the individual.

3.2 Self-determination and human rights

The approaches of the developing countries to international human rights law cannot be understood in isolation from the larger third world project. Basically, the question was, how could the emerging law of international human rights be formulated and deployed for the purpose of achieving the political goals of the third world? The most immediate goal confronting the third world at the time was that of promoting decolonisation and eradicating racism. Further, and related to this, the apartheid regime in South Africa had become a target of concerted action by the third world, whose strategy involved the elaboration of basic equality principles to deal with the issue of racial discrimination.

---

24 Article 27(1) of the African Charter expands the range of actors and the duties owed to them: '[e]very individual shall have duties towards his family and society, the State and other legally recognized communities and the international community.' African Charter on Human and Peoples' Rights (hereafter African Charter) (adopted 27 June 1981, entered into force 21 October 1986) OAU Doc. CAB/LEG/67/3 rev. 5. The American Declaration of the Rights and Duties of Man, adopted in 1948 contains an entire chapter enumerating the 'duties' of the individual, including duties to society, and the family. See American Declaration of the Rights and Duties of Man, (adopted 2 May 1948) OAS Res. XXX, OAS Doc. OEA/Ser. L. V/II.82doc.6rev.1 at 17 (1992) Chapter 2.

Several scholars have recently examined the participation of third world states in the formation of human rights law at the time, following the adoption of the UDHR, and they have demonstrated that third world states, and particularly prominent third world diplomats, played a major role in the debates that took place in the Third (Human Rights) Committee of the United Nations.[25] The main concern of the developing countries in the 1950s was to insist on the 'right to self-determination' as a human right,[26] the insistent argument being that self-determination was inseparable, a crucial prerequisite for the enjoyment of other individual human rights.[27] Correspondingly, a General Assembly Resolution, adopted in 1952 asserted that 'the right of peoples and nations to self-determination is a prerequisite to the full enjoyment of all fundamental human rights'.[28] The connection between self-determination and human rights was pursued by the third world in many different venues, such as the Bandung Conference, which focused on and asserted its support for the 'fundamental principles of human rights', while insisting that 'self-determination is a fundamental prerequisite for the enjoyment of all fundamental Human Rights'.[29] The Bandung Conference also condemned racial segregation.[30] The emphasis of the developing countries on self-determination, which was not mentioned in the Universal Declaration, resulted in the formulation of Article 1(1) of both the International Covenant on Economic, Social and Cultural Rights (ICESCR) and the International Covenant on Civil and Political Rights (ICCPR) affirming the right of peoples to self-determination.[31] Scholars have debated whether the right to self-determination should be regarded properly as a 'human right', as human rights deal distinctively with the protection of the individual against the excesses of the government.[32] Nevertheless, irrespective of the conceptual issues involved, the inclusion of the right to self-determination in the Covenants suggests that it should, for our purposes, be regarded as such, and particularly so in any account of the approaches of the developing countries towards human rights, precisely because an aspect of those approaches had to do with challenging classical understandings of Western-derived human rights law.

The campaign of developing countries against racial segregation and discrimination was directed principally against South Africa. The International Convention on the Elimination of All Forms of Racial Discrimination (CERD) was one of its products. Notably, the CERD came into being before the ICCPR and ICESCR. Further, the campaign against South Africa, based mainly on the principle of non-discrimination, was waged in virtually all the organs of the United Nations, including the General Assembly, the Security Council and the International Court of Justice.[33] South Africa, in defence of its policies, cited Article 2(7) of

---

25 The Third Committee is the Committee established by the General Assembly of the United Nations to deal with 'Social Humanitarian and Cultural Affairs', and this included human rights issues.
26 Burke (n. 21) 41.
27 Ibid., 41–42.
28 The Rights of Peoples and Nations to Self-determination, GA Res. 637(VII) (16 December 1952).
29 Asian African Conference, Bandung, April 18–24, Final Communiqué (1955) para. C.1 (Human Rights and Self-Determination).
30 Ibid. C.2.
31 The anti-colonial aspects of this right are emphasised by Art. 1(3), which particularly refers to the Non-Self Governing Trust and Territories.
32 See S. Moyn, *The Last Utopia: Human Rights in History* (Belknap Press of Harvard University Press, 2010) 100.
33 The *South West Africa Cases* in the ICJ was an attempt to realise the principles of self-determination and racial equality. For the full text of the case, see ICJ, *South West African Cases* (*Ethiopia v South Africa; Liberia v South Africa*) (Advisory Opinions and Orders) 1966, http://www.icj-cij.org/docket/files/47/4955.pdf, accessed 29 January 2012.

the UN Charter, which prohibited the UN from interfering in matters 'within the domestic jurisdiction of the state'. Most significantly, in the light of subsequent events, the developing countries insisted that this was an invalid argument, and that South Africa had to comply with fundamental international human rights norms. In the end, the preoccupations of the developing countries with issues of race and colonialism have persisted; the recent and ill-fated Durban initiatives against racism were in many ways extensions of these concerns.[34] It is, however, notable that the developing countries have been very reluctant to endanger their sovereignty in any way by extending the right to self-determination to minorities and indigenous peoples.[35]

3.3 The right to development

The developing countries' attempts to use human rights to further their political projects is again suggested by the attempts of developing countries to use human rights for the purposes of promoting economic development. Following decolonisation, the developing countries launched a major campaign to achieve economic development, most markedly in their demands for the creation of a New International Economic Order (NIEO). Several aspects of that initiative intersected with the international human rights law. The most significant among these was the passing of the UN Declaration on the Right to Development (1986). Again, this caused uncertainty because, like certain provisions of the ICESCR, certain provisions within it, such as Article 2(1), suggested that the human rights obligations extended beyond borders, that is, rich states had duties to ensure the well-being of people in poorer states. The right to self-determination was politically, if not conceptually linked with various rights relating to permanent sovereignty over natural resources that were a part of the effort to create an NIEO.[36]

The right to development was, in many ways, an elaboration of the idea hinted at in Article 28 of the Universal Declaration, asserting that: 'Everyone is entitled to a social and international order in which the rights and freedoms set forth in this Declaration can be fully realized.' The right to development was characterised as promoting 'economic self-determination' to accompany the political self-determination that was already in place.[37]

---

34 For the World Conference against Racism, Racial Discrimination, Xenophobia and Related Intolerance see http://www.un.org/WCAR/ (last accessed on 24 February 2013).

35 Article 27 of the ICCPR (International Covenant on Civil and Political Rights, 1966) (adopted 16 December 1966, entered into force 23 March 1976) 999 UNTS 171) and the UN Declaration on the Rights of Persons Belonging to National or Ethnic, Religious and Linguistic Minorities (adopted 18 December 1992) GA Res. 47/135, Annex, UN Doc. A/RES/47/135, focus on the rights of individuals who belong to minorities; the UN Declaration on the Rights of Indigenous Peoples (adopted 2 October 2007) UNGA Res. 61/295, UN Doc. A/Res/61/295, Arts 3 and 4, mentions self-determination, but in a highly qualified manner. See K. Engle, 'On Fragile Architecture: The UN Declaration on the Right of Indigenous Peoples in the Context of Human Rights' (2011) 22(1) *European Journal of International Law* 141–63.

36 For instance, the preambular paragraph 15 of the Declaration on the Rights to Development states that the General Assembly is '[a]ware that efforts at the international level to promote and protect human rights should be accompanied by efforts to establish a new international economic order'. UN Declaration on the Right to Development, 1986 (adopted 4 December 1986) GA Res. 41/128 UN Doc. A/RES/41/128. Article 4 of the Declaration on the Right to Development asserts that '[s]tates have the duty to take steps individually and collectively, to formulate international development policies with a view to full realization of the right'. Ibid. Art. 4.

37 R. Normand and S. Zaida, *Human Rights at the UN: the Political History of Universal Justice* (Indiana University Press, 2008) 298.

Keba Mbaye of Senegal, widely regarded as the author of the right to development, and many of the most distinguished jurists from developing countries, such as Georges Abi-Saab and Mohammed Bedjaoui, have commented that the right to development was implicit in the other rights that had already been recognised: 'the right to development . . . is a necessary precondition for the satisfaction of the social and economic rights of the individual.'[38] The meaning and coherence of the right to development was highly contested by scholars adhering to Western concepts of human rights. And the issue of how to give meaning and content to the right has remained problematic, although it has been evoked in various situations, including proposals for debt relief. Nevertheless, the right to development remains an ongoing topic, if only because the issue of development remains a central preoccupation of the international system. Thus, questions inevitably remain unresolved as to the relationship between international development efforts and the right to development. An enduring, if not prominently noted, consequence of the efforts to create a right to development, is the ongoing campaign for solidarity rights, often categorised as 'third generation rights'.[39]

3.4 Human rights and enforcement

The question of how human rights were to be enforced was one of the most controversial confronting this new project. It was one thing for governments to concede, with some reluctance, that their treatment of their own citizens was a legitimate subject of international scrutiny and concern. It was quite another, on the other hand, to provide real mechanisms by which human rights could be enforced by individuals at the international level. The history of the drafting of the Universal Declaration and other major instruments reveals that developing countries and their representatives took the initiative in attempting to formulate effective enforcement mechanisms. Indeed, developing countries improvised the 1503 Procedure,[40] which enabled the Sub-Commission on Prevention of Discrimination and Protection of Minorities to receive petitions from individuals; the origins of this, and the related 1235 Procedure[41] were inspired in many ways by the ongoing issues of colonialism and racism. Indeed, the process can be compared with the petition system established under the Trusteeship Council,[42] whose specific purpose was to carefully monitor the Administrating Power as it prepared dependent peoples for self-governance. The dominance of developing country states in the UN system enabled these initiatives.

The approach of the developing countries to enforcement, nevertheless, took quite a different turn when developing countries themselves came under increased scrutiny for human rights violations. The aspirations of third world peoples for justice and a better future in the new, decolonised world order were bitterly disappointed by the emergence of dictatorial third world regimes that established themselves by the 1970s and 1980s, and with the eruption of ethnic conflict within many of these states. These authoritarian leaders, many of

---

38 G. Abi-Saab, 'The Legal Formulation of A Right to Development', in H.J. Steiner, P. Alston and R. Goodman (eds), *International Human Rights in Context: Law, Politics, Morals,* 3rd edn (Text and Materials, OUP, 2008) 1445–46. Mohammed Bedjaoui went further, in asserting that 'it is the alpha and omega of human rights'. M. Bedjaoui, 'The Right to Development' in ibid. 1447.

39 K. Vasek, 'For the Third Generation of Human Rights: The Rights of Solidarity' in ibid. 1442–43.

40 Economic and Social Council Resolution 1503 (XLVIII) of 27 May 1970.

41 Economic and Social Council Resolution 1235 (XLII) of 6 June 1967.

42 UN Charter, Art. 87(2).

whom had been at the forefront of the nationalist struggle, turned on their own people and asserted the primacy of sovereignty over human rights – an ironic reversal of the stances taken against colonial regimes and the apartheid regime of South Africa. Many of these dictatorships, further, were supported by the major forces involved in the Cold War. During this period much of the scholarship in third world countries focused on the issue of how the basic civil and political rights of the third world peoples could be protected, on one hand, and the role of human rights in the foreign policies of the major Western actors, on the other hand. Developing countries have become increasingly wary of the international human rights enforcement mechanisms, particularly in situations where this could involve intervention and the use of force in the name of human rights. In more recent times, the dominance of developing countries in bodies such as the UN Human Rights Council has resulted, in the view of many non-governmental organisations and Western governments, in the undermining of international human rights law.

3.5 Human rights and the end of history

The collapse of the Berlin Wall and the end of the Cold War affected the third world approaches to human rights law in at least two major respects. First, the collapse of the Wall was widely interpreted as 'The End of History'.[43] Liberal democracy had won, and all that remained for the developing countries was to work towards making this model a reality. Whatever the intellectual limitations of Fukuyama's central thesis, it captured the broad thinking of the international human rights community. Second, the collapse of the Berlin Wall further inaugurated and intensified the phenomenon of globalisation. International human rights law, with its prescription of universal standards, embodies many of the characteristics of globalisation. Globalisation took a particular form, the promotion of neo-liberal economic policies that broadly sought to expand the reach of the market and reduce the role of the state. Somewhat paradoxically, even as the collapse of the Wall presaged the beginning of a 'New World Order', the 1990s also witnessed massive human rights atrocities, particularly in the Balkans and Rwanda. More encouragingly, democratic rule replaced authoritarian regimes in many Latin American countries, and the release of Nelson Mandela signalled the end of apartheid in South Africa.

The intensification of globalisation, suggested by the creation of the World Trade Organization in 1995, and the general expansion in the reach and activities of multinational corporations, presented a new set of challenges to human rights and the peoples of the third world. Human rights law struggled to realign and apply itself to the newly revived areas of international economic law, such as international investment law and international trade law which had a profound impact on the lives and rights of the peoples of the third world. Further, institutions such as the World Bank were drawing upon international human rights law in various ways in their efforts to promote 'the rule of law and good governance'.[44] As

---

43 F. Fukuyama, 'The End of History?' (Summer 1989) *The National Interest* 3–27.
44 J.T. Gathii, 'Retelling Good Governance Narratives on Africa's Economic and Political Predicaments: Continuities and Discontinuities in Legal Outcomes between Markets and States Symposium – Critical Race Theory and International Law' (2000) 45(5) *Villanova Law Review* 971–1036.

Upendra Baxi persuasively argued, a 'market friendly' version of human rights resulted.[45] This neo-liberal rendition of human rights and its claims to promote development contrasted markedly with the approach of the developing countries when they attempted to fuse rights with development through the right to development, which seemed to be less effective than the neo-liberal project of good governance and rule of law that also deployed international human rights law to advance the market.

It was not only with regard to globalisation and good governance, however, that human rights became fused with some broader political and economic project. Simplifying considerably, the period from the 1990s onwards witnessed not simply the continuing proliferation of human rights instruments, such as The International Convention on the Protection of the Rights of All Migrant Workers and Members of Their Families (1990)[46] and the Convention on the Rights of the Child (1989), but also the infusion of human rights in a number of other major political projects: these included the right to democratic governance and all the programmes associated with this, transitional justice and its related field, international criminal law, which received intense international interest as a result of the creation of the International Criminal Court, and post-conflict reconstruction. Further, human rights became intimately connected with the revival of a new and more refined version of humanitarian intervention, the 'Responsibility to Protect',[47] which emerged from the experiences of Kosovo and Rwanda. The new field of 'transitional justice', that relied heavily on human rights principles, derived from the experiences of Latin American countries and the system established by South Africa to deal with the history of apartheid.

All these projects claimed, in one way or another, to be furthering and expanding human rights, but difficult questions remained as to the implications of human rights being used in all these different ways. The fact that these initiatives sought to consolidate themselves by invoking international human rights law, suggested that human rights had acquired a special legitimating force. It had become the principal language by which to explore issues of justice and international relations. The truth and reconciliation initiatives of the Latin American and South African governments played a landmark role in the creation of the field of 'transitional justice', but generally, the most important human rights initiatives from the 1990s onwards, such as the 'Responsibility to Protect', have emerged from the West. The major initiative of the developing countries regarding self-determination has been, in many ways, reversed as developing countries have proved reluctant to recognise the rights of minorities or the rights of indigenous peoples, where those rights involve self-determination. The preoccupation of the developing countries with sovereignty continues in this way. The right to development has been now allied with the project on the Millennium Development Goals;[48] but the neo-liberal

---

45 U. Baxi, 'Voices of Suffering and the Future of Human Rights Symposium: International Human Rights at Fifty: a Symposium to Commemmorate the 50th Anniversary of the Universal Declaration of Human Rights' (1998) 8(2) *Transnational Law and Contemporary Problems* 125–70 at 163–64.
46 UNTS vol. 2220, 3; UN doc. A/RES/45/158.
47 See World Summit Outcome, General Assembly A/60/L.1, 15 September 2005.
48 Declaration on Right to Development, GA Res. 41/128 (adopted 4 December 1986), UN Millennium Development Goals, available at http://www.un.org/millenniumgoals/, accessed on 8 January 2012; for a critique, see P. Alston, 'Ships Passing in the Night: The Current State of the Human Rights and Development Debate Seen through the Lens of the Millennium Development Goals' (2005) 27(3) *Human Rights Quarterly* 755–829: B. Ibhawoh, 'The Right to Development: The Politics and Polemics of Power and Resistance' (2011) 33(1) *Human Rights Quarterly* 76–104.

development policy remains, despite its travails, the dominant operational paradigm for the achievement of development. The attempts of the developing countries to further promote the right to development[49] and right to solidarity within the UN system are still ongoing.[50]

The developing countries were not the prominent actors in the formulation and expansion of many of these initiatives, although they were fashioned to deal with political and legal issues arising from these countries, whether it was South Africa or Rwanda or Timor-Leste. Human rights, both in their explicit and secondary forms, fused with these other initiatives, became extraordinarily powerful and intrusive.

3.6 Cultural relativism

The question of cultural difference and cultural relativism emerged once again in the 1990s. This has always been a problem: studied in an historical perspective, the debate has gone through a number of phases. First, in the early phase, developing countries, as part of the decolonisation programme, insisted on the universality of rights; scholars acknowledged the difference between 'Western rights' and local traditions; but they often insisted on the commonalities between human rights and their own traditions, often focusing on even broader concepts such as 'the protection of human dignity' to establish such commonalities.[51] In the later phase, the resistance to rights by third world states in the 1970s onwards was based on the assertion of sovereignty and an emphasis on the importance of economic and social rights, that is, development. Put simply, development took precedence over rights: to the extent that rights promoted development, they were welcome, but if the two goals were in tension with each other, then development prevailed. Human rights scholars such as Abdullahi An-Na'im and Francis Deng[52] have produced important works examining the implications of cultural difference and have developed a model of cross-cultural approaches to international human rights law, suggesting a model of a dialogue between different cultures and, importantly, insisting on the fact that cultures are not static, and that they have different internal resources enabling changing responses to new circumstances. As An-Na'im argues, the fact that international human rights law was initially Western does not negate the point that it is a valuable and important way in which to preserve human dignity.[53] Importantly, further, scholars have pointed to the ways in which customary law and traditional norms can prove effective ways of protecting the well-being of women, for instance, because these norms are a part of the lived social reality of the people involved.[54]

---

49 See for example, 'Promotion and Protection of All Human Rights, Civil, Political, Economic, Social and Cultural Rights Including the Right to Development', Human Rights Council, General Assembly, UN Doc. A/HRC/12/27 (22 April 2009).

50 See for example, Human Rights Council, 'Report of the Independent Expert on Human Rights and International Solidarity' (5 July 2010) 15th Session (2010) UN Doc. A/HRC/15/32.

51 See for instance, Weeramantry (n. 2).

52 F. Deng, 'A Cultural Approach to Human Rights among the Dinka', in A.A. An-Na'im and F.M. Deng (eds), *Human Rights in Africa: Cross-Cultural Perspectives* (The Brookings Institution, 1990) 261. Deng writes of a 'bridge between cultural contexts . . . [that] would also enrich the process of universalization in the promotion and protection of human rights'. Ibid. 288–89.

53 A.A. An-Na'im, 'Conclusion', in A.A. An-Na'im (ed.), *Human Rights in Cross-Cultural Perspectives: A Quest for Consensus* (University of Pennsylvania Press, 1992) 427–30.

54 C.I. Nyamu, 'How Should Human Rights and Development Respond to Cultural Legitimization of Gender Hierarchy in Developing Countries?' (2000) 41(2) *Harvard International Law Journal* 381–418 at 383.

The developing countries were relatively united by the common cause of decolonisation and the creation of an NIEO. In the course of time, however, the attitudes of the developing countries towards human rights shifted, as the developing world itself underwent transformation and division. Certain countries in East and South-East Asia were astonishingly successful in achieving impressive levels of economic growth. These were the countries that were most vociferous in asserting the 'Asian values' argument, which was in many respects a revival, in a more concentrated form, of the argument that society was based on duties and the community, rather than individual rights. These arguments were made by a few Asian leaders,[55] but they were in many ways an expression of the emergence and economic success of these countries, and of an exasperation about Western arguments insisting on the universality of a particular vision of human rights. Arguably, important countries in the West itself were 'cultural relativists' – an examination of the reservation that the United States entered into when ratifying the ICCPR, for instance, clearly demonstrates that the United States had, in effect, amended the treaty to accept obligations that corresponded with its own understanding of rights.[56]

In Latin America, by contrast, the States had united with each other to create their own human rights system that included the Inter-American Court of Human Rights, which handed down many notable judgments that were innovations in the sphere of human rights law worldwide.[57] The Inter-American system of human rights suggested a model in which the universal human rights would be enforced by a regional system, that would be all the more effective because it somehow better represented the understandings and culture of the countries which were bound.

In Africa, the African Charter of Human and Peoples' Rights outlined an African understanding of rights, and the African Commission on Human and Peoples' Rights represented, yet again, a regional focus on rights. By this stage, then – the 1990s – the whole term 'developing countries' had become even more problematic, given the significant differences, in economic status and political realities, of these countries. The contrast was starkly suggested by different approaches to the whole issue of humanitarian intervention. Asian countries remain resolutely sceptical of the 'Responsibility to Protect' initiative; in Africa, by contrast, humanitarian intervention is legalised by Article 4(h) of the Constitutive Act of the African Union.

4 The future of human rights in developing countries

Human rights is increasingly expanding its reach, particularly as it now serves as an important element of new initiatives regarding transitional justice, international criminal law, the Responsibility to Protect, post-conflict reconstruction and the promotion of the rule of law. This has given rise to a new set of debates regarding, for instance, the relationship between human rights and international humanitarian law in situations of internal armed conflict. The

---

55 Y. Ghai, 'Human Rights and Governance: The Asia Debate' *1995 Australian Yearbook of International Law*, 1–34.

56 See the 'reservations', 'understandings' and 'declarations' of the United States in respect to its ICCPR ratification at http://treaties.un.org/pages/ViewDetails.aspx?src=TREATY&mtdsg_no=IV-4&chapter=4&lang=en (last accessed on 24 February 2013).

57 For instance, expanding the reach of rights into the private sphere: V. Rodriguez, 'Inter-American Court of Human Rights, 1988, Ser. C, No. 4' (1998) 9 *Human Rights Law Journal* 212.

overall framework that is created is one that may be termed 'Humanity's Law'.[58] Complex issues remain as to whether 'human rights' should be the principal vocabulary by which to discuss questions of international justice; especially as they remain focused, by and large, on relations between the state and its citizens, a framework that inhibits discussions of international justice and redistribution, fields that are now dominated by private law regimes dealing with international trade and investment. Accompanying each of the initiatives inspired by human rights, furthermore, are entire industries devoted to promoting transitional justice or state reconstruction or democratic governance or international criminal tribunals. What results is the 'rule of experts', the management of extremely complex issues by experts,[59] whose authority resides in the claim that they possess knowledge of fundamental international standards which will provide a solution, appropriately modified for local conditions, to very difficult issues.[60]

International human rights norms are now affecting the lives of peoples in the developing countries in a number of ways. Apart from their existence at the international level, they have been incorporated into constitutions, as in the case of South Africa, and they are found in regional instruments. Human rights law, then, is being made and interpreted and applied and extended in myriad locations, each with their complex backgrounds and unpredictable effects. This could be seen as a process by which human rights are localised, their abstract injunctions made relevant and effective through their application in particular contexts. The risk remains that human rights will be undermined through this process of 'vernacularisation', but it is perhaps essential for its success. Quite apart from this, they are now an inescapable part of everyday political debate, and are invoked by government officials, non-governmental organisations and international organisations. The 'War on Terror' waged by the United States has posed a profound challenge to international human rights law, and it remains to be seen whether developing states will employ comparable legal techniques that in effect undermine fundamental rights in the name of security.

Recent scholarship which has been inspired by the experiences of the peoples in the developing countries, rather than that of states, has approached these crucial questions from a somewhat different vantage point, that is, to what extent can human rights empower the most disadvantaged who must contend with both international forces and the violence inflicted by their own states. A number of scholars have focused on understanding what difference human rights makes to the peoples of the third world, in their lived realities.[61] How can human rights be recharacterised when viewed from this epistemology, that is 'human rights from below'? The focus of this scholarship is on a different set of actors who might be termed 'subaltern', and which include 'new social movements'.[62] The central issue, here, is how human rights may be used by such actors to empower themselves and achieve social justice. This approach

---

58 R.G. Teitel, *Humanity's Law* (OUP, 2011); for the argument that 'humanity' has become the basis of all notions of progress and justice, see Moyn (n. 32).

59 V. Nesiah, 'The Specter of Violence that Haunts the UDHR: The Turn to Ethics and Expertise' (2009) 24(1) *Maryland Journal of International Law* 135–54 at 136.

60 D. Kennedy, 'Challenging Expert Rule: The Politics of Global Governance: Address' (2005) 27 *Sydney Law Review* 5–28.

61 B. Rajagopal, *International Law From Below: Development, Social Movements, and Third World Resistance* (CUP, 2003); U. Baxi, *The Future of Human Rights*, 2nd edn (OUP, 2006); O.C. Okafor, *The African Human Rights System, Activist Forces, and International Institutions* (CUP, 2007).

62 See Rajagopal (n. 61).

corresponds with the anthropological and 'law and society research' explorations of human rights, which have enhanced understandings of how human rights and its operations may be better understood in their sociological contexts.[63] The question of how human rights can be used to protect the dignity of women has been and continues to be a central theme of contemporary human rights law.[64]

It is through the experience of these actors that the strengths and limits of international human rights law may be interpreted and assessed afresh. By identifying the centrality of these actors to the human rights project further, it might be possible to undermine the claims made by third world states regarding issues such as cultural relativism, even while challenging the claims to authority made by the discourse of 'expertise'. It is these actors who can add a different and powerful voice to the ongoing discussion on human rights.

This work corresponds with the work done by anthropologists who seek to understand what role human rights plays in these settings, how human rights norms, even if they are not completely and transparently enforceable, nevertheless change the terms of political discourse. The question, here, is how can the most disadvantaged appropriate and define human rights in ways that would make a real difference to their everyday lives?

5 Conclusions

The attitudes of the developing countries towards human rights can best be understood in the broader context of political developments and changing international relations. The key concerns of developing countries, namely, decolonisation, sovereignty and development, have played a crucial role in shaping developing country attitudes to human rights law. Even so, however, no easy generalisations may be made about developing countries and human rights, as different developing countries, and regions have evolved in quite distinctive ways. Human rights is a particular political project, and developing country approaches to human rights have been animated by their own political projects – decolonisation, development and sovereignty. It is unsurprising, given this approach, that developing countries have been unmoved by arguments about conceptual purity that human rights are a means by which individuals may be protected from the abuses of the state.

But to focus only on 'developing country' approaches to human rights is to negate one of the main goals of human rights law, which is to empower and give voice to the people: the people who are after all the foundation of sovereignty, and in whose name and for whose benefit the projects of decolonisation, sovereignty and development are supposedly advanced. These earlier projects were based on various assumptions and a political vision in which, for instance, decolonisation, nationalism and sovereignty were pitted against colonialism and neo-colonialism in its various forms. A focus on third world peoples rather than states, however, reveals that authoritarian nationalism could pose as much of a danger to the well-being of these peoples as neo-colonialism. Dramatic events, such as the Arab Spring, suggest a need to reinterpret and reinvigorate old principles – the idea that 'all people have the right to self-determination' where self-determination does not mean freedom from colonial rule

63 See e.g. M. Goodale and S.E. Merry (eds), *The Practice of Human Rights: Tracking Law Between the Global and the Local* (Cambridge Studies in Law and Society, CUP, 2008).
64 See for instance, Nyamu (n. 54); C.A. Choudhury, '(Mis)Appropriated Liberty: Identity, Gender Justice and Muslim Personal Law Reform in India' (2008) 17(1) *Columbia Journal of Gender and Law* 45–110.

but from dictatorship. The peoples of developing countries face dangers from a number of different sources: from a hostile international system that often reproduces neo-colonial structures, on the one hand, and on the other from authoritarian rulers who commit massive violence in the name of sovereignty and nationalism, even while often effectively acting on behalf of the foreign agents and instrumentalities they condemn. The enduring question then is how human rights can be developed to protect human dignity in the face of these threats. The task ahead is for the peoples of developing countries, through their political struggles, to deploy, reconstruct and animate human rights, providing them with a meaning and content that may transform abstract international principles into a vehicle not only of empowering themselves, but also enriching the field of human rights in general.

Select bibliography

A. An'naim (ed.), *Human Rights in Cross-Cultural Perspectives* (University of Pennsylvania Press, 1992).

U. Baxi, *The Future of Human Rights* (Oxford University Press, 2002).

R. Burke, *Decolonization and the Evolution of Human Rights* (University of Pennsylvania Press, 2010).

M. Goodale and S.E. Merry (eds), *The Practice of Human Rights: Tracking Law Between the Local and the Global* (Cambridge University Press, 2007).

J. Morsink, *The Universal Declaration of Human Rights: Origins, Drafting and Intent* (University of Pennsylvania Press, 2000).

M. Mutua, *Human Rights: A Political and Cultural Critique* (University of Pennsylvania Press, 2002).

B. Rajagopal, *International Law From Below* (Cambridge University Press, 2003).

C.G. Weeramantry, *Justice Without Frontiers: Furthering Human Rights* Vol. I (Kluwer Law, 1997).

J.M. Woods and H. Lewis (eds), *Human Rights and the Global Marketplace: Economic, Social and Cultural Dimensions* (Transnational Publishers, 2005).

8

The contemporary challenges to international human rights

Radhika Coomaraswamy

At a recent bilateral meeting at the United Nations, the representative from a country which was facing mounting criticism about its human rights record said: 'human rights is a dead concept, it has become part of the arsenal of Western imperialism. It is politics by other means.' A few months earlier, as the Special Representative on Children and Armed Conflict, I was in Bangui, the capital of the Central African Republic (CAR), and met three generations of women in one family who stated that they were raped by Jean Pierre Bemba's troops when they marched into CAR from the Democratic Republic of the Congo in 2002. These women were at the headquarters of a local non-governmental organisation (NGO) that was meticulously preparing for the women to go to The Hague to testify before the International Criminal Court.[1] The women were excited and felt that justice was going to be done and that they would have their day in court.

This is the duality of human rights in the contemporary world. At one level, even in multilateral fora, the discourse of human rights is being challenged by powerful member states and some theorists from the developing world. At another level, human rights have begun to inform the lives of so many people, invoked by citizens and communities everywhere whenever they feel that freedom or justice is being denied.

This chapter will argue that in the contemporary world, human rights doctrine and practice face three challenges. The first is the challenge of universality and the need to ensure resonance in all societies. It will particularly look at substantive questioning of human rights, including with regard to the 'Asian values' discourse, and the allegation that double standards prevent universal application, as well as the lack of universality when it comes to the rights of women. The second challenge relates to the fact that warfare is changing and many of the foundations of human rights based on civil and political rights are being challenged and transformed. Finally, increasingly non-state actors are playing an important role in political

---

1 Jean Pierre Bemba Gombo (Bemba) was the head of the Movement for the Liberation of Congo (MLC). The MLC went into the Congo in 2002 and has been accused of committing war crimes and crimes against humanity. Bemba has been indicted by the ICC: *The Prosecutor v Jean Pierre Bemba Gombo*, ICC-01/05–01/08.

and social development. Human rights, with its state focus, may be unable to fully respond to the types of injustices that people face in their daily lives.

1 Universality

1.1 Asian values

From its inception, the Universal Declaration of Human Rights, shepherded by Eleanor Roosevelt and adopted by the United Nations in the 1940s,[2] faced challenges from theorists and member states alike. In the 1980s, when the doctrine was formulated into treaties and when the Commission on Human Rights began to be more proactive, resistance continued. One of the notable challenges came from Asian scholars and Asian member states that claimed that human rights were contrary to Asian values.[3] The Bangkok Declaration of 1993 was the high point of this movement, where Asian states accepted the principles of human rights, but at the same time reaffirmed the principles of sovereignty, non-interference and the priority of economic development.[4]

With the rise of Asian economic power, there is a resurgence of the doctrine of Asian values that had receded after the growth of democratic movements in South Korea, Indonesia and the Philippines. Valuing strong central government over pluralism, social harmony over dissent, development over civil liberties and the community over the individual, many Asian leaders, pointing to the prosperity of China, are again today positing Asian values as an alternative model that calls into question the universality of human rights.[5]

Amartya Sen, who has spent a great deal of time assessing the pluralism inherent in some parts of Asia, has challenged the core premises and ideas of what are termed Asian values.[6] Sen argues that 'Asian values' assume one normative standard for Asia, whereas there is a great deal of diversity in Asia and among nation states. He points out that in all of the world's traditions, Western or Eastern, there is a stream of thought that is for strong authoritarian leaders and other streams of thought that value pluralistic and democratic traditions. His study of India is an example of the triumph of the latter traditions over the former.[7] His argument goes to the core of the challenge to those political and philosophical writings that identify clashes among civilisations and seek to essentialise civilisations along particular values and themes. The truth is that there is diversity, contradiction and contestation within all civilisations, and leaders and theorists may choose to glorify core elements that seek to drive their agenda, ignoring other traditions.

Asia in particular is ill-suited to these generalisations. It is true that Asia has been home to modern authoritarian governments, but developments in Taiwan, South Korea, the Philippines

---

2 Universal Declaration of Human Rights (adopted 10 December 1948) UNGA Res. 217 A(III).
3 F. Zakaria, 'Culture is Destiny: A Conversation with Lee Kwan Yew' (1994) 73(2) *Foreign Affairs*,109.
4 Final Declaration of the Regional Meeting for Asia of the World Conference on Human Rights, UN Doc. A/CONF.157/ASRM/8 A/CONF.157/PC/59 (7 April 1993).
5 HE Mahinda Rajapaksa, President of Sri Lanka, 'Statement at the General Debate of the 66th Session of the United Nations General Assembly' (23 September 2011), available at: http://gade-bate.un.org/66/sri-lanka, accessed on 5 March 2012.
6 A. Sen, 'Human Rights and Asian Values', The Sixteenth Morgenthau Memorial Lecture on Ethics and Foreign Policy, Carnegie Council on Ethics and Foreign Affairs (1997), available at http://www.carnegiecouncil.org/media/254_sen.pdf, accessed on 5 March 2012.
7 A. Sen, *The Argumentative Indian: Writings on Indian History, Culture and Identity* (Picador, 2006).

and Indonesia point to the fact that people have strong democratic and pluralistic aspirations. In addition, social movements in Asia are very powerful and there are many organisations and individuals who challenge the state on a whole variety of issues, many of them human rights issues. These dynamic NGOs and grass-roots organisations can be identified in most Asian countries, and would be the first to challenge the assertion that Asian values are anti human rights.

Another substantive critique of human rights comes from communitarian philosophers such as Charles Taylor who are the theorists of pluralism, multiculturalism and the protection of vulnerable communities.[8] For him as well as others, international universal standards cannot be imposed, and the right to self-determination of communities requires that local traditions define the quality of life in communities. For many of these theorists, diversity trumps individual rights, and the rights of communities carry equal weight to accepted universal standards. The importance of a calibrated approach to the balance between universal standards and local realities must be acknowledged. I have tried to deal with this dilemma in the specific context of women's rights in a later section.

1.2 Double standards

The other challenge to the universality of human rights comes not from those who question its substance, but from those who feel that the current politics of human rights is full of double standards, and serves to reinforce the hegemony of the West. Mahmood Mamdani has in many ways become the leading figure of this movement, though he is supported by a great many post-modern theorists and writers. In his book *Saviours and Survivors*,[9] he focuses on the Darfur crisis in Sudan to challenge international human rights and international humanitarian practice.

Mamdani sees the world as moving from a sovereign-based international system to a new humanitarian order, where state sovereignty takes second place to human rights and humanitarian action. In this latter model, individuals who are victims of abuses within countries are wards, part of a regime of trusteeship administered by those who control the international system. He refuses to accept the basic concepts of the neutrality of humanitarian space or the legal autonomy of regimes such as human rights. For him everything is about politics. Contrasting the response of the international system to the Darfur crisis with its response to the Iraq invasion, he highlights the double standards inherent in the international human rights and humanitarian project. Mamdani is not arguing for authoritarian models, but the only human rights responses that he feels are legitimate are those that emerge from within societies. He highlights the South African Truth and Reconciliation Commission as a good example of home-grown justice. He is opposed to any international intervention based on human rights or humanitarian law which he feels, given the dominant power structure, is an extension of colonialism.[10]

Many theorists, especially from the third world, question whether the movement from a sovereignty-based model of international relations to a human rights and humanitarian model is truly a progressive movement. The institutional structure of the United Nations is based on

8 For a good discussion of these issues, see C. Taylor and A. Gutman (eds), *Multiculturalism: Examining the Politics of Recognition* (Princeton University Press, 1994).
9 M. Mamdani, *Saviours and Survivors: Darfur, Politics and the War on Terror* (Pantheon, 2010).
10 Ibid. 206.

member states, and during the initial phase of its development, sovereignty was an essential part of its foundation. However, over the course of the next five decades, the veil of sovereignty was constantly pierced to protect individuals and groups living within nation states.

The first such effort was in the 1960s over the question of apartheid in South Africa.[11] The UN Commission on Human Rights in Geneva moved from norm-setting to naming and shaming on this question. The second such movement was in the late 1970s and early 1980s, after the spate of disappearances and extrajudicial killings in Latin America, with the setting up of the Working Group on Disappearances in 1980. Since then the thematic mechanisms of the Human Rights Commission and later the Human Rights Council have grown exponentially. Now there are over 35 such mechanisms. This movement toward a rights-oriented approach is the result of countless struggles from all over the world. To dismiss human rights as Western or colonial is to take away from these worldwide struggles of people searching for justice and freedom and who in waging these struggles looked for international recognition and solidarity. The so-called 'Arab Spring' is the latest such manifestation.

Despite these developments, the recent resistance to human rights in developing country discourse has paralleled an increasing championing of human rights by Europe and North America as one of the pillars of their foreign policy. Nationalist elites who came of age during the colonial period and who took over leadership after the colonial era watch this championing with great scepticism. Sovereignty therefore became the discourse of nationalists who seized state power in the immediate post-colonial era and who wish to protect that state from outside interference, and sometimes internal disturbances. Protecting the power and influence of the third world state from metropolitan overreach has become a cause célèbre for some of them.[12] Much of this rhetoric has resonance with their populations who also remember the bitter history of colonialism.

However, where nationalist elites have become dictatorial or despotic, the discourse of sovereignty is often only a cover for gross human rights abuses. This has become increasingly true in the contemporary world. By pointing the finger at the West, they absolve themselves of local crimes and abuses. They are able to rouse parts of their population and make international alliances to protect their power base. Their rhetoric at the international level has led to a false dichotomy between third world nationalism on the one hand and human rights on the other.

The false dichotomy between third world nationalism and human rights is augmented by a belief that there are double standards in the application of human rights globally. The difference in the international community's response to specific situations has led many to conclude that double standards operate and that human rights and humanitarian law have become politics by other means.

In some sense this argument is disingenuous. Though double standards exist at the international level, they also operate at the national level in the very countries that may level a charge. Certain individuals of wealth and political privilege often enjoy impunity under national legal systems. In the United States, research has shown that the African American community is subject to double standards in the implementation of laws.[13] The answer to

---

11 R. Gardner, *In Pursuit of World Order* (Praeger, 1965).

12 See B. Mathews, 'The Limits of International Engagement in Human Rights Situations, Case Study of Sri Lanka' (2009) 82(4) *Pacific Affairs* 577.

13 J.G. Miller, *Search and Destroy: African American Males in the Criminal Justice System* (Cambridge University Press, 1997).

these issues is not to get rid of the criminal law as a whole and let the criminals go free. The response must surely be to consistently and collectively work toward removing double standards so that there is one standard of justice for all. It would be fruitless to argue that just because there are double standards impunity should prevail and we should have no standards at all to guide our actions.

The central question for an international response in these situations is not whether violations take place. In all wars or criminal justice operations there are certain cases of violations. The real dilemma is whether remedies or recourse exist for these violations. International action only kicks in if there are no remedies or if these remedies have been exhausted.[14] The mere occurrence of a war crime or a human rights violation does not trigger scrutiny. If redress and remedies exist locally, the world will leave national sovereigns alone. In fact, modern theorists argue that one aspect of sovereignty is the protection of civilian populations and it is only when sovereignty fails that international action becomes relevant.[15]

Double standards do sometimes operate at the international level, even if remedies are not exhausted primarily because the two organs of the United Nations responsible in effect for human rights – the Human Rights Council and the Security Council – are made up of member states and their decision-making style is distinctly political. Any advocacy to remove double standards would then necessarily move toward the creation of an International Court of Human Rights and to ensure universal jurisdiction at the International Criminal Court. If we truly wish to eradicate double standards we may have to change the multilateral architecture. The answer to double standards is not fewer human rights, but actually more human rights that are well grounded in strong institutions which emphasise objective, non-political and impartial decision-making.

The response of humanitarian actors on the ground to the issue of double standards is to work on a case-by-case basis.[16] This strategy may be a better guide to the vindication of international human rights than other more abstract approaches. If space is created in any particular situation for the achievement of human rights, they attempt to seize the space to push for rights vindication. Their approach is that whenever we can, we must, realising that there are situations where human rights vindication is less possible. It is an approach grounded in years of humanitarian experience without theoretical abstraction. To save one child is surely better than saving no children just because there are double standards. Giving justice to one is surely better than giving justice to none. The struggle to eradicate double standards must continue, but not at the expense of actual justice for real people.

The belief that a purely sovereignty-based international system with less regulation is more protective of vulnerable third world societies is also a fallacy. A sovereignty-based system reinforces an international system based on the balance of power, where power and politics are the sole determining influences. It is therefore no wonder that the theories of John Bolton on an exceptional United States have much in common with third world detractors of human

---

14 See A.A. Cancado Trindade, 'Exhaustion of Local Remedies in International Law Experiments Granting Procedural Status to Individuals in the First Half of the Twentieth Century' (1977) 24 *Netherlands International Law Review* 373.

15 See D. Rothchild, F. Deng, W. Zartman, S. Kimaro and T. Lyons, *Sovereignty as Responsibility: Conflict Management in Africa* (Brookings Institution, 1996); Report of the Secretary General, 'Implementing the Responsibility to Protect' (2009) UN Doc. A/63/677.

16 The work of the ICRC is an example of this point.

rights and humanitarian law.[17] A norms-based system rooted in the UN Charter and international law – including human rights and humanitarian law – provides greater protection for vulnerable nation states and peoples than the realist dream of a balance of power based on sovereign nation states.

1.3 Women's rights

The most disturbing challenge to the universality of human rights is in the area of women's rights. To accept women as equal, empowered individuals is not always a norm, and even in situations where it is the norm, it is very often not the practice. Many countries have made reservations to the Convention of the Elimination of Discrimination against Women[18] (CEDAW). Tribal and village elders often refuse equality for women and even civil society groups in the aftermath of the Arab Spring found women's right to be expendable. The lack of universal support for basic tenets of women's equality and personal dignity has frustrated many activists from around the world through the years.

The future course of action to further universal acceptance may lie in deciding which battles should be fought at the international level and which issues should be left to local level activism. There are some practices against women that resemble torture, extrajudicial killing or enslavement – the *'jus cogens'* crimes.[19] These include female genital mutilation, honour killings, the burning of widows, the killing of witches, the mutilation of breasts and the pledging of young girls as slaves to priests. These practices can no longer be tolerated in a world united around the UN Charter and the Universal Declaration of Human Rights. International institutions should be united in strategies to eradicate these practices. There should be universal condemnation and a zero tolerance attitude toward such practices, as well as toward sexual violence and domestic violence generally. Policies should be advocated that combine punishment of offenders with appropriate health and education strategies for the survivors and their communities. International intervention is necessary, welcome and required, and should be in coalition with national and regional women's groups.

However, there are a whole plethora of tribal, customary and religious laws that deal with women's property and private lives that also discriminate against women.[20] These laws are intertwined with local level social and economic life. The same strategies that may be applied to *jus cogens* violations may not succeed and may in fact create a backlash. The norms of CEDAW should be seen to govern and international actors must continue to advocate for these changes. Countries that have signed CEDAW without reservations should be made to account and those who have reservations should be asked to reconsider. Through awareness-raising, training, and material support, these norms should be disseminated. However, in this context, the movement for actual change at the national level has to be led by local level activists who better understand how best to proceed and what substantive changes can be made and in what time period. Such movements may be supported internationally, but the initiative must come from within.

17 J. Bolton, *Surrender is Not an Option: Defending America at the United Nations and Abroad* (Simon & Schuster, Threshold Editions, 2007).
18 Convention on the Elimination of Discrimination against Women (adopted 18 December 1980, entered into force 3 September 1981) 1249 UNTS 13.
19 ILC, 'Report of the International Law Commission on the Work of its 53rd Session' (23 April–1 June and 2 July–10 August 2001), UN Doc. A/56/10,208.
20 In South Asia they are called 'personal laws'; in Africa they are often called customary laws.

To make fundamental changes in these systems it may be necessary to evolve innovative solutions. One may work toward enacting legislation that allows for the right of couples to opt out of such laws in favour of one governed by CEDAW, or work toward a minimum core of rights that women should enjoy regardless of religious, ethnic or tribal affiliation. These decisions would have to be made at the local level, to maximise support and minimise any further deterioration in the condition of women. Around the world, such local initiatives have resulted in changes to the family law systems.[21] This type of change may be slower, but is in the long term more effective, since inevitably there has to be community level 'buy-in' to the process, if it is to succeed.[22]

2 Unsettling civil and political rights

Civil and political rights were in fact the original human rights found in the Declaration of the Rights of Man and the many political manifestos of the nineteenth and twentieth centuries.[23] By the end of the twentieth century, a large number of countries had signed the Convention against Torture[24] and the International Covenant on Civil and Political Rights[25] (ICCPR). The Rome Statute had come into force and the Human Rights Committee was dispensing with individual cases. At the national level, many states had incorporated the provisions of the ICCPR as part of their Constitutions. Judiciaries all over the world were creating interesting and innovative case law to ensure that these rights were implemented[26] and many civil society groups were created to ensure that justice was done. While debates continued on the justiciability of economic and social rights, the area of civil and political rights was a settled area of the law with a strong history and legacy.

The events of 11 September 2001 seem to have unsettled the very foundations of political and civil rights. The changing nature of warfare has given many the excuse to move beyond the prohibitions and protection contained in international law. The new conflicts included terrorist attacks aimed at civilians by transnational non-state actors. These actors perpetrated violence across borders, and this armed violence was not the traditional exchanges between armed groups and the state, but acts aimed at terrorising the civilian population. The nature of the actors and the character of the warfare sent traditional assumptions of civil and political rights into disarray.[27]

---

21 See the website of Women Living Under Muslim Laws (WLUML), available at <www.wluml.org>.

22 For a fuller version of this argument see R. Coomaraswamy, 'Identity Within: Cultural Relativism, Minority Rights and the Empowerment of Women' (2003) 34 *George Washington International Review* 483.

23 D. Van Kley, et al., *The French Idea of Freedom: The Old Regime and the Declaration of Rights of Man, 1789* (Stanford University Press, 1997).

24 The Convention against Torture and Other Cruel, Inhuman or Degrading Treatment or Punishment (adopted 10 December 1984, entered into force 26 June 1987) 1465 UNTS 85.

25 International Covenant on Civil and Political Rights (adopted 16 December 1966, entered into force 23 March 1976) 999 UNTS 171.

26 See for example, P.N. Bhagwati, 'Judicial Activism and Public Interest Litigation' (1985) 23 *Columbia Journal of Transnational Law* 561.

27 A good book that discusses the challenges is D. Wippman et al. (eds), *New Wars, New Laws? Applying the Laws of War in 21st Century Conflicts* (Hotel Publishing, 2005).

States have reacted differently to this kind of armed violence, but most have adopted what may be termed draconian provisions to deal with its impact.[28] The primary question remains: how does one define this violence? Is it armed conflict or is it a series of criminal acts? Is it governed by international humanitarian law or by the more detailed provisions of international human rights law? The confusion of legal frameworks has resulted in the removal of traditional protections under human rights law and has led to national processes that bypass essential safeguards. In addition, the intensity of the violence, with civilians as the target, has made some question the bases of these frameworks, even the non-derogable ones such as the Convention against Torture, arguing that we must rethink these protections in the interest of the safety and security of the population.

In this context we have seen some extraordinary actions. For example, on 30 September 2011, the radical cleric Anwar Al Awlaki was killed by a missile fired by a drone aircraft operated by US forces in Yemen. He was a US citizen.[29] If Mr Awlaki was said to be involved in armed conflict against the United States, even though this was outside the traditional scenario of hostilities governed by international humanitarian law, his killing may be seen as a legitimate act of violence against a combatant. Any collateral damage to civilians or property would also be acceptable.

Some have argued that if he was not actually engaged in hostilities at the moment he was killed, he would not be a combatant. Only those 'directly participating in conflict' may be killed.[30] US legal advisors obviously think otherwise. Under the latter way of thinking, any member of Al Qaeda, whether he is armed or asleep, would be a combatant and liable to be killed. This may be said to be an extraordinary reading of international humanitarian law. If on the other hand, he was regarded not as a combatant but as a criminal running afoul of the law, then his killing would be governed by human rights law, as opposed to international humanitarian law. His death would be seen as an extrajudicial killing in violation of the right to life – one of the gravest human rights violations.

Another extraordinary development has been the detention of individuals in Guantànamo. Given the peculiar nature of Al Qaeda members as transnational actors unattached to a state party, the United States has refused prisoner of war status to the Guantànamo detainees, and labels them 'enemy combatants'. There is no such status under the Geneva Conventions that is protected.[31] However, by designating them as combatants, these individuals may be detained until the end of hostilities, which, given the nature of these terrorist activities, may be an indefinite period of time.[32] Their right to counsel and appeal are also somewhat unclear.[33] In addition, since these are transnational actors, there is also no geographical limitation; as many as sixty countries may be included in the 'War on Terror'.[34]

28 See M.T. McCarthy, 'Recent Developments: USA Patriot Act', (2002) 39 *Harvard Journal On Legislation* 435.
29 BBC News, 'Islamist Cleric Anwar al Awlaki killed in Yemen' (30 September 2011), available at: www.bbc.co.uk/news/world-middle-east-15121879, accessed on 5 March 2012.
30 ICRC, however, states that a 'clear and uniform definition of direct participation in hostilities has not been developed', see J.M. Henckaerts et al., *Customary International Humanitarian Law* (Cambridge University Press, 2005) at 23.
31 See for example, F.J. Hampson, 'Detention, The War on Terror and International Law', in H.M. Hensel (ed.), *The Law of Armed Conflict: Constraints on the Contemporary Use of Force* (Ashgate, 2007).
32 See N. Balendra, 'Defining Armed Conflict' (2008) 29(6) *Cardozo Law Review* 2461 at 2506–08.
33 Ibid.
34 See R.E. Brooks, 'War Everywhere: Rights, National Security Law and the Law of Armed Conflict in the Age of Terror' (2004) 153 *University of Pennsylvania Law Review* 675.

The particular nature of Al Qaeda and international terrorist networks therefore poses a major challenge to international human rights and humanitarian law. Instead of choosing between them, the response of international legal scholars has been to push for the concurrent application of humanitarian law and human rights law. The International Court of Justice has clearly stated that 'the protection of the International Covenant on Civil and Political Rights does not cease in times of war, except by operation of Article 4 of the Covenant whereby certain provisions may be derogated from in times of national emergency'.[35] The UN Human Rights Committee in its General Comment 31 of 2004 is also quite explicit: human rights obligations do apply in situations of armed conflict, and both spheres should be seen as complementary.[36]

However, as is quite clear from the examples cited above, there are situations where the frameworks may be contradictory, leading to very different results. Though there is no settled law in this area, scholars have argued for principles that better protect individuals. At first, it has been argued that where there is actual inconsistency between the two frameworks, the principle of *lex specialis* applies. That is, where a matter is being regulated by a general standard and at the same time by a more specific rule, then the latter takes precedence over the former.[37] In situations of armed conflict this was initially taken to mean automatic application of international humanitarian law as a whole in armed conflict situations.

Given the actual realities on the ground, legal authorities and scholars have begun to narrow the application of international humanitarian law in favour of the more protective norms of human rights law. The 1996 Advisory Opinion of the ICJ in the *Legality of the Threat or Use of Nuclear Weapons* case recognises that, within armed conflict, some matters may be exclusively matters of international humanitarian law, and some matters may be exclusively matters of human rights law.[38] The International Law Commission also states that there is no automatic application of international humanitarian law, and such matters should be determined on a case-by-case basis.[39]

Speaking specifically of detention under humanitarian law, the International Committee of the Red Cross (ICRC) has recognised that humanitarian law must be given specific content by other bodies of law. For example, the principles of fair trial under Article 14 of the ICCPR should augment the provisions of common Article 3 of the Geneva Conventions.[40] Some have argued that *lex specialis* should be applied in a way that the more stable the situation on the ground, the greater the effective control, and the more the human rights paradigm becomes applicable. The less stable the situation and the lack of effective control by the authorities, the more international humanitarian law should apply.[41] Others have argued that in applying *lex specialis*, the term

---

35 See *Legality of the Threat or Use of Nuclear Weapons* (Advisory Opinion) [1996] ICJ Rep. 226 [25]; *Legal Consequences of the Construction of A Wall* (Advisory Opinion) [2004] ICJ Rep. 136 [106].

36 UNHRC, 'General Comment No. 31: The Nature of the General Legal Obligation Imposed on State Parties to the Covenant', (2004) UN Doc. CCPR/C/21/Rev.1/Add. 13, para. 11.

37 Report of the Study Group of the International Law Commission, 'Fragmentation of International Law: Difficulties Arising From the Diversification and Expansion of International Law' (2006) UN Doc. A/CN.4/L.682, paras 56–57.

38 *Legality of the Threat or Use of Nuclear Weapons* (n. 35) para. 25.

39 Study Group of the International Law Commission (n. 37) para. 58.

40 J. Pelec, 'Procedural Principles and Safeguards for Internment/Administrative Detention in Armed Conflict and Other Situations of Violence', (2005) 87 *International Review of the Red Cross* 858.

41 OHCHR 'Outcome of the Expert Consultation on the Issue of Protecting the Human Rights of Civilians in Armed Conflict' (2009) UN Doc. A/HRC/11/31, para. 14.

armed conflict should be interpreted narrowly in situations where human rights laws will be derogated from, and even within situations of armed conflict, any derogation from human rights should also be read narrowly.[42] We should welcome the attempt by scholars and legal bodies to narrow the areas where human rights are not applicable in situations of armed conflict or those that resemble armed conflict. These developments have to be successful if civil and political rights are to regain their previous strength and importance.

It is not only action but also the discourse on civil and political rights in the past decade which poses some challenges for the future. Alan Dershowitz in his book *Why Terrorism Works: Understanding the Threat, Responding to the Challenge*[43] advocates judicially sanctioned non-lethal torture for the extraction of information that would prevent a terrorist attack. Called the 'ticking bomb' scenario, law enforcement officials would have to obtain a judicial warrant from a court to inflict torture. This 'shock the conscience' proposal is put forward as a means of minimising torture as it actually happens, and for protecting the victims. The arguments justifying this practice are *utility* – torture one person but save many lives – and *necessity* – violating the law to prevent a greater harm.[44]

Until 2001, the prohibition against torture was such a widely held belief that many considered it *jus cogens*, a norm of international law that cannot be derogated from.[45] This norm born of an international consensus was based, as the Convention against Torture states, on 'the inalienable rights that derive from the inherent dignity of the human person'.[46] Article 2 of the Convention against Torture states that no 'exceptional circumstances whatsoever, whether a state of war or a threat of war, internal political stability or any other public emergency may be invoked as a justification of torture'.[47] Even US courts using the 'shock the conscience' standard have regularly held that this type of police action violates due process.[48]

The fact that a leading scholar, once a prominent human rights lawyer, has put forward this argument is an indication of the perilous state of civil and political rights. Not only is such an argument morally repulsive, not only does it go to the heart of judicial integrity, there is no proof that torture actually works in eliciting the type of information wanted by law enforcement officials.[49] The institutionalisation of torture will also have a corrosive effect on all aspects of the criminal justice system.[50] The belief that anything can be done for the sake of security is a mindset that has enormous consequences for the lives of individual citizens. Experience from recent decades has pointed to alternative ways of increasing security and safety without violating human dignity. Law enforcement officials should spend more time on devising alternative methods of gathering information without delving into practices that truly shock the conscience.

If we allow for judicially sanctioned barbaric acts we go to the very foundation of the rule of law and the protection of human rights. There have been times in world history when

---

42 Balendra (n. 32) 2487–503.
43 A. Dershowitz, *Why Terrorism Works: Understanding the Threat, Responding to the Challenge* (Yale University Press, 2002).
44 For a philosophical analysis of this issue, see V. Bufacchi et al., 'Torture, Terrorism, and the State: a Refutation of the Ticking Bomb Argument' (2006) 23(3) *Journal of Applied Philosophy* 355.
45 ILC (n. 19) 208.
46 Convention against Torture (n. 24) preamble.
47 Ibid., Art. 2.2.
48 See *Rochin v California*, 342 US 165,172 (1952).
49 H.H. Koh, 'A World Without Torture' (2005) 43 *Columbia Journal of Transnational Law* 641.
50 A.O. Rourke et al., 'Torture, Slippery Slope, Intellectual Apologists and Ticking Bombs: an Australian Response to Bagaric and Clarke' (2006) 40 *University of San Francisco Law Review* 85.

people were quartered, stamped on by elephants, torn apart, disembowelled, crucified and stoned to death. The mark of the modern world has been the elimination of these practices that inflict physical pain and suffering on fellow human beings. To betray this norm is to challenge fundamental assumptions and to return us to levels of barbarism from which we are still trying to emerge.

3 Non-state actors

Human rights, as originally conceived, focused on obligations of states toward individuals, either in guaranteeing their freedom or in providing services for the achievement of rights. Increasingly there is a realisation that a great deal of suffering and injustice in the world is the result of actions perpetrated by private parties or armed groups. This has resulted in practice where there is an attempt to ensure human rights obligations on the part of non-state actors.

According to Andrew Clapham in his definitive work on the human rights obligations of non-state actors,[51] there are four categories of non-state actors: (i) large corporations (ii) private sector companies involved in public sector work such as prisons, communications and water; (iii) perpetrators in cases of violence against women, such as domestic violence, sexual violence and trafficking; and (iv) non-state armed groups. I will focus on the last category, the human rights obligations of non-state armed groups in situations of armed conflict.

In the past, non-state armed groups were not responsible for human rights or humanitarian violations except under the criminal law of the country concerned. If they graduated to an insurgency with some control over territory and were recognised as such by governments, then they were bound by the rules of armed conflict.[52] Increasingly it is recognised that common Article 3 of the Geneva Conventions and Protocol II of 1977 and the Rome Statute impose obligations on parties regardless of any recognition given by states.[53] What is necessary is a situation of armed conflict, something that has been discussed elsewhere in this chapter.

This interpretation of international obligations has paralleled an increasing attempt to hold non-state actors accountable for violations of human rights and humanitarian law. Leading this attempt has been the Security Council of the United Nations. Security Council resolutions increasingly call on all parties to comply with their obligations under international humanitarian and human rights law.[54]

The Council has gone further, and one of its initiatives on children and armed conflict has made some groundbreaking attempts to make non-state actors accountable. Given the increased involvement of children in armed conflict around the world, the UN General Assembly commissioned a three-year study on children and armed conflict which was eventually headed by Graça Machel. The study, completed in 1996, called for increased Security Council involvement and resulted in the creation of the post of a Special Representative on Children and Armed Conflict.[55]

51 A. Clapham, *Human Rights Obligations of Non-State Actors* (Oxford University Press, 2006).
52 A. Cassese, *International Law*, 2nd edn (Oxford University Press, 2005) 125.
53 See Y. Sandoz et al., *Commentary on the Additional Protocols of 8 June 1997 to the Geneva Conventions of 13 August 1949* (ICRC, 1987).
54 Clapham (n. 51) 281–83.
55 UNGA, 'Report of the Expert of the Secretary-General, Graça Machel: The Impact of Armed Conflict on Children' (1996) UN Doc. A/51/306.

Since that seminal report, the Security Council has had a focused engagement on children and armed conflict. An annual report is submitted by the Secretary-General describing specific incidents and perpetrators who commit grave violations against children under humanitarian law: the killing and maiming of children contrary to international law; sexual violence against children; the recruitment and use of children; denial of humanitarian access; abductions; and attacks on schools and hospitals. The Council has also created a working group to deal specifically with this theme and installed monitoring and reporting mechanisms in countries on the agenda of the working group.[56]

Since 2001, the Secretary-General has provided to the Security Council a list of parties which named and shamed those who recruit and use children as child soldiers.[57] Since 2009, a list of parties who kill and maim children contrary to international law,[58] and since 2011, a list of parties who attack schools and hospitals,[59] are also being submitted. Most of the parties on the lists are non-state actors. By being placed on these lists, persistent violators become eligible to be subject to sanctions. Sanctions have been imposed against parties in Côte d'Ivoire and the Democratic Republic of Congo.[60]

The Security Council process then recognises that non-state actors have legal obligations not to commit grave violations against children. In addition, the only way a party can get off the lists provided by the Secretary-General is to enter into an action plan with the United Nations, which requires the parties to take certain measures and allow for UN verification. If the action plan is successfully implemented, the party is delisted. The action plan is signed by the head of the United Nations in the country and the United Nations Children's Fund (UNICEF) representative, as well as by the parties concerned. The precise legal character of the action plan is unclear, but according to Clapham and Zegveld all agreements witnessed by the UN and with parties that have 'requisite' status are governed by international law.[61] By the term 'requisite', it is implied that they have the status of an armed group under international humanitarian law.

These innovations by the Security Council with regard to children and armed conflict have become a model for other areas of Security Council concern such as sexual violence in situations of conflict,[62] another area where the main perpetrators are non-state actors. The imposition of international obligations on non-state actors by the Security Council is also complemented by the actions of the International Criminal Court where the recruitment of child soldiers by a non-state actor was the first case that the Court chose for prosecution.[63]

The recognition that a great deal of suffering and injustice in the world is due to the actions of non-state actors is a welcome development. The attempt to bring them into a rule of law framework and to impose obligations cannot be seen as anything but positive,

56 UNSC Res. 1612 (2005) UN Doc. S/RES/1612.
57 UNSC Res. 1379 (2001) UN Doc. S/RES/1379.
58 UNSC Res. 1882 (2009) UN Doc. S/RES/1882.
59 UNSC Res. 1998 (2011) UN Doc. S/RES/1998.
60 For example, in December 2010, the Security Council imposed targeted measures including travel bans and freezing of assets on Colonel Innocent Zimurinda for grave violations against children.
61 Clapham (n. 51) 272–73; L. Zegveld, *Accountability of Armed Groups in International Law* (Cambridge University Press, 2002) 49.
62 On 2 February 2010, the Secretary-General of the United Nations appointed Margot Wallstrom as Special Representative of the Secretary-General on Sexual Violence in Conflict on a mandate given by the Security Council.
63 *The Prosecutor v Thomas Lubanga Dyilo*, ICC-01/04–01/06.

especially with regard to children. Some member states do resist this process because they are concerned that the dialogues and agreements will convey legitimacy on the non-state actors, whom many see as worse than criminals. Nevertheless, the attempt to bring these non-state actors into the regime of human rights law and international humanitarian law must be seen as laudable, if we are to have a long-term vision for the relevance of human rights.

4 Conclusion

This chapter attempts to outline three areas where international human rights, and to some extent international humanitarian law, is facing challenges with regard to doctrine and practice. The first is a challenge to its universality both in substance and application; the second is the erosion of civil and political rights in the twenty-first century; and finally the impetus to hold non-state actors accountable for violations and atrocities.

Of these challenges, the challenge to universality is the most urgent, for it is also a recognition that there is an ongoing battle for the hearts and minds of populations around the world, to convince them that the protection of human rights must be the centerpiece for any new world order. The discourse for human rights that has spearheaded many changes all over the world also has its detractors. In this struggle over ideas, member states may be less important than civil society and people's movements on the ground whose energy will have to be mobilised. Some may argue that it is a battle between idealist and realist frames of reference for the conduct of international affairs. And yet, as daily commentaries in the media foretell, the implications for the situation on the ground are enormous. These battles for the universal recognition of human rights must be waged, for they are nowhere near won.

Select bibliography

A. Clapham, *Human Rights Obligations of Non-State Actors* (Oxford University Press, 2006).

J.M. Henckaerts and L. Doswald-Beck, *Customary International Humanitarian Law* (Cambridge University Press, 2005).

M. Mamdani, *Saviours and Survivors: Darfur, Politics and the War on Terror* (Pantheon, 2010).

A. Sen, *The Argumentative Indian: Writings on Indian History, Culture and Identity* (Picador, 2006).

D. Wippman and M. Evangelista, *New Wars, New Laws? Applying the Laws of War in 21st Century Conflicts* (Hotel Publishing, 2005).

9

Human rights and foreign policy: syntheses of moralism and realism

Bruno Stagno Ugarte

'From enthusiasm to imposture, the step is perilous and slippery.'

Edward Gibbon[*]

Reflecting on the consequences of the fall of the Berlin Wall in 1989, Zbigniew Brzezinski declared that 'human rights have become the genuine historical inevitability of our times'.[1] Looking forward, and in light of the remarkable yet still unfinished awakening of Arab societies after the spark lit in Tunisia in December 2010, it would seem that recent events are once again giving credence to the inevitable role that human rights and fundamental freedoms will play in the field of foreign affairs in the future.

Since the adoption of the Charter of the United Nations in 1945, which inter alia tasked the organisation with promoting 'universal respect for, and observance of, human rights and fundamental freedoms for all',[2] and the adoption in 1948 of the Universal Declaration of Human Rights,[3] states have negotiated and ratified many international or regional human rights instruments. The incorporation of human rights obligations has been voluntary, and although unequal, surprisingly universal despite the association of human rights with predominantly Western concerns.[4] Refutations based on the hypocrisy of former colonial

---

[*] E. Gibbon, *The History of the Decline and fall of the Roman Empire*, ed. J.B. Bury with an Introduction by W.E.H. Lecky (New York: Fred de Fau and Co., 1906), in 12 vols.

1 Z. Brzezinski, *The New Dimensions of Human Rights* (Fourteenth Morgenthau Memorial Lecture on Ethics and Foreign Policy, Carnegie Council on Ethics and International Affairs, New York, 1995) 7.

2 Charter of the United Nations (1945) 1 UNTS XVI, Art. 55.

3 UNGA Res. 217 A(III) (10 December 1948).

4 The 1989 Convention on the Rights of the Child was the most universal human rights instrument at time of writing, with 193 states parties. Other instruments nearing universality include the 1979 Convention on the Elimination of Discrimination against Women, with 187 states parties, followed by the 1966 International Convention on the Elimination of all Forms of Racial Discriminations, with 175 states parties, and the 1966 International Covenants on Political and Civil Rights and on Economic, Social and Cultural Rights, with 167 and 160 states parties, respectively. See the Status of Treaties (MTDSG) Human Rights section (Chapter IV) of the United Nations Treaty Collection available at treaties.un.org for updated information.

powers lecturing newly independent countries on human rights have slowly but surely taken a back seat, as the latter have signed and ratified human rights instruments acting on their sovereign volition.[5] Arguments for 'African solutions to African problems',[6] 'Asian values'[7] or other claims for cultural relativism notwithstanding, the dignity and integrity of the individual have progressively cut across cultural and geographical divides and pierced through the inviolability of national sovereignty.

Today, different views on the correct approach to human rights issues certainly persist, including on what is the appropriate role of human rights in foreign policy. Irrespective of whether it is to limit the reach of human rights or to unleash their promise, all states have with the passage of time incorporated a human rights dimension into their foreign policy. Even states that are dismissive of those 'imperceptible limitations hardly worth mentioning known as international law',[8] end up incorporating a reactive and negative approach to human rights into foreign policy in an effort to curtail if not their codification at least their implementation. Yet, all human rights instruments are based on intergovernmental negotiations, where the nature, scope and precise language employed to enshrine each human right is intensely negotiated. This implies participation of all negotiating states, even if, in the end, they refrain from becoming signatories or parties to the relevant instrument. Independently of each state's intent behind the negotiations or to abide by the obligations emanating from the human rights instruments, the engagement with the subject matter in the course of the negotiations requires a formulation of the human rights component to foreign policy.

1 Human rights and foreign policy space: tenet or afterthought?

Foreign policy requires priority-setting, with some issues gaining precedence over others and at times entirely crowding out other issues from what is by definition a limited policy space. Every state and every government has a certain policy space within which it can pursue its foreign policy. Although this space is limited and constrained, it does not have definite contours, as circumstances and capacities change and can either lead to an expansion or contraction of the policy space available. Within it, the quantity and priority of issues are inversely related, while the sum of resources apportioned to each issue generally increases as one scales up the priority axis, as schematically shown in Figure 1.

Human rights are rarely a priority issue, although they have become ever more present in the overall foreign policy formulations of a growing number of states and governments. Historically speaking, human rights are a newcomer to the priority-setting that is integral to foreign policy formulation. But even in those cases where human rights are considered a

---

5 In 1994, for example, the then Deputy Prime Minister of Malaysia, Anwar Ibrahim, complained that 'to allow ourselves to be lectured and hectored on freedom and human rights after one hundred years of struggle to regain our liberty and human dignity, by those who participated in or benefited from our subjugation, is willingly to suffer impudence'. A. Ibrahim 'The Pacific Century' (2 June 1994) *Far Eastern Economic Review*, at 20.

6 As introduced in the Declaration of the Assembly of Heads of State and Government on the Establishment within the OAU of a Mechanism for Conflict Prevention, Management and Resolution (the Cairo Declaration), AHG/DECL.1–3 (XXIX) (28–30 June 1993) and later developed within the principle of non-indifference enshrined in the Constitutive Act of the African Union (1 July 2000), Arts 4(h) and 4(j).

7 F. Zakaria, 'Culture is Destiny: A Conversation with Lee Kuan Yew' (1994) 73(2) *Foreign Affairs* 109–26.

8 C. von Clausewitz, *On War* (Michael Howard and Peter Paret eds and transls, PUP, 1989) 75.

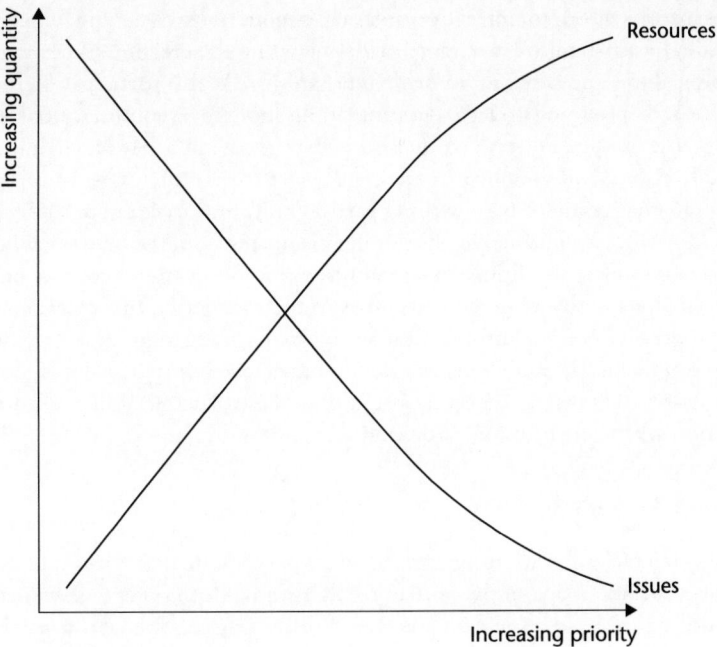

Figure 1 Policy space and the interplay of issues and resources

Note: Although depicted as a quasi-linear relationship for illustration means, issues and resources can actually follow multiple curves.

priority, the approach to the issue can vary significantly as states and governments pursue their national interests. As recognised by Lawrence, 'not only have different states acted on different principles, but the action of the same state at one time has been irreconcilable with its action at another.'[9] Schematically, along a human rights continuum that spans different positions, it could be argued that there are in essence three base positions for a foreign policy with a human rights component.[10] Focusing on governments that are positively inclined to a human rights agenda, the three base positions could be described as follows: normative positioning; generic operative positioning; and case-specific operative positioning.[11]

1.1 Normative positioning

Normative positioning entails that the human rights component of a foreign policy is limited to the legal codification of emerging norms, contributing to the expansion of the normative foundation for human rights with the intent to seek universality for the norms. This usually

9 T.J. Lawrence, *The Principles of International Law* (Macmillan, 1895) 117.

10 For a similar approach based on two contexts, please see G. Ulrich, 'Framework for the Analysis of Human Rights Diplomacy', in M. O'Flaherty and others, *Human Rights Diplomacy: Contemporary Perspectives* (Martinus Nijhoff, 2011) 19–42.

11 On the concept of 'normative power', see I. Manners, 'Normative Power Europe: The International Role of the EU', European Community Studies Association Biennial Conference, Madison, WI, 13 May 2001, 1–30.

encompasses participation in intergovernmental negotiations to codify emerging human rights norms in multilateral treaties, potentially including the creation of new treaty-bodies, complaint procedures and other monitoring mechanisms. As this participation is of a normative type, primarily premised on legal determinations more than political calculations, it does not directly target a specific state. Although it may focus on a particular human right or fundamental freedom, and thereby may indirectly relate to specific cases, codification creates obligations that are binding only on willing parties (ratifying, acceding or succeeding states).

Regardless of whether normative positioning originates from the belief that human rights are a cause or a common condition,[12] a moral possession or an aspiration, it is not disruptive of the twin principles of sovereign equality and sovereign integrity. In fact, even governments that play a progressive role in enshrining new rights and obligations at times crawl back on the new developments through reservations or restrictive interpretation of such rights or obligations before the ratification or accession to a particular treaty in order to limit their implementation within their own jurisdiction.

1.2 Operative positioning

Conceptually, operative positioning can be of two types, mainly distinguishable by the generic or case-specific scope of the human rights agenda. Both types seek to persuade third parties to protect human rights or dissuade them from taking action that is contrary to human rights. However, if a foreign policy advances human rights norms in a generic sense, without targeting any specific states and remaining within the comfort zone of enunciating and operationalising human rights principles and procedures in the abstract, it is less likely to have any bilateral repercussions. On the other hand, if it advances human rights norms in a case-specific sense, signalling out particular country situations, then it is more likely to have bilateral repercussions and could potentially come into conflict with other bilateral priorities. Whenever relations between the parties permit, case-specific positioning will most likely seek to provide encouragement and support to a government struggling to address human rights violations. The opportunity to provide such support exponentially decreases if bilateral relations sour or the government in question is manifestly failing or unwilling to protect its people. In such cases, condemnation and coercion can take over the place of encouragement. Case-specific positioning may therefore contain, albeit as an instrument of last resort, some coercive element in an effort to make its prescriptions enforceable. The coercive elements can vary widely, but can include anything from diplomatic to economic measures, and in extreme cases, the potential threat of use or actual use of force.[13]

In reality, the two types of operative positioning may not be so easily distinguishable, as a government may, for example, provide support for the activation of either special or complaint procedures or other mechanisms meant to determine compliance with treaty-body obligations, thereby zeroing in on a particular country situation, albeit doing so under the 'cover' provided by multilateralism. In refraining from a bilateral action but participating in a multilateral effort to seek compliance with obligations arising from human rights treaties, the

---

12 C. Vance, 'Human Rights and Foreign Policy' (Address before the University of Georgia Law School, Law Day Ceremonies, US Department of State's Press Release No. 194, 30 April 1977) 2.
13 See P.R. Beahr and M. Castermans-Holleman, *The Role of Human Rights in Foreign Policy* (Palgrave Macmillan, 2004).

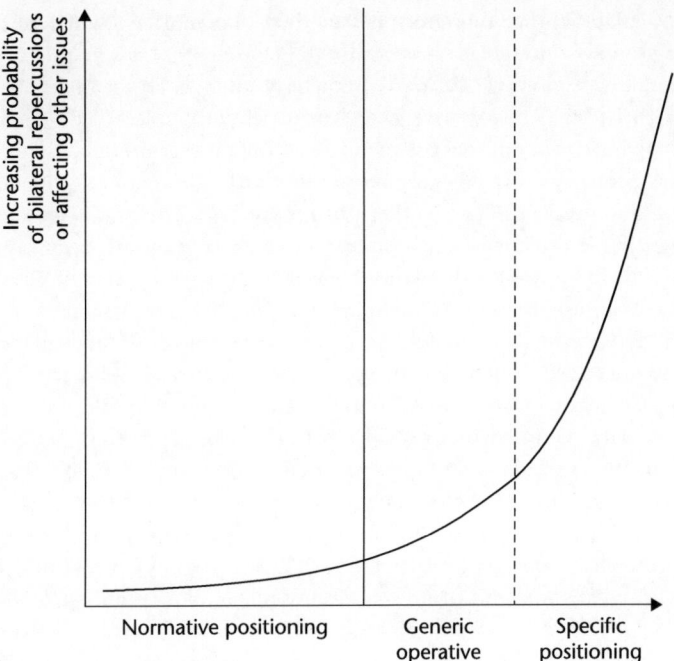

Figure 2   The increasing cost of specificity

The line separating normative from operative positioning is for mere illustration. The line separating the two basic types of operative positioning is even more tenuous and is therefore represented by a dotted line.

government in question stands in the more comfortable middle ground of operative positioning (see Figure 2).

Operative positioning can also be of a rhetorical nature or, as the name suggests, of an operational nature. When it is of a rhetorical nature, it is frequently out of recognition that the advocated position is simply unenforceable and therefore serves only for declaratory or stridency purposes. However, the fact that rhetoric can be rather effortless does not mean that it is costless. In fact, as the stridency of rhetorical formulations or the specificity of operational formulations increases, so does the probability that it will have bilateral repercussions and that it may affect other foreign policy issues or priorities. Moreover, as Morgenthau once cautioned, there is a limit to 'how often you can use this kind of rhetoric without following up with action, without destroying the plausibility of the rhetoric itself'.[14]

When operative positioning is associated with measures that seek to produce a change in the party concerned, it requires considerable efforts and becomes costly, externally because of the chorus of detractors that will denounce a violation of the principle of non-intervention, but also domestically if it potentially displaces other concurrent interests. In view of these costs, governments allegedly committed to a human rights agenda at times turn to 'façades of

14 H.J. Morgenthau, 'Human Rights and Foreign Policy' (First Distinguished CRIA Lecture on Morality and Foreign Policy, Council on Religion and International Affairs, New York, 1979) 16.

action' or 'charade[s] designed more to appease critics of complacency than to secure change, a calculated diversion from the fact that nothing of consequence is being done'.[15] The silence or prudence employed vis-à-vis China is frequently cited as an example of other interests trumping human rights concerns and giving in to the principle of non-intervention. The recent NATO operation to enforce the mandate of the protection of civilians authorised by United Nations Security Council Resolution 1973 (2011) provides a poignant counterexample. The operation was derided by other third parties as a case of mission creep to achieve a regime change, but it also effectively brought to an end – just months after Libya was invited to attend the 2009 G8 Summit – all relations between the participating NATO states and the Qaddafi regime in a number of areas, including commercial and financial transactions.

Although adherence to the principle of non-intervention in the internal affairs of other states[16] may initially take part in determining the role that human rights are to play in foreign policy, 'it is not an adequate conclusion.'[17] In an interdependent world, in which threats are no longer necessarily confined to national borders and human rights bear the promise of universality, non-intervention is no longer the default position. The emergence of concepts such as the groundbreaking idea of sovereignty as responsibility,[18] from which the recently minted norm of the responsibility to protect arose, is a clear evidence of the erosion of one of the bedrock principles of international relations. This is not an entirely new phenomenon, since the 'civilising mission' or 'white man's burden' or 'humanitarian intervention' have played a significant role in the past in creating exceptions to the principle, albeit mostly in a colonial or post-colonial setting. What is new is the acquiescence of states in accepting limitations to sovereignty, partaking in what would appear to be an act of self-immolation[19] that runs counter to the very idea of sovereignty inherent in states.[20]

2 Realism or moralism: human rights as synthesis

The policy space available for the conduct of human rights diplomacy depends on the overall inclination of foreign policy towards one of two conceptual extremes: moralism or realism. Moralism, as applied to foreign policy, encompasses the belief that certain human rights and fundamental freedoms are universal entitlements which are meant to be enjoyed by every society regardless of their value systems, and therefore in need of protection and promotion abroad, as the case may be. The universal character of these entitlements, or the presumption of their alleged universality, overrides concerns of national sovereignty. Realism, as applied to foreign policy, encompasses the belief in the national interest defined in terms of power, guiding against 'two popular fallacies: the concern with motives and the concern with ideological preferences'.[21]

---

15 K. Roth, 'A Façade of Action: The Misuse of Dialogue and Cooperation with Rights Abusers', in Human Rights Watch, *World Report 2011* (HRW, 2011) 2.
16 See Article 2(7) of the Charter of the United Nations.
17 R.J. Vincent, *Foreign Policy and Human Rights* (CUP, 1986) 6.
18 F.M. Deng and others, *Sovereignty as Responsibility: Conflict Management in Africa* (The Brookings Institution, 1996).
19 T.M. Franck, *Fairness in International Law and Institutions*, 3rd edn (OUP, 2002) 483.
20 J.J. Mearsheimer, *The Tragedy of Great Power Politics* (Norton, 2001) 30.
21 H.J. Morgenthau, *Politics Among Nations: The Struggle for Power and Peace,* 6th edn (Kenneth W. Thompson ed., McGraw-Hill, 1993) 5.

In the United States, the Carter administration stands out for its incorporation of human rights as a fundamental tenet of its foreign policy formulations. However, recognising the limits of moralism, President Jimmy Carter stated that 'this does not mean that we can conduct our foreign policy by rigid moral maxims. We live in a world that is imperfect and that will always be imperfect, in a world that is complex and confused and that will always be complex and confused. I understand fully the limits of moral suasion.'[22]

Prime Minister David Lloyd George reputedly stated that he was 'a man of principles, but one of my principles is expediency'.[23] This generally applies to foreign policy priorities, as human rights are generally promoted and defended until a matter of urgency or higher priority requires their partial or total suspension or abrogation. Human rights rarely trump higher-order policy objectives of a political, military or commercial nature. Considerations of utility and opportunity frequently come into play, upsetting or changing priorities. When higher-order policy objectives come into conflict with human rights concerns, it is frequently argued that the former are too important to be held hostage by a single issue.

As in most dialectic relations, the extremes more often come to some type of synthesis rather than remain in their pure form. Virtually all foreign policies are in fact in flux between both extremes. As human rights have gained prominence over time, it makes perfect sense for realist foreign policies to take account of this. Morgenthau anticipated this in stating that:

> The kind of interest determining political action in a particular period of history depends upon the political and cultural context within which foreign policy is formulated. The goals that might be pursued by nations in their foreign policy can run the whole gamut of objectives any nation has ever pursued or might possibly pursue.[24]

One of the foremost exponents of realist thought, Kenneth W. Thompson, acknowledged the policy space that morality could occupy within a realist foreign policy by stating that '[m]oralism is the tendency to make one's moral value supreme and to apply it indiscriminately without regard to time and place; morality, by comparison, is the endless quest for what is right amidst the complexity of competing and sometimes conflicting, sometimes compatible, moral ends'.[25] It should come as no surprise, therefore, that most foreign policy positions are entrenched in pragmatism, entailing a certain degree of relativism of time and place and competing interests that temper the more extreme manifestations or aspirations of universalism.

Regardless of the type of government, and even in consolidated democracies, the 'whole of government efforts fall along a spectrum'.[26] Differences in policies, strategies, sequences or priorities between ministries, or even between departments within a single government ministry or agency, tend to be the rule rather than the exception, with experience suggesting that 'a whole of government ethos rarely emerges at once, but rather is the outcome of an iterative process'.[27] The inter-ministry and inter-agency bureaucratic process by which policy is constructed usually also has a synthesising effect, toning down antithetical positions.

22 J. Carter, *Public Papers of the Presidents of the United States: Jimmy Carter,* vol. I (US Government Printing Office, 1977) 954.

23 A. Eban, 'Interest and Conscience in Diplomacy' (1986) 23(3) *Society* 14–22.

24 Morgenthau, *Politics Among Nations* (n. 21) 8–9.

25 K.W. Thompson, *Moralism and Morality in Politics and Diplomacy* (University Press of America, 1985) 5.

26 S. Patrick and K. Brown, *Greater than the Sum of its Part? Assessing 'Whole of Government' Approaches to Fragile States* (International Peace Academy, 2007) 129.

27 Ibid.

Within the moralism and realism continuum, some are prompt to suggest that smaller and weaker states are more prone to include human rights concerns in their foreign policy formulations. This is allegedly based on their having comparatively fewer interests to defend and less bilateral or economic power, and being more naturally inclined to a rules-based international order. However, although Thucydides had already highlighted the fact that the weak must suffer what they must,[28] an international rules-based system does not necessarily entail respect for human rights which operate at the societal and individual level and not at the supranational level. Not all smaller or weaker states advocate for human rights, although most do adhere strongly to the principle of the sovereign equality of states. Nor do larger or stronger states have a weaker position in defence of human rights. The size of the state is not a determining factor.

There is, however, a reasonable correspondence between the democratic credentials of a government and the role human rights may play in its foreign policy formulations. 'State action . . . takes on significance from its context',[29] both internal and external. Internally, as British Foreign Secretary William Hague has put it, 'foreign policy is domestic policy written large.'[30] As it could be expected that a democracy allows for the attainment and enjoyment of most human rights, it follows that the government in question will not be raising issues that would otherwise be uncomfortable for its internal state of affairs. Governments lacking democratic credentials are usually uncomfortable in openly raising human rights issues abroad which have the potential to backfire domestically. However, democracies are not necessarily exempt from advancing human rights while simultaneously seeking less altruistic objectives that may in fact run counter to the very notion of human rights. Practices and images that are now associated with names likes Abu Ghraib are recent cases in point.

Externally, not all democracies are equally committed to the advancement of human rights in other latitudes and longitudes. Few, if any, actually 'roam the four continents in search of liberties to protect'.[31] Those that may do so usually see some degree of correspondence between national and global interests,[32] and 'roam' into distant geographic confines because they have no overriding interests to defend or are seeking additional leverage. In the former case, they are not national Don Quixotes tilting at windmills[33] but governments that can afford to act on principle because the potential costs and benefits of doing so are worth the effort. In the latter case, they are national Januses applying moral leverage as a means for an end totally unrelated to the advancement of human rights.

Even within the realm of human rights and fundamental freedoms, most foreign policy formulations tend to focus on acute threats to the human rights enshrined in the International Covenant on Civil and Political Rights[34] and less so its counterpart International Covenant on Economic, Social and Cultural Rights.[35] It could be argued that more diplomatic effort

---

28 'They that have odds of power exact as much as they can, and the weak yield to such conditions as they can get.' See Thucydides, *The History of the Grecian War*, in T. Hobbes (transl.), *The English Works of Thomas Hobbes of Malmesbury*, vol. IX (William Molesworth ed., Bohn, 1843) 99.

29 M. Walzer, *Just and Unjust Wars* (Basic Books, 1977) 77.

30 W. Hague 'Human Rights are Key to our Foreign Policy' *The Daily Telegraph* (London, 31 August 2010).

31 A. Sen, *Human Rights and Asian Values* (Sixteenth Morgenthau Memorial Lecture on Ethics and Foreign Policy, Carnegie Council on Ethics and International Affairs, New York, 1997) 30.

32 A. Brisk, *Global Good Samaritans: Human Rights as Foreign Policy* (OUP, 2009) 4.

33 F.E. Smith, *International Law* (James Wylie ed., JM Dent, 1911) 63–64. Quoted by S. Chesterman, *Just War or Just Peace? Humanitarian Intervention and International Law* (OUP, 2003) 38.

34 (1966) 999 UNTS 171.

35 (1966) 993 UNTS 3.

has been spent in advancing what is frequently called the democratic entitlement than economic development. In fact, some states that have been at the forefront in advocating for the democratic entitlement do not even recognise the right to development.[36] Alternatively, foreign policy formulations at times also focus on emblematic individual cases which cast light on a particular violation or situation of concern – as has been the case with Amina Lawal, Mohamed Bouazizi or Liu Xiaobo, among many others – yet also tend to concentrate on systematic or episodic violations of an egregious nature. However, the balance of consequences on other potential interests may even trump action on the most egregious violations. This is most often the case when gross violations are being committed by a government that is otherwise considered to be an ally. The Cold War period offered too many examples of the East–West confrontation stymieing reactions to systematic or episodic violations of human rights committed by allies, while exacerbating reactions to those perpetrated by foes.

Although this is less the case today, condemnation of allies in the public domain is rather uncommon. Selectivity and double standards are fixtures of the international order. Clausewitz, among others, already recognised this when identifying that 'the entire difficulty lies in this: to remain faithful in action to the principles we have laid down for ourselves'.[37] While there was an immediate and concerted effort to isolate and hold accountable the de facto government of Moussa Dadis Camara in Guinea after the killing of 157 protesters and the wounding of a further 1,250 on 28 September 2009,[38] there was no comparable reaction to violations that have led to much higher thresholds of violence in less peripheral countries. Just months before, the international community literally stood by as the government of Sri Lanka cornered and liquidated the 26-year-old Liberation Tigers of Tamil Eelam (LTTE) separatist insurgency, with at least 40,000 innocent civilians killed in the crossfire.[39] At the time of writing, with more than 60,000 civilians killed and countless thousands injured, besieged or displaced by the ongoing military crackdown of the Bashar Al-Assad regime,[40] Syria offers another stark contrast. However distasteful selectivity is, most proponents of a foreign policy human rights agenda will argue that inaction in one case due to insurmountable political constraints should not translate into inaction everywhere. The best should not be trumped by the perfect.

3 Redefining sovereignty as responsibility

Since the end of the Cold War, there have been two potentially seismic adjustments to national sovereignty. The first seismic shift was the recognition, at the 1998 Rome Conference on the International Criminal Court (ICC), that whenever and wherever a national jurisdiction proves to be 'unwilling or unable genuinely to carry out the investigation or prosecution'[41] of

---

36 The right to development was first internationally recognised in the Declaration on the Right to Development, GA Res. 41/128 (4 December 1986). The relevant resolution was voted affirmatively by 146 member states, with eight abstaining (Denmark, Federal Republic of Germany, Finland, Iceland, Israel, Japan, Sweden, United Kingdom) and one casting a negative vote (United States).

37 Clausewitz (n. 8) 17.

38 D. Lewis and S. Samb, 'Guinea Death Toll Jumps to 157 – Rights Group', *Reuters* (Conakry, 29 September 2009).

39 Report of the Secretary-General's Panel of Experts on Accountability in Sri Lanka, 31 March 2011, 41.

40 M. Price, J. Klinger and P. Ball, *Preliminary Statistical Analysis of Documentation of Killings in the Syrian Arab Republic*, Benetech Human Rights Program, 2 January 2013, 1.

41 Rome Statute of the International Criminal Code (1998, last amended 2002) A/CONF.183/9, Art. 17(1a).

the crimes over which the ICC has jurisdiction,[42] the Court can do so under the principle of complementarity. Although the diplomats participating in the Rome Conference did not share a common position on the unassailability of national sovereignty, a consensus emerged nonetheless. As per the Rome Statute, this displacement of national jurisdiction for the international jurisdiction of the ICC can come about in three ways: through a referral by another state party or the concerned government recognising that the state does not have the capacity to do so,[43] through a referral by the Security Council acting under Chapter VII of the UN Charter,[44] or *proprio motu* by a determination to that effect by the ICC Prosecutor.[45] Although the last two routes are clearly offensive to those who adhere to a strict interpretation of national sovereignty, 122 states[46] have become parties to the Rome Statute and thereby acquiesced to Articles 13(b) and 15(1). Even the first route, which is less intrusive in that it allows the government to make the determination as to the most appropriate jurisdiction, can at times lead to intense discussion and opposition.[47] Nonetheless, at the time of writing, five out of the seven open cases under consideration by the ICC had been referred to it by states acting under their own volition. All of them were developing countries.[48]

The second seismic shift was the acknowledgement, first by the General Assembly of the United Nations[49] and later on by the United Nations Security Council,[50] of the emerging norm of the responsibility to protect. Similarly addressing gross violations arising from a government being unable or unwilling to protect its populations from genocide, war crimes, ethnic cleansing and crimes against humanity, the responsibility to protect potentially

---

42 Art. 5 of the Rome Statute establishes that the Court has jurisdiction with respect to the following crimes: (a) the crime of genocide; (b) crimes against humanity; (c) war crimes; and (d) the crime of aggression.

43 Arts 13(a) and 14 of the Rome Statute.

44 Ibid. Art. 13(b).

45 Ibid. Art. 15(1).

46 As at 1 March 2013.

47 International Crisis Group, 'Kenya: Impact of the ICC Proceedings' (2012) Africa Briefing No. 84. C. Kress, 'Self-Referrals and Waivers of Complementarity - Some Considerations in Law and Policy', 2 J. Int'l Crim. Just. (2004) 944.

48 In alphabetical order: Central African Republic, Côte d'Ivoire, Democratic Republic of the Congo, Kenya and Uganda.

49 On 16 September 2005, the General Assembly adopted Resolution 60/1 (2005) containing the World Summit Outcome Document, which in paragraphs 138 and 139 recognised the responsibility to protect. Paragraph 138 states the responsibility becoming every individual state 'to protect its populations from genocide, war crimes, ethnic cleansing and crimes against humanity . . . [and to ensure] the prevention of such crimes, including their incitement, through appropriate and necessary means'. Paragraph 139 recognises that 'the international community, through the United Nations, also has the responsibility to use appropriate diplomatic, humanitarian and other peaceful means, in accordance with Chapters VI and VIII of the Charter, to help to protect populations from genocide, war crimes, ethnic cleansing and crimes against humanity. In this context, we are prepared to take collective action, in a timely and decisive manner, through the Security Council, in accordance with the Charter, including Chapter VII, on a case-by-case basis and in cooperation with relevant regional organisations as appropriate, should peaceful means be inadequate and national authorities are manifestly failing to protect their populations from genocide, war crimes, ethnic cleansing and crimes against humanity.'

50 On 28 April 2006, the Security Council first acknowledged the responsibility to protect in Resolution 1674 (2006) on the protection of civilians in armed conflict. Operative paragraph 4 of the Resolution 'reaffirms the provisions of paragraphs 138 and 139 of the 2005 World Summit Outcome Document regarding the responsibility to protect populations from genocide, war crimes, ethnic cleansing and crimes against humanity.'

envisages enforcement action, including the threat of use or actual use of force, as a measure of last resort. The decisions taken by the General Assembly and the Security Council are both relevant as virtually unanimous acknowledgements of the norm by all participating member states, 192 in the case of the former and 15 in the latter,[51] albeit without generating any binding legal obligations.[52] The fact that this emerging norm, unlike the Rome Statute, does not create any legal obligations is not a liability, as 'its ultimate value will be assessed by its potential to influence policy decisions.'[53] Despite intense negotiations which led to the watering down of the language in the respective resolutions from the adoption to the (re)affirmation of the norm, governments defending the unassailability of national sovereignty lost out. With the advent of the Arab Spring, and the situation in Libya in particular, the responsibility to protect would receive its first baptism under fire with the Security Council referencing it alongside enforcement measures. Resolutions 1970 (2011) and 1973 (2011) openly endorsed the norm and provided a unique framework for its implementation, allowing for the use of all necessary means.[54]

Although judicial complementarity and the responsibility to protect have made significant inroads into foreign policy formulations, progress has not been linear. Just as the responsibility to protect was first implemented by the Security Council in a country-specific situation, the staunchest proponents of its application on Libya were some months later the most opposed to NATO becoming accountable for any collateral damage arising from its aerial sorties. Moreover, while the Security Council unanimously decided to refer the gross crimes committed in Libya to the ICC for investigation and eventual prosecution, once the demise of the Qaddafi regime was ensured, the Council has failed to recall the obligations of the successor governments, i.e. the National Transitional Council or the General National Congress vis-à-vis the ICC under the relevant resolutions. Similarly, regarding the referral of the situation in Darfur, following the indictments and the issuance of arrest warrants for President Omar Al-Bashir and other alleged perpetrators of gross crimes in Darfur, some states parties to the Rome Statute have failed to arrest Al-Bashir during his visits to their countries, while other countries have endorsed an African Union declaration that seeks to 'suspend any actions against President Al Bashir by the International Criminal Court'.[55]

Further seismic adjustments along the lines of judicial complementarity or the responsibility to protect cannot be ruled out in the near future. Recent events are giving credence to the fact that the twenty-first century is not only confirming the inevitability of human rights as anticipated by Brzezinski but is also apparently ushering in an era of accountability, as

---

51 General Assembly Resolution 60/1 (2005) was adopted without a vote and Security Council Resolution 1674 (2006) was adopted unanimously. Back in 2005, the General Assembly had 192 member states.

52 On 12 February and 17 September 1999, the Security Council unanimously first acknowledged the wider thematic issue of the protection of civilians in armed conflict in respectively adopting a presidential statement (S/PRST/1999/6) and Resolution 1265 (1999). Both are significant in that they expressed the willingness of the Council 'to respond to situations of armed conflict where civilians are being targeted or humanitarian assistance to civilians is being deliberately obstructed'.

53 N. Deller, 'Challenges and Controversies', in J. Genser and I. Cotler (eds), *The Responsibility to Protect: The Promise of Stopping Mass Atrocities in Our Time* (OUP, 2012) 76.

54 See SC Res. 1970 (26 February 2011) preambular para. 9 and SC Res. 1973 (17 March 2011) para. 4.

55 African Union, 'Solemn Declaration of the Assembly of State and Government of the African Union on Sudan' (16th Ordinary Session) (30–31 January 2011) para. 6. Since then, other declarations and resolutions have renewed the call for the application of Article 16 of the Rome Statute.

foreshadowed by the UN Secretary-General Ban Ki-moon.[56] Regardless, the inviolability of sovereignty has been breached. Although it may be safe to say that human rights are destined to progressively occupy a more commanding place in foreign policy in general, it could be argued that this will mainly apply to symmetric relations, i.e. state to state relations. Asymmetric threats, most notably terrorism, will probably be confronted with less nobility, as has been the case throughout history and most recently since the 9/11 terrorist attacks. As, and if, the asymmetric threats continue to proliferate or metastasise, more and more governments may press for a dividing line to the drawn between like and unlike actors. Whereas they may be willing to abide by human rights standards vis-à-vis other governments, they may prove increasingly unwilling to do so when countering asymmetric actors that do not abide by any rules. Moreover, the latter pose a larger challenge for diplomacy in general, in that they have at times become subject matter for foreign policy but are not recognised as legitimate actors of foreign policy.[57] Whereas states have willingly and repeatedly crossed the Rubicon of sovereignty with other states, it is still too early to expect states to apply the same human rights standards in their interactions confronting threatening non-state actors. This, it would seem, is one Rubicon too far to cross at present.

Select bibliography

P.R. Beahr and M. Castermans-Holleman, *The Role of Human Rights in Foreign Policy,* 3rd edn (Palgrave Macmillan, 2004).

A. Brisk, *Global Good Samaritans: Human Rights as Foreign Policy* (OUP, 2009).

Z. Brzezinski, *The New Dimensions of Human Rights,* Fourteenth Morgenthau Memorial Lecture on Ethics & Foreign Policy (Carnegie Council on Ethics and International Affairs, 1995).

D.P. Forsythe, *Human Rights in International Relations,* 2nd edn (CUP, 2006).

R.A. Müllerson, *Human Rights Diplomacy* (Routledge, 1997).

M. O'Flaherty, and others, *Human Rights Diplomacy: Contemporary Perspectives* (Martinus Nijhoff, 2011).

K. Roth, 'A Façade of Action: The Misuse of Dialogue and Cooperation with Rights Abusers', in Human Rights Watch, *World Report 2011* (HRW, 2011).

R.J. Vincent, *Foreign Policy and Human Rights* (CUP, 1986).

56 Ban Ki-moon, 'An Age of Accountability' (Address to the Review Conference of the Rome Statute of the ICC, Kampala, 31 May 2010), available at: www.un.org/sg/statements/?nid=4585, accessed on 2 August 2012.

57 The (as of time of writing) stalled negotiations between the United States and the Taliban via a representative office in Doha, Qatar, offers an interesting deviation from this rule. See M. Semple, 'How to Talk to the Taliban: An Office in Qatar Changes the Rules of the Game', *Foreign Affairs* (9 January 2012).

10

The use of international human rights law by civil society organisations

Andrew Clapham

Civil society organisations deploy human rights law every day. It is a weapon of choice for holding governments and others to account for human rights violations. Of course there will be appeals to the values that underpin human rights, such as respect for human dignity and demands for democracy and transparency, but the contemporary normative framework is heavily reliant on human rights law. This law is used in advocacy, campaigning, fact-finding reports, complaints to international bodies, briefs to courts, and to develop the scope and efficacy of the international human rights institutional framework. There are also signs that civil society is starting to use this law to govern its own behaviour.

1 Civil society organisations in different formal contexts

The contemporary meaning of civil society organisations (CSOs) encompasses a wide variety of entities, ranging from small groups of volunteers providing free legal advice, food or shelter, through to religious organisations, trade unions, environmental groups, relief organisations, charitable foundations, think tanks, educational institutions, industry-wide organisations and of course, in the present context, one also thinks of large established human rights organisations such as Amnesty International, Human Rights Watch, the Fédération internationale des ligues des droits de l'Homme (FIDH) and the International Commission of Jurists. While there is no accepted definition of civil society organisation or non-governmental organisation, in various contexts there will be specific criteria which will need to be satisfied in order to exercise certain rights.

1.1 Multistakeholder initiatives

In some circumstances there will be formal requirements for a CSO to be allowed to participate in a particular process. For example, in multistakeholder initiatives, such as those relating to 'Better Cotton' or human rights principles for private security companies, CSOs may be defined in order to limit the pool of eligible organisations. This is to ensure that the members of a constituency exercising rights within the regime have the relevant background, and are truly independent from the other stakeholders. So in the context of the

Better Cotton Initiative, a CSO is defined as 'any organization that runs not-for-profit activity related to the cotton supply chain'.[1] And in the private security context, CSOs wishing to become members:

> shall be independent, non-profit organizations with a demonstrated institutional record at the local, national, or international level of the promotion and protection of human rights, international humanitarian law or the rule of law. Independence shall be assessed by reference to relationships with other stakeholder pillars, such as via specific, relevant or substantial funding, or through active working relationships. Civil society members commit to promote the Purpose of the Association.[2]

The point is that because the general concept of a CSO is seen as so wide as to potentially cover just about any non-governmental entity, certain regimes have developed restrictive criteria to limit which CSOs can participate in such regimes. Because participation may bring voting rights, as well as the right to trigger certain procedures, these criteria may be quite carefully policed by the other members.

1.2 Intergovernmental complaints procedures

Similarly, some intergovernmental regimes have limited which organisations may bring complaints of violations of particular international human rights. So, under the relevant Protocol to the European Social Charter, complaints can be brought by:

(a) the European Trade Union Confederation (ETUC), BusinessEurope (formerly UNICE) and the International Organisation of Employers (IOE);
(b) international non-governmental organisations (INGOs) with participatory status with the Council of Europe which are on a list drawn up for this purpose by the Governmental Committee;[3]
(c) representative national organisations of employers and trade unions within the jurisdiction of the Contracting Party against which they have lodged a complaint; and

---

1 Better Cotton Initiative Statutes approved with revision of 10 June 2010, Art. 5.2.4.
2 Articles of Association of the International Code of Conduct for Private Security Service Providers' Association 23 February 2013, Art. 3.3.3.
3 Resolution 2003(8) of the Council of Europe's Committee of Ministers states that: 'Participatory status may be granted by the Council of Europe to INGOs: (a) which are particularly representative in the field(s) of their competence, fields of action shared by the Council of Europe; (b) which are represented at European level, that is to say which have members in a significant number of countries throughout greater Europe; (c) which are able, through their work, to support the achievement of that closer unity mentioned in Article 1 of the Council of Europe's Statute; (d) are capable of contributing to and participating actively in Council of Europe deliberations and activities; (e) which are able to make known the work of the Council of Europe among European citizens.' Resolution 2003(9) covers the status of partnership between the Council of Europe and national non-governmental organisations; note also the European Convention on the Recognition of the Legal Personality of International Non-Governmental Organisations (1986) and Recommendation CM/Rec(2007)14 of the Committee of Ministers to member states on the legal status of non-governmental organisations in Europe.

(d) where the relevant state has agreed, any other representative national non-governmental organisation within its jurisdiction which has particular competence in the matters governed by the Charter.[4]

As of 1 January 2012 there were 77 international NGOs (category (b) above) entitled to submit complaints under this procedure. Only Finland has accepted that national NGOs (category (d) above) may make complaints under this procedure. Reviewing 10 years of complaints, one leading human rights scholar describes the procedure as 'remarkably fast, with a decision on the merits generally adopted within 18 months of the initial filing of the complaint. It is inexpensive and easily accessible for the organisations concerned.'[5]

The African Union similarly has a system for allowing 'relevant Non Governmental Organizations (NGOs) with observer status' to complain directly to the African Court of Human and Peoples' Rights, not only as victims, but also on behalf of others.[6] This is a potentially powerful route for NGOs to use in order to ensure compliance with human rights treaties as judgments of the Court are considered legally binding on the states concerned.[7] So far, only Burkina Faso, Mali, Malawi, Tanzania and Ghana have made the requisite declarations allowing for such complaints, and up until now the Court remains rather underutilised by CSOs, although recently several orders for provisional measures have been issued against Libya and Kenya as a result of cases brought via the Commission.[8]

The Inter-American Commission on Human Rights can receive petitions from 'any nongovernmental entity legally recognised in one or more member states of the Organization' of American States.[9] Again there is no need for the organisation to be the actual victim and so it is sometimes said that in this system NGOs can play a role in an *action popularis*. However, there is no right to complain directly to the Inter-American Court of Human Rights. Lastly, we should mention that non-governmental organisations (undefined) can file applications directly with the European Court of Human Rights if they allege that they are the victims of a violation of one or more of the rights included in the European Convention of Human Rights and its Protocols. The Court applies a wide understanding of non-governmental organisation in this context, so 'NGOs, companies (even if dissolved), . . . trusts, professional associations, trade unions, political parties and religious organisations may all submit applications to the Court'.[10]

---

4 Arts 1 and 2, Additional Protocol to the European Social Charter Providing for a System of Collective Complaints (1995).

5 O. De Schutter, 'The European Social Charter', in C. Krause and M. Scheinin (eds), *International Protection of Human Rights: A Textbook* (Abo Akademi Institute for Human Rights, 2009) 425–42 at 436.

6 Art. 5(3) Protocol to the African Charter on Human and Peoples' Rights on the Establishment of an African Court on Human and Peoples' Rights (1998).

7 See http://www.african-court.org/en/index.php/about-the-court/jurisdiction-2/basic-facts: 'The Judgment of the Court is legally binding and the Executive Council of the African Union is charged with monitoring the implementation of the judgment on behalf of the Assembly.'

8 See http://www.african-court.org/en/index.php/judgments/orders; for the states that have made declarations, see http://au.int/en/organs/cj.

9 Art. 44 of the American Convention on Human Rights (1969).

10 P. Leach, *Taking a Case to the European Court of Human Rights*, 3rd edn (OUP, 2011) at 109 (footnotes omitted). Local authorities would be precluded from bringing cases, but a national broadcaster (Radio France) was held to qualify as a non-governmental organisation due to the manner of the regulations governing it. Ibid. at 114; see also A.K. Lindblom, *Non-Governmental Organizations in International Law* (CUP, 2006) at 247–55.

1.3 Participation in the work of intergovernmental organisations

The Charter of the United Nations foresaw consultative status for non-governmental organisations and the detailed arrangements adopted in the Economic and Social Council (ECOSOC) apply, not only for that Council and its subsidiary bodies such as the Commission on the Status of Women and the Commission on Crime Prevention and Criminal Justice, but also for the Human Rights Council, which is a subsidiary body of the UN General Assembly. Different NGOs are entitled to variegated rights under the ECOSOC arrangements.[11] These include the right to be present in meetings, to make oral statements and to circulate short documents. There are three categories: general, special and roster.[12] There are various conditions set out in Resolution 1996/31, one of which relates to funding.[13] Consultative status is granted, renewed, suspended or withdrawn based on recommendations from by a governmental body known as the Committee on NGOs.[14] Olivier de Frouville's detailed study has highlighted the rise of so-called GONGOs (governmental NGOs). He points out that in recent years there has been a 'progressive introduction of servile NGOs into the United Nations bodies . . . accompanied by attacks on NGOs considered too critical of the concerned state'.[15] The Human Rights Council and the General Assembly regularly hear reports from the Special Rapporteur on Human Rights Defenders who has a broad mandate related to implementation of the General Assembly's 1998 Declaration on this topic.[16] In 2012 the General Assembly considered a report which focused on a review of the type of legislation affecting human rights CSOs: 'including anti-terrorism and other legislation relating to national security; legislation relating to public morals; legislation governing the registration, functioning and funding of associations; access to information legislation and official-secret legislation; defamation and blasphemy legislation; and legislation regulating Internet access'.[17]

The African Union (AU) sets out a very detailed set of criteria that need to be met for 'observer status',[18] but goes a step further towards real participation by allowing for membership of the AU's advisory organ, the Economic, Social and Cultural Council (ECOSOCC).

---

11 See ECOSOC Res. 1996/31, paras 21–6.

12 Ibid. For example: '23. Organizations that have a special competence in, and are concerned specifically with, only a few of the fields of activity covered by the Council and its subsidiary bodies, and that are known within the fields for which they have or seek consultative status shall be known as organizations in special consultative status.'

13 'The basic resources of the organization shall be derived in the main part from contributions of the national affiliates or other components or from individual members. Where voluntary contributions have been received, their amounts and donors shall be faithfully revealed to the Council Committee on Non-Governmental Organizations. Where, however, the above criterion is not fulfilled and an organization is financed from other sources, it must explain to the satisfaction of the Committee its reasons for not meeting the requirements laid down in this paragraph. Any financial contribution or other support, direct or indirect, from a Government to the organization shall be openly declared to the Committee through the Secretary-General and fully recorded in the financial and other records of the organization and shall be devoted to purposes in accordance with the aims of the United Nations.' At para. 13.

14 See http://www.un.org/esa/coordination/ngo/committee.htm (last accessed 23 February 2013).

15 O. de Frouville, 'Domesticating Civil Society at the United Nations', in P.M. Dupuy and L. Vierucci (eds), *NGOs in International Law: Efficiency or Flexibility?* (Elgar, 2008) 71–115 at 92–93.

16 See further http://www.ohchr.org/EN/Issues/SRHRDefenders/Pages/SRHRDefendersIndex. aspx.

17 See A/67/292.

18 EX.CL/195 (VII), Annex IV, July 2005 'Criteria for Granting Observer Status and for a System of Accreditation within the AU'.

Membership is open to a wide group of CSOs, which includes but is not limited to the following:

(a) social groups such as those representing women, children, the youth, the elderly and people with disability and special needs;
(b) professional groups such as associations of artists, engineers, health practitioners, social workers, media, teachers, sport associations, legal professionals, social scientists, academia, business organisations, national chambers of commerce, workers, employers, industry and agriculture as well as other private sector interest groups;
(c) non-governmental organisations (NGOs), community-based organisations (CBOs) and voluntary organisations; and
(d) cultural organisations.[19]

These, and similar arrangements for consultative status developed in other organisations,[20] allow some CSOs to maintain continual contact with diplomats, officials from the secretariat of the relevant intergovernmental bodies, other CSOs and the specialist press that covers the relevant issues. The present author would suggest that consultative status is particularly important in terms of the opportunities it opens up for access to decision makers and the chance to influence the process in person. This presence 'in the room' will play a particular role where CSOs are seeking to influence the drafting of a text, whether it be recommendations in a periodic country review, a resolution, set of guidelines, or even a treaty. It is in this context that there is the chance to offer instant approval or disapproval of various formulations and make textual suggestions.

The formal opportunities offered by consultative status are significant, but such status is not usually essential in order to use the political and legal procedures created by international law. Moreover, international lawyers have shied away from concluding that such participation or consultation allows NGOs to be seen as subjects of international law or international legal persons.[21] Such a doctrinal debate is probably rather unhelpful. The rights and obligations of NGOs will depend on the legal context rather than some overarching theory.[22]

A related debate concerns whether the actions of NGOs can be seen as generating new rules of international law. Although some have imagined that international law-making may fundamentally change, so that some non-state actors actually generate binding international law on a limited group of actors,[23] for the time being we can simply admit that NGOs exert considerable influence on the development of international law. We are speaking here not merely of providing pressure for new norms but of generating new appreciations of existing norms. Vaughan Lowe explains as follows:

19 ECOSOCC Statutes Art. 3(2).
20 For the UN agencies and programmes as well as the WTO, see S. Ripinsky and P. Van den Bossche, *NGO Involvement in International Organizations* (BIICL, 2007), see also Lindblom (n. 10) esp. 197ff. for the OAS.
21 Lindblom (n. 10) ch. 3.
22 See for example the rights of NGOs under the European Convention on Human Rights discussed above. The obligations of NGOs are discussed in the last section of this chapter.
23 A.C. Arend, *Legal Rules and International Society* (OUP, 1999) at 176–85.

Following a conservative approach to international law one would say that States and States alone are capable of generating legal obligations by the making of treaties and customary international law. But, since interstitial norms do not derive their force from the process of treaty or customary law formation, there is no reason why only states should participate in their generation. For example, Greenpeace may study and explain the content of the concept of sustainable development. If that explanation is persuasive, in the sense that a rhetorical, topical argument addressed to the invisible college of international lawyers is persuasive, it is likely to take root. There is, in principle, no limit to the category of persons who may contribute to the development of interstitial norms.[24]

2 Monitoring existing norms

The day-to-day work of many CSOs consists in simply gathering information, checking it against existing international human rights law, and writing reports detailing the violations. This is the way that human rights law is used by many human rights CSOs day-to-day. Of course it may be more effective to rely simply on national law, constitutional principles or regional international human rights treaties, or even an appeal to human dignity and basic moral behaviour, but today human rights claims are invariably accompanied by evidence that there has been a violation of human rights law, rather than an appeal to morality, ethics or the philosophy of human rights. In some cases where the direct application of international human rights law is considered problematic (such as reporting on rebel groups),[25] there may be nuanced appeals to 'principles' of human rights and humanitarian law, but the framework adopted by human rights CSOs remains, on the whole, a legal one.

International CSOs obviously find it more convenient to focus on the international law rather than national law applicable in the state concerned. First, this enables them to claim that they are judging all states by the same standards and that states are bound by these standards under international law. Relying on international commitments also makes it impossible for governments to claim that the issue is exclusively a matter of national jurisdiction and that CSO reports represent interference in the state's internal affairs. Second, few international CSOs are in a position to develop detailed expertise in the national legal orders of the states they are monitoring. Of course where the reports are critical of fair trial guarantees, or issues of access to justice, there will have to be a careful critique of the inadequacy of the national law, but in many cases the issue will be simply a question of holding up the state's behaviour to the international standards and pointing to the violations.

---

24 V. Lowe, 'The Politics of Law-Making: Are the Method and Character of Norm Creation Changing?', in M. Byers (ed.), *The Role of Law in International Politics: Essays in International Relations and International Law* (OUP, 2000) 207–26 at 219. Lowe points to the 'emergence of normative concepts operating in the interstices between those primary norms [that mandate or forbid certain activities]. These emergent concepts we may call "interstitial norms" or "modifying norms" or "meta-principles", because they do not themselves have a normative force of the traditional kind but instead operate by modifying the normative effect of other, primary norms of international law.' Ibid. at 213.

25 See further *Rules of Engagement: Protecting Civilians through Dialogue with Armed Non-State Actors* (2011) available at http://www.adh-geneva.ch/docs/publications/Policy studies/Rules-of-Engagement-EN.pdf. See also A. Clapham, 'Human Rights Obligations of Non-state Actors in Conflict Situations' (2006) 88(863) *International Review of the Red Cross*, 491–523.

National and international CSOs will nevertheless often simply address human rights violations through the prism of national law, although in many cases the national law may in turn be based on an international human rights treaty. In some situations a CSO may actually be challenging national law for its failure to conform to the state's international obligations under international human rights law. Often such challenges will develop around a state's reporting to the UN under the relevant human rights treaty. It is to that topic that we now turn.

3 Working with the human rights treaty bodies and the Universal Periodic Review

Many human rights treaties are monitored by expert bodies that work closely with CSOs.[26] While some bodies, such as the Committee on the Rights of the Child, have formalised their interaction with CSOs,[27] others simply rely on informal briefings and written communications. CSOs are involved at various phases of the process. They may be consulted by the government that is preparing a periodic report to the monitoring body. They may prepare their own 'shadow' or 'alternative' report to inform the members of the expert body and confront the government with alternative interpretations of the facts and the law. They may use the media to focus national attention on the UN or regional body's examination, or seek to concentrate the expert body on a particular aspect of the applicable law. They will often be present for the oral examination of the state's report, and the questions will inevitably draw on the information and priorities communicated by the relevant CSOs.[28] After the body has published its concluding observations, CSOs may then take these conclusions back to the national legislature or executive and seek to effect a change in policy or a repeal of the law.[29] Indeed, some of the treaty bodies, due to their own lack of follow-up capacity, rely on CSOs to take a leading role in any implementation of the recommendations made during the periodic reporting process. More generally CSOs through their regular monitoring and reporting work are particularly well placed to inform the experts of the human rights challenges facing the state being examined. Anne Marie Clark has highlighted what she calls the 'interpretive capacity' of CSOs in this context. She emphasises a:

> mastery of the conceptual process necessary to collate facts and normative standards. It requires well informed NGOs to reinforce normative standards by relating specific details to general concepts. Where facts are shockingly incongruous with known standards of behaviour, as is often the case when 'new' human rights violations are discovered, the interpretation of fact in a way that cohered with previous norms or

---

26 See further C. Krause and M. Scheinin (eds), *International Protection of Human Rights: A Textbook*, (Abo Akademi Institute for Human Rights, 2009) Chs 6–14, 17–23, 26–27; P. Alston, *The United Nations and Human Rights* (OUP, 1992).

27 See 'Guidelines for the participation of partners (NGOs and individual experts) in the pre-sessional working group of the Committee on the Rights of the Child' (CRC/C/90, Annex VIII).

28 See further E. Riedel, 'The Development of International Law: Alternatives to Treaty-Making? International Organizations and Non-State Actors', in R. Wolfrum and V. Röben (eds), *Developments of International Law in Treaty Making* (Springer, 2005) 301–18.

29 For examples see A. Clapham, 'The UN Human Rights Reporting Procedure: An NGO Perspective', in J. Crawford and P. Alston (eds), *The Future of UN Human Rights Treaty Monitoring*, (CUP, 2000) 175–98 at 176–87.

precedents promotes the application of existing norms and the development of new standards.[30]

Since 2008 CSOs have had a new arena in which to raise issues of international human rights law. The UN Human Rights Council established Universal Periodic Review (UPR), whereby the Council reviews every UN member state's compliance with its human rights obligations and commitments.[31] As the Council embarked on this review process, the President of the Council saw this in terms of a three-fold universality.[32] In this understanding the review is universal because every UN member state will be reviewed; the review is universal in the sense that all states can participate in the review; and the review reflects the universality of human rights because all rights (civil and political as well as economic and social and cultural) are examined. The cycle covering the whole world now takes four-and-a-half years, with forty-two states being examined each year. Each review lasts three-and-a-half hours in the Council's Working Group on the UPR, with an extra hour dedicated to the outcome document in the plenary session. CSOs accredited to the UN can only intervene orally in the plenary session.

Questions posed by UN member states are collated before the actual review based in part on three key UPR documents: (a) information prepared by the state concerned (20 pages maximum); (b) a compilation prepared by the Office of the High Commissioner for Human Rights (OHCHR) based on the reports of treaty bodies, special procedures and other relevant official United Nations documents (10 pages maximum); (c) a summary prepared by OHCHR of credible and reliable information provided by other relevant stakeholders (10 pages maximum).[33] This last document is compiled from multiple CSO 'stakeholder submissions' sent to the OHCHR. At the same time, CSOs post their entire reports on the internet, and lobby states to include their issues in the question and answer dialogue that makes up the review in the working group.

The Human Rights Council has now completed one full review cycle, and views are mixed on whether this process is actually leading to significant improvements on the ground, or whether it may even be paving the way for a watering down of the standards and scrutiny developed over the years by the treaty bodies and other monitoring arrangements.[34]

30 A.M. Clark, *Diplomacy of Conscience: Amnesty International and Changing Human Rights Norms* (Princeton University Press, 2001) at 16.

31 For the details see the document annexed to the resolution adopted by the Human Rights Council (HRC) as Resolution 5/1 of 18 June 2007; see also HRC Decision 6/102 follow-up to HRC resolution 5/1; HRC 8/PRST/1; Follow-up to President's statement HRC 8/1 PRST/9/2; A/HRC/RES/16/21; and HRC decision 17/119.

32 Private conversation with the President of the Council, Ambassador Doru Romulus Costea, 10 January 2008.

33 'United Nations Human Rights Council: Institution-Building', document annexed to the resolution adopted by the Human Rights Council as Resolution 5/1 of 18 June 2007. Also included in the report of the Human Rights Council to the General Assembly, UN Doc. A/HRC/5/21, 7 August 2007, para. 15.

34 C. Tomuschat, 'Universal Periodic Review: a New System of International Law with Specific Ground Rules', in U. Fastenrath, R. Geiger, D.-E. Khan, A. Paulus, S. von Schorlemer and C. Vedder (eds), *From Bilateralism to Community Interest: Essays in Honour of Judge Bruno Simma* (OUP, 2011) 609–28; M.C. Bassiouni and W.A. Schabas (eds), *New Challenges for the UN Human Rights Machinery. What Future for the UN Treaty Body System and the Human Rights Council Procedures?* (Intersentia, 2012); R.K.M. Smith, 'More of the Same or Something Different? Preliminary Observations on the Contribution of Universal Periodic Review with Reference to the Chinese Experience' (2011) 10(3) *Chinese Journal of International Law*, 565–86.

Perhaps the test will be whether the second cycle reveals concrete improvements and a further holding to account. So far, many CSOs have relished the opportunity to provide documentation to the UN on country situations, have their key points sometimes reproduced in the compilation document, and reference governments' promises made in public and webcast around the world. One might also mention that those CSOs that speak on the record in plenary sessions similarly achieve a level of publicity and exposure due to the live broadcast and archives of the video footage. CSOs that this author spoke to suggested that the UPR provides domestic CSOs with a useful post-review lobbying tool at the national level. This is due to the formal engagement of senior officials in the review process, which concludes at the UN with the state under review undertaking to implement accepted recommendations as well as making voluntary pledges with regard to various human rights improvements within the country.

The present arrangements for CSO interaction with the treaty monitoring procedures and the work of the UN's Human Rights Council represent a huge improvement on the original rudimentary arrangements. CSOs no longer have to deliver their reports surreptitiously to the UN experts, in unmarked brown paper envelopes; experts and government representatives are no longer shy about revealing the source of their information; and the UN Secretariat seeks out the views of CSOs and highlights their concerns. While the CSO contribution to the more legalistic treaty body monitoring process may allow for greater attention to complex issues and individual cases, it remains the case that many CSOs will find the UPR process allows for a sense of greater accountability and interaction. The government ministers and officials, that were filmed defending the human rights record of the state under review, apparently remain particularly amenable to dialogue with CSOs before and after their live review before the international community.

4 Representation, complaints and expert briefs

CSOs can use international human rights law before national and international bodies. First, CSOs may take on the representation of victims before national courts where international human rights law will complement the national law or even form the basis of the complaint. Victims or their lawyers may be unfamiliar with the international legal order, while CSOs may have developed specialist expertise. Similarly groups such as AIRE Centre (Advice on Individual Rights in Europe) specialise in supporting suitable applications to the European Court of Human Rights.[35] CSOs such as TRIAL and Interights also now have a track record of coordinating and assisting complainants before the UN Human Rights Committee.[36] As the new protocols for the Convention on the Elimination of Discrimination against Women, Economic Social and Cultural Rights Covenant, the Child Rights Convention the and the Convention on Persons with Disabilities gradually expand the scope for individual complaints, we can expect to see CSOs choosing to support certain complaints that are considered important for the development of the treaty bodies' 'jurisprudence'.

Second, as we saw above, in some contexts the international human rights treaty may allow for a CSO to complain directly before an international forum. This may mean tackling a structural issue, rather than supporting a particular victim. So, for example, the International

---

35 See http://www.airecentre.org/ (last accessed on 23 February 2013).

36 See http://www.trial-ch.org/en/about-trial.html and http://www.interights.org/home/index. html (last accessed on 23 February 2013).

Commission of Jurists and Interights have respectively brought complaints to the Committee of Social Rights established under the European Social Charter with regard to child labour in Portugal and homophobic education in Croatia.[37] Similarly, issues of the right to housing and environmental degradation were raised in the complaint brought by the Social and Economic Rights Action Center and the Center for Economic and Social Rights against Nigeria before the African Commission on Human Peoples' Rights.[38] This activity is resource-intensive and demands relatively high levels of expertise. As explained above, other regimes such as the European Convention on Human Rights only allow for complaints by *victims* of human rights violations. Human rights organisations, trades unions, political parties and corporations have therefore all been admissible applicants before the Court. A vegetarian association successfully complained that it had been denied airtime on Swiss television,[39] while Animal Defenders International was unsuccessful in its complaint that it had been denied freedom of expression due to the ban on political advertising in the UK.[40] Multiple cases have been heard concerning complaints by political parties and associations that have been denied the freedom of association.

Of course not all rights can be simply transposed onto the CSO. A number of early applications ruled out the idea that non-physical entities have a right to freedom of conscience, although churches and religious organisations have a right to manifest religion,[41] and a religious foundation was held unable to claim the right to education.[42] Non-state actors have no right to marry (no fundamental right to merger!). Nor can non-human non-state actors complain of torture or inhuman or degrading treatment under the European Convention.[43] But the key point remains that organisations are capable of bearing some international rights and that this has been accepted with regard to a limited number of human rights more generally.[44]

A more recent UN treaty allowing for complaints about discrimination against women states that a complaint can be brought on behalf of individuals or groups of individuals with the consent of the alleged victim (unless the author can justify acting on their behalf without their consent).[45]

---

37 *ICJ v Portugal*, Complaint No. 1/1998; *INTERIGHTS v Croatia*, Complaint No. 45/2007: R.R. Churchill and U. Khaliq, 'The Collective Complaints System of the European Social Charter: An Effective Mechanism for Ensuring Compliance with Economic and Social Rights', (2004) 15 *European Journal of International Law* 417–56.

38 *Social and Economic Rights Action Center and Center for Economic and Social Rights v Nigeria*, 155/96, Decision of the African Commission of Human and Peoples' Rights, October 2001.

39 *Case of Vgt Verein Gegen Tierfabriken v Switzerland*, Judgment of 28 June 2001.

40 *Case of Animal Defenders International v The United Kingdom*, Judgment of 22 April 2013.

41 See e.g. *Kustannus Oy Vapaa Ajattelija AB (Publishing Company Freethinker Ltd) et al v Finland,* Applic. 20471/92, 15 April 1996; *Verein 'Kontakt-Information-Therapie (KIT) and Siegfried Hagen v Austria*, 11921/86, 12 October 1988; *X v Switzerland*, 27 February 1979.

42 *Ingrid Jordebo Foundation of Christian Schools and Ingrid Jordebo v Sweden*, 6 March 1987.

43 *KIT v Austria* (n. 41).

44 For some comparative constitutional law examples of human rights claims brought by non-physical persons see M.K. Addo, 'The Corporation as a Victim of Human Rights Violations', in M.K. Addo (ed.), *Human Rights Standards and the Responsibility of Transantional Corporations* (Kluwer Law International, 1999) 187–96; see also M. Emberland, *The Human Rights of Companies: Exploring the Structure of ECHR Protection* (OUP, 2006).

45 Optional Protocol to the Convention on the Elimination of All Forms of Discrimination Against Women (CEDAW) (1999) Art. 2. See for example *Ms. A. S. (represented by the European Roma Rights Center and the Legal Defence Bureau for National and Ethnic Minorities) v Hungary*, Communication No. 4/2004.

In this context we should mention that a number of treaties allow for CSOs to trigger investigations by international human rights bodies. For example, the Torture Convention (CAT) not only allows for individual complaints, but also allows for the Committee established under the Convention to initiate an inquiry where it has received 'reliable information which appears in it to contain [*sic*] well-founded indications that torture is being systematically practised in the territory of a State Party'.[46] A similar provision exists with regard to discrimination against women where a similar inquiry procedure can be triggered by CSOs where 'the Committee receives reliable information indicating grave or systematic violations' of the Convention.[47] CSOs are likely to be considered as providing reliable information where the Committee has relied on such sources in the past in the context of reviewing the reports of states that are parties to the treaty regime (discussed below).[48] In turn the results of such inquiries and their findings can become central to CSO campaigns to highlight such violations in inter-governmental fora or in the media.[49]

Lastly, in this context, we should refer to the UN Human Rights Council's procedure, formerly known as the '1503' procedure (after the ECOSOC resolution that established it) that allows for complaints from CSOs which reveal 'consistent patterns of gross and reliably attested violations of all human rights and all fundamental freedoms occurring in any part of the world and under any circumstances'.[50] Communications are admissible, provided that they are not manifestly politically motivated and their object is consistent with human rights. They must provide a factual description of the alleged violations and the relevant human rights norms. They must be submitted by a person or a group of persons claiming to be the victims of violations of human rights, or by anyone, including CSOs, with knowledge or evidence of the violations concerned. The communication cannot be exclusively based on reports disseminated by mass media and cannot refer to a case already being dealt with by a special procedure, a treaty body or other United Nations or similar regional complaints procedure in the field of human rights. Domestic remedies must be exhausted. This procedure has enabled some CSOs to bring political pressure on certain governments in the past, but the process remains opaque and is now highly politicised.[51]

---

46 Convention Against Torture and Other Forms of Cruel, Inhuman or Degrading Treatment or Punishment (1984) Art. 22.

47 Optional Protocol to CEDAW Art. 8. See now Report on Mexico produced by the Committee on the Elimination of Discrimination against Women under Article 8 of the Optional Protocol to the Convention, and reply from the Government of Mexico, CEDAW/C/2005/OP.8/MEXICO, resulting from information brought as a result of information provided by Equality Now and Casa Amiga.

48 See for example UN Doc. A/51/44 at para. 219. The Committee included in its list of sources Amnesty International, the Egyptian Organization for Human Rights, the World Organization against Torture, and stated that 'other non-governmental sources have occasionally provided information during this inquiry.' At para. 201.

49 See further A. Clapham, 'Defining the Role of Non-Governmental Organizations with Regard to the UN Human Rights Treaty Bodies', in A.F. Bayefsky (ed.), *The UN Human Rights Treaty System in the 21st Century* (Kluwer, 2000) 193–94 at 187–90.

50 United Nations Human Rights Council: institution-building document annexed to the resolution adopted by the Human Rights Council as Resolution 5/1 of 18 June 2007. Also included in the report of the Human Rights Council to the General Assembly, UN Doc. A/HRC/5/21, 7 August 2007 para. 85ff.

51 See further D. Weissbrodt et al., *International Human Rights: Law, Policy, and Process*, 4th edn (Lexis Nexis, 2009) at 239ff.

Thirdly, CSOs have developed a role in informing courts of the relevant international human rights law pertinent to the case before them. CSOs may have insights which go beyond the experience of the lawyers and judges directly involved in the case, or the CSO may simply be proffering an interpretation which seeks to develop international human rights law. Of course a court will not be obliged to follow the CSO interpretation and may not even acknowledge the influence that it has had on the judgement. An interesting example of the influence of an *amicus curiae* brief is the brief prepared by Amnesty International in the context of the *McCann and others v United Kingdom* case before the European Court of Human Rights. This case concerned the shooting of three people suspected of preparing a terrorist bomb attack in Gibraltar. The claim brought by their next of kin was based on the right to life. The *amicus* brief provided arguments based on UN norms which went into more detail concerning the use of force and firearms and the necessary inquest procedures than were apparent from the right-to-life provisions in the European Convention.[52] CSOs have also filed *amicus* briefs using international law to bolster the arguments of the side they are supporting.[53]

5 Campaigning for new norms, institutions and frameworks

CSOs have not only relied on international law, but have also campaigned for new norms of international law. The anti-slavery movement, women's groups, workers' organisations, the anti-apartheid movement, religious groups and organisations working on minority rights have all been influential in creating the present human rights framework.[54] If one looks at particular treaties we should acknowledge that the Genocide Convention of 1948 was inspired by the efforts of Raphael Lemkin and his World Movement to Outlaw Genocide.[55] The Declaration and eventual Convention against Torture can be traced to a number of drafts prepared by CSOs (including the International Association of Penal Law and the International Commission of Jurists) and a campaign orchestrated by Amnesty International, and launched with a London concert by Joan Baez in 1973.[56] The Protocol to that Treaty (creating a new Sub-Committee to visit places of detention) was in part the brainchild of Jean Jacques Gautier of the Swiss Committee against Torture (later the Association for the Prevention of Torture).[57] The development of the prohibition on disappearances and the eventual Convention on Enforced Disappearances can be similarly traced to dogged work on the part of human rights organisations and FEDEFAM (Latin American Federation of Associations for Relatives of the Detained-Disappeared). Most recently the Convention on the Rights of Persons with Disabilities benefited from considerable input from the International Disability Caucus (IDC), a consortium of about fifty CSOs.

---

52 *McCann and Others v United Kingdom*, Judgment of the European Court of Human Rights, 5 September 1995, esp. para. 157.
53 For recent examples see the briefs to the US Supreme Court in the Alien Tort Statute litigation against Shell in 2012, available at http://www.americanbar.org/publications/preview_home/10–1491.html.
54 See generally P.G. Lauren, *The Evolution of International Human Rights: Visions Seen,* 3rd edn (University of Pennsylvania Press, 2011).
55 W. Schabas, *Genocide in International Law: The Crime of Crimes* (CUP, 2000) ch. 1.
56 See for more detail Clark (n. 30) ch. 3.
57 *Jean-Jacques Gautier et la prévention de la torture: de l'idée à l'action (Recueil de textes)* (Geneva, APT, 2003).

The influence of CSOs in this context can be explained by a threefold phenomenon. First, by documenting the situation on the ground, and working to remedy the situation, CSOs are often best placed to know what legal lacunae need to be filled, and what sort of obligations should be contained in a legal text. Second, treaties and declarations are adopted in diplomatic fora, and certainly with regard to the early efforts to write human rights law there was a sense that only a few diplomats had the requisite expertise to draft such human rights texts unassisted.[58] Third, CSOs provide the momentum and in some cases create the political will for the eventual adoption of the text and ratification of the treaty by states. In particular, national CSOs and international organisations with widespread membership are critical to the mobilisation of national parliamentarians and governments over issues which would otherwise not generate much national interest or debate.[59] One should perhaps be aware of the tension here between CSOs providing expertise and advice while simultaneously publishing damning reports about the governments they are seeking to persuade.[60]

More recently, CSOs have developed global coalitions to campaign for new norms such as the bans on landmines and cluster munitions, and for new institutions such as the International Criminal Court.[61] These campaigns have been successful and high-profile, with Jody Williams and the International Campaign to Ban Landmines being awarded the Nobel Peace Prize in 1997. Some commentators have now started to question the legitimacy of this form of law-making, asking us to consider the legitimacy and accountability of such movements, casting them as 'global transnational elites' and going on to ask whether it is democratic to have law-making so influenced by unelected NGOs.[62] In some situations individuals from various CSOs have 'changed hats' and served on governmental delegations, providing expertise and capacity for smaller (and larger) governmental delegations at diplomatic conferences leading to the adoption of treaties.[63] The most recent such campaign relates to the Arms Trade Treaty, designed to tackle potential transfers of conventional weapons to states where they would be used to commit atrocity crimes or there is an overriding risk they will be used to commit serious violations of human rights violations.[64] Here there is no question of generating new human rights or institutions or outlawing types of weapons; rather the CSOs are using human rights law not only to reinforce primary universal human

---

58 See the comments by Margo Picken quoted in Clark (n. 30) at 35; see further K. Martens, 'Professionalised Representation of Human Rights NGOs to the United Nations' (2006) 10(1) *International Journal of Human Rights* 19–30.

59 Consider in this context the work of Parliamentarians for Global Action and the Inter-Parliamentary Union.

60 Clark (n. 30) at 128.

61 See the work of the International Coalition to Ban Landmines, Control Arms, and the International Coalition for the International Criminal Court.

62 K. Anderson, 'The Ottawa Convention Banning Landmines, the Role of International Non-Governmental Organizations and the Idea of International Civil Society' (2000) 11(1) *European Journal of International Law* 91–120.

63 See further M. Glasius, 'Expertise in the Cause of Justice: Global Civil Society Influence on the Statute for an International Criminal Court', in M. Glasius, M. Kaldor and H. Anheirer (eds), *Global Civil Society 2002* (OUP, 2002) 137–68; S. Sur, 'Vers une Cour pénale internationale: la Convention de Rome entre les ONG et le Conseil de sécurité', *Revue générale de droit international Public* (1999) 29–45.

64 See Arms Trade Treaty (2013), in annex to UN doc. A/RES/67/234 adopted by the UN General Assembly 2 April 2013, 154 votes in favour, 3 against and 23 abstentions; Art. 6(3). The three negative votes were Syria, the Democratic People's Republic of Korea and Iran.

rights obligations on states, but also to develop a framework of secondary due diligence obligations.

The formal arrangements for CSOs to participate in these and similar exercises are complex and have developed in a rather ad hoc way depending on the relevant secretariat and the approach of the Chair and the Bureau.[65] But the variations in the formal arrangements are in fact unlikely to alter radically the role and relevance of CSOs in these contexts. It is no longer possible to imagine a multilateral treaty-drafting process sealed off from the views and influence of CSOs.

6 Accountability of civil society organisations themselves

As we saw at the beginning of this contribution, the concept of a non-governmental organisation has been adapted to cover a wide range of organisations. As NGOs have become more visible, questions have been asked not only about the concept of a 'global civil society',[66] but also as to the legitimacy of the plethora of organisations springing up every day. We have already come across the concept of a GONGO, but there are a number of other labels now bandied about. Kumi Naidoo, currently Executive Director of Greenpeace, has highlighted how:

> Challenges to civil society's legitimacy come from many quarters. They are often voiced by national political leaders, and occasionally by prominent voices at global institutions. It is frequently said that civil society groups don't represent the views of anyone but themselves and that if they are accountable at all, it is usually 'upward' to their funders, rather than 'downward' to those they purportedly serve. Those that offer this critique sometimes evoke a range of derogatory acronyms to describe certain kinds of wannabe NGOs: BONGOs (business-organised NGOs), PONGOs (politically-organised NGOs), BRINGOs (Briefcase NGOS), DONGOs (donor-organised NGOs), GONGOs (government-organised NGOs), MONGOs (My own NGO), and RONGOs (royally-organised NGOs).
>
> My personal favourite are these three . . . In the Middle East they have a thing called RONGOs, which are royally-organized NGOs set up by Princes and Princesses, people within the royal infrastructure in the Middle East. And the other one called BRINGOs which are briefcase NGOs. This is the same enthusiastic person walking around with a briefcase with a funding proposal in it, hoping it will get funded. And my super personal favourite is MONGOs which is my own NGO. And MONGOs are where people set up NGOs as their personal property and treat it as personal property.[67]

65 For the Arms Trade Treaty see the provisional rules of procedure rules 57 and 63, which limits participation to open meetings and oral statements in a specially designated meeting. See UN Doc. A/CONF.217/L.1; for the details related to NGO inclusion in negotiations at the General Assembly leading to the resolution creating the UN High Commissioner for Human Rights, see A. Clapham, 'Creating the High Commissioner for Human Rights: The Outside Story' (1994) 5 *European Journal of International Law* 556–68.

66 K. Anderson and D. Rieff, 'Global Civil Society: A Sceptical View,' in H. Anheier, M. Glasius and M. Kaldor (eds), *Global Civil Society 2004/5* (Sage, 2005) 27–39.

67 'What Are the Challenges Faced by Civil Society Organizations' (2004) 1(1) *civilsociety.hr*, available at http://zaklada.civilnodrustvo.hr/upload/File/old_eng/magazine/broj01/eng_casopis_01.pdf.

Surprisingly little attention has been given to elaborating mechanisms for ensuring the accountability of CSOs. Peter Spiro has separated out what he calls the internal and external dimensions of accountability: 'Internal accountability is absent where organizational leaderships can act without regard for the preferences of organizational members or other followers. External accountability is absent where actors are able to depart without penalty from the terms of process bargains.'[68] We might add a third dimension: there are real possibilities that CSOs themselves may abuse human rights, and this demands accountability towards their victims. Examples of such human rights abuses by CSOs include the incidents related to sexual favours for food in CSO-run refugee camps, discriminatory or racist publications, and of course issues related to working conditions within a CSO. These problems bring us to a last use of international human rights law by CSOs.

Faced with accusations of human rights abuses by CSOs themselves, a number of CSOs have developed various initiatives which rely on the principles of international human rights law to elaborate a normative regime to ensure better standards of behaviour and a degree of accountability.[69] These initiatives may involve certification for compliance with various standards and codes of conduct and the reliance on the principles and values that underlie human rights law is evident. It would be ironic if CSOs failed to see how calls for respect for human dignity, transparency and accountability will be undermined where those same values are not taken seriously by CSOs themselves.

Select bibliography

R. Brett, 'Non-Governmental Organizations and Human Rights', in C. Krause and M. Scheinin (eds), *International Protection of Human Rights: A Textbook* (Abo Akademi Institute for Human Rights, 2009) 621–35.

W.E. DeMars, *NGOs and Transnational Networks: Wild Cards in World Politics* (Pluto Press, 2005).

P.-M. Dupuy and L. Vierucci (eds), *NGOs in International Law: Efficiency or Flexibility?* (Elgar, 2008).

K. Martens, *NGOs and the United Nations: Institutionalization, Professionalization and Adaptation* (Palgrave, 2005).

T. Paffenholz, 'Civil Society', in V. Chetail (ed.), *Post-Conflict Peacebuilding: A Lexicon* (OUP, 2009) 60–73.

T. Treves, M. Frigissi di Rattalma, A. Tanzi, A. Fodella, C. Pitea and C. Ragni (eds), *Civil Society, International Courts and Compliance Bodies* (TMC Asser Press, 2005).

C.E. Welch (ed.), *NGOs and Human Rights: Promise and Performance* (University of Pennsylvania Press, 2001).

68 P.J. Spiro, 'NGOs and Human Rights: Channels of Power', in S. Joseph and A. McBeth (eds), *Research Handbook on International Human Rights Law* (Elgar, 2010) 115–38 at 134.
69 Humanitarian Accountability Partnership International; and the Sphere Project's *Humanitarian Charter and Minimum Standards in Disaster* Response, 3rd edn (Practical Action Publishing, 2011).

11

International human rights in field operations: a fast-developing human rights tool

Michael O'Flaherty and Daria Davitti

1 Introduction

The ever-increasing deployment by the United Nations of human rights field operations in conflict and post-conflict environments reflects the growing acknowledgement of the circular nexus of human rights violations and the causes of armed conflict and other emergency situations.[1] This recognition, and the recent focus on human rights mainstreaming at the field level,[2] have provided the context for the deployment of human rights experts by other intergovernmental organisations besides the UN, as well as by international human rights and humanitarian non-governmental organisations (NGOs). Although the considerations contained in this chapter are relevant to most of these actors, the primary analytical focus rests on the work of human rights field operations of the UN (HRFOs), and on the core functions and key partnerships that shape their efforts to address the ever-changing challenges that they encounter.

2 Historical overview

The deployment of specifically mandated UN human rights field teams began in 1991.[3] The early 1990s saw the deployment of a human rights component within the UN mission in

---

1 M. O'Flaherty, 'Human Rights Field Operations', in G. Alfredsson et al. (eds), *International Human Rights Monitoring Mechanisms: Essays in Honour of Jakob Th. Moeller,* 2nd edn (Martinus Nijhoff Publishers, 2009) 205.

2 OHCHR, 'High Commissioner's Strategic Management Plan 2010–2011' (2010) 51–55.

3 Although already in 1978 the UN mission in Namibia had responsibility for election monitoring, development of electoral legislation, repatriation of refugees and release of political prisoners, the first human rights mission was deployed in El Salvador, mandated with monitoring the implementation of the San Jose Peace Agreement. For Namibia, see SC Res. 431 (27 July 1978) and SC Res. 435 (29 September 1978). For El Salvador, see R. Brody, 'The United Nations and Human Rights in El Salvador's "Negotiated Revolution"', (1995) 8 *Harvard Human Rights Journal* 153–78; D. García Sayán, 'The Experience of ONUSAL in El Salvador', in A. Henkin (ed.), *Honoring Human Rights* (Kluwer Law International, 2000) 21–46; T. Whitfield, 'Staying the Course in El Salvador', in A. Henkin (ed.), *Honoring Human Rights* (Kluwer Law International, 2000) 319–44.

Cambodia[4] and the first exclusively human rights-focused mission in Haiti.[5] These first missions were mainly New York-led, established under the authority of, or in consultation with, the Security Council and/or the General Assembly, but without the involvement of the then UN Centre for Human Rights based in Geneva. The Centre, since renamed the Office of the High Commissioner for Human Rights (OHCHR) in 1998, had itself deployed human rights monitors in the former Yugoslavia;[6] had taken over the UN human rights programme in Cambodia from the UN Transitional Authority (UNTAC) in 1993; and in 1994, following the Rwandan genocide, had established one of the biggest human rights mission at the time.[7] All of these missions were funded by voluntary contributions and established notwithstanding the Centre's lack of experience and infrastructure in this area. Commentators soon indicated concerns in relation to the management of these missions, particularly in terms of their sustainability; the need for the Centre and the High Commissioner for Human Rights to assume a guiding role; the functions to be undertaken; and the need to ensure that all UN peace missions addressed human rights in a more systematic manner.[8]

With the 1996 UN Reform Programme,[9] the Secretary-General moved to address some of these concerns within the context of a general move to operationalise the notion of human rights as a cross-cutting responsibility in all the work areas of the UN. As part of this reform, the Centre for Human Rights adopted a policy of seeking, as far as possible, to insert human rights components in New York-led missions.[10] Human rights components within peacekeeping and, to a lesser extent, peacemaking operations, also became increasingly crucial for New York departments. Within this context, human rights components were deployed in UN missions such as Liberia,[11] Angola,[12] Sierra Leone,[13]

---

4 D. McNamara, 'UN Human Rights Activities in Cambodia: An Evaluation', in Henkin (n. 3) 47–72; B. Adams, 'UN Human Rights Work in Cambodia: Efforts to Preserve the Jewel in the Peacekeeping Crown', in Henkin (n. 3) 345–82.

5 W.G. O'Neill, 'Human Rights Monitoring versus Political Expediency: The Experience of the OAS/UN Mission in Haiti' (1995) 8 *Harvard Human Rights Journal* 101–28; W.G. O'Neill, 'Gaining Compliance Without Force: Human Rights Field Operations', in S. Chesterman (ed.), *Civilians in War* (Lynne Reinner, 2001); I. Martin, 'Paper versus Steel: The First Phase of the International Civilian Mission in Haiti', in Henkin (n. 3) 73–118; C. Granderson, 'Institutionalizing Peace: The Haiti Experience', in Henkin (n. 3) 383–412.

6 O'Flaherty (n. 1) 207.

7 W. Clarance, 'The Human Rights Field Operation in Rwanda: Protective Practice Evolves on the Ground' (1995) 2(3) *International Peacekeeping* 291–308; I. Martin, 'After Genocide: The UN Human Rights Field Operation in Rwanda', in Henkin (n. 3) 253–88; T. Howland, 'Mirage, Magic or Mixed Bag? The United Nations High Commissioner for Human Rights' Field Operation in Rwanda' (1999) 21(1) *Human Rights Quarterly* 1–55.

8 I. Martin, 'A New Frontier: The Early Experience and Future of International Human Rights Field Operations' (1998) 16(2) *Netherlands Quarterly of Human Rights* 121–39 at 134; W. Clarance, 'Field Strategy for the Protection of Human Rights' (1997) 9(2) *International Journal of Refugee Law* 229–54; D. Little, 'Protecting Human Rights During and After Conflicts: The Role of the United Nations' (1996) 4(1) *Tulsa Journal of Comparative and International Law* 87–98.

9 K. Annan, 'Renewing the United Nations: A Programme for Reform' (1997) UN Doc. A/51/950.

10 O'Flaherty, (n. 1) 208.

11 B. Nowrojee, 'Joining Forces: United Nations and Regional Peacekeeping – Lessons from Liberia' (1995) 8 *Harvard Human Rights Journal* 129–52; A. Clapham and E. Martin, 'Smaller Missions Bigger Problems', in Henkin (n. 3) 289–318.

12 T. Howland, 'UN Human Rights Field Presence as Proactive Instrument of Peace and Social Change: Lessons from Angola' (2004) 26(1) *Human Rights Quarterly* 1–28.

the Democratic Republic of Congo (DRC),[14] Ethiopia and Eritrea,[15] and where the UN had assumed transitional authority, namely Kosovo[16] and East Timor.[17] In some instances components were also established within the missions to promote the rule of law and the rights of the child, and to address gender issues, all objectives that clearly overlapped with the areas of interest of the human rights components. Similarly, civilian police components also started operating under human rights mandates, as in the case of post-conflict Bosnia and Herzegovina.[18]

Simultaneously, OHCHR-led missions continued to be launched in, for instance, Colombia, DRC and Burundi, in order to respond to the needs of specific initiatives of the UN Commission on Human Rights or intended work areas, such as human rights technical cooperation. These OHCHR programmes sometimes complemented the human rights operations of peace missions, as was the case of the OHCHR programme in Sierra Leone which supported the truth and reconciliation process.

A more systematic approach to human rights field operations emerged in 2000 with the *Report of the Panel on United Nations Peace Operations* ('Brahimi Report'),[19] which emphasised the need for mission-wide team approaches to uphold the rule of law and respect for human rights.[20] It also described the human rights component of peace operations as 'indeed critical to effective peace-building' and emphasised the need to engage in both human rights monitoring and capacity building. The Brahimi Report was published simultaneously with the finalisation of a Memorandum of Understanding (MOU) between OHCHR and the Department of Peacekeeping Operations (DPKO), which established a formal relationship for the design and operation of peacekeeping missions. The Brahimi Report proposed a management model that envisaged the involvement of OHCHR throughout the design and oversight of all UN peace operations.[21] The Report's proposal was tested in 2002 with the design of a new 'integrated mission' in Afghanistan, where the human rights monitoring function was meant to be 'mainstreamed' throughout the mission, thus resulting in the absence of a dedicated human rights monitoring unit. Following criticism of this model,[22]

13 See M. O'Flaherty, 'Sierra Leone's Peace Process: The Role of the Human Rights Community,' (2004) 26(1) *Human Rights Quarterly* 29–62

14 A. Hilding Norberg, 'Challenges of Peace Operations' (2003) 10(4) *International Peacekeeping* 94–103; O'Flaherty (n. 13).

15 T. Neethling, 'Whither Peacekeeping in Africa: Revisiting the Evolving Role of the United Nations' (2009) 18(1) *African Security Review* 1–20.

16 W. Betts et al., 'The Post-Conflict Transitional Administration in Kosovo and the Lessons Learned in Efforts to Establish a Judiciary and Rule of Law' (2001) 22(3) *Michigan Journal of International Law* 371–90.

17 D. Criswell, 'Durable Consent and a Strong Transitional Peacekeeping Plan: The Success of UNTAET in Light of the Lessons Learned in Cambodia' (2002) 11(3) *Pacific Rim Law and Policy Journal* 577–612; B. Kondoch, 'The United Nations Administration of East Timor' (2001) 6(2) *Journal of Conflict and Security Law* 245–66.

18 M. O'Flaherty, 'International Human Rights Operations in Bosnia and Herzegovina', in Henkin (n. 3) 227–52; M. O'Flaherty and G. Gisvold (eds), *Post-war Protection of Human Rights in Bosnia and Herzegovina* (Martinus Nijhoff, 1998).

19 Report of the Panel on United Nations Peace Operations (2000) UN Doc. A/55/305 S/2000/809.

20 Ibid. 6.

21 Ibid. 41.

22 M. O'Flaherty, 'Future Protection of Human Rights in Post-Conflict Societies: The Role of the United Nations', (2003) 3(1) *Human Rights Law Review* 53–76.

subsequent integrated missions, including in Iraq, Liberia and Ivory Coast, reverted to the deployment of dedicated human rights units.[23]

The process of human rights mainstreaming received further impetus with the 2002 report of the Secretary-General entitled *Strengthening of the United Nations: An Agenda for Further Change.*[24] The report, which emphasised the promotion and protection of human rights as 'a bedrock requirement for the realisation of the Charter's vision of a just and peaceful world',[25] was followed by the *Action 2 Plan of Action*, designed to further integrate human rights throughout all UN humanitarian, development and peacekeeping work, including through a human rights-based approach to programming.[26] The 2002 Secretary-General's Report mandated OHCHR to 'ensure that human rights are incorporated into country level analysis, planning and programme implementation',[27] and to 'train country teams, assess and disseminate best practice, and develop monitoring mechanisms for measuring the impact of its human rights programming'.[28] OHCHR responded by deploying human rights experts as UN country team advisers, including in conflict-affected countries such as Sri Lanka and Nepal.[29] In 2003 a UN country team human rights capacity-building operation was established in Angola following the departure of the peace mission, and a similar operation was deployed in Timor Leste in 2006[30] to provide technical support for the newly instituted office of the Ombudsman (*Provedor*), as well as for the government, the parliament and civil society. In 2003 the United Nations Development Group (UNDG) elaborated a definition of a human rights-based approach for the UN system, the *UN Common Understanding of a Human Rights-Based Approach to Development Cooperation.*[31] Various tools and guidelines were then developed for its operationalisation across the UN.[32]

Academic and policy-level interest in human rights field operations has been high in recent years, with attempts to identify the parameters of human rights fieldwork and the principal challenges to be addressed. In particular, recommendations for a comprehensive review of the sector were advanced, with the view to ensure enhanced performance of field operations and deployment dictated by current field needs rather than by political considerations.[33] These recommendations were partly echoed by the 2005 Secretary-General's report, *In Larger Freedom*, which identified human rights as one of the UN pillars, alongside security and development.[34] In response, then High Commissioner Louise Arbour published a Plan of

---

23 In the specific case of Iraq, human rights were first integrated in UN programming in 2002 through secondment of OHCHR staff to the Office of the UN Humanitarian Coordinator for Iraq (UNOHCI); OHCHR, 'Annual Appeal 2004' (2004) 53.
24 Strengthening of the United Nations: An Agenda for Further Change (2002) UN Doc. A/57/387.
25 Ibid. 45.
26 *Strengthening Human Rights-Related United Nations Action at Country Level: National Human Rights Promotion and Protection Systems Plan of Action* (2003), available at: http://www.un.org/events/action2/action2plan.pdf, accessed 14 December 2011.
27 Strengthening the United Nations: An Agenda for Further Change (n. 24) 51.
28 Ibid.
29 M. O'Flaherty, *The Human Rights Field Operation: Law, Theory and Practice* (Ashgate, 2007) 7.
30 OHCHR, Annual Appeal 2004, 32–33, quoted in O'Flaherty (n. 29).
31 H. Alizadeh, 'A Proposal for How to Realize Human Rights at the National and Regional Level: A Three-Pillar Strategy' (2011) 33(3) *Human Rights Quarterly* 826–55 at 836.
32 Ibid.
33 M. O'Flaherty, 'Human Rights Monitoring and Armed Conflict: Challenges for the UN' (2004) 3 *Disarmament Forum* 47–58 at 54.
34 Report of the Secretary-General, 'In Larger Freedom: Towards Development, Security and Human Rights for All', (59th Session) (2005) UN Doc. A/59/2005, 17.

Action for OHCHR, in which she committed to an increased sustained presence of OHCHR on the ground, with a preference for 'stand-alone' offices rather than integrated models.[35] Notably, despite the commonplace deployment of human rights components within peace missions, the Plan of Action dedicated little attention to such operations, probably because of the growing disenchantment with the integrated-mission model.[36] Indeed, criticisms were increasingly raised in relation to the way in which such missions unacceptably subordinated human rights to political considerations, and restricted the autonomy and resources of their human rights components.[37] The UN Secretary-General decision 'Human Rights in Integrated Missions'[38] addressed some of these concerns by clarifying, inter alia, that OHCHR had a central role in providing expertise, guidance and support to human rights components, which in turn were to discharge core human rights functions and help mainstream human rights across all mission activities. These guidelines were reinforced in the 2006 'Guidance on Integrated Missions',[39] where the head of the human rights component was also identified as a full member of the UN country team.

Human rights mainstreaming continues to be a UN priority,[40] although there remain questions relating to the specific role of OHCHR in achieving this, particularly in relation to a clearer policy and strategy to translate human rights protection principles into effective protection measures at the field level.[41] As further outlined below, a number of UN agencies have already gone some distance in integrating human rights approaches in their work and, through the Protection Cluster approach, in coordinating their protection roles also with relevant NGOs. These recent developments have increasingly shaped the work and character of human rights field operations, engendering new partnership configurations and presenting additional challenges, especially in relation to the protection of civilians in armed conflict.

3 The professionalisation of human rights fieldwork

As O'Flaherty and Ulrich have observed,[42] a human rights field sector has emerged over time comprising a significant cadre of officers, deployed to a wide range of challenging locations and all united in the goal of the promotion and protection of human rights. They argue that the issue of whether this sector constitutes a distinct new profession may be assessed by means of the application of a tripartite test: whether the sector has a set of shared values, whether a body of scientific knowledge exists, and whether frameworks, systems and procedures are in place to apply that knowledge. O'Flaherty and Ulrich argue that, while it is not difficult to

---

35 L. Arbour, *The OHCHR Plan for Action: Protection and Empowerment* (OHCHR 2005). The first OHCHR stand-alone field operations were opened at the beginning of 2005 in Uganda and Nepal; O'Flaherty (n. 1) 211.
36 Arbour (n. 35) 16.
37 OHCHR, 'Internal Review on Human Rights and Integrated Missions: Responses from Head of Human Rights Components' (18 July 2005) on file with authors.
38 UN Secretary-General's Policy Committee on Human Rights in Integrated Missions (October 2005) Decision No. 2005/24.
39 *UN Secretary-General's Note of Guidance on Integrated Missions* (17 January 2006), available at: http://reliefweb.int/node/22464, accessed 14 December 2011.
40 Alizadeh (n. 31) 837–38.
41 Ibid. 827.
42 For a detailed commentary on HRFOs' professionalisation, see M. O'Flaherty and G. Ulrich, 'The Professionalization of Human Rights Field Work' (2010) 2(1) *Journal of Human Rights Practice* 1–27 at 17.

identify core elements for the shared set of values and scientific knowledge, the identification of frameworks, systems and procedures is less straightforward. In this regard they point to the findings of a project that O'Flaherty directed during 2004–08, 'Consolidating the Profession: The Human Rights Field Officer'.[43] This project sought to identify the professional parameters of human rights fieldwork and to generate empirical and qualitative findings, analysis and guidance aimed at enhancing the process of professionalisation.[44] In order to clarify the applied frameworks, two questionnaires were distributed, one in 2004 to 80 current and former senior staff of field missions,[45] and one in 2008 to 44 respondents,[46] none of whom had participated in the 2004 exercise. Almost all of the 2008 respondents (42 out of 44) were working in a function directly related to a human rights field mission of an international or regional organisation (primarily UN and Organization for Security and Cooperation in Europe (OSCE)), either as head of such a mission, as a human rights officer/adviser, or as a desk officer in the headquarters supporting such a mission. Both questionnaires highlight common vocational priorities and clearly discernible trends in identifying the essential role and functions of human rights officers deployed by an international organisation to a conflict or post-conflict situation. Among the core functions identified by the respondents, certain key components emerged as recurrent elements in both surveys, namely: monitoring the human rights situation, reporting human rights abuses, and assisting local actors through capacity building and partnerships. Other functions, such as providing assistance and human rights-based advice to other international actors, support to peace processes and transitional justice mechanisms were also mentioned, as they clearly also pertain to the range of functions of relevance to field officers. Interestingly, the 2008 findings revealed a greater emphasis placed on advocacy and intervention activities as core functions. Advocacy, in fact, emerged as the function perceived to be most important by respondents to the 2008 survey. Overall the surveys indicated some common core work areas, albeit the functions of the field officer/ operation remained varied and tended to change depending on the specific context encountered on the ground as well as the presence of other key actors in the field.

On the basis of the 2004 survey findings, O'Flaherty argued for the existence of nine principal work areas: monitoring, reporting, advocacy/intervention, capacity building, engaging with humanitarian and development partners, support to peace processes, transitional justice, in-mission sensitisation, and participation in UN governance of transitional territories.[47] His findings were tested within the framework of the research project during a series of consultations with field officers and this eventually resulted in the drafting of a set of Guiding Principles for Human Rights Field Officers Working in Conflict and Post-conflict Environments, including a Statement of Ethical Commitments of Human Rights

---

43 For all available documents related to the various phases of the project, see 'Annex: The Proceedings of the Project', in M. O'Flaherty and G. Ulrich (eds), *The Professional Identity of the Human Rights Field Officer* (Ashgate, 2010).

44 M. O'Flaherty and G. Ulrich, 'The Professional Identity and Development of Human Rights Field Workers', in M. O'Flaherty and G. Ulrich (eds), *The Professional Identity of the Human Rights Field Officer* (Ashgate, 2010) 9.

45 On file with authors. For a summary of the findings, see O'Flaherty and Ulrich (eds), *The Professional Identity of the Human Rights Field Officer* (n. 43) 337.

46 On file with authors.

47 M. O'Flaherty, 'Human Rights Field Operations: An Introductory Analysis' in O'Flaherty, *The Human Rights Field Operation: Law, Theory and Practice* (n. 29).

Professionals.[48] The Guiding Principles collate O'Flaherty's nine activities into five principal functions for human rights field officers: monitoring, reporting, advocacy, capacity building and partnership.

According to the Guiding Principles, monitoring is integral to all other functions of the officers, and includes all activities whereby the field officers 'gather, analyse and use information on the human rights situation to prevent further violations and to establish responsibility for violations already committed'.[49] Monitoring has the ultimate purpose 'to improve respect for human rights. It involves developing a solid base of information on the human rights situation (types of violations, victims, persons responsible, and why abuse is occurring), as well as working relationships with authorities, non-governmental organisations and other actors, and knowledge of the terrain.'[50]

Reporting, described in the project as essential to human rights protection, has five principal functions: recording a current human rights situation and its evolution over time; ensuring that government authorities and other relevant actors respect human rights and are accountable when violations occur; informing the decisions of the international community and mobilising action; supporting the rights of victims and their families to justice, restitution, compensation or reparations; and use in criminal prosecutions and other accountability mechanisms.[51]

Advocacy, the third function, is considered a cross-cutting element of all human rights field activity. Advocacy is 'principled, respectful, timely and targeted',[52] and aimed at ensuring that governments and other actors meet their human rights obligations. The fourth function, capacity building, is defined as 'an essential aim of human rights fieldwork: it can function as a key protection tool if strategically integrated in the overall field operation strategy. It strengthens national entities' . . . ability to respect and protect human rights. Capacity building promotes comprehensive institutional reform since institutions failed to protect rights in the past and need to operate differently now.'[53] The Guiding Principles also identify one additional core function, that of partnerships. For the purposes of this chapter, however, partnerships are analysed separately in the following section, where specific attention is dedicated to the way in which officers engage with different actors in the field, depending on the circumstances and actions to be undertaken.

4 Partnerships

The Guiding Principles define partnerships as a crucial element that underpins and defines human rights fieldwork. Human rights field operations (HRFOs), in fact, crucially rely on close cooperation, consultation and communication with other UN agencies, and

---

48 *The Guiding Principles for Human Rights Field Officers and Statement of Ethics* (and their relevant annotations), available at: http://www.hrfoguidingprinciples.org/English/annotations.html, accessed 14 December 2011.
49 Ibid.; W.G. O'Neill, 'The Guiding Principles for Human Rights Field Officers Working in Conflict and Post-Conflict Environments: A Commentary', in O'Flaherty and Ulrich (eds), *The Professional Identity of the Human Rights Field Officer* (n. 43) 33–48.
50 Guiding Principles (n. 48).
51 Ibid.
52 Ibid.
53 Ibid.

international, regional and national actors, with the best partnerships being those 'promoting the primacy of local actors'.[54]

In contemporary practice, by far the most significant context for partnership is that of humanitarian emergencies.[55] HRFOs are increasingly deployed in such situations, which 'include situations of armed conflict, natural disasters and combined situations with both elements of conflict and natural disaster',[56] and their willingness and ability to engage with a growing number of humanitarian actors, as well as with parties to the conflict, is crucial. Partnership of human rights and humanitarian actors, however, has had a troubled history primarily due to concerns among the humanitarians that human rights approaches may be inconsistent with humanitarian principles and that they may lead to the politicisation of aid.[57] The UN has taken a number of initiatives to overcome such resistance on the basis that human rights approaches serve to strengthen rather than undermine humanitarian work.[58]

In 2005 the Inter-Agency Standing Committee (IASC), following the outcomes of a Humanitarian Response Review,[59] agreed to the implementation of the 'cluster approach' in selected countries and for all subsequent humanitarian emergencies. The aims of the cluster approach, as defined by IASC, are as follows:

> [S]trengthen humanitarian response by demanding high standards of predictability, accountability and partnership in all sectors or areas of activity. It is about achieving more strategic responses and better prioritization of available resources by clarifying the division of labour among organizations, better defining the roles and responsibilities of humanitarian organizations within the sectors, and providing the Humanitarian Coordinator with both a first point of call and a provider of last resort in all the key sectors or areas of activity. The success of the cluster approach will be judged in terms of the impact it has on improving the humanitarian response to those affected by crises.[60]

The establishment of the cluster approach has come to shape the way in which HRFOs engage in partnerships with humanitarian actors in their daily activities. At the field level, the cluster approach has the objective of strengthening the coordination and capacity of the various actors present on the ground, by strategically harmonising and prioritising their response. Each cluster has one designated lead, responsible and accountable for ensuring an

---

54 Ibid.
55 OHCHR, 'Office-Wide Strategy on OHCHR Engagement in Humanitarian Action', copy on file with authors.
56 Ibid. 2.
57 M. O'Flaherty, 'The Human Rights Field Operation in Partnership for Humanitarian Relief and Reconstruction', in O'Flaherty, *The Human Rights Field Operation: Law, Theory and Practice* (n. 29).
58 Inter-Agency Standing Committee, 'Human Rights Guidance Note for Humanitarian Coordinators' (7 June 2006); A. Donini, 'Between a Rock and a Hard Place: Integration or Independence of Humanitarian Action?' (2011) 93(881) *International Review of the Red Cross* 141–57; A. Donini et al., 'Humanitarian Agenda 2015: The State of the Humanitarian Enterprise' (March 2008), available at: https://wikis.uit.tufts.edu/confluence/display/FIC/Humanitarian+Agenda+2015+—+The+State+of+the+Humanitarian+Enterprise, accessed 20 December 2011.
59 Office for the Coordination of Humanitarian Affairs, *Humanitarian Response Review* (August 2005), available at: www.oneresponse.info/. . ./Humanitarian%20Response%20Review.pdf, accessed 14 December 2011.
60 IASC, 'Guidance Note on Using the Cluster Approach to Strengthen Humanitarian Response' (24 November 2006).

appropriate and efficient humanitarian operational response. Together with UNHCR and UNICEF, OHCHR is one of the protection-mandated agencies taking the lead of the Protection Cluster at the field level.

In recognition of its lead role, OHCHR has clarified its own objectives within humanitarian emergency contexts. It takes as its starting point the mandate of the High Commissioner for Human Rights, as found in General Assembly Resolution 48/141, whereby it should: (1) promote and protect the effective enjoyment by all of civil, cultural, economic, political and social rights; (2) coordinate the human rights promotion and protection activities throughout the United Nations system; (3) enhance international cooperation for the promotion and protection of all human rights.[61] It observes that, in situations of armed conflict, the mandate is complemented by relevant Security Council resolutions which address specific national contexts and/or thematic issues, such as protection of civilians, impunity, women, and children in armed conflict.[62]

Drawing on these sources, OHCHR identifies[63] three main areas of human rights field protection work in humanitarian crises: addressing the causes and consequences of the humanitarian crises through the main HRFOs' functions outlined above; mainstreaming human rights throughout all humanitarian actions, focusing on both processes and outcomes; and engaging, although only in certain limited situations, in quick impact projects with national counterparts (e.g. by funding short-term activities aimed at strengthening human rights).[64] It is argued that the skills and expertise of HRFOs can therefore add value to the protection cluster along the range of activities which pertain to these three main areas of engagement, especially as they can provide a consolidated methodology for human rights monitoring and reporting. They also ensure a focus on the affected population as a whole, rather than on specific vulnerable segments of it (e.g. refugees and IDPs, women and children), since their human rights-based approach to humanitarian action demands a focus on the rights and needs of individuals or groups who are particularly vulnerable and in special need of protection in any given circumstances. Furthermore, the human rights-based approach advocated by HRFOs should promote respect for the principles of participation, equality and non-discrimination, accountability and upholding the rule of law. It is observed that these principles remain of the utmost importance at all stages of humanitarian programming, from planning and preparedness, to response and recovery actions.[65] Furthermore, in conflict situations, HRFOs bring the particular added value of being able to address the relationship between human rights and international humanitarian law, especially in relation to the protection of civilians, for example, by carrying out human rights fact-finding investigative missions as part of the humanitarian response.[66] In addition, the HRFOs' expertise in developing the capacity of national counterparts, including state actors, civil society as well as the local population, and in promoting the accountability of duty-bearers has also proven of fundamental importance within the framework of the cluster

---

61 High Commissioner for the Promotion and Protection of All Human Rights, GA Res. 48/141 (20 December 1993).
62 *SC Resolutions*, available at: http://www.un.org/documents/scres.htm, accessed 14 December 2011.
63 OHCHR Strategy (n. 55).
64 Ibid.
65 UN Office for the Coordination of Humanitarian Affairs, *Strategic Plan: OCHA in 2012 and 2013, Plan and Budget* (December 2011), available at: http://www.unocha.org/ocha2012–13/strategic-plan, accessed 20 December 2011.
66 OHCHR Strategy (n. 55).

approach.[67] This expertise can be further enhanced by their ability to easily access, through OHCHR, the Human Rights Council's special procedures mechanisms and the work of the human rights treaty bodies.[68]

The effectiveness of HRFOs' leadership within the humanitarian cluster approach remains to be definitively ascertained, although there exist some encouraging assessments. For instance, recent findings from Northern Uganda are positive. The work carried out there by the protection sub-cluster on gender-based violence, led by OHCHR, has been evaluated favourably, especially in terms of strategic coordination; strengthening of monitoring procedures; harmonisation of training; and improved coordination of referrals between health and legal organisations.[69]

5 Other emerging issues and challenges

As the number of human rights field missions continues to increase rapidly, so also do the types of human rights protection challenges encountered both in emergency and non-emergency contexts.[70] It is however possible to identify certain common issues that HRFOs are called to address in their fieldwork. Many of these challenges, in fact, reflect the nature of indeterminacy and flux experienced by the countries in which HRFOs are deployed, such as general resistance and/or hostility from state actors in acknowledging and addressing human rights violations; lack of legal and other governmental structures appropriate to ensure redress; a prevailing situation of impunity; weak independent civil society organisations and/or national human rights institutions (NHRI) with whom to cooperate to establish solid monitoring, reporting and advocacy activities; and unavailability of baseline disaggregated data to be used as a starting point for further research and reporting.[71]

In addition to these general challenges, there are more specific challenges directly related to the ability of relevant actors in the field to engage with the UN human rights mechanisms, especially the treaty bodies, special procedures and Universal Periodic Review (UPR) process.[72] These are invaluable instruments to address the human rights issues encountered on the ground but are only sporadically used in an effective manner.[73] Shortcomings are apparent in the way in which relevant government stakeholders, civil society organisations, NHRIs, as well as HRFOs and UN agencies, are involved at the different stages of consultations and

---

67 Ibid.; K. Mancini Beck, 'Training to Strengthen Protection of IDP Rights' (2008) Special Issue *Forced Migration Review* 36–37.
68 R. Brett, 'A Curate's Egg: UN Human Rights Council: Year 3, 19 June 2008 to 18 June 2009' (Quaker UN Office 2009), available at: http://www.quno.org/humanrights/UN-CHR/councilLinks.htm, accessed 14 December 2011.
69 J. Landegger et al., 'Strengths and Weaknesses of the Humanitarian Cluster Approach in Relation to Sexual and Reproductive Health Services in Northern Uganda' (2011) 3 *International Health* 108–14.
70 Alizadeh (n. 31) 839.
71 Ibid., 829.
72 M. Cherif Bassiouni and W. Schabas (eds), *New Challenges for the UN Human Rights Machinery: What Future for the UN Treaty Body System and the Human Rights Council Procedures?* (Intersentia, 2012); R. Brett, 'Digging Foundations or Trenches? UN Human Rights Council Year 2' (Quaker UN Office 2008), available at: http://www.quno.org/humanrights/UN-CHR/councilLinks.htm, accessed 14 December 2011.
73 Alizadeh (n. 31) 839.

cooperation with the UN mechanisms.[74] The scope for action by HRFOs in relation to these mechanisms is considerable.[75] So far, their levels of engagement vary widely depending on the UN mechanism concerned; for instance, HRFOs already coordinate with Special Procedures, before and during their field visits, by providing relevant information and ensuring that the visits address significant thematic sub-issues. Limitations, however, appear at the follow-up stage of the work, when recommendations by the Special Procedures mandate holders are not adequately prioritised and integrated in the work of the HRFOs. It is recognised that HRFOs could have a stronger role in supporting state actors in the implementation of the recommendations, not least through the UN Country Teams. They could also strengthen the capacity of NHRIs and civil society organisations to establish direct links with the mandate holders.

HRFOs are also already involved in the UPR process, although the level of engagement varies from mission to mission. Their work mainly consists of supporting NHRIs and NGOs to participate in the consultations for the drafting of the national report to the Human Rights Council.[76] However, in many cases the UPR process remains a 'one-way system', whereby a lack of activities for the implementation of recommendations is again apparent.[77] HRFOs, for instance, could act as a driving force in establishing an ongoing consultative process (perhaps within the UN country teams or within the protection clusters) on the UPR outcome recommendations, so that different actors can jointly assist the government in the implementation phase.[78] It is when it comes to the work of the human rights treaty bodies that engagement from the field appears less consistent, if not altogether absent. As 'reporting under the treaty bodies is a *process* rather than an *event*',[79] HRFOs could play a stronger role in technically supporting the government and other relevant national actors both during the reporting process and for the timely implementation of treaty bodies' recommendations.[80] As also reiterated in the High Commissioner's Strategic Management Plan 2010–11,[81] the success of the UN human rights mechanisms in countries where there is a human rights field presence depends very much on the way in which these are able to encourage greater synergies between local and international actors, ensure meaningful participation in the various review processes, and later assist in following up on relevant recommendations.

Another area which has recently witnessed considerable development and could therefore benefit from more significant engagement at the field level is that of the promotion of human

74 Ibid.; OHCHR, Working with the Office of the United Nations High Commissioner for Human Rights: A Handbook for NGOs (2006) Publication no. HR/PUB/06/10.

75 Alizadeh (n. 31) 831–32.

76 Ibid., 851–52.

77 Ibid.

78 For further suggestions of how field presences could support the implementation of UPR recommendations, see ibid., 852–53.

79 Ibid., 847; M. O'Flaherty, 'Reform of the UN Human Rights Treaty Body System: Locating the Dublin Statement' (2010) 10(2) *Human Rights Law Review* 319–35; M. O'Flaherty and C. O'Brien, 'Reform of the UN Human Rights Treaty Monitoring Bodies: A Critique of the Concept Paper on the High Commissioner's Proposal for a Unified Standing Treaty Body' (2007) 7(1) *Human Rights Law Review* 141–72. The full text of The Dublin Statement on the Process of Strengthening of the United Nations Human Rights Treaty Body System is reprinted in (2010) 28(1) *Netherlands Quarterly of Human Rights* 116–56.

80 Alizadeh (n. 31) 847–48.

81 OHCHR, *High Commissioner's Strategic Management Plan 2010–2011* (2009) 42–50, available at: www.ohchr.org/Documents/Press/SMP2010–2011.pdf, accessed 14 December 2011.

rights compliance in the business sector. In particular, following the recent launch of the tripartite framework 'Protect, Respect and Remedy'[82] and the related Guiding Principles for business and human rights,[83] HRFOs could have a key role in raising awareness of the duties and responsibilities of relevant state and non-state actors, as well as of the availability of remedies for the victims of corporate abuse. More specifically, and in line with the increased OHCHR focus on the realisation of economic, social and cultural rights in the field,[84] there is a potential for greater HRFO involvement in supporting governments at the negotiation stages of international investment agreements (IIAs) or investment contracts. This could be especially relevant in key sectors having a greater impact on the human rights of local communities, such as natural resources, large infrastructure projects and public utilities. HRFOs could also offer legal and technical expertise to train NHRIs and local NGOs in monitoring the human rights impacts of business activities, especially in conflict and emergency contexts. This could be achieved, for instance, by carrying out human rights impact assessments, both before and after the negotiations of IIAs and investment contracts, thus ensuring the participation of various vulnerable groups in society in matters affecting their lives as well as the establishment of credible accountability mechanisms in the longer term.[85]

6 Conclusion

The overview offered in this chapter reveals the varied and multidisciplinary nature of the work carried out by human rights field professionals. It also shows that, despite the challenges that human rights field presences face on a daily basis, much has been achieved in the short history of intergovernmental human rights fieldwork. There are clear indications of a growing standardisation and professionalisation of the sector, with the UN in general, and OHCHR in particular, playing an important role in propelling that process forward. We can conclude that the human rights field operation is a potent tool for human rights protection with a potential that, as yet, is only partially realised.

Select bibliography

R. Brett, 'A Curate's Egg: UN Human Rights Council: Year 3, 19 June 2008 to 18 June 2009' (Quaker UN Office 2009) available at: http://www.quno.org/humanrights/UN-CHR/councilLinks.htm, accessed 14 December 2011.

M. Cherif Bassiouni and W. Schabas (eds), *New Challenges for the UN Human Rights Machinery: What Future for the UN Treaty Body System and the Human Rights Council Procedures?* (Intersentia, 2012).

82 Report of the Special Representative of the Secretary-General on the issue of human rights and transnational corporations and other business enterprises, 'Protect, Respect and Remedy: A Framework for Business and Human Rights' (7 April 2008) UN Doc A/HRC/8/5.

83 Report of the Special Representative of the Secretary-General on the issue of human rights and transnational corporations and other business enterprises, 'Guiding Principles on Business and Human Rights: Implementing the United Nations "Protect, Respect and Remedy" Framework' (21 March 2011) UN Doc. A/HRC/17/31.

84 OHCHR, 'Report of the UN High Commissioner for Human Rights on the Question of the Realization in All Countries of Economic, Social and Cultural Rights' (21 March 2011) UN Doc. A/HRC/17/24; OHCHR, 'High Commissioner's Strategic Management Plan 2010–2011' (n. 2).

85 D. Davitti, 'On the Meanings of International Investment Law and International Human Rights Law: The Alternative Narrative of Due Diligence', 12(3) *Human Rights Law Review* (2012) 421–53.

A. Henkin (ed.), *Honoring Human Rights* (Kluwer Law International, 2000).

M. O'Flaherty, 'Future Protection of Human Rights in Post-Conflict Societies: The Role of the United Nations' (2003) 3(1) *Human Rights Law Review* 53–76.

M. O'Flaherty (ed.), *The Human Rights Field Operation: Law, Theory and Practice* (Ashgate, 2007).

M. O'Flaherty and G. Ulrich (eds), *The Professional Identity of the Human Rights Field Officer* (Ashgate, 2010).

Part III

Interaction of human rights with other key regimes and bodies

12

The relationship between international humanitarian law and international human rights law

Françoise J. Hampson

1 Introduction

To look at recent contributions to the debate about the relationship between international humanitarian law (IHL)[1] and human rights law (HRsL), one would think that the solution to the problem is easy. The difficulty is that each author uses the same words with a different meaning[2] and/or applies them differently. The debate started in the 1970s and, at that time, it was principally those from an IHL background who addressed the issue.[3] Not surprisingly,

---

1 This area of law has, since 1977, increasingly been called international humanitarian law (IHL). This is potentially misleading, especially with regard to an important distinction when considering the relationship between IHL and human rights law (HRsL). Until 1977, the laws of war or the law of armed conflict (LOAC) described the whole body of law designed for and specifically applicable to armed conflicts. LOAC consisted of two strands. The first was rules dealing with the conduct of hostilities or means and methods of warfare, also known as the law of The Hague. The second strand consisted of rules on the protection of the victims of war, also known as international humanitarian law, or the law of Geneva. The two strands functioned in significantly different ways. The law of Geneva, like HRsL, tended to be designed to prohibit a certain result. It achieved this by requiring or prohibiting certain behaviour. The law of The Hague addressed the mind of the military operator at the time at which he acted. It required him to take certain things into account. It is usually not possible to determine whether a breach of Hague Law has occurred without knowing what the suspected perpetrator knew, thought he knew or ought to have known. It cannot be determined solely on the basis of the result. In this text, the term IHL will be used to refer to the whole of the law of armed conflict. See generally, F.J. Hampson, 'Direct Participation in Hostilities and the Interoperability of the Law of Armed Conflict and Human Rights Law', in Pedrozo and Wollschlaeger (eds), *International Law and the Changing Character of War*, International Law Studies, vol. 87, Naval War College (2010), 187 at 193–95. Where it is necessary to distinguish between the two strands, they will be referred to as the law of The Hague and the law of Geneva.

2 E.g. *lex specialis*; see below, at 4. The approach of the International Court of Justice (ICJ).

3 For example, K.D. Suter, 'An enquiry into the meaning of the phrase "Human Rights in Armed Conflicts"' (1976) 15(3–4) *Revue de Droit Penal Militaire et de Droit de la Guerre* 393; Henry Meyrowitz, 'Le Droit de la Guerre et les droits de l'homme' (1972) 5 *Revue du Droit Public et de la Science Politique en France et à l'Etranger* 1059; G.I.A.D. Draper, 'The Relationship between the Human Rights

most of them reached the conclusion that HRsL only applied in peacetime, as a result of which there was no need to consider the relationship between the two fields of law. At that time, human rights lawyers were more focused on examining human rights in situations of emergency and/or the question of derogation.[4] They paid scant attention to the esoteric, little-known field of IHL. It was unusual for the problem to be addressed by the very limited human rights machinery in existence at that time. The one exception, the Report of the European Commission of Human Rights in the joined first and second inter-state cases between Cyprus and Turkey, attracted surprisingly little attention.[5] By the early 1990s, attention was focused not on the relationship but on the alleged gap between restricted human rights applicability and the point at which IHL becomes applicable. The *Turku/Åbo Declaration* was a statement of norms, drawn from both HRsL and IHL, which was said to apply in all circumstances.[6] It was based on the assumption of a gap in applicability, which assumption was open to challenge and which was subsequently virtually closed in 2001 by General Comment No. 29 of the Human Rights Committee under the International Covenant on Civil and Political Rights (ICCPR).[7] The question of the relationship between the two fields of law has only really come to the fore over the past ten years.[8]

Regime and the Law of Armed Conflict' (1971) 1 *Israel Yearbook on Human Rights* 191. By way of contrast, see Dietrich Schindler, 'Human Rights and Humanitarian Law: Interrelationships of the Law' (1982) 31 *American University Law Review* 935 and F.J. Hampson, 'Using International Human Rights Machinery to Promote Respect for International Humanitarian Law', (1992) 31 *International Review of Military Law & Law of War* 117.

4 E.g. Questiaux, N., 'Study of the Implication for Human Rights of Recent Developments on Situations Known as States of Siege or Emergency', UN Doc. E/CN.4/Sub.2/1982/15 (1982); Higgins, R., 'Derogations Under Human Rights Treaties', (1976–77) 48 *British Yearbook of International Law* 281; Hartman, J.F., 'Derogation from Human Rights Treaties in Public Emergencies', (1981) 22 *Harvard International Law Journal* 1, 11.

5 *Cyprus v Turkey* Applications Nos 9780/74 and 6950/75 Report of the Commission, 10 July 1976; see Hampson (n. 3).

6 Declaration of Minimum Humanitarian Standards, reprinted in Report of the Sub-Commission on Prevention of Discrimination and Protection of Minorities on its Forty-sixth Session, Commission on Human Rights, 51st Sess., Provisional Agenda Item 19, at 4, UN Doc. E/CN.4/1995/116 (1995) (Declaration of Turku), Turku/Åbo 2 December 1990. Available at: http://web.abo.fi/instut/imr/publications/publications_online_text.htm.

7 Human Rights Committee, General Comment No. 29: States of Emergency (Art. 4), CCPR/C/21/Rev.1/Add.11, 31 August 2001.

8 See, for example, Provost, R., *International Human Rights And Humanitarian Law* (CUP, 2002); Arnold, R., and Quénivet, N., *International Humanitarian Law And Human Rights Law: Towards A New Merger In International Law* (Leiden, Martinus Nijhoff, 2008); Ben-Naftali, O. (ed.) *International Humanitarian Law and International Human Rights Law: Pas De Deux* (OUP, 2011). In the way of articles, see Meron, T., 'The Humanization of Humanitarian Law', (2000) 94 *American Journal of International Law* 239, 243; Watkin, K., 'Controlling the Use of Force: A Role for Human Rights Norms in Contemporary Armed Conflict', (2004) 98 *American Journal of International Law* 1, 34; Lubell, N., 'Challenges in Applying Human Rights Law to Armed Conflict', (2005) 87 *International Review of the Red Cross* 737; Abresch, W., 'A Human Rights Law of Internal Armed Conflict: The European Court of Human Rights in Chechnya', (2005) 16 *European Journal of International Law* 741; Krieger, H., 'A Conflict of Norms: The Relationship between Humanitarian Law and Human Rights Law in the ICRC Customary Law Study', (2006) 11 *Journal of Conflict & Security Law* 265, 269; McGoldrick, D., 'Human Rights and Humanitarian Law in the UK Courts', (2007) 40 *Israel Law Review* 527; Cassimatis, A., 'International Humanitarian Law, International Human Rights Law, and the Fragmentation of International Law', (2007) 56 ICLQ 623; Droege, C., 'The Interplay between International Humanitarian Law and International

There has been a singular failure to engage experts in IHL, particularly those from the armed forces, in the debate. The answer to the relationship question has practical implications for members of the armed forces and the police in their own country or serving outside it, for the legal advice to be given by foreign ministry lawyers, for the UN where the problem arises during the course of a UN-mandated operation, for those working for NGOs and inter-governmental organisations (IGOs) in the field, for international and regional human rights monitoring and enforcement machinery and for lawyers trying to advise potential clients. Each of these groups comes to the issue from a different perspective. The answer has to be capable of being applied in situations of conflict and delivering what is seen as an acceptable solution by all those players. A solution which does not satisfy such a test will not result in greater application of HRsL. It will result, at best, in the exclusive application of IHL. This will result in deadlock between states and human rights bodies.[9]

Why is it proving so difficult to come up with an appropriate solution? It is submitted that a large part of the problem is the inadequate thinking that has gone into addressing the whole question of how to deal with the co-applicability of two or more fields of law. The relationship between IHL and HRsL is but one example of a much wider problem. This chapter seeks to identify some of the questions that need to be addressed before attempting to provide an answer to the specific question of the relationship between IHL and HRsL. Since the author's thesis is that a range of separate research questions are involved, she can hardly be expected to produce answers! Consideration will first be given to a range of horizontal collisions of areas of law before identifying possible different general approaches. The specific problem of the relationship between IHL and HRsL will then be discussed. Finally, the questions raised by attempting to apply one of the approaches to this specific relationship will be discussed.

Human Rights Law in Situations of Armed Conflict', (2007) 40 *Israel Law Review*, 310; Droege, C., 'Elective Affinities? Human Rights and Humanitarian Law', (2008) 90 *International Review of the Red Cross* 501; McCarthy, C., 'Human Rights and the Laws of War under the American Convention on Human Rights', (2008) *European Human Rights Law Review* 762; Verdirame, G., 'Human Rights in Wartime: A Framework for Analysis', (2008) *European Human Rights Law Review* 689; Sassòli, M., and Olson, L., 'The Relationship between International Humanitarian and Human Rights Law where it Matters: Admissible Killing and Internment of Fighters in Non-International Armed Conflicts' (2008) 90 *International Review of the Red Cross* 599; Hampson, F., 'The Relationship between International Humanitarian Law and Human Rights Law from the Perspective of a Treaty Body', (2008) 90 *International Review of the Red Cross* 549; Milanovic, M., 'Norm Conflict in International Law: Whither Human Rights?', (2009) 20 *Duke Journal of Comparative & International Law* (2009) 69; Tomuschat, C., 'Human Rights and International Humanitarian Law', (2010) 21(1) *European Journal of International Law* 1; Kretzmer, D., 'Targeted Killing of Suspected Terrorists: Extra-Judicial Executions or Legitimate Means of Defence', (2005) 16(2) *European Journal of International Law* 171. These materials need to be examined in the light of subsequent case law, notably that of the European Court of Human Rights, as to which, see below. See also OHCHR, *International Legal Protection of Human Rights in Armed Conflict* (New York, OHCHR, 2011), HR/PUB/11/01, available at: http://www.ohchr.org/Documents/Publications/HR_in_armed_conflict.pdf. It is not clear whether military lawyers were involved in the writing of this report.

9 Israel and the United States dispute the applicability of HRsL when IHL is applicable (whether or not it is in fact applied). They also dispute the extraterritorial applicability of HRsL. See Hampson, F.J., 'Other Areas of Customary Law in Relation to the Study', in Wilmshurst, E. and Breau, S. (eds), *Perspectives on the ICRC Study on Customary International Humanitarian Law* (CUP, 2007) 50 at 68–72.

2 Horizontal collisions between areas of law

Before turning to the case law and international precedent and practice, it is useful to consider the relationship at the level of general principles. Two preliminary issues are raised by this sub-heading: why *horizontal* collisions and why *areas* of law, rather than individual rules? The law often has to deal with the relationship between the general and the specific. There may be general rules for contracts of an *uberrimae fidei* character but specific rules in sectors such as banking and insurance. There may be general rules regarding banking but specific rules relating to retail or investment banking. We are used to general rules on the landlord/tenant relationship but specific rules address residential tenancies, tenancies of commercial property and agricultural tenancies. The relationship between the general and the specific is a vertical one. On the ground floor, one finds the general regime. The answer may be found there unless, in the circumstances, it is necessary to take one of the various staircases up to a different floor. The general is the default position, unless it is displaced by a specific provision. It seems highly unlikely that there would be a conflict between the areas of law themselves, since the specific prevails over the general.[10] Any conflict is likely to be based on whether the situation falls within the general or special regime. It is not clear whether there is a presumption in favour of the default position unless . . . or whether, possibly over time, there comes to be a presumption in favour of one or other form of specific regime. An example of such a general/specific relationship within an area or special regime of international law might be human rights in emergency situations (i.e. where derogation has been invoked).

This type of general–specific relationship within an area of law is not what is at issue in the type of relationships with which this chapter is concerned. Rather, two completely independent areas of law over time extend their area of applicability, as a result of which both may be applicable in a specific situation. This is a horizontal collision – a result of the coexistence of special regimes. IHL is not HRsL in situations of armed conflict or emergency. It is a discrete body of rules, with its own distinct purpose and objectives and whose origin significantly predates HRsL, at least at the international level.

Why *areas* of law? In a particular situation, it may appear that two specific rules are in conflict. An example from the relationship under examination here will provide an illustration. The armed forces of state A during an armed conflict with the forces of state B shoot dead an individual in the uniform of state B, whilst he is asleep and unarmed. Under IHL, a combatant has the right to kill an opposing combatant, unless he is wounded, sick or surrendering (i.e. *hors de combat*). Under HRsL, resort to potentially lethal force has, under the law and order paradigm, to be as a last resort and has to be based on the risk posed to others by the behaviour at the time of the person targeted. The collision appears to be between two rules, but this is misleading. In fact, the collision is between the assumptions and understandings of IHL as a whole and the presumptions and interpretation of HRsL as a whole. A failure to recognise that what is at issue is the relationship between areas or fields of law, rather than specific rules, is likely to lead to a range of blind alleys.

Horizontal collisions of areas of law can be found in both domestic and international law. What follows are merely illustrative examples. The first two come from English private law. A problem arose when a victim of negligent performance of a contract wished to sue. Should

---

10 The perspicacious reader will recognise that this appears to raise the question of *lex specialis derogat legi generali*. This will be discussed further below.

he bring proceedings based on the tort of negligence or for breach of contract? The question in this context is how should a court set about addressing the question? To the best of the author's knowledge, there is no guidance as to how to do so. Should it be left to the plaintiff to choose or does the court have a proactive role? If the defendant challenges the plaintiff's choice, presumably the court has to determine the question. What overall goal is to be pursued and what elements are relevant? How important was it to the search for a solution that both were areas of common law?

The second example concerns the distribution of real property upon the dissolution of marriage. Here, the conflict was much more dramatic. The rules relating to ownership of such property were mainly statutory and based on the evolution of norms over centuries. The nature of real property made for a requirement of certainty and rigidity. The relatively recent phenomenon, at least on a large scale, of dissolution of marriage, with an attendant need to address the distribution of assets, required guiding principles rather than rules. It was important to achieve a fair result and that required flexibility in either the rules themselves or their application. Was the ownership of the matrimonial home to be subject to flexibility and fairness or was it different from other assets? If any change were to be introduced to the rules, should it be limited to the matrimonial home or extended to other forms of real property?

There may be a difference between these two collisions. The first is essentially of interest only to lawyers. It concerns the operation of the legal system. Whilst it might affect the result in some cases, in many cases it is unlikely to do so. The solution adopted in the second case would have an impact on millions. It involves an issue of social policy. Does that affect the process for determining how to arrive at an answer or the elements that may be regarded as relevant? It would be useful if researchers in different countries would study such horizontal collisions with a view to establishing how the authorities set about determining how to determine the overall goal and how they established what elements needed to be taken into account. Whilst the areas of collision are likely to vary between different countries, it would be interesting to see whether there is any commonality of approach as to how to handle them.

One reason for referring to domestic examples is that most national legal systems have had longer to evolve than the much younger international legal system. Horizontal collisions are likely to be the product of the evolution of a legal system. This is not to suggest that an automatic transfer can be made from the national to the international level. If it is the case, however, that horizontal collisions of areas of law occur during the evolution of all legal systems, then it may be the case that lessons can be learned from the national sphere of relevance to the experience in the international system. The ILC study of fragmentation includes some, but limited, reference to collisions between different special regimes but there is a need for more detailed analysis of such collisions in international law.[11] They may vary significantly as between themselves and require different tools for their resolution.

Horizontal collisions are also increasingly common in international law. Until 1945, the evolution of international law was relatively slow. Since then, there has been a dramatic expansion in the fields of activity addressed by international law and the rate of change within those legal fields has speeded up enormously. This combination may be the ideal breeding ground

---

11 ILC, *Report of the Study Group on the Fragmentation of International Law: Difficulties Arising from the Diversification and Expansion of International Law (Koskenniemi)*, UN Doc. A/CN.4/L.682, 13 April 2006.

for horizontal collisions between areas of law. Whilst many of the collisions involve HRsL, there are exceptions. One example is the conflict between sovereignty, specifically over natural resources, and environmental concerns.[12] HRsL has notoriously collided with state or sovereign immunity.[13] This raises an interesting possibility. Is there a difference between rules which enable the functioning of an international legal system, such as rules on sources, treaty law, state responsibility and various forms of immunity, and substantive rules about an area of activity? Do collisions with system rules have to be resolved in favour of the system in order to ensure its integrity and coherence?[14] HRsL also collides with rules regulating international trade. That particular conflict surfaces in myriad ways, illustrating that the problem arises between areas of law rather than particular rules. It also raises the question of how the existence of specific monitoring mechanisms, as opposed to ones of general competence such as the International Court of Justice (ICJ), affects the handling of collisions.[15] One respect in which international law differs from national legal systems is in the role played by international judicial bodies in determining the law. State practice and state views of the international law play a role for which there is no equivalent at the domestic level. Judicial and quasi-judicial bodies play a more important role in the interpretation of HRsL than is common in other areas of international law. Is this a partial explanation for the number of horizontal collisions involving HRsL or is the content of HRsL the key to that question?

The institutional architecture of international law may well affect the tools available for handling horizontal collisions, but it would seem unlikely that it affects the existence of the problem. At the domestic level, there are tools available for delivering the solution to a collision, once it is determined what the solution should be. Unless jurisdictional questions arise between different types of courts, the court itself may produce an answer. The greater the policy implications, the more likely it may be that a legislature will have to be involved. At the international level, fewer problems first surface before a judicial body. They are more likely to arise as a foreign ministry lawyer seeks to brief the government or during the course of a negotiation. At the same time, there are fewer legal tools for resolving problems. Specialist judicial bodies are unlikely to have the competence to apply more than one area of law. The possibility of drafting a multilateral treaty is hardly the equivalent of a national legislature. At the very least, this means that it is likely to take longer to find solutions. What is the impact of the length of time taken to find a solution on the solution itself? Does the time for reflection increase the suitability and sophistication of the solutions found or does the prolonged uncertainty just increase the confusion and increase the impact of the collision?

---

12 E.g concerns over the destruction of the rain forest and control of logging in Brazil and Indonesia.
13 *Al-Adsani v UK* 35763/97 (judgment of 21 November 2001); *Jurisdictional Immunities of the State (Germany v Italy, Greece intervening)*, ICJ, judgment of 3 February 2012. See generally, Campbell McLachlan, 'The Principle of Systemic Integration and Article 31(3)(c) of the Vienna Convention', (2005) 54 ICLQ 279.
14 This is one of the concerns addressed by the debate regarding the fragmentation of international law; see ILC Study (n. 11). This raises the important question of the relationship between the fragmentation question and horizontal collisions in international law. See generally, Lindroos, A., 'Addressing Norm Conflicts in a Fragmented Legal System: The Doctrine of *Lex Specialis*', (2005) 74 *Nordic Journal of International Law* 27 and Prud'homme (n. 26, below).
15 Since 1945, there has been a dramatic increase in the number of mechanisms with limited competence, such as the Law of the Sea Tribunal, the WTO dispute settlement mechanism, and a range of human rights mechanisms. Their limited competence may make it difficult for them to recognise, far less resolve, horizontal collisions with other areas of law.

It would be useful if a range of studies were undertaken of horizontal collisions in international law, looking not only at the substantive issues but also at how the available tools have been used by the wide range of players involved.

3 Possible general approaches

There would appear to be three possible general approaches to the relationship: trumping; demarcation and integration. In the case of trumping, field B would be required to yield to field A, or vice versa, whenever the two were in conflict. Who would take such a decision? On what basis? Presumably all players within the international legal system either need to agree or else need to accept the decision, even if they disagree with it. How is this to be achieved? We have already seen that trumping appears to operate as between HRsL and general rules which govern the operation of the international legal system.[16] Is that the only example; one made necessary by the overarching nature of the latter?[17] Does the principle apply only to conflicts between areas of law or does it extend to all areas of overlap, including those where there is a difference in specificity or emphasis?

The second possible general approach would be demarcation. Within the overlapping areas, some issues would be allocated to field A and others to field B. The more the issues in question are central to a field, the more it would harm the field as a whole to allocate an issue to the other field. The decision on when to open fire, discussed above, is central to both IHL and HRsL. Whilst theoretically attractive, demarcation may well be impracticable, save in exceptional circumstances. A possible example of exceptional circumstances is the allocation of the matrimonial home upon dissolution of marriage. By characterising it as the matrimonial home, it might be possible to distinguish between that and other real property and that and other assets, thereby demarcating between property and family law. That would make it possible to deal with matrimonial property in a particular way. It is difficult to see how demarcation could deal with the collision between IHL and HRsL. Even an issue such as choice of weapon, which looks distinctly IHL-ish, is important in HRsL, which may require the use of weapons prohibited under IHL.[18]

The third possible approach is total or partial integration. Partial integration could be combined with one of the other approaches. In the case of integration, both fields would be recognised as relevant and important. An attempt would be made to meld them together. Where there is a similarity of approach in the two fields, it might be relatively easy to iron out differences of nuance or interpretation. In other areas, choices would need to be made. The choice, however, would be located within a context of integration. Difficulties in integration

---

16 See n. 12 and accompanying text.

17 Where a collision concerns the relationship between rules in a particular field of international law and rules regarding the operation of the international legal system, it may be acceptable to states that the result should be determined by a court, since it is a purely legal question, albeit one with significant implications. Is it the case that states would be more reluctant to allow a court to determine how a collision between rules in two different fields of international law should be resolved?

18 Tear gas has a role to play as an instrument of riot control, and hollow-point or dum-dum bullets as a tool of law enforcement, where there is a real risk that the bullet might pass through the intended target and kill other people. Neither can be used under IHL. More obviously IHL authorises the use of a range of weapons which could not be used as part of law enforcement. See *Gulec v Turkey*, Application No. 21593/93 (judgment of 27 July 1998); *Finogenov & others v Russia*, Application Nos 18299/93 and 27311/03 (judgment of 20 December 2011) (Moscow Theatre Siege).

would arise if there were gaps in either field or uncertainty as to the content of the law. Integration would not mean that the respective legal fields would lose their distinctive character. Rather, each field would be modified to take account of the other, as reflected in the 'principle of systemic integration'.[19] The delivery of integration would pose a range of challenges. It would be vital that the underlying rationale, assumptions and functioning of each system was taken into account in determining how rules in that field function in practice.[20] That might seem straightforward, but most lawyers are more familiar with the specific rules in their field, and rarely consider the underlying operational principles of the particular field.[21]

The purpose in identifying possible approaches is not to impose a theoretical construct on horizontal collisions but rather to clarify the nature of the solution adopted. The examination of the specific relationship between IHL and HRsL will start by examining the pronouncements of the ICJ and discussing the principle of *lex specialis*. This will be followed by a discussion of illustrative examples of the practice of Special Procedures, commissions of inquiry and treaty bodies. The chapter will conclude with a discussion of integration in the context of the relationship between IHL and HRsL.

4 The approach of the International Court of Justice (ICJ)

The ICJ has addressed the relationship between IHL and HRsL on three occasions, in two advisory opinions and one contentious case.[22] It has been clear and consistent in what it has said. The same cannot be said for what it might *mean* by what it has said. Nor has it addressed the principles to be applied generally when two substantive areas collide.

In the context of this issue, HRsL applies in all circumstances, subject only to derogation and jurisdiction over territory or persons.[23] This must mean that a human rights body does not lose jurisdiction by virtue simply of the existence of an armed conflict and/or of the applicability of IHL but it presumably can only handle issues addressed by HRsL. Given that HRsL consists of general principles applicable in a wide variety of very different situations, this is hardly a constraint. It is certainly capable of covering the decision to open fire, the precautions that need to be taken when doing so and the choice of weapons.[24] On the relationship itself, the ICJ stated:

> As regards the relationship between international humanitarian law and human rights law, there are thus three possible situations: some rights may be exclusively matters of international humanitarian law; others may be exclusively matters of human rights law;

---

19 E.g. see McLachlan (n. 13).
20 On the way in which IHL functions, see n. 1.
21 'The significance of a special regime often lies in the way its norms express a unified object and purpose. . . . Each rule-complex or 'regime' comes with its own principles, its own form of expertise and its own "ethos"'; ILC Study (n. 13), para. 13.
22 ICJ, *Legality or Threat of Use of Nuclear Weapons, Advisory Opinion*, 8 July 1996, para. 25 ; ICJ, *The Legal Consequences of the Construction of a Wall in the Occupied Palestinian Territory*, Advisory Opinion, 9 July 2004, para. 106; ICJ, *Case Concerning Armed Activity on the Territory of the Congo (Democratic Republic of the Congo v Uganda)*, Judgment of 19 December 2005, paras 216–20.
23 ICJ, *The Legal Consequences* (n. 22), at paras 105 and 106.
24 *McCann & others v UK*, Application No. 18984/91 (judgment of 27 September 1995); *Ergi v Turkey*, 66/1997/850/1057 (judgment of 28 July 1998); *Gulec v Turkey*, Application No. 21593/93 (judgment of 27 July 1998); *Isayeva, Yusopova and Bazayeva v Russia*, Application No. 57947–49/00 (judgement of 24 February 2005); *Isayeva v Russia*, Application no. 57950/00 (24 February 2005).

yet others may be matters of both these branches of international law. In order to answer the question put to it, the Court will have to take into consideration both these branches of international law, namely human rights law and, as *lex specialis*, international humanitarian law.[25]

The first difficulty is how any matter can be exclusively a question of IHL, since the ICJ in the previous paragraph had reaffirmed that HRsL applies in all circumstances, subject only to derogation. The second difficulty is what is meant by *lex specialis*. It cannot be that IHL trumps HRsL, since that applies in all circumstances. It cannot be that there is to be a demarcation between the two fields, since that would result in two possible situations, not three. Does this mean that the *lex specialis* principle is a tool for achieving or managing integration?

Lex specialis appears to be better suited to vertical relationships between the general and the specific, rather than to horizontal collisions.[26] Nevertheless, in the most general terms, it is clear what the ICJ is getting at. IHL has been specifically developed to address conduct in war. This could even be expressed in terms of a vertical relationship. If HRsL is the general law dealing with the relationship between those exercising authority and those subject to its exercise, IHL is the body of rules which deals with that relationship during armed conflict. The problem is that this seriously distorts what IHL is essentially about.[27] It also ignores the autonomous and indeed prior existence of IHL. In vertical relationships, the specialist area depends upon the general to fill in the gaps. IHL is free-standing. The ICJ presumably means that in situations in which both IHL and HRsL are applicable, priority must be given to the purpose-made rules. That being said, the notion that HRsL, as the *lex generalis*, might fill in any gaps is one that will require further discussion below.

The ICJ does not address the applicability of the two legal regimes and any link between that and the three situations identified. Clearly only HRsL applies to situations in which IHL is not applicable, but does the second situation identified by the ICJ only arise where that is the case or does HRsL alone apply to some issues even during armed conflict? Does the *lex specialis* principle prima facie apply whenever IHL is applicable, unless IHL alone applies? According to the assumptions made by many writers, the applicability of rules on the means and methods of fighting have been dramatically extended over the past 15 years, principally through the articulation of customary IHL.[28] If this interpretation were applied to the relationship, it would be inconsistent with the existing scope of protection of HRsL, embodied in decisions which were not challenged by the respondent state on the basis of the applicability of IHL.

25 ICJ, *The Legal Consequences* (n. 22), at para. 106.
26 See generally Prud'homme, N., '*Lex Specialis*: Oversimplifying a More Complex and Multifaceted Relationship?', (2007) 40 *Israel Law Review* 355; see also n. 10, above.
27 IHL is about the avoidance of *unnecessary* suffering, death and destruction by providing a balance between military necessity and considerations of humanity. It envisages not only the killing of fighters but also that innocent civilians may be killed without such killing being unlawful. It is not about limitations on the exercise of power as such, although the exercise of power is obviously involved.
28 E.g. Henckaerts, J.-M. and Doswald-Beck, L., *Customary International Humanitarian Law* (CUP, 2006). The clearest evidence of customary IHL, particularly rules applicable in non-international armed conflicts, is to be found in that ICRC Study, the case law of the ICTY and ICTR and the provisions of Art. 8(2)(c) and (e) of the Statute of the International Criminal Court. For an analysis of one particular implication, relevant to this discussion, see Hampson (n. 1).

What, however, does 'priority' mean? It cannot mean using IHL *instead of* HRsL, for in that case HRsL would not be applicable in all circumstances. Does it mean that there is only a breach of HRsL where there would be a breach of IHL, or does that amount to the same thing as the previous possibility? If the pronouncement in the Advisory Opinion is opaque, perhaps greater clarity is to be found in the application of the principle in a contentious case. Unfortunately, in the *DRC v Uganda* case, the ICJ simply found that the same acts violated Additional Protocol I of 1977 to the Geneva Conventions of 1949 and the ICCPR. The ICJ did not explain how it reached that conclusion. Did the Court examine separately the possible violation of both treaties or did it just look at the former? Was the violation of the Protocol *necessary* to the finding of a violation of the Covenant? Would it have been possible for the Court to find no violation of the Protocol but a violation of the Covenant?

Two issues raised earlier are relevant in this context. The first concerns the tools available at the international level for resolving horizontal collisions and the second the role of judicial and quasi-judicial mechanisms in resolving collisions. An ICJ advisory opinion may be authoritative but it is not binding on anyone. Judgment in a contentious case only binds the parties. This question of the authority of the ICJ's pronouncements on the relationship between IHL and HRsL matters because at least two states deny the applicability of HRsL in situations in which IHL is applicable.[29]

It might appear that there is plenty of scope for research on the *lex specialis* principle. At the risk of appearing flippant, it is submitted that there are sufficient doctorates on that subject. More useful research would be on horizontal collisions in international law and the tools available and substantive principles relevant to their determination. What needs to be researched now is the operationalisation of the ICJ's pronouncement on the relationship between IHL and HRsL, not the pronouncement itself.

5 Illustrative examples of the practice of human rights and related (quasi-)judicial mechanisms

This section seeks to examine how an illustrative sample of human rights and related (quasi-) judicial mechanisms handle the relationship between IHL and HRsL. The same cannot be done for IHL mechanisms, since the only one that exists, other than on an ad hoc basis, has never been used.[30] It should be emphasised that the examination is not exhaustive. What have the mechanisms said about the relationship and has it been affected by the ICJ pronouncements? The human rights mechanisms chosen include two Special Procedures, the Special Rapporteur on Extra-judicial, Summary or Arbitrary and Execution, and the Working Group on Arbitrary Detention, with occasional references to other Special Procedures.[31]

---

29 Israel and the United States (n. 9).

30 International Humanitarian Fact-Finding Commission under Art. 90 of Additional Protocol I of 1977 to the four Geneva Conventions of 1949. On IHL fact-finding in situations of conflict generally, see Hampson, F.J., 'Fact-Finding and the International Fact-Finding Commission', in Fox and Meyer (ed.), *Effecting Compliance*, Vol. II of Armed Conflict and the New Law (British Institute of International & Comparative Law, 1993), 53.

31 One reason for not including the mandate on the prohibition of torture is that torture is prohibited in all circumstances under both IHL and HRsL. Whilst that should reduce conflicts, there may be differences in the definition of torture and a greater degree of specificity under HRsL with regard to secondary rules designed to buttress the prohibition, such as the need to conduct effective investigations and the non-use of evidence obtained through torture in criminal proceedings.

Three related quasi-judicial mechanisms are considered, which might be considered to be commissions of inquiry. The reason for selection is that they were all examining conduct during conflict and they were created by a human rights body. They are the commissions of inquiry on Lebanon, the Goldstone Report on Gaza and the Bassiouni Report on Libya, all established by the Human Rights Council. The Commissions of Inquiry are in a different position from the human rights mechanisms. The former are likely to have a mandate that expressly or by necessary implication includes both IHL and HRsL. The mandate of human rights mechanisms might be expected to be limited to finding a violation of HRsL. Five treaty bodies are also considered: the Human Rights Committee, the Inter-American Commission and Court of Human Rights and the former European Commission and the European Court of Human Rights.

5.1 Human rights mechanisms – Special Procedures

Very little attention has been paid to the work of Special Procedures in this context of IHL and HRsL. Systematic research across time and across mandates, including country-specific mandates, would be extremely useful. In addition to the distinction between thematic and country mandates, it may be necessary to distinguish between mandates seen as addressing economic and social rights and those dealing with civil and political rights. It may also be necessary to track the evolution of mandates over time. That includes understanding the circumstances in which different mandates were created and changes in the mandate holder. Within the work of a given mandate and mandate holder, it may also be necessary to distinguish between general reports, reports on missions and specific reports requested by the Commission on Human Rights and, more importantly, the Human Rights Council.[32]

The material examined below has been chosen with a view to identifying what the Special Procedures say and what they do about the relationship between IHL and HRsL. That includes trying to see whether the approach is coherent, both across different mandates and within the same mandate. The goal is to seek to identify some of the questions that may need to be the subject of research. To repeat, what follows is not a comprehensive analysis of the work of Special Procedures in this area. That is precisely why comprehensive research is advocated.

With the exception of the Working Group on Arbitrary Detention, most Special Procedures are usually not in a position to determine the existence of a violation in an individual case.[33] Their comments on implementation within a state tend to be of a more general

---

32 As a matter of impression, the Human Rights Council has made much greater use than the former Commission on Human Rights of the possibility of requesting a report from a specified group of Special Procedures to address possible violations, particularly in the context of Israel's actions in the Occupied Palestinian Territories and Lebanon. Alongside that, the Human Rights Council has established what look like Commissions of Inquiry with regard to that situation and Libya. It is not clear on what basis the Human Rights Council chooses between the two possible mechanisms.

33 In the case of serious human rights violations which, in certain circumstances, can constitute crimes against humanity, the state most commonly disputes the facts alleged by the complainant, rather than accepting the facts but claiming that they do not violate HRsL. The Special Procedures are not equipped to resolve disputes on the facts. They can merely set out the competing claims. In the case of arbitrary detention, however, the problem is often the law on the basis of which the detainee is held. The law itself may well violate the prohibition of arbitrary detention, thereby enabling the Working Group to reach a conclusion in an individual case.

character. This has made it possible for them to avoid articulating their view as to the relationship between IHL and HRsL, in contrast to bodies which determine individual cases and which have to consider the impact of the applicability of IHL on HRsL. That said, Special Procedures have examined respect for the relevant right(s) during armed conflict. The extent to which it matters how Special Procedures deal with the relationship depends on the wider question of the authority of their work. Whilst formally the reports of Special Procedures are not binding, their work is more important than this suggests. The elaboration of their mandates may shape the view of treaty bodies as to the scope of a human rights norm. States could challenge an interpretation of the mandate and/or a human rights norm before the Human Rights Council or the General Assembly but, in practice, they more commonly challenge conclusions and the manner in which they were arrived at than the mandate or its interpretation.[34] Two reports have been examined in this context, both produced by a group of Special Procedures mandate holders.

Four mandate holders submitted a report on the impact of the conflict in Lebanon between Israel and Hezbollah in 2006.[35] The mission was undertaken at their own initiative, in response to a suggestion of the President of the Human Rights Council.[36] The objectives are set out in paragraph 2:

> [They] were (i) to assess, from the perspective of international human rights and human-itarian law as covered by their respective mandates, the impact on the civilian popula-tions of the armed conflict that affected southern Lebanon and other parts of the country and northern Israel between 12 July and 14 August 2006; (ii) to advise the authorities on fulfilling their responsibility to protect and assist affected civilians in accordance with their human rights obligations and in light of the challenges faced by the respective Governments; and (iii) to make recommendations to United Nations agencies and other relevant actors on how best to address the protection needs of the people concerned, especially the most vulnerable among them.

When setting out the applicable legal framework, the Special Procedures stated that HRsL remains applicable, subject to derogation. In the case of the International Covenant on

---

34 The best example is the United States, which has challenged the Special Rapporteur's interpretation of the mandate dealing with summary, arbitrary and extra-judicial executions, see below, but which has never sought to amend the mandate at the time of its renewal. It is possible that the United States has thought about seeking to amend the mandate but that it thought such an initiative would have no prospect of success.

35 Report of the Special Rapporteur on extrajudicial, summary or arbitrary executions, Philip Alston; the Special Rapporteur on the right of everyone to the enjoyment of the highest attainable standard of physical and mental health, Paul Hunt; the Representative of the Secretary-General on human rights of internally displaced persons, Walter Kälin; and the Special Rapporteur on adequate housing as a component of the right to an adequate standard of living, Miloon Kothari, Mission to Lebanon and Israel, A/HRC/2/7, 2 October 2006. The Human Rights Council also established a Commission of Inquiry into the same conflict; Report of the Commission of Inquiry on Lebanon pursuant to Human Rights Council resolution S-2/1, A/HRC/3/2, 23 November 2006: 'The Commission, according to paragraph 7 of resolution S-2/1, was mandated: (a) to investigate the systematic targeting and killings of civilians by Israel in Lebanon; (b) to examine the types of weapons used by Israel and their conformity with international law; and (c) to assess the extent and deadly impact of Israeli attacks on human life, property, critical infra-structure and the environment'; ibid., para. 1; see further below, Commissions of Inquiry.

36 Ibid., para. 3.

Economic, Social and Cultural Rights, where there is no provision for derogation, the conflict context may affect the resources available.[37] On the relationship between HRsL and IHL, the report stated: 'In respect of certain human rights, more specific rules of international humanitarian law may be relevant for the purposes of their interpretation.'[38] This does not make it clear when IHL will be used in this way, nor the practical effect of the relevance of IHL. The analysis of targeting and weapon use is based on IHL.[39] The analysis of the impact of the conflict on the civilian population appears to be based primarily on HRsL.[40] It is not clear that a distinction was drawn between the negative consequences of unlawful attacks and the negative consequences of all attacks. There is an urgent need for research into how bodies, whether based on the UN Charter or on treaties, dealing with economic, social and cultural rights should take account of the fact of armed conflict or the possible relevance of IHL. In their final report, the Special Procedures concluded that 'serious violations of both human rights and humanitarian law have been committed by Israel'.[41] It is not clear that they had the authority, either inherently or in terms of their own definition of their objectives, to reach a finding of violation of IHL.

On 12 January 2009, the Human Rights Council passed a resolution urging all parties to the conflict in Gaza to respect their obligations under international human rights law and humanitarian law.[42] The resolution requested a specified group of Special Procedures 'to urgently seek and gather information on violations of the human rights of the Palestinian people and submit their reports to the Council at its next session'.[43] This appears to have been a request for evidence gathering rather than evaluation, since the Council had already declared there to have been grave violations in the very title of the resolution. The subsequent report sets out the applicable legal framework in a broadly similar way to the report on the conflict in Lebanon.[44] Again, it is not clear that certain of the mandate holders distinguished between the impact of lawful and unlawful attacks under IHL.[45] The Special Rapporteur on

---

37 Ibid., para. 15.
38 Ibid., para. 16.
39 Ibid., paras 38–58.
40 Ibid., paras. 59–67.
41 Ibid., para. 99. The Report also asks for information regarding the nature of prima facie civilian targets and the anticipated collateral or incidental effects of attacks; ibid. para. 103b. This indicates one of the problems with using human rights machinery to monitor compliance with IHL. Compliance with the rules on the conduct of hostilities can only be monitored with the cooperation of the possible violator because it depends on what that party knew or ought to have known; see n. 1.
42 Human Rights Council Resolution S-9/1, The grave violations of human rights in the Occupied Palestinian Territory, particularly due to the recent Israeli military attacks against the occupied Gaza strip, 12 January 2009.
43 Ibid, para. 12.
44 Combined Report of the Special Rapporteur on the right of everyone to the enjoyment of the highest attainable standard of physical and mental health, the Special Representative of the Secretary-General for Children and Armed Conflict, the Special Rapporteur on violence against women, its causes and consequences, the Representative of the Secretary-General on the human rights of internally displaced persons, the Special Rapporteur on adequate housing as a component of the right to an adequate standard of living, and on the right to non-discrimination in this context, the Special Rapporteur on the right to food, the Special Rapporteur on extrajudicial, arbitrary or summary executions, the Special Rapporteur on the right to education, and the Independent Expert on the question of human rights and extreme poverty, Human Rights Situation in Palestine and Other Occupied Arab Territories, A/HRC/10/22, 10 March 2009, paras 9–25.
45 E.g. ibid., paras 32, 38–39, 46, 54 and 65.

Extrajudicial, Summary or Arbitrary Executions analysed the killings in terms of IHL. In contrast to the other Special Procedures, he referred not to grave violations but to 'strong and credible reports of war crimes and other violations of international norms' which required investigation.[46]

These two reports raise the following questions which require further research. Can or must Special Procedures take account of IHL when conducting their investigations? Where IHL is relevant, can a Special Procedure reach a conclusion of violation of HRsL based on the result, without first determining whether the perpetrator breached IHL? Where the conduct was not in breach of relevant IHL, can its effects (including foreseeable effects) be in breach of HRsL? Do the Special Procedures have the authority to find a violation of IHL or only of HRsL?

Two of the Special Procedures have, to some extent, had to deal overtly with the relationship with IHL. The Working Group on Arbitrary Detention can reach conclusions in individual cases since often the problem is posed not by disputed facts but by the law being applied. In the case of international armed conflicts (IACs), it has shown itself to be aware of the detention regimes for prisoners of war (Geneva Convention III) and for civilians (Geneva Convention IV). There is a problem in non-international armed conflicts (NIACs), where the treaty law contains no reference to the grounds or modalities of administrative detention but where there is said to be a body of customary law rules. In NIACs within the detaining state, reliance may be placed on domestic law, possibly including emergency legislation and derogation under one or more human rights treaties. A significant problem arises in the case of extraterritorial NIACs, such as the situation in Iraq after the end of the occupation and the situation after the installation of President Karzai in Afghanistan. Should the applicability of IHL have any effect on the application of the normal rules of HRsL, or should the former only affect the latter where there is a specific inconsistent rule of IHL? Does the answer to that question have to apply across the board or could it vary depending on the human right at issue? Under HRsL, there are unusually specific rules regulating detention, including the ability to modify them by derogation. Does that or should that have an effect on the ease with which rules should be modified on account of the applicability of IHL? Does it make a difference whether the IHL rule is part of treaty law or allegedly part of customary law?

The Working Group on Arbitrary Detention has addressed detention in situations of conflict in a range of general observations and opinions in individual cases. Its most comprehensive treatment of the question is to be found in its report submitted in 2005.[47] The Working Group stated that applicable legal standards are to be found in both IHL and HRsL. It confirmed that the two bodies of rules are complementary and not mutually exclusive.[48] It accepts that, where IHL is applicable, it is the *lex specialis*. It cited the 1993 methods of work to the effect that it would not deal with detention in international armed conflicts because the *lex specialis* provides for grounds of detention in Geneva Conventions III and IV and to avoid duplication with the work of the International Comittee of the Red Cross (ICRC).[49] This abnegation of responsibility might be thought to sit uncomfortably with the view that HRsL remains applicable in armed conflicts. It might be more consistent with the principles set out by the ICJ for the Working Group to accept the Geneva Conventions as grounds of detention, but to

---

46 Ibid., paras. 91–92 and 98.
47 Report of the Working Group on Arbitrary Detention, E/CN.4/2006/7, 12 December 2005, paras 68–75.
48 Ibid, para. 70.
49 Ibid, paras 73–74.

investigate whether the detention was in conformity with the provisions of the two Geneva Conventions, for example, with regard to the provisions for review. The claimed need to avoid duplication with the ICRC is surprising. The role of the ICRC is significantly different and does not include public reporting. The Working Group, however, has introduced a refinement to its self-denying ordinance. It will examine detention in international armed conflicts where detainees are not getting the benefit of the provisions of Geneva Conventions III and IV.[50] An example of such a situation is the detainees in Guantánamo Bay. The US denied that they were entitled to prisoner of war status and did so by executive decision, not individual legal decision as required by the third Geneva Convention.[51] The view that HRsL should be applied where a state does not provide the guarantees of Geneva Convention III ignores the applicability of IHL, including Geneva Convention IV and Article 75 of Additional Protocol I.

The Working Group determines for itself whether IHL is applicable. In particular, it has stated that detention in the 'global war on terror' is not covered by IHL unless it occurs in the course of an armed conflict.[52] In this context, are the rules determining applicability rules of IHL, or in effect rules regarding the jurisdiction of the human rights body? If the former, does the Working Group have the authority to apply them? If the latter, it presumably has the inherent authority to determine whether it has jurisdiction, and how the relevance of IHL addressed?[53]

In its 2005 Report, the Working Group identified four situations in which it might have to deal with this issue.[54] It accepted that what it called situations of internal conflict involve the applicability of IHL. It then went on to point out that treaty law applicable in non-international armed conflicts (NIACs) does not address grounds of detention.[55] The first question is whether the Working Group would consider using customary IHL. It is alleged that there are customary rules regulating detention in NIACs.[56] The second question is what the Working Group would do, faced with the use of internment in an extraterritorial NIAC.

Whilst the analysis of the Working Group on Arbitrary Detention is not free of difficulties and possible inconsistencies, it has addressed the relationship between IHL and HRsL relatively specifically.

The other Special Procedure to be noted in this context is the Special Rapporteur on Extra-Judicial, Summary and Arbitrary Executions. In this case, the reason the Special Rapporteur needs to address the relationship is on account of the radically different norms applicable to killings under a law and order paradigm compared to under a law of armed conflict paradigm. Early on in the mandate, the question was often fudged.[57] There was no

---

50 Ibid, para. 75.
51 Report of the Working Group on Arbitrary Detention, E/CN.4/2003/8, 16 December 2002, para. 64. The Working Group states that, in the event of the detainees not being given the benefits of Geneva Convention III, their detention would fall to be considered under the International Covenant on Civil and Political Rights. It is surprising that again no consideration was given to the detention provisions of Geneva Convention IV.
52 For an example in an individual case, see Opinions adopted by the Working Group on Arbitrary Detention, A/HRC/7/4/Add.1, 16 January 2008, 29–37, at 31 (Al-Marri).
53 It is not always easy to determine whether IHL is applicable; Hampson (n. 8).
54 N. 44 above, para. 71.
55 Ibid., para.72.
56 Henckaerts and Doswald-Beck (n. 28).
57 e.g. Report of the Special Rapporteur, Mission to Afghanistan, E/CN.4/2003/3/Add.4, 3 February 2003. At para. 36 there is a reference to crimes against humanity but not to war crimes. When referring to an attack against a wedding party, at paras 43–44, the facts are set out but there is no reference to IHL rules or principles. Until Philip Alston became Special Rapporteur, most of the mandate-holders fudged the question of the possible applicability and relevance of IHL.

clear articulation of the relationship, extremely limited citation of specific IHL rules (as opposed to principles), and no clarity as to how the *lex specialis* affected the articulation of HRsL. Philip Alston, Special Rapporteur from 2004 to 2010, addressed some of those questions head-on.[58] In his report submitted in 2004, Alston first referred to IHL in the context of executions.[59] He then addressed the use of allegedly excessive force in Fallujah, Iraq. The US denied that such military operations during the course of an armed conflict come within the mandate of the Special Rapporteur. Alston stated:

> The fact is that it [humanitarian law] falls squarely within the mandate. All major relevant resolutions in recent years have referred explicitly to that body of law. Most recently, the General Assembly, in resolution 59/197 of 20 December 2004, dealing with the mandate of the Special Rapporteur, urged Governments 'to take all necessary and possible measures, in conformity with international human rights law and international humanitarian law, to prevent loss of life ... during ... armed conflicts' (para. 8 (b)). Consistent with this approach, every single annual report of the Special Rapporteur since at least 1992 has dealt with violations of the right to life in the context of international and non-international armed conflicts.[60]

He established the applicability of HRsL by relying on observations of the Human Rights Committee and the ICJ.[61] He dealt with the United States' claim that the applicability of IHL means the non-applicability of HRsL by relying on ICJ pronouncements and general principles of international law.[62] This still left unaddressed the possible impact of the applicability of IHL to the scope of HRsL in the particular situation.

In his next report, Alston dealt with the issue of the obligation to investigate possible breaches of IHL.[63] He first referred to the existence of the obligation under IHL.[64] He then referred to the obligation under HRsL. He suggested that this would apply in NIACs, since there are no IHL treaty provisions on the issue.[65] Alston suggests that IHL is only used as the *lex specialis* where there is a conflict between IHL and HRsL. Is this too narrow a view of the impact of the applicability of IHL on HRsL? Is it simultaneously too wide, in that it would appear to permit the use of an armed conflict paradigm even at the low threshold for the applicability of common Article 3 of the Geneva Conventions?[66] He does envisage taking account of the fact of armed conflict when determining what type of investigation is practicable in such situations.[67] He refers to the problem experienced by investigators and monitors external to the state if they are not provided with the evidentiary basis on which the decisions about the attack were made.[68]

---

58 These questions often overlapped with the question of the extraterritorial applicability of human rights law, which is not addressed in this chapter but which needs to be taken into account since it has huge implications for the practical impact of the relationship between IHL and human rights law.
59 Report of the Special Rapporteur, E/CN.4/2005/7, 22 December 2004, para. 43.
60 Ibid, para. 45, footnote omitted.
61 Ibid, paras 46–47.
62 Ibid, paras 48–52.
63 Report of the Special Rapporteur, E/CN.4/2006/53, 8 March 2006, paras 33–43.
64 Ibid, para. 34.
65 Ibid.
66 Hampson (n. 1) at 196–98, 202–204.
67 Ibid., para. 36.
68 Ibid., para. 43; see further below.

The following year, the Special Rapporteur had to return to the general question of the relationship between IHL and HRsL, owing to US objections. He addressed three issues: alleged exclusivity of one set or rules or the other; the authority of the then Commission on Human Rights to address IHL; and the mandate of the Special Rapporteur.[69] He also considered the implications of the United States' position. He then discussed in detail a specific issue, dealing with an uncontroversial area of IHL which concerns the rules on the protection of victims of war, rather than those on the means and methods of fighting: mercy killings in armed conflicts.[70] He made express reference to particular rules of IHL, both those in the Geneva Conventions to which the United States is a party and to a rule in Additional Protocol I (Article 5), to which the United States is not a party but which is generally regarded as customary law.

The Special Rapporteur's most controversial report was perhaps the one on targeted killings.[71] When establishing the applicable legal framework, Alston first deals with situations of armed conflict. Where there are clear IHL rules, he accepts that they are the *lex specialis*. He then suggests that: 'To the extent that IHL does not provide a rule, or the rule is unclear and its meaning cannot be ascertained from the guidance offered by IHL principles, it is appropriate to draw guidance from human rights law.'[72] Alston identifies the applicable principles from the rules for international armed conflicts (IACs) and then suggests that they apply in both international and non-international conflicts.[73] However, he does not define NIACs. The treaty regime distinguishes between two different types of NIACs: those covered by common Article 3 of the Geneva Conventions which has a low threshold of applicability and a very limited range of norms, effectively only covering the protection of victims of war. That would include the execution of detainees but not the conduct of military operations. Additional Protocol II has a much higher threshold of applicability and does address, in a very limited way, the conduct of military operations. To apply IAC rules or principles in a common Article 3 situation would mean reducing the current level of protection afforded by HRsL.[74] This study of the Special Rapporteur involves the most systematic and sophisticated use by a Special Procedure of IHL.[75]

---

69 Report of the Special Rapporteur, A/HRC/4/20, 29 January 2007, paras 18–28.
70 Ibid., paras 29–38.
71 Report of the Special Rapporteur, *Study on Targeted Killings*, A/HRC/14/24/Add.6, 28 May 2010.
72 Ibid, para. 29, footnote omitted.
73 Ibid, para. 30.
74 The distinction between common Art. 3 and Additional Protocol II is made later in the report (para. 50) in the context of the applicability of IHL, rather than the substantive rules applicable in different types of conflict. There is then a separate section on who can be targeted under IHL (paras 57–69). In that context, Alston acknowledges the problem posed by using a continuous combat function test to determine whether a person can be treated as a long-term fighter in NIACs and therefore targeted at any time, irrespective of the threat he poses at the time. See generally, Hampson (n. 66).
75 Other reports in which IHL issues were discussed include A/HRC/2/7 and A/HRC/11/2/Add.4. Mission reports in which the obligations of states under IHL were considered include Central African Republic (A/HRC/14/24/Add.5), Afghanistan (A/HRC/11/2/Add.4, paras. 9 and 23–24), and Israel and Lebanon (A/HRC/2/7, paras. 30 and 68–70). He also discussed the obligations of non-state armed groups in Afghanistan (A/HRC/11/2/Add.4, para. 71), the Central African Republic (A/HRC/11/2/Add.3, para. 6), Colombia (A/HRC/14/24/Add.2), the Democratic Republic of the Congo (A/HRC/14/24/Add.3), Sri Lanka (E/CN.4/2006/53/Add.5, paras. 26, 30 and 33) and the Philippines (A/HRC/8/3/Add.2, para. 5).

IHL is unlikely to have the same impact on different mandates of Special Procedures. Nevertheless, there needs to be a commonality of approach. It is far from clear that that is the case. Systematic research is needed on this issue.

5.2 Commissions of inquiry established by the Human Rights Council

This section only considers independent commissions established by the Human Rights Council. Certain UN political organs presumably have the capacity to establish similar mechanisms. In addition, there seems to be a capacity to fact-find within the UN itself. For example, the Secretary-General appointed a group of three experts in 1993, one of whom was Amos Wako, to establish which group was responsible for the Carter Camp massacre, near Harbel in Liberia.[76] The Office of the High Commissioner for Human Rights has, on occasion, conducted investigations and reported to the Human Rights Council or even the Security Council. It would be useful if research were conducted into both independent and in-house investigations carried out at the behest of the UN Secretary-General or the High Commissioner. Is the goal just to establish facts or to establish whether the law has been violated? Is the mandate limited to HRsL or does it also include IHL? In the case of in-house investigations, is there a tension between an investigatory role and other functions? International bodies other than the UN have also made use of commissions of inquiry to examine conduct during an armed conflict.[77]

The Human Rights Council has established independent commissions of inquiry on five occasions – for Lebanon, Gaza, Libya, Syria and DPRK. The first question is why, given that it already has available to it the reports of Special Rapporteurs. That was particularly striking in the case of Lebanon, where, as discussed above, a group of Special Rapporteurs had submitted a report to the Council. All five situations involved conduct in conflict. The mandate of the Commission of Inquiry on Lebanon was:

(a) to investigate the systematic targeting and killings of civilians by Israel in Lebanon;
(b) to examine the types of weapons used by Israel and their conformity with international law; and
(c) to assess the extent and deadly impact of Israeli attacks on human life, property, critical infrastructure and the environment.[78]

It is obviously objectionable that the conduct of only one party was to be examined and the conclusion sought was contained in the mandate. By necessary implication, the relevant law was both HRsL and IHL. The flaws in the mandate also hindered the application of IHL. In

---

76 *The Carter Camp Massacre: Results of an investigation by the panel of inquiry appointed by the Secretary-General into the massacre near Harbel, Liberia, on the night of June 5/6 1993*, United Nations, New York, September 10, 1993. Amos Wako was, at that time, the Special Rapporteur on Summary, Arbitrary and Extra-Judicial Executions.

77 E.g. Independent International Fact-Finding Mission on the Conflict in Georgia (Tagliavini Report). The Mission was headed by a diplomat, not a lawyer, but legal expertise, including IHL expertise, was available to the Mission. In addition to looking at the *ius in bello*, it looked at facts relevant to a *ius ad bellum* determination. The Mission was created by and reported to the Council of the EU.

78 Report of the Commission of Inquiry on Lebanon pursuant to Human Rights Council resolution S-2/1, A/HRC/3/2, 23 November 2006, para. 1.

order to evaluate the lawfulness of Israeli targeting, it was necessary to understand the structure, functioning and behaviour of Hezbollah.[79] The violation of the rules on targeting is not determined by the result but is based on what was known or ought to have been known by the party in question. Many of the conclusions of the report of the Commission of Inquiry raise the question of whether IHL was applied in the way in which IHL should be applied and whether the application of HRsL was appropriately modified by the *lex specialis*, especially in relation to economic and social rights.

Similar concerns are raised by the Commission of Inquiry on Gaza, chaired by Judge Richard Goldstone.[80] The original mandate provided that the independent international fact-finding mission was:

> [T]o investigate all violations of international human rights law and international humanitarian law by the occupying Power, Israel, against the Palestinian people throughout the Occupied Palestinian Territory, particularly in the occupied Gaza Strip, due to the current aggression, and calls upon Israel not to obstruct the process of investigation and to fully cooperate with the mission.[81]

The body was called a fact-finding mission but it was required to investigate violations of the law. Again, the mandate appears to assume the existence of violations. It also assumed that Gaza remained occupied. It only mandated the investigation of the conduct of one party. That aspect of the mandate was modified by the fact-finding mission. In its report, the Commission stated that its mandate was:

> [T]o investigate all violations of international human rights law and international humanitarian law that might have been committed at any time in the context of the military operations that were conducted in Gaza during the period from 27 December 2008 and 18 January 2009, whether before, during or after.[82]

Under either articulation of the mandate, the applicable law was expressly HRsL and IHL. One member of the panel was a former legal adviser in the Irish defence forces (i.e. there was IHL expertise). Again, there were two principal problems with the report. The first was the willingness to reach conclusions as to the violations of rules of IHL dealing with the means and methods of warfare. Even assuming that the true facts were found by the Commission, and it should be noted that it itself referred to the problem of residents of Gaza not being prepared to implicate local fighters, that is not the test. The test is what was known or ought to have been known by the Israeli defence forces. Since Israel did not cooperate with the Commission, its members were not in a position to know why and on what informational basis certain objects were targeted.

The second problem was how HRsL should be applied in the context of armed conflict. In the case of physical and mental health, for example, it is obvious that armed conflict will have an adverse effect on both. Since armed conflict is not necessarily unlawful, HRsL has to

---

79 The Commission itself commented on this problem; ibid., paras 6–7.
80 *Report of the United Nations Fact Finding Mission on the Gaza Conflict*, Executive Summary, A/HRC/12/48 (Advance 1), 23 September 2009 (Goldstone Report).
81 Human Rights Council Resolution S-9/1, 12 January 2009, para. 14.
82 Goldstone Report (n. 80), para. 1.

accommodate an increase in the adverse consequences for physical and mental health. This does not mean that HRsL is irrelevant, but it does require that a means be found to distinguish between regrettable and adverse but legitimate consequences and unlawful consequences. It is noteworthy that after the report attracted considerable criticism, much of it political, Judge Goldstone himself appeared to retract some of the conclusions.[83]

The third such investigation was the one into events in Libya (the Bassiouni Commission). On 25 February 2011, the Human Rights Council called for the 'dispatch [of] an independent, international commission of inquiry . . . to investigate all alleged violations of international human rights law in Libya, to establish the facts and circumstances of such violations and of the crimes perpetrated'.[84] The mandate did not refer to IHL but, at that time, the situation in Libya was in the process of evolving from one of massive demonstrations to organised armed violence. The Commission was given a short period of time in which to report. In its report, the Commission said that it considered the actions of all parties in the light of HRsL, IHL on account of the evolution of the situation, and International Criminal Law (ICL) on account of the referral of the situation to the ICC by the Security Council.[85] The Commission was cautious in its handling of the evidence and in drawing conclusions. It was nevertheless able to conclude that violations of HRsL had occurred and that issues of concern under IHL had occurred which required further investigation.[86]

The commissions of inquiry created by the Human Rights Council raise various questions worthy of further research. The first is why they are created, given the existence of Special Procedures. Is it relevant that some of them had a mandate which included violations of IHL? Had the mandates not included IHL, could the Commissions nevertheless have referred to IHL, if it was the body of law applicable to the issue at hand? Does the Human Rights Council have the authority to determine violations of IHL?[87] If a subsidiary organ of the UN regularly exceeds its mandate without objection by the body to which it reports, in this case the General Assembly, does that imply a de facto extension of the mandate which, over time, may become a *de jure* mandate? Is there any requirement, when creating a mechanism to establish the facts and possible violations of the law in a particular situation, that the Human Rights Council be even-handed and require that the conduct of all the parties be examined? Can a commission of inquiry amend the mandate itself, with or without the approval of the President of the Human Rights Council, so as to make it even-handed? Are there any principles regarding the time available to the Commission in which to report? What 'quality control' mechanisms are available, if any, to ensure that a commission applies the law in an appropriate fashion? Are any necessary?

---

83 'Reconsidering the Goldstone Report on Israel and war crimes', *Washington Post*, 2 April 2011, www.washingtonpost.com/opinions/reconsidering-the-goldstone-report-on-israel-and-war-crimes/2011/04/01/AFg111JC_story.html. The other members of the Commission do not appear to have retracted their findings.

84 *Report of the Human Rights Council on its Fifteenth Special Session*, A/HRC/S-15/1, 25 February 2011, resolution, para. 11.

85 *Report of the International Commission of Inquiry to investigate all alleged violations of international human rights law in the Libyan Arab Jamahiriya*, A/HRC/17/44, 1 June 2011, at 2.

86 The Commission requested clarification of certain targeting issues from NATO. NATO took the decision to cooperate with the Commission and provided such information as it felt able. That probably contributed significantly to the way in which targeting issues were handled in the final report.

87 General Assembly Resolution 60/251 which established the Human Rights Council gave it a mandate to deal with human rights, including 'situations of violations of human rights, including gross and systematic violations' with regard to which it could make recommendations; A/RES/60/251, para. 3.

5.3 Human rights treaty bodies

At the international level, human rights treaty bodies have three principal functions. They receive reports from states on domestic implementation and observance of treaty commitments, in relation to which, following a discussion with the state in question, they produce concluding observations. They issue general comments, exploring the scope of particular provisions or concepts. They also, in some cases, address individual complaints of violation, resulting in a non-binding but authoritative opinion. In theory, they also often have the capacity to address inter-state complaints of violation but they have almost never been called upon to do so. At the regional level, individual and, to a lesser extent, inter-state petitions play a much more important role. As already indicated, the principal focus will be on a limited number of bodies.[88] The mandate of such bodies is limited to HRsL. They can therefore not be expected to find violations of IHL, but the question remains of how the applicability of IHL affects their application of HRsL. It should not be thought that this question is capable of either an obvious or an easy answer.[89] It should also be remembered that treaty obligations only bind the state. The treaty bodies cannot therefore be expected to address violations of IHL by non-state actors, even where they would also constitute HRsL violations if committed by a state. Some of the academic discussion relating to the work of the human rights treaty bodies regarding the relationship between IHL and HRsL occurs in a different context, that of the scope of the extraterritorial applicability of HRsL.[90]

The Human Rights Committee appears to have made no reference to IHL in the course of ordinary reporting. It did ask for ad hoc reports from Croatia, Bosnia and the Federal Republic of Yugoslavia (Serbia and Montenegro) during the course of the conflicts which marked the disintegration of Yugoslavia. The questions to which the Human Rights Committee asked for responses were articulated in terms of HRsL. No reference was made to IHL.[91]

88 Certain treaties, by virtue of their express terms, are clearly applicable during armed conflict (e.g. Convention against Torture, which also applies extraterritorially; second optional Protocol to the Convention on the Rights of the Child on the use of persons under the age of 18 in armed forces). Other treaties concern a norm that, at least to some extent, is non-derogable when the norm is also found in a general civil and political rights treaty which provides for derogation (e.g. Convention on the Elimination of Racial Discrimination; Convention on the Elimination of Discrimination against Women; Convention on Enforced Disappearances). Whilst the scope of the norm during armed conflict may change, the essence of a non-derogable norm remains applicable. Yet other treaties fail to provide for derogation and do not address norms found in general treaties with a derogation clause (e.g. International Covenant on Civil and Political Rights). The equivalent Special Procedures have not yet found a coherent and systematic way of dealing with the norm in a conflict situation, so as to distinguish between regrettable but not unlawful consequences of action in armed conflict and unlawful consequences; see n. 37.

89 Hampson (n. 8).

90 Milanovic M., *Extraterritorial Application of Human Rights Treaties* (OUP, 2011). Gibney, M. and Skogly, S., *Universal Human Rights and Extraterritorial Obligations* (University of Pennsylvania Press, 2010), whilst dealing with the overlap between HRsL and refugee law and environmental law, does not address the overlap with IHL.

91 E.g. Concluding Observations of the Human Rights Committee: Yugoslavia. 28/12/1992; CCPR/C/79/Add.16, 28 December 1992; Concluding Observations of the Human Rights Committee: Croatia. 28/12/1992; CCPR/C/79/Add.15, 28 December 1992; Concluding Observations of the Human Rights Committee: Bosnia and Herzegovina. 28/12/1992; CCPR/C/79/Add.14, 28 December 1992.

In its General Comments, the Human Rights Committee has addressed both the circumstances in which a state may derogate and the effects of derogation.[92] In General Comment No. 29 (2001), there is a reference to the applicability of IHL.[93] There is no discussion of how the applicability of IHL might affect the application of HRsL, beyond the reference to the fact that a state cannot derogate from a right protected under IHL. General Comment 31 (2006) addresses the nature of the general legal obligation imposed on states parties to the Covenant. It refers to the fact that states owe human rights obligations to those 'within the power or effective control of the forces of a state party acting outside its territory'.[94] It states that the Covenant applies in situations in which IHL is applicable:

> While, in respect of certain Covenant rights, more specific rules of international human-
> itarian law may be specially relevant for the purposes of the interpretation of Covenant
> rights, both spheres of law are complementary, not mutually exclusive.[95]

This appears to imply that the only relevance of IHL is to clarify interpretation of a Covenant right. It is not clear whether this includes restricting the scope of the right as applicable in peacetime.

In individual cases, the Human Rights Committee has made no reference to IHL. The events giving rise to certain cases occurred against the backdrop of an armed conflict but the cases usually involve an alleged violation committed against a person in the control of the forces of the state.[96] In the case of extra-judicial execution or torture, the conduct would be a violation of both common Article 3 of the Geneva Conventions as well as the Covenant. It is not clear that the Committee has yet had to deal with a case where the answer under IHL and HRsL would be different.

The Inter-American Commission and Court of Human Rights have dealt with the relationship between the two bodies of rules at some length but principally at the theoretical

---

92 General Comment No. 29 States of Emergency *(article 4)*: CCPR/C/21/Rev.1/Add.11, 31 August 2001.
93 'During armed conflict, whether international or non-international, rules of international humani-
    tarian law become applicable and help, in addition to the provisions in article 4 and article 5, para-
    graph 1, of the Covenant, to prevent the abuse of a state's emergency powers. The Covenant requires
    that even during an armed conflict measures derogating from the Covenant are allowed only if and
    to the extent that the situation constitutes a threat to the life of the nation. If states parties consider
    invoking article 4 in other situations than an armed conflict, they should carefully consider the
    justification and why such a measure is necessary and legitimate in the circumstances.' Ibid., para.
    3. In addition, the Human Rights Committee pointed out that the requirement that derogation
    measures not be inconsistent with the state's other international obligations means that they cannot
    be inconsistent with IHL; ibid., paras 9, 11. The Human Rights Committee said that derogation
    could not be justified, even if the right is potentially derogable, where it is guaranteed by IHL; ibid.,
    para. 16.
94 General Comment No. 31: The Nature of the General Legal Obligation Imposed on States Parties
    to the Covenant, CCPR/C/21/Rev.1/Add.13, 26 May 2006, para. 10.
95 Ibid., para.11.
96 E.g. the death, ill-treatment or disappearance of a person in the control of state agents. Such ques-
    tions usually involve Geneva Law (protection of victims), rather than Hague Law (means and
    methods for the conduct of hostilities).

level.[97] The Court has stated clearly that the two organs cannot find a violation of IHL but can take it into account when determining whether there is a violation of the American Convention on Human Rights.[98] Reference has been made principally to common Article 3 of the Geneva Conventions, which the Court states resembles non-derogable HRsL.[99] It is arguable that, in some of the cases with which it has dealt, Additional Protocol II to the Geneva Conventions would have been relevant. That contains rules on the conduct of hostilities, including permissive rules in possible conflict with non-derogable HRsL.[100] A useful research exercise would be to consider whether the application of IHL treaty law or customary law would have made a difference in any of the cases considered by the Commission and/or Court.

The former European Commission and former and current European Court of Human Rights are at the other end of the spectrum. After an initial, disastrous, foray into the field, the European institutions have done a very good imitation of an ostrich in their avoidance of the issue. That is about to change. In the joined first and second cases brought by Cyprus against Turkey, following the invasion in 1974 of part of the territory of the former by the latter, the Commission had to consider the detention regime applicable to detained Cypriot soldiers.[101] The majority only looked at the Convention. Turkey had neither communicated a derogation to the Secretary-General of the Council of Europe, nor taken any domestic measure of derogation in relation to Cyprus. That meant that Article 5 of the Convention, which provides an exhaustive list of permitted grounds of detention and does not include administrative detention or internment, applied without the benefit of derogation. The detention of prisoners of war in an international armed conflict was therefore unlawful![102] It may be argued that all Turkey had to do to make the detention lawful was to derogate.[103] The

---

97 The Inter-American Commission of Human Rights also produces country reports. They will not be further considered here but would be worth researching to determine whether IHL has been taken into account or, if not, whether it would have made any difference if it had been. Similarly, no consideration is given to individual cases addressed by the Commission under its competence under the OAS Charter and the American Declaration on Human Rights. That is a basis on which it can exercise jurisdiction over states which have not ratified the American Convention on Human Rights, such as the United States.

98 *Las Palmeras v Colombia*, Inter-American Court of Human Rights, Preliminary Objections, Judgment of February 4, 2000; *Bámaca Velásquez Case,* Inter-American Court of Human Rights, Judgment of November 25, 2000, See generally, McCarthy (n. 8).

99 Unusually, in *Abella v Argentina*, Case 11.137, Report No. 55/97, OEA/Ser.L/V/II.95 Doc. 7 rev. at 271 (1997), the Inter-American Commission on Human Rights used customary law rules on the means and methods for the conduct of hostilities but found insufficient evidence of the alleged violation of the alleged IHL rules (firing over a white flag; use of unlawful weapons).

100 Where a rule relates to the conduct of hostilities but prohibits certain conduct, it is less likely to be in conflict with human rights law: e.g. the prohibition of attacks against civilians or the prohibition of indiscriminate attacks, but it should be noted that the definition of proportionality under IHL is significantly different and looser than that under human rights law.

101 *Cyprus v Turkey*, Applications Nos. 9780/74 and 6950/75 Report of the Commission, 10 July 1976.

102 Trechsel and Sperduti dissenting argued that IHL was applicable as a matter of law. Geneva Convention III expressly provides for the detention of POWs. That answered the question as to lawful authority to detain and lawful grounds of detention but did not deal with the treatment actually meted out to the POWs. They found it sufficient to say that the ICRC had access to the POWs.

103 That does, however, assume that it is possible to derogate with regard to a situation outside the borders of the derogating state.

case is striking because, in other contexts, the Strasbourg Court has stated that the Convention has to be interpreted in the context of international law as a whole.[104]

That case is the most stark example of a failure to take any account of IHL, since it involves a regime particular to IHL.[105] If ever IHL is relevant as the *lex specialis*, it might have been thought to be in the case of the detention of prisoners of war. Since then, the possible relevance of IHL has arisen in situations in which its applicability was a matter of dispute, most notably in the case of Northern Ireland and South-East Turkey.[106] More recently, the European Court of Human Rights has had to address the situation during and after the second Chechen War. It has again avoided any reference to IHL. It may be argued that in certain cases, most notably *Isayeva & others v Russian Federation,* the possible relevance of IHL was recognised. The Court was willing to take account of the *fact* of the conflict[107] but did not refer to IHL, even though a third party intervention made express reference to the rules applicable in non-international armed conflict.[108] The Court has on occasion used vocabulary that appears to be drawn from IHL but has not referred to that body of rules.[109] It is submitted that a situation in which the Court takes account of the fact of armed conflict and uses the vocabulary of IHL but does not make specific reference to that body of rules gives rise to considerable

104 *Al-Adsani v UK,* 35763/97, judgment of 21 November 2001; see n. 13 and accompanying text.
105 Another, more complicated, situation arose in the case of *Al-Jedda v United Kingdom,* No. 27021/08, judgment of 7 July 2011, where the UK had detained an individual in Iraq on security grounds. The UK had not derogated with regard to Iraq. The UK sought to argue that the detention was authorised under a Security Council resolution. The difficulty was the resolution *authorised* detention but did not require it. Arguably, a Security Council resolution can only displace a HRsL obligation under Art. 103 of the UN Charter where it requires the action in question to be undertaken. There is no evidence that the UK relied on a purely IHL argument, i.e. that administrative detention is authorised under customary IHL in a non-international armed conflict; HRsL needs to be applied in a fashion consistent with the rest of international law. That includes customary IHL which, furthermore, is *lex specialis.* It is not known how the Court would have reacted to the argument. The point is that it was not put to the Court in those terms. See generally, Pejic, J., 'The European Court of Human Right's *Al-Jedda* Judgment: the Oversight of International Humanitarian Law', 2011 93(883) *International Review of the Red Cross,* 837–51.
106 Both the United Kingdom and Turkey denied that the situations in Northern Ireland and South-East Turkey respectively crossed the threshold of applicability of common Article 3 of the Geneva Conventions.
107 'In the absence of corroborated evidence that any unlawful violence was threatened or likely, the Court retains certain doubts as to whether the aim can at all be said to be applicable. However, given the context of the conflict in Chechnya at the relevant time, the Court will assume in the following paragraphs that the military reasonably considered that there was an attack or a risk of attack from illegal insurgents, and that the air strike was a legitimate response to that attack.' *Isayeva, Yusopova and Bazayeva v Russia,* Application No. 57947–49/00, judgment of 24 February 2005, para. 181. See also *Isayeva v Russia,* Application no. 57950/00, 24 February 2005, paras 182–91; 'No martial law and no state of emergency has been declared in Chechnya, and no derogation has been made under Article 15 of the Convention (see § 133). The operation in question therefore has to be judged against a normal legal background', para. 191.
108 Ibid., paras 162–67.
109 Ibid., paras 182–91, references to the giving of warnings, the use of heavy combat weapons within the boundaries of a populated area, and evacuation of civilians. See also *Ergi v Turkey,* 66/1997/850/1057, judgment of 28 July 1998, para. 79, need to avoid and in any event minimise the incidental loss of civilian life.

uncertainty for states and for lawyers seeking to advise clients.[110] The 'fog of war' has become the 'fog of law'. This attitude appears set to change. In its admissibility decision in the case of *Georgia v Russia (No. 2)*, the Court stated that, at the merits stage, it would address the relationship between IHL and HRsL.[111] That would appear unavoidable. The case arises out of the brief conflict between the two states in August 2008 and concerns both rules on how fighting is carried out and rules on the protection of victims; in IHL terms, both the law of The Hague and the law of Geneva.

It is clear that the relationship between IHL and HRsL is currently causing a problem, particularly for human rights treaty bodies. It is less clear that there is agreement as to the nature of the problem, the goal to be achieved or especially the means of getting there.

6 The ways forward?

Three preliminary issues need to be taken into account. First, it is necessary to distinguish between the applicability of IHL to a *situation* and its applicability to an *incident*. A theoretical example may help to illustrate the point. A demonstration is held, against the backdrop of a significant level of violence directed by two organised armed groups against one another and by one of them against state institutions and officials. At one point, a soldier policing the demonstration thinks that he hears a shot. In order to know in what circumstances he may open fire, it is necessary to know whether IHL is even potentially applicable. If not, a law and order paradigm will apply. The answer to that question requires an examination of not one but two issues. First, is IHL applicable to the *situation* generally? If not, it is most unlikely that it will apply to the demonstration. Second, if and only if IHL is applicable to the situation generally, it is also necessary to ask whether it is applicable to the demonstration. Even during an armed conflict, there are places and times where a law and order paradigm is applicable. No one would suggest that, when dealing with a common or garden burglar, the state's security forces would be entitled to open fire under an armed conflict paradigm. A demonstration might be argued to be prima facie a law and order question unless there is a specific reason for believing that it is part of the armed conflict.

The second point, only relevant in certain circumstances, is to remember that the relationship between IHL and HRsL is not the same question as the scope of the extraterritorial applicability of HRsL. The reason for possible confusion, at least at the European level, is that many European states have only had experience of the IHL/HRsL question in the context of extraterritorial military operations, most notably in Iraq and Afghanistan.

The final preliminary point is the distinction between the fact of the conflict and the applicability of IHL. Under 'ordinary' HRsL, it is possible for bodies monitoring to take

---

110 In *Finogenov & others v Russia* (Moscow Theatre Siege) 18299/93 & 27311/03, judgment of 20 December 2011, the Court stated, 'As a rule, any use of lethal force must be no more than 'absolutely necessary' for the achievement of one or more of the purposes set out in paragraph 2 (a), (b) and (c) of Article 2 of the Convention . . . That being said, the Court may occasionally depart from that rigorous standard of "absolute necessity" . . . It is prepared to grant them a margin of appreciation, at least in so far as the military and technical aspects of the situation are concerned, even if now, with hindsight, some of the decisions taken by the authorities may appear open to doubt. In contrast, the subsequent phases of the operation may require a closer scrutiny by the Court; this is especially true in respect of such phases where no serious time constraints existed and the authorities were in control of the situation'; paras 210–14

111 38263/08, Decision of 19 December 2011.

account of the fact of conflict without the need to derogate or to consider the applicability of IHL. Many rights contain a limitation clause. The relevant interest (e.g. the right to demonstrate) is protected but may be subject to such limitations as are necessary in a democratic society for the attainment of specifically identified goals, on condition that the restriction is proportionate to the aim being pursued. The more troubled the backdrop, the more likely it is that the state will be able to justify a restriction on the exercise of the right. A similar result may be achieved in the case of certain rights which do not contain a limitation clause. So for example, the due process clauses in human rights treaties require the proceedings as a whole to be fair. Whilst there is likely to be a bottom line, fairness may be affected by the prevailing situation. Only a limited number of rights are inflexible. That is not coterminous with being non-derogable. The prohibition of arbitrary killing is non-derogable but what is arbitrary may be different in situations of armed conflict and peacetime.[112]

The next issue is to identify the goal being pursued. For any state that believes that HRsL may be applicable to some extent during armed conflict and which therefore believes that there is currently a problem in knowing when IHL may also be relevant, clarity and forseeability may be goals.[113] A second goal may be the operationalisation of the *lex specialis* principle. If this implies the integration, in some sense, of the two sets of rules, it is necessary to determine when and how they are to be integrated. It is also necessary to know what is being integrated. Is it just the treaty rules in each field or is it the totality of the rules, including customary law and the case-law of human rights bodies? This may appear to be an innocuous question but it will make a very real difference in practice to the problem of integration. Geneva Law as a whole and Hague Law prohibitions should not pose too many difficulties. The real problem are those rules which permit action to be taken which is usually unlawful. They may be termed Hague permissive rules. An example would be targeting by reference to status, rather than behaviour. In non-international armed conflicts, the majority of such rules are customary in character.

Assuming that there is agreement that some form of integration is to be sought, when would it apply? How much of each body of rules would be integrated; would it be all or nothing? Finally, in what manner would the rules be integrated?

Some commentators have concentrated on when reference should be made to IHL. It has been suggested that IHL should not be used at all in low intensity NIACs.[114] Reliance should be placed exclusively on HRsL. Whilst it is undoubtedly the case that human rights bodies have been applying HRsL alone for decades in situations in which there is a strong argument that common Article 3 was applicable, it would appear inappropriate to take the same approach when the non-state fighters mount sustained and concerted military operations.[115] Such situations would include the Spanish Civil War and, arguably the situation in Syria at the time of

---

112 The International Covenant on Civil and Political Rights and the American Convention on Human Rights prohibit arbitrary killings. Art. 2 of the European Convention, by contrast, lists exhaustively the only grounds on which there may be resort to potentially lethal force, unless the derogation clause has been invoked. On the face of it, this makes Art. 2 inflexible but see n. 103 above.

113 For those states which think that the applicability of IHL has the effect of 'turning off' the applicability of HRsL, there is no relationship about which it might be desirable to have clarity and foreseeability.

114 I.e. within common Art. 3 of the Geneva Conventions but not within Additional Protocol II of 1977.

115 Kretzmer (n. 8) at 201–204.

writing. Another suggestion has been that it depends on the proximity to the fighting.[116] This can change in an instant. In the example given above of a demonstration, assuming that the overall situation was one in which IHL was applicable, if there was in fact no shot, only HRsL would be applicable. On the other hand, if a shot was fired, the demonstration would have become proximate to the fighting. Not only would such an analysis require constantly changing patterns of applicability but those patterns would often depend on the actions of the non-state actors. It may be relatively easy to decide whether a planned operation by the security forces is directly related to hostilities. It will be more difficult to determine when it is a matter of responding to a constantly changing situation. The author's preference would be to allow some relevance to Geneva Law and Hague Law prohibitions whenever IHL is applicable but only to allow some effect to Hague Law permissive rules in a non-international armed conflict where the non-state fighters are able to mount sustained and concerted operations against the state's security forces. This will require them to have a chain of command, which will permit the delivery and enforcement of instructions. It will also generally, but not inevitably, involve control of territory.

Even if there is agreement as to the relevance of IHL, to what extent and in what manner is it to be used? It has been suggested that IHL should be used where it provides greater specificity.[117] Whilst this is superficially attractive, it neglects a range of issues. First, it hardly represents a principled basis for the use of IHL. Second, if IHL is used to clarify HRsL, it appears to suggest that HRsL and not IHL is the *lex specialis*. Third, it raises the question of 'greater specificity than what'; human rights treaty law and treaty provisions enriched by the wealth of case-law? IHL will not often be more specific than that. The most obvious areas where IHL may be more specific than HRsL are the detention regime of prisoners of war and the protection of the wounded and sick, including medical personnel and medical facilities. Another suggestion has been to pick whichever is the more specific rule.[118] IHL requires review of administrative detention but contains limited information as to the characteristics of the body carrying out the review. HRsL, on the other hand, requires review by a court and there is a significant body of case-law on the characteristics of a court.[119] It is submitted that such to-ing and fro-ing between different regimes is completely unworkable in practice. It would be constantly changing, depending on the evolution of the case law. A possible solution for some issues, not all, would be for states to use the provisions applicable in IACs as a model. In the case of detention, for example, Geneva Convention IV would appear to offer a possible model for detention in NIACs outside national territory. HRsL could then be used to identify the issue which would need to be addressed (e.g. access to information regarding the reasons for detention; access to legal advice; access to family members and friends; access to medical assistance in case of need; periodicity of review etc.) but the solution adopted would not necessarily be the peacetime human rights solution. So, for example, if limited information can be provided regarding the reasons for detention, owing to the risk of compromising sources, it should at least be possible to require the review body to consider, two weeks before periodic review of detention, whether more information can be released than previously. As is clear, there is no consensus as to how to achieve integration.

116 A possible implication of *Finogenov & others v Russia* (n. 110).
117 See text accompanying n. 92 above.
118 Droege (n. 8).
119 E.g. see *De Wilde, Ooms and Versyp v Belgium*, 2832/66, 2835/66, 2899/66, judgment of 18 June 1971; *X v UK*, A 46 (1981); 4 EHRR 188.

Neither is there agreement as to the procedure to be adopted to move forward. The Danish government embarked on a consultation exercise with states over a period of five years to address just the issue of detention.[120] The Copenhagen Process: Principles and Guidelines leave many questions unanswered (e.g. transfer of a detainee to either the host state authorities or the authorities of other states, inside or outside the territory in question). Non-governmental organisations have been critical of the result. It is not clear to what extent this is due to their having been excluded from the process. Sir Daniel Bethlehem, former legal adviser to the British Foreign and Commonwealth Office, is heading up an initiative to encourage states to make a declaration that they will apply the IHL rules applicable in international armed conflict even in non-international conflicts. It is not clear how this would affect the relationship between IHL and HRsL. Another suggestion has been for a small group of experts to produce a series of leaflets on all relevant issues. They would be drafted with the specificity of the UN Standard Minimum Rules for the Treatment of Prisoners.[121] They would offer a menu. In other words, if there is only a limited amount of disturbance, package A is expected regarding the issue. If the level of violence is more marked, then the state can use packages B or C. If IHL is applicable but the operations are not sustained and concerted, package D would be applicable and so on. The idea would be to guide human rights bodies, and others. These bodies would determine the level of disruption and how that impacts on the relevant aspect of the right in question. They would then get an idea of what it is reasonable to expect. It would be important that the leaflets should not be formally adopted by anybody. They would be a possible soft law guide. If they proved useful, over time they would provide foreseeability for states. That would clarify the situation for armed forces and other personnel in the theatre.

There is no limit to the number of possible proposals with regard to the way in which IHL and HRsL are to be integrated and the process or procedure whereby that is to be achieved. On condition that a proposal is capable of being applied in practice by all relevant actors, it should receive a fair hearing. Whilst these issues may not be research questions in the traditional sense, they represent an area where detailed and considered work is urgently needed. Armed forces need both front line troops and many other specialists further back who make it possible for the front line forces to function. Operationalising the integration of IHL and HRsL may be the front line but this chapter has shown that there are plenty of other questions which need further work in order to reduce some of the difficulties caused by the horizontal collision of IHL and HRsL. Any examination of these questions needs to be undertaken by experts in IHL and HRsL working together. Human rights lawyers should not claim an expertise in IHL unless they are genuinely regarded as 'bi-lingual' by both constituencies. It is possible that the failure to involve specialists in IHL, and more particularly military lawyers, in recent discussions is responsible for some of the problems, chaos and occasionally deadlock being experienced by those who have to address the relationship between IHL and HRsL.

---

120 The process was known as the Copenhagen Process. Its outcome, 'The Copenhagen Process: Principles and Guidelines', can be found at http://um.dk/da/~/media/UM/Danish-site/Documents/Politik-og-diplomati/Nyheder_udenrigspolitik/2012/Copenhangen%20Process%20Principles%20and%20Guidelines.pdf.
121 UN doc. A/RES/45/100 (14 December 1990).

Select bibliography

R. Arnold and N. Quénivet, *International Humanitarian Law And Human Rights Law: Towards A New Merger In International Law* (Leiden, Martinus Nijhoff, 2008).

O. Ben-Naftali (ed.), *International Humanitarian Law and International Human Rights Law: Pas De Deux* (OUP, 2011).

A. Cassimatis, 'International Humanitarian Law, International Human Rights Law, and the Fragmentation of International Law', (2007) 56 *International and Comparative Quarterly* 623.

D. Kretzmer 'Targeted Killing of Suspected Terrorists: Extra-Judicial Executions or Legitimate Means of Defence', (2005) 16 (2) *European Journal of International Law* 171.

N. Prud'homme, '*Lex Specialis*: Oversimplifying a More Complex and Multifaceted Relationship?', (2007) 40 *Israel Law Review* 355.

C. McLachlan, 'The Principle of Systemic Integration and Article 31(3)(c) of the Vienna Convention', (2005) 54 *International and Comparative Quarterly* 279.

13

International criminal law and tribunals and human rights

William Schabas

In the space of a little more than 24 hours, during the second week of December 1948, the United Nations General Assembly adopted two fundamental legal instruments: the Convention on the Prevention and Punishment of the Crime of Genocide[1] and the Universal Declaration of Human Rights.[2] Both were proclaimed without a negative vote, although there were eight abstainers on 10 December when the Universal Declaration was adopted. At that time, René Cassin spoke of the Genocide Convention as a specific application of the Universal Declaration of Human Rights.[3] Much later, Alain Pellet described the Genocide Convention to the International Law Commission as 'a quintessential human rights treaty'.[4] On the website of the United Nations Treaty Collection, the Genocide Convention appears under the rubric of 'human rights' where, as the first such instrument chronologically, it is at the top of the list.[5]

The two texts seem closely related, although the negotiations of each took place more or less in parallel and in relative isolation from the other. Occasionally, diplomats in the General Assembly's Third (Human Rights) Committee, where the Universal Declaration was being hammered out, remarked on the drafting of the Genocide Convention in the Sixth (Legal) Committee.[6] Meanwhile, those who negotiated the Genocide Convention thought that attacks upon minority groups falling short of outright physical extermination were better

---

1 Convention on the Prevention and Punishment of the Crime of Genocide (adopted 9 December 1948, entered into force 12 January 1951) (1951) 78 UNTS 277.
2 Universal Declaration of Human Rights (adopted 10 December 1948) UNGA Res. 217A(III).
3 UNCHR, Summary Record of the Three Hundred and Tenth Meeting UN Doc E/CN.4/SR.310, p. 5; UNCHR, Summary Record of the Three Hundred and Eleventh Meeting (27 May 1952) UN Doc E/CN.4/SR.311, at 5.
4 International Law Commission (ILC), 'Report of the International Law Commission on the work of its forty-ninth session' (12 May–18 July 1997) UN Doc A/52/10, para. 76. See also: *Prosecutor v Kayishema and Ruzindana* (Judgment) ICTR-95–1-T (21 May 1999), para. 88.
5 United Nations Treaty Collection, *Chapter IV: Human Rights*, available at: http://treaties.un.org/pages/Treaties.aspx?id=4&subid=A&lang=en., accessed on 25 August 2012.
6 UNGA Official Records of the General Assembly, Third Session (1948), pp. 102, 244, 419, 584, 854, 890, 912.

addressed within the framework of the Declaration, where a broad provision upon minority rights was being considered. In the end, the Third Committee dropped the minority rights text, leaving a gap in the international legal framework of the United Nations that to some extent has never been properly filled.[7]

Both Committees wrestled with the legacy of the Nuremberg trial. The negotiators of the Genocide Convention were conscious of the danger that the definition would be too closely linked to the crimes against humanity formulation applied at the International Military Tribunal because this might then exclude international criminal liability for atrocities perpetrated in times of peace. Those working on the Universal Declaration contended with the general principle of non-retroactivity of criminal law. Too rigid a formulation might suggest disapproval of the Nuremberg proceedings.

Not everyone welcomed the potent synergy of the Universal Declaration and the Genocide Convention. Raphael Lemkin, who had invented the term 'genocide' in 1944 and campaigned ardently for its codification, viewed the Universal Declaration as a dangerous distraction from what he considered to be the main task. Lemkin apparently also resented news coverage of the UN General Assembly referring to 'two UN achievements' that year.[8] Hersch Lauterpacht dismissed the Universal Declaration as a relatively worthless exercise of no legal consequence. Lauterpacht was intensely disappointed that the General Assembly had failed to agree upon a full-blown human rights treaty that might then provide a real parallel to the corresponding Genocide Convention.[9]

Much later, Benjamin Whitaker, who was Special Rapporteur of the UN Sub-Commission on the Prevention of Discrimination and the Protection of Minorities, said genocide was 'the ultimate human rights problem'.[10] Each of the two instruments was seminal in its own field. The Universal Declaration of Human Rights is the foundation of all modern human rights treaties and to this day provides the core legal framework for mechanisms such as the Universal Periodic Review, undertaken by the United Nations Human Rights Council since 2008.[11] The Genocide Convention also influenced the drafting of future international criminal law treaties. Perhaps more importantly, its acknowledgement of the international criminal court project in Article 6 ultimately bore fruit, a half-century later, in the successful negotiation of the Rome Statute of the International Criminal Court.

The two disciplines, human rights and international criminal law, are obviously associated in many ways besides their common ancestry, something which was certainly more than a mere coincidence. A simplistic attempt at distinguishing them might focus on the fact that international human rights law is addressed to the obligations of a state towards those subject to its jurisdiction whereas international criminal law targets individual perpetrators. Yet while human rights treaties are confined to the obligations of states, human rights law speaks to corporations and individuals as well. Article 29(1) of the Universal Declaration recalls that '[e]veryone has duties to the community in which alone the free and full development of his personality is possible', underscoring the observation that the duty-bearers of human rights

7 W. Schabas, 'Les droits des minorités: Une déclaration inachevée', in *Déclaration universelle des droits de l'homme 1948–98, Avenir d'un idéal commun* (La Documentation française, 1999), at 223–42.

8 S. Power, *A Problem from Hell: America and the Age of Genocide* (Basic Books, 2000) 333.

9 H. Lauterpacht, 'The Universal Declaration of Human Rights' (1948) 25 British Ybk Intl L 354–81.

10 UNCHR (Sub-Commission) (1984) UN Doc. E/CN.4/Sub.2/1984/SR.3, para. 6.

11 UNHRC, 'Institution-building of the United Nations Human Rights Council' (18 June 2007) A/HRC/RES/5/1, 5/1, Annex, I.A.1(b).

are not states alone.[12] As for international crimes, they are 'committed by men, not by abstract entities, and only by punishing individuals who commit such crimes can the provisions of international law be enforced', as the Nuremberg judgment famously declared.[13] Not that the state is entirely absent, because it is inconceivable that genocide could take place without its involvement.[14] The Elements of Crimes of the International Criminal Court state that genocide must be committed 'in the context of a manifest pattern of similar conduct directed against that group or was conduct that could itself effect such destruction',[15] implying if not explicitly requiring that criminal conduct be pursuant to a plan or policy of a state. In other words, although international human rights law seems directed mainly at the state, whereas international criminal law looks to the individual perpetrator, human rights law also applies to individuals and international criminal law requires some role for the state.

Because they were both generated within the framework of the UN law-making process and couched under the normative umbrella of the Charter of the United Nations, a comfortable relationship between the Universal Declaration and the Genocide Convention may be presumed. They were adopted by the same legislator, of identical composition, within hours of each other, and with essentially the same unanimity. No similar remark can be made of another cognate, international humanitarian law, whose place within the United Nations system was actually disputed by members of the International Law Commission at its first sessions.[16]

Several international treaties might be described as belonging both to human rights and international criminal law. A number of major United Nations conventions that arguably belong under the rubric of international criminal law, because they impose obligations to prosecute with respect to apartheid, torture and enforced disappearances, all reference the relevant provisions of the Universal Declaration in their preambles.[17] The Rome Statute of the International Criminal Court, on the other hand, rather studiously avoids too close an association with international human rights law. Its preamble cites the Charter of the United Nations but not the Universal Declaration of Human Rights.

1 Impunity and the obligation to prosecute

In the decades that followed 1948, the human rights systems and international criminal law evolved in parallel, with some notable exceptions such as the International Convention on the

---

12 See, for example, Security Council Resolution 310 (1972) calling upon all states with nationals and corporations operating in Namibia to use all available means to ensure that such nationals and corporations conform, in their policies of hiring Namibian workers, to the basic provisions of the Universal Declaration of Human Rights. On the subject generally, see Andrew Clapham, *Human Rights in the Private Sphere* (Clarendon Press, 1996).

13 *France et al. v Goering et al.* (1946) 22 IMT 411, 466.

14 *Prosecutor v Kayishema and Ruzindana* (Judgment) ICTR-95-1-T (21 May 1999), para. 94.

15 International Criminal Court, 'Elements of Crimes,' *Official Records of the Assembly of States Parties to the Rome Statute of the International Criminal Court, First Session, New York, 3–10 September 2002* (United Nations publication, Sales No. E.03.V.2 and corrigendum), part II.B.

16 Yearbook of the ILC, 'Report to the General Assembly on the Work of the First Session' (12 April–9 June 1949), 51–53; UN Doc. A/CN.4/13, para. 18.

17 International Convention on the Suppression and Punishment of the Crime of Apartheid (adopted 30 November 1973, entered into force 18 July 1976) [1015 UNTS 243, preambular para (PP)] 2; Convention against Torture and Other Cruel, Inhuman or Degrading Treatment or Punishment (adopted 10 December 1984, entered into force 26 June 1987) 1465 UNTS 85, PP 4; International Convention for the Protection of All Persons from Enforced Disappearance (adopted 20 December 2006, entered into force 23 December 2010) UN Doc. A/61/488, PP 2.

Suppression and Punishment of the Crime of Apartheid adopted in 1973. The Convention tackled the quintessential human rights challenge of the time with a package of obligations involving individual criminal responsibility and a duty upon states to prosecute offenders. The General Assembly's Declaration on the Protection of All Persons from Being Subjected to Torture and Other Cruel, Inhuman or Degrading Treatment or Punishment, adopted in 1975, combined classic human rights obligations to prevent torture with a duty to 'ensure that all acts of torture as defined in Article 1 are offences under its criminal law'.[18]

This was not an easy link to make for many in the human rights movement who had traditionally viewed the criminal justice system with diffidence and suspicion. The focus was on violations of the right to a fair trial and on abuses of detention regimes. Success was marked by acquittals, successful appeals and release from prison. It was hardly accidental that one of the first great human rights non–governmental organisations, Amnesty International, chose to identify itself with 'amnesty', something that today seems inconceivable. Certainly the link between criminal justice and the protection of human rights had always been implicit. For example, it was trite to affirm that the right to life was protected by the criminalisation of murder. But it took a number of decades for the human rights movement to see criminal law as a tool for the protection of vulnerable groups and individuals and not just as an instrument used by repressive regimes.

This development became more pronounced in the 1980s when experts in bodies like the UN Sub-Commission for the Prevention of Discrimination and the Protection of Minorities began to use terms like 'impunity' and 'accountability', and to focus on justice for victims of human rights violations.[19] International human rights tribunals made innovative pronouncements about the rights of victims to have crimes investigated and prosecuted.[20] Meanwhile, the UN International Law Commission, which was struggling to complete the Code of Crimes Against the Peace and Security of Mankind, on which it had begun work some 40 years earlier, decided to abandon entirely the notion of crimes against humanity in favour of '[s]ystematic or mass violations of human rights'.[21] These developments were also reflected in the adoption, by international human rights organisations, of international criminal justice as an important area of activity. In 1998, Amnesty International played an instrumental role in attempts to prosecute former Chilean dictator Augusto Pinochet. Human rights is a broad church, of course, and there are many who, while they accept the importance of accountability, prefer softer alternatives to criminal justice, such as truth and reconciliation commissions and similar mechanisms.

The normative justification for the engagement of international human rights law with international criminal justice and its institutions appears to be largely rooted in the entitlement of victims to justice and accountability. However, international criminal law is not concerned with all victims of violent crime. Its remit, as defined by treaty and customary international law, is almost entirely confined to widespread and systematic violations perpetrated in association with a state or state-like entity. Sovereign states would surely resist any

---

18 UNGA Res. 3452 (XXX) (9 December 1975), Art. 7.
19 'Preliminary report submitted by Theo van Boven, Special Rapporteur, Study concerning the right to restitution, compensation and rehabilitation for victims of gross violations of human rights and fundamental freedoms' ('Preliminary report') (26 July 1990) UN Doc. E/CN.4/Sub.2/1990/10.
20 *Velasquez Rodriguez v Honduras*, Judgment, Inter-American Court of Human Rights Series C, No. 4 (29 July 1988,).
21 ILC, 'Report of the International Law Commission on the work of its forty-third session' (29 April–19 July 1991) UN Doc. A/46/10, at 96.

attempt to expand the internationalisation of criminal justice so as to encompass all forms of violent crime. Yet from the standpoint of the victim of a violation of fundamental rights, can there be a reasonable distinction resulting from the context of a crime so that a woman who is raped finds an entitlement to international criminal justice only if the violence can be described as part of a larger attack amounting to crimes against humanity?

In recent years, international human rights law has taken the view that there is indeed a duty upon states to see that all serious crimes against the person are investigated and prosecuted.[22] In other words, from the standpoint of international human rights law and the entitlement of victims it does not appear to make much of a difference whether the violence results from an organised state-led attack, or is the result of an isolated, opportunistic social deviant. Nevertheless, the obligation upon states imposed by human rights law to investigate and prosecute serious crimes appears to be confined to acts perpetrated within their jurisdiction unless the acts are associated with the contextual elements of international crimes and are therefore subject to universal jurisdiction. This inequality of treatment is not a simple thing to explain to victims. Taken from the standpoint of international human rights law alone, it is an incoherent result. Such incoherence is perhaps the inevitable consequence of uneven evolution within the two fields – human rights and international criminal law.

Confusion creeps in because of a tendency to blur the applicable principles. For example, the argument developed within international human rights law by which amnesty for serious crimes is deemed unacceptable, relies upon the recognition of the rights of victims to justice.[23] Yet it is also said that prohibition of amnesty is confined to international crimes or so-called *jus cogens* violations. But why, if victims of human rights violations are entitled to justice, should it make any difference whether the crime meets the international definition? If amnesty is prohibited for *jus cogens* crimes, such as genocide, crimes against humanity and war crimes, why is it not also ruled out for murder and rape? This is where the complementarity and even synergy between human rights and international criminal law appears to stumble.

2 The subject-matter of international crimes and their relationship to human rights norms

Many crimes fall within the ambit of international criminal law. Not all of them bear an obvious relation to the protection and promotion of human rights. A century ago, international law recognised obligations to punish and repress, and the possibility of the exercise of universal jurisdiction, to offences such as piracy, trafficking in pornography and counterfeit currency, and disrupting undersea telecommunications cables. Such crimes were designated 'international' because challenges to their repression required international cooperation and agreement on jurisdictional matters. These were not crimes about which it could be said that they 'shocked the conscience of humanity'.

With the end of the Second World War, a new generation of international crimes was recognised whose common denominator was contiguous with the protection of human

---

22 *MC v Bulgaria*, ECtHR, Application No. 39272/98, Judgment of 4 December 2003.
23 *Barrios Altos v Peru*, Judgment (Inter-American Court of Human Rights, 30 November 2001), paras 41–44; *Marguš v Croatia*, Application No. 4455/10, ECtHR, Judgment of 13 November 2012, para. 74.

rights. Raphael Lemkin recognised this in the draft resolution on genocide he prepared for the UN General Assembly in October 1946:

> *Whereas* the punishment of the very serious crime of genocide when committed in time of peace lies within the exclusive territorial jurisdiction of the judiciary of every state concerned, while crimes of a relatively lesser importance such as piracy, trade in women, children, drugs, obscene publications are declared as international crimes and have been made matters of international concern . . .[24]

In the past, crimes had been internationalised in order to facilitate arrest and prosecution of international outlaws, like pirates, who were the enemies of all states: *hostis humani generis*, as Grotius called them.[25] The newer international crimes were being internationalised precisely because they were committed by states or with their complicity. Perpetrators went unpunished not because they could hide on the high seas but because they were protected by states and were indeed the implements of ruthless policies directed against civilian populations.

By the end of the 1940s, three broad categories of international crime were recognised: genocide, as defined in Article 2 of the 1948 Genocide Convention; crimes against humanity, according to Article VI(c) of the Charter of the Nuremburg Tribunal; and war crimes, set out in Article VI(b) of the Charter as well as in the grave breach provisions of the 1949 Geneva Conventions. Later, with the continuous enrichment of international human rights norms, criminalisation was associated with other violations that became stand-alone categories of crimes against humanity, notably apartheid, torture and enforced disappearance. War crimes evolved away from battlefield offences involving combatants who had broken the rules of lawful killing towards a body of law targeted at the protection of civilians, in occupied territories for international armed conflict and within the territories of the concerned state for non-international armed conflict. With confirmation that war crimes could be perpetrated in non-international armed conflict, a consequence of the judicial law-making of the International Criminal Tribunal for the former Yugoslavia[26] and something later confirmed in Article 8 of the Rome Statute, war crimes became relatively indistinguishable from serious violations of human rights.

Some tension remains in the relationship between human rights and international criminal law with respect to the latter's subject matter.[27] At the Rome Conference, some delegations campaigned for the recognition of international drug trafficking, terrorism, and the crime of aggression as categories of offences that belonged within the jurisdiction of the International Criminal Court.[28] Drug trafficking clearly seems closer to the first generation of international

---

24 First draft resolution on genocide, GA Res. 96(I), UN Doc. A/BUR/50. The General Assembly decided to include the point in its agenda (UN Doc. A/181), and the matter was referred to the Sixth Committee (UN Doc. A/C.6/64).

25 *In re Piracy Jure Gentium, Special Reference* [1934] AC 586 (PC).

26 *Prosecutor v Tadi* (Decision on the Defence Motion for Interlocutory Appeal on Jurisdiction) IT-94-1-AR72 (2 October 1995).

27 See, e.g., *Situation in the Democratic Republic of the Congo* (Separate and partly dissenting opinion of Judge Georghios M. Pikis) ICC-01/04 (13 July 2006), para. 32

28 'Proposal Submitted by Barbados, Dominica, Jamaica, and Trinidad and Tobago on Article 5', UN Doc. A/CONF.183/C.1/L.48; 'Barbados, Dominica, India, Jamaica, Sri Lanka, Trinidad and Tobago and Turkey: proposal regarding Article 5 and the draft Final Act', UN Doc. A/CONF.183/C.1/L.71.

crime to which Lemkin referred in his draft 1946 General Assembly resolution. Terrorism is in more of a grey area, with lingering controversy about its place within the protection and promotion of human rights. Like most crimes, it has its innocent victims, and they may contend that fundamental rights have been breached. However, like pirates and those who tamper with undersea cables, terrorists are generally the enemies of humanity. A system of international treaties addressed to the repression of terrorist crimes has little to do with the protection of human rights. Indeed, the 'war on terror' is often more a source of violations of human rights than a means to their protection.[29]

Given a lack of consensus at the Rome Conference with respect to both terrorism and drug crimes, the matter of their inclusion in the Statute of the International Criminal Court was left to a subsequent Review Conference.[30] But little changed when these crimes returned to the agenda in preparation for the 2010 Kampala Review Conference, and it was decided not to address them. The central project of the Kampala Conference was the incorporation of provisions concerning the crime of aggression.

3 The crime of aggression, peace and human rights

In 1941, at the dawn of the modern human rights movement, Franklin D. Roosevelt spoke of the 'four freedoms'.[31] His succinct formulation is repeated in the preambles of the Universal Declaration of Human Rights and the two Covenants: 'freedom of speech and belief and freedom from fear and want'. But although freedom of speech, belief and want resonate through precise provisions of those instruments, the place of freedom from fear within human rights law has not been as clear. Roosevelt's message was that we have a right to live in a secure, peaceful environment. Article 28 of the Universal Declaration comes closest to recognising this: 'Everyone is entitled to a social and international order in which the rights and freedoms set forth in this Declaration can be fully realized.' When linked with the prohibition of aggressive war, there is a potent synergy between human rights and international criminal law.

Even in international criminal law, the place of the crime of aggression has not always been as secure as that of the other categories of crimes where the human rights pedigree is more clearly evident. Thus, although crimes against peace were prosecuted at Nuremberg (described by the judges as 'the supreme international crime'),[32] they were remarkably absent when the UN Security Council established the ad hoc tribunals for the former Yugoslavia and Rwanda. At the 1998 Rome Conference, there was insufficient consensus on the subject, not so much a result of difficulties of definition as of reconciling exercise of the Court's jurisdiction over aggression with an alleged monopoly on the topic attributed to the Security Council by the Charter of the United Nations. The matter was postponed until the first Review Conference, which was held in 2010. A package of amendments was adopted by consensus that should enter into force in 2017.[33]

---

29 E.g. see Martin Scheinin's chapter on counter-terrorism and human rights in this volume.
30 P. Robinson, 'The Missing Crimes', in A. Cassese, P. Gaeta and J.R.W.D. Jones (eds), *The Rome Statute of the International Criminal Court: A Commentary* (OUP, 2002) 497–525.
31 William Schabas (ed.), *The Universal Declaration of Human Rights, The* travaux préparatoires, Vol. I (Cambridge University Press, 2013) lxxiii.
32 *France et al. v Goering et al.* (1948) 22 IMT 427.
33 ICC, The Crime of Aggression, RC/Res. 6 (11 June 2010).

The major international human rights NGOs, generally highly devoted to the creation and work of the International Criminal Court, were surprisingly indifferent to the issue of the crime of aggression. Amnesty International said it had not:

> taken a position on the definition of the crime of aggression because its mandate – to campaign for every person to enjoy all of the human rights (civil and political and economic, social and cultural rights) enshrined in the Universal Declaration of Human Rights and other international human rights standards – does not extend to the lawfulness of the use of force.[34]

Human Rights Watch took a more pragmatic, policy-oriented view:

> Human Rights Watch's institutional mandate includes a position of strict neutrality on issues of *jus ad bellum*, because we find it the best way to focus on the conduct of war, or *jus in bello*, and thereby to promote our primary goal of encouraging all parties to a conflict to respect international humanitarian law. Consistent with this approach, we take no position on the substance of a definition of the crime of aggression.[35]

In a footnote to its explanation, Human Rights Watch added: 'The only exceptions that Human Rights Watch has made to this policy is to call for military intervention where massive loss of human life, on the order of genocide, can be halted through no other means, as was the case in Bosnia and Rwanda in the 1990s.'[36]

The footnote in the Human Rights Watch statement may provide a useful clue to understanding some of the reticence in this area. A militaristic tendency has crept into human rights discourse in recent years, encouraged by talk of 'humanitarian intervention' and the 'responsibility to protect'. Of course, human rights law has never been pacifistic, in the sense of a principled and intransigent opposition to the use of force under all circumstances. The preamble of the Universal Declaration says that human rights must be protected by the rule of law so that 'man is not to be compelled to have recourse, as a last resort, to rebellion against tyranny and oppression'. But there has been a growing willingness to contemplate military interventions as the ultimate solution to serious human rights violations. In these discussions, it seems that an appeal to US military intervention (or, often, an *ex post facto* rationalisation), albeit framed in reluctant language, is rarely very distant.

Another influence may be the debates about the relationship between peace and justice in the context of prosecutorial strategy at the International Criminal Court. In situations where there is an arguable case that peace negotiations may be jeopardised by prosecution, such as northern Uganda and even Darfur, there has been political pressure on the International Criminal Court from bodies like the African Union to back off in respect for the interests of promoting peace. Encouraged by human rights NGOs, the Prosecutor of the Court has taken the view that the quest for peace should not condition his decisions about selection of situations and cases. In a policy paper issued in September 2007, the Prosecutor cited paragraph 3 of the preamble to the Rome Statute ('Recognizing that such grave crimes threaten the

---

34 Amnesty International, 'International Criminal Court: Concerns at the seventh session of the Assembly of States Parties' (2008) Index: IOR 40/022/2008, at 22.
35 Human Rights Watch, 'Memorandum for the Sixth Session of the International Criminal Court Assembly of States Parties' (2007), at 13.
36 Ibid.

peace, security and well-being of the world'), noting that '[t]he ICC was created on the premise that justice is an essential component of a stable peace'.[37] He wrote that 'there is a difference between the concepts of the interests of justice and the interests of peace and that the latter falls within the mandate of institutions other than the Office of the Prosecutor'. Furthermore, 'the broader matter of international peace and security is not the responsibility of the Prosecutor; it falls within the mandate of other institutions.'[38]

Yet there is also much to be said for the view that the rationale of the International Criminal Court is to promote peace, just as it was for the ad hoc tribunals. The latter were, after all, created by the UN Security Council in pursuit of its mandate to promote international peace and security, with Chapter VII of the Charter invoked in support. According to the first annual report of the International Criminal Tribunal for the former Yugoslavia: '[I]t would be wrong to assume that the Tribunal is based on the old maxim *fiat justitia et pereat mundus* (let justice be done, even if the world were to perish). The Tribunal is, rather, based on the maxim propounded by Hegel in 1821: *fiat justitia ne pereat mundus* (let justice be done lest the world should perish). Indeed, the judicial process aims at averting the exacerbation and aggravation of conflict and tension, thereby contributing, albeit gradually, to a lasting peace.'[39] These words suggest that the pursuit of peace lies at the heart of international justice.

The danger is that the crime of aggression directs human rights and international criminal law in different directions, as it appeared to do at the Kampala Conference, which can be averted through greater attention to the underdeveloped role of peace within human rights discourse. It is certainly unfortunate that the Universal Declaration does not affirm a right to peace expressly. Perhaps that is because the drafters viewed human rights and the quest for peace as being inextricably linked, but considered peace to be a condition for the attainment of human rights rather than a right requiring precise enumeration and definition. The initial 48-article draft of the Declaration prepared by John Humphrey of the UN Secretariat began by noting that the preamble would refer to the four freedoms and was to start by stating the principle that 'that there can be no peace unless human rights and freedoms are respected'.[40]

The first sentence of the preamble to the Universal Declaration reads: 'Whereas recognition of the inherent dignity and of the equal and inalienable rights of all members of the human family is the foundation of freedom, justice and peace in the world . . .'. The immortal four freedoms of Franklin D. Roosevelt, which include 'freedom from fear', are cited, as Humphrey initially planned. The preamble also says that 'it is essential to promote the development of friendly relations between nations'. Article 26 declares that education is to 'further the activities of the United Nations for the maintenance of peace'.

There is also a structural argument. The Universal Declaration of Human Rights is an emanation of the Charter of the United Nations. Originally, the Charter was to have included a 'bill of rights'. That would have left no doubt about the link between peace and human rights. To the disappointment of many states, delegates to the San Francisco Conference

---

37 ICC, Office of the Prosecutor, *Policy Paper on the Interests of Justice*, available at: http://www.icc-cpi. int/nr/rdonlyres/772c95c9-f54d-4321-bf09-73422bb23528/143640/iccotpinterestsofjustice.pdf, accessed 26 August 2012.
38 Ibid.
39 First Annual Report of the International Criminal Tribunal for the former Yugoslavia (1994) UN Doc. A/49/342-S/1994/1007, annex, para. 18.
40 Draft Outline of International Bill of Rights, Commission on Human Rights Drafting Committee (1947) UN Doc. E/CN.4/AC.1/3, p. 2.

could not agree on how to incorporate a catalogue of fundamental rights in the Charter itself. They settled on general references to human rights in several provisions of the Charter, notably Articles 1 and 55, as well as the preamble, leaving the work of codification to the Commission on Human Rights in accordance with Article 68. That mandate was fulfilled on 10 December 1948 with the adoption of the Universal Declaration of Human Rights. To contend that the Universal Declaration is somehow neutral on the issue of aggressive war is to dissociate that document from the context of its adoption and its place within the post-Second World War legal order, which is founded on the prohibition of recourse to force to settle international disputes.

There is much support for the concept of a 'peoples' right to peace'. For example, this is recognised by the African Charter of Human and Peoples' Rights, adopted in 1981 ('All peoples shall have the right to national and international peace and security'). In 1984 the UN General Assembly adopted a resolution entitled 'The Peoples' Right to Peace'. The text proclaimed that 'the peoples of our planet have a sacred right to peace' and that 'the preservation of the right of peoples to peace and the promotion of its implementation constitute a fundamental obligation of each state'.[41] There was a series of resolutions in the Commission on Human Rights[42] and in the General Assembly[43] and the matter has been taken up again within the Human Rights Council.[44] The word 'peoples' has been dropped and it has become, simply, the 'right to peace' for which a UN declaration is currently being prepared.[45] There is a North–South divide on this issue, with Western states decidedly unfriendly to such initiatives, perhaps because they see this as an encroachment upon the prerogatives of the Security Council. The right to peace provides a unifying principle that assists in uniting human rights and international criminal law, as well as the other cognate, international humanitarian law. The right to peace has strong potential to assist in putting other rights into perspective.

4 *Nullum crimen sine lege*

The most direct bridge between international human rights instruments and international criminal law relates to the issue of retroactive criminal prosecution. Article 15(2) of the International Covenant on Civil and Political Rights (there is a similar provision in the European Convention on Human Rights) provides:

> Nothing in this article shall prejudice the trial and punishment of any person for any act or omission which, at the time when it was committed, was criminal according to the general principles of law recognized by the community of nations.

---

41 Declaration on the Right of People to Peace, GA Res. 39/11 (12 November 1984), annex, paras 1–2.
42 Promotion of the right of peoples to peace, Commission on Human Rights Res. 2002/71 (25 April 2002).
43 Promotion of peace as a vital requirement for the full enjoyment of all human rights by all, GA Res. 60/163 (2 March 2006).
44 Promotion on the right of peoples to peace, HRC Res. 8/9 (18 June 2008); Promotion of the right of peoples to peace, HRC Res. 14/3 (23 June 2010); Promotion of the right of peoples to peace, AHRC Res. 17/16 (15 July 2011).
45 Draft Declaration on the Right to Peace, HRC Res. 20/L.15, para. 1.

The purpose was to ensure that the general prohibition of retroactive criminality did not cast any aspersions on the Nuremberg judgment and that of other post-Second World War prosecutions.[46] It seems that some members of the Commission on Human Rights were concerned that the text of Article 11(2) of the Universal Declaration of Human Rights was inadequate in this respect.[47]

Retroactivity is an issue that has obsessed international criminal justice since its earliest days. At the international criminal tribunals, this has been a source of unceasing controversy. With the adoption of the Rome Statute and the development of an international criminal justice regime whose application promises to be universal, the issue of retroactive punishment ought to be largely laid to rest. The principle of *nullum crimen* is set out in Article 23 of the Rome Statute, but this hardly seems necessary because the International Criminal Court can only exercise jurisdiction over crimes defined in its own texts on a prospective basis, that is, for crimes perpetrated after the Statute has entered into force. Indeed, in the initial cases before the Court, the issue has hardly arisen, in contrast with the experience at all of the earlier international criminal tribunals.

But arguments about retroactive prosecution persist at both the judicial and political levels. The development of international criminal law is accompanied by constant attempts to reassess the past. Although human longevity makes prosecution for many offences that occurred years ago increasingly unlikely, because the perpetrators continue to die off or become unfit to stand trial, many difficulties remain. In 2008 Spanish prosecutor Baltazar Garzón launched an investigation into the crime against humanity of enforced disappearance committed in the years immediately following the Spanish Civil War, raising questions as to whether international law applicable in the early 1940s recognised that crimes against humanity could be committed in peacetime. The same point has arisen recently with respect to trials concerning post-Second World War atrocities in the Baltic states, and the acts of the Khmer Rouge in Cambodia during the 1970s. An important decision of the Grand Chamber of the European Court of Human Rights, *Kononov v Latvia* of 17 May 2010, ruled favourably upon the legality of a trial held in the 1990s of a pro-Soviet partisan for the summary execution of Nazi sympathisers at the height of the Second World War.[48]

There is a lingering unease about retroactivity at the Nuremberg and Tokyo trials. According to the judgment of the International Military Tribunal, 'it is to be observed that the maxim *nullum crimen sine lege* is not a limitation of sovereignty, but is in general a principle of justice'.[49] The French version of the judgment is more qualified: '[n]ullum crimen sine lege ne

---

46 *Kononov v Latvia*, Application No. 36376/04, ECtHR, Judgment of 24 July 2008, para. 115(b), citing *X. v Belgium*, Application No. 268/57 [1960] *Yearbook* 241; *Touvier v France*, Application No. 29420/95 (1997) 88 DR 148; *Papon v France (No. 2)* (dec.), Application No. 54210/00, ECHR 2001-XII (extracts).

47 Kenneth S. Gallant, *The Principle of Legality in International and Comparative Criminal Law*, (Cambridge University Press, 2009) 178–88; David Weissbrodt, *The Right to a Fair Trial under the Universal Declaration of Human Rights and the International Covenant on Civil and Political Rights* (Martinus Nijhoff, 2001) 78–83.

48 *Kononov v Latvia*, Application No. 36376/04 [GC], ECtHR, Judgment of 17 May 2010; also see: *Korbely v Hungary*, Application No. 9174/02 [GC], ECtHR, Judgment of 19 September 2008; *Kolk and Kislyiy v Estonia*, Application No. 23052/04, ECtHR, Decision of 17 January 2006.

49 *France et al. v Goering et al.* (1948) 22 IMT 462.

limite pas la souveraineté des États; elle ne formule qu'une règle généralement suivie.' The judgment continues:

> To assert that it is unjust to punish those who have in defiance of treaties and assurances attacked neighbouring States without warning is obviously untrue, for in such circumstances the attacker must know that he is doing wrong, and so far from it being unjust to punish him, it would be unjust if his wrong were allowed to go unpunished . . . [The Nazi leaders] must have known that they were acting in defiance of all international law when in complete deliberation they carried out their designs of invasion and aggression.[50]

In other words, the Tribunal admitted that there was a whiff of retroactivity to prosecution for crimes against peace, but said leaving such wrongs unpunished would be unjust. The *nullum crimen* rule was thus a relative one, subject to exception in light of circumstances. With respect to war crimes, the Tribunal was able to point to some precedent supporting international prohibition of certain behaviour, including the Hague Convention of 1907.

In place of the rather flexible approach at Nuremberg, and perhaps somewhat in reaction to it, international human rights law proposes a seemingly intransigent prohibition of retroactive prosecution unless it can be shown that the crime existed under national or international law. The norm is deemed to be non-derogable and, for this reason, it has sometimes been classified among the *noyau dur* of human rights. Yet in practice, human rights tribunals have often manifested the same malleable approach to *nullum crimen* that was adopted by the International Military Tribunal and that was endorsed by the likes of Hans Kelsen, B.V.A. Röling, and Hersch Lauterpacht. They have tended to reject the militant positivism proposed by the Nuremberg defendants.

For example, the European Court of Human Rights has held that uncodified crimes may be prosecuted providing they are sufficiently foreseeable and accessible. This is not really all that different from the remarks of the war crimes tribunal, cited above: 'the accused knew or should have known that in matters of international concern he was guilty of participation in a nationally organized system of injustice and persecution shocking to the moral sense of mankind.' It is an approach that might seem to lean to a natural law approach, in its fealty to morality as a basis for human conduct.

Cases from the United Kingdom dealing not with international crimes but with the ordinary crime of spousal rape provide important authority here.[51] This concept had not traditionally been part of the common law, which defined the crime of rape as an act perpetrated by a man against a woman other than his wife. In the 1980s common law judges in England started to find defendants guilty of raping their wives. The convicted men petitioned the European Court of Human Rights, arguing that the law had been changed without them being properly informed. The Court dismissed the applications, saying the criminal prohibition of rape, even with respect to a spouse, was both foreseeable and accessible. The Court was persuaded in its opinion by the fact that the crime in question was offensive to 'human

---

50 Ibid.
51 *CR v United Kingdom*, ECtHR, Ser. A, No. 335-B, para. 41; *SW v United Kingdom*, ECtHR, Ser. A, No. 335-B, Judgment of 22 November 1995, para. 36.

dignity and human freedom'.[52] In other words, it might well have applied the non-retroactivity rule in a stricter fashion had the case concerned a more technical or administrative offence that did not engage core values.

The liberal approach to *nullum crimen* taken by the European Court of Human Rights appears to have influenced judges at the ad hoc international criminal tribunals. In one of the more detailed treatments of this issue, a Trial Chamber of the International Criminal Tribunal for the former Yugoslavia was asked to declare that the concept of superior responsibility as a mode of liability amounted to retroactive law. The Trial Chamber turned to the case law of the European Court of Human Rights, noting that Article 7 of the Convention 'allows for the "gradual clarification" of the rules of criminal liability through judicial interpretation'.[53] It said that it was 'not necessary that the elements of an offence are defined, but rather that general description of the prohibited conduct be provided',[54] citing in support several rulings of the European Court, including one of the spousal rape decisions, which it quoted *in extenso*. Subsequently, the Appeals Chamber of the Special Court for Sierra Leone relied upon this passage in its discussion of *nullum crimen* in the child soldiers case.[55]

A year after the *Hadžihasanović* jurisdictional motion, the Appeals Chamber of the International Criminal Tribunal for the former Yugoslavia invoked the words of the International Military Tribunal to the effect that *nullum crimen* was 'first and foremost a "principle of justice" '. Also citing the spousal rape cases of the European Court, the Appeals Chamber said:

> This fundamental principle [*nullum crimen*] 'does not prevent a court from interpreting and clarifying the elements of a particular crime'. Nor does it preclude the progressive development of the law by the court. But it does prevent a court from creating new law or from interpreting existing law beyond the reasonable limits of acceptable clarification. This Tribunal must therefore be satisfied that the crime or the form of liability with which an accused is charged was sufficiently foreseeable and that the law providing for such liability must be sufficiently accessible at the relevant time, taking into account the specificity of international law when making that assessment.[56]

The Appeals Chamber referred again to the European Court's position that the concepts of 'foreseeability' and 'accessibility' of a norm will greatly depend on 'the content of the instrument in issue, the field it is designed to cover and the number and status of those to whom it is addressed'. On the specificity of international criminal law, the Appeals Chamber returned to Nuremberg, and the the *Alstötter* case, explaining the difficulties of applying the *ex post facto* rule to such prosecutions.[57]

---

52 *CR v United Kingdom*, ECtHR, Ser. A, No. 335–B, para. 42.

53 *Prosecutor v Hadžihasanović et al.* (Decision on Joint Challenge to Jurisdiction) IT-01–47-PT (12 November 2002), para. 58.

54 Ibid.

55 *Prosecutor v Norman* (Decision on Preliminary Motion Based on Lack of Jurisdiction (child recruitment) SCSL-04-14-AR72(E) (31 May 2004), para. 25.

56 *Prosecutor v Milutinović et al.* (Decision on Dragoljub Ojdanić's Motion Challenging Jurisdiction – Joint Criminal Enterprise) IT-99-37-AR72 (21 May 2003), para. 38 (references omitted).

57 *Prosecutor v Milutinović et al.* (Decision on Dragoljub Ojdanić's Motion Challenging Jurisdiction – Joint Criminal Enterprise) IT-99-37-AR72 (21 May 2003), para. 39.

5 Rights of victims and reparations

One of the most concrete manifestations of the influence of human rights discourse on international criminal law is in the area of reparations for victims. As early as 1989, the UN Sub-Commission for the Prevention of Discrimination and the Protection of Minorities prepared a report on the 'restitution, compensation and rehabilitation for victims of gross violations of human rights'.[58] The language was taken up in Article 75(1) of the Rome Statute, which is entitled 'Reparations for victims':

> The Court shall establish principles relating to reparations to, or in respect of, victims, including restitution, compensation and rehabilitation. On this basis, in its decision the Court may, either upon request or on its own motion in exceptional circumstances, determine the scope and extent of any damage, loss and injury to, or in respect of, victims and will state the principles on which it is acting.

The Rome Statute envisages that orders of reparation be made against convicted persons. When the Statute was adopted, there was a widely held view that the Court would prosecute warlords and tyrants who had stashed unimaginable sums of money in Swiss bank accounts. But experience as the ad hoc tribunals has shown that virtually all defendants are sufficiently indigent as to qualify for legal aid. The Trial Chamber hearing the first case at the International Criminal Court considered that it was 'inappropriate to impose a fine in addition to the prison term, given the financial situation of Mr Lubanga. Despite extensive enquiries by the Court, no relevant funds have been identified.'[59]

Alternatively, reparations may be paid out of the Trust Fund for Victims, established pursuant to Article 79 of the Rome Statute. Located within the Part of the Statute dealing with penalties, it was conceived of in the Statute as a repository for 'money and other property collected through fines or forfeiture'. To date, it has received a small income in the form of voluntary contributions from states parties and a few individuals. The operating costs of the Fund are charged to the general budget of the Court. This makes it less easy to see that if the operating costs were subtracted from its income, the Fund would be bankrupt. There will probably be much acclaim when the Court makes its first orders of reparation to victims drawn from the Trust Fund. It is doubtful, however, if this is really the best (and most cost-effective) way to address the issue of reparation and compensation for victims. An important part of assessing the relationship between human rights and criminal law is appreciating the limits of both sectors.

6 Concluding comments

This short essay has not endeavoured to present a comprehensive overview of the relationship between international criminal law and human rights. Rather, it has proposed a discussion of some of the nodal points, where the two disciplines intersect and interact, not always without a degree of friction. Perhaps the most obvious relationship of all, which is the application of fair trial norms drawn from human rights law to the work of the international criminal

---

58 Preliminary report (n. 19).
59 *Prosecutor v Lubanga* (Decision on Sentence pursuant to Article 76 of the Statute) ICC-01/04-01/06 (10 July 2012), para. 106.

tribunals, has been eschewed. In one sense this is a huge topic, and its omission might be deemed an unpardonable gap in any discussion. In reality, the procedural fairness discussion sheds little light on the relationship between human rights and international criminal law. The principles and norms are broadly similar to those applicable to national justice systems, with slight distinctions. There are shocking violations of fair trial standards accepted at the domestic level in the cases before the international criminal tribunals. Probably the most notorious problem is the right to trial without unreasonable delay. The first trial at the International Criminal Court took more than six years from arrest to sentence.[60] At the International Criminal Tribunal for Rwanda, two accused men spent 12 years in detention before and during their trial before eventually being acquitted. The hearing concluded in December 2008 but the judgment was not issued until September 2011. The two innocent men remained in detention for 32 months while the judges drafted a verdict declaring them to be not guilty. In the final judgment, they dismissed arguments that fundamental rights had been violated, holding 'that a delay of 12 years from arrest to judgment does not, *per se,* constitute undue delay for the purposes of the Statute'.[61]

International criminal law and human rights both emerged from the crucible of the Second World War. Profound changes were underway in the world order as the hitherto impenetrable wall of sovereignty began to give way to certain fundamental human values. The two strands came together in December 1948 when the United Nations General Assembly adopted the Universal Declaration of Human Rights and the Convention on the Prevention and Punishment of the Crime of Genocide. Several decades of parallel and uneven development were to follow. The revival of international criminal justice in the 1990s was very much a consequence of progress within the human rights movement, by that time increasingly attentive to issues of victims, accountability and impunity.

A final observation of a more personal nature: there is an extraordinary cross-fertilisation of individual professionals who move back and forth across the divide between human rights and international criminal law. Many of the greatest judges at the international tribunals were distinguished veterans of human rights institutions, including Antonio Cassese, Theodor Meron, Fausto Pocar and Stefan Trechsel. Moving in the other direction, the last two UN High Commissioners for Human Rights came to the position from distinguished careers in international criminal justice: Louise Arbour had been Prosecutor at the ad hoc tribunals for the former Yugoslavia and Navi Pillay had been a judge at the International Criminal Court and the Rwanda Tribunal, where she served as President for a term. Perhaps nothing else better illustrates the close bonds between these two fields.

Select bibliography

H. Lauterpacht, 'The Universal Declaration of Human Rights' (1948) 25 *British Ybk Intl L* 354–81.

S. Power, *A Problem from Hell: America and the Age of Genocide* (Basic Books, 2000) 333.

W, Schabas (ed.), *The Universal Declaration of Human Rights, The* travaux préparatoires, Vol. I (Cambridge, Cambridge University Press, 2013).

---

60 Ibid.
61 *Prosecutor v Bizimungu et al.* (Judgment and Sentence) ICTR-99-50-T (30 September 2011), para. 74.

14

International refugee and human rights law: partners in ensuring international protection and asylum

*Cornelis (Kees) Wouters**

1 Introduction

International refugee law finds its roots in the atrocities of war and conflict,[1] in the recognition of human dignity,[2] and in the equality and inalienability of rights of all human beings.[3] International refugee law and international human rights are closely linked and are necessary partners in ensuring a strong framework of international protection, i.e. protection afforded in the absence of protection from one's own country. In human rights law, a wealth of standards and instruments has been developed accompanied by a variety of entities monitoring and/or supervising their interpretation and application at the national, regional and global level.[4] In the field of international refugee law, few explicit norms have emerged and instruments have developed with only one actor – the UN High Commissioner for Refugees (UNHCR) – being tasked in its Statute to supervise the application of international conventions.[5]

---

* The views expressed are the personal views of the author and may not necessarily be shared by the United Nations or by UNHCR. The author is grateful to Najla Akef for her assistance in writing this chapter and to Blanche Tax for her advice and feedback.

1 GA Res. 319 A (IV) (3 December 1949).

2 Charter of the United Nations (1948) 1 UNTS XVI, preamble, recital 2.

3 Universal Declaration of Human Rights, GA Res. 217 A (III) (10 December 1948) preamble, recital 1.

4 J. Fitzpatrick, 'Human Rights and Forced Displacement: Converging Standards', in A. Bayefsky and J. Fitzpatrick (eds), *Human Rights and Forced Displacement* (Martinus Nijhoff Publishers, 2000) 3.

5 UN General Assembly, *Statute of the Office of the United Nations High Commissioner for Refugees*, 14 December 1950, A/RES/428(V), para, 8(a), available at: http://www.unhcr.org/refworld/docid/3b00f0715c.html. UNHCR's Statute does not specify which conventions, but it includes the following conventions: the 1951 Convention Relating to the Status of Refugees, 189 UNTS 137, available at: http://www.refworld.org/docid/3be01b964.html; the 1967 Protocol Relating to the status of Refugees, 606 UNTS 267, available at: http://www.unhcr.org/refworld/ docid/3ae6b3ae4. html; and the 1969 OAU Convention governing specific aspects of refugee problems in Africa, 1001 UNTS 45, available at: http://www.unhcr.org/refworld/docid/3ae6b36018.html.

Since the end of the 1980s, there has been growing awareness that there are no impene-trable boundaries between human rights law, international humanitarian law, international criminal law and refugee law.[6] International human rights and refugee law have become complementary and mutually reinforcing legal regimes. There is no hierarchical relationship between these strands of international law; they are interconnected.[7] The interconnection between international human rights and refugee law is most visible in two areas: first, in the reasons why people seek protection, and second, in the enjoyment of such protection. Human rights violations in the context of armed conflict and other situations of violence or in the context of oppressive regimes are a major cause of people seeking refuge and protection in another country, and define the notion of persecution or other forms of harm. The failure or inability of a person's country of nationality or habitual residence to fulfil its responsibility to ensure the human rights of its inhabitants is a matter of international concern and responsi-bility. At the core of this responsibility lies the principle of non-refoulement, i.e. in general terms the prohibition of return, which was traditionally only part of international refugee law, but has been extensively developed under international human rights law. Second, inter-national human rights and refugee law jointly provide a framework for states to respond to situations in which people flee human rights violations elsewhere. This joint framework defines the entitlements people have while receiving international protection outside their country of origin and consequently dictates the corresponding state obligations.

This chapter examines the aforementioned ways in which international human rights and refugee law are interconnected and the challenges this connection is facing. The chapter first discusses the evolution of the interaction by reviewing how human rights law has and continues to have a significant influence on how persecution or other forms of harm are defined and how the principle of non-refoulement has largely been developed through human rights law rather than refugee law. The chapter then addresses the importance of human rights law in determining the entitlements refugees have; using and addressing the right to asylum as an overarching and justiciable right. Finally, this chapter addresses some of the contemporary challenges the interconnection between international human rights and inter-national refugee law is facing.

2 The cornerstone of international protection: the principle of non-refoulement and the protection from harm

2.1 The principle of non-refoulement

In 1950, UNHCR was established by the UN General Assembly to provide international protection to refugees and to seek permanent solutions for the problem of refugees by assisting governments.[8] The cornerstone of international protection was the principle

---

6 J. Sztucki, 'Who Is a Refugee? The Convention Definition: Universal or Obsolete?' in F. Nicholson and P. Twomey (eds), *Refugee Rights and Realities: Evolving International Concepts and Regimes* (CUP, 1999) 56.

7 UNHCR, 'Expert Meeting on Complementarities between International Refugee Law, International Criminal Law and International Human Rights Law: Summary Conclusions' (2011) available at: http://www.unhcr.org/refworld/docid/4e1729d52.html, accessed on 19 October 2012.

8 Statute of the Office of the United Nations High Commissioner for Refugees, GA Res. 428 (V) (14 December 1950) Annex, Art. 1.

of non-refoulement. People whose lives or freedom are at risk in their own country may seek protection elsewhere. States in turn have the responsibility to provide such people with protection in accordance with the principle of non-refoulement.

The principle of non-refoulement traditionally refers to the prohibition of refoulement codified in Article 33(1) of the 1951 Convention Relating to the Status of Refugees (1951 Refugee Convention).[9] In the context of refugee protection the principle is affirmed in Article II(3) of the OAU Convention Governing the Specific Aspects of Refugee Problems in Africa (OAU Refugee Convention)[10] and Conclusion 4 of the 1984 Cartagena Declaration on Refugees.[11] The OAU Refugee Convention was concluded under the auspices of the Organisation of African Unity but is still part of the architecture of today's African Union. The Cartagena Declaration was the result of a pragmatic and protection-motivated process, largely driven by academics and practitioners in response to the Central American refugee crises. Both regional refugee instruments were drafted inter alia to reflect regional realities, including foreign domination, internal armed conflict, mass human rights violations and large-scale and indiscriminate violence, and to move away from the 1951 Refugee Convention emphasis on individualised harm in the form of persecution and to protect people who flee in large numbers.[12] The principle of non-refoulement is limited to refugees, i.e. those who meet the definition of a refugee as formulated primarily in Article 1A(2) of the 1951 Refugee Convention and further extended in Article I(2) of the OAU Refugee Convention and Conclusion 3 of the 1984 Cartagena Declaration. The principle of non-refoulement has also been developed in international human rights law. In Article 3(1) of the 1984 Convention Against Torture and Other Cruel, Inhuman or Degrading Treatment or Punishment (Convention Against Torture),[13] an explicit prohibition of refoulement is formulated to protect any individual from being returned to a country where there is a risk of him or her being subjected to torture. Similarly, Article 16(1) of the 2006 International Convention for the Protection of Persons from Enforced Disappearance (Convention Against Enforced Disappearance)[14] explicitly prohibits the expulsion, return, surrender or extradition of any person to another state when he or she is at risk of enforced disappearance.

Regional human rights instruments also include the principle of non-refoulement, for example in Article 22(8) of the American Convention on Human Rights[15] and Article 19(2) of the Charter of Fundamental Rights of the European Union.[16] Furthermore, while the

9 Convention Relating to the Status of Refugees (1951) 189 UNTS 137. According to Art. 33(1) of the 1951 Refugee Convention, no state party 'shall expel or return ("*refouler*") a refugee in any manner whatsoever to the frontiers of territories where his life or freedom would be threatened on account of his race, religion, nationality, membership of a particular social group or political opinion.'

10 OAU Convention Governing the Specific Aspects of Refugee Problems in Africa (1969) 1001 UNTS 45.

11 Cartagena Declaration on Refugees (1984) OAS Doc. OEA/Ser.L/V/II.66/doc.10, rev. 1, 190–93.

12 Marina Sharpe, *The 1969 OAU Refugee Convention and the Protection of People Fleeing Armed Conflict and Other Situations of Violence in the Context of Individual Refugee Status Determination*, January 2013, available at: http://www.refworld.org/docid/50fd3edb2.html. On the Cartagena Declaration the author is grateful for input received from Dr Michael Reed-Hurtado.

13 Convention against Torture and Other Cruel, Inhuman or Degrading Treatment of Punishment (1984) 1465 UNTS 85.

14 International Convention for the Protection of All Persons from Enforced Disappearance, GA Res. 61/177 (20 December 2006).

15 American Convention on Human Rights (1969) 1144 UNTS 123.

16 Charter of Fundamental Rights of the European Union [2000] OJ C364/1.

prohibitions of torture and other forms of cruel, inhuman or degrading treatment or punishment laid down in Article 7 of the International Covenant on Civil and Political Rights (ICCPR)[17] and Article 3 of the European Convention on Human Rights and Fundamental Freedoms (ECHR)[18] do not explicitly protect from refoulement, the supervising bodies have interpreted these articles as providing protection from refoulement.[19] Prohibitions on refoulement have also been developed and adopted in other fields of international law, including international humanitarian law and international criminal law, i.e. in treaties concerning the protection of victims of armed conflicts and in extradition treaties.[20]

The principle of non-refoulement applies to any conduct resulting in the removal, expulsion, deportation, return, extradition, rejection at the frontier or non-admission, etc. that would place a person at risk of a certain harm. The harm is most clearly defined in the context of the Convention Against Torture and the Convention Against Enforced Disappearance. For example, the prohibition of refoulement under Article 3 of the Convention Against Torture protects individuals from being subjected to torture as defined in Article 1 of the Convention. The principle of non-refoulement in the context of international human rights law is developed by the case law and views of supervisory judicial and quasi-judicial bodies, linking the principle to a specific human right with the aim of preventing a violation of that human right. While these prohibitions of refoulement restrict the scope of the protection to situations where people are at risk of being subjected to a violation of a specific human right, what amounts to a violation or what comes within the scope of the human rights at stake is often broadly interpreted.

The principle of non-refoulement in international human rights law is most clearly developed in the context of the prohibition of torture and cruel, inhuman or degrading treatment or punishment. What amounts, in particular, to cruel, inhuman and degrading treatment or punishment is either not explained or is broadly interpreted. For example, in most refoulement cases adjudicated under Article 3 of the ECHR, the European Court of Human Rights has not explicitly examined the treatment to which the claimant was subjected or classified such treatment. The Court merely assessed and concluded that the anticipated treatment would meet a certain level of severity.[21] The assessment is largely concerned with evaluating the risk of the applicant being subjected to ill-treatment upon return. Further, it is increasingly accepted that other human rights may also include a prohibition on refoulement. This includes first and foremost other 'absolute' human rights, i.e. rights that have been formulated in absolute terms; not allowing for any exceptions for reasons of public interest or national security, and for which no derogations are permitted in times of war or public

---

17 International Covenant on Civil and Political Rights (1966) 999 UNTS 171.

18 Convention for the Protection of Human Rights and Fundamental Freedoms (as amended).

19 UN Human Rights Committee, General Comment No. 20, 'Article 7' (44th session) (1992), para. 9; UN Human Rights Committee, General Comment No. 31, 'The Nature of the General Legal Obligation Imposed on States Parties to the Covenant' (80th session) (2004) UN Doc CCPR/C/21/Rev.1/Add.13, para. 12; *Soering v United Kingdom*, App No. 14038/88 (ECtHR, Judgment of 7 July 1989); *Cruz Varas and Others v Sweden*, App No. 15576/89 (ECtHR, Judgment of 20 March 1991).

20 For example, Art. 45 of the 1949 Geneva Convention (IV) relative to the Protection of Civilian Persons in Time of War protects civilians from being 'transferred to a country where [they] may have reason to fear persecution for [their] political opinions or religious beliefs.' Art. 3(2) of the 1957 European Convention on Extradition and Art. 4(5) of the 1981 Inter-American Convention on Extradition protect people from being extradited when fearing persecution for reasons such as race, religion, nationality or political opinion.

21 K. Wouters, *International Legal Standards for the Protection from Refoulement* (Intersentia, 2009) 238–39.

emergencies. This includes in particular the right to life under Article 6 ICCPR[22] and Article 2 ECHR.[23] However, non-absolute human rights may also include a prohibition of refoulement, in particular when there is a risk of a flagrant denial of a human right. The European Court of Human Rights for example considered already in 1989 in the case of *Soering v United Kingdom* that an obligation of non-refoulement may exist in exceptional circumstances involving a risk of suffering a flagrant denial of a fair trial.[24] It was not until its judgment in 2012 in the case of *Othman v UK* that the Court concluded that a flagrant denial of justice may arise upon return of the applicant when it considered that 'a flagrant denial of justice will arise when evidence obtained by torture is admitted in criminal proceedings'.[25]

The principle of non-refoulement developed in the context of international refugee law is far less clear. Article 33(1) of the 1951 Refugee Convention protects refugees from a threat to life or freedom, and Article II(3) of the OAU Refugee Convention adds the notion of physical integrity. While neither of these instruments define or elaborate on the meaning of persecution and physical integrity, it is commonly accepted that both concepts are informed by international human rights and humanitarian law, as will be outlined below.

2.2 The meaning of persecution

Article 33(1) of the 1951 Refugee Convention protects a refugee from threats to his or her life or freedom. In contrast, the definition of a refugee in Article 1A(2) of the Convention uses the words 'being persecuted'. It was the intention of the drafters that the words 'life and freedom' should be given a broad interpretation and that a risk of any kind of persecution should be considered a threat to life or freedom.[26] The terms 'life and freedom' cannot be used to delineate the term 'persecution'; it is the other way round.[27]

Persecution is not defined in the 1951 Refugee Convention. It appears the drafters of the Convention omitted a definition deliberately in order to introduce a flexible concept.[28] Furthermore, persecution will depend on the circumstances of each case.[29] The flexible and factual character of the term 'persecution' precludes a clear definition; it must be open to continuously changing notions of such concepts as ill-treatment, serious harm and

---

22 GC 31 (n. 19) para. 12.
23 *Bader and Others v Sweden*, App No. 13284/048 (ECtHR, Judgment of November 2005).
24 *Soering v United Kingdom*, Appl No. 14038/88 (ECtHR, Judgment of 7 July 1989), para. 113.
25 *Othman (Abu Qatada) v United Kingdom*, App No. 8139/09 (ECtHR, Judgment of 17 January 2012), para. 282.
26 A. Grahl-Madsen, *The Status of Refugees in International Law, Volume I, Refugee Character* (A.W. Sijthoff, 1966) 196.
27 Ibid. 196: 'We may look at Article 1 in order to determine the scope of Articles 31 and 33, but not vice versa.' See also UNHCR, 'Handbook and Guidelines on Procedures and Criteria for Determining Refugee Status under the 1951 Convention and the 1967 Protocol Relating to the Status of Refugees' (reissued 2011) HCR/1P/4/ENG/REV.3, 13, para. 51, available at: http://www.unhcr.org/refworld/docid/4f33c8d92.html, accessed on 21 October 2012, which mentions that a threat to life or freedom is always persecution and that persecution may also include other serious human rights violations.
28 Grahl-Madsen (n. 26) 193; See also D.E. Anker, *Law of Asylum in the United States*, 3rd edn (Refugee Law Center, 1999) 171; D.J. Miller, 'Holding States to their Convention Obligations: The United Nations Convention against Torture and the Need for a Broad Interpretation of State Action' (2003) 17(2) *Georgetown Immigration Law Journal* 299–324 at 310.
29 UNHCR Handbook (n. 27) para. 52.

discrimination.[30] What amounts to persecution is in essence determined by the level of severity or seriousness of certain harm that in turn is determined by the type, nature and scale of the human rights violation(s) that constitute the harm.

The need for a flexible concept has over the years proven to be relevant and useful. For example, many parts of the world have seen large numbers of refugees fleeing an armed conflict and other situations of violence. Such situations are characterised by widespread violence often pursued for a multiplicity of motivations and with discriminate impact on civilians or specific groups in society. As UNHCR puts forward in its Note on Interpreting Article 1 of the 1951 Refugee Convention:

> It is sometimes argued that the 1951 Refugee Convention does not provide a suitable legal framework for addressing present-day refugee problems, as these often occur in the context of war and armed conflicts . . . [H]owever . . . even in war or conflict situations, persons may be forced to flee on account of a well-founded fear of persecution for Convention reasons and war and violence are themselves often used as instruments of persecution.[31]

Meanwhile, states in Africa and Latin America have sought to develop regional instruments explicitly extending the definition of a refugee to include people fleeing war, mass human rights violations, or situations of generalised violence or public disorder. In Africa this led to the adoption of the OAU Refugee Convention and the inclusion of a broader refugee definition, and in the Latin American region many states have incorporated a similar broader refugee definition stipulated in Conclusion 3 of the 1984 Cartagena Declaration into their national legislation. As mentioned above, this was inter alia due to regional realities whereby large groups of people flee objective harmful situations of war, violence and massive human rights violations.[32] According to Hathaway, the broader refugee definitions acknowledge 'that fundamental forms of abuse may occur not only as a result of the calculated acts of the government of refugee's state or origin, but also as a result of that government's loss of authority'.[33] As a result the emphasis is more on the objective circumstances in the country of origin than on the individual well-founded fear of persecution.

Scholars have long argued which human rights are relevant to determine the scope of persecution, for example, to what extent a distinction must be made between derogable and non-derogable rights, between civil and political rights and economic, social and cultural rights, and between rights protecting a person's physical integrity and those protecting a person's well-being.[34] As a result, the process for assessing international protection needs – the refugee status determination process, or 'asylum procedures' – often focuses on identifying

---

30 See UNHCR written intervention in the case of *Sepet (FC) and Another (FC) v Secretary of State for the Home Department* [2003] UKHL 15 (8 January 2003) 9 para. 3.7, available at: http://www.unhcr.org/refworld/docid/3e5ba7f02.html, accessed on 20 October 2012.

31 UNHCR, 'Interpreting Article 1 of the 1951 Convention Relating to the Status of Refugees' (2001) 6, para. 20, available at: http://www.unhcr.org/refworld/docid/3b20a3914.html, accessed on 21 October 2012.

32 UNHCR, *Summary Conclusions on International Protection of Persons Fleeing Armed Conflict and Other Situations of Violence; Roundtable 13 and 14 September 2012, Cape Town, South Africa*, 20 December 2012, available at: http://www.refworld.org/docid/50d32e5e2.html.

33 J.C. Hathaway, *The Law of Refugee Status* (Butterworths, 1991) 17.

34 See Wouters (n. 21) 61–67, analysing various schools of thought addressed in the works of Grahl-Madsen and Hathaway.

the applicable human rights standard, rather than the severity or seriousness of the harm. Focusing too much on identifying the applicable human rights standard is problematic for a number of reasons. First, it does not do justice to the evolution of human rights or of the – purposefully left undefined – term persecution. Second, there is a tendency to distinguish between the core and the margins of a human right when assessing the severity or seriousness, and third – and more importantly – it does not do justice to the predicament of the individual and his/her right to be protected from being subjected to harm that seriously may affect his or her life, freedom and well-being in a serious manner. Fortunately the distinction between the core and margins of a human right has been considered to be irrelevant in a judgment by the UK Supreme Court in the case of *RT (Zimbabwe) and others v Secretary of State for the Home Department*,[35] and in a judgment of the Court of Justice of the European Union (CJEU).[36] In the case of *Germany v Y and Z* the CJEU considered that:

> It is unnecessary to distinguish acts that interfere with the 'core areas' ('forum internum') of the basic right to freedom of religion, which do not include religious activities in public ('forum externum'), from acts which do not affect those purported 'core areas'.[37]

In the same judgment, the CJEU unfortunately 'legalises' the predicament of the individual in need of international protection, by using a strictly textual interpretation of what constitutes persecution within the meaning of Article 9(1) of the EU Qualification Directive. The CJEU stated that:

> It is apparent from the wording of Article 9(1) of the Directive that there must be a 'severe violation' of religious freedom having a significant effect on the person concerned in order for it to be possible for the acts in question to be regarded as acts of persecution. Acts amounting to limitations on the exercise of the basic right to freedom of religion within the meaning of Article 10(1) of the Charter which are provided for by law, without any violation of that right arising, are thus automatically excluded as they are covered by Article 52(1) of the Charter [of Fundamental Rights of the European Union].[38]

In particular, the word 'automatically' is worrying, as it implies that the lawfulness or unlawfulness of acts in terms of human rights will determine the level of severity required for the act to amount to 'persecution'. However, severity is not determined by the unlawfulness of the act, but rather by the effect of the act, by its nature and/or repetition, on the individual. The severity or seriousness may lie in the fact that a specific human right may be violated, or that the situation as a whole to which an individual is subjected is severe enough to amount to persecution. For example, a threat to life or freedom as well as other serious human rights violations may constitute persecution,[39] but circumstances which in themselves would not amount to a serious human rights violation may do so when taken together (cumulative

---

35 *RT (Zimbabwe) and others v Secretary of State for the Home Department* [2012] UKSC 38.
36 Joined cases C-71/11 and C-99/11 *Bundesrepublik Deutschland v Y, Z* [2012] CJEU.
37 Ibid. para. 62.
38 Ibid paras. 59–60.
39 UNHCR Handbook (n. 27) para. 51.

grounds).[40] Further, discrimination will amount to persecution only if it leads to consequences of a substantially prejudicial nature for the person concerned making life intolerable, for example, when it results in serious restrictions on the person's right to earn his livelihood, to practise his religion, or to access normally available educational facilities,[41] when it concerns racial discrimination[42] or where discriminatory measures are, in themselves, not serious, but may cumulatively be severe enough to produce a feeling of apprehension and insecurity as regards his or her future existence.[43]

Respect for human rights and the principle of non-discrimination are core aspects of the 1951 Refugee Convention and international refugee law.[44] The refugee definition and the notion of persecution thus need to be interpreted and applied with due regard for the principle of non-discrimination, including on the basis of age, sex, gender, sexual orientation, gender identity or any other relevant statuses or characteristics people have. Discrimination will amount to persecution where measures of discrimination, individually or cumulatively, lead to consequences of a substantially prejudicial nature for the person concerned.[45] Assessing whether the cumulative effect of such discrimination rises to the level of persecution is to be made by reference to objective facts and circumstances, including country of origin information as well as the overall circumstances of the case, including the age, gender, opinions, feelings and psychological make-up of the applicant.[46] Past persecution is not a prerequisite for refugee status under the 1951 Refugee Convention, and in fact the well-foundedness of the fear of persecution is a prospective test, to be based on the assessment of the predicament that the applicant would have to face if returned to the country of origin.[47]

2.3 Absolute protection

The principle of non-refoulement as developed in the context of international human rights law is absolute in character, as the objective is to prevent serious human rights violations. This means no exceptions are allowed for such reasons as past criminal conduct or the public order, health, morals or national security of the state concerned, and no derogation is possible from the principle in times of war or other public emergencies threatening the life of the nation. Under international refugee law the principle of non-refoulement is not absolute. Article 33(2) of the 1951 Refugee Convention allows for exceptions to be made if

---

40 Ibid. para. 53.
41 Ibid. para. 54.
42 Ibid. para. 69.
43 Ibid. para. 55.
44 1951 Refugee Convention (n. 9) preamble and Art 3.
45 UNHCR Handbook (n. 27) paras 54–55; See also *Kadri v Mukasey*, US 543 F.3d 16 (1st Cir. 2008) available at: http://www.unhcr.org/refworld/docid/498b0a212.html, accessed on 21 October 2012. The case was remanded for consideration of the standard for economic persecution, referring to *In re T-Z-*, 24 I & N. Dec. 163 (US Board of Immigration Appeals, 2007), which had found that '[non-physical] harm or suffering . . . such as the deliberate imposition of severe economic disadvantage or the deprivation of liberty, food, housing, employment, or other essentials of life may rise to persecution.'
46 UNHCR Handbook (n. 27) paras 51–53.
47 See e.g. *HJ (Iran) and HT (Cameroon) v. Secretary of State for the Home Department*, [2010] UKSC 31 available at: http://www.unhcr.org/refworld/docid/4c3456752.html; *Bromfield v Mukasey*, US 543 F.3d 1071, (9th Cir. 2008) 1076–77; *RRT Case No. 1102877*, [2012] RRTA 101, para. 91, available at: http://www.unhcr.org/refworld/docid/4f8410a52.html, accessed on 21 October 2012.

the refugee poses a threat to the security of the country of asylum or because s/he has been convicted by final judgment of a particularly serious crime and constitutes a danger to the community of the country of asylum.[48] Applying Article 33(2) of the 1951 Refugee Convention does not mean that the person concerned is no longer a refugee, but merely that s/he cannot claim the benefits of the prohibition of refoulement contained in the first paragraph of Article 33. As a result, the person concerned continues to have a well-founded fear of being persecuted and as such is at risk of being subjected to treatment proscribed by international human rights law.

While the refugee may be removed in accordance with Article 33(2) of the 1951 Refugee Convention, s/he may not be removed in accordance with prohibitions of refoulement developed under international human rights law. As a consequence, the refugee remains entitled to the benefits of the 1951 Refugee Convention at large, in particular those provisions of the Convention which do not require lawful presence or residence. Moreover, the applicability of Article 33(2) of the 1951 Refugee Convention becomes questionable. If a refugee cannot be removed on the basis of other absolute prohibitions of refoulement developed under international human rights law, applying Article 33(2) of the 1951 Refugee Convention will no longer be proportionate to its aim of alleviating or negating the danger to the country of asylum.[49] Interestingly, contrary to the 1951 Refugee Convention, the 1969 OAU Refugee Convention does not allow for exceptions to be made to the principle of non-refoulement and is in line with the absolute character that the principle has attained.

There is an important irony to point to when looking at the absolute character of the prohibition of refoulement and the interconnection between international refugee and human rights law. While people are in need of international protection because of human rights violations, the perpetrators of these violations may equally be in need of international protection. The international law framework includes states' obligations to protect perpetrators of human rights violations and also requires that they are held accountable for their conduct. States therefore cannot avoid identifying those who are responsible for human rights violations amongst those seeking international protection and hold them accountable while ensuring international protection for them.[50]

3 The content and quality of international protection

3.1 The rights of refugees under international refugee law

The 1951 Refugee Convention sets out the rights to which refugees are entitled in their country of asylum. These rights concern a refugee's juridical status, her/his gainful employment, the welfare of the refugee, including housing, education and social assistance, and rights concerning administrative assistance, freedom of movement, identity papers, travel documents and so on. The Convention, however, does not grant all rights immediately to all refugees but distinguishes between: refugees in general; refugees who are present in the

---

48 1951 Refugee Convention (n. 9) Art. 33(2).
49 I have made this argument before in Wouters (n. 21) 564.
50 Elizabeth Santalla Vargas, 'Ensuring Protection and Prosecution of Alleged Torturers: Looking for Compatibility of Non-Refoulement Protection and Prosecution of International Crimes', (2006) 8 *Eur. J. Migration & L.* 41.

country of asylum; refugees whose presence is lawful; and, finally, refugees who are lawfully residing in the country of asylum.

3.2 The rights of refugees under international human rights law

International human rights law identifies the duties undertaken by state parties to respect and ensure some of the most basic and instinctive rights afforded to human beings such as the right to life, liberty and security of the person.[51] In addition, human rights also provide individuals with certain other basic civil and political rights, and economic, social and cultural rights. Although certain rights are afforded only to certain groups of individuals, most human rights are afforded to everyone simply because they are human beings and within the jurisdiction of the state.

In contrast, international refugee law has an entirely different function. The 1951 Refugee Convention provides a legal framework for international protection to those compelled to flee because their human rights are at risk of being abused in their state of nationality. Yet, through the application of the 1951 Refugee Convention and through the specific context in which we compartmentalise individuals fleeing persecution, we tend to forget that refugees, regardless of their status and their whereabouts, are afforded and must benefit from human rights because they are, after all, human beings.

4 The right to asylum

4.1 Background and evolution

While the principle of non-refoulement is at the centre of international protection, it comes full circle through the right to asylum. The 1948 Universal Declaration of Human Rights (UDHR) provides in Article 14 for a right to seek and enjoy asylum. In turn, the preamble of the 1951 Refugee Convention refers to the UDHR and affirms the importance of the principle that human beings shall enjoy fundamental rights and freedoms without discrimination.[52] The term 'asylum' has no determined meaning in international law and appears to have a dual character.[53] The grant of asylum as a sovereign right of states seems well accepted. In general, it refers to protection offered by states in their territory or elsewhere to an individual who came to seek the state's protection in the absence of protection from his/her own state.[54] As Goodwin-Gill puts it, 'the UN General Assembly urges the grant of asylum and observance of the principle of asylum, and States' constitutions and laws offer the promise of asylum, yet nowhere is this act of States defined.'[55]

Asylum as a enforceable right for individuals is far less acknowledged. Deriving in nature from many basic human rights such as 'freedom from slavery, torture, arbitrary execution or imprisonment',[56] the right to asylum has grown to be recognised as an international human

---

51 UDHR (n. 3) Art. 3.
52 1951 Refugee Convention (n. 9).
53 M.T. Gil-Bazo, 'The Charter of Fundamental Rights to the European Union and the Right to be Granted Asylum in the Union's Law' (2008) 27(3) *Refugee Survey Quarterly* 33–52 at 38.
54 Institute du Droit International, *L'Asile en Droit International Public* (11 Septembre 1950) quoted in Grahl-Madsen (n. 26) 3.
55 G. Goodwin-Gill and J. McAdam, *The Refugee in International Law,* 3rd edn (OUP, 2007) 355.
56 D. Steingbock, 'The Refugee Definition as Law: Issues of Interpretation', in F. Nicholson and P. Twomey (eds), *Refugee Rights and Realities: Evolving International Concepts and Regimes* (CUP, 1999) 21.

right, implicitly rooted in various human rights instruments. The right to asylum is increasingly grounded in international law, albeit in instruments of regional scope. Starting with the right to seek and enjoy asylum in Article 14 of the Universal Declaration of Human Rights[57] and in Article XXVII of the American Declaration of the Rights and Duties of Man,[58] it is now contained in various binding legal instruments, including in Article II of the OAU Refugee Convention,[59] Article 22(7) of the American Convention on Human Rights,[60] Article 12(3) of the African Charter on Human and Peoples' Rights[61] and in Article 18 of the Charter of Fundamental Rights of the EU.[62] In addition, many countries have incorporated the right to asylum in their constitutions.[63]

The manner in which a state exercises its sovereignty has a direct effect upon the ability of refugees to seek and enjoy international protection in that state. The right to asylum as a sovereign right of states is often incumbent upon that particular state adhering to human rights instruments and refugee law instruments. Whilst states have a legitimate right to manage immigration and control regarding their territory – the entry, stay and removal of foreigners – this right is limited by human rights obligations and the responsibility of states to protect people who lack the national protection of their own state.[64]

The right to asylum would be illusory if it were subject to rigorous and unlimited state sovereignty, thus creating a meaningless and discretionary opportunity to seek and receive protection. This can further be supported by the fact that most human rights instruments refer to the 'right *to* asylum' rather than the 'right *of* asylum'; a right *to* something implies that it belongs *to* someone and this someone can only be an individual whereas a right *of* something is more fitted for state obligations.[65] Such a distinction is a determining factor in arguing that the right to asylum has developed into an individual enforceable right.

As with most individual rights, the right to asylum would be meaningless if the individual claiming it was unable to enforce its application through a claim or entitlement before a court of law, so as to ensure the enjoyment of this particular right. Developing from a sovereign state right, to an individual enforceable right, to a justiciable right, the right to asylum is now, more than ever, part of the legal structure of many countries and can be subject to adjudication in court.

4.2 The content of the right to asylum

The right to asylum, as recognised in international and regional refugee and human rights instruments, encompasses a number of fundamental rights, both substantive and procedural,

---

57 UDHR (n. 3).
58 American Declaration of the Rights and Duties of Man, Res. XXX, Final Act of the Ninth International Conference of American States (Pan American Union) (Bogotà, 30 March–2 May 1948) 38.
59 OAU Refugee Convention (n. 10).
60 ACHR (n. 15).
61 African Charter on Human and Peoples' Rights (1981) 1520 UNTS 217.
62 EU Charter (n. 16).
63 According to the Oceana database 'Constitutions of the Countries of the World', of the 188 Constitutions included, 65 contain an explicit right to asylum, available at: http://www.oceanalaw.com/gateway/gateway.asp?ID=31&SessionID=%7BB41EB37E-BF74-4455-AC52-706FD5AEBFD7%7D, accessed on 21 October 2012. Overview available with the author.
64 UNHCR, 'The State of the World's Refugees: In Search of Solidarity' (summary, 2012) 3, available at: http://www.unhcr.org/4fc5ceca9.pdf, accessed on 21 October 2012.
65 Gil-Bazo (n. 53) 38.

including the principle of non-refoulement, respect for human dignity, due process guarantees and freedom from torture and other ill-treatment. International human rights law, which generally applies to all persons within a state's territory and jurisdiction, provides the overarching framework for the protection of asylum-seekers and refugees.

Central to the realisation of the right to asylum is the principle of non-refoulement, the cornerstone of international refugee protection. This principle is codified, inter alia, in Article 33(1) of the 1951 Refugee Convention. The principle of non-refoulement applies to any conduct resulting in the removal, expulsion, deportation, return, extradition, rejection at the frontier or non-admission, etc. that would place a refugee at risk. The principle of non-refoulement is not subject to territorial restrictions; it applies wherever the state in question exercises jurisdiction.[66] Further to the 1951 Refugee Convention, the principle of non-refoulement as stated above is codified in regional refugee law instruments,[67] forms a rule of customary international law,[68] and is complemented by non-refoulement obligations contained in and developed under international human rights law, prohibiting the removal of a person to a real risk of torture or other cruel, inhuman or degrading treatment or punishment or other forms of serious harm.[69] The principle of non-refoulement applies to all refugees, including those who have not been formally recognised as such, and to asylum-seekers who may be refugees, but whose status has not yet been determined.[70]

Thus, while the right to asylum in international law encompasses a number of fundamental rights, it is nevertheless an independent right intended to ensure individual safety and security, with the prospect of continuing to live free from harm. While the principle of non-refoulement is a fundamental right and the cornerstone of international refugee protection, the right to asylum in international law goes beyond the prevention of refoulement, and includes not only admission to a safe territory and access to fair and effective procedures for determining status and protection needs, but also the attainment of a durable solution.[71]

4.3 Contemporary challenges

In its 2012 'State of the World's Refugees' report, UNHCR expresses its concern that the institution of asylum is threatened.[72] From a legal point of view the relevant question is

---

66 *Hirsi Jamaa and Others v Italy*, App. No. 27765/09 (ECtHR, Judgment of 23 February 2012); UNHCR, *Advisory Opinion on the Extraterritorial Application of Non-Refoulement Obligations under the 1951 Convention relating to the Status of Refugees and its 1967 Protocol* (26 January 2007) paras 24, 26, 32–43; UNHCR, *Submission by the Office of the United Nations High Commissioner for Refugees in the case of Hirsi and Others v Italy* (March 2010) paras 4.1.1–4.2.3.

67 See OAU Refugee Convention (n. 10) Art II(3); and 1984 Cartagena Declaration (n. 11).

68 UNHCR, 'UNHCR Note on the Principle of Non-Refoulement' (1997); UNHCR, 'Declaration of States Parties to the 1951 Convention and or its 1967 Protocol Relating to the Status of Refugees' (2002) HCR/MMSP/2001/09, para. 4; and E. Lauterpacht and D. Bethlehem, 'The Scope and Content of the Principle of Non-Refoulement: Opinion', in E. Feller, V. Türk and F. Nicholson (eds), *Refugee Protection in International Law: UNHCR's Global Consultations on International Protection* (CUP, 2003) 163–64.

69 CAT (n. 13) Art. 3(1); ICCPR (n. 17) Art. 7; ACHR (n. 15) Art. 5(2) and Art. 22(8); Inter-American Convention to Prevent and Punish Torture (1985) 25 ILM 519, Art. 13.

70 UNHCR Handbook (n. 27) para. 28.

71 UNHCR, 'Note on international protection: report of the High Commissioner' (2011) UN Doc. A/AC.96/1098, paras 2 and 3. See also 'Final Act of the United Nations Conference of Plenipotentiaries on the Status of Refugees and Stateless Persons' (25 July 1951) UN Doc A/CONF.2/108/Rev.1, Recommendation D.

72 UNHCR (n. 64) 9.

whether the right to asylum was ever adequately developed and implemented. In 1951, Van Heuven Goedhart, the first High Commissioner for Refugees, noted the problem that 'the world has not yet given practical expression to the conception laid down in the UDHR that every man exposed to political persecution has a claim to asylum and to protection of the law, to the right to work and to the exercise of a profession, to benefits of social security and to full freedom of movement'.[73] Van Heuven Goedhart mentioned, among other elements, too many economic and national interests standing in the way of a full and unrestricted fulfilment of the institution of asylum. His hopes for positive change were vested in the 1951 Refugee Convention.

More than half a century later much has been achieved. As outlined above, a strong international legal regime encompassing inter alia refugee law and human rights law instruments has been developed. Nonetheless, states seem reluctant to fully protect those who are in need of international protection. The challenge differs in the 'developed' and the 'developing' world. In the 'developed' world, refugees face the challenge of convincing states that they are refugees.[74] Governments continue to implement restrictive laws, policies and practices aimed at deterring people from seeking refuge, at least in their respective country or region – for example, through joint border monitoring and operational management.[75] An often cumbersome and highly individualised administrative procedure is put in place to decide who will be recognised and protected as a refugee and who will not. However, once recognised, refugees are granted a variety of rights at par with nationals and going beyond, to which they are immediately entitled under the 1951 Refugee Convention. In the 'developing' world, states have a long-standing practice of receiving – as they are often in the vicinity of 'refugee-producing' countries – and recognising on a prima facie basis large numbers of refugees. However, they do not have the will or resources to provide full protection. As a result, refugees are protected from refoulement, but their human rights and further entitlements are limited.[76]

A lack of political will, exacerbated by certain communities' disenchantment with hosting refugees, as well as increasing government concerns about transnational threats, including terrorism, crime and irregular mixed movements, have complicated – or even jeopardised – protection responses. Humanitarian crises and conflict have been exacerbated by the simultaneous impact of population growth, climate change, and food, water and energy insecurity. Growing levels of poverty and unemployment have proven to be sources of social and political unrest. In this environment, a strong commitment from states is needed to uphold the institution of asylum.

Select bibliography

E. Feller, V. Türk and F. Nicholson (eds), *Refugee Protection in International Law: UNHCR's Global Consultations on International Protection* (CUP, 2003).

G. Goodwin-Gill and J. McAdam, *The Refugee in International Law* 3rd edn (OUP, 2007).

A. Grahl-Madsen *The Status of Refugees in International Law, Volume I, Refugee Character* (A.W. Sijthoff, 1966).

73 G.J. van Heuven Goedhart, 'People Adrift' (1953) 7(1) *Journal of International Affairs* 7–49 at 7.

74 J. Hathaway, *The Rights of Refugees under International Law* (CUP, 2005) 1.

75 This refers to, for example, FRONTEX in the European Union, which is the European Agency for the Management of Operational Cooperation at the External Borders of the Member States of the European Union.

76 UNHCR (n. 64) 9.

J. Hathaway, *The Law of Refugee Status* (Butterworths, 1991).

J. Hathaway, *The Rights of Refugees under International Law* (CUP, 2005).

F. Nicholson and P. Twomey (eds), *Refugee Rights and Realities: Evolving International Concepts and Regimes* (CUP, 1999).

K. Wouters, *International Legal Standards for the Protection from Refoulement* (Intersentia, 2009).

15

Human rights and international trade

Sheldon Leader*

1 Introduction

What difference do human rights potentially make to the logic and practice of international trade and – running in the opposite direction – what difference does trade make to the way in which human rights are understood and deployed? The importance of these questions is highlighted by the fact that, as one authority has observed, the relationship between these two domains 'is one of the central issues confronting international lawyers at the beginning of the twenty-first century'.[1] The challenge, of course, reaches well beyond lawyers to all of those individuals and institutions ultimately responsible for pulling these two domains into a viable relationship.

There is mutual suspicion on both sides of the divide between the practices of trade and human rights, manifested by the heat of recent academic debate and by confrontations on the street. Each side worries that the other might sabotage its best-laid plans. Yet the international community has less and less tolerance for this stand-off. It demands an effective and workable synthesis, allowing the two disciplines to widen and to coordinate their agendas. This chapter is concerned with this prospect. It raises two broad issues: which role, if any, human rights have to play in shaping the rules of trade; and how should we understand the relative priority among, and balances between, rights in trading relations? If analysis can provide an appropriate map for working out the problem of priorities and balances, then it might be possible to locate respect for human rights among the central objectives of international trade – as the UN expects it to be – while at the same time preserving the ability of a robust system of trade to pursue many of its traditional goals as well.[2]

---

* A version of this chapter first appeared in P. Macrory and A. Appleton (eds), *Understanding the WTO: Perspectives from Law, Politics, and Economics* (Springer, 2005).

1 P. Alston, 'Resisting the Merger and Acquisition of Human Rights by Trade Law: A Reply to Petersmann', (2002) 13(4) *European Journal of International Law* 815–44 at 818.

2 J. Oloka-Onyango and D. Udagama, *Human Rights as the Primary Objective of International Trade, Investment and Finance Policy and Practice*, a paper submitted in accordance with UN Sub-Commission Resolution 1998/12 E/CN.4/Sub.2/1999/11; UN Sub-Commission on the Promotion and Protection of Human Rights, *Liberalization of Trade in Services and Human Rights*, E/CN.4/Sub.2/2002/9, June 25, 2002, ¶ 7; cf. UN Commission On Human Rights, Fifty-Ninth Session, *The Fundamental Principle of Non-discrimination in the Context of Globalization*, E/CN.4/2003/50, December 2002.

2 The challenge of rival political philosophies

How should international norms regulate a world in which some societies assign priority to market-oriented liberty and property rights, with a relatively lower rank given to any human rights that would limit market freedom; while others arrange their priorities in the opposite way; along with many other different solutions located in between? Can a trading system bring these actors together in an impartial way? The system aspires to bridge these differences while avoiding, in principle, a structure in which the values of the strong members dominate those of the weak. It may well fall far short of this ideal as things stand, but that criticism tacitly endorses the benchmark of political impartiality as one way of measuring progress by the system. It is this benchmark that is our concern here, for there is more to it than meets the eye.

We can properly focus on the impartial relationship between trade and human rights only if we try to follow the approach taken by the UN Committee charged with interpreting the International Covenant on Economic, Social and Cultural Rights (ICESCR). In deciding whether or not one of the rights has been violated, the Committee insists that the Covenant:

> cannot accurately be described as being predicated exclusively upon the need for, or the desirability of a socialist or a capitalist system, or a mixed, centrally planned, or laissez-faire economy, or upon any other particular approach.[3]

This does not mean that we can shelve the politically divisive issues in working out the proper relationship between international trade and human rights. Some such issues have to be confronted. However, we can be optimistic about reaching consensus on them only if we can build on a platform that gives all participants – the weak as well as the strong – the conviction that their priorities have the chance of making an impact on trading rules. There is a difference between forcing a compromise onto a trading partner, and forcing that partner to abandon a set of priorities among values it thinks are fundamentally important to its social health. The trading system must navigate in this terrain.

3 Linking the WTO's objectives to human rights

The World Trade Organization (WTO) is not a party to any human rights treaties. However, the stated goals of the organisation, which can be found in its preamble, provide a useful potential entry point for those guarantees. There are seven overlapping goals within the preamble. While they are run together in the text, it is useful to separate them as commitments to:

1. raising standards of living;
2. ensuring full employment;
3. ensuring a large and steadily growing volume of income and effective demand;
4. expanding the production of, and trade in, goods and services;
5. allowing the optimal use of the world's resources in accordance with the objective of sustainable development;

---

3 Committee on Economic, Social and Cultural Rights, 'General Comment 3, Concerning the Nature of States Parties' Obligations Under Art. 2 (1) of the Covenant' § 8, (1994) UN Doc HRI\ GEN\1\Rev.1 at 45.

6. seeking both to protect and preserve the environment, consistent with the contracting parties' respective needs and concerns at different levels of economic development; and

7. assuring developing countries, especially the least developed, a share in the growth in international trade commensurate with the needs of their economic development.

In addition, the preamble describes an eighth objective, and one which serves the other objectives:

8. the members aim at 'contributing to these objectives by reciprocal and mutually advantageous arrangements directed to substantial reduction of tariffs'. It will do this by developing '. . . an integrated, more viable and durable multilateral trading system'.

3.1 Embedded and imported rights

Human rights are not explicitly mentioned here. However, they can be linked to the text, depending on how it is read. Some of the rights are embedded in some of the objectives, as necessary for their attainment. Take, as an example, the commitment to 'sustainable development' in the fifth item of the preamble. As a report from the United Nations Development Programme (UNDP) argues:

Development is unsustainable where the rule of law and equity do not exist; where ethnic, religious or sexual discrimination are rampant; where there are restrictions on free speech, free association and the media; or where large numbers of people live in abject and degrading poverty. [4]

That is, societies must be in a position to remove internal obstacles to their ability to renew themselves. If the least well off are provided with these rights, then the UN argues that they will be less likely to deplete their own key resources such as land, water or human capital, in the effort to survive.[5] Certain rights are therefore embedded in the goal of sustainable development.

While important, this way of picking out certain rights that the WTO must respect has its limits. It treats human rights as means to ends rather than as goals worthy of pursuit in their own right. To continue with our example, if a commitment to give effect to certain human rights is grounded on, and flows from, a particular feature of development – its sustainability – then if the WTO were to take seriously any given right it would have to be convinced that the right plays a demonstrable role in helping a society to renew its basic resources, both

---

4 UNDP, Human Rights and Sustainable Development, Section C (Nov. 1997), available at: http://mirror.undp.org/magnet/e-list/hr.htm#N1C, accessed on 23/02/2013.

5 E. Barbier, 'The Concept of Sustainable Economic Development', (1987) 14(2) *Environmental Conservation* 101–10 ('the primary objective is reducing the absolute poverty of the world's poor through providing lasting and secure livelihoods that minimize resource depletion, environmental degradation, cultural disruption and social instability'). R. Goodland and G. Ledoc, 'Neoclassical Economics and Principles of Sustainable Development', (1987) 38(1) *Ecological Modelling* 19–46 ('Sustainable development is a policy which optimizes the economic and societal benefits available in the present, without jeopardizing the likely potential for similar benefits in the future.'). See also UNDP, *Integrating Human Rights with Sustainable Human Development: A UNDP Policy Document* (1998).

material and non-material. That does not fully cover the wider goals of a human rights agenda, such as that of the ICESCR, which is aimed at progressively improving access to certain basic social goods because of their intrinsic worth, quite apart from their ability to contribute to a society's ability to husband and renew its resources.[6]

For several other objectives announced in the preamble, it is not possible to find human rights embedded in them. Any connection to such rights therefore has to come from importing the relevant guarantees into the text. For example, the institution can pursue the first objective on the list, raising aggregate or even average standards of living, without necessarily satisfying the right of *all* relevant portions of society to an adequate standard as would be called for by the ICESCR.[7] It is notoriously possible to increase the average standard while allowing the level enjoyed by the least well off to fall. Any concern for the least well off engages entitlements to distributive justice. Prima facie, this falls within the province of WTO members' domestic policy, be they states or regional groupings such as the European Union, and is not the business of the WTO.

However, the trade treaties draw a balance between the objective of furthering trade and various permissions given to member states to refuse to trade. In the latter case, the member might be motivated by a concern that the terms on which a good or service is entering the country might damage the well-being of the least well off. The question that then arises is, to what extent do the trade treaties have to be sensitive to the demands of social and economic rights as part of the legitimate reason that members can have for the refusal to trade? That is, to what extent is it appropriate to take the rights standards that bind members and import them into the legitimate concerns of the WTO as it interprets the relevant treaties? Is it possible to go further and call on the WTO itself to formulate policies with the avowed intention of actually facilitating (rather than simply not obstructing) the task of members in meeting their required social and economic targets?

Would it be necessary to amend the organisation's Articles in order to open up these possibilities? That depends on how the Articles are interpreted.[8]

3.2 Techniques of interpretation: functional versus civic inclusion

An interpretation of WTO treaties can develop in two distinct directions. One of these takes what can be called a functional view of power, and another takes a civic view.[9] The difference can best be appreciated by going back to the eight objectives in the preamble. The first seven are general objectives: they are shared by a number of other national and international organisations along with the WTO. The eighth is a special objective. That is, it specifies the particular way in which the WTO is meant to pursue its general objectives: its commitment to achieve a 'substantial reduction of tariffs' and 'an integrated, more viable, and durable

---

6 This freestanding quality of the right can be seen in ICESCR Art. 11.
7 Ibid.
8 For an excellent consideration of the interpretive options, see G. Marceau, 'WTO Dispute Settlement and Human Rights', (2002) 13(4) *European Journal of International Law* 753–814.
9 The functional outlook described here is different from functionalism as it normally figures in the literature on trade. See e.g. Ernst-Ulrich Petersmann, *Time for Integrating Human Rights into the Law of Worldwide Organizations*, Working Paper 7/01 Jean Monnet Program, Harvard Law School (2001) text associated with his fn. 6. Compare this with the distinction between civic and functional approaches in S. Leader, 'Three Faces of Justice and the Management of Change', (2000) 63 *Modern Law Review* 55–83 passim.

multilateral trading system'. Now, according to the functional approach, it is the special and not the general objectives of the institution that fix the appropriate scope of its responsibilities. Its duties are, for the functionalist, to the actors who are directly involved in the process of this movement to integrated trade, and no further.

Thus, even if it could be shown that opening markets to certain goods and services damages the prospects of certain local populations, the functionalist claims that this is not enough to attach the responsibility for those effects to the WTO. The proper concern of the organisation, from this perspective, is not to achieve *comprehensive* fairness, but only to achieve the limited sorts of fairness that its commitment to non-discrimination among goods and service providers involves. Debra Steger, former Director of the WTO Appellate Body Secretariat, has recently articulated this view. She refuses to include concerns about users of services or of goods within the scope of WTO responsibility, confining herself to their producers. 'The WTO's mandate,' she says:

> is to promote freer trade and market access through the application of the principles of non-discrimination. Although I would equate the principle of non-discrimination with the fight against protectionism, nowhere in the GATT is the term 'fairness' used. That does not mean that the GATT is 'unfair'; it simply means that 'fairness' in trading relations is not a GATT principle or norm – non-discrimination is.[10]

This is a position standing in sharp contrast with that which embraces users and producers, as well as potential beneficiaries and victims of both. Several recent reports by the UN take this wider view, as do commentators such as Steve Charnovitz and Ernst-Ulrich Petersmann.[11] They implicitly endorse what can be called a civic approach. This does not tie the WTO's responsibility to its special objectives, but roots these objectives within wider concerns. To illustrate this difference, consider the WTO rules that affect access to education or health, or affect the full range of labour rights. Based on the civic approach, if those impacts are significant then the organisation is responsible for them. Based on the functional approach, the organisation might not be responsible for these same impacts. For the functionalist, there is an additional issue of institutional identity at stake: the special mission of the WTO distinguishes it from a state, and in turn for example from the International Labour Organization (ILO) and World Health Organization (WHO). A *member* of the WTO may well be held accountable for implementing policies that violate its own commitments to basic rights, but it does not follow for the functionalist that the WTO is therefore also accountable.[12]

Even if the members, working collectively as the WTO, make demands on one of their number to open its markets, the way in which the latter then copes with any negative effects

10 D. Steger, 'The "Trade and . . . ." Conundrum – A Commentary', (2002) 96(1) *American Journal of International Law* 135–45 at 139.

11 See S. Charnovitz, 'Triangulating the World Trade Organization', (2002) 96(1) *American Journal of International Law* 28–52 at 41: 'The capacity of horrendous working conditions to render trade unfair was acknowledged by the parties to the Covenant of the League of Nations . . . Whether the addition to the WTO Agreements of a provision on workers' rights would enhance fairness or erode it depends upon what that provision would require. Yet it can hardly be doubted that the labour issue fits the trade fairness frame.' Petersmann (n. 9), text associated with his fn. 16.

12 For this approach in international economic law, see F. Gianviti, 'Economic, Social and Cultural Rights and the International Monetary Fund', Working Paper for the UN Committee on Economic, Social and Cultural Rights (2001) UN DOC. E/C 12/2001/WP.5, para. 6 ff. See also the discussion of functionalists in Charnovitz (n. 11) at 48.

of such an opening is, for the functionalist, not the proper concern of the organisation. It is an issue that calls on the member's particular range of responsibilities that are wider than those of the trading body. It may, for example, be appropriate that the member seeks the international assistance to which the ICESCR refers so as to obtain the technical advice, and possibly the resources, necessary to protect any human right that would be jeopardised as a by-product of opening its markets.[13] This would call, inter alia, for contributions from specialised agencies of the UN to provide the requisite assistance – to fill the gap that might be opened up by market integration. The civic approach is fundamentally different. It is not primarily concerned with the distinct or special *roles* of states and other institutions, but instead focuses on their overlapping *power*. If the policies of a given member, and those of all members working as the WTO, have equivalent effects on a population, then on applying the civic view, the responsibility of each member singly and their responsibility collectively could well be similar.

This is one of the fundamental points of division in the free trade vs fair trade debate. The parties to that confrontation are not, whatever the appearances, divided about whether 'fairness' as a value does or should form part of the WTO's existing principles. This is true despite the way in which Steger has expressed her point. For the principle of non-discrimination to which she refers is itself a species of fairness and, as Brian Languille has pointed out, some degree of concern for fairness – in this case fairness to states but the point could be extended to individuals or groups impacted – is therefore built into the very fabric of free trade.[14] The real clash between the fair trade and free trade advocates is over the *scope* of the demand for fairness.

Telling against the civic view of appropriate scope is the fact that the WTO is clearly not a state, and therefore would not seem to have the same range of responsibilities as does a state. But telling against the functional alternative is the possibility that member states may be caught between the twin pressures of market integration and human rights concerns, each sometimes pointing in opposite directions. It does not seem right, or realistic, to offload the negative affects of trade onto other international organisations meant to assure respect for labour, health or environmental standards. That creates tension and rivalry among international organisations that should be complementing the work of one another. A clash of international demands becomes particularly aggravated when a state finds that the steps it takes to satisfy a requirement of one of the trade treaties places it in possible violation of one of the human rights treaties.

3.3 Human rights and refusals to trade

The trade treaties administered by the WTO all create space within which a member can refuse to import a given good or service, or can override a claim of intellectual property,

---

13 International Covenant on Economic Social and Cultural Rights 1966 Art. 2(1), 'Each state party to the present Covenant undertakes to take steps, individually and *through international assistance and cooperation . . .* with a view to achieving progressively the full realization of the rights recognized in the present Covenant' (emphasis added). For an example of such damage as a by-product, consider the UN's analysis of the possible effects of trade policy on the ability of the least well off to gain access to education and health facilities. See 'Liberalization of Trade in Services' (n. 2), para. 60.

14 A point ably demonstrated in B. Languille, 'Labour Standards in the Globalised Economy and the Free Trade/Fair Trade Debate', in W. Sengenberger and D. Campbell (eds), *International Labour Standards and Economic Interdependence* (ILO, 1994), 329–39.

because of the demands of its domestic policy.[15] Depending on how the existing rules are read, human rights can figure as acceptable reasons for such a refusal to accept market integration. There are two possible scenarios, which we shall illustrate by focusing on the General Agreement on Tariffs and Trade (GATT). In one, prompted by what can be called outwardly directed concerns, country X refuses to import goods or services from country Y because it is concerned that Y is violating the human rights of its own population. In another, prompted by inwardly directed concerns, X refuses to import from Y because it is concerned about the effect that the entry of such goods and services might have on the human rights of its, X's, population.

As an example of the outwardly directed concern, Y might have acted so abusively that it is considered by the UN Security Council to be a threat to international peace and security, as South Africa was when it practised apartheid. If so, Article 41 of the UN Charter provides for the legitimate use of economic sanctions. Article XXI(c) of the General Agreement on Tariffs and Trade (GATT) (1947) in turn permits members to refuse to import goods from that country for reasons of international peace and security. Similarly, objections to the importing of products that have been made by prison labour might overlap with human rights concerns, and this refusal is permitted under Article XX(e).[16] What about objections that X might raise to Y's non-respect of the basic trade union rights of its labour force? What about its objections to abuses of other human rights?[17] While these fall outside the explicit grounds mentioned in the treaties, there is potential room within their more general terms. For example, Article XX(a) of GATT permits refusals to trade when this is 'necessary to protect public morals'. Steve Charnovitz has suggested that, under suitable constraints, this clause could accommodate refusals to trade based on human rights violations, given the centrality of such standards at the core of the moral standards of many societies.[18]

There is a danger in this outwardly directed strategy, however. One country, particularly if it is powerful, might be able to unilaterally impose its own understanding of human rights requirements on another. It might do this for protectionist reasons, or for reasons that arise from a good faith interpretation of the importance of a given right with which its trading partner disagrees. Given free reign, refusals to trade for such reasons would cause the system to fragment. The WTO decisions show some sensitivity to this possibility. While, as was said, human rights issues have not yet been directly raised in past cases, decisions have made it clear that the WTO will allow a member to refuse to import from another because of outwardly directed concerns about issues such as the protection of endangered species, and not simply because of concerns about its own domestic situation. However, the Appellate Body in the famous *Shrimp-Turtle* case has also made it clear that before a country can refuse to trade on such Article XX grounds, it must have made good faith efforts to negotiate with other

---

15 See inter alia GATT, Art. XX; GATS, Art. XIV; and TRIPS, Art. VIII.

16 Concerns about prison labour and about human rights potentially overlap. Note, however, that the original purpose of this provision was protection of prisoners but not respect for human rights per se.

17 An example is the abuse of human rights in Myanmar, and the reaction of Massachusetts with the 'Burma' law. The law restricts the authority of the Commonwealth of Massachusetts to buy goods and services from companies that do business with Burma/Myanmar. Mass. Gen. Laws Ann. Ch. 7, §§ 22G–22M (West 1998 Supp.). The matter was not dealt with by a Panel, but it is not difficult to imagine circumstances in which an issue like this would reach that stage.

18 See S. Charnovitz, 'The Moral Exception in Trade Policy', (1998) 38 *Virginia Journal of International Law* 689.

countries a common understanding of the content of any such standard.[19] The negotiation need not be with all interested parties, and indeed it might not result in an agreement before the embargo is imposed, but the coverage of parties must be substantial enough to be convincingly multilateral, and the efforts to reach agreement must be made in good faith.

Turning to inwardly directed concerns, the member refusing to accept a WTO demand for entry into its market, or a demand for shaping its intellectual property rights, can also rely on the same provision in the GATT and its equivalent in the General Agreement on Trade in Services (GATS) and Trade-Related Aspects of Intellectual Property Rights (TRIPS). It is worth noting in particular the scope for inwardly directed human rights concerns potentially available in Article 8 of TRIPS. As they give effect to the agreement's core provisions, members may adopt measures 'necessary to protect public health and nutrition, and to promote the public interest in sectors of vital importance to their socio-economic . . . development . . . [p]rovided that such measures are consistent with the provisions of this Agreement.'[20] The Doha Declaration on TRIPS and Public Health gave added emphasis to the need to interpret the agreement such that it gives scope to members' 'right to protect public health and . . . to promote access to medicines for all'.[21] If there is room for a member's *right* to protect public health, then there must equally be room for a member's *obligation* to protect public health – an obligation arising, inter alia, from the ICESCR.

At this stage, we can see why the trading system is likely to have a built-in resistance to a human rights claim, when these claims prompt members to refuse to accept goods, services, or the recognition of intellectual property rights. As was true of the example of derogations from TRIPS, they are all claims to carve out an exception to demands that a trading partner go along with market integration.[22] As a result, the system looks at human rights much as it does other non-tariff barriers. It may reluctantly admit them but on condition that, like other barriers, they do 'least damage' to the core objective to free trade from among alternatives available. In other words, when they prompt refusals to trade, human rights demands face the rigours of a policy of negative integration. Quite apart from any views trade officials or adjudicators might have about the proper place for such rights in a trading system, this is an institutional influence on the way in which they see the problem. The result might radically

---

19 For a statement of these principles, see the views by the Appellate Body in *United States – Import Prohibition of Certain Shrimp and Shrimp Products* ('*Shrimp-Turtles I*'), WT/DS58/AB/R (1998), followed by *United States – Import Prohibition of Certain Shrimp and Shrimp Products – Recourse to Article 21.5 of the DSU by Malaysia* ('*Shrimp-Turtles II*') *WT/DS58/AB/RW* (2001). See also J. Scott, 'On Kith and Kine (and Crustaceans)', in J. Weiler (ed.), *The EU, the WTO, and the NAFTA* (OUP, 2000), 162 ff.

20 In the same spirit, though with different detail, are Art. XX(b) of GATT and Art. IV(b) of GATS.

21 Declaration on the TRIPS Agreement and Public Health (2001), WTO Doc, WT/MIN(01)/DEC/2, available at: http://www.wto.org/english/thewto_e/minist_e/min01_e/mindecl_trips_e.pdf accessed on 23/02/2013.

22 When a refusal to import a good is accompanied by local production of the same or a similar good, then there is prima facie a violation of the ban by Art. III:4 on according domestic goods better treatment than is given to imported goods. This can happen in the situations we are considering, since the country refusing an import because of the policies or conditions surrounding the production of a good in another country, or because of its impact on the basic rights of its own citizens, might not have the same objections to similar goods produced in its own borders. At that point, while the member might look benignly on local producers, there is a case to answer under Art. III:4. The member will only be able to overcome the presumption against such differential treatment by relying on Art. XX.

shrink the force of any given human right – taking it well below the promise it offers in other quarters, where it does not have to be provided in a version that is the least restrictive of trade. This is one factor that fuels the feeling of many sceptics that international trade is inherently corrosive of social standards. It is a product of a functionalist vision of the mission and responsibility of the WTO. We shall explore more of the civic alternative in a moment.

4 The problem of collateralism

Whereas many states aim to hold the whole range of human rights in an equitable balance with one another – limiting the exercise of some so as to make room for others – this balance can lose a central place in the work of certain international organisations: organisations that have the most power to influence the domestic policies of those same states. In place of the sort of equilibrium among rights that democratic states seek, we find that some rights receive automatic preference over others in some international organisations: the latter becoming collateral concerns of the organisation, while the former are deemed to lie at the core of its objectives.

If the WTO is thought to draw its legitimacy from the its particular mandate to promote an integrated trading system – what was identified earlier as objective 8 in the preamble – then it can seem reasonable to conclude that this core function should generate the basic rights that deserve its prior attention. Others will become collateral concerns. Thus, those who make and interpret the norms of the organisation might fully accept that they should respect the obligations on member states arising from social, economic and cultural rights. However, they might also insist that while these ICESCR rights constrain what the WTO does, they cannot constrain it in the way they would constrain a state. When a hard choice has to be made between the objectives of market integration and concerns to protect those who might lose out from such integration, then on this view the WTO must stick by its special function and shape the rights involved so as to impede as little as possible its central mission.

True, the rules of the various agreements managed by the WTO do build in room for allowing its members to assign ultimate priority to certain non-trade concerns, as we have seen with Article XX of the GATT. However, this deference to national priorities is sometimes accorded by the WTO at a price. The member state might be required to compromise on its preferred content and method of achieving those non-trade objectives more than it would in other settings. The social and economic rights in the ICESCR are seen as incapable of rising to more than a secondary concern in an organisation that defines its tasks in what was earlier called functionalist terms.

The result is what we are familiar with: the perceived bias towards market liberalism in WTO policies. This priority flows as much from the institutional constraints faced by the organisation as it does from deeper convictions on matters of political economy in the hearts of those running it. The price paid is a high one, since the system loses its ability to show member states that, while it might put pressure on their domestic agenda, it does so in a politically impartial way, and in doing so truly respects their other international human rights commitments. Things could conceivably be different.

5 From collateralism towards an impartial order for trade relations

It is possible to frame the work of the WTO in a way that reduces the damage done by collateralism. States are certainly not forbidden by their entry into the organisation to pursue a strong domestic human rights agenda. Yet, this is a permission that is more formal than real for many weaker states and economies. It can be turned into a live option by appropriate balances within the trade treaties.

In order to explore this possibility, we can draw on our earlier distinction between civic and functional principles. These, we saw, provide fundamentally different starting points in deciding on the standards that should guide the formulation and interpretation of trading rules. Those different starting points in turn lead to two distinct ranges of human rights that the organisation might respect. A civic order incorporates a wide range, since it looks for continuity in regulating principles across a large spectrum of different institutions, from the nation state through to international bodies. A functional order – which underpins collateralism – is different in that it divides up the terrain, looking for unique matches between particular organisations and their particular domains of responsibility. We can now go further with this distinction, using it to see the different ways of balancing disparate concerns in a trading regime.

6 Approaching the balance between trade and non-trade interests

We will assume that respect for *some* human rights calls for the opening up of markets to trading relations, while respect for *other* human rights calls for closing or limiting access to those markets. Everything turns on the balance between the two sets of considerations. How does a civic order approach such a balance? Whereas in a functional order the special, defining objectives of an organisation fix priorities among rights, in a civic order human rights are assigned priorities for reasons that are independent of the specific functions assigned to the organisation. Even if the WTO has the special objective of promoting free trade this does not, on civic principles, dictate the relative weight of rights that the organisation must respect. There is no reason for trading rules to give priority to a service provider's claim for market access over a state's claim to close its markets to such a service in order to protect a competing and fundamentally important priority. Instead, a civic order calls – in a distinctive way – for mutual adjustment between the rights.

We can see what is distinctive in a civic approach by comparing it with the functional approach to the well-known 'necessity' requirement in the balance between trade and non-trade interests. When systems are confronted by competing rights, calling for their impartial adjustment, they often resort to the device of saying that one right may be limited if doing so is necessary for the fair exercise of the other. For example, the International Covenant on Civil and Political Rights (ICCPR) requires respect for the right to freedom of expression, and then permits the right to be restricted if doing so is necessary for achieving, inter alia, respect for the rights of others and the protection of public morals.[23] Similar phrases also figure in the structure of the GATT,[24] the GATS[25] and TRIPS,[26] as a qualification to their ability to protect public health, public morality, and other fundamental interests.

In all such treaties, 'necessary' does not mean what it seems to mean. That is, one does not have to show that any given measure is indispensable to the protection of the countervailing objective, such that there is no alternative measure that would protect it. There are usually several such routes available to protecting something like public morality, each sufficient to

23 International Covenant on Civil and Political Rights 1966 Art. 19(2) and (3).
24 Art. XX(a).
25 Art. XIV(a).
26 Art. 27(2).

yield the result while none is literally the only way to go about it. Instead, the notion of necessity points at something quite different: it identifies the core objectives of the treaty in question, and then asks whether a member state's overriding of those objectives by its domestic policy does the least damage to that treaty commitment, as compared with alternative possible domestic measures. The implicit question is not, for example, 'do you need to protect your public morality?', but rather 'is this the way of protecting public morality that imposes the least cost on the ability of the treaty to do what it is designed to do?' We can call this the 'least impact' feature of necessity.

In a functional order, this approach demands that domestic priorities protecting public morals, and human, animal, plant life or health, all be pursued in a way that does least damage to international trade. There is clear room in the trade agreements for domestic priorities to prevail, but this is a potential that is largely lost – say the critics – when the member state is forced to select that version of its priorities that is most friendly to the commercial interests of international providers of goods and services.[27] As Esty puts it, 'a policy approach that intrudes less on trade is almost always conceivable and therefore in some sense "available" '.[28] As a result the non-trade exception is eviscerated. In considering this critique, we should notice that the 'least trade - restrictive' demand does not necessarily flow from the fact that these agreements place the intrinsic merits of free trade above the protection of morals or human life. Instead, this priority is a result of a functional reading of the agreements. As was indicated in the earlier discussion of functional interpretation, it is the special, and not the shared, general objectives of the WTO that set the priorities among the interests the organisation is to satisfy. That is, the market integration goals that give the institution its particular role among international organisations are primary, and any other interests that are contained in the shared and general objectives – which the WTO pursues along with many other organisations – are to be given a place that does least to upset the special objectives. It follows, based on this approach, that the shared and general aim of promoting, say, sustainable development, to which the WTO is committed along with other international bodies, should be interpreted so as to least trouble the special objective of market integration via free trade. Shared and general objectives are to be adjusted in favour of special ones and not vice versa, says the functionalist.

Before looking further into the civic alternative, notice that the direction in which functional adjustment moves can cut quite deeply into domestic priorities. This is because functional alternatives do not just put pressure on the means selected to achieve certain policy goals, they can also affect the content of those goals. We can see this by contrasting two WTO cases, *Thai Cigarettes*[29] and *Asbestos*.[30]

In the *Thai Cigarettes* case, Thailand limited imports of tobacco, while permitting their domestic manufacture and sale. The limitation partly took the form of a refusal to grant licences to import, raising a complaint under GATT. Thailand sought to defend the measures,

---

27 See e.g. M. Albert, 'A Q&A on the WTO, IMF and World Bank and Activism' (2000), available at: http://www.zcommunications.org/a-q-and-a-on-the-wto-imf-world-bank-and-activism-by-michael-albert, accessed on 23/02/2013.

28 D. Esty, *Greening the GATT 48* (1994), cited by M.J. Trebilcock and R. Howse, *The Regulation of International Trade 140* (Routledge, 2001).

29 Report of the GATT Panel, *Thailand – Restrictions on Importation of and Internal Taxes on Cigarettes*, GATT No. DS10/R, BISD 37S/200, adopted on November 7, 1990.

30 *European Communities – Measures Affecting Asbestos and Asbestos-Containing Products* Appellate Body WT/DS135/11.

inter alia, as necessary for the protection of human health within the terms of GATT Article XX(b). It claimed to be concerned to keep domestic demand from growing beyond its present level.[31] The entry of foreign producers would, it argued, lead to expertly targeted marketing that would increase consumption among parts of the population who smoked far less than their foreign counterparts.[32] This result, it said, would damage the GATT's own objectives as set out in its preamble. For, smoking:

> lowered the standard of living, increased sickness and thereby led to billions of dollars being spent every year on medical costs, which reduced real income and prevented an efficient use being made of resources, human and natural.[33]

The US countered that these reasons were a thinly disguised attempt to carve out special protection for Thai producers.[34] It also argued – and this is central for our purposes – that Thailand would be able to protect public health by a less trade-restrictive method: regulations requiring that the potentially harmful ingredients in different sorts of cigarettes, domestic or foreign, be clearly indicated to the consumer.[35] The panel decided in favour of the US. It found that labelling and ingredient disclosure regulations, as well as price rises induced by non-discriminatory taxation strategies, were less trade-restrictive methods of reducing domestic demand.[36] Thailand's measures were therefore not necessary for the protection of public health.[37]

Of interest here is the *character* of the non-trade objective that a member state can pursue, such as the protection of public health or the environment. Objectives such as these do not stand on their own. The level at which they are pursued domestically is tied up with other social values demanding satisfaction. One society, placing a high value on consumer sovereignty, will also accept the greater risks to public health that go with allowing people to make up their own minds about a product. Another society will aim at a higher level of health protection because it feels less constrained by the value placed on informed consumer choice. The second was true of Thailand. Assuming for these purposes their bona fides when they denied protectionist motives, they did not trust the average consumer to react appropriately to warning labels on cigarette packages, nor to price increases. In short, they took a paternalist approach to the proper balance between achieving certain health objectives and respecting freedom of consumer choice.

The GATT panel did not reject this paternalist approach as a matter of ethical principle. That would not be within its brief. It rejected the approach because of the need to find the solution with the least impact on trade. The effect – if not in intention – substituted a different weighting for the value of free consumer choice, and this in turn yielded a different level of health protection that would probably be attained. Labelling requirements place public health objectives more in the hands of individuals deciding the level of risk they will run. Within a population, the pattern of choice is likely to result in more smoking-related illness than would an outright ban on imports. It is a lesser level of protection, but one that gives greater

---

31 Ibid. § 28.
32 Ibid. § 54.
33 Ibid. § 21.
34 Ibid. § 23.
35 Ibid. § 23.
36 Ibid. § 77, 78.
37 Ibid. § 75 – setting the issue in terms of 'necessity'.

place to other important values in keeping with what was identified earlier as the proportion-ality element, rather than the 'least impact' element, in the requirement that a measure must be necessary for the promotion of a non-trade objective.

From a functionalist perspective, this decision makes sense. If one's point of departure is that the WTO's distinctive mission is to bring about 'an integrated, more viable and durable multilateral trading system', then this is the dominant concern, and the panel should require members to arrange their local values so as to do least damage to that objective.

A different approach can be seen in the *Asbestos* case.[38] There, the WTO was willing to allow France to ban imports of asbestos and products containing asbestos. It found, inter alia, that the prohibition was 'necessary' to protect human life or health within the terms of GATT Article XX(b). It specifically said, 'WTO members have the right to determine the *level* of protection of health that they consider appropriate in a given situation.'[39] Canada had argued that the French could not unilaterally fix the level of risk to health to be avoided, but this was precisely what the Appellate Body said did fall within the prerogative of a WTO member.[40]

The approach to levels of health protection in *Asbestos* certainly gives more room to domestic priorities than does the approach taken in *Thai Cigarettes*. However, this result might be thought to have gone too far in the opposite direction. By way of analogy, the inter-national human rights system sets itself to protect freedom of expression, and the system allows that right to be balanced against a member state's need to protect national security.[41] If the state were allowed to unilaterally set the level of national security it wanted, and then to fix restrictions on speech that were necessary to attain *that level*, the result of fixing the ultimate objective so high could easily shrink freedom of expression to a vanishing point.

An impasse threatens here. Too little deference to the priorities of WTO members risks unduly narrowing the room for them to make basic value choices; and too great a deference to those priorities risks unduly narrowing the place of the right to freedom of economic activity, insofar as this is considered to be a fundamental right. Both of these are routes that this analysis has set itself to avoid, for the sake of an approach that is not a hostage to the sometimes deep political cleavages among trading partners. An impartial solution might lie in looking more closely at the proper adjustments between trade and non-trade interests.

7 Rethinking the directions of adjustment between trade and non-trade interests

Elements of a different approach can be borrowed from the constitutional traditions of modern democracies, though they do require some alteration in this context, since we need to keep in mind the fundamental differences between organisations like the WTO on the one hand, and the state on the other. On a functional approach to the balance between trade and non-trade interests, as has been seen, the basic rights located in the shared and general objec-tives of the WTO – such as those embedded in the promotion of sustainable development – must always be adjusted so as to have least impact on the rights furthered by its unique, special objective: the promotion of free trade. In a civic order, the adjustment runs in the opposite direction. It is the general objectives that are primary, even if they are widely shared with

---

38 Ibid.
39 Ibid. §§ 165, 168 (emphasis added).
40 Ibid. § 168.
41 ICCPR, Art. 19(2) and (3).

other institutions, and the special objectives that must be read so as to do least damage to them. Respect for the human rights furthered by free trade, as well as for those potentially damaged by free trade, are all to be shaped in the light of the general objectives, with no automatic priority for one set over the other. Instead, any one of the basic rights can be adjusted in favour of any of the others. This is so even if, once mutual adjustment is accomplished, one of the rights does take ultimate priority.

To draw an analogy from another constitutional domain, the preservation of life is ultimately more important than is the interest in freedom of movement along the highway. But it is not true that each and every level of risk of death is more important to prevent than is any given level of freedom of movement. Evidence shows that the death rate on highways is reduced by a significant but decreasing number for every mile per hour of reduction in permitted speed. Assume that the reduction is 10,000 deaths in a given population for every mile of reduction between 100 and 90 mph; 1,000 from 50–40 mph; and 100 from 40–20 mph, and 10 between 20–10 mph. Even though the preservation of life is more important than is freedom of movement along the highway, it does not follow that the right to freedom of movement must always be adjusted downwards so as to have the least impact on the death rate. At a certain point a polity may, and sometimes must, *reverse the direction of compromise*, limiting the attention paid to the risk of death in favour of the right to freedom of movement, however clearly a certain number of deaths is linked to a further reduction in speed.[42]

Looking at the same point in a trade setting, consider the example of a country that wants to ban imports of a certain product on grounds of risk to health, but allows local producers to manufacture and market a like product. Assume that it wishes to exclude the imports because their pricing and packaging will substantially increase their consumption per person. Now consider two such products: the higher per capita consumption of one carries a marginally higher risk of threat to life-threatening illness, and another that carries a substantially higher risk of a life-threatening illness. An example of the former could be a food that, beyond a certain level of consumption, tends to cause obesity which in turn can marginally increase the incidence of certain diseases such as cancer; and an example of the latter could be another food which, beyond a certain level of consumption, radically increases the incidence of that cancer. Assume finally that, as in *Thai Cigarettes*, it is not practical or desirable for a country to totally ban the domestic consumption of these products, the local variety of which are much less attractive to the population.

In the first situation, if the local production and sale of such food is allowed, then it seems appropriate for the WTO to demand that all regulations aimed at controlling the level of its consumption be effected in the least trade-restrictive way: such as by non-discriminatory labelling requirements that carry appropriate warnings. Leaving the choice of the imported product up to the consumer – where it and its domestic cousin carry the appropriate warning label – would be likely to yield a greater number of cases of obesity than would an outright ban of the import. Nevertheless, it would be a way of balancing the two competing concerns of sustaining non-discriminatory access to markets and protecting this domain of public health. The latter objective can be pursued with vigour, but via compulsory warnings and advice on labels.

In the second situation, if the state allows increased consumption of a product which leads to a substantial threat to life, it might be in violation of relevant international conventions for

---

42 This argument builds on some points made by Jeremy Waldron, 'Rights in Conflict' (1989) 99(3) *Ethics* 503, 509–12; 516–18.

a failure to act.[43] How should the trading system approach the options in front of it? Once again, the choices range from labelling requirements through to outright bans on imports. Here, it is submitted, the state should be allowed to choose the import-reducing measure that will do most to reduce the risk to life which it is obliged by other international conventions to pursue. The direction of adjustment is reversed: rather than finding a method of protecting human life that has the least negative impact on trade; the state would be allowed here to adjust the flow of trade in a way that has the least impact on human life.

It is not, of course, easy to draw lines between degrees of risk of harm arising from the import of different sorts of goods and services, and hence to know when it would be appropriate to alter the direction of adjustment between trading and non-trading interests in the light of human rights requirements. However, the bodies charged with the primary duty of interpreting the meaning of these basic rights do provide us with guidelines: either in the form of norms coming from organisations that specialise in a particular domain, such as the ILO or WHO; or from bodies with a more general mandate, such as the General Comments and Statements on the meaning of provisions in the ICESCR made by the Committee on Economic Social and Cultural Rights. These can be drawn upon by WTO panels in order to see when a member should be given the scope by the trading treaties to adjust the requirements of trade so as to do least damage to a non-trading interest, and when it should be required to adjust the non-trading interest to the requirements of trade.

The important thing is to move away from a *blanket* commitment to a 'least trade-restrictive' reading of the 'necessity' requirement. There are indeed principles established in some WTO cases that take us in this direction, acknowledging the right of a state to restrict imports in order to meet its international obligations, and allowing the level at which that commitment is to be fixed to flow from that undertaking rather than be compromised by the 'least trade-restrictive' demand.[44] Unless this is done, a commitment to the least trade-restrictive solution can sit like a lid on top of a wide range of states' engagements to their subjects. The result is something we are familiar with: the complaint worldwide that the WTO weakens the ability of member states to pursue policies that are valuable in themselves, but which when pursued might make the promotion of free trade more difficult. The approach considered here aims to keep an equitable balance of the full range of basic rights at stake in trading relations. This is the approach called for by civic principles of interpretation.

There are signs of this strategy in more recent WTO jurisprudence. In the *China Publications* case, the Appellate Body considered a trade-restrictive measure aimed at protecting public morals.[45] It accepted that the state was entitled to set for itself a high level of protection of a value such as that embodied in the concept of public morality. This had to be preceded by establishing that the value in question was indeed a particularly important one for it to pursue.[46] Once the importance and desired level of protection of the value were clear, there would then be an evaluation by the WTO of the material contribution that a given trade-restrictive measure made to the state's objective. The greater the contribution, the more likely

---

43 For an example in which the failure by the state to secure individuals against a reasonably preventable danger to health and safety that was so grave as to amount to a violation of the right to life under Art. 2 of the European Convention on Human Rights, see *Oneryildiz v Turkey,* App. No. 48939/99 (Judgment of 18 June 2002).

44 See the *'Shrimp/Turtle'* case (n. 19).

45 'China – Measures Affecting Trading Rights and Distribution Services For Certain Publications and Audio-visual Entertainment Products' (December 2009) WTO Doc. WT/DS363/AB/R 21.

46 Ibid. para. 241.

that the Panel or Appellate Body would find the measure to be 'necessary'. There could also be a consideration of less trade-restrictive alternatives to the measure being imposed by the challenged state, but this would factor in only if such alternatives would deliver the same level of material contribution to the value which the state was protecting.[47] On the other hand, when a challenged measure does not make a clearly material contribution to the core value, then it becomes more vulnerable to being overridden by the WTO's pressure to find a less trade-restrictive means of regulation.

7.1 Factoring in Trading Interests

It is important that we do not lose sight of our initial willingness to place human rights on both sides of the divide between trade and non-trade interests. Those offering goods and services, as well as those potentially damaged by the terms on which those offers are made, have these basic rights potentially at stake. This means that when a WTO Dispute Settlement Panel is considering, for example, whether or not a member state has violated TRIPS by refusing to grant a local patent to the inventor of an important drug (as is normally required by Article 27 of the TRIPS Agreement), then the Panel should take into account the inventor's fundamental property rights as provided for by Article 15(1)(c) of the ICESCR. However, the inventor's property right under TRIPS will also count as a property right in the human rights instrument only if it is brought within the full set of other relevant rights, and adjusted against them. Sometimes, as was argued above, the direction of adjustment must from the dominant objective of the treaty towards having least impact on an objective lying outside the treaty. If these balances are made part of the approach, then the UN Sub-Commission on the Promotion and Protection of Human Rights is likely to conclude that all facets of the applicable intellectual property rights have been respected.[48]

This cannot be adequately done in the functionalist mode, requiring as it does that those who might suffer from an abuse of intellectual property rights should have their own rights regularly adjusted so as to do least damage to the interests of those who claim their property rights under TRIPS. The member state is allowed by the WTO-administered treaties to give ultimate priority to certain non-trade interests, including the space provided by Article 8 of TRIPS. Mutual compromise among rights, along the lines sketched in the previous section, would be the better route.

8 Conclusion

What has been discussed in this chapter is the need to give concrete meaning to the UN's claim that human rights should be the 'primary objective' of trade, investment and financial policy.[49] In doing so, we have tried to navigate between two poles of a dilemma. On the one

---

47 Ibid. para. 243.

48 The Sub-Commission's report 'affirms that the right to protection of the moral and material interests resulting from any scientific, literary or artistic production of which one is the author is a human right, subject to limitations in the public interest, in accordance with Article 27, ¶ 2, of the Universal Declaration of Human Rights and Article 15, ¶ 1(c), of the International Covenant on Economic, Social and Cultural Rights Sub-Commission on Human Rights Resolution 2000/7 ¶ 1'.

49 UN Human Rights Commission, Resolution of September 4, 1998, available at: http://www.pdhre.org/involved/uncommission.html, accessed 23/02/2013.

hand, it is essential to respect the fact that the WTO is qualitatively different from a state: it has a mandate to promote free trade that is stronger and more narrowly focused than are the agendas of its constituent members. On the other hand, if the WTO is encouraged to focus too narrowly on its particular mandate, this can disrupt the wider domestic agendas of its members, so pulling them away from their attempt to achieve a fair balance of all relevant human rights. We have tried to reconcile these two elements by insisting that there is one thing that the trading body and member states have in common: they must both respect the *relationships of equitable balance* among human rights in the same way. This need for a fair balance means several concrete things. It means that the members of the organisation should consider a wider range of rights than allowed by a functional understanding of the WTO's powers. It also means that none of these rights, including trade-related rights, is to be given systematic priority over other rights. Instead, the priorities to be achieved are more varied, depending on the rights concerned and on the circumstances surrounding their realisation – a variety of solutions that a civic approach encourages.

The civic approach might also permit the trading system to respond to the criticism that it is only willing to take account of non-trade interests as exceptions to its core objectives.[50] The argument here is designed to move the system beyond this occasional and exceptional status for such values. It calls for two possible directions of adjustment – shaping trading rules to be least restrictive of non-trading interests in some cases, and shaping the protection of non-trading interests to be least trade-restrictive in others. This might make it possible to move beyond some of the traditional rhetoric in debates. There is, for example, the fear that linking trade to a human rights agenda will wrongly mix politics and economics. For some, this translates into a worry that the economic agenda at the centre of the WTO will dominate the domestic political agendas of member states. This chapter has considered how it might be possible to avoid this result, while preserving a distinct and robust role for the WTO as a trade body. There are also those who fear that linking trade and human rights draws the WTO into politics, and that this is to be avoided. However, there is no such thing as a free trade agenda that does not carry within it some priorities with political significance. Whichever way the WTO turns, its decisions will have an effect on available political options. The same is true for international human rights: however they are interpreted, they will also have an impact on political choices. What we need in both cases is a way of setting an international benchmark for what is minimally acceptable in the relationship between the two domains. We can no longer allow the standards set by international trade and those set by international human rights to function separately. Human rights can frame world trade, so that trade can in turn be a motor for bringing about what these rights promise.

Select bibliography

L. Compa and S. Diamond (eds), *Human Rights, Labour Rights, and International Trade* (University of Pennsylvania Press, 1996).

T. Cottier (ed.), *Human Rights and International Trade* (OUP, 2005).

F. Francioni (ed.), *Environment, Human Rights, and International Trade* (Hart Publishing, 2001).

F. Garcia, 'Trade and Justice: Linking the Trade Linkage Debates', Symposium on Linkage as Phenomenon: An Interdisciplinary Approach, (1998) 19(2) *University of Pennsylvania Journal of International Economic Law*, 391.

50 'The fundamental nature of these entitlements as rights requires an approach that sets the promotion and protection of human rights as objectives of trade liberalization, not as exceptions': 'Liberalization of Trade in Services' (n. 2) at para. 7.

F. Garcia, 'The Global Market and Human Rights: Trading Away the Human Rights Principle' (1999) 25(1) *Brooklyn Journal of International Law*, 51–98.

L. Helfer, 'Adjudicating Copyright Claims under the TRIPS Agreement: The Case for a European Human Rights Analogy' (1998) 39 *Harvard International Law Journal*, 357–441.

R. Housman, 'Democratising International Trade Decision-Making', Symposium on 'Greening the GATT' (1994) 27(3) *Cornell International Law Journal*, 699.

S. Joseph, *Blame it on the WTO? A Human Rights Critique* (OUP, 2011).

A. Seita, 'Globalization and the Convergence of Values' (1997) 30 *Cornell International Law Journal*, 429.

R. Siegel, *Employment and Human Rights: The International Dimension* (University of Pennsylvania Press, 1994).

16

International finance and investment and human rights

Peter T. Muchlinski

This chapter maps out the main human rights issues and responsibilities facing financial lenders. Financial lenders are defined here as institutions whose primary function is the provision of loan capital for public or private economic purposes. They include multilateral lenders, specifically the World Bank Group (WBG) and the International Monetary Fund (IMF), collectively referred to as the International Financial Institutions (IFIs),[1] and private commercial banks. Other financial services providers, such as insurance companies, pension funds and portfolio equity investors, are not considered, because their main function is not the provision of loan capital but other specific financial services and/or equity investment. Nor are multilateral or national investment guarantee bodies, such as the Multilateral Investment Guarantee Agency (MIGA) or the UK Export Credits Guarantee Department (ECGD), included as they are primarily political risk insurers.

This chapter focuses on financial lenders as financial lending has significant social and environmental, as well as economic, impacts – a matter well recognised among such lenders. Both the IFIs and commercial banks have established procedures for the examination of the social and environmental impacts of their lending decisions and practices. For private lenders this has become an issue of reputational risk, given that lending to clients, whose activities may infringe social and environmental standards, can lead, and has led, to public criticism and concerted campaigning from non-governmental organisations (NGOs). In the case of IFIs, shifts in policy from purely economic development considerations, towards more socially and environmentally sensitive development considerations have necessitated the integration of these wider issues into the process of project lending by the WBG and into financial stabilisation programmes undertaken by the IMF. Equally, the rise in the use of public–private partnerships (PPPs) as a means of funding major infrastructure projects has involved private

---

1 The World Bank Group consists of the International Bank for Reconstruction and Development (IBRD), the International Development Agency (IDA), the International Finance Corporation (IFC) and the International Centre for Settlement of Investment Disputes (ICSID). For a general overview, see Andreas F. Lowenfeld, *International Economic Law*, 2nd edn (OUP, 2008) Pt VII 'The International Monetary System'.

lenders and IFIs in arrangements with the host state that often involve major social and environmental considerations and responsibilities.

That said, by comparison, human rights–focused analysis is much less advanced in both banks and IFIs. In 2004 a study on human rights and banking, undertaken by F&C Asset Management and KPMG, asked the question: 'Are human rights relevant to the financial sector?' Based on a survey of the experiences and practices of nine international banks, the study concluded that 'the answer received from all participants was an indisputable "Yes" ', and that 'awareness is most certainly growing' but that 'this is still a very new area for the sector. Whilst human rights issues are being addressed in nascent policies and risk assessment procedures, the sector's approach is far from comprehensive and remains largely *ad hoc*.'[2]

As will be discussed below, banks have made considerable progress in relation to human rights responsibilities since 2004, but this is still a relatively short period of experience. In addition the development of wider human rights responsibilities for business enterprises is still in its infancy. Only in 2011 did the UN adopt the Guiding Principles on Business and Human Rights Implementing the United Nations 'Protect, Respect and Remedy' Framework (UN Guiding Principles; the UN Framework), the first comprehensive international instrument to address this issue that has gained official recognition in the UN system.[3] The corporate responsibility to respect human rights contained within the UN Guiding Principles is a non-binding obligation under international law given the lack of international personality for corporate actors.[4] Equally, at the level of municipal law there are few binding obligations upon business enterprises to observe human rights norms, though this is slowly changing. For example, in the United States recent laws have introduced human rights disclosure and reporting requirements for companies in relation to 'conflict diamonds' and human trafficking and slavery.[5]

---

2 F&C Asset Management and KPMG, *Banking on Human Rights: Confronting Human Rights in the Financial Sector* (KPMG, 2004), at 35, available at http://us.kpmg.com/microsite/FSLibraryDotCom/docs/Banking%20on%20Human%20Rights_FC_KPMG.pdf. The nine banks involved were: ABN-Amro, Barclay's, Credit Suisse group, HSBC, Morgan Stanley, Rabobank, Royal Bank of Scotland, Standard Chartered and UBS.

3 UN Human Rights Council, Seventeenth Session 21 March 2011, 'Guiding Principles on Business and Human Rights: Implementing the United Nations "Protect, Respect and Remedy" Framework', UN Doc. A/HRC/17/31, available at http://www.ohchr.org/documents/issues/business/A.HRC.17.31.pdf (Guiding Principles). Adopted by UN Human Rights Council Res. 17/4 (6 July 2011) UN Doc. A/HRC/RES/17/4, available at http://www.business-humanrights.org/media/documents/un-human-rights-council-resolution-re-human-rights-transnational-corps-eng-6-jul-2011.pdf.

4 See UN Guiding Principles at General Principles: 'Nothing in these Guiding Principles should be read as creating new international law obligations, or as limiting or undermining any legal obligations a State may have undertaken or be subject to under international law with regard to human rights.' On the legal status of corporate actors in international law see further Peter Muchlinski, 'Corporations in International Law', in Rudiger Wolfrum (ed.), *The Max Planck Encyclopedia of Public International Law*, online edition (OUP, 2008), available at http://www.mpepil.com/subscriber_articles_by_author2?author—uchlinski, Peter&letter—.

5 See Dodd-Frank Wall Street Reform and Consumer Protection Act 2010, s. 1502, available at http://www.sec.gov/about/laws/wallstreetreform-cpa.pdf, and the Transparency in Supply Chains Act 2010 (California), available at http://info.sen.ca.gov/pub/09–10/bill/sen/sb_0651–0700/sb_657_bill_20100930_chaptered.html (entered force 1 January 2012).

A Federal Bill to the same effect was introduced before the US Congress (112th Congress 1st Session): Business Transparency on Trafficking and Slavery Act, available at http://www.gpo.gov/fdsys/pkg/BILLS-112hr2759ih/pdf/BILLS-112hr2759ih.pdf.

The IFIs have been discussing human rights concerns for a longer time than commercial lenders. They began actively to consider the human rights impacts of their practices during the late 1990s. Nonetheless, the role of human rights as determining factors in assessing projects and programmes remains an open issue. While IFIs have acknowledged a role for human rights considerations as a factor informing their work, they have never accepted an express *legal* duty to follow human rights norms either in their substantive operations or in the running of their organisations.

The present chapter will address the main issues relating to human rights and financial lending in the light of the new UN Framework on business and human rights. Briefly described, the UN Framework, as contained in the UN Guiding Principles, revolves around a state duty to protect human rights, the above-mentioned corporate responsibility to respect human rights and access to an adequate remedy for human rights infringements by corporate actors.[6] The state duty to protect is a key element in the developing debate over the human rights responsibilities of IFIs. As organisations composed of member states, the majority of which have accepted their duties to respect, protect and promote human rights under the main international human rights instruments (the 'International Bill of Rights'[7]), the IFIs are implicated in the state's duty to protect human rights and in the oversight of business enterprises in the exercise of their responsibility to respect when they are involved in IFI projects and policy delivery. This question will be considered in section 16.1 as one aspect of the wider range of issues raised by the human rights responsibilities of IFIs. The corporate responsibility to respect human rights is a central issue in relation to the human rights responsibilities of banks. In particular it requires the exercise of human rights due diligence as a means of discharging the responsibility to respect. Its implications will be discussed in section 16.2 of the chapter. The third element of the UN Framework, access to remedy, will be discussed in relation to the specific questions of remediation raised in the differing contexts of IFI and commercial bank activity and will form an integral part of the discussions in both sections 16.1 and 16.2.

1 IFIs and human rights responsibilities

The debate over whether, and if so, to what extent, IFIs have human rights responsibilities has moved from an initial denial of any such obligations towards the current position where human rights considerations clearly play a role in IFI activities but where that role is not based on any formal legal acceptance of human rights obligations. This will be discussed in the first sub-section in the context of changing IFI practice that has led to some regard for human rights issues in the work of IFIs. The second sub-section will consider whether there should be a legally binding duty placed upon IFIs to observe human rights and how this can be

---

6 For further discussion of the UN Framework see Wesley Cragg, 'Ethics, Enlightened Self-Interest, and the Corporate Responsibility to Respect Human Rights: A Critical Look at the Justificatory Foundations of the UN Framework' (2012) 22(1) *Business Ethics Quarterly* 9–36; and Peter Muchlinski, 'Implementing the New UN Corporate Human Rights Framework: Implications for Corporate Law, Governance and Regulation' (2012) 22(1) *Business Ethics Quarterly* 145–77.

7 The International Bill of Human Rights consists of the Universal Declaration of Human Rights 1948, the International Covenant on Economic, Social and Cultural Rights 1966, and the International Covenant on Civil and Political Rights 1966 and its two Optional Protocols. See UN Fact Sheet No. 2 (Rev. 1), *The International Bill of Human Rights*, available at http://www.ohchr.org/Documents/Publications/FactSheet2Rev.1en.pdf.

justified, while the third sub-section will deal with issues of remediation in relation to IFI activities.

1.1 IFIs, human rights and policy change

There is no express reference to human rights responsibilities in the constitutive instruments of the WBG organisations or the IMF. Thus Article I of the World Bank's Articles of Agreement places economic reconstruction and development at the heart of the Bank's purposes.[8] This is supplemented by the aims of promoting foreign investment and balanced trade, the provision of project loans, and considering the impact of international investment on business conditions in the territories of members.[9] Similarly, the main purposes of the International Development Association (IDA) and the International Finance Corporation (IFC) are to promote the economic development of their less-developed members though financing and other economic and business support functions,[10] while the International Centre for Settlement of Investment Disputes (ICSID) functions to offer dispute settlement facilities for investor–state investment disputes '[c]onsidering the need for international cooperation for economic development, and the role of private international investment therein'.[11]

The IMF Articles of Agreement describe the purposes of the Fund as being the 'promotion of international monetary cooperation through a permanent institution which provides the machinery for consultation and collaboration on international monetary problems'. This is to be achieved by facilitating the expansion and balanced growth of international trade, thereby promoting and maintaining 'high levels of employment and real income and to the development of the productive resources of all members as primary objectives of economic policy'. In addition the Fund will promote exchange stability, assist in the establishment of a multilateral system of payments in respect of current transactions, and make the general resources

---

8 Articles of Agreement of the World Bank Art. I(i): the Bank is to 'assist in the reconstruction and development of territories of members by facilitating the investment of capital for productive purposes, including the restoration of economies destroyed or disrupted by war, the reconversion of productive facilities to peacetime needs and the encouragement of the development of productive facilities and resources in less developed countries', available at http://web.worldbank.org/WBSITE/EXTERNAL/EXTABOUTUS/0,,contentMDK:20049563~pagePK:43912~menuPK:58863~piPK:36602,00.html#I1.

9 Ibid. Art. I(ii)–(v).

10 International Development Association Articles of Agreement, Art. I: 'The purposes of the Association are to promote economic development, increase productivity and thus raise standards of living in the less-developed areas of the world included within the Association's membership, in particular by providing finance to meet their important developmental requirements on terms which are more flexible and bear less heavily on the balance of payments than those of conventional loans . . .', available at http://web.worldbank.org/WBSITE/EXTERNAL/EXTABOUTUS/IDA/0,,contentMDK:20052360~menuPK:115747~pagePK:83988~piPK:84004~theSitePK:73154,00.html; International Finance Corporation Articles of Agreement, Art. I: 'The purpose of the Corporation is to further economic development by encouraging the growth of productive private enterprise in member countries, particularly in the less developed areas . . .', available at http://www1.ifc.org/wps/wcm/connect/corp_ext_content/ifc_external_corporate_site/about+ifc/articles+of+agreement/about+ifc+-+ifc+articles+of+agreement+-+article+i.

11 ICSID Convention on the Settlement of Investment Disputes Between States and Nationals of Other States, Preamble, available at http://icsid.worldbank.org/ICSID/StaticFiles/basicdoc/CRR_English-final.pdf.

of the Fund temporarily available to members under adequate safeguards in order to correct maladjustments in their balance of payments.[12]

Upon a narrow reading of these instruments it appears that human rights considerations play no appreciable part in the work of the IFIs. Indeed their mandates are geared, respectively, towards economic development and financial stability in the global economy, and thus only considerations relevant to the operation of these mandates can be taken into account.[13] In addition the World Bank, IDA and IFC Articles introduce an identical 'political affairs' exception to the legitimate operating parameters of these institutions, which requires that only 'economic considerations' weighed impartially shall be relevant to their decisions.[14]

Nonetheless, human rights considerations have made some headway in the operations of these institutions. At a conceptual level both legal and developmental arguments have been used to justify this. Thus according to former General Counsel of the WBG, Ibrahim Shihata, the Articles of Agreement should be read teleologically so that wider considerations can be taken into account when necessary. Shihata accepts that 'the World Bank's mandate should enable the organization to assist member countries and to improve the economic standards of their peoples'.[15] However, he saw these efforts as being limited to issues of economic and social rights.[16] Shihata stopped short of advocating that the World Bank should take an active role in the advancement of political rights in donor countries but accepted that, in certain extreme cases, the lack of political rights could affect the economic climate in which the Bank was offering its support and thus make this unviable.[17]

12 IMF Articles of Agreement, Art. I, available at http://www.imf.org/external/pubs/ft/aa/pdf/aa.pdf.

13 See Daniel D. Bradlow, 'The World Bank, the IMF, and Human Rights' (1996) 6 *Transnational Law and Contemporary Problems* 47–90 at 54 and 72.

14 For example the World Bank Articles of Agreement, Art. IV (10): '*Political Activity Prohibited*. The Bank and its officers shall not interfere in the political affairs of any member; nor shall they be influenced in their decisions by the political character of the member or members concerned. Only economic considerations shall be relevant to their decisions, and these considerations shall be weighed impartially in order to achieve the purposes stated in Art. I.' See too IDA Articles of Agreement, Art. V, s. 6 and IFC Articles of Agreement Art. III (9). Similarly, Art. III, s. 5(b) restricts political considerations in Bank financing: '(b) The Bank shall make arrangements to ensure that the proceeds of any loan are used only for the purposes for which the loan was granted, with due attention to considerations of economy and efficiency and without regard to political or other non-economic influences or considerations.' See too IDA, Art. V, s. 1(g).

15 Ibrahim F.I. Shihata, 'Human Rights, Development, and International Financial Institutions' (1992) 8(1) *American University International Law Review* 27–36 at 31.

16 Ibid.

17 In a 1991 legal opinion Shihata wrote '[v]iolation of political rights may . . . reach such proportions as to become a Bank concern, either due to significant direct economic effects or if it results in international obligations relevant to the Bank, such as those mandated by binding decisions of the United Nations Security Council'; see Legal Memorandum of the Vice President and General Counsel of IBRD, 'Issues of "Governance" in Borrowing Members – The Extent of Their Relevance Under the Bank's Articles of Agreement' (5 Feb. 1991) cited in Shihata (n. 15) 32. In an earlier Opinion, Shihata also wrote 'political events which have a bearing on the economic conditions of a member or on the member's ability to implement a project or the Bank's ability to supervise the project may be taken into consideration by the Board'; see *Prohibition of Political Activities Under the IBRD Articles of Agreement and Its Relevance to the Work of the Executive Directors*, sec. M87–1409, 8 (23 Dec. 1987) cited in Ibrahim F.I. Shihata, 'The World Bank and Human Rights: An Analysis of the Legal Issues and the Record of Achievements' (1988) 17(1) Denv. J. Int'l L. & Pol'y 39–67 at 46.

By contrast, a subsequent successor to Dr Shihata as General Counsel, Roberto Dañino, expressed in a landmark legal opinion to the Executive Directors a more unequivocal view of how the Articles of Agreement should be interpreted.[18] While accepting that only economic considerations were of relevance to Bank decisions, he notes that the host of social, environmental and political elements that may affect economic growth all have to be taken into account by the Bank.[19] These factors include human rights. Unlike Shihata, Dañino argues that both economic, social and cultural rights and civil and political rights can be taken into account depending on the circumstances of each case.[20]

Furthermore, Dañino does not see the political prohibition as a barrier to human rights considerations. This was introduced so that the WBG institutions refrained from endorsing or mandating a particular form of government, political bloc or political ideology. But this did not prevent the Bank from considering non-economic issues, including human rights, which have economic consequences or implications, provided this was done in a non-partisan, non-ideological and neutral manner, and so long as these were related to projects supported by the Bank.[21] Dañino concludes, going beyond the advice of Ibrahim Shihata, that:

> [T]he Articles of Agreement permit, and in some cases require, the Bank to recognize the human rights dimensions of its development policies and activities since it is now evident that human rights are an intrinsic part of the Bank's mission.[22]

Dañino adds that 'in egregious situations, where extensive violations of human rights reach pervasive proportions, the Bank should disengage if it can no longer achieve its purposes'.[23]

By contrast, legal opinion concerning the IMF's responsibilities in relation to human rights is more cautious. According to former General Counsel to the IMF, Francois Gianviti, as a monetary agency functioning primarily at the macroeconomic level, the Fund has different responsibilities from the WBG which function as development agencies at the level of individual sectors. Its functions concentrate upon financial stability. That said, the work of the Fund does impact indirectly on certain economic, social and cultural rights contained in the International Covenant on Economic, Social and Cultural Rights (ICESCR).[24] This is achieved by the Fund's promotion of a stable system of exchange rates, current payments free of restrictions and a policy of promoting economic growth and providing support for balance of payments problems. Thus 'the Fund helps provide the economic conditions that are a precondition for the achievement of the rights set out in the Covenant.'[25] However, Gianviti

---

18 Roberto Dañino, 'Legal Opinion on Human Rights and the Work of the World Bank – Senior Vice President and General Counsel January 27, 2006' (copy on file with author), available at http://www.ifiwatchnet.org/?q=en/node/335.

19 Ibid. para. 10.

20 Ibid. para. 13.

21 Ibid. para. 14.

22 Ibid. para. 25.

23 Ibid. para. 22.

24 International Covenant on Economic, Social and Cultural Rights UNTS Vol. 993 (1976), available at http://treaties.un.org/doc/publication/UNTS/Volume%20993/v993.pdf.

25 Francois Gianviti, 'Economic, Social and Cultural Human Rights and the International Monetary Fund', in Philip Alston (ed.), *Non-State Actors and Human Rights* (OUP, 2005) at 137. See too the discussion of Gianviti's views in Andrew Clapham, *Human Rights Obligations of Non-State Actors* (OUP, 2006) at 145–49, where Clapham challenges this narrow view of the human rights responsibilities of the IMF.

is clear that the Fund has no legal obligation to observe the Covenant, as it is not a signatory of that treaty and it cannot be bound by its terms as a result of its relationship agreement with the UN, which renders the Fund a specialised agency of the UN. Nor does the Covenant represent binding customary international law such that the Fund could be expected to observe its contents independently of the Covenant.[26]

From the above it is clear that a stronger legal case has been made for the WBG having human rights responsibilities as compared to the IMF, a case based largely on the different functions of each set of IFIs. That said, the second relevant conceptual development rests with the changing idea of development itself. In particular in the last 20 or so years this concept has been explicitly linked to human rights and personal freedom in that pure economic development without corresponding human development is no longer seen as an adequate policy goal.[27] This shift has had a significant impact on the work of the IFIs and on the expectations placed upon them by civil society groups and by policy-makers. In 1998 the World Bank asserted that:

[P]ublic discourse on human rights and development too often ignores their fundamental two-way relationship. The world now accepts that sustainable development is impossible without human rights. What has been missing is the recognition that the advancement of an interconnected set of human rights is impossible *without development*.[28]

The linkage between development and human rights was also highlighted by Roberto Dañino as a reason for a stronger responsibility on the part of the WGB for human rights.[29] Both sets of IFIs have followed the development and human rights approach to varying degrees corresponding to their distinctive functions. The WBG's poverty reduction programmes have allowed the WBG institutions to cover many human rights-based questions through 'safeguard policies' for the protection of the environmental and social interests

26 Gianviti (n. 25) 118–30. See further the Agreement Between the United Nations and the International Monetary Fund Art. 1(2): 'The Fund is a specialized agency established by agreement among its member governments and having wide international responsibilities, as defined in its Articles of Agreement, in economic and related fields within the meaning of Article 57 of the Charter of the United Nations. By reason of the nature of its international responsibilities and the terms of its Articles of Agreement, the Fund is, and is required to function as, an independent international organization.' See http://www.imf.org/external/pubs/ft/sd/index.asp?decision=DN15.

27 See generally Stephen P. Marks, 'Human Rights and Development', in Sarah Joseph and Adam McBeth (eds), *Research Handbook on International Human Rights Law* (Edward Elgar Publishing, 2010) at 167; Varun Gauri and Siri Gloppen, *Human Rights Based Approaches to Development: Concepts, Evidence, and Policy*, World Bank Policy Research Working Paper 5938 (The World Bank Development Research Group Human Development and Public Services Team, January 2012), available at http://www-wds.worldbank.org/external/default/WDSContentServer/WDSP/IB/2012/01/09/000158349_20120109120516/Rendered/PDF/WPS5938.pdf; Laure-Hélène Piron with Tammie O'Neil, *Integrating Human Rights into Development: A Synthesis of Donor Approaches and Experiences* (OECD DAC Network on Governance (GOVNET), 2005), available at http://www.odi.org.uk/resources/docs/4404.pdf. For a conceptual approach see Amartya Sen, *Development as Freedom* (OUP, 1999).

28 World Bank, *Development and Human Rights: the Role of the World Bank* (World Bank, 1998) available at http://www.fao.org/righttofood/KC/downloads/vl/docs/HR%20and%20devlopment_the%20role%20of%20the%20WB.pdf.

29 Dañino (n. 18) para. 8.

of the communities in which the Bank operates. These require environmental impact assessments, protection of natural habitats and pest management, preventing adverse impacts on physical cultural resources, the protection of indigenous peoples and the avoidance, so far as feasible, of involuntary settlement as a result of Bank-sponsored projects.[30]

Equally, despite the different functions of the IMF, the Fund too has taken on board the need to focus on poverty reduction issues that arise in the course of discharging its mandate, with the result that member countries may seek to include human rights concerns into their Fund-supported poverty reduction programmes.[31] Of especial significance in this regard is the formal abandonment in the late 1990s of traditional 'structural adjustment' programmes by the WBG and IMF.

'Structural adjustment' is characterised by an emphasis on economic growth strategies based upon controls over public spending and management of the public sector, privatisation of state-owned enterprises, deregulation of barriers to trade and investment and the encouragement of private sector business. These policies, often referred to as the 'Washington Consensus', were seen as universally applicable to any country and were required as conditions of project lending by the WBG and stabilisation and balance of payments policies by the IMF.[32] They also opened the door to cooperation between the IFIs and private commercial interests whose influence over the design and terms of Bank and Fund financial arrangements grew, as witnessed by the increase in Bank support for PPPs as a means of funding major infrastructure projects,[33] and by the involvement of 'supplementary financiers' from private financial institutions in IMF financing to countries facing balance of payments crises.[34]

'Structural adjustment' became something of a bogey among development-oriented NGOs in the 1990s.[35] Such market-oriented approaches were criticised as undermining state sovereignty and placing too much power in the hands of IFI officials and private sector actors.[36] In addition structural adjustment policies were perceived as being potentially harmful to the promotion and protection of human rights as cuts in public expenditure could lead to increases in poverty and unemployment as access to social services and public sector jobs

---

30 For detailed discussion see Adam McBeth, *International Economic Actors and Human Rights* (Routledge, 2010), at 197–210.
31 See for example Sérgio Pereira Leite (Assistant Director, Office in Europe IMF), 'The International Monetary Fund and Human Rights', *Le Monde* (September 4, 2011), available at http://www.imf.org/external/np/vc/2001/090401.htm. This article is the first document to appear when 'human rights' is typed into the IMF search engine. There is little else that appears which deals directly with human rights. See too McBeth (n. 30) 184.
32 See McBeth (n. 30) 186–87; Celine Tan, *Governance Through Development: Poverty Reduction Strategies, International Law and the Disciplining of Third World States* (Routledge, 2011), at 46–47; and see Ioannis Glinavos, *Neoliberalism and the Law in Post-Communist Transition: The Evolving Role of Law in Russia's Transition to Capitalism* (Routledge, 2010), at 48–53 on the origins of the 'Washington Consensus.' See too Mac Darrow, *Between Light and Shadow: The World Bank, the International Monetary Fund and International Human Rights Law* (Hart Publishing, 2006), at 68–87.
33 See further the work of the donor funded body Public-Private Infrastructure Advisory Facility (PPIAF) to which the WBG institutions act as donors alongside other intergovernmental bodes and national governments, available at http://www.ppiaf.org/ppiaf/page/about-us.
34 Tan (n, 32) 48.
35 McBeth (n. 30) 185.
36 Tan (n. 32) 48–52.

declined.[37] Equally the UN's Millennium Development goals of 2000 placed a human-based approach to development at the heart of poverty alleviation for the twenty-first century.[38] In response the IFIs accepted that a purely economic approach to poverty reduction was inadequate, given its potential social costs.[39] Accordingly the IFIs introduced a process known as Poverty Reduction Strategy Papers (PRSPs).[40] The basic idea is that donor countries are encouraged to formulate a poverty reduction strategy as a condition for the receipt of assistance from the IFIs. This must include consideration of the poverty and social impacts of the strategy, though this does not include any express consideration of human rights standards and impacts. The evaluation of PRSPs from the perspective of effective poverty reduction and increased local 'ownership' of adjustment policies has been, on the whole, negative.[41] According to Tan, while the process of assessing official development financing has changed, the underlying substantive conditions for obtaining such financing have not and developing countries still retain little or no control over negotiations with their financiers.[42] Thus the shift to PRSPs can be properly described as a change of policy which formally requires greater attention to social issues but in practice remains rooted in the same basic economic conditionalities that characterised the earlier structural adjustment-oriented programmes and projects.

In more recent years the IFC has made significant efforts to deal with human rights-related issues. For example, in the late 1990s it introduced a policy of not funding projects harmful to child labour.[43] In 2006 the IFC introduced a comprehensive change in its social and environmental impact policy by way of new review procedures to be applied to social and environmental matters (the Sustainability Framework).[44] These reviews are carried out by the client rather than the IFC itself but the IFC must be satisfied that the assessment has identified the relevant risks and that the client can manage them. If not then finance is refused.[45] The 2006 edition of the Sustainability Framework applies to all investments assessed up to 31 December 2011.

On 1 January 2012 the second edition of the Framework was introduced following an 18-month consultation process with stakeholders around the world.[46] The principal modifications require assessment of the social and environmental implications of supply chain

37 McBeth (n. 30) 187–91; on labour implications see C.S. Venkata Ratnam, *Trade Unions and Structural Adjustment: A Guide for Trade Union Participation* (ACTRAV, International Labour Office, 1996), available at http://www.ilo.org/wcmsp5/groups/public/---ed_dialogue/---actrav/documents/publication/wcms_111437.pdf.

38 See further http://www.un.org/millenniumgoals/bkgd.shtml; Darrow (n. 32) 18.

39 See further World Bank (n. 28).

40 See McBeth (n. 30) 191–94; Tan (n. 32) ch. 3; Darrow (n. 32) 87–91.

41 McBeth (n. 30) 191–94.

42 Tan (n. 32) 205.

43 See IFC, *IFC's Policy Statement on Forced Labour and Harmful Child Labour* (IFC, March 1998), available at http://www.ifc.org/ifcext/enviro.nsf/AttachmentsByTitle/pol_ChildLabor/$FILE/ChildForcedLabor.pdf; IFC, *Good Practice Note: Addressing Child Labor in the Workplace and Supply Chain* (IFC, June 2002), available at http://www.ifc.org/ifcext/enviro.nsf/AttachmentsByTitle/p_childlabor/$FILE/ChildLabor.pdf.

44 IFC, *International Finance Corporation's Performance Standards on Social & Environmental Sustainability* (IFC 30 April 2006), available at http://www.ifc.org/ifcext/enviro.nsf/AttachmentsByTitle/pol_PerformanceStandards2006_full/$FILE/IFC+Performance+Standards.pdf.

45 McBeth (n. 30) 211.

46 See IFC, *Sustainability Framework – 2012 Edition* (IFC, 2012), available at http://www1.ifc.org/wps/wcm/connect/topics_ext_content/ifc_external_corporate_site/ifc+sustainability+framework/2012+edition/2012-edition#PerformanceStandards.

management, resource efficiency and climate change, business and human rights (including human rights due diligence), and the securing of 'Free, Prior and Informed Consent' from indigenous peoples affected by investment projects, in line with the 2007 United Nations Declaration on the Rights of Indigenous Peoples. In relation to human rights due diligence, the IFC launched its new human rights impact assessment guide for corporations in 2010.[47] The IFC Guide provides guidance on all elements of human rights due diligence, as advanced in the above-mentioned UN 'Protect, Respect and Remedy' Framework. The approach of the IFC Guide will be discussed in section 16.2 when the due diligence responsibilities of commercial banks will be considered.

From the above it is clear that human rights issues do play a part in the work of the WBG and (to a lesser extent) the IMF. The objectives provisions in the Articles of Agreement have not been a barrier to the consideration of human rights impacts where this is relevant to the effective assessment and execution of policies and projects. This is so as a result of a purposive approach to the interpretation of these provisions and by reason of the adoption of a more human-centred concept of development by the IFIs in practice. However, neither set of institutions will accept a legally binding obligation to use human rights standards as the basis for their review of projects and policies. They remain, at heart, economic institutions run by economists and not constitutional review bodies run by lawyers.[48] Nonetheless, a number of arguments can be made for the introduction of such a binding obligation.

1.2 A positive legal duty to observe human rights?

A positive legal obligation to undertake a human rights-based analysis of IFI projects, policies and operations is seen as important by its advocates, as it focuses attention on the rights of those individuals and communities affected by a lending project or policy.[49] This provides a benchmark for assessment that cannot be side-stepped by an exercise of discretion or ignored as irrelevant on purely economic grounds. In addition it can form the basis of remedial claims should such rights be infringed,[50] and a human rights-based approach can make the operation

---

47 IFC and IBLF, *Guide to Human Rights Impact Assessment and Management (HRIAM)* (IFC & IBLF, 2010), available at http://www.guidetohriam.org/app/images/documents/Guide%20to%20 HRIAM%20booklet%20English.pdf.

48 On the limited influence of lawyers, as compared to economists, in the World Bank as an explanation for the rejection of binding legal duties relating to human rights, see Galit A. Sarfaty, 'Why Culture Matters in International Institutions: The Marginality of Human Rights at the World Bank', (2009) 103(4) *American Journal of International Law* 647–83. For a discussion of institutional factors as a barrier to the evolution of a human rights approach to development issues at the World Bank, see: Kirk Herbertson, Kim Thompson and Robert Goodland, *A Roadmap for Integrating Human Rights into the World Bank Group* (World Resources Institute, 2010), available at http://www. wri.org/publication/roadmap-for-integrating-human-rights-into-world-bank-group.

49 See generally the 'Tilburg Guiding Principles on World Bank, IMF and Human Rights', in Willem van Genugten, Paul Hunt and Susan Mathews (eds), *World Bank, IMF and Human Rights* (Wolf Legal Publishers, 2003), at 247–55, also available at: http://ssrn.com/abstract=957195; Robert T. Coulter, Leonardo A. Crippa and Emily Wann, *Principles of International Law for Multilateral Development Banks: The Obligation to Respect Human Rights* (Indian Law Resource Centre, January 2009), available at http://indianlaw.org/sites/default/files/Principles%20Memo%20FINAL%20 ENG_0_0.pdf.

50 See McBeth (n. 30) 239–41; Bradlow (n. 13) 78–88; Darrow (n. 32) 5–7 (who stresses avenues of accountability beyond legal claims that human rights-based approaches require including monitoring, reporting and public debate and participation).

of the institutional processes in the IFIs more open and accountable.[51] The resulting obligation is generally seen as encompassing both positive duties to promote and protect human rights as well as a negative duty to refrain from activities that worsen an existing human rights situation.[52] Some go so far as to require that the IFIs shall not enter projects or conclude financial agreements that contravene applicable international human rights law.[53]

The existence of a positive legal duty to observe human rights standards in the operations of IFIs has been defended from a number of legal perspectives. First, as international institutions enjoying legal personality, IFIs are under an obligation to observe customary international law, including customary international human rights law.[54] Secondly, as specialised agencies of the UN, the IFIs are bound to follow the basic policy goals of the UN Charter as a result of the terms of the relationship agreements between them and the UN.[55] These include the duty to observe human rights as stated in Article 55 of the UN Charter, which also outlines the economic and social policy goals of the UN.[56] Thirdly, given the general obligation of the member states to observe human rights, the IFIs cannot do anything that might undermine those obligations. This argument assumes that all member states are parties to the relevant international human rights instruments. Where this is not the case then the IFIs' responsibilities would vary with respect to different members.[57]

A variant of the member state responsibility argument exists in principle 10 of the UN Guiding Principles:

> States, when acting as members of multilateral institutions that deal with business related issues, should:
>
> (a) Seek to ensure that those institutions neither restrain the ability of their member states to meet their duty to protect nor hinder business enterprises from respecting human rights;
>
> (b) Encourage those institutions, within their respective mandates and capacities, to promote business respect for human rights and, where requested, to help states meet their duty to protect against human rights abuse by business enterprises, including through technical assistance, capacity-building and awareness-raising;

---

51 See Bradlow (n. 13) 89.
52 See McBeth (n. 30) 65–71; Bradlow (n. 13) 64; Tilburg Principles (n. 49) principles 23–31; Coulter et al., *Principles of International Law* (n. 49) principle 1. By contrast, Skogly sees the obligation as limited to the negative duty alone: Sigrun I. Skogly, *The Human Rights Obligations of the World Bank and the International Monetary Fund* (Cavendish Publishing, 2001), at 145.
53 See Tilburg Principles (n. 49) principles 30 (WBG) and 31 (IMF), which advocate changes to the Articles of Agreement in this regard.
54 See Skogly (n. 52) 84–87; Darrow (n. 32) 126; Bradlow (n. 13) 63.
55 See Skogly (n. 52) 118–20; Darrow (n. 32) 127–29; Bradlow (n. 13); McBeth (n. 30) 68–71.
56 Charter of the United Nations (1945) 1 UNTS XVI, Art. 55: 'With a view to the creation of conditions of stability and well-being which are necessary for peaceful and friendly relations among nations based on respect for the principle of equal rights and self-determination of peoples, the United Nations shall promote: (a) higher standards of living, full employment, and conditions of economic and social progress and development; (b) solutions of international economic, social, health, and related problems; and international cultural and educational cooperation; and (c) universal respect for, and observance of, human rights and fundamental freedoms for all without distinction as to race, sex, language, or religion', available at http://www.un.org/en/documents/charter/chapter9.shtml.
57 See Sarfaty (n. 48) 658.

(c) Draw on these Guiding Principles to promote shared understanding and advance international cooperation in the management of business and human rights challenges.

This falls short of accepting a binding duty on the multilateral institution in question, in that the Guiding Principles are not addressed directly to IGOs, but does see a duty on the member states to further business respect for human rights as an element of institutional policy. In this regard the recent developments at the IFC on human rights impact assessments for companies in line with the requirements of the UN Framework, discussed below, may be seen as an example of this principle at work.

1.3 Remedying human rights claims

The third element of the UN Framework on business and human rights concerns remediation. The state duty to ensure adequate remedies for human rights abuses includes non-state-based grievance mechanisms. Principle 28 of the UN Guiding Principles provides that: 'States should consider ways to facilitate access to effective non-State-based grievance mechanisms dealing with business-related human rights harms.'[58]

Under this heading, the Guiding Principles list grievance mechanisms administered by a business enterprise alone or with stakeholders, by an industry association or a multi-stakeholder group. Such mechanisms are non-judicial, 'but may use adjudicative, dialogue-based or other culturally appropriate and rights-compatible processes'.[59] Also mentioned are regional and international human rights bodies. Thus IGOs are not excluded in principle as foci for such mechanisms, though the IFIs are not expressly mentioned. In the practice of the IFIs there already exist some rudimentary mechanisms for the settlement of grievances and these can consider human rights-related issues, though they are under no express obligations in this regard.

Thus the World Bank Inspection Panel can receive complaints relating to projects and make an inspection which results in the making of recommendations to resolve the complaint. In relation to human rights issues these would have to come within the substantive elements of the 'safeguards policies' which, as noted above, have only an indirect human rights element.[60] The Inspection Panel has discussed human rights related questions in a number of cases though the sample is as yet too small to be instructive of any general policy.[61] Nonetheless, the Inspection Panel remains a possible avenue for the development of human rights-based claims so long as these come within the terms of non-compliance with a World Bank policy.[62]

---

58 UN Guiding Principles (n. 3).
59 Ibid. Commentary to principle 28.
60 See McBeth (n. 30) 222–23; Darrow (n. 32) 224–26. See further the Inspection Panel website, available at http://web.worldbank.org/WBSITE/EXTERNAL/EXTINSPECTIONPANEL/0,, menuPK:64132057~pagePK:64130364~piPK:64132056~theSitePK:380794,00.html.
61 See e.g. the Manila Sewerage Project case, the China Western Poverty Reduction Project (Qinghai) case and the Chad–Cameroon Pipeline Project case, all discussed in McBeth (n. 30) 223–27. See too Steven Hertz and Anne Perrault, *Bringing Human Rights Claims to the World Bank Inspection Panel* (CIEL, BIC, International Accountability Project, October 2009), available at http://www.bicusa. org/en/Document.101841.aspx.
62 McBeth (n. 30) 226.

In addition to the Inspection Panel, the IFC and MIGA also provide an ombudsman function through the Compliance Advisor/Ombudsman (CAO).[63] The CAO works to address the concerns of individuals or communities affected by IFC/MIGA projects, enhance the social and environmental outcomes of IFC/MIGA projects and foster greater public accountability of IFC and MIGA. The audit criteria include IFC/MIGA policies, performance standards, guidelines, procedures and requirements whose violation might lead to adverse social or environmental consequences. Audit criteria may have their origin, or arise from, the environmental and social assessments or plans, host country legal and regulatory requirements (including international legal obligations), and the environmental, social, health, or safety provisions of the World Bank Group, IFC/MIGA, or other conditions for IFC/MIGA involvement.[64] The approach is one of mediation and dispute resolution and so it is less likely than the Inspection Panel to make normative pronouncements on the human rights implications of a dispute before it.[65]

As regards the IMF, it has no equivalent mechanism to the Inspection Panel or the CAO. It does have an Independent Evaluation Office (IEO), whose function is to conduct independent and objective evaluations of Fund policies and activities. Under its Terms of Reference, it is fully independent from the Management of the IMF and operates at arm's length from the Board of Executive Directors. It is intended to serve as a means to enhance the learning culture within the Fund, strengthen the Fund's external credibility, promote greater understanding of the work of the Fund throughout the membership, and support the Executive Board's institutional governance and oversight responsibilities.[66] It does not have any explicit human rights mandate. According to the Tilburg Principles, human rights considerations should be integrated in the IEO's Terms of Reference, mandate and functioning and, more generally 'the IMF should review its accountability mechanisms, in order to provide for settlement of complaints, brought by affected individuals and communities, challenging IMF programs and policies.'[67]

Thus there are at present few avenues for redress at the institutional level for human rights claims. This is compounded by the fact that litigation before municipal courts against the World Bank or the IMF is highly unlikely to succeed given the immunities form suit that the IFIs enjoy under their Articles of Agreement and in the practice of municipal courts.[68] Equally the investor–state dispute settlement mechanism under ICSID is of very limited use. The IFIs cannot be parties to ICSID proceedings, as they are not parties to the ICSID Convention, and the types of disputes coming before ICSID Tribunals rarely involve human rights claims as they are complaints brought by investors against a host state for actions that are alleged to violate applicable investor guarantees in international investment protection agreements or investment contracts to which the host state is a party.[69]

---

63 See CAO website at http://www.cao-ombudsman.org/ and the CAO, *Operational Guidelines* (CAO April 2007), available at http://www.cao-ombudsman.org/about/whoweare/documents/EnglishCAOGuidelines06.08.07Web.pdf.

64 CAO Operational Guidelines (n. 63) 21.

65 McBeth (n. 30) 231.

66 Independent Evaluation Office (IEO), 'Terms of Reference – Purpose', available at http://www.ieo-imf.org/ieo/pages/IEOPreview.aspx?mappingid=y3p1dhO74YQ%3d&img=i6nZpr3iSlU%3d.

67 Tilburg Principles (n. 49) paras 41 and 42; and see McBeth (n. 30) 232–33; Darrow (n. 32) 227–30 (who questions the independence of the IEO from the IMF Board).

68 See further Skogly (n. 52) 176–80.

69 According to Clapham, the ICSID procedure could evolve to consider claims of human rights infringements by host states and by foreign investors: Clapham (n. 25) 155–57.

2 Commercial banks and human rights responsibilities

The UN Guiding Principles do not single out commercial banks as a distinctive type of business enterprise for the purposes of the corporate responsibility to respect human rights.[70] However, there is no doubt that John Ruggie, the Special Representative of the Secretary General of the UN for Business and Human Rights (SRSG), the principal author of the UN Guiding Principles, considered banks to have particular responsibilities in relation to their lending practices. In his 2009 Report, the SRSG noted:

> The principles of human rights due diligence and its core elements should be internalized by all businesses, regardless of their nature or size. But the specific activities that companies must undertake to discharge this responsibility will vary in ways not yet fully understood. . . . For example, a bank's human rights due diligence for a project loan will differ in some respects from that of the company operating the project. Nevertheless, banks do have human rights due diligence requirements in this context, and human rights risks related to the projects are also risks to the banks' liability, returns and reputation. Beyond banks lies an even more complex array of other lenders, investors, and asset managers. Precisely how their respective due diligence differs requires further clarity.[71]

The stress on liability, returns and reputation echoes the concerns of the banks themselves as shown by recent human rights statements issued by leading international banks. For example, the Barclays Group 'Statement on Human Rights' asserts that 'where our involvement may associate Barclay's with actual or perceived violations of human rights, the issue should be referred to the Group Brand and Reputation Committee.'[72] Equally, where Barclays discovers, or is made aware, that it has been associated with human rights violations, the bank shall take steps to remedy the situation, taking account of the interests of those whose rights are being violated. Appropriate action in mitigation will be taken and this may include exiting a particular business relationship, or constructive engagement with others to promote good practice.[73]

---

70 For an argument in favour of such distinctive treatment see Banktrack, *Human Rights Responsibilities of Private Sector Banks* (Banktrack, July 2010), available at http://www.banktrack.org/manage/ ems_files/download/the_human_rights_responsibilities_of_banks/310715_hr_responsibilities_ of_banks_submission_to_dr_ruggie.pdf.

71 UN Human Rights Council, 'Report of the Special Representative to the Secretary General (SRSG) on the Issue of Human Rights and Transnational Corporations and Other Business Enterprises: Business and Human Rights: Towards Operationalizing the "Protect, Respect, and Remedy" Framework' (22 April 2009) UN Doc A/HRC/11/13, paras 72–73, available at http:// www2.ohchr.org/english/bodies/hrcouncil/docs/11session/A.HRC.11.13.pdf.

72 Barclays Group, *Statement on Human Rights* (Barclays December 2010), at para. 3.3.4, available at http://group.barclays.com/cs/Satellite?blobcol=urldata&blobheader=application%2Fpdf&blobhe adername1=Content-Disposition&blobheadername2—DT-Type&blobheadervalue1=inline%3B+ filename%3DBarclays-Statement-on-Human-Rights.pdf&blobheadervalue2=abinary%3B+charse t%3DUTF-8&blobkey=id&blobtable—ungoBlobs&blobwhere=1231873782808&ssbinary=true. See too *Banking on Human Rights* (n. 2) 9.

73 Barclays Group Statement (n. 72) 3.1.4.

2.1 The nature of human rights risk for banks

The UN Framework distinguishes between direct and indirect human rights impacts.[74] Both types of impact can arise out of the operations of banks. The most common direct impact is on the rights of workers employed by the enterprise. According to a major survey of patterns of human rights abuses by companies, carried out by the SRSG in 2008, in relation to workplace rights all sectors have been involved in allegations with cases such as denial of access to medical facilities to combat HIV/AIDS, discrimination in hiring practices and inadequate conditions of work and life.[75] However, indirect impacts are more common in the banking sector given that the lending function to clients is the most likely way that a bank will become implicated in human rights abuses.[76]

Several types of human rights risks are identifiable in this regard. The first is the risk that the bank may finance a company implicated with workplace rights abuses. For example the SRSG's survey found that:

> One group of financial firms was alleged as the main investors in a company that used forced labour; another group was alleged to financially support a large retailer that is known for discrimination, forced and child labour, excessive work hours, unsafe work conditions, and frustrating employee efforts to organize.[77]

In addition, identifiable workplace rights risks include supply chain risks, where loans are made to manufacturing companies in low skill, labour-intensive sectors often operating in export processing zones in developing countries.[78] A particular concern for banks has arisen in relation to the treatment of offshore call centre staff and cleaners in developing countries.[79]

A second type of human rights risk is sovereign risk, where loans are made to governments with poor human rights records. The SRSG's survey noted cases where banks had lent to a government for a project that was allegedly ousting indigenous communities from cultivated farmland or made loans to a corrupt government known for widespread human rights abuses.[80] A third type of risk involves project finance, where major infrastructure projects are funded in emerging markets with potentially high impact on local communities and/or where finance is extended on a non-recourse basis with the bank reliant on the project's cash

---

74 See UN Guiding Principles (n. 3) principle 13: 'The responsibility to respect human rights requires that business enterprises: (a) Avoid causing or contributing to adverse human rights impacts through their own activities, and address such impacts when they occur; (b) Seek to prevent or mitigate adverse human rights impacts that are directly linked to their operations, products or services by their business relationships, even if they have not contributed to those impacts.'

75 UN Human Rights Council, 'Addendum to the Report of the SRSG on the Issue of Human Rights and Transnational Corporations and Other Business Enterprises: Corporations and Human Rights – A survey of the scope and pattern of alleged corporate-related human rights abuse (23 May 2008) UN Doc A/HRC/8/5/Add.2, available at http://daccess-dds-ny.un.org/doc/UNDOC/GEN/G08/136/61/PDF/G0813661.pdf?OpenElement.

76 See *Banking on Human Rights* (n. 2) 9–10.

77 SRSG (n. 75) para. 58.

78 See *Banking on Human Rights* (n. 2) 11.

79 Ibid. 9.

80 SRSG (n. 75) paras 85–86.

flows for repayment, and where a human rights controversy can impact on the long-term financial viability of the project due to the risk of non-repayment.[81] A fourth type of human rights risk arises out of the incorrect valuation of capital markets transactions where existing or potential human rights risks that can materially affect the value of the transaction are not identified.[82] In addition banks have to be vigilant against the link that often exists between human rights abuses and money laundering when engaging in private banking activities and ensuring that asset management activities are conducted through socially responsible investment funds.[83]

2.2 Banks and human rights due diligence

Under the UN Framework, the core element of the corporate responsibility to respect human rights is due diligence. This requires that the enterprise assesses the extent of the human rights risks that it faces in a given project and, having identified those risks, sets in motion a strategy to avoid or at least to mitigate their impact. Such an assessment is to be made in the context of a wider human rights policy adopted by the enterprise which ensures that human rights concerns are fully integrated into the enterprise's management system and processes and which allows the enterprise to monitor human rights risks.[84]

According to Principle 17 of the UN Guiding Principles, human rights due diligence:

(a) Should cover adverse human rights impacts that the business enterprise may cause or contribute to through its own activities, or which may be directly linked to its operations, products or services by its business relationships;

(b) Will vary in complexity with the size of the business enterprise, the risk of severe human rights impacts, and the nature and context of its operations;

(c) Should be ongoing, recognizing that the human rights risks may change over time as the business enterprise's operations and operating context evolve.[85]

Due diligence is normally associated with the buying or selling of company assets, the lending of finance for a specific project, the assessment of a potential joint venture partner, the listing of a company on the stock exchange to verify its ability to carry out its prospectus and the privatisation of state enterprises or state bodies.[86] In all these cases investment risk is involved and due diligence seeks to minimise that risk through a thorough investigation of the assets and liabilities of the firm or investor in question. Thus its extension to human rights risks appears to be a novel departure as this is not a normal aspect of what is generally understood as commercial risk, in that, as the SRSG points out, it requires a shift from

---

81 See *Banking on Human Rights* (n. 2) 11.
82 Ibid.
83 Ibid. 12.
84 See UN Guiding Principles (n. 3) principles 16 and 17.
85 Ibid., principle 17.
86 See generally Linda S. Spedding, *Due Diligence Handbook: Corporate Governance, Risk Management and Business Planning* (CIMA Publishing, 2009).

considering the risk to the company to considering the risk to potential victims of corporate action.[87]

This approach is not new to commercial lenders. For some years a number of banks and other financial institutions (known as Equator Principles Financial Institutions, or EPFIs[88]) have adhered to the Equator Principles (EPs) which seek to ensure that projects financed by such entities are developed in a manner that is socially responsible and which reflects sound environmental management practices.[89] The EPs are adopted voluntarily by financial institutions and are applied where total project capital costs exceed $10 million. The EPs are primarily intended to provide a minimum standard for due diligence to support responsible risk decision-making.[90] The EPs are strongly influenced by the social and environmental assessment standards developed by the World Bank and the IFC which form the substantive basis for assessments under the EPs.[91] However, the EPs go beyond these instruments to the extent that they list the 'protection of human rights and community health, safety and security (including risks, impacts and management of project's use of security personnel)' as potential social and environmental issues to be taken into account in the assessment.[92] The EP review is undertaken by an independent social or environmental expert not directly associated with the borrower with a view to assisting the EPFI in its due diligence and in assessing EP compliance.[93]

The EPs represent a pioneering attempt to ensure greater social and environmental sensitivity on the part of EPFIs when considering the risks surrounding a major finance project. They are closely related to developments at the IFC given their reliance on IFC Performance Standards. The recent adoption by the IFC of human rights impact assessment principles, and its adherence to the UN Framework in this regard will affect the evolution of due diligence assessments under the EPs and more generally for financial lenders.

---

87 See further UN Human Rights Council, 'Report of the SRSG on the Issue of Human Rights and Transnational Corporations and Other Businesses: Business and Human Rights – Further steps toward the operationalization of the "protect, respect, and remedy" framework' (9 April 2010) UN Doc. A/HRC/14/27, at paras 81–83, available at http://198.170.85.29/Ruggie-report-2010.pdf.

88 There are currently 73 adopting financial institutions (71 Equator Principles Financial Institutions and 2 Associates), see http://www.equator-principles.com/index.php/members-reporting/members–and-reporting.

89 See The Equator Principles (June 2006) (EPs), available at http://www.equatorprinciples.com/resources/equator_principles.pdf. The EPs apply to 'project finance' which is defined in the EPs at preambular para. 1 n. 1 as: 'a method of funding in which the lender looks primarily to the revenues generated by a single project, both as the source of repayment and as security for the exposure. This type of financing is usually for large, complex and expensive installations . . . In such transactions, the lender is usually paid solely or almost exclusively out of the money generated by the contracts for the facility's output, such as the electricity sold by a power plant. The borrower is usually an SPE (Special Purpose Entity) that is not permitted to perform any function other than developing, owning, and operating the installation. The consequence is that repayment depends primarily on the project's cash flow and on the collateral value of the project's assets': Basel Committee on Banking Supervision, International Convergence of Capital Measurement and Capital Standards ('Basel II'), November 2005, available at http://www.bis.org/publ/bcbs118.htm.

90 See 'About The Equator Principles' available at http://www.equator-principles.com/index.php/about-the-equator-principles.

91 EPs (n. 89) principle 3.

92 Ibid. exhibit II(d).

93 Ibid. principle 7.

The IFC recommends that human rights risk assessment take place as part of the seven-step process identified by the IFC as a method for complying with the corporate responsibility to respect under the UN Framework.[94] The process of assessment gives effect to the due diligence requirement of the UN Framework. It is to be carried out in the light of consultations within the company and with experts outside. According to the IFC Guide the scope of a human rights risks and impact assessment should consider, at the very minimum:

> The key human rights risks associated with the country of operation; The human rights risks of key business relationships, including associated facilities and third party organisations; The human rights risks and impacts relating to the business activity itself; The range of stakeholders (potential and actual) that are directly or indirectly affected by the business activity; The nature and level of the risks and impacts, at different key stages of the project's lifecycle.[95]

When conducting the assessment, companies should consider developing an understanding of any unintended consequential human rights impacts, negative or positive, arising from the business activity, identify the long-term consequences of loss of rights, for example, reduced access to education or disruption of water supply, and look for evidence of human rights risks in the host country, region, industry sector or business activity, which may signal likely patterns of human rights impact in the company's business activity.[96]

To assess how the business activity is impacting the rights of affected stakeholders, the company should consider the business risks and impacts and any business opportunities associated with each relevant human right and identify the source of the risks and impacts taking account of:

> the root causes, trigger points, and key actors of the risks and impacts (e.g. the business activity itself, a possible contractor, supplier and/or government involvement etc.) . . . individuals, groups, and communities who are subject to actual or potential business activity-related risks and/or adverse human rights impacts (e.g. workers, local communities, indigenous peoples, vulnerable and disadvantages individuals, groups or communities, consumers, customers, etc.) . . . [and] . . . identify key stages during the project's lifecycle (e.g. design, construction, operation, decommissioning and closure etc.) where human rights risks and impacts may have occurred or will likely occur.[97]

---

94 *Guide to HRIAM* (n. 47). See at 12, http://www.guidetohriam.org/guide-to-human-rights-impact-assessment-and-management-: the seven steps are: 'PREPARATION – Determine the company's human rights due diligence approach Scope the company's human rights impact assessment. INDENTIFICATION – Identify the key human rights risks and impacts; set the baseline. ASSESSMENT – Assess the human rights risks and impacts; analyse the assessment findings. ENGAGEMENT – Engage with stakeholders to verify the human rights risks and impacts; develop a grievance mechanism that considers human rights issues. MITIGATION – Develop appropriate mitigation action plans; present the mitigation action plans and recommendations to management. MANAGEMENT – Implement the mitigation action plans and recommendations; integrate human rights within the management system. EVALUATION – Monitor, evaluate and report on the company's capacity to address human rights; review the evaluation and make appropriate adjustments if necessary.'
95 Ibid. 46.
96 Ibid. 47.
97 Ibid.

The assessment will take account of human rights as an indivisible whole. Accordingly no prior assumptions are to be made as to which human rights risks have priority and the main risks need to be clarified according to their number and type, their impacts, their precise nature in relation to the business activity, whether they are past, ongoing or potential impacts, the number of affected stakeholders and their underlying conditions such as, for example, lack of enforcement, oversight or poor training.[98] Finally, where disadvantaged and vulnerable individuals, groups or communities have been identified as significantly negatively impacted by the business activity, further assessments should be carried out to ensure the company does not exacerbate the existing situation in future policies or practices.[99]

The IFC Guide is one of a number of recent initiatives that use the UN Framework, illustrating its growing influence in this field. Notable too is the inclusion, for the first time, of a human rights chapter containing a due diligence requirement in the 2011 revision of the OECD Guidelines for Multinational Enterprises as well as a general responsibility on multinational enterprises to apply due diligence analysis to all the main social and environmental standards in the OECD Guidelines.[100] The concept also figures in the International Organization for Standardization ISO 26000 standard on corporate social responsibility.[101]

2.3 Issues of remedies for human rights claims

The UN Guiding Principles require that business enterprises should establish or participate in effective operational-level grievance mechanisms for individuals and communities who may be adversely impacted so that grievances can be addressed early and remediated directly.[102] According to the Commentary to the Guiding Principles:

> [S]uch mechanisms need not require that a complaint or grievance amount to an alleged human rights abuse before it can be raised, but specifically aim to identify any legitimate concerns of those who may be adversely impacted. If those concerns are not identified and addressed they may over time escalate into more major disputes and human rights abuses.[103]

Such mechanisms can complement wider stakeholder engagement and collective bargaining processes, but cannot substitute for either as '[t]hey should not be used to undermine the role of legitimate trade unions in addressing labour-related disputes, nor to preclude access to judicial or other non-judicial grievance mechanisms.'[104]

Financial lenders have been involved in such procedures. Indeed the EPs require that EPFIs set up a grievance mechanism as part of their project management systems for their higher risk projects. According to Article 6 of the EPs such a mechanism should ensure that consultation,

---

98 Ibid. 48.

99 Ibid.

100 OECD, *Guidelines for Multinational Enterprises 2011 Edition* (OECD 2011), at part 1 ch. VI 'Human Rights' para. 5 & ch. II 'General Policies' paras 10–12, available at http://www.oecd.org/dataoecd/43/29/48004323.pdf.

101 See http://www.iso.org/iso/iso_catalogue/management_and_leadership_standards/social_responsibility/sr_discovering_iso26000.htm§d-6.

102 UN Guiding Principles (n. 3) principle 29.

103 UN Guiding Principles (n. 3) Commentary to principle 29.

104 Ibid.

disclosure and community engagement continues throughout construction and operation of the project, allowing the borrower 'to receive and facilitate resolution of concerns and grievances about the project's social and environmental performance raised by individuals or groups from among project-affected communities'.[105] The borrower is required to inform the affected communities about the mechanism in the course of its community engagement process and ensure that the mechanism addresses concerns promptly and transparently, in a culturally appropriate manner, and is readily accessible to all segments of the affected communities.[106]

Such informal mechanisms will in no way supplement or replace more legal forms of redress, particularly litigation. However, they will enable a more cooperative environment to develop between the bank and the main human rights stakeholders in a project financed by the bank, thereby reducing the chances of legal confrontation. The effective management of human rights risks can reduce a bank's exposure to potentially costly litigation on the basis of discrimination clams or complicity in human rights abuses.[107]

That such a litigation risk exists is undeniable. For example, in the case of *Khulumani v Barclays Bank*, Barclays, Citigroup and Deutsche Bank were sued under the US Alien Tort Claims Act (ATCA) for human rights violations arising out of their operations in South Africa during the period of apartheid. The plaintiffs alleged that the banks not only benefited from business during apartheid in South Africa, but also directly supported apartheid by providing the financial support for 'the expansion of the apartheid police and security apparatus'. The claim was dismissed by the District Court. On appeal by the plaintiffs the US Court of Appeal for the Second Circuit overturned the District Court by a majority and held that aiding and abetting liability existed under international law and extended to 'substantial assistance' or 'practical assistance' to the perpetrator of human rights violations. This liability extended to corporate actors. Accordingly the case could continue.[108] Whether this head of liability will continue is open to debate now that the principle of aiding and abetting liability has been challenged before the US Supreme Court.[109]

The US Supreme Court issued a writ of certiorari on 17 April 2013.[110] One striking aspect of this decision is that the US Supreme Court avoided answering the original question, whether the law of nations does recognise corporate liability. Instead, it focused on the extra-territorial application of the ATCA and held that the presumption against extraterritoriality applies to claims under the ATCA, and nothing in the statute rebuts that presumption. Although some commentators have interpreted this decision as the end of human rights litigation against global corporations in the US,[111] it appears that the US Supreme Court's

---

105 EPs (n. 89) Art. 6.
106 Ibid.
107 See *Banking on Human Rights* (n. 2) 32.
108 *Khulumani v Barclays Bank* 504 F 3d 254, 2007 US App LEXIS 24370 (United States Court of Appeals, Second Circuit), available at http://caselaw.findlaw.com/us-2nd-circuit/1089266.html.
109 In the case of *Kiobel v Royal Dutch Shell* the petition for certiorari was granted by the US Supreme Court on 17 October 2011. See for further background Harvard University International Human Rights Clinic at http://harvardhumanrights.wordpress.com/criminal-justice-in-latin-america/alien-tort-statute/kiobel-v-royal-dutch-petroleum-co/.
110 *Kiobel et al. v Royal Dutch Petroleum Co. et al.*, 569 US _ (2013).
111 Jen Alic, *Shell vs. Kiobel: Green Light for Multinational Human Rights Abuses*, Oilprice.com, April 22, 2013, available at http://oilprice.com/Energy/Energy-General/Shell-vs.-Kiobel-Green-Light-for-Multinational-Human-Rights-Abuses.html; Amol Mehra, *Supreme Court Undermines Human Rights*, Providence Journal, April 25, 2013, available at http://blogs.providencejournal.com/ri-talks/this-new-england/2013/04/amol-mehra-supreme-court-undermines-human-rights.html.

avoidance of the question relating to corporate liability under the ATCA actually leaves the door ajar to further claims against Multinational enterprises (MNEs).[112] Future plaintiffs would have to demonstrate a strong nexus of their claim with the US jurisdiction. This will certainly narrow the number of claims brought against foreign MNEs, but may have the benefit of legitimising litigation against corporations before the US district courts. Nonetheless, even if future US courts cut down corporate liability principles under ATCA, other avenues for redress through civil and criminal law will remain.[113]

3 Concluding remarks

This chapter has provided an overview of the main human rights issues facing financial lenders. Both IFIs and commercial banks face similar issues of human rights impacts as in each case the lenders have influence over clients and can, in principle, affect client behaviour by reason of their ability to facilitate access to finance. The main difference is that banks are not as likely as IFIs to be involved in major development finance projects (though they may act as partners in such activities) but will lend on a smaller scale to other commercial enterprises.

As noted above, the legal responsibilities of these lenders are far from settled. The IFIs accept that their work has human rights implications and they will consider these on a case-by-case basis in the light of their operating mandates, which allow for consideration of social and environmental impacts. But they will not accept a general legal duty to determine their policies, or the approval of specific projects, following a human rights impact analysis. That would require a change in the Articles of Agreement, a matter that the member states will not accept at this stage. Equally, as shown above, the capacity for mounting a legal challenge against IFI decisions on the basis of a human rights claim is limited.

By contrast, the commercial banks are more vulnerable to legal claims based on human rights, as recent ATCA cases show. They may also be subjected to human rights claims based on general principles of civil and criminal law where appropriate. On the other hand, as the above-mentioned IFC initiatives indicate, commercial lenders may be expected to put in place an effective human rights impact assessment process which will include a corporate human rights policy, due diligence analysis of human rights risks in given projects, and procedures for improving accountability and monitoring of human rights impacts, as well as mitigation policies in cases where infringements have occurred.

Selected bibliography

Banktrack, *Human Rights Responsibilities of Private Sector Banks* (Banktrack, July 2010), available at http://www.banktrack.org/manage/ems_files/download/the_human_rights_responsibilities_of_banks/310715_hr_responsibilities_of_banks_submission_to_dr_ruggie.pdf.

D.D. Bradlow, 'The World Bank, the IMF, and Human Rights' (1996) 6 *Transnational Law and Contemporary Problems* 47–90.

---

112 Justice Kennedy, who joined the majority opinion in full, also concurred separately. He held that 'the opinion for the Court is careful to leave open a number of significant questions regarding the reach and interpretation of the Alien Tort Statute.' See also Katie Redford, *Commentary: Door Still Open for Human Rights Claims after Kiobel*, SCOTUSblog, 17 April, 2013, available at http://www.scotusblog.com/2013/04/commentary-door-still-open-for-human-rights-claims-after-kiobel/.

113 See further Peter Muchlinski, 'The Provision of Private Law Remedies against Multinational Enterprises: a Comparative Law Perspective', (2010) 4(2) *Journal of Comparative Law* 148–70.

R. Dañino, 'Legal Opinion on Human Rights and the Work of the World Bank – Senior Vice President and General Counsel January 27, 2006' (copy on file with author), available at http://www.ifiwatchnet.org/?q=en/node/335.

M. Darrow, *Between Light and Shadow: The World Bank, the International Monetary Fund and International Human Rights Law* (Hart Publishing. 2006).

The Equator Principles (June 2006) (EPs), available at http://www.equator-principles.com

F&C Asset Management & KPMG, *Banking on Human Rights: Confronting Human Rights in the Financial Sector* (KPMG, 2004), available at http://us.kpmg.com/microsite/FSLibraryDotCom/docs/Banking%20on%20Human%20Rights_FC_KPMG.pdf.

IFC, *Sustainability Framework – 2012 Edition* (IFC 2012), available at http://www1.ifc.org/wps/wcm/connect/topics_ext_content/ifc_external_corporate_site/ifc+sustainability+framework/2012+edition/2012-edition#PerformanceStandards.

IFC and IBLF, *Guide to Human Rights Impact Assessment and Management (HRIAM)* (IFC & IBLF, 2010), available at http://www.guidetohriam.org/guide-to-human-rights-impact-assessment-and-management-.

A. McBeth, *International Economic Actors and Human Rights* (Routledge, 2010), ch. 5.

I.F.I. Shihata, 'Human Rights, Development, and International Financial Institutions' (1992) 8(1) *American University International Law Review* 27–36.

UN Human Rights Council, Seventeenth Session 21 March 2011, 'Guiding Principles on Business and Human Rights: Implementing the United Nations "Protect, Respect and Remedy" Framework', UN Doc. A/HRC/17/31, available at http://www.ohchr.org/documents/issues/business/A.HRC.17.31.pdf.

World Bank, *Development and Human Rights: the Role of the World Bank* (World Bank, 1998) available at http://www.fao.org/righttofood/KC/downloads/vl/docs/HR%20and%20devlopment_the%20role%20of%20the%20WB.pdf.

17

International environmental law and human rights

Karen Hulme

1 Introduction

In March 2012 the Human Rights Council created the three-year post of Independent Expert on 'the issue of human rights obligations *related to* the enjoyment of a safe, clean, healthy and sustainable environment'.[1] This development comes almost 20 years after the attempt by Ms Fatma Zohra Ksentini, Special Rapporteur on Human Rights and the Environment for the Sub-Commission on Prevention of Discrimination and Protection of Minorities, to urge the adoption of a human right to a satisfactory environment and the recommendation that human rights bodies examine this relationship between human rights and the environment.[2] Quite clearly, from its wording, the mandate of the Independent Expert seems to have him picking up from where Ksentini left off in 1994, notably in studying the relationship and in identifying best practice.[3] Might this then represent the first step towards the adoption of that which has hitherto remained elusive: a universal human right to a healthy environment? And if it were to come to pass, is such a right capable of meeting the needs of the environment, rather than just mankind?

1.1 Conservation rethought

When we think about the notion of 'conservation' we tend to envisage protected areas of natural beauty, or scientific programmes designed to save species on the brink of extinction. We do not perceive ourselves – human beings that is – as falling within the notion of 'conservation'. One reason for this omission may be a definitional one – that conservation is

---

1 *Human Rights and the Environment*, A/HRC/RES/19/10, 19 April 2012, para. 2 (emphasis added). In July 2012 Mr John Knox was appointed to the post; see his first report as Rapporteur, John H. Knox, *Report of the Independent Expert on the Issue of Human Rights Obligations Relating to the Enjoyment of A Safe, Clean, Healthy and Sustainable Environment*, 24 December 2012, A/HRC/22/43.
2 Final Report Prepared by Mrs Fatma Zohra Ksentini, Special Rapporteur, Sub-Commission on Prevention of Discrimination and Protection of Minorities, *Human Rights and the Environment*, E/CN.4/Sub.2/1994/9 (6 July 1994).
3 *Human Rights and the Environment* (n. 1) para. 2(a)(b).

generally understood to be concerned with maintaining an environment or species to further its use for human exploitation. A second may be because our planetary number is greater than ever. Yet, over the next century it is predicted that the impacts of climate change will threaten our human habitats, food and water sources, health and, ultimately, life.[4] And so while it is trite to suggest that mankind is at a crossroads in terms of our ability to deal more effectively with the threat of climate change – a crossroads at which we have been stalled for at least two decades now – it is probably not too much of an exaggeration to suggest that mankind itself is in need of 'conservation'. Because it is not just climate change that threatens our existence and well-being, it is also the daily exploitation of our planet's resources, and it is the drive of our desire for what we perceive to be 'development' that combine to threaten people (and often other species) everywhere with disease and suffering. From the human rights perspective, the phenomenon of climate change poses possibly the greatest legal and political challenge since the acceptance of the two 1966 International Covenants, and was undoubtedly a major catalyst for the Human Rights Council's decision to appoint an Independent Expert.[5]

This contribution is tasked with examining human rights in the broader context of its interaction with international environmental law. Clearly there have been many developments in the field of environmental human rights in the past decade, and while some of these will be articulated in section 2, the first section is dedicated to environmental law as a discipline. Such an examination of environmental law is necessary in order to discover its rationale, the values it enshrines as well as its limits. The final section is dedicated to future challenges and possible directions.

1.2 Environmental protection

It is a common misconception among those who are unfamiliar with environmental law that that body of law is based on some utopian concept of nature, and that the rationale for nature protection is centred on some idealistic view of nature having intrinsic value (i.e. a value in and of itself, for itself, without reference to its many values to people). Only in the last 30 years or so has the law come to embrace such non-anthropocentric values, and so it remains to be dominated by the self-interested motives of people (and states), including the recognition of mankind's survival needs of ensuring a viable environment as well as its other economic and utility-based values. Thus in protecting particular species or ecosystems, or in prohibiting the manufacture or use of toxic or hazardous chemicals, environmental laws are truly about protecting mankind: protecting our food and water sources from over-exploitation and contamination, controlling diseases and harmful air pollution, conserving the biodiversity that provides our medicines for today and in the future, and even protecting our leisure activities such as touristic beauty spots and the waters of boating lakes.

One aspect of this dominance of the legal landscape by anthropocentric reasoning is often suggested to be due to the dominance of the 'Western' legal traditions and states in treaty

---

4 Intergovernmental Panel on Climate Change, *Climate Change 2007: The Physical Science Basis*, Contribution of Working Group I to the Fourth Assessment Report of the IPCC (Cambridge University Press, 2007).
5 Human Rights Council resolutions on human rights and climate change, HRC Res. 10/4 (25 March 2009) A/HRC/RES/10/4; HRC Res. 7/23 (28 March 2008) A/HRC/RES/7/23; and HRC Res. 18/22 (17 October 2011) A/HRC/RES/18/22; see also OHCHR, *Report on the Relationship Between Climate Change and Human Rights*, 15 January 2009, A/HRC/10/61.

negotiations, which states are in turn dominated by Christian theology. For Lynn White, professor of medieval history, Christianity was perceived to be the most anthropocentric of all religions, in viewing man as having dominion over nature.[6] Descartes adopted the instrumentalist view of the German astronomer Kepler who saw nature as a machine, incapable of original thought, but open to manipulation and control by man.[7] Philosophers Kant and Bacon added to this anthropocentric viewpoint by dismissing nature's ability for reason or to feel pain, and thus elevating the status of humans as above nature.[8] For Locke, Rousseau, Descartes and Nietszche, among others, man's special place in the world derived from their observation of his unique ability for rationality, an attribute that they denied existed in other species.[9] On the other hand, Bentham, Ryder and Singer were among those philosophers who disputed the unfeeling nature of animals, and termed it 'speciesism' (a reference to discrimination) to assign rights to one set of creatures but not another.[10] Such recognitions need not extend to the notion of so-called 'rights for nature', but the recent constitutional amendments of this kind in Bolivia[11] and Ecuador[12] are worth watching, especially in the light of recent Ecuadorian case law reaffirming the 'effectiveness of the right'.[13]

Environmental law thus tends to mirror the anthropocentric approach of the human rights notion of indivisibility,[14] in that a healthy environment is a necessary basis from which most other human rights are possible; thus a healthy environment is vital in achieving the human rights to development, food, water, health, even the right to life itself.[15]

As with the minimum core commitments for economic, social and cultural rights, international environmental law obligations are generally set for progressive realisation. Furthermore, the notion of differentiated obligations, notably that state obligations are set in

---

6 L. White Jr., 'The Historical Roots of Our Ecological Crisis', in R.L. Fischman, M.I. Lipeles and M.S. Squillace (eds), *An Environmental Law Anthology* (Anderson Publishing Co., 1996) 2–8, 5; R.F. Nash, *The Rights of Nature: A History of Environmental Ethics* (University of Wisconsin Press, 1989) 50–52; and L.H. Leib, *Human Rights and the Environment: Philosophical, Theoretical and Legal Perspectives* (Martinus Nijhoff, 2011) 12–15. For a contrary view of Christianity see D. Pepper, *Modern Environmentalism: An Introduction* (Routledge, 1996) 151–55.

7 Pepper (n. 6) at 137–43; A. Gillespie, *International Environmental Law, Policy and Ethics* (Clarendon Press, 1997) 9.

8 Pepper (n. 6) at 143–48; Leib, (n. 6) 17; Gillespie, (n. 7) 9–15.

9 Gillespie (n. 7) 10.

10 Nash (n. 6) 204; Leib (n. 6) 29–31; R.D. Ryder, *Speciesism, Painism and Happiness: A Morality for the Twenty-First Century* (Societas Imprint Academic, 2011); P. Singer, *Animal Liberation* (Pimlico, 1995) 9.

11 The Rights of Mother Earth, 2011. A translation is available at http://f.cl.ly/ items/212y0r1R0W2k2F1M021G/Mother_Earth_Law.pdf (accessed on 7 August 2012).

12 Arts 71–74, 2008 Constitution of Ecuador, available at http://pdba.georgetown.edu/Constitutions/ Ecuador/english08.html (accessed on 7 August 2012).

13 See *R.F. Wheeler and E.G. Huddle v Attorney General of the State of Loja*, 2011, detailed in Professor Erin Daly's blog, available at http://blogs.law.widener.edu/envirolawblog/2011/07/12/ecuadorian-court-recognizes-constitutional-right-to-nature/ (accessed on 10 August 2012), and referenced in D.R. Boyd, *The Environmental Rights Revolution: A Global Study of Constitutions, Human Rights and the Environment* (UBC Press, 2012) 140.

14 1993 Vienna Declaration and Programme of Action, Adopted by the World Conference on Human Rights, Vienna, 1993, (1993) 32 ILM 1661–87, para. 5 (such that 'All human rights are universal, indivisible and interdependent and interrelated').

15 See both para. 1 and Principle 1 of the 1972 Declaration of the United Nations Conference on the Human Environment (Stockholm) (1972) 26 *Yearbook of the United Nations* 319.

relation to their capacity for pollution prevention, now forms a core principle within environmental law, and was a necessary compromise in the initial climate change negotiations.[16] Two further observations are worthy of mention at this point. First, and possibly more than any other area of law, international environmental protection epitomises the need for inter-state cooperation. The regulation of international spaces or the 'global commons', such as the marine environment of the high seas, the atmosphere and Antarctica as well as migratory and endangered species, biodiversity and hazardous pollutants could not function without a large body of state cooperation and support for the need to protect the global environment.[17] Secondly, while international environmental law may have developed initially in quite a fragmented way to protect individual habitats and prevent particular threats, the past 30 years have witnessed the move to an approach of holistic ecosystem conservation and management.[18] How far, then, are environmental rights capable of helping to meet that goal?

2 Human rights and the environment

The links between human rights and the environment began properly in the 1960s with early notions of development. With her now infamous warning in 1962 of the hidden dangers of chemical pesticides and their system-level ability to upset the natural balance of nature and food webs, including the human food chain, renowned marine biologist Rachel Carson in her book *Silent Spring* advocated that: 'To the bird watcher, the suburbanite who derives joy from the birds in his garden, the hunter, the fisherman or the explorer of wild regions, anything that destroys the wildlife of an area for even a single year has deprived him of pleasure to which he has a legitimate right.'[19] Carson's recognition of such rights was premature, as was the incorporation of 'rights' language at the 1972 Stockholm Conference where it was declared that a healthy environment is 'essential to the enjoyment of basic human rights even the right to life itself'.[20] In the wake of Carson's warning of impending ecosystem collapse came a torrent of similar publications emphasising the environmental destructiveness of mankind's economic model of development. Of note are the Club of Rome's postulations in 1972 of *The Limits to Growth*,[21] Hardin's 'The Tragedy of the Commons'[22] in 1968 together with Erlich's *The Population Bomb*,[23] the International Union for the Conservation of Nature's (IUCN) *World*

---

16 This is a reference to the notion of 'common but differentiated responsibilities'; see Art. 3, 1992 United Nations Framework Convention on Climate Change (UNFCCC) (1992) 1771 UNTS 107.
17 For example note the 1982 United Nations Convention on the Law of the Sea (1982) 1833 UNTS 3.
18 Note the notion of 'wise use' of wetlands at Arts 2(6) and 3 of the 1971 Ramsar Convention on Wetlands of International Importance especially as Waterfowl Habitat (1971) 996 UNTS 245, and Art. 6 of the 1992 Convention on Biological Diversity (1992) 31 ILM 822.
19 R. Carson, *Silent Spring* (Readers Union/Hamish Hamilton, 1964) 71.
20 Stockholm Declaration (n. 15) para. 1. Note, the word 'healthy' is used only as an example; other descriptors include clean, safe and favourable. According to Boyd (n. 13) 62, 'healthy' environment is used by 63 states (out of 92 which include a substantive right to environment).
21 D.H. Meadows, D.L. Meadows, J. Randers and W.W. Behrens III, *The Limits to Growth: A Report for the Club of Rome's Project on the Predicament of Mankind* (Universe Books, 1974).
22 G. Hardin, 'The Tragedy of the Commons' (1968) 162 *Science* 1243–48.
23 P.R. Erlich, *The Population Bomb* (Ballantine Books, 1968), and see T. Malthus, *An Essay on the Principle of Population* (J. Johnson, 1798) available at http://129.237.201.53/books/malthus/population/malthus.pdf (accessed on 7 August 2012).

Conservation Strategy[24] in 1980 and finally the Brundtland Commission's *Our Common Future*[25] in 1987, the last of which postulated a concept of sustainable development – notably the fusion of the three concepts of economic development, environmental protection and human rights. And with the rejection of Sub-Commission Special Rapporteur Ksentini's proposal in 1994 for a universal human right to a 'secure, healthy and ecologically sound environment',[26] the evolution of an international environmental human rights regime has been relatively slow and piecemeal.

Today the three legal approaches to environmental human rights are well established, namely (1) the reinterpretation or 'greening' of relevant existing rights, (2) procedural environmental rights and (3) a substantive right to a healthy environment. With no universal right or approach, regional regimes and individual states have been free to choose their own fit, leading to fragmentation and disparity in environmental rights owed around the globe. An early adopter of the substantive right approach, the African Charter[27] regime, however, suffers from compliance failure.[28] In a rebuke to criticisms of the weak and vague nature of Article 24 of the African Charter, on the right of all peoples to 'a general satisfactory environment favourable to their development', the Commission, in the regime's only case on environmental harm, confirmed that 'there is no right in the African Charter that cannot be made effective'.[29] As has similarly been found within those states whose constitution includes a similar substantive right to environment, the Commission seemed comfortable in giving form to the right by requiring the state 'to take reasonable and other measures to prevent pollution and ecological degradation, to promote conservation, and to secure an ecologically sustainable development and use of natural resources.'[30] Leaving aside effectiveness and compliance issues, from an environmental perspective this elaboration of the right clearly goes beyond the industrial pollution dimension of property protections and right to family life and home found in the European Convention regime,[31] and even the reinterpretation of the right to life in both the European regime and individual states such as India and Bangladesh.[32] The reference to (sustainable) development is clearly central to the African Charter system and the wording of Article 24 itself. Yet, it is the reference to conservation and the prevention of ecological degradation in the *SERAC* judgment that is most interesting from a human rights perspective. Such terminology appears to evince a more holistic ecological management focus aligned with current environmental thinking. Understandably,

24 *World Conservation Strategy* (IUCN-UNEP-WWF, 1980).
25 Report of the United Nations World Commission on Environment and Development (WCED), *Our Common Future* (Oxford University Press, 1987).
26 Final Report (n. 2) at Annex, Draft Principle 2, Draft Principles on Human Rights and the Environment.
27 1981 African Charter on Human and Peoples' Rights (1982) 21 ILM 58–68.
28 See F. Viljoen and L. Louw, 'State Compliance with the Recommendations of the African Commission on Human and Peoples' Rights' (2007) 101 AJIL 1–34.
29 Communication 155/96, *The Social and Economic Rights Action Centre (SERAC) and Another v Nigeria* (2001) AHRLR 60 para. 68. See generally K. Ebeku, 'The Right to a Satisfactory Environment and the African Commission' (2003) 3 *African Human Rights Law Journal* 149.
30 *SERAC v Nigeria*, (n. 29) para. 52.
31 Note the cases of *Lopez-Ostra v Spain* App. No. 16798/90, ECHR 9 December 1994; *Fadayeva v. Russia* App. No. 55723/00, ECHR 9 June 2005; *Guerra and Others v. Italy* App. No. 116/1996/735/932, ECHR, 19 February 1998; *Taskin v Turkey* App. No. 46117/99, ECHR 10 November 2004.
32 *Öneryildiz v Turkey* App. No. 48939/99, ECHR 30 November 2004; *M.C. Mehta v Union of India* (2002) 4 SCC 356; *Dr M. Farooque v Bangladesh* 49 DLR (AD) 1997 at 1.

some might continue to fear the relationship between conservation and human rights, for, historically and especially in Africa, human rights have often been sidelined for obligations of environmental protection. The recent case of *Centre for Minority Rights Development (Kenya) and Another on behalf of Endorois Welfare Council v Kenya*[33] demonstrates this uneasy relationship when indigenous cultures and their environmental impacts are little understood.

At the forefront of greening the right to life are probably India, Bangladesh and Pakistan.[34] India's story is one of the triumph of judicial activism but it does have its detractors, often critical of the judicial allocation of public resources[35] and the trampling of human rights in the name of anti-pollution.[36] In the now infamous case of *Kumar v State of Bihar* (1991),[37] the Indian Supreme Court reinterpreted the constitutionally protected right to life to include 'the right to enjoyment of pollution-free water and air for full enjoyment of life'.[38] India's suspension of civil liberties in the 1970s by the Indira Ghandi regime was apparently the immediate catalyst for the Supreme Court's judicial activism in the area of human rights.[39] Expanding the remit of public interest litigation (PIL) the Supreme Court opened up the courts to India's citizens to litigate, and with prominent PIL lawyers taking the lead, the Supreme Court has managed to broaden human rights protections to include a right to a healthy environment. India's path to development, via heavy industrial pollution, and, in particular, the 1984 Bhopal disaster and a weaker legislative approach to environmental protection, were thus all catalysts for such judicial activism. And as early as 1995 the Indian Supreme Court recognised in the right to life 'the protection and preservation of the environment, ecological balance, freedom from pollution of air and water, and sanitation, without which life cannot be enjoyed'.[40] Most famously in the Delhi air pollution litigation, the Supreme Court's continuing mandamus orders have constantly monitored state compliance with the Court's orders for compulsory catalytic converters on new vehicles, the conversion of all public transport to compressed natural gas, vehicle emissions testing and the closure of polluting facilities in the city.[41] Taking a broader, environmental approach to the management of forestry and wildlife conservation, the Court has heard continual applications in the *Godavarman*[42] case since 1996, and today the case law has covered issues of deforestation, mining,[43] logging,[44] impacts of clearing forest for a 'recreational park' on a bird sanctuary,[45] and the reintroduction of

---

33 Communication 276/03, (2009) AHRLR 75 (ACHPR 2009).

34 For a good appraisal see Boyd (n. 13) 175–86; see also J.R. May and E. Daly, 'Vindicating Fundamental Environmental Rights: Judicial Acceptance of Constitutionally Entrenched Environmental Rights' (2009) 11 *Oregon Review of International Law* 365–439.

35 A. Rosencranz and S. Lélé, 'Supreme Court and India's Forests' (2008) *Economic and Political Weekly* 11–14; S. Divan and A. Rosencranz, *Environmental Law and Policy in India*, 2nd edn (Oxford University Press, 2001) 148.

36 *Almitra Patel v Union of India* (2000) 2 SCC 679.

37 *Subhash Kumar v State of Bihar* (1991) 1 SCC 598.

38 Ibid., at 7.

39 A. Rosencranz and M. Jackson, 'The Delhi Pollution Case: The Supreme Court of India and the Limits of Judicial Power' (2003) 28 *Colum. J. Envtl. L.* 223–54, at 229–30.

40 *Virender Gaur v State of Haryana* (1995) 2 SCC 577.

41 *M.C. Mehta v Union of India* (2002) 4 SCC 356, and see Rosencranz and Jackson (n. 39); Boyd (n. 13) 175–83.

42 *T.N. Godavarman Thirumulpad v Union of India* (1996) 9 SCC 982.

43 *T.N. Godavarman Thirumulpad v Union of India & Ors* (2008) 2 SCC 222, para. 19; *T.N. Godavarman Thirumulpad v Union Of India & Ors* [2011] INSC 587.

44 *T.N. Godavarman Thirumulpad v Union of India* (1996) 9 SCC 982.

45 *T.N. Godavarman Thirumulpad v Union Of India & Ors* [2010] INSC 1058 para. 66.

endangered species.[46] Other cases address water issues such as water resource management,[47] clean-up of river pollution[48] and the prevention of pollution to the drinking water of reservoirs.[49] Yet, while Indian law is now infused with procedural environmental rights and a powerful public interest litigation lobby, many question whether these singular environmental victories have brought real improvement to the overall quality of India's environment.[50]

In the European context, 'greening' of human rights has been the preferred approach, and in light of the judicial activism displayed in the Court's environmental rights jurisprudence, the Committee of Ministers has consistently rejected the need for a stand-alone substantive right to environment.[51] A substantive right may, however, not be such a distant dream, if the Court's recent judgment in *Di Sarno v Italy* (2012)[52] is anything to go on. Here the Court appears to recognise within Article 8 of the European Convention of Human Rights[53] a 'right of the persons concerned to respect for their private life and their home and, more generally, *to enjoy a healthy and protected environment*.[54] Although often viewed as an intermediate or transitional stage, the greening approach of the European Court of Human Rights has thus notched up some notable achievements, including some that extend beyond the industrial pollution paradigm. In the *Budayeva and Others v Russia* (2008)[55] case, the Court gave us a glimpse of how it might handle future incidences of climate change impacts, such as floods and mudslides. The Court was undoubtedly at pains to limit the liabilities of the state under Article 2 (the right to life) in cases of natural disasters to only foreseeable and clearly identifiable impacts, especially of recurring calamities affecting a distinct human habitation.[56] The case involved several deaths and injuries caused by a mudslide, attributable to state failure to repair a dam. Although a frequently recurring natural disaster in this Russian town, and despite advance warning from the Russian Agency tasked with monitoring the river and dam, the state issued no emergency warning.[57] Thus, recognising the severity of the incident and the applicability of Article 2 to 'any activity, whether public or not',[58] the Court's focus was clearly on an expansive reading of the right to life, to extend beyond the sphere hitherto established of industrial risks or dangerous activities. Yet, with the ferocity and frequency of climate change impacts ever looming on the horizon, was the Court nevertheless still too

---

46 *T.N. Godavarman Thirumulpad v Union Of India & Ors* [2012] INSC 114.

47 *Re Networking of Rivers* [2012] INSC 147; *M.K. Balakrishnan & Ors v Union Of India & Ors* [2009] INSC 840.

48 *Tirupur Dyeing Factory Owners Ass. v Noyyal River Protection Ass. & Ors* [2009] INSC 1624.

49 *A.P. Pollution Control Board II v Prof. M.V. Nayudu & Ors* [2000] INSC 679.

50 Boyd (n. 13) 179–83

51 Drafting an additional protocol to the European Convention on Human Rights concerning the right to a healthy environment, Recommendation 1885 (2009), Reply from the Committee of Ministers, adopted at the 1088th meeting of the Ministers' Deputies (16 June 2010), available at http://assembly.coe.int/Main.asp?link=/Documents/WorkingDocs/Doc10/EDOC12298.htm (accessed on 10 August 2012).

52 *Di Sarno v Italy* App. No. 30765/08 (ECHR, 10 January 2012).

53 Convention for the Protection of Human Rights and Fundamental Freedoms (as amended) (1950) ETS No. 005.

54 *Di Sarno* (n. 52) para. 110 (emphasis added).

55 *Budayeva and Others v Russia* App. Nos. 15339/02, 21166/02, 20058/02, 11673/02 and 15343/02 (ECHR, 20 March 2008).

56 Ibid., paras 135–37.

57 Ibid., para. 29.

58 Ibid., para. 130.

cautious in its approach? It was a unanimous verdict for a breach of Article 2, but what if the mudslides had not been so common an occurrence, or an inadequate warning failed to prevent injury or death?

From an environmental protection perspective, all the regional courts, but especially the European Court, have provided an invaluable tool in the promotion of existing environmental law standards. Not only has the proliferation of environmental procedural rights been achieved through the regional human rights courts,[59] but also the recognition of Environmental Impact Assessments,[60] mining and industrial licensing requirements and contaminant safety standards.[61] Since breach of the relevant environmental standards, or licensing requirements, is often a precursor for the finding of a human rights violation, the courts' jurisprudence tends to reinforce the need for state compliance with the applicable environmental requirements.[62] In the 2005 *Fadeyeva v Russia*[63] case the European Court was actually quite strict in its finding of a violation of Article 8, concerning protection of the right to family life and home, where progress had been made in halving the contaminant level from a steel plant, but must ultimately be viewed as correct as the plant was operating in violation of Russian environmental protection laws. Yet, despite the courts' frequent attempts at reinforcing existing environmental laws, the compliance gap remains, even in European zone states such as Russia.[64]

The cross-fertilisation of ideas and standards between the regional courts, especially the Inter-American and African systems, has seen particular developments in indigenous land rights.[65] Indeed, on both continents the right to environment has developed probably most notably as a valuable tool for the recognition of the holistic nature of the land and environmental rights of indigenous and tribal communities.[66] It was the Inter-American Court in the

---

59 Notably in the form of the 1998 Aarhus Convention on Access to Information, Public Participation in Decision-Making and Access to Justice in Environmental Matters (1999) 38 ILM 517–33; see *Taskin v Turkey* App. No. 46117/99 (ECHR, 10 November 2004); *Case of the Saramaka People v Suriname*, 28 November 2007, IACHR, paras 133–54.

60 Outside the human rights context, the ICJ in the *Pulp Mills* case found that the obligation of conducting an EIA to be part of general international law (especially in the sense of a transboundary context of a shared resource) see *Pulp Mills on the River Uruguay (Argentina v Uruguay), Merits*, ICJ Reports 2010, 14, at para. 204.

61 See e.g. *Guerra and Others v Italy* App. No.116/1996/735/932 (ECHR, 19 February 1998); *Lopez-Ostra v Spain* App. No. 16798/90 (ECHR, 9 December 1994); *Fadeyeva v Russia* App. No. 55723/00 (ECHR, 9 June 2005).

62 A. Boyle, 'Human Rights or Environmental Rights? A Reassessment' (2007) 18 *Fordham Environmental Law Review* 471–511, 487.

63 *Fadeyeva* (n. 61).

64 Industrial pollution in breach of the European Convention: Measures required by a European Court judgment, CM/Inf/DH (2007)7 13 February 2007, available at https://wcd.coe.int/ViewDoc.jsp?id=1094807&BackColorInternet=9999CC&BackColorIntranet=FFBB55&BackColorLogged=FFAC75 (accessed on 7 August 2012).

65 In *Maya Indigenous Communities v Belize*, Case 12.053, Report No. 78/00, OEA/Ser.L/V/II.111 Doc. 20 rev. at 129 (2000), for example, the Commission acknowledges that Belize is not a state party to ILO Convention (No. 169) but that 'it considers that the terms of that treaty provide evidence of contemporary international opinion concerning matters relating to indigenous peoples', fn. 123; *Endorois v Kenya* (n. 33); and see *SERAC v Nigeria* (n. 30) para. 57 where the Commission recognises the duty of governments to protect citizens from acts of private citizens, and quotes ECHR and IACHR case law.

66 See *Endorois v Kenya*, ibid.; *SERAC v Nigeria*, ibid.; *Case of the Yakye Axa Indigenous Community v Paraguay*, 17 June 2005, IACHR.

2007 *Case of the Saramaka People v Suriname*[67] which first took a more holistic approach to the indigenous (property) right of access to their natural resources to include the contemplation by the state not only of the impact of granting minerals concessions on resources directly used by the groups, notably the minerals themselves, but also the ecosystem level impacts that the mining or extraction of these minerals would cause.[68] Thus, the state must assess more holistically the impact of such mineral extraction concessions on the waters, the wildlife and other food sources of the group.

2.1 The world we're in

It is difficult to assess the progress and effectiveness of the environmental rights movement. Progress has certainly been made and on a global scale. The variety of approaches adopted by states and regional human rights bodies is creating a rich jurisprudence. The fragmented manner in how environmental rights are being developed seems to be aiding, not restricting, these rights to permeate the full spectrum of human rights discourse. The three-pronged approach of greening, substantive and procedural rights coupled with judicial/litigator activism and ingenuity have established environmental rights as an acceptable, even necessary part of human rights. And it is undoubtedly the climate change dialogue that has driven environmental rights developments over the past 10 years and catalyzed the human rights-based approach to climate change, which seeks to infuse human rights into adaptation planning.[69] Advances have clearly been made in holding states to account, for both their own actions and their omissions in failing to regulate industry, but there is still some way to go in holding corporate actors to account and to inspire confidence in policies of finance institutions such as the World Bank. On the other hand, despite the disappointing 2012 UN Conference on Sustainable Development Rio+20 on the 'green economy', the notions of sustainable development and environmental justice[70] continue to impact national decision-making on big development projects.

3 Future directions

Of all the developments and possible future developments in this area of law, this section will focus on three aspects that are of emerging importance in this field; these are (1) the notion of resilience, (2) the worrying trend of land grabs, and (3) developments in the acceptance of principles of international environmental law.

---

67 28 November 2007, IACHR.

68 Ibid., paras 155–58.

69 *Integrating Climate Change Considerations in the Country Analysis and the United Nations Development Assistance Framework (UNDAF): A Guidance Note for United Nations Country Teams* (UN Development Group, 2010).

70 The recognition in South Africa for example of environmental justice issues led the new South African government to include environmental rights in the constitution. See E. Emesch, 'Human Rights Dimensions of Contemporary Environmental Protection', in M. Odello and S. Cavandoli (eds), *Emerging Areas of Human Rights in the 21st Century: The Role of the Universal Declaration of Human Rights* (Routledge, 2011), 66–86, at 70.

3.1 Resilience

With the global focus on the impacts of climate change and the management of mitigation and adaptation, the notion of 'resilience' has emerged. Not to be confused with sustainability and sustainable development, which centre on limiting the exploitation of resources today to ensure the maintenance of adequate resources for future generations,[71] 'resilience' measures the abilities of a system (for example an ecosystem) to adapt to external pressures, such as the impacts of climate change, and maintain its integrity.[72] As with sustainability, resilience theory can also be criticised for its anthropocentrism, but its value lies in its emphasis on promoting good environmental governance and the ecological integrity of the environment, and in promoting those features of cultures and communities which minimise their impact on the environment,[73] while promoting biodiversity and good environmental governance.

Resilience theory is also applied to human communities showing adaptability in the face of climatic shocks, environmental degradation or resource depletion, such as indigenous and tribal peoples and cultures and communities that work closely with the land such as small-scale farmers or fishermen in developing countries and small-island states.[74] It will be these same key communities, of course, that will be most vulnerable to both immediate and long-term impacts of climate change, and thus for whom a strong environmental rights mechanism is most important.[75] Probably of most relevance are participatory rights to enable such strongly resilient communities, and hence the kind of communities that will aid in the transition to a climate-changed future, to maintain their resilience in the face of external threats such as big development projects or resource extraction on their lands or nearby lands, or otherwise impacting their way of life.[76] Education of such communities is also important and hence their right to information regarding such threats as climate change is important, but also educating such communities in their broader human rights.

Furthermore, the environmental rights need to be strongly integrated with those human rights closest in spirit to environmental rights, namely the human rights to water, food and health, and of course ultimately to the right to life. Unfortunately, all three economic, social and cultural rights are still very weak under current international law provision, and so real progress needs to be made in these rights in order to strengthen the protection of the environment for the benefit of all concerned. Real water and food security – and hence the right to both, is not going to be delivered without the protection of the quality of the soils and waters of the world, as well as their quantity. With its focus on resilient communities and resource management, the infusing of resilience theory into the human rights dialogue could

71 *Our Common Future* (n. 25) at 'Chairman's Foreword'.
72 C.S. Holling, 'Resilience and Stability of Ecological Systems' (1973) 4 *Annual Review of Ecology and Systematics* 1–23.
73 See L.C. Gerhardinger, G. Martins, A. Moreira, C. Curti and C. Seixas, 'Socioecological Resilience at Céu do Patriarca Ecovillage – South Brazil' (2011) Ecocultures Working Paper: 2012–14, University of Essex, UK, available at http://www.Ecocultures.org/2012/05/socioecological-resilience-at-ceu-do-patriarca-ecovilage-south-brazil/ (accessed on 10 August 2012).
74 See the websites http://www.resalliance.org and http://gen.ecovillage.org/ (accessed on 10 August 2012).
75 It is lamentable that many small island states most vulnerable to climate change impacts are not parties to the major human rights instruments.
76 See 'the resilience shown historically by Arctic indigenous peoples is now being severely tested': IPCC, *Climate Change 2007* (n. 4) 655, and see chapters generally on Africa, ecosystems, coastal systems and low-lying areas.

certainly strengthen these economic, social and cultural rights, as well as others of participation, education and development, while promoting environmental protection. The key is thus to explore the resilience practices of ecocultures around the globe, and, if not to learn from them, certainly maintain them.[77]

The UN Special Rapporteur on the Right to Food is reflecting resilience thinking when he advocates a 'Green Revolution',[78] emphasising the urgent need for a new green agricultural paradigm of agroecology – the notion of sustainable agriculture achieved through the science of ecology, or in simple terms using the interactions of the natural world to improve the environment.[79] A good example of agroecology is the planting of crops interspersed with certain grasses which act as a natural pesticide.[80] Thus if we could now infuse resilience theory into environmental rights, adaptation planning and the human rights dialogue more broadly, maybe we could at least ensure that we are retaining and promoting those community and environmental aspects that are resilient to climate change shocks, instead of losing them forever.

3.2 Land grabs

Since 1987 and the Brundtland Commission's recognition of the environmentally damaging impacts of poverty and the cycle of human and environmental impoverishment that results, the principle of sustainable development has become embedded in all dimensions of human rights and environmental planning.[81] Yet it has not been the role of the principle to halt large dam projects, mineral exploitation or oil exploration.[82]

The principle appears to have had even less influence on the global land grab which has taken hold over the past decade. This new phenomenon of foreign land-grabbing, the 'foreignisation of space' as one author refers to it,[83] includes the sale or leasing of land by companies, wealthy individuals or foreign states.[84] Particularly prevalent since the 2008 food

---

77 Worldwatch Institute, *State of the World 2009: Into a Warming World* (W.W. Norton & Company, 2009), ch. 5 on Building Resilience.

78 O. De Schutter and G. Vanloqueren, 'The New Green Revolution: How Twenty-First-Century Science Can Feed the World' (2011) 2(4) *Solutions* 33–44.

79 J. Pretty, A.D. Noble, D. Bossio, J. Dixon, R.E. Hine, F.W.T. Penningdevries and J.I.L. Morison, 'Resource-Conserving Agriculture Increases Yields in Developing Countries', (2006) 40 *Environmental Science and Technology* 4, 1114–19.

80 See ibid., and J. Pretty, C. Toulmin and S. Williams, 'Sustainable Intensification in African Agriculture' (2011) 9(1) *International Journal of Agricultural Sustainability* 5–24; Report submitted by the Special Rapporteur on the right to food, Olivier De Schutter to the Human Rights Council, A/HRC/16/49 (20 December 2010), 16–20.

81 See 1992 UN Declaration on Environment and Development, Rio de Janeiro, 12 August 1992 (UN Doc. A/CONF.151/26/REV.1); *Case Concerning the Gabčikovo-Nagymaros Project* (Hungary/ Slovakia) 25 September 1997, ICJ, Judgment, available at http://www.icj-cij.org/docket/ files/92/7375.pdf (last accessed 10 August 2012) at 75.

82 Note for example such large-scale projects as Brazil's Belo Monte Dam and Canada's Athabasca Tar Sands. Particularly as regards the latter project, Polly Higgins has called for an international crime of ecocide. See P. Higgins, *Eradicating Ecocide: Laws and Governance to Stop the Destruction of the Planet* (Shepheard-Walwyn (Publishers) Ltd, 2010).

83 A. Zoomers, 'Globalisation and the Foreignisation of Space: Seven Processes Driving the Current Global Land Grab' (2010) 37(2) *Journal of Peasant Studies* 429–47.

84 Ibid.; and W. Anseeuw, L.A. Wily, L. Cotula and M. Taylor, *Land Rights and the Rush for Life: Findings of the Global Commercial Pressures on Land Research Project* (The International Land Coalition, 2012).

security crisis, it is not just large tracts of land for food production that is contributing to the percentage of land under foreign control. Other reasons for the acquisition of land include the extraction of minerals, growing biofuels, development of tourist complexes and nature reserves – including wildlife (i.e. biodiversity hot spots) or wilderness areas, but also areas of reforestation under the climate change regime's REDD (Reducing Emissions through Deforestation and Forest Degradation) agenda.[85]

From the human rights perspective such land grabs rarely result in labour benefits as the local population are often unskilled for such roles, especially for example in new IT ventures, but also for agricultural work.[86] Where land rights have been granted to individuals, they may be keen to sell their land for a profit but they will then only be able to purchase land of a lesser quality, and hence they will then struggle to maintain their livelihood.[87] For those without land rights the situation is their further marginlisation as they may be displaced forcibly from the land without compensation. Land–grabbing by foreign states to secure their own food security is particularly disturbing in countries where there is already a food shortage, and this aspect has caused much condemnation of certain land deals.[88] Furthermore, it is not possible today to separate food security from the problems inherent in the impacts of climate change.

The UN Special Rapporteur on the Right to Food[89] has again responded to the land grab issue with the promotion of the Food and Agriculture Organization's *Voluntary Guidelines on the Responsible Governance of Tenure of Land, Fisheries and Forests in the Context of National Food Security*,[90] and his own principles outlined in the report, *Large-scale Land Acquisitions and Leases: A Set of Core Principles and Measures to Address the Human Rights Challenge*.[91] The Rapporteur's principles include that the 'need to preserve food security within the host country' is taken into account 'proactively' in any investment agreements,[92] the promotion of 'labour–intensive' farming methods using local labour,[93] that the rights of pastoralists are respected,[94] including the requirement of the free, prior and informed consent for indigenous communities,[95] and finally recognises the potential for sustainable farming as it is 'vital that high environmental standards are complied with'.[96] The Rapporteur refers to the 2009 Declaration by the UN

---

85 For information see http://www.un–redd.org/ (accessed on 10 August 2012); Zoomers, (n. 83) and Anseeuw et al (n. 83).

86 Zoomers, (n. 83) 441.

87 Ibid.

88 L. Cotula, S. Vermeulen, R. Leonard and J. Keeley, *Land Grab or Development Opportunity? Agricultural Investment and International Land Deals in Africa* (IIED; FAO and IFAD, 2009).

89 De Schutter and Vanloqueren (n. 78).

90 Rome, 2012, FAO and Committee on World Food Security, available at http://www.fao.org/docrep/016/i2801e/i2801e.pdf (accessed on 8 August 2012).

91 O. De Schutter, *Large-scale Land Acquisitions and Leases: A Set of Core Principles and Measures to Address the Human Rights Challenge*, 11 June 2009, available at http://ap.ohchr.org/documents/dpage_e.aspx?si=A/HRC/13/33/Add.2 (accessed on 8 August 2012). An abridged report was also presented to the Human Rights Council, see A/HRC/13/33/Add.2 (28 December 2009).

92 De Schutter report, ibid., 5.

93 Ibid., 6.

94 Ibid., 7.

95 Ibid., 7, see also Art. 19 of the 2007 United Nations Declaration on the Rights of Indigenous Peoples, 7 September 2007, A/61/L.67.

96 De Schutter report (n. 91) 6.

Commission on Sustainable Development,[97] which recognised that 'sustainable agricultural practices as well as sustainable forest management can contribute to meeting climate change concerns',[98] and that 'sustainable soil, land, livestock, forest, biodiversity and water management practices, and resilient crops are essential'.[99] Thus, fundamental for those caught up in land grabs will be an integrated approach of environmental rights – including this focus on the maintenance of a viable environment itself, and ordinary human rights. Of particular relevance then are the rights of education and participation, but also the need to ensure strong land rights in order to deliver the rights to food, development and, ultimately, the right to self-determination.[100]

3.3 Principles of international environmental law

In his recent book, Boyd presents the most comprehensive study to date of the constitutionalisation of environmental rights.[101] He surveys the constitutions and jurisprudence of 193 states, and as his book title suggests, the picture that emerges is nothing short of an 'environmental rights *revolution*'. Quoting some of Boyd's statistics, three-quarters of states now have a constitutional right or duty to the environment (some 147 states out of 193),[102] 92 of which have a substantive right to environment.[103] A negative point, however, is the fact that 24 of the 49 states without a constitutional right or duty to the environment are small-island states.[104] As suggested earlier, this domestic constitutionalisation of environmental rights in states, and within states in a federal system,[105] has led to a fragmented yet rich application of such human rights. With little international guidance on the issue, it was left to individual states and regional human rights mechanisms to develop a position specific to the environmental values rooted in their own traditions and cultures. This, almost personal, evolution of environmental rights while capturing the essence of choice, does, however, somewhat fly in the face of the universality of human rights.

Thus there is broad consensus on the need to provide some measure of environmental rights; however, these are to be achieved within a particular state or regional human rights system. Yet, as the European Court has indicated, such rights do not entail a right to nature protection.[106] Indeed, in the European context there appears to be a general lack of

---

97 *The Commission on Sustainable Development*, Resolution 17/1, *Policy Options and Practical Measures to Expedite Implementation in Agriculture, Rural Development, Land, Drought, Desertification and Africa*, Report on the seventeenth session (16 May 2008 and 4–15 May 2009) Economic and Social Council Official Records, 2009 Supplement No. 9, E/CN.17/2009/19.

98 Ibid., para. 5.

99 Ibid.

100 S. Vermeulen and L. Cotula, 'Over the Heads of Local People: Consultation, Consent, and Recompense in Large-scale Land Deals for Biofuels Projects in Africa' (2010) 37 (4) *Journal of Peasant Studies* 899–916, 900. Note the issue of participation rights in the legal challenge of the Lamu Port – Southern Sudan – Ethiopia Transport project in Kenya. See http://www.ciel.org/HR_Envir/Lamu_6June2012.html (accessed on 10 August 2012).

101 Boyd (n. 13).

102 Ibid., 47.

103 Ibid., 59.

104 Ibid., 49.

105 J.C. Tucker, 'Constitutional Codification of an Environmental Ethic' (2000) 52 *Florida Law Review* 299–327.

106 See *Fadeyeva v Russia* (n. 61) para. 68.

environmental awareness displayed in the majority opinions of what the true value of nature entails. The Court's reference to a wetland ecosystem as a 'swamp' in the *Krytatos v Greece* case[107] shows the work to be done in this area. Clearly, the protection sought may well have been outside the remit of the rights under the Convention,[108] even the greener version of those rights, but if the Court is unaware of the true value of the environment and such ecosystems, how are the judges to know if they should at least be thinking about including such concerns in their judgments? A greater awareness of the need for clean energy in the face of climate change did show the Court's greener side in the *Fägersköld v Sweden* case,[109] and even in the *Krytatos* case the Court did suggest that it might protect a forest.[110] But, so far, there is very little in the European Court's jurisprudence on such broader issues as biodiversity, or the environmental notion of inter-generational equity and the precautionary principle.[111] The African and Inter-American jurisprudence thus appears to be richer in environmental terms than that produced by the European Court. Again, leaving aside the compliance gap, the African Commission showed such depth in its environmental understanding and the ecological values it espoused in the *SERAC v Nigeria* case,[112] and also the *Endorois v Kenya* case,[113] particularly in the precedent-setting requirement for environmental clean-up of damaged lands.[114] As the *SERAC* case demonstrates, there is a need to consider a broader range of remedies to compensate for breaches of environmental rights.

Yet, as Boyd points out, while much progress has been made in environmental rights, the Earth is little closer to achieving environmental sustainability.[115] As the regional jurisprudence demonstrates, however, there are certainly pockets of good practice, where real integration of rights is taking place and where a solid environmental ethos is informing the dialogue. At the national level there have been some interesting developments in Ecuador, where the newly created rights of nature were upheld to find the state in violation by allowing road-building to cause siltation of the Vilcabamba River, and consequent damage to riverside lands.[116] The Ecuadorian court upheld the precautionary principle and the notion of intergenerational equity.[117] The precautionary principle has also been recognised in the case law of the Costa Rican Constitutional Court, which in a 2011 case recognised that the right to a healthy and ecologically balanced environment gives special protection to biodiversity and groundwater.[118]

---

107   *Krytatos v Greece* App. No. 41666/98 (ECHR, 22 May 2003).
108   According to the Court the applicants had not proved how the alleged damage to the birds and other protected species living in the swamp directly affected their right under Art. 8.
109   *Fägersköld v Sweden* App. No. 37664/04, Admissibility Decision, ECHR.
110   *Krytatos* (n. 107) para. 53. The Court suggested the destruction of a nearby forest was a 'situation which could have affected more directly the applicants' own well-being'. Judge Zagrebelsky in his partly dissenting opinion saw 'no major difference' between the destruction of a forest and the 'extraordinary swampy environment'.
111   Note the seven dissenting judges in case of *Balmer-Schafroth and others v Switzerland* (67\1996\686\876), 26 August 1997, ECHR who referred to the precautionary principle and *Tatar v Romania* App. No. 67021/01 (ECHR, 27 January 2009), para. 120.
112   N. 29, para. 52.
113   N. 33.
114   See *SERAC v Nigeria* (n. 29) where the Commission ordered the comprehensive clean-up of lands and rivers damaged by the oil operations.
115   Boyd (n. 13) 9.
116   See the *Wheeler and Huddle* case and Daly's blog (n. 13).
117   Ibid. While a landmark case, the decision reportedly remains unimplemented.
118   *Luis Arturo Morales Campos, Recurso de amparo*, expediente 11-002110-0007-CO (10 May 2011).

Equally notable was the 2008 judgment[119] which found that species extinction violates the right to a healthy environment, a decision which created protection for the highly endangered leatherback turtles from the annual harvest at Las Baulas National Park.[120] And the notion of intergenerational equity was recognised in the groundbreaking *Mendoza* case in Argentina in 2008,[121] where the Supreme Court ordered the public authorities to clean up the river basin due to the health problems caused by the heavily polluted river, and recognised the rights of future generations.[122] That integrated dialogue is also occurring across the human rights and environmental divide between intergovernmental organisations, NGOs and treaty bodies. In its 2011 Discussion Paper entitled *Our Planet, Our Health, Our Future: Human Health and the Rio Conventions: Biological Diversity, Climate Change and Desertification*,[123] the World Health Organization acknowledged the central role of biodiversity as the 'foundation for human health',[124] commenting that 'biodiversity underpins the functioning of the ecosystems on which we depend for our food and fresh water; aids in regulating climate, floods and diseases; and provides recreational benefits and offers aesthetic and spiritual enrichment'.[125] The Discussion Paper referenced the *2010 Global Biodiversity Outlook 3*[126] conclusion that since the rate of biodiversity loss is not slowing down but is actually intensifying in some cases, this is 'bringing us closer to a number of potential tipping points that would catastrophically reduce the capacity of ecosystems to provide these essential services'.[127] The World Health Organization consequently endorses the Aichi Biodiversity Targets,[128] especially Target 14 which refers to ecosystem services to human health and well-being with the objectives of promoting the integration of ecosystem management considerations into health policy and promoting ecosystem integrity in order to secure water and food security and protection from diseases.[129] Less prominent but also included in the WHO Discussion Paper is the objective of Aichi Target 15, which refers to the enhancement of ecosystem resilience, which appears most prominently in the discussion on adaptation to climate change.[130]

All of this discussion points to the need for strong recognition and implementation of the broadest possible interpretations of environmental rights. The evidence from the human

---

119 *Clara Emilia Padilla Gutiérrez, Recurso de amparo*, expediente 07-005611-0007-CO (16 December 2008).

120 See also the earlier judgment in *Caribbean Conservation Corporation and Others v Costa Rica (Green Turtles)* (Decision 01250-99) 15 February 1999; A. Palmer and C. Robb, *International Environmental Law Reports, Volume 4 International Environmental Law in National Courts* (Cambridge University Press, 2005) 186–96.

121 *Mendoza Beatriz Silva et al. v State of Argentina et al. on damages (damages resulting from environmental pollution of Matanza/Riachuelo river)*, File M. 1569. XL (8 July 2008).

122 For a full analysis of the case see K. Staveland-Sæter, *Litigating the Right to a Healthy Environment: Assessing the Policy Impact of 'The Mendoza Case'* (Chr. Michelsen Institute, 2011).

123 World Health Organization 2011, available at http://www.who.int/globalchange/publications/reports/health_rioconventions.pdf (accessed on 8 August 2012).

124 Ibid., 2.

125 Ibid.

126 *Global Biodiversity Outlook 3* (Montreal, Secretariat of the Convention on Biological Diversity, 2010).

127 Ibid., 5, 71–81. See also *Global Environment Outlook (GEO-5)* (UNEP, 2012), available at http://www.unep.org/geo/pdfs/geo5/GEO5_report_full_en.pdf (accessed on 7 August 2012) 134–66.

128 COP 10 Decision X/2, X/2. Strategic Plan for Biodiversity 2011–2020, available at http://www.cbd.int/sp/targets/ (accessed on 7 August 2012).

129 *Our Planet* (n. 123) 20.

130 Ibid., 20

rights community shows some real areas of best practice, but this practice is patchy at best on the acceptance of such broader notions of ecological governance. Notably, the UN Special Rapporteurs on the Rights to Food and Water are generally lonely voices in recognising such a broad environmental approach.[131] Recent reports on the Right to Health,[132] for example, have made no such inclusion.

Thus, while we can continue to advocate an anthropocentric approach to environmental protection via human rights, we must look to incorporate and integrate more fully such a broadened environmental outlook, to include biodiversity and ecosystem resilience, if we are truly to conserve both the non-human and the human population for future generations. Unfortunately, such an opportunity was not grasped at the Rio+20 UN Conference on Sustainable Development of 2012, where again no progress was made on a substantive human right to environment. The Rio+20 Outcome Document, *The Future We Want*,[133] did, however, reference a very broad outlook on the notion of sustainable development, including the acknowledgement of the 'need to further mainstream sustainable development at all levels integrating economic, social and environmental aspects and recognising their interlinkages'.[134] The Conference also reaffirmed the need to achieve sustainable development by, inter alia, 'promoting integrated and sustainable management of natural resources and ecosystems that supports inter alia economic, social and human development while *facilitating ecosystem conservation, regeneration and restoration and resilience* in the face of new and emerging challenges'.[135]

4 Conclusions

The topic of human rights and environmental protection is exceedingly fast-moving at present. The fragmented approach to the topic has led, in this author's opinion, to a rich jurisprudence that would perhaps have been lost had a substantive, global right to environment emerged from the Ksentini Report in 1994. There are many examples of best practice, and as Boyd recognises, there now appear to be efforts being made at harmonisation of approaches,[136] or at least there is an equally rich dialogue and cross-fertilisation of ideas between courts and other bodies. Will the newly created post of Independent Expert garner sufficient support for such a stand-alone right? Only time will tell on this aspect, but as this chapter has suggested, there is still some way to go from an environmental law perspective in really infusing those environmental rights, across the whole spectrum, with key ecological and social perspectives of resilience and key environmental principles. That this is a necessary dimension to environmental rights is shown most forcefully in climate change adaptation planning, as without a resilience approach it is likely that good environmental practices will be lost. Indeed, the UN Special Rapporteur on the Right to Food has highlighted how valuable such resilience approaches can be for the realisation of human rights more broadly. On the other hand, a major threat to many communities at present is foreign land acquisition. The scale and

---

131 For the right to water see, CESCR, General Comment No. 15, E/C.12/2002/11 (20 January 2003), para. 28(e).
132 Report A/HRC/17/25 (12 April 2011) focusing on development and the right to health.
133 A/CONF.216/L.1 (19 June 2012).
134 Ibid., preambular para. 3.
135 Ibid., preambular para. 4 (emphasis added).
136 Boyd (n. 13) 108.

locations of land grabs as well as the human rights impacts on the communities affected are a worrying trend, and are only likely to exacerbate existing vulnerabilities and cause further problems of environmental (in)justice. Again an integrated and effective environmental rights approach is needed in order to safeguard the environment for future generations.

Select bibliography

D.R. Boyd, *The Environmental Rights Revolution: A Global Study of Constitutions, Human Rights and the Environment* (UBC Press, 2012).

J.J. Bruckerhoff, 'Giving Nature Constitutional Protection: A Less Anthropocentric Interpretation of Environmental Rights'(2007–8) 86 *Texas Law Review* 615–46.

J. Fairhead, M. Leach and I. Scoones, 'Green Grabbing: A New Appropriation of Nature?' (2012) 39(2) *Journal of Peasant Studies* 237–61.

B.E. Hill, S. Wolfson and N. Targ, 'Human Rights and the Environment: A Synopsis and Some Predictions' (2003–2004) 16 *Georgetown International Environmental Law Review* 359–402.

J.H. Knox, *Report of the Independent Expert on the Issue of Human Rights Obligations Relating to the Enjoyment of A Safe, Clean, Healthy and Sustainable Environment*, 24 December 2012, A/HRC/22/43.

L.A. Wily, 'Looking Back to See Forward: The Legal Niceties of Land Theft in Land Rushes' (2012) 39(3–4) *Journal of Peasant Studies*, 751–75.

A. Zoomers, 'Globalisation and the Foreignisation of Space: Seven Processes Driving The Current Global Land Grab' (2010) 37(2) *Journal of Peasant Studies* 429–47.

18

Customary law and human rights

Evadné Grant

1 Introduction

Few would disagree with the view that human rights discourse has become the dominant ethical language of our time.[1] This discourse presupposes universal applicability of human rights norms, described in the preamble of the Universal Declaration of Human Rights (UDHR) as a 'common standard of achievement for all peoples and all nations'. But, in a world characterised by diversity, where people live in very different societies and cultures, the assertion of universality has given rise to a great deal of controversy.

Acknowledging the tension between the claim to universality and the reality of diversity, the World Conference on Human Rights in Vienna agreed that:

> While the significance of national and regional particularities and various historical, cultural and religious backgrounds must be borne in mind, it is the duty of states, regardless of their political, economic and cultural systems, to promote and protect all human rights and fundamental freedoms.[2]

At the same time cultural diversity itself is explicitly acknowledged and protected by international human rights law. Many of the rights commonly protected under both national and international human rights regimes include rights to express differences and to pursue different ways of life. Perhaps the clearest expression of support for cultural diversity is to be found in the 2005 Convention on the Protection and Promotion of the Diversity of Cultural Expressions.[3] The Convention makes a clear connection between cultural diversity and human rights:

---

1 U. Baxi, *The Future of Human Rights* (OUP, 2002) 1.
2 World Conference on Human Rights, 'Vienna Declaration and Programme of Action' (1993) UN Doc. A/CONF.157/23, para. 5.
3 UNESCO Convention on the Protection and Promotion of the Diversity of Cultural Expressions (adopted Paris 20 October 2005, entered into force 18 March 2007).

> Cultural diversity can be protected and promoted only if human rights and fundamental freedoms, such as freedom of expression, information and communication, as well as the ability of individuals to choose cultural expressions, are guaranteed.[4]

But the Convention also acknowledges the underlying tension between cultural diversity and human rights by specifically stating that the provisions of the Convention are not to be invoked in order to infringe human rights.[5]

Customary law is one of the manifestations of culture and its diversity. It is a little-appreciated fact that, especially in the global South, far more people rely on customary laws to regulate family relationships and resolve disputes than on formal state law.[6] But while the right to use customary law is itself protected under international human rights law as a cultural right, many systems of customary law endorse norms and practices which violate international human rights norms such as the right to due process and the right to equality.[7]

This chapter explores the sometimes fraught relationship between the idea of universal human rights and the acceptance of cultural diversity, focusing on customary law as an important component or representation of culture. It begins by considering customary law as an aspect of culture and the place of cultural rights in international human rights law. It subsequently focuses on the South African experience of constitutional protection of customary law subject to a bill of rights to illustrate the tension between customary law and human rights norms, and attempts to resolve conflicts in that context. In the final section, a number of different responses to the tension between international human rights law and customary law are critically assessed.

2 Culture and customary law

Culture is a notoriously slippery concept.[8] While the term is commonly used to refer to artistic, musical, literary or philosophical activity, customary law is usually associated with culture in the sense of the totality of a society, group or people's store of knowledge, practices, morals, laws, customs and artefacts that give social groups their unique characters.[9] Defining culture in this way is, however, misleading, as it suggests that culture is static,

---

4 Art. 2(1).

5 Ibid.

6 See F. Banda, *Women, Law and Human Rights: An African Perspective* (Hart, 2005) 85; M. Ndulo, 'African Customary Law, Customs, and Women's Rights' (2011) 18 *Indiana Journal of Global Legal Studies* 87 at 88.

7 See C.I. Nyamu, 'How Should Human Rights and Development Respond to Legitimization of Gender Hierarchy in Developing Countries?' (2000) 41 *Harvard International Law Journal* 381; Ndulo (n. 6) 87; J.E. Bond, 'Culture, Dissent, and the State: The Example of Commonwealth African Marriage Law' (2011) 14 *Yale Human Rights and Development Law Journal* 1.

8 See B. Oomen and S. Templeman, 'The Power of Definition', and W. Mannens, 'A Structure Called Culture', both in Y. Donders (ed.), *Law and Cultural Diversity: Proceedings of a Workshop Organised by the Working Group 'Law and Cultural Diversity' in Co-operation with the School of Human Rights Research, the Netherlands, 25 September 1998* (Netherlands Institute of Human Rights, 1999) 7, 27; J. Symonides, 'Cultural Rights', in J. Symonides (ed.), *Human Rights: Concept and Standards* (Ashgate and UNESCO, 2000) 175, 179.

9 See T.W. Bennett, *Human Rights and African Customary Law under the South African Constitution* (Juta, 1995) 23. See also L.V. Prott, 'Cultural Rights as Peoples' Rights in International Law', in J. Crawford (ed.), *The Rights of Peoples* (Clarendon, 1988) 93, 94; Oomen and Templeman (n. 8) 8; T.W. Bennett, *Customary Law in South Africa* (Juta, 2004) 78.

homogenous and discrete. In reality, cultural practices, values and norms are the product of human agency, in constant flux and not always uniformly shared. Communities and groups belonging to different cultures often share the same social space, influencing each other.[10] As Preis suggests:

> A theoretical shift must be made from the static view of culture to the analysis of culture as practice, a practice embedded in local context and in the multiple realities of everyday life.[11]

Customary law is one aspect of culture. In essence customary law is the law of a particular community which is derived from the social practices of that community and is considered to be obligatory.[12] Like the culture of which it is a part, customary law usually coexists with other legal systems or bodies of law. While it is necessary for the purposes of discussion to refer to customary law in general, clearly there is no universal system of customary law. As cultures differ, customary laws differ, even within the same region or country.[13]

Legal pluralism refers to a situation in which more than one body of law or legal system applies in the same society.[14] As a consequence of colonialism but also, increasingly, economic globalisation, legal pluralism is a fact of daily life for millions of people around the world.[15] Yet, as Twining notes:

> [L]egal pluralism is generally marginalised and viewed with scepticism in legal discourse. Perhaps the main reason for this is that for over 200 years Western legal theory has been dominated by conceptions of law that tend to be monist (one internally coherent legal system), statist (the state has a monopoly of law within its territory), and positivist (what is not created or recognised as law by the state is not law).[16]

One of the enduring legacies of colonialism in Africa, in particular, is the pluralistic systems of law which apply in most African countries.[17] Most systems of customary law in Africa

---

10 A.B.S. Preis, 'Human Rights as Cultural Practice: An Anthropological Critique' (1996) 18 *Human Rights Quarterly* 286 at 289.

11 Ibid. 290. See also A.A. An-Na'im, 'Towards a Cross-Cultural Approach to Defining International Standards of Human Rights: The Meaning of Cruel, Inhuman, or Degrading Treatment or Punishment', in A.A. An-Na'im (ed.), *Human Rights in Cross-Cultural Perspectives: A Quest for Consensus* (University of Pennsylvania Press, 1992) 19, 27.

12 See Bennett, *Customary Law in South Africa* (n. 9) 1; Ndulo (n. 6) 88; E.S. Nwauche, 'The Constitutional Challenge of the Integration and Interaction of Customary and Received English Common Law in Nigeria and Ghana' (2010) 25 *Tulane European and Civil Law Forum* 37 at 40.

13 Because of the nature of customary law, it is arguable that it is not possible to talk about systems of customary law.

14 S.E. Merry, 'Legal Pluralism' (1988) 22 *Law and Society Review* 869 at 870. See also Bennett, *Customary Law in South Africa* (n. 9) 27; W. Menski, *Comparative Law in a Global Context: The Legal Systems of Asia and Africa*, 2nd edn (CUP, 2006) 83; R. Perry, 'Balancing Rights or Building Rights? Reconciling the Right to Use Customary Systems of Law with Competing Human Rights in Pursuit of Indigenous Sovereignty' (2011) 24 *Harvard Human Rights Journal* 71 at 73.

15 P.S. Berman, 'Global Legal Pluralism' (2006–07) 80 *Southern California Law Review* 1155.

16 W. Twining, *Globalisation and Legal Theory* (Butterworths, 2000) 232 (footnotes omitted).

17 See Ndulo (n. 6) 87; Banda (n. 6) 14.

were, at least in their original form, unwritten.[18] The oral tradition resulted in considerable local diversity as the law applicable to different communities took different forms. Being oral, it was also possible for customary laws to change without the need for formalities, making them easily adaptable to changing circumstances. Thus rather than being in existence from time immemorial, as is required for the recognition of custom in English law, customary law is often referred to as 'living' law.[19] Like the culture that it mirrors, customary law is dynamic, subject to contestation and adaptation in response to internal and external pressures, including the influence exerted by other cultures and legal regimes.[20]

This does not mean that customary laws are devoid of certainty or continuity. Oral regimes make use of a variety of techniques to maintain continuity. For example, rules are encapsulated in myths, proverbs, maxims and rhymes. Folk tales may be acted out at ceremonial occasions or recalled by elders during trials. Physical features such as rivers and mountains may be used to locate rights to land.[21] However, these techniques rely to a large extent on group cohesion, location and opportunities for repetition to continue to operate as reminders of the rules. Migration, urbanisation, physical changes in the landscape brought about by economic development and the use of written sources have all brought about fundamental changes in the conditions necessary for maintaining the oral tradition. The impact of such changes is ongoing, with serious implications for the maintenance of customary laws in many communities.[22]

Although all societies can be said to be legally plural to a greater or lesser extent, colonialism left a particular imprint on pre-colonial customary laws, the consequences of which are still being worked out today.[23] Although pre-colonial laws were recognised in most colonies, this was always at best a compromise, and certainly never entailed recognition of customary law on an equal basis with the law of the colonial power. In most countries which were subject to British colonial rule, English common law was imposed,[24] with customary law only recognised as applying to the indigenous population. Recognition was moreover usually subject to an overriding requirement, expressed in terms of what is widely referred to as the 'repugnancy' rule, that customary laws should not be repugnant to 'general principles of humanity observed throughout the civilized world',[25] further underlining the inferior status of such laws. Although the recognition of customary law was mostly confined to private law

---

18 Bennett, *Customary Law in South Africa* (n. 9) 2; Bennett, *Human Rights and African Customary Law* (n. 9) 60; Menski (n. 14) 396.

19 Bennett, *Customary Law in South Africa* (n. 9) 7; E. Grant, 'Human Rights, Cultural Diversity and Customary Law in South Africa' (2006) 50 *Journal of African Law* 2 at 16.

20 Preis (n. 10) 289.

21 Bennett, *Customary Law in South Africa* (n. 9) 3–4.

22 Ibid. 5.

23 Similar issues arise in countries that were not colonised but where common or civil law was imported. See S.E. Merry, 'Anthropology, Law and Transnational Processes' (1992) 21 *Annual Review of Anthropology* 357.

24 One of the few exceptions was South Africa, where Roman Dutch law was recognised when the British took occupation of the Cape Colony in 1806. See Bennett, *Human Rights and African Customary Law* (n. 9) 18.

25 This particular formulation of the repugnancy rule is to be found in Ordinance 3 of 1849 (Natal) cited in Bennett, *Customary Law in South Africa* (n. 9) 38. Different formulations of the repugnancy rule were used in different countries and at different times. See N. Peart, 'Section 11(1) of the Black Administration Act No. 38 of 1927: The Application of the Repugnancy Clause' [1982] *Acta Juridica* 99; Banda (n. 6) 16; Nwauche (n. 12) 46; Ndulo (n. 6) 95.

and to specific issues which were considered to be of marginal importance to the colonial authorities, such as marriage and succession, the colonial authorities also took control of local dispute settlement procedures, which played an important part in establishing and consolidating colonial political control.[26]

Perhaps the most fundamental change made to customary law during the colonial era was the reduction of oral laws to writing.[27] As noted above, their oral character resulted in customary laws being localised and varied in content and application. This did not suit the needs of the colonial authorities who wanted known and uniform laws following the European model. The process of capturing customary laws in writing had a number of consequences. Seen through the eyes of writers schooled in European law, local concepts were translated not only into European languages, but also into recognisable juristic forms which often did not capture their true nature.[28] Structure was imposed on previously flexible arrangements, structure derived from Western legal systems, which had no connection with the operation of customary laws. The identity of those involved in the project of codification of customary law is also significant. The traditional leaders, who were the keepers of the oral law consulted by those whose task it was to record customary laws, were predominantly male, as were those who wielded power in the colonial administrations.[29] As Bennett notes, 'the overall tendency of colonial and post-colonial governments in Africa was to endorse the indigenous African system of patriarchy'[30] an endorsement which extended to the version of customary law which became accepted as official customary law in former colonies.

While cultures coexist and influence each other, the way in which customary laws were influenced by dominant colonial legal systems was particularly profound. Recognition of customary law was entirely at the behest of the colonial power and filtered through the concepts of the imposed and dominant legal system. The recognition of particular customary laws but not others, and the application of the repugnancy rule, in effect determined the scope of application of customary law. The imposition of a centralised court system with state-appointed actors and codification which recast customary laws in terms familiar to European lawyers, often profoundly changed both the character and the content of customary laws, distorting their underlying values and aims.[31] While commentators may disagree about the extent to which customary law is a construction of the colonial era, what does seem clear is that the effect of colonialism was to rob customary law of its character as living law and to ossify versions of customary laws in many regions which served the interests of a narrow segment of the community.[32]

The demise of colonialism brought its own quandaries. Banda observes in relation to decolonisation in Africa that 'there was the much romanticized notion of restoring "customary law" and "African culture" to their former glory'.[33] In practice, however, most newly

---

26 M. Chanock, *Law, Custom, and Social Order: The Colonial Experience in Malawi and Zambia* (Heinemann, 1998) 60.
27 The process of codification in the South African context is discussed in detail in Bennett, *Customary Law in South Africa* (n. 9) 34–42.
28 Ibid. 55; Grant (n. 19) 15.
29 See Banda (n. 6) 18.
30 Bennett, *Customary Law in South Africa* (n. 9) 31.
31 See for example the discussion of the customary law of succession in relation to the case of *Bhe v Magistrate Khayelitsha* [2004] ZACC 17 below.
32 Banda (n. 6) 19.
33 Ibid.

independent states opted for integration of the courts administering colonial and customary law, and the retention of much of the colonial legal system.[34] The version of customary law which often continued to be applied was the court/state/man-manufactured hand-me-down colonial era version.[35]

3 Customary law and international human rights law

Although cultural rights are recognised as a specific category in international human rights law, they have received much less attention than civil, political, social and economic rights.[36] Few human rights textbooks devote specific attention to cultural rights.[37] Moreover, discussion of cultural rights is complicated by the fact that such rights derive from different sources and are recognised as both individual rights and as group rights. In seeking to understand cultural rights, it is therefore necessary to consider not only the International Bill of Rights, but also minority rights, the right to self-determination and the rights of indigenous peoples.

Article 22 of the UDHR recognises cultural rights together with economic and social rights, specifically linking such rights to dignity and the development of personality: 'Everyone, as a member of society . . . is entitled to realization . . . of the economic, social and cultural rights indispensable for his dignity and the free development of his personality.' The only other provision in the UDHR which mentions cultural rights is Article 27(1): 'Everyone has the right freely to participate in the cultural life of the community, to enjoy the arts and to share in scientific advancement and its benefits.'

In spite of its name, the International Covenant on Economic Social and Cultural Rights (ICESCR) provides little further elaboration, merely recognising in Article 15 the right 'to take part in cultural life'. Article 15 goes on to provide for rights to the benefits of scientific progress and the protection of the rights of artists and inventors. References to cultural rights are also to be found in Article 13 of the International Covenant on the Elimination of All Forms of Discrimination against Women (CEDAW), which provides for the rights of women to participate in 'recreational activities, sports and all aspects of cultural life' on the basis of equality, and in Article 31 of the Convention on the Rights of the Child (CRC), which recognises the right of children to 'participate freely in cultural rights and the arts'.[38] The American Declaration of the Rights and Duties of Man (1948) and the Additional Protocol to the American Convention on Human Rights in the Area of Economic, Social and Cultural Rights (1988) both recognise the right of participation in 'the cultural life of the community'.[39] These instruments all associate culture with science, art and literature.

A different perception is evident in Article 27 of the International Covenant on Civil and Political Rights 1966 (ICCPR), which relates cultural rights particularly to minorities, and provides:

34 Ibid. 20; Nwauche (n. 12) 38.
35 Banda (n. 6) 22.
36 See Symonides (n. 8) 179; A. Eide, 'Cultural Rights and Minorities: On Human Rights and Group Accommodation', in K. Hastrup (ed.) *Legal Cultures and Human Rights: The Challenge of Diversity* (Kluwer Law International, 2001) 25, 27; Prott (n. 9) 96–97.
37 See, however, Symonides (n. 8) 179.
38 Art. 5 of the International Convention on the Elimination of All forms of Racial Discrimination provides for equal participation in cultural activities.
39 Art. 13 of the American Declaration and Art. 14 of the Additional Protocol to the American Convention.

In those States in which ethnic, religious or linguistic minorities exist, persons belonging to such minorities shall not be denied the right, in community with the other members of their group, to enjoy their own culture, to profess and practise their own religion, or to use their own language.[40]

The formulation of cultural rights in Article 27 of the ICCPR also differs from the UDHR and ICESCR in that the rights are those of individuals by virtue of belonging to particular minority groups, and the rights are to be exercised with other members of the group. Culture in this context is associated with religion and language rather than art and science. Similarly, Article 17 of the African Charter on Human and Peoples' Rights (ACHPR) of 1981 associates the right to participate in the cultural life of his community with education and the protection of morals and traditional values recognised by the community. Article 29 of the ACHPR also places a duty on individuals to 'preserve and strengthen positive African cultural values'.

Because of its reference to minorities, Article 27 of the ICCPR is often linked to the right to self-determination recognised in both customary international law[41] and in treaty law.[42] In terms of common Article 1(1) of the ICCPR and ICESCR, the right to self-determination entails the right of 'all peoples . . . to freely pursue their economic, social and cultural development'. In contrast to the rights of minorities as expressed in Article 27, the right to self-determination is a right held by peoples rather than individuals. This definition is echoed in all subsequent international and regional human rights instruments that recognise a right to self-determination.[43] In the immediate post-war period, self-determination was conceived of as primarily a response to colonialism. As a result of constant restatement, consistent state practice and *opinio juris*, many commentators view the right of colonial peoples to self-determination as a *jus cogens* norm.[44] However, it has been argued that in the post-colonial period the right to self-determination should be confined to internal self-determination which entails, in particular, the right of groups within an independent state to live according to their own customs and traditions.[45]

Finally, the protection of cultural rights can be said to be an aspect of the protection afforded to indigenous peoples in international law. There is no settled definition of indigenous peoples in international law, but the term is commonly used to refer to the descendants of the original inhabitants of lands before conquest and colonisation who consider themselves

---

40 Elaboration of the rights of minorities is provided in the Declaration on the Rights of Persons Belonging to National or Ethnic, Religious and Linguistic Minorities, GA Declaration 47/135 (18 December 1992).

41 *Legal Consequences for States of the Continued Presence of South Africa in Namibia (South-West Africa) Notwithstanding Security Council Resolution 276 (1970)* (Advisory Opinion) 1971 ICJ Reports 16 at 31.

42 See Art. 1 of the UN Charter; Common Art. 1 of the ICCPR and the ICESCR.

43 The ACHPR contains an extended definition in Art. 20.

44 R. McCorquodale, 'Rights of Peoples and Minorities', in D. Moeckli, S. Shah and S. Sivakumaran, *International Human Rights Law* (OUP, 2010) 365, 372.

45 *Reference re Secession of Quebec* [1998] 2 SCR 217 [126]; A. Cassese, *International Law* (OUP, 2001) 106; J.D. van der Vyver, 'Cultural Identity as a Constitutional Right in South Africa' 2003(1) *Stellenbosch Law Review* 51 at 58. See also J. Klabbers, 'The Right to Be Taken Seriously: Self-Determination in International Law' (2006) 28 *Human Rights Quarterly* 186 at 198; J. Klabbers, *International Law* (CUP, 2013) at 118.

to be culturally distinct from the dominant population.[46] Lobbying by indigenous groups for a code of indigenous rights finally resulted in the adoption of the UN Declaration on the Rights of Indigenous Peoples in 2007.[47] Article 3 of the Declaration is of particular importance in clarifying that indigenous people have the right to self-determination. The Declaration also recognises the right of indigenous peoples:

> to promote, develop and maintain their institutional structures and their distinctive customs, spirituality, traditions, procedures, practices and, in the cases where they exist, juridical systems or customs, in accordance with international human rights standards.[48]

Perry proposes that this clearly establishes the right of indigenous peoples to use customary systems of law.[49] The Declaration confirms that indigenous peoples have the right to full enjoyment of all human rights both as individuals and as groups.[50] Although the Declaration is not a binding instrument, based on acceptance of the Declaration by the overwhelming majority of states and other state practice, it is widely acknowledged that the right of self-determination (in the internal sense) of indigenous peoples has been established.[51] However, as discussed above, the main implication of this is that indigenous peoples have the right to live according to their own customs and traditions. That the Declaration specifies the right of indigenous peoples to use customary systems of law is therefore arguable based on an elaboration of the right to self-determination.

While international human rights law thus provides specific protection for the right to culture, the tension between culture and the protection of other human rights is also plainly recognised. In terms of Article 5 of CEDAW, states parties undertake to take action:

> To modify the social and cultural patterns of conduct of men and women, with a view to achieving the elimination of prejudices and customary and all other practices which are based on the idea of the inferiority or the superiority of either of the sexes.

There is likewise a clear recognition in the Protocol to the African Charter on Human and Peoples' Rights on the Rights of Women in Africa (2003)[52] of the existence of cultural patterns of conduct and practices which are harmful to women or discriminatory, and the need for states to take action to modify or eliminate them.[53] The Protocol goes further than CEDAW in specifically prohibiting harmful cultural practices, singling out female genital mutilation.[54]

---

46 See J.R. Martinez-Cobo (Special Rapporteur of the Sub-Commission on Prevention of Discrimination and Protection of Minorities), 'Study of the Problem of Discrimination Against Indigenous Populations, Volume 5: Conclusions, Proposals and Recommendations' (1987) UN Doc. E/CN.4/Sub.2/1986/7/Add.4, para. 378–80. See also R. Falk, 'The Rights of Peoples (In Particular Indigenous Peoples)', in J. Crawford (ed.), *The Rights of Peoples* (Clarendon, 1988) 17, 18; Bennett, *Human Rights and African Customary Law* (n. 9) 14.
47 UN Doc. A/RES/61/295 (13 September 2007). The Resolution was adopted by 143 votes in favour, four against and with 11 abstentions.
48 Art. 34.
49 Perry (n. 14) 71.
50 Art. 1.
51 McCorquodale (n. 44) 374.
52 See Banda (n. 6) 79. The Protocol entered into force in November 2005.
53 See for example Art. 1(2) and Art. 4(2)(d).
54 Art. 5.

What appears from this necessarily brief overview is that international human rights law provides for some form of protection of culture for both individuals and groups. What exactly is protected is variously expressed as 'cultural rights', the right to participate in the cultural life of the community, or 'the right to pursue cultural development'. Given the complexity of defining culture, as already discussed, it is clearly futile to attempt an abstract definition of what protection of culture in any of these forms entails. Few would, however, dispute that the right to use customary law could fit into any of the above categories. It can therefore be concluded that there are a number of different bases for the recognition of the right to use customary law in international human rights law. At the same time, there is a clear acknowledgement in international human rights law, articulated for example in both CEDAW and the Protocol on the Rights of Women in Africa, that cultural practices may conflict with the right to equality and other rights, particularly of women. Resolving this conflict is one of the main challenges in maintaining and protecting customary law.

4 Customary law under the South African Constitution

As already noted, legal pluralism is one of the legacies of colonialism, especially in Africa. As a consequence, the constitutions of many states on the African continent recognise customary law and provide for its application together with received law and, in many countries, religious laws too.[55] At the same time, many African constitutions guarantee equality and prohibit discrimination on various grounds including gender. However, while some constitutions subject culture and customary law to a human rights test, many exempt the application of customary law from the requirements of non-discrimination provisions within their bills of rights.[56]

Given the troubled history of racial segregation and minority rule in South Africa, the multicultural makeup of South African society, and the nature of the constitutional negotiations, the need to balance the interests of diverse groups and communities was of special importance in the drafting of the 1996 South African Constitution. Perhaps more than in any other country that had been subjected to colonial domination, the experience of apartheid dictated a particular sensitivity to the need for equality to be at the heart of the new constitutional system. Specific recognition and protection is given in the Bill of Rights within the Constitution[57] to the diversity of languages[58] and cultures[59] of the various communities that make up the population of the country. The way in which this protection is formulated in the Bill of Rights suggests an intention to implement the international norm contained in Article 27 of the ICCPR.[60] Moreover, the Constitution secures an influential role for international law in the interpretation of the Bill of Rights providing specific direction to the courts to consider international law in interpreting the provisions of the Bill of Rights.[61]

---

55 Nwauche (n. 12) 38; Ndulo (n. 6) 87.

56 Banda (n. 6) 33; Ndulo (n. 6) 89; Bond (n. 7) 34.

57 Chapter 2 of the Constitution.

58 S. 6. The right to be educated in the official language of choice is provided for in s. 29.

59 S. 30, discussed below.

60 Van der Vyver (n. 45) 52. Bennett notes that Art. 27 applies only to minorities, but argues that the right to self-determination and the doctrine of aboriginal rights provide the international law background to the right to culture in South Africa. Bennett, *Customary Law in South Africa* (n. 9) 84.

61 S. 39(1). S. 233 extends the requirement to use international law as an aid to interpretation of all legislation by incorporating the interpretive presumption of compliance of national legislation with international law.

The Constitution in sections 30 and 31 provides for cultural rights. In terms of section 30, '[e]very person shall have the right to use the language and to participate in the cultural life of their choice.' Section 31 reflects the formulation of Article 27 of the ICCPR:[62] 'Persons belonging to a cultural, religious or linguistic community may not be denied the right, with other members of that community . . . to enjoy their culture, practise their religion and use their language.'[63] In addition to general provision for the enjoyment of cultural rights, particular provision is made for the use of customary law. Section 211(3) states that '[t]he courts must apply customary law when that law is applicable, subject to the Constitution and any legislation that specifically deals with customary law'.[64]

However, neither the general right to culture nor the right to use customary law is unlimited. Sections 30, 31 and 211 all require the exercise of these rights to be consistent with the Constitution.[65] Moreover, the supremacy of the Bill of Rights is highlighted in section 39(2) which obliges the courts to 'promote the spirit, purport and objects of the Bill of Rights' in interpreting legislation and developing common and customary law. Placing the issue beyond doubt, section 39 declares that the Bill of Rights 'does not deny the existence of any other rights or freedoms that are recognised or conferred by common law, customary law or legislation' but only 'to the extent that they are consistent with the Bill'.

The subjection of the right to culture and customary law to the Constitution and in particular to the Bill of Rights met with fierce resistance prior to the adoption of the 1996 Constitution.[66] Opposition was led by the Congress of Traditional Leaders of South Africa (CONTROLESA), who objected to what was seen by many as the imposition of Western values.[67] In turn, women's groups opposed any exemption of customary law and cultural practices from compliance with the provisions of the Bill of Rights, arguing that a failure to address well-documented disadvantages suffered by women under customary law[68] could not be justified in the new South Africa, under a constitution which is explicitly based on the values of 'human dignity, equality and freedom'.[69]

---

62 The terms minority and ethnic in Art. 27 of the ICCPR have been omitted. The question of which groups in South Africa can claim to be minorities is controversial. See K. Lehman, 'Aboriginal Title, Indigenous Rights and the Right to Culture' (2004) 20 *South African Journal on Human Rights* 86 at 105.

63 S. 181 also makes provision for the creation of a Commission for the Promotion and Protection of the Rights of Cultural, Religious and Linguistic Communities. See also ss. 185–86.

64 S. 211(1) also recognises the 'institution, status and role of traditional leadership, according to customary law . . . subject to the Constitution'. For a discussion of the position of traditional leaders under the 1996 Constitution, see M. Pieterse, 'Traditional Leaders Win Battle in Undecided War' (1999) 15 *South African Journal on Human Rights* 179 at 185. See also s. 15(3) which permits the recognition of 'systems of personal and family law under any tradition'.

65 Ss. 30 and 31 require consistency with the Bill of Rights while s. 211 requires consistency with the Constitution.

66 See the *Certification* case, *Ex Parte Chairperson of the Constitutional Assembly: Re Certification of the Constitution of the Republic of South Africa* 1996 (4) SA 744 (CC); 1996 (10) BCLR 1253 (CC) [189ff].

67 See F. Kaganas and C. Murray, 'The Contest between Culture and Gender Equality under South Africa's Interim Constitution' (1994) 21 *Journal of Law and Society* 409 at 410; T. Nhlapo, 'Cultural Diversity, Human Rights and the Family in Contemporary Africa: Lessons from the South African Constitutional Debate' (1995) 9(2) *International Journal of Law, Policy and the Family* 208 at 215.

68 V. Bronstein, 'Reconceptualizing the Customary Law Debate in South Africa' (1998) *South African Journal on Human Rights* 388 at 390; Bennett, *Human Rights and Customary Law* (n. 9) 90–91, 126–28.

69 S. 39 of the Constitution of South Africa.

The significance of the right to equality in the South African Constitution has already been noted.[70] The right, as expressed in section 9 of the Constitution, is wide-ranging, guaranteeing non-discrimination on an extensive list of grounds, including gender and culture.[71] It is also noteworthy that unlike the right to culture, the right to equality is not specifically limited by a proviso that the right is to be exercised subject to the Bill of Rights. The importance of equality is highlighted in section 1 of the Constitution, which specifies not only the achievement of equality but also non-racialism and non-sexism as founding values of South African democracy.[72] The founding values are given specific application in section 39 which instructs that interpretation of the Bill of Rights 'must promote the values that underlie an open and democratic society based on human dignity, equality and freedom'.[73] Limitation of the rights in the Bill of Rights is permitted in terms of section 36 only to the extent that the limitation is 'reasonable and justifiable in an open and democratic society based on human dignity, equality and freedom'.[74]

As highlighted by women's groups during the constitutional negotiations, many aspects of customary law as applied in South Africa at the time were clearly discriminatory.[75] Subsequent legislative reform removed some of the most obviously discriminatory aspects[76] and research undertaken by the South African Law Reform Commission (SALRC) identified further areas requiring amendment in order to ensure compliance with the Bill of Rights.[77] However, before reform of the customary law of succession could be implemented,[78] the compatibility of the customary law principle of male primogeniture with the right to equality was raised before the Constitutional Court in the case of *Bhe v Magistrate of Khayelitsha*.[79] The principle of male primogeniture dictated that, as a general rule, only a male relative of the deceased

---

70 *Bhe v Magistrate Khayelitsha* (n. 31); *Shibi v Sithole* [2004] ZACC 18; *South African Human Rights Commission and Another v President of the Republic of South Africa* 2005 (1) BCLR 1 (CC) [71]. See also Moseneke J in *Minister of Finance v Van Heerden* 2004 (6) SA 121 (CC); 2004 (11) BCLR 1125 (CC) [22]; O'Regan J in *Brink v Kitshoff NO* 1996 (4) SA 197 (CC); 1996 (6) BCLR 752 (CC) [33].

71 For a discussion of the equality jurisprudence, see J. Small and E. Grant, 'Dignity, Discrimination and Context: New Direction in South African and Canadian Human Rights Law' (2005) 6 *Human Rights Review* 25; E. Grant and J. Small, 'Disadvantage and Discrimination: The Emerging Jurisprudence of the South African Constitutional Court' (2000) 51 *Northern Ireland Legal Quarterly* 174.

72 See also s. 7 which introduces the Bill of Rights.

73 S. 39(1)(a).

74 S. 36 (1).

75 Bronstein (n. 68) 392.

76 See the Recognition of Customary Marriages Act 120 of 1998. For a discussion see M. Mamashela, 'New Families, New Property, New Laws: The Practical Effects of the Recognition of Customary Marriages Act' (2004) 20 *South African Journal on Human Rights* 616; V. Bronstein, 'Confronting Custom in the New South African State: An Analysis of the Recognition of Customary Marriages Act 120 of 1998' (2000) 16 *South African Journal on Human Rights* 558.

77 See South African Law Commission, *Project 90: The Harmonisation of the Common Law and the Indigenous Law: Report on Conflicts of Law*, September 1999; South African Law Commission, *Project 90: The Harmonisation of the Common Law and the Indigenous Law: Report on Traditional Courts and the Judicial Function of Traditional Leaders*, 21 January 2003; South African Law Reform Commission, *Project 90: Discussion Paper 93 Customary Law: Succession* 2000.

78 Legislative proposals were twice rejected by parliament. See South African Law Reform Commission, *Project 90: Discussion Paper 93 Customary Law: Succession* (2000), 5–6; L. Mbatha, 'Reforming the Customary Law of Succession' (2002) 18 *South African Journal on Human Rights* 259 at 284.

79 (n. 70). Discussed in Grant (n. 19) 10.

qualified as intestate heir. In the case of a family in which the parents were in a monogamous relationship, the eldest son inherited. In the absence of male descendants, the father of the deceased became heir, otherwise the nearest male descendant, related to the deceased through the male line, inherited.[80]

In the case of *Bhe*,[81] Ms Bhe and one of her daughters had lived with her partner[82] in a shack on property which he had acquired with the help of state housing subsidies.[83] On the death of her partner, the partner's father was appointed sole heir in accordance with customary law. Faced with the loss of the family home, Ms Bhe, on behalf of her daughters, challenged the application of the male primogeniture rule in the High Court on the basis that it offended the constitutional equality guarantee. The Constitutional Court concluded unanimously that the exclusion of women from inheritance on the grounds of gender was in breach of the right to equality as well as violating the right to human dignity guaranteed under section 10 of the Constitution.[84] However, the ruling that the male primogeniture rule was inconsistent with the right to gender equality left another more difficult question to be decided. If the customary law principle of male primogeniture was not to determine succession, what rule was to be substituted? The answer to this question had potentially important consequences for the future role of customary law in South Africa.

The Constitutional Court was faced with three choices. First, it could leave it to the legislature to resolve the question of how intestate succession cases such as this should be decided.[85] Secondly, it could direct that the Intestate Succession Act should apply, thus essentially replacing the customary law rules with the principles of South African common law on which the legislation is based. Or, thirdly, it could develop customary law in order to bring it into compliance with the right to equality.[86]

The argument presented and largely accepted by the Court in *Bhe* was that the version of customary law which was subject to challenge was a distortion of customary law. It was a version which had become accepted during the colonial period but which did not reflect the underlying values of the culture on which it was based and which had not been allowed to continue to develop to take account of changing economic and social conditions.[87] In particular, it was argued that the understanding of family, property and succession in customary law differed fundamentally from the way in which those concepts were understood

---

80 Para. 77 of the judgment. Different arrangements applied to polygynous marriages. See Mbatha (n. 78) 261; Bennett, *Customary Law in South Africa* (n. 9) 336.

81 (n. 31).

82 It was not disputed that the couple were unmarried, but the Court found that the evidence as to whether the couple were in a customary union was inconclusive. It therefore decided that it was necessary to consider the position of the children as having been born outside of marriage or a customary union [13]. In considering whether the male primogeniture rule was incompatible with the right to equality protected in terms of s. 9 of the Constitution, the Court therefore assessed whether the rule was discriminatory on the grounds of both 'sex' and 'birth.' Discrimination on the grounds of 'birth' was interpreted to include differentiation on the grounds of being born extra-maritally (para. 59).

83 Para. 14 of the judgment.

84 Paras 91–92 (Langa A.C.J.), 210 (Ngcobo J). The Constitutional Court also held that the male primogeniture rule discriminated against children who were born outside of marriage (para. 93).

85 The Court could either make a declaration of invalidity, leaving a gap which the legislature would have to fill, or it could suspend the declaration of invalidity pending legislative reform of the measure.

86 S. 39.

87 Paras 89–90.

in Roman-Dutch and English law. Rather than being based on the idea of the transfer of individual ownership, the aim of the customary law of succession was to preserve family property in order to support the family unit.[88] Succession in customary law therefore entailed not merely inheriting the family property, but also responsibility for supporting dependent members of the family.[89] Evidence was also presented of changes in the way in which some communities viewed succession, including cases where the widow of the deceased was permitted to administer family property by agreement with the family.[90] It was therefore argued that the most appropriate outcome of the case would be for the Court to either develop the male primogeniture rule in order to bring customary law into compliance with the Constitution, or to introduce the necessary Constitutional principles into the customary law system to permit it to develop within the community, along the lines of existing exceptions which were consistent with the right to equality.[91]

However, although both the majority and minority judgments acknowledged the distorting effect of 'official' customary law and the necessity for living customary law to be allowed to develop and to be applied, neither took up the opportunity in this instance to do so. The majority of the Court opted for legislative change, although in the short term, until legislation could be put in place, it directed that the Intestate Succession Act should apply.[92] In the view of the majority, this was the best solution in the circumstances, because of the need for immediate protection of the interests of large numbers of vulnerable women. Development of customary law, according to the majority judgment, would be too slow in these particular circumstances. In a dissenting judgment, Ngcobo J expressed the view that the substitution of the Intestate Succession Act was misplaced and that customary law should be developed to bring it into compliance with the Constitution by removing the male primogeniture rule and allowing women to inherit under customary law.[93]

The protection of culture, as well as specific provision made for the application of customary law in the South African Constitution, demonstrates an unambiguous commitment to the maintenance of cultural diversity. By making provision for the application of both South African common law and customary law on an equal basis, the Constitution clearly envisages legal pluralism. However, the solution which was most consistent with this goal was rejected by the majority of the Constitutional Court in *Bhe*. Thus while the decision was wholly consistent with the constitutional commitment to equality, the suitability of the solution imposed by the Court is open to question. In spite of this, the recognition in *Bhe* of the need to apply living customary law, rather than unquestioningly accepting the documented 'official' version, provides an important starting point for future development of customary law.

The recognition of living customary law was given further impetus in the case of *Shilubana and others v Nwamitwa*.[94] The case arose from a dispute about the right to succeed as Chief (Hosi) of the Valoyi traditional community. The applicant was the eldest daughter of a former Chief who had died in 1968 without a male heir. She had not been considered eligible for appointment as Chief at the time because of her gender, and consequently her uncle had

---

88 Paras 168–69.
89 Bennett, *Human Rights and African Customary Law* (n. 9) 126.
90 Paras 84–87 (Langa DCJ); 190, 217 (Ngcobo J).
91 Paras 109–110.
92 Langa DCJ, Chaskalson CJ, Madala J, Mokgoro J, Moseneke J, O'Regan J, Sachs J, Skweyiya J, Van der Westhuizen J and Yacoob J concurring.
93 Para. 222.
94 [2008] ZACC 9; 2008 (2) SA 66 (CC).

become Chief. In the aftermath of the passing of the 1996 South African Constitution, the Valoyi Royal Family, with the participation of her uncle, the Chief, decided to confer Chieftainship on the applicant. At the time she had not wanted to displace her uncle as Chief and the Royal Council therefore decided that her uncle would continue as Chief for an unspecified period of time. On his death in 2001, the Royal Family confirmed Ms Shilubana as Chief. It was this decision which was challenged by the respondent, the eldest son of the now deceased Chief. The argument of the respondent was that he was the rightful heir being the eldest son of the Chief and that the Royal Family had no authority to appoint someone else as Chief.

In a unanimous judgment, the Constitutional Court emphasised that the right to use customary law and the right of a traditional authority to function subject to the customary law that applies to the community it serves was recognised by the Constitution.[95] Moreover, it acknowledged that living customary law was an 'independent and original source of law'[96] recognised by the Constitution and on a par with South African common law. However, what needed to be clarified was how living customary law was to be determined by the Court. First, the Court distinguished customary law from custom as a source of law. The accepted test for determining the existence of custom as a source of law in South Africa is that a practice must be 'certain, uniformly observed for a long period of time and reasonable'.[97] The Court noted that this test is inappropriate for customary law not only because customary law is an independent source of law recognised by the Constitution, and as such does not have to be proved,[98] but also because the test precludes change. While the history of a particular customary rule is an important starting point in establishing its content, history alone cannot determine the content of customary law since change is part of the nature of customary laws.[99] Moreover, the Court stressed the need to contextualise the historical investigation in order to mitigate the distortions introduced by viewing customary law through the lens of the common law.[100] But the historical investigation is merely the first step in determining the content of living customary law. Evidence of contemporary practice is the second requirement, taking into account that customary law is by nature flexible and constantly evolving. According to the Constitutional Court, 'the free development by communities of their own law to meet the needs of a rapidly changing society must be respected and facilitated'.[101] Finally, in the view of the Court, flexibility must be balanced against the need for certainty and the overriding importance of the Bill of Rights. The Court also drew a distinction between development of customary law by a customary community and development of customary law by the courts in order to comply with the Constitution.[102]

On the facts of the case, the Constitutional Court held that there was not enough evidence to conclude that the current practice of the Valoyi community permitted the appointment of Ms Shilubana as Chief.[103] However, the Court accepted that the traditional authorities had made changes to their customs in order to satisfy the requirements of the Constitution.[104]

---

95 Ibid., para. 42.
96 Ibid., para. 54.
97 *Van Breda and others v Jacobs and others* 1921 AD 330 para. 334, cited in *Shilubana* (n. 94) para. 52.
98 *Shilubana* Ibid., para. 56.
99 Ibid., para. 55.
100 Ibid., para. 44.
101 Ibid., para. 45.
102 Ibid., para. 48.
103 Ibid., para. 71.
104 Ibid., paras 73–75.

Since there were no counterbalancing considerations,[105] the Court concluded that it was incumbent on it to recognise the right of the traditional authorities to change customary law in order to ensure compliance with the Constitution.[106]

The decision confirms that it is living customary law that is to be applied by the courts, rather than the official customary law to be found in the literature.[107] It also offers timely clarification of how the content of living customary law is to be established in practice, creating a sound foundation for further development.

The South African Constitution provides an important example of how culture in general and customary law in particular can be located in a constitutional structure based on the recognition of human rights and the protection of human dignity. As illustrated in the cases of *Bhe* and *Shilubana*, there is little doubt that where the application of customary law is subject to a Bill of Rights, it is necessary for customary rules to yield to the requirements of equality and human dignity. At the same time, the cases show the potential for development, adaptation and strengthening of customary law within a human rights-based constitutional order.

5 Addressing the tension between customary law and human rights

The tension between customary law and human rights elucidated in the preceding discussion is commonly characterised as incompatibility between culture and human rights. However, since the right of individuals and groups to exercise their cultural rights is itself protected in international human rights law, one could equally plausibly construct the issue as one of a conflict between rights. There is of course no universally accepted method or procedure for resolving such conflicts in international human rights law. Human rights are considered to be 'universal, indivisible, interdependent and interrelated'.[108] A different way to view the problem of conflict between culture and human rights is to think of it as involving a clash of cultures. It has been argued above that, rather than being static and isolated, culture is in fact fluid, subject to constant debate and negotiation in interaction with other cultures.[109] Preis suggests that a potentially useful way to understand how human rights interact with culture is to consider human rights as a culture in its own right:

> Human Rights increasingly form part of a wider network of perspectives which are shared and exchanged between the North and South, centers and peripheries, in multiple, creative and sometimes conflict-ridden ways. Human Rights have become 'universalized' as values subject to interpretation, negotiation and accommodation. They have become 'culture'.[110]

As noted above, accepting that culture is dynamic does not mean that there is no coherence or stability. An-Na'im argues that 'one of the apparent paradoxes of culture is the way it combines stability with dynamic continuous change'.[111] This can be illustrated by reference to the customary law of succession. As has already been discussed in relation to the case of *Bhe*, in many African societies succession laws were historically connected with the need to

---

105 Ibid., paras 77–78.
106 Ibid., para. 75.
107 See also *Gumede v President of the Republic of South Africa* [2008] ZACC 23 paras 17–20.
108 World Conference on Human Rights (n. 2) para. 5.
109 Preis (n. 10) 289.
110 Ibid. 290.
111 An-Na'im (n. 11) 27.

preserve family property, which in turn was necessary for the survival of the family and its members.[112] Changes in the rules of succession may result from a variety of factors, including changes in the economic conditions which render the old imperatives redundant. But as long as the need to provide for the survival of the family remains, the adjustment of the rules will continue to serve those priorities. Reconceiving human rights as a culture is therefore not to imply that human rights are simply changeable at will. The cornerstone of human rights, as expressed in the UN Charter, Article 1 of the UDHR and numerous international human rights instruments,[113] is respect for human dignity, the notion that each person matters in view of his or her humanity.[114] The global institutionalisation of human rights in the UN system and regional human rights systems provides a framework and points of reference. But interpretations of the rights vary over time and in different contexts, since what it means to live a life of dignity is constantly evolving and being re-evaluated in different societies.[115]

From this perspective, human rights arguments are not simply Western ideas that are being imposed on previously pure and monolithic cultures. As already contended, cultures coexist everywhere, overlapping and influencing each other. Within these complex networks of intersecting standpoints, human rights discourses are increasingly being used in order to raise concerns and challenge existing practices, even in previously remote and isolated societies.[116]

The permeation of human rights ideas into a variety of cultural contexts is evident from the number of former colonial states that have ratified major international human rights treaties and the drafting of regional human rights instruments such as the African Charter on Human and Peoples' Rights. In relation to one of the key areas of conflict between culture and human rights, namely women's claim to equality, it is arguable that the ratification of CEDAW by a significant number of countries that recognise customary law and, more specifically in the African context, the drafting of the Protocol to the African Charter on Human and Peoples' Rights on the Rights of Women, suggest increasing influence of human rights culture in a wide range of countries which use customary systems of law.[117] The influence of human rights culture can also be seen in the inclusion of equality and other human rights guarantees in a variety of constitutions and numerous examples of legislative intervention to promote gender equality in the laws of countries which recognise customary systems of law.[118] For example, Tanzania's Law of Marriage Act 1971 was hailed as a landmark for imposing requirements designed to provide women with a range of rights within marriage, regardless of whether the marriage was governed by customary, religious or statutory law.[119] In addition, the use of international human rights instruments by the judiciaries in many African states is significant.[120] While the incorporation of human rights norms into national constitutions and laws and the application of those norms in the courts are not in themselves enough to guarantee the protection of human rights, they do play an important role in facilitating the acceptance of

---

112 Nhlapo (n. 67) 211; Bennett, *Customary Law in South Africa* (n. 9) 334.
113 See E. Grant, 'Dignity and Equality' (2007) 7(2) *Human Rights Law Review* 299 at 302.
114 C. Gearty, *Principles of Human Rights Adjudication* (OUP, 2004) 84; see P. Capps, *Human Dignity and the Foundations of International Law* (Hart, 2009) 107.
115 Gearty (n. 114) 86–88.
116 Preis (n. 10) 289.
117 See Bond (n. 7) 39.
118 See M.E. Adjami, 'African Courts, International Law and Comparative Case Law: Chimera or Emerging Human Rights Jurisprudence?' (2002) 24 *Michigan Journal of International Law* 103 at 113; Bond (n. 7) 34.
119 Bond (n. 7) 52.
120 Adjami (n. 118) 124.

human rights ideas in those states. In this way, judicial adherence to international human rights norms aids the process of acceptance of those norms within the communities they serve. It is also arguable that these developments have been and continue to be driven by local activists, with the implication that human rights ideas are being taken up in local communities.[121]

The interplay of human rights and other cultural perspectives is demonstrated in significant detail in the South African context. The 1996 Constitution was the product of intensive negotiation involving a range of interest groups representing a variety of cultural perspectives.[122] The inclusion of a Bill of Rights in the Constitution, and the explicit Constitutional commitment to the protection of human dignity and freedom is testament to the influence of human rights culture.[123] But it is perhaps in the serious engagement by the South African Constitutional Court with the difficult issues surrounding the implementation of the right to use customary law within such a constitutional framework, that the process of cultural exchange is most apparent. This is clear, not only from the careful consideration given to the question of balancing culture and equality by the Constitutional Court in the cases discussed, but also from the submissions made by a range of interested parties who were admitted as *amici curiae*.[124] Participation is encouraged and both official bodies as well as civil society organisations made submissions in both cases discussed.[125]

It is therefore arguable that human rights culture already coexists to a significant degree with other cultures in societies across the world. In spite of the protestations of those who purport to protect cultural practices against outside influences, there are very few societies in which human rights ideas have not taken root.[126] The language of human rights has become familiar and has been adopted by communities everywhere. The result of this exchange has already been the adaptation of many customary laws, especially in relation to their effect on women. Of course the extent to which human rights culture has been incorporated into laws and practices depends to a large extent on the attitude of the powerful within the communities in question.[127] As Merry cautions, '[r]ights need to be presented in local cultural terms to be persuasive but they must challenge existing relation of power in order to be effective.'[128]

Since it often powerful elites who impose their interpretation of cultural norms on the whole community, An-Na'im argues that it is necessary to challenge their power of interpretation by engagement in 'internal cultural discourse to offer alternative interpretations' which support the disadvantaged, as well as cross–cultural dialogue.[129] Both internal cultural discourse and dialogue between cultures is an ongoing process in many societies in which customary laws operate. The South African cases discussed above show how groups with differing perspectives on human rights and customary law engage in dialogue in the courts.

---

121 See F. Banda, 'Global Standards: Local Values' (2003) 17 *International Journal of Law, Policy and the Family* 1 at 8; J.E. Bond, 'Gender Discourse and Customary Law in Africa' (2010) 83 *Southern California Law Review* 509 at 540.

122 See H. Corder, 'Towards a South African Constitution' (1994) 57(4) *The Modern Law Review* 491 at 496; Grant (n. 19) 7.

123 See Corder (n. 122) 514.

124 Constitutional Court of South Africa Part V Rule 10 Amici curiae.

125 *Shilubana* (n. 94) para. 18; *Bhe* (n. 31) paras 11, 29.

126 Adjami (n. 118) 118.

127 An-Na'im (n. 11) 27–28.

128 S.E. Merry, 'Human Rights and Gender Violence', in H.J. Steiner, P. Alston and R. Goodman, *International Human Rights in Context: Law Politics Morals*, 3rd edn (OUP, 2008) 524.

129 An-Na'im (n. 11) 28.

The viewpoints expressed in court are themselves the products of dialogue within different communities,[130] and the discourse continues outside the court facilitated by the media.[131] Moreover, cross-cultural dialogue is a two-way process. While the South African cases illustrate the infiltration of human rights culture into customary law, there is equally scope for customary law to stimulate new thinking about the implementation of human rights. For example, notions of familial support which underlie many aspects of customary laws in Africa provide a basis for different ways of conceptualising marriage, family relationships and support for the extended family.[132]

In spite of evidence of dialogue within communities and between cultures, participation is often uneven, with disadvantaged groups often less well represented than others.[133] In many societies in which customary law is applied, the voices of women are absent or at least muted. In order to engage disadvantaged groups, especially women, in the development of customary law, it is necessary to provide mechanisms which facilitate participation. Recognition of the need to encourage participation by marginalised groups can be found, for example, in the Statutes and Protocols of a range of African Union bodies which specify the inclusion of women as members.[134] The Protocol to the African Charter on the Rights of Women in Africa goes further, by incorporating a right for women 'to participate at all levels in the determination of cultural policies'.[135] In South Africa, the Constitution has been important in establishing gender equality and familiarity with the language of human rights and identification with the norms. In addition, as has been seen, litigation can play a key role in encouraging and legitimating changes to customary law. Litigation can assist in providing a forum for debate about the development of customary law in light of other protected rights and facilitate participation of marginalised or vulnerable groups. The case of *Shilubana* shows, for example, how access for women's groups was facilitated by the provision made for participation by organisations or individuals in proceedings before the Constitutional Court as friends of the Court.[136]

While such mechanisms are important in encouraging dialogue, it is questionable whether existing measures are always sufficient to ensure a level of engagement and cross-cultural dialogue to bridge the gap between human rights and customary law especially given the power differential between traditional leaders and disadvantaged groups. Bond argues, that the development of customary law as a natural consequence of interaction between cultures will not in all cases guarantee the protection of women and other vulnerable groups, and that it is ultimately necessary to provide a legislative floor to guarantee the rights of women in societies that apply customary law.[137] A similar view was taken by the majority of the South African Constitutional Court in the *Bhe* case, leading to the decision that in order to protect vulnerable groups, it was necessary for legislation to be passed and that until this happens, the application of existing legislation was the best way to provide protection. But as argued above

---

130 See the cases discussed by Adjami (n. 118) 124.
131 See for example W. Foster, 'Alone and Overlooked' *Mail and Guardian Online* 5 November 2007, available at: http://mg.co.za/printformat/single/2007-11-05-alone-and-overlooked/, accessed on 11 January 2012.
132 See Bond (n. 7) 56.
133 See for example the discussion of participation of women in the Organization of African Unity in R. Murray, *Human Rights in Africa: From the OAU to the African Union* (CUP, 2004) 135.
134 Ibid. 136.
135 Art. 17; see Bond (n. 121) 546.
136 Constitutional Court Rule 10 (n. 124); see *Shilubana* (n. 94) [18].
137 Bond (n. 7) 52.

in relation to the decision in *Bhe*, the needs of communities must be carefully assessed before deciding on a legislative solution.

6 Conclusion

Customary laws play an important part in maintaining and invigorating the cultural identity of many communities. The importance of preserving cultural diversity and providing space for members of diverse communities to practise their culture is clearly recognised by providing for the protection of the right to culture within the framework of international human rights law. The right to culture is reinforced by the protection provided for in a range of other related rights such as freedom of expression, freedom of association, non-discrimination, education and freedom of religion among others. These rights make it possible for individuals and communities to participate in the culture of their choice on an equal footing and to express their cultural identity freely.

While the right to culture is protected within the framework of international human rights law, there is also a clear recognition of the potential for tension between culture and human rights especially the right to equality. As has been illustrated by reference to South Africa, this tension is often addressed within constitutional systems by requiring that the right to culture be exercised subject to other rights protected under the constitution. This makes judicial resolution of clashes between culture and equality possible. However, as the South African cases show, resolution is much more complicated than merely choosing equality over customary law. Protecting the right to culture requires careful consideration of ways of supporting the development of customary law in ways that will ensure protection for the widest range of other rights.

Ultimately, however, formal recognition of rights must be accompanied by real community engagement with human rights culture. This requires both internal debate and cross-cultural discourse involving all sectors of the community, in particular disadvantaged and vulnerable groups. Facilitating participation this debate is crucial in order to bridge the gap between culture and human rights.

Select bibliography

A.A. An-Na'im, 'Towards a Cross-Cultural Approach to Defining International Standards of Human Rights: The Meaning of Cruel, Inhuman, or Degrading Treatment or Punishment', in A.A. An-Na'im (ed.), *Human Rights in Cross-Cultural Perspectives: A Quest for Consensus* (University of Pennsylvania Press, 1992).

F. Banda, *Women, Law and Human Rights: An African Perspective* (Hart, 2005).

T.W. Bennett, *Customary Law in South Africa* (Juta, 2004).

E. Grant, 'Human Rights, Cultural Diversity and Customary Law in South Africa' (2006) 50 *Journal of African Law* 2.

S.E. Merry, 'Legal Pluralism' (1988) 22 *Law and Society Review* 869.

M. Ndulo, 'African Customary Law, Customs, and Women's Rights' (2011) 18 *Indiana Journal of Global Legal Studies* 87.

E.S. Nwauche, 'The Constitutional Challenge of the Integration and Interaction of Customary and Received English Common Law in Nigeria and Ghana' (2010) 25 *Tulane European and Civil Law Forum* 37 at 40.

B. Oomen and S. Templeman, 'The Power of Definition', and W. Mannens, 'A Structure called Culture', both in Y. Donders (ed.), *Law and Cultural Diversity: proceedings of a workshop organised by the Working Group 'Law and Cultural Diversity' in co- operation with the School of Human Rights Research, the Netherlands, 25 September 1998* (Netherlands Institute of Human Rights, 1999).

19

Reservations to treaties and the integrity of human rights

Alain Pellet*

Curiously there are probably few subjects in classical general international law which ignite such impassioned debates as the apparently extremely technical subject of reservations to treaties. One is 'pro' or 'contra' reservations for reasons which clearly come closer to a 'religious war' than to rational considerations: for some, reservations are an absolute evil because they cause injury to the integrity of the treaty; for others, to the contrary, they facilitate a broader adhesion and, thus, universality. This debate – which has principally surfaced with regard to human rights treaties – is fixed since the 1951 International Court of Justice (ICJ) Advisory Opinion and its terms and scope are clearly represented by the opposition between the majority and the dissenting judges in that case.[1]

While not exclusively unfolding in the field of human rights, these are at the very heart of the classic dialectic according to which, on the one hand, reservations, in a way, 'bilateralise' the relations between the parties to multilateral treaties and therefore 'fragment' the treaty regime, while, at the same time, they facilitate a wider acceptance of the core elements of the treaties in question and, therefore serve the global community interest. Although reservations strengthen 'the universality of human rights', the dominant view among human rights activists is that they endanger the 'unity of human rights' and therefore constitute an absolute evil. They are not – nor are they a threat to the global consistency of human rights treaty regimes, at least when the rules applicable to reservations are correctly perceived and applied.

These rules are now embodied in the Guide to Practice on Reservations to Treaties (hereafter 'Guide to Practice'), adopted by the International Law Commission (ILC) in 2011.[2] This

---

* This chapter is in large part directly inspired from my joint contribution with Daniel Müller, 'Reservations to Human Rights Treaties: Not an Absolute Evil', in U. Fastenrath and others (eds), *From Bilateralism to Community Interest – Essays in Honour of Judge Bruno Simma* (OUP, 2011) 521–51.

1 Comp. Advisory Opinion, *Reservations to the Convention on the Prevention and Punishment of the Crime of Genocide*, ICJ Reports 1951, 24 (hereafter: *Reservations to the Genocide Convention*), and Joint dissenting opinion of Judges Guerrero, Sir Arnold McNair, Read and Hsu Mo, ibid., 47; see also Dissenting opinion of Judge Alvarez, ibid., 51 and 53.

2 Report of the International Law Commission, *GAOR 66th Session Supp 10*, (2011) UN Doc. A/66/10/Add.1.

non-binding instrument[3] clarifies the rules on reservations to treaties which are embodied in Articles 19 to 23 of the 1969 Vienna Convention on the Law of Treaties[4]. While still contemplating a unitary regime, it fills in large parts the latters' lacunae and realises a globally fair balance between the legitimate requirements for the unity of treaty regimes and the needs to widen the participation to multilateral treaties with universal or regional purposes, with particular regard to the unity of international treaty law itself. In other words, the law applicable to reservations embodied in the Guide to Practice preserves both the unity of international law (section 19.1) and that of human rights (section 19.2).

1 The unity of international law preserved

It is worth noting from the outset that, even though the members of the ILC have been sensitive to the 'voices of human rights' during the elaboration of the Guide to Practice, and have taken account and benefit of the important and quite well-established practice of states, monitoring bodies and international human rights courts and tribunals in order to clarify and fill the gaps of the Vienna regime, the expression 'human rights' appears in none of the guidelines of the Guide to Practice.[5] This means that the Commission considered that, as a matter of principle, there is no justification for deviating from the general regime applicable to reservations to treaties in the field of human rights.

1.1 The 'flexible regime' of reservations

And for good reasons: the rules applicable to reservations constituting the 'Vienna regime', as developed in the Guide to Practice, have realised the best possible balance between the prerequisites of universality and of the integrity of the treaty. Undoubtedly, that is what the Guide to Practice strives for, irrespective of the particular nature or content of the treaty concerned. The specificities of certain types of treaties put forward by the advocates of parochial approaches of specialised fields of international law and, singularly, by 'human rightists',[6] do not constitute a valid argument against the applicability of the general regime of reservations under the 1969 Vienna Convention[7] which is flexible enough to provide the appropriate solutions in respect to human rights as well as for any other kind of treaties.

---

3 The Guide to Practice was be discussed by the Sixth Committee of the UN General Assembly during its 67th Session (2011–12). For a topical summary of the debate prepared by the UN Secretariat, see UN Docs A/CN.4/650 (2012) and A/CN.4/650/Add.1 (2012).

4 The 1986 Convention on the law of treaties between states and international organisations or between international organisations is very similar to the 1969 Convention in most respects, including on the rules applicable to reservations. Many guidelines in the Guide to Practice are copied from the more complete 1986 Convention.

5 As explained in para. (1) of the Introduction to the Guide to Practice, this lengthy instrument (630 pp.) 'consists of guidelines that have been adopted by the Commission . . . accompanied by commentaries', (n. 2) 34.

6 On the notion of 'human rightism', see A. Pellet, ' "Human Rightism" in International Law' (2000) 10 *Italian YB Intl L* 3.

7 The 1986 Convention on the law of treaties between states and international organisations or between international organisations is very similar to the 1969 Convention in most respects, including on the rules applicable to reservations.

The Human Rights Committee nevertheless affirmed:

> Although treaties that are mere exchanges of obligations between States allow them to reserve *inter se* application of rules of general international law, it is otherwise in human rights treaties, which are for the benefit of persons within their jurisdiction.[8]

In making this assumption, the Committee fails to acknowledge that these instruments, even though they are designed to protect individuals, are still treaties which are '"built" like all other multilateral treaties':[9] it is true that they benefit individuals directly, but only because – and after – states have expressed their willingness to be bound by them. The rights of the individual, under the treaty, derive from the state's consent to be bound by such instruments.[10] Reservations must be envisaged in that context, and the order of factors cannot be reversed by stating – as the Committee does – that the *treaty* rule exists as a matter of principle and is binding on any state even if it has not consented to it.[11] If, as the Committee maintains, states can 'reserve *inter se* application of rules of general international law', there is no legal reason why the same should not be true of human rights treaties; in any event, the Committee does not give any such reason.

However, a recurrent argument put forward by the 'human rightist' approach to reservation to treaties is based on the premise that the reciprocity principle on which, they believe, the Vienna regime is based cannot operate with regard to human rights instruments. Indisputably, human rights instruments are not mainly governed by reciprocity. This has prominently been recognised by the ICJ[12] and the regional courts of human rights.[13]

As such, absence of reciprocity neither constitutes a specificity of human rights instruments (it is also present in in other categories of treaties establishing obligations owed to the

---

8 UNHRC 'General Comment No. 24', in *GAOR 50th Session Supp 40* (1995) UN Doc. A/50/40, 120, para. 8.

9 B. Simma and G.I. Hernández, 'Legal Consequences of an Impermissible Reservation to a Human Rights Treaty: Where Do We Stand?' in E. Cannizzaro (ed.), *The Law of Treaties Beyond the Vienna Convention, Essays in Honour of Professor Giorgio Gaja* (OUP, 2011) 60–85.

10 The rights in question may belong to individuals 'inherently' or by virtue of customary (including peremptory) principles – but this is quite a different issue. Thus, Dame Rosalyn Higgins might well be right in affirming that human rights treaties 'reflect rights inherent in human beings, not dependent upon grant by the state'. R. Higgins, 'Human Rights: Some Questions of Integrity' (1989) 52 MLR 11; see also B. Simma and G.I. Hernández (n. 9). However, this does not, as such, influence the nature of the binding force of the treaty instrument or the extent of consent to that instrument given by the parties including the reserving state.

11 *Reservations to the Genocide Convention* (n. 1) 21. See also *Delimitation of the Continental Shelf between the United Kingdom of Great Britain and Northern Ireland, and the French Republic* (1977) 18 RIAA 42 (paras 60–61); W.W. Bishop, Jr., 'Reservations to Treaties' (1961) 103 *Recueil des Cours de l'Académie de Droit International* 255; Ch. Tomuschat, 'Admissibility and Legal Effects of Reservations to Multilateral Treaties' (1967) 27 ZaöRV 466; D. Müller, Commentary to Art. 20 (1969), in O. Corten and P. Klein (eds), *The Vienna Conventions on the Law of Treaties: A Commentary* (OUP, 2011) 496–98, paras 18–22.

12 *Reservations to the Genocide Convention* (n. 1) 23.

13 *Loizidou v Turkey* (preliminary objections), App. No. 15318/89, (ECtHR, 1995) Series A no. 310, para. 70, quoting *Ireland v United Kingdom* App. no. 5310/71 (1978) Series A no. 25, para. 239. See also Inter-American Court of Human Rights (IACtHR), Advisory Opinion OC-2/82, 24 September 1982, *The Effect of Reservations on the Entry into Force of the American Convention on Human Rights (Arts 74 and 75)*, IACtHR Series A No. 2; and HCR, General Comment No. 24 (n. 8) 123, para. 17.

community of contracting states[14]), nor is it incompatible with the Vienna regime as such. However, this specificity does not make the general reservations regime inapplicable as a matter of principle. Of course, as a consequence of the actual nature of the 'non-reciprocal' clauses to which the reservations apply, 'the reciprocal function of the reservation mechanism is almost meaningless.'[15] However, besides the fact that reciprocity is not entirely absent from human rights treaties, it must be noted that the reciprocity element of the effect of reservations is not indispensable for the correct operation of the Vienna rules. Any rule of law applies only when it is applicable, and the same is true for the reciprocity principle: if and when a valid reservation is made to a non-reciprocal provision, Article 21(1)(b) or Article 21(3) simply does not (entirely) operate for the accepting or the objecting party.[16]

This does not mean that human rights treaties have no special characteristics, but simply shows that, despite their specificity, the Vienna rules apply to reservations to those treaties.

This should come as no surprise: one must not omit that the 1951 Advisory Opinion, which marked the starting point of the radical transformation of the reservation regime and influenced dramatically the work of the ILC in the 1960s was given about reservations to the 1948 Convention on the Prevention and the Punishment of the Crime of Genocide. It is precisely the special nature of this treaty which led the Court to distance itself from what was undeniably the dominant[17] system at the time, namely unanimous acceptance of reservations, and to favour a more flexible system. In other words, it was difficulties connected with reservations to a highly 'normative' human rights treaty that gave rise to the definition of the present regime. The Court expressly referred to the special character of that Convention, i.e., its 'purely humanitarian and civilizing purpose', and to the fact that state parties did 'not have any interests of their own',[18] arguments which have been constantly put forward by those who want to prove the inadaptability of the Vienna regime to human rights treaties. Should there have been particularities of human rights treaties with regard to reservations, they would consequently already have been incorporated into the regime of the Vienna Convention. The ILC questioned the possibility of exceptions to this general regime but did not deem necessary to include any.[19]

---

14 This applies as well to treaties on commodities, on the protection of the environment, to some demilitarisation or disarmament treaties or to private international law treaties providing uniform law.

15 R. Higgins, 'Human Rights: Some Questions of Integrity' (n. 10) 9. It would, of course, be untenable to sustain that the objections by the various European states to the United States reservation on the death penalty discharge them from their obligations under Articles 6 and 7 of the Covenant on Civil and Political Rights in their relations with the United States; this is surely not the intention of the objecting states in making their objections (see W.A. Schabas, 'Reservations to Human Rights Treaties: Time for Innovation and Reform' (1995) 32 *Canadian YB of Intl L* 65; G.G. Fitzmaurice, 'Reservations to Multilateral Conventions' (1953) 2 ICLQ 15–16).

16 Exactly as reservations purporting to limit the territorial application of a treaty are, by definition, deprived of any possible reciprocal application; in such a case, the reciprocal effect of the reservation has 'nothing on which it can "bite" or operate.' See G. Fitzmaurice, *The Law and Procedure of the International Court of Justice* (Grotius Publications, 1986) 412.

17 As is convincingly shown by the joint dissenting opinion quoted above (n. 1) 32–42.

18 Ibid. 23.

19 The question of the specificity of human rights treaties was abundantly discussed during the elaboration of the Vienna Convention and, even in more depth, during that of the Guide to Practice. It is noteworthy that, when it deemed it necessary, the ILC and the Vienna Conference did not hesitate to establish particular regimes for treaties relating to specific matters (see Art. 20(2) and (3)).

Moreover, the Human Rights Committee itself, in its General Comment No. 24, considers that, in the absence of any express provision on the subject in the Covenant on Civil and Political Rights, 'the matter of reservations . . . is governed by international law'[20] and makes an express reference to Article 19 of the 1969 Vienna Convention. Admittedly, it considers this provision as providing only 'relevant guidance';[21] nevertheless it accepts the applicability of the 1969 Vienna Convention to the Covenant as part of customary international law.[22] Finally, the Committee concludes:

> Even though, unlike some other human rights treaties, the Covenant does not incorporate a specific reference to the object and purpose test, that test governs the matter of interpretation and acceptability of reservations.[23]

It is thus apparent that the object and purpose test,[24] the foundation of the Vienna regime concerning reservations, which originated directly from the specific nature of human rights instruments – without however being limited to these kinds of treaties – is fully applicable to human rights treaties. Indeed it has expressly been referred to in the reservations provisions of these instruments themselves,[25] in the recommendations of human rights treaty bodies,[26] and by states making objections to reservations deemed incompatible with the object and purpose of human rights instruments.[27] It is therefore undeniable that 'there is a general agreement that the Vienna principle of "object and purpose" is the test'.[28] It is also worth noting that the jurisprudence and the practice relating to human rights instruments have considerably developed the Vienna regime further.[29]

---

20 General Comment No. 24 (n. 8) 120, para. 6.

21 Ibid.

22 Ibid.

23 Ibid.

24 See below (nn. 44–45) and accompanying text.

25 See Art. 75 of the American Convention on Human Rights, and IACtHR, Advisory Opinion (n. 13). See also Art. 28(2) of the 1979 Convention on the Elimination of All Forms of Discrimination against Women (which repeats the wording of Art. 20(2) of the 1966 Convention on the Elimination of All Forms of Racial Discrimination and hence pre-dates the adoption of the 1969 Vienna Convention) ('A reservation incompatible with the object and purpose of the present Convention shall not be permitted'); Art. 51(2) of the 1989 Convention on the Rights of the Child; Art. 91(2) of the 1990 International Convention on the Protection of the Rights of All Migrant Workers and Members of Their Families; Art. 46(1) of the 2006 Convention on the Rights of Persons with Disabilities ('Reservations incompatible with the object and purpose of the present Convention shall not be permitted').

26 See the Reports of the fourth and fifth meetings of persons chairing the human rights treaty bodies: UN Doc. A/47/628 (1992) para. 60; and UN Doc. A/49/537 (1994) para. 30. See also the Report of the meeting of the working group on reservations to the nineteenth meeting of chairpersons of the human rights treaty bodies and the sixth inter-committee meeting of the human rights treaty bodies, UN Doc. HRI/MC/2007/5 (2007) para. 19, points 4 and 6 of the recommendations.

27 See examples provided in the commentary to guideline 4.5.1, ILC Report 2011 (n. 2) 511–17, paras 8–23.

28 R. Higgins, 'Introduction', in J.P. Gardner (ed.), *Human Rights as General Norms and a State's Right to Opt Out – Reservations and Objections to Human Rights Conventions* (BIICL, 1997) xxi. See also the conclusions of the joint meeting of 15–16 May 2007 of the International Law Commission and representatives of human rights treaty bodies and regional human rights bodies in A. Pellet, *Fourteenth Report on Reservations to Treaties* (2009), UN Doc. A/CN.4/614, Annex, para. 27.

29 On the objectivising role of the monitoring treaty bodies, see below section 19.2.2.

1.2 The effects of invalid reservations clarified

As far as the other parties having accepted the treaty obligations in their entirety are concerned, they are completely protected by the consent principle. Indeed, and this is one of the most striking innovations of the Vienna regime, they are still free to accept[30] or to object[31] to a permissible reservation formulated by another state; and, if they feel the need, they can even go as far as to exclude the application of the entire treaty in regard to the reserving state,[32] which does not help to preserve the unity of human rights but instead excludes the reserving state from the circle of the parties. For this reason, this possibility is rarely resorted to.[33]

One of the most fundamental lacunae of the Vienna Convention regime on reservation is constituted by the absence of any clear provision guiding the legal effects to be attributed to a non-valid, impermissible reservation.[34] In fact, the Vienna regime of reservations is applicable only to permissible reservations, in particular because it would be incoherent for a codification convention to establish permissibility conditions on the first hand (Article 19) and then continue to deal with permissible and impermissible reservations indistinctively.[35] The ILC Guide to Practice carefully makes the difference: guideline 4.3.8 (Right of the author of a valid reservation not to comply with the treaty without the benefit of the reservation) squarely excludes that an objection with 'super-maximum' purpose[36] could deprive the author of the valid reservation of its right 'to comply with the provision of the treaty without the benefit of its reservation'. However, if it is true that the Vienna regime does not establish clear rules on the legal consequences of the formulation of an impermissible reservation, the entire regime is indeed not applicable to such impermissible reservations and it is therefore unnecessary to distinguish in this regard between reservations to human rights instruments and reservations to 'ordinary' treaties.

30 Acceptance is necessary in order for the reservation to produce is effects. See Arts 20(4)(a) and (c), and 21(1) of the Vienna Convention. See also the guidelines in sections 4.1 (Establishment of a reservation with regard to another state or international organisation) and 4.2 (Effects of an established reservation) of the ILC Guide to practice.

31 Arts 20(4)(b) and 21(3) of the Vienna Convention. See also guideline 2.6.2 (Right to formulate objections), and the relevant guidelines of section 4.3 (Effect of an objection to a valid reservation).

32 Art. 20(4)(b) of the Vienna Convention. See also guidelines (n. 2) 2.6.6 (Right to oppose the entry into force of the treaty vis-à-vis the author of the reservation) and 4.3.5 (Non-entry into force of the treaty as between the author of a reservation and the author of an objection with maximum effect).

33 For examples of such maximum-effect objections, see ILC Report 2011 (n. 2) 415, footnote 1939.

34 For a detailed analysis of the *travaux préparatoires* of both Vienna Conventions and the issue of impermissible reservations, see A. Pellet, *Fifteenth Report on Reservations to Treaties* (2010), UN Doc. A/CN.4/624/Add.1 (2012) paras. 386–402. See also G. Gaja, 'Il regime della Convenzione di Vienna concernente le riserve inammissibili', in *Studi in onore di Vincenzo Starace* (Ed. Scientifica, 2008) 349–61; B. Simma, 'Reservations to Human Rights Treaties— Some Recent Developments', in G. Hafner, G. Loibl, A. Rest, L. Sucharipa-Behrmann and K. Zemanek (eds), *Liber-Amicorum Professor Seidl-Hohenveldern in Honour of his 80th birthday* (Kluwer Law International, 1998) 659, 667–68; Ch. Tomuschat, 'International Law: Ensuring the Survival of Mankind on the Eve of a New Century' (1999) 281 *Recueil des Cours de l'Académie de Droit International* 321.

35 See the commentary of guideline 4.3.6 (Effect of an objection on treaty relations) (n. 2) 486–87, paras 19–22.

36 That is 'objections in which the authors deem not only that the reservation is not valid but also that, as a result, the treaty as a whole applies ipso facto in the relations between the two States'. See ILC Report 2011 (n. 2) 419, para. 17 of the commentary of guideline 3.4.2 (Permissibility of an objection to a reservation).

In order to fill this particular gap, the ILC relied quite extensively on state practice and the pronouncements of human rights monitoring bodies and human rights courts and tribunals, without implying that the solution finally adopted would be applicable only to impermissible reservations to human rights instruments. However, the relevant guidelines should contribute to enhancing the integrity of human rights treaty regime.

Thus, guideline 4.5.1 on the 'Nullity of an invalid reservation' fills up one of the most important gaps of the Vienna regime. It states:

> A reservation that does not meet the conditions of formal validity and permissibility set out in Parts 2 and 3 of the Guide to Practice is null and void, and therefore devoid of any legal effect.[37]

This 'new' rule in the law of reservations does not come out of the blue. The absence of any legal effect and the nullity of an impermissible reservation were recognised more than two decades ago by the European Court of Human Rights in *Belilos v Switzerland*,[38] and *Loizidou v Turkey*.[39] In both cases, the Court, after noting the impermissibility of the reservations formulated by Switzerland and Turkey, applied the European Convention on Human Rights as if the reservations had not been formulated and, consequently, had produced no legal effect.

In its General Comment No. 24, the Human Rights Committee also came to the conclusion – without relying on the law of treaties but on the specificities of the Covenant – that an impermissible reservation should be disregarded as a nullity.[40] Despite the unfavourable responses to this General Comment made by the United States of America, the United Kingdom and France, none of the three states challenged the position that a non-valid reservation cannot have any legal effect on the treaty provisions.[41] The Committee subsequently confirmed the conclusion reached in General Comment No. 24 in its decision in *Rawle Kennedy v Trinidad and Tobago*.[42] The Inter-American Court of Human Rights followed up with its decision in *Hilaire v Trinidad and Tobago*.[43]

The findings of human rights bodies, courts and tribunals – which have influenced the ILC's work on the question of impermissible reservations – are furthermore confirmed by important state practice which is, interestingly, not limited to human rights instruments.[44]

---

37 Ibid. 509.
38 *Belilos v Switzerland*, App. No. 10328/83, (ECtHR, 1988) Series A No. 132, para. 60 (Preliminary objections).
39 *Loizidou* (n. 13) paras 89–98.
40 General Comment No. 24 (n. 8), pp. 151–52: 'The normal consequence of an unacceptable reservation is not that the Covenant will not be in effect at all for a reserving party. Rather, such a reservation will generally be severable, in the sense that the Covenant will be operative for the reserving party without benefit of the reservation' (para. 18). See also Françoise Hampson's final working paper on reservations to human rights treaties (2004) UN Doc. E/CN.4/Sub.2/2004/42, para. 57.
41 See the observations of the United States of America, *GAOR 50th Session Supp 40* (1995) UN Doc. A/50/40, 154–58; the United Kingdom (ibid., 158–64) and France, *GAOR 51st Session Supp 40* (1996) UN Doc. A/51/40, 104–106.
42 *Rawle Kennedy v Trinidad and Tobago*, Communication No 845/1999 (1999) UN Doc. CCPR/C/67/D/845/1999, para. 6.7.
43 *Hilaire v Trinidad and Tobago*, IACtHR, Series C No. 80 (2002), para. 98 (Preliminary Objections). See also *Benjamin et al. v Trinidad and Tobago*, IACtHR, Series C No. 81 (2002), para. 89 (Preliminary Objections).
44 See ILC Report 2011 (n. 2), paras 9, 15, 22 of the commentary to guideline 4.5.1 (Nullity of an invalid reservation); see also below (n. 50).

One must admit that many objections are formulated by states in respect of reservations that are considered impermissible, either because they are prohibited by the treaty or because they are incompatible with its object and purpose, without however precluding the entry into force of the treaty.[45] This practice is both surprising and debatable: it does not give any effect to the impermissibility of the reservation. Sweden, speaking on behalf of the Nordic countries, rightly explained during the Sixth (Legal) Committee of the General Assembly's discussion of the report of the Commission on the work of its fifty-seventh session:

> A reservation incompatible with the object and purpose of a treaty was not formulated in accordance with article 19, so that the legal effects listed in article 21 did not apply. When article 21, paragraph 3, stated that the provisions to which the reservation related did not apply as between the objecting State and the reserving State to the extent of the reservation, it was referring to reservations permitted under article 19. It would be unreasonable to apply the same rule to reservations incompatible with the object and purpose of a treaty. Instead, such a reservation should be considered invalid and without legal effect.[46]

In this perspective, the ILC adopted in 2011 guideline 4.5.3 (Status of the author of an invalid reservation in relation to the treaty) which offers a suitable solution to one of the most disputed issues concerning reservations to treaties: the severability of an impermissible reservation. For a long time, that issue represented one of the most raging disputes between human rights treaty bodies, on the one hand, and defenders of the Vienna reservations regime, on the other hand. Even though the severability presumption has been adopted by human rights bodies[47] and mainly advocated in the 'human rightist' doctrine, it serves more general purposes.

This approach has developed and is confirmed by the practice, followed, inter alia, by the Nordic states,[48] of formulating what have come to be called objections with 'super-maximum' effect.[49] Even if these objections with 'super-maximum' effect have appeared in particular as a response to invalid reservations to human rights treaties, they are nevertheless not limited to reservations to such treaties.[50]

---

45 See the examples given in paras 1–2 of the commentary to guideline 3.4.2 (Permissibility of an objection to a reservation) ILC Report 2011 (n. 2) 413–16 and paras 20–38 of the commentary to guideline 4.3.6 (Effect of an objection to treaties relations) 486–91.

46 UN Doc. A/C.6/60/SR.14 (2004), para. 22. See also Malaysia UN Doc. A/C.6/60/SR.18 (2004), para. 86; and Greece (2004) UN Doc. A/C.6/60/SR.19, para. 39, as well as the report of the meeting of the working group on reservations to the nineteenth meeting of chairpersons of the human rights treaty bodies and the sixth inter-committee meeting of the human rights treaty bodies, UN Doc. HRI/MC/2007/5 (11 June 2007), para. 18: '[I]t cannot be envisaged that the reserving State remains a party to the treaty with the provision to which the reservation has been made not applying.'

47 See n. 37 and accompanying text.

48 Concerning this practice, see e.g. J. Klabbers, 'Accepting the Unacceptable? A New Nordic Approach to Reservations to Multilateral Treaties' (2000) 69 *Nordic J of Intl L* 183–86.

49 For a definition, see n. 36. On the general issue, see Simma (n. 34) 667–68. See also A. Pellet, *Eighth Report on Reservations to Treaties*, UN Doc. A/CN.4/535/Add.1 (2003) para. 96; and *Fifteenth Report on Reservations to Treaties*, UN Doc. A/CN.4/624 (2010) paras 364–68.

50 For an extensive list of objections with 'super-maximum' effects, see A. Pellet, *Fifteenth Report on Reservations to Treaties*, UN Doc. A/CN.4/624/Add.1 (2010) paras 437–39.

The principal objection to the severability doctrine is the consent principle governing the entire law of treaties, in general, and the law of reservations, in particular.[51] But this principle is not one-sided, in that if the consent of the author of the reservation must be preserved, so must the will of the other parties to the treaty, which should not be placed before a *fait accompli* by the reserving state. Remarkably the two 'quantitatively equal' groups of states which expressed themselves in 2010 in the Sixth Committee both agreed 'that the intention of the author of the reservation was the key criterion for determining whether the author was bound by the treaty or not, and that the author of the reservation was best placed to specify what that intention was.'[52] But they were divided in respect to the 'positive presumption' retained provisionally by the Commission, in line with the practice of the human rights monitoring bodies, in favour of the principle of severability of the invalid reservation from the rest of the treaty. Based on the proposals made by some states during that debate, in 2011 the ILC adopted a compromise solution, preserving the 'positive presumption', but emphasising even more the role of the will of the reserving state.

Considering that 'the key to the problem is simply the will of the author of the reservation: does the author intend to be bound by the treaty even if its reservation is invalid – without benefit of the reservation – or is its reservation a *sine qua non* for its commitment to be bound by the treaty?',[53] the ILC adopted guideline 4.5.3 which provides:

1. The status of the author of an invalid reservation in relation to a treaty depends on the intention expressed by the reserving State or international organization on whether it intends to be bound by the treaty without the benefit of the reservation or whether it considers that it is not bound by the treaty.

2. Unless the author of the invalid reservation has expressed a contrary intention or such an intention is otherwise established, it is considered a contracting State or a contracting organization without the benefit of the reservation.

3. Notwithstanding paragraphs 1 and 2, the author of the invalid reservation may express at any time its intention not to be bound by the treaty without the benefit of the reservation.

4. If a treaty monitoring body expresses the view that a reservation is invalid and the reserving State or international organization intends not to be bound by the treaty without the benefit of the reservation, it should express its intention to that effect within a period of twelve months from the date at which the treaty monitoring body made its assessment.

---

51 See e.g. France's comments to Human Rights Committee's General Comment No. 24, *GAOR 51st Session Supp 40*, UN Doc. A/51/40 (1996) 106, para. 13. This approach finds some support in the 1951 Advisory Opinion of the Court (*Reservations to the Genocide Convention* (n. 1) 29, in the practice of the Secretary-General (*Summary of Practice of the Secretary-General as Depositary of Multilateral Treaties*, UN Doc. ST/LEG/7/Rev.1, 57 (1994), paras 191–93), and in state practice (see the examples given in A. Pellet, *Fifteenth Report on Reservations to Treaties* (2010), UN Doc. A/CN.4/624/ Add.1, paras 450–51). And the ILC seemed to favour such an approach in its 1997 Preliminary Conclusions (Preliminary conclusions of the International Law Commission on reservations to normative multilateral treaties including human rights treaties adopted by the Commission, in (1997) ILC YB, vol. II(2) 57, point 5).

52 ILC Report 2011 (n. 2) 533, para. 21 of the commentary of guideline 4.5.3, see UN Doc. A/C.6/65/ SR.19 (2010).

53 Ibid. 534, para. 22 of the commentary to guideline 4.5.3.

As the Commission has noted in its commentary:

> This position offers a reasonable compromise between the underlying principle of treaty law – mutual consent – and the principle that reservations prohibited by the treaty or incompatible with the object and purpose of the treaty are null and void.[54]

This solution is largely in line with the 'Strasburg approach' and with the Recommendation made in June 2006 by the Working Group on Reservations of the human rights treaty bodies:

> The consequence that applies in a particular situation depends on the intention of the State at the time it enters its reservation. This intention must be identified during a serious examination of the available information, with the presumption, which may be refuted, that the State would prefer to remain a party to the treaty without the benefit of the reservation, rather than being excluded.[55]

2 The integrity of human rights treaties preserved

The traditional unanimity principle[56] was straightforward: if not all other contracting states accepted the reservation (at least tacitly), the reserving state could not become a party to the treaty. It is to be noted that such a principle did not preserve the integrity of the treaty since, when unanimously accepted, a derogatory regime originated from the reservation; however, it made universality more unlikely. The flexible regime as initiated in the Americas during the first part of the nineteenth century, endorsed (with some changes) by the ICJ in 1951, accepted – although reluctantly – by the ILC in 1962, and finally established by the 1969 Vienna Convention,[57] certainly strikes a better balance by preserving the essential integrity of the treaty. Moreover, the existence and growing weight of monitoring bodies enhances the objective appraisal of the validity of reservations.

---

54 *GAOR 66th Session Supp 10* (2011) A/66/10/Add.1, 537, para. 32 of the commentary to guideline 4.5.3.

55 UN Doc. HRI/MC/2006/5 (2006) para. 19(7). In December 2006, the working group slightly changed its recommendation: 'As to the consequences of invalidity, the Working Group agrees with the proposal of the Special Rapporteur of the International Law Commission according to which an invalid reservation is to be considered null and void. It follows that a state will not be able to rely on such a reservation and, unless its contrary intention is *incontrovertibly* established, will remain a party to the treaty without the benefit of the reservation' (emphasis added). See UN Doc. HRI/MC/2007/5 (2007), para. 19(7). The new formulation places the emphasis solely on the presumption that the state entering an invalid reservation has the intention to remain bound by the treaty without the benefit of the reservation as long as its contrary intention has not been 'incontrovertibly' established; but this goes too far. See also A. Pellet, *Fourteenth Report on Reservations to Treaties*, UN Doc. A/CN.4/614 (2009), para. 54.

56 *Reservations to the Genocide Convention* (n. 1) 21.

57 On this long saga, see the Preliminary Report on the Law and Practice relating to Reservations to Treaties, by A. Pellet, Special Rapporteur, A/CN.4/470 (1995) ILC YB, vol. II (1), 127–36, paras 10–61; and Pellet, commentary to Article 19 (n. 11) 645–73, paras 2–67.

2.1 The essential integrity of human rights treaties preserved

It has to be admitted, however, that, for its part, the Vienna regime does not guarantee an absolute integrity of treaties. The concept of reservations is incompatible with the very notion of integrity.[58] By definition, a reservation 'purports to exclude or to modify the legal effect of certain provisions of the treaty'.[59] The only way to preserve this integrity completely is to prohibit any reservations whatsoever, a solution which is perfectly consistent with the Vienna regime,[60] and which is sometimes resorted to in human rights treaties.[61]

The fact remains that, where a treaty is silent – and most human rights treaties are silent on this issue – the rules on reservations set out in the Vienna Convention, while not fully addressing the concerns of those who would defend the absolute integrity of normative treaties, guarantee, to all intents and purposes, that the very essence of the treaty is preserved since, according to Article 19(c):

> A State may, when signing, ratifying, accepting, approving or acceding to a treaty, formulate a reservation unless . . . the reservation is incompatible with the object and purpose of the treaty.

This provision is much more than 'a mere doctrinal assertion, which may serve as a basis for guidance to States regarding acceptance of reservations'.[62] Even if one must admit that 'the object and purpose of a treaty are indeed something of an enigma',[63] the ILC has now made clear that a reservation is to be considered not in conformity with the object and purpose of a treaty 'if it affects an essential element of the treaty that is necessary to its general tenour, in

---

58 As the International Court of Justice noted, '[i]t does not appear, moreover, that the conception of the absolute integrity of a convention has been transformed into a rule of international law'. See *Reservations to the Genocide Convention* (n. 1) 24.

59 Art. 2(1)(d) of the 1969 Vienna Convention. See also n. 2 guideline 1.1.1 (Object of reservations) of the Guide to practice: 'A unilateral statement formulated by a State or an international organization at the time when that State or that organization expresses its consent to be bound by a treaty, by which its author purports to limit the obligations imposed on it by the treaty, constitutes a reservation.'

60 See Art. 19(a) of the Vienna Convention. See also LC Report 2011 (n. 2) guideline 3.1 (Permissible reservations) and 3.1.1 (Reservations prohibited by the treaty).

61 See e.g. the Supplementary Convention on the Abolition of Slavery, the Slave Trade and Institutions and Practices Similar to Slavery of 7 September 1956 (Art. 9); the Convention against Discrimination in Education of 14 December 1960 (Art. 9, para. 7); Protocol No. 6 to the European Convention on Human Rights on the abolition of the death penalty of 28 April 1983 (Art. 4); or the European Convention against Torture of 26 November 1987 (Art. 21); which all prohibit any reservations to the treaty.

62 J.M. Ruda, 'Reservations to Treaties' (1975) 146 *Recueil des Cours de l'Académie de Droit International* 190. For similar points of view, see J. Combacau, *Le droit des traités*, Que sais-je?, No. 2613 (PUF, 1991) 60; or 'Logique de la validité contre logique de l'opposabilité dans la Convention de Vienne sur le droit des traités', in *Le droit international au service de la paix, de la justice et du développement – Mélanges Michel Virally* (Pedone, 1991) 200; P-H. Imbert, *Les réserves aux traités multilatéraux* (Pedone, 1979) 134–37; P. Reuter, *Introduction au droit des traités*, 3rd edn (PUF, 1995) 74; or K. Zemanek, 'Some Unresolved Questions Concerning Reservations in the Vienna Convention on the Law of Treaties', in *Essays in International Law in Honour of Judge Manfred Lachs* (Nijhoff, 1984) 331–33.

63 I. Buffard and K. Zemanek, 'The Object and Purpose of a Treaty: An Enigma?' (1998) 3 *Austrian Rev of Intl & Eur L* 322.

such a way that the reservation impairs the *raison d'être* of the treaty.'[64] Thus interpreted, Article 19(c) constitutes 'the fundamental criterion for the permissibility of a reservation',[65] and the linchpin of the flexible system laid out by the Vienna regime.[66] The 'object and purpose' criterion limit the sovereign freedom[67] of states to formulate reservations to a treaty.[68]

The fact that '[t]he claim that a particular reservation is contrary to object and purpose is easier made than substantiated'[69] was certainly one of the major critiques of the minority in the *Reservations to the Genocide Convention* Advisory Opinion. In their joint dissenting opinion, they expressed the fear that 'object and purpose' could not 'produce final and consistent results'.[70] However, notwithstanding the inevitable 'margin of subjectivity' in the appreciation of the object and purpose of a treaty, the criterion has considerable merit and undoubtedly constitutes a useful guideline capable of resolving the issue of permissibility in a reasonable manner.

Within the area of human rights, most lively debates have taken place in this regard, particularly over reservations made to general treaties such as the European and Inter-American Conventions, the African Charter, or the International Covenants on Economic, Social and Cultural Rights and on Civil and Political Rights. In the case of the latter, the Human Rights Committee stated in its famous (and debatable) General Comment No. 24 that:

> In an instrument which articulates very many civil and political rights, each of the many articles, and indeed their interplay, secures the objectives of the Covenant. The object and purpose of the Covenant is to create legally binding standards for human rights by defining certain civil and political rights and placing them in a framework of obligations which are legally binding for those States which ratify; and to provide an efficacious supervisory machinery for the obligations undertaken.[71]

This statement of principle constitutes one of the major arguments invoked in order to ban all reservations to human rights treaties, because, taken literally, this position would render

---

64 ILC Report 2011 (n. 2) guideline 3.1.5 (Incompatibility of a reservation with the object and purpose of the treaty). More generally, guidelines 3.1.5.1 to 3.1.5.7 aim at better assessing the notion of 'object and purpose' of the treaty.

65 ILC Report 2011 (n. 2) 351, para. 1 of the commentary to guideline 3.1.5 (Incompatibility of a reservation with the object and purpose of the treaty).

66 See Pellet (n. 11) 443, para. 95.

67 The ILC pointed out that '[a]lthough the view has sometimes been expressed that it was excessive to speak of a 'right to reservations', even though the Convention proceeds from the principle that there is a presumption in favour of their permissibility. This, moreover, is the significance of the very title of article 19 of the Vienna Conventions ("Formulation of reservations"), which is confirmed by its chapeau: "A State may . . . formulate a reservation unless . . .". It should, however, be noted that by using the verb "may", the introductory clause of article 19 recognizes that States have a right, but it is only the right to "formulate" reservations.' ILC Report 2011 (n. 2) 333, para. 5 of the commentary to guideline 3.1 (Permissible reservations), footnotes omitted.

68 See *Reservations to the Genocide Convention* (n. 1) 24.

69 L. Lijnzaad, *Reservations to UN-Human Rights Treaties: Ratify and Ruin?* (Nijhoff, 1995) 82–83.

70 Joint dissenting opinion (n. 1) 44. See also the ILC's resistance to adopt the criterion established by the ICJ, (1951) ILC YB, vol. II, 128, para. 24.

71 General Comment No. 24. (n. 8) 120, para. 7. See also Hampson (n. 40) para. 50: 'The difficulty in the case of human rights law is that the object is not the acceptance of a large number of separate obligations. Rather, there is a single goal (respect, protection and promotion of human rights) which is to be achieved by adherence to a large number of separate provisions.'

invalid any general reservation bearing on any one of the rights protected by the Covenant. However, the Committee itself does not go that far and recognises that reservations may usefully encourage a wider acceptance of the Covenant.

In order to take account of the specific difficulty raised in this regard by reservations to general human rights treaties, the ILC had at first envisaged devoting a particular guideline to the specific issues concerning the determination of the object and purpose of 'general human rights treaties'.[72] However, realising that there was no reason to individualise human rights treaties since the same considerations came into play for all treaties containing numerous interdependent rights and obligations,[73] the Commission eventually adopted guideline 3.1.5.6,[74] which:

[A]ttempts to strike a particularly delicate balance between these different considerations by combining three elements:

- The interdependence of the rights and obligations;
- The importance that the provision to which the reservation relates has within the general tenour of the treaty; and
- The extent of the impact that the reservation has on the treaty.

The first element, the *interdependence of the rights and obligations* affected by the reservation, lays emphasis on the goal of achieving global realization of the object and purpose of a treaty and aims at preventing the dismantling of its obligations, that is, their disintegration into bundles of obligations, the individual, separate realization of which would not achieve the realization of the object of the treaty as a whole.

The second element qualifies the previous one by recognizing – in keeping with practice – that nonetheless certain rights protected by these instruments are less essential than others – in particular, than the non-derogable ones. The *importance of the provision* concerned must, of course, be assessed in the light of the 'general tenour' of the treaty, an expression taken from guideline 3.1.5.

Lastly, the reference to 'the extent of the *impact that the reservation has*' upon the right or the provision to which it relates allows for the inference that, even in the case of essential rights, reservations are possible if they do not preclude protection of the rights in question and do not have the effect of excessively modifying their legal regime.[75]

---

72 Draft Guideline 3.1.5.5 ('To assess the compatibility of a reservation with the object and purpose of a general treaty for the protection of human rights, account shall be taken of the indivisibility, interdependence and interrelatedness of the rights set out in the treaty as well as the importance that the right or provision which is the subject of the reservation has within the general thrust of the treaty, and the gravity of the impact the reservation has upon it.') *GAOR 62nd Session Supp 10* UN Doc. A/62/10 (2007) 113–16.

73 The ILC thus confirms the unity of the reservations regime.

74 Guideline 3.1.5.6 (Reservations to treaties containing numerous interdependent rights and obligations): 'To assess the compatibility of a reservation with the object and purpose of a treaty containing numerous interdependent rights and obligations, account shall be taken of that interdependence as well as the importance that the provision to which the reservation relates has within the general tenour of the treaty, and the extent of the impact that the reservation has on the treaty.'

75 ILC Report 2011 (n. 2) 386–87, paras 6–9 of the commentary to guideline 3.1.5.6, footnotes omitted (emphasis added).

Thus conceived, the 'object and purpose' test constitutes an objective criterion which is aimed at setting a uniform standard against which the validity of any reservation must be assessed, that is it constitutes the bookmark of the community interest – at least the interest of the community of the parties to the treaty – to be preserved. All reservations must pass this threshold; if they do not, they are impermissible and, consequently, null and void,[76] irrespective of any acceptance or objection by the other contracting states.[77] Thus, the regime is designed to preserve the essence of the collective will of the parties, that is the quintessence of the community interest embodied in the conventional instrument.

On the other hand, the flexibility of the Vienna regime, and in particular the way it recognises the freedom of a state to formulate valid reservations to a treaty, encourages the aim to universality of multilateral treaties much better than the traditional 'unanimity' system largely prevailing before the 1969 Vienna Convention. Such a purpose certainly comports with the objective of most multilateral human rights instruments which inherently yearn for universal application.[78] '[T]he possibility of formulating reservations may well be seen as a strength rather than a weakness of the treaty approach, in so far as it allows a more universal participation in human rights treaties.'[79] And, as has been recognised, 'the lodging of carefully tailored reservations may also be taken as a sign that the reserving State takes the respective human rights treaty seriously.'[80] In this respect, Article 19(c) of the Vienna Convention acts as the balancing factor in limiting the freedom to formulate reservations only to some degree, while leaving some room for states to modulate their consent with regard to secondary or accessory issues.[81]

2.2 The essential integrity of human rights treaties controlled

The preservation of the integrity of human rights is enhanced by the existence of monitoring bodies, which certainly is a particularity of modern human rights treaties. Their existence makes an objective determination of the validity of reservations possible and eliminates one of the most important uncertainties with regard to the application of the Vienna regime.

76 See the beginning of section 19.1.2 above.
77 See e.g. D.W. Bowett, 'Reservations to Non-Restricted Multilateral Treaties' (1976–1977) 48 *British YB of Intl L* 88.
78 See *Reservations to the Genocide Convention* (n. 1) 21–22.
79 M. Coccia, 'Reservations to Multilateral Treaties on Human Rights' (1985) 15 *Cal W Intl L J* 3. The author refers to O. Schachter, M. Nawaz and J. Fried, *Toward Wider Acceptance of United Nations Treaties* (Arno Press, 1971) 148, and adds: 'This UNITAR study shows statistically that "the treaties . . . which permit reservations, or do not prohibit reservations, have received proportionally larger acceptance than the treaties which either do not permit reservations to a part or whole of the treaty, or which contain only one substantial clause, making reservations unlikely".'
80 Simma and Hernández (n. 9); see also Simma (n. 34) 660.
81 For recent illustrations in the jurisprudence of the ICJ: *Armed Activities on the Territory of the Congo (New Application: 2002) (Democratic Republic of the Congo v Rwanda), Jurisdiction and Admissibility*, ICJ Reports 2006, 32, para. 67. See also *Armed Activities on the Territory of the Congo (New Application: 2002) (Democratic Republic of the Congo v Rwanda), Provisional Measures, Order of 10 July 2002*, ICJ Reports 2002, 246, para. 72.

In General Comment No. 24, the Human Rights Committee considered that:

> Because of the special character of a human rights treaty, the compatibility of a reservation with the object and purpose of the Covenant must be established objectively, by reference to legal principles.[82]

It is certainly desirable that the compatibility of a reservation with the object and purpose of a treaty be determined objectively. That this can rarely be the case because of the particular structure of the international society is a different question. And even in the case of human rights treaties the assessment of the permissibility of a reservation cannot always be made by a monitoring body; this is the case when no such body is instituted by the treaty and/or, possibly, when the responsibility to make this assessment has been expressly entrusted to the state parties.[83]

However, whereas the existence of monitoring bodies is certainly a particularity of human rights treaties, it is neither a necessary element of these instruments, nor an 'exclusive' particularity,[84] and certainly not an argument to modify the generally applicable reservations regime which bears upon the substantive principles to be applied by the competent authority to assess the validity of the reservation – whether a state, an international organisation, a judge or a monitoring body. But the control of the compatibility of a reservation to the object and purpose of the treaty constitutes a guarantee of a more objective assessment of this objective test. Monitoring constitutes consequently a clear progress in the application of the Vienna rules and therefore contributes to ensuring the integrity of human rights by permitting an objective assessment of the compatibility of a given reservation to the object and purpose of the treaty.

3 Conclusion: human rights and treaty law reconciled?

In their Joint Separate Opinion appended to the ICJ judgment in *DRC v Rwanda*, Judges Higgins, Kooijmans, Elaraby, Owada and Simma rightly stressed:

> 22. Human Rights courts and tribunals have not regarded themselves as precluded by this Court's 1951 Advisory Opinion from doing other than noting whether a particular State has objected to a reservation. This development does not create a 'schism' between general international law as represented by the Court's 1951 Advisory Opinion, a 'deviation' therefrom by these various courts and tribunals.

> 23. Rather, it is to be regarded as developing the law to meet contemporary realities, nothing in the specific findings of the Court in 1951 prohibiting this. Indeed, it is clear that the practice of the International Court itself reflects this trend for tribunals and courts themselves to pronounce on compatibility with object and purpose, when the need arises.[85]

This is a fair description of the process which led to taking more seriously the *rule* contained in Article 19(c) of the Vienna Convention, in which the practice of human rights bodies

---

82 General Comment No. 24 (n. 8) 124, para. 18.
83 See e.g. Art. 20(2) of the 1965 Convention on the Elimination of All Forms of Racial Discrimination.
84 Disarmament or environment treaties quite often also create other kinds of monitoring bodies although they operate differently.
85 *Armed Activities on the Territory of the Congo* (n. 81) 71, paras 22–23.

played a leading, if not exclusive, role, and which led to the adoption by the ILC of a set of well-balanced rules usefully filling the gaps and dispelling the uncertainties in the Vienna reservations regime.

However, reservations are like the Aesopian language: they can be the worst or the best instrument for promoting community interests, including in the domain of human rights. If there is a risk that they put in danger the integrity of treaties and transform a multilateral convention into a bundle of bilateral relations, they are also, when used with good judgment and moderation, an efficient factor of integration and of strengthening adhesion to community values. The regulation promoted in the ILC Guide to Practice endeavours to minimise the evil while maximising the good, with the hope of putting an end to Manichean unfounded views.

Select bibliography

I. Boerefijn, 'Impact on the Law on Treaty Reservations' in M.T. Kamminga and M. Scheinin (eds), *The Impact of Human Rights Law on General International Law* (OUP, 2009) 63–97.

P.-H. Imbert, *Les réserves aux traités multilatéraux* (Paris, Pedone, 1979).

A. Pellet, 'Commentary to Article 19', in O. Corten and P. Klein (eds), *The Vienna Conventions on the Law of Treaties. A Commentary* (OUP, 2011) 405–88.

A. Pellet and D. Müller, 'Reservations to Human Rights Treaties: Not an Absolute Evil', in U. Fastenrath, R. Geiger, D-E. Khan, A. Paulus, S. von Schorlemer and C. Vedder (eds), *From Bilateralism to Community Interest – Essays in Honour of Judge Bruno Simma* (OUP, 2011) 521–51.

R. Riquelme Cortado, *Las reservas a los tratados, Lagunas y Ambigüedades del Regimen de Viena* (Universidad de Murcia, 2004) 433.

W. Schabas, 'Reservations to Human Rights Treaties: Time for Innovation and Reform' 32 *Canadian Ybk of Intl L* (1995) 39–81.

B. Simma and G.I. Hernández, 'Legal Consequences of an Impermissible Reservation to a Human Rights Treaty: Where Do We Stand?' in E. Cannizzaro (ed.), *The Law of Treaties Beyond the Vienna Convention. Essays in Honour of Professor Giorgio Gaja* (OUP, 2011) 60–85.

I. Ziemele (ed.), *Reservations to Human Rights Treaties and the Vienna Convention Regime: Conflict, Harmony or Reconciliation* (Nijhoff, 2004).

See also the bibliography provided in the Guide to Practice (*GAOR 66th Session Supp. 10* (A/66/10/Add.1) 603–30, esp. 616–22.

20

The International Labour Organization and international human rights system

Lee Swepston

Scholars and activists often neglect a vital aspect of human rights: the role of labour law and the International Labour Organization (ILO). Yet labour law is often the most immediate and practical way to promote and to enforce human rights, entering directly into contact with the concerns that most people encounter on a daily basis. The right to freedom from discrimination is fundamental. But people can be most affected in practical terms when they are unable to get a job and to support their family because of the colour of their skin, their sex or their religion. Not being able to join a political association makes nonsense of the right to freedom of speech and association. But not being able to join or form the trade union of choice means that workers are unable to bargain for improved working conditions, safety and health and a living wage.

1 The connection between human rights and workers' rights and the origins of the ILO

Many of the first manifestations of human rights were in the realm of workers' rights. In the fourteenth century, the plague killed a third of the population of Europe. In doing so it created the first labour market, by loosening the ties that bound most skilled workmen to feudal estates and by contributing to the birth of towns. The shortage of skilled workers meant that those who remained could market their work and bargain for privileges and rights they had never had before.[1] Thus began a pattern of workers combining to assert their rights, leading gradually to the formation of trade unions as early as the seventeenth century in Europe.

The first manifestation of human rights in the international arena was focused on work: the slave trade was prohibited, in 1815, by the Congress of Vienna, and Great Britain also campaigned to suppress it in practice. Within half a century, slavery was extinguished – at least by law – in Europe and the Americas. But when nations decided to establish permanent international organisations to maintain peace, human rights were far from their minds.

---

1 See, for example, B. Tuchman, *A Distant Mirror: The Calamitous 14th Century* (Alfred A. Knopf, 1978).

At the end of the First World War, the Treaty of Versailles[2] established the first two international organisations: the League of Nations and the ILO. The League was established to maintain military and political peace, and the ILO was established to combat social unrest and to promote social justice. Neither was created with a rights mandate, and indeed the founders – the leaders of the United States, Great Britain and France – consciously avoided any human rights language. In spite of their own national traditions of recognising human rights, the British and the French knew that the recognition of human rights without regard to race or colour would call into question their colonial empires, and President Wilson knew that the recognition of racial equality would prevent the ratification of the Treaty in the US Senate. The only mention of rights in the Treaty was in the section that formed the first constitution of the ILO, which referred to the right to freedom of association and to collective bargaining.[3]

The ILO had a very different design and mandate from the League and, subsequently, from the United Nations, as will be explored further below. While only representatives of states could take part in the League's discussions and decision-making, the ILO allowed representatives of workers and employers from each member state to take part in the decision-making process. This tripartism, as it is called, is both a source of the strength of the ILO and a limitation on its ability to take action. The other major difference from the League was that the ILO was conceived as a standard-setting organisation, to carry on the work begun in the late nineteenth century by a small group of European states. Today the ILO has an advisory and assistance mandate based directly on the standards it adopts, once again very different from other intergovernmental organisations.

2 The place of the ILO in the international human rights system

The ILO has a curious history in international human rights, so much so that many of those working in human rights neglect – indeed, may be ignorant of – its proper place in the system. The ILO itself was behind both its own initial absence from international human rights discussions and its return to the field.

As previously mentioned, the ILO was different from the League of Nations (and the UN) as far as human rights were concerned, in that it was essentially conceived as a standard-setting organisation. With nearly 200 Conventions and an equal number of Recommendations[4] adopted since 1919, the ILO's body of law is both substantial and continually updated. ILO standards have an interesting characteristic among human rights instruments in that, subject to a few exceptions, most have not been placed within a 'rights'

---

2 The Treaty of Peace between the Allied and Associated Powers and Germany (adopted 28 June 1919, entered into force 10 January 1920) 225 CTS 188.

3 See G. Rodgers, E. Lee, L. Swepston and J. van Daele, *The ILO and the Quest for Social Justice, 1919–2009* (ILO, 2009), in particular ch. 2.

4 Conventions are the main instruments used by the ILO for human rights. They can be ratified by states, and place obligations on such states. Recommendations are instruments unique to the ILO. Adopted in the same way as Conventions, they often – but not always – supplement Conventions with more detailed guidance on implementation. They may also be adopted as free-standing instruments if the subject of the Recommendation is not yet ready to be adopted as a Convention. Recommendations cannot be ratified, but act as guidance for states and the ILO's social partners and carry authority as they are adopted at the International Labour Conference. In addition, the Constitution of the International Labour Organisation ((adopted 9 October 1946, entered into force 20 April 1948) 15 UNTS 35, as amended (ILO Constitution)) allows the ILO's Governing Body to require reports on their implementation (see Art. 19(6)(d) of the ILO Constitution).

framework.[5] From the beginning of its work, the ILO took a utilitarian approach to standards, adopting standards intended to give better outcomes in the world of work than would be achieved without them. ILO standards tend to spell out governments' obligations, rather than the rights that individuals should enjoy. As an example, the ILO's main instrument on child labour, the Minimum Age Convention, 1973 (No. 138),[6] never mentions rights or child labour as a concept, but instead carefully lays out the ages at which and the conditions under which children and young persons may enter the workforce. For all this, it is the basic international instrument on the right of children to be free from child labour, going into far greater and more practical detail than the Convention on the Rights of the Child,[7] which devotes one Article to child labour.[8]

This approach has contributed to ILO standards often being considered a poor stepchild of human rights law. However, in 1944, before the UN system had been created, the ILO met in Philadelphia under the sponsorship of President Roosevelt to discuss its future following the end of the Second World War as the only surviving fragment of the League of Nations architecture. It had already begun before the war to undermine the culture of exploitation of colonial peoples that enabled colonialism, through its regulation of the conditions of work of 'native' peoples and its call for the gradual abolition of forced labour[9] – until then an accepted practice in the colonies. But, in 1944, it adopted the Declaration of Philadelphia to provide a moral basis for its future work, and in so doing became the first international organisation to adopt a philosophy based on human rights and equality.[10] Part II of the Declaration stated:

> Believing that experience has fully demonstrated the truth of the statement in the Constitution of the International Labour Organization that lasting peace can be established only if it is based on social justice, the Conference affirms that:
>
> (a) all human beings, irrespective of race, creed or sex, have the right to pursue both their material well-being and their spiritual development in conditions of freedom and dignity, of economic security and equal opportunity;

5 Notably the ILO's instruments on freedom of association and collective bargaining, and Convention No. 182 concerning the prohibition and immediate action for the elimination of the worst forms of child labour (adopted 7 June 1999, entered into force 19 November 2000) 2133 UNTS 161 (Convention No. 182).

6 Convention No. 138 concerning minimum age for admission to employment (adopted 26 June 1973, entered into force 19 June 1976) 1015 UNTS 297 (Convention No. 138).

7 Convention on the Rights of the Child (1989) (adopted 20 November 1989, entered into force 2 September 1990) 1577 UNTS 3 (CRC).

8 Like other comparisons with UN instruments in this chapter, this is not meant as a criticism but as an illustration of the different roles played by UN instruments, which set out general principles and are of broad coverage, and ILO standards, which regulate many of the same questions but in a narrower context and in much greater depth. In fact, analysis shows that when examining the application of Art. 32 of the CRC, the UN Committee on the Rights of the Child relies heavily on Convention No. 138 and its companion, Convention No. 182, and recommends that governments ratify them and then solicit the technical cooperation of the ILO to implement them.

9 See the discussion in ch. 2 of Rodgers, Lee, Swepston and van Daele (n. 3) regarding the ILO's Native Labour Code, which was the first attempt to regulate conditions of work in colonial situations, until then carried out in conditions of forced labour and exploitation without any controls in place.

10 International Labour Conference (26th Session) Declaration concerning the aims and purposes of the International Labour Organisation (Philadelphia, 10 May 1944) (Declaration of Philadelphia).

(b) the attainment of the conditions in which this shall be possible must constitute the central aim of national and international policy;

(c) all national and international policies and measures, in particular those of an economic and financial character, should be judged in this light and accepted only in so far as they may be held to promote and not to hinder the achievement of this fundamental objective.

The UN was created in 1945, and the ILO became its first specialised agency. While the UN was finding its voice with the adoption of the Universal Declaration of Human Rights in 1948[11] – several articles of which were based on the ILO Constitution and the Declaration of Philadelphia – and beginning to codify human rights in treaty form, the ILO was adopting its own core human rights instruments. The UN adopted its first human rights convention, the Convention on the Elimination of All Forms of Racial Discrimination, in 1965, followed, in 1966, by the two Covenants that, together with the UDHR, form the International Bill of Human Rights.[12] In comparison, from 1948 to 1958, the ILO adopted two Conventions[13] on freedom of association and collective bargaining (No. 87 in 1948 and No. 98 in 1949), two Conventions on equality and non-discrimination at work (No. 100 in 1951 and No. 111 in 1958), its second Convention on forced labour (No. 105 in 1957), and the first of its two Conventions on indigenous and tribal peoples (No. 107 in 1957).[14]

All of these Conventions contained concepts, and even language, later adopted by the UN in its human rights instruments. Care was taken in these UN instruments not to diminish the protection provided in the ILO standards, but instead to adapt it more generally to wider human rights concerns.

However, by the time the UN began adopting its basic standards on human rights in the mid-1960s, the Cold War had set in, and the division between civil and political rights on the one hand, and economic, social and cultural rights on the other, was embedded in the ICCPR and ICESCR. The ILO at that point left human rights to the UN and pursued, on a far less politicised basis, the development and supervision of its own standards on basic human rights concepts, which it began to refer to exclusively as 'labour standards'. In doing so, and with the aid of its tripartite structure and strong supervisory system, it largely (but not entirely) opted out of the ideological wars around which human rights were really human rights and academic debates about the division between individual and collective rights and the justiciability of economic, social and cultural rights as opposed to civil and political rights. At the same time, however, it absented itself from the awareness of the growing human rights

---

11 Universal Declaration of Human Rights, GA Res. 217 A(III) (10 December 1948) (UDHR).

12 International Convention on the Elimination of All Forms of Racial Discrimination (1965) (adopted 21 December 1965, entered into force 4 January 1969) 660 UNTS 195 (ICERD); International Covenant on Economic, Social and Cultural Rights (1966) (adopted 19 December 1966, entered into force 3 January 1976) 993 UNTS 3 (ICESCR); International Covenant on Civil and Political Rights (1966) (adopted 19 December 1966, entered into force 23 March 1976) 999 UNTS 171 (ICCPR).

13 See nn. 5 and 6 above and section 20.3.4 below for the full titles of these fundamental ILO standards.

14 Convention (No. 107) concerning the protection and integration of indigenous and other tribal and semi-tribal populations in independent countries (adopted 26 June 1957, entered into force 2 June 1959) 328 UNTS 247 (Convention No. 107).

community.[15] It was not until the mid-1990s, as the world began adjusting to a post-Cold War discussion of human rights and to globalisation, that the ILO began referring to itself as a human rights organisation.

Regardless of whether it is described as a human rights organisation, the ILO has a practical, day-to-day involvement in human rights in many fields, going beyond the limited impression one might have from its name. Its mandate is in fact social affairs, and is not restricted to labour questions alone. The ILO's competence includes a wide range of rights in addition to those that might be considered purely labour issues. It has designated four subjects as fundamental human rights: freedom of association and collective bargaining; protection from child labour; protection from forced labour; and protection from discrimination.[16] The ILO deals with these rights and various other subjects, including safe and healthy working conditions, social security, minimum age for work, vocational guidance and training, protection of wages, occupational safety and health, employment of women, migrant workers, indigenous and tribal peoples, and labour administration. It has also set up special promotional mechanisms to deal with these fundamental human rights.

The ILO has made – and continues to make – important contributions to human rights. First, it has set the basic standards on subjects such as forced labour, freedom of association, child labour and discrimination. These standards have been incorporated into the ICCPR and ICESCR (as mentioned above) and all the regional human rights standards. Indeed, Articles 6 to 10 of ICESCR are a brief condensation of basic principles set out in various ILO standards adopted prior to 1966.

Second, the ILO's prior discussions and definitions have been incorporated into the UN's core human rights instruments, although there are differences in the way the UN has approached such issues. As an example, the definition of racial discrimination in Article 1(1) of ICERD reads:

---

15 This writer, who was responsible for the projection of the ILO's human rights messages to the UN and elsewhere from the mid-1980s until 2007, could never trace a conscious decision to take this stance. By the time I joined the ILO in 1973, this attitude of separation from UN human rights concerns was so well installed, by officials who had long retired, that it was simply accepted. When the ICESCR and ICCPR entered into force in 1976, the ILO established the position of Human Rights Coordinator, whose job consisted very largely of ensuring that the UN's human rights work did not undermine ILO concepts, instead of promoting an ILO vision of human rights. Klaus Samson, the first ILO Human Rights Coordinator, made his points so effectively that the ILO was physically excluded from meetings of the Human Rights Committee (HRC) for many years at the instigation of the 'socialist' members, in what he later informed me was an attempt to ensure that the ILO's less ideological approach to an unrestricted right to freedom of association in particular did not intrude on UN deliberations. When Samson asserted his right to attend under the Agreement between the United Nations and the International Labour Organization ((signed 30 May 1946, entered into force 14 December 1946) 1 UNTS 184), according to his later account to me, he was physically escorted from the room by UN Security. This was not, of course, minuted in the proceedings of the HRC. For some years afterwards, an invitation was extended to the ILO to submit written information, which was barely taken into account. After the end of the Cold War, when the ILO requested an invitation to attend the HRC's sessions, no one on the staff of the UN or on the HRC recalled why the ILO was no longer invited; the invitation was duly extended from the early 1990s, and the ILO began to take its place at HRC meetings.

16 See section 20.3.4 below for detail as to how this designation was reached.

In this Convention, the term 'racial discrimination' shall mean any distinction, exclusion, restriction or preference based on race, colour, descent, or national or ethnic origin which has the purpose or effect of nullifying or impairing the recognition, enjoyment or exercise, on an equal footing, of human rights and fundamental freedoms in the political, economic, social, cultural or any other field of public life.

This was obviously closely based on the definition of discrimination adopted a few years earlier in the ILO's Discrimination (Employment and Occupation) Convention, 1958 (No. 111),[17] Article 1 of which reads, in part:

For the purpose of this Convention the term *discrimination* includes—

(a) any distinction, exclusion or preference made on the basis of race, colour, sex, religion, political opinion, national extraction or social origin, which has the effect of nullifying or impairing equality of opportunity or treatment in employment or occupation.

There are small differences between the two definitions, including as to their scope, but these do not change their basic wording or meaning. As in a number of other cases, the fact that the ILO had previously adopted very similar language eased the drafting and the adoption of such language in the UN instrument.

Another striking instance of UN human rights instruments being influenced by earlier ILO standards is the language in Article 8(3) of the ICESCR and nearly identical language in Article 22(3) of the ICCPR:

Nothing in this article shall authorise States Parties to the International Labour Organization Convention of 1948 concerning Freedom of Association and Protection of the Right to Organise to take legislative measures which would prejudice, or to apply the law in such a manner as would prejudice, the guarantees provided for in that Convention.

There is no other instance, in any of the UN's human rights instruments, of a specific deferral to an instrument of another international organisation.

Other instances can also be found of the influence of ILO standards on UN human rights instruments. This includes the reference in Article 32 of the CRC to 'having regard to the relevant provisions of other international instruments', which were specified in discussions leading to the adoption of the CRC as being the ILO standards on minimum age and child labour.[18]

17 Convention (No. 111) concerning discrimination in respect of employment and occupation (adopted 25 June 1958, entered into force 15 June 1960) 362 UNTS 31.
18 Office of the United Nations High Commissioner for Human Rights, 'Legislative History of the Convention on the Rights of the Child', vol. II (2007) UN Doc. HR/PUB/07/1 at 693–708, http://www.ohchr.org/Documents/Publications/LegislativeHistorycrc2en.pdf, accessed 15 February 2012.

3 ILO standards and supervision[19]

Human rights are implemented by the ILO principally through the adoption of international labour standards. The ILO adopts these Conventions and Recommendations at the annual International Labour Conference,[20] and closely supervises how countries apply the Conventions they decide to ratify. By early 2012, there had been nearly 7,800 ratifications of the 189 ILO Conventions.

3.1 Adoption of standards

ILO standards are adopted in a different way from most international standards. Without going into detail,[21] workers' and employers' representatives play a role equal to that of governments, and at times in the process can even outvote governments. This lends a realism to ILO standards that goes beyond the more distant relationship diplomats often have with the problems addressed by international instruments. In addition, the invariable schedule of less than three years from the decision to discuss a standard until its adoption concentrates negotiations and changes the dynamics of discussions towards seeking decisions at each stage.

3.2 Ratification of ILO standards

Unlike other international instruments, ILO Conventions may not be ratified with reservations. However, many ILO standards have flexibility built into them, which allows ratifying states to choose their level of obligation and method of implementation – a sort of preselected list of allowable reservations.

3.3 Supervision of standards

Briefly, the ILO's reporting system is based on its Constitution and not on individual Conventions. States must submit reports on all Conventions they have ratified at intervals of one to five years, depending on the character of the Convention and on certain other circumstances. Governments' reports must be sent to national employers' and workers' organisations, who have standing to comment on them and may even submit their own reports if governments do not do so. Reporting rates are very high compared to other international procedures. For instance, the 2011 report of the ILO Committee of Experts stated that for that session:

---

19 For more detailed descriptions, see: ILO, *Rules of the Game: A Brief Introduction to International Labour Standards*, revised edn (ILO, 2009) http://www.ilo.org/global/publications/WCMS_108393/lang—en/index.htm, accessed 15 February 2012; or L. Swepston, 'The International Labour Organisation and Human Rights', in C. Kraude and M. Scheinen (eds), *International Protection of Human Rights: A Textbook* (Institute for Human Rights, Abo Akademi University, 2009).

20 See Arts 19–37 of the ILO Constitution. Most standards are adopted at the regular annual sessions, but standards relevant to maritime work are adopted at special sessions of the International Labour Conference devoted exclusively to this issue.

21 See ILO, *Rules of the Game* (n. 19) and L. Swepston, 'Adoption of Standards by the International Labour Organisation: Lessons and Limitations', in *Human Rights Standards: Learning from Experience* (International Council on Human Rights Policy, 2006) http://www.ichrp.org/en/projects/120?theme=12, accessed 15 February 2012.

2,745 reports were requested from governments. Of these, 1,866 had been received by the Office by the end of the present session of the Committee. This figure corresponds to 67.98 per cent of the reports requested (compared to 68 per cent last year).[22]

These figures do not reveal that an even greater percentage of reports are received within a few months of when they are due, yielding a very high reporting rate compared to other international supervisory procedures. This is due, at least in part, to the influence of workers' and employers' organisations.

All of these reports are examined by the ILO's Committee of Experts on the Application of Conventions and Recommendations, an expert body of 20 members appointed by the Director-General with the approval of the Governing Body. In comparison to the UN supervisory bodies, committees are not set up for each separate Convention. In addition, as members of the ILO Committee are appointed rather than elected from among ratifying states, this tends to produce members who are more technically qualified to examine governments' reports than elected members can be. Members of the ILO Committee include lawyers, judges of national courts and of the International Court of Justice, professors, and other experts appointed in their individual capacities.

The Committee of Experts makes detailed comments on governments' reports, in the form of direct requests (which are not 'published' in the formal sense but which do become public some months after they are made) and observations (which are published in the Committee's annual report and communicated to the International Labour Conference for review). The Conference forms a tripartite Committee on the Application of Standards, in which non-governmental parties have a voting majority. This Committee has called a number of governments before it to discuss comments from the Committee of Experts on their reports and, on occasion, has expressed concern over or approved the actions of governments (again, a review process not available under UN human rights instruments).

The ILO also has complaints procedures, although unlike other international procedures these are not open to individuals. Workers' and employers' organisations may file representations[23] and governments, delegates to the International Labour Conference and the Governing Body itself may file complaints[24] alleging violations of ratified Conventions. Under a special procedure, complaints about violations of the right to freedom of association may be filed by employers' and workers' organisations against governments that are members of the ILO even when they have not ratified the relevant Conventions.[25]

One of the outcomes of the supervisory and complaints procedures is assistance from the International Labour Office, the ILO secretariat. This assistance is most often directed toward the implementation of standards, whether as a consequence of ratification and supervisory

---

22 ILO, *Report of the Committee of Experts on the Application of Conventions and Recommendations*, Report III(1A) (2011) at para. 34, http://www.ilo.org/global/standards/WCMS_151490/lang--en/index. htm, accessed 15 February 2012 (emphasis removed).

23 Arts 24–34 of the ILO Constitution.

24 Arts 26–34 of the ILO Constitution.

25 ILO, 'Annex I: Special procedures for the examination in the International Labour Organization of complaints alleging violations of freedom of association' in *Freedom of Association: Digest of Decisions and Principles of the Freedom of Association Committee of the Governing Body of the ILO*, 5th edn (ILO, 2006) at 231, http://www.ilo.org/public/libdoc/ilo/2006/106B09_305_engl.pdf, accessed 15 February 2012. These complaints are examined by the Committee on Freedom of Association or the Fact-Finding and Conciliation Commission on Freedom of Association.

criticism or with a view to ratification. One example is the International Programme for the Prevention of Child Labour (IPEC), the ILO's largest technical assistance programme, which, together with other international organisations, has secured large reductions in child labour around the world.[26]

3.4 Declaration of Fundamental Principles and Rights

As indicated earlier, the ILO for many years did not identify itself as a human rights organisation. In 1998, the ILO moved firmly into the human rights arena when it adopted the Declaration of Fundamental Principles and Rights at Work, to address the influence of globalisation and the lack of ratification by some member states of fundamental ILO standards.[27] The Declaration proclaims that all member states – even if they have not yet ratified the relevant Conventions – have an obligation by the very fact of their membership of the ILO to apply the following basic principles arising from the ILO Constitution:

(i)   freedom of association and the effective recognition of the right to collective bargaining;
(ii)   the effective abolition of child labour;
(iii)   the elimination of all forms of forced or compulsory labour; and
(iv)   the elimination of discrimination in respect of employment and occupation.

These principles were selected for two reasons: first, because they had already been designated as targets for ratification and implementation during the World Summit for Social Development (Copenhagen, 1995) and, second, because they were considered by the ILO to be 'enabling standards' which if implemented would open the way to providing other protections. These principles have been codified in eight ILO Conventions, thereafter designated by the ILO as its core human rights instruments:

(i)   Freedom of Association and Protection of the Right to Organise, 1948 (No. 87);[28]
(ii)   Right to Organise and Collective Bargaining, 1949 (No. 98);[29]
(iii)   Forced Labour, 1930 (No. 29);[30]
(iv)   Abolition of Forced Labour, 1957 (No. 105);[31]
(v)   Equal Remuneration, 1951 (No. 100);[32]

---

26 See ILO, *The End of Child Labour: Within Reach, Global Report under the Follow-up to the ILO Declaration on Fundamental Principles and Rights at Work*, 2006; and ILO: Accelerating action against child labour, 2010 .
27 International Labour Conference (86th Session) Declaration on Fundamental Principles and Rights at Work (Geneva, 18 June 1988).
28 Convention (No. 87) concerning freedom of association and protection of the right to organise (adopted 9 July 1948, entered into force 4 July 1950) 68 UNTS 17.
29 Convention (No. 98) concerning the application of the principles of the right to organise and to bargain collectively, as modified by the Final Articles Revision Convention, 1961 (adopted 1 July 1949, entered into force 18 July 1951) 96 UNTS 257.
30 Convention (No. 29) concerning forced or compulsory labour, as modified by the Final Articles Revision Convention, 1946 (adopted 28 June 1930, entered into force 1 May 1932) 39 UNTS 55.
31 Convention (No. 105) concerning the abolition of forced labour (adopted 25 June 1957, entered into force 17 January 1959) 320 UNTS 291.
32 Convention (No. 100) concerning equal remuneration for men and women workers for work of equal value (adopted 29 June 1951, entered into force 23 May 1953) 165 UNTS 303.

(vi)   Discrimination (Employment and Occupation), 1958 (No. 111);[33]

(vii) Minimum Age, 1973 (No. 138); and[34]

(viii) Worst Forms of Child Labour, 1999 (No. 182).[35]

Under this Declaration, member states that have not ratified all of these core human rights instruments have to report annually to the ILO, stating what obstacles exist to their implementation.

    The Declaration is cast in a promotional rather than a supervisory vein, and does not result in findings against states in the same way that the regular supervisory procedure for ratified Conventions does. It was intended from the beginning to promote the ratification and application of these Conventions, and in this it has been very successful, with ratifications of all of them approaching universality.[36]

    In 2008, this Declaration was supplemented by the Declaration on Social Justice for a Fair Globalisation, which added the basic principles of governance of labour markets to the ILO's highest priorities, representing another aspect of importance to human rights.[37]

4 Looking ahead

The ILO has consistently been one of the most inventive and flexible of the international organisations. It has reinvented itself since the end of the Cold War to tackle the challenges of a globalised world that seems to be in a state of perpetual financial crisis. It continues to adopt standards on outstanding questions not adequately covered by international regulation (e.g., the HIV and AIDS Recommendation, 2010 (No. 200) and the Domestic Workers Convention, 2011 (No. 189)).[38]

    One of the major challenges for the ILO, as for the entire international system, is migration for work. This is perhaps the greatest failure of the international human rights system, by the ILO, the UN and national and regional bodies. Virtually everyone agrees on what the rules ought to be, but the states to which such workers migrate, in particular, refuse to bind themselves to apply these rules. However, international migration will continue to grow and will continue to be vital to established economies to compensate for their ageing populations and shortfalls in social security funding.

    Another unsolved challenge is the informal economy, which contains as many as 90 per cent of workers in some countries. Workers cannot be protected if they are not effectively covered by law. This calls for a renewed emphasis on governance as an essential element of human rights protection and balanced development everywhere, in the face of continuing resistance by business to regulation.

33 N. 17.

34 N. 6.

35 N. 5.

36 The most highly ratified of these standards is Convention No. 29, with 175 ratifications by the beginning of 2012 out of the ILO's 183 members. The least well ratified of these standards is Convention No. 87, with 150 ratifications by the beginning of 2012, reflecting the continuing reluctance of many states to accept independent and potentially powerful trade unions within their borders. The other standards have 160 or more ratifications.

37 International Labour Conference (97th Session) Declaration on Social Justice for a Fair Globalization (Geneva, 10 June 2008).

38 ILO Recommendation R200: HIV and AIDS Recommendation (Recommendation concerning HIV and AIDS and the World of Work) (99th Conference Session, Geneva, 2 June 2010); Convention (No. 189) concerning decent work for domestic workers (adopted 16 June 2011) 50 ILM 699.

With respect to its internal governance, the ILO is unlikely to allow greater participation by non-occupational non-governmental organisations (NGOs). Not only do the employers' and workers' representatives want to preserve their pre-eminence, but it is also probably more effective if their ability to act inside the system is not compromised by less focused organisations. While this is not a prescription for the entire international system, where the still-limited participation of civil society has brought positive results, in this one organisation it seems wiser not to dilute NGO participation.

Overall, the ILO should continue to pursue the goal of 'Decent Work' proclaimed at the beginning of the century – that is, increasing employment while ensuring that employment is created in conditions of dignity, adequate income and respect for human rights.

5 Concluding comments on the ILO and human rights

The ILO has significant differences from other parts of the international human rights system, making it both more and less effective. What is clear, however, is that leaving the ILO – and, more broadly, labour rights – out of a human rights approach will leave an incomplete picture and may unnecessarily prevent both the provision of relevant information to, and the taking of action by, the ILO.

5.1 Tripartism

One of the greatest strengths of the ILO is the tripartite system – the fact that non-governmental elements from every state, and even international occupational NGOs, can intervene and have a right of standing in ILO processes is unheard of in any other inter-governmental organisation. Workers' and employers' organisations are members of the ILO Governing Body and of delegations to the International Labour Conference, and participate directly in standard-setting and in complaints and other supervisory mechanisms. By comparison, the UN and other intergovernmental organisations allow NGOs to submit information, to be heard and to take part in standard-setting – but in the corridors, with no right to make proposals directly in their own names or to vote.

However, the ILO accords these rights only to occupational organisations (i.e. trade unions and employers' organisations). These bodies do not necessarily see themselves as human rights bodies and do not always address the broader human rights spectrum. In addition, employers' organisations often (although, rather surprisingly, not always) take a more conservative view of rights than do workers' organisations. NGOs with a broader human rights mandate, such as Human Rights Watch or Amnesty International, and national human rights organisations, only have the same access to the ILO standard-setting and supervisory machinery as they have in the UN, normally through trade unions.[39]

---

39 This has happened most frequently with indigenous NGOs who get access to meetings concerning the supervision of the ILO's two Conventions on Indigenous and Tribal Peoples (Convention No. 107 (n. 14) and Convention (No. 169) concerning Indigenous and Tribal Peoples in Independent Countries (adopted 27 June 1989, entered into force 5 September 1991) 1650 UNTS 383). The ILO's adoption of these two instruments, the only international Conventions to specifically address the rights of indigenous and tribal peoples (although, of course, other human rights instruments also apply to them) reflects the fact that many broader human rights themes are addressed by ILO standards beyond those specifically designated as human rights standards.

Therefore, even though trade unions form the largest NGO system in the world, they normally do not address broader human rights questions.[40] This has two results. It means that those NGOs who consider themselves to be human rights defenders often neglect the informational and procedural advantages of working with trade unions and the labour-related aspects of situations with which they are concerned. It also means that the ILO itself is often presented with a narrower analysis of human rights views and problems than would be desirable. It is unlikely that this will change in the near future, although the ILO is building more practical links with national NGOs operating on the ground by entering into partnerships for carrying out technical assistance.

5.2 Governance structures

When the ILO was established, in 1919, the world was resolutely nation–state oriented, and workers' and employers' organisations normally worked within national boundaries only. Today, governments in many regions have delegated some of their traditional functions to international and regional bodies. The European Union is the most prominent example, with legislative functions in many areas having been transferred to the EU, to the effect that its member states are often even unable to ratify international conventions until the EU has adopted relevant legislative instruments and consistency is assured among its members.

At the same time, globalisation has rendered business multinational. National boundaries are therefore no longer an obstacle to those business patterns that often challenge the governance structures that previously held in check the actions of purely national business entities. National employers' organisations, and even national governments, are unable to address concerns regarding the operations of multinational organisations.[41] Trade unions have gone the other direction, losing both membership and influence, as they have not yet made the successful transition to confronting and bargaining with multinational enterprises and multi-government entities. Another factor is the growth of the 'informal economy' in many parts of the world, leaving many businesses and workers essentially beyond the reach of national law.

Thus the ILO's governance structures have to some extent been undermined or, in any case, no longer fit the original state-based model. The UN and other multilateral organisations suffer from the same problems, of course. Trade unions and employers' organisations are less representative than they once were. However, they remain more representative than other NGOs whose mandate may be based on the UDHR or other UN human rights instruments but who are, unlike elected workers' and employers' organisations, self-appointed.

---

40 It should, however, be noted that many problems related to the right to freedom of association, prohibition on forced labour, prohibition on child labour and prohibition on discrimination in the workplace, to take a few prominent examples, are an important part of the wider human rights picture, and often are the best entry points into addressing these problems.

41 The ILO has adopted a Tripartite Declaration, which addresses these questions in a non-supervisory context (International Labour Conference (204th session) Tripartite Declaration of Principles concerning Multinational Enterprises and Social Policy (Geneva, 16 November 1977), as amended at the International Labour Conference (279th session) (Geneva, November 2000) and the International Labour Conference (295th Session) (Geneva, March 2006)). It has worked with and supported the work of Professor John Ruggie, Special Representative of the UN Secretary-General on human rights and transnational corporations and other business enterprises. As Professor Ruggie has brilliantly illustrated, international law remains largely inadequate to address human rights concerns related to multinational corporations.

5.3 Supervision

The ILO supervises treaty obligations on a more direct and detailed basis than any other international organisation, albeit on a narrower range of issues. The ILO also has the advantage of the sheer number and detail of its treaties and obligations. The nine core human rights instruments of the UN have truly broad coverage and some of them approach universal ratification. However, other UN instruments, even basic ones such as the Slavery Convention adopted by the League of Nations and the Supplementary Convention on the Abolition of Slavery adopted by the UN, are not directly supervised by any organ of the UN.[42] ILO Conventions, on the other hand, are far more detailed, though usually much narrower in scope, than UN instruments, and there are more of them on any given topic. Each of the nearly 7,800 ratifications of the 189 ILO Conventions are subject to detailed reporting and examination.

In another respect, as well, the ILO machinery is far more detailed and attentive to law than the UN. UN Conventions are subject to supervision only if provided for in the relevant treaty (although this has now been provided for in all of the nine core UN human rights instruments). By comparison, all ILO Conventions are subject to supervision. In addition, ILO supervision is carried out by a single unified machinery consisting of the Committee of Experts, constitutional complaints procedures and review by the International Labour Conference, yielding a unity of view not always available in other international organisations.

This review is not intended to say that the ILO is a more effective human rights organisation than the UN. The two have different, though complementary, missions and capacities. The ILO's supervisory effectiveness and the detail of its instruments could only have been achieved within the limited arena of labour-related rights, with the participation of directly interested parties. A broad based human rights organisation could not have achieved the necessary consensus for the ILO's model of tripartism, strict supervision and detailed instruments. Indeed, the basic ILO adoption and supervisory structures were established between 1919 and 1926, when intergovernmental organisations were very much at an experimental stage and their management concentrated in a much smaller group of states than they are today. In many ways, the ILO's very isolation from the human rights debates that have dominated the UN allowed it to develop detailed human rights protections in a far less ideologically charged arena. The divisions with respect to human rights matters among governments during the Cold War and in the era of liberation movements were overcome within the ILO by the essential unity on most issues of its workers' and employers' organisations, which hold half the ILO's voting power.[43]

The ILO and international labour law are thus indispensable to a fully developed view of human rights, while remaining to a certain extent outside general discussions on international human rights. The absence of the ILO for many years from the academic and political consideration of human rights has left it to deal with different types of issues, which can

---

42 Slavery Convention (adopted 25 September 1926, entered into force 9 March 1927) 60 LNTS 254; Supplementary Convention on the Abolition of Slavery, the Slave Trade, and Institutions and Practices Similar to Slavery (adopted 7 September 1956, entered into force 30 April 1957) 266 UNTS 3.

43 The end of the Cold War has resulted in more dissension between workers and employers on some issues, particularly the right to freedom of association, but these differences remain far smaller than those between East and West during the Cold War.

be subject to both more and less intensive discussion depending on time and other matters. While the ILO influenced the foundation of many of the human rights concepts adopted by the UN and other organisations, some governments remain suspicious of the ILO on human rights issues precisely because it cannot be controlled by the political considerations applying to other systems.

Select bibliography

ILO, *Rules of the Game: A Brief Introduction to International Labour Standards*, revised edn (ILO, 2009) http://www.ilo.org.

Reports of the Committee of Experts on the Application of Conventions and Recommendations, published annually as Report III(1A) to the International Labour Conference, http://www.ilo.org.

G. Rodgers, E. Lee, L. Swepston and J. van Daele, *The ILO and the Quest for Social Justice, 1919–2009* (ILO, 2009).

L. Swepston, 'The International Labour Organisation and Human Rights', in C. Kraude and M. Scheinen (eds), *International Protection of Human Rights: A Textbook* (Institute for Human Rights, Abo Akademi University, 2009).

21

The International Court of Justice and human rights

Awn Shawkat Al-Khasawneh*

1 Introduction

It is commonplace to state that, in a formal sense, in the field of international human rights law, the role of the International Court of Justice is restricted. This is due not only to the lack of individual *locus standi* but also to a relatively low number of jurisdictional clauses in human rights instruments, the application of which may be further limited through reservations[1] or procedural preconditions for recourse to the Court (such as prior recourse to negotiation or other dispute-settlement procedures).[2]

Nonetheless, while the ICJ clearly is not a human rights court, it is the principal judicial organ of the United Nations and must, as such, fulfil its role in accordance with the objectives of the United Nations Charter, including by promoting and protecting human rights. As a court of general subject-matter jurisdiction, the ICJ has the competence to address any question of international law brought to it by states and, in certain circumstances, international organisations. As the Court itself confirmed, '[t]he mere fact that it is not the rights of States which are in issue in the proceedings cannot suffice to deprive the Court of a competence expressly conferred on it by its Statute.'[3]

Indeed, since the beginning of the ICJ's work, its contentious and advisory proceedings have occasionally touched upon the rights of individuals under international law and its decisions today routinely address a wide range of human rights issues. The Court is thus steadily affirming its place on the list of international judicial bodies concerned with human rights,

---

* I would like to acknowledge the great help and contribution of my associate legal officer Dominika Švarc. Without her assistance the completion of this text would not have been possible.

1 See, for example, *Armed Activities on the Territory of the Congo (New Application: 2002) (Democratic Republic of the Congo v Rwanda) (Jurisdiction and Admissibility)* [2006] ICJ Rep. 31–33, paras 64–70 and 34–35, paras 74–79.

2 Ibid. pp. 38–41, paras 87–93; see also *Application of the International Convention on the Elimination of All Forms of Racial Discrimination (Georgia v Russian Federation) (Preliminary Objections)* [2011] ICJ Rep. 48–65, paras 122–84.

3 *Application for Review of Judgement No. 158 of the United Nations Administrative Tribunal (Advisory Opinion)* [1973] ICJ Rep. 171–72, para. 14.

and has made an important contribution to the development and coherence of substantive human rights law as well as its structural framework, and to the strengthening of mechanisms for its enforcement.

This chapter examines the extent of this contribution in three selected areas. The first section considers the Court's contribution to clarifying and strengthening the normative status of human rights norms in general international law, particularly through its discourse of *erga omnes* obligations and norms of *jus cogens*. The second section examines the Court's approach to the interpretation of human rights treaties and its position regarding the scope of application of human rights treaties. Finally, the third section looks at the role of the Court in the enforcement of human rights, including through its interaction with other judicial bodies and other mechanisms concerned with human rights.

2 The normative status of human rights norms

2.1 'Elementary considerations of humanity'

The Court has made many valuable pronouncements on the status of human rights norms. In its very first contentious case, at a time when human rights law was still in a very rudimentary form, the Court underscored the importance of 'general and well-recognized principle' of 'elementary considerations of humanity'.[4]

2.2 The Universal Declaration of Human Rights and the UN Charter

The Court has also contributed to the debates on the legally binding nature *vel non* of the human rights clauses of the UN Charter and the Universal Declaration of Human Rights (UDHR). The clearest pronouncement as to the binding nature of the human rights clauses of the UN Charter was made in the *Namibia* advisory opinion, where the Court held that 'denial of fundamental human rights is a flagrant violation of the purposes and principles of the [UN] Charter'.[5]

Although the Court has not explicitly commented upon the binding nature of the UDHR, in the *Tehran Hostages* case, the Court apparently considered the UDHR as having sufficient legal status to justify its invocation by the Court (*proprio motu*) in the context of the state's obligations under general international law. In establishing the responsibility of Iran towards the United States for continued detention of the US diplomatic and consular staff in Tehran, the Court stated that:

> Wrongfully to deprive human beings of their freedom and to subject them to physical constraint in conditions of hardship is in itself manifestly incompatible with the principles of the [UN Charter], as well as with the fundamental principles enunciated in the [UDHR].[6]

---

4 *Corfu Channel (United Kingdom of Great Britain and Northern Ireland v Albania) (Merits)* [1949] ICJ Rep. 22; see also, subsequently, *Military and Paramilitary Activities in and against Nicaragua (Nicaragua v United States of America) (Merits)* [1986] ICJ Rep. 112, para. 215 and pp. 113–14, para. 218; *Legality of the Threat or Use of Nuclear Weapons (Advisory Opinion)* [1996] ICJ Rep. (I) 257, para. 79; *Jurisdictional Immunities of the State (Germany v Italy)* (Judgment) [2012] ICJ Rep. 22, para. 52.

5 *Legal Consequences for States of the Continued Presence of South Africa in Namibia (South West Africa) notwithstanding Security Council Resolution 276 (Advisory Opinion)* [1970] ICJ Rep. 57, para. 131.

6 *United States Diplomatic and Consular Staff in Tehran (United States of America v Iran),* (Judgment) [1980] ICJ Rep. 42, para. 91.

2.3 Customary status of human rights norms

As early as 1951, the Court noted that the principles underlying the Genocide Convention are part of customary international law, 'recognized by civilized nations as binding on States, even without any conventional obligation', whilst the Convention itself confirms and endorses 'the most elementary principles of morality'.[7] Most recently, in the *Diallo* case, the Court similarly confirmed, in an *obiter dictum*, the customary nature of the prohibition of inhuman or degrading treatment.[8]

2.4 Obligations erga omnes

The Court has also introduced and importantly contributed to the evolution of the concept of *erga omnes* obligations. In the famous *obiter dictum* in the *Barcelona Traction* case, it recognised that the principles and rules of international law concerning the basic human rights engender obligations *erga omnes*, which are owed to 'the international community as a whole', as opposed to the obligations 'arising vis-à-vis another State in the field of diplomatic protection'.[9] These obligations are 'by their very nature . . . the concern of all States' and may '[i]n view of the importance of the rights involved' be invoked by any state.[10]

The Court has so far explicitly confirmed that these obligations derive from, inter alia, 'the outlawing of acts of aggression, and of genocide, as also from the principles and rules concerning the basic rights of the human person, including protection from slavery and racial discrimination'[11] as well as from the right to self-determination[12] and certain fundamental principles of international humanitarian law.[13]

Although the Court itself has not yet ruled on an *'erga omnes'* case,[14] its recognition of the concept has had a significant impact on the strengthening of the normative position of

7   *Reservations to the Convention on the Prevention and Punishment of the Crime of Genocide (Advisory Opinion)* [1951] ICJ Rep. 23; see also *Application of the Convention on the Prevention and Punishment of the Crime of Genocide (Bosnia and Herzegovina v Yugoslavia) (Preliminary Objections)* [1996] ICJ Rep. (II) 615–16, para. 31; *Armed Activities (New Application: 2002), Jurisdiction and Admissibility* (n. 1) pp. 31–32, para. 64; *Application of the Convention on the Prevention and Punishment of the Crime of Genocide (Bosnia and Herzegovina v Serbia and Montenegro (Judgment)* [2007] ICJ Rep. (I) 110–11, para. 161.

8   *Ahmadou Sadio Diallo (Republic of Guinea v Democratic Republic of the Congo)* (Judgment) [2010] ICJ Rep. 30–31, para. 87.

9   *Barcelona Traction, Light and Power Company, Limited (Belgium v Spain) (Second Phase – Judgment)* [1970] ICJ Rep. 32, paras 33–34.

10 Ibid.

11 Ibid p. 32, para. 34. The Court subsequently affirmed its adherence to the concept of *erga omnes* in *East Timor (Portugal v Australia) (Judgment)* [1995] ICJ Rep. 102, para. 29; *Genocide Case, Preliminary Objections* (n. 7) pp. 615–16, para. 31; *Armed Activities (New Application: 2002), Jurisdiction and Admissibility* (n. 1) pp. 31–32, para. 64 and pp. 51–52, para. 125; *Genocide Case, Merits* (n. 7) pp. 104, 110–11 and 120, paras 147, 161 and 185; *Legal Consequences of the Construction of a Wall in the Occupied Palestinian Territory (Advisory Opinion)* [2004] ICJ Rep. (I) 199, paras 155–57.

12 *East Timor* (n. 11) p. 102, para. 29; *The Wall* (n. 11) p. 199, paras 155–56.

13 *The Wall* (n. 11) p. 199, paras 155–57.

14 While the Court's cases occasionally relate to questions of 'public interest' (such as the *Nuclear Tests* cases, or the pending proceedings between Belgium and Senegal), the applications to the Court are still typically formulated in terms of the applicant's special interest in the subject-matter before the Court; see C.J. Tams and A. Tzanakopoulos, 'Barcelona Traction at 40: the ICJ as an Agent of Legal Development' (2010) 23 (4) *Leiden Journal of International Law* 781 at 792–93.

international human rights in the contemporary legal order.[15] The Court's finding in *Barcelona Traction* was expressly relied upon by the Inter-American Court of Human Rights (IACtHR) in its advisory opinion interpreting Article 64 of the American Convention on Human Rights (ACHR), where the Court confirmed that the obligation to respect certain basic human rights is *erga omnes*[16] and by the Trial Chamber in the International Criminal Tribunal for Former Yugoslavia (ICTY) in *Kupreškić*, when considering the absolute and *erga omnes* nature of the fundamental rules of international humanitarian law.[17]

2.5 Jus cogens

Whilst the Court has been at the forefront of the development of the concept of *erga omnes* obligations, it has long been reluctant to pronounce on the concept of *jus cogens* despite having had several opportunities to do so.[18] Although the notion has been invoked by several judges in individual opinions since the times of the Permanent Court of International Justice,[19] and by other international courts and tribunals since the 1990s,[20] the Court itself has avoided even utilising the term '*jus cogens*'. Notably, in the *Nuclear Weapons* advisory opinion, the Court referred to the fundamental rules of international humanitarian law as 'intransgressible principles of international customary law';[21] however, although the Court noted that 'it has been maintained in these proceedings that these principles and rules of humanitarian law are part of *jus cogens* as defined in Article 53 of the Vienna Convention on the Law of Treaties', it avoided any pronouncement on the question as it did not consider it to be a part of the request before it.[22]

---

15 For a discussion of the effect of the *Barcelona Traction* case on the evolution of the *erga omnes* concept, see, Tams and Tzanakopoulos (n. 14) at 791–94.

16 *Interpretation of the American Declaration of the Rights and Duties of Man Within the Framework of Article 64 of the American Convention on Human Rights*, IACtHR, OC-10/89 (1989) (Advisory Opinion), para. 38.

17 *Prosecutor v Kupreškić (Judgment)* ICTY-95-16-T (14 January 2000), para. 519.

18 See, e.g., *North Sea Continental Shelf (Federal Republic of Germany/Denmark; Federal Republic of Germany/Netherlands) (Judgment)* [1969] ICJ Rep. 42, para. 72; *Nuclear Weapons* (n. 4), pp. 257–58, paras. 79–83; *Arrest Warrant of 11 April 2000 (Democratic Republic of the Congo v Belgium) (Judgment)* [2002] ICJ Rep. 23–26.

19 One of the earliest utilisations of the term *jus cogens* was made by Judge Schücking in his Separate Opinion in the *Oscar Chinn* case decided by the PCIJ in 1934 *(Oscar Chinn (Britain v Belgium) (Judgment)* PCIJ Rep. (1934) Series A/B No. 17, p. 149). In the jurisprudence of the ICJ, see, among many examples, the *South West Africa* cases *(Ethiopia v South Africa; Liberia v South Africa) (Second Phase – Judgment)* [1966] ICJ Rep. 1966, Dissenting Opinion of Judge Tanaka, p. 298; *Barcelona Traction* (n. 9) Separate Opinion of Judge Ammoun, pp. 304 and 311–12; *Arrest Warrant* (n. 18) Dissenting Opinion of Judge Al-Khasawneh, p. 98, para. 7; *Questions Relating to the Obligation to Prosecute or Extradite (Belgium v Senegal) (Provisional Measures Order)* [2009] ICJ Rep. 2009, Dissenting Opinion of Judge Cançado Trindade, p. 188, para. 66; *Accordance with International Law of the Unilateral Declaration of Independence in Respect of Kosovo (Advisory Opinion)* [2010], Separate Opinion of Judge Cançado Trindade, p. 64, para. 215; *Diallo, Merits* (n. 8) Separate Opinion of Judge Cançado Trindade, pp. 42–43, para. 163; *Jurisdictional Immunities* (n. 4) Dissenting Opinion of Judge Cançado Trindade.

20 *Prosecutor v Furundzija* (Judgment) ICTY-95-17/1-T (10 December 1998), paras. 144, 153–56; *Al-Adsani v United Kingdom* App. No. 35763/97 (ECtHR, Judgment of 21 November 2001), paras. 57–65.

21 *Nuclear Weapons* (n. 4) p. 257, para. 79. The ICTY expressly invoked this statement of the Court in, inter alia, *Prosecutor v Hadžihasanović et al (Decision on Joint Defence Interlocutory Appeal of Trial Chamber Decision on Rule 98bis Motions for Acquittal)* ICTY-01-47-AR73.3 (11 March 2005), para. 28.

22 *Nuclear Weapons* (n. 4) p. 258, para. 83.

At long last, the Court expressly acknowledged the existence of *jus cogens* norms in positive international law in the *Armed Activities (New Application: 2002)* case, where it placed the prohibition of genocide into that category of norms.[23] While the Court has so far refrained from defining the material scope of *jus cogens* in a comprehensive manner, it did provide some clarity in this regard in its recent judgment in the *Jurisdictional Immunities* case. In the context of examining the relationship between the norms of *jus cogens* and the jurisdictional immunity of states in foreign courts, the Court '[assumed] for this purpose that the rules of the law of armed conflict which prohibit the murder of civilians in occupied territory, the deportation of civilian inhabitants to slave labour and the deportation of prisoners of war to slave labour are rules of *jus cogens*',[24] that is to say rules 'from which no derogation is permitted'.[25] In the same judgment, the Court also affirmed that whilst its earlier judgment in the *Arrest Warrant* case made no express reference to *'jus cogens'* in respect of the violations of rules of international human rights and humanitarian law amounting to crimes against humanity and war crimes, these rules 'undoubtedly possess[ed] the character of *jus cogens*'.[26]

Some judges, in their individual opinions, have considered that the category of *jus cogens* norms includes: (a) the norms concerning human rights protection in general;[27] (b) the right to self-determination;[28] (c) the prohibition of torture;[29] (d) the prohibition of ethnic cleansing, summary or extra-legal executions, and forced disappearance of persons;[30] (e) the principle of equality and non-discrimination;[31] and (f) the 'principles of humanity' and 'dictates of the public conscience' invoked by the Martens clause.[32]

2.6 The limits of the concepts of erga omnes and jus cogens

The Court has consistently taken the view that the substantive rules of *erga omnes* and the rules of *jus cogens* have no effect on the procedural rules determining the scope and the extent of the Court's jurisdiction and the conditions for the exercise of that jurisdiction. Thus, in the *East Timor* case, the Court, considering that 'the *erga omnes* character of a norm and the rule of consent to jurisdiction are two different things', held that 'when its judgment would imply an evaluation of the lawfulness of the conduct of another State which is not a party to the case' it could not act 'even if the right in question [was] a right *erga omnes*'.[33]

---

23 *Armed Activities (New Application: 2002), Jurisdiction and Admissibility* (n. 1) pp. 31–32, para. 64; see also, subsequently, *Genocide Case, Merits* (n. 7) pp. 110–11, para. 161.
24 *Jurisdictional Immunities, Merits* (n. 4) p. 38, para. 93. While in the *Arrest Warrant case*, the Court itself avoided using the term *'jus cogens'*, Judge ad hoc van den Wyngaert and I expressly invoked the *jus cogens* nature of the crimes against humanity and war crimes in our respective dissenting opinions (*Arrest Warrant* (n. 18) Dissenting opinion of Judge Al-Khasawneh, p. 98, para. 7 and Dissenting Opinion of Judge ad hoc van den Wyngaert, pp. 155–56, para. 28.
25 *Jurisdictional Immunities, Merits* (n. 4) pp. 38–39, para. 95.
26 Ibid.
27 *South West Africa* (n. 19) Dissenting Opinion of Judge Tanaka, p. 298.
28 *Namibia* (n. 5) Separate Opinion of Vice-President Ammoun, pp. 89–90.
29 *Questions relating to the Obligation to Prosecute or Extradite* (n. 19) Dissenting Opinion of Judge Cançado Trindade, p. 188, para. 66; *Kosovo* (n. 19) Separate Opinion of Judge Cançado Trindade, p. 64, para. 215.
30 *Kosovo* (n. 19).
31 *Diallo, Merits* (n. 8) Separate Opinion of Judge Cançado Trindade, pp. 42–43, para. 163; *Jurisdictional Immunities of the State (Germany v Italy) (Provisional Measures Order)* [2010], Dissenting Opinion of Judge Cançado Trindade, pp. 37–38, paras. 134–35.
32 *Jurisdictional Immunities, Provisional Measures* (n. 4) p. 39, para. 139.
33 *East Timor* (n. 11) p. 102, para. 29.

In more general terms, the Court affirmed, in the *Armed Activities* case, that 'the mere fact that rights and obligations *erga omnes* or peremptory norms of general international law *(jus cogens)* are at issue in a dispute cannot in itself constitute an exception to the principle that its jurisdiction always depends on the consent of the parties'.[34] According to the Court, no peremptory norm requires states to consent to jurisdiction where the compliance with a peremptory norm is at stake.[35]

A similar line of reasoning based on the dichotomy between the substantive rules and the procedural rules was adopted in a series of cases dealing with the question of state immunity.

In the *Arrest Warrant* case, the Court held that incumbent Foreign Ministers (and by implication other high-level state officials) enjoy absolute immunity from criminal jurisdiction in a foreign state, even when charged with a war crime or a crime against humanity,[36] which, as the Court affirmed in the *Jurisdictional Immunities* case, undoubtedly possessed the character of *jus cogens*.[37] In a much-criticised[38] *obiter dictum*, the Court affirmed that this immunity continues to apply to Foreign Ministers even after they have left the office, in respect of those acts committed in an 'official capacity' as opposed to those committed 'in a private capacity'.[39] Several judges, including myself, have rejected the Court's argument that 'immunity does not mean impunity' and advocated for the denial of immunity for core international crimes in pursuit of greater personal accountability and the fight against impunity.[40]

Similarly, in the *Jurisdictional Immunities* case, the Court concluded that the *jus cogens* status of the substantive rule which the state is alleged to have violated does not deprive it of its customary law entitlement to immunity from the jurisdiction of the courts of other states.[41] In other words, even though the application of a particular jurisdictional rule might operate so as to render unavailable certain procedural means by which a *jus cogens* rule could be enforced, this does not alter the applicability of the rules pertaining to the international

---

34 *Armed Activities (New Application: 2002), Jurisdiction and Admissibility* (n. 1) pp. 51–52, para. 125; see also pp. 31–32, para. 64 and p. 35, para. 78; *Armed Activities on the Territory of the Congo (New Application: 2002) (Democratic Republic of the Congo v Rwanda)* (Provisional Measures Order) [2002] ICJ Rep. 245–46, para. 71.

35 *Armed Activities (New Application: 2002), Jurisdiction and Admissibility* (n. 1) p. 33, para. 69; see also p. 35, para. 78.

36 *Arrest Warrant* (n. 18) p. 24, para. 58.

37 *Jurisdictional Immunitites of the State, Merits* (n. 4) pp. 38–39, para. 95, referring to the *Arrest Warrant* (n. 18) p. 24, para. 58.

38 See, among others, A. Cassese, 'When May Senior State Officials Be Tried for International Crimes? Some Comments on the *Congo v Belgium* Case' (2002) 13 *European Journal of International Law* 4 853–75.

39 *Arrest Warrant* (n. 18) pp. 25–26, para. 61.

40 *Arrest Warrant* (n. 18) Dissenting Opinion of Judge Al-Khasawneh, p. 98, para. 7; see also Dissenting Opinion of Judge ad hoc van den Wyngaert, pp. 152–56, paras. 24–28. For some doctrinal discussions on this matter see, e.g., A. Orakhelashvili, 'State Immunity and International Public Order Revisited' (2006) 49 *German Yearbook of International Law* 327–65, particularly at 353–63; L.M. Caplan, 'State Immunity, Human Rights, and *Jus Cogens*: A Critique of the Normative Hierarchy Theory' (2003) 97 *American Journal of International Law* 4, 741–81.

41 Whilst the Court emphasised that its holding in the *Jurisdictional Immunities* case relates only to the immunity of the state itself and not to the separate issue of the immunity of state officials in criminal proceedings in foreign courts (*Jurisdictional Immunities, Merits* (n. 4) p. 37, para. 91), the *Arrest Warrant* decision nonetheless confirms that the Court adopts the same approach at least in respect of the individual criminal responsibility of high-level state officials.

responsibility of the state or its officials for any violation.[42] In supporting this conclusion, the Court referred to the relevant domestic and international law and practice, inter alia, to the decisions of the European Court of Human Rights in *Al-Adsani v United Kingdom* and *Kalogeropoulou and others v Greece and Germany*, which likewise considered that the *jus cogens* status of a norm does not displace the state's jurisdictional immunity in foreign courts.[43]

By contrast, in his eloquent dissenting opinion, Judge Cançado Trindade emphasised the need to prevent impunity in cases of perpetration of international crimes and considered that the gravity of the breaches of human rights and of international humanitarian law removes any bar to jurisdiction – there should be no immunity in cases of international crimes, which belong to the domain of *jus cogens*.[44]

3 Interpretation and application of human rights treaties

3.1 Interpretation of human rights treaties

3.1.1 General rules of interpretation

The Court's case law confirms that the interpretation of human rights treaties is guided by the rules and methods of interpretation under general international law, as laid down in Articles 31–33 of the Vienna Convention on the Law of Treaties[45] (VCLT).[46]

The special emphasis on the 'object and purpose', reflected in Article 31 of the VCLT, is of particular relevance in the context of human rights treaties. In its advisory opinion on the *Reservations to the Genocide Convention*, the ICJ held that the object and purpose of the Convention, which was 'manifestly adopted for a purely humanitarian and civilizing purpose', would be the crucial criterion limiting both the freedom of states to make reservations to the Convention as well as their freedom to object to them.[47] The Court also noted that 'in this type of treaty, the contracting states do not have their own interests; they only have an overall common interest: to attain the purposes that are the *raison d'etre* of the Convention.'[48]

This approach has been endorsed also by the European Court of Human Rights (ECtHR) and the Inter-American Court of Human Rights (IACtHR), which have repeatedly

---

42 *Jurisdictional Immunities, Merits* (n. 4) pp. 38–39, paras 93–95 and p. 40, para. 100; see also, in a somewhat different context of the immunity of state officials from criminal jurisdiction of foreign courts, *Arrest Warrant* (n. 18) p. 25, para. 60; *Certain Questions of Mutual Assistance in Criminal Matters (Djibouti v France) (Judgment)* [2008] ICJ Rep. 244, para. 196.

43 *Jurisdictional Immunities, Merits* (n. 4) p. 37, para. 90, citing *Al-Adsani v United Kingdom* (n. 20) para. 61 and *Kalogeropoulou and others v Greece and Germany*, App. No. 59021/00 (ECtHR, Decision of 12 December 2002).

44 *Jurisdictional Immunities, Merits* (n. 4) Dissenting Opinion of Judge Cançado Trindade.

45 Vienna Convetion on the Law of Treaties (1969) 1155 UNTS 331.

46 *Genocide Case, Merits* (n. 7) pp. 109–10, para. 160; *The Wall* (n. 11) p. 174, para. 94; *Avena and Other Mexican Nationals (Mexico v United States of America) (Judgment)* [2004] ICJ Rep. (I) 48, para. 83; *LaGrand (Germany v United States of America) (Judgment)* [2001] ICJ Rep. 501, para. 99.

47 *Reservations to the Genocide Convention* (n. 7) pp. 23–24.

48 Ibid. p. 23. This statement was explicitly relied upon by the IACtHR when noting the unique character of human rights treaties in the case *Baena Ricardo et al. (270 workers) v Panama*, IACtHR, Ser. C No. 104, (2003) (Competence), para. 97.

emphasised that the reference to the object and purpose of a treaty assumes a particular importance in the interpretation of human rights treaties establishing obligations aimed at protection of human rights, and not subjective and reciprocal rights for states parties.[49]

3.1.2 Dynamic interpretation

Although the Court has not altogether rejected the intertemporal principle of interpretation of treaties, which emphasises the intention of the drafters,[50] the Court has normally followed the evolutionary (dynamic) approach to interpretation in respect of treaties directly or indirectly concerning human rights.[51] As confirmed in the *Namibia* advisory opinion, a treaty should be interpreted 'within the framework of the entire legal system prevailing at the time of the interpretation'.[52] Both the IACtHR and the ECtHR have expressly relied upon this finding of the Court in their observations that evolutionary interpretation is particularly relevant in respect of human rights treaties.[53]

In its most recent advisory opinion on *International Fund for Agricultural Development*, the Court referred to the various comments of the United Nations Human Rights Committee (HRC) on the principle of equality before the courts and tribunals articulated in Article 14, paragraph 1, of the International Covenant on Civil and Political Rights (ICCPR) as reflective of the normative development of the principle of equality in judicial proceedings, and concluded, on this basis, that this principle 'must now be understood as including access on an equal basis to available appellate or similar remedies unless an exception can be justified on objective and reasonable grounds'.[54]

3.1.3 Coherence of interpretation

In an important passage in the recent *Diallo* case, the Court attributed considerable weight to the interpretative jurisprudence of other jurisdictions in the field of human rights law. Finding support for its own interpretation of the ICCPR provision concerning the prohibition of arbitrary expulsion of aliens in the jurisprudence of the HRC, the Court explained:

> Although the Court is in no way obliged, in the exercise of its judicial functions, to model its own interpretation of the Covenant on that of the Committee, it believes that it should ascribe great weight to the interpretation adopted by this independent body that was established specifically to supervise the application of that treaty. The point here is

---

49 *Restrictions to the Death Penalty (Arts. 4(2) and 4(4) of the American Convention on Human Rights)*, IACtHR, Ser. A No. 3, OC-3/83 (1983) (Advisory Opinion), para. 50; *Soering v United Kingdom* App. No. 14038/88 (ECtHR, Judgment of 7 July 1989), para. 87; *Caesar v Trinidad and Tobago*, IACtHR, Ser. C, No. 123 (2005) (Merits, Reparations and Costs), (Separate Opinion of Judge Cançado Trindade), pp. 1–2, paras. 4–14.

50 See, e.g., *South West Africa* (n. 19) para. 16.

51 Which is reflected to a considerable extent in Art. 31(3)(c) of the VCLT.

52 *Namibia* (n. 5) pp. 31–32, para. 53.

53 *Interpretation of the American Declaration of the Rights and Duties of Man* (n. 16) para. 37; *Tyrer v the United Kingdom* App. No. 5856/72 (ECtHR, Judgment of 25 April 1978), para. 31; *Loizidou v Turkey (Preliminary Objections)* App. No. 15318/89 (ECtHR, Judgment of 23 March 1995), para. 71.

54 *Judgment No. 2867 of the Administrative Tribunal of the International Labour Organization Upon a Complaint Filed against the International Fund for Agricultural Development (Advisory Opinion)* [2012], p. 16, para. 39 and p. 18, para. 44.

to achieve the necessary clarity and the essential consistency of international law, as well as legal security, to which both the individuals with guaranteed rights and the states obliged to comply with treaty obligations are entitled.[55]

Similarly, the Court observed that 'when [it] is called upon . . . to apply a regional instrument for the protection of human rights, it must take due account of the interpretation of that instrument adopted by the independent bodies which have been specifically created, if such has been the case, to monitor the sound application of the treaty in question'.[56] The Court cited the jurisprudence of the African Commission on Human and People's Rights (AComHPR) as supportive of its own interpretation of Article 12(4) of the African Charter on Human and Peoples' Rights (ACHPR), but did not stop there – it also found support in the jurisprudence of the ECtHR and the IACtHR interpreting similar provisions of the European Convention on Human Rights and the American Convention on Human Rights concerning the expulsion of aliens.[57]

3.2 Reservations to human rights treaties

As mentioned above, in its advisory opinion on *Reservations to the Genocide Convention*, the Court considered the 'object and purpose' test as crucial in determining the validity *vel non* of a specific reservation to the Genocide Convention.[58] The test was subsequently included in Article 19, paragraph 3, of the VCLT and is today widely considered as reflecting customary international law.

In *Reservations to the Genocide Convention*, the Court was not asked to pronounce on the compatibility of particular reservations to the Genocide Convention with its object and purpose, nor whether its finding as to the role of states in making and responding to reservations precluded it from making such pronouncement in the future. Yet, its opinion was long perceived as establishing that the final assessment of compatibility should be left to the states parties to the specific treaty themselves.[59] However, human rights courts and treaty-monitoring mechanisms have never regarded themselves as precluded by the Court's finding of 1951 from making their own assessments as to the compatibility of specific reservations to human rights treaties.[60]

Although this practice has been frequently seen as creating a schism in the jurisprudence on the law of treaties, the Court itself recently confirmed the opposite in the case concerning

---

55 *Diallo, Merits* (n. 8) p. 24, para. 66.
56 Ibid. p. 25, para. 67.
57 Ibid. para. 68.
58 *Reservations to the Genocide Convention* (n. 7) p. 24.
59 See, e.g., the interpretation of the Court's advisory opinion by the UNHRC, in its General Comment No. 24, 'Issues relating to reservations made upon ratification or accession to the Covenant or the Optional Protocols thereto, or in relation to declarations under article 41 of the Covenant' (52nd session) (1994) UN Doc. CCPR/C/21/Rev.I/Add.6, para. 16. See also the concerns expressed by Judge Cançado Trindade in *Caesar v Trinidad and Tobago* (n. 49) pp. 7–8, paras 21–27.
60 See, amongst other, *Belilos v Switzerland* App. No. 10328/83 (ECtHR, Judgment of 29 April 1988); *Loizidou v Turkey (Preliminary Objections)* (n. 53); *The Effect of Reservations on the Entry into Force of the American Convention on Human Rights (Arts. 74 and 75)*, IACtHR, Ser. A No. 2, OC-2/82, (1983) (Advisory Opinion); UNHRC, General Comment No. 24 (n. 59); UNHRC, *Rawle Kennedy v Trinidad and Tobago*, Communication No. 845 (1999) UN Doc. CCPR/C/67D/845/1999.

Armed Activities (New Application: 2002), where it made its own assessment as to the compatibility of Rwanda's reservation to Article IX of the Genocide Convention with the object and purpose of the Convention.[61] In a joint separate opinion, several judges explicitly endorsed the above-mentioned practice of the HRC and the regional human rights courts concerning their authority to pronounce on the compatibility of reservations.[62]

3.3 The scope of application of human rights treaties

The recent jurisprudence of the Court has contributed importantly to the contemporary discussions concerning the scope of application of human rights treaties, particularly as to whether they apply extraterritorially and whether they apply in situations of armed conflict and occupation.

3.3.1 Extraterritorial application

In its advisory opinion on *The Wall*, the Court noted that while the jurisdiction of a state is primarily territorial, 'it may sometimes be exercised outside the national territory'. It then held that the ICCPR, the International Covenant on Economic, Social and Cultural Rights (ICESCR) and the Convention on the Rights of the Child (CRC) were applicable within the Occupied Palestinian Territory (OPT).[63] As regards the ICCPR, the Court considered it 'natural', in light of the 'object and purpose' of the Covenant, that it was 'applicable in respect of acts done by a State in the exercise of its jurisdiction outside its own territory'.[64] It further pointed out that such interpretation was consistent with the practice of the HRC.[65] Similarly, in determining the applicability of the ICESCR to the OPT, the Court referred to the views of the Committee on Economic Social and Cultural Rights, that the state party's obligations under the Covenant apply to all territories and populations under its effective control.[66] In the *Armed Activities* case, the Court interpreted its finding in *The Wall* as more generally stating that 'international human rights instruments are applicable "in respect of acts done by a State in the exercise of its jurisdiction outside its own territory" '.[67]

Most recently, in its order indicating the provisional measures in the case between Georgia and the Russian Federation, the Court held that the International Convention on the Elimination of All Forms of Racial Discrimination (ICERD) contains 'no restriction of a general nature . . . relating to its territorial application' and that the provision of Articles 2 and 5, which were at issue, are generally applicable, 'like other provisions of instruments of that nature', to the actions of a state party outside its territory.[68]

---

61 *Armed Activities (New Application: 2002), Provisional Measures* (n. 34) pp. 245–46, para. 72; *Armed Activities (New Application: 2002), Jurisdiction and Admissibility* (n. 1) pp. 32, para. 67.

62 *Armed Activities (New Application: 2002), Jurisdiction and Admissibility* (n. 1) Joint Separate Opinion of Judges Higgins, Kooijmans, Elaraby, Owada and Simma, p. 69, paras 15–16.

63 *The Wall* (n. 11) pp. 178–81, paras 107–14.

64 Ibid. p. 180, paras 109 and 111.

65 Ibid. pp. 179–80.

66 Ibid. p. 180, para. 112.

67 *Armed Activities on the Territory of the Congo (Democratic Republic of the Congo v Uganda) (Merits)* [2005] ICJ Rep. 2005, pp. 242–43, para. 216. These findings of the Court were extensively cited by the ECtHR in *Al-Skeini and Others v the United Kingdom* App. No. 55721/07 (ECtHR, Judgment of 7 July 2011), para. 90.

68 *Application of the International Convention on the Elimination of All Forms of Racial Discrimination (Georgia v Russian Federation) (Provisional Measures Order)* [2008] ICJ Rep. 386, paras 108–109.

3.3.2 Application in situations of armed conflict and occupation

The ICJ has further confirmed the continued applicability of human rights instruments in times of armed conflict and in the context of occupation, as well as the relationship of complementarity between international human rights law and international humanitarian law.

In its advisory opinion on *Nuclear Weapons*, the Court held that 'the protection of the [ICCPR] does not cease in times of war, except by operation of Article 4 of the [ICCPR] whereby certain provisions may be derogated from in a time of national emergency'.[69] The Court continued to explain, with regard to the right of life, that the test in interpretation of human rights provisions in armed conflict is the applicable *lex specialis*, namely, international humanitarian law:

> In principle, the right not arbitrarily to be deprived of one's life applies also in hostilities. The test of what is an arbitrary deprivation of life, however, then falls to be determined by the applicable *lex specialis*, namely, the law applicable in armed conflict which is designed to regulate the conduct of hostilities [and not by the terms of the Covenant itself].[70]

In *The Wall* advisory opinion and the *Armed Activities* case, the Court expanded this conclusion to human rights treaties in general, stating that 'the protection offered by human rights conventions does not cease in case of armed conflict, save through the effect of the provisions for derogation of the kind to be found in Article 4 of the [ICCPR]'.[71]

As to the relationship between international humanitarian and human rights law, the Court explained that:

> [S]ome rights may be exclusively matters of international humanitarian law; others may be exclusively matters of human rights law; yet others may be matters of both these branches of international law. In order to answer the question put to it, the Court will have to take into consideration both these branches of international law, namely human rights law and, as *lex specialis*, international humanitarian law.[72]

4 The role of the International Court of Justice in the enforcement of human rights

4.1 Finding of a violation and determination of appropriate remedies

Despite the many jurisdictional obstacles, the ICJ has occasionally had the opportunity to directly enforce human rights through a finding of state responsibility for violations and through the determination of appropriate remedies.

---

69 *Nuclear Weapons* (n. 4) p. 240, para. 25.
70 Ibid. This decision was explicitly relied upon by the ICTY in, *inter alia, Prosecutor v Gotovina, et al. (Decision on Several Motions Challenging Jurisdiction)* ICTY-06-90-PT (19 March 2007), para. 24.
71 *The Wall* (n. 11) p. 178, para. 106.
72 Ibid.; see also, subsequently, *Armed Activities, Merits* (n. 67) pp. 242–43, para. 216. These findings were directly relied upon by the ECtHR in *Al-Skeini and Others* (n. 67) , para. 90.

Whilst the majority of the contentious cases before the Court have been formulated in the traditional language of inter-state responsibility, applications were occasionally brought to the Court within the framework of diplomatic protection on behalf of the individual to be protected and were formulated in terms of the direct rights of the individual.[73] The Court has also expressly stated that the scope of diplomatic protection in respect of natural persons included, inter alia, 'internationally guaranteed human rights'.[74]

4.1.1 Finding of a violation

In the *LaGrand* and *Avena* cases, the Court recognised that the obligations under Article 36, paragraph 1, of the Vienna Convention on Consular Relations (VCCR) created individual rights for the detained person, which may be invoked in the Court by the national state of that person,[75] and that, consequently, the reference to 'rights' in Article 36, paragraph 2, of the VCCR must be read as applying not only to the rights of the sending state, 'but also to the rights of the detained individual'.[76] Accordingly, in the *LaGrand* case, the Court held that by not informing the LaGrand brothers of their rights under Article 36 of the VCCR, the US had violated its obligations under this provision with regard to Germany *and* with regard to the LaGrand brothers.[77]

Human rights violations featured prominently in the Court's advisory opinion on *The Wall*, where the Court found, inter alia, that Israel had violated provisions of the ICCPR, the ICESCR and the CRC, as well as its obligation to respect the right of the Palestinian people to self-determination, alongside the various violations of international humanitarian law.[78]

Similarly, in the *Armed Activities* case, the Court held that Uganda had violated, inter alia, the provisions of the ICCPR, the CRC and the Optional Protocol thereto, and the ACHPR.[79] Two years later, in the *Genocide* case, the Court found that genocide was committed in Srebrenica in 1995[80] and that Serbia had violated its obligation to prevent and punish genocide under the Genocide Convention.[81]

In its recent judgment in the *Diallo* case, the Court considered whether certain domestic administrative and judicial procedures complied with international human rights obligations. The Republic of Guinea brought the case against the Democratic Republic of the Congo (DRC) 'on behalf of Mr Diallo', alleging a 'violation of his rights as a result of his arrest,

---

73 *Vienna Convention on Consular Relations (Paraguay v United States of America) (Provisional Measures Order)* [1998] ICJ Rep. 248; *LaGrand, Merits* (n. 46) p. 466; *Avena, Merits* (n. 46) p. 12; *Diallo, Merits* (n. 8).

74 *Ahmadou Sadio Diallo (Republic of Guinea v Democratic Republic of the Congo) (Preliminary Objections)* [2007] ICJ Rep. (II) 599, para. 39.

75 *LaGrand, Merits* (n. 46) p. 494, para. 77; *Avena, Merits* (n. 46) pp. 35–36, para. 40 and pp. 65–66, para. 140. For more on the impact of these decisions on the law of consular protection, see, e.g., C. Hoppe, 'Trends and Trials: The Implementation of Consular Rights a Decade after *LaGrand*', in U. Fastenrath et al. (eds), *From Bilateralism to Community Interest: Essays in Honour of Judge Bruno Simma* (OUP, 2011).

76 *LaGrand, Merits* (n. 46) p. 497, para. 89.

77 Ibid. pp. 514–517, para. 128(3)–(4).

78 *The Wall* (n. 11) pp. 183–84, para. 120; p. 184, para. 122; p. 189, para. 132; pp. 191–92, para. 134.

79 *Armed Activities, Merits* (n. 67) p. 244, para. 219; pp. 279–83 para. 345(3).

80 *Genocide Convention, Merits* (n. 7) p. 166, para. 297.

81 Ibid. p. 229, para. 450 and pp. 237–39, para. 471(5)–(6).

detention and expulsion' by the DRC in 1995–1996.[82] The Court held that the DRC had violated the prohibitions on arbitrary arrest, detention and expulsion under Articles 9(1)-(2) and 13 of the ICCPR and under Articles 12(4) and 6 of the ACHPR, as well as Mr Diallo's right to consular notification under Article 36(1) of the VCCR.[83]

4.1.2 The obligation to make 'full reparation'

The Court has also confirmed that violations of human rights (and humanitarian law) create an obligation on the part of the wrong-doing state to provide 'full reparation', including monetary compensation, to states or individuals for damage flowing from such violations.[84]

Although in the traditional framework of inter-state claims, the injured state remains the sole claimant and recipient of reparation, even where injury was incurred by its national(s), the Court has made clear that reparation for human rights violations ultimately accrues to the benefit of individual victims. Thus, in the *Wall* advisory opinion, the Court stated that Israel was 'under an obligation to return the land, orchards, olive groves and other immovable property seized from any natural or legal person for purposes of construction of the wall in the Occupied Palestinian Territory' and that '[i]n the event that such restitution should prove to be materially impossible, Israel ha[d] an obligation to compensate *the persons in question* for the damage suffered'.[85] The Court also considered that Israel 'ha[d] an obligation to compensate, in accordance with the applicable rules of international law, all natural or legal persons having suffered any form of material damage as a result of the wall's construction'.[86]

Similarly, in the *Armed Activities* case, where the Court held that reparations were due to the DRC for all damages caused by Uganda's violations of its international obligations, it also made clear that those violations 'resulted in injury to the DRC *and to persons on its territory*', imposing upon Uganda an obligation to make reparations accordingly.[87] The Court remains seized of the case and will decide on the appropriate reparation if the parties fail to reach an agreement in this regard.[88]

In the *Diallo* case, the Court not only decided that compensation is due to an injured state in respect of damages suffered by the injured state's national as a result of human rights violations,[89] but also fixed the amount of such compensation after the parties had failed to agree on this matter within the time-limit set by the Court. Thus, in its judgment of 19 June 2012, the Court determined that the DRC is under an obligation to pay to Guinea $85,000

---

82 *Diallo, Preliminary Objections* (n. 74) p. 5998, para. 40; see also *Diallo, Merits* (n. 8) p. 19, para. 43.

83 *Diallo, Merits* (n. 8) pp. 49–50, para. 165. For a discussion of other issues raised in this complex case, particularly the issue of companies and investor rights, see, e.g., E. Bjorge, 'Ahmadou Sadio Diallo (*Republic of Guinea v Democratic Republic of the Congo*)' (2011) 105(3) *American Journal of International Law* 534–40.

84 The principle of full reparation was first set out by the Permanent Court of International Justice in the *Factory at Chorzów* case (*Case Concerning the Factory at Chorzów (Germany v Poland) (Merits)*, PCIJ Rep. (1928) Series A No. 17, p. 47) and was subsequently consistently reaffirmed by the ICJ, most recently in the *Diallo* case *(Diallo, Merits* (n. 8) p. 48, para. 161). For more on this issue, see, for example, G. Zyberi, 'The International Court of Justice and Applied Forms of Reparation for International Human Rights and Humanitarian Law Violations' (2011) 7(1) *Utrecht Law Review* 204–15.

85 *The Wall* (n. 11) p. 198, para. 153 (emphasis added).

86 Ibid.

87 *Armed Activities, Merits* (n. 67) p. 257, para. 259.

88 Ibid. p. 257, paras 260–61.

89 *Diallo, Merits* (n. 8) pp. 49–50, operative para. 165, subpara. (7).

for non-material injury suffered by Mr Diallo and \$10,000 for material injury resulting from the wrongful arrests, detentions and expulsion by Guinea of Mr Diallo in 1995–1996.[90] In determining the appropriate compensation, the Court took into account the practice of other international courts and tribunals, including the ECtHR, the IACtHR, the UNHRC, and the AComHPR.[91] In line with that practice, the Court affirmed that non-material injury is 'an inevitable consequence' of human rights violations such as those at stake in this case, and that such injury can thus be established even without specific evidence;[92] accordingly, the amount of compensation due for such injury 'necessarily rests on equitable considerations'.[93] By contrast, the Court, similarly to the practice of the regional human rights courts, took a stricter view in respect of material injury, and rejected for the most part Guinea's claims in this regard due to Guinea's failure to prove such damage and/or its causal nexus with the human rights violations in question.[94]

4.1.3 Protection of human rights through provisional measures

Another important manner in which the ICJ has contributed to the enforcement of human rights has been through the exercise of its power to indicate binding provisional measures.[95] In most cases provisional measures for the protection of human rights were indicated precisely because compliance with those human rights formed the very subject-matter of the dispute, in particular in situations involving imminent risk to human life.

Thus, in each of the three consular protection cases (*Breard*, *LaGrand* and *Avena*), the Court ordered the United States to ensure that the individuals in question were not executed pending the Court's final decision on the merits.[96] Unfortunately, none of the three orders prevented the United States authorities from carrying out the planned executions, notwithstanding the Court's explicit confirmation in the *LaGrand* case that its orders on provisional measures are legally binding.[97]

---

90 *Ahmadou Sadio Diallo (Republic of Guinea v Democratic Republic of the Congo), Compensation owed by the Democratic Republic of the Congo to the Republic of Guinea (Judgment)* [2012], pp. 21–22, operative para. 61, subparas (1)–(2).

91 Ibid. p. 8, para. 13; p. 10, para. 18, pp. 11–12, para. 24; p. 14, para. 33; p. 16, para. 40; p. 18, para. 49; pp. 19–20, para. 56.

92 Ibid. pp. 10–11, para. 21.

93 Ibid. pp. 11–12, para. 24.

94 Ibid. pp. 13–19, paras. 29–55.

95 For an elaborated discussion of the protection of human rights through the provisional measures of the ICJ, see R. Higgins, 'Interim Measures for the Protection of Human Rights', in J. Charney, D. Anton and M. O'Connell (eds), *Politics, Values and Functions: International Law in the 21st Century: Essays in Honor of Professor Louis Henkin* (Martinus Nijhoff Publishers, 1997); Y. Yoshiyuki, 'The Protection of Human Life through Provisional Measures Indicated by the International Court of Justice' (2002) 15(2) *Leiden Journal of International Law* 345–66; see also the analysis in the dissenting opinion of Judge Cançado Trindade in *Questions relating to the Obligation to Prosecute or Extradite (Belgium v Senegal)* (Provisional Measures Order) [2009], Dissenting Opinion of Judge Cançado Trindade, particularly pp. 171–75, paras. 15–25.

96 *Vienna Convention on Consular Relations, Provisional Measures* (n. 73) p. 258, para. 41; *LaGrand (Germany v United States of America) (Provisional Measures Order)* [1999] ICJ Rep. (I) 16, para. 29; *Avena and Other Mexican Nationals (Mexico v United States of America) (Provisional Measures Order)* [2003] ICJ Rep. 2003, pp. 91–92, para. 59.

97 *LaGrand, Merits* (n. 46) p. 506, para. 109.

In more general terms, in *Armed Activities* the Court ordered both parties, inter alia, to 'take all measures necessary to ensure full respect within the zone of conflict for fundamental human rights and for the applicable provisions of humanitarian law'.[98] In the *Genocide* case, the Court issued two provisional measures orders, requesting the Federal Republic of Yugoslavia to immediately 'take all measures within its power to prevent commission of the crime of genocide', in particular to ensure that no genocidal acts are committed by 'any military, paramilitary or irregular armed units which may be directed or supported by it, as well as any organizations and persons which may be subject to its control, direction or influence'.[99]

Most recently, in the case between Georgia and the Russian Federation, the Court ordered both parties: (a) to refrain from any act of racial discrimination; (b) to abstain from sponsoring, defending or supporting racial discrimination by any persons or organisations; (c) to do all in their power to ensure, without distinction as to national or ethnic origin, the security of persons, the right of persons to freedom of movement and residence within the border of the state and the protection of the property of displaced persons and of refugees; and (d) to do all in their power to ensure that public authorities and public institutions under their control or influence do not engage in acts of racial discrimination.[100]

The protection of human rights is taken into account by the Court when indicating provisional measures even in cases where human rights norms are not strictly part of the subject-matter of the dispute. For instance, in the recent case between Cambodia and Thailand, the Court indicated certain provisional measures, considering that the risk of irreparable prejudice was posed to the rights asserted by Cambodia, 'resulting from the military activities in that area and, in particular, from the loss of life, bodily injuries and damage caused to the Temple and the property associated with it'.[101]

4.2 Interaction with other human rights mechanisms

The Court has been gradually contributing to the larger unity and coherence in international human rights law (and international law in general) by increasingly referring to both legal and factual findings of the ECtHR,[102] IACtHR,[103] AComHPR[104] and international criminal

---

98 *Armed Activities on the Territory of the Congo (Democratic Republic of the Congo v Uganda) (Provisional Measures Order)* [2000] ICJ Rep. 129, para. 47.

99 *Application of the Convention on the Prevention and Punishment of the Crime of Genocide (Bosnia and Herzegovina v Yugoslavia) (Provisional Measures Order)* [1993] ICJ Rep. 1993, pp. 24–25, para. 52(A); *Armed Activities, Merits* ibid. pp. 349–50, para. 61(1)–(2).

100 *Application of the International Convention on the Elimination of All Forms of Racial Discrimination (Provisional Measures)* (n. 68) pp. 398–99, para. 149.

101 *Request for Interpretation of the Judgment of 15 June 1962 in the Case Concerning the Temple Of Preah Vihear (Cambodia v Thailand) (Provisional Measures Order)* [2011], p. 15, para. 55. See also *Land and Maritime Boundary between Cameroon and Nigeria (Cameroon v Nigeria) (Provisional Measures Order)* [1996] ICJ Rep. (I) 23 para. 42; *United States Diplomatic and Consular Staff in Tehran (United States of America v Iran) (Provisional Measures Order)* [1979] ICJ Rep. 1979, pp. 20–21, para. 47(A)(ii–iii).

102 *Diallo, Merits* (n. 8) p. 25, para. 68; *Jurisdictional Immunities, Merits* (n. 4) pp. 31–33, 37 and 39, paras. 72–73, 76, 78, 90 and 96.

103 *Diallo, Merits* (n. 8) p. 25, para. 68.

104 *Diallo, Merits* (n. 8) p. 25, para. 67.

tribunals,[105] as well as to other treaty-monitoring mechanisms such as the HRC[106] and even the Special Rapporteurs of the UN Commission on Human Rights.[107] In addition, the Court has occasionally relied on the factual findings of non-governmental organisations such as Amnesty International and Human Rights Watch.[108]

Whilst the Court explicitly noted that it was not obliged to follow the opinions and conclusions of judicial and other mechanisms dealing with human rights, it has nonetheless frequently (explicitly or implicitly) emphasised their importance and mostly cited their findings with approval.[109] As explained above,[110] the Court has attributed particular weight to the interpretative jurisprudence of other jurisdictions in the field of human rights, emphasising the need for coherent interpretation of human rights treaties in order to achieve 'the necessary clarity and the essential consistency of international law, as well as legal security, to which both the individuals with guaranteed rights and the states obliged to comply with treaty obligations are entitled.'[111]

In turn, regional human rights courts and other human rights treaty-monitoring mechanisms have likewise utilised and benefitted from the Court's work. Even in the absence of any formal institutional hierarchy among international judicial institutions, the ICJ undoubtedly carries a special weight in the global system as the principal judicial organ of the United Nations and the only universal international judicial body with general subject-matter jurisdiction.

While its jurisprudence of course cannot be imposed on other international fora, it has nonetheless been frequently relied upon by the regional human rights courts and other treaty-monitoring mechanisms, both in respect of general international law matters (such as the question of formation of customary international law[112]) as well as in respect of specific human rights issues, including matters such as: the *erga omnes* status of certain human rights;[113] the

---

105 Most extensively, the Court relied on a number of legal and factual findings of the ICTY in the *Genocide Case* (*Merits* (n. 7) pp. 121–27, paras. 188, 190, 195, 198–201; pp. 138–206, paras. 232–395; pp. 224–25, para. 437). In the same case, the Court also relied on legal findings of the International Criminal Tribunal for Rwanda (ibid., pp. 126, 167 and 191, paras. 198, 300 and 358).

106 *The Wall* (n. 11), pp. 179–80, paras. 109–10; *Diallo, Merits* (n. 8) p. 24, para. 66 and p. 28, para. 77; *Judgment No. 2867 of the Administrative Tribunal of the International Labour Organization* (n. 54) p. 16, para. 39.

107 *The Wall* (n. 11) pp. 189–91, para. 130; *Armed Activities, Merits* (n. 67), pp. 204–205, para. 70, pp. 239–40, paras. 206 and 209; *Genocide Case, Merits* (n. 7) p. 144, para. 246, pp. 148–49, paras. 258 and 260, pp. 176–81, paras. 323–31, and p. 183, para. 338.

108 *Genocide Case, Merits* (n. 7) p. 180, para. 330 and p. 184–85, para. 341.

109 In fact, the only human rights–related case in which the Court explicitly took issue with the position of another jurisdiction was the *Genocide* case, and even there the divergence of views between the ICJ and the ICTY concerned a point of general international law, namely the appropriate standard for attribution of the actions of a non-state actor to a state under the law of state responsibility. The Court explicitly rejected the standard of 'overall control' adopted by the ICTY in the *Tadi* case, and insisted on its own, more restrictive standard of 'effective control' developed in the *Nicaragua* case (see *Genocide, Merits* (n. 7) pp. 209–11, paras. 402–407).

110 See above, section 21.3.1.3.

111 *Diallo, Merits* (n. 8) p. 24, para. 66.

112 See, e.g., *Baena Ricardo et al. (270 Workers) v Panama*, IACtHR, Ser. C No. 104, (2003) (Competence) p. 32, para. 102.

113 IACtHR, *Interpretation of the American Declaration of the Rights and Duties of Man* (n. 16) para. 38; ICTY, *Prosecutor v Kupreškić* (n. 17) para. 519.

interpretation of human rights treaties;[114] and the obligation of 'full reparation' for human rights violations.[115]

5 Conclusion

Although the ICJ is not a human rights court, it is a court of general jurisdiction over questions of international law, of which human rights law forms part. It is also the principle judicial organ of the United Nations and has, as such, an important role in fulfilling the fundamental principles and objectives of the organisation, including the protection and promotion of human rights.

Indeed, as this chapter reveals, human rights issues are increasingly part of the Court's docket and its decisions have made a tangible contribution to the development and the interpretive clarity of concepts, principles and rules of international human rights law. The Court has also helped to clarify the relationship between international human rights law and other branches of international law and has affirmed that states have positive obligations under international human rights law – both territorially and extraterritorially, not only in times of peace but also in situations of armed conflict and belligerent occupation. All these pronouncements have helped to strengthen the overall protection of human rights and their place in the contemporary international legal order. The Court has also contributed significantly to the enforcement of human rights, through findings of violations and confirmation that 'full reparation' for a human rights violation is due both to the injured state and the injured individual(s), as well as through indication of provisional measures to protect human rights at immediate risk of irreparable damage.

Finally, the Court's increasing interaction with other human rights institutions contributes to greater unity and coherence of international human rights law and helps in Consolidating the international protection of human rights. The Court's jurisprudence reveals more uniformity than divergence of views among the proliferating international judicial institutions and other mechanisms concerned with human rights, confirming that international human rights law is not a series of fragmented regimes, but rather an increasingly unified system of rules and mechanisms for international protection of human beings.

Select bibliography

L.M. Caplan, 'State Immunity, Human Rights, and *Jus Cogens* : A Critique of the Normative Hierarchy Theory' (2003) 97 *American Journal of International Law* 4, 741–81.

---

114 See, e.g., IACtHR, *Interpretation of the American Declaration of the Rights and Duties of Man* (n. 16) para. 37; ECtHR, *Tryer v the United Kingdom* (n. 53) para. 31; ECtHR, *Loizidou v Turkey (Preliminary Objections)* (n. 53) para. 71.

115 See, e.g., *Velásquez-Rodríguez v Honduras*, IACtHR, Ser. C No. 7, (1989) (Reparations and Costs), para. 26; *Papamichalopoulos v Greece (Article 50)* App. No. 14556/89 (ECtHR, Judgment of 31 October 1995), para. 36; Permanent Court of Arbitration, *Final Award, Eritrea's Damages Claims Between the State of Eritrea and the Federal Democratic Republic of Ethiopia*, available at: http://www.pca-cpa.org/upload/files/ER%20Final%20Damages%20Award%20complete.pdf, accessed on 12 January 2012, pp. 7–8, paras 24–26.

R. Higgins, 'Interim measures for the protection of human rights', in J. Charney, D. Anton and M. O'Connell (eds), *Politics, values and functions: international law in the 21st century: essays in honor of Professor Louis Henkin* (Martinus Nijhoff Publishers, 1997).

A. Orakhelashvili, 'State Immunity and International Public Order Revisited' (2006) 49 *German Yearbook of International Law* 327–65.

C.J. Tams and A. Tzanakopoulos, 'Barcelona Traction at 40: the ICJ as an Agent of Legal Development' (2010) 23 (4) *Leiden Journal of International Law* 781.

22

The UN Security Council and international human rights obligations

Towards a theory of constraints and derogation

Scott Sheeran and Catherine Bevilacqua

1 Introduction

1.1 Confusion and absence of a general framework

The question of how international human rights relate and interact with the work of the UN Security Council (UNSC) arises frequently in theory and practice. The relationship between human rights and the Security Council is most often perceived as tense, for example, with states arguing that they were obliged to limit or sideline human rights in deference to 'higher' obligations deriving from a Security Council mandate and the Charter of the United Nations.[1]

---

1 An emblematic assertion in the recent *Nada v Switzerland* case is the state respondent's oral statement at the hearing on 23 March 2011: 'States have no margin of manoeuvre, neither when it comes to implementation of the restrictions nor in the choice of the individual to whom they should apply . . . What Switzerland does strongly challenge . . . is the idea that Switzerland had the freedom in legal or political terms not to institute a regime which had been established and which was being monitored by fifteen Member States of the Security Council and was binding on all of the 192 Members of the UN pursuant to Chapter VII of the Charter in the fight against terrorism.' Transcript of English interpretation, webcast at: http://www.echr.coe.int/Pages/home.aspx?p=hearingsandw=1 059308_23032011andlanguage=en (accessed on 22 June 2013). In *Nada v Switzerland* – 10593/08 – HEJUD [2012] ECHR 1691, ECHR (2012) and earlier case law, the state respondent argued that the obligation to fulfil a UN Security Council mandate prevails over human rights treaty obligations under Art. 103 of the UN Charter; see for example *Kadi v Council and Commission (Common foreign and security policy)* [2005] EUECJ T-315/01, EUECJ (2005) (hereafter *Kadi 2005*) paras 12, 17, 26, 34 and in particular 153–56, a position reflected also in *Kadi v Council and Commission (Common foreign and security policy)* [2008] EUECJ C-402/05, EUECJ (2008) (hereafter *Kadi 2008*); UN Human Rights Committee, *Nabil Sayadi and Patricia Vinck v Belgium* (2008) CCPR/C/94/D/1472/2006, state party's observations on the merits para 8.1; *R. (Al-Jedda) v Secretary of State for Defence* [2007] UKHL 58, [2008] 1 AC 332, [2008] 2 WLR 31, 12 December 2007 (hereafter *Al-Jedda HL*), para. 30, cited also in *Al-Jedda v United Kingdom*, App. No. 27021/08, 7 July 2011 (hereafter *Al-Jedda ECtHR*) para 20. See also M. Milanovic, '*Al-Skeini* and *Al-Jedda* in Strasbourg' (2012) 23(1) *European*

The absence of clear guidance on this alleged normative conflict is the most high-profile symptom of a deeper gap in theory. At the time of the UN Charter's adoption in 1945, there was little substance to its references to 'human rights'.[2] The relationship between the Security Council and international human rights law (IHRL) is yet to be directly considered by the International Court of Justice (ICJ). Conflictual or not, the relationship has not been captured in a coherent legal theory. How human rights norms relate to Security Council powers in general remains unsettled.

The absence of a general framework gives rise to greater tension than warranted between international human rights law and Security Council mandates. The analogy with a national legal system – with constitutional human rights and compulsory legal adjudication – is ill-suited to the UN legal order.[3] Without clarity concerning the overall legal framework, human rights have largely failed to penetrate practice in a positive manner, and despite an increasing prominence of human rights on the international agenda, an opportunity is lost to promote respect through the Security Council as both a political and legal necessity.

1.2 Anatomy of debated issues

The dominant starting point of the discussion on the Security Council and human rights is the idea that tension exists between different legal obligations. This is borne out in three main types of UNSC resolutions and practice relating to human rights obligations. The first type concerns economic sanctions and their impact on economic, social and cultural rights, especially the right to health, in situations such as Iraq and more recently Iran.[4] The second consists of the targeted sanctions arising from counter-terrorism measures against legal and

Journal International Law 133–37; *Behrami and Behrami v France, Saramati v France, Germany and Norway,* Eur C HR, App. Nos 71412/01 and 78166/01, 2 May 2007 (hereafter *Behrami*) paras 97, 102, 106, 113 as cited in M. Milanovic, 'Norm Conflict in International Law: Whither Human Rights?' (2009) 20 *Duke Journal of Comparative and International Law,* 69, 84 and fn. 68.

2 UN Charter (1945) Arts 1(3) and 55. It was not until the Universal Declaration of Human Rights (1948) that the term began to have content within the UN system.

3 There is no compulsory jurisdiction for the UN's primary legal organ, the ICJ, except where recognised by states through a declaration under Art. 36 of its Statute, paras 2–3; see also Art. 2(7) of the UN Charter.

4 International Covenant on Economic Social and Cultural Rights (1966) Art. 12; see the Maastricht Principles on Extraterritorial Obligations of States in the area of Economic, Social and Cultural Rights (2011), in particular Principle 22 on the scope of extraterritorial obligations arising from sanctions and equivalent measures; see also O. De Schutter, A. Eide, A. Khalfan, M. Orellana, M. Salomon and I. Seiderman, 'Commentary to the Maastricht Principles on Extraterritorial Obligations of States in the Area of Economic, Social and Cultural Rights' (2012) 34 *Human Rights Quarterly,* 1131; A. Tzanakopoulos, 'The Countermeasure of Disobedience: Implementing the Responsibility of International Organisations', in M. Ragazzi (ed.), *The Responsibility Of International Organizations: Essays In Memory Of Sir Ian Brownlie* (Martinus Nijhoff Publishers, forthcoming); on Iraq, Sub-Commission on the Promotion and Protection of Human Rights, 'Review of further developments in fields with which the sub-commission has been or may be concerned: The adverse consequences of economic sanctions on the enjoyment of human rights' (The Bossuyt Report) (Fifty-second Session) (21 June 2000) E/CN.4/Sub.2/2000/33 paras 52–53; K. Van Brabant, 'Can Sanctions Be Smarter? The Current Debate', Report on Conference of 16–17 December 1998, the Humanitarian Policy Group and the Relief and Rehabilitation Network at the Overseas Development Institute, London, p. 6; UN Security Council Resolution 1929 (9 June 2010) UN Doc. S/RES/1929 (2010); Report of the Secretary General on the situation of human rights in the Islamic Republic of Iran: Advance Unedited Version (28 February 2013) UN Doc. A/HRC/22/48 para. 52.

real persons, such as the Taliban-Al Qaida sanctions list under resolution 1267 and, to a lesser degree, the general counter-terrorism resolution 1373.[5] The third relates to UN peacekeeping and UN-authorised peace enforcement operations and their human rights implementation, as well as accountability for arbitrary detention, sexual exploitation and abuse, amongst others.[6]

Given a focus on tension as the central issue, the critical question becomes whether that tension should be resolved in favour of a predominance of human rights obligations or Security Council powers under the Charter. This question has been discussed, both centrally and peripherally, in largely separate debates in the scholarly and jurisprudential spheres.[7] The polarisation within the scholarly debate might be aptly portrayed by Koskenniemi's paradigm of 'apology and utopia'.[8] At one end, legal realists contend expressly or implicitly that the Security Council is driven largely by considerations of policy and negotiation, rather than law, in exercising its political responsibility for international peace and security, which reflects the idea that international law furnishes a retroactive, 'apologetic' explanation;[9] at the other, legal formalist approaches declare the firm boundaries placed by IHRL on the Security Council's powers, which however have little resonance in practice.[10]

---

5 UN Security Council Resolution 1267 (1999) UN Doc. S/RES/1267 (1999) establishing the sanctions regime and related UN Security Council committee and list (para. 6), renamed Al-Qaida Sanctions List in 2011; *Kadi* 2005 and *Kadi* 2008 (n. 1); The Office of the Ombudsperson created by UN Security Council Resolution 1904 (17 December 2009) UN Doc. S/RES/1904 (2009) and renewed in subsequent resolutions has a mandate to review requests for removal from the Sanctions List of the Sanctions Committee; M. Bothe, 'Security Council's Targeted Sanctions against Presumed Terrorists: The Need to Comply with Human Rights Standards' (2008) 6(3) *Journal of International Criminal Justice* 541–55. L. van den Herik and N. Schrijver, 'Delisting Challenges in the Context of UN Targeted Sanctions Regimes: A Legal Perspective', in T. Biersteker and S. Eckert, *Addressing Challenges to Targeted Sanctions: An Update of the 'Watson Report'* (2009) 34–45 (Appendix A), available at: http://www.watsoninstitute.org/pub/2009_10_targeted_sanctions.pdf (accessed on 26 June). On SC Res. 1373, e.g. see *People's Mojahedin Organization of Iran v Council of the European Union*, Judgment, Case No. T-284/08, 4 December 2008 and preceding ECJ judgments; M. O'Connell, 'Debating the Law of Sanctions', 13 EJIL 63 (2002); M. Craven, 'Humanitarianism and the Quest for Smarter Sanctions', (2002) 13 EJIL 43; M. Reisman and D. Stevick, 'The Applicability of International Law Standards to United Nations Economic Sanctions Programmes', (1998) 9 EJIL 86.

6 See Human rights due diligence policy on United Nations support to non-United Nations security forces UN Doc. A/67/775–S/2013/110; Report of the Panel on United Nations Peace Operations (Brahimi Report) UN Doc. A/55/305 S/2000/809; Institute for Justice and Democracy in Haiti claim against the UN on account of cholera outbreaks in the island: Petition for Relief, http://ijdh.org/wordpress/wp-content/uploads/2011/11/englishpetitionREDACTED.pdf; *S.C. against UNMIK* (Case No. 02/09), Decision of the UNMIK Human Rights Advisory Panel (6 December 2012); Report of the Secretary-General's Special Advisor, Prince Zeid Ra'ad Zeid al-Hussein on 'A comprehensive strategy to eliminate future sexual exploitation and abuse in United Nations peacekeeping operations' (24 March 2005) UN Doc. A/59/710.

7 See E. de Wet, 'The Role of Human Rights in Limiting the Enforcement Power of the Security Council: A Principled View', in E. de Wet and A. Nollkaemper (eds), *Review of the Security Council by Member States* (Intersentia, 2003).

8 M. Koskenniemi, *From Apology to Utopia: the Structure of International Legal Argument* (CUP, 2005).

9 See M. Wood, 'The Interpretation of Security Council Resolutions', *Max Planck Yearbook of United Nations Law* (1998) 73–95. Wood illustrates the uniquely political process resulting in a Security Council resolution including with binding effect, as compared to other documents with legal force under international law.

10 de Wet (n. 7); A. Orakhelashvili, 'The Impact of Peremptory Norms on the Interpretation and Application of United Nations Security Council Resolutions' (2005) 16(1) EJIL 59–88, 64–66. More generally, see G. Nolte, 'The Limits on the Security Council's Powers and its Functions in the International Legal System', in M. Byers (ed.), *The Role of Law in International Politics* (OUP, 2000), 322.

The literature is divided between two main alternative approaches to the question. First, a more legal realist perspective, such as Sir Michael Wood's, takes as a starting point the reality of UNSC decision-making: UNSC resolutions 'are frequently not clear, simple, concise or unambiguous. They are often drafted by non-lawyers, in haste, under considerable political pressure, and with a view to securing unanimity within the Council.'[11] Wood points to the relevant context for the resolution as one of the key tools for interpretation.[12] Further, the extent to which Security Council resolutions should be interpreted according to general international law or treaty-law 'depends in the last analysis on the intentions of the Security Council'.[13] In Wood's view, '[i]f it appears that the Council was intending to lay down a rule irrespective of the prior legal obligations of States, in general or in particular, then that intention would prevail.'[14] Wood points to the primacy of an obligation towards the Security Council under Article 103 of the UN Charter, noting that the Charter is of fundamental importance including its Purposes and Principles.[15]

Second, a more aspirational human rights perspective, such as that of Erika de Wet, suggests that 'the UN Charter did not intend the Security Council to be unbound by law' and even implies respect for human rights norms 'when undertaking action to maintain international peace and security'.[16] However, even this 'principled' position takes as its premise the reality of a UNSC that is powerful in practice: '[w]hen we talk about the discretion of the Security Council to limit general international law, the question is not whether such a discretion exists, but rather how broad this discretion would be. In fact, one could turn the question around and ask whether the Security Council would be limited by international law at all.'[17] De Wet goes on to establish constraints on such powers, yet without dismissing the idea that the Security Council's 'special role' may require leniency with regard to restrictions on human rights, 'justifiable in the light of the gravity of the threat' which the Council addresses.[18] Though at opposite ends of the spectrum, the two approaches focus on the same starting point: that the Security Council has special powers, and implicitly may enjoy unique flexibility with regard to obligations.

The jurisprudence, quite separately, weaves its own patchy discourse on the subject. The debate emerging from the cases, similar to state and UN practice and the relevant scholarship, is whether the UNSC has the power to suspend or dismiss human rights and whether there is any exception to such power, other than norms *jus cogens*. Additionally, a key question concerns the authority to determine a correct interpretation of Security Council decisions vis-à-vis international human rights law. The narrower question of how to handle norm conflict between state obligations under the Charter and UNSC decisions and international human rights law is also central.[19] The idea of norm conflict raises the question of the UN's

---

11 Wood (n. 9) 73, 82. See generally M. Reisman, 'The Constitutional Crisis in the United Nations', (1993) 87 AJIL 83–100, at 88–92,
12 Ibid.
13 Ibid. 78, 92.
14 Ibid.
15 Ibid. This approach is consistent with many states' perspectives (indeed Wood is a former legal adviser to the UK Foreign and Commonwealth Office). Art. 103 provides that: 'In the event of a conflict between the obligations of the Members of the United Nations under the present Charter and their obligations under any other international agreement, their obligations under the present Charter shall prevail.'
16 de Wet (n. 7).
17 Ibid. 8 (footnotes omitted).
18 Ibid. 18.
19 Milanovic (norm conflict) (n. 1).

legal authority with respect to other legal frameworks outside of the Charter. International and regional courts and human rights treaty bodies such as the UN Human Rights Committee have assessed differently the extent of their own, largely limited, competence to interpret UNSC resolutions.[20] Nevertheless, within their own limitations such bodies have upheld minimum standards of fundamental rights.[21] This suggests a common tendency towards the idea that human rights constrain the Security Council to some degree. Yet it equally demonstrates the need for a clearer framework to apply to implementation and practice.

Although not well known in the literature, the most constructive and nuanced explanation of the UNSC and IHRL relationship is offered in the individual opinion of Sir Nigel Rodley in the UN Human Rights Committee's communication of *Sayadi and Vinck v Belgium*.[22] Rodley sets out a series of interpretive 'presumptions' that the Security Council does not intend actions pursuant to its decisions to violate IHRL. He indicates this is especially the case for norms *jus cogens* and non-derogable human rights under the International Covenant on Civil and Political Rights (ICCPR),[23] and where such rights are derogable, any departures from them would be 'conditioned by the principles of necessity and proportionality'.[24] The important part of his opinion is that he expressly tackles the issue of derogation and states of emergency (a concept reflected, for example, in Article 4 of the ICCPR) which hitherto has not been well developed in the literature or cases. However, Rodley does not go as far as a 'strict interpretation', in his own words, which would find 'that the Security Council cannot act in a way that requires disrespect for those rights and freedoms'.[25]

1.3 Security Council and human rights: addressing gaps between theory and practice

In light of the problems in law and practice, this chapter articulates a theory of the relationship between the Security Council and human rights to assist the implementation of IHRL and interpretation of Council resolutions. The analysis is divided into two parts.

The first part (sections 2 and 3) considers the theoretical framework for powers and constraints upon the Security Council under international law, and in particular sheds light on the constraint posed by human rights. On the one hand, the UNSC is empowered under the Charter to make decisions which are legally binding upon UN members. On the other hand, the UNSC has obligations under IHRL in accordance with the UN Charter and customary international law. A presumption that the Security Council does not intend for states to violate human rights can be confirmed in UNSC practice.

The second part (sections 4 and 5) articulates how the framework resolves tension between obligations of human rights and Security Council resolutions under the Charter at the level of implementation and practice, including the issue of 'norm conflict'.

---

20 E.g. see *Nada* (n. 1); *Kadi* 2005 and 2008 also the 2010 judgment and appeals (n. 1); *Sayadi and Vinck* (n. 1); *Al-Jedda* HL (n. 1); *Al-Jedda* ECtHR (n. 1).

21 E.g. see *Nada* (n. 1); *Sayadi and Vinck* (n. 1).

22 *Sayadi and Vinck* (n. 1) 36–38.

23 Art. 4, ICCPR (1966) 999 UNTS 171 (which sets out the regime of derogation of rights in a public emergency threatening the life of the nation). E.g. see generally S. Sheeran, 'Reconceptualising States of Emergency under International Human Rights Law: Theory, Legal Doctrine, and Politics', (2013) 34(2) *Michigan Journal of International Law* 101–68.

24 *Sayadi and Vinck* (n. 1) 37.

25 Ibid. 36.

1.4 A new premise – the central role of derogations in formulating the legal theory

The unresolved and pertinent question is not whether human rights constrain the Security Council, but to what extent, and how they do so. Today, even the staunchest realist might shirk from claiming that international human rights norms do not apply at all to UNSC decisions. There is a degree of common ground in the otherwise discordant debates that the UNSC must be bound by human rights in some way.[26] However, in practice, human rights obligations are still set aside in a manner undermining their universality.

This analysis therefore takes as its premise that international human rights law constitutes an important and real element of constraint on the significant power of the Security Council. As will be shown, the UN Charter itself asserts beyond doubt that limits exist to the powers of the UNSC. The real question is exactly how far human rights constrain the UNSC in theory and practice. In this regard, and as indicated above, the debate is underdeveloped and stuck in an unhelpful dialectic. A concept of 'derogation' in emergency situations is central to unlocking a sensible theory of the Security Council and human rights obligations.[27] Rodley recognised this in *Sayadi and Vinck*, but it is necessary to go further. The application of a form of the derogation concept of international human rights law to the Security Council's powers allows an understanding in which states' human rights obligations are not 'disrespected' or overridden per se by the Council and Charter. Rather, if the Charter's legal order includes a concept of derogation, it will permit Article 103 to be understood as another means, similar to Article 4 of the ICCPR, according to which rights are temporarily limited by operation of law in a public emergency situation.

Accordingly, this analysis will examine first the framework for powers and limitations of the Security Council in general, and then turn to the basis for human rights in particular to act as a constraint, with a focus on UNSC derogations and international human rights obligations.

POWERS, CONSTRAINTS AND THE ROLE OF HUMAN RIGHTS

2 Powers and limitations of the UN Security Council

2.1 Security Council 'powers': problems within the premise

Before turning to the specific question of human rights, it is necessary to consider the general framework governing the Security Council. The UN Charter offers a relatively clear framework for the UNSC's role, authority and powers.[28] The Security Council has 'primary responsibility'[29] for one of the principal purposes of the United Nations as established in Article 1(1) of the Charter,[30] namely, the maintenance of international peace and security.

---

26 E.g. see Wood (n. 9).

27 For an explanation of the derogation concept in human rights treaties, see Sheeran (n. 23) 1–10.

28 B. Simma (ed.), *The Charter of the United Nations: A Commentary*, 2nd edn (OUP, 2002) 437–582; V. Lowe, A. Roberts, J. Welsh and D. Zaum (eds), *The United Nations Security Council and War: The Evolution of Thought and Practice since 1945* (OUP, 2008); Wood (n. 9); de Wet (n. 7).

29 UN Charter Art. 24(1); see Simma (n. 28) 442–52; L. Goodrich and E. Hambro, *Charter of the United Nations* (World Peace Foundation, 1946) 120–21.

30 Specifically, UN Charter Art.1(1) establishes inter alia as a primary purpose for the UN '[t]o maintain international peace and security, and to that end: to take effective collective measures for the prevention and removal of threats to the peace, and for the suppression of acts of aggression or other breaches of the peace.'

The Security Council's reason for existence is a core responsibility of the Organisation. Its framework of action is articulated in terms of duties in fulfilment of that responsibility.

The emphasis primarily on Security Council 'powers' (and any constraints thereon) arises from all sides of the debate about human rights and the Council. This emphasis stems from the unique status of this organ within the UN system, conceived at the political level and consisting, from a legal standpoint, of the Security Council's near-exclusive ability within the UN to make decisions which are legally binding upon states.[31] The source of the legal obligation upon the 193 states which are members of the UN is the Charter. Membership is predicated upon states' acceptance of the obligations contained in the Charter and on the judgment of the Organisation that they are able and willing to carry out those obligations.[32]

The Security Council's powers and duties are explicitly linked to each other through the UN Charter principles and provisions establishing its authority. The UNSC is at once both empowered and constrained by the law. As Judge Sir Robert Jennings stated in the *Lockerbie* case in which the UNSC's powers were a central issue:

> [A]ll discretionary powers of lawful decision-making are necessarily derived from the law, and are therefore governed and qualified by the law. This must be so if only because the sole authority of such decisions flows itself from the law. It is not logically possible to claim to represent the power and authority of the law, and at the same time, claim to be above the law.[33]

If that UNSC power is not subject to the law contained in the Charter there will also be an absence of legitimacy,[34] which is essential to the United Nations.

The emphasis on 'powers' does not dismiss Security Council duties altogether. Yet it does construct a contrast between 'powers' and obligations, which harks back to the simplistic premise of 'tension' to be resolved between the Council and human rights obligations. Shifting focus not just from whether to 'how,' but to a more integrated account, can yield a conceptual gain. Clarity on the connection within the Charter between powers and obligations will highlight the specific link between human rights and the Security Council.

2.2 Powers and duties in general under the UN Charter

2.2.1 Security Council powers

To fulfil a purpose key to the Organisation's reason for existence – the maintenance of peace and security – the Security Council enjoys a degree of power superior to other UN organs. Of the six principal organs established under the UN Charter,[35] the UNSC alone is

---

31 See generally Simma (n. 28) 442–75; Security Council Report, 'Security Council Actions under Chapter VII: Myths and Realities', *Special Research Report No. 1* (23 June 2008); de Wet (n. 7).

32 UN Charter Art. 4(1); Goodrich and Hambro (n. 29) 80–82 .

33 *Questions of Interpretation and Application of the 1971 Montreal Convention arising from the Aerial Incident at Lockerbie (Libya v U.S.)*, Provisional Measures, Order of 14 April 1992, ICJ Rep. 1992, 114. (Judge Jennings dissenting opinion) 110. See also, on interlocking in law of authority and power, R. Higgins, *Problems and Process – International Law and How We Use It* (OUP, 1994) 4.

34 E.g. T. Franck, *The Power of Legitimacy among Nations* (OUP, 1990); J. Coicaud and V. Heiskanen (eds), *The Legitimacy of International Organizations* (UNU Press, 2001).

35 UN Charter, Art. 7.

empowered to make legally binding decisions requiring enforcement action with respect to threats against peace.[36] UN members 'agree that in carrying out its duties under this responsibility the Security Council acts on their behalf', thereby ensuring 'prompt and effective action'.[37] With respect to a UNSC finding of illegality, the ICJ confirmed in the *Namibia Advisory Opinion* that '[i]t would be an untenable interpretation to maintain that, once such a declaration had been made by the Security Council under Article 24 of the Charter, on behalf of all member States, those members would be free to act in disregard of such illegality or even to recognize violations of law resulting from it'; rather, 'Members of the United Nations would be expected to act in consequence of the declaration made on their behalf.'[38]

In each specific circumstance, the Security Council may establish whether all or some members must act, and how, including with respect to Chapter VII enforcement action under Articles 41 and 42.[39] Further to the determination of the existence of a threat under Chapter VII, the Security Council has the power to 'make recommendations, or decide what measures shall be taken in accordance with Articles 41 and 42, to maintain or restore international peace and security.'[40] According to Article 41 the UNSC 'may decide what measures not involving the use of armed force are to be employed to give effect to its decisions'. Its specific powers are laid down in Chapters VI, VII, VIII, and XII of the UN Charter.[41] Yet the ICJ stated in the *Namibia* opinion that the Security Council's authority to take action is not restricted to those specific powers; instead it also has general powers to carry out its responsibilities defined under 24(1), 'commensurate with [the] responsibility for the maintenance of peace and security' conferred upon it by members.[42] This is consistent with the concept of 'implied powers', which is accepted in UN Charter interpretation.[43] As Alvarez indicates for UN peacekeeping operations, they are based on a broad interpretation of the 'general powers'

36 A qualification is necessary as the ICJ has held that 'the responsibility conferred is "primary", not exclusive. This primary responsibility is conferred upon the Security Council, as stated in Art. 24, "in order to ensure prompt and effective action" ... The Charter makes it abundantly clear, however, that the General Assembly is also to be concerned with international peace and security ... Thus while it is the Security Council which, exclusively, may order coercive action, the functions and powers conferred by the Charter on the General Assembly are not ... merely hortatory ... Moreover, these powers of decision of the General Assembly under Arts 5 and 6 are specifically related to preventive or enforcement measures.' *Certain expenses of the United Nations (Article 17, paragraph 2 of the Charter)*, Advisory Opinion of 20 July 1962: ICJ Rep. 1962, 163–64.

37 UN Charter Art. 24(1); Simma (n. 28) 442–52.

38 *Legal Consequences for States of the Continued Presence of South Africa in Namibia (South West Africa) notwithstanding Security Council Resolution 276 (1970), Advisory Opinion*, ICJ Rep. 1971, 16, 52 §112, see also 54 §119. The ICJ had made an analogy with respect to one of its own decisions 'declaring a situation as contrary to a rule of international law: 'This decision entails a legal consequence, namely that of putting an end to an illegal situation.' See *Namibia Advisory Opinion*, 54 §117, citing *Haya de la Torre Case*, Judgment of June 13th, 1951: ICJ Rep. 1951, 71, 82.

39 UN Charter Art. 48(1).

40 UN Charter Art. 39. See Simma (n. 28) 717–28; T. Gill, 'Legal and Some Political Limitations on the Power of the UN Security Council to Exercise its Enforcement Powers under Chapter VII of the Charter', 26 *Netherlands Yearbook of International Law* (CUP, 1995) 33–138.

41 UN Charter Art. 24(2).

42 *Namibia Advisory Opinion* (n. 38) 16, 52 §110.

43 J. Alvarez, 'Constitutional Interpretation in International Organizations', in J. Coicaud and V. Heiskanen (n. 34) 121; F. Seyersted, *United Nations Forces in the Law of Peace and War* (Sijthoff, 1966) 133–34; *Reparation for Injuries Suffered in the Service of the United Nations, Advisory Opinion* [1949] ICJ Rep., 174.

of the Security Council acting under Chapter VII or under its general grant of authority in Articles 24 and 25.[44]

2.2.2 Purposes and principles

The UN Charter forms the basis for all Security Council action, as demonstrated above.[45] The Purposes and Principles of the Organisation, contained in Articles 1 and 2 respectively, determine the scope of Security Council's powers – both those explicit and implied.[46] The obligation upon the Security Council in particular to act in accordance with Purposes and Principles in discharging its duties is clear in Article 24(2). Article 25 indicates that UN member states are under an obligation to carry out Security Council decisions 'in accordance with the . . . Charter.'[47] This phrase can be seen as a direct reference to the Charter's status as the source of UN members' obligation to carry out decisions (through that same Article 25 in particular). It also indicates that such obligation deriving from Security Council resolutions must be met in accordance with the Purposes and Principles.

Taken together, the chapeaux of Article 1 and Article 2 underscore that the obligations under these two Articles apply not just to UN members, but to the Organisation and therefore its organs such as the Security Council. The chapeau of Article 2 establishes an obligation upon 'the Organization and its Members' to 'act in accordance with the Principles' (Article 2) in pursuit of Purposes (Article 1). UN organs such as the Security Council, as well as individual member states, are subject to the Principles. The distinction is absent from the chapeau of Article 1, which refers generally to the 'United Nations'. Because Article 1 lists overall constitutive purposes rather than how (and therefore by whom) they should be pursued, the more general formulation seems appropriate. It also shows the significance of a distinction in the Article 2 chapeau.

On the legal relevance of Articles 1 and 2 to the Security Council, Wood comments that '[t]he Purposes and Principles are very general statements that are not defined and are subject to a wide range of interpretation, and some by their nature do not seem to have specific legal content'.[48] He adds that '[t]heir fulfillment, and the relative importance to be attached to

---

44 J. Alvarez, *International Organizations as Law-Makers* (OUP, 2005) 191.

45 The UN Charter is 'of fundamental importance', also because of 'its Purposes and Principles and because it is the basis for all the Security Council's activities'. Wood (n. 9) 92–93.

46 Inversely, the more general Articles on the Organisation's 'functions, responsibilities and grants of powers' relate these to the Purposes and Principles 'either by express reference . . . or by employing language derived from the text of Articles 1 and 2.' Repertory of Practice of UN Organs (1945–1954), vol. 1 'Art. 1', para. 2, see http://untreaty.un.org/cod/repertory/art1/english/rep_orig_vol1-art1_e.pdf#gemode=none.

47 See Simma (n. 28). The legally binding obligation imposed upon UN members by Art. 25 is underscored in opinions and judgments of the ICJ: '[W]hen the Security Council adopts a decision under Article 25 in accordance with the Charter, it is for member States to comply with that decision, including those members of the Security Council which voted against it and those Members of the United Nations who are not members of the Council. To hold otherwise would be to deprive this principal organ of its essential functions and powers under the Charter.' See *Namibia Advisory Opinion* (n. 38) 53–54, §116, citing *Reparation* opinion (n. 43) 178. Further, '[a] binding determination made by a competent organ of the United Nations to the effect that a situation is illegal cannot remain without consequence. [T]here is an obligation, especially upon Members of the United Nations, to bring that situation to an end.' *Namibia Advisory Opinion* (n. 38) 54 §117.

48 M. Wood, *The UN Security Council and International Law*, Hersch Lauterpacht Memorial Lectures, University of Cambridge (8 November 2006) para. 20. Wood acknowledges the importance of the Purposes and Principles, (n. 9) 92–93 and quote in (n. 45).

them are essentially matters for policy choice, not for courts or lawyers'.[49] Yet the view that the Purposes and Principles are largely a concern of policy rather than law does not appear consistent with pronouncements of the ICJ and by scholars. For example, in the *Certain Expenses* Advisory Opinion, the ICJ considered and confirmed the legality of Security Council resolutions that established UN peacekeeping operations, and stated that they 'must be tested by their relationship to the purposes of the United Nations'.[50] In discussing the broad scope of Security Council powers, the ICJ specified in the subsequent *Namibia* opinion that '[t]he only limitations are the fundamental principles and purposes found in Chapter 1 of the Charter'.[51] As Rudiger Wolfrum among others comments, the position of the Purposes and Principles in the Charter, taking into consideration the history of Article 1, suggests that they are legally binding.[52]

As the Appeals Chamber of the International Criminal Tribunal for the former Yugoslavia (ICTY) stated in the *Tadic* case, even though the Security Council has the power to determine the existence of a threat which would justify Chapter VII measures, 'it has to remain, at the very least, within the limits of the Purposes and Principles of the Charter' in its determination.[53] The ICTY in determining the scope of its own mandate (i.e. deriving from a Chapter VII resolution) had to engage in questions of UNSC resolution interpretation and the suggestion that establishment of the ad hoc international criminal tribunal was ultra vires. More generally, the UN Secretariat has stated that from a constitutional perspective, the decisions of UN organs taken under Articles of the Charter other than Articles 1 and 2 may be regarded as constituting the implementation of those other Articles.[54] However, such decisions, including by the Security Council, may be considered 'evidence of the application and interpretation in practice of the Purposes which the Organization seeks to achieve and of the Principles in accordance with which the Organization and its Members, in pursuit of the Purposes of the Charter, are obligated to act'.[55]

49 Ibid.
50 Ibid.
51 *Namibia Advisory Opinion* (n. 38) 16, 52 §110.
52 Simma (n. 28) 40 (see 'Purposes and Principles', History of Committee 1); de Wet (n. 7) 198, 'while the framers' intent might be questioned, Article 1(3) has the same structural standing as peace and security'. De Wet also notes (at 8–9) that Art. 1(1) contains the phrase 'in accordance with the principles of justice and international law' only in the second sentence on dispute settlement, omitting it in the first, which addresses 'collective measures for the prevention and removal of threats to the peace'. However, she concludes that the *travaux préparatoires* demonstrate that 'the Security Council could not deviate from international law in an unrestricted fashion when maintaining international peace and security'. Cf. Koskenniemi (n. 8) 327, 336–37 ('the principles and purposes of the Charter are many, ambiguous and conflicting').
53 *Prosecutor v Dusko Tadic*, 2 October 1995, ICTY, Decision on the Defense, Motion for Interlocutory Appeal on Jurisdiction, Case No. IT-94-1-AR72. para. 29.
54 Further, '[t]his reciprocal relationship is often given expression in the decisions of organs in the form of references, made in a preamble or in an operative paragraph, to the Purposes and Principles of the Charter, or to parts of them, together with a citation of the Articles allocating powers and assigning functions and responsibilities.' See 'Article 1', Repertory of Practice of UN Organs (1945–1954), vol. 1, para. 2. The Repertory 'is a legal publication containing analytical studies of the decisions of the principal organs of the United Nations . . . prepared by the Secretariat . . . to throw light on questions of application and interpretation of the Charter which have arisen in practice.' See http://www.un.org/law/repertory/.
55 Ibid.

2.2.3 Respect for human rights as a UN purpose

Human rights are explicitly entrenched in the UN Charter.[56] Among the purposes of the UN is 'to achieve international cooperation . . . in promoting and encouraging respect for *human rights* and for *fundamental freedoms* for all without distinction as to race, sex, language, or religion'.[57] The reaffirmation of 'faith in human rights [and] in the dignity and worth of the human person' is a constitutive aim of the United Nations, declared in the Charter's Preamble.

De Wet, who has written extensively on this issue, suggests that the Security Council is required to respect the core content of fundamental human rights, as set out in the Purposes under Article 1(3) of the Charter.[58] Similarly, Verdirame considers that a 'general obligation to respect human rights' arises from a combination of Articles 1 and 2 of the Charter.[59] In de Wet's view, norms of international human rights law are 'core elements of the principles and purposes of the United Nations and, in light of Article 1, enforcement measures under Chapter VII may not undermine the essence of basic human rights, as well as self-determination or norms of international humanitarian law'.[60]

UN member states as a whole have not gone quite so far. The 1993 UN Vienna Declaration and Programme of Action on human rights refers to the UN's promotion and protection of human rights and fundamental freedoms not as a legal obligation but as a 'priority objective . . . in accordance with its purposes and principles'.[61] The Declaration identifies that the UN's promoting and protecting of human rights 'should be conducted in conformity with the purposes and principles . . . and international law',[62] but not that other Charter activities (e.g. of the UNSC) should be in conformity with human rights. The Declaration appears to restrict 'the consistent and objective application of international human rights instruments' to the activities of 'organs and specialized agencies related to human rights'.[63] While the Declaration obviously could not go beyond the existing treaty and customary international law, it also did not take a progressive position in that regard. How human rights constrain Security Council powers is discussed more fully in sections 3 and 4 below. First, the basis for international human rights law constraints on the Security Council must be established.

3 International human rights law constraints on the UN Security Council

3.1 International human rights as a constraint: inherent limitations

Many human rights are not absolute in nature. Such rights need to be balanced against the goals of society and the state as a whole. Few rights, such as the prohibition against

---

56 UN Charter, Arts 1(3), 55(c).

57 Ibid, Art. 1(3) (emphasis added).

58 E. de Wet, *The Chapter VII Powers of the UN Security Council* (Hart Publishing, 2004) 198; cf. Martti Koskenniemi, 'The Police in the Temple. Order, Justice and the UN: A Dialectical View' (1995) 6 *European Journal of International Law* 327, 336–37.

59 G. Verdirame, *The UN and Human Rights: Who Guards the Guardians?* (CUP, 2011) 74.

60 Ibid. 187, 193.

61 UN Vienna Declaration and Programme of Action, Adopted by the World Conference on Human Rights in Vienna on 25 June 1993, para. 4.

62 Ibid para. 7.

63 Ibid. para. 4. The opposite can be and is equally true of so-called soft law instruments.

torture, are not subject to any limitations under any circumstances.[64] McGoldrick states that the 'idea of limitations is based on the recognition that most human rights are not absolute but rather reflect a balance between individual and community interests'.[65] Not all scholars agree with this view, however, as McHarg notes: 'There is thus something of a paradox in a legal scheme which is supposed to protect the individual against the collective, itself sanctioning limitations to rights on collective interest grounds.'[66] Limitations nonetheless are accepted as an inherent feature of international human rights obligations. This is reflected in the structure of the Universal Declaration, which has a general limitations provision in Article 29:

(1) Everyone has *duties to the community* in which alone the free and full development of his personality is possible.

(2) In the exercise of his rights and freedoms, everyone shall be subject only to such limitations as are determined by law solely for the purpose of securing due recognition and respect for the rights and freedoms of others and of meeting the just requirements of *morality, public order* and the *general welfare* in a democratic society.

(3) These rights and freedoms may in no case be exercised contrary to the *purposes* and *principles* of the United Nations.[67]

Limitations address the need to balance individual human rights against collective goals such as 'morality', 'public order' and 'national security', terms that are not easily defined by law. This balancing is not unique to limitations, but is also part of the regime of derogation in times of public emergencies. Limitations and derogations tend to overlap, with many of the same legal principles applicable (for example, proportionality, non-discrimination).[68] In the case of a human rights treaty, such as the ICCPR, the limitations are contained in individual articles and rights, and in the regime of derogation, for example in Article 4 of the ICCPR. Limitations and derogations belong to the important context for understanding the scope of human rights obligations.

3.2 Constraints within and beyond the UN framework

While the source of obligation on the UN is not without controversy, several alternative grounds may give rise to an obligation in relation to human rights, each by a different legal

---

64 See ICCPR, Art. 7; e.g. Art. 4, ICCPR; Sheeran (n. 23) 118–19.

65 D. McGoldrick, 'The Interface Between Public Emergency Powers and International Law', (2004) 2 *Int'l J. of Const. L.* 380 at 383.

66 A. McHarg, 'Reconciling Human Rights and the Public Interest: Conceptual Problems and Doctrinal Uncertainty in the Jurisprudence of the European Court of Human Rights', (1999) 62 *Mod. L. Rev.* 671, 672.

67 See Universal Declaration of Human Rights, GA Res. 217 (III) A, UN Doc. A/RES/217(III) (10 Dec. 1948); see also Special Rapporteur of the Sub-Comm'n on Prevention of Discrimination and Protection of Minorities, *The Individual's Duties to the Community and the Limitations on Human Rights and Freedoms Under Article 29 of the Universal Declaration of Human Rights*, UN Doc. E/CN.4/Sub.2/432/Rev.2 (1983) (by Erica-Irene A. Daes).

68 McGoldrick (n. 65) 383–84.

means.[69] This analysis does not privilege one explanation in particular, but illustrates the different possibilities. The main grounds confirm that human rights do place a constraint on the Security Council. First, as indicated, the Charter commits the Security Council to human rights through a requirement of consistency with its Purposes and Principles. Second, beyond the UN Charter, a basis for constraint exists through the application of customary international law in relation to human rights to the Organisation. Human rights constraints constitute actual legal obligations upon the UN, on the basis of the Organisation's legal personality. UN practice corroborates both of these grounds. The further basis of human rights constraints may be sought in the concept of inherent human dignity, which lends IHRL a special status under international law.

Finally, a different, non-binding basis for a constraint derived from human rights is a simple presumption that the Security Council does not intend to require states to violate human rights. This 'interpretative presumption', as Milanovic has called it, falls short of any legal force. It is a guideline for interpretation of Security Council resolutions grounded in a reasonable inference, serving a pragmatic purpose of dispelling to a significant degree ambiguity and arbitrariness.[70] Rodley articulated just such a principle in *Sayadi and Vinck*.[71] Different thresholds are discussed in a fuller treatment of interpretation below.

3.3 Human rights as constraint within the charter

As seen above, the Charter upholds respect for 'human rights and for fundamental freedoms' among its key purposes in its preamble and Article 1(3). At a conceptual level, 'human rights' are a broader notion, encapsulating also 'fundamental freedoms'; the former are protections which flow from the idea of equality grounded in a shared human nature and dignity, while the latter denote norms protecting individuals from interference by the state.[72] From a strictly legal perspective, human rights are similarly considered to constitute protections of the individual in relation to the power of the state.[73] The concept of human rights, however, encompasses not just freedoms but protection of a more comprehensive range of rights, from economic, social and cultural rights guaranteeing not freedoms but, for example, access, to the state obligation of 'due diligence to prevent, punish, investigate or redress the harm caused by . . . private persons or entities' and the provision of effective remedies. It follows that references to an obligation to 'act in accordance with the Charter' must be understood to include the Charter's commitment to the overarching framework of human rights.

As Humphrey stated, human rights references pervade the Charter like a 'golden thread'.[74] Article 1(3) of the UN Charter sets out the Purpose that concerns human rights, while

---

69 For discussion of different bases, see F. Megret and F. Hoffman, 'The UN as a Human Rights Violator? Some Reflections on the UN's Changing Human Rights Responsibilities' (2003) 25(2) *Human Rights Quarterly* 314–34; S. Sheeran, 'A Constitutional Moment?: United Nations Peacekeeping in the Democratic Republic of Congo', (2011) 8 *International Organizations Law Review* 55; N. White and D. Klaasen (eds), 'Introduction', in *The UN, Human Rights and Post Conflict Situations* (Juris Publishing, 2005) x; see discussion in Alvarez (n. 44) 171.

70 Milanovic (n. 1).

71 *Sayadi and Vinck* (n. 1).

72 See Simma (n. 28) 919–41, in particular discussion and references at 921.

73 Nigel Rodley, 'Can Armed Opposition Groups Violate Human Rights', in K.E. Mahoney and P. Mahoney (eds), *Human Rights in the Twenty-first Century: A Global Challenge* (Martinus Nijhoff Publishers, 1993), 297–318. For a broader definition, see A. Clapham, *Human Rights Obligations of Non-State Actors* (OUP, 2006).

74 J. Humphrey, *No Distant Millennium: The International Law of Human Rights* (UNESCO, 1989).

Article 55 in the 'International Economic and Social Cooperation' section provides that the UN shall promote 'universal respect for, and observance of, human rights and fundamental freedoms'. Human rights are mentioned in the Charter's Preamble and Articles 1(03), 13(1), 55(c), 56, 62(2), 68 and 76(c). These provisions elaborate on the general obligation for the Organisation and member states to respect and promote human rights, as well as endowing the main organs with the power to address human rights questions. The UN Human Rights Committee has stated that 'there is a United Nations Charter obligation to promote universal respect for, and observance of, human rights and fundamental freedoms'.[75]

The scope of 'human rights' referred to in the Charter can be determined by reference to IHRL, using human rights treaties as interpretive sources.[76] The preambles of the ICCPR and the UN International Covenant on Economic, Social and Cultural Rights (ICESCR) refer explicitly to UN Charter principles and the Charter-based obligation upon states 'to promote universal respect for, and observance of, human rights and freedoms'.[77] The treaty articles establishing human rights obligations are thus firmly grounded in the UN Charter framework. This supports the idea that the Charter establishes many of these norms as binding on the Organisation, including the Security Council and Secretariat.

Further, as suggested above in the consideration of the general framework of constraints upon the Security Council, the obligation to act (or require action by member states) consistent with UN Purposes applies not just to members but to the Organisation and therefore the UNSC. This is reinforced indirectly by Article 24(2), which creates an obligation upon the Security Council to discharge its duties 'in accordance with the Purposes and Principles of the United Nations', including the respect of human rights. Similarly, Article 25, providing for the binding force upon members of Security Council decisions, establishes that members 'agree to accept and carry out' those decisions 'in accordance with the present Charter', including Article 1(3).

Article 2 states that 'the Organization and its Members, *in pursuit of the Purposes* stated in Article 1, *shall act in accordance with*' a series of Principles, including in Article 2(4) that '[a]ll Members shall refrain in their international relations from the threat or use of force against the territorial integrity or political independence of any state, *or in any other manner inconsistent with the Purposes of the United Nations*',[78] including Article 1(3) relating to human rights. In other words, all members have an obligation to refrain from using force in a manner inconsistent with the Organisation's Purpose of promoting and encouraging respect for human rights. This constraint becomes important with respect to the Security Council and its action taken under Article 39, binding upon states under Article 25.

It is possible to infer the Organisation itself cannot require members to use force in a way inconsistent with UN Purposes, that is, in violation of human rights. A Security Council decision requiring an IHRL violation would constitute a violation of a UN Charter obligation. However, as indicated above, also with respect to limitations and derogations,

---

75 UN Human Rights Committee, General Comment No. 31, (26 May 2004) UN Doc. CCPR/C/21/Rev.1/Add. 13 (2004) para. 2. Note that this paragraph contains the only specific mention of 'fundamental freedoms', while the General Comment refers otherwise to human rights throughout.

76 Universal Declaration of Human Rights (1948), ICCPR (1966), ICESCR (1966), International Convention on the Elimination of Racial Discrimination (1965), Convention on the Elimination of All Forms of Discrimination Against Women (1979), Convention on the Rights of the Child (1989) and Convention Against Torture (1984); de Wet (n. 58) 199–200 and (n. 7) 13–14.

77 ICCPR and ICESCR Preamble.

78 UN Charter Art. 2(4).

understanding the exact scope of obligations may sometimes be difficult. In particular, the limited legal personality of the UN as compared to the sovereign nature of a state inflects the reading of scope. Accordingly, IHRL applying to the Organisation may lead to a different range of obligations than as applying to a state. Article 2(7) on non-intervention could also prima facie be read as a constraint on the Organisation, and Security Council in particular, with respect to impact on human rights (both negatively and positively) at least outside the context of Chapter VII measures.[79]

The obligations extend beyond the negative requirement not to commit human rights violations. A positive obligation upon the UN to respect human rights may be inferred under the Charter, as is the case generally for states under IHRL.[80] A foundation stone in IHRL is the obligation to 'ensure' respect of the rights for all people within a state's territory and subject to its jurisdiction.[81] The Security Council can violate a Charter obligation to respect IHRL through a resolution requiring action that would violate human rights. States could have parallel responsibility if they carried out such action. This is consistent with the particular nature of the UN's legal personality, according to which the Organisation's rights and obligations under international law are limited and 'depend on the UN's *purposes* and functions as specified or *implied* in the Charter and developed in practice'.[82] Human rights fall squarely within that limited space, depending on UN purposes in both specified and implied form, and developed through UN practice as shown above.

3.4 Human rights as constraint beyond the Charter

3.4.1 Human rights through customary international law

It is well accepted that international organisations may be bound *mutatis mutandis* by customary international law,[83] and the ICJ has affirmed this for the Organisation.[84] It is also understood

---

79 N. Tasagourias 'Consent, Neutrality/Impartiality and the Use of Force in Peacekeeping', 11(3) *Journal of Conflict and Security Law*, 465; Simma (n. 28) 164–67. Art. 2(7) of the UN Charter provides: 'Nothing contained in the present Charter shall authorise the United Nations to intervene in matters which are essentially within the domestic jurisdiction of any state or shall require the Members to submit such matters to settlement under the present Charter; but this principle shall not prejudice the application of enforcement measures under Chapter VII.'

80 *Velasquez Rodriguez v Honduras, Preliminary Objections*, Judgment of June 26, 1989, Inter-Am.Ct.H.R. (Ser. C) No. 1 (1994) para. 172 (referring to 'the lack of due diligence to prevent the violation or to respond to it as required by the Convention'); ICCPR, Art. 2(1) and UN Human Rights Committee, General Comment No. 31 (n. 75) paras 3 and 10.

81 General Comment 31 (n. 75) The UN Human Rights Committee has stated that the general obligation to respect and *ensure* under Art. 2(1) of the ICCPR includes that 'States Parties must ensure that individuals also have accessible and effective remedies to vindicate those rights' and a failure to investigate or to 'ensure that those responsible are brought to justice' (which includes NSAs) may constitute a state violation of the ICCPR.

82 *Reparation* opinion (n. 43) 178.

83 R. Higgins, *The Development of International Law through the Political Organs of the United Nations* (OUP, 1963) 2; A. Clapham, *Human Rights Obligations of Non-State Actors* (OUP, 2006) 19; C. Tomuschat, *International Law: Ensuring the Survival of Mankind on the Eve of a New Century: General Course on Public International Law* (Martinus Nijhoff, 2001), vol. 281 RCADI, 34–35; P. Sands and P. Klein, *Bowett's Law of International Institutions*, 6th edn (Sweet & Maxwell, 2009) 458–59.

84 *Reparations* case (n. 43) 179; ICJ, *Interpretation of the Agreement of 25 March 1951 between the WHO and Egypt, Advisory Opinion*, 1980 ICJ Reports 73, 89 and 90 (ICJ 1980); Verdirame (n. 59) 56.

that customary international law can be a source of human rights obligations for the Organisation.[85] As mentioned above, the exact scope of obligations upon the UN as an international organisation may be unclear. Accordingly, the application of customary international law might be modified so that Organisation is bound at least by those norms relevant to its activities or 'functionality'.[86]

The development of customary international law applicable to the UN requires *opinio juris* and practice and therefore will have a similar basis to an implied power under the UN legal order. As the law's content is still determined by the scope of the Charter and its practice, a customary international law obligation is not meaningfully independent of the UN system and its practice.[87] The scope of obligations will be essentially the same, whether based on the Charter or customary international law. Even so, customary international law constitutes an alternative basis for human rights obligations. A customary international law obligation on the UN is consistent with, and builds upon, the constraint internal to the UN Charter discussed above. It provides a robust external legal obligation upon the Security Council. The applicability of customary international human rights law expands the scope of obligations applicable to the Security Council beyond the Charter and treaty law.

3.4.2 UN practice: confirmation of the human rights constraint

UN practice confirms that the Organisation, and therefore the Security Council as a primary organ, are constrained by obligations of IHRL. A range of UN documents and internal legal advice from the UN Office of Legal Affairs consistently affirms as a general matter that the Organisation is obligated by human rights, under both the Charter and customary international law.[88] The UN Office of Legal Affairs' internal advice on a key peacekeeping issue of UN support to government forces committing human rights violations stated clearly 'the Organization's obligations under *customary international law* and from the *Charter* to uphold, promote and encourage respect for human rights, international humanitarian law and refugee law'.[89] The internal advice, and the 2011 Human Rights Due Diligence Policy on UN support to non-UN security forces which followed, spelt out obligations upon UN peacekeeping missions fully consistent with IHRL. Such obligations were not limited to avoiding participation in violations, but extended to a possible positive duty to protect against them.[90]

The 2008 UN Peacekeeping Operations, Principles and Guidelines ('Capstone Doctrine') states in its section dedicated to human rights that '[i]nternational human rights law is an

---

85 Alvarez (n. 44) 171; Sheeran (n. 69); Megret and Hoffman (n. 69).

86 Sheeran (n. 69) 80–81; Moshe Hirsch, *The Responsibility of International Organizations Towards Third Parties: Some Basic Principles* (Springer, 1995) (where 'functionality' refers to the test set out by the ICJ in the *Certain Expenses* advisory opinion (n. 36)).

87 J. Cerone, 'Reasonable Measures in Unreasonable Circumstances: a Legal Responsibility Framework for Human Rights Violations in Post-conflict Territories under UN Administration', in Nigel White and Dirk Klaasen (eds), *The UN, Human Rights and Post Conflict Situations* (Juris Publishing, 2005) 62.

88 E.g. see discussion in Sheeran (n. 23).

89 See letter dated 1 April 2009 from UN Office of Legal Affairs to the UN Department of Peacekeeping Operations, available at Geoffrey Gettleman, 'UN Army told not to join Congo Army in Operation', *New York Times*, 9 December 2009 (emphasis added), <http://www.nytimes.com/2009/12/10/world/africa/10congo.html>, 9 November 2010.

90 Ibid.

integral part of the normative framework for United Nations peacekeeping operations'.[91] The 'Capstone Doctrine' confirms the importance of respecting and promoting human rights, with specific reference to IHRL: 'United Nations peacekeeping operations should be conducted in full respect of human rights and should seek to advance human rights through the implementation of their mandates . . .'.[92]

In light of the UN's increasing role in transitional justice processes, in 2010 the Secretary-General adopted a Guidance Note on the United Nations Approach to Transitional Justice.[93] The Note states that:

> The *normative foundation* for the work of the UN in advancing transitional justice is the Charter of the United Nations, along with four of the pillars of the modern international legal system: *international human rights law*, international humanitarian law, international criminal law, and international refugee law.[94]

This translates to a UN position on transitional justice issues whereby the Organisation may potentially commit, or, more commonly, be complicit in, a violation of human rights norms. The Guidance Note consequently states that the UN 'will neither establish nor provide assistance to any tribunal that allows for capital punishment, nor endorse provisions in peace agreements that include amnesties for genocide, war crimes, crimes against humanity, and gross violations of human rights'.[95] These brief examples support the general conclusion that the UN as an Organisation is constrained by human rights obligations.

3.4.3 Inherent human dignity

Underpinning the special status of human rights, and indeed the special nature of IHRL under international law, is not just consent, but the normative power of an idea. Beyond consent and legal positivism, the status ascribed to human rights stems from a deeper philosophical concept and idea of human dignity, captured by natural rights theory and articulated in key documents such as the UN Charter, Universal Declaration of Human Rights and Bill of Rights.[96] The Preamble of the UN Charter, for example, reads:

> We the peoples of the United Nations determined . . . to reaffirm faith in fundamental human rights, in the dignity and worth of the human person, in the equal rights of men and women . . . and to establish conditions under which justice and respect for the

---

91 UN Peacekeeping Operations, Principles and Guidelines (Capstone Doctrine), 1.2, 14–15, http:// pbpu.unlb.org/pbps/Library/Capstone_Doctrine_ENG.pdf.

92 Capstone Doctrine, ibid. 15. The Capstone Doctrine also cites the Universal Declaration on Human Rights as a key reference for human rights standards (p. 14), as does another core document establishing UN practice, 'We are United Nations Peacekeeping Personnel' (UN Doc. A/61/645, Annex III).

93 UN Secretary-General, Guidance Note of the Secretary-General: United Nations Approach to Transitional Justice (March 2010), available at www.unrol.org/doc.aspx?d=2957 (accessed on 20 June 2013).

94 Ibid. 3.

95 Ibid. 4.

96 G. Verdirame, 'Human Rights in Political and Legal Theory' and N. Rodley, 'Non State Actors and Human Rights' both in this volume.

obligations arising from treaties and other sources of international law can be maintained
. . . have resolved to combine our efforts to accomplish these aims.

Human rights, and the inherent dignity of the human being, are fundamental elements of modern law and society as reflected in the views of numerous legal theorists.[97] Higgins goes as far as to posit that human rights treaties 'reflect rights inherent in human beings, not dependent upon grant by the state'.[98] This status relates to the assertion of human rights as positivist norms within the UN constitutional order.[99]

Jus cogens, a peremptory norm of general international law from which no derogation is permitted, is by definition accepted and recognised by the international community.[100] Likewise, it is accepted that the Security Council must not violate *jus cogens*, and that it is inconceivable both on the basis of policy and law that the Security Council could act inconsistently with those rights prescribed as non-derogable in the ICCPR. This is reflected in state practice and intent expressed in treaty language, as well as jurisprudence.[101] The definition of torture, the prohibition of which is recognised under international law as *jus cogens* as well as treaty law, captures precisely this notion of inherent human dignity. The ICTY Appeals Chamber in the *Tadic* case stated that peremptory norms are binding on the Security Council, and Judge Lauterpacht asserted the same in his separate opinion in the *Genocide Convention* case.[102] According to legal scholar Cassese, it follows that Security Council resolutions inconsistent with *jus cogens* norms must be interpreted consistently, or held partly or wholly invalid.[103] Regional court rulings have also upheld a broader framework of fundamental rights (e.g. *Kadi*) and have influenced discussions within the Security Council.

BALANCING AND SAFEGUARDS ON POWERS

4 UN Security Council and human rights in practice: interpretive constraints and norm conflict

The previous section considered the conceptual framework for the relationship between the Security Council and international human rights norms. This section considers how that framework applies at the level of interpretation and also how to understand the scope or limitation of human rights obligations. An absence of clarity about the relationship between human rights norms and the UNSC has led to arbitrariness and widely differing approaches,

---

97 On social contract or social compact theory, see J. Rawls, *A Theory of Justice* (Belknap Press, 1971); J. Rousseau, *Du contrat social ou Principes du droit politique* ('Of The Social Contract, Or Principles of Political Right') (1762); J. Locke, 'Second Treatise of Civil Government' (1690).

98 R. Higgins, 'Human Rights: Some Questions of Integrity' (1989) 15 Commonwealth Law Bulletin 598, at 607.

99 S. Sheeran, 'The Relationship of International Human Rights Law and General International Law: Hermeneutic Constraint or Pushing the Boundaries?' in this volume.

100 Vienna Convention on the Law of Treaties (1969), Art. 53.

101 Individual opinion of Committee member Sir Nigel Rodley (concurring), *Sayadi and Vinck* (n. 1) 36–37, citing the European Court of Human Rights (*Behrami and Behrami v France* and *Saramati v France, Germany and Norway* (2007)); and *Kadi* 2005 (n. 1). See also Wood (n. 9).

102 *Tadic* (n. 53) para. 296; *Reservations to the Genocide Convention, Advisory Opinion* [1951] ICJ Rep. 15, paras. 100 and 102.

103 A. Cassese, *International Law*, 206

as discussed above. The main challenge facing a theory of the Security Council and human rights is to be both intellectually coherent and practically applicable.

4.1 Human rights as interpretive constraint

This chapter has examined the different bases for human rights obligations upon the Security Council. It has established that respect for human rights is generally integral to the UNSC's authority and powers. From this finding arises an important principle of interpretation: at a minimum, the UN and Security Council in particular is *presumed not to intend* that human rights will be violated due to its decision or require members to violate human rights obligations. This stems from a presumption of legal consistency with the Charter, and is supported by UN legal advice, relevant scholarship, and by a certain degree of consensus as reflected in international tribunal rulings and state practice, as well as in discussions in the Security Council.[104] From this presumption arises a constraint on possible interpretations of Security Council decisions. These shall always be interpreted in a manner which would not be contrary to, or indeed would be consistent with, human rights obligations.[105]

To establish the meaning of a Security Council resolution or decision is not always straightforward.[106] However, a measure pursuant to a UNSC resolution requiring a violation of IHRL cannot in theory be a correct interpretation. The connection between Security Council powers and constraints under the UN Charter, as well as human rights obligations upon the Organisation in general, translate into a constraint on the scope of Security Council powers.

Accordingly, for a clear binding decision under Chapter VII or Articles 24 and 25 of the Charter,[107] interpretation is a crucial method to establish what action is required. In general, the interpretive presumption will not be required, as only in limited cases could it reconcile a clear Security Council decision to violate human rights (which in any event will not usually be the case). Where the Security Council resolution's meaning is not explicit or without ambiguity, or has scope for varied interpretations, states or other implementing actors that interpret a Council decision would have to 'err' on the side of respect for human rights, with little ability to claim that any violations were conducted as an obligation under the resolution. That was in effect the position taken and implemented by the Secretariat, a primary organ of the UN, in a recent UN peacekeeping situation. That situation concerned withdrawal of UN support, provided under a Security Council Chapter VII resolution, to Congolese government armed forces which were committing violations of human rights and international humanitarian law.[108]

The scope of application of the interpretive constraint is not limited to binding decisions. On the contrary, insofar as the Charter obligations upon the Security Council are general, the interpretive constraint applies to the interpretation of all Security Council resolutions.

---

104 *Kadi* 2008 (n. 1), *Al-Jedda* HL and ECtHR (n. 1), *Nada* (n. 1).
105 See Milanović, ('norm conflict) (n. 1), discussed below.
106 Wood (n. 9).
107 For discussion of when a Security Council resolution is binding, see Security Council Report (n. 31) 9–11.
108 This was for support by MONUC peacekeeping operation in the Democratic Republic of the Congo to government forces, see Sheeran (n. 69).

This is significant. Whether or not a particular mandate is established through binding powers is not unequivocal in every case, much less what specific measures such a mandate entails. Irrespective of such ambiguity, a human rights obligation and therefore the interpretive constraint apply and guide implementation.

This presumption of 'non-intent' as it relates to the interpretive constraint must be distinguished from a purely pragmatic interpretive presumption. Milanović argues for an 'interpretative presumption' whereby Security Council resolutions should be presumed and interpreted to be compatible with human rights, 'as far as possible' and 'in the absence of a clear statement by the Council to the contrary.' The 'interpretative presumption' is designed primarily to address the immediate problem of interpretation. Its basis is in the presumption against norm conflict in international law, the fact that the Security Council's powers are after all limited, and Security Council statements compatible with such a presumption, as well as the equal standing of human rights and 'peace and security'.[109] This standard falls short of the presumption discussed here, which instead admits no exceptions in accordance with the status of human rights under the Charter and under international law.

The difference can be seen when the interpretive constraint set by human rights meets not with a choice between reasonable and competing interpretations, but with an irreconcilable violation required by the Security Council.[110] Here, the distinction between the two otherwise similar approaches diverges. A purely pragmatic 'interpretative presumption' defers to the Security Council's 'powers'. Instead, the interpretive constraint flowing from a deeper presumption of non-intent, based in a reading of the Charter as discussed and a finding of obligation, offers a different response grounded in that broader theoretical framework. Rodley anticipates this approach in his individual opinion; though he deliberately stops short of suggesting the existence of binding obligations, the principles he proposes reflect those flowing here from the theoretical framework of an interpretive constraint.[111] The tools offered by the interpretive constraint to the practitioner are discussed in the remaining sections.

4.2 Interpreting tension between obligations

Interpretation is the main tool to resolve apparent tension between obligations. Security Council resolutions often employ ambiguous rather than clear-cut language. In practice, it is uncommon for a violation to be unambiguous in a Security Council decision. Security Council decisions tend not to require a measure so narrow and specific as to constitute a clear violation of human rights. This is consistent with the presumption and obligation under the Charter of respect towards human rights, but also simply flows from the fact that UNSC resolutions tend to establish a general mandate without detailing every aspect. This is for reasons both political, as the negotiation and quest for consensus,[112] and legal and practical, in cases where the UNSC is only in a position to authorise and delegate action (e.g. UN-authorised use of force by non-UN forces as in the *Al-Jedda* case[113]). The interpretive constraint offered by human rights is therefore key to establishing the legality and scope of a Security Council resolution or decision.

---

109 Milanovic (norm conflict) (n. 1) 98–99.
110 Ibid.
111 Individual opinion *Sayadi and Vinck* (n. 101).
112 The quest for consensus or even unanimity can lead to 'deliberate ambiguity', Wood (n. 9) 82.
113 *Al-Jedda* HL (n. 1); *Al-Jedda* ECtHR (n. 1).

Yet tension between obligations under a Security Council resolution (i.e. measures promoting peace and security) and a human rights treaty or customary international law cannot always be resolved through interpretation of ambiguities, and through the interpretive constraint in favour of human rights. Sometimes, tension is not the result of ambiguity but of a real and irreconcilable conflict of norms and objectives. The European Court of Justice decision in *Kadi* involved such a clear conflict of human rights obligations with a European Community (EC) regulation promulgated pursuant to UNSC resolution 1267 (i.e. the Taliban–Al Qaida sanctions list). The Court applied a strongly dualist approach by effectively holding that the European legal system and EC regulation could be reviewed separately from, and without prejudice to, the UN system and Charter obligations.[114] On this basis, the Court was able to determine that the relevant EC regulation violated the applicable European human rights obligations without dealing with the state's claim that it was obligated to carry out the measure under UNSC resolution 1267 and Article 103 of the Charter.[115]

In *Sayadi and Vinck*, the Human Rights Committee was faced with a similar irreconcilable conflict between human rights obligations and the obligations pursuant to resolution 1267, and the majority also opted for a strongly dualist approach and separation of legal regimes in order to find a violation of the ICCPR:

> While the Committee could not consider alleged violations of other instruments such as the Charter of the United Nations, or allegations that challenged United Nations rules concerning the fight against terrorism, the Committee was competent to admit a communication alleging that a State party had violated rights set forth in the Covenant, regardless of the source of the obligation implemented by the State party.[116]

In targeted sanctions cases where the only possible interpretation is a conflict between human rights and the Security Council's decision, the court or treaty body has usually responded with essentially a strictly dualist approach to the treaty obligations and obligations under the UN Charter and Article 103.[117] These cases and their legal consequences for member states have forced the Security Council to eventually respond by improving (though not resolving) the process of review available to listed individuals through the institution of an Ombudsperson's office.[118] This strongly suggests that one avenue for effective checks and balances on the Security Council, absent judicial review, is a slow process of indirect review through regional and national legal decisions, which translates into pressure from UN member states on the Security Council. However, the approach in *Kadi* and *Sayadi and Vinck* does not provide a complete answer. As indicated by Shearer in his dissenting view in *Sayadi and Vinck*, the Committee's rationale 'appears to regard the Covenant as on a par with the United Nations Charter, and not as subordinate to it'.[119] It therefore involves a legal fiction of sorts, and one

---

114 *Kadi* 2008 (n. 1).
115 *Kadi* 2008 (n. 1) para. 297–99; see van den Herik and Schrijver (n. 5) 35–37.
116 *Sayadi and Vinck* (n. 1) para. 7.2. Marko Milanović, 'The Human Rights Committee's Views in *Sayadi v Belgium*: A Missed Opportunity', *Goettingen Journal of International Law* (2009) 1 (3), 519–38
117 E.g. *Kadi* 2008 (n. 1); *Sayadi and Vinck* (n. 1); *HM Treasury v Mohammed Jabar Ahmed and ors (FC); HM Treasury v Mohammed al-Ghabra (FC); R. (on the application of Hani El Sayed Sabaei Youssef) v HM Treasury* [2010] UKSC 2 *(United Kingdom); Abousfian Abdelrazik v The Minister of Foreign Affairs and the Attorney General of Canada* (Federal Court of Canada) T-727–08, 2009 FC 580 (2009).
118 The Ombudsperson's Office (n. 5)
119 *Kadi* 2008 (n. 1).

which may not be applied consistently (e.g a court of treaty body may in fact wish to rely on a Charter obligation).

Instead, the significance of an interpretive constraint is not only to navigate interpretative choices, but also to speak to an explicit conflict between human rights and a Security Council decision. The interpretive constraint presupposes a robust presumption of non-intent. Such a presumption does not merely serve interpretation *en lieu* of a clearer framework on human rights and the Security Council. As shown, the interpretive constraint and pre-sumption of non-intent arises from a Charter obligation to respect human rights. As a result, it does not fall away when human rights norms conflict with measures required by Security Council decisions. The interpretive constraint offers an approach derived from the human rights framework on limitations and derogations, which may mediate the clash and respect the presumption of non-intent. This approach is discussed fully in the final section.

4.3 Test of legal validity

In the cases beyond ambiguity or reconcilable conflicts, the Security Council could require action directly in violation of human rights. The interpretive constraint offers a further inter-pretive principle: if the only possible interpretation of a decision requires a violation of human rights, this would generally signal the legal invalidity of such a decision or relevant parts thereof, since the Security Council would be acting *ultra vires* under the Charter. This conclusion reflects the interdependence of the Security Council's powers and the Charter framework discussed above. The interpretive constraint thus not only tries to ensure correct interpretation but also serves to define the legal validity of the Security Council decision.

The significant challenge with this approach is the absence of an authoritative interpreter who could make an objective determination. The ICJ lacks mandatory jurisdiction within the UN legal order, including over Security Council decisions.[120] Instead, a key proposition of Charter interpretation is that a generally acceptable interpretation made by an organ is 'binding' or 'authoritative'.[121] This principle of effectiveness has been used to interpret deci-sions of organs in the absence of contrary indications. Koskenniemi thus reluctantly suggests that 'what the Council says *is* the law'.[122]

Regardless of other considerations, trying to objectively determine illegality holds an intrinsic value. As one of the current authors has stated elsewhere, 'the UN legal order and its organs . . . have the potential to correct non-compliance through the classification of inter-national responsibility, rather than the implementation of the consequences of responsibility on the international plane.'[123] These consequences arising from the labelling of illegality, whether by states or their tribunal and courts and if sufficiently persuasive to others, are an important mitigation of the Security Council's lack of formal accountability.[124]

---

120 UN Charter, ICJ Statute (n. 3).
121 C.F. Amerasinghe, *Principles of the Institutional law of International Organizations* (CUP, 1996) 63; Alvarez (n. 44) 79.
122 Koskenniemi (n. 58) 327
123 Sheeran (n. 69) 134.
124 This is arguably what occurred with the US-led resolutions that attempted to provide immunity to nationals of non-state parties to the Rome Statute in SC Res. 1422 (2002).

4.4 The question of norm conflict

The concept of norm conflict is most often used to explain possible or occurring human rights violations within the context of Security Council-driven action. The issue of alleged conflict between human rights obligations under IHRL and Charter obligations toward the UN Security Council has been treated in several prominent cases in regional courts, particularly the European Court of Human Rights.[125] States generally argued that their obligation under the Charter, and the superiority of that legal obligation, left them no choice but to comply with Security Council decisions under Chapter VII, even where compliance led necessarily to violations of human rights treaty obligations. Court or treaty body decisions or rulings themselves varied but in general were limited by a lack of jurisdictional authority or competence to address the matter, and compounded by Article 103 of the Charter.

The conflict between human rights and obligations pursuant to a Security Council resolution is framed as one between different norms, that is often it is a clash between distinct legal orders or objectives. Most often, Article 103 is invoked to justify a resolution of the conflict in favour of obligations under the Security Council resolution. This is considered to be the case equally for states' obligations under customary international law, and not just other treaties.[126] Jus cogens is the only agreed limit to the pre-eminence of Charter obligations under Article 103.[127]

The resolution of 'conflict' in favour of compliance with binding Security Council decisions over human rights obligations is the typical argument made by states before international courts and treaty bodies. Crucially, the conflict is characterised as a conflict of norms, namely of the UN legal order and the relevant international human rights treaty and customary international law. States invoke Article 103 of the UN Charter, which resolves a conflict between obligations under the Charter and 'other international agreements' in favour of the Charter. The classification as norm conflict also influences and constrains the forum of adjudication. The *Certain Expenses* advisory opinion and *Tadic* case are two examples of the few cases in which tribunals, the ICJ and ICTY Appeal Chamber respectively, engaged actively in interpreting Security Council resolutions with a view to considering their legality.[128] More usual is a reluctance, as in the ICJ *Lockerbie* cases, to determine the legality of Security Council decisions.[129] The European Court of Human Rights and international human rights treaty bodies have jurisdiction over specific treaties and consider known treaty obligations against external UN obligations which they do not have the authority to interpret. For the purposes of those discussions, it may formally be the case that these conflicts can only be interpreted as norm conflicts, lacking a clear judgment – for example from the ICJ on the role of human rights in the Charter and with respect to Security Council obligations.

Yet a question that is captured in the idea of norm conflict has broader relevance. Surely, given the special mandate of the Security Council and the status of the UN Charter under international law, the Council must have executive powers (e.g. as compared to other organs

---

125 For discussion, see Milanovic (norm conflict) (n. 1); M. Milanovic, 'European Court Decides Al-Skeini and Al-Jedda', EJIL: TALK! (7 July 2011), available at: http://www.ejiltalk.org/european-court-decides-al-skeini-and-al-jedda/ (accessed on 25 June 2013).

126 Simma (n. 28) 1298–99.

127 See P. Sands and P. Klein, *Bowett's Law of International Institutions*, 6th edn (Sweet & Maxwell, 2009) 458–59; Wood (n. 48) paras 36–37; While not dealing with *jus cogens*, but rather various human rights including the core of a right to a remedy, see *Kadi* 2008 (n. 1).

128 *Tadic* (n. 53); *Certain Expenses* (n. 36).

129 *Lockerbie* case (n. 33)

of the UN) concerning constraints even in relation to human rights? This would appear to be the meaning of Article 103, in combination with Articles 24 and 25 and Chapter VII of the Charter. It could be argued that human rights need to be limited and balanced against the goals of the community. How that balance might be reflected with respect to the objectives of the Organisation as opposed to state parties under human rights treaties requires clarification.

The interpretive constraint derives from the limits of those Security Council powers, and confirms that human rights are essential to the Purposes and Principles of the entire UN enterprise. This, however, does not respond to the question as posed, namely in terms of a 'norm conflict' between the UN legal order and international human rights law. The emphasis in the case law is placed on the conflict itself and on which norm prevails, and less on whether there is a conflict or, more importantly, the extent of the conflict.[130] One answer has been given: there is no norm conflict because human rights also belong to the UN legal order as obligations internal to the Charter, interpreted through IHRL. Allegations of norm conflict are symptoms of a lack of interpretive guidance, and of the jurisdictional limitations of regional courts, forced to judge greater authority.

There is a further crucial point. In theory, a violation of human rights obligations will always signal invalidity, whether it is the result of decision-makers' reasonable interpretation or whether it flows unequivocally from a Security Council resolution or decision. In practice, the legality of the UNSC resolution or decision may also be driven by states' reactions and understanding or perceptions of the legality, for example, as discussed above in relation to individual sanctions. Compatible with this principle and fact, an exceptional circumstance could exist in which the Security Council legitimately and lawfully makes a decision constraining human rights, of the type of limitation afforded to states under derogation regimes provided in human rights treaties. Such an approach would apply whether or not a norm conflict is identified, that is, whether or not the tension is considered internal to the Charter rather than between two different legal orders. This issue is deeply relevant to practice on the UNSC and human rights and requires full consideration.

5 Exceptional measures: derogations as safeguard

5.1 Real conflict of obligations

To conceive of the interpretive constraint framework as the absolute primacy of human rights over Security Council imperatives would be a flawed assessment of the real political importance of the Council. Such a suggestion also evokes a false juxtaposition of human rights and Security Council powers, resolved in favour of the former. The human rights paradigm, which gives rise to the interpretive constraint, makes provision for exceptional circumstances. Under international human rights treaty law, there are derogations provisions to regulate exceptional situations. There is no convincing reason why some form of 'derogation' should not apply to action taken by the Security Council and pursuant to its binding decisions. Since IHRL applies to the Security Council, it would be hard to argue that there is no provision for exceptional measures. This follows from the specific mandate of the Security Council, the

---

130 The comparison of the different Lords decisions in *Al-Jedda*, and the European Court of Human Rights decision illustrate this spectrum of perspectives well. See *Al-Jedda* HL (n. 1); *Al-Jedda* ECtHR (n. 1). See Milanovic (*Al-Jedda*) (n. 1).

role of human rights in interpreting its resolutions, and the fact that a more restrictive framework would not apply to the Security Council versus an individual state, which may benefit from derogations under treaty law.

Situations raising the issue of exceptions can be found in each of the above-mentioned typical areas of conflict between Security Council decisions and human rights: (i) overseas military deployments, (ii) economic sanctions and (iii) targeted sanctions. The various decisions in the *Al-Jedda* case illustrate the problem.[131] The case concerned, inter alia, the UK claim that it had not violated the prohibition of arbitrary detention in detaining Mr Al-Jedda pursuant to a Security Council mandate under Chapter VII.[132] With some exceptions, the general trend in individual opinions in the UK House of Lords decision was that Mr Al-Jedda was subject to human rights protections, but some of these (e.g. arbitrary detention) were interpreted to have restricted application in light of the Security Council mandate and state obligations under the Charter. If the UK had derogated under the European Convention, the result would have been similar in legal terms. Lord Bingham, in a view supported by two other Law Lords (i.e. a majority), stated that the UK was able to exercise the authority to detain under Security Council resolution 1546, but had to ensure rights under Article 5 (right to liberty and security) were not infringed 'to any greater extent than is inherent in such detention'.[133] Baroness Hale was more precise and illuminating:

> The right is qualified but not displaced. This is an important distinction, insufficiently explored in the all or nothing arguments with which we were presented. We can go no further than the UN has implicitly required us to go in restoring peace and security to a troubled land. The right is qualified only to the extent required or authorised by the resolution. What remains of it thereafter must be observed. This may have both substantive and procedural consequences.

The European Court of Human Rights, by contrast to the House of Lords, effectively decided there was no norm conflict (a valid position in a technical sense as the UK was *authorised* not *required* to detain). It held that there was no derogation by the state, therefore the full obligations of the Convention applied.[134] This legal rationale is problematic for both theoretical and practical reasons. It does not recognise or permit a capacity of the Security Council to derogate or limit rights (even justifiably). The full application of the Convention to an exceptional situation (i.e. a conflict setting in Iraq) is unrealistic and therefore ultimately leads to a narrower scope and impact of application of human rights. This latter point is borne out in the European Court's cases concerning Iraq. State parties were required to respect human rights of those they detained, but not in the context of other security activities.[135] The European Court in *Al-Skeini v UK* thus held that 'whenever the state through its agents *exercises control and authority over an individual*, and thus jurisdiction, the state is under an obligation . . . to secure to that individual the rights and freedoms . . . of the Convention'.[136]

Economic sanctions and targeted sanctions also offer examples of a framework for balancing, limitation and derogation. In the case of economic sanctions, the UN Committee

---

131 Ibid.
132 Ibid.
133 *Al-Jedda* HL (n. 1) (along with Lord Carswell and Lord Brown) para. 39.
134 *Al-Jedda* HL (n. 1).
135 E.g. see *Al-Skeini and Others v the United Kingdom* (55721/07) (2011) 53 EHRR 18.
136 Ibid para. 137.

on Economic, Social and Cultural Rights stated in its General Comment No. 8 (1997) that the rights 'cannot be considered to be inoperative, or in any way inapplicable, solely because a decision has been taken that considerations of international peace and security warrant the imposition of sanctions'.[137] While strictly speaking outside its jurisdiction, the Committee recognised that an international organisation may be responsible for sanctions and relevant human rights obligations.[138] The Committee did not address the issue of balancing or derogation, other than to reiterate that 'decisions to reduce the suffering of children' and other vulnerable groups 'or minimize other adverse consequences can be taken without jeopardizing the policy aim of sanctions'.[139]

The main attempt to articulate a balancing or derogation for economic sanctions can be found in the Maastricht Principles on Extraterritorial Obligations of States in the area of Economic, Social and Cultural Rights, a recent scholarly codification project.[140] The commentary to Principle 22 on 'Sanctions and other equivalent measures' provides that: 'Sanctions must be in *proportion* to the objectives of ensuring compliance with international obligations while the negative impacts of the sanctions on human rights should be minimised to the greatest extent possible.'[141] This too suggests an approach of limitation, balancing and derogation that may be considered necessary in an exceptional situation (e.g. the development of a nuclear threat, as in Iran).

In the case of targeted sanctions, there is a wealth of jurisprudence, for example, *Kadi* and *Sayadi and Vinck*, and *A, K, M, Q & G v HM Treasury* (the 'Al Qaida Order' case').[142] Targeted sanctions are a difficult issue for national courts as many of the usual requirements for due process and judicial review are circumscribed or suspended pursuant to binding Security Council resolutions under the Charter.[143] *Sayadi and Vinck*, specifically Rodley's separate opinion mentioned above, contains one of the few articulations of the idea of limitation, balancing and derogation between Security Council decisions and human rights obligations.

5.2 Derogations: a general concept

5.2.1 Essential function of human rights derogations

The derogation regimes under human rights treaties have features specific to treaty law which do not carry over to customary international law or to the Security Council in particular.[144]

---

137 Committee for Economic, Social and Cultural Rights, General Comment No. 8, The relationship between economic sanctions and respect for economic, social and cultural rights (1997) UN doc. E/C.12/1997/8, para. 7.
138 Ibid. para. 11.
139 Ibid. para. 15.
140 Maastricht Principles and Commentaries (n. 4). .
141 Ibid. commentary to Principle 22.
142 *Kadi* 2008 (n. 1); *Sayadi and Vinck* (n. 1); *HM Treasury v Mohammed Jabar Ahmed and ors (FC); HM Treasury v Mohammed al-Ghabra (FC); R. (on the application of Hani El Sayed Sabaei Youssef) v HM Treasury* [2010] UKSC 2.
143 E.g. see Bothe (n. 5).
144 The main treaties and provisions for derogation are ICCPR, Art. 4; American Convention on Human Rights Art. 27, (1969) 1144 UNTS 123; European Convention on Human Rights Art. 15, (1950), 213 UNTS. 221.

However, they are a useful illustration of the basic purpose and function of derogation under international human rights law. To derogate means to 'take away a part from', or 'fall away from a standard'.[145] The institutionalised suspension of laws has its origin in the Roman practice of installing a dictator, empowered to suspend the law temporarily in order to respond to a crisis.[146] In legal terms, a derogation is a temporary and extraordinary suspension or restriction of specific rights due to exceptional circumstances. Its purpose is to preserve the rule of law and safeguard human rights during a state response to an emergency. By setting the terms for constraints, the derogations clause prevents arbitrariness, while allowing a state to respond adequately to the exceptional circumstances. Under treaty law, 'derogation clauses express the concept that states of emergency do not create a legal vacuum. The derogation regime aims at striking a balance between the protection of individual human rights and the protection of national needs in times of crisis by placing reasonable limits on emergency powers.'[147] For this reason, the derogation clause has been termed 'the "cornerstone" of the entire system for protecting human rights'.[148]

The two legal issues at the heart of derogation regimes provided in human rights treaties are: first, whether a situation constitutes a 'public emergency which threatens the life of the nation', and second, whether the measures are 'strictly required by the exigencies of the situation'.[149] The latter question is associated in the jurisprudence primarily with a discussion of proportionality of the measures to the emergency situation.[150]

At its core, the derogations concept is not especially bound to treaty law but rather constitutes a safeguard regulating an exceptional situation. The concept of derogation is based on the recognition as stated above that human rights must be balanced against legitimate community objectives. During 'normal' circumstances, the balancing and limitations inherent in the articulation of individual rights apply, and in times of 'exception', a specific regime applies for derogation of specific rights, according to well-defined criteria such as temporariness and proportionality of measures.[151]

In terms of derogations to human rights treaties, both substantive and procedural aspects of derogations are noteworthy. The treaties contain important procedural means for the implementation of derogations, in particular, declaration at the national level and notification at the international level of the state's public emergency and measures of

---

145 From the Latin: 'de- + rogare, ask, question, propose (a law). *Derogation*. F. or L. Partial abrogation of a law.' *Oxford Dictionary of English Etymology* (OUP, 1966), p. 258.

146 Norberto Bobbio, *La dittatura degli antichi, Democrazia/dittatura, Enciclopedia Einaudi* Vol.4 (Einaudi Torino, 1978), 535–58, 551–53; see also J. Oraá, *Human Rights in States of Emergency in International Law* (Clarendon Press, 1992) 7; Sheeran (n. 23).

147 J. Hartman, 'Derogations from Human Rights Treaties in Public Emergencies' (1981) 22 *Harvard International Law Journal*, 2, 1, 11; see fnn. 1 and 2.

148 Remarks of Prado Vallejo, UN Human Rights Committee member, in CCPR/C/SR.351 (1982), para. 32, cited in J. Oraá, *Human Rights in States of Emergency in International Law* (1992), 1.

149 ICCPR, Art. 4; see also Human Rights Committee, General Comment No. 29: States of Emergency, UN Doc. CCPR/C/21/Rev.1/Add.11 (2001) paras 2, 4 ('Before a State moves to invoke article 4, two fundamental conditions must be met: the situation must amount to a public emergency which threatens the life of the nation, and the State party must have officially proclaimed a state of emergency').

150 Sheeran (n. 23) 117; J. Fitzpatrick, *Human Rights in Crisis: The International System for Protecting Rights During States of Emergency* (University of Pennsylvania Press, 1994) 55.

151 Sheeran, (n. 23) 108.

derogation.[152] This information provides transparency and accountability for the decision to derogate, and reflects that in any situation the limitation of human rights is to be taken seriously. Rodley notes instead that with respect to action pursuant to a Security Council decision, 'the absence of compliance with such procedural rules by a State party to an international human rights agreement cannot be taken as evidence that derogation has not happened or cannot be effected'.[153]

The application of a derogations-type framework to Security Council decisions serves an important and indeed necessary function. An unregulated exception for the Security Council would undermine the entire system of human rights, including the concept of an interpretive constraint. The derogation approach protects IHRL by regulating exceptions with legal standards. From a theoretical perspective, scholars such as Agamben hold the view that the exceptional situation is 'an integral part of positive law because the necessity that grounds it acts as an autonomous source of law'.[154] Inversely, by permitting exceptions, it protects the Security Council and states acting on its behalf. A derogations approach is also a concession to the reality of Security Council practice and the kind of measure which may be required. That concession, however, does not go beyond the 'concession' to individual states, because the derogation essentially maintains the balance between legitimate powers to address an exceptional threat, and the threat posed by measures taken regarding the general framework of human rights.

5.2.2 Core features of Security Council derogations

There are two main questions to resolve in a framework of derogations applying to the Security Council: whether the Security Council and states have essentially the same inherent capacity to derogate from human rights in exceptional situations, and second, if so, whether the Chapter VII threshold is analogous to that under the human rights treaties for derogation. Derogations applying to Security Council decisions stem from a broader or less clearly articulated framework than treaty-law derogations. While sharing an underlying common purpose, the precise objective of states derogating differs from that of the Security Council.

Inherent differences become evident in terms of the threshold for the applicability of a derogation. The initial premise for Security Council action versus a state derogation under treaty law is different and so must be the nature of derogations in each case. The concept of 'public emergency' (e.g. something that threatens the life of the nation), which refers to the state and is the first requirement to justify a derogation, does not have an exact analogue in the context of the Security Council. In practice, courts and treaty bodies have interpreted 'public emergency' quite broadly under the human rights treaties, and it has included international

---

152 E.g. ICCPR, European Convention on Human Rights and Inter-American Convention on Human Rights (n. 145). See Sheeran (n. 23) 117, 129, 131; General Comment No. 29 (n. 150) paras 10(3), 17. General Comment No. 29 does not provide that notification of the substantive articles derogated is a requirement of notification. However, the UN Human Rights Committee's guidelines for Art. 40 periodic reports provide that for Art. 4, '[f]ull explanations should be provided in relation to every article of the Covenant affected by the derogation.' Human Rights Committee, *Guidelines for the Treaty-Specific Document to Be Submitted by States Parties Under Article 40 of the International Covenant on Civil and Political Rights*, U.N. Doc. CCPR/C/2009/1 (2010) 39.

153 *Sayadi and Vinck* (n. 1) 37.

154 G. Agamben, *The State of Exception* (K. Attell trans.) (University of Chicago Press, 2005) 23. For references to contrary views, see Sheeran (n. 23) 110–13.

and civil war, serious internal disturbances and terrorism threats.[155] The 'existence of any threat to the peace, breach of the peace' is the basis for the Security Council, through Article 39 of the UN Charter, to initiate binding measures under Chapter VII. Over time, this has expanded from obvious threats to international peace and security, such as inter-state conflict, to civil war, humanitarian crises, threats of terrorism, and even gross human rights violations.[156]

Broadly speaking, underlying derogation by the Security Council and a state is essentially the same principle or concern – a threat to the life of the organised community. The key differences are found in the nature of the community (international vs. national), the position of the derogator (Security Council vs. a government), and the scope of powers of the derogator (peace and security vs. comprehensive powers of the state). The Security Council has a narrower jurisdiction for derogation, as under the Charter it might be difficult for it to pass Chapter VII resolutions in respect of a severe natural disaster (e.g. a tsunami), which by contrast a state may be able to do within its jurisdiction. However, the actual capacity to limit or derogate human rights should be broadly the same, whether for example the situation in question is a military operation in Iraq, or an asset freeze against individuals in Belgium. There is no obvious logic as to why this should not be the case. If states are able to and are required under human rights treaties to carry out counter-terrorism measures without derogating,[157] such as asset freezes and other measures, why should the Security Council be able to require states to do what they could not? This seems to be borne out in the position of international courts and treaties, with the UN Human Rights Committee, European Court of Human Rights, European Court of Justice and UK Supreme Court[158] all having demonstrated reluctance to uphold the significant limitation of human rights pursuant to UNSC-targeted sanctions regimes. This is similar for states that have tried to derogate significantly under treaty law for the purpose of counter-terrorism measures, as the normal law enforcement paradigm may be sufficient.[159] This would offend human rights, and the finely crafted balances that have developed, but also the general principle that states ought not to use an international organisation to do what they could not do themselves.

This is not to say, however, that the Security Council will not deal with the limitation and derogation of human rights in situations that have no analogy for states (the converse will also be true). That is natural in light of the contextual differences pointed out above – the Security Council is quite different to the government of a state. The inherent capacity is the same, and the right balance can be achieved by drawing on analogies where appropriate.

It might be argued that the temporary nature of the concept of a public emergency justifying a treaty law derogation is not entrenched in the concept of a threat to international peace and security, as it has a more indefinite scope and is not inherently bound to a particular timeframe. However, the temporality element is a guide and not an end unto itself, and

---

155 For discussion of definition in the ICCPR's negotiation and in jurisprudence, see respectively M. Bossuyt, *Guide to the 'Travaux Préparatoires' of the International Covenant on Civil and Political Rights* (Martinus Nijhoff, 1987) 85–86; and Sheeran (n. 23) 137–48.

156 Simma (n. 28) 724–25.

157 See discussion on the *Belmarsh* detainees case (*A and Others v United Kingdom* App. No. 3455/05 (ECtHR, 2009)) in Sheeran (n. 23) 145–46.

158 *Sayadi and Vinck* (n. 1), *Nada* (n. 1), *Kadi* 2008 (n. 1), and *A, K, M, Q and G v HM Treasury* (n. 143).

159 For a post-9/11 example, see *A and Others* (n. 158). The UK government, after losing in the House of Lords (as it would eventually in the ECtHR), legislated to remove the offending measures from its emergency powers regime, and therefore found a way to deal with the issue without invoking ECHR Art. 15 (derogation) at all.

seldom if ever applied as a firm requirement in the cases under the human rights treaties.[160] There are states of emergency that were in place for terrorist threats, such as in Northern Ireland and Turkey, which legitimately lasted for years.[161] The fact that a civil war runs for 20 years, as in Somalia, does not make it a 'normal' situation for the purposes of application and derogation of human rights.

The answer to whether invoking Chapter VII is a threshold analogous to a public emergency threatening the life of the nation, can be inferred from the above. Derogations occur, by definition, in a situation in which the state has judged it necessary not to implement human rights obligations to the fullest extent. That is the sole purpose for the derogation, and is not the case with binding legal decisions of the Security Council under Chapter VII or Articles 24 and 25 of the Charter. The fact of a threat to international peace and security, even as broadly understood today, is not tantamount to a determination that human rights cannot and should not apply as they would normally in resolution of that threat to peace and security. The example provided of targeted sanctions above supports this position. The threshold for derogation needs to be judged contextually, and not rigidly or automatically assumed on the basis of a binding Security Council resolution. As a contextual question it is difficult to assess in abstract, as is the case for a 'public emergency',[162] making the interpretive constraint in favour of human rights all the more appropriate.

5.3 Derogations: interpreting UN Charter Article 103

The approach to derogations in the Security Council context shows that balancing is of essence. Implemented in light of the interpretive constraint, UNSC derogations preserve the balance between human rights and community considerations. In general, the conceptual framework for the Security Council and human rights proposes a shift from a binary choice between two adversarial sides to a more nuanced understanding of the relationship between human rights and the Council, which offers better tools and guidance to navigate and strike the balance. It also opts into the idea of a legal framework rather than extra-legal powers, and ensures a more realistic and broader scope of application for human rights obligations. The most recent jurisprudence fully advocates this approach, notably in the European Court of Human Rights judgment in *Nada v Switzerland*, which found that 'Switzerland enjoyed some latitude, which was admittedly limited but nevertheless real, in implementing the relevant binding resolutions of the UN Security Council'.[163] The European Court focused in *Nada* on factors often central to its derogation cases, inter alia the proportionality of measures, 'relevant and sufficient' reasons from national authorities, and adaptation of the measures (i.e. sanctions regime) to the individual's circumstances within the state's margin of appreciation.[164]

---

160 The ECtHR has stated it 'has never, to date, explicitly incorporated the requirement that the emergency be temporary, although the questions of proportionality of the response may be linked to the duration of the emergency.' *A and Others* (n. 158) para. 178. While the HRC states in general that measures should be 'exceptional and temporary in nature' (General Comment No. 29 (n. 150) para. 2), its views on individual communications do not evidence the temporary nature as a requirement; see Sheeran (n. 23) 137–40.
161 See Fitzpatrick (n. 151) 197.
162 Sheeran (n. 23) 158–59, 161 ('The idea of some kind of concrete abstract threshold for establishing a state of emergency is alluring but ultimately misleading.')
163 *Nada* (n. 1) §180.
164 Ibid. §185.

A 'derogations approach' also offers a new understanding of Article 103 of the UN Charter. It is proposed here that, in relation to human rights, Article 103 may be understood as a derogation provision, not displacing but rather limiting human rights obligations according to a legal framework which preserves the Security Council's powers to carry out its mandate, while minimising their negative impact on human rights in accordance with the Charter. This would seem persuasive, because it systematises an approach which courts, treaty bodies and others are already promoting in theory or practice, by objecting to the suspension of fundamental rights, including judicial guarantees. It would seem useful, because it preserves the status quo which the courts and states are unwilling (or unable) to challenge, namely, the primacy of the UN Charter legal order, and states' legal personality as subjects under international human rights law.

Article 103 regulates the relationship between Charter obligations – therefore including binding Security Council decisions – and all other obligations under international agreements, including those of human rights, and customary international law.[165] To 'prevail', taken in its plain English meaning, is not to displace or suspend the conflicting interest (or obligation) entirely, but to 'have greater power'. The ICJ interpreted Article 103 in the *Lockerbie* case, establishing that Security Council decisions in particular prevail also over any other demands upon the UN institutions.[166] The Court found that Article 25 extended prima facie to the decision in the relevant resolution, and that 'in accordance with Article 103 of the Charter, the obligations of the Parties in that respect prevail over their obligations under any other international agreement, including the Montreal Convention'.

In the case of two conflicting treaty obligations as in the *Lockerbie* scenario, it is clear that the more powerful Charter obligation must lead to the complete displacement of the other obligation, for both cannot coexist. Yet in the case of international human rights law obligations, this outcome is not obvious or inherent to the nature of those obligations. On the contrary, the Charter principles themselves, in accordance with which binding decisions are to be enacted, state the primary importance of respect for and promotion of human rights and fundamental freedoms. An interpretation of Article 103 as 'absolute displacement of a conflicting obligation' in all cases is how this provision would normally and necessarily apply to a treaty obligation. Yet the conflict posed by a treaty obligation is of a fundamentally different nature from the conflict posed by human rights obligations. Human rights are a part of the plurality of values and norms upon which the United Nations is constituted, including the Security Council itself. The Charter is not merely a treaty but rather has attained a quasi-constitutional status in the international legal order.[167] Article 103 is the *conditio sine qua non* condition for that status. Regardless of the scope of its application, Article 103 illustrates how the derogations regime as part of the Charter's legal order with effect under general international law could provide a safeguard for human rights even where the UN member states implementing Security Council decisions are not parties to particular international agreements.

---

165 Simma (n. 28).

166 *Lockerbie* (n. 33) 126, §39. Libya also declared the resolution itself as unlawful, regarding 'the decision of the Security Council as contrary to international law, and considers that the Council has employed its power to characterise the situation for purposes of Chapter VII simply as a pretext to avoid applying the Montreal Convention.'

167 de Wet (n. 7) 92–116.

5.4 Jurisprudence: review and verdict

The process of 'review' of general derogations is clearly different from a treaty law review. A derogation under the Charter and general international law (as opposed to treaty law) is more fully shaped by the horizontal nature of international law, and lacks monitoring mechanisms with clear jurisdiction to review and adjudicate as a check and balance of Security Council powers. As mentioned above, the ICJ does not have a mandatory judicial review role. Each organ has the capacity to determine its own jurisdiction or powers under the Charter. The Charter therefore does not reflect a fully developed constitutional theory of checks and balances.[168]

The assessment of Security Council resolutions in light of human rights obligations is generally interpretive, and the evaluation of derogations may similarly be interpretive and discursive. An illustration of this, as noted, might be the individual sanctions regime, which the Security Council attempted to improve following decisions from regional courts that were implicitly or even expressly critical.[169] The objective determination of legality is useful for correcting non-compliance through classification of international responsibility. The influence thereof on state acceptance of Security Council actions is recognised by the ICJ in its determination of legality. The drawn-out process of review of different resolutions and cases, testing actions through the legal discourse, is perhaps the best available review process. It is also evidence of a discursive shift in favour of interpretive constraints and safeguards to human rights.

This approach is broadly consistent with core tenets of the UN Charter's legal order including that each organ will determine its own competence. Under this approach, the Security Council will not make an a priori determination of derogation in any given binding resolution, as is required for a state making a derogation under the human rights treaties. This is not precluded by the UNSC as a matter of law, but it is not expected in practice. The same procedural clarity may therefore not exist for the UNSC as for state derogations. However, the interpretive approach will confer a greater flexibility and texture to the human rights constraint, and shift indirect interpretative power away from the UNSC towards member states and other UN organs, thereby enhancing the constraint and check and balance.

6 Conclusion

It has been shown that the UN Security Council's use of its powers is formally compatible with human rights norms. At the same time, the impact of UN Security Council binding decisions on human rights is most often restrictive and in reality may sometimes lead to violations. Yet there is some agreement in the literature and case law that the Security Council must be bound by human rights in some way. The problem is a clear gap 'between theories of how international human rights law binds the United Nations, and explanations of how the United Nations might violate human rights'.[170] This chapter therefore proposes a conceptual framework which could serve to navigate the relationship between the UN Security

---

168 M. Reisman, 'Constitutional Crisis in the United Nations' (1993) 87(1) AJIL 83. As Judge Weeramantry stated in his dissenting opinion in the *Lockerbie* case, the central role of the Security Council in the UN 'system of governance' does not allow us to speak of a true separation of powers in the Organisation. *Lockerbie* case (n. 33) Judge Weeramantry (dissenting opinion) 165.
169 The Office of the Ombudsperson (n. 5)
170 Megret and Hoffman (n. 69) 320.

Council and human rights obligations under the Charter and customary international law. Similar to the approach of other commentators, it set at its centre the interpretive presumption for Security Council decisions in favour of human rights norms. Human rights are found to constitute an interpretive constraint with respect to Security Council resolutions.

The second and equally essential component of the conceptual framework is derogation, which has barely featured in the scholarship to date. Derogations are to be applied through the prism of that interpretive constraint. A concept of derogation in emergency situations is key to arriving at an applicable theory on the Security Council and human rights obligations. This fertile theoretical ground has evaded a clear articulation in doctrine and practice to date, especially concerning the 'hard cases'. The concept of derogation applies to the Security Council and the conceptual basis, although not the legal framework, is very similar in nature to derogation under the human rights treaties. The threshold or justification for Security Council derogation of human rights is contextual and independent of the legally binding nature of a Chapter VII or other resolution. Through this approach, Article 103 is not only the technical basis for the application of a Security Council derogation, but also the means, in combination with the interpretive constraint offered by a presumption in favour of human rights, to move to a more effective and constructive approach and result. While this theory cannot move the mountains of real politics and power, it can make a modest but important difference to the respect for human rights by the UN Security Council and those acting according to its binding decisions under the Charter.

Select bibliography

J. Alvarez, 'Constitutional Interpretation in International Organizations', in J. Coicaud and V. Heiskanen (eds), *The Legitimacy of International Organizations* (UNU Press, 2001).

E. de Wet, *The Chapter VII Powers of the UN Security Council* (Hart Publishing, 2004)

M. Milanovic, 'Norm Conflict in International Law: Whither Human Rights?' (2009) 20 *Duke Journal of Comparative and International Law*, 69.

G. Nolte, 'The Limits on the Security Council's Powers and its Functions in the International Legal System', in M. Byers (ed.), *The Role of Law in International Politics* (OUP, 2000).

S. Sheeran, 'A Constitutional Moment?: United Nations Peacekeeping in the Democratic Republic of Congo', (2011) 8 *International Organizations Law Review* 55.

S. Sheeran, 'Reconceptualising States of Emergency under International Human Rights Law: Theory, Legal Doctrine, and Politics', 34(2) *Michigan Journal of International Law* (2013) 101–68.

M. Wood, 'The Interpretation of Security Council Resolutions', *Max Planck Yearbook of United Nations Law* (1998) 73–95.

G. Verdirame, *The UN and Human Rights: Who Guards the Guardians?* (CUP, 2011).

Part IV

Evolution and prospects of regional approaches to human rights

23

The European system and approach

Philip Leach

1 Introduction

What is the place of human rights within an increasingly constitutionalised system of European law? This chapter seeks to analyse some of the more significant developments in recent years and discuss potential future progressions in the European context, taking account of the evolution of standards, mechanisms and case law within the Council of Europe and the European Union, and looking ahead to the accession by the European Union to the European Convention on Human Rights.[1]

Whilst acknowledging the important contributions of the Committee for the Prevention of Torture (CPT) and other Council of Europe mechanisms, the chapter focuses first on the position and impact of the European Court of Human Rights, before addressing the intensification of the influence of fundamental rights principles within the European Union. The recurring themes are the inter-relationship between national and supranational legal orders, the relevance of the principles of subsidiarity and national sovereignty, the risk of divergence as between the two European courts and systems of law, and the efficacy of the continent's response to human rights violations which have systemic causes.

2 The Council of Europe[2]

Although much of the analysis of the regional human rights approach in Europe has centred on the European Convention[3] and Court of Human Rights, it is important to acknowledge

---

1 The chapter does not of course purport to be a comprehensive analysis – more a brief reflection on selected themes and trends. I am very grateful to Shanta Bhavnani for her invaluable research assistance.
2 All bodies, offices and institutions referenced in this section form part of the structure of the Council of Europe unless otherwise stated.
3 The European Convention on Human Rights and the European Social Charter represented the continent's primary response to the 1948 Universal Declaration of Human Rights in the fields of civil and political rights and socio-economic rights, respectively, but in the course of its standard-setting more than 200 conventions have been adopted under the auspices of the Council of Europe,

the range of mechanisms operating within the Council of Europe applying diverse methodologies, which include the verification of compliance with state undertakings made at accession (by the Parliamentary Assembly), state reporting and monitoring processes (such as under the Framework Convention for the Protection of National Minorities), complaints mechanisms (under the European Social Charter), in-country monitoring visits (by the CPT), the provision of expert advice (by the Venice Commission), political and diplomatic pressure (by the Commissioner for Human Rights) and technical assistance (via the Directorate General for Human Rights).

This multiplicity of devices is indicative of the fact that it is often the case that a multi-faceted approach (combining legal, political and diplomatic mechanisms) will be necessary in order to tackle the more intractable human rights problems experienced across the continent. By way of example, take the issue of the repression of the media in Azerbaijan, as illustrated by the treatment of the newspaper editor Eynulla Fatullayev who was prosecuted, convicted and imprisoned for eight and a half years as a result of articles he had written which were critical of the Government of Azerbaijan. His case was taken up by, amongst others, a monitoring group reporting to the Committee of Ministers[4] and by the European Commission against Racism and Intolerance (ECRI).[5] Furthermore, in 2010 the European Court of Human Rights found Fatullayev's conviction to be grossly disproportionate and, exceptionally, ordered the authorities to release him.[6] The Committee of Ministers then took up the execution of that judgment. When Mr Fatullayev was subsequently released in May 2011 following a presidential decree of pardon, the Secretary-General of the Council of Europe (CoE), Thorbjørn Jagland, wrote to President Aliyev to express the CoE's willingness to work with the authorities in Azerbaijan to reform legislation as well as administrative and judicial practices.[7] Both the Parliamentary Assembly[8] and the Commissioner for Human Rights[9] have urged the Azerbaijani authorities to reform criminal defamation laws. Those reforms are still a work in progress, but this example illustrates a situation in which a state has been put under concerted pressure by the combined and mutually enforcing actions of Council of Europe mechanisms.

reflecting in recent years in particular the struggle against human trafficking (Council of Europe Convention on Action Against Trafficking in Human Beings (2005) Council of Europe Treaty Series No. 197) and violence against women (Council of Europe Convention on Preventing and Combating Violence against Women and Domestic Violence (2011) Council of Europe Treaty Series No. 210).

4 CoE (Committee of Ministers) 'Report on a visit by a delegation from the Ago Group to Armenia and Azerbaijan 20–25 November 2009' (4 December 2009) CM (2009) 180.

5 CoE (European Commission Against Racism and Intolerance) 'Final report on Azerbaijan adopted by ECRI at its 54th plenary meeting 23–25 March 2011' (14 April 2011) CM (2011) 54 add 1.

6 *Fatullayev v Azerbaijan* App. No. 40984/07 (ECtHR, Judgment of 22 April 2010).

7 Letter from Thorbjørn Jagland to President Aliyev, 30 May 2011, available: http://www.coe.int/lportal/c/document_library/get_file?uuid=cb3099fa-7102–40f4-acad-c11566f121f3andgroupId= 10227 (accessed on 2 July 2012).

8 CoE (Parliamentary Assembly) 'The Functioning of Democratic Institutions in Azerbaijan' PACE Resolution 1614 (2008).

9 CoE (Commissioner for Human Rights) 'Report by the Commissioner for Human Rights, Mr Thomas Hammarberg, on his Visit to Azerbaijan 3–7 September 2007' (20 February 2008) CommDH (2008) 2; CoE (Commissioner for Human Rights) 'Observations on the Human Rights Situation in Azerbaijan' (29 September 2011) CommDH (2011) 33.

2.1 Committee for the Prevention of Torture

The work of the European Committee for the Prevention of Torture and Inhuman and Degrading Treatment or Punishment (CPT) has been hailed as 'the most advanced and penetrating form of supervision so far devised'.[10] In carrying out scrutiny of places of detention from a multidisciplinary perspective (frequently in the course of unscheduled visits), and in standard-setting,[11] the CPT has undoubtedly improved the treatment of people held in European prisons.[12] Although inspired by the draft optional protocol to the UN Convention Against Torture proposing a global systems of visits, the CPT has been operational since 1989, some years before the UN Subcommittee on Prevention of Torture (SPT) was established in 2007. Applying primarily a preventive philosophy, the CPT has relatively successfully sought constructive dialogue with states (protected by a policy of confidentiality), and accordingly states parties have proved increasingly willing to allow the CPT's reports to be published.[13] Where it finds a lack of cooperation, the CPT will make a stand by issuing a public statement – as it has done in respect of Turkey and Russia, highlighting the widespread practice of torture and other forms of severe ill-treatment of detainees in police custody in Turkey in the mid-1990s[14] and the use of torture by members of law enforcement agencies and security forces in Chechnya in the 2000s.[15] Jim Murdoch has lauded its achievements:

> That so much has been achieved so rapidly in Europe in the protection of detainees against ill-treatment (particularly from the vantage point of 1989 rather than 1945) is astonishing. The willingness of states to allow the spotlight of scrutiny to penetrate places of detention, to permit publication of critical findings (as tested against exacting standards), and to subject themselves to monitoring to ensure that defects have been remedied is unparalleled.[16]

Other observers of the CPT's work have been more equivocal – Malcolm Evans and Rod Morgan, for example, have noted the 'conspicuous success' of the CPT's 'considerable achievements', but found that it had exercised 'at best a marginal influence on the domestic policy of

10 A Cassese, 'A New Approach to Human Rights: the European Convention for the Prevention of Torture' (1989) 83(1) *American Journal of International Law* 128–53 at 151.
11 See CoE (CPT) CPT Standards CPT/Inf/E (2002) 1 – Rev. 2011, available at: http://www.cpt. coe.int/en/documents/eng-standards.pdf (accessed on 2 July 2012). See also R. Morgan and M. Evans, *Protecting Prisoners – The Standards of the European Committee for the Prevention of Torture in Context* (OUP, 1999).
12 See N. Rodley and M. Pollard, *The Treatment of Prisoners under International Law*, 3rd edn (OUP, 2009), 231–38 and 245.
13 However, Evans and Morgan have been critical of the extent and quality of the dialogue with states after the CPT's reports have been published. See: M. Evans and R. Morgan, *Preventing Torture – A Study of the European Convention for the Prevention of Torture and Inhuman or Degrading Treatment or Punishment* (Clarendon Press, 1998), 341–46.
14 CoE (CPT) 'Public Statement on Turkey' (15 December 1992) CPT/Inf (93) 1; CoE (CPT) 'Public Statement on Turkey' (6 December 1996) CPT/Inf (96) 34.
15 CoE (CPT) 'Public Statement Concerning the Chechen Republic of the Russian Federation' (10 July 2001) CPT/Inf (2001) 15; CoE (CPT) 'Public Statement Concerning the Chechen Republic of the Russian Federation' (10 July 2003) CPT/Inf (2003) 33; CoE (CPT) 'Public Statement Concerning the Chechen Republic of the Russian Federation' (13 March 2007) CPT/Inf (2007) 17.
16 J. Murdoch, 'The Impact of the Council of Europe's "Torture Committee" and the Evolution of Standard-setting in Relation to Places of Detention' (2006) 6(1) *European Human Rights Law Review* 158–79 at 178.

member states, and then only in a very few cases'.[17] Harding has highlighted the limitations of the CPT in covering 47 states and has questioned the effectiveness of sporadic, sample inspections.[18]

2.2 European Court of Human Rights

Within the European human rights system it is the European Court of Human Rights (European Court, or ECtHR), and its application of the European Convention on Human Rights (European Convention, or ECHR), which has undoubtedly had the most significant impact and profile during the Council of Europe's 60-year history.[19] The Convention was drafted in the immediate aftermath of the Second World War, in response to grave and wide-spread human rights atrocities. Its development, and that of the Court, reflected an aspiration for greater European unity and enhanced democracy, and the need to establish an early warning system to prevent a descent into totalitarianism ever happening on the continent again.[20]

The Strasbourg Court's effectiveness has been grounded on the high level of state take-up, the periodic addition of new substantive rights (including the abolition of the death penalty and a free-standing prohibition of discrimination),[21] the incorporation of the Convention into domestic law by Council of Europe states, the depth of the Court's case law in particular areas, and the extent to which its judgments have led to changes in domestic laws and practice.[22] Since 11 states came together in 1949 to adopt the Statute of Council of Europe[23] and then ratify the European Convention on Human Rights in the early 1950s, accession has increased the number of state parties almost five-fold, including, in the 1990s, many of the states which had formerly been part of the Soviet Union. With membership at 47 since 2006, only Belarus remains out in the cold. Although the admission of certain states into the Council of Europe at particular junctures has been criticised, the fact that virtually all European states have been willing to join it and accordingly to be subject to the resulting obligations – at least in principle, if not always in practice – is itself significant, and lends the

---

17 Evans and Morgan (n. 13), 344 and 381.
18 R. Harding, 'Regulating Prison Conditions: Some International Comparisons', in J. Petersilia and K. Retiz (eds), *The Oxford Handbook of Sentencing and Corrections* (OUP, 2012), 448.
19 See, for example: H. Keller and A. Stone Sweet (eds), *A Europe of Rights – The Impact of the ECHR on National Legal Systems* (OUP, 2008) ('The European Convention on Human Rights is the most effective human rights regime in the world' at 3); M. O'Boyle, 'On Reforming the Operation of the European Court of Human Rights' (2008) 13(1) *European Human Rights Law Review* 1–11 ('one of the major developments in European legal history and the crowning achievement of the Council of Europe' at 1); R. Blackburn and J. Polakiewicz (eds), *Fundamental Rights in Europe: The ECHR and its Member States, 1950–2000* (OUP, 2001) ('the most effective and influential international human rights instrument in the world' at ix).
20 On the development of the Court and its jurisprudence from the 1960s to the 1990s see: E. Bates, *The Evolution of the European Convention on Human Rights: From its Inception to the Creation of a Permanent Court of Human Rights* (OUP, 2010).
21 The substantive rights in the Convention have been supplemented by additional protocols to the Convention: Protocol No. 1 (1952) European Treaty Series No. 9; Protocol No. 4 (1963) European Treaty Series No. 46; Protocol No. 6 (1983) European Treaty Series No. 114; Protocol No. 7 (1984) European Treaty Series No. 117; Protocol No. 12 (2000); European Treaty Series No. 177; and Protocol No. 13 (2002) European Treaty Series No. 187.
22 See Blackburn and Polakiewicz (n. 19).
23 Statute of the Council of Europe (1949) Council of Europe Treaty Service No. 001.

organisation further credibility and gravitas in the pursuit of achieving common minimum standards applicable across the *espace juridique* of the continent. In their study of the impact of the Convention on national systems within 18 Council of Europe states, Keller and Stone Sweet refer to 'thousands of discrete legal and policy outcomes [which] have been altered as a result of the influence of Convention rights'.[24] They argue that even the original contracting states had no real conception as to how the Convention would influence their national legal orders, and they conclude that the Court's impact, admittedly variable across states, has increased over the years.[25]

It should also be acknowledged that the significant increase in state accession to the Convention, especially since the 1990s, has meant an evolution in the Court's role. It continues to perform the vital function of enhancing standards of rights protection as regards states where compliance with the Convention is relatively strong, but it has also increasingly been required to adjudicate on cases of egregious human rights violations and on very large numbers of systemic or widespread violations (both of which are discussed further below), which in the main (although not exclusively) concern newer member states from central and eastern Europe.

As the oldest of the regional human rights courts, it is perhaps unsurprising that the weight and extent of its jurisprudence in distinct areas (such as in relation to the field of criminal justice and the duty on the state to hold effective investigations into fatal incidents) has enabled the European Court to engage in gradations and nuances of its case law, the equivalent of which cannot be found elsewhere.

The Strasbourg Court has notably proved resolute in seeking to uphold fundamental democratic principles in a myriad of circumstances, for example, taking a stand over the dissolution of political parties,[26] election irregularities,[27] restrictions imposed on minority rights associations[28] and the banning of marches or demonstrations.[29] What is more, the Court has repeatedly emphasised the central importance of freedom of speech (particularly political speech)[30] in democratic societies, including statements that may be offensive, shocking or disturbing to some.[31] It has upheld the right of the media and civil society to scrutinise and criticise political leaders,[32] bolstered pluralistic and independent public

---

24 Keller and Stone Sweet (n. 19) 677.

25 Ibid.

26 *United Communist Party of Turkey and others v Turkey* [GC], App. No. 19392/92 (ECtHR, Judgment of 30 January 1998); *Yazar and others v Turkey* App. Nos 22723–5/93 (ECtHR, Judgment of 9 April 2002); *Democracy and Change Party and others v Turkey*, App. Nos 39210/98 and 39974/98, (ECtHR, Judgment of 26 April 2005); *Demokratik Kitle Partisi and Elçi v Turkey* App. No. 51290/99 (ECtHR, Judgment of 3 May 2007); *HADEP and Demir v Turkey* App. No. 28003/03 (ECtHR, Judgment of 14 December 2010).

27 *Georgian Labour Party v Georgia*, App. No. 9103/04 (ECtHR, Judgment of 8 July 2008).

28 *Stankov and the United Macedonian Organisation Ilinden v Bulgaria*, App. Nos 29221/95 and 29225/95 (ECtHR, Judgment of 2 October 2001); *Association of Citizens Radko and Paunkovski v the former Yugoslav Republic of Macedonia*, App. No. 74651/01 (ECtHR, Judgment of 15 January 2009).

29 *Alekseyev v Russia*, App. Nos 4916/07, 25924/08 and 14599/09 (ECtHR, Judgment of 22 October 2010).

30 *Castells v Spain*, App. No. 11798/85 (ECtHR, Judgment of 23 April 1992).

31 *Handyside v United Kingdom*, App. No. 5493/72 (ECtHR, Judgment of 7 December 1976); *Ukrainian Media Group v Ukraine*, App. No. 72713/01 (ECtHR, Judgment of 29 March 2005).

32 *Lingens v Austria*, App. No. 9815/82 (ECtHR, Judgment of 8 July 1986); *Fatullayev v Azerbaijan* (n. 6) (discussed further above).

broadcasting services,[33] sought to protect the confidentiality of journalistic sources,[34] and closely probed instances of prior restraint of the media[35] and the application of heavy-handed defamation laws.[36] The Court has fought against the unjustifiable severity of sanctions imposed on journalists (especially imprisonment)[37] and has found against states for failing to provide adequate protection of journalists under threat.[38] The European Convention does not, however, provide absolute protection – accordingly, steps taken by national authorities in response to the incitement of racial hatred, hate speech and the glorification of violence have been upheld.[39]

There are, inevitably, a number of substantive areas where the Court's jurisprudence has been the subject of forceful criticism. Such critiques have concerned, for example, its disregard for the rights of minorities,[40] its cautious interpretation of the prohibition of discrimination,[41] its approach to the right to freedom of religion (notably in relation to Islam),[42] its inconsistency as to the parameters of extra-territorial jurisdiction[43] and the application of the Court's 'margin of appreciation' doctrine.[44]

2.2.1 Egregious violations

The European Court has been required to adjudicate on egregious violations of the Convention in the context of situations of conflict, notably by the security forces in south-east Turkey in the 1990s, and the Russian armed forces in Chechnya in the 2000s. In respect

33 *Informationsverein Lentia and others v Austria*, App. Nos 13914/88 et al. (ECtHR, Judgment of 24 November 1993); *Manole and others v Moldova*, App. No. 13936/02 (ECtHR, Judgment of 17 September 2009).

34 *Goodwin v United Kingdom* [GC], App. No. 17488/90 (ECtHR, Judgment of 27 March 1996); *Sanoma Uitgevers B.V. v Netherlands* [GC], App. No. 38224/03 (ECtHR, Judgment of 14 September 2010).

35 *Observer and Guardian v United Kingdom*, App. No. 13585/88 (ECtHR, Judgment of 26 November 1991).

36 *Gorelishvili v Georgia*, App. No. 12979/04 (ECtHR, Judgment of 5 June 2007).

37 *Cumpǎnǎ and Mazǎre v Romania* [GC], App. No. 33348/96 (ECtHR, Judgment of 17 December 2004).

38 *Özgür Gündem v Turkey*, App. No. 23144/93 (ECtHR, Judgment of 16 March 2000); *Dink v Turkey*, App. No. 2668/07 (ECtHR, Judgment of 14 September 2010).

39 *Sürek v Turkey (No. 1)* [GC], App. No. 26682/95 (ECtHR, Judgment of 8 July 1999); *Leroy v France*, App. No. 36109/03 (ECtHR, Judgment of 2 October 2008); *Balsytè-Lideikienè v Lithuania*, App. No. 72596/01 (ECtHR, Judgment of 4 November 2008); *Féret v Belgium*, App. No. 15615/07 (ECtHR, Judgment of 16 July 2009).

40 the well-known dissenting opinion of Judge Bonello in *Anguelova v Bulgaria*, App. No. 38361/97 (ECtHR, Judgment of 13 June 2002).

41 P. Leach, *Taking a Case to the European Court of Human Rights*, 3rd edn (OUP, 2011), 6.570–6.575.

42 K. Boyle, 'Human Rights, Religion and Democracy: the Refah Party Case' [2004] 1 (1) *Essex Human Rights Review* 1–16.

43 M.. Schaefer, '*Al-Skeini* and the Elusive Parameters of Extraterritorial Jurisdiction' [2011] 5 *European Human Rights Law Review* 566–81.

44 E. Benvenisti, 'Margin of Appreciation, Consensus and Universal Standards' [1999] 31 *International Law and Politics* 843–54.

of both of these regions,[45] and also in relation to northern Cyprus,[46] the Court has tackled the phenomenon of enforced disappearances, building on the earlier case law of the Inter-American Court of Human Rights.[47] In these regions of conflict, the Court has played a very important role in casting a spotlight on the nature and extent of human rights violations, often in the absence of effective prevention or monitoring work by other regional or international human rights mechanisms. There are, however, real limitations in the Court's oversight. It would be right to acknowledge, for example, that there has been a remarkably high rate of findings of substantive violations of the right to life in the Chechen cases (in other words, that state agents were found to be directly responsible). However, in many of the disappearance cases, the Court's processes have not enabled the victim's relatives to find out, for example, whether in fact the victim has died (rather than being presumed dead), or how, when or where they died, or which identifiable state agency or agents were responsible.[48] Elsewhere, the Court has had selective success in securing the release of individuals unlawfully detained by separatist groups in Georgia[49] and Moldova.[50] Moreover, the Court has confirmed that the extraterritorial jurisdiction of the Convention does extend to human rights violations perpetrated by member states' armed forces acting beyond the boundaries of the Council of Europe, such as the operations of the British army in Iraq.[51] In cases from Northern Ireland, Turkey and Russia, in particular, the Court has developed an extensive jurisprudence on the constituent elements of what is considered to be an effective, independent and timely investigation into fatalities and ill-treatment.[52]

In spite of mounting international political pressure post-9/11, the Court has held firm in maintaining the absolute prohibition on torture.[53] In the *Abu Qatada* judgment,[54] the Court for the first time held that an applicant's deportation (to Jordan) would violate the right to a fair hearing and amount to a 'flagrant denial of justice',[55] because of the real risk of the admission at his Jordanian trial of evidence obtained by torturing witnesses. However, in the same decision, the Court also concluded that there would be no violation of Article 3[56] on the basis that assurances made by the Jordanian government in a memorandum of understanding (backed up by independent monitoring) removed any real risk of ill-treatment.[57] Another

45 *Timurta v Turkey*, App. No. 23531/94 (ECtHR, Judgment of 13 June 2000); *Bazorkina v Russia*, App. No. 69481/01 (ECtHR, Judgment of 27 July 2006); *Imakayeva v Russia*, App. No. 7615/02 (ECtHR, Judgment of 9 November 2006); *Aslakhanova and Others v Russia*, App. Nos 2944/06 and 8300/07, 50184/07, 332/08, 42509/10 (ECtHR, Judgment of 18 December 2012).

46 *Cyprus v Turkey* [GC], App. No. 25781/94 (ECtHR, Judgment of 10 May 2001); *Varnava and others v Turkey* [GC], App. No. 16064/90 (ECtHR, Judgment of 18 September 2009).

47 C. Sandoval, 'The Inter-American System of Human Rights and Approach' in this volume.

48 See P. Leach, 'The Chechen Conflict: Analysing the Oversight of the European Court of Human Rights' (2008) 6 *European Human Rights Law Review* 732–61.

49 *Assanidze v Georgia* [GC], App. No. 71503/01 (ECtHR, Judgment of 8 April 2004).

50 *Ilaşcu and others v Moldova and Russia* [GC], App. No. 48787/99 (ECtHR, Judgment of 8 July 2004).

51 *Al-Saadoon and Mufdhi v United Kingdom* App. No. 61498/08 (ECtHR, Judgment of 2 March 2010); *Al-Skeini v United Kingdom* [GC] App. No. 55721/07 (ECtHR, Judgment of 7 July 2011); *Al-Jedda v United Kingdom* [GC] App. No. 27021/08 (ECtHR, Judgment of 7 July 2011).

52 See Leach (n. 41), 6.46–6.63.

53 *Saadi v Italy* [GC] App. No. 37201/06 (ECtHR, Judgment of 28 February 2008) (a case in which the UK government as third party intervenor sought, unsuccessfully, to dilute the absolute protection provided by Art. 3).

54 *Othman (Abu Qatada) v UK* App. No. 8139/09 (ECtHR, Judgment of 17 January 2012).

55 Ibid. §§ 281–85

56 The prohibition of torture and inhuman or degrading treatment or punishment.

57 *Othman v UK* (n. 54), §§ 190–205.

landmark judgment was the *El-Masri* decision concerning the practice of extraordinary rendition.[58] There, the Court found the Macedonian government responsible for the torture and secret rendition of a terrorist suspect, and that his transfer into the custody of the US authorities exposed him to the risk of further ill-treatment contrary to Article 3 of the Convention.

Another area of distinction of the Strasbourg Court is a procedural one – its relatively progressive approach to obtaining and considering evidence. Evidential problems inevitably arise in the context of the work of an international court with a remit covering 47 states, and have resulted in the Court itself despatching its judges to hear witnesses in order to establish the facts,[59] in reversing the burden of proof in relation to ill-treatment and deaths in custody[60] and in the Court drawing inferences from a respondent state's failure to disclose key domestic documents.[61]

2.2.2 Interpreting the Convention

The limitations of the European Convention on Human Rights certainly need to be acknowledged. As a treaty concerned only with civil and political rights, it lacks even the limited range of socio-economic rights that were written into the equivalent treaties in the Inter-American[62] and African systems.[63] Nor does it incorporate third-generation rights,[64] or the broader range of civil and political rights that have been reflected in later human rights treaties, such as children's rights.[65] These (important) limitations aside, there are two principles of interpretation which, above all else, have been applied by the Court in a progressive way to ensure that the Convention and its case law have not become outdated or irrelevant. The first is the teleological notion that the Convention represents a 'living instrument'. Thus its standards must be assessed through conceptions that are of the present day – not historical. In this way the Convention continues to evolve and enables the Court to take account of, for example, changes in societal attitudes and perceptions,[66] of scientific and technological developments,[67] and indeed refinements in related fields of international law.[68] This evolutive approach to the law is an essential feature of an international human rights court, and arguably indeed of any court.[69]

---

58 *El-Masri v the Former Yugoslav Republic of Macedonia* [GC] App. No. 39630/09 (ECtHR, Judgment of 13 December 2012).

59 Notably in respect of the Kurdish cases from south-east Turkey in the 1990s. See P. Leach, C. Paraskeva and G. Uzelac, *International Human Rights and Fact-Finding: An Analysis of the Fact-Finding Missions Conducted by the European Commission and Court of Human Rights* (Human Rights and Social Justice Research Institute, London Metropolitan University, 2009).

60 *Salman v Turkey* [GC] App. No. 21986/93 (ECtHR, Judgment of 27 June 2000).

61 *Musayeva v Russia* App. No. 12703/02 (ECtHR, Judgment of 3 July 2008).

62 American Convention on Human Rights (1969) OAS Treaty Service No. 36, Art. 26 and the Protocol of San Salvador (1988) OAS Treaty Service No. 69.

63 African Charter on Human and Peoples' Rights (1982) 21 ILM 58, Arts 15–18.

64 See, by contrast, Arts 19–24 of the African Charter, ibid.

65 See, for example, Art. 18 ibid. and Art. 19 of the American Convention on Human Rights (n. 62).

66 *Marckx v Belgium* App. No. 6833/74 (ECtHR, Judgment of 13 June 1979).

67 *S.H. and others v Austria* [GC] App. No. 57813/00 (ECtHR, Judgment of 3 November 2011).

68 *Sergey Zolotukhin v Russia* [GC] App. No. 14939/03 (ECtHR, Judgment of 10 February 2009).

69 See, for example, Baroness Hale, 'Common Law and Convention Law: The Limits to Interpretation' (2011) 5 *European Human Rights Law Review* 534–43.

The second interpretative principle is the notion of 'positive obligations' – including those which are not explicitly referred to in the Convention itself, but which have been implied by the Court through its case law. For example, by applying an expansive interpretation of the right to life and of physical integrity, and of the prohibition of torture and inhuman or degrading treatment, the Court has considerably strengthened the protection of some of the most vulnerable people on the continent. Grounded on the positive obligations to prevent and protect, the Court has upheld complaints that national authorities have failed to take adequate steps to protect individuals against foreseeable threats by others,[70] including victims of domestic violence[71] and trafficking.[72] The Court has also highlighted legislative deficiencies which have led to the inadequate protection of victims of rape[73] and domestic servitude.[74]

For some, the European Court's expansive, evolutive approach means it has strayed into the realm of judicial law-making – indeed the Court is periodically criticised (as are all international human rights bodies) by those who perceive unjustifiable incursions into state sovereignty. However, one of the Court's central jurisprudential principles in interpreting Convention rights is to allow states a discretion (the 'margin of appreciation'), the breadth of which is variable, depending on the particular context. Thus, where a particularly important facet of an individual's existence or identity is at stake, the margin allowed to the state will be more restricted, but where cases are considered to raise sensitive moral or ethical issues, the margin will be wider.[75]

2.2.3 Redress and systemic violations

The European Court has been cautious and tentative in its consideration of redress, applying during its first four decades an essentially declaratory approach in its judgments, and limiting itself to awarding damages. As a result it has been left behind by the Inter-American Court, which although it was established 20 years after the European Court, has already developed a rich and progressive jurisprudence on reparations, taking account of the victim's life plan (*proyecto de vida*) and encompassing symbolic and collective remedies.[76] However, in more recent years the European Court has proved to be rather more progressive, and indeed interventionist, by including in its judgments binding obligations on respondent governments to take particular measures, such as returning property,[77] holding re-hearings of trials deemed

---

70 *Osman v United Kingdom* [GC] App. No. 23452/94 (ECtHR, Judgment of 28 October 1998).

71 See e.g., *Opuz v Turkey* App. No. 33401/02 (ECtHR, Judgment of 9 June 2009); *E.S. and others v Slovakia* App. No. 8227/04 (ECtHR, Judgment of 15 September 2009); *A v Croatia* App. No. 55164/08 (ECtHR, Judgment of 14 October 2010); *Hajduová v Slovakia* App. No. 2660/03 (ECtHR, Judgment of 30 November 2010); *Eremia and Others v Moldova* App. No. 3564/11 (ECtHR, Judgment of 28 May 2013).

72 *Rantsev v Cyprus and Russia* App. No. 25965/04 (ECtHR, Judgment of 7 January 2010).

73 *MC v Bulgaria* App. No. 39272/98 (ECtHR, Judgment of 4 December 2003); *C.N. and V. v France* App. No. 67724/09 (ECtHR, Judgment of 10 October 2012); *I.G. v Moldova* App. No. 53519/07 (ECtHR, Judgment of 15 May 2012).

74 *Siliadin v France* App. No. 73316/01 (ECtHR, Judgment of 26 July 2005); *C.N. v United Kingdom* App. No. 4239/08 (ECtHR, Judgment of 13 November 2012).

75 Two examples: *Evans v UK* [GC] App. No. 6339/05 (ECtHR, Judgment of 10 April 2007); *A, B and C v Ireland* [GC] App. No. 25579/05 (ECtHR, Judgment of 16 December 2010).

76 Sandoval (n. 47).

77 See, e.g., *Papamichalopoulos and others v Greece* App. No. 14556/89 (ECtHR, Judgment of 31 October 1995); *Brumarescu v Romania* [GC] App. No. 28342/95 (ECtHR, Judgment of 23 January 2001).

to be unfair,[78] requiring detainees held unlawfully to be released[79] and ordering the reinstatement of a judge who was unfairly dismissed.[80]

Of even greater significance has been the Court's development of a new approach to systemic human rights violations – those which relate to widespread or structural issues affecting thousands. Since 2004, by invoking its 'pilot judgment procedure' the Court has developed an approach of explicitly identifying the source of large-scale structural problems (usually malfunctioning legislation or a defective legal system) and establishing a binding obligation on the government to resolve the issue (without, however, specifying *how* it should be done).[81] This may include an obligation to legislate – and to do so within a specified time period. The majority of pilot judgments to date have concerned disputes over property – particularly arising from the non-enforcement of domestic court judgments and the excessive length of legal proceedings. The respondents have predominantly been states from eastern Europe (Poland,[82] Romania,[83] Bulgaria[84]) and the former Soviet bloc (Ukraine,[85] Russia[86] and Moldova[87]), but western and central European states have also been targeted by pilot judgments, as a consequence of various systemic failings: Germany,[88] Turkey[89] and Greece[90] (all length of proceedings), Bosnia and Herzegovina[91] (lost foreign currency savings), the UK[92] (the disenfranchisement of convicted prisoners) and Slovenia[93] (denial of the rights of the 'erased', who lost their permanent residence status after independence).

These innovations have been introduced, at least in part, because of the massive backlog of cases pending at the European Court, many of which are 'clone' cases.[94] Where states and their respective national authorities fail to resolve the issues which are adjudicated upon by

---

78 See, e.g., *Lungoci v Romania* App. No. 62710/00 (ECtHR, Judgment of 26 January 2006); *Maksimov v Azerbaijan* App. No. 38228/05 (ECtHR, Judgment of 8 October 2009).

79 *Assanidze v Georgia* (n. 44); *Ilaşcu and others v Moldova and Russia* (n. 50); *Aleksanyan v Russia* App. No. 46468/06 (ECtHR, Judgment of 22 December 2008); *Tehrani and others v Turkey* App. Nos 32940/08, 41626/08, 43616/08 (ECtHR, Judgment of 13 April 2010); *Fatullayev v Azerbaijan* (n. 6).

80 *Oleksandr Volkov v Ukraine* App. No. 21722/11 (ECtHR, Judgment of 9 January 2013).

81 See further P. Leach, H. Hardman, S. Stephenson and B. Blitz, *Responding to Systemic Human Rights Violations: An Analysis of Pilot Judgments of the European Court of Human Rights and their Impact at National Level* (Intersentia, 2010).

82 *Broniowski v Poland* [GC] App. No. 31443/96 (ECtHR, Judgment of 22 June 2004); *Hutten-Czapska v Poland* [GC] App. No. 35014/97 (ECtHR, Judgment of 19 June 2006).

83 *Maria Atanasiu and others v Romania* App. Nos 30767/05 and 33800/06 (ECtHR, Judgment of 12 October 2010).

84 *Dimitrov and Hamanov v Bulgaria* App. Nos 48059/06 and 2708/09 (ECtHR, Judgment of 10 May 2011).

85 *Yuriy Nikolayevich Ivanov v Ukraine* App. No. 40450/04 (ECtHR, Judgment of 15 October 2009).

86 *Burdov v Russia* (No. 2) App. No. 33509/04 (ECtHR, Judgment of 15 January 2009); *Ananyev and others v Russia* App. Nos 42525/07 and 60800/08 (ECtHR, Judgment of 10 January 2012).

87 *Olaru and others v Moldova* App. Nos 476/07, 22539/05, 17911/08 and 13136/07 (ECtHR, Judgment of 28 July 2009).

88 *Rumpf v Germany* App. No. 46344/06 (ECtHR, Judgment of 2 September 2010).

89 *Ümmühan Kaplan v Turkey* App. No. 24240/07 (ECtHR, Judgment of 20 March 2012).

90 *Vassilios Athanasiou and others v Greece* App. No. 50973/08 (ECtHR, Judgment of 21 December 2010); and *Michelioudakis v Greece* App. No. 54447/10 (ECtHR, Judgment of 3 April 2012).

91 *Suljagić v Bosnia and Herzegovina* App. No. 27912/02 (ECtHR, Judgment of 3 November 2009).

92 *Greens and M.T. v United Kingdom* App. Nos 60041/08 and 60054/08 (ECtHR, Judgment of 23 November 2010).

93 *Kurić and Others v Slovenia* [GC] App. No. 26828/06 (ECtHR, Judgment of 26 June 2012).

94 There were 124,900 cases pending as at 30 April 2013.

the Court at the national level, more cases raising exactly the same issue (sometimes in their thousands) pile up in Strasbourg.[95] The Court's more prescriptive position is therefore justified, and in some cases states have responded reasonably swiftly to pilot judgments by introducing legislative changes aimed at the resolving the problems.[96] However, the Court's increasing interventionism has also been met with growing recalcitrance in some quarters – both from and within states. One example concerned the issue of prisoner voting in the UK. As the UK authorities had failed to alter the ban (enshrined in legislation) on convicted prisoners voting while they remain in prison, following the 2005 Grand Chamber judgment in *Hirst*,[97] the European Court issued a pilot judgment in 2010, requiring remedial legislation to be brought forward within six months.[98] That an international court could intervene on such a question met with strong ministerial[99] and parliamentary[100] disapproval.

2.2.4 Reforming the European Court

There is clearly a pressing need to make further reforms of a system which is buckling under more than 124,000 pending cases, and equally to take steps to improve implementation at the national level. There have also been calls to improve the process for the selection of Strasbourg judges, to ensure that only those suitable for the highest judicial office are elected to the Court. As it is the states which put forward a list of three candidates to the Parliamentary Assembly, this is primarily a matter of ensuring there are rigorous, objective national

95 See, for example, *Yuriy Nikolayevich Ivanov v Ukraine*, (n. 85). This was the 300th judgment against Ukraine on the issue of the non-enforcement of domestic court judgments, and at the time there were another 1,400 similar cases pending (see §§ 83–86 of the judgment).

96 Take, for example, the Polish response to *Broniowski* (n. 82) and the Russian response to *Burdov (No. 2)* (n. 86). However, in February 2012 the Court began to process cases again concerning the non-enforcement of domestic decisions in Ukraine because the requisite general measures had not been introduced following the *Ivanov* pilot judgment (n. 85) (see: Coe (ECtHR) Press Release 'Court decides to resume examination of applications concerning non-enforcement of domestic decisions in Ukraine' (29 February 2012) ECHR 086 (2012)), and in June 2012 the Romanian authorities were given an additional nine months within which to introduce general measures to respond to the *Athanasiu* pilot judgment (n. 90).

97 *Hirst v UK (No. 2)* [GC] App. No. 74025/01 (ECtHR, Judgment of 6 October 2005).

98 *Greens and M.T. v UK* (n. 92). The time period was extended during the consideration of the *Scoppola* case (*Scoppola v Italy (No. 3)* [GC] App. No. 126/05 (ECtHR, Judgment of 22 May 2012)), after which the Court confirmed that the six months time limit stipulated in *Greens* started to run from the date of the *Scoppola* judgment – see CoE (ECtHR) Press Release 'Court says that it is up to member states to decide how to regulate the ban on prisoners voting' (22 May 2012) ECHR 222 (2012).

99 The Prime Minister, David Cameron, was reported to have said he felt 'physically sick' at the prospect of giving prisoners the vote (see, for example, T. Whitehead, 'European Court gives Cameron ultimatum on prisoner votes' *The Daily Telegraph* (13 April 2011), available: http://www.telegraph.co.uk/news/uknews/law-and-order/8446557/European-court-gives-Cameron-ultimatum-on-prisoner-votes.html# (accessed on 5 June 2012)). The Secretary of State for Justice, Kenneth Clark, warned against Strasbourg being 'too ready to substitute its own judgment for that of national parliaments and courts' (Speech by Rt Hon. Kenneth Clarke QC MP, Secretary of State for Justice, Lord Chancellor, 26 April 2011, High Level Conference on the Future of the European Court of Human Rights, Izmir, 26–27 April 2011).

100 A House of Commons backbench motion in February 2011 to the effect that 'legislative decisions of this nature should be a matter for democratically-elected lawmakers', and supporting the existing ban on sentenced prisoners from voting, was carried by 234 votes to 22. See also D. Raab, *Strasbourg in the Dock: Prisoner Voting, Human Rights and the Case for Democracy* (Civitas, 2011).

selection procedures (certainly to ensure that they are non-politicised), backed up by close, objective scrutiny at the European level, which enables the rejection of states' lists where this proves necessary.[101]

The debate about the need to reform the Strasbourg Court has continued for several decades, driven predominantly by the problems created by the excessive case load. This process led to Protocol 11 in 1998 which abolished the filtering role played by the former European Commission of Human Rights, and also resulted in Protocol 14 which brought about various operational changes in 2010, including: a new admissibility criterion (the 'significant disadvantage' requirement); enabling single judges to declare cases inadmissible; allowing committees of three judges to decide on the admissibility and merits of applications on which there is already well-established case law; the appointment of judges for a single, nine-year term; and providing for 'infringement proceedings' where a state fails to comply with a judgment. In February 2010 a Ministerial conference was held at Interlaken in Switzerland to discuss further reform of the Court, culminating in the adoption of the Interlaken Declaration which incorporated an 'Action Plan' for reforms up to 2019.[102] This envisaged that between 2012 and 2015 the Committee of Ministers would assess to what extent the implementation of Protocol No. 14 and the Interlaken Action Plan had improved the situation of the Court, and on the basis of that evaluation the Committee of Ministers would decide whether further action would be required.

However, amidst the numerous proposals about operational changes, the essence of the debate is about what function the Court can, or should, perform. Although the Convention's preamble envisaged a collective obligation on European states to ensure compliance with the Convention, the reality is that the Court's work over the last five decades has been concerned with thousands of individual applications. In recent years, there has been a tendency for the debate to be polarised between those who emphasise the importance of the right of individual petition, and the principle of access to justice, and those who argue that the Court should only deal with the most 'important' cases, acting akin to a constitutional court for the region and setting standards for the continent as a whole. Through the adoption of an explicit prioritisation policy in 2010, and the development of the pilot judgment procedure since the mid-2000s, the Court has already taken important steps in developing a more focused and collective approach. There needs to be a rather more nuanced recognition (moving away from an 'either/or' debate) of the various distinctive tasks which the Court can and should carry out, encompassing Grand Chamber decisions on significant legal questions and upholding the right of individual petition, particularly in developing areas of law and in relation to egregious or systemic human rights violations. This is an approach which acknowledges the Convention system as 'an authoritative, dynamic, and transnational source of law'[103]

---

101 For example, there was media criticism of the politicisation of the election of the UK judge to succeed Sir Nicolas Bratza in June 2012. See: J. Rozenberg, 'Paul Mahoney: politics trumps merit' *The Guardian* (27 June 2012), available: http://www.guardian.co.uk/law/2012/jun/27/paul-mahoney-strasbourg (accessed on 5 July 2012); O. Bowcott, 'Paul Mahoney appointed UK's new judge in Strasbourg' *The Guardian* (27 June 2012), available: http://www.guardian.co.uk/law/2012/jun/27/paul-mahoney-european-court-judge (accessed 5 July 2012).

102 High Level Conference on the Future of the European Court of Human Rights, Interlaken Declaration (19 February 2010), available at: http://www.eda.admin.ch/eda/en/home/topics/eu/euroc/chprce/inter.html (accessed on 2 July 2012).

103 Keller and Stone Sweet (n. 19) 25.

for the continent, but also one which is predicated on effective national implementation, a key feature of the Brighton Declaration adopted in April 2012.[104]

3 The European Union

The 'other' European institution – the European Union (EU) – had its origins in the Treaty of Paris of 1952 (establishing the European Coal and Steel Community) and the Treaties of Rome of 1957 (establishing the European Economic Community and the European Atomic Energy Community), and was primarily concerned with European economic integration. In the early years, the Court of Justice of the European Union (Court of Justice, or CJEU) sought to uphold the primacy of Community law over domestic laws, which proved to be problematic where national constitutional provisions included human rights standards, but Community law did not.[105] However, in the subsequent decades, human rights approaches were permitted more of a central place within the EU, as the Court of Justice moved to acknowledge the place of fundamental rights within general principles of EU law,[106] increasingly relying on Strasbourg jurisprudence.[107] The Court of Justice has been especially active in the fields of equal treatment and anti-discrimination law,[108] its hand strengthened by the two discrimination directives adopted in 2000, as well as subsequent gender equality legislation.[109] Other areas where the Court of Justice has applied human rights norms include family

104 CoE, Brighton Declaration, High Level Conference on the Future of the European Court of Human Rights (19–20 April 2012), available: http://www.coe.int/en/20120419-brighton-declaration (accessed 2 July 2012).

105 *Bundesverfassungsgerichtshof*, Decision of 19 May 1974, Bverfge 37, 271; 2 C.M.L.R. 540, 551 (1974) – the *'Solange I'* decision.

106 Case C-29/69 *Stauder v City of Ulm* (1969) ECR 419; Case C-11/70 *Internationale Handelsgesellschaft v Einfuhr- und Vorratsstelle Getreide* (1970) ECR 1125; Case C-4/73 *Nold II* (1974) ECR 508. See too the discussion in E. Defeis, 'Human Rights and the European Court of Justice: An Appraisal' (2007) 31(5) *Fordham International Law Journal* 1104–07. Alston and Weiler have suggested that 'The European Court of Justice deserves immense credit for pioneering the protection of fundamental human rights within the legal order of the Community when the Treaties themselves were silent on this matter' in P. Alston and J. Weiler, 'An "Ever Closer Union" in Need of a Human Rights Policy' (1998) 9(4) at *European Journal of International Law* 658–723, at 709.

107 Case 374/87 *Orkem SA* (1989) ECR 3283 and Case C-274/99 P *Connolly* (2001) ECR I-1611. However, the CJEU has been subject to criticism for making only limited reference to non-European standards. See, for example, I. Butler and O. De Schutter, 'Binding the EU to International Human Rights Law' (2008) 27(1) *Yearbook of European Law* 277–320.

108 Case 149/77, *Defrenne v SA Belge de Navigation Aerienne (SABENA)* (1978) ECR 1365 (gender discrimination); Case C-144/04, *Mangold v Helm* (2005) ECR I-9981 (age discrimination); Case C-555/07 *Kücükdeveci v Swedex Gmbh & Co KG* (2010) 2 CMLR 33 (age discrimination).

109 Directive 2000/43 implementing the principle of equal treatment between persons irrespective of racial or ethnic origin [2000] OJ L180/22; Directive 2000/78 establishing a general framework for equal treatment in employment and occupation [2000] OJ L303/16; Directive 2004/113 implementing the principle of equal treatment between men and women in the access to and supply of goods and services [2004] OJ L373/37; Directive 2006/54 on the implementation of the principle of equal opportunities and equal treatment of men and women in matters of employment and occupation [2006] OJ L204/23.

life,[110] criminal justice,[111] freedom of expression,[112] free movement[113] and anti-terrorism provisions.[114]

At the treaty level, it was not until the Maastricht Treaty in 1992 that formal recognition was given to human rights as part of EU law.[115] That was followed by the Treaty of Amsterdam in 1997, which promulgated the 'Copenhagen criteria' for EU accession, which includes the obligation to be a stable democracy, and to respect human rights, the rule of law, and the protection of minorities. The Treaty of Amsterdam also conferred the power on the EU to adopt legislation to combat discrimination within the fields of its existing competencies.

There are increasingly prominent questions about the justiciability and likely future impact of the Charter of Fundamental Rights of the European Union, which has become a developing reference point as a normative standard within the EU. Originally proclaimed in 2000, its provisions apply to all EU institutions and bodies, and it is increasingly being referred to by the Court of Justice. Unlike the European Convention on Human Rights, it incorporates economic and social rights, and third-generation rights, thus codifying, for example, the right to engage in work, the rights of the elderly and the right to a high level of environmental protection, as fundamental rights within the EU context. Where an EU institution fails to comply with the Charter, the Court of Justice has the power to review the legality of the act in question, and the Commission has the power to institute proceedings. After considerable wrangling over the status of the Charter, the Lisbon Treaty of 2009 confirmed its binding legal status.[116] Thus the Court of Justice is able to hold member states directly to account in respect of breaches of the Charter, as they are required to respect its provisions when implementing EU law.[117]

There remains uncertainty as to what impact the relatively new legal status of the Charter will have. The Court of Justice has found the Charter to have 'the same legal value' as the Treaties.[118] Commentators have accordingly pointed to the Charter's greater prominence, although the sources of fundamental rights previously relied on within the EU (notably the ECHR) will remain important both directly and indirectly.[119] How significant is it that fundamental rights are no longer simply considered to be general principles of EU law, but have been codified as citizens' rights? Weiß, for example, has detected a shift in legitimacy for

---

110 Case C-60/00, *Carpenter v Secretary of State for the Home Department* (2002) 2 CMLR 64.
111 *Orkem* (n. 107); Case C-450/06, *Varec SA v Belgium* (2008) ECR I-581.
112 *Connolly* (n. 107).
113 Case 36/75, *Rutili v Minister for the Interior* (1975) ECR 1219.
114 Case C-402/05 P, *Kadi v European Council* (2008) ECR I-6351.
115 Art. F(2) of the Treaty on European Union (TEU): 'The Union shall respect fundamental rights as guaranteed by the European Convention for the Protection of Human Rights signed in Rome on 4 November 1950 and as they result from constitutional traditions common to the Member States, as general principles of Community Law.'
116 Art. 6(1) TEU.
117 Pursuant to Art. 51(1) of the Charter. See the discussion of the implications of this provision in K. Mathisen, 'The impact of the Lisbon Treaty, in particular Article 6 TEU, on Member States' obligations with respect to the protection of fundamental rights', University of Luxembourg Law Working Paper Series, Paper number 2010–01 (29 July 2012).
118 *Kücükdeveci* (n. 108) 22.
119 See, for example, Mathisen (n. 117).

the EU 'towards the European citizenry'.[120] Some commentators have suggested that the codification and constitutionalisation of fundamental rights within the EU has meant a greater visibility which has assisted in the development of political forms of monitoring (such as the European Parliament's annual reports on fundamental rights),[121] or that it has led to a transformation in culture and practice of the European institutions themselves (notably the European Parliament and European Commission).[122] What significance will the 'parallel coexistence' of three different legal sources of human rights within the EU have after Lisbon (fundamental rights arising from general principles of EU law, Charter rights and ECHR rights)?[123] Questions have also been raised about the consequences of there being differences between the Charter and the European Convention on Human Rights as to how the same (or similar) rights are phrased.[124]

The increasing influence of fundamental rights within the EU has led some commentators to suggest we are witnessing a 'rights revolution'.[125] Other developments could be prayed in aid of such a view, including the establishment of a monitoring body – the Fundamental Rights Agency (FRA) – in 2007, and funding streams, such as the European Initiative for Democracy and Human Rights (EIDHR),[126] as well as the adoption of new standards, such as guidelines on human rights defenders (2008),[127] on violence against women and girls (2008)[128] and on human rights dialogues with third countries (2009).[129] In 2012 the EU for the first time adopted a Strategic Framework on Human Rights and Democracy,[130] and appointed an EU Special Representative on Human Rights (the EU's first thematic Special Representative).[131]

120 W. Weiß, 'Human Rights in the EU: Rethinking the Role of the European Convention on Human Rights After Lisbon' (2011) 7(1) *European Constitutional Law Review* 64–95 at 67.
121 P. Alston and O. de Schutter (eds), *Monitoring Fundamental Rights in the EU – the Contribution of the Fundamental Rights Agency* (Hart Publishing, 2005), 3–5.
122 O. De Schutter, *International Human Rights Law* (CUP, Cambridge, 2010), 25.
123 See the discussion in Weiß (n. 120) 64–95.
124 P. Layden and T. Lock (UK National Rapporteurs), 'Protection of Fundamental Rights post-Lisbon: The Interaction between the EU Charter of Fundamental Rights, the European Convention on Human Rights (ECHR) and National Constitutions', United Kingdom National Report (2011) at 27–29. Art. 52 (3) of the Charter provides: 'In so far as this Charter contains rights which correspond to rights guaranteed by the Convention for the Protection of Human Rights and Fundamental Freedoms, the meaning and scope of those rights shall be the same as those laid down by the said Convention. This provision shall not prevent Union law providing more extensive protection.'
125 See e.g. M. Dawson, E. Muir and M. Claes, 'Enforcing the EU's Rights Revolution: the Case of Equality' (2012) 3 *European Human Rights Law Review* 276–91.
126 This became the European Instrument for Democracy and Human Rights in 2006. See http://ec.europa.eu/europeaid/how/finance/eidhr_en.htm (accessed on 2 July 2012).
127 Available: http://www.consilium.europa.eu/uedocs/cmsUpload/16332-re01.en08.pdf (accessed on 2 July 2012).
128 Available http://eeas.europa.eu/human_rights/guidelines/women/docs/16173_08_en.pdf (accessed on 2 July 2012).
129 Available http://eeas.europa.eu/human_rights/guidelines/dialogues/docs/16526_08_en.pdf (accessed on 2 July 2012).
130 Council of the European Union 'EU Strategic Framework and Action Plan on Human Rights and Democracy' (25 June 2012) 11855/12, available: http://www.consilium.europa.eu/uedocs/cms_data/docs/pressdata/EN/foraff/131181.pdf (accessed on 2 July 2012).
131 Mr Stavros Lambrinidis took office in September 2012. See http://eeas.europa.eu/policies/eu-special-representatives/index_en.htm (accessed on 6 June 2013). See also *Statement on Salafranca Report: EUSR on Human Rights*, A 265/12, Strasbourg (12 June 2012).

It may well be true to say that the promotion of democracy, human rights and the rule of law are now seen as core constituent elements of the EU's constitutional framework and yet there is resistance in some quarters. Commentators, such as von Bogdandy, have expressed scepticism that the concept of human rights should become the EU's *raison d'être*, over and above its focus on the common market – he argues that the development of a predominant human rights policy for the EU could threaten the subsidiarity principle and national legal autonomy.[132] Other commentators have challenged the apparent inevitability of the strengthening of the human rights agenda within the EU. De Búrca paints a more nuanced picture:

> Rather than a story of unidirectional progress, what characterizes the development of the EU human rights system in recent years is a dialectical tension manifested in the complex interaction between a range of 'mobilizing' actors – including civil society organizations, transnational networks and supranational actors like the EU Commission and Court – seeking to strengthen the institutions and mechanisms for human rights protection, and 'resistant' governmental actors on the other hand seeking to curb and deter these.[133]

Others have warned of increasing levels of complexity:

> An NGO or individual seeking to use EU law to bolster their fight against EU breaches of fundamental rights . . . faces a potentially bewildering array of mechanisms and rights to choose from.[134]

There is also evidence to suggest that public understanding of the EU's role in the human rights field still seems to be very limited.[135]

Scholars have highlighted the failure of the EU to develop a 'fully-fledged human rights policy'[136] and expressed concern about an over-reliance upon judicial remedies. It is also possible to contrast the priority given to human rights in the EU's external relations[137] with that of its internal policies, suggesting that double standards may be being applied.[138] De

---

132 A. von Bogdandy, 'The European Union as a Human Rights Organization?: Human Rights and the Core of the European Union' 37(6) (2000) *Common Market Law Review*, 1307–38.

133 G. de Búrca, 'The Road Not Taken: The EU as a Global Human Rights Actor', (2011) 105(4) *American Journal of International Law* 649–93 at 650.

134 See, for example, Dawson, Muir and Claes (n. 125), 277.

135 For example, in 2010, the European Commission received more than 4,000 letters from the public regarding fundamental rights, but about three-quarters of these concerned cases outside the remit of EU law. See: *2010 Report on the Application of the EU Charter of Fundamental Rights*, COM(2011) 160 final (30 March 2011), at 3.

136 Alston and Weiler (n. 106), 662 and 668.

137 The impact of the aspiration to secure membership of the EU has often been acknowledged as driving up human rights standards – albeit in circumstances which are extremely difficult to quantify. See e.g., Murdoch (n. 16), 159.

138 See, for example, Alston and Weiler (n. 106), 663. Shoraka argues that as regards minority rights, the EU exercises double standards as between the newer member states from eastern Europe and the older member states in the west: K. Shoraka, *Human Rights and Minority Rights in the European Union* (Routledge, 2010). See also: Amnesty International, *The EU and Human Rights: Making the Impact on People Count* (AI 2009), which argued that 'The absence of an overall human rights framework . . . has led to the EU not acknowledging the misconduct of its own member states' (at 47). Von Bogdandy has argued for a 'triple human rights standards' within the EU, to reflect, in part, differences of approach to foreign states and Member states: von Bogdandy (n. 132), 1319.

Búrca, for example, has questioned the willingness of European states to be held to account in human rights terms, detecting 'an insistent emphasis by Member States on restricting the extent to which the EU and its institutions can scrutinize or monitor the policies of the Member States'.[139]

3.1 Accession of the EU to the European Convention on Human Rights

The human rights mechanisms in Europe are expected to be harmonised and strengthened by the impending accession of the EU to the ECHR, a development which was originally proposed in the late 1970s.[140] All of the 27 EU member states are also parties to the ECHR and its ratification is an explicit condition of accession to the EU. However, it is anomalous that the EU and its institutions (such as the European Commission, European Parliament and the Court of Justice) are not themselves directly bound by the ECHR. To rectify this situation, the EU has committed itself – in the Treaty of Lisbon in 2009 – to become a party to the ECHR,[141] which will enable individuals to bring complaints to the European Court of Human Rights against the EU institutions (about alleged violations of the ECHR). Accession will also allow the EU to become a party in cases directly or indirectly concerned with EU law before the European Court of Human Rights, thus enabling it to defend, as required, the provisions in question. For Alston and Weiler, this development will enable 'the sensibilities and experiences of the [EU] to form an integral part of the evolving jurisprudence and extra-juridical activity of the European Convention system'.[142] Hitherto, the European Court of Human Rights has only permitted itself a limited role in reviewing certain acts of the EU. The European Court's position vis-à-vis international organisations is that where a state transfers sovereign power to a supranational body, this is considered justified provided that the organisation in question is considered to protect fundamental rights to an extent that is at least equivalent to that provided by the ECHR. If such equivalent protection is considered to be provided by the organisation, it is presumed that a state has not breached its obligations under the Convention simply by implementing its legal obligations flowing from membership of that organisation (a presumption which can be rebutted). In the *Bosphorus* case, the European Court found that this rebuttable presumption applies to the EU.[143] This standpoint can be

---

139 G. de Búrca, 'The Evolution of EU Human Rights Law', in P. Craig and G. de Búrca (eds), *The Evolution of EU Law*, 2nd edn (OUP, 2011), 485.

140 European Commission, Memorandum adopted by the Commission (4 April 1979) *Bulletin of the European Communities*, Supp. 2/79.

141 Art. 6(2) of the Treaty of Lisbon. See also the equivalent – Art. 59(2) of the ECHR.

142 Alston and Weiler (n. 106), 686.

143 *Bosphorus Hava Yollari Turizm Ve Ticaret AS v Ireland* [GC] App. No. 45036/98 (ECtHR, Judgment of 30 June 2005). See also: *Connolly v 15 Member States of the European Union* App. No. 73274/01 (ECtHR, Decision of 9 December 2008); *La Société Etablissement Biret et CIE S.A. v 15 Member States of the European Union* App. No. 13762/04 (ECtHR, Decision of 9 December 2008); *Beygo v 46 Member States of the Council of Europe* App. No. 36099/06 (ECtHR, Decision of 16 June 2009); *Cooperative Producentenorganisatie Van De Nederlandse Kokkelvisserij U.A. v Netherlands* App. No. 13645/05 (ECtHR, Decision of 20 January 2009). See further: *Lopez Cifuentes v Spain* App. No. 18754/06 (ECtHR, Decision of 7 July 2009) (re International Olive Council); *Lenzing AG v Germany* App. No. 39025/97 (ECtHR, Decision of 9 September 1998) and *Rambus Inc. v Germany* App. No. 40382/04 (ECtHR, Decision of 16 June 2009) (both cases re European Patent Convention).

criticised as being too deferential, and one result of EU accession to the ECHR is likely to be a stricter scrutiny being exercised by the European Court. In any event, EU accession is expected to have the effect of reducing the likelihood of diverging European standards[144] (or overlapping and competing jurisdictions[145]) and should lead to a more integrated mutual development of the case law of the European Court and the Court of Justice.[146]

EU accession to the ECHR may also have important consequences as to process. A significant feature of accessing the Court of Justice has been the preliminary rulings procedure, according to which national courts can put questions to the Court of Justice as to the interpretation or validity of EU law.[147] To date there has been no equivalent mechanism in Strasbourg, but it is intended that a new Protocol to the ECHR will for the first time enable the European Court to issue 'advisory opinions' on the ECHR to national courts.[148] Such a development certainly accords with the Council of Europe's dominant agenda of improving implementation at the national level – by placing further emphasis on decisions being taken by domestic courts, and thereby reducing the need to be reliant upon a protracted process at the regional level, even after the national courts have issued their rulings. Other important questions of process arising from EU accession to the ECHR which remain to be resolved include the designation of a co-respondent, the extent to which there should be prior involvement of the Court of Justice, and the allocation of responsibility after the ECtHR has issued its judgment.[149]

4 Conclusion

The European human rights system has changed beyond recognition during its 60-year existence. Although this chapter recognises the mutually reinforcing contributions of the various Council of Europe human rights mechanisms, it is the European Court of Human Rights which continues to take centre stage. As the debate persists about the need for reform of the Strasbourg Court, this contribution calls for duality in its objectives – both honouring its keystone, the right of individual petition, and further developing its jurisprudence of constitutional significance.

The Strasbourg Court has developed a nuanced approach to interpreting the European Convention on Human Rights as a living instrument, and a progressive stance as regards the evolving imposition of positive obligations on states. In the future, the Court is likely to enhance its focus on collective or representative litigation (especially in response to systemic

---

144 See, e.g. the discussion of differences between the CJEU and the ECtHR in Weiß (n. 120), 7, 64–95, 77–80.
145 See e.g., Mathisen (n. 117), 31.
146 See the discussion about developing legal harmony and certainty in J. Callewaert, 'The European Convention on Human Rights and European Union Law: A Long Way to Harmony' (2009) 6 *European Human Rights Law Review* 768–83. Callewaert identifies the privilege against self-incrimination and the detention of asylum seekers as being areas where the CJEU and ECtHR have developed diverging standards in recent years.
147 Pursuant to Art. 267 TFEU.
148 See clause 12(d) of the Brighton Declaration (n. 104).The advisory opinion process will be set out in Protocol No. 16 to the ECHR. See the draft Explanatory Report at http://www.coe.int/t/dghl/standardsetting/cddh/DH_GDR/DH-GDR(2012)020_Draft%20Explanatory%20 Report_Protocol%20no%20%2016_ECHR%20(3).pdf (accessed on 6 June 2013).
149 See e.g. Layden and Lock (n. 124) 32–34.

human rights failings), extend further its scope of redress and give additional emphasis to egregious violations (arising for example out of armed conflict).

Whether it is accurate or not to talk of a 'rights revolution' within the European Union, the position of fundamental rights has certainly been significantly enhanced in recent years, marking something of a shift of emphasis towards citizens' rights and culminating in the conferring of binding legal status on the Charter of Fundamental Rights in 2009. However, commentators have pointed to states' resistance to additional human rights protections and not infrequently complain of 'double standards' being applied internally within the EU and externally.

Expectations are high as regards the impact of EU accession to the European Convention on Human Rights. It is predicted to lead to a harmonising and strengthening of European human rights mechanisms, reducing the risk of diverging standards being promulgated by the two European courts and leading to a stricter degree of scrutiny by the Strasbourg Court over EU institutions.

Select bibliography

E. Bates, *The Evolution of the European Convention on Human Rights: From its Inception to the Creation of a Permanent Court of Human Rights* (OUP, 2010).

G. de Búrca, 'The Evolution of EU Human Rights Law', in P. Craig and G. de Búrca (eds), *The Evolution of EU Law*, 2 edn (OUP, 2011).

D. Harris, M. O'Boyle, E. Bates, and C. Buckley, *Harris, O'Boyle & Warbrick—Law of the European Convention on Human Rights*, 2 edn (OUP, 2009).

H. Keller and A Stone Sweet (eds), *A Europe of Rights – The Impact of the ECHR on National Legal Systems* (OUP, 2008).

P. Leach, H. Hardman, S. Stephenson, and B. Blitz *Responding to Systemic Human Rights Violations: An Analysis of Pilot Judgments of the European Court of Human Rights and their Impact at National Level* (Intersentia, 2010).

Open Society Justice Initiative *From Judgment to Justice – Implementing International and Regional Human Rights Decisions* (Open Society Foundations, 2010).

24

The Inter-American System of Human Rights and approach

Clara Sandoval*

1 Introduction

The Americas has one of the most interesting yet contested regional human rights systems in the world: the Inter-American System of Human Rights (the IASHR, or the System). This chapter looks at its achievements and challenges over the period of more than 50 years since the Inter-American Commission on Human Rights (IACommHR) was created, and more than 30 years since the first judges of the Inter-American Court (IACtHR) were appointed. The Commission and the Court are known as the two institutions of the System.

An overview of what has been done, why, when and how, is necessary to identify the lessons that need to be learned as well as the major contributions of the system to the promotion and protection of human rights in the hemisphere and to the development of international human rights law.

To this end, the first part of the chapter puts the System in context; it introduces the Organisation of American States (OAS); the key players of the System, its aims and powers. The second part looks at its achievements by considering both the work done by the Commission and the Court, and the different tools they have at hand to protect human rights. The third part focuses on its challenges. While there are many things to celebrate about the System, it is also important to consider those areas where the System faces strong limitations, therefore failing to carry out its mandate. Lastly, the chapter concludes with some reflections on to where the system is heading. It puts the System in perspective and looks into the future.

* I am grateful to various persons who either commented on various drafts of this chapter or provided me with information I needed. In particular, I am grateful to Oscar Parra, Camilo Sánchez, Michael Duttwiler, Sabine Michalowski, Diana Guarnizo, Judith Schonsteiner and Indiana Jimenez.

2 The Inter-American System of Human Rights in context

2.1 Concept of a System and the IASHR

The Oxford English Dictionary defines a system as a 'set or assemblage of things connected, associated, or interdependent, so as to form a complex unity'.[1] This definition does not fully capture the unique features of the Inter-American mechanisms for the protection of human rights. The IASHR has two key institutions: the Commission and the Court. However, they do not always work in an interdependent manner.

The Commission is a main body of the OAS, and is mandated to protect and promote human rights in the hemisphere. It is connected to the Court when its quasi-judicial powers or capacity to request an advisory opinion from the Court are at stake. Otherwise, the Commission is a self-standing institution that would exist even without the Court.

The Court, on the other hand, was created by the American Convention on Human Rights (the American Convention or the Convention) – the key human rights treaty in the Americas – and is not a main body of the OAS. The Court has contentious jurisdiction only over the states that have become party to the Convention and explicitly accepted the jurisdiction of the Court. The Court cannot exercise its contentious jurisdiction unless the Commission refers a case to the Court or requests provisional measures. So, the real System, understood for its interdependent and complex unity, only exists in relation to the judicial functions of both the Commission and the Court.

It is also important to note that beyond the Commission and the Court – the IASHR in the strict sense – there are other institutions within the OAS that can play an important role in the promotion and protection of human rights in the hemisphere and that should also be understood as part of the IASHR in the broad sense. For example, the OAS Permanent Council, the Inter-American Juridical Committee, and some specialised organisations like the Pan-American Health Organisation (PAHO) or the Inter-American Commission of Women (CIM) are crucial to advancing human rights protection. They have or could play important monitoring or advisory roles. A narrow understanding of the institutions that constitute the IASHR has a negative impact on the promotion and protection of human rights in the Americas since key bodies that would be essential to this end are simply ignored.

2.2 What we have

2.2.1 The OAS

It is not possible to conceive of a regional human rights system without the existence of an international organisation that makes it possible. In the Americas the IASHR exists because of the OAS, a regional organisation established in 1948; today it has 35 member states. While the OAS did not envisage the existence of the System when the Charter of the Organization of American States (the OAS Charter) was signed, it facilitated its establishment.

The OAS Charter does not include the promotion and protection of human rights as one of its purposes,[2] which included strengthening peace and security, non-intervention, poverty

---

1 *Oxford English Dictionary* (OUP, 1989).
2 OAS Charter, Art. 1, (1948) 119 UNTS 3.

eradication, development and representative democracy at its heart. Nevertheless, the Charter refers to rights, and particularly labour rights, in other provisions. For example, Article 3 recognises the fundamental rights of persons without discrimination and Article 45 incorporates the right to work or freedom of assembly or association. The Charter has been amended over the years allowing human rights to gain more importance. For example, when the OAS was established, it did not envisage the creation of the Commission. This only happened more than a decade later, in 1959, as a result of a Meeting of Consultation of Ministers of Foreign Affairs.[3] Nevertheless, the Commission did not have Charter status until it was amended in 1967 by the Protocol of Buenos Aires.[4]

In 1948, however, the states represented in Bogotá at the International Conference that created the OAS agreed on the enactment of Resolution XXX, otherwise known as the American Declaration on the Rights and Duties of Man (the Declaration). While this Resolution was a mere declaration without binding status, it was the first codification of human rights and duties in the hemisphere. It predates the Universal Declaration of Human Rights and includes civil and political and economic, social and cultural rights.

The legal status of the Declaration remains contested by some states in the region like the United States.[5] Nevertheless, when the Commission began to work, it carried out its mandate by applying the Declaration, as this was expressly ordered by its Statutes.[6] At the time, there were no human rights treaties in the System for the Commission to inform its mandate. Today, the Commission continues to monitor human rights protection in states that have not become party to the American Convention by applying the standards of the American Declaration; and state practice in the Americas reflects the belief that the majority of OAS member states consider it as a binding instrument.[7]

The OAS has promoted the enactment and ratification of several human rights treaties that complement the American Convention and the Declaration. These treaties are the Protocol to the American Convention to Abolish the Death Penalty (1990) (the Convention on Death Penalty) and the Protocol of San Salvador in the Area of Economic, Social and Cultural Rights (1988); the Inter-American Convention to Prevent and Punish Torture (1985); the Inter-American Convention on Forced Disappearance of Persons (1994); the Inter-American Convention on the Prevention, Punishment and Eradication of Violence against Women (1994) (Belém do Pará Convention); the Inter-American Convention on the Elimination of All Forms of Discrimination against Persons with Disabilities (1999); the Inter-American Convention Against all Forms of Discrimination and Intolerance; and the Inter-American Convention Against Racism, Racial Discrimination, and Related Forms of Intolerance. The last two Conventions were signed in June 2013 and at the moment of writing this chapter are not yet in force.

---

3 Meeting of Consultation of Ministers of Foreign Affairs, Resolution III, Santiago de Chile, 1959.
4 Third Special Inter-American Conference, *Protocol of Buenos Aires*, Article XII, OAS Treaty Series, No. 1-A, 27 February 1967.
5 *Interpretation of the American Declaration of the Rights and Duties of Man Within the Framework of Article 64 of the American Convention on Human Rights*, IACtHR (Advisory Opinion OC-10/89) (14 July 1989) Ser. A No. 10, para.12.
6 Statute of the Inter-American Commission on Human Rights, Art. 9, Doc. OEA/Ser.L/V/II, 26 September 1960.
7 *Interpretation of the American Declaration of the Rights and Duties of Man Within the Framework of Article 64 of the American Convention on Human Rights*, IACtHR (Advisory Opinion OC-10/89) (14 July 1989) Ser. A No. 10, paras 2, 11–18.

All these treaties, except the Convention on Death Penalty, go beyond the recognition of rights and state duties and indicate the ways in which the System, in the broad sense, should help in the implementation of their provisions. For example, the Belém do Pará Convention gives the CIM a monitoring role over the Convention as well as the power to request advisory opinions from the Court.[8] It also grants the Commission the power to receive petitions claiming violations of Article 7 of the Convention that incorporates the state duties.

2.2.2 The Inter-American Commission on Human Rights

The Commission is composed of seven members who are elected in their personal capacity by the OAS General Assembly for a period of four years and who can be re-elected only once.[9] While the Commission is a main body of the OAS, the commissioners are not permanently based at its headquarters in Washington. They only meet as necessary during the Commission's ordinary and extraordinary sessions.

According to the OAS Charter, the Commission should 'promote the observance and protection of human rights and to serve as a consultative organ of the Organization in these matters'.[10] It carries out its mandate through three main activities: the individual and inter-state petition system; monitoring the human rights situation in OAS member states through *on-site* visits and other means and by devoting attention to key areas/countries of concern through special reports or technical assistance.[11] Individuals and states have access to the Commission through either of the main activities. In relation to the individual and inter-state petition system, it should be noted that any person, group of persons or non-governmental organisations (NGOs) duly recognised in any of the OAS member states can file a petition with the Commission claiming a violation of any of the rights established in the American Declaration or the Convention and, depending on the treaty in question, of other regional human rights treaties. However, they do not have direct access to the Court. Exhaustion of domestic remedies is necessary unless such remedies are not effective or adequate to deal with alleged violation.

As in the United Nations, since 1990 the Commission has also established thematic rapporteurships that help it carry out its mandate. As of 2012 the Commission has rapporteurships on themes like the rights of women; the rights of indigenous peoples; persons deprived of their freedom and human rights defenders.[12] In October 2011 the Commission also decided to establish a Unit on the Rights of Lesbian, Gay, Bisexual, Trans and Intersex Persons that might evolve into a rapporteurship in the future. In November 2012 a Unit on Economic, Social and Cultural Rights was also established. The office of the special rapporteur on freedom of expression was established in 1997. This post is held by a person who is not a commissioner. In contrast with the other rapporteurships, this is a permanent and independent office of the Commission that is funded by external funds.

---

8 Convention of Belém do Pará, Arts 10–11, (1994) 33 ILM 1534.
9 OAS General Assembly, Statute of the Inter-American Commission on Human Rights, Arts 2–6, Resolution 447, October 1979.
10 OAS Charter (n. 2) Art. 106.
11 Statute of the Inter-American Commission on Human Rights, Arts 18–20, OAS General Assembly Resolution 447 (1979), and Rules of Procedure of the IACommHR Arts 14–21, IACommHR 137th regular period of sessions (November 2009). Some Articles of the Rules of Procedure of the IACommHR were amended in March 2013. Such changes will enter into force in August 2013. The articles mentioned here were not amended.
12 More information is available at: http://www.oas.org/en/iachr/mandate/composition.asp#tab3.

As of March 2012, the United States, Canada, the Bahamas, Belize, Guyana, St Kitts and Nevis, Saint Lucia, St Vincent, the Grenadines and Cuba have not become party to the Convention. Almost all of these countries have common law systems. The Commission monitors the human rights situation in all of these states applying the standards of the American Declaration while in relation to the rest of the states, almost all of which have civil law systems and part of the so-called Latin America, it applies the American Convention. Two countries have denounced the Convention: Trinidad and Tobago in 1998 and Venezuela in 2012. The denunciation takes effect one year after official notice has been given by the state to the Secretary General of the organisation.[13] Trinidad and Tobago and Venezuela continue to be bound by the American Declaration.

2.2.3 The Inter-American Court of Human Rights

Unlike the European Court of Human Rights, where each member state of the Council of Europe has one judge sitting at the Court, the Inter-American Court is composed of seven judges, nationals of any of the OAS member states, and not only of the states that have become party to the Convention. They are elected by the OAS General Assembly and work in their personal capacity for a period of four years and can be re-elected only once.[14] The Court has its headquarters in Costa Rica but the judges, as with the Commission, only meet during the ordinary and extraordinary sessions of the Court. They are not working as judges full time.

The Court has contentious and advisory jurisdiction.[15] While the Court can only exercise its contentious jurisdiction in relation to those states that have become party to the Convention and accepted explicitly the jurisdiction of the Court, its advisory jurisdiction goes beyond the states parties to the Convention. In fact, any OAS member state, can request the Court to interpret a provision of the Convention, of any other human rights treaty concerning the protection of rights in the Americas region, or regarding the compatibility of a domestic law with the Convention or any other relevant human rights treaty.[16]

The Court can exercise its contentious jurisdiction over inter-state complaints or individual petitions but only if the Commission refers a case to the Court. So, in contrast with the European system, no state or individual can go directly to the Court claiming violations of rights protected under the Convention and/or any other relevant and applicable regional human rights treaty. Once the Commission refers a case to the Court, the alleged victims gain *locus standi in judicio* and can act autonomously before the Court through their legal representatives. This gives place to a very peculiar feature of the litigation before the Court since besides the state and the victims – the two parties of the litigation – the Commission also has some rights before the Court as it represents the public order.[17]

2.2.4 The OAS member states

The key players of the System are the 35 members of the OAS. They make the System possible thanks to their political and economic support but they are also one of its main problems since some of them constantly attack or threaten the work of the System, as has been the situation

---

13 American Convention on Human Rights, Art. 78, (1969) 1144 UNTS 123.
14 American Convention on Human Rights, Arts 52–54, ibid.
15 Ibid, Art. 52–64.
16 Ibid, Art. 64.
17 Inter-American Court of Human Rights, Rules of Procedure, Arts 35 and 40, 2009.

in the last two years with the so-called Bolivarian Alliance for the Americas (ALBA), headed by Venezuela, Ecuador, Nicaragua and Bolivia, and supported by others including Brazil and Colombia, trying to weaken in serious ways the mandate and financial situation of the Inter-American Commission on Human Rights.[18]

The System has had to adapt to a changing political landscape in the region. During the initial years of the OAS, the region was divided between capitalist and communist states. States were led by dictatorships or repressive regimes and they were not supportive of human rights. The key goal was to suppress any type of leftist ideology by any means possible. Then, disappearances, torture and extrajudicial executions were the rule and happened systematically.[19] The Commission was the institution of the System forced to respond to these mass atrocities during the first decades of the System, as is noted in the coming pages. Later, the Court also dealt with these violations, as happened when it decided *Velásquez Rodríguez v Honduras*, its first contentious case. Then, the Commission and the Court built the legal foundations for the treatment of such human rights violations, particularly enforced disappearances, under international law.

This political context began to change in the 1980s when countries like Argentina began their transitions to democracy. Such transitions continued during the 1990s and are still visible today in countries like Colombia. Today the region is in theory led by elected democratic governments where liberal tendencies are predominant, but where moderate to radical socialist tendencies are also visible in countries such as Brazil, Ecuador, Venezuela or Bolivia. Cuba is the only remaining communist country in the Americas.

While the occurrence of gross human rights violations, like enforced disappearances, has decreased; poverty, inequality and discrimination have spread across the region. These structural problems threaten various human rights including economic, social and cultural rights.[20] Nevertheless, the apparent political changes towards democratisation and liberalism that have taken place in the Americas have made these problems invisible. And while disappearances might have decreased in some countries, authoritarianism remains an embedded practice in most of the OAS member states but it merges in sophisticated ways with democracy, rule of law and with liberalism.[21]

In this changing political context, the System has had to face threats and challenges from different states in the region. For instance, while Cuba remains in theory a member of the OAS, the Cuban Government was suspended from the System in 1962 by the Meeting of Ministers of Foreign Affairs due to its communist approach.[22] Since then Cuba considers that the Commission does not have any jurisdiction over its human rights situation, diminishing the

---

18 Conferencia de Estados Parte de la Convención Americana de Derechos Humanos, Declaración de Guayaquil, 11 March 2013, http://www.conectas.org/arquivos/DECLARA%C3%87%C3%83O%20 GUAYAQUIL_conferencia_estados_partes%202013%20(1).pdf.

19 C. Medina, *The Battle of Human Rights: Gross, Systematic Violations and the Inter-American System* (International Studies in Human Rights, Kluwer, 1988).

20 V. Abramovich, 'From Massive Violations to Structural Patterns: New Approaches and Classical Tensions in the Inter-American Human Rights System' (2009) 11 *SUR International Journal on Human Rights* 7–37 at 9 and 16.

21 See for example the book by M. Garcia, *La Eficacia Simbólica del Derecho* (Uniandes, 1993).

22 *Octava Reunión de Consulta de Ministros de Relaciones Exteriores, Resolución VI, 'Exclusión del Actual Gobierno de Cuba de su Participación en el Sistema Interamericano'*, in *Acta Final*, 21 to 31 January 1962, 293–295, available at: http://www.oas.org/consejo/sp/RC/Actas/Acta%208.pdf, accessed on 15 June 2012.

impact it could have in Cuba. This is interesting given that Cuba was one of the few Caribbean countries to become a party to the Charter since 1948. The OAS has tried to improve its relationship with Cuba. To this end, its General Assembly decided in 2009 to lift the suspension of Cuba and to welcome it again to the Organisation.[23] Cuba rejected this approach.

As for other countries in the region, it should be noted that Canada became party to the OAS Charter in 1990 after a period of friendly distance from the Organisation, but it has not become party to the Convention or accepted the jurisdiction of the Court. Equally, the US has been party to the OAS Charter since 1951, signed the Convention in 1977, but has not ratified it and has not accepted the jurisdiction of the Court. Mexico and Brazil became party to the Convention in 1981 and 1992 respectively, but only accepted the jurisdiction of the Court in 1998. Consequently, the Court has no jurisdiction over the US, the most powerful country in the region, nor over Canada, but has gained jurisdiction over Brazil and Mexico, two economically emerging powers.

Although Venezuela became party to the Convention and accepted the jurisdiction of the Court very early on – in 1977 and 1981 respectively – the late President Hugo Chavez consistently attacked the System. He decided to denounce the Convention in September 2012.[24] Equally, countries like Peru have threatened to denounce the Convention and to withdraw their acceptance of the Court's jurisdiction. Trinidad and Tobago denounced the Convention in 1998, as a result of a dispute with the System over unreasonable delays in applying the death penalty to persons in death row.[25]

In addition, it should be noted that while OAS member states appear to uphold human rights protection internationally, their lack of economic and political support to the System puts this in question. Indeed, the System works without the necessary resources (financial and human) required for responding in an adequate manner to the challenges of human rights protection in the Americas.

2.2.5 Other players in the System

The System's work is possible thanks to a very strong civil society in some of its countries. Indeed, in countries like Argentina or Colombia, NGOs were able to articulate their political efforts from very early on, and to use the System to advance human rights protection. NGOs like the Argentinean Centre for Socio-Legal Studies (CELS) founded in 1979 or the Colombian Commission of Jurists (CCJ) founded in 1988 began to use the System since they were established to advance human rights protection.

While these NGOs have been key players in the System, the globalisation of human rights law as a language of social change soon began to be articulated by other social actors that in turn established new NGOs that interact with the System in one way or another, as is the case of the Centre for Justice and International Law (CEJIL), established in 1991, and which is the leading NGO litigating before the System. So, nowadays different NGOs, from local to international ones, are using the tools that the System offers to advance human rights protection.

23 OAS General Assembly, AG/Doc.5005/2009, 3 June 2009.
24 Inter-American Commission on Human Rights, Press Release, *IACHR Regrets Decision of Venezuela to Denounce the American Convention on Human Rights*, 12 September 2012, http://www.oas.org/en/iachr/media_center/PReleases/2012/117.asp accessed in March 2013.
25 N. Parassram, 'The Legal Implications of Trinidad and Tobago's Withdrawal from the American Convention on Human Rights', (2001) 16(3) *American University International Law Review* 848–90.

This has been the case mainly in Latin American states, the US and Canada. It should also be noted that academics from across the region, some of whom also work for human rights NGOs like CELS or *De-Justicia*, have been crucial to advancing understanding about the System and to help generate awareness of its importance. The role played by civil society organisations during the latest reform of the Commission was fundamental to block the reforms proposed by the ALBA states and other ones in the region which, as already indicated, aimed to weaken this body in serious ways.[26]

However, civil society remains weak in Caribbean states. In fact, if one takes as an indicator of this situation the amount of petitions presented to the Commission against the OAS member states per year, one sees that Latin American countries, the US and Canada are the states most subject to complaints before the System while the lowest number of complaints, or no complaints whatsoever, are submitted against Caribbean states such as Dominica, Barbados or Grenada.[27] Therefore, the development of civil society in the OAS member states, as well as their interest in the IASHR, is uneven.

3 The achievements of the System

3.1 The achievements of the Commission

The Commission has carried out remarkable work promoting human rights in the OAS member states despite its lack of economic and human resources. This has been possible due to the commitment of some of its commissioners and staff as well as to the tools it has been given to fulfil its mandate. In particular, in-situ visits and country and thematic reports, tools given to the Commission under Article 18 of its Statute,[28] have been essential to this end.

On-site observations in OAS member states require the consent of the state while the preparation of reports does not.[29] So, even if states do not allow the Commission to carry out a visit, it can still write a country report using the information it gathers from NGOs, individual complaints and other means, although the state must be given the opportunity to make observations it deems pertinent on the draft report. Equally, after an on-site visit a report may be released, and reports usually include recommendations for the state concerned.

When Chile was ruled by Augusto Pinochet, who overthrew the government of President Allende in September 1973, an on-site visit took place and four country reports were released by the Commission. These were the tools available to respond to the very serious and systematic human rights violations then taking place in Chile, a country that at the time had just signed the Convention. The Commission sent its Executive Secretary to assess the situation. The Secretary was able to visit the country and recommended the Commission to carry out

---

26 N. Sánchez, 'El Balance Político de la Reforma al Sistema de Derechos Humanos de la OEA', http://www.americasquarterly.org/content/nelson-camilo-sanchez accessed in March 2013.
27 See the statistics section of the Commission's Annual Report to the OAS General Assembly. For example, contrast the Annual Report of 2010 with the Annual Report of 1999, and in both it is visible that no petitions were filed by Granada or Dominica. So, despite the lapse of time and the increasing impact of the System in the OAS member states, countries like Granada or Dominica are not engaging with the System and this might be explained, in part, due to a weak civil society.
28 Arts 53 to 57 of the Rules of Procedure of the Commission further regulate this power, indicating the type of activities that the members of the Special Commission can carry out as well as the support that the state should provide.
29 IACommHR, Rules of Procedure, Arts 39 and 60, 2011.

an on-site visit. Chile granted permission to the Commission to carry out the visit between 22 July and 2 August 1974. A first report on the human rights situation in Chile was then written in 1974,[30] including the recommendation to Chile to conduct an impartial investigation into torture and detention cases. This report was sent to the OAS General Assembly and to the UN Commission on Human Rights (the forerunner to the UN Human Rights Council). Both of these bodies also took action. The General Assembly requested the Commission to continue monitoring the human rights situation in Chile and the UN Commission on Human rights established different ad hoc mechanisms to do the same, such as the Ad-hoc Working Group to inquire into the Human Rights Situation in Chile and later on in 1979 a Special Rapporteur on the Human Rights Situation in Chile among others.[31]

The Commission then produced a second report on Chile in 1976,[32] without carrying out an on-site visit. The Commission tried to rely on written reports presented by the Chilean government based on information it requested, but Chile did not cooperate as required. As a result, the Commission had to rely on other information it had gathered based on the argument that the OAS General Assembly had authorised it to use 'all pertinent methods' to assess the situation in an adequate manner.[33] A third report was then written by the Commission in 1977,[34] again without an on-site visit. Nevertheless, the Chilean government replied to the questionnaires sent by the Commission. The Commission made new recommendations to Chile. A final report to cover the dictatorship years in Chile was written by the Commission in 1985.[35] The on-site visit and the four reports were essential to document the human rights violations taking place in Chile and to put pressure on Chile to change this record.

Another country report within the System that has been groundbreaking under international law was the one produced by the Commission in 1980, regarding the human rights situation in Argentina, where a dictatorship reigned between 1976 and 1983 and enforced disappearances were the rule, among other gross human rights violations.[36] This report followed an on-site visit carried out by the Commission to Argentina in September 1979. It included a chapter titled 'the problem of the disappeared', which considered its legal dimensions, its patterns, those affected including the next of kin of the disappeared and even the laws enacted in Argentina to deal with the consequences of a disappearance. This report chapter set up the foundations for understanding the human rights dimensions of the crime of enforced disappearance.

As the cases of Chile and Argentina illustrate, the Commission's reporting mechanism has been far-reaching. Indeed, it has published more than 60 country reports in its history.[37] Nevertheless, in recent years an important change in the quality and focus of its reporting

---

30 IACommHR, *Report on the Status of Human Rights in Chile*, OEA/Ser.L/V/II.34.doc.21.corr.1, 25 October 1974.

31 UN Commission on Human Rights, Resolution 11 (XXXV), 6 March 1979.

32 IACommHR, *Second Report on the Situation of Human Rights in Chile*, OEA/Ser.L/V/II.37.doc.19. corr.1, 28 June 1976.

33 Ibid. para 11.

34 IACommHR, *Third Report on the Situation of Human Rights in Chile*, OEA/Ser.L/V/II.40.doc.10, 11 February 1977.

35 IACommHR, *Report on the Situation of Human Rights in Chile*, OEA/Ser.L/V/II.66.doc.17, 9 September 1985.

36 IACommHR, *Report on the Situation of Human Rights in Argentina*, OEA/Ser.L/V/II.49, 11 April 1980.

37 A full list of those country reports can be found at: http://www.oas.org/en/iachr/reports/country. asp, last visited in March 2013.

mechanism has been visible. The production of general country reports has decreased but the production of thematic reports or country-thematic reports has increased to more than 40 since 1998. This shift is to be welcomed given the need to address problems that affect the region as a whole or a particular OAS member state.[38] Thematic reports have been important, for example, to generate awareness and knowledge of women rights, indigenous rights and economic, social and cultural rights among states and relevant stakeholders in the region. For instance, the Commission has produced various reports on women's rights, dealing with the status of women in the Americas: in particular places like Ciudad Juárez in Mexico, in Haiti or in armed conflicts like in Colombia; on access to justice; to maternal health services and to information on reproductive health among others.[39] These reports reflect the great legal knowledge of some members of the Commission who had taken on the task to help the System to clarify international standards that bind OAS member states. For example, former commissioners like Juan Méndez or Victor Abramovich were responsible for important thematic reports on migrant workers, women's rights, and economic, social and cultural rights.

The Commission has also carried out an important work through its quasi-judicial powers. Indeed, it has decided important cases,[40] helped to settle others[41] and referred others to the Court. Nevertheless, what makes the Commission so unique in its work, and what justifies its existence, is precisely that it has the power to look after the human rights situation in the Americas region and not only in relation to states that have ratified the American Convention using other tools than the quasi-judicial one. This latter power, while important, constitutes just one dimension of its multifaceted tools.[42]

3.2 The achievements of the Court

Despite the fact that the Court has only decided some 130 cases on the merits since it was established – in contrast with, for example, 1,157 judgments handed down by the European Court in the year 2011[43] – it has taken many opportunities to develop international and regional human rights standards, creating, in such a way, inspirational jurisprudence for

---

38 Examples of country-thematic reports are the Commission's *Report on Access to Justice and Social Inclusion: The Road Towards Strengthening Democracy in Bolivia*, OEA/Ser.L/V/II.doc.34, 28 June 2007 and its *Follow-up Report*, OEA/Ser.L/V/II.135.doc.40, 7 August 2009 and its *Report on Democracy and Human Rights in Venezuela*, OEA/Ser.L/V/II.doc.54, 30 December 2009.

39 IACommHR, *Report on the Status of Women in the Americas*, OEA/Ser.L/V/II.100.doc.17, 13 October 1998; *Report on the Situation of the Rights of Women in Ciudad Juárez, Mexico: The Right to be Free from Violence and Discrimination*, OEA/Ser.L/V/II.117.doc.44, 7 March 2003; *Report on Violence and Discrimination Against Women in the Armed Conflict in Colombia*, OEA/Ser.L/V/II.doc.67, 18 October 2006; *Report on Access to Justice for Women Victims of Violence in the Americas*, OEA/Ser.L/V/II.doc.68, 20 January 2007; and *Report on Access to Maternal Health Services from a Human Rights Perspective*, OEA/Ser.L/V/II.doc.69, 7 June 2010, among others.

40 IACommHR, Report 54/01, Petition 12.051, *Maria Da Pehna Maia Fernandes (Brasil)*, 16 April 2001 or Report 66/06, Petition 12.001, *Simeone André Diniz (Brasil)*, 21 October 2006.

41 IACommHR, Report 71/03, Petition 12.191, friendly settlement, *María Mamérita Mestanza Chávez (Peru)*, 22 October 2003 or Report 21/07, Petition 161–02, friendly settlement, *Paulina del Carmen Ramírez Jacinto* (Mexico), 9 March 2007.

42 A. Dulitzky, 'The Inter-American Human Rights System Fifty Years Later: Time for Changes' (2011) *Quebec Journal of International Law* (Special edition) 127–64 at 142.

43 European Court of Human Rights, *Analysis of Statistics 2011* (January 2012), p. 4, available at: http://www.echr.coe.int/NR/rdonlyres/11CE0BB3–9386–48DC-B012-AB2C046FEC7C/0/STATS_EN_2011.PDF, accessed on 25 June 2012.

international and domestic courts worldwide. This has been possible given the scope of some provisions of the American Convention, the holistic integration of international law in its reasoning, the nature of the cases at stake and the commitment of eminent judges at the Court. This section illustrates this achievement with different examples, but given space constrains important contributions of the Court to international law are not covered.

The scope of some provisions of the Convention, like that of Article 29 (Restrictions Regarding Interpretation), have been important for the Court's holistic interpretations of the rights and freedoms that it recognises. This Article indicates that states parties to the Convention cannot interpret it in a way that restricts the rights and freedoms it recognises or that precludes other rights or guarantees that are inherent to people or derived from representative democracy as a form of government or 'excluding or limiting the effect that the American Declaration . . . and other international acts of the same nature may have'.

The Court has used Article 29 in different ways to enhance human rights protection.[44] For example, the Court used it to recognise that the right to property under the American Convention also includes the right to communal and ancestral property of indigenous peoples, arguing that it should use 'an evolutionary interpretation of international instruments for the protection of human rights'.[45] The Court also used Article 29 to recognise that the next of kin of the disappeared have a right under Article 8(1) of the Convention – the right to a fair trial – to know the truth of what happened to their loved ones through effective investigation, prosecution and punishment of the perpetrators as well as to adequate reparation for the harm suffered.[46] The Court argued that the Article 'must be given a broad interpretation based on both the letter and the spirit of this provision' and referred to Article 1.2 of the UN Declaration on the Protection of all Persons Against Forced Disappearances to note that it also recognised the suffering of the next of kin of the disappeared. Both of these interpretations have been groundbreaking under international law. The first uses an individual right, the right to property, to recognise collective rights of indigenous peoples. The second is part of one of the key transitional justice pillars; that gross human rights violations and serious breaches of international humanitarian law should be investigated, prosecuted and punished and that reparation should be provided in adequate form.[47]

Equally, the Court has been in constant engagement with international and regional law and has been ready to incorporate it in its reasoning through a progressive interpretation of the Convention or other applicable instruments. For example, on children rights, the Court has appealed to what it considers to be the applicable international *corpus juris* on the subject. In the case of the *Juvenile Re-education Institute v Paraguay*, the Court used treaties ratified by Paraguay such as the UN Convention on the Rights of the Child or the Protocol of San Salvador, as well as the views of the Committee on the Rights of the Child, to illustrate that states have an enhanced obligation to provide, for example, a life with dignity to all children even while they are in detention.[48] Something similar has taken place in relation to the rights

---

44 *Apitz Barbera and Others v Venezuela*, IACtHR (5 August 2008) (Preliminary Exceptions, Merits, Reparations and Costs), paras 216–23.

45 *Mayagna (Sumo) Awas Tingni Community v Nicaragua*, IACtHR (31 August 2001) (Merits, Reparations and Costs), paras 148–55.

46 *Blake v Guatemala*, IACtHR (24 January 1998) (Merits), paras 96–97.

47 *Velásquez Rodríguez v Honduras*, IACtHR (29 June 1988)(Merits), para. 166.

48 *Juvenile Re-education Institute v Paraguay*, IACtHR (2 September 2004) (Preliminary Objections, Merits, Reparations and Costs), paras 147–176.

of internally displaced persons. The Court has interpreted Article 22 of the Convention, on freedom of movement and residence, using the Guiding Principles on Internal Displacement[49] prepared by Francis Deng as Representative of the UN Secretary-General on Internally Displaced Persons in 1998. Their use has been recommended by the UN Commission on Human Rights and the UN General Assembly.[50]

The Court has also been able to help in the development of international law, given the nature of the cases it has had to decide. For many years the Court knew of systematic gross human rights violations, such as disappearances, when there was no international treaty applicable on the subject. It was the Court that was called on to fill this gap.

Building on the work done by the Commission, the Court began to do so with *Velásquez Rodríguez v Honduras*, a case that was foundational because it defined an enforced disappearance from a human rights perspective.[51] In this case, the Court lowered the standard and burden of proof of those alleging the violations given the systematic nature of the violation, and it defined the scope of the duty to prevent under Article 1.1 of the Convention when indicating that the state has the:

> duty to prevent [which] includes all those means of a legal, political, administrative and cultural nature that promote the protection of human rights and ensure that any violations are considered and treated as illegal acts, which, as such, may lead to the punishment of those responsible and the obligation to indemnify the victims for damages.[52]

Given the many amnesties and pardon laws enacted in OAS member states to prevent the investigation of gross human rights violations, the Court has been asked, in paradigmatic cases, to decide on whether such laws have breached the American Convention. The Court has been unanimous in maintaining that amnesties and statutes of limitations are in breach of the American Convention because this treaty establishes the obligation to investigate, prosecute, punish and provide adequate reparation.[53]

It should also be mentioned that the Court has developed what is considered to be the most groundbreaking jurisprudence on reparations for gross human rights violations under international law.[54] Indeed, the Court has crafted important substantive and procedural principles to award reparations that are based on international law principles on reparations, such as that reparation should be adequate and that it aims for *restitutio in integrum*.[55] Nevertheless, it has adapted those principles to respond in an adequate manner to human rights violations.

---

49 *Guiding Principles on Internal Displacement* (E/CN.4/1998/53/Add.2), 1998.
50 *Mapiripán Massacre v Colombia*, IACtHR (15 September 2005) (Merits, Reparations and Costs), para. 171 or *Chitay Nech et al v Guatemala* (25 May 2010) (Preliminary Objections, Merits, Reparations and Costs), para. 140.
51 *Velásquez Rodríguez v Honduras* (n, 47), paras 149–58.
52 Ibid. para 175.
53 Such as *Barrios Altos v Peru*, IACtHR (14 March 2001) (Merits), para. 41; *Almonacid Arellano et al v Chile*, IACtHR (26 September 2006) (Preliminary Objections, Merits, Reparations and Costs) paras 98–128; *Gomes Lund and others (Guerrilha do Araguaia) v Brasil*, IACtHR (24 November 2010) (Preliminary Objections, Merits, Reparations and Costs), paras 126–82.
54 R. Goldman, 'History and Action: The Inter-American Human Rights System and the Role of the Inter-American Commission on Human Rights' (2009) 31(4) *Human Rights Quarterly* 856–87 at 857.
55 This has been the position of the Court since its first judgment on reparations. See *Velásquez Rodríguez v Honduras*, IACtHR (21 July 1989) (Reparations), paras 26, 175.

Among the substantive principles that it has established is the principle of due recognition of victimhood, according to which the words 'injured party' of Article 63.1 of the Convention (the article that allows the Court to order reparations) should be understood to include, if applicable, not only direct victims of human rights violations but also indirect ones such as next of kin (understood broadly and in a culturally sensitive manner), the family unit, dependents and the community if applicable.[56]

Another significant principle is that of transformative reparations. In *Cotton Field v Mexico* the Court advanced a significant redefinition of its concept of adequate reparation. It did so by highlighting that when the violations occur in a context of structural discrimination, reparation cannot simply return victims to the situation they were in before the violation took place (one of discrimination); instead, reparations should aim to transform or change the pre-existing situation.[57] While this is an important contribution of the Court to what international law ought to be, the Court failed in *Cotton Field* or in subsequent cases to apply it to the reparations it awarded.[58] As a consequence, this visionary jurisprudence, while important, 'may hinder rather than advance respect for human rights'[59] since its international law grounds are not well developed, and the Court does not really use the principle to award 'transformative' reparations.

The Court has demonstrated flexibility in its approach to the principles of reparation. Procedural reparation principles include, among others, the principle of flexible approach to standard and burden of proof on reparations. For example, the general rule is that the person who alleges the harm has to prove his/her identity by way of a birth certificate and/or statements before a notary public. However, the Court is ready to lower this standard when the person cannot present the required documentation because the state failed to provide the necessary means to identify the person. In such situations the Court permits the person to prove his/her status through other means as established by the Court.[60]

While the reparations jurisprudence is significant, the Court has not used its substantive and procedural principles to challenge the structural conditions that allowed the violations to take place. Indeed, an area that remains to be developed in the future is its understanding of rehabilitation and guarantees of non-repetition.[61]

4 The challenges of the System

This chapter has provided an overview of the working of the System and has hinted at some of the areas where it faces challenges. This section considers some of the obstacles faced so as to look into the future.

---

56 C. Sandoval, 'The Concepts of Injured Party and Victim of Gross Human Rights Violations in the Jurisprudence of the Inter-American Court of Human Rights: A Commentary on their Implications for Reparations', in C. Ferstman et al. (eds), *Reparations for Victims of Genocide, War Crimes and Crimes Against Humanity: Systems in Place and Systems in the Making* (Martinus Nijhoff Publishers, 2010) 243–82.

57 *Cotton Field v Mexico*, IACtHR (16 November 2009) (Admissibility, Merits and Reparations), para. 450.

58 C. Sandoval and R. Rubio-Marín, 'Engendering the Reparations Jurisprudence of the Inter-American Court of Human Rights: The Promise of the Cotton Field Judgment' (2011) 33 *Human Rights Quarterly* 1062–91.

59 J. Cavallaro and S. Brewer, 'Reevaluating Regional Human Rights Litigation in the Twenty First Century: The Case of the Inter-American Court' (2008) 102(4) *American Journal of International Law* 768–827 at 817.

60 *Massacre of Plan de Sánchez v Guatemala*, IACtHR (19 November 2004) (Reparations) paras 62 and 67.

61 Abramovich (n. 20) 26.

4.1 Lack of universal acceptance of its treaties

While the American Declaration remains applicable by the Commission to all OAS member states and in particular to those that have not become party to the American Convention, it should be noted that there is no universal acceptance of OAS human rights treaties. Out of seven regional human rights treaties only the Belém do Pará Convention has 32 out of 35 possible state parties. This treaty is followed by the American Convention with 23 state parties (22 once the denunciation of the Convention by Venezuela takes effect). All other treaties have approximately half or fewer state parties than the number possible. This shows the lack of commitment of OAS member states to respect and ensure human rights in the Americas, but also complicates the work of the Commission and the Court since they are not able to use important tools to carry out their mandates in the same manner and with consistency across the region.

The problem is not only lack of ratification but also lack of implementation of the mechanisms and obligations incorporated in the seven treaties. For example, the Protocol of San Salvador, on economic, social and cultural rights, entered into force in November 1999. However, it has taken more than a decade to design and implement the monitoring mechanisms (including indicators) of Article 19 of the treaty so that the OAS can effectively monitor compliance with the obligations of the Protocol.[62]

A visible problem when considering ratification of human rights treaties in the Americas is also that the Americas region appears to be two different worlds. The majority of ratifications come from the so-called Latin-American countries, while those that do not ratify tend to be common law countries. Legal cultures and institutions strongly influence the acceptance or rejection of regional human rights obligations.

4.2 The System is in need of serious reform

The Inter-American System has experienced important reforms since its establishment. However, they have tended to be procedural reforms rather than holistic ones. A serious reflection is yet to take place on the role of the Inter-American System to advance human rights protection in OAS member states in a globalising world, or on how to effect social change through the System in the future.[63] This is not to say that procedural reforms are not important, but it rather suggests that such reforms should always be conceived and pursued bearing in mind the goals of the System and the improvement of human rights protection in the Americas.

It is difficult to summarise in this chapter all the reforms that are needed. However, some of those reforms concern the potential of the System to carry out its multifaceted mandate, while others concern its capacity to respond to the new human rights challenges faced in the region. Of paramount importance to both concerns is to get the OAS member states to agree that Commissioners and Judges should be appointed to work on a permanent basis and with adequate remuneration.

---

62 Some progress has been made in recent years in this regard. Some indicators to measure compliance with some rights under the Protocol have been adopted while others are currently open to consultation. More information is available at the website of the Committee on Juridical and Political Affairs of the Permanent Council of the OAS: http://www.oas.org/consejo/sp/cajp/fortalecimiento.asp.

63 Dulitzky (n. 42) 140.

4.3 Lack of human and economic resources to carry out its work

The Commission and the Court are understaffed and underfunded, which puts the system, in a strict sense, at the verge of collapse,[64] given that demand for its services has increased notoriously without a proportional increase in the human or financial resources to respond to such demand. At the same time, the expectations of civil society and victims about what can be achieved using the System are higher than ever, despite the fact that the System lacks what it needs to carry out is multifaceted mandate in an adequate manner.

From a financial point of view, for example, the ordinary budget of the OAS that funds the work of the Court has not increased as required and is only able to cover approximately 50 per cent of the total costs of the Court. This makes the Court the international tribunal with the lowest available budget in the world.[65] As the OAS contribution is not sufficient to fund the work of the Court, the other 50 per cent comes from voluntary contributions from OAS member states, other states and from international cooperation.[66] This lack of sufficient funding jeopardises the work of the Court as it is unable to plan its work effectively. Also, voluntary state contributions put into question the Court's independence.

This lack of financial funding is troublesome given that the work of the Court has and will continue to increase. The Court is expecting approximately 100 cases per year in contrast to the average 12 cases it has received so far.[67] In 2012 the Secretariat of the Court had 50 members of staff to carry out its administrative and legal work. Among them there were eight senior lawyers and nine junior lawyers dealing with cases. The increase in cases would require not only permanent judges working at the Court but also a better pool of legal staff to support their work. Current funding makes this impossible.

4.4 Judicialisation of the System

One of the strengths of the System is the multifaceted functions of the Commission. However, non-judicial tools, such as its capacity to monitor effectively human rights respect, protection and promotion in the Americas, have been diminished given the strong emphasis given to litigation of human rights violations before the Commission and the Court. While that is an important venue to advance some human rights causes, civil society in the Americas overestimates what is achievable through it. As Dulitzky points out there has been 'very few if any profound reflections on whether the individual petition system is the best response to meet the human rights needs of the region'.[68]

Importantly, not all human rights are directly justiciable before the System. This is the case for most economic and social rights.[69] Therefore, the judicial venue might not be the best tool to achieve their protection and if used, it can be counterproductive as states fail to take such recommendations/orders seriously. This is problematic given that some of the most serious

---

64 Goldman (n. 54) 882.
65 IACtHR, *Lineamientos 2011–2015: Fortaleciendo la Justicia Interamericana, a través de un Financiamiento Previsible y Armónico (Lineamientos)*, 8 June 2011, 13.
66 IACtHR, *Annual Report 2011*, 66–67.
67 *Lineamientos* (n. 65) 12.
68 Dulitzky (n. 42) 140.
69 See for example, *Additional Protocol to the American Convention on Human Rights in the Area of Economic, Social and Cultural Rights 'Protocol of San Salvador'*, Art. 19.6, OAS Treaty Series No. 69, 17 November 1988.

problems in the Americas region concern lack of respect, protection and promotion of these rights. Therefore, important jurisprudence is enacted, expectations are raised, but in practice nothing changes because states are not willing to implement the judgments. Furthermore, such judgments might not be the best way to trigger the structural changes that are needed to respect and ensure these rights.

Equally, in the Americas, effective protection of human rights becomes illusory when the System takes an unreasonable period of time to process a petition. As shown by Dulitzky, the average time taken by the Commission to decide on admissibility is 3.10 years, and on the merits 6.16 years. After this, and if certain requirements are fulfilled, the case may go to the Court to be decided in approximately 19 months.[70] Therefore, a judgment by the Court is only handed down after a decade or more of litigation. This is not timely justice. This length of time does not include the years that are needed to achieve full implementation of judgments.

The judicialisation of the System has another problem, which is achieving compliance by states with the recommendations made by the Commission or the orders by the Court. So, while the System, particularly the Court, has developed important reparation measures, its capacity to trigger important changes domestically and to provide adequate redress to victims is diminished because states fail to comply with the measures or do so partially. For example, one of the clear problems in the Americas region is the lack of willingness and/or ability of the national judicial systems to investigate, prosecute and if applicable punish perpetrators of human rights violations. While the Commission and the Court consistently call on states to comply with this obligation, the rate of compliance remains very low.[71]

4.5 Dealing with key systemic problems in the Americas – new forms of authoritarianism, inequality, poverty and discrimination

A key challenge of the System is how to respond to new human rights violations that take place in a context of inequality, poverty, discrimination and/or authoritarianism. While the System has important tools to respond to these problems, and to contribute to their solution, its response to these problems has been rather minimalistic. The Commission, in particular, should play a greater role in advancing awareness of these issues and in helping states to deal with them.

5 Conclusions

It is undeniable that the Inter-American System has advanced human rights protection in the Americas despite the lack of support of OAS member states. This is visible in areas like gross human rights violations and transitional justice. The impact of the System, however, cannot be overestimated. The System is not the solution to all human rights problems in the Americas region but it is an important and complementary tool to get OAS member states to fulfil their human rights obligations under the American Convention, the Amereican Declaration and other applicable treaties.

---

70 Ibid., 135–36.
71 A. Huneeus, 'Courts Resisting Courts: Lessons from the Inter-American Court's Struggle to Enforce Human Rights' (2011) 44(3) *Cornell International Law Journal* 493–533 at 495 and 504.

Today, the System faces a new age with a different region: It is not a young System any more. The politics in the Americas and the nature of human rights violations have also changed; the actors of the System (states and civil society) are far more complex and sophisticated in their behaviour than before, and the demand for the System's services is increasing exponentially. In this context, and without an adequate structure and human and economic support to promote human rights protection in the region, the System will not be able to replicate its achievements of the past in areas where its work is urgently needed, like in relation to poverty and discrimination. The time has come to rethink the role and approach of the System, and to consider effective ways to help OAS member states to comply with their human rights obligations.

Select bibliography

V. Abramovich, 'From Massive Violations to Structural Patterns: New Approaches and Classical Tensions in the Inter-American Human Rights System' (2009) 11 *SUR International Journal on Human Rights* 7–37.

J. Cavallaro and S. Brewer, 'Reevaluating Regional Human Rights Litigation in the Twenty First Century: The Case of the Inter-American Court' (2008) 102(4) *American Journal of International Law* 768–827.

A. Dulitzky, 'The Inter-American Human Rights System Fifty Years Later: Time for Changes' (2011) *Quebec Journal of International Law* (Special edition) 127–64.

R. Goldman, 'History and Action: The Inter-American Human Rights System and the Role of the Inter-American Commission on Human Rights' (2009) 31(4) *Human Rights Quarterly* 856–87.

A. Huneeus, 'Courts Resisting Courts: Lessons from the Inter-American Court's Struggle to Enforce Human Rights' (2011) 44(3) *Cornell International Law Journal* 493–533.

C. Sandoval, 'The Concepts of Injured Party and Victim of Gross Human Rights Violations in the Jurisprudence of the Inter-American Court of Human Rights: A Commentary on their Implications for Reparations', in C. Ferstman et al. (eds), *Reparations for Victims of Genocide, War Crimes and Crimes Against Humanity: Systems in Place and Systems in the Making* (Martinus Nijhoff Publishers, 2010).

C. Sandoval and R. Rubio-Marín, 'Engendering the Reparations Jurisprudence of the Inter-American Court of Human Rights: The Promise of the Cotton Field Judgment' (2011) 33 *Human Rights Quarterly* 1062–91.

25

The impact and influence of the African regional human rights system on domestic law

*Frans Viljoen**

1 Introduction

Although the African system is the youngest of the three 'main' regional human rights systems, it has now come of age.[1] Indeed, the African Charter on Human and Peoples' Rights (African Charter) in 2011 celebrated 30 years since its adoption (in 1981), and 25 years since its entry into force (on 21 October 1986),[2] and its quasi-judicial supervisory arm, the African Commission on Human and Peoples' Rights (African Commission), in 2012 marked 25 years since its establishment in 1987. While there may be much to celebrate, this is also a good time to take stock, and in particular to ask what the impact (or influence) of the African regional human rights system has been over this quarter century. As the African Court on Human and Peoples' Rights (African Human Rights Court) has only been in existence for a much shorter period, and as of the end of 2012 had not decided any case on the merits,[3] the Court is omitted from the discussion. Although the African Committee of Experts on the Rights and Welfare of the Child (African Children's Committee) also forms part of the 'African human rights system',[4]

* My appreciation to Magnus Killander for his insightful comments.

1 On the African regional human rights system, generally, see R. Murray, *Human Rights in Africa: From the OAU to the African Union* (CUP, 2004) and F. Viljoen *International Human Rights Law in Africa* (2012) (OUP, 2012).

2 African [Banjul] Charter on Human and Peoples' Rights, adopted June 27, 1981, OAU Doc. CAB/LEG/67/3 rev. 5, 21 I.L.M. 58 (1982), entered into force Oct. 21, 1986. See F. Ouguergouz, *The African Charter on Human and Peoples' Rights: A Comprehensive Agenda for Human Dignity and Sustainable Development in Africa* (The Hague, Martinus Nijhoff, 2003).

3 For the judgments of the Court on jurisdictional issues, see www.african-court.org (accessed on 12 August 2013). In its only significant decision, against Libya, the Court ordered provisional measures (*African Commission v Libya*, AfCHPR, Application 4/2011, Order for Provisional Measures, 25 March 2011).

4 It is the supervisory body of the African Charter on the Rights and Welfare of the Child, adopted in 1990, and entered into force in 1999.

its relative novelty and limited activities restrict its relevance to the topic under discussion.[5]

The 'impact' of the African human rights system, as it has evolved so far, derives mainly from the core obligation of state parties to 'give effect' to the rights guaranteed in the African Charter.[6] In line with the principle that postnational norms are subsidiary to and serve to steer and supplement rather than replace national norms, states are allowed some leeway about the specific measures they should take to produce the desired domesticating 'effect'.

It may be assumed that it was the combined effect of the centrality of the obligation to give domestic effect and the open-endedness of the specified means ('legislative or other measures') that inspired the African Commission to devote one of its first 'resolutions' to the 'Integration of the Provisions of the African Charter on Human and Peoples' Rights into National Laws of States'.[7] Both the Legislature and Executive are implicated in the requirement to 'introduce' the substantive provisions of the Charter into the 'Constitutions, laws, rules and regulations and other acts relating to human and peoples' rights' of states parties. A subsequent resolution urged the Judiciary 'to play a greater role in incorporating' the Charter and the Commission's jurisprudence into their judgments.[8] In this resolution, the Commission also clarifies its understanding that it is not only the three organs of state that have a role to play. In order to develop a legal culture conducive to domestication, legal practitioners should 'place greater reliance on the Charter', and law societies, judicial associations and NGOs should 'initiate specialised and comprehensive training for judicial officers, [and] lawyers at national and sub-regional levels'. In addition to these civil society actors, legal scholars also have an important role to play. Finally, a media actively involved in reporting accurately yet critically on the practical effect of regional human rights also has much to contribute to national levels of awareness about, knowledge of and insight into such a system.

Against the background above, this contribution aims at providing some insight into the impact or influence of the African regional system (principally the African Charter, but also the Protocol to the Charter on the Rights of Women in Africa (Women's Protocol), adopted in 2003 and entering into force in 2005)[9] through measures taken by state parties. With its focus mainly on the legal dimension of the system's impact, this contribution does not purport to account for the broader impact (for example, in the arena of international politics, its role in the erosion of state sovereignty) or the system's important influence on civil society.

2 Direct and indirect impact

When talking about 'impact', one should be cautious not to raise expectations too high, or to overstate one's case. 'Impact' is understood here as a form of influence on particular aspects of

---

5 The African Children's Committee was established in 2001. For more information, see www. acerwc.org (accessed on 13 August 2012). By the end of 2012, the Committee has decided only one case (*Institute for Human Rights and Development in Africa an Another (on behalf of Children of Nubian Descent) v Kenya*, 22 March 2011.

6 Art. 1, African Charter.

7 Adopted in April 1989, 5th ordinary session, Banjul, The Gambia.

8 Resolution on the Role of Lawyers and Judges in the Integration of the Charter and the Enhancement of the Commission's work in National and sub-Regional Systems, adopted at the Commission's 19th session, 26 March to 4 April 1996, Ouagadougou, Burkina Faso.

9 Protocol to the African Charter on Human and Peoples' Rights on the Rights of Women in Africa 2003.

a person's life world, namely those spheres affected by law. In other words, this contribution focuses on the 'legal effects' of the Charter and Protocol, rather than on the 'actual', statistically or empirically verifiable changes brought about by them, or following in their wake. The crucial question is whether the African regional system has in some way affected domestic legal culture,[10] or has been 'incorporated' into domestic practice by relevant actors.[11] Even if this limited scope of investigation does not relate to the fullness of human life, such an approach seems to be more in tune with the nature of these treaties as instruments imposing legal obligations. It also allows the emphasis to fall on the state or government officials, as well as other actors who play a role in constructing the domestic legal culture. They are all implicated in and expected to facilitate the system's impact or influence, based on the assumption that the influence of regional norms would manifest itself in the 'institutionalization and habitualization' of these treaties through the patterns of conduct of domestic actors.[12]

A distinction is drawn between *direct impact* and other forms of more *indirect impact* (or 'influence'). *Direct impact* entails specific instances of compliance by states *in response to specific directives* (requests or commands) from a treaty body, such as findings in respect of an individual communication or recommendation contained in the concluding observations on state reports. *Indirect impact* speaks to the ways in which a relevant treaty has left its mark on the domestic scene in the absence of a specific treaty body directive. Indirect impact or influence may take many forms, ranging from the more obvious and discernible (such as legislation or policies conforming with treaty provisions) to the more subtle and unobtrusive (such as changes in societal attitudes in line with the letter or spirit of a treaty). Here, the assessment of the indirect impact of the African human rights system is limited to aspects of the legal system.

Studies of the 'impact' of human rights treaties or the 'difference' they make often take a panoramic view, for example by comparing the situation in one of more states before and after ratification of one or more treaties, on the basis of a set of indicators.[13] However, by basing itself on information provided by country-based researchers, who undertook desk studies and conducted interviews on the basis of a guiding questionnaire,[14] this research targets the micro (rather than macro) level, and uses a qualitative (rather than quantitative) methodology.[15]

3 Domestic impact and influence of the African regional human rights system

3.1 Direct impact (through state compliance)

Little research has been undertaken about the direct impact of the African human rights system. The limited existing studies conclude that the findings of the Commission

---

10 R. Goodman and D. Jinks 'Measuring the Effects of Human Rights Treaties' (2003) 13 *European Journal of International Law* 171 at 182
11 Goodman and Jinks, ibid. 172.
12 T. Risse and S.C. Ropp, 'International Human Rights Norms and Domestic Change: Conclusions' in T. Risse, S.C. Ropp and K. Sikkink (eds), *The Power of Human Rights: International Norms and Domestic Change* (CUP, 1999) 234 at 256.
13 See e.g. O. Hathaway, 'Do Human Right Treaties Make a Difference?' (2002) 35 *Yale Law Journal* 1935.
14 Centre for Human Rights, *The Impact of the African Charter and Women's Protocol in Selected African States* (Pretoria, PULP, 2012).
15 Also see C. Heyns and F. Viljoen, 'The Impact of the United Nations Human Rights Treaties on the Domestic Level' (2001) 23 *Human Rights Quarterly* 483.

in individual communications had not generally been fully complied with;[16] and other recommendations have mostly not been responded to.[17] These studies reveal the dearth of available information, the difficulties associated with getting reliable information about compliance measures, and the complexity of establishing a causal link between steps taken by states and the treaty body's direction (finding or recommendation).

Findings of violations in individual communications present the most trying test for directed impact. So far, however, relatively few communications have been finalised by the African Commission. The arena in which direct impact has been most pronounced is the amendment of legislation in Nigeria during the second period of military rule (Second Junta) between 1983 and 1998, and in particular the period after General Sani Abacha foiled the democratic elections organised in 1993, until his death in 1998.[18]

In 1987, the Babangida military regime promulgated the 1987 Civil Disturbances (Special Tribunal) Decree, setting up a special tribunal to try persons accused of causing civil disturbances. Under the Decree, a special tribunal was made up of a superior court judge and four other members, one of whom had to be a serving member of the Armed Forces. The African Commission's 1995 decision,[19] finding the Decree in violation of the African Charter, became part of the rallying cries of Nigerian activists campaining for legal reform. As a result of combined pressure, on 5 June 1996, in the midst of the Abacha dictatorship, the Decree was amended.[20]

The African Commission further found many decrees adopted in the context of the 'stolen election' of 1993 to be in violation of the Charter. One such example is the State Security (Detention of Persons) (Amendment) Decree 14 of 1994, which not only allowed for the detention without trial for three months of anyone critical of the government, but also foreclosed judicial recourse to the remedy of habeas corpus. In October 1998, the African Commission held that this Decree violated the right against arbitrary arrest in the Charter.[21] To be faithful to chronology, it should be assumed that civil society used the *fact of submission* of the communication, rather than the finding, as part of its campaign culminating in the repeal of the Decree in June 1996.[22] In addition to these examples, a number of other decrees were the subject of Commission decisions and were later repealed, mostly only at the end of the period of military government or as part of the transition to democracy.[23]

---

16 See F. Viljoen and L. Louw, 'State Compliance with the Recommendations of the African Charter on Human and Peoples' Rights, 1993–2004' (2007) 101 *American Journal of International Law* 1.

17 F. Viljoen, 'State Compliance with the Recommendations of the African Commission on Human and Peoples' Rights', in M.A. Baderin and M. Ssenyonjo (eds), *International Human Rights Law: Six Decades after the UDHR and Beyond* (Burlington, Ashgate, 2010).

18 O.C. Okafor, *The Africa Human Rights System: Activist Forces and International Institutions* (CUP, 2007).

19 *Constitutional Rights Project (in respect of Lekwot and Others) v Nigeria*, ACHPR, Communication 87/93,1995 reported in 2000 AHRLR 183.

20 The amendment specifically granted a right of appeal and removed the Armed Forces member of the tribunal. For a more detailed account of the process leading up to the repeal of the Decree, see Okafor (n. 18) 128–30.

21 See *International Pen and Others (on behalf of Saro-Wiwa) v Nigeria*, ACHPR 1998, reported in 2000 AHRLR 212.

22 See, however, Okafor (n. 18 above) 131, describing the amendment as an example of how the Commission's efforts helped 'to produce a very valuable form of correspondence between its decisions and the legislative actions of the Nigerian military government'.

23 E.g. the Constitution (Suspension and Modification) Decree 1984, the State Security (Detention of Persons) Decree 1984 and the Military Courts (Special Powers) Decree 1984.

In other instances, compliance took the form of executive conduct, for example, the release of detainees. In yet another case emanating from the Abacha period, *Centre for Free Speech v Nigeria*,[24] four journalists were tried in secret by a military tribunal, without access to lawyers or the right to appeal against their conviction. Finding that their rights under the Charter had been violated, the Commission urged the government to release the journalists. They were eventually released.[25]

A combination of factors accounts for the peculiar impact of the Charter and Commission in Nigeria over this period. For one, a vibrant civil society, including NGOs with a very explicit human rights mandate and a lively and organised legal profession, were in place when the military took charge. The Commission's unequivocal findings, civil society campaigns and international reaction were all informed by the unapologetically abusive nature of the regime. Much more than any previous military government or one-party regime, the Abacha regime's atrocities stood out like a very sore thumb contrasting with the main trend towards greater democratisation in Africa. When the regime was replaced by a democratically elected government, the wholesale rejection of the legal remnants of this period was therefore uncontroversial.

Since the advent of the African Human Rights Court, the importance of establishing compliance with the Commission's findings has gained importance. Individuals may only exceptionally approach the Court directly, when the relevant state party to the Protocol establishing the Court has made an optional declaration to that effect.[26] For complainants in all other state parties, the route is still through the Commission.[27] Referral to the Court is therefore mostly dependent on the exercise of the Commission's discretion to (directly) refer the case to the Court. However, in exercising its discretion, the Commission is guided by the following: once the Commission has found a state in violation of the Charter, it allows that state six months to comply with its finding.[28] Once non-compliance has been established, the Commission may refer the case to the Court.

In respect of provisional measures, the same position applies, but the period allowed for compliance is shortened to 15 days.[29] So far, the Commission has only referred two matters: one against Libya,[30] and one concerning a request for provisional measures in respect of the Ogiek community in Kenya. In the first, the Court ordered provisional measures, and in the second, the matter as of the end of 2012 was still pending.[31] In some other cases, such as the *Endorois* case, also decided against Kenya,[32] the period of six months has long expired,

---

24 ACHPR 1999 reported in 2000 AHRLR 250.

25 See Viljoen and Louw (n. 16) 10.

26 Art. 34(6), Protocol to the African Charter on the Establishment of an African Court on Human and Peoples' Rights. Five states have by the end of 2012 made this declaration: Burkina Faso, Ghana, Malawi, Mali and Tanzania.

27 Contrast Art. 5(1) with Art. 5(3) of the Protocol to the African Charter on the Establishment of an African Court on Human and Peoples' Rights; and see the African Human Rights Court's judgment in *Yogogombaye v Senegal*, Application 1/2008, 15 December 2009, paras 34–37, in which the Court found that it lacked jurisdiction to hear a case that was submitted directly to it against a state party to the Court Protocol that had not made the Art. 34(6) declaration.

28 Rules of Procedure of the African Commission on Human and Peoples' Rights 2010, r. 118(1).

29 Ibid. r. 118(2), read with r. 98(4).

30 *African Commission v Libya* (n. 3).

31 Application 6/2012, *African Commission v Kenya* (2012).

32 *Centre for Minority Rights and (Endorois Welfare Council) v Kenya* (2009) AHRLR 75 (ACHPR 2009).

but the Commission's lack of a reliable mechanism to assess compliance and the ongoing promises of the respondent state to give effect to the Commission's finding have hampered referral.

3.2 Indirect impact or influence

The indirect impact or influence of the African Charter and Women's Protocol is traced in respect of constitution-making, legislation and court judgments. Although a discussion of these aspects gives a sense of the regional system's influence on the legal system, it is incomplete as it does not cover the system's effect on policy, executive acts, the legal profession and the media. It should be pointed out that the Charter, and in particular the Women's Protocol, have become integrated into the mandates and activities of NGOs and that the influence of the Charter has perhaps been strongest in respect of legal education, legal scholarship and academic writing.

3.2.1 Constitution

As many African states adopted new constitutions in the post-1990 era, subsequent to becoming state parties to the African Charter, these constitutions provide an opportunity to assess the influence of the Charter on important legal texts in these countries. However, the absence of any explicit reference to the Charter in most of these constitutions renders speculative any conclusion about causal relationships of 'influence'.

Still, there are clear indications that the African Charter played at least some part in the adoption of the Constitutions as the 'third wave of democracy' reached the continent's shores.[33] Benin is one such country. While under a military dictatorship, in 1986, Benin ratified the African Charter. Subsequent political developments led to a national conference and the adoption of a new Constitution in 1990. The 1990 Constitution, different to the previous Constitution, explicitly incorporates the Charter by providing that 'all the duties and rights in the African Charter are part of the present Constitution'.[34] In addition, the full text of the African Charter is annexed to the Constitution. In terms of this constitutionalised affirmation of the monist position, an individual may invoke the Charter as the source of remedy under the domestic law of Benin.

The amendment of the Kenyan Constitution in 1997 to add 'sex' to the grounds for non-discrimination was, according to a Court of Appeal judgment, in part inspired by the ratification by Kenya of the African Charter in 1992.[35] Under the 2010 Constitution, Kenya adopted the monist position that 'any treaty or convention ratified by Kenya shall form part of the law of Kenya under this Constitution'.[36] As Kenya had ratified the Charter, it is thus clearly 'part of' domestic Kenyan law.

33 See S.P. Huntington, *The Third Wave: Democratization in the Late Twentieth Century* (University of Oklahoma Press, 1991); and C. Young, 'Democratization in Africa', in R. Joseph (ed.), *State, Conflict, and Democracy in Africa* (Boulder, Lynne Rienner, 1999).

34 Art. 7 of the 1990 Constitution.

35 *Rono v Rono*, describing the amendment as evidence that the country was moving 'in tandem' with 'emerging global culture, particularly in gender issues' (*Rono v Rono KeCA* 2005 (2005) AHRLR 107).

36 Art. 2(6) of the 2010 Constitution.

Some post-1990 Constitutions paint a more ambiguous picture. In 2000, Côte d'Ivoire adopted a new Constitution, replacing the version of 1960.[37] The influence of the African Charter, ratified by Côte d'Ivoire in 1992, can be discerned from the preambular proclamation of 'adherence' to the Charter (alongside the Universal Declaration of Human Rights), and the relatively extensive list of human rights and freedoms (contrasted with their total absence from the previous (1960) Constitution). On the one hand, many of the human rights provisions in the 2000 Constitution correspond to both the Universal Declaration and the African Charter, and a number of them even mirror the specific formulations of the Charter quite closely. Examples of such provisions are (i) the obligation on the state to protect 'the aged and the handicapped';[38] (ii) the right to a 'healthy environment';[39] and (iii) the inclusion of an extensive list of *individual duties*.[40] On the other hand, it should be noted that the content of these *individual duties* are formulated quite differently from those in the Charter, and therefore do not reflect the corresponding Charter provisions.

Some post-1990 Constitutions, such as that of Lesotho, show very little indication of having been influenced by the Charter. Lesotho ratified the Charter in 1992, and adopted a new Constitution in 1993. Although this Constitution contains some rights that are also provided for in the Charter, the very detailed provisions of the Lesotho Constitution are formulated vastly differently to those of the Charter. The only close resemblance is in relation to the Charter provision dealing with the right to conduct public affairs 'directly or through freely chosen representatives'.[41] The Lesotho Constitution omits Charter provisions such as the right to receive information, and relegates the 'socio-economic' rights of the Charter to non-justiciable 'Principles of State Policy'.[42]

3.2.2 Adoption of legislation

In theory, the Charter forms an automatic part of the domestic law of 'monist' states upon its ratification and official publication. In practice, however, the effect of the Charter has been negligible in these states, with the exception of Benin, where the Charter was in fact explicitly incorporated. The most obvious way in which the Charter or Protocol can be given domestic effect in 'dualist' states is through their domestication in national legislation. Only Nigeria did so, when its National Assembly passed the 'African Charter on Human and Peoples' Rights (Ratification and Enforcement) Act' a few months prior to ratifying the Charter.[43]

The Charter's influence on legislation is difficult to trace. In a very abstract sense, many laws are adopted that give effect to the rights in the Charter (for example, the criminal law on murder protects the right to life). However, without a clear indication either in the drafting history, the preamble or in the specific formulation of the law, a concrete connection is very difficult to establish. Naturally, viewed from the domestic perspective, it does not matter

---

37 See also the 1990 Constitution of Chad, which shows great resemblance to the features mentioned here.
38 Art. 6 of the 2000 Constitution; Art. 18(4) of the African Charter.
39 Art. 19 of the 2000 Constitution; Art. 24 of the African Charter.
40 Arts 23–28 of the 2000 Constitution; Arts 27–29 of the African Charter.
41 Art. 13 of the African Charter; Art. 20(1)(a) of the Lesotho Constitution.
42 Arts 27 and 28 of the Lesotho Constitution, providing for health and education as Principles of State Policy.
43 Preamble, African Charter Act cap. A9 Laws of the Federation of Nigeria.

what the source or inspiration of a law is; it only matters if it embodies human rights principles, or whether it is otherwise progressive. The influence of the Charter should therefore not be restricted to instances of explicit reference. Despite not mentioning the Charter or Commission by name, some legislation clearly corresponds with a priority theme or concern of the Commission. One such example is the Congolese Law on the Promotion and Protection of Indigenous Populations,[44] the first piece of national legislation adopted to deal with the rights of indigenous peoples.

Even though it is much more recent, there are more indications of the domestication of the Women's Protocol. One of the most visible traces of the influence of the Protocol on the domestic law of state parties is the adoption of legislation pertaining to domestic violence against women.[45]

While some state parties in Southern Africa already had domestic violence legislation in place before ratifying the Women's Protocol (as in the case of South Africa), a few others adopted such legislation subsequent to their becoming party to the Protocol. Mozambique ratified the Protocol in 2003, and in 2009 passed the Domestic Violence against Women Act.[46] Although the law itself is silent on the specific role of the Protocol in its adoption, it should be noted that the Forum Mulher, an umbrella organisation in Mozambique bringing together women's activists and organisations, in its proposal for such a law makes specific reference to the Protocol.[47] As this civil society proposal initiated the drafting process, it can thus be deduced that the Protocol played a pertinent role in the process of the law's adoption. The adoption of this Law underlines the complexity of causal claims: while the Act reflects the norms in the Women's Protocol, it should be kept in mind that Mozambique also ratified the Convention on the Elimination of All Forms of Discrimination against Women (CEDAW) and the SADC Protocol on Gender and Development.[48] At least as far as CEDAW is concerned, the submission and examination of Mozambique's initial and second periodic report seems to have contributed to the adoption of the legislation mentioned earlier.[49]

Malawi, which became a state party to the Protocol in 2005, in 2006 adopted domestic violence legislation.[50] Namibia, a state party to the Protocol since 2004, adopted the Combating of Domestic Violence Act No. 3 of 2003, and Zambia, having ratified the Protocol in 2006, adopted the Gender Based Violence Act.[51] Domestic violence legislation also

---

44 Act No. 5–2011 of 25 February 2011.
45 Art. 4 of the Women's Protocol requires states to enact and enforce legislation to prohibit violence against women in public and private.
46 Act 29 of 209, adopted 29 September 2009.
47 For a copy of the Act in the official bulletin of Mozambique (in Portuguese), see http://www.wlsa.org.mz/lib/pdf/Lei_VD_2009.pdf (accessed on 1 May 2013).
48 SADC Protocol on Gender and Development (17 August 2008) available at http://www.sadc.int/files/8713/5292/8364/Protocol_on_Gender_and_Development_2008.pdf (accessed on 1 May 2013).
49 Concluding comments after examination of the initial and second periodic report, UN Doc. CEDAW/C/MOZ/CO/2, 11 June 2007, para. 25. The Committee calls upon the state party to adopt the draft law against domestic violence as soon as possible, and to ensure that violence against women and girls, including domestic violence, marital rape, sexual harassment, and all forms of sexual abuse, constitutes a criminal offence; that perpetrators are prosecuted, punished and rehabilitated; and that women and girls who are victims of violence have access to immediate means of redress and protection.
50 Prevention of Domestic Violence Act No. 5 of 2006, Cap. 7:05; it commenced only in 2011.
51 This Act was assented to in 2011 by President Banda.

followed upon the ratification of the Protocol in other regions of the continent. Benin, for example, having ratified the Protocol in 2005, adopted legislation dealing with violence against women in 2011.[52] Having ratified the Protocol in 2004, Rwanda in 2008 adopted the Law on Prevention and Punishment of Gender Based Violence. Underscoring the complexity of tracing indirect impact back to a specific source, the preamble to this law makes mention of a long list of international instruments, including the African Charter and CEDAW, but it does not mention the Women's Protocol.

State parties to the Protocol adopt legislation not only relating to domestic violence, but also relevant to aspects of family law. Mozambique, for example, adopted the 2004 Family Code,[53] in which new legal standards for parental responsibilities, guardianship, adoption and inheritance rights are provided. The Code also sets the age of marriage for both boys and girls at 18 years. Benin ratified the Protocol in September 2005, and adopted women's rights laws immediately preceding and subsequent to that date: in 2004, it adopted the Family Code,[54] and in 2005 the Sexual Harassment Act.[55] Lesotho ratified the Protocol in 2004, and adopted the Legal Capacity of Married Persons Act in 2006. This far-reaching Act abolishes *de jure* discrimination against women in many spheres of life; in particular, it lifts restrictions on women's status and reviews the restrictive marital power that previously extended to almost all spheres of a women's life in Lesotho. Under Rwanda's 2012 Penal Code, exemptions from liability for performing an abortion were for the first time introduced into Rwandan law.[56] The influence of the Protocol is strongly suggested by the resemblance between the Protocol grounds (Article 14(2)(c)) and those in the Penal Code (Article 165); and by the fact that the amendment to the Penal Code was followed by the government's withdrawal of its reservation to the relevant Protocol provision.

3.2.3 Use in case law

The African regional human rights system may feature in the jurisprudence of African domestic courts either as the direct source of a remedy, or as an interpretive guide. Only the courts of Nigeria, and to a very limited extent, those of Benin and the Gambia, have found violations of the African Charter.[57] Despite its formal status as an 'integral part of the law' in other 'monist' states in Africa,[58] the Charter has not been used as a directly enforceable right in any court decision outside Benin.

---

52 The National Assembly of Benin on 27 September 2011 adopted Law 2011–26 on the prevention and curbing of violence against women (Loi no. 2011–26 portant prévention et répression des violences faites aux femmes).

53 Act 10 of 2004.

54 Loi no. 2002–07 du 24 août 2004 portant Code des Personnes et de la Famille en République du Bénin.

55 Loi no. 2006–19 du 05 septembre 2006 portant répression du harcèlement sexuel et protection des victimes.

56 Organic Law 01/2012 of 2/5/2012 instituting the Penal Code.

57 See cases discussed in e.g. Viljoen (n. 1) ch. 12, and in M. Killander (ed.), *International Law and Domestic Human Rights Litigation in Africa* (Pretoria University Law Press, 2010), in addition to the few cases discussed in this contribution.

58 In fact, this situation is part of a broader pattern of practice, which makes the distinction between 'dualist' and 'monist' states increasingly unimportant. See e.g. Viljoen (n. 1) 518–25.

In Nigeria, the courts have maintained that the Charter has a status superior to all domestic legislation (but is inferior to the Constitution).[59] This approach enabled Nigerian courts to hear human rights cases, based on the African Charter (Act), despite the ousting of the courts' jurisdiction by the Decrees adopted during the military government.[60] Since the story of the relationship between the Nigerian courts and the African Charter has been told elsewhere, I will not attempt to provide a narrative here.[61]

As Benin has fully incorporated the Charter into domestic law, the Constitutional Court of Benin could be expected to make findings that the African Charter had been violated, when appropriate. Thus far, the Court has mostly found a violation of the Charter in conjunction with, and essentially merely reinforcing, a constitutional provision. In only a handful of cases did the Court make a finding exclusively on the basis of the Charter. Two of these cases are now highlighted. In the first, the *Okpeitcha* case, the Court found that because he 'ceased to ensure the upkeep and education of his children and thus of his family', Mr Okpeitcha had violated Article 29(1) of the African Charter,[62] which places the obligation on an individual to 'preserve the harmonious development of the family'. In the second case, DCC 05-114 of 20 September 2005, the Court found a violation of Article 7(1)(a) and (d) of the African Charter.[63] This case clearly illustrates the value of the Charter as a supplementary source on which to base a violation. The complainant in this case alleged that files concerning his criminal appeals to the Cour d'Appel had been stalled and were not referred to the Court for between five and eleven years. Finding in his favour, the Court had recourse to the provisions of the Charter dealing with the right to an appeal and to a trial within a reasonable period, in the absence of any corresponding provision in the Constitution of Benin.

The Charter has been more influential on African judiciaries as a guide to interpretation of national law. Although reliance on the Charter is growing, for example in South Africa,[64] reliance on the findings of the African Commission is still extremely limited.

Despite the lack of any explicit judicial anchor on which to base reliance on the Charter or the Commission's jurisprudence, the Gambian Supreme Court made reference to both. In *Sabally v Inspector General of Police*,[65] the Gambian Supreme Court declared unconstitutional a retroactive amnesty law. In arriving at its decision, the Gambian Supreme Court referred to both the African Charter[66] and the African Commission's case law.[67] The Court described the Charter as 'an instrument to which The Gambia incidentally is also a State party', and observed that 'the principles laid down' in the Charter and the case law 'are pertinent and

---

59 See e.g. *Abacha v Fawehinmi* [2006] 6 NWLR (part 660) 228.
60 See e.g. *Comptroller Nigerian Prisons v Dr Femi Adekanye* (1999) 10 NWLR 400.
61 Okafor (n. 18).
62 *Okpeitcha v Okpeitcha* BnCC 2001 (2002) AHRLR 33
63 *Taïrou v Tribunal de Kandi* BeCC 2005. available at http://www.courconstitutionnelle.gouv.bj/activitesuite.php?recordID=246 (accessed on 21 September 2012).
64 Because much has been written about the South African courts and their approach to international law, including the African Charter, the South African judiciary is not discussed here.
65 GaSC Referral from the High Court on constitutional review; Civil ref. no. 2/2001 (Supreme Court); ILDC 11 (GM 2001) 5 December 2001, (2002) AHRLR 87.
66 Paras 11 and 12 of the decision, referring to Communication no. 145/95 brought by the Constitutional Rights Project, the Civil Liberties Organisation and Media Rights Agenda against Nigeria (*Constitutional Rights Project and Others v Nigeria* ACHPR 1999 (2000) AHRLR 227).
67 Art. 7 of the African Charter.

relevant to the instant case'.[68] In *Denton v Director General National Intelligence Agency*,[69] the Gambian High Court held that detention beyond the constitutionally prescribed limit of 72 hours and initial arrest not only violated the Gambian Constitution,[70] but also the African Charter.[71] Justice Monageng, at the time a sitting member of the African Commission, placed reliance on the Commission's findings.[72] Although the Court found a violation of Article 6 of the Charter (the right to liberty and security of the person, and not to be arbitrarily arrested or detained), this provision is an almost perfect mirror image of Article 19(1) of the Gambian Constitution. In other words, the finding of violation of the Charter does not provide for protection unavailable under domestic law.

Even prior to the adoption of the 2010 Constitution, courts in Kenya have taken the initiative in eroding the divide between dualism and monism. In *Rono v Rono*,[73] the Court of Appeal held that the Charter,[74] together with other international human rights obligations, needs to be relied on to supplement domestic law, and on this basis found that distribution of an estate under customary law constituted sex discrimination. In *Martha Karua v Radio Africa Ltd t/a Kiss FM Station and two others*,[75] the question before the Kenyan Courts was whether a public official may bring a civil suit for defamation against a radio station. The Court found that a proper balance between the official's claim to dignity and the radio station's claim to freedom of speech leads to the conclusion that such a suit may be brought to vindicate alleged violations of a person's dignity even if that person holds high public office. The Court arrived at this conclusion by noting that the right to freedom of speech is limited under international human rights instruments, including the African Charter, the ICCPR, the American Convention and the European Convention.[76] Disappointingly, the Court made extensive reference to the jurisprudence of the European and Inter-American Courts (and even domestic courts) but not to the jurisprudence of the African Commission.

Lesotho judges are emblematic of judicial hesitance to rely on the Charter in their decisions even for interpretive purposes. In a rare exception, the Court of Appeal in *Director of Public Prosecutions v Sole and Another*[77] made a single reference to the African Charter, but this reference was all but lost in the much more extensive reliance on other international human rights law, including the European Convention, the jurisprudence of the European Court of Human Rights and the jurisprudence of the South African and other domestic courts. In another case,[78] however, the Court rejected a challenge against an affirmative action measure reserving a third of local government seats for women on the basis that those measures were in line with Lesotho's international obligations under the CEDAW and the Women's Protocol.

---

68 Para. 13.
69 Gambian High Court Decision on Application for Declaratory Relief, Civil HC 241/06/MF/087/F1; ILDC 881 (GM 2006).
70 Art. 19(6) of the Gambian Constitution.
71 Art. 6 of the African Charter.
72 Para. 58: *Jawara v The Gambia* (2000) AHRLR 107 (ACHPR 2000), para. 59: communication 101/93 and the Commission's Resolution on the Rights to Freedom of Association.
73 KeCA 2005 (2005) AHRLR 107.
74 Art. 18(3) of the Charter.
75 [2006] eKLR, judgment of 21 July 2006.
76 See reliance placed on e.g. the decisions of the European Court of Human Rights in *Handyside v UK* and *Lingens v Austria*, and the Court's finding in the part headed 'Conclusion'.
77 Case no. CRI/T/111/99, available at http://www.lesotholii.org/ls/judgment/court-appeal/2001/101 accessed on 21 September 2012.
78 *Molefi Ts'epe v The Independent Electoral Commission and Others LeCA 2005* (2005) AHRLR 136.

What made reliance on the Protocol quite extraordinary is the fact that, although Lesotho had at the time ratified this treaty, it had not yet entered into force.

4 Factors enhancing and limiting impact or influence

Although there are notable exceptions, and emerging trends, one is left with the overall impression that the African regional human rights system has had a very limited direct impact and that its influence (or 'indirect impact') has in the main not been very significant.

4.1 Reasons for lack of direct impact

One of the reasons for the lack of direct impact is the legal status of the Commission's findings, which states consider to be 'non-binding' under international law.[79] At least one state, Botswana, relied explicitly on this reason to 'justify' its non-compliance with a finding of the Commission against it.[80] The Commission responded by referring the instance of non-compliance to the AU's political organs (particularly, the Executive Council).

Many other factors may, however, also influence state behaviour, such as the political cost of compliance, the 'legal culture' within the state, including the existence of a domestic culture of non-compliance with judicial orders, the mobilising role and strength of civil society, and the lack of precision in the order or recommendation. On this basis, it may be concluded that compliance with judgments of the African Human Rights Court would not *necessarily* (that is, merely because they are legally binding) surpass compliance with findings of the Commission.

It should also be considered that the *potential for* direct influence increases or diminishes in correlation to the number of complaints or cases submitted and decided within the system. Thus far, very few Africans have submitted complaints to the African regional human rights bodies. By 2012, the African Commission had received just over 400 complaints, and in that period it had finalised some 180 cases, about half of which were found inadmissible.[81] The African Children's Committee has received much fewer cases, and has finalised only one of them during the decade of its existence. Only a handful of cases have been submitted directly to the African Human Rights Court by individuals in some of the five states where this is possible.[82]

The reasons for the dearth of cases relate to the treaty body, the potential complaints and the deficiencies in and perceptions of the domestic legal system.

---

79 The bases of this understanding is that, under the African Charter, (i) the findings of the African Commission are merely 'recommendatory' (and not legally binding) (Arts 55–58), and (ii) the Assembly has to authorise the publication of these findings, and may thus withhold its approval (Art. 59). Few states have explicitly refused to comply with findings.

80 Combined 32nd and 33rd Activity Report of the African Commission on Human and Peoples' Rights, AU Doc. EX.CL/782(XXII) Rev. 2, January 2013, para. 24. For the first time, the Commission drew the attention of the Executive Council to the refusal of a state party to implement a finding by the Commission. This transpired in respect of Communication 313/05, *Kenneth Good v Botswana*. Through Diplomatic Note Ref: 10/12 BEA5/21 C VIII (4) AMB of 23 March 2012, Botswana informed the Commission as follows: 'The Government has made its position clear; that it is not bound by the decision of the Commission.'

81 See African Human Rights Case Law Analyser, http://caselaw.ihrda.org/acmhpr/ search/?o=174%7C792 (accessed on 13 August 2012).

82 Cases have been submitted against Burkina Faso, Malawi and Tanzania, and the first hearing has been held in one of the cases against Tanzania.

As for the treaty body, for many years, the Charter and the work of the Commission remained invisible and unknown. The African Commission did very little to disseminate its findings widely. It has also been taking a very long time to finalise cases, due to its practice of dealing with complaints in three phases ('seizure', admissibility and merits), and because it too easily and frequently postpones cases at the request of states or due to its own operational inefficiencies. In recent years, the Commission has neglected its protective mandate in favour of promotional activities,[83] which have mushroomed over time and now comprise not only promotional visits, but also at least one special mechanism allocated to each Commissioner. The additional burden on Commissioners derives from an important difference between the UN and African human rights systems: under the UN system, the members of human rights treaty bodies and individuals holding special mechanisms are distinct and do not overlap; in the African system, the same Commissioners who are acting as treaty body members are also responsible for special mechanisms.

Most Africans at the receiving end of human rights violations (whom we may call 'potential litigants') have no idea of the existence of an African regional human rights system. The lack of knowledge and awareness is embedded in low levels of general literacy, weak and unprofessional civil society organisations, and negligible legal literacy. Legal recourse is expensive, alien and inaccessible. In the limited instances where legal avenues are explored, the most logical – and most appropriate – option is in the first instance to rely on domestic legislation and the national Constitution. As far as some lawyers or NGOs may have knowledge of the African system, their perception of the system would to a great extent correspond with that of the community. Lawyers may in particular be reluctant to embark on a long and burdensome route holding little promise of enforcement.[84]

Many problems beset the exhaustion of local remedies. In a context and a continent where the state's penetration of the national polity still remains incomplete, and formal legal avenues have long been viewed as remote, ordinary Africans are not likely to view the wrongs done to them or describe their grevances as 'human rights violations'. Built on patterns inherited from the colonial period, the post-colonial African state apparatus evolved to serve a 'bureaucratic bourgeoisie',[85] a governing elite that dispenses privilege on patrimonial grounds. The law and legal systems are adjuncts placed under the elite's control, albeit with the semblance of impartiality. As a result, 'potential litigants' may view the law and the legal apparatus with distrust as being alien and culturally illegitimate, or feel that their prospects of success are slim as no specific remedy actually exists at the domestic level. In many African states, the court systems and administration of justice is very weak or even dysfunctional.[86] While it is correct to retort that the Commission may exempt 'litigants' from exhausting local remedies that are

---

83 In 2010 and 2011, for example, the Commission decided only one case per year on the merits.
84 See the possibilities presented for individuals in ECOWAS member states, where the domestic remedies requirements does not apply: see e.g. ECOWAS Court of Justice, *Karaou v Niger*, judgment ECW/CCJ/JJD/06/08, judgment of 27 October 2008; (2008) AHRLR 183 (ECOWAS 2008), para. 45.
85 R.L. Sklar and C.S. Whitaker, *African Politics and Problems in Development* (Boulder and London, Lynne Reinner, 1991) 215.
86 A 2003 study edited by An-Na'im painted a dismal picture of the justice system in much of Africa: 'Court dockets are crowded, courtroom facilities are inadequate, delays are frequent, and there is a general lack of access to case reporters and other sources of legal precedent necessary for adequate judicial performance in common law jurisdictions.' (A.A. An-Na'im *Human Rights under African Constitutions: Realizing the Promise for Ourselves* (Philadelphia, University of Penn Press, 2003) 23.

not available, sufficient and effective, the problem is one of perception – even lawyers have internalised the defeatist view that the Commission presents a remote and unlikely form of recourse.

The reasons for the (even more severe) dearth of cases submitted to the Children's Committee are largely similar to those outlined above. However, those grounds have been exacerbated by the totally inadequate institutional support provided to the Committee, rendering the Committee ineffectual and invisible.[87]

Although a few cases are pending, the African Human Rights Court has not yet decided a case against any of the states that have accepted the right of direct access to the Court.[88] The main constraint is possibly the requirement that domestic remedies still have to be exhausted, combined with the temporal scope of the Court's jurisdiction.[89] Because exhaustion may take quite some time, cases recently instituted at the domestic level may take a number of years before being 'ripe' for submission to the Court.

It cannot be left unmentioned that not a single case has yet been decided under the Women's Protocol, and that no state has yet presented its state report under the Women's Protocol.[90] Perhaps the relative newness of this Protocol can explain why the clarity and progressive content of these norms, together with the support of lawyers and women's rights civil society organisations, have not inspired more litigation. Or perhaps the lack of cases underscores the difficulty of challenging deep-rooted patterns of patriarchy.

4.2 Reasons for limited indirect impact or influence

4.2.1 Limited effect on constitution-making

An expectation of influence of the Charter has been raised by the circumstance that many states adopted new constitutions in the post-1990 era, usually some time after becoming state parties to the Charter. However, these expectations were confounded by the analysis of these Constitutions, which shows little correlation between the 1981 Charter and the post-1990 texts. The limited effect of the African Charter may be ascribed to the language of the Charter, on the one hand, and the disjuncture between the moment of becoming a party and the moment of constitution-making, on the other.

In the context of the Africa's 'third wave of democracy' the Charter reads like an antiquated and outdated document. Its 'claw-back clauses',[91] lack of a right to privacy, weak

---

87 However, some significant improvements took place in recent years, see e.g. Viljoen (n. 1) 408–9.
88 The Court considered the first matter on the merits against any of these states (*Reverend Christopher Mtikila v Tanzania*) in June 2012.
89 With the exception of 'continuous violations', the Court's temporal jurisdiction is demarcated by the date of the entry into force of the Court Protocol (on 25 January 2004), and for subsequent state parties by the date marking three months after the deposit of the instrument of ratification by that state (Art. 65 of the Court Protocol).
90 The report required of states party to the Women's Protocol is not a separate report, but should form an integral part of the report submitted by that state under the African Charter (see J. Biegon, 'Towards the Adoption of Guidelines under the African Union Protocol on Women's Rights, A Review of the Pretoria Gender Expert Meeting, 6–7 August 2009' (2009) 9 *African Human Rights Law Journal* 615).
91 Arts 9, 10 and 12(1) of the African Charter.

provisions on representative democracy[92] and the dubious formulation of a number of individual duties[93] rendered the Charter out of tune and a less than ideal normative beacon for states endeavouring to embrace an age of optimism about democracy and responding to the dictates of structural adjustment.

The potential effect of the Charter was also blunted by the relatively lengthy period in most countries between becoming party to the Charter and the corresponding revision of the national constitution. By the time of the various African constitutional conferences and peoples' congresses devoted to constitutional reform, which started in 1989, the Charter was not in the forefront of the constitutional drafters' minds, and did not feature prominently in the sources on which relevant rights-based provisions were based.[94] This situation of diminished influence was exacerbated in those countries where the African Charter was adopted under one-party rule or during military dictatorship.[95] Factors such as a lack of public consultation and failure to create awareness tainted the initial perception of the Charter at the moment of national ratification, and to some extent continue to colour popular perceptions of the Charter. While the process of becoming a party to the Women's Protocol may have been much more open and participatory, its effect can only be assessed in relation to the small number of Constitutions adopted or amended after 2006. In any event, the detailed wording of many of the Protocol's provisions may make them better candidates for inclusion in domestic legislation as justiciable constitutional rights.

4.2.2 Limited legislative influence

Due to factors such as the legacy of colonialism, military government, one-party states and the dominance of liberation movements turned political parties, parliamentary institutions across the continent are weak, under-resourced, not properly representative, and overly dependent on the executive.[96] This situation denies parliaments effective participation in the adoption, implementation and supervision of international human rights treaties. The lack of domesticating legislation may also be ascribed to the lack of initiative, rigour or debates in parliaments. Parliaments almost never debate international human rights treaties prior to ratification, and have no role in supervision of treaty obligations, for example through involvement in state reporting or domestic implementation.

As a generalisation, law-making in African states may be described as a lengthy and drawn-out process. Bills are often pending for many years before they are adopted. In Benin, for example, it took about a decade to get the Family Code of 2004 adopted. Another illustration of unnecessary delay is found in Mozambique, where a 2006 proposal for domestic violence legislation was eventually adopted, three years later, more or less in line with the

---

92 Art. 13 of the African Charter.
93 Art. 29, ibid.
94 On the sources used during the Charter's drafting, see the M'Baye 'Draft African Charter' in C. Heyns (ed) *Human Rights law in Africa 1999* (The Hague, Kluwer Law International, 2002) 65.
95 As was previously mentioned, Benin became a state party to the Charter in 1986, at the height of the dictatorship; it was joined in that year by Libya, Sudan and Zimbabwe, none of which at the time had much claim to democratic credentials.
96 M.O.A. Alabi, 'The Legislatures in Africa: A Trajectory of Weakness' (2009) 3 *African Journal of Political Science and International Relations* 233.

original submission. The delay was explained with reference to 'the complexity of the matter and lack of time'.[97]

4.2.3 Limited influence on judiciary

Judges do not frequently rely on the African Charter or Women's Protocol in their judgments, and only on the rarest of occasions do they refer to the jurisprudence of the African Commission.

One reason for this state of affairs is the lack of an explicit textual mandate. However, as a number of instances clearly illustrate, an explicit textual mandate is not determinative of the issue.[98] While such clarity may provide a foothold for a judicial leap into activism, as has been the case in post-1994 South Africa, experience has also shown that even in 'dualist' states without any explicit legal mandate, such as the Gambia, some judges have placed reliance and even based findings on the African Charter and the Commission's case law. Also, the same courts that are reluctant to enter into judicial dialogue with the African system, are often much more likely to place reliance on the UN treaties that the state has ratified, the Universal Declaration, and even the European and American Conventions and the case law of their Courts, notwithstanding that the state can clearly never be a party and thus be bound by these standards. The finding in the Kenyan case of *Rono v Rono* provides further proof that adherence to the 'dualist' tradition does not preclude reliance on international instruments, including the African Charter. In that case, the legal basis for reliance was located in international 'soft law', in the form of the Bangalore Principles of Judicial Conduct of 2002.[99]

A second reason for the infrequent use of the regional human rights system lies in the inadequate articulation of these issues and infrequent inclusion of these sources in legal counsel's arguments. Judicial reliance is often hampered by a lack of reliance sought by legal practitioners arguing in cases, combined with a stark adherence to the principle that judges should not decide outside the scope of the briefs presented to them. Although the form and content of legal education has changed and now more frequently include human rights and even ference to the African regional system, many lawyers learnt their trade in different times. Their failing may rather be ascribed to the failure of the legal profession to ensure that its members are regularly updated and exposed to regional human rights law.[100]

Some specific factors inform the almost total absence of reliance on or even reference to the Commission's jurisprudence in national cases. Judges may be reluctant to follow the non-binding 'precedent' of a quasi-judicial body. Often, the case law of the Commission may also not be of much assistance, given the small number of cases decided on the merits,

---

97 AfriMAP and the Open Society Initiative for Southern Africa, *Mozambique Democracy and Political Participation: A Review* (2009) p. 38, avaliable at http://www.afrimap.org/english/images/report/AfriMAP-Moz-PolPart-EN.pdf (accessed on 21 September 2012).

98 See e.g. Art. 26(2) of Angola's 2010 Constitution, which provides that fundamental rights must be interpreted in accordance with the Universal Declaration, the African Charter and other ratified treaties. However, Angolan courts have not yet made reference to any of these instruments.

99 A copy of the Bangalore Principles is contained in UN ECOSOC res. 2006/23 (2006).

100 See e.g. M. Killander and H. Adjolohoun, 'International Law and Domestic Human Rights Litigation in Africa: An Introduction', in M. Killander (ed.), *International Law and Domestic Human Rights Litigation in Africa* (2010) 19.

and the often crude factual circumstances that give rise to findings lacking in subtlety or reflecting a careful balancing of competing rights or interests of comparable weight. For many years, the case law was also not easy to find and access, but in recent years it has become much more accessible.[101] Not knowing about the existence of or where to find case law has become a matter of lack of knowledge and information. A further factor is the general reluctance of civil law judges to rely on case law, given their traditional preoccupation with codified texts.

4.2.4 Relatively greater influence of the Women's Protocol

The Women's Protocol seems to have generated greater impetus for legislative and policy reform than the Charter. The reasons why this instruments has, compared to the African Charter, had much more of an immediate impact are related to the different processes of its drafting and adoption, its acceptance by states, and to the more detailed and precise nature of state obligations.

The Women's Protocol is the product of an inclusive process, in which the women's movement and African Commission took the initiative and played an important part.[102] In contrast, the Charter was to a much greater extent a state-initiated and government expert-driven project. The Women's Protocol was adopted by the African Union, in which human rights promotion and protection is a central organisational tenet. This was not the case in the OAU, under whose auspices the Charter was adopted. A sense of optimism and euphoria linked to the novelty and the promise of the AU as an organisation *different to the OAU*, which prevailed at the time of the Protocol's adoption, may also have left its mark on the provisions of the Protocol. Also at the domestic level, ratification by states was a much more participatory, public and inclusive process. While the rights under the African Charter are often framed as one-liners, the Protocol, by its very nature as a complement to the Charter focusing on women's issues, specifies and particularises these rights in much more elaborate and detailed formulations.[103]

5 Conclusion and future trends and priorities

5.1 Contextual approach to states

To a large extent, the African regional system's negligible impact may be ascribed to the immensity of human rights violations, combined with infrastructural and institutional weaknesses at the domestic level, in many African states. As much as the greatest impact-potential of the Charter and Protocol may logically lie in the countries where the problems are the greatest, or the human rights violations the severest, it is also in these very situations where the regional system seems to be at its least effective. One is thus faced with the paradox that

---

101 See the African Human Rights Law Reports (AHRLR), http://www1.chr.up.ac.za/index.php/ahrlr-downloads.html; the African Human Rights Case Law Analyser, http://caselaw.ihrda.org; and the Commission's website, http://www.achpr.org/communications/.

102 F. Banda, *Women, Law and Human Rights: An African Perspective* (Oxford, Hart, 2005) 67.

103 Compare, for example, Art. 16 (on 'health') of the Charter with Art. 14 of the Protocol (dealing with 'health and reproductive rights', including partner disclosure or notification of HIV status and medicalised abortion.

the greatest need for influence and impact corresponds with the greatest failure of impact and influence.[104]

To best understand the (lack of) impact of the African human rights system in this context, one should see states as located, and constantly shifting, along a sliding scale.[105] At one extreme, there are states in which the assumptions traditionally associated with a regional human rights system are in place. First, states share a set of core values, such as respect for the rule of law, democracy and observance of human rights, and largely implement or observe these values in practice. Second, the relationship between the regional and domestic legal system is one of functional subsidiarity, concretised in the main obligation on state parties to give effect to treaty provisions, leaving the treaty body to supervise and correct the state's efforts; and in the requirement of exhaustion of domestic remedies. Third, the domestic remedies requirement implies the existence of a functioning judiciary able to redress basic human rights violations. Before the entrance of the new members from Central and Eastern Europe, the Council of Europe system largely conformed to this image.

At the other extreme are the states in which these assumptions are not in place at all. First, states differ fundamentally about the core values, particularly as far as their practical application is concerned, and do not in practice observe the basic tenets of the rule of law. Second, the unwillingness or inability of state institutions to take any significant measures to give effect to the treaty renders illusory the notion of subsidiarity between national and international law. Third, domestic remedies are not available or accessible due to the extent and nature of violations in the state, or a dysfunctional administration of justice. The states at this end of the spectrum include those in which massive violations occur with great regularity, such as the Sudan and the DRC during most of the first decade of the twenty-first century; those where no semblance of the role or rule of law exists, such as present-day Eritrea; and those states least engaged with the human rights system.

Understanding the reasons for the lack of participation by the least engaged states may give some further insight into the factors limiting the influence of the African regional system. A clear indicator of minimal engagement is the failure to submit even an initial state report to the African Commission. Some of the most prominent non-reporting states, such as Liberia, Sierra Leone and Somalia, have experienced periods of prolonged political instability and widespread violence.[106] The urgency of these situations called the attention of these states to a different set of priorities, geared towards the peaceful resolution of conflict, and addressing its causes and immediate aftermath. The Commission's ineffectiveness in dealing with situations of human rights violations on a massive scale and its inability to respond speedily to urgent situations are likely to have reduced the likelihood of states prioritising the role of the Commission or the Charter in trying to overcome the situations of instability in their

---

104 See the related contention that 'treaty effects' are most likely in 'partially democratic transitional regimes' and not in 'stable democracies' or in 'stable autocracies' (B.A. Simmonds, *Mobilizing for Human Rights: International Law in Domestic Politics* (CUP, 2009) 153.

105 Take the case of Nigeria: it has moved from a military dictatorship (in 1998) to a leading African democracy, but the religious-based violence in Jos (in Plateau State) during 2010 shows that moments of instability may arise at any time even within a 'democratic' state. In that situation, the Commission used the 'political' aspect of its mandate when it requested the consent of the Nigerian government to conduct a fact-finding mission (30th Activity Report of the African Commission, AU Doc. EX.CL/717(XX), para. 258).

106 For a long time, Côte d'Ivoire was also on this list; it submitted its first report to the Commission in July 2012, combining all reports due for almost two decades, since 1994.

countries. Instead of dealing with these states on the same terms as other states, the Commission may have gained from adjusting its approach to confront more directly the political (rather than the legal) side of the situation. The Commission should not adopt a 'one size fits all' approach. Merely earmarking a situation as one of 'non-compliance' makes little contribution if the underlying causes are not contextualised. The Commission's role has to be rethought with reference to where a particular state is on the continuum, or, differently phrased, under which set of assumptions it operates. It should also tap into the insight that the possibilities of treaty impact may be enhanced where states are in a process of transition from authoritarianism/non-engagement to democracy/engagement.[107]

Against this background, it is contended that the African human rights system should align its interventions and priorities according to the position a state occupies along this continuum by adopting either a more 'legal' or more 'political' approach. A more formal legal approach, involving the consideration of individual communications and the examination of state reports, may be best suited to situations of greater stability, greater commitment to the rule of law and where stronger domestic institutions exist. In the least engaged states, a much more political approach may be called for, requiring the regional judicial and quasi-judicial institutions to liaise closely with and put pressure on the AU's political organs to take action. Fact-finding reports by the African Commission, establishing massive violations giving rise to genocide, crimes against humanity and war crimes, may for example be an important source on which the AU's Peace and Security Council (PSC) and Assembly may base a decision to intervene under Article 4(h) of the Constitutive Act. The Commission is, in any event, under an obligation to bring any relevant information to the attention of the PSC.[108] In what would amount to a revival of the procedure under Article 58 of the African Charter, the AU Assembly should be alerted to all other situations revealing, in the Commission's view, a series of serious or massive violations (in particular, those not meeting the Article 4(h) threshold). The Commission's 2010 Rules of Procedure also highlight the role of the AU's political organs (the Chairperson of the Assembly, the Executive Council and the Chairperson of the AU Commission) in 'emergency' situations.[109] The referral by the African Commission of the situation of internal conflict in Libya early in 2011 and the adoption of provisional measures by the Court may, against this background, be viewed as an attempt to fuse the regional system's legal and political aspects.[110] However, compliance with the Court's order was largely dependent on the political context, and rendered the Court's judgment mostly symbolic.

The emphasis on the political aspect of the Commission's mandate does not mean that its protective mandate is irrelevant in situations of massive violations. In these situations the complainant is often exempted from exhausting local remedies, causing the regional institution in effect to become a court of first instance, although it should be clear that AU institutions cannot replace national institutions. A series of individual communications, supported by a broader social movement, can go some distance to draw attention to the

---

107 See n. 82 above.
108 Art. 19, Protocol Relating to the Establishment of the Peace and Security Council of the African Union Adopted by the 1st Ordinary Session of the Assembly of the African Union, Durban, 9 July 2002. Acting under Art. 19, the Commission referred the situation of religious-based violence in Jos (Plateau State, Nigeria) to the PSC (30th Activity Report of the African Commission, AU Doc. EX.CL/717(XX), para. 258).
109 Rule 80(1).
110 See n. 3 above.

underlying deficiencies of a national legal and political order, but these findings will matter most if they feed into processes of political and structural reform. In this way, the legal and political aspects of the Commission's mandate remain linked and mutually supportive to enhance the domestic impact of the African regional human rights system.

5.2 Relationship between the Commission and the Court

It is unrealistic to expect that all the deficiencies plaguing the African Commission will be rectified in near future. The mere establishment of the Court is also no reason for optimism, as it is experiencing its own problems.

One way of improving the impact of the African human rights system may be to ensure effective and functional complementary between the Commission and the Court. In devising the details of the referral system, the Commission should be guided by the following factors: reducing delay, avoiding duplication and ensuring the most effective outcome in urgent cases. Applying these factors, the Commission's competence under Rule 118(4) to refer cases to the Court 'at any stage of the proceedings' should not necessarily lead to de novo trials before the Court. In order to avoid duplication, the Commission may, adopting an improved approach to fact-finding, consider such cases first on admissibility, thus acting as a 'filtering mechanism', before referring cases to the Court. In order not to further exacerbate the likely delays already experienced, the Court should be disinclined to interfere with the Commission's admissibility finding. In particular, the Court should not allow states to introduce jurisdictional and admissibility arguments which it did not raise before the Commission. However, in urgent matters the Commission should refer the matter for the Court's speediest possible binding judgment, including on provisional measures. In making sense of its competence under Rule 118(4), the Commission should not take account of the criteria used by the Inter-American Commission,[111] such as considering the development of regional jurisprudence, but should prioritise the need for immediate resolution of the issue by the Court. The Commission should elaborate and publicise the criteria that would guide referrals to the Court under Rule 118(4). On a more general basis, the Commission should improve its capacity for fact-finding, so as to limit the necessity for de novo hearings before the Court.

5.3 Emergence of sub-regional fora in response to lack of domestic impact

Any discussion about the impact of the continental human rights system takes place against the background of a recent and peculiarly African phenomenon, the emergence of sub-regional economic communities (RECs) as 'human rights systems'. This broadening of priorities beyond matters related to trade and regional economic cooperation within African RECs is not unrelated to the impact, or, more accurately, the (im)possibility of direct impact of the African regional human rights system. A combination of lack of confidence in the African Commission's protective ability and the impossibility of approaching the African Human Rights Court seems to have inspired Zimbabwean litigants to approach the SADC Tribunal.[112]

---

111 Art. 45 of the Rules of Procedure of the Inter-American Commission on Human Rights, as amended in 2011.
112 See *Campbell v Zimbabwe* ACHPR 2008 ((2008) AHRLR 199 (SADC 2008); Zimbabwe ratified the African Charter, but did not become a state party to the Protocol establishing the African Human Rights Court.

The Economic Community of West African States (ECOWAS) unequivocally became a 'rival' and perhaps more 'attractive' human rights system by not only allowing the ECOWAS Court to consider violations of the African Charter by state parties,[113] but also dispensing with the need to exhaust local remedies.[114] The evolution of a parallel human rights system at the sub-regional level in West Africa seems to be linked to the institutional weakness, protracted procedure and non-binding recommendations of the African Commission, on the one hand, and the burdensome access to the African Human Rights Court due to the exhaustion of local remedies requirement, on the other. These developments suggest a shift of gravity away from the regional/continental to the sub-regional, presumably on the assumption that the direct impact and influence of a human rights system may be more effective in a sphere closer and more immediate to the people of a smaller, more homogenous unit, where interests more closely intersect and the potential consequence of political and economic pressure on recalcitrant states may result in greater adherence to commonly agreed minimum standards. However, the recent SADC Summit decision to restrict the competence of the SADC Tribunal to deal only with inter-state cases, underlines that there is no guarantee that a smaller regional arrangement will be a better guarantor of human rights.[115]

Select bibliography

R. Murray, *Human Rights in Africa: From the OAU to the African Union* (CUP, 2004).

O.C. Okafor, (2007) *The Africa Human Rights System: Activist Forces and International Institutions* (CUP, 2007).

F. Ouguergouz, *The African Charter on Human and Peoples' Rights: A Comprehensive Agenda for Human Dignity and Sustainable Development in Africa* (The Hague, Martinus Nijhoff, 2003).

F. Viljoen, *International Human Rights Law in Africa* (OUP, 2012).

113 See Art. 9(4) of the Protocol on the ECOWAS Court of Justice: 'The Court has jurisdiction to determine case of violation of human rights that occur in any Member State', as amended in 2005; read with Art. 4(g) of the ECOWAS Treaty, as amended in 1995, which stipulates that the protection of the rights in the African Charter is one of the fundamental principles of ECOWAS.

114 Art. 10(d) of the Protocol on the ECOWAS Court of Justice (as amended in 2005), listing the admissibility requirements, does not make reference to the exhaustion of local remedies.

115 SADC Summit Communique, August 2012: 'a new Protocol on the [SADC] Tribunal should be negotiated and that its mandate should be confined to interpretation of the SADC Treaty and Protocols relating to disputes between Member States.'

26

The South East Asian system for human rights protection

Vitit Muntarbhorn

The notion of South East Asia, for the purpose of this study, is both geographical and functional.[1] Geographically, it implies the part of Asia – the South East Asian corner – that lies between the Indian Ocean and the Pacific Ocean. The South East Asian branch of the United Nations (UN) human rights office – the Office of the UN High Commissioner for Human Rights (OHCHR) – is located in Bangkok and is mandated to cover 11 countries: Cambodia, Brunei, Indonesia, Laos, Malaysia, Myanmar, Singapore, Timor Leste, Thailand, the Philippines and Vietnam.

The conglomeration of 11 very different countries leads to the intriguing question as to whether it is possible for them to become some kind of 'system' for the purpose of human rights protection, transcending the nation state and unifying, to a lesser or greater extent, for a common purpose. The term 'system' would also seem to suggest the need for an identifiable organisation, mechanism or network established for the attainment of that purpose. That systemic challenge, of course, cannot exist in a void and requires an understanding of the pluralistic context that is South East Asia.

In this regard, it may firstly be noted that those 11 countries are culturally very diverse, ranging from one country with (possibly) the world's biggest Muslim community – Indonesia – to a plethora of religions and communities in the other 10 countries. There is also demographically one of the world's smallest countries in the region – Timor Leste. Then there is a varied political panorama, from the democracies of Indonesia, Thailand, the Philippines and Timor Leste, to the 'guided' democracies of Malaysia, Singapore and Cambodia. There are also two countries, Laos and Vietnam, which are shifting from communism to a controlled socialist market economy. On another front, Brunei is under an absolute monarchy and

---

1 For general reading on South East Asia, ASEAN and human rights, see: Working Group for an ASEAN Human Rights Mechanism (Working Group), *ASEAN and Human Rights: a Compilation of ASEAN Statements on Human Rights* (Working Group 2003); S. Siddique and S. Kumar, *The 2nd ASEAN Reader* (Institute of Southeast Asian Studies, 2003); R.C. Severino, *Southeast Asia in Search of an ASEAN Community: Insights from the Former ASEAN Secretary-General* (Institute of Southeast Asian Studies, 2006). See also ASEAN's website, available at: www.aseansec.org. For links with the UN see OHCHR's website, available at: www.ohchr.org.

Myanmar is now in a 'wait and see situation,' transitioning from its introverted authoritarian rule to potential democracy.

Another challenge to unification has to do with the fact that, historically, most of these countries were under colonial rule. After the Second World War and the demise of colonialism, the Cold War emerged largely because of an ideological battle between capitalism and communism which was played out by proxy in the region. This pitted many of the 11 South East Asian countries against each other – particularly Thailand, the Philippines, and later Malaysia, Singapore and Brunei, against communist groups in Laos, Vietnam and Cambodia. Burma, which was later renamed Myanmar, became increasingly hermetic and later was faced with a superimposed junta rule. Meanwhile, Timor Leste, which was initially under Portuguese colonial rule, was subsumed by Indonesian rule until Indonesia, faced with its own economic crash, withdrew at the end of the 1990s.

This accounts for the fact that the first attempt at unification in the region in the 1950s was the South East Asia Treaty Organization (SEATO), an anti-communist, political and self-defence pact, established in 1954.[2] This was backed particularly by the US, UK and Australia, and included Thailand and the Philippines as members. In effect, it was segmented in geography (precisely because only a limited number of South East Asian countries were involved) and in content (precisely because it was merely a security bloc of a nominal kind). It was never active at the field level and was dissolved in 1977.

Third, the precariousness of the political situation gave rise to various wars in the region which superseded the end of the Second World War. Significantly, in the 1960s the war which was waged by the US, its allies and various South East Asian countries against communist groups in Vietnam was in full swing and had major spill-over effects in Cambodia and Laos. Various neighbouring South East Asian countries started to feel the need to coalesce so as not to be too dependent on the West and this propelled them to come together in 1967 to form what would be the first South East Asian organisation of an enduring kind – the Association of South East Asian Nations (ASEAN).[3] It was initiated by means of the Bangkok Declaration and initially comprised five members: Indonesia, Malaysia, Singapore, Thailand and the Philippines, later to be joined by Brunei. Yet, human rights were not on its agenda.

The organisation was a political organisation at heart, quietly acting as a security bloc vis-à-vis the neighbouring communist bloc and with a war raging at its borders. ASEAN became all the more politically relevant in the 1970s when in 1975 the US withdrew from the region and Vietnam, Laos and Cambodia came under full communist control. The decade which ensued was one where war and instability raged in South East Asia, particularly with internal conflicts between different governments in Cambodia and the fight for a Cambodian seat at the UN. It was only in the early 1990s that peace arrived in the South East Asian region, and the possible convergence with former enemies became a reality, as ASEAN expanded its membership to include Cambodia, Laos and Vietnam. In addition, Myanmar joined ASEAN in the 1990s to complete the South East Asian political jigsaw. Thus, before the new millennium, ASEAN had become a 10-member organisation. Now that the region is into its second decade after the turn of the millennium, there is another stepping-stone of note: Timor Leste recently applied to join ASEAN.

2 US Department of State, *Southeast Asia Treaty Organization (SEATO), 1954*, available at: http://history.state.gov/milestones/1953–1960/SEATO, accessed on 16 January 2012.
3 V. Muntarbhorn, *Legal Cooperation Among ASEAN Countries* (Institute of Security and International Studies 1997). See also publications listed in n. 1 above.

Fourth, another development ensued in the 1990s, propelled by the 1993 World Conference on Human Rights held in Vienna, in which South East Asian countries participated. The recommendation from the conference was for all regions to establish regional human rights protection systems and for all countries to establish national human rights institutions. As will be seen below, this encouraged ASEAN to contemplate the possibility of a regional human rights mechanism.

Moreover, the call for national institutions was taken up especially in South East Asia with the creation of national human rights institutions, particularly the National Human Rights Commission(s) and office(s) of the Ombudsman/Ombudsperson. Internationally, the criteria for these institutions is that they: are to be set up by the state, should be independent of the executive branch of government and need to be pluralistic in composition. As a consequence, various countries in South East Asia have set up these national institutions, particularly the National Human Rights Commissions in the Philippines (preceding even the 1993 World conference), Indonesia, Thailand and Malaysia, and these have been recognised as fulfilling the international criteria mentioned.[4] In 2004 Timor Leste set up its Ombudsman ('Provedoria'), which also enjoys international blessing. Meanwhile, Cambodia has various human rights committees, although these are not internationally recognised as independent from the executive branch. In 2011, interestingly, Myanmar also established a National Human Rights Commission, but this is not considered independent by the international community.[5] The proliferation of these institutions again invites the question as to whether these institutions may be seen as a kind of system if they converge for a common purpose and network accordingly.

Fifth, from the angle of human rights protection, it is worth bearing in mind that it is preferable to look to various checks and balances rather than a single institution to safeguard those rights, precisely because a monopoly may lead to abuse of power. This implies that the regional system is not a substitute for the national system, and vice versa, and the presence of a national institution working on human rights is not a substitute for the plurality of checks and balances required. While the system referred to here is principally one to be set up by the state/government, in its operationalisation it should be independent of that state/government for purposes of human rights protection. This is paralleled by the principle that the primary responsibility for human rights protection rests with the state, and where the state fails in its responsibility to protect human rights, the international system may offer assistance to protect those rights. Although this study is not on the civil society system operating in the region, the contribution of civil society should not be underestimated and is an important part of the check and balance system in the region. The presence of the UN in Bangkok is also an essential part of this process.

1 South-East Asian system?

As a preamble to examination of the institutional aspects of the South East Asian system, it is worth bearing in mind that the notion of human rights itself is still much debated in the

---

4 For a detailed discussion, see: V. Muntarbhorn, *Unity in Connectivity? Evolving Human Rights Mechanisms in the ASEAN Region* (Martinus Nijhoff, The Hague, 2013). See also: B. Burdekin, *National Human Rights Institutions in the Asia Pacific Region* (Martin Nijhoff, 2007).

5 A. Malatest, *Myanmar Government Forms Human Rights Commission*, available at: http://jurist.org/paperchase/2011/09/myanmar-government-forms-human-rights-commission.php, accessed on 16 January 2012.

region. Some governmental quarters (particularly the non-democratic elements) question the universality of human rights, claiming that there are various values in the region which diverge from universal standards. According to them, universal standards should take into account regional/national practices, alias 'particularities', and if there is a conflict between them, those regional/national practices should prevail over the former.[6] Moreover, there is an emphasis on the divisibility of human rights – based on a preference for economic, social and cultural rights[7] – rather than indivisibility of human rights based on the interconnected nature of civil, political, economic, social and cultural rights which are the cornerstone of international human rights law. In reality, this is an incarnation of the 'Asian values' referenced by some Asian governments, particularly before the economic crash in the Asian region in the mid-1990s, which find themselves now transmuted into the South East Asian setting as 'ASEAN values'. More specifically, those so-called values underline economic rights (such as the right to food and an adequate standard of living) rather than political rights such as freedom of expression and peaceful assembly; respect for authority based on strong and stable government, society and family rather than the aspirations of the individual; and justify the status quo based on broad state powers vis-à-vis the rights of individuals. There is also an emphasis on the responsibilities and duties of individuals in their relationship with the state rather than the rights of individuals as a priority.[8]

The above position on the part of some South East Asian governments is a reminder that there remain in this region traits of ethnocentrism or cultural relativism which may lead to a conflict between universal human rights standards, on the one hand, and their acceptance and reception at the regional and national levels, on the other hand. In 2008–09, this friction appeared in the drafting of the Terms of Reference of the ASEAN Intergovernmental Commission on Human Rights (referred to below in detail) and is exemplified by the nebulous wording of the final Terms of Reference adopted by ASEAN in 2009, which states that the mandate of that body includes, per Article 1(4): 'To promote human rights within the regional context, bearing in mind national and regional particularities and mutual respect for different historical, cultural and religious backgrounds, and taking into account the balances between rights and responsibilities.'[9]

The issue reared its head again in the 2011–12 period (during which this study was prepared) with the process initiated by the ASEAN countries to draft an ASEAN Human

---

6 See, for example, the potential conflict between universality of human rights and particularities in the Asia-Pacific (Governmental) Human Rights Declaration adopted in Bangkok, with participation from ASEAN states, just before the 1993 Vienna World Conference on Human Rights. Its Art. 8 states as follows: 'Recognise that while human rights are universal in nature, they must be considered in the context of a dynamic and evolving process of international norm-setting, bearing in mind the significance of national and regional particularities and various historical, cultural and religious backgrounds'. Contrast that with the Asia-Pacific (Nongovernmental) Human Rights Declaration 1993, which emphasises universality without referring to particularities. For text of both declarations, see: *Our Voice: Bangkok NGO Declaration on Human Rights* (Asia Cultural Forum on Development 2003).

7 This is the (questionable) reality given that currently only three countries in the ASEAN group are democratic, the others being non-democratic, semi or demi democracies, or in transition to democracy!

8 See further: V. Muntarbhorn, *Dimensions of Human Rights in the Asia Pacific Region* (National Human Rights Commission of Thailand 2002).

9 See ASEAN, *ASEAN Intergovernmental Commission on Human Rights (Terms of Reference)* (ASEAN Secretariat, 2009).

Rights Declaration pursuant to the Terms of Reference mentioned. While the final text of the potential Declaration was still being discussed in mid-2012 (and was pending), elements of cultural relativism favoured by various governmental quarters in the negotiation process included/include the following.[10] First, they favour explicit references to regional/national practices or particularities where universal human rights are raised. Second, they are wary of a comprehensive list of political rights based upon universal instruments, such as the Universal Declaration of Human Rights 1948 and the International Covenant on Civil and Political Rights 1966. They also wish to subject such rights to broad limitations and constraints such as national security and public morality or public morals. Third, they are prone to qualify the existence and realisation of human rights by subjecting them to national law. This position thus subordinates universal standards to their concretisation (if at all) through the instrument of national law, thus implying that rights are given or conferred by the state (a subjective approach) rather than guaranteed by the state against a backdrop of international standards and monitoring (an objective approach). Let us now turn to the institutional aspects of human rights in the South East Asian region.

The South East Asian system may be seen as comprising two components: National Human Rights Institutions (unified by the South East Asia National Human Rights Institutions Forum), and the ASEAN System: the ASEAN Intergovernmental Commission on Human Rights and its sectoral bodies.

1.1 National human rights institutions and the South East Asian Human Rights Institutions Forum (SEANF)

As already mentioned, there are now internationally recognised national human rights institutions in five South East Asian countries: the Philippines, Indonesia, Thailand, Malaysia and Timor Leste.

What is the nature of their work? As with most national human rights institutions, they promote and protect human rights at the national and local levels. As an example, the mandate of The Philippine Commission on Human Rights, a body established by the 1987 Constitution, illustrates the point, which is set out in section 18 of the Constitution:

(1) Investigate, on its own or on complaint by any party, all forms of human rights violations involving civil and political rights;

(2) Adopt its operational guidelines and rules of procedure, and cite contempt for violations thereof in accordance with the Rules of Court;

(3) Provide appropriate legal measures for the protection of human rights of all persons within the Philippines, as well as Filipinos residing abroad, and provide for preventive measures and legal aid services to the underprivileged whose human rights have been violated or need protection;

(4) Exercise visitorial powers over jails, prisons, or detention facilities;

(5) Establish a continuing program of research, education, and information to enhance respect for the primacy of human rights;

(6) Recommend to the Congress effective measures to promote human rights and to provide for compensation to victims of violations of human rights, or their families;

---

10 For some of the happenings in 2011–12, see: V., *Development of the ASEAN Human Rights Mechanism.* European Parliament: EXPO/B/DROI/2012/15. September 2012.

(7) Monitor the Philippine Government's compliance with international treaty obligations on human rights . . .[11]

In general, all these national institutions have the power to protect human rights by monitoring the human rights situation, receiving complaints from individuals and their representatives, investigating and fact-finding, recommending remedies and pressuring for change. One useful power in practice is the ability to visit prisons and this can lead to indirect monitoring and to increased transparency in those facilities. These national institutions may also play the role of mediator, even though they are not judicial institutions.

What of their appointment and operations? In some countries, the appointment of the members of the national institutions is too close to the executive branch. While the promotional angle of their work, such as through human rights education and awareness-raising is relatively easy, the protection work is a continual challenge. In addition, they have to face perpetrators from officialdom, particularly the police, security forces and the army, where impunity runs deep. Moreover, they are not courts of law and most do not have powers to litigate and prosecute perpetrators in the courts; rather they can only make recommendations. They often have to depend on a third party, such as the prosecutors' office, to do so, but action from the latter is often tardy or ineffective.

In efforts to develop a system, these national human rights institutions in South East Asia came together in 2007 and formed a network consisting of the four Commissions listed above. The ASEAN National Human Rights Institutions, as they are known, adopted a Declaration of Cooperation with the following tenets:

1. The four national human rights commissions shall do whatever possible to carry out jointly, either on bilateral or multilateral basis, programmes and activities in areas of human rights identified and agreed upon at the meetings.
2. Regional Strategies for the promotion and protection of human rights shall be gradually developed within and among the four national human rights commissions including advising their respective governments to take necessary steps to establish an appropriate human rights mechanism and/or any organ in the ASEAN Charter.
3. Formalisation of cooperation should be further enhanced. More specific terms of references shall continue to be discussed among the four national human rights commissions.
4. The four national human rights commissions shall meet regularly, at least once a year. Host could be rotated on an alphabetical basis or as otherwise agreed upon.
5. The four national human rights commissions shall welcome and be open to considering any cooperation or joint efforts with other like-minded organizations, be

---

11 For the Constitution see Commission on Human Rights of the Philippine's website, available at: http://www.chr.gov.ph/MAIN%20PAGES/about%20us/01consti_creation.htm, accessed 10 February 2012. See also: Commission on Human Rights of the Philippines (Commission), *Resource Book on the Commission on Human Rights of the Philippines* (Commission, no date), for the Constitution and other documents.

they governmental or non-governmental or academic institutions , to pursue their commitments to promote respect for and protection of human rights in their respective countries, in the region and in the international community.[12]

They have adopted a plan of action to cover issues such as anti-terrorism, economic, social, and cultural rights, human right education, human trafficking and migrant workers, and they meet periodically. They have now modified their focus on anti-terrorism to concentrate on internal security laws. That network is also opening up to more South East Asian links and has now set up the South East Asia National Human Rights Institutions Forum (SEANF). SEANF may admit, as members, human rights bodies in other countries which do not yet have national human rights commissions. For example, it has interlinked with the Ombudsman of Timor Leste.

In 2010, the SEANF adopted a Memorandum of Understanding against Trafficking of Women and Children.[13] The aims were to prevent and combat trafficking and promote cooperation between the institutions. Legal aid is also to be provided. Projected activities include curricula development for law enforcement, the judiciary, the academe and pertinent ministries. An important element will be to promote effective identification of the victims and differentiate them from illegal immigrants. Interestingly, some monitoring of implementation is also provided for. The members are also required to submit a report to the annual meeting of the SEANF.

1.2 The ASEAN system: the ASEAN Intergovernmental Commission on Human Rights and the sectoral bodies

1.2.1 The ASEAN Intergovernmental Commission on Human Rights (AICHR)

It is worth recalling at the outset that ASEAN is not a human rights organisation. Yet, there are some possible entry points for the promotion and protection of human rights. Pursuant to the 1993 World Conference, ASEAN Foreign Ministers made a statement that they would consider the possibility of a human rights mechanism. The idea was shelved by the governments for many years but civil society repeatedly raised the need for such a mechanism. After confidence-building initiatives at various seminars between governments and civil society, several lead countries began to press for the creation of a formal human rights mechanism. In 2004, an ASEAN plan of action called for the establishment of an ASEAN Commission on the rights of women and children. In 2007, ASEAN adopted its first declaration oriented

---

12 The ASEAN National Human Rights Institutions (NHRI) Forum, *Declaration of Cooperation* (NHRI 2007), available at: http://www.aseannhriforum.org/attachments/011_declaration_of_cooperation.pdf, accessed 10 February 2012. The declaration 'Not[ed] in particular the five human rights areas of common concern already identified during the 1st consultation meeting of the four national human rights commissions held in Bangkok on 19 October 2004, namely the implementation of the economic, social, and cultural rights and right to development, enhancement of human rights education, human rights aspects of trafficking in persons especially women and children, protection of the human rights of migrants and migrant workers, and the suppression of terrorism while respecting human rights.'
13 SEANF, 'Memorandum of Understanding against Trafficking of Women and Children' (30 March 2010, Philippines), see http://www.aseannhriforum.org/en/joint-projects/anti-trafficking/54-sea-nf-members-sign-mou-on-anti-trafficking-.html, accessed on 12 July 2012.

towards human rights – the ASEAN Declaration on the Rights of Migrant Workers, discussed below, to be followed up by a committee on the issue. Importantly, in 2007 ASEAN also adopted the ASEAN Charter to act as a kind of constitution for the region. Article 14 of this Charter stipulates that an ASEAN human rights body shall be established.[14]

Subsequently, a High Level Panel was set up to draft the terms of reference (TOR) of the body, and as a result the TOR was adopted in 2009, leading to the establishment of the ASEAN Intergovernmental Commission on Human Rights (AICHR).[15] This approach is perceived to be modest, in the sense that it is based on a step-by-step process, evolving gradually. Thus even though the AICHR is mandated to promote and protect human rights in the region, it focuses more on the promotion of rights as seen below. Incidentally, the AICHR is composed of one representative per country. There is no system in place to monitor their independence, though they are expected to act impartially.

The mindset behind the AICHR can be seen in these initial provisions of the terms of reference (TOR). The purposes of the AICHR are set out in Article 1:

1.1. To promote and protect human rights and fundamental freedoms of the peoples of ASEAN;

1.2. To uphold the right of the peoples of ASEAN to live in peace, dignity and prosperity;

1.3. To contribute to the realization of the purposes of ASEAN as set out in the ASEAN Charter in order to promote stability and harmony in the region, friendship and cooperation among ASEAN Member States, as well as the well-being, livelihood, welfare and participation of ASEAN peoples in the ASEAN community building process;

1.4. To promote human rights within the regional context, bearing in mind national and regional particularities and mutual respect for different historical, cultural and religious backgrounds, and taking into account the balance between rights and responsibilities;

1.5. To enhance regional cooperation with a view to complementing national and regional efforts on the promotion and protection of human rights; and

1.6. To uphold international human rights standards as prescribed by the Universal Declaration of Human Rights, the Vienna Declaration and Programme of Action, and international human rights instruments to which ASEAN Member States are parties.[16]

The principles to be upheld are stipulated in Article 2 of the TOR, and they include not only fundamental freedoms, human rights, democracy and the rule of law, but also sovereignty and non-interference in the internal affairs of ASEAN member states. The AICHR mandate in Article 4 of the TOR is expressed as follows:

4.1. To develop strategies for the promotion and protection of human rights and fundamental freedoms to complement the building of the ASEAN Community;

14 ASEAN Charter (ASEAN Secretariat 2008).
15 *ASEAN Intergovernmental Commission on Human Rights (Terms of Reference)* (n. 9); see also: T. Hsien-Li, *The ASEAN Intergovernmental Commission on Human Rights* (CUP, 2011).
16 *ASEAN Intergovernmental Commission on Human Rights (Terms of Reference)* (n. 9).

4.2. To develop an ASEAN Human Rights Declaration with a view to establishing a framework for human rights cooperation through various ASEAN conventions and other instruments dealing with human rights;

4.3. To enhance public awareness of human rights among the peoples of ASEAN through education, research and dissemination of information;

4.4. To promote capacity building for the effective implementation of international human rights treaty obligations undertaken by ASEAN Member States;

4.5. To encourage ASEAN Member States to consider acceding to and ratifying international human rights instruments;

4.6. To promote the full implementation of ASEAN instruments related to human rights;

4.7. To provide advisory services and technical assistance on human rights matters to ASEAN sectoral bodies upon request;

4.8. To engage in dialogue and consultation with other ASEAN bodies and entities associated with ASEAN, including civil society organizations and other stakeholders, as provided for in Chapter V of the ASEAN Charter;

4.9. To consult, as may be appropriate, with other national, regional and international institutions and entities concerned with the promotion and protection of human rights;

4.10. To obtain information from ASEAN Member States on the promotion and protection of human rights;

4.11. To develop common approaches and positions on human rights matters of interest to ASEAN;

4.12. To prepare studies on thematic issues of human rights in ASEAN;

4.13. To submit an annual report on its activities, or other reports if deemed necessary, to the ASEAN Foreign Ministers Meeting; and

4.14. To perform any other tasks as may be assigned to it by the ASEAN Foreign Ministers Meeting.[17]

It is evident that the AICHR mandate maintains a delicate balance between the promotion and protection of human rights. The preoccupation of several ASEAN states with the principle of non-interference in the internal affairs of a state explains their approach to a regional human rights mechanism. The mandate of the AICHR thus reveals that there is no provision for investigations, fact-finding and country visits to follow up cases. Nor is there a procedure to receive complaints from individuals. This is a marked difference from the powers of the national human rights institutions discussed earlier. Yet, various provisions open the door to elements of protection, albeit indirectly and expressed in non-confrontational terms. Of particular relevance are the references to: 'engage in dialogue and consultation with other ASEAN bodies' (Article 4.8); 'consult with other national, regional and international institutions' (Article 4.9); 'obtain information' (Article 4.10); 'prepare studies' (Article 4.12); 'submit an annual report on its activities, or other reports if deemed necessary' (Article 4.13).[18] Of course, these have to be tested in practice to gauge the extent that the AICHR will be creative on this front.

17 Ibid.
18 Ibid.

What has the AICHR done since its formation? First, it prepared an initial work plan emphasising key priority areas to focus on. This plan concentrates on the following issues: corporate social responsibility, migration, human trafficking, child soldiers, women and children in conflicts and natural disasters, juvenile justice, right to information in criminal justice, right to health, right to education, right to life and right to peace. It has also been asked to advise on the issue of mandatory testing for HIV.

Second, it has already decided on a complaint from various individuals concerning alleged human rights violations in the Philippines. Third, it has had difficulties trying to evolve its rules of procedure and no such rules have been adopted as yet. Finally, it has held meetings additional to the two per annum proposed in the TOR in order to coordinate and has at times been represented at various seminars in the region. It has also approved training programmes on human rights.

Currently, AICHR's main preoccupation is the preparation of an ASEAN Human Rights Declaration. The AICHR's key concern was to try to finalise a draft by the end of 2012 and to ensure it does not fall below international standards. One of the fears of civil society is that the less liberal ASEAN countries will push for many references to particularities, such as ASEAN values implying the predominant role of the government over individuals' rights and freedoms, and the preference for economic rights over political rights, which will lower international standards and undermine the universality and indivisibility of human rights.

The AICHR's seventh meeting was held in Bali in December 2011. It also met for the first time with the sectoral body on women and children to discuss the issue of aligning their work.[19] All in all, these stepping stones are more to do with promotion than protection of human rights. The AICHR is due to be reviewed after five years, and this will be an opportunity for the higher organs of ASEAN, such as the ASEAN Summit and the ASEAN Foreign Ministers, to consider a more concrete protection mandate for the AICHR, if the political will is present.

1.2.2 The Sectoral Bodies:[20] the ASEAN Commission on the Promotion and Protection of the Rights of Women and Children and the ASEAN Committee on the Implementation of the ASEAN Declaration on the Promotion and Protection of the Rights of Migrant Workers

1.2.2.1 The ASEAN Commission on the Promotion and Protection of the Rights of Women and Children (ACWC)

The idea of an ASEAN Commission on the rights of women and children was aired in an ASEAN action plan in 2004. Moreover, all the countries of South East Asia are state parties to the Convention on the Elimination of All Forms of Discrimination against Women (CEDAW) and the Convention on the Rights of the Child (CRC).

Yet, the TOR of this ASEAN body were drafted after the initiation of the TOR for what was to become the AICHR. The TOR of the ASEAN Commission on the promotion and

---

19 ASEAN, *Press Release of the Seventh Meeting of the ASEAN Intergovernmental Commission on Human Rights (AICHR)*, available at: http://www.aseansec.org/26752.htm, accessed on 13 January 2012.

20 'Sectoral bodies' is the ASEAN term for the various mechanisms that deal with specific issues, rather than human rights generally. They refer to specific groups such as women, children and migrant workers.

protection of the rights of women and children (ACWC) was finalised and approved by the ASEAN Summit in 2010. The Commission is composed of 20 members, two per country, one of whom represents the concerns of women and the other who represents the concerns of children.

The Purposes of the ACWC are stated in Article 2:

2.1. To promote and protect the human rights and fundamental freedoms of women and children in ASEAN, taking into consideration the different historical, political socio-cultural, religious and economic context in the region and the balances between rights and responsibilities.

2.2. To uphold, promote, protect, respect and fulfill the rights of women and children in ASEAN to live in peace, equality, justice, dignity and prosperity.

2.3. To promote the well-being, development, empowerment and participation of women and children in the ASEAN community building process which contribute to the realization of the purposes of ASEAN as set out in the ASEAN Charter.

2.4. To enhance regional and international cooperation with a view to complementing national and international efforts on the promotion and protection of the rights of women and children.

2.5. To uphold human rights as prescribed by the Universal Declaration of Human Rights, the Vienna Declaration and Programme of Action, Convention on the Elimination of All Forms of Discrimination against Women (CEDAW), Convention on the Rights of the Child (CRC), Beijing Platform for Action (BPFA), World Fit for Children, International Humanitarian Law and other international human rights instruments and regional declarations related to women's and children's rights to which ASEAN Member States are parties.

2.6. To promote stability and harmony in the region, friendship and cooperation among ASEAN Member States.[21]

In the mandate, there are innovative features which may be seen as more proactive than the AICHR TOR. These are seen as follows in Article 5:

5.1. To promote the implementation of international instruments, ASEAN instruments and other instruments related to the rights of women and children.

5.2. To develop policies, programs and innovative strategies to promote and protect the rights of women and children to complement the building of the ASEAN Community.

5.3. To promote public awareness and education of the rights of women and children in ASEAN.

5.4. To advocate on behalf of women and children, especially the most vulnerable and marginalized, and encourage ASEAN Member States to improve their situation.

5.5. To build capacities of relevant stakeholders at all levels, e.g. administrative, legislative, judicial, civil society, community leaders, women and children machineries, through the provision of technical assistance, training and workshops, towards the realization of the rights of women and children.

---

21 ASEAN Commission for the Promotion and Protection of the Rights of Women and Children (ACWC), *Terms of Reference*, available at: http://www.asean.org/documents/TOR-ACWC.pdf, accessed on 16 January 2012.

5.6. To assist, upon request by ASEAN Member States, in preparing for CEDAW and CRC Periodic Reports, the Human Rights Council's Universal Periodic Review (UPR) and reports for other Treaty Bodies, with specific reference to the rights of women and children in ASEAN.

5.7. To assist, upon request by ASEAN Member States, in implementing the Concluding Observations of CEDAW and CRC and other Treaty Bodies related to the rights of women and children.

5.8. To encourage ASEAN Member States on the collection and analysis of disaggregated data by sex, age etc., related to the promotion and protection of the rights of women and children.

5.9. To promote studies and research related to the situation and well-being of women and children with a view to fostering effective implementation of the rights of women and children in the region.

5.10. To encourage ASEAN Member States to undertake periodic reviews of national legislations, regulations, policies, and practices related to the rights of women and children.

5.11. To facilitate sharing of experiences and good practices, including thematic issues, between and among ASEAN Member States related to the situation and well-being of women and children and to enhance the effective implementation of CEDAW and CRC through, among others, exchange of visits, seminars and conferences.

5.12. To propose and promote appropriate measures, mechanisms and strategies for the prevention and elimination of all forms of violence of the rights of women and children, including the protection of victims.

5.13. To encourage ASEAN Member States to consider acceding to, and ratifying, international human rights instruments related to women and children.

5.14. To support the participation of ASEAN women and children in dialogue and consultation processes in ASEAN related to the promotion and protection of their rights.

5.15. To provide advisory services on matters pertaining to the promotion and protection of the rights of women and children to ASEAN sectoral bodies upon request.

5.16. To perform any other tasks related to the rights of women and children as may be delegated by the ASEAN Leaders and Foreign Ministers.[22]

The ACWC was established in the first half of 2010. What has it done to date? First, it has prepared its work plan. This focuses on the following issues: trafficking of women and children; affects of HIV on women and children; the social impact of climate change; disabilities; the child protection system; an integrative approach for children in need of special protection; quality education; child care; the child's right to participation; the participation of women in politics; and economic rights of women. Second, it also finalised its rules of procedure. Third, it met the AICHR recently to discuss aligning its work with that body. Finally, it has attempted to broaden its funding base by seeking philanthropic support. At its third meeting in Solo, Indonesia in September 2011, it proposed a future meeting with philanthropists and foundations which may potentially support work on women and children.[23]

22 Ibid.
23 ASEAN, *ACWC to Seek Philanthropists' Funding Support in Its Endeavour to Help Victims of Violence through an ASEAN Network of Social Service Centres*, available at: http://www.aseansec.org/26613. htm, accessed on 13 January 2012.

1.2.2.2 The ASEAN Committee on the Implementation of the ASEAN Declaration on the Promotion and Protection of the Rights of Migrant Workers (ACMW)

In 2007 the ASEAN Declaration on the Promotion and Protection of the Rights of Migrant Workers was adopted by the Member States.[24] This laid the groundwork for an ASEAN Committee on this issue. The TOR were finalised in 2007 and a committee was then established. The Declaration lays down standards for the treatment of migrant workers, particularly as they relate to source and destination countries. The Committee's mandate is to help implement the Declaration rather than the promotion and protection of migrant rights in the broader sense. In shape and content, it is more of a governmental body that coordinates work on this front with one representative per country, drawn from the various ministries of labour in the region. Essentially, its key task is to draft an ASEAN instrument (possibly a Convention) on the rights of migrant workers, which is now being discussed.

The TOR state the purpose of the Committee on migrant workers is as follows:

> The Committee, in accordance with the national laws, regulations, and policies of Member Countries, will serve as the focal point within ASEAN to coordinate the following:
>
> 1. Ensuring the effective implementation of the commitments made under the Declaration; and
> 2. Facilitating the development of an ASEAN instrument on the protection and promotion of the rights of migrant workers.[25]

The functions of the Committee on migrant workers are identified as follows in the TOR:

> Subject to the national laws, regulations, and policies of the Member Countries, the functions of the Committee will be as follows:
>
> 1. Explore all avenues to achieve the objectives of the Declaration;
> 2. Facilitate sharing of best practices in the ASEAN region on matters concerning the promotion and protection of the rights of migrant workers;
> 3. Promote bilateral and regional cooperation and assistance on matters involving the rights of migrant workers;
> 4. Facilitate data sharing on matters related to migrant workers, for the purpose of enhancing policies and programmes to protect and promote the rights of migrant workers in both sending and receiving countries;
> 5. Encourage international organizations, ASEAN Dialogue Partners and other countries to respect the principles and extend support and assistance to the implementation of the measures contained in the Declaration;

---

24 ASEAN, *Declaration on the Protection and Promotion of the Rights of Migrant Workers*, available at: http://www.aseansec.org/19264.htm, accessed on 16 January 2012.

25 ASEAN, *Establishment of the ASEAN Committee on the Implementation of the ASEAN Declaration on the Protection and Promotion of the Rights of Migrant Workers*, available at: http://www.asean.org/20768.htm, accessed 10 February 2012; OHCHR, *Frequently Asked Questions on ASEAN and Human Rights*, available at: http://bangkok.ohchr.org/files/Regional_Dialogue_ASEAN_Background_Paper.pdf, accessed 16 January 2012; see also: ASEAN, *Asean Committee on the Implementation of the ASEAN Declaration on the Protection and Promotion of the Rights of Migrant Workers (ACMW): Work Plan*, available at: http://www.aseansec.org/23062.pdf, accessed on 16 January 2012.

6. Promote harmonization of mechanisms between both sending and receiving countries that promote and protect the rights of migrant workers to implement the ASEAN commitment reflected in paragraph 17 of the Declaration;
7. Work closely with the ASEAN Secretariat in the preparation of the report of the Secretary-General of ASEAN to the ASEAN Summit; and
8. Work towards the development of an ASEAN instrument on the protection and promotion of the rights of migrant workers.[26]

It held its first meeting in September 2008 and held a fourth meeting in Jakarta in April 2011.[27] Its work plan has four tenets: protection and promotion of the rights of migrant workers against exploitation; enhancing labour migration governance in ASEAN countries; regional cooperation to fight human trafficking in ASEAN; and development of an ASEAN instrument on the protection and promotion of the rights of migrant workers. Its role may be seen to be more facilitative than substantive. In this regard, it does not have a genuine protection role in the sense that its powers do not cover the possibility of investigating complaints and taking communications from individuals with a view to advocating redress.

2 Observations

In retrospect, it can be said that the South East Asian system is nascent rather than well-established. The most long-standing element of the system is the presence of national human rights institutions, but their formation of a network is a recent innovation and the SEANF is still in the process of initiating implementation of its commitments. Interestingly, the SEANF to date has had no access to the ASEAN system, even though this would seem to be a logical move, especially noting the added value of protection national human rights institutions can bring by explicitly monitoring the human rights situation, investigating alleged violations, fact-finding, receiving communications from individuals and making recommendations in regard to cases needing redress.

Meanwhile, the ASEAN system has grown to comprise AICHR (the general human rights body), ACWC (women and children) and ACMW (migrant workers), all of which are still trying to find their way in terms of initiating and implementing their work plans. Even though they do not have the protection role similar to that of the national human rights institutions, their presence at the regional level is important since their mandates help to raise the profile of human rights in the region and legitimise the taking up of human rights issues at ASEAN.

In the future, it is recommended that to move forward with human rights protection in South East Asia the national human rights institution SEANF and the ASEAN system need to meet periodically to share their experiences and coordinate their work. The national human rights institutions themselves also need to be strengthened in terms of their access to the courts and their call for redress against impunity. Meanwhile, SEANF has the potential to bridge the gap between the various human rights institutions in South East Asia and support the setting up of similar institutions in countries which do not yet have them. It is crucial that these institutions are encouraged to work effectively, are accessible and importantly, are independent from the executive branch of government.

---

26 Ibid.
27 Task Force on ASEAN Migrant Workers, *ASEAN Negotiating Rules to Protect Migrant Workers*, available at: http://workersconnection.org/articles.php?more=140, accessed on 16 January 2012.

On the regional front, the various ASEAN mechanisms that now exist need to prove that they undertake their work well in relation to (at the very minimum) the promotion of human rights in the region, whether through support for education, awareness - raising, mobilisation and related actions. The various ASEAN instruments that have evolved from these mechanisms, especially the emerging ASEAN Human Rights Declaration, should not backtrack from international standards and commitments, and should be supportive of the international human rights system. Given that the current protection role of the ASEAN mechanisms is limited, the next phase for developing their substantive role will surely be to strengthen their mandates, particularly on monitoring, investigations, fact-finding and reception of complaints from individuals, coupled with redress and action against impunity.

Ultimately, the bottom line for the system is that in order for human rights to be realised and implemented, they must first be effectively protected. Indeed, human rights protection is the pivotal challenge - here, there or anywhere.

Select bibliography

B. Burdekin, *National Human Rights Institutions in the Asia Pacifi c Region* (Martin Nijhoff, 2007).

T. Hsien-Li, *The ASEAN Intergovernmental Commission on Human Rights* (CUP, 2011).

V. Muntarbhorn, *Legal Cooperation Among ASEAN Countries* (Institute of Security and International Studies 1997).

V. Muntarbhorn, *Unity in Connectivity? Evolving Human Rights Mechanisms in the ASEAN Region* (MartinusNijhoff, The Hague, 2013).

S. Siddique and S. Kumar, *The 2nd ASEAN Reader* (Institute of Southeast Asian Studies, 2003).

R.C. Severino, *Southeast Asia in Search of an ASEAN Community: insights from the former ASEAN security-general* (Institute of Southeast Asian Studies, 2006).

27

The League of Arab States and human rights

Mervat Rishmawi

1 Introduction

The League of Arab States (LAS) was the first regional inter-governmental organisation, created in 1945 by seven newly independent Arab states.[1] These were subsequently joined by 15 others, therefore constituting the current 22 members of LAS.[2] LAS has its headquarters in Cairo in Egypt, although some of its meetings are held in other locations.

As LAS was created on the backdrop of independence recently acquired by Arab states, the Charter of the Arab League (LAS Charter)[3] reflects this fact. Article 2 states that the main purpose of LAS is to:

> [D]raw closer the relations between member States and co-ordinate their political activities with the aim of realizing a close collaboration between them, to safeguard their independence and sovereignty, and to consider in a general way the affairs and interests of the Arab countries.

Article 2 also provides that among the purposes is to ensure a close cooperation of member states in the following matters: economic and financial; communication; culture; nationality, passports and visas; social welfare; and health.

The structure of LAS institutions, processes and rules, especially in relation to human rights, has witnessed little development since the establishment of the organisation. While

---

1 The first members of LAS, which established the organisation, were Egypt, Iraq, Transjordan (renamed Jordan after 1946), Lebanon, Saudi Arabia, Syria and Yemen. The initial meeting in which a decision was taken to create the organisation was in 1944, and this is sometimes cited as the date of the inception of LAS.
2 The 22 members of LAS (in order of joining the organisation) are: Egypt, Iraq, Jordan, Lebanon, Saudi Arabia, Syria, Yemen, Libya, Sudan, Morocco, Tunisia, Kuwait, Algeria, Oman, Qatar, United Arab Emirates, Bahrain, Mauritania, Somalia, Palestine (represented by the Palestine Liberation Organization – PLO), Djibouti, and Comoros.
3 Arab League Charter (adopted 22 March 1945), available at: http://www.unhcr.org/refworld/publisher,LAS,,,3ae6b3ab18,0.html/, accessed 14 July 2012.

there are signs of changes within LAS, the directions where these changes may go, as well as their real impact on the ground, is not yet clear. It is therefore suggested that two factors point to the need for a fresh look at LAS as an intergovernmental organisation, and its potential role in promoting and protecting human rights. These are the following:

(a) A reform process, which started over 20 years ago aiming partly to strengthen the performance of LAS in relation to human rights, is moving slowly. The Tunisia Summit in 2004 resolved that it is essential for LAS to engage in a reform process which must be internally driven, and that such reform process should focus on human development and the needs of Arab citizens.[4] The Tunisia Summit dealt with a number of important reform issues that relate to the development of the Arab joint system, as well as issues related to security. The summit adopted the revised Arab Charter on Human Rights, and adopted a reformed Arab Economic and Social Council.[5] In 2005, the revised Arab Charter on Human Rights was adopted. In 2006, an Arab Peace and Security Council was established. This is still to be activated.[6] Several other decisions related to economic and social development have been adopted since 2004. Incremental reform steps were taken, including past amendments to the Charter in relation to the role and structure of the LAS Council and the decision-making process, in addition to the creation of the Arab Parliament (see further below). In 2011, the Secretary General of LAS appointed a Commission to provide comprehensive proposals for such reform.[7]

(b) Recent events in the Middle East (including what is commonly referred to as the 'Arab Spring') have changed some of the approaches of LAS towards human rights concerns within Arab states. However, at the same time, actions and decisions taken by LAS in this context exposed the lack of coherent policies and approaches towards human rights and democracy, as well as a rift between some of its member states.

Hitherto, the Charter of LAS has not referred to human rights. A proposal to add a sentence in the Charter referring to respect and promotion of human rights has been delayed by a decision of the Council in 2010, until decisions are taken on what is referred to 'the

---

4 Many standards and other documents of LAS provide for the protection of rights of Arab citizens, not the rights of every person within the jurisdiction of the state as is provided by international human rights treaties. See for example Art. 2 of the International Covenant on Civil and Political Rights and Human Rights Committee, 'General Comment No. 31: The Nature of the General Legal Obligation Imposed on States Parties to the Covenant' (2004) UN Doc CCPR/C/21/Rev.1/Add. 13, para. 10.

5 Tunisia Summit Final Statement (2004), available at: http://www2.ohchr.org/english/law/compilation_democracy/league.htm, accessed on 14 July 2012.

6 Council of the League of Arab States Resolution 18/331 'Statutes of Arab Peace and Security Council', 29 March 2006 (Arabic).

7 The Commission is yet to issue its findings and recommendations. None of its documentation has been made public so far. A number of NGOs in the Middle East and North Africa have submitted a vision for priorities for such reforms from a human rights perspective. See for example, 'Memorandum on the Development of Joint Arab Action' signed by 37 organisations working in the field of human rights in nine Arab countries, including four regional organisations to the Secretary General of LAS and Chairman of the Committee for the development of joint Arab action at the Arab League, charged with preparing a plan for LAS reform to be presented to the next Arab Summit. Text of the memorandum is available through: http://www.cihrs.org/?p=1892&lang=en, accessed on 14 July 2012.

development of joint Arab action mechanisms', which refers to a wide reform of the Arab League.[8]

This chapter therefore aims to provide an exposé of LAS as an intergovernmental organisation at a crossroads. It has taken some steps recently, but it lacks coherent and consistent directions and policies in relation to human rights. The focus of the chapter is purely the bodies and instruments that are particularly related to human rights. To do this, the chapter starts with a short introduction to the main bodies of LAS, followed by a discussion of the development of the main human rights standards, with a reference to how these relate to international human rights law. The chapter ends with illustrations of positions that LAS has adopted in relation to the 'Arab Spring'.

Recognising that there is very little literature analysing LAS's work from a human rights perspective, especially in English, this chapter can only provide an overview in order to capture important points which partly delineate recent developments in the organisation. It does not attempt to be a comprehensive analysis.

2 Main bodies of LAS relevant to human rights

Like other intergovernmental organisations, the bodies of LAS fall in three groupings:

(a) political bodies (e.g. the Summit, Council, Ministerial Councils, Commission on Human Rights);
(b) expert bodies (e.g. the Arab Human Rights Committee); and finally
(c) the Secretariat and its different Departments and Units.

While such distinction is present in theory, the dominance of political considerations and centres of power – which may vary depending on the subject or the country – is still a dominant factor influencing much of the dynamics within these structures and between them.

2.1 Political bodies

LAS is composed of the Council, specialised Ministerial Councils and Committees, and specialised agencies.[9] The Council, which is formed of representatives from each member state, is the chief decision-making organ. In a recent Summit resolution, it was decided that the Council can meet at three levels: (a) summits of heads of states; (b) ministers of foreign affairs; or (c) permanent representatives to LAS. In the same resolution, it was decided that summits of LAS are to be held regularly every year (while previously summits were not regulated or institutionalised).[10]

Article 4 of the LAS Charter also provides for the creation of special committees which are responsible for studying subjects of common significance and for drafting agreements. LAS

---

8 This decision has subsequently been reiterated by various bodies of LAS. See for example LAS Council Resolution 7202, Council Regular Session 133, 3 March 2010, adopting Recommendations of the Arab Commission on Human Rights, Regular Session 28, 26–30 January 2010.

9 For LAS organisational structure, see http://www.lasportal.org/ (under 'About Us'), accessed on 3 May 2012.

10 LAS Summit Decision 198, 'Decision Adding an Annex to the Charter of the League Concerning the Regular Convening of Summits of the League', 22 October 2000.

also has Ministerial Councils for various issues including justice, interior, social welfare, media and information. These have adopted many important decisions pertaining to human rights, as will be discussed below. Use of force for settlement of disputes among member states, aggression or threat of aggression against a member state, are prohibited. Therefore the Charter establishes a procedure of arbitration and mediation.[11] The LAS Charter also provides for the withdrawal and exclusion of a member state from the organisation.[12]

The Arab Economic and Social Council ('Arab ECOSOC') was established by LAS in 1953. In January 2005, Arab ECOSOC adopted Resolution 1540 on 'Criteria for Attendance of Civil Society Organisations in Meetings of ECOSOC and its Bodies'.[13] In 2009, 2011 and 2013 special 'Economic and Social Development Summits' were convened. In 1968, the Council approved the creation of a permanent body to be called the Arab Commission on Human Rights, also known as the Arab Standing Committee for Human Rights or the Permanent Arab Commission on Human Rights.[14] This is formed of one representative from each LAS member state, who attends as a state representative and not as an independent expert. In September 2007, the Commission adopted its own Rules of Procedures (while before that it applied rules of procedures that applied to the technical committees), which were endorsed by the LAS Council of Ministers.[15] According to the Rules of Procedures, the main role of the Commission is to:

(a) establish rules of cooperation among LAS member states in the field of human rights;
(b) formulate an Arab position on human rights issues that are under discussion at the regional and international levels, including positions on draft treaties;
(c) draft human rights treaties to be presented to the LAS Council of Ministers or the Summit for ratification;
(d) study Arab agreements pertaining to human rights in order to give an opinion on their compatibility with international human rights principles and standards; and
(e) promote cooperation in the field of human rights education.

The Commission also studies matters referred to it by the LAS Council, Secretary General or member states.

The Rules provide that on the nomination of representatives, states should give due consideration to expertise in human rights but does not require it. The Commission does not have a mechanism to receive or examine periodic reports from states on human rights situations. It also does not have thematic or country special procedures. A group of experts, initially created as a sub-commission, is appointed to assist the Commission in its work, by preparing proposals (see further below).

The Arab Commission on Human Rights was the first body within LAS to adopt a mechanism to allow non-governmental organisations (NGOs) to attend its sessions. In 2003, the

---

11 LAS Charter (n. 3) Arts 5–6.
12 Ibid., Art. 18.
13 Many elements of these criteria were adapted for the criteria of observer status of the Arab Commission on Human Rights (see below).
14 Not to be confused with the Arab Commission for Human Rights, an NGO founded in 1998.
15 See Mervat Rishmawi, 'Human Rights Commission of the Arab States' in *Max Planck Encyclopaedia of Public International Law* (OUP/Max Planck Institute for Comparative Public Law and International Law, 2010).

Commission adopted the procedures and criteria for granting observer status for NGOs.[16] While the Commission states that it engages with NGOs, in reality the observer status is very limited. NGOs have only limited and untimely access to documentation, and have limited access to sessions and deliberations. They are not allowed to make statements on agenda items. Although many NGOs have applied to obtain this observer status, only 23 from across the Arab countries have obtained this status as the criteria are very restrictive. They include that the NGO must be registered in an Arab country, which is often not possible due to the restrictive associations' laws in many Arab countries. In fact, a large number of active human rights NGOs in Arab countries have either been denied registration by their national governments, or have not been able to register due to restrictive laws.[17]

The Commission has very few major achievements to record. It adopted the revised version of the Arab Charter on Human Rights (discussed below), although it has made significant negative changes to the draft. It has also adopted the Arab Human Rights Education Plan.[18] The structure of the Commission as a political body and its narrow mandate are considered major hindrances towards its active engagement in human rights concerns in the region. The Commission is serviced by a special Human Rights Directorate in the Secretariat of LAS.

2.2 The Parliament and the Court

A newly established Arab Parliament is still in its nascent phases. The LAS Charter also allows for the establishment of an Arab Court of Justice, but this is yet to materialise. The Baghdad Summit in March 2012 adopted the Statute of the Arab Parliament, which was previously endorsed by the Council of Ministers of Foreign Affairs.[19] The Arab Parliament is an addition to the structure of LAS through an added article to the LAS Charter which provides: '[a]n Arab Parliament shall be established in the framework of LAS, and its rules of procedure, composition, functions and areas of competence shall be defined'.[20] The Statute makes the Parliament a relatively weak body. It is not given the mandate to draft agreements, but can approve agreements referred to the Parliament. Issues for discussion can be referred to it by the Council or any of the other Councils of Ministers or Committees. Its work focuses on issuing recommendations that have to be approved by a Ministerial Council or a Summit.

---

16 See 'The Arab League and Human Rights: Challenges Ahead' – Regional Seminar held in Cairo on 16–17 February 2013, FIDH, 27–28, available at http://www.fidh.org/for-an-effective-arab-league-human-rights-protection-system-las-secretary-12932, accessed on 5 June 2013.

17 This is documented and criticised widely by UN mechanisms and NGOs. See for example the Euro-Mediterranean Human Rights Network, 'Freedom of Association in the Euro-Mediterranean Region: A Threatened Civil Society' (2010), available at: http://www.euromedrights.org/en/publications-en/emhrn-publications/emhrn-publications-2010/4758.html, accessed on 14 July 2012.

18 The text of the Plan is available in Arabic on the Childs Rights International Network's website at: http://www.crin.org/resources/infodetail.asp?id=19376, accessed on 14 July 2012.

19 LAS Summit Decision 559, Regular Session 23, 29 March 2012 (the Statute is annexed to the decision). This became Art. 19 of the amended Charter of the League of Arab States.

20 LAS Summit Decision 290, 'Development of the Joint Arab Collaboration System: Amendments to some Articles of the Charter of the League of Arab States', Regular Session 17, 23 March 2005; and LAS Summit Decision 292, 'Development of the Joint Arab Collaboration System: Establishment of an Interim Arab Parliament', Regular Session 17, 23 March 2005. The Article about the Parliament became Art. 19 in the revised Charter of LAS.

The Parliament can question Ministerial Councils, the Secretary General, senior staff of the Secretariat or the specialised agencies, who must respond to such questions. Importantly, the Parliament is mandated to develop Arab cooperation in the field of human rights and present recommendations accordingly.[21] Also the Parliament has a primary role in leading efforts to unify Arab legislation and to give guidance in that regard. The Parliament is composed of four members for each member state of LAS. These individuals are either to be elected directly from their national parliaments, or otherwise chosen or appointed from their own national parliament or similar national assemblies. The Arab Parliament now has a Committee on Legal and Human Rights Affairs.

Although Article 19 of the original LAS Charter (Article 20 of the amended LAS Charter) provides for the creation of an Arab Court of Justice,[22] this has yet to materialise. The first attempt to create a regional judicial body was presented to LAS in 1950 by Lebanon. The Council decided to present the proposal to its Political Committee and to form a Committee to suggest a statute for the Court and any amendments to the Charter of the League.[23] The idea was then abandoned for some decades, and only discussed again in 1990 at the extraordinary session of LAS at Summit level. At this session, it was agreed that the Council of Ministers of Foreign Affairs must conclude a study of the draft Statute of the Arab Court of Justice. In 1996, the Summit agreed to establish the Arab Court of Justice in principle and charged Ministers of Foreign Affairs with the completion of the final draft of its Statute.[24] A draft Statute was finalised shortly after that and submitted to the Council of LAS, but the consideration of the draft has been periodically postponed by the Council. In 2005, the Secretary General made a number of proposals to the Summit in relation to reform of LAS, including a proposal of the Statute of the Arab Court of Justice. Interestingly, the proposal of the Secretary General in 2005 gave the Court the jurisdiction to look into disputes pertaining to human rights.[25] The Summit reviewed the proposals and tasked the Secretary General to establish specialised committees with two representatives from each member state to consider the proposal for the Court and for an Arab Security Council.[26] There has been no progress in in relation to creation an Arab Court of Justice as at the time of this writing.

However, in 2011, Bahrain proposed the creation of an Arab Court on Human Rights within the LAS system. This was discussed in the Council at the level of Ministers of Foreign Affairs, and then at the Summit level.[27] An evaluation of the idea was prepared by experts, and the idea was discussed further in a special conference of member states, hosted by Bahrain. The outcome of this came before of the Summit in March 2013, which took a decision to endorse the idea of establishing the Court. Discussion is underway at the time of writing on

---

21 See LAS Summit Decision 559, 'Adoption of the Statute of the Arab Parliemant', Regular Session 23, 29 March 2013.
22 (n. 3).
23 LAS Council Resolution 316, Regular Session 12, 13 April 1950, and then in 1952, the question was raised again but was postponed. LAS Council Resolution 381, Regular Session 15, 3 October 1951, and LAS Council Resolutions 432, Regular Session 16, 14 September 1952,
24 LAS Summit Decision 196, 'Arab Court of Justice, Honour Charter for Security and Cooperation, League of Arab States Mechanism for Conflict Prevention and Arab Union Proposal', 23 June 1996.
25 LAS Summit Decision 294, 'Development of the Joint Arab Action System: Further Study of the Proposed Arab Court of Justice and Arab Security Council', Regular Session 17, 23 March 2005.
26 Ibid.
27 Council Resolution 7372, 13 September 2011, and Council Resolution 7489, 10 March 2012.

whether the Arab Charter on Human Rights is now a suitable normative framework for the Court, or whether the Arab Charter on Human Rights will need to be revised first. Further discussion on mandate, rules of procedures, composition of the Court and other such matters will also have to take place.[28]

In 1990, the Council of LAS recommended the establishment of an Arab Centre for Human Rights, and asked the Secretariat to elaborate a proposal for that objective. However, in 1988, the Arab ECOSOC had recommended that LAS should reduce its expenditure. Therefore, the idea of the Centre was abandoned and a Human Rights Directorate was established in 1992. The main role of this Directorate today is to service the Commission and it is also meant to carry out activities in the field of human rights.

2.3 Expert bodies

2.3.1 The Arab Human Rights Committee and the Arab Charter on Human Rights

The Arab Human Rights Committee is the treaty-body that is entrusted with supervising the implementation of the Arab Charter on Human Rights. The Arab Charter was adopted by the Summit in Tunisia in 2004.[29] This is a revised version of an old treaty that was adopted by LAS in 1994 but it did not enter into force due to insufficient ratification.[30] The 1994 version was widely criticised for falling far below international standards.[31]

The process of revising the Charter was important in itself. A previously existing Memorandum of Intent between LAS and the UN Office of the High Commissioner for Human Rights (OHCHR) was used by OHCHR and the civil society to convince LAS to appoint a team of independent experts to provide their recommendations for the drafting of the revised Charter.[32] This Committee was therefore formed of members from Arab countries in various UN human rights mechanisms.[33] This Committee reviewed the provisions of the 1994 version of the Charter and relied in its redrafting on international human rights standards as well as regional instruments, studies and suggestions by its members in their own areas of expertise, and oral and written interventions by national,

---

28 LAS Summit Decision 573, 'Establishment the Arab Court on Human Rights', Regular Session 24, 26 March 2013.

29 Arab Charter on Human Rights (adopted 22 May 2004, entered into force 15 March 2008), available at: http://www1.umn.edu/humanrts/instree/loas2005.html, accessed on 14 July 2012.

30 Adopted by Council Resolution 5437, 15 September 1994.

31 See for example M. Rishmawi: 'The Arab Charter on Human Rights: A Comment', in 'Islam and Human Rights', 10(1) *Interights Bulletin* (1996).

32 'Effective Functioning of Human Rights Mechanisms: Regional Arrangements for the Promotion and Protection of Human Rights – Report of the Secretary-General', 22 December 2004, UN Doc. E/CN.4/2005/104, paras 38–40.

33 The members of the committee were: Hatem Kotrane, Tunisia, member of the Committee on the Rights of the Child (CRC) and independent expert to examine the question of a draft Optional Protocol to the International Covenant on Economic, Social and Cultural Rights; Ibrahim al-Shaddi, Saudi Arabia, CRC Committee member; Leila Zerrougui, Algeria, Chairperson of the Working Group on Arbitrary Detention and member of the Sub-Commission on the Promotion and Protection of Human Rights; Ghalia Mohammed Bin Hamad Al-Thani, Qatar, CRC Committee member; and Ahmed Tawfiq Khalil, Egypt, member of the Human Rights Committee. Leila Zerrougui was chair of the Committee.

regional and international NGOs.[34] The final draft produced by the experts was welcomed widely by the civil society in the region. The draft was presented to the Arab Commission on Human Right for adoption. However, unfortunately, the Commission made fundamental changes rendering the document in conflict with international law in some important areas, and lacking in important guarantees in others. Nevertheless, the Commission maintained some very important provisions from the experts' draft, which in any case makes the 2004 version of the Charter a much better document than the 1994 version, despite its many shortcomings.[35]

It is not possible here to include a full review of the revised Arab Charter of Human Rights; however, some highlights will be helpful.[36] On the positive aspect, Article 1 starts with emphasising the importance of human rights, including stressing the principle that 'all human rights are universal, indivisible, interdependent and interrelated'.[37] The Charter recognises many important rights including the rights to health, education, fair trial, prohibition of torture and ill-treatment, the independence of the judiciary, the right to liberty and security of person, equality before the law, courts and tribunals. Other political rights include the right to political participation including the right to take part in the conduct of public affairs.

Despite these positive elements and many others, the Charter excludes some important rights and guarantees, and also includes provisions which are inconsistent with international law. The following are only selected examples. The Charter does not prohibit cruel, inhuman or degrading treatment or punishment, nor does it recognise the rights to non-citizens in many areas, for example, health and education, as it limits many rights to citizens (unlike international and other regional treaties which recognise most rights to everyone under the jurisdiction of the state). One of the examples where the Charter is in clear conflict with international law is in relation to freedom of thought, conscience, and religion. The Charter allows for regulating these rights according to national law (Article 30). International law, on the other hand, allows for restrictions only on the manifestation aspect of a religion, thought, conscience or belief, but not on the freedom to hold an opinion, religion or belief, as is evident for example in Articles 18(3) and 19(3) of the International Covenant on Civil and Political Rights (ICCPR).[38] The ICCPR does not provide for regulating (i.e. limiting) by national law the right to hold an opinion, religion or belief. Article 19(3) of the ICCPR provides: 'The exercise of the rights provided for in paragraph 2 of this article carries with it special duties and responsibilities. It may therefore be subject to certain restrictions.'

Moreover, the Charter leaves the regulation of many important rights to national legislation. For example, Article 7(1) permits the imposition of the death penalty against

---

34 For background information about the revision process of the Charter, see M. Rishmawi, 'The Revised Arab Charter on Human Rights: A Step Forward?' (2005) 5(2) *Human Rights Law Review* 361–76.

35 For a full documentation of the process see (in Arabic) Mo'taz alFigiri (ed.), *La Himaya Li Ahad (No Protection to Anyone): the Role of the League of Arab States in Protecting Human Rights* (2006).

36 For a thorough analysis of the Arab Charter on Human Rights, see M. Rishmawi, 'The Revised Arab Charter on Human Rights' in C. Krause and M. Scheinin (eds), *International Protection of Human Rights: A Text Book* (Turku/Abo, second revised edition, 2012).

37 Arab Charter on Human Rights (n. 29) Art. 1(4).

38 International Covenant on Civil and Political Rights (adopted 16 December 1966, entered into force 23 March 1976) 999 UNTS 171.

children if national law allows it, while international law prohibits the imposition of the death penalty on children under the age of 18 in all circumstances. Indeed, Article 6(5) of the ICCPR provides that: 'Sentence of death shall not be imposed for crimes committed by persons below eighteen years of age'; and Article 37(a) of the Convention on the Rights of the Child[39] (CRC) provides that: 'Neither capital punishment nor life imprisonment without possibility of release shall be imposed for offences committed by persons below eighteen years of age.' The Charter in Article 33(1) also leaves regulation of rights and responsibilities of men and women in marriage and divorce to national law. Article 23(4) of the ICCPR and Article 16 of the Convention on the Elimination of All Forms of Discrimination against Women[40] (CEDAW) require states to take measures to ensure equality in rights and responsibilities, and not only to regulate these in law. National law therefore has to be consistent with international law.[41]

It can therefore be concluded that the Charter ended up being a document that mirrors the human rights record of some dominant Arab states and the degree to which they accept international human rights treaties, as reflected in the reservations entered by them to international instruments (e.g. ICCPR, CRC, CEDAW). Unlike other regional mechanisms, the Arab Charter on Human Rights does not have individual or collective complaint mechanisms. This is particularly important in the light of the lack of any specific procedures within the Arab League human rights system to consider complaints related to human rights (for example in special procedures). Unlike other international and regional treaties, the Charter does not include clear provisions detailing state obligations. Instead, Article 44 provides this in very general terms stating '[t]he states parties undertake to adopt, in conformity with their constitutional procedures and with the provisions of the present Charter, whatever legislative or non-legislative measures that may be necessary to give effect to the rights set forth herein.'

The Arab Charter entered into force on 15 March 2008, two months after seven Arab states ratified it, pursuant to paragraph 2 of Article 49 of the Charter. By May 2013 11 states, half of the Arab states members in LAS, had ratified the Charter.[42] According to Article 48, initial reports are to be submitted after one year of entry of the Charter into force in the state party, and periodic reports every three years for review by the Arab Human Rights Committee. By the end of May 2013 Jordan, Algeria, Bahrain and Qatar had submitted their initial reports, although initial reports of all other state parties were already overdue. The Committee has reviewed the reports of Jordan, Algeria and Bahrain by May 2013, and issued its conclusions and recommendations regarding Jordan and Algeria (in Arabic), according to Article 48 of the Charter.[43]

---

39 Convention on the Rights of the Child (adopted 20 November 1989, entered into force 2 September 1990) 1577 UNTS 3.

40 Convention on the Elimination of All Forms of Discrimination against Women (adopted 18 December 1979, entered into force on 3 September 1981) UNGA Res. 34/180.

41 See further CEDAW Committee, 'General Recommendation No. 21: Equality in Marriage and Family Relations' (1994) UN Doc. A/47/38, paras 16–17.

42 Jordan, Bahrain, Algeria, Palestine, Syria, Libya, United Arab Emirates, Saudi Arabia, Yemen, Qatar and Lebanon, see ICNL, NGO Law Monitor: League of Arab States, available at: http://www.icnl.org/research/monitor/las.html.

43 For details about the Arab Charter on Human Rights, ratifications, state reports, sessions and work of the Arab Committee on Human Rights, see website of the League of Arab States at http://www.arableagueonline.org/wps/portal/las_ar/home_page, accessed on 1 April 2012.

The Arab Charter on Human Rights is the first, and so far the only, treaty in LAS to have an independent supervisory mechanism embodied in the treaty itself. The Secretary General of LAS, on the occasion of the fourth anniversary of the Arab Human Rights Day, recognised that the Arab Charter for Human Rights falls short of meeting international human rights standards, and that revising and amending it has become a pressing requirement that cannot be overlooked.[44]

2.3.2 The Committee of Experts assisting the Arab Commission on Human Rights

A Committee of Experts was established in 2007 to assist the Arab Commission on Human Rights.[45] It was initially established as a sub-Commission on Human Rights, mandated to develop a proposal for the Human Rights Education Plan for 2009–14, and then follow up the Plan and its implementation. The name of the sub-commission was changed in 2010 into a Committee of Experts of the Arab Commission on Human Rights. The mandate of the Committee of Experts was expanded to include preparation of studies upon the request of the Commission or the Secretariat and to make other proposals for the Commission on its own initiative.[46]

In 2012, the Council of LAS approved the recommendation of the Commission to end the work of the Committee of Experts, and ask an expert committee to supervise the implementation of the Human Rights Education Plan.[47] The Committee of Experts produced a Plan of Action and guidelines for implementation of the Plan in a form of a manual based on their expertise and information from governments. On 29 March 2007, the Summit of the Arab League approved the Arab Human Rights Education Plan for 2009–14.[48] The Plan's goal is stated to be to raise future generations that believe in a respect for human rights based on the basic principles of human rights: universality, complementarily and interdependency, equality and participation. The Plan provides that it is based on the main international and Arab human rights instruments besides the main values of Islam, Christianity and Judaism. The objectives of the Plan are:

1. integrating human rights values into education in the Arab world at all levels;
2. capacity-building to ensure specialisation in human rights education;
3. providing a suitable environment for the implementation of the Plan; and
4. encouraging social involvement.

The Plan identifies a number of bodies that should be involved in furthering human rights education in each Arab country including a wide range of governmental institutions and ministries. It also stresses the importance of the work of civil society.

---

44 See statement by Nabil al-Arabi, LAS Secretary General: 'al-Arabi calls for dignified life for Arab peoples in the occasion of the Arab Human Rights Day', 15 March 2012.
45 Pursuant to LAS Council Resolution 391, 29 March 2007.
46 See agenda item 5 of the Report of the Commission for Human Rights, 26–30 January 2010, approved in LAS Council Resolution 7202, Regular Session 133, 2–3 March 2010.
47 LAS Council Resolution 7488, Regular Session 137, 10 March 2012, approving recommendations of Session 32 of the Arab Commission on Human Rights.
48 (n. 18).

3 LAS and international law

The Charter of the League of Arab States does not include reference to human rights. Attempts to make such inclusion in the past were always delayed until there is reform of the organisation. There are few instances in the past, before the latest developments within the context of the events in the Middle East in the last three years, which became commonly referred to as the 'Arab Spring', when LAS made reference to international law in its documents and decisions. For example, following the outbreak of hostilities between Israel and Hezbollah on 12 July 2006, the Ministerial Council convened extraordinarily on 15 July 2006 and issued two resolutions.[49] Both resolutions refrained from addressing Hezbollah's role or responsibilities in the conflict, but respectively condemned the Israeli aggression against the Palestinian territories and the Israeli aggression against Lebanon, and stated that the Israeli actions contravened international resolutions, laws and norms.

Before that, at an emergency Summit in August 1990, 12 of the 20 states present condemned the Iraqi invasion of Kuwait. In 2003, the Council of LAS voted 21–1 to adopt a resolution demanding the immediate and unconditional removal of US and British soldiers from Iraq (Kuwait cast the only dissenting vote). Shortly after the US-led invasion of Iraq on 19 March 2003, the Council of LAS adopted a resolution in which it condemned what it called the US–British aggression against Iraq, considered the action a violation of the UN Charter and customary international law, and a threat to international peace and security.[50] The resolution also demanded immediate and unconditional withdrawal of US and British troops, and held the latter responsible on a legal and moral basis. Notably, the resolution urged all Arab states to refrain from participating in any military action that affects the sovereignty and security of Iraqi territories or any other Arab state. Other resolutions followed to reiterate a similar position.

In September 2003, the Council adopted a resolution which reflected a clear shift in the stance of LAS regarding violations of international law committed by the previous regime in Iraq. Before that, LAS normally did not condemn violations by any Arab leaders or government policies or refrained from addressing violations in Arab countries by member states. This resolution considered the Iraqi transitional government a positive step towards the establishment of an internationally recognised national legitimate government and condemned gross violations of human rights and international law committed by the previous Iraqi regime against its people and detainees from Kuwait and other nationalities.[51] The resolution also called for bringing members of the former regime to justice.

3.1 LAS and the ICC

One of the important issues that LAS has been following closely is the situation in Darfur, Sudan. The Council of LAS affirmed on many occasions the importance of

---

49 LAS Council Resolution 6656, 'The Israeli Aggression against the Palestinian Territories', 15 July 2006, available in English in UN Doc. S/2006/582; LAS Council Resolution 6657, 'Critical New Developments relating to the Israeli Military Aggression against Lebanon', 15 July 2006, available in English in UN Doc. S/2006/582.

50 LAS Council Resolution 6266/119/2, 'The American/British Aggression against Fraternal Iraq and Its Implications for the Security and Safety of Neighbouring Arab States and Arab National Security', 24 March 2003, available in English in UN Doc. A/57/776.

51 LAS Council Resolution 6325, 'Development of Situation in Iraq', Regular Session 20, 9 September 2003.

the acceptance of Sudan of peacekeeping forces, that the situation should be resolved through Arab and African avenues, and rejected what it called 'the internationalisation of the situation in Sudan'.[52] LAS agreed to support the deployment of a peacekeeping force by the African Union, contributing to the personnel deployed in the force and supporting it financially. However, following the decision of the International Criminal Court (ICC) Prosecutor to issue the arrest warrant against President Omar Al-Bashir of Sudan, several bodies of LAS, including the Summit, issued resolutions rejecting the decision, stressing the integrity of Sudan, and claiming that the decision of the UN Security Council with regard to the situation in Darfur violated the UN Charter.[53] LAS also stated that the decision of the ICC Prosecutor violated the principle of state sovereignty; that the decision to issue an arrest warrant against a sitting head of state was a dangerous precedent which violated the Vienna Convention on Diplomatic Relations (1961) and principles of international customary law, and LAS requested member states to reconsider their position regarding the ICC.[54]

However, this strong position against the ICC came under challenge following changes in Tunisia and Egypt. A conference hosted in Doha, Qatar jointly by the ICC and LAS in May 2011 witnessed many statements on the importance of combating impunity and cooperating with the ICC. Arrest warrants had already been issued by the ICC against the previous president of Tunisia, as well as Qaddafi and members of his family. This was not disputed at all by LAS or any of its members. However, at the same time, LAS endorsed the solution of the Yemen situation according to a plan which was proposed by the Gulf Cooperation Council (GCC), and which included guarantees that President Saleh of Yemen will not stand trial for possible crimes he may be responsible for if he is to step down and leave the country. Saleh lives now in Saudi Arabia. Jordan, Djibouti and Comoros were the first Arab states to ratify the Rome Statute of the ICC. Tunisia, after the fall of the previous regime, announced its accession to the Rome Statute. Nabil al Arabi, the current LAS Secretary General, while Foreign Minister of Egypt, also announced the intention of Egypt to do the same, although this is yet to materialise.[55]

LAS has a number of model laws that are prepared by its legal department and endorsed by its political bodies. One such law is the Model Law on Crimes within the Jurisdiction of the ICC (2005).[56] While some of the provisions of this Model Law are largely consistent with the ICC Rome Statute, other provisions raise concerns. For example, Article 3 of the Model Law stipulates that the formulation of what it refers to as 'irrelevance of Official Capacity' – ('The person's official rank may not be used as a reason to exempt them from responsibility or mitigate the punishment') – is left to national law, pursuant to the legal

---

52 See for example LAS Council Resolution 7093, Regular Session 132, 9 September 2009, and earlier LAS Summit Decision 465, 30 March 2009.
53 See for example LAS Summit Decision 465, Regular Session 21, 30 March 2009. See also *Prosecutor v Al Bashir* (Warrant of Arrest) ICC-02/05–01/09–1 (4 March 2009). E.g. see P. Gaeta, 'Does President Al Bashir Enjoy Immunity from Arrest?', 7 *Journal of International Criminal Justice*, (2009) 315–32.
54 LAS Summit Decision 465 (n. 53).
55 See Human Rights Watch: 'Egypt: Important Commitment to Ratify Rome Statute', 29 April 2011.
56 See unofficial translation provided by the Coalition for the International Criminal Court, 'Decree regarding the Arab Model Law on Crimes within ICC Jurisdiction' (2005), available at: http://www.iccnow.org/documents/ArabLeague_ModelImplementationLaw_29Nov05_en.pdf, accessed on 14 July 2012.

system of each state.[57] The Model Law also provides that the death penalty can be imposed for crimes within the jurisdiction of the law, for example, in relation to genocide, crimes against humanity, war crimes and crimes of aggression.[58]

3.2 Universality of human rights

In 1998, the Arab Commission on Human Rights elaborated what it called the Guidelines on Universality of Human Rights.[59] The Guidelines affirm religious and cultural specificity and state sovereignty and seem to justify the selected respect for universal human rights on this pretext, as is often reflected through the engagement of Arab states in international mechanisms. The Guidelines provide that:

- the importance of considering religious, cultural and social specificity of the Arab states as contributions to the universality of human rights; at the same time, stressing that cultural specificity should not mean cultural alienation and shutting oneself away from other civilisations;
- human rights should not be used as a pretext for interference in internal affairs;
- the need for reaching an Arab understanding of human rights that is based on the concepts and principles of Islam;
- freedom of expression should be respected in a way that does not contradict Islamic Shari'a; and
- affirming the right of Arab states to enter reservations to international treaties.

It should be noted that the Charter of the League of Arab States itself does not refer to Islam. However, many of its associated documents, including human rights standards, refer to Islam as guidance. For example, the preamble of the Arab Charter on Human Rights provides that member states adopt the Charter '[i]n furtherance of the eternal principles of fraternity, equality and tolerance among human beings consecrated by the noble Islamic religion', and also 'having regard to the Cairo Declaration on Human Rights in Islam'. Many of the rights and guarantees that are provided in the Model Law for the Rights of Arab Child of the League of Arab States (see below) are largely framed within concepts in Islamic Shari'a in relation to many issues. This is the same in relation to punishment of crimes within the context of ICC and Rome Statute.

3.3 Children's rights

The main LAS instrument on treaty children's rights is the Charter of the Rights of the Arab Child (1983). It refers in its title to the rights of the Arab child, rather than being an Arab charter for the rights of all children in Arab countries.

The Charter of the Rights of the Arab Child has been criticised widely for being inconsistent with international law, particularly the CRC to which all Arab states are party

---

57 Ibid. Art. 3 which states that '[t]he person's official rank may not be used as a reason to exempt them from responsibility or mitigate the punishment'.

58 Ibid. Arts 10–13.

59 Adopted under item 1 by the Arab Commission on Human Rights, Regular Session 14, 23–24 February 1998.

except for Somalia and Palestine. According to the document, state reports are not to be presented to a specialised committee of experts, but are to be provided to the General Secretariat of LAS on measures they have taken to give effect to the Charter. There is no clear time-frame or format for such reports. The Committee of Experts of the Arab Commission on Human Rights was asked in 2009 to look into updating the treaty. However, the Secretariat recommended instead that states' reports to the CRC Committee on their implementation of the CRC and its two Optional Protocols must be strengthened. In the 2012 Summit, LAS adopted the Marrakech Declaration, which affirmed commitment to the CRC and its Protocols and adopted tools for advancing rights of children accordingly.[60] No mention or decision was made in connection with updating the Charter of the Rights of the Arab Child. It seems that this idea has been abandoned.

3.4 Freedom of expression

As mentioned earlier, the Arab Charter on Human Rights allows for imposing restrictions not only on the manifestation aspect of thought, conscience and belief, but on the freedom itself. The original draft by the Committee of Experts was consistent with international law. The changes were introduced when the draft was brought before the Arab Human Rights Commission, a political body. This indicates that such changes were introduced for political considerations. The Arab Convention on the Suppression of Terrorism[61] (see below) is also a threat to protection of freedom of thought and expression.

In February 2008, LAS introduced the Arab Satellite Broadcasting Charter: Principles for Regulating Satellite Broadcasting Transmission in the Arab World.[62] The document asserts in its Preface the necessity to preserve what it calls the 'Arab identity' and 'Arab culture' as well as 'Islamic culture and values'. Although these Principles state that their aim is to regulate broadcasting transmission and reception in Arab countries and 'to ensure the right to express opinions',[63] the document actually imposes a number of restrictions on the content of the material broadcast on the pretext of respect for human dignity and individual privacy, as well as prohibition on material that would incite hatred, violence and terrorism. While this is to be welcomed, the problem is in the how these general principles are reflected in the details of the provisions. For example, the document permits freedom of expression, but within the limits of broad and undefined notions like 'full responsibility, for the protection of the supreme interests of the Arab countries and the Arab World'.[64] The document also includes a number of provisions that mirror those that currently exist in Arab codes and which have been used consistently to silence critics of the state, among others. This includes provisions

---

60 LAS Summit Decision 565, Regular Session 23, 29 March 2012. LAS adopted the 2010 Marrakech Declaration of Arab Conference on Rights of the Child, see http://www.unicef.org/media/media_57288.html, accessed on 10 May 2013.
61 Arab Convention on the Suppression of Terrorism (adopted 22 April 1998), available at: http://www.unhcr.org/refworld/publisher,LAS,,,3de5e4984,0.html, accessed on 14 July 2012.
62 Arab Satellite Broadcasting Charter (2008). Text and unofficial English translation available at: http://www.arabmediasociety.com/?article=648, accessed on 14 July 2012. See Art. 19, 'Arab Charter for Satellite TV: A setback for freedom of expression' (2008), available at: http://www.article19.org/pdfs/press/egypt-adoption-of-the-arab-charter-for-satellite-tv.pdf, accessed on 14 July 2012.
63 Ibid. Art. 1.
64 Ibid. Art. 5(1).

relating to prohibition of the so-called defamation against leaders, religion, national symbols, and damaging social harmony and national unity.[65]

Finally, it should be noted that Arab states have played a negative role in the last few years within the UN Human Rights Council in an attempt to weaken international standards in relation to freedom of expression, including attempts to weaken the mandate of the UN Special Rapporteur on Freedom of Opinion and Expression. For example, Arab states repeatedly attempted to include undefined and broad concepts like 'defamation of religion', and 'respect for traditional values' in resolutions that relate to freedom of expression through proposals of the Organisation of Islamic States (OIC). While such attempts have not succeeded so far, the threat remains.[66]

3.5 Minorities and non-citizens

It is common that the language of resolutions, texts or instruments adopted by LAS is framed in relation to rights of Arab citizens or Arabs. There is very little attention to and recognition of rights of non-Arabs, including non-citizens. This is pertinent as some Arab countries, especially in the Gulf, have a large number of migrant workers. Also, ethnic and religious minorities, who may also not be Arab citizens, live in many parts of Arab countries. As discussed above, the Arab Charter on Human Rights limits several of its rights to citizens, rather than everyone within the jurisdiction of the state.

The League of Arab States has its own refugee convention: The Arab Convention on the Status of Refugees in the Arab Countries (1994).[67] The Convention provides that states parties 'shall undertake to exert every possible effort, to ensure that refugees are accorded a level of treatment no less than that accorded to foreign residents on their territories',[68] and that states must not discriminate against refugees as to race, religion, gender and country of origin, political or social affiliation.[69] The Convention does not include any specific provisions relating to rights, including rights to education and health. A separate protocol to the Charter of LAS was adopted in 1965, 'the Casablanca Protocol for the Treatment of Palestinian Refugees in Arab States'[70] to specifically regulate the status of Palestinian refugees. This protocol is considered to be one of the earliest regional attempts at refugee protection. The

---

65 A number of defamation cases, which resulted mostly in arbitrary detention and accompanied by various human rights violations, have been brought against critics of the state, journalists, bloggers and human rights activists. Concerns over these arrests and detentions have been raised by several UN mechanisms. See for example UNHCR, 'Report of the Special Rapporteur on the promotion and protection of the right to freedom of opinion and expression: Summary of cases transmitted to Governments and replies received' (27 May 2011) UN Doc. A/HRC/17/27/Add.1.

66 See Art. 19 and the Cairo Institute for Human Rights Studies, 'The Demise of "Defamation of Religions"? Human Rights Council Should Support Resolution On Religious Discrimination' (22 March 2011), available at: http://www.unhcr.org/refworld/pdfid/4d94294c2.pdf, accessed on 1 April 2012.

67 Arab Convention on the Status of Refugees in the Arab Countries (adopted by LAS, 1994), available at: http://www.unhcr.org/refworld/publisher,ARAB,,,4dd5123f2,0.html, accessed on 14 July 2012.

68 Ibid. Art. 5.

69 Ibid. Art. 7.

70 Protocol for the Treatment of Palestinians in Arab States (adopted 11 September 1965), available at: http://www.unhcr.org/refworld/country,,LAS,,SDN,456d621e2,460a2b252,0.html, accessed on 14 July 2012.

protocol mainly regulates entry and freedom of movement, but does not include specific provisions on many civil, political, economic, social and cultural rights.

Both the 1994 Arab Convention on the Status of Refugees and the 1964 Casablanca Protocol provide narrower protection than that provided under the 1951 UN Convention Relating to the Status of Refugees,[71] which in any case excludes from its protection Palestinian refugees who receive assistance from the United Nations Relief and Works Agency for Palestine Refugees in the Near East.[72] There is no treaty body that oversees the implementation of the Arab Convention on the Status of Refugees. According to Article 15 of the Convention, this is entrusted to the Secretary General of LAS, who may request information from states, including on laws, regulation and decisions. The Secretariat of LAS also includes a department that works on the situation of refugees.

3.6 Combating terrorism

The Arab Convention on the Suppression of Terrorism was adopted by the Council of Ministers of Justice in 1998.[73] To date it has been ratified by at least 16 of the member states. While it includes many provisions that are consistent with international law and standards, the Convention also includes many problematic provisions. It contains a very broad and widely criticised definition of terrorism.[74] It defines terrorism as:

> Any act or threat of violence, whatever its motives or purposes, that occurs in the advancement of an individual or collective criminal agenda and seeking to sow panic among people, causing fear by harming them, or placing their lives, liberty or security in danger, or seeking to cause damage to the environment or to public or private installations or property or to occupying or seizing them, or seeking to jeopardize national resources.[75]

Therefore, not only an act itself, but a threat of an act which may constitute an act of freedom of expression consistent with international law can be considered an act of terrorism. The Convention, while allowing arrest and detention, does not require that due process and fair trial guarantees be respected in respect of alleged terrorists. The Convention also allows for the imposition of the death penalty in cases that are not strictly limited to most serious crimes as is required by Article 6 of the ICCPR. It places further restrictions on freedom of expression and association. For example, provisions of the Convention could be interpreted to allow for censorship and interference with freedom of expression in the general civilian media, imposed

71 Convention relating to the Status of Refugees (adopted 28 July 1951, entered into force 22 April 1954) 189 UNTS 137.
72 Ibid. Art. 1(d) which states that the Convention 'shall not apply to persons who are at present receiving from organs or agencies of the United Nations other than the United Nations High Commissioner for Refugees protection or assistance.'
73 For a thorough analyses of the Arab Convention on the Suppression of Terrorism, including in relation to freedom of expression, see Amnesty International, 'The Arab Convention for the Suppression of Terrorism: A serious threat to human rights' (2002) IOR 51/001/2002. Available at: http://www.amnesty.org/fr/library/asset/IOR51/001/2002/en/d032efbb-d8a7-11dd-ad8c-f3d4445c118e/ior510012002en.html, accessed on 14 July 2012.
74 Ibid.
75 Arab Convention on the Suppression of Terrorism (n. 61) Art. 2.

or required by what is called in the Convention the 'security media services', on the pretext of 'security', which is not defined. The treaty also requires exchange of information and cooperation between states in the field of combating terror.

The definition of terrorism in the Arab Convention and many of its provisions is a replica of Egyptian legislation on the matter.[76] The UN Special Rapporteur on the promotion and protection of human rights and fundamental freedoms while countering terrorism has expressed concern over the Egyptian legislation, noting that the definition of terrorism in addition to violent acts extends to include 'any threat or intimidation' with the aim of 'disturbing the peace or jeopardizing the safety and security of the society' and contains a wide range of purposes, such as 'to prevent or impede the public authorities in the performance of their work or thwart the application of the Constitution or of laws or regulations'.[77] The Rapporteur expresses concern that this definition, including the substantial and intentional elements as well as its purposes, is notably broad and runs the risk of including acts that do not comprise a sufficient relation to violent terrorist crimes. Of particular concern to the Special Rapporteur are the offences beyond most serious crimes which may subject to the death penalty, based on the definition. The Special Rapporteur also expressed concern over the impact of the legislation on restricting freedom of expression, as well as work of human rights defenders and critics of the state.

The Arab Convention on the Suppression of Terrorism does not have supervision or reporting mechanisms. The Council of Arab Ministers of the Interior were entrusted with monitoring the implementation of this Convention. It is reported that under the auspices of Council of Ministers of Interior, several meetings of ministers and experts were convened to discuss ways to improve both cooperation among them and national responses to terrorism, as well as 'anti-terrorism panels'. For example, the Council hosted the sixth meeting of the Arab Anti-Terrorism Panel on 27–28 June 2008, where participants called on Arab states to implement the UN Global Counter-Terrorism Strategy, noting the emphasis the Strategy placed on capacity-building and technical assistance.[78] It is important to note that meetings of Council of Ministers of Interior are generally not accessible to NGOs, and the documentation and resolutions are not available on LAS's website.

---

76 The Penal Code in Law No. 974 of 18 July 1992, Arts 86–102 establish a number of terrorism-related offences and their corresponding penalties. The definition of terrorism, as provided for in Art. 86, extends to include 'any threat or intimidation' with the aim of 'disturbing the peace or jeopardizing the safety and security of the society' in addition to violent acts. Furthermore, it contains a wide range of purposes, such as 'to prevent or impede the public authorities in the performance of their work or thwart the application of the Constitution or of laws or regulations'. See more on this in UNHCR, 'Report of the Special Rapporteur on the promotion and protection of human rights and fundamental freedoms while countering terrorism' (14 October 2009) UN Doc. A/HRC/13/37/Add.2, para. 11.

77 UNHCR, 'Report of the Special Rapporteur on the promotion and protection of human rights and fundamental freedoms while countering terrorism' (14 October 2009) UN Doc. A/HRC/13/37/Add.2, para. 11.

78 E. Rosand, A. Millar, J. Ipe and M. Healey, 'The UN Global Counter-Terrorism Strategy and Regional and Subregional Bodies: Strengthening a Critical Partnership' (Center on Global Counterterrorism Cooperation, 2008), available at: http://www.globalct.org/images/content/pdf/reports/strengthening_a_critical_partnership.pdf, accessed on 14 July 2012. For UN Global Counter-Terrorism Strategy (2006) UN Doc. A/RES/60/288, see http://www.un.org/terrorism/strategy-counter-terrorism.shtml, accessed on 10 May 2013.

In 2006, the Council of Ministers of the Interior adopted a programme in the field of training and cooperation to combat terrorism that is largely based on the Arab Convention. The Arab Bureau of Criminal Policing, an LAS body, is mandated to collect regular information and reports from states about their implementation of the treaty and their efforts in this regard.

4 LAS and the Arab Spring

The position of LAS on human rights violations leads to, and in the context of the events during what is referred to as the 'Arab Spring' reveals, an inconsistent approach by the organisation to the various countries' human rights situations. Importantly, the Arab Spring reveals that the positions taken are not necessarily driven by a coherent and consistent human rights policy, but are largely politically motivated.[79] Further, what is very important to note is that the steps taken by LAS in the context of the increasing human rights violations concerns were taken by the political bodies of LAS, and not by the human rights bodies.

From the start of the events in Tunisia, Egypt and other Arab countries, several general statements were issued by the previous Secretary General, calling on states to respect freedom of speech and peaceful assembly, to resort to dialogue and to refrain from the use of excessive and lethal force towards the demonstrators who were exercising their legitimate rights.

4.1 Egypt

Initially, LAS called for an inquiry into violent events in Tahrir Square in Cairo, Egypt[80] when demonstrators were violently attacked and welcomed the announcement of President Mubarak that he would not run for another term of office. LAS then issued a statement congratulating the Egyptian people on their peaceful revolution, which is expected to have an impact on the rest of the region, the statement said.[81]

4.2 Libya[82]

In February 2011, LAS suspended Libya's right to participate in all the bodies and meetings of the organisation in protest at violence against civilians.[83] On 12 March 2011, the Council of the League, meeting in an extraordinary session, while recognising the position of the Gulf

---

79 The Arab League's conflicting positions are believed by commentators to be due to the disproportionate long-standing influence of Saudi Arabia over the pan-Arab organisation; while in the past: regional policies were largely determined by an axis consisting of the US and Israel on one hand, and Egypt and Saudi Arabia on the other, with the former two using the latter two to implement their policies. See for example Inter Press Service, A. Morrow and K. Moussa Al-Omrani, 'Two-faced Arab League losing ground' (23 April 2011), available at: http://www.ipsnews.net/2011/04/two-faced-arab-league-losing-ground/, accessed on 14 July 2012.
80 Statement of the Secretary General of the League of Arab States, 3 February 2011.
81 Statement of the Secretary General of the League of Arab States, 3 February 2011.
82 The reaction of LAS towards Libya's emerging situation was different from that of Tunisia and Egypt. In addition to the reaction of the Libyan Regime to demonstrators with brutal force, at the time of the revolution in 2011, the Libyan leader Muammar al-Qaddafi had made an enemy of almost every Arab regime, and Libyan authorities have historically stood against many initiatives within LAS.
83 LAS Council Statement no. 136, Extraordinary Session, 22 February 2011.

Cooperation Council (GCC), the European Union and the African Union on the situation in Libya, and on basis of the recent previous resolution of LAS on the Libya, decided to ask the UN Security Council to impose a 'no-fly zone' as a preventative measure to protect the civilians. The Council also decided that LAS will cooperate and coordinate with the Interim National Council.[84]

Full membership status was restored on 27 August 2011 when the Libyan Transitional Council was considered the representative of the Libyan people in LAS.[85] UN Security Council Resolution 1973, which builds on LAS resolutions, authorises 'all necessary measures' to protect civilians in Libya, while excluding a foreign occupation force of any form on any part of Libyan territory.[86] A coalition of North Atlantic Treaty Organization (NATO) allies and Arab partners began an operation which is said to be for 'enforcing an arms embargo, maintaining a no-fly zone and protecting civilians and civilian populated areas from attack or the threat of attack in Libya'.[87]

4.3 Bahrain

The Council approved the initiative of the King of Bahrain to resolve conflict through dialogue, rejected any foreign interference in its internal affairs, but justified the entry of the Gulf Shield Forces (primarily from Saudi Arabia) into Bahrain on the basis of the joint security and defence agreement between GCC members. LAS did not condemn the excessive use of force against demonstrators. It only expressed its sorrow for the falling of victims.[88] LAS welcomed the establishment of the Bahrain Independent Commission of Inquiry but did not comment on the outcome of the Commission's investigation, conclusions and report, which has blamed the government for the use of lethal force, as well as pointing to the shared responsibility of the government and the opposition in the escalation of events.[89]

84 LAS Council Resolution 7360, Extraordinary Session, 12 March 2011.
85 LAS Council Resolution 7370, Extraordinary Session, 27 August 2011.
86 UNSC Res. 1973 (17 March 2011) UN Doc. S/RES/1973.
87 See NATO, 'NATO and Libya', available at http://www.nato.int/cps/en/natolive/topics_71652. htm, accessed on 14 July 2012. It is argued that that the decisions taken against Libya within LAS were to facilitate other interests, mainly of NATO, which wanted to avoid the Iraq scenario. This is why it was essential for NATO to have the Arab decisions and backing first so that it could say that it was only implementing the wish of Arab governments.
88 See Agence France-Presse, 'Arab uprisings put off Baghdad summit until 2012' (5 May 2011): 'An Arab summit due to be held in Baghdad next week has been postponed until March 2012, the Arab League chief and Iraq's foreign minister announced on Thursday, after Gulf calls for it to be scrapped'.
89 The Independent Commission of Inquiry concluded that, 'there is no doubt that what occurred in February/March [2011], and subsequently, was the result of an escalating process in which both the Government and the opposition have their share of responsibility in allowing events to unfold as they did.' The Commission adds that '[t]he forceful confrontation of demonstrators involving the use of lethal force and resort to a heavy deployment of Public Security Forces led to the death of civilians. This caused a marked increase in the number of persons participating in protests and led to a palpable escalation in their demands.' See 'Report of the Bahrain Independent Commission of Inquiry' (Manama, Bahrain, 23 November 2011) paras 1690–91. Available at http://www.bici.org. bh/BICIreportEN.pdf, accessed on 14 July 2012.

4.4 *Yemen*

LAS's position on Yemen has been weak, calling for a peaceful transition of power, condemning 'crimes against civilians' and requesting concerted efforts to safeguard national unity and the right to freedom of expression.[90] On 23 March 2011, the LAS Council condemned 'crimes against civilians' in Yemen and urged the government to deal with the people's demands in a 'peaceful manner', called for concerted efforts to safeguard national unity and the right to free expression. A call for dialogue and 'democratic methods' to deal with the demands of the Yemeni people in a peaceful manner was also launched.[91]

In April 2012, LAS announced its support for the initiative of the GCC to reach a peaceful solution to the crisis in Yemen. This marked a setback to international justice as the GCC initiative embodied in it a formula for impunity for President Saleh, where he was allowed to leave the country in exchange for transfer of power, with guarantees that he would not be brought to justice.[92]

4.5 *Syria*

LAS met in relation to the situation of Syria in a number of regular and irregular sessions, considered a record for LAS as the bodies of the organisation have never considered the human rights situation in a member state so frequently. The approach of LAS towards Syria was more elaborate and marks a shift towards a more proactive role. Beyond condemnation of the use of lethal force and calls for respect for freedom of speech and peaceful assembly, LAS initially approved a four-step agreement with Russia which included: a call for cessation of violence by all parties; the acceptance of an independent monitoring mechanism; the rejection of international intervention; and enabling access to humanitarian assistance.

In October 2011, LAS agreed with the Syrian President a plan which called for: the cessation of violence by all parties; release of all detainees arrested in the context of the crisis; removal of all arms from residential areas; and allowing LAS organisations and all media to access Syria freely.[93] In November 2011, in the light of Syria's lack of cooperation with the above the LAS Council voted to suspend Syria's right to participate in its meetings and impose sanctions if the Syrian regime failed to stop violence against protesters. The same resolution provided for the imposition of economic and political sanctions.[94]

LAS decided to send an observer mission to Syria,[95] which was widely criticised by NGOs and some LAS bodies including the Parliament and the Arab Human Rights Committee for lacking clear guidance and equipment. The Council also adopted a resolution in which it asked the Secretary General to contact international organisations concerned with human rights, 'including the United Nations', if the bloodshed in Syria continued.[96] On 12 February 2012, the Council of LAS adopted a resolution in which it called on the UN Security Council to adopt a resolution to deploy an Arab–International peacekeeping force to oversee a

---

90 LAS Council Statement 140, 22 March 2011.
91 LAS Council Resolution 7597, Regular Session 139, 6 March 2013.
92 LAS Summit Decision 555, Regular Session 23, 29 March 1202.
93 LAS Council Resolution 7436, Irregular Session, 2 November 2011.
94 LAS Council Resolution 7438, Extraordinary Session, 12 November 2011.
95 Pursuant to LAS Council Resolution 7438, Extraordinary Session, 12 November 2011.
96 LAS Council Resolution 7438, 12 November 2011, para. 2.

ceasefire agreement.[97] The same resolution affirms the continuation of the economic blockade which LAS adopted against Syria, and ends the mandate of its observer mission. By June 2012, the report of the mission had not been made public. The resolution also affirms that crimes committed by the government regime and forces are crimes under international law that must be punished.

On 23 February 2012, Kofi Annan was appointed Joint Special Envoy of the UN and LAS to provide good offices aimed at bringing an end to all violence and human rights violations, and promoting a peaceful solution to the Syrian crisis.[98] As annexed to Security Council Resolution 2042 of 14 April 2012, the Security Council adopted the six-point plan proposed by the Joint Envoy.[99] These requirements included that the Syrian Government ensure timely provision of humanitarian assistance; intensify the pace and scale of release of arbitrarily detained persons; ensure freedom of movement throughout the country for journalists; and respect freedom of association and the right to demonstrate peacefully.

On 21 April 2012, the Security Council adopted Resolution 2043 that set up the UN Supervision Mission in Syria (UNSMIS), initially for a period of 90 days and a deployment of up to 300 unarmed military observers and a civilian component.[100] However, on 16 June 2012, UNSMIS has suspended its activities owing to an intensification and escalation of armed violence across the country which was deemed to be limiting ability of the Mission to observe, verify, report as well as assist in local dialogue and stability projects as specified in its mandate.

On 3 July, the Arab League hosted a conference in Cairo for the various opposition groups in Syria. The participants affirmed that the political solution for the crisis in Syria starts with the Syrian president and those close to him leaving power. Participants affirmed their support to the Free Syrian Army, and to work towards unifying the leadership of the revolution.

In a very important and unprecedented decision, the Council then called on the Syrian president to leave power. It offered the assistance of the Arab League in securing for him and his family a safe exit. It called for forming a transitional government to lead a peaceful democratic transition.[101]

In a subsequent resolution the Council considered the crimes committed by the Syrian regime and its militias known as the Shabihha as crimes against humanity and called on the UN Security Council to ensure bringing those responsible to justice. At the same time it condemned violence and crimes against civilians by any party. The Council also welcomed the appointment of al-Akhdar al-Ibrahimi as a joint UN–Arab League envoy.[102]

In December 2012, in a statement, the Arab League Ministerial Committee on Syria welcomed the outcome of the meeting held by the Syrian National Coalition for the Revolution Forces and the Syrian opposition in Cairo and encouraged the establishment of a unified military command of the forces of the Syrian revolution, as well as establishing a framework for joint action between all the revolutionary actors through dialogue in order to manage the transition period as the legitimate representative of the Syrian people.[103]

In 2013, the League started to focus more on the issue of Syrian refugees. In January 2013, the League stressed the importance of implementation of previous resolutions for the support

97 LAS Council Resolution 7446, Extraordinary Session, 12 February 2012.
98 In accordance with UNGA Res. 66/253 (16 February 2011) UN Doc A/RES/66/253.
99 UNSC Res. 2042 (14 April 2012) UN Doc. S/RES/2042.
100 UNSC Res. 2043 (21 April 2012) UN Doc. S/RES/2043.
101 LAS Council Resolution 7510, Irregular Session, 22 July 2012.
102 LAS Council Resolution 7523, Regular Session 138, 5 September 2012.
103 Statement by the Arab Ministerial Committee on the situation in Syria 9 December 2012.

of neighbouring countries in their efforts to host and assist Syrian refugees, asked the Secretariat of LAS to coordinate with relevant UN agencies and bodies and with other relevant bodies to support Syrian refugees in order to ensure the provision of food, medical, health, water and other such services, and reaffirmed the importance of protection of Palestinian refugees.[104]

In the subsequent Regular session of the Council in March 2013, the Council asked the Syrian National Coalition to form an Executive Committee in order to occupy the seat of Syria in the League of Arab States and all its bodies, and to represent Syria in the Summit of LAS in Doha on 26–27 March 2013. An Arab League statement issued at the end of the meeting said that Arab states are free to offer military aid to rebels fighting President Assad. This was not included in the resolution itself.[105]

In the Summit of the League in March 2013, the Summit decided that the National Coalition for Syrian Revolutionary and Opposition Forces, as the sole representative of the Arab League and the counterpart of negotiations and discussions with the Arab League, will occupy the Seat of Syria in the Arab League and the meetings of its bodies until elections are carried to choose a representative government.[106]

5 Conclusion

It is important to understand LAS as an organisation that was formed by and consists of recently independent Arab states which lacked experience in governance. They were keen to maintain balance between intergovernmental cooperation, state sovereignty and equality between states. This therefore resulted in a policy of decision-making by consensus, which has stalled the organ-isation for many decades until it was changed in 2004–05. Together with possible changes in regional dynamics, this has contributed to the slow reform of LAS. The dynamics within the organisation seem to be changing, and new steps have been taken, especially in the last few years. Although predominantly driven by political interests, these steps and changes will influence the direction of the organisation in the future. It is not clear how much these will be translated into coherent human rights promotion and protection policies, and if so, how long will that take.

The movement of LAS towards more consistency with international law, human rights and the practice of other intergovernmental organisations will depend on the internal polit-ical dynamics in the region, and on the level of influence other bodies are willing to exert on LAS to catch up and not lag behind. Only time will tell.

Select bibliography

M. al Figiri (ed.), *La Himaya Li Ahad (No Protection to Anyone): the Role of the League of Arab States in Protecting Human Rights* (2006) (in Arabic).
FIDH, 'The Arab League and Human Rights: Challenges Ahead' – Regional Seminar held in Cairo on 16–17 February 2013, FIDH, 27–28, available at http://www.fi dh.org/for- an-effective- arableague-human- rights- protection-system- las-secretary-12932, accessed on 5 June 2013.
M. Rishmawi, *Human Rights Commission of the Arab States' in Max Planck Encyclopaedia of Public International Law* (OUP/Max Planck Institute for Comparative Public Law and International Law, 2010).
M. Rishmawi: 'The Arab Charter on Human Rights: A Comment', in 'Islam and Human Rights', 10(1) Interights Bulletin (1996).

104 LAS Council Resolution 7581, Irregular Session, 11 March 2013.
105 LAS Council Resolution 7595, Regular Session 139, 6 March 2013.
106 LAS Summit Decision 580, Regular Session 24, 26 March 2013.

28

The relationship of the UN treaty bodies and regional systems

Lorna McGregor

1 Introduction

Other chapters in this Handbook examine the regional human rights systems individually as well as the roles of the UN treaty bodies in the promotion and protection of human rights.[1] The purpose of this chapter is not to duplicate those efforts, but to address the interaction between these institutions and whether it strengthens or weakens the unity of international human rights law.

For reasons of space, this chapter concentrates on the relationship between the regional human rights and UN treaty bodies when acting in a judicial or quasi-judicial capacity. As the Arab and ASEAN human rights systems have yet to establish judicial bodies of this nature, the chapter is limited to the courts and commissions within the African, American and European systems. While regional courts such as the East African Court of Justice, Court of Justice of the Economic Community of West African states (ECOWAS), European Court of Justice and Southern African Development Community (SADC) Tribunal consider human rights issues in specific cases, their mandate is also much wider. Accordingly – and again for reasons of space – this chapter focuses on the relationship of the dedicated regional human rights bodies (the African Commission and Court on Human and Peoples' Rights, the European Court of Human Rights and the Inter-American Commission on and Court of Human Rights) to the six UN treaty bodies currently able to hear individual and inter-state communications.[2] Collectively, this chapter refers to these judicial and quasi-judicial bodies as 'international human rights bodies'.

This chapter considers their relationship from two perspectives. First, the majority of international and regional treaties contain the general legal principles of *lis pendens* and *res judicata*. These principles prevent international human rights bodies from hearing the same

1 See Chs 22–26 and Ch. 37.
2 The Committee on Enforced Disappearance, Committee on the Elimination of All Forms of Discrimination against Women, Committee on the Elimination of Racial Discrimination, Committee on the Rights of Persons with Disabilities, Committee against Torture and the Human Rights Committee.

matter if it is already pending or has been examined by another procedure of international investigation or settlement. However, in certain cases it is still possible that more than one international human rights body may hear the same case. As will be discussed, sometimes this may be justified where one international human rights body is unable to hear the whole complaint due to restrictions on its subject-matter jurisdiction. In other instances, however, it may inappropriately result in the state being judged twice; cause compliance challenges where the decisions rendered are contradictory; and put pressure on the already constrained resources of international human rights bodies.

Second, a number of international treaties contain the same or similar rights. While, strictly speaking, they are only mandated to interpret the terms of their own treaty, the overlap in substantive protection means that their decisions also contribute to the broader interpretation of international human rights law. Echoing a wider debate in public international law, the number of tribunals capable of interpreting and applying international human rights law gives rise to concerns of fragmentation where they reach different results or employ different reasoning in similar cases. The second part of this chapter engages with these challenges and explores practical ways in which the risk of fragmentation can be reduced through greater engagement with each other's jurisprudence and peer-to-peer dialogue.

2 The possibility that more than one body will hear the same complaint

A number of states have authorised more than one international human rights body to hear complaints against them. In such a situation, applicants may attempt to adjudicate their case before more than one international forum, particularly if they consider the first decision rendered to be unfavourable. To warrant against this possibility, the majority of international treaties incorporate the general legal principles of *lis pendens* and *res judicata*.[3] The principle of *res judicata* signifies the end of litigation, whereas the principle of *lis pendens* refers to proceedings that have been initiated but not yet completed by another court.[4] A number of human rights treaties provide that a complaint will be deemed inadmissible if it has been or is being examined under another procedure of international investigation or settlement – for example, Article 22(4)(a) of the Convention against Torture and Other Forms of Cruel, Inhuman and Degrading Treatment or Punishment (CAT), Article 4(2) of the Optional Protocol to the Convention on the Elimination of All Forms of Discrimination against Women (OP CEDAW), Article 3(2)(c) of the Optional Protocol to the International Covenant on Economic, Social and Cultural Rights (CESCR), Article 2(c) of the Optional Protocol to the Convention on the Rights of Persons with Disabilities (CRPD) and Article 77(3)(a) of the International Convention on the Protection of the Rights of All Migrant Workers and Members of Their Families.

Article 5(2)(a) of the Optional Protocol to the International Covenant on Civil and Political Rights (ICCPR) and Article 31(2)(c) of the International Convention for the Protection of All Persons from Enforced Disappearance (ICPPED) only provide that a

---

3   See UN Committee on the Elimination of Racial Discrimination, *Anna Koptova v Slovak Republic* (2000) UN Doc CERD/C/57/D/13/1998, para. 6.3.
4   For a full discussion of these terms, see A. Reinisch, 'The Use and Limits of *Res Judicata* and *Lis Pendens* as Procedural Tools to Avoid Conflicting Dispute Resolution Outcomes' (2004) 3 *The Law and Practice of International Courts and Tribunals* 37–77 at 43.

complaint is admissible if the same matter is not being examined under another procedure of international investigation or settlement. Thus, they can receive complaints which have already been examined by another procedure of international investigation or settlement as long as that body has already disposed of the matter either through a finding of inadmissibility or a decision on the merits. However, a number of states have entered a reservation to Article 5(2)(a) of the Optional Protocol to the ICCPR to prevent two international decisions on the same complaint and according to Phuong, the Human Rights Committee (HRC) tries to interpret the rule restrictively in order to minimise the possibility of duplication.[5] States that have made a declaration authorising the Committee on Enforced Disappearance to hear individual complaints have not made similar reservations to the ICPPED. The only UN treaty body that is not restricted by either of these principles is the Committee on the Elimination of Racial Discrimination which can hear complaints even if they are already being or have been decided upon by another international human rights body.

At the regional level, Article 46(1)(c) of the American Convention on Human Rights (ACHR) deems a complaint admissible provided 'that the subject of the petition or communication is not pending in another international proceeding for settlement'. Article 47(d) also provides that 'the petition or communication [must not be] substantially the same as one previously studied by the Commission or by another international organization'. Article 35(2)(b) of the European Convention on Human Rights (ECHR) provides that a complaint will be rejected if it 'is substantially the same as a matter that has already been examined by the Court or has already been submitted to another procedure of international investigation or settlement and contains no relevant new information'. Finally, Article 56(7) of the African Charter on Human and Peoples' Rights provides that complaints will be admissible where they '[d]o not deal with cases which have been settled by these States involved in accordance with the principles of the Charter of the United Nations, or the Charter of the Organization of African Unity or the provisions of the present Charter'. Viljoen notes that '[w]hile the African Charter allows for the simultaneous submission of communications to both the African Commission and a UN treaty body . . . the complainant has to abide by the first decision or finding'.[6]

The incorporation of the principles of *lis pendens* and *res judicata* into the rules and practice of most international human rights bodies is important for a number of reasons. First, it provides legal certainty for both parties to the dispute. Second, it protects states from subjection to complaints in multiple forums and from being required to comply with two potentially inconsistent judgments.[7] Third, it is a matter of 'judicial economy'[8] in that it protects international human rights bodies from having to decide upon cases that have already been considered by another international body, which reflects a key practical concern in light of the resource constraints and backlogs each faces. Fourth, it minimises forum shopping.[9] Fifth,

---

5 C. Phuong, 'The Relationship between the European Court of Human Rights and the Human Rights Committee: Has the 'Same Matter' Already been 'Examined'?' (2007) 7(2) *Human Rights Law Review* 385–95 at 387.

6 F. Viljoen, 'Communications under the African Charter: Procedure and Admissibility', in M. Evans and R. Murray (eds), *African Charter on Human and Peoples' Rights: The System in Practice: 1986–2006* (CUP, 2008) 126.

7 L.R. Helfner, 'Forum Shopping for Human Rights' (1999) 148(2) *University of Pennsylvania Law Review* 285–400 (1999) at 325.

8 Reinisch (n. 4) 44.

9 Helfner (n. 7) (for a full discussion of the potential for forum shopping and its impact on the integrity of international human rights law, arguing that 'forum shopping, if properly regulated, can materially benefit international human rights law' at 292).

as discussed in the next section of this chapter, it also lessens the prospect of divergent decisions and interpretations of international human rights law in similar cases.

Equally, the submission of a complaint to more than one international body may be necessary in certain instances where the limited subject-matter jurisdiction of an international human rights body prevents it from examining the whole complaint. Helfner also argues in favour of re-litigating a complaint even where one forum is available to hear the whole complaint, where it would 'minimize the erroneous denial of fundamental rights claims'[10] and redress what he perceives as the inequality between the parties particularly in experience of litigating before international human rights bodies.[11]

Where the principles of *lis pendens* or *res judicata* apply, the scope for two international human rights bodies to hear the same complaint turns on the interpretation of the terms (or their equivalent) 'another procedure of international investigation or settlement'; 'same matter'; and 'examination'. The remainder of this section explores how these terms have been interpreted by different international human rights bodies and the possibility for duplication that arises as a consequence.

2.1 The interpretation of 'another body of international investigation or settlement'

The first issue that requires resolution is whether the international body that is or has already considered the case is the type of body foreseen by the principles of *lis pendens* and *res judicata*. As detailed throughout this Handbook, a range of political, legal, monitoring and advocacy bodies at the international level work to promote and protect human rights. These bodies can take up individual cases and due to the different functions and methodologies each employs, multiple treatment may enhance the prospects for the resolution of the case and the guarantee of its non-repetition in the future. As Leach points out, '[t]his multiplicity of devices is indicative of the fact that it is often the case that a multi-faceted approach (combining legal, political and diplomatic mechanisms) will be necessary in order to tackle the more intractable human rights problems.'[12]

Despite the number of international bodies that can address an individual case, as a general rule, only those that are capable of determining state responsibility will be considered to engage the principles of *lis pendens* and *res judicata*. Thus, if a case is referred to by a treaty body when acting in its monitoring capacity through state party reporting, as part of the Universal Periodic Review, or by the Human Rights Council's country or thematic special procedures which 'examine, monitor, advise and publicly report on human rights situations',[13] this will usually be insufficient to render a case inadmissible before an international human rights body acting in a judicial or quasi-judicial manner. For example, the Office of the United Nations Human Commissioner for Human Rights (OHCHR) explains the role of the UN Working Group on Enforced and Involuntary Disappearances (one of the Human Rights Council's thematic special procedures) in the examination of individual cases as:

---

10 Helfner (n. 7) 347.

11 Ibid. at 348 (although this may not always be a persuasive argument given the experience of many NGO representatives in litigating cases at the international level).

12 See P. Leach, 'The European System and Approach' in this Handbook.

13 OHCHR website *Special Procedures of the Human Rights Council*, available at: http://www.ohchr.org/EN/HRBodies/SP/Pages/Welcomepage.aspx, accessed on 27 July 2012.

to assist families in determining the fate and whereabouts of their disappeared relatives ... The Working Group's role ends when the fate or whereabouts of the disappeared person have been clearly established as a result of investigations ... At that point the Working Group no longer concerns itself with the question of determining responsibility for specific cases of disappearance or for other human rights violations which may have occurred in the course of a disappearance; its work in this respect is of a strictly humanitarian nature.[14]

By characterising its work on individual cases as 'humanitarian', this does not preclude the submission of a case to an international human rights body for the purpose of determining state responsibility. Thus, in a case concerning allegations of enforced disappearance, the HRC explained that:

extra-conventional procedures or mechanisms established by the Commission on Human Rights or the Economic and Social Council, and whose mandates are to examine and publicly report on human rights situations in specific countries or territories or on major phenomenon of human rights violations worldwide, do not constitute procedures of international investigation or settlement within the meaning of article 5, paragraph 2(a), of the Optional Protocol. The Committee recalls that the study of human rights problems of a more global character, although it might refer to or draw on information concerning individuals, cannot be seen as being the same matter as the examination of individual cases within the meaning of article 5, paragraph 2(a) of the Protocol.[15]

Another UN Human Rights Council special procedure, the Working Group on Arbitrary Detention (WGAD), may be an exception to this general principle. Leach observes that the European Court on Human Rights (ECtHR) has found a complaint inadmissible on the basis that it had already been submitted to the WGAD, which in its view could be analogised to the HRC as it 'could accept individual applications, its proceedings were adversarial and its recommendations were determinative of state liability, were capable of bringing the violations in question to an end and were also subject to a monitoring procedure'.[16] The HRC has so far declined to take a position on whether the WGAD constitutes another form of international investigation or settlement for the purposes of admissibility. For example, in *Arredondo v Peru*, it noted that while the case had also been referred to the WGAD:

[t]he Committee decides to reach no decision on whether this matter falls within the scope of article 2, paragraph 5(a) of the Optional Protocol, since it has received information from the Working Group that it realized the existence of the present communication and has referred the case to the Committee without any expression of its views.[17]

---

14 OHCHR, Fact Sheet No. 6/Rev.3, 'Enforced or Involuntary Disappearances' 15.
15 UN Human Rights Committee, *Madoui v Algeria* (2008) UN Doc. CCPR/C/94/D/1495/2006 (2008) para. 6.2.
16 P. Leach, *Taking a Case to the European Court of Human Rights* (OUP, 2011) 148.
17 UN Human Rights Committee, *Arredondo v Peru* (2000) UN Doc. CCPR/C/69/D/688/1996 para. 10.2. See also, UN Human Rights Committee, *Musaeva v Uzbekistan* (2012) UN Doc. CCPR/C/104/D/1914 para. 82.

Another procedure lacking in clarity for these purposes is that established under Economic and Social Council (ECOSOC) Resolution 1503. The International Commission of Jurists helpfully explains the questions surrounding this procedure in its description that:

> Although the '1503 procedure' was known as a procedure for individual complaints, it was in fact established to enable the Commission and Sub-Commission to consider in a confidential manner, information from nongovernmental sources about situations that showed 'a consistent pattern of gross and reliably attested violations of human rights and fundamental freedoms'. Although individuals can submit complaints, the procedure is not designed to protect the rights of individual victims, nor to be a mechanism to provide redress and reparation to victims. Rather, the procedure is a way to the establish mechanisms to monitor a situation and/or to provide technical assistance to a government. The complainant (the author of the communication) plays no role in the procedure after having submitted the original complaint. The '1503 procedure' is non-accusatorial, confidential and non-adversarial in style.[18]

The African Commission on Human and Peoples' Rights (ACommHPR) has previously found that a case considered under this procedure triggered the principle of *res judicata* without providing any reasoning for this assessment.[19] However, the ECtHR has not reached the same conclusion.[20] Accordingly, the principles of *lis pendens* and *res judicata* work to preserve the complimentary political, advocacy and monitoring functions of international human rights bodies when considering individual cases but seek to avoid duplication when such bodies act in a (quasi) judicial manner.

2.2 The interpretation of the 'same matter'

The 'same matter' generally refers to the same parties, facts and alleged violations.[21] However, as set out below, the interpretation and application of the 'same matter' (or 'substantially the same matter' as set out in the American and European Conventions) is far from straightforward and gives rise to the greatest possibility of duplication by international human rights bodies.

2.2.1 Interpretation of the same parties

To engage the principles of *lis pendens* and *res judicata* the parties to the case must be the same. This aspect of the rule not only protects states from multiple proceedings against it at the international level but also ensures that individuals are able to have their complaints heard even if a similar case has already been decided by an international human rights body. For example, in *Kayhan v Turkey*, the applicant challenged the state party's ban on the wearing of headscarves in schools before the Committee on the Elimination of All Forms of

---

18 International Commission of Jurists, 'Establishing a Complaint Procedure in the Human Rights Council – Moving beyond the "1503 procedure"' (2006), available from www.icj.org.
19 *Amnesty International v Tunisia*, ACommHPR, Comm. No. 69/92 (1994), para. 2. See also Viljoen (n. 6) 127–28.
20 *Celniku v Greece*, ECtHR, Application No. 21449/04, Judgment of 5 July 2007, para. 40.
21 *Baena-Ricardo et al. v Panama*, Petition No. 11,325, IACtHR (1999) (Preliminary Objections), para. 53.

Discrimination against Women (CEDAW). The state party contested the admissibility of the case on the basis that the ECtHR had already decided the issue in *Leyla Sahin v Turkey*. The CEDAW rejected this challenge, finding that while the issue was similar, the parties were different, implying that Ms Kayan could not be prevented from accessing justice at the international level simply because someone else had already challenged the ban in another forum.[22]

Similarly, the HRC still admitted a case that was under consideration by the Inter-American Commission on Human Rights (IACommHR) on the basis that the parties were different.[23] The factors that appeared persuasive to the Committee in this case were that the applicant had 'no prior knowledge' of the complaint before the IACommHR; 'in spite of extensive inquiries on his part, he had been unable to find out who may have submitted that case to IACHR'; and the IACommHR had confirmed to the HRC that the complaint had been submitted by an 'unrelated third party'.[24] Again, this decision is significant as it provides important protection to the applicant who otherwise would have been unable to have his case heard.

Equally, the formality of the rule still leaves space for duplication even if the parties were part of the same case before national courts. The starkest illustrations of this point are the HRC case of *Leirvåg and others v Norway* and the ECtHR case of *Folgerø v Norway*. In these cases, eight sets of parents challenged a domestic law on compulsory religious education before the Norwegian courts. Following the Supreme Court's dismissal of the complaint, they separated into two groups with one complaining to the HRC and one to the ECtHR. Norway challenged the admissibility of the complaints in both forums on the basis that they had been joined at the national level and were 'to a large extent identical. Thus it appears that the authors stand together, but that they are seeking a review by both international bodies of what is essentially one case.'[25] Both the HRC and the ECtHR rejected this admissibility challenge as the applicants were factually 'distinct'.[26] Accordingly, where cases involve more than one complainant it is possible that more than one international body will be seized of the complaint even if the facts and alleged violations are the same.

2.2.2 Interpretation of the same alleged violations

Where the parties and the facts are the same, the international human rights body must still consider whether the alleged violations are the same to satisfy the principles of *lis pendens* and *res judicata*. Treaties can frame certain rights differently. However, the principles of *lis pendens* and *res judicata* generally do not require identical wording unless the scope of the right is significantly different.

This may arise with regard to complaints that involve allegations of violations of the right to equality and non-discrimination. This is because the right to equality and non-discrimination is treated differently by different treaties. For example, Article 14 of the

22 UN Human Rights Committee, *Fanali v Italy* (1983) UN Doc CCPR/C/18/D/75/1980, para. 7.2; UN Committee on the Elimination of Discrimination Against Women, *Kayhan v Turkey* (2006) UN Doc CEDAW/C/34/D/8/2005, para. 7.3.
23 UN Human Rights Committee, *Miguel Angel Estrella v Uruguay* (1990) UN Doc. CCPR/C/OP/2.
24 Ibid. para. 4.2.
25 UN Human Rights Committee, *Leirvåg and others v Norway* (2004) UN Doc. CCPR/C/82/D/1155/2003, para. 8.2.
26 Ibid. para. 13.3. *Folgerø v Norway*, App. No. 15472/02, (ECtHR, Admissibility, 2004) at section B(2) (finding that the complainants must be identical).

ECHR treats the right to non-discrimination as an accessory right, meaning that it can only be invoked in relation to one of the other substantive rights set out in the Convention itself.[27] By contrast, Article 26 of the ICCPR provides a free-standing right to equality and non-discrimination. As Phuong explains, where the ECtHR has considered a case under Article 14, the HRC 'often concludes that the [European] Court could not have examined the author's independent right to equality and non-discrimination'[28] and therefore still admits the case. However, she also points out that the Committee is alive to the possibility that parties may allege a violation of Article 26 in order to overcome the barrier of the principle of *res judicata*. Therefore, it carefully scrutinises claims on this basis in order to ensure that the 'allegation based on Article 26 truly constitutes a free-standing claim of discrimination. If it does not, it considers that the new allegation of a violation of Article 26 does not exceed the scope of the claim already made under another article of the ICCPR.'[29]

This issue may also arise before the CEDAW and the Committee on the Rights of Persons with Disabilities if it can be successfully argued that their governing conventions frame the right to equality and non-discrimination differently to other international treaties. This argument has already been presented to the CEDAW in *Cristina Muñoz-Vargas y Sainz de Vicuña v Spain* in which the complainant argued that:

> the two communications brought before the Human Rights Committee were based on article 26 of the International Covenant on Civil and Political Rights (right to equality), which was more restrictive than articles 1 and 2(f) of the Convention. The purpose of the Convention is to eradicate discrimination suffered by women in all spheres of life, without any limitations (article 1). Therefore, the same matter has not been examined under another procedure of international investigation or settlement. For the same reasons, the petition brought before the European Court of Human Rights should also not be considered as the same matter as a communication brought before the Committee on the Elimination of Discrimination against Women.[30]

However, the Committee found the case inadmissible on other grounds and found no 'reason to find the communication inadmissible on any other grounds.'[31] Therefore, it is unclear whether this argument could be successfully made.

The second issue that arises is whether applicants may split up their complaints in order to have them heard by different bodies. Certain UN treaty bodies only have a narrow subject-matter jurisdiction with the result that they may only be able to consider particular aspects of a wider complaint. For example, the Committee against Torture can only deal with complaints of torture and other ill-treatment even if the broader allegations raise questions relating to the freedom of expression or association or the right to liberty and security of person. Even the HRC and the regional bodies with wider mandates will not always be capable of examining the full complaint, for example, if it involves allegations of violations of certain economic,

---

27 See Phuong (n. 5) 388 (contrasting the HRC's practice on Art. 26 ICCPR with the ECtHR's on Art. 14). Notably, this issue may not arise with regards to Protocol 12 to the ECHR which provides a free-standing prohibition of discrimination but which has not been ratified by all states).

28 Ibid.

29 Ibid. 389.

30 UN Committee on the Elimination of Discrimination Against Women, *Cristina Muñoz-Vargas y Sainz de Vicuña v Spain* (2007) UN Doc. CEDAW/C/39/D/7/2005, para. 8.3.

31 Ibid. para. 11.6.

social and cultural rights, gender rights or rights of persons with disabilities. Inevitably this may result in multiple complaints before international human rights bodies due to the applicant's lack of options in the absence of a body capable of adjudicating the whole complaint.

However, in other cases one body may be available to hear the full complaint but the applicant may seek to act strategically by splitting up the complaint with the view to achieving multiple international decisions against the state.[32] For example, in *Pauger v Austria*, the applicant had already successfully complained to the HRC, which found a violation of Article 26 ICCPR.[33] The European Commission still found the subsequent complaint admissible on the basis that 'he [had] complained about issues related to the proceedings before the Austrian authorities and courts' under Article 6(1) and not non-discrimination.[34] Similarly, if the second complaint is wider than the first, the international human rights body may still find it admissible. For example, in *Smirnova & Smirnova v Russia,* the ECtHR admitted a complaint that was pending before the HRC as the HRC complaint only concerned one of the applicants and was not 'substantially the same' as:

> the first applicant's complaints in that case were directed against her arrest on 26 August 1995 and, in particular, the question whether this arrest was justified, the impossibility to challenge it in the courts, and the alleged inadequate conditions of detention. The scope of the factual basis for the first applicant's application to the Court, although going back to the arrest of 26 August 1995, is significantly wider. It extends to the whole of the proceedings which terminated in 2002, and includes the first applicant's arrest on three more occasions since 26 August 1995.[35]

2.2.3 The interpretation of 'examination'

The final issue that arises with regard to the principles of *lis pendens* and *res judicata* is the interpretation of whether the complaint is being 'examined'. Clearly, a previous decision on the merits or the agreement of a friendly settlement will satisfy this aspect of the principles. For the ACommHPR this is the only possible reading of the Charter as it refers to 'settled' cases, as was confirmed by the ACommHPR in *Bob Ngozi Njoku v Egypt.*[36]

However, this reading does not necessarily apply to other international human rights bodies as the UN treaty bodies only refer to 'examined' cases; the ECHR refers to 'submitted' cases; and the ACHR refers to 'previously studied' complaints. This language could be interpreted to mean that decisions on admissibility alone could satisfy the principles of *lis pendens* and *res judicata* even if the grounds for the admissibility decision by the first body were not shared by the second body (such as the ECtHR's six-month rule which is not employed by other international human rights bodies) or the facts were no longer the same (for example,

---

32 See Helfner (n. 7) proposing reforms to ward against splitting up claims while still allowing complainants to access more than one international human rights forum where one alone is incapable of dealing with the full claim.

33 *Pauger v Austria,* App. No. 16717/90 (ECtHR, Judgment of 28 May 1997), paras. 27–28.

34 Ibid. para. 65 (although the Court did not reconsider this issue as the state party did not raise it before the Court, para. 66).

35 *Smirnova & Smirnova v Russia,* ECtHR, Application No. 46133/99 and 48183/99, Admissibility Decision of 3 October 2002.

36 *Bob Ngozi Njoku v Egypt,* ACommHPR, Comm. No. 40/90 (1997), para. 55.

where the first complaint was rejected for a failure to exhaust domestic remedies which are subsequently exhausted prior to the second complaint). Phuong explains that the HRC has not found that a complaint has been 'examined' where the admissibility decision by the first international human rights body was based on 'purely procedural' grounds. However, she observes that if the ground for inadmissibility can be read to have any substantive content, such as a finding that the complaint is manifestly ill-founded, the HRC will usually reject the complaint. She highlights the dangers of this approach by noting that:

> Due to the increasing workload of the ECtHR, Committees of three judges have started to issue one-paragraph decisions on the admissibility of complaints whereby the ECtHR finds that the facts of the case 'do not disclose any appearance of a violation of the rights and freedoms set out in the Convention or its Protocols'. What is slightly disturbing in the wording of these decisions is the term 'appearance'. It suggests that the Committee of three judges has examined the complaint very briefly and concluded that there did not *appear to be* any violation, rather than that there *was* no violation. Nonetheless, one could argue that the Court has still 'examined' the complaint, although it may not have done so in the most thorough manner.[37]

This section has therefore examined the relationship and interaction between the regional human rights and UN treaty bodies and their general attempt to avoid duplicated proceedings, though this may sometimes materialise.

3 The relationship between the jurisprudence

Each international human rights body is formally only mandated to interpret and apply the terms of its own treaty. In theory, therefore, they simply co-exist with each autonomously contributing to the general promotion and protection of human rights through the adjudication of disputes arising from their governing treaties and within their jurisdiction. However, as set out in the previous section of this chapter, in certain cases more than one international human rights body may consider the same case. In addition, certain rights are replicated or are very similar in more than one convention with the result that multiple adjudicative bodies flesh out their meaning and scope under international human rights law more broadly. Where the decisions are consistent with each other and the bodies cross-reference each other's jurisprudence, the bodies collectively deepen and strengthen international human rights law. Equally, as this section details, where international human rights bodies reach different outcomes or employ divergent reasoning in the consideration of similar cases, this can potentially threaten the unity of international human rights law and lead to its fragmentation. It also produces what Helfner frames as a 'true conflict (. . .) where a signature to the two agreements cannot comply with both treaty obligations at the same time'.[38]

3.1 Fragmentation as an issue germane to international law generally

In response to the general proliferation of international tribunals and the development of specialised sub-regimes of public international law, a number of scholars have raised concerns

---

37 Phuong (n. 5) 391.
38 Helfner (n. 7), 325.

about the threat to the unity and legal certainty in public international law.[39] In a study for the UN International Law Commission, Professor Koskenniemi explained that:

> fragmentation does create the danger of conflicting and incompatible rules, principles, rule-systems and institutional practices[40] ... The problem [with the emergence of specialised regimes such as human rights], as lawyers have seen it, is that such specialized law-making and institution-building tends to take place with relative ignorance of legislative and institutional activities in the adjoining fields and of the general principles and practices of international law. The result is conflicts between rules or rule-systems, deviating institutional practices and, possibly, the loss of an overall perspective on the law.[41]

Equally, the Report recognises the reality of fragmentation as deriving from 'the rapid expansion of international legal activity into various new fields and the diversification of its objects and techniques'.[42] Scholars have also pointed out that divergent interpretations of the same principles of public international law by different tribunals does not necessarily need to be viewed negatively where it gives rise to inter-judicial dialogue and engagement in the field's development. For example, one of the leading writers on fragmentation, the late Jonathan Charney, noted that:

> tribunals may differ on the rules of international law. I find much value in this situation. The variety of views on what the rules of international law are, the debates over those judicial decisions when they may differ, and the resolution of the issues will help the international community discover what may be the most acceptable interpretations of international law. This is a healthy process. International tribunals are aware of what other international tribunals may decide, and if those tribunals are not aware, counsel will inform them. As a consequence, this debate will continue across the broad spectrum of tribunals, and hopefully will result in optimal rules of international law that are fully thought through and analyzed.[43]

As noted above, international human rights law is often cited as contributing to fragmentation due to its nature as a specialised regime of international law.[44] Less attention has been paid, however, to the risk of fragmentation within international human rights law as a result of the proliferation of tribunals capable of interpreting and applying it but without necessarily coordinating.[45] This risk and its possible mediation are explored in the remainder of this chapter.

---

39 See for example M. Young (ed.), *Regime Interaction in International Law: Facing Fragmentation* (CUP, 2011).
40 UN General Assembly, International Law Commission, 'Fragmentation of International Law: Difficulties Arising from the Diversification and Expansion of International Law: Report of the Study Group of the International Law Commission, Finalized by Martti Koskenniemi', UN Doc. A/CN.4/L.682 (2006), para. 14.
41 Ibid. para. 8.
42 Ibid. para. 14.
43 J. Charney, 'The "Horizontal" Growth of International Courts and Tribunals: Challenges and Opportunities?' (2002) 96 *ASIL Annual Meeting Proceedings* 369 at 370.
44 M. Craven, 'Legal Differentiation and the Concept of the Human Rights Treaty in International Law' (2000) 11(3) *European Journal of International Law* 489–519 at 490.
45 L. Lixinski, 'Choice of Forum in International Human Rights Adjudication and the Unity/Fragmentation Debate: Is Plurality the Way Ahead?' (2009) 9 *University College Dublin Law Review* 23–45 at 29.

3.2 Fragmentation in international human rights law

To some extent fragmentation and divergent interpretations of international human rights law are inevitable due to the number of international human rights bodies that have been established and the commonalities in the rights provided in their governing treaties. While it might be inevitable in certain situations, the International Court of Justice in *Ahmadou Sadio Diallo (Republic of Guinea v Democratic Republic of Congo)* emphasised the importance of aiming for unity in order to ensure clarity, consistency and legal security.[46] Such an approach would ensure that fragmentation only occurs where there are real points of disagreement on the interpretation of a right in common.

In order to minimise fragmentation in this way, knowledge and engagement with each other's jurisprudence is necessary, as referenced by Charney above. Helfner emphasises that this safeguards against fragmentation arising 'by chance or inadvertence'[47] and argues in favour of what he characterises as 'horizontal dialogue' of which the 'core feature . . . is open acknowledgment of *the existence* of relevant precedents from other treaty systems as a way to enhance the precision, certainty, and reasoned decision-making that are essential features of a coherent body of human rights law'.[48] This is where the challenges with international human rights bodies lie as historically, they rarely acknowledged or engaged with each other's jurisprudence. Many examples can be provided as evidence of this point, but in the space available the following cases illustrate the traditional lack of interaction between the different international human rights bodies when deciding similar cases.

In the cases of *Leirvåg* and *Folgerø* referenced above, the HRC issued its decision before the ECtHR. However, the Grand Chamber only noted the HRC's decision in its description of the factual background to the case and did not engage with its finding.[49] This was the case even though the decisions were reasonably similar in finding a violation of Article 18(4) ICCPR requiring states 'to undertake to have respect for the liberty of parents and, when applicable, legal guardians to ensure the religious and moral education of their children in conforming with their own convictions',[50] and Article 2 of Protocol 1 to the ECHR on the right to education, including the obligation on states to:

> respect the right of parents to ensure such education and teaching in conformity with their own religious and philosophical convictions undertake to have respect for the liberty of parents and, when applicable, legal guardians to ensure the religious and moral education of their children in conformity with their own convictions.[51]

Similarly, in *Carlos Correia de Matos v Portugal,* the HRC heard a case that had previously been decided upon by the ECtHR.[52] The ECtHR had previously found that Article 6(3)(c) on the right to defend himself in court without legal counsel had not been violated.[53] The HRC

---

46 Judgment of 30 November 2010, para. 66.
47 Helfner (n. 7) 335.
48 Ibid. 350.
49 *Folgerø* (n. 26) paras 43–46.
50 Ibid. para. 15
51 Ibid. para. 105.
52 UN Human Rights Committee, *Carlos Correia de Matos v Portugal* (2006) UN Doc. CCPR/ C/86/D/1123/2002/Rev.1.
53 For a full discussion of these cases see Phuong (n. 5) 391.

found that the equivalent provision in the ICCPR, Article 14(3)(d), had been violated. However, in doing so, it made no reference to the ECtHR's decision or why it disagreed with it.[54] In an individual opinion, three members (Palm, Ando and O'Flaherty) expressed concern that 'two international instances – instead of trying to reconcile their jurisprudence with one another – come to different conclusions when applying exactly the same provisions to the same facts'.[55] One of this Handbook's editors, Professor Sir Nigel Rodley, in his own separate opinion criticised the HRC for 'the cavalier way in which the Committee chooses to ignore the reasoned approach of the European Court of Human Rights, applying the same law to the same facts'.[56]

The two cases presented to the ECtHR and the HRC on whether a prohibition on wearing a headscarf violated the right to manifest one's religion again provide stark illustration of this point. In *Leyla Sahin v Turkey,* the applicant petitioned the ECtHR following her exclusion from university as she had violated a ban on wearing a headscarf. The ECtHR issued its Chamber decision on 29 June 2004. In finding that there had been no violation of Article 9 on the right to manifest one's religion or Article 14 on the right to equality and non-discrimination, the Court only took into account its own jurisprudence.[57] On 18 January 2005, the HRC then issued its decision in the similar case of *Raihon Hudoyberganova v Uzbekistan*.[58] In this case, the HRC found that the applicant's 'right to freedom of thought, conscience and religion was violated as she was excluded from University because she refused to remove the headscarf that she wore in accordance with her beliefs' and an 'individual's freedom to have or adopt a religion'.[59] In support of its decision, the Committee cited its own General Comment 22, but with the exception of Professor Wedgewood in her individual opinion, did not reference the ECtHR's decision in the year prior or the reason for reaching a different decision. The Grand Chamber of the ECtHR then issued its decision in *Leyla Sahin* on 10 November 2005, upholding its Chamber decision. In a 54-page judgment, however, it failed to acknowledge or engage with the HRC's views despite their issuance only months earlier.[60]

More recently, however, international human rights bodies have begun to demonstrate a greater willingness to engage with comparative jurisprudence, although this typically only arises if a party or third party intervener presents the jurisprudence rather than *proprio motu*. For example, in the 2011 decision of *Yevdokimov & Rezanov v Russian Federation* on the question of whether prisoners have the right to vote, the HRC not only acknowledged the previous decision on the same issue before the ECtHR in *Hirst (No. 2) v The United Kingdom*[61] but also engaged with the tests applied in the case.[62] It also stated that:

> [t]he Committee notes the state party's reference to earlier decisions of the European Court of Human Rights. However, the Committee is also aware of the Court's judgment

54 Ibid. 393.
55 *Carlos Correia de Matos v Portugal* (n. 52).
56 Ibid.
57 *Leyla Sahin v Turkey,* App. No. 44774/98 (ECtHR, Judgment of 29 June 2004).
58 UN Human Rights Committee, *Raihon Hudoyberganova v Uzbekistan* (2005) UN Doc CCPR/C/82/D/931/2000.
59 Ibid. para. 6.2.
60 *Leyla Sahin v Turkey,* App. No. 44774/98 (ECtHR, Judgment of 10 November 2005).
61 *Hirst v The United Kingdom (No. 2)*, App. No. 74025/01 (ECtHR, Judgment of 6 October 2005).
62 UN Human Rights Committee, *Yevdokimov and Rezanov v Russian Federation* (2011) UN Doc. CCPR/C/101/D/1410/2005.

in the case *Hirst v. United Kingdom* in which the Court affirmed that the principle of proportionality requires sufficient link between the sanction and the conduct and circumstances of the individual concerned.[63]

Other members also engaged with the test applied by the ECtHR in their dissenting opinion, commenting that:

> General Comment 25 states that the right to vote and to be elected is not an absolute right and that restrictions may be imposed on it, provided they are not discriminatory or unreasonable. It also states that if conviction for an offence is a basis for suspending the right to vote, the period for such suspension should be proportionate to the offence and the sentence. The norm which follows from General Comment 25 should be used in interpreting whether a violation of the Covenant has occurred in the case before us, instead of some form of extended proportionality test, as might be inferred from the European Court of Human Rights in the case *Hirst v. United Kingdom* and which seemingly has inspired the majority.[64]

Some bodies have also begun to engage in dialogue with peers from other bodies such as the recent meeting between the ECtHR and the HRC at the former's seat in Strasbourg.[65] At this meeting, members of both bodies discussed their practice and approach to interim measures, freedom of expression, the prohibition of discrimination and enforced disappearance. The UN High Commissioner for Human Rights in her latest report on the reform of treaty bodies also highlighted such engagement as an important aspect of treaty body reform.[66] Similarly, the second meeting of the chairpersons of treaty bodies took place in Addis Ababa in part in order to 'strengthen linkages and enhance synergies between international and regional human rights mechanisms and institutions, as well as with their stakeholders' and to meet with the 'African human rights mechanisms . . . to discuss complementarities between the international and regional human rights systems'.[67] The summary report notes that one point discussed at a round table was:

> how to ensure that the jurisprudence of the African Court on Human and Peoples' Rights, the Committee of Experts on the Rights and Welfare of the Child, the African Commission on Human and Peoples' Rights, and sub-regional courts is consistent with that of the United Nations human rights treaty bodies, and how to identify examples of diverging jurisprudence, as well as sharing of experiences.[68]

---

63 Ibid. para. 7.5.
64 Individual opinion by Committee members, Mr Krister Thelin and Mr Michael O'Flaherty (dissenting).
65 Visit by a Delegation of the United Nations Human Rights Committee to the European Court of Human Rights (29 June 2012).
66 *Strengthening the United Nations Human Rights Treaty Body System: A Report by the United Nations High Commissioner for Human Rights*, Navanethem Pillay (June 2012), 69, available at: http://www2. ohchr.org/english/bodies/HRTD/docs/HCReportTBStrengthening.pdf.
67 UN General Assembly, 'Implementation of Human Rights Instruments: Note by the Secretary-General', UN Doc A/67/28442 (2012) Advanced Unedited Version, summary and para. 16.
68 Ibid. para. 26.

One recommendation that emerged from the round table was the establishment of a 'forum for regional and international courts to meet regularly to discuss topical issues'[69] and to seek 'coherence and avoid . . . the fragmentation of international human rights law'.[70] Other recommendations included 'attendance of representatives of the African mechanisms during the annual meetings of treaty body Chairpersons and treaty body sessions, and the attendance of treaty body members during the meetings of the African Commission';[71] 'regular contacts at the level of the secretariats';[72] 'efforts by the [international and regional bodies] . . . to take into consideration and reference their respective jurisprudence so as to seek coherence and avoid the fragmentation of international human rights law'.[73]

4 Conclusion

The number of international human rights bodies capable of hearing individual complaints continues to increase, particularly at the UN level once the Committee on Economic, Social and Cultural Rights and the Committee on the Rights of the Child start to hear individual complaints. This increases the opportunities for individuals to access justice at the international level and enhances the development of a core body of jurisprudence on international human rights law. In order to maximise the opportunities offered by such proliferation as well as provide certainty and clarity to all stakeholders, coordination and dialogue between the different bodies presents a crucial aspect of their working methodology both in relation to their interpretation of the principles of *lis pendens* and *res judicata* and the substantive rights in common in their governing treaties.

Equally, while this is a desirable approach, it is by no means straightforward. All supranational human rights bodies currently face significant resource constraints with the result that it is not always easy to remain aware of judicial developments elsewhere and to ensure that sufficient time is provided for the body as a collective to consider the significance of comparative jurisprudence to its decisions, particularly when not raised by the parties or third party interveners (the role of which not all international human rights bodies recognise). Moreover, the ACommHPR and the UN treaty bodies typically issue short decisions that do not always reference their own jurisprudence, let alone those of other bodies. A full engagement with the jurisprudence of other bodies would require lengthier decisions which may not always be possible, particularly as these bodies sit on a part-time basis and with small secretariats. By contrast, the Inter-American Court of Human Rights may face a similar problem due to its recent commitment to shortening its decisions in order to make them more accessible. The ECtHR may also experience difficulties in engaging with other bodies' jurisprudence in light of thousands of its own decisions. Accordingly, within the ongoing individual reform projects, greater consideration is required of how to support and enable regional human rights and UN treaty bodies to engage with each other's practice from a practical and realistic perspective without further overburdening them.

---

69 Ibid. para. 27.
70 Ibid. para. 28. See also, Annex II.
71 Annex II, para. 1.
72 Ibid. para. 15.
73 Ibid. para. 16.

Select bibliography

J. Charney, 'The "Horizontal" Growth of International Courts and Tribunals: Challenges and Opportunities?'(2002) 96 *ASIL Annual Meeting Proceedings* 369.

L.R. Helfner, 'Forum Shopping for Human Rights' (1999) 148(2) *University of Pennsylvania Law Review* 285–400 (1999) at 325.

C. Phuong, 'The Relationship between the European Court of Human Rights and the Human Rights Committee: Has the 'Same Matter' Already been 'Examined'?' (2007) 7(2) *Human Rights Law Review* 385–95.

A. Reinisch, 'The Use and Limits of Res Judicata and LisPendensas Procedural Tools to Avoid Conflicting Dispute Resolution Outcomes' (2004) 3 *The Law and Practice of International Courts and Tribunals* 37–77.

M. Young (ed.) *Regime Interaction in International Law: Facing Fragmentation* (CUP, 2011).

Part V

Key contemporary issues and challenges for the future

29

Non-state actors and human rights

Sir Nigel Rodley

1 Introduction

Traditionally, human rights were conceived as that set of principles that constituted the *limits* of organized state power to compel the individuals subject to that power. More recently the notion has become understood as denoting that set of principles that *mediate* the relationship between the same power and those subject to it. This position recognises that human rights must be seen as embracing not only negative obligations on the state (limits) but also some positive obligations. A further qualification of the notion has been the at least theoretical acceptance that if another entity – a non-state actor (NSA) – exercises 'effective power' analogous to that of the state, then such an entity should logically be seen as capable of being obliged to respect the human rights of those subject to that power.[1] We may call this the 'modified traditional view'.

Against the (modified) traditional view, there are those who advocate 'new ways of looking at human rights'.[2] Andrew Clapham, the most prominent of them, proposes 'a paradigm shift in our understanding of the power and utility of human rights'.[3] He contemplates a need to 'pull human rights inside out', indeed to 'turn human rights on their heads'.[4] This would permit us to include 'corporations, mercenaries, international organizations, criminal organizations and terrorists within the category of those capable of committing human rights violations'.[5] Now, 'human rights obligations can fall on states, individuals and non-state actors'.[6]

The human rights obligations of intergovernmental organisations (IGOs) will not be dealt with at length. As will be seen in the following section, to describe IGOs, that is, interstate

---

1 E.g. see N. Rodley, 'Can Armed Opposition Groups Violate Human Rights?', in K. Mahoney and P. Mahoney (eds), *Human Rights in the Twenty-First Century* (Dordrecht, Martinus Nijhoff, 1993), 297, 299–300.
2 A. Clapham, *Human Rights Obligations of Non-State Actors* (Oxford, OUP, 2006), 50 (hereafter 'Clapham').
3 Ibid. 56.
4 Ibid.
5 Ibid. 43.
6 Ibid. 58.

bodies, at all as non-state actors is misleading, and IGOs simply do not pose the same conceptual or legal problems as do (other) NSAs. Mercenaries will simply be left aside as being of limited conceptual interest, since the activities of mercenary organisations fall within the responsibility of the state or other party to a conflict on behalf of which they are acting and, indirectly, like any transnational corporation, potentially with the responsibility of the parent state(s).

The point of addressing criminal organisations as a potential category of human rights violator is not clear. Presumably, the reference is to organised common criminality, for example trafficking (in drugs or human beings), kidnapping or 'racketeering'. Such activities are also frequently resorted to by terrorist and armed opposition groups to finance their activities.[7] The responsibility or otherwise of the latter as human rights violators will be addressed. The point of considering non-politically-motivated organised crime within the human rights paradigm is not explained and hardly self-evident. Clapham himself does not further address the category, either from a theoretical point of view or within the context of international human rights law (IHRL). Nor does he offer us a suggestion of what might be the added value of considering organised criminality as a species of human rights violation.[8]

What follows in this chapter is, first, a reflection on the nature of NSAs; second, a consideration of the conceptual and legal arguments at stake generally; and, third, an examination of specific categories of suggested non-state human rights violators, notably, (a) terrorist and other armed opposition groups, (b) corporations, and (c) individuals, with particular reference to domestic violence.

2 Non-state actors

The notion of non-state actor (NSA) is, as Alston has warned us, so broad as to be misleading.[9] There is and can be nothing relevant in common between every individual and every entity that is not a state. The warning is important, because many writers are tempted to argue that because some entity that is not a state may have or be accorded some specific rights and duties, then the same is or may be true for every other entity. The most far-fetched would be the argument that since an intergovernmental organisation like the United Nations can have rights and responsibilities under international law, there is the basis for considering any NSA as being in the same position.[10]

It has been evident since the *Reparations Case*[11] that the UN has indeed been endowed with sufficient personality to enjoy the rights and be subject to the responsibilities that are necessary for it to discharge its functions under the Charter. However, this means little, if anything, more than that states can pool their powers to create a separate international person exercising powers that can only be realised by cooperation. Thus, we have public functions, exercised

---

7 See, generally, R. Dudai and K. McEvoy, 'Thinking Critically about Armed Groups and Human Rights Praxis' (2012) 4 *Journal of Human Rights Practice* 1, 19

8 Dudai and McEvoy consider that such groups are in position as a possible 'next frontier' of interest for human rights groups, though the focus is more on state responsibility for their acts and potential liability under international criminal law rather than on direct responsibility under IHRL, ibid. 22–23.

9 P. Alston, 'The "Not-a-Cat" Syndrome: Can the International Human Rights Regime Accommodate Non-State Actors?', in P. Alston (ed.), *Non-State Actors and Human Rights* (Oxford, OUP, 2005), 3.

10 This seems to be the implication of Clapham's treatment of the matter: Clapham (n. 2) 63–69.

11 *Reparation for Injuries Suffered in the Service of the United Nations*, ICJ Reports (1949) 174.

by a public body, created by the archetypal international law actor to affect their joint will. Such a (traditional) development is plainly irrelevant to the project of considering other potential actors to be endowed with the legal personality required to have international legal rights and responsibilities. Indeed, the very categorisation of an *interstate* body as a *non-state* actor is arguably a contradiction in terms.

However, a reason to note the argument is that it seems to have a dual function: not only is it invoked to show (or to imply) that there are potentially no limits on what or who may have international legal personality, it then further asserts that the personality can or does extend to the realm of rights and duties under the international law specifically applicable to human rights (IHRL). In fact, even here, no violence is done to the traditional understanding of the human rights notion by acknowledging that, when states give IGOs effective power that would make each of them capable of violating human rights, then the new collective entity can be placed in exactly the same position.

This does not mean that the notion of IGOs, even the UN, having human rights obligations has, *in fact* been easily accepted. This is not the case, but it has become, first slowly, then increasingly recognised. The UN Secretariat has come to acknowledge that the UN may be bound by general principles of international humanitarian law[12] and IHRL.[13] Whether the same goes for other IGOs depends on their mandate and the powers they have to enforce it. The point is that whether or not any particular IGO has been given functions that could lead it to incur responsibility under IHRL, no theoretical challenge is posed to the idea of the centrality of the state to public international law (PIL) in general and IHRL in particular is done when it does happen. Therefore, it does not follow that other NSAs and, even less, individuals, are in the same position.

Moreover a traditional understanding of the human rights idea does not demand embracing the view that NSAs and individuals cannot, *ipso jure* be endowed with rights and duties under PIL. This would be untenable. For instance, the ICSID convention as long ago as 1965 created the framework for corporations (and, indeed, individual foreign investors) to compel arbitration of disputes with states.[14] After an evolution of some half a century, the European Convention on Human Rights has been adapted to give individuals directly enforceable rights against states parties to the European Court of Human Rights.[15]

As to the idea that individuals may have obligations under international law, it is a trite observation that this is the case. If there were any doubt after the Nuremberg trials that individuals – or at least individuals acting as state agents – could be in direct violation of

12 UN Secretary-General, Secretary-General's Bulletin: Observance by United Nations Forces of International Humanitarian Law, 6 August, 1999, UN doc. ST/SGB/1999/13.

13 Remarks of the UN Legal Counsel, Nicolas Michel, to the Security Council meeting on 'Strengthening International law: rule of law and maintenance of international peace and security', UN doc. S/PV.5474 (2006) 3–5; UN Secretariat, 'Human Rights Due Diligence Policy on UN support to non-UN security forces (HRDDP)' (July 2012), which confirms 'the Organization's Purposes and Principles in the Charter and *its obligations under international law to respect*, promote and encourage respect for *international* humanitarian, *human rights* and refugee *law*' (emphasis added); see A. Bianchi, 'Assessing the Effectiveness of the UN Security Council's Anti-terrorism Measures: The Quest for Legitimacy and Cohesion' (2007) 17 *EJIL* 881.

14 World Bank, International Convention for the Settlement of Investment Disputes between States and Nationals of Other States (ICSID Convention).

15 D. Harris, M. O'Boyle and C. Warbrick, *Law of the European Convention on Human Rights*, 2nd edn (Oxford, OUP, 2009), 4–5, 811–12.

international law,[16] there can be none now we have the International Criminal Court (ICC). Aggression may be committed by individual state agents; genocide, crimes against humanity and war crimes may be committed by state agents and by others associated with a (non-state) party to an armed conflict or with an organisation engaging in crimes against humanity.[17]

This means that the issue is not whether or not it is possible for NSAs (and individuals) to have rights and duties under international law, rather it is *whether or not they actually possess them for any particular purpose.* And even if they do, are these properly called rights and, more importantly for our purposes, obligations under the international law of human rights? And, if not, should they be?

These questions in turn beg a further question: while states may well be able to endow natural or juridical persons with rights and duties (often equated to legal personality), can it happen at the international level other than by a manifestation of interstate will? That is, have power relations, other than those involving state or interstate bodies, so evolved – can they so evolve – as to require international law to recognise such personality, despite the will of states and even in the face of general interstate opposition?

For this is the implicit, if not explicit, condition precedent for some of the claims made on behalf of NSA legal personality which challenge the state-oriented nature of international law. A positive answer to this question would necessarily entail the development of a set of techniques to determine what the rights and obligations are that are wholly alien to those that international lawyers presently use. The so-called sources of international law[18] would be by-passed, for they are overwhelmingly state-centred, requiring state-will or state-recognition. So far, there seems to be no alternative route map available or even proposed to determine the content of the law. Nor does one seem likely to become available, as long as states themselves are unwilling to allow it to happen – for they certainly have the means and the power to prevent it. The advocates who suggest that alternative loci of power may be identified, fail to come to grips with the trumping power of the (inter-) state system.

3 Conceptual issues

There seems little disagreement that the original idea of human rights was one which was understood to mean those rights that the individual could assert against the organised power of the state.[19] It is an idea that grew in the West, as feudalism was replaced by mercantilism and religion began to lose its position as a counterweight to royal power that was being succeeded by the emergent, industrialising state. Indeed, it was the state that claimed a monopoly of the use of force with a view to protecting all from each other. It was the

---

16 According to one approach, the Allies who set up the International Military Tribunal that delivered justice to the top Nazi leaders was merely a pooling among themselves of a jurisdiction each of them could have exercised separately.

17 No organisational affiliation as such is required in the definitions of genocide in the 1948 Convention on the Prevention and Punishment of the Crime of Genocide (Art. 2) nor in the Rome Statute of the International Criminal Court (Art. 6); however, in the Elements of Crimes adopted pursuant to Art. 9 of the Rome Statute, one element is that '[t]he conduct took place in the context of a manifest pattern of similar conduct directed against that group or was conduct that could itself effect such destruction.' For crimes against humanity and war crimes, see below.

18 Usually considered to be reflected in the points of reference listed in Art. 38 of the Statute of the International Court of Justice.

19 M. Freeman, *Human Rights: An Interdisciplinary Perspective*, 2nd edn (Polity, 2011), 15–36.

Leviathan that would tame the dangerous, predatory jungle.[20] But it too required taming, and from Locke[21] to Rousseau[22] and Thomas Paine,[23] from Magna Carta and the English Bill of Rights to the Virginia Bill of Rights[24] and the *Déclaration des droits de l'homme et du citoyen*,[25] the idea of an individual human *domaine réservé* was born and consecrated.[26] The human gift of conscience was now not only of equal worth and respect as the duty to obey the sovereign,[27] it was now, in some limited but basic respect, superior to that duty, whether the sovereign be hereditary or institutional/constitutional.

The notion later evolved to include not only the negative obligations of the state to remain within the sphere delimited by human rights, but as noted in the introduction, some (limited) positive obligations.[28] Commentators have seen in such an evolution so fundamental a departure from the original notion of human rights that a paradigm change was emerging.[29] There are two key reasons why this is not the case. First, although sight of it may have been lost, part of the new deal with the rise of the modern state was the obligation on the state to protect people from each other. Where it fails to do that, for reasons implicating a lack of political will (as opposed to practical difficulties), then the failure spills over into the human rights sphere. The important thing here is that the failure involves an element of culpability. The test for the existence of that culpability is typically called 'due diligence', the absence of the exercise of which becomes attributable to the state. Second, it is a convention of international law (as it is of diplomacy) that there should be very strong evidence to permit a conclusion that harmful and unlawful acts not overtly committed by state agents should necessarily be

---

20 The Leviathan was Hobbes' image for that 'man or assembly of men' to whom each vulnerable individual member of society would surrender 'all their power and strength' for 'our peace and defence'. T. Hobbes, *Leviathan* (1651) ch. XVII: http://ebooks.adelaide.edu.au/h/hobbes/Thomas/h681/index.html, accessed 23 November 2012.

21 e.g. John Locke, *A Letter Concerning Toleration* (1689, trans. William Popple), www.constitution.org/jl/toerati.htm.

22 J.-J. Rousseau, *The Social Contract* (1762, trans. GDH Cole 1782, http://www.constitution.org/jjr/socon.htm, accessed 9 December 2012), especially Book I, ch. 4 on the limits of sovereign power (that democratically reflects the General Will).

23 T. Paine, *Rights of Man* (1791), http://www.ushistory.org/paine/rights/, accessed 9 December 2012.

24 (English) Bill of Rights (1689), http://www.parliament.uk/about/living-heritage/evolutionof parliament/parliamentaryauthority/revolution/collections/billofrights/image-3/; Virginia Bill of Rights (1776), http://www.ddleague-usa.net/vbor.htm, accessed 9 December 2012.

25 *Déclaration des droits de l'homme et du citoyen* (1789), http://www.assemblee-nationale.fr/histoire/dudh/1789.asp, accessed 9 December 2012.

26 See L. Henkin, *The Rights of Man Today* (London, Stevens and Sons, 1978) 3–13. On the history of human rights generally, see M. Ishay, *The History of Human Rights: From Ancient Times to the Globalization Era* (University of California Press, Berkeley/Los Angeles/London, 2004), esp. 63–116.

27 The primacy of conscience is sometimes erroneously sourced to Antigone, who had to choose between obedience to her king and her obligation to bury her brother: B. Weston, 'Human Rights', in R. Claude and B. Weston (eds), *Human Rights in the World Community* (Philadelphia, University of Pennsylvania Press, 1989) 13. In fact, even though she chose to do the latter, Sophocles at any rate does not seem to make clear that this was the morally superior stance: Sophocles, *Antigone* (442 BCE, trans. R.C. Jebb, <http://classics.mit.edu/Sophocles/antigone.html>, accessed 9 December 2012.

28 See, e.g. Human Rights Committee General Comment 31 (The Nature of the General Legal Obligation on States Parties to the Covenant), UN doc. CCPR/C/21/Rev.1/Add.13 (2004), para. 8.

29 E.g. R. McCorquodale and R. La Forgia, 'Taking Off the Blindfolds: Torture by Non-State Actors' (2001) *Human Rights Law Review* 189.

attributed to the state.[30] Yet, it is well understood that states will encourage, facilitate and even commit clandestinely acts that they cannot admit to having committed. In such a scenario, it has been necessary to contemplate a scheme analogous to the drawing of inferences of responsibility from what would in ordinary trial terms be called circumstantial evidence. Thus, by developing a positive obligation on a state, say, to investigate effectively suspicious deaths and to prosecute the perpetrators, we are indirectly permitting ourselves, when no such investigation or prosecution happens, to link the state's responsibility to such deaths, even though it may be diplomatically or legally unacceptable to assign direct responsibility. In any event, what is clear is that the general principle in respect of the conduct of those acting unlawfully against the public order, such as organised, insurrectional movements, committed during the continuing struggle with the constituted authority, is that their actions are not attributable to the state under international law.[31]

There is at another level a third reason for not encouraging the sort of paradigm change the advocates would urge. It is something as basic as the need for clarity, for words to be understandable and for important meanings not to be lost, much less cavalierly discarded. For example, it would have been a loss for human consciousness if the fascist chauvinistic enterprise known as National Socialism (Nazism) had succeeded in cornering the market for socialist projects in a nationalistic context. Similarly, humanity's understanding of political systems has doubtless benefited from the failure of one-party dictatorship (Soviet communism) to brand itself as 'democratic'. It seems curious that the new paradigm advocates either genuinely do not regard the notion of something that mediates the relationship of the individual to the state (traditionally and currently called 'human rights') as important enough to figure in human thinking and discourse, or that they do not offer a replacement term to capture that meaning.

Accordingly, it becomes unclear what purpose our new paradigm would serve. Common criminals (murderers, batterers, thieves) remain, after all, criminal. Their behaviour is universally condemned. No clear answer is given as to what the value-added is of calling them human rights violators. The same applies to terrorists. Surely the opprobrium associated with the words 'terrorist' and 'terrorism' should satisfy those seeking to focus on and condemn the behaviour in question?

One perfectly understandable answer might be speculated, namely, that the success of the human rights idea since the second half of the twentieth century make identification with it desirable. It is not so much that they wish to dignify the perpetrators as violators of the right to life or of the prohibition of torture and similar ill-treatment or as flouters of the right to

---

30 The test, according to Art. 8 of the ILC's Draft Articles on State Responsibility is that the group 'is in fact acting on the instructions of, or under the direction or control of' the state concerned. This is the (controversial) test laid down by the World Court in *Military and Paramilitary Activities in and against Nicaragua* (*Nicaragua v United States of America*), *Merits*, ICJ Reports 1986, 64, para. 115; and vigorously reaffirmed in *Application of the Convention on the Prevention and Punishment of the Crime of Genocide* (*Bosnia and Herzegovina v Serbia and Montenegro*, *Judgment* ICJ Reports 2007, 43, paras. 398–407; the reaffirmation came in the light of a challenge to the test made by the Appeals Chamber of the International Criminal Tribunal for the Former Yugoslavia (ICTY) in its *Tadić* judgment (ICTY, IT-94-I-A, judgment, 15 July 1999); the ICJ roundly rejected the challenge at paras 402–407.

31 International Law Commission, Draft Articles on the Responsibility of States for Internationally Wrongful Acts, Report of the International Law Commission on the work of its 53rd session, UN doc. A/56/10 (2001), 49: Commentary to Art. 10 (para. (2)).

property or infringers of the liberty and security of the person, it is rather that it is felt that the victims of these crimes should also be thought of as victims of human rights violations. No disrespect to their grievous pain and suffering is intended, if one describes this phenomenon as a bandwagon tactic. If being a victim of a human rights violation somehow attracts more attention to what one has undergone and gives greater vindication to the worthiness of their story, then it is natural enough to want to wear this cloak on top of the others offered by the existing terminology. However, it is simply not a good reason to abandon the specificity of the nomenclature. It is doing a disservice to the victims of human rights violations (as generally understood) and to the victims of terrorism and other criminality simply to treat being the victim of a human rights violation as a status symbol.

Another reason, indeed one explicitly offered, is that, by treating the non-traditional phenomena as human rights violations, it is then possible to enlist the help of international mechanisms to address them.[32] It is difficult to follow the intellectual leap according to which the existence of an instrument dealing with X justifies renaming Y as X so as to bring Y within the purview of that instrument. Of course, in the case of international machinery for dealing with human rights, the existing methodology used for addressing state behaviour would be inapt for dealing with the behaviour of non-state actors, as will become apparent in the following section.

4 Categories of non-state actor

4.1 Terrorists and armed opposition groups

Before we address directly the responsibility of terrorists and members of armed opposition groups (and the range of entities that these may involve), it is necessary to be aware of the existence of three areas of international law, each with its own specificity, but all capable of addressing under appropriate circumstances the same acts. In order of their entry into the lexicon of international law, they are:

1. international humanitarian law (IHL);
2. international criminal law (ICL); and
3. international human rights law (IHRL).

4.1.1 International humanitarian law

IHL is the law applicable to the parties to an armed conflict. An international armed conflict (IAC) is traditionally one carried out between states. The rules laid down by IHL are addressed to and binding on the states in conflict with each other. For example, they are required to treat prisoners of war from an adverse party according to a detailed formula aimed at protecting them from further harm, once they have become non-combatants. Some of the rules are considered so serious that breach of them by individual soldiers will attract individual criminal responsibility, for example the torture of prisoners of war to gain intelligence about

---

32 Clapham (n. 2) 285.

the intentions of the adverse party (a 'grave breach' of Geneva Conventions, a species of war crime).[33]

IHL also addresses 'armed conflict not of an international character' or 'non-international armed conflicts' (NIAC). Traditionally this was a civil war in which there are two organised, well-structured sides, usually each claiming to be or to have the right to be the government. The rules are more limited than those for IAC and it was not until recently that they were recognised as binding not only on the parties to the conflict as such, but also as far as the most serious practices are concerned, on the individuals involved on their behalf.[34] The threshold of organisation and territorial control necessary for an armed group to be considered a party to such a conflict is variable.[35] There remains the existence of a level of violent armed opposition that by any definition does not constitute NIAC for IHL purposes: these are known as 'internal disturbances and tensions' and they are not governed by IHL.[36] These are the situations that are most at issue in terms of the extent to which IHRL applies to the non-government side(s) (there is little dispute that governments are bound by IHRL).

It is also necessary to consider the phenomenon of transnational terrorism of the sort that rightly horrified the world when operatives of Al-Qaeda attacked the United States of America on 11 September 2001. To the extent that the contest between Al-Qaeda and those following it, on the one hand, and the USA – perhaps not alone – on the other, is an armed conflict at all, it is not an IAL between two states. Nor is it an NIAC in the sense of an intra-state civil war-style conflict. Whether or not is should be seen at all as an armed conflict, rather than a particular species of organised crime, is itself controversial.[37] To the extent that

---

33 The Geneva Conventions (GC) of 12 August 1949 on the protection of victims of war. See Geneva Convention for the Amelioration of the Condition of the Wounded and Sick in Armed Forces in the Field (12 August 1949), Arts 49–50; Geneva Convention for the Amelioration of the Condition of the Wounded, Sick and Shipwrecked Members of Armed Forces at Sea (12 August 1949), Arts 50–51; Geneva Convention Relative to the Protection of Civilian Persons in Time of War (12 August 1949), Arts 129–130; Geneva Convention Relative to the Treatment of Prisoners of War (12 August 1949), Arts 146–147, and Additional Protocol I to the Geneva Conventions of 12 August 1949 on International Armed Conflict (1977), Art. 85.

34 See the ICTY *Tadić* judgment above (n. 30); and Rome Statute of the International Criminal Court Art. 8(2)(c).

35 Common Art. 3 to the four Geneva Conventions does not lay down a clear threshold, other than that more be involved than 'internal tensions and troubles', whereas Additional Protocol II to the Geneva Conventions of 12 August 1949 on Armed Conflict Not of an International Character only applies in situations where a non-governmental party controls territory and has a substantial degree of organisation (Art. 1).

36 See Additional Protocol II, Art. 1(2); Rome Statute Art. 8(2)(d).

37 It has notoriously been the US position since 11 September 2001 that the USA is at war with 'Al-Qaeda and its affiliates'. The position is implicitly, but diplomatically, confirmed in its fourth report to the Human Rights Committee under the ICCPR: UN doc. CCPR/C/USA/4, para. 506 ff, in particular through its continued reliance on military commissions to try certain detainees with this background (paras 578–582); note, however, the address to the Oxford Union by Jeh C. Johnson, the Legal Adviser to the US Department of Defense, who sees the prospect of a reversion to a law enforcement paradigm, once a 'tipping point' has been reached when Al-Qaeda and its affiliates are no longer able to launch 'a strategic attack on the United States': J. Garamone, 'Johnson Gives Legal Background for War against Al-Qaida', American Forces Press Release, 30 November 2012, http://www.defense.gov/news/newsarticle.aspx?id=118667, accessed 2 December 2012; see also H. Koh, 'How to End the Forever War?', Oxford Union, Oxford, UK, 7 May 2013, http://opiniojuris.org/wp-content/uploads/2013-5-7-corrected-koh-oxford-union-speech-as-delivered.pdf, accessed 17 May 2013.

it is indeed a conflict subject to IHL, there is also no clarity as to whether it should be seen as a species of IAC or NIAC.[38] It may be that the argument is academic, in the sense that there are no treaty rules expressly applicable to such an IAC (not between states) and the only other potentially applicable treaty rules are those applicable to NIACs, the core of which are also recognised as constituting 'general principles of international humanitarian law'[39] applicable to any armed conflict.

4.1.2 International criminal law

International criminal law (ICL) is not at all concerned with the responsibility of the state or of any other entity as such. Its focus is avowedly individual criminal responsibility. Examples of candidates for consideration as international crimes that have been identified over time are piracy and various forms of transnational terrorism, such as aircraft hijacking and hostage-taking. For some, these were not a manifestation of the law targeting individuals as much as authorising or requiring states to exercise criminal jurisdiction extra-territorially when such exercise might have been legally prohibited or at least dubious. As indicated earlier, the Rome Statute for the International Criminal Court has put beyond doubt that certain activities by individuals may make them liable to trial in a court established at the universal level for the offences listed and defined in that Statute.

As already foreshadowed, there is overlap between the three fields of law. In particular, at this point, Article 8 of the Rome Statute includes war crimes under IHL constituting grave breaches of the Geneva Conventions in IACs and the most important of these are now also applicable to NIACs.[40] As noted below, crimes against humanity also overlap with IHRL.

4.1.3 International human rights law

In structure and terminology IHRL is more in the mainstream of international law, even though its content, except in respect of (internal) NIAC, is decidedly anomalous, dealing as it does with issues that do not of themselves necessarily have material transnational ramifications. It is simply about the responsibility of the state for its own behaviour. If it commits a breach of human rights obligation, it is expected to make reparation. As in the case of the traditional branch of state responsibility – injury to aliens – that reparation will typically consist of compensation and occasional measures of satisfaction such as acknowledgment of the responsibility. For some serious violations, such as torture, violations of the right to life involving extra-legal killing and enforced disappearance, it will also require bringing perpetrators to justice[41] and even, by treaty, being required to exercise universal jurisdiction over such perpetrators.[42]

---

38 In the US Supreme Court case of *Hamdan v Rumsfeld* 548 US 557 (2006), it was treated as an armed conflict not of an international character and, accordingly, within the scope of Art. 3 common to the Geneva Conventions.
39 ICJ, *Military and Paramilitary Activities* above (n. 30) para. 255, uses this formulation.
40 See above (n. 33).
41 See Human Rights Committee General Comment 31 (n. 28), para. 18.
42 See, e.g., Convention against Torture and Other Cruel, Inhuman or Degrading Treatment or Punishment (UNCAT), adopted by GA res. 39/46 (1984), Arts 4–7; ICJ, *Questions Relating to the Obligation to Prosecute or Extradite (Belgium v Senegal) Judgment*, 20 July 2012, International Convention for the Protection of All Persons from Enforced Disappearance, adopted by GA res. 61/177 (2006), Arts 9–11.

Again there is significant overlap between IHRL and both IHL and ICL. For example, an act of torture may violate all three. If it is committed by a government against someone within its jurisdiction it will be a violation of IHRL. If it is committed by any party to an armed conflict it will be a war crime under IHL and if it is committed outside of armed conflict, as part of an organised attack against a civilian population on a systematic or wide-spread scale, it may be a crime against against humanity under ICL. As a violation of IHRL, the responsible government will be expected prosecute the perpetrator(s). Those perpetrators not associated with a government will at least expect to be brought to justice by those they are confronting if captured. In any event, persons responsible for the war crime or the crime against humanity of torture will be amenable to the direct application of international justice by an international tribunal with the requisite jurisdiction, such as the ICC.

The key point here is that a person who may be a criminal directly under international law does not by that mere fact become a human rights violator. Under IHRL it is the state that typically violates it, either by direct commission (through its agents) or by failure to take the necessary measures to prevent the harm in question, such as by not exercising the required due diligence. For instance, failure by the state to take such measures as it could reasonably be expected to take to prevent harm inflicted by terrorists or armed opposition groups could entail the state's responsibility for a human rights violation stemming from the harm inflicted.

The disputed question is whether it is or would be appropriate to consider any organisation to which a terrorist or armed opposition group member belongs as a human rights violator and, indeed, whether the individual perpetrators should be so treated.

From a legal theoretical point of view there is no obstacle in respect of such armed or terrorist groups having sufficient control over persons and territory as to permit them to be considered parties to an armed conflict. This is not because, by being responsible for breaches of IHL, they automatically qualify as IHRL violators. Rather it is because they will be exercising 'effective power' of the sort that triggers the relevance of the human rights paradigm, as discussed earlier.[43] An example of this would be the Committee against Torture's finding in the *Elmi* case that Somali warlords were effectively exercising state functions. McCorquodale and La Forgia, have described the Committee's decision as a fiction.[44] From this they inferred the basis of a development away from the traditional position. However, there is nothing fictional about the test of effective power as the touchstone of human rights responsibility. Far from being a 'straw in the wind' of a new paradigm, it is rather a vindication of the old well-rooted one.[45] Just as the exercise of 'effective power or control' is the touchstone of state responsibility under IHRL,[46] the underlying theory is applicable *pari passu* to NSAs. This does not mean that IHRL has necessarily gone this far, but it would not be conceptually unjustifiable for it to do so, as *Elmi* illustrates.

---

43 Rodley, 'Armed Opposition Groups' (n. 1). It should be noted that Zegveld has nevertheless questioned what is the value added of using IHRL: L. Zegveld, *The Accountability of Armed Opposition Groups in International Law* (Cambridge, CUP, 2002), 53. Clapham's response seems to be that the human rights machinery can then be invoked: see above (n. 32) and accompanying text.

44 McCorquodale and La Forgia (n. 29), 217, discussing Committee against Torture, *Elmi v Australia*, UN doc. CAT/C/22/D/120/26.

45 It should be recalled that the General Assembly, when adopting the Declaration on the Protection of All Persons from Being Subjected to Torture and Other Cruel, Inhuman or Degrading Treatment or Punishment, did so for the Declaration to serve 'as a guideline for all states *and other entities exercising effective power*'. GA res. 3452 (XXX) (emphasis added) (1975).

46 Human Rights Committee General Comment 31 (n. 28), para. 10.

There is an outstanding question as to whether an organised group involved in the perpetration of crimes against humanity is also capable in theory of violating human rights. Certainly many categories of crime against humanity are also human rights violations.[47] Apart from the fact that the drafts of the Rome Statute deliberately refrained from providing for the ICC's jurisdiction over entities (as opposed to individuals), it should be recalled that crimes against humanity need to be committed within the framework of 'a widespread or systematic attack directed against any civilian population'.[48] Moreover, it needs to be committed 'in furtherance of a state or *organisational* policy to commit such attack'.[49] Together, their elements – attack; widespread or systematic; against a population; by an organisation sufficiently structured to have a policy – come close to replicating an armed conflict setting. It may well be that any such organisation will indeed be exercising some serious measure of effective power. To that extent, again from a legal theoretical perspective, the human rights paradigm could be pertinent.

What, then, is the actual legal position? Evidently, there is no international human rights treaty that purports to impose obligations on entities other than states. They are instruments adopted by and addressed to states, imposing obligations on those states that ratify them. On one occasion thought was given to the idea of including torture by a non-state actor as within the remit of a convention aiming at repressing the practice. The idea was dropped.[50] The machinery they established to monitor or enforce compliance with their terms aims solely at identifying state responsibility. Even the interpretation of the Committee against Torture in the *Elmi* case, mentioned earlier, concerned return of a person to a state (Somalia), albeit one without a state-wide government.

So, if we cannot look to treaties or the courts or other bodies established by such treaties to promote or ensure compliance with them, then we must look elsewhere. For practical purposes this means customary international human rights law and institutions established by the international community to check state compliance with it.

4.1.3.1 Normative instruments

Most 'soft law' instruments capable of reflecting customary international law refrain from imposing direct legal obligations on groups (or individuals), albeit there may be reference to duties and responsibilities that are acknowledged as setting boundaries to a person's scope for exercise of his or her human rights. Article 29 of the Universal Declaration of Human Rights (UDHR) on general limitations, to the extent that the UDHR may be considered a legally binding instrument, is of this nature.[51]

In 1998, the UN General Assembly adopted the Declaration of the Rights and Responsibilities of Individuals, Groups and Organs of Society to Promote and Protect Universally Recognized Human Rights and Fundamental Freedoms (commonly known as the Declaration on Human Rights Defenders).[52] This could have provided an opportunity to articulate, not only the rights, but also the obligations of non-state actors (and individuals) in this field. It is no secret that some states (not usually associated with vigorous international

---

47 See Rome Statute of the ICC, Art. 7(1).
48 Ibid.
49 Ibid.
50 See N. Rodley and M. Pollard, *The Treatment of Prisoners under International Law,* 3rd edn (Oxford, OUP, 2009) 89.
51 Rodley, Armed Opposition Groups' (n. 1), 305
52 GA res. 53/144 (1998).

action for human rights) wanted to make full use of this opportunity.[53] The text that emerged unmistakably rejected this approach. Thus, while 'the prime responsibility and *duty* to promote and *protect* human rights and fundamental freedoms lie with the state', there is a 'right and responsibility of individuals, groups and associations to promote respect for and foster knowledge of human rights and fundamental freedoms'. The emphasised words make clear where the duty to observe human rights (as compared with *promoting* respect for them) lies: it is on the state. Subsequent Articles lay down various obligations on the state. Similarly, Article 2 vests in the state a prime responsibility and duty to '*protect*, promote and *implement* all human rights and fundamental freedoms'.[54] This may be contrasted with Article 18(2) which provides: 'Individuals, groups, institutions and non–governmental organisations have an important role to play and a responsibility in *safeguarding* democracy, *promoting* human rights and fundamental freedoms and contributing to the promotion and advancement of democratic societies, institutions and processes.' The absence of any language suggesting a legal obligation on groups and individuals is evident, as is the absence of any kind of obligation to *protect or comply with* human rights, as opposed to *promoting* (*respect for*) human rights.

4.1.3.2 Institutional action

Support for the thesis that terrorist groups could be human rights violators appeared in some resolutions of the Commission on Human Rights and the General Assembly. Thus, the Commission on Human Rights in a resolution on human rights and terrorism described itself as '[s]eriously concerned at the violations of human rights perpetrated by terrorist groups'.[55] It also condemned 'the violations of the right to life, liberty and security', seemingly resulting from these terrorist acts. This very language caused it to be the subject of a vote, with a substantial minority voting against or abstaining.[56] Similar language in a General Assembly resolution also led to a divided vote.[57]

When it came to appointing a special rapporteur on 'the promotion and protection of human rights while countering terrorism', the offending language disappeared and the resolution was adopted by consensus.[58] The same was true of the parallel resolution of the General Assembly.[59]

Ben Emmerson, the distinguished British Queen's Counsel who became the second Special Rapporteur on the topic, followed the line of these resolutions in his first report. In an introductory thematic section, curiously entitled 'State obligations corresponding to the human rights of victims of terrorism', he asserted that '[a] purely legalistic perspective, which insists that only states and comparable entities can violate human rights, must now be regarded as an outdated and retrograde analysis'.[60] The assertion was made to reflect a 'victim-oriented approach' and was justified by a footnote reference to Clapham.[61] He then went on to

---

53 Recollection of the author who represented Amnesty International at several sessions of the UN Commission on Human Rights working group charged with drafting the text.
54 Emphasis added.
55 Commission on Human Rights res. 2003/37.
56 30 for, 12 against, 11 abstentions.
57 GA res. 59/195 (2004); 127 for, 50 against, 8 abstentions.
58 Commission on Human Rights res. 2005/80.
59 GA res. 60/158 (2005).
60 A/HRC/20/14, para. 13.
61 Ibid., fn. 8, referring to A. Clapham, 'Human Rights Obligations of Non-State Actors in Conflict Situations', (September 2006) 88 *International Review of the Red Cross*, No. 863.

advocate the elaboration of an international instrument on the rights of victims of terrorism that would recognise the victims as persons whose fundamental human rights have been violated.[62] The rest of his report retains the traditional focus of state responsibility. In this, as well as in his second report, he accomplishes the task authoritatively. It may be that, having aligned himself with an understandably victim-oriented approach to his mandate, leading him to venture observations *de lege ferenda*, he will continue to discharge his mandate in the traditional way.[63]

The traditional way is not an approach dictated by inadvertence. In 1997, the annual meeting of special procedures had discussed the issue and concluded:

> [T]hat, when dealing with the consequences of the acts, methods and practices of terrorist groups in their reports to the Commission, the holders of human rights mandates should adopt a victim-oriented approach. The meeting recalled that abuses by terrorist groups could not be considered as a justification for human rights violations by the state. Furthermore, all measures to counter terrorists must be in conformity with international human rights standards.[64]

It is evident from this and the summary of the discussion[65] that there was scant enthusiasm for the proposition that terrorist groups as such could be human rights violators. Nor does there seem to be any action undertaken by the relevant special procedures that aim to engage the direct responsibility of terrorist or similar groups.[66] Indeed, it is not easy to see how this could be done in any consistent way: after all, to what office or official would the *notes verbales* containing urgent appeals or the allegations of violations be sent? At what address? What might be the reaction of the UN member states in question of diplomatic correspondence with terrorists? The less-than-evident answers to these questions – with their factual, political and legal implications – would need resolving before systematic action could be taken. The unlikelihood of any such resolution also undermines even the opportunistic argument that by calling terrorist atrocities human rights violations it would bring them within the mandated activities of the special procedures.[67]

Finally a word about organised crime. As already indicated there has been no sustained conceptual justification for considering organised criminality as a form of human rights

---

62 Ibid., para. 14.
63 The reaction of the International Commission of Jurists, while lauding the report generally, was critical of the approach regarding terrorist group responsibility for human rights violations, expressing 'concern that the report inappropriately conflates the distinct legal regimes governing responsibilities of terrorist criminals and the obligation of states to protect persons from such acts': ICJ, Statement on the Report of the Special Rapporteur on Human Rights and Counter-terrorism in the 20th session of the Human Rights Council: http://www.icj.org/icj-statement-on-un-experts-report-on-terrorism-victims-and-human-rights/, accessed 2 December 2012.
64 Commission on Human Rights, 53rd session, note by the High Commissioner for Human Rights transmitting the report of the third meeting of the special rapporteurs/representatives/experts and chairpersons of working groups of the special procedures of the Commission on Human Rights and of the advisory services programme, UN doc. E/CN.4/1997/3 (1996), para. 76.
65 Ibid., paras 44–48.
66 Two are cited by Dudai and McEvoy (n. 7), 5–6: they seem to invoke situations in which the groups in question were arguably parties to an armed conflict and exercising effective power, such as the Tamil Tigers in Sri Lanka.
67 See text accompanying n. 32 above.

violation. Indeed, its very intuitive inaptness supports the traditionalist argument.[68] It is certainly the case that there are NSAs that engage in activities such as drug-trafficking or kidnapping for ransom that are typical of organised crime in various contexts, notably to raise funds.[69] Again, from the traditional position, this simply confirms that the attempt to bring in politically motivated organised criminality while necessarily excluding it when practised for traditional venal motives, is as incoherent as it would be to treat the mafia as a human rights issue. The point could not be better illustrated than by a paragraph of the first report of the Special Rapporteur on human rights and counter-terrorism. After the passage quoted above about terrorists as human rights violators, he later advises states confronted with terrorism that:

> [N]o distinction is to be drawn ... between terrorism and other crimes against the person or against property. The Special Rapporteur adopts and reiterates the approach of his predecessor that all acts of terrorism should be categorised as ordinary crimes, and dealt within the legal and institutional framework of the ordinary criminal law.[70]

How this approach is to be reconciled with treating terrorists as human rights violators is not explained.

To sum up, there are profound conceptual grounds for resisting the temptation to treat as human rights violators terrorist and other armed groups not exercising effective power, not least the desirability of preserving the very meaning of human rights as pertaining to the relationship between those possessing and those subject to that power. There is no serious evidence that this paradigm has shifted as a legal proposition. Evidently, that could change if states wished it to, just as the traditional meaning of marriage as a heterosexual union is giving way to one involving a similar union by persons of either sexual orientation. The case for it at the time of writing is at best speculative, barely going beyond advocacy. And, from the conceptual perspective, this advocacy is misguided. On the other hand, the underlying justification of the advocates' case is to identify the real need for all public actors and commentators, perhaps especially traditional human rights advocates, to be unstinting in expressing their revulsion at and condemnation of the sorts of terrorist atrocity that, when committed by governments, are properly denounced as the gravest of human rights violations. The victims and, more, the potential victims of such atrocities deserve no less.

4.2 Human rights and corporate responsibility

At first glance the idea that corporations could violate human rights is even more implausible than that armed groups could. But history tells us it is not conceptually impossible. The role of corporations such as the British East India Corporation in settling and indeed governing colonial territories is reminder enough. However, in such cases there was a direct exercise of effective power. Even here, there could have been no question that the British state would have been ultimately responsible for the acts of the corporation it had created and authorised to undertake direct acts of governance.

---

68 See Rodley (n. 49).
69 See Dudai and McEvoy (n. 7), 19–23.
70 Cited above (n. 60) para. 24.

Those who argue for contemporary recognition of corporate responsibility for human rights violations point to the vast economic power that large, often transnational, corporations can deploy to override the will of governments.[71] But it is only in the area of governance that the argument could be relevant, that 'effective power' as properly understood could be deployed.[72]

In reality there is an enormous variety of activities that could bring a business enterprise (the sort of corporation really meant here) into contact with human rights issues. They can range from the purely economic, such as terms and conditions of employment, to the more neuralgic domain of requiring protective security if their operations are under physical threat from dissident groups. In the latter type of case, a range of nuanced relationships may exist. For instance, the enterprise may have private security protection whose operatives engage in acts that, if committed by the state, would clearly be human rights violations, or it could call in the security forces of the state, in full knowledge that the measures that would be undertaken by those forces would involve serious human rights violations, such as arbitrary detention, torture or even extra-legal killings. In all such situations, there is little controversy that, at least conceptually, the territorial state retains prime responsibility for protecting human rights, whether by exercising the due diligence necessary to prevent the harms committed by the corporation, via its agents or contractors, or by refraining from committing the violations, via the actions of its own agents. After considering the extent of this responsibility, in practice, there will be a brief consideration of any direct responsibility of the corporation.

The starting point in identifying what might be the relevant law must now be the Guiding Principles on Business and Human Rights endorsed by the Human Rights Council in 2011.[73] The first principle – one of the few that uses the imperative 'must' rather than the hortatory 'should' – provides: 'states must protect against human rights abuse within their territory and/or jurisdiction by third parties, including business enterprises. This requires taking appropriate steps to prevent, investigate, punish and redress such abuse through effective policies, legislation, regulations and adjudication.' As the commentary states, this stems from the duty of states under IHRL 'to protect against human rights abuse by third parties, including business enterprises'.[74] It would appear that, by speaking of human rights abuses generally the full range of human rights are contemplated.[75] In this it seems to go beyond the more cautious formulation of the Human Rights Committee, which affirmed:

---

71 See, e.g., J. Paust, 'Human Rights Responsibilities of Private Corporations', (2002) 35 *Vanderbilt Journal of International Law* 801, 802.

72 As Knox coolly responds to Paust above, '[t]hose making this argument tend to look only at economic size, not at indicia of power like armies, police forces, prosecutors, and courts, which governments generally have and corporations do not': J. Knox, 'Horizontal Human Rights Law' (2008) 102 *American Journal of International Law* 1, 19, fn. 85.

73 Human Rights Council res. 17/4 (2011). The Guiding Principles were drafted by Professor John Ruggie, the Secretary-General's Special Representative (appointed pursuant to Council res. 2005/69) and contained in his final report to the Council: A/HRC/17/31, Annex (2011).

74 Final report, ibid.

75 See also Principle 12, which reads: The responsibility of business enterprises to respect human rights refers to internationally recognised human rights – understood, at a minimum, as those expressed in the International Bill of Human Rights and the principles concerning fundamental rights set out in the International Labour Organization's Declaration on Fundamental Principles and Rights at Work.

The Covenant itself envisages in some articles certain areas where there are positive obligations on States Parties to address the activities of private persons or entities. For example, the privacy-related guarantees of article 17 must be protected by law. It is also implicit in article 7 that States Parties have to take positive measures to ensure that private persons or entities do not inflict torture or cruel, inhuman or degrading treatment or punishment on others within their power. In fields affecting basic aspects of ordinary life such as work or housing, individuals are to be protected from discrimination within the meaning of article 26.[76]

More controversial is the extent to which the state of a 'parent' corporation has the same responsibility for acts committed in a foreign state, for instance, by a subsidiary of that corporation incorporated under the law of that foreign state.[77] Here, the Principles are decidedly more tentative. According to Principle 2: 'states should set out clearly the expectation that all business enterprises domiciled in their territory and/or jurisdiction respect human rights throughout their operations'. Indeed, the Commentary to this Principle is explicit: 'At present states are not generally required under [IHRL] to regulate the extraterritorial activities of businesses domiciled in their territory and/or jurisdiction.' Nevertheless, by the following year the Human Rights Committee felt it could adopt its first concluding observation on the issue in respect of Germany, in language closely tracking that of Principle 2.[78] In the light of such developments and others outside the UN, such as the OECD Guidelines,[79] it could well be that the world could be on its way from encouraging to requiring state control of relevant extra-territorial activities of business enterprises. Arguably, insofar as most business enterprises are corporations, that is, creations of the legal systems of states, the obligation of due diligence by the state of incorporation, at home and abroad, is even more apposite than for individuals (see below). The practice of states in permitting that reality to be concealed, as though corporations were some sort of natural phenomena, should not be allowed to succeed in misleading us.

There remains the question of whether individual business enterprises can be considered as having direct responsibility for complying with human rights, that is, can a corporation violate IHRL? Many of the conceptual arguments applicable to the same issue regarding terrorists and armed opposition groups apply, *pari passu,* to business enterprises and need not be repeated. The central factor of effective control should be recalled. An element that differs is that, in principle, such enterprises, far from acting against the interests of the pertinent state like terrorists, are as already noted creatures of the state. Thus, state responsibility is broadly available or potentially available to provide a remedy to victims.[80]

---

76 Human Rights Committee General Comment 31 above (n. 28). Another article that speaks of the positive obligation to protect is Art. 6 (right to life).

77 R. McCorquodale and P. Simons, 'Responsibility Beyond Borders: State Responsibility for Extra-Territorial Violations by Corporations of International Human Rights Law' (2007) 70 *Modern Law Review* 598.

78 The state party is encouraged to set out clearly the expectation that all business enterprises domiciled in its territory and/or its jurisdiction respect human rights standards in accordance with the Covenant throughout their operations.

79 OECD, *OECD Guidelines for Multinational Enterprises* (OECD Publishing, 2011), http://dx.doi.org/10.1787/9789264115415-en.

80 Knox (n. 72), 29.

There is limited evidence that international law has vested direct responsibility in such bodies.[81] Certainly, there are increasingly numerous national decisions that go in this direction. However, on their own, these can be seen more as manifestations of the exercise of state responsibility, as much as, or even rather than, state practice as evidence of an international legal doctrine imposing individual/corporate liability. Indeed, the better explanation of even the national decisions is that the corporations in question were acting complicitously rather than as direct violators.[82]

The Guiding Principles certainly do not aid the case for direct responsibility of business entities for human rights violations. The use of the word 'abuse' rather than violation in Principle 1 quoted above[83] is no accident. It is the term typically used to describe the acts of concern in a way that distinguishes them from 'violations' committed by states (or other entities exercising effective power). The key Guiding Principles are:

11. Business enterprises should respect human rights. This means that they should avoid infringing on the human rights of others and should address adverse human rights impacts with which they are involved . . . .

13. The responsibility to respect human rights requires that business enterprises:

(a) Avoid causing or contributing to adverse human rights impacts through their own activities, and address such impacts when they occur;
(b) Seek to prevent or mitigate adverse human rights impacts that are directly linked to their operations, products or services by their business relationships, even if they have not contributed to those impacts.

The call ('should') to avoid 'adverse human rights impacts' is studiously different from a legal obligation to comply with IHRL. In this, the language can be compared with that of the ill-fated Norms on the Responsibilities of Transnational Corporations and Other Business Enterprises with Regard to Human Rights adopted by the former Sub-Commission on Promotion and Protection of HR, but unceremoniously abandoned by the Commission on HR.[84] According to the first of the Norms:

1. States have the primary responsibility to *promote, secure the fulfilment of, respect, ensure respect of and protect human rights* recognised in international as well as national law, including ensuring that transnational corporations and other business enterprises respect human rights. Within their respective spheres of activity and influence, transnational corporations and other business enterprises have the obligation *to promote, secure the fulfilment of, respect, ensure respect of and protect human rights* recognised in international as well

---

81 A rare example is the ICSID Convention provision permitting investors to compel arbitration of disputes with a host state, as well as the reverse, see above (n. 14).
82 Clapham (n. 2), 252–66.
83 Other Guiding Principles using the term 'human rights abuses' are nos 4, 7, 10, 23, 25, 26 and 27.
84 UN doc. E/CN.4/Sub.2/2003/12/Rev.2 (2003); Sub-Commission on prevention of Discrimination and Protection of Minorities res. 2003/16. See D. Weissbrodt and M. Kruger, 'Human Rights Responsibilities of Businesses as Non-State Actors', in P. Alston (ed.), *Non-State Actors and Human Rights*, above (n. 9), 315; P. Miretzki and S-D. Bachman, 'The UN "Norms on the Responsibility of Transnational and Other Business Enterprises with Regard to Human Rights": A Requiem' (2012) 17 *Deakin Law Review* 5.

as national law, including the rights and interests of indigenous peoples and other vulnerable groups.

The emphasised words clearly evidenced an intent to vest direct responsibility on both the state *and* business enterprises to *comply* with IHRL. The change in approach found in the Guiding Principles is stark and unmistakable.

On the other hand, it is perhaps by previously avoiding the notion of *direct legal* responsibility, that Principle 11 can be understood as applying extra-territorially as well as within the 'home' state's territory and/or jurisdiction. As the Commentary to Principle 11 explains: 'The responsibility to respect human rights is a *global standard* of expected conduct for all business enterprises *wherever they operate*'. The emphasised words clearly complement the notion of state responsibility so cautiously articulated in Principle 2 quoted earlier.

While it is therefore clear that business enterprises, notably those acting transnationally, have no direct legal responsibility under IHRL, there is every reason to focus on the responsibility of the state of the (parent) corporation to ensure that the latter does not become an accomplice to human rights abuses. Similarly, civil society can accomplish much in mobilising protests, through consumer boycotts, shareholder initiatives and suchlike, against the *moral* misbehaviour of corporations complicit in human rights abuses.[85]

4.3 Responsibility of individuals/domestic violence

As already indicated, there is nothing controversial about the proposition that certain harms committed by individuals may entail individual responsibility under international law. That responsibility may be direct under international law, in the case of crimes against humanity and war crimes, or indirect insofar as the exercise of state responsibility requires the bringing of the perpetrators to justice under IHRL. In the latter case, it is evident that the human rights violation is committed by the state that fails to take appropriate measures to prevent or redress the violations.

Nothing could be further from, nor more subversive of, the human rights paradigm than to consider that individuals could be vested with 'effective power' in the sense that the term is and deserves to be understood. Stronger human beings can always coerce and harm weaker ones. The legal system is there primordially to protect the weaker. It is when it fails to do so that the human rights idea becomes relevant. A bully can terrorise a household, a gang of bullies can cause mayhem to a neighbourhood. We are nevertheless still only dealing with bullies and possible crimes, not human rights violators.

The issue has arisen principally in the context of domestic violence (overwhelmingly male violence against women and children). The claim is that the traditional human rights paradigm is insufficiently gender-sensitive to take account of such behaviour.[86] There may have been some truth to this in an earlier phase of human rights thinking and action. It is less applicable in the twenty-first century. For instance, the Human Rights Committee

---

85 See R. McCorquodale, *International Law Beyond the State: Essays on Sovereignty, Non-State Actors and Human Rights* (London, CMP Publishing, 2011) 232–37; R. Steinhardt, 'Corporate Responsibility and the International Law of Human Rights: The New *Lex Mercatoria*', in Alston (ed.) above (n. 9).

86 E.g., C. Romany, 'State Responsibility Goes Private: A Feminist Critique of the Public/Private Distinction in International Human Rights Law', in R. Cook (ed.), *Human Rights of Women: National and International Perspectives* (Philadelphia, University of Pennsylvania Press, 1994) 85.

consistently expresses concern at the existence and persistence of domestic violence in states all over the world, typically citing ICCPR Article 3 (gender discrimination) and Article 7 (torture and cruel, inhuman or degrading treatment or punishment). The issue here, as previously stressed, is one of whether the state is exercising the requisite due diligence to address the problems.

One question that has arisen is whether domestic violence can constitute torture,[87] within the meaning of the UNCAT definition which is generally understood to be the appropriate definition for customary international law and *jus cogens* prohibition of torture.[88] It is not clear whether the claim is made on the basis, and for the purpose, of establishing state responsibility (and the appropriate modes of reparation, including punishment of the perpetrator) or of establishing direct individual responsibility.

Starting with the seemingly more plausible approach, that of state responsibility, there is, as noted, no problem with the idea that the overall prohibition of 'torture or cruel, inhuman or degrading treatment' can be violated when a state fails to exercise the requisite due diligence. However, on closer analysis a problem arises with regard to the specific aspect of torture. For the relevant 'severe pain or suffering' contemplated by the definition to constitute *torture*, it must be committed for a particular kind of purpose and be inflicted, tolerated or acquiesced in by a public official. Each of these elements militates against the idea that acts of domestic violence, however torturous they might be in ordinary parlance (horrifying examples are only too frequently to be found in our news media), can violate the international law human right not to be subjected to torture. However negligent state officials might be in addressing manifestations of such violence, thereby engaging the state's responsibility, the purposive element will be rare. As to the crucial purposive element required for a finding of torture, the relevant officials will certainly not have the purpose of obtaining information or a confession. Probably the most relevant of the stated purposes will be the purpose of 'discrimination of any kind'. To muster the evidence required to demonstrate the presence of such a purpose will usually present an insurmountable challenge. In the improbable case that the police are instructed by some superior level of officialdom not to respond to allegations of male domestic violence against women, then both the relevant purposive element and the public official element would combine to categorise the treatment as torture. Indeed, it would be possible to identify and, at least in theory, prosecute the officials responsible for the instruction. That one is drawn into far-fetched territory such as this calls in doubt the initial project of treating cruel domestic violence as torture within the meaning of international law prohibitions.

A variation on the theme is offered by those who would argue that the very inclusion of the link to public officialdom involves a male-gendered approach. We are told that in much

---

87 R. Copelon, 'Recognizing the Egregious in the Everyday: Domestic Violence as Torture' (1994) 25 *Columbia Human Rights Law Review* 291. Art. 1(1) of the UNCAT above (n. 42) contains the following definition: 'For the purposes of this Convention, the term "torture" means any act by which severe pain or suffering, whether physical or mental, is intentionally inflicted on a person for such purposes as obtaining from him or a third person information or a confession, punishing him for an act he or a third person has committed or is suspected of having committed, or intimidating or coercing him or a third person, or for any reason based on discrimination of any kind, when such pain or suffering is inflicted by or at the instigation of or with the consent or acquiescence of a public official or other person acting in an official capacity. It does not include pain or suffering arising only from, inherent in or incidental to lawful sanctions.'

88 Rodley and Pollard (n. 50) 84–122.

of the world, the home is the relevant unit and, indeed, it is the male who exercises effective power.[89]

A problem with this line of argument is that it seems to accept as legitimate that which is not legitimate. If the home is a prison, then the traditional human rights project is there to condemn the states in question for letting it happen or, worse, enforcing it. Meanwhile, the logic would lead us back to a situation where anyone who coerces anyone else to do anything, however unlawful or criminal, becomes a human rights violator. Meanwhile, had the public official dimension not been contained in the UNCAT definition of torture, the UK would have had to release General Pinochet when he was being held in anticipation of extradition to Spain. The British courts would have had to grant him the immunity claimed by the government of Chile. The only reason the House of Lords could ignore that claim, according to its own reasoning, was that it was inconceivable that the Convention would have contemplated the applicability of an immunity that was co-extensive with the offence.[90]

Dubious as the case may be for domestic violence being treated as torture, it must be recalled that none of this relieves the state of its responsibility to exercise due diligence to prevent, repress and redress it. Otherwise, the state will not be able to avoid incurring responsibility for the grave human rights violation of cruel, inhuman or degrading treatment.

5 Conclusion

The eighteenth-century notion of human rights as representing the limits of state power over those subject to that power contains an important idea that does not deserve to be lost. A modified conception takes account of the fact that acts of omission – human rights as mediating the relationship of the state with the same subjects – is consistent with the core notion. So is recognition that other entities may exercise effective power analogous to that of the state and thus, at least conceptually, fall within the human rights paradigm.

The alternative idea, claiming to be victim-oriented, that human rights should be understood in terms of the harm done, regardless of the character of the perpetrator, means that human rights as an idea will be indistinguishable from most kinds of serious crime or terrorism. The perceived advantages of this paradigm – use of a term that has acquired a positive resonance (it was not always the case) and jurisdiction of international human rights machinery – are evidently opportunistic and fail the test of value added or practical applicability.

In any event, international human rights law has not adapted to the proposed new paradigm. IHL and ICL may catch acts committed by parties to an armed conflict or members of such parties or organisations involved in crimes against humanity that would, if committed by a state, involve state responsibility under IHRL (including in many cases a duty to bring individual perpetrators to justice). That does not make the non-state parties or their members violators of IHRL. In any event, they will remain – as they well deserve to be known – as criminals and/or terrorists.

If corporations or major business enterprises were endowed with state-like power, there is no conceptual reason why they could not fall under the rubric of human rights. In fact, they

---

89 Romany (n. 86).
90 *R v. Bartle and the Commissioner of Police for the Metropolis Ex Parte Pinochet* (1999) 38 ILM 432, *per* Lord Millett at 651; see N. Rodley, 'Gross Violations of Human Rights: the *Pinochet* Case in Perspective', (2000) 69 *Nordic Journal of International Law* 11.

do not typically exercise such power, nor has IHRL recognised them in any other way. That does not mean that they cannot act in such a way as to be complicit in human rights violations committed or tolerated by the state in which the acts are committed. It is the responsibility of that state to prevent such behaviour (as well as to refrain from it itself). There is much to be said for the recognition of state responsibility for acts adversely affecting enjoyment of human rights of its own corporations committed abroad. International law has not so far consolidated such a responsibility but it could be in the offing. It is certainly encouraged by the UN Guiding Principles.

As to individual responsibility under IHRL, it is neither conceptually appropriate nor is there a hint of its recognition under IHRL. There is undoubtedly state responsibility for failure to exercise due diligence to prevent or repress serious harm that, if directly inflicted by the state, would constitute a violation of IHRL. That includes the perpetration of domestic violence. However, individuals are not held directly responsible under IHRL for such violence. It is a curious brand of feminism that implies that IHRL is not being gender neutral when treating arbitrary detention, torture, enforced disappearance and murder of women as seriously as such violations against men. It is hardly respectful of the women so treated, of those women and men who have worked on their behalf and of those feminists who had to struggle so hard for women to have an equal role in the public sphere, a role which increasing numbers worldwide are, however belatedly, getting the opportunity to enjoy.

None of the above should be taken as indicating that international law would be inherently unable to take on these tasks. It can assign rights and responsibilities to natural and legal persons if it wishes to. Rather, the point here is that it has not done so and it would be inappropriate to the authenticity of the human rights paradigm for it do so.

Instead of seeking to denature the concept of human rights and distort IHRL to fit the ambition, it may be thought that priority should be given to shaming states that do not exercise due diligence to protect persons in their jurisdiction from serious private harm and to create a culture that is as intolerant of ill-treatment of and discrimination against women as it is supposed to be of ill-treatment and discrimination on grounds of race; to encouraging states to ensure that they bring to heel its corporations which are complicit in abuses abroad; to recognising the often grievous harm inflicted by terrorists while still holding states to a human-rights-respecting standard in countering terrorism; and to exposing those corporations that pursue profit at the expense of individual lives and life projects. This is a viable, victim-oriented approach that remains respectful of the essence of human rights.

Select bibliography

P. Alston, 'The "Not-a-Cat" Syndrome: Can the International Human Rights Regime Accommodate Non-State Actors?', in P. Alston (ed.), *Non-State Actors and Human Rights* (Oxford, OUP, 2005).

A. Clapham, *Human Rights Obligations of Non-State Actors* (Oxford, OUP, 2006).

R. Copelon, 'Recognizing the Egregious in the Everyday: Domestic Violence as Torture' (1994) 25 *Columbia Human Rights Law Review* 291.

J. Knox, 'Horizontal Human Rights Law' (2008) 102 *American Journal of International Law* 1.

R. McCorquodale and R. La Forgia, 'Taking Off the Blindfolds: Torture by Non-State Actors' (2001) *Human Rights Law Review* 189.

R. McCorquodale and P. Simons, 'Responsibility Beyond Borders: State Responsibility for Extra-Territorial Violations by Corporations of International Human Rights Law' (2007) 70 *Modern Law Review* 598.

N. Rodley, 'Can Armed Opposition Groups Violate Human Rights?', in K. Mahoney and P. Mahoney (eds), *Human Rights in the Twenty-First Century* (Dordrecht, Martinus Nijhoff, 1993).

C. Romany, 'State Responsibility Goes Private: A Feminist Critique of the Public/Private Distinction in International Human Rights Law', in R. Cook (ed.), *Human Rights of Women: National and International Perspectives* (Philadelphia, University of Pennsylvania Press, 1994) 85.

D. Weissbrodt and M. Kruger, 'Human Rights Responsibilities of Businesses as Non-State Actors', in P. Alston (ed.), *Non-State Actors and Human Rights* (Oxford, OUP, 2006).

L. Zegveld, *The Accountability of Armed Opposition Groups in International Law* (Cambridge, CUP, 2002).

30

Implementation of economic, social and cultural rights

Paul Hunt, Judith Bueno de Mesquita, Joo-Young Lee
and Sally-Anne Way

The implementation of economic, social and cultural rights (ESCR) has a number of interrelated dimensions. In this chapter, we outline two of them: first, how the ESCR provisions of human rights treaties are given effect in domestic laws and institutions, including litigation before national courts and court orders requiring the authorities to take appropriate measures to fulfil their legal obligations. Although very important, this dimension of ESCR implementation is unlikely to engage most of those working in sectors such as health, food, housing, education, water and sanitation. For them, implementation has a second dimension. Take children's health rights as an example. For a policy-maker or practitioner in children's health, the implementation of children's rights refers to the specific, practical and operational interventions needed to deliver children's access to immunisation programmes, safe drinking water, adequate nutrition, reliable health information, health care and so on. For health professionals, the implementation of children's rights implicates the design, delivery and financing of clinical and public health interventions, such as practical outreach programmes, which are needed to ensure equitable access for all children, including those living in remote and impoverished communities. If human rights experts advise health professionals on the implementation of children's health rights, and they only survey laws, litigation and court orders, they are likely to be heard with polite mystification. While these opening remarks have illustratively referred to health rights, the same point arises in relation to all ESCR.

In our view, implementation of ESCR encompasses laws, litigation and judicial remedies, as well as the operational delivery of ESCR in communities and beyond. Accordingly, this chapter provides a brief introduction to both of these interrelated dimensions of ESCR implementation.

Section one provides an overview of the evolution of ESCR since 1945. Section two introduces the protection of ESCR through domestic law, judicial accountability and effective remedies. Section three considers the implementation of ESCR by way of policies and other operational interventions. Before a brief conclusion, section four outlines new tools and techniques that are needed for both dimensions of implementation.

1 Overview of the evolution of economic, social and cultural rights

A brief history of the post-Second World War development of international human rights suggests four approximate and overlapping phases that mark significant shifts in the global community's approach to ESCR.

The first phase was the holistic vision of human rights that emerged at the end of World War II, when ESCR were included in the Universal Declaration of Human Rights (1948) (UDHR) on equal terms with civil and political rights.[1] While the inclusion of these rights in the UDHR was innovative at the time, it was not as controversial as is commonly perceived.[2] The post-1945 development of the international human rights framework was not only a response to the horrors of Nazism, but also built on the conviction that the misery and deprivation of the 1920s and 1930s had fuelled the rise of fascism. However, although ESCR were included in the non-binding UDHR without great controversy, the debate became more heated within the UN when it came to translating these rights into binding treaty law acceptable to all states. In 1952, the UN General Assembly reversed its earlier position and voted to separate civil and political rights, and ESCR, into two separate covenants.[3]

With the hardening of ideological tensions between the liberal and socialist states during the Cold War, a second phase can be identified: the emergence of Western states' opposition to the idea of ESCR. As a result, for much of the Cold War it became very difficult to have an informed, balanced, sensible discussion about the nature and implementation of ESCR.[4]

In a third phase, a new human rights literature emerged during the 1980s and early 1990s, which posited that ESCR were 'real' rights in the same sense as civil and political rights, and that their recognition, protection and promotion could and should properly be the subject of international law.[5] This literature challenged the view that the implementation of civil and political rights could be cost-free, pointing to the enormous resources devoted to the electoral, police and justice systems. It also demonstrated that the implementation of both civil and political rights, and ESCR, placed negative and positive obligations on the state; in other words, all human rights not only required the state to refrain from some actions but also to take positive measures.

In 1985, the UN Economic and Social Council (ECOSOC) finally established an independent, international monitoring mechanism for state reporting on the International Covenant on Economic, Social and Cultural Rights (ICESCR):[6] the UN Committee on

---

1 Universal Declaration of Human Rights, UNGA Res. 217 A(III) (10 December 1948).
2 G. Alfredsson and A. Eide, *The Universal Declaration of Human Rights: A Common Standard of Achievement* (Martinus Nijhoff Publishers, 1999); D. Whelan and J. Donnelly, 'The West, Economic and Social Rights, and the Global Human Rights Regime: Setting the Record Straight' (2007) 29 *Human Rights Quarterly* 908–949.
3 For a detailed overview of the history, see D. Whelan, *Indivisible Human Rights: A History* (University of Pennsylvania Press, 2010).
4 M.C.R. Craven, *The International Covenant on Economic, Social, and Cultural Rights: A Perspective on Its Development* (Clarendon Press, 1998).
5 Whelan (n. 3) 5; H. Shue, *Basic Rights: Subsistence, Affluence, and U.S. Foreign Policy*, 2nd edn (Princeton University Press, 1996); A. Eide, 'The Right to an Adequate Standard of Living including the Right to Food', in A. Eide, C. Krause and A. Rosas (eds), *Economic, Social and Cultural Rights: A Textbook* (Martinus Nijhoff, 1995) 89–105, P. Alston, 'International Law and the Human Right to Food', in P. Alston and K. Tomaševski (eds), *The Right to Food* (Martinus Nijhoff, 1984) 9–68.
6 International Covenant on Economic, Social and Cultural Rights (1966) 993 UNTS 3 (ICESCR).

Economic, Social and Cultural Rights (CESCR).[7] In contrast, however, to the UN Human Rights Committee (which monitors the International Covenant on Civil and Political Rights (ICCPR)[8]), the CESCR was not initially empowered with the possibility to receive individual complaints. Meanwhile, in Africa, the Americas and Europe, enhanced protections for ESCR were established by new regional treaties and protocols, most notably the African Charter on Human and Peoples' Rights (1981), the Additional Protocol to the American Convention on Human Rights in the Area of Economic, Social and Cultural Rights (1988) and the Revised European Social Charter (1996).[9]

With the end of the Cold War, and by the time of the World Conference on Human Rights in Vienna during 1993, the international consensus on ESCR had shifted to the extent that the resulting Vienna Declaration and Programme of Action (Vienna Declaration) stated:

> All human rights are universal, indivisible and interdependent and interrelated. The international community must treat human rights globally in a fair and equal manner, on the same footing, and with the same emphasis.[10]

Thus, the Vienna Declaration reconfirmed that ESCR were 'real' rights, and that the ICESCR placed binding, legal obligations on states parties. However, the discussion about the justiciability of ESCR then intensified. This discussion often revolved around the argument that it is difficult to adjudicate ESCR due to the 'vague' nature of states parties' obligations under Article 2(1) of the ICESCR, which requires progressive realisation of the rights in the ICESCR subject to resource availability.

In a fourth phase, over the last two decades, the alleged 'vagueness' of ESCR has been addressed by conceptual progress, which has given substance to both Article 2(1) and the rights included in the ICESCR, as well as other international and regional treaties protecting ESCR. Much of this work has been carried out by the CESCR and other UN treaty bodies in their General Comments and Recommendations; by the reports of UN Special Rapporteurs on ESCR; by academic and other civil society experts in the Limburg Principles, Maastricht Guidelines and similar initiatives;[11] and by regional human rights mechanisms.

---

7 The CESCR was established under ECOSOC Resolution 1985/17 of 28 May 1985 to carry out the monitoring functions assigned to the ECOSOC in Part IV of the ICESCR. See ECOSOC, 'Review of the composition, organization and administrative arrangements of the Sessional Working Group of Governmental Experts on the Implementation of the International Covenant on Economic, Social and Cultural Rights', Res. 1985/17 (28 May 1985).

8 International Covenant on Civil and Political Rights (1966) 999 UNTS 171 (ICCPR).

9 African Charter on Human and Peoples' Rights (1981) (1982) 21 ILM 58; Additional Protocol to the American Convention on Human Rights in the Area of Economic, Social and Cultural Rights (1988) OAS Treaty Series No. 69 (Protocol of San Salvador); European Social Charter (Revised) (1996) CETS No. 163.

10 'Vienna Declaration and Programme of Action', World Conference on Human Rights (Vienna 14–25 June 1993) (25 June 1993) UN Doc. A/CONF.157/23 para. 5.

11 'The Limburg Principles on the Implementation of the International Covenant on Economic, Social and Cultural Rights' (1986) UN Doc. E/CN.4/1987/17 (8 January 1987); 'The Maastricht Guidelines on Violations of Economic, Social and Cultural Rights' (1997) UN Doc. E/C.12/2000/13 (2 October 2000). The Limburg Principles focus on the nature and scope of states parties' obligations under the ICESCR, while the Maastricht Guidelines clarify the nature and scope of ESCR violations, along with appropriate responses and remedies with respect to such violations.

For example, the CESCR's General Comment 3, on the nature and scope of states parties' obligations under Article 2(1) of the ICESCR, clarifies that the concepts of progressive realisation and resource availability do not diminish the obligations of states parties under the ICESCR.[12] It highlights that the ICESCR includes 'obligations . . . of immediate effect', which are not contingent on resources or time, but must be implemented immediately.[13] These include the obligation of non-discrimination, and the 'core obligation' to achieve 'minimum essential levels' of ESCR as a first priority in the use of the state's resources (the so-called 'minimum core obligation').[14] In a range of General Comments on specific rights in the ICESCR, the CESCR has developed a tripartite framework under which states parties have obligations to 'respect, protect and fulfil' ESCR.[15] This has allowed the discussion to move beyond the traditional dichotomy of positive and negative rights. These General Comments on specific rights in the ICESCR have also articulated standards to improve the availability, accessibility, acceptability, adaptability and quality (the precise formulation varies a little from one General Comment to another) of goods and services relevant to the ESCR in question.[16] The UN Committee on the Elimination of All Forms of Discrimination against Women (CEDAW) and the UN Committee on the Rights of the Child have also adopted important General Recommendations and Comments, which help to clarify the nature of states' obligations in relation to ESCR.[17] In numerous detailed reports on specific ESCR, UN Special Rapporteurs have applied, deepened and refined the insights provided by the UN treaty bodies.[18] Regional human rights mechanisms have also engaged with concepts developed by the UN treaty bodies and Special Rapporteurs in order to clarify the nature of regional ESCR protections.[19]

Substantive legal work has also been undertaken to clarify standards for the obligations of international assistance and cooperation under Article 2(1) of the ICESCR. In recent General Comments, the CESCR has emphasised that the duty to provide international assistance and cooperation is particularly incumbent on states 'in a position to assist' and that it should be directed primarily towards states unable to secure minimum core obligations through their

12 CESCR General Comment No. 3, 'The Nature of States Parties' Obligations (Art. 2, para. 1, of the Covenant)' (Fifth Session) (1990) UN Doc. E/C.12/1990/8, Annex III.

13 Ibid. para. 1.

14 Ibid. paras 1 and 10.

15 See, for example, CESCR General Comment No. 12, 'The Right to Adequate Food (Art. 11)' (Twentieth Session) (1999) UN Doc. E/C.12/1999/5. The tripartite framework drew from the seminal work of Asbjørn Eide in his report on the right to food (UN Sub-Commission on the Promotion and Protection of Human Rights), 'Report of the Special Rapporteur on the Right to Adequate Food as a Human Right' (1987) UN Doc. E/CN.4/Sub.2/1987/23). Also see Shue (n. 5).

16 See, for example, CESCR General Comment No. 14, 'The Right to the Highest Attainable Standard of Health (Article 12 of the International Covenant on Economic, Social and Cultural Rights)' (Twenty-Second Session) (2000) UN Doc. E/C.12/2000/4.

17 See, for example, CEDAW General Recommendation No. 24, 'Women and Health (Article 12)' (Twentieth Session) (1999) UN Doc. A/54/38/Rev.1; CRC General Comment No. 15, 'The Right of the Child to the Enjoyment of the Highest Attainable Standard of Health (Article 24)' (Sixty-Second Session) (2013) UN Doc. CRC/C/GC/15.

18 See, for example, the Reports of the UN Special Rapporteur on the Human Right to Safe Drinking Water and Sanitation.

19 See, for example, African Commission on Human and Peoples' Rights, 'Draft Principles and Guidelines on Economic, Social and Cultural Rights in the African Charter on Human and Peoples' Rights' (Fiftieth Ordinary Session) (2011), available at http://www.achpr.org/instruments/economic-social-cultural/, accessed on 21 February 2013.

own resources.[20] At the same time, the CESCR has emphasised that this duty to cooperate is not only a positive obligation to provide assistance, but also a negative obligation to refrain from causing harm.[21] More recently, building on the CESCR's analysis, a group of independent international legal experts adopted the Maastricht Principles on Extraterritorial Obligations of states in the Area of Economic, Social and Cultural Rights (2011).[22] These principles aim to clarify further the legal obligations of states beyond their own borders. The principles set out how the tripartite framework of obligations to respect, protect and fulfil ESCR apply beyond a state's own borders, with the aim of emphasising how states can be held accountable for the adverse effects of their actions or omissions on the enjoyment of ESCR of people in other countries. However, many states – notably high-income countries – continue to resist the idea of legally binding obligations of international assistance and cooperation, or extraterritorial obligations, with respect to ESCR.

Important efforts are also underway – primarily within civil society – to clarify the complex ESCR obligation on states to devote 'maximum available resources'[23] to the realisation of these rights, as well as to develop the tools to measure this concept, for example through budget analysis.[24] Measuring the progressive realisation of ESCR in relation to the resources available to a state has also generated substantial methodological work on the use of indicators and benchmarks and more complex quantitative methods of analysis.[25] We briefly consider some of these developments later in this chapter.

This fourth phase of conceptual development has deepened the understanding of ESCR, and lowered the barriers to their justiciability. In 2008, the UN General Assembly adopted an Optional Protocol to the ICESCR.[26] As the Optional Protocol entered into force on 5 May 2013, it finally allow the CESCR to receive individual and collective complaints, initiate inquiries into alleged violations, and adjudicate state-to-state complaints. As this chapter will show, an increasing number of cases are being litigated before national courts under the framework of ESCR, to the extent that, as Malcolm Langford observes, '[t]he sheer weight of the jurisprudence makes it difficult to argue against the possibility of social rights

---

20 See, for example, CESCR General Comment No. 15, 'The Right to Water (Arts. 11 and 12 of the International Covenant on Economic, Social and Cultural Rights)' (Twenty-Ninth Session) (2003) UN Doc. E/C.12/2002/11 paras 31–38.

21 Ibid.

22 'Maastricht Principles on Extraterritorial Obligations of States in the Area of Economic, Social and Cultural Rights' (2012)', available at http://icj.wpengine.netdna-cdn.com/wp-content/uploads/2012/12/Maastricht-ETO-Principles-ENG-booklet.pdf, accessed on 21 February 2013. See also O. De Schutter et al., 'Commentary to the Maastricht Principles on Extraterritorial Obligations of States in the Area of Economic, Social and Cultural Rights' (2012) 34 *Human Rights Quarterly* 1084–169.

23 ICESCR Art. 2.1: 'Each State Party to the present Covenant undertakes to take steps, individually and through international assistance and co-operation, especially economic and technical, to *the maximum of its available resources*, with a view to achieving progressively the full realization of the rights recognized in the present Covenant by all appropriate means, including particularly the adoption of legislative measures.' (Emphasis added.)

24 R. Balakrishnan et al., *Maximum Available Resources & Human Rights: Analytical Report* (Center for Women's Global Leadership, Rutgers University, 2011).

25 See A. Corkery and S.A. Way, 'Integrating Quantitative and Qualitative Tools to Monitor the Obligation to Fulfil Economic, Social and Cultural Rights: the OPERA Framework' (2012) 3 *Nordic Journal of Human Rights* 324–49.

26 Optional Protocol to the International Covenant on Economic, Social and Cultural Rights, UNGA Res. A/RES/63/117 (10 December 2008).

justiciability'.[27] Today, the debate has moved beyond justiciability to encompass issues such as remedies, enforcement and the role of non-judicial forms of accountability. Also, the practical operationalisation of ESCR – in villages and communities, fields and farms, clinics and hospitals, schools and universities, offices and factories – is attracting more attention today than ever before. These are among the issues to which this chapter now turns.

2 The protection of ESCR in domestic law

The ICESCR adopts a flexible approach to implementation, requiring states parties to give effect to its provisions 'by all appropriate means'.[28] The CESCR has spelt out that states parties have an obligation to adopt appropriate legislative, administrative, budgetary, judicial, promotional and other measures.[29]

Informed by Western liberal traditions, the legislative framework for the protection of rights in many countries evolved over generations to protect civil and political rights to a greater extent than ESCR.[30] However, by ratifying the ICESCR, as well as other international human rights treaties recognising ESCR, states parties have undertaken to adopt legal measures as a means to implement their obligations under the ICESCR.[31] The CESCR has emphasised the importance of domestic legal recognition of ESCR:

> [T]he Covenant norms must be recognized in appropriate ways within the domestic legal order, appropriate means of redress, or remedies, must be available to any aggrieved individual or group, and appropriate means of ensuring governmental accountability must be put in place.[32]

The ICESCR does not stipulate the specific means by which states parties must implement it within the domestic legal order and, in practice, states have adopted a variety of arrangements. In some countries, such as Argentina, Colombia and Norway, the ICESCR itself has been incorporated into the domestic legal order.[33] Constitutional protections of ESCR have become increasingly widespread. In 2004, Gauri estimated that, of 165 countries

---

27 M. Langford, 'The Justiciability of Social Rights: From Practice to Theory', in M. Langford (ed.), *Social Rights Jurisprudence: Emerging Trends in International and Comparative Law* (CUP, 2009) 29.
28 ICESCR Art. 2.1.
29 See, for example, CESCR General Comment No. 14 (n. 16) para. 33; CESCR General Comment No. 21, 'Right of Everyone to Take Part in Cultural Life (Art. 15, para. 1(a), of the International Covenant on Economic, Social and Cultural Rights)' (Forty-Third Session) (2009) UN Doc. E/C.12/GC/21 para. 48; CESCR General Comment No. 18, 'The Right to Work (Article 6 of the International Covenant on Economic, Social and Cultural Rights)' (Thirty-Fifth Session) (2005) UN Doc. E/C.12/GC/18 para. 22.
30 P. Hunt, *Reclaiming Social Rights: International and Comparative Perspectives* (Dartmouth, 1996).
31 ICESCR Art. 2.1.
32 CESCR General Comment No. 9, 'The Domestic Application of the Covenant' (Nineteenth Session) (1998) UN Doc. E/C.12/1998/24 para. 2.
33 Section 75, para. 22 of the Constitution of Argentina grants ICESCR along with other major international human rights treaties constitutional status. Art. 93 of the Consitution of Colombia states that international human rights treaties ratified by Colombia including ICESCR must prevail domestically. The Act relating to the Strengthening of the Status of Human Rights in Norwegian Law (the Human Rights Act of 1999) has incorporated ICESCR, as well as the European Convention on Human Rights and ICCPR, and accorded them priority over any other domestic legislation.

with written constitutions, 116 made reference to a right to education and 73 to a right to health care.[34] Some constitutions, such as those of South Africa (1996), Brazil (1988) and Kenya (2010), recognise a wide range of ESCR as fundamental and justiciable rights on a par with civil and political rights. In other constitutions, such as those of India (1949) and Ireland (1937), ESCR are not for the most part considered fundamental and justiciable rights on a par with civil and political rights, but are instead considered non-justiciable directive principles of public policy. This latter model affords more limited legal protection. However, as discussed shortly, creative interpretation by the judiciary in some countries, such as India, has led to the indirect protection of ESCR by reading them into fundamental and justiciable rights, such as the right to life.[35]

Some states, such as the United Kingdom and the United States, have failed to give explicit constitutional or other legal recognition to many ESCR. Even so, where ESCR are not specifically recognised within the domestic legal order, national law can provide important protections. The consistency of this protection is, however, likely to be patchy if not framed explicitly in terms of rights and duties. In 2004, for example, Eleanor Kinney and Brian Clarke found that, while over 65 per cent of national constitutions included protections for health and health care, not all of these commitments were framed in terms of rights and duties.[36] Others included statements of aspiration, or programmatic statements specifying, for example, approaches to financing or delivery of care. Other constitutional or legal provisions not directly focusing on ESCR can sometimes provide protection. In the United Kingdom, for example, the Human Rights Act 1998 gave domestic legal effect to the European Convention on Human Rights (ECHR).[37] While the ECHR and its Protocols only afford limited direct protection to some economic rights and the right to education, developing jurisprudence of the European Court of Human Rights has extended indirect protection to certain elements of other ESCR, including adequate housing and health.[38] Moreover, the Human Rights Act has been successfully used in some British cases to enhance domestic protection for ESCR, particularly for vulnerable groups.[39] To take another example, in a recent US Supreme Court decision on the Patient Protection and Affordable Care Act, which extends health care insurance coverage in the United States, Chief Justice Roberts wrote in the majority opinion:

> The Affordable Care Act's requirement that certain individuals pay a financial penalty for not obtaining health insurance may reasonably be characterized as a tax, . . . Because the Constitution permits such a tax, it is not our role to forbid it, or to pass upon its wisdom or fairness.[40]

---

34 V. Gauri, 'Social Rights and Economics: Claims to Health Care and Education in Developing Countries' (2004) 32(3) *World Development* 465–77 at 465.

35 S. Muralidhar, 'India: The Expectations and Challenges of Judicial Enforcement of Social Rights', in Langford (n. 27) 102–24.

36 E.D. Kinney and B.A. Clark, 'Provisions for Health and Health Care in the Constitutions of the Countries of the World' (2004) 37 *Cornell International Law Journal* 285–355 at 287.

37 Convention for the Protection of Human Rights and Fundamental Freedoms (1950) CETS No. 005 (ECHR).

38 E. Palmer, *Judicial Review, Socio-Economic Rights and the Human Rights Act* (Hart, 2007) ch. 2.

39 Ibid. ch. 6.

40 *National Federation of Independent Business et al. v Sebelius, Secretary of Health and Human Services et al.*, 2012 US Lexis 4876 (2012); A. Liptak, 'Supreme Court Upholds Health Care Law, 5–4, in Victory for Obama' (*New York Times*, 28 June 2012), available at http://www.nytimes.com/2012/06/29/us/supreme-court-lets-health-law-largely-stand.html?pagewanted=all, accessed on 21 February 2013.

2.1 Judicial accountability

In the 60 years between the UN General Assembly's adoption of the UDHR and the adoption of the Optional Protocol to the ICESCR, debate on ESCR has often focused on whether or not they are justiciable; in other words, whether or not they can and should be subject to judicial or quasi-judicial determination. As this chapter has suggested, the argument against justiciability was informed by an oversimplified and now outdated understanding of alleged differences between categories of human rights; civil and political rights were often characterised as generating negative and cost-free duties, while ESCR were presented as giving rise to positive and costly duties. It has been often suggested that resource distribution among competing social policy objectives should be decided by a democratically elected legislature rather than unelected judges.[41] The CESCR has rebutted such arguments by pointing out that:

> While the respective competences of the various branches of government must be respected, it is appropriate to acknowledge that courts are generally already involved in a considerable range of matters which have important resource implications.[42]

This statement is supported by Cécile Fabre's observation that courts in the United States, Canada and Europe have made decisions about resource allocation when adjudicating upon civil and political rights.[43] The South African Constitutional Court explicitly reasoned, during the certificate hearing on the new, 1996 Constitution, that:

> [M]any of the civil and political rights entrenched in the [new text] will give rise to similar budgetary implications without compromising their justiciability. The fact that socio-economic rights will almost inevitably give rise to such implications does not seem to us to be a bar to their justiciability.[44]

Whether or not it is democratically legitimate for courts to decide cases concerning public policy and resource allocation partly depends on what democracy is understood to mean. From the perspective of deliberative democracy, for example, the courts may play a positive role in providing a forum where the disadvantaged and marginalised in representative politics can have their voices heard, thereby fostering democratic participation.[45] Courts can facilitate

---

41 A. An-Na'im, 'To Affirm the Full Human Rights Standing of Economic, Social & Cultural Rights', in Y. Ghai and J. Cottrell (eds), *Economic, Social and Cultural Rights in Practice: The Role of Judges in Implementing Economic, Social and Cultural Rights* (Interights, 2004).

42 CESCR General Comment No. 9 (n. 32), para. 10.

43 C. Fabre, 'Constitutionalising Social Rights' (1998) 6(3) *The Journal of Political Philosophy* 263–84 at 282.

44 *Certification of the Constitution of the Republic of South Africa, 1996 (CCT 23/96)* [1996] ZACC 26; 1996(4) SA 744; 1996 (10) BCLR 1253 (CC) (Constitutional Court of South Africa, 6 September 1996), para. 78.

45 R. Gargarella, 'Dialogic Justice in the Enforcement of Social Rights: Some Initial Arguments', in A.E. Yamin and S. Gloppen (eds), *Litigating Health Rights: Can Courts Bring More Justice to Health?* (Harvard University Press, 2011) 238; R. Gargarella, 'Theories of Democracy, the Judiciary and Social Rights', in R. Gargarella, P. Domingo and T. Roux (eds), *Courts and Social Transformation in New Democracies: An Institutional Voice for the Poor?* (Ashgate, 2006) 28; C.R. Sunstein, *Designing Democracy: What Constitutions Do* (OUP, 2001) 223.

a reasoned debate, and transparency in the process of decision-making and implementation, by holding the government to account for its decisions.[46] In this manner, judicial enforcement of ESCR has the potential for promoting democratic deliberation without displacing the decision-making function of the political branches of government.[47]

Recent decades have witnessed a rapidly growing number of ESCR cases in a wide range of national and regional courts, particularly in Latin America, South Asia, South-East Asia, Eastern Europe, South Africa, the Middle East and some Western countries.[48] In recent years, Latin American courts have adjudicated thousands of ESCR cases, with Colombian courts hearing 140,000 cases on health rights in 2008 alone.[49] In India, since 1950, there have been more than 200 cases involving the right to health care and 170 cases involving the right to education at the High Court level and above.[50] National decisions demonstrating the justiciability of ESCR were referred to extensively in the discussions that led to the adoption of the Optional Protocol to the ICESCR. The establishment of this new complaints procedure is likely, in turn, to encourage some national courts to be more receptive to adjudicating ESCR.

Unsurprisingly, the burgeoning ESCR jurisprudence across the world has exposed variations in how courts have interpreted these human rights. For example, there are differences between jurisdictions in their approach to minimum core obligations. In *Grootboom*, the South African Constitutional Court only required the state to take '*reasonable* measures . . . to provide relief for people who have no access to land, no roof over their heads, and who are living in intolerable conditions or crisis situations'.[51] The Court has largely maintained this 'reasonableness' approach in its subsequent ESCR jurisprudence.[52] In contrast, while assessing the reasonableness of policies and programmes in light of the progressive nature of ESCR obligations, the Colombian Constitutional Court has applied, when necessary, the notion of 'minimum conditions for a dignified life',[53] which is akin to the international human rights concept of minimum core obligations.

---

46 D.M. Brinks and V. Gauri, 'A New Policy Landscape: Legalizing Social and Economic Rights in the Developing World', in V. Gauri and D.M. Brinks (eds), *Courting Social Justice: Judicial Enforcement of Social and Economic Rights in the Developing World* (CUP, 2008) 342–49.

47 Gargarella, 'Dialogic Justice in the Enforcement of Social Rights: Some Initial Arguments' (n. 45) 238; Gargarella, 'Theories of Democracy, the Judiciary and Social Rights' (n. 45) 28; Sunstein (n. 45) 223.

48 See Langford (n. 27); F. Coomans (ed.), *Justiciability of Economic and Social Rights: Experiences from Domestic Systems* (Intersentia, 2006); International Commission of Jurists, *Courts and the Legal Enforcement of Economic, Social and Cultural Rights: Comparative Experiences of Justiciability* (ICJ, 2008).

49 See Yamin and Gloppen (n. 45).

50 V. Gauri and D.M. Brinks, 'Introduction: The Elements of Legalization and the Triangular Shape of Economic, Social and Cultural Rights', in Gauri and Brinks (n. 46) 31.

51 *Government of the Republic of South Africa v Grootboom, 2000 (CCT 11/00)* [2000] ZACC 19; 2001 (1) SA 46; 2000 (11) BCLR 1169 (Constitutional Court of South Africa, 4 October 2000) paras 83–84 and 99 (emphasis added).

52 R. Dixon, 'Creating Dialogue about Socioeconomic Rights: Strong-form versus Weak-form Judicial Review Revisited' (2007) 5 *International Journal of Constitutional Law* 391–418 at 398.With respect to the model of 'reasonableness review' developed by the Constitutional Court of South Africa, see S. Liebenberg, 'South Africa: Adjudicating Social Rights under a Transformative Constitution', in Langford (n. 27) 83–86.

53 See, for example, Cases T-207/95, T-254/93, T-539/94 and T-431/94. M. Sepúlveda, 'Colombia: The Constitutional Court's Role in Addressing Social Injustice', in Langford (n. 27) 147–48.

Yamin rightly observes that 'the role of courts and the possibilities for effecting social change through courts are inextricably embedded in social contexts'.[54] Brinks and Gauri recognise that ESCR litigation may distort public service budgets in favour of privileged litigants who have resources to access the courts.[55] While there is evidence of this occurring in some Brazilian cases,[56] it is suggested that a more nuanced judicial application of human rights standards, especially those of non-discrimination and substantive equality, can avoid court orders deepening disadvantage and reinforcing privilege. Collating empirical analysis of ESCR litigation in six countries, Brinks and Gauri conclude that under appropriate conditions 'legalization can bring some measure of dignity to those in our world who continue to live in conditions of extreme poverty and deprivation'.[57]

In short, the potential for ESCR litigation to promote social justice may vary between countries. It also depends upon judges, as well as advocates appearing before them, recognising that human rights standards, including non-discrimination and substantive equality, have the potential to erode, disadvantage and promote social justice.

2.2 Effective remedies

As this chapter has shown, today it is widely accepted that ESCR are justiciable and, in numerous jurisdictions, courts routinely hear ESCR cases. However, settlement of the justiciability question has led to another important legal issue that is only just beginning to attract the attention it deserves. If a court finds a violation of ESCR, what are the court orders needed to ensure an effective remedy? For the most part, court orders to remedy human rights violations have been designed for violations of civil and political rights. There are obvious historical reasons for this. Are such court orders adequate for violations of ESCR? Or do ESCR violations sometimes have features that require an effective remedy that is unavailable in the judicial armoury largely assembled for violations of civil and political rights? While constraints of space do not permit in-depth responses to these challenging questions, this chapter offers a few observations.

The five forms of reparation set out in the UN Basic Principles and Guidelines on the Right to a Remedy and Reparation for Victims of Gross Violations of International Human Rights Law and Serious Violations of International Humanitarian Law provide an important starting point: restitution, compensation, rehabilitation, satisfaction and guarantees of non-repetition.[58] Moreover, they resonate with advice provided by the CESCR.[59]

A recurrent challenge in the context of ESCR violations is not only to provide redress for an individual in relation to a specific violation but also, in appropriate cases, to tackle the structural or systemic causes of such a violation. In other words, implementation of ESCR

---

54 A.E. Yamin, 'Power, Suffering, and Courts: Reflections on Promoting Health Rights Through Judicialization', in Yamin and Gloppen (n. 45) 335.
55 Gauri and Brinks (n. 50) 6.
56 See O.L.M. Ferraz, 'Brazil: Health Inequalities, Rights, and Courts: The Social Impact of the Judicialization of Health', in Yamin and Gloppen (n. 45); J. Biehl et al., 'Judicialisation of the Right to Health in Brazil' (2009) 373 *The Lancet* 2182–84.
57 Gauri and Brinks (n. 50) 35.
58 Basic Principles and Guidelines on the Right to a Remedy and Reparation for Victims of Gross Violations of International Human Rights Law and Serious Violations of International Humanitarian Law, UNGA Res. A/RES/60/147 (21 March 2006).
59 See, for example, CESCR General Comment No. 14 (n. 16) para. 59.

may require institutional reform and the redistribution of resources.[60] Thus, courts may wish to order immediate redress for individual litigants, as well as a structural or systemic remedy that aims to provide justice to a large number of people.[61] Of course, courts that find violations of civil and political rights sometimes face analogous remedial challenges. Indeed, for many years, when confronted with such systemic failures, some courts used structural remedies to bring about far-reaching institutional reforms.[62] For example, the pioneering decision of the US Supreme Court in *Brown v Board of Education of Topeka (Brown II)*,[63] which mandated racial desegregation in public schools, demanded institutional reforms with implications for equal opportunities in education.[64]

Structural remedies for systematic failures in relation to ESCR are a growing trend in a number of countries.[65] In one case, for example, the Colombian Constitutional Court mandated the government to develop a plan of action and budget to address the deplorable living conditions of internally displaced persons, which should 'guarantee the protection of at least the survival-level content ("essential core") of the most basic rights – food, education, health care, land, and housing'.[66] In another case, the same Court joined 22 *tutelas* (writs of constitutional protection) concerning structural failures in the health system, and called for the government to reform the health care system in line with its unfulfilled commitments, as well as to provide a remedy for the individual cases before the Court.[67] In the *People's Union for Civil Liberties v Union of India* case before the Indian Supreme Court, the applicant filed a 'writ petition' concerning the failure of several states, despite surplus food in their stocks, to make available adequate food to very large numbers of people suffering from several years of drought.[68] In this case, the Court ordered a series of remedies, including the provision of

---

60 For instance, consider the issues of access to fair trial, decent prison conditions and safety on the street.

61 K. Roach, 'The Challenges of Crafting Remedies for Violations of Socio-economic Rights', in Langford (n. 27) 57–58.

62 A. Chayes, 'The Role of the Judge in Public Law Litigation' (1976) 89 *Harvard Law Review* 1281–316 at 1284: '[T]he trial judge has increasingly become the creator and manager of complex forms of ongoing relief, which have widespread effects on persons not before the court and require the judge's continuing involvement in administration and implementation.' Although his observation related to the United States, it may have a wider relevance to other modern regulatory states.

63 349 US 294 (1955).

64 D.E. Hirsch, 'A Defense of Structural Injunctive Remedies in South African Law' (2007) 9(1) *Oregon Review of International Law* 1–66 at 26–27. Hirsch notes that since the case of *Brown II*, 'numerous courts [in the United States] have employed structural injunctive remedies in a variety of ways to foster public school desegregation, to reform state prisons and mental hospitals, and to address legislative reapportionment and other institutional reform of housing authorities and employment discrimination' (footnotes omitted).

65 C. Rodríguez-Garavito, 'Beyond the Courtroom: The Impact of Judicial Activism on Socioeconomic Rights in Latin America' (2011) 89 *Texas Law Review* 1669–98 at 1671–73; Brinks and Gauri (n. 46).

66 Rodríguez-Garavito (n. 65) 1682. See Case T-025/04 (Colombian Constitutional Court, Judgment of 22 January 2004).

67 Case T-760 (Colombian Constitutional Court, Judgment of 31 July 2008). For discussion, see A.E. Yamin, O. Parra-Vera and C. Gianella, 'Colombia: Judicial Protection of the Right to Health: An Elusive Promise?', in Yamin and Gloppen (n. 45) 117–22.

68 *People's Union for Civil Liberties v Union of India & Ors*, Writ Protection (Civil) No. 196 of 2001, Supreme Court Order of 28 November 2001. Information about the case and the text of all related court orders are available at http://www.righttofoodindia.org/orders/interimorders.html, accessed on 28 February 2013.

cooked midday meals for all children at schools in keeping with a pre-existing policy.[69] In *Eldridge v British Columbia (Attorney General)*, the Supreme Court of Canada, relying upon the Canadian Charter of Rights and Freedoms, held that the failure to provide sign language interpreters for patients within the publicly funded health care system violated the equality rights of individuals who are deaf.[70]

Structural remedies in relation to ESCR may require a continuing dialogic process between courts and government, accompanied by civil society engagement and oversight.[71] Subject to context, this process may have several steps: the court declares a violation and sets out objectives to be achieved by the government in accordance with human rights law; the court calls for the government to revise, as appropriate, laws, policies and programmes to address the situation in question; the court exercises continuing supervisory jurisdiction and, after an agreed period of time, calls the government to account for the effective implementation of the remedy; and the court issues new orders in light of progress to ensure full remedial compliance.[72] Given that there can be a range of legitimate options, the court should give the government sufficient flexibility to choose the exact means to ensure compliance with the judicial order.[73]

In conclusion, with the increasing number of such cases coming before the courts, more attention should be devoted to devising effective remedies for violations of ESCR. This will require some judicial creativity and should be informed by existing practice and sound scholarship.

3 Implementation by way of policies and other operational interventions

This section moves on from the implementation of ESCR through domestic law to address the importance of implementing ESCR through policies, plans, programmes and other operational interventions, such as facilities, goods and services required to deliver ESCR. These latter methods are often determinative of whether or not ESCR are implemented in practice. An important development in this respect is the increasing emphasis on explicitly integrating human rights into policies and other operational interventions. This is often referred to as a human rights-based approach, and can help prevent the intended or unintended neglect of human rights considerations in the policy-making arena.

Although national governments hold the primary duty for realising rights, work on integrating human rights into government policies was initially primarily undertaken in the field of development, notably by the United Nations and donor agencies. While there are variations between the human rights-based approaches of different organisations,[74] in broad terms they have focused on defining and applying general human rights principles, such as participation, non-discrimination and accountability, as well as norms and obligations associated with particular human rights relevant to a given policy or programme.

---

69 Ibid. Also see Muralidhar (n. 35) 116–17.
70 [1997] 3 SCR 624.
71 Dixon (n. 52); Roach (n. 61); Hirsch (n. 64) 21–25; Rodríguez-Garavito (n. 65).
72 Hirsch (n. 64) 21–22; Rodríguez-Garavito (n. 65) 1691.
73 Roach (n. 61) 52–57; Hirsch (n. 64) 23–25; Rodríguez-Garavito (n. 65) 1676.
74 See, for example, L.-H. Piron and T. O'Neill, *Integrating Human Rights into Development: A Synthesis of Donor Approaches and Experiences* (Overseas Development Institute, 2005).

Today, building on this invaluable experience, there are renewed attempts to make human rights-based approaches more specific, detailed and – above all – operational. For example, the Office of the United Nations High Commissioner for Human Rights (OHCHR) has recently developed technical guidance that applies human rights to different stages of the policy cycle relating to maternal mortality and morbidity.[75] Other analysis has focused on identifying specific interventions related to ESCR, which must be provided for in policies and programmes and implemented in practice. By way of illustration, the following paragraphs (taken from an article by Cottingham, Germain and Hunt detailing how human rights can help to shape policies and other operational interventions with respect to family planning) briefly outline the priority operational measures that are required by human rights standards and principles in order for governments to eliminate the unmet need for family planning:

> *National and sub-national plans for sexual and reproductive health education, information, and services, including family planning*: Design plans, through a participatory process, to provide universal access (not only for married but also for unmarried people, adolescents, others marginalised by income, occupation, or other factors); to encompass all appropriate public, private, national, and international actors; and to include certain features, such as objectives and how they are to be achieved, timeframes, a detailed budget, financing, reporting, indicators and benchmark measures.
>
> *Removal of legal and regulatory barriers:* Remove barriers that impede access to sexual and reproductive health education, information, and services, including family planning, particularly by disadvantaged groups.
>
> *Commodities:* Make available the widest feasible range of safe and effective modern contraceptives, including emergency contraception, as enumerated in a national List of Essential Medicines based on the WHO Model List and delivered through all appropriate public and private channels.
>
> *Community-based and clinic-based health workers:* Train adequate numbers of health workers who are skilled and supervised to provide good quality sexual and reproductive health services, including full and accurate contraceptive information and modern contraceptives, using the local language and exercising respect for privacy, confidentiality, diversity, and other basic ethical and human rights values.
>
> *Health facilities:* Provide health facilities that are clean, provide seating and privacy for user–provider interaction, are adequately stocked and equipped, adhere to published hours of services, and inform users of their rights.
>
> *Financial access:* Provide state subsidies and community insurance schemes to allow access for people who would not otherwise be able to afford services.
>
> *Monitoring and accountability:* Establish mechanisms that provide effective, accessible, transparent, and continuous review of the quality of services; assess progress toward equitable access and other objectives; and check that the commitments of all stakeholders are met.[76]

Cottingham, Germain and Hunt also highlight that:

75 UN Human Rights Council, Twentieth Regular Session 18 June–6 July 2012 'Technical Guidance on the Application of A Human Rights-based Approach to the Implementation of Policies and Programmes to Reduce Preventable Maternal Morbidity and Mortality: Report of the Office of the United Nations High Commissioner for Human Rights' (2 July 2012) UN Doc. A/HRC/21/22.

76 J. Cottingham, A. Germain and P. Hunt, 'Use of Human Rights to Meet the Unmet Need for Family Planning' (2012) 380 *The Lancet* 172–80.

Governments have a legal obligation to do all they reasonably can to put these operational measures in place as a matter of urgent priority. If they fail to do so without compelling justification, they are in breach of their legally binding international human rights commitments in relation to health, contraceptive information and services, and women's equality. For this reason, human rights are a strong device that could be more widely used by governments to shape, and secure support for, effective and inclusive policies, but also by health-care providers and advocates to improve the quality of services and achieve universal access to reproductive health, including family planning.[77]

Although the examples given here are from the health sector, in other fields such as food, education, housing, water and sanitation, policy-makers and practitioners are also endeavouring to transform general and abstract human rights into specific, practical and operational priorities with a view to accelerating the implementation of ESCR.

4 New tools and techniques

In recent years, a range of tools and techniques, including indicators, benchmarks, budget analysis and impact assessments, have been developed to enhance the effective implementation of ESCR. These methods can strengthen policy-making and other operational interventions, as well as monitoring and accountability of duty-bearers in relation to their legal obligations with respect to ESCR. In short, these methods have an indispensable role to play in relation to measuring and monitoring the different dimensions of ESCR implementation.

To date, civil society groups, international organisations and human rights accountability mechanisms have most commonly used these methods in relation to ESCR. Although governmentsare the primary duty-bearers of human rights, they have less often used these important tools and techniques to deepen ESCR implementation.

4.1 Indicators and benchmarks

In 1993, the Vienna Declaration recommended the examination of 'a system of indicators to measure progress in the realization of the rights set forth in the International Covenant on Economic, Social and Cultural Rights'.[78] Sector-specific indicators have been developed by a range of actors for the rights to health,[79] housing,[80] food[81] and

---

77 Ibid. 177–78.

78 Vienna Declaration (n. 10) para. 98.

79 G. MacNaughton and P. Hunt, 'A Human Rights-Based Approach to Health Indicators', in M. Baderin and R. McCorquodale (eds), *Economic, Social and Cultural Rights in Action* (OUP, 2007); G. Backman, P. Hunt et al., 'Health Systems and the Right to Health: An Assessment of 194 Countries' (2008) 372 *The Lancet* 2047–85.

80 For example, UN-HABITAT and OHCHR, 'Monitoring Housing Rights: Developing a Set of Indicators to Monitor the Full and Progressive Realisation of the Human Right to Adequate Housing' (Expert Group Meeting on Housing Rights Monitoring, Geneva, November 2003), available at http://ww2.unhabitat.org/programmes/housingrights/documents/Monitoring-Housing-Rights.pdf, accessed on 1 March 2013.

81 For example, Food and Agricultural Organisation of the United Nations (FAO), 'Methods to Monitor the Human Right to Adequate Food', Vols 1 and 2 (2008), available at http://www.fao.org/docrep/011/i0349e/i0349e00.htm and http://www.fao.org/righttofood/publications/publications-detail/en/c/129281/, accessed on 1 March 2013.

water,[82] while some projects have also sought to develop broader methodologies for indicators in relation to ESCR in general.[83] Proposed indicators vary but include many common features. They comprise selected quantitative and qualitative indicators matched to the framework of norms and obligations of the relevant rights. Many of the indicators are drawn from those which are commonly used to monitor progress in development, and are selected on the basis of a reasonably precise relationship with ESCR norms. Given the centrality of equality and non-discrimination to human rights, these indicators can require disaggregation on more grounds than are commonly used by the development community. New indicators important to human rights may also supplement these existing indicators, for example on participation and accountability, which are key human rights concerns.

Although indicators alone cannot give a complete picture of the implementation of ESCR, they are crucial tools for monitoring and holding states accountable for the progressive realisation of ESCR. UN treaty bodies, UN Special Rapporteurs and courts have drawn on indicators for this purpose. Indicators also serve an underlying policy, and sometimes a legislative, function by highlighting progress and exposing obstacles. For example, they can help to identify where policy, resource or legal adjustments are required. Some indicators are designed specifically to be applied directly as part of the policy-making process rather than in any formal accountability setting. For example, the World Health Organization and the Harvard School of Public Health have developed an assessment tool, based on a set of indicators, which uses human rights concepts and methods to strengthen laws, regulations and policies in line with states' human rights obligations and to help overcome barriers to sexual and reproductive health.[84] Data is gathered and analysed as part of a government-led multi-stakeholder process:

> The completed analysis across the full range of topics included under sexual and reproductive health, provides a comprehensive picture of the state's efforts to improve sexual and reproductive health as well as a human rights analysis of national laws, regulations and policies, and the barriers that exist.[85]

This assessment tool, replete with indicators, can be applied within a process of policy reform.

4.2 Budget analysis

Budget analysis is an important tool for holding states parties to the ICESCR accountable for their legally binding obligation to devote maximum available resources to the realisation of

---

82 V. Roaf, A. Khalfan and M. Langford, Centre on Housing Rights & Evictions (COHRE), 'Monitoring Implementation of the Right to Water: A Framework for Developing Indicators' (2005) Global Issue Papers No. 14, available at http://www.boell.de/downloads/internationale-politik/righttowaterindicators.pdf, accessed on 1 March 2013.

83 Center for Economic and Social Rights (CESR), 'The OPERA Framework: Assessing Compliance with the Obligation to Fulfil Economic, Social and Cultural Rights' (New Horizons in Economic and Social Rights Monitoring, Madrid, March 2012), available at http://www.cesr.org/downloads/the.opera.framework.pdf, accessed on 1 March 2013; Inter-American Commission on Human Rights, 'Guidelines for Preparation of Progress Indicators in the Area of Economic, Social and Cultural Rights' (19 July 2008) OEA/Ser.L/V/II.132 Doc. 14.

84 J. Cottingham et al., 'Using Human Rights for Sexual and Reproductive Health: Improving Legal and Regulatory Frameworks' (2010) 88 *Bulletin of the World Health Organization* 551–55.

85 Ibid.

ESCR. Budget analysis has focused on assessing, for example, the levels of allocated and actual public expenditure within a given sector, as well as which groups are benefiting and which are not.[86] Analysis has been undertaken in relation to the current global economic crisis, including austerity measures in countries such as Ireland, the United Kingdom and Greece, to reveal their impact on ESCR, particularly among vulnerable groups.[87]

4.3 Enhancing accountability for the implementation of ESCR

The previous sections of this chapter have focussed on one critically important form of human rights accountability: judicial accountability. However, this is accountability of last resort. There are other powerful forms of accountability, such as quasi-judicial, administrative, political and social accountability.[88] The tools and techniques already outlined in this section can help to measure and monitor the realisation of ESCR and thus can contribute to collecting the evidence for holding governments to account not only in courts, but through other quasi-judicial, administrative, political and social accountability mechanisms.

The international human rights community is drawing on the accountability tools and techniques developed by different sectors and professions, to enhance accountability for ESCR. Impact assessments, for example, can be used to analyse laws, policies and programmes for human rights compatibility. Assessments may be conducted *ex ante* or *ex post* to identify, assess, prevent or respond to the likely or actual harm of a particular initiative on the enjoyment of human rights.[89] To take another example, health professionals have established, in numerous jurisdictions, maternal death audits or reviews.[90] Suitably adjusted, these audits or reviews could serve as vehicles for holding authorities accountable for their human rights obligations in relation to maternal health. This is unlikely to occur, however, without open-minded collaboration between experts from different professions.

The human rights community is also extending traditional techniques used to hold states to account for civil and political rights to the field of ESCR. Subject to their mandate, powers and resources, national human rights institutions can provide quasi-judicial accountability in relation to ESCR measures. Established in 1986, for example, the Australian Human Rights Commission conducted a number of public inquiries on ESCR issues, including homelessness as it affects children and young people.[91] More recently, the Kenyan National Commission on Human Rights launched an initiative that led to *The Report of the Public Inquiry into Violations of Sexual and Reproductive Health Rights in Kenya*, published in 2012.[92] National human rights

---

86 CESR (n. 83).
87 See, for example, P. O'Connell, 'Let Them Eat Cake: Socio-Economic Rights in an Age of Austerity', in A. Nolan, R. O'Connell and C. Harvey (eds), *Human Rights and Public Finance: Budgets and the Promotion of Economic and Social Rights* (Hart, 2013) (forthcoming); D. Elson, 'The Reduction of the UK Budget Deficit: A Human Rights Perspective' (2012) 26(2) *International Review of Applied Economics* 177–90.
88 See P. Hunt and T. Gray (eds), *Maternal Mortality, Human Rights and Accountability* (Routledge, 2013) (forthcoming).
89 CESR (n. 83); G. MacNaughton and P. Hunt, 'A Human Rights-based Approach to Social Impact Assessment', in F. Vanclay and A.M. Esteves (eds), *New Directions in Social Impact Assessment: Conceptual and Methodological Advances* (Edward Elgar, 2011).
90 WHO, *Beyond the Numbers: Reviewing Maternal Deaths and Complications to Make Pregnancy Safer* (Geneva, 2004).
91 Hunt (n. 30) 190–95.
92 Hunt and Gray (n. 88).

institutions have a rich potential to enhance effective accountability and implementation in relation to ESCR.

5 Conclusion

In this chapter, we have introduced two interrelated dimensions of ESCR implementation: giving effect to ESCR through domestic laws and institutions; and through practical and operational interventions. Human rights lawyers are more likely to be comfortable with the first, while experts from sectors such as health, food, housing, water, sanitation and education are more likely to be able to relate to the second. However, it is vital that both dimensions of ESCR implementation attract multidisciplinary attention and collaboration. Judges and legal practitioners need advice from sectoral experts if they are to address, in a coherent and compelling manner, issues such as minimum core obligations, the reasonableness of an ESCR-related policy, the interpretation of indicators and benchmarks, and the fairness of a sector budget. Equally, policy-makers and practitioners working in education, food, housing and so on, need to understand how national and international human rights law can shape, deepen and reinforce their operational interventions. Only by different professions working closely together will it be possible to realise the different dimensions of ESCR implementation.

Select bibliography

R. Balakrishnan et al., *Maximum Available Resources and Human Rights: Analytical Report* (Center for Women's Global Leadership, Rutgers University, 2011).

D.M. Brinks and V. Gauri, 'A New Policy Landscape: Legalizing Social and Economic Rights in the Developing World', in V. Gauri and D.M. Brinks (eds), *Courting Social Justice: Judicial Enforcement of Social and Economic Rights in the Developing World* (CUP, 2008).

A. Corkery and S.A. Way, 'Integrating Quantitative and Qualitative Tools to Monitor the Obligation to Fulfil Economic, Social and Cultural Rights: the OPERA Framework' (2012) 3 *Nordic Journal of Human Rights* 324–49.

J. Cottingham, A. Germain and P. Hunt, 'Use of Human Rights to Meet the Unmet Need for Family Planning' (2012) 380 *The Lancet* 172–80.

P. Hunt and T. Gray (eds), *Maternal Mortality, Human Rights and Accountability* (Routledge, 2013) (forthcoming).

M. Langford (ed.), *Social Rights Jurisprudence: Emerging Trends in International and Comparative Law* (CUP, 2009).

H. Shue, *Basic Rights: Subsistence, Affluence, and U.S. Foreign Policy*, 2nd edn (Princeton University Press, 1996).

D. Whelan, *Indivisible Human Rights: A History* (University of Pennsylvania Press, 2010).

A.E. Yamin and S. Gloppen (eds), *Litigating Health Rights: Can Courts Bring More Justice to Health?* (Harvard University Press, 2011).

31

The relationship of religion and human rights

Malcolm Evans

1 Religion and human rights: a many-faceted relationship

Questions of 'religion and . . .' are prone to generate controversy. Consider, for example, the so-called 'science and religion' debate, focusing on whether 'science' and 'religion' (or, perhaps more accurately, whether approaches or understandings based on 'science' and 'religion') are 'compatible' with each other.[1] Juxtaposing religion with something else tends immediately to summon up a hermeneutic of opposition which, rather than facilitate an exploration of the nature of the relationship at hand, calls into question the legitimacy of there being a relationship at all. Nowhere does this seem to be truer than in the context of religion and human rights.

From the very outset of its being recognised as a part of the 'canon' of international human rights law, the freedom of religion has been the subject of a 'double' pressure, both from within and from without. From within, it has been under pressure to be aligned with freedoms pertaining to non-religious forms of belief.[2] The idea that religious belief per se should be the subject of particular protections as a human right has never gained particular traction, and some of the consequences of this alignment of religion and belief for the purposes of international human rights protection will be considered later. In general, however, it might be said that the freedom of religion is 'internally moderated' by this parallelism with other forms of conscience – freedoms. This tends to mean that rather than the focus being

---

1 For perhaps the most prominent example of this controversy in popular writing see R. Dawkins, *The God Delusion* (London, Black Swan, 2007), which prompted a series of debates and responses, including works by A. McGrath and A.C. McGrath, *The Dawkins Delusion: Atheist Fundamentalism and the Denial of the Divine* (London, SPCK, 2007); K. Ward, *Why There Is almost Certainly a God: Doubting Dawkins* (Oxford, Lion, 2008) and, most recently A. McGrath, *Why God Won't Go Away: Engaging with the New Atheism* (London, SPCK, 2011).

2 This is reflected in the freedom being cast as the freedom of 'thought, conscience and religion' and that there be protection of manifestations of 'religion and belief'. The European Court of Human Rights has frequently held that Art. 9 of the ECHR includes non-religious patterns of belief, commenting that 'it is a precious asset for . . .'. See also UN Human Rights Committee, General Comment No. 22, Art. 18 (48th session) (1993) UN Doc. CCPR/C/21/Rev.1/Add.4, para. 1.

on the freedom of religion itself, attention is more often focused on the manner in which other human rights ideals – such as thought, expression, association, equality and non-discrimination – find their outworking in the context of religious belief and belief systems.

The external constraint – the constraint from without – is the view that there is a question mark over the legitimacy of freedom of religion being protected as a human right at all. It is quite remarkable that many of those who fervently support it, let alone those who fervently oppose it, embrace the idea that there is not only a right 'to' the freedom of religion, but also the mirror-image right (nowhere formally articulated) to the 'anti-right': the right to be free 'from' religion.[3] To the extent that this means no one ought to be forced into accepting forms of religion or religious practices this is (or ought to be) unexceptional. However, and as will be seen, it has been taken to mean a great deal more than this. It is difficult to think of any other freedom-right which has an anti-right of this nature associated with it in quite this fashion. For example, the freedom of expression is not said to imply a right to freedom from expression, or the freedom of association a freedom from association, and so on. Religion, it seems, is different.

Over the years some within the human rights world have been distinctly cool – and others outwardly hostile – about religion in the context of human rights. Arguably, this has been of relatively little consequence until quite recently, due to the relative lack of engagement with the freedom of religion by those working within the field of human rights. Following 9/11, however, religion became a more prominent feature in international relations, resulting in a greater politicisation of religion within the human rights field. For some, this meant that if one wanted to return to a safer and more secure world, one means of doing so would be to depoliticise the freedom of religion – and that returning it to the obscurity from whence it came would be an ideal way of bringing this about. In short, if, in international affairs and in the human rights sphere, 'religion is trouble', then 'no-religion' is trouble averted.

There is much that could be said against this argument, but perhaps the most telling objection concerns its underlying premise. Rather than the 'marginal' concept of religion becoming less obscure within the more prominent worldviews derived from human rights thinking, it may well be that the opposite is the case: that in the last 10 years or so it is relatively the marginal concept of human rights which has become less obscure within the more prominent worldviews derived from religion. Once again, however, perceiving the relationship in this manner smacks of opposition, of dualism between ideas and clashes of right and wrong. The author has been party to many serious discussions in which evidence of egregious violations of basic religious rights of believers have been countered with examples of situations in which *other* religious believers have not been particularly accommodating of the rights of others, perhaps of women or of those who are lesbian, gay, bisexual and transgender (LGBTs), or have sought to restrict the right of others to express themselves through the use of blasphemy laws, and so on. It is as if it were acceptable to say 'Yes, we know that X is being persecuted for their beliefs, but if we protect them in the enjoyment of their religious beliefs, we will be failing to properly protect the human rights of others'. Such logical non sequiturs and unproven consequentialism would quickly be rejected in other areas of human rights thinking: a state is not generally accused of endorsing

---

3 See, for example, UN HRC General Comment No. 22 (n. 2) para. 2: 'Article 18 protects theistic, non-theistic and atheistic beliefs, as well as the right not to profess any religion or belief.'

criminal conduct or of prejudicing the rights of victims of crime, because of its insistence that those charged with criminal offences receive a fair trial. All the more so is it strange that there should be such a reluctance to protect the rights of religious believers lest it be thought that in doing so one supports and encourages their beliefs.

Be that as it may, mutual doubt and hesitation permeate the relationship between religion and human rights, and it does need to be recalled that for many years, many within the organised religious world rejected the theoretical underpinnings of human rights thinking as being inimical to their theological understandings,[4] and for some this remains the case today. Once again, a sense of dualism pervades the arena. For many, human rights must be compatible with their faith, whilst for others it is faith which must be rendered compatible with human rights. Much of the doctrinal work in this area – and particularly as regards Islam and human rights – has focused on how religious belief and human rights can be 'reconciled' through the reinterpretation of one's faith, or in adhering to strands within one's faith tradition which accord with contemporary human rights standards.[5] Yet it ought not to be thought that this process has only involved Islam. For example, although it takes a different form and reflects different historical, political, social and theological factors, a similar process is occurring in Europe, focusing on what might be called the secularising of the public space.[6] Given the nature of, certainly, Western Christian doctrine, the so-called debate about the role of religion in public life seems to fulfil a very similar function to the debate concerning schools of interpretation within Islamic thinking. In both, the central issue is not 'about' secularity or neutrality or about theological inquiry, it is about forging an approach capable of resolving the tensions between religion and human rights.[7]

Once again, however, we find ourselves drawn back to the 'religion and . . .' question, which is why both these lines of enquiry, and others like them, are ultimately so unsatisfactory. This is not to say that they are unhelpful. Such discussions can be profoundly helpful in clarifying lines of thinking and the issues which underlie them. Yet they can only assist in addressing the 'tension' to the extent that those engaged in the discussions concerning, say, role of religion in public life or the acceptability of principles of theological interpretation, continue to share a sufficiency of common space. One has to have agreement on what comprises the 'public' as opposed to the 'private' sphere; on what falls within the scope of public life and what does not;[8] on what religious texts are to be subject to interpretation of whatever nature, and so on. The real problem lies in the perception that there are ultimately limits to the common space within which shared discourse can generate positive outcomes.

---

4 By way of example, see the recent overview of the development of Catholic doctrinal thinking concerning Human Rights by C. McCrudden, 'Legal and Roman Catholic Conceptions of Human Rights: Convergence, Divergence and Dialogue' (2012) 1 *Oxford Journal of Law and Religion* 185.

5 Of the many works exploring such approaches from a legal perspective, see in particular the work of A. An-Na'im, e.g. *Islam and the Secular State: Negotiating the Future of Sharia* (Cambridge, MA, Harvard University Press, 2008) and M. Baderin (ed.), *Islam and Human Rights: Selected Essays of Adbullahi An-Na'im* (Farnham, Ashgate Publishing, 2010). See also M. Baderin, *International Human Rights and Islamic Law* (Oxford, OUP, 2003).

6 See, for example, R. Trigg, *Religion in Public Life: Must Faith be Privatized?* (Oxford, OUP, 2007).

7 That there might be tensions is both explored in and graphically illustrated in the title of N. Ghanea, A. Stephens and R. Waldron, *Does God Believe in Human Rights* (The Hague, Martinus Nijhoff, 2007).

8 For example, is buying a postage stamp in a state-run post office to be understood as a public event? If so, then does the religious clothing worn by the person buying the stamp become a matter of legitimate public concern?

If all one is doing is redefining the parameters of the 'problem', one is merely relocating the source of future tension, rather than identifying a means of addressing it.

Need it be this way? It is often overlooked that the originators of contemporary international human rights thinking – as with so many other aspects of international humanitarianism – did not only derive inspiration or motivation from their religious beliefs, but that the protection of religious believers originally lay at the heart of the enterprise,[9] though this has tended to become lost from view. It has also been argued by some that there is something of the 'religious' about the espousal of human rights,[10] which perhaps finds some reflection in the contemporary trend towards grounding both religion and human rights in the concept of dignity.[11] Whatever one's view on this, it does offer a rather different approach to the relationship between religion and human rights. Rather than an approach based on identifying a means of accommodation which is mutually acceptable to the various camps concerned (an approach which of course also reinforces the sense of there being a separation between them, a gulf to cross, a bridge to build), it points to an approach which is founded upon their commonalities. This is not to suggest that religion and human rights are, in some sense, the same. They are not. But they do share an overlapping function, this being a shared concern with how people are to relate to each other within a governed society. The starting point, then, for a useful exploration of the relationship between religion and human rights begins not with religion, nor with human rights, but with recognition of the contribution which each makes to that common enterprise. That each may seek to do more besides is neither here nor there.

This is not without implications, and most troublesome of which might be that it accords legitimacy upon both religion and human rights and seeks to understand them as operating within a shared space. It has already been mentioned that this is a claim which many in religious circles have long denied, and which is still contested by some religious believers. It is also deeply controversial for many of a non-religious persuasion who find it difficult to accept the rationality or reality of religious belief and who are not inclined to accept any implications of religious legitimacy which might have a material bearing upon them. Yet religion and human rights demonstrably exist as forces within the shared space of human governance. The future lies not in trying to understand the one in terms of the other, but in trying to understand each in terms of each other: not as forces pulling in opposite directions but as forces directed at a common endeavour, albeit not necessarily always doing so in a mutually supportive fashion and neither of which is immune from misunderstanding, misapplication or mistake. To borrow and adapt a phrase, however, it involves taking religion and rights seriously. This chapter is a contribution to a section of a book concerning key contemporary challenges facing international human rights law. The remainder of this chapter will now seek to apply this approach in the context of a number of areas of current practical controversy in order to lend practicality to these rather abstract introductory reflections.

---

9 See generally M. Evans, *Religion and International Law in Europe* (Cambridge, CUP, 1997). For the interplay between religion and international law more generally, see M. Janis and C. Evans, *Religion and International Law,* 2nd edn (The Hague, Martinus Nijhoff, 2004). For an older work predating the 'human rights' era on this see N. Bentwich, *The Religious Foundations of Internationalism* (London, Allen & Unwin, 1933).

10 See, for example, M. Perry, *The Idea of Human Rights* (Oxford, OUP, 1997), ch. 1.

11 For a penetrating analysis of this trend, see C. McCrudden, 'Human Dignity and the Judicial Interpretation of Human Rights' (2008) 19 *European Journal of International Law* 655.

2 The architecture of protection

2.1 The current scheme of international 'protection' of the freedom of religion and belief

There is an understandable tendency for international lawyers to look to the provisions of international human rights law when considering the scope of protection afforded internationally to a human right. Whilst this might be appropriate when considering the normative content of a right, it is increasingly understood that it is less so when it comes to questions of implementation, or realisation, of the right. Paradoxically, it is at a time when the oversight mechanisms associated with human rights instruments are proliferating as never before[12] that their centrality to the business of international human rights protection is coming under increasingly critical scrutiny.[13] As regards the freedom of religion or belief, however, this is hardly so pressing a concern, as one of the most notable features of the development of the international human rights regime since the Universal Declaration of Human Rights (UDHR) in 1948 has been the remarkable lack of progress concerning a right which in the run-up to its adoption was considered by many to be one of the most significant of the rights proclaimed. Indeed, it bears mentioning that the Preamble to the Declaration by United Nations of 1 January 1942, prefiguring not the UDHR but the UN Charter itself, stated that 'complete victory . . . is essential to defend life, liberty, independence and religious freedom, and to preserve human rights and justice',[14] placing religious freedom at the heart of the enterprise of allied victory and the post Second World War reconfiguring of the world order. This has not been followed up with particular alacrity within the sphere of human rights.

The story is well known, and space precludes a lengthy account. In summary, Article 18 of the Universal Declaration of Human Rights provides that:

> Everyone has the right to freedom of thought, conscience and religion; this right includes freedom to change his religion or belief, and freedom, either alone or in community with others and in public or private, to manifest his religion or belief in teaching, practice, worship and observance.

This conceptualises the freedom as a classic individual right, operating in two spheres. The first is an internal 'sphere', usually referred to as the 'forum internum' and representing the absolute right of a person to intellectual autonomy by guaranteeing the freedom of thought, conscience and religion. This is supplemented by the right to manifest religion or belief in a

---

12 For example, Optional Protocols have recently added individual communications procedures to several UN human rights treaties, including the Optional Protocol to the Convention on Economic, Social and Cultural Rights (adopted by GA Res. 63/117, 10 December 2008: for text see Doc. A/63/435, 11 December 2009) and, most recently, the Third Optional Protocol to the Convention on the Rights of the Child (adopted by GA Res. 66/141, 19 December 2011).

13 See the increasing focus on the work of National Human Rights Institutions (e.g. R. Murray, *The Role of National Human Rights Institutions at the International and Regional Levels: The Experience of Africa* (Oxford, Hart Publishing, 2007) and the role of National Preventive Mechanisms under some recent international instruments, including the Optional Protocol to the UN Convention against Torture (2002), 2375 UNTS 237 and the UN Convention on the Rights of Persons with Disabilities (2006) 2515 UNTS 3.

14 See R.B. Russell, *A History of the United Nations Charter* (Washington DC, The Brookings Institute, 1958), p. 975.

number of ways in both public and private, usually expressed as the external sphere, or the 'forum externum'. The freedom of thought, conscience and religion is an absolute right, which cannot be derogated from even in times of public emergency. The right of manifestation is, however, more circumscribed and is capable of being subject to proportionate restrictions in order to protect a range of other interests, including the rights and freedoms of others. This basic pattern for protection is found in the UDHR,[15] the International Covenant on Civil and Political Rights,[16] the European Convention on Human Rights[17] and other regional instruments (albeit with some small but significant differences).[18] Although specific provisions exist in a number of other major international human rights instruments concerning the freedom of religion to be enjoyed by particular groups, such as children, minorities or indigenous peoples,[19] it is the architecture of the right as found in UDHR Article 18 and those instruments based upon it which provide the dominant legal and intellectual apparatus for engaging with the freedom of religion and belief.

Yet it was not meant to be this way. It was in 1956 that the UN decided to undertake further work on the freedom of religion or belief, a process that culminated in a Report in 1960 which set out 18 draft 'principles'.[20] In 1962 the UN decided to develop a declaration and a convention on the freedom of religion or belief. Strangely, work on the Convention moved ahead first, made little progress and was shelved in 1967, and has not been returned to since. A declaration was finally adopted in 1981, the Declaration on the Elimination of All Forms of Intolerance and of Discrimination Based on Religion or Belief.[21] The 30th Anniversary of the Declaration in 2011 passed by with relatively little attention. By any standards, this does not suggest particular activism within the international community to strengthen and develop the right over time. Within the UN system there is one formal mechanism devoted to the right, the Special Rapporteur on the Freedom of Religion and Belief. This mandate was one of the earliest to be established in 1986, and has been regularly renewed ever since.[22] In common with many other UN Special Procedures, the mandate-holders have been able to become more active in recent times as a result of greater practical and political support for their work. Nevertheless, one mandate – holder cannot develop and uphold the freedom of religion and belief single-handedly. The UN Human Rights Committee operating under the ICCPR complements this within the treaty body system, and the Human Rights Council is also increasingly engaging with issues concerning the

---

15 Art. 18, for which see above.
16 International Convenant on Civil and Political Rights, Art. 18 (1966) 999 UNTS 171.
17 European Convention on Human Rights and Fundamental Freedoms, Art. 9 (1950) ETS No. 5.
18 See, for example, American Convention on Human Rights, Art. 12, (1969) OAS TS No. 36; African Charter on Human and Peoples' Rights, Art. 8, (1981) 1520 UNTS 363 (this departing more than any other from this model). But see also the Arab Charter for Human Rights (2004), in (2005) 12 Int H. Rights Rep. 893, which does not adopt this approach at all.
19 See UN Convention on the Rights of the Child, Art. 14 (1989), 1577 UNTS 3; Declaration on the Rights of Persons Belonging to National or Ethnic or Religious Minorities, *passim*, GA Res. 47/135 (18 December 1992); Declaration on the Rights of Indigenous Peoples, Art. 12, GA Res. 61/995 (13 September 2007).
20 The Krishnaswami Report, UN Doc. E/CN.4/Sub.2/200/Rev.1.
21 Adopted by GA Res. 36/55 (25 November 1981). For an overview and analysis of the work of the UN during the period leading up to its adoption, see B. Tahzib, *Freedom of Religion or Belief: Ensuring Effective International Action* (Dordrecht, Martinus Nijhoff, 1995); M. Evans, *Religion and International Law in Europe* (Cambridge, CUP, 1997), ch. 9.
22 The mandate was originally established by UN Commission on Human Rights Res. 1986/20 and was most recently renewed by Human Rights Council Res. 14/11 (18 June 2010).

freedom of religion or belief, but as will be seen shortly, the general political context is not entirely auspicious. There has, then, been a comparative dearth of normative development within the UN system.

On the other hand, outside of the UN system, the European Court of Human Rights has over the last 20 years produced an increasingly rich, and richly controversial, body of jurisprudence on the freedom of religion or belief, aspects of which will be touched on below.[23] As a result, it is largely this body of material which has driven the subject forward, since other regional systems have had relatively little engagement with the issue under their respective human rights instruments. An exception is the Organization for Security and Cooperation in Europe, which has developed an extensive series of Commitments pertaining to the freedom of religion and belief[24] and has established the only other quasi-formally constituted international body tasked with addressing issues pertaining to the freedom of religion and belief, in the form of the Office of Democratic Institutions and Human Rights' Advisory Council and Advisory Panel.[25] Other expert bodies established under other regional systems, such as the Council of Europe's Commission for Democracy through Law (the Venice Commission), also do considerable work on an ad hoc basis, including joint work with the OSCE Advisory Council. Many other international organs, of course, engage with the freedom, but there are few others which are structurally centred upon it. There are of course other tiers which comprise elements of the protective framework, including NGOs and national commissions with international foci, perhaps the most significant of which is the US Commission on International Religious Freedom.[26] As a consequence of this pattern of development (or of non - development) at the broader international level, international jurisprudential thinking has often been driven by European perceptions and preoccupations.

With the exception of the ECHR and, perhaps, the UN Special Rapporteur, the international machinery of protection can then appear generally weak, unfocused or disengaged. If it is, there may be good reasons. The overriding reason is the enduring sensitivity of the subject and a lack of consensus around key aspects of the normative framework. There is little point in seeking to develop elaborate international enforcement mechanisms when there is not even baseline consensus concerning key aspects of what it is that is to be enforced. For example, it appears that no such consensus exists around even so fundamental a question as the right of an individual to change their religion, despite this being expressly provided for in the UDHR and having been advocated by the organs of oversight for many years.[27] In the

---

23 For some examples of the many works surveying its output, see, inter alia, C. Evans, *Religious Freedom under the European Convention on Human Rights* (Oxford, OUP, 2001); P. Taylor, *Freedom of Religion: UN and European Human Rights Law and Practice* (Cambridge, CUP, 2005); M. Evans, 'From Cartoons to Crucifixes', in E. Reed and M. Dumper (eds), *Civil Liberties, National Security and Prospects for Consensus: Legal, Philosophical and Religious Perspectives* (Cambridge, CUP, 2012). Resonating with the title of this section of this chapter, see also C. Evans, 'Individual and Group Religious Freedom in the European Court of Human Rights: Cracks in the Intellectual Architecture' (2010–11) 26 *Journal of Law and Religion* 321.

24 See U. Gibson and K.S. Lord, 'Advancements in Standard Setting: Religious Liberty and OSCE Commitments', in T. Lindohlm, W. Cole Durham Jr and B. Tahzib-Lie (eds), *Facilitating Freedom of Religion or Belief: A Deskbook* (The Hague, Martinus Nijhoff, 2004).

25 For details see http://www.osce.org/odihr/44455, accessed on 25 January 2012.

26 Established by the International Religious Freedom Act, 1998, P.L. 105–292 (as amended). For the work of the Commission see http://www.uscirf.gov/home.html, accessed on 25 January 2012.

27 See, for example, UN HRC General Comment No. 22 (n. 2), para. 5.

face of this, it is unsurprising that the political ramifications of developing the freedom of religion as a human right are often considered to be too difficult to overcome.

2.2 Defamation of religion: a challenge diverted[28]

Moreover, and more ominously, there has been an increasingly vocal lobby challenging the premise that the freedom of religion is to be enjoyed within the context of human rights protection at all, it being argued that religion provides the context within which human rights are to be understood and experienced. In some ways, this is the mirror image of the theoretical approach mentioned earlier in which religious belief is to be reinterpreted in the light of emergent human rights standards. The difference is that whilst the latter has been an academic and intellectual movement, the former has taken the form of hard politics, and has coalesced around the 'debate' on 'defamation of religions'.

One of the weaknesses of the architecture of protection outlined above is the extent to which it focuses on the freedom of religion and belief as an individual right. That it is an individual right is beyond question, but it is also beyond doubt that it also has a collective dimension as well: indeed, UDHR Article 18 itself refers to the right to manifest in public as well as in private. However, this does not mean that international human rights law should be used – by individuals or by religious bodies – to promote or to protect particular religious values or beliefs. Nor should it, in general, be used to restrain others from behaviour which adherents to a given belief deem to be inappropriate. The starting point for human rights law should be the right of persons to hold, and to act in accordance with their beliefs, individually and collectively. Generally speaking, it is only if the level of comment, criticism or patterns of behaviour reaches an intensity which prejudices their capacity to do so, that there will be grounds for intervention.

Nevertheless, this has not prevented concerted efforts being made within international fora for recognition to be given to the very opposite idea – that human rights thinking means that the state should be entitled to use its legal powers to restrict those who seek to 'defame' religion, not just in the sense of criticising but in the broader sense of failing to respect the values of the religious system in question. It is on the basis of such thinking that some seek to justify action against those who oppose apostasy or blasphemy laws, as well as imposing restrictions upon or taking action against those whose lifestyles and mores do not accord with those espoused by their religion. The precise parameters of the idea have always been rather vague, but this has not stopped the UN from adopting a resolution each year from 1999 to 2010 supporting the idea (albeit with ever-declining majorities).[29] Since these Resolutions were couched in the language of the promotion of tolerance and respect, whilst combating negative stereotyping, it is easy to see why these resolutions resonated with many. But over time their repressive potential has been realised and, in response to this, the language used began to shift away from 'defamation of religions' and towards the widely accepted language associated with combating incitement to religious hatred.

In March 2011 it appeared that the 'defamation debate' was finally put to rest when the Organization of the Islamic Conference, the body which has been co-ordinating the

---

28 Elements of this section draw on M. Evans, 'Advancing Freedom of Religion or Belief: Agendas for Change', (2012) 1 *Oxford Journal of Law and Religion* 5.

29 For overviews see G. Bennett, 'Defamation of Religions: the End of Pluralism?' (2009) 23 *Emory International Law Review* 69; L. Langer, 'Recent Development: The Rise (and Fall?) of Defamation of Religions', (2010) 35 *Yale Journal of International Law* 257.

defamation resolutions, failed to put a resolution on this topic forward to the UN Human Rights Council, but presented and secured the adoption, without a vote, of a resolution on 'Combating intolerance, negative stereotyping and stigmatization of, and discrimination, incitement to violence, and violence against persons based on religion or belief'.[30] Inter alia, the Resolution calls on states 'To foster religious freedom and pluralism by promoting the ability of members of all religious communities to manifest their religion, and to contribute openly and on an equal footing to the society' (paragraph 6(b)), but its principal focus was on the need to tackle incitement to religious hatred.

HRC Resolution 16/18 marks a significant change in approach, both practically and conceptually, away from the 'defamation' approach and it has been endorsed at the highest political levels.[31] But there is a danger of losing sight of the point that the 'defamation' debate was not about defamation per se. Rather, it was about the legitimacy of the state intervening to protect or promote particular forms of belief through disadvantaging, stigmatising, pressurising or even persecuting those whose beliefs or behaviours did not accord with the dominant view. Moving the debate on to issues concerning incitement to religious hatred may seem – and may indeed prove to be – a positive step. There is, however, a major difficulty with approaches based on incitement, and this concerns the point at which it is legitimate to intervene: at one end of the spectrum lies intervention in order to prevent the imminent risk of violence; at the other lies intervention in order to prevent forms of expression or activities which challenge, question or merely contravene the values of others.[32]

It seems, then, that the growing realisation that 'defamation of religions' was more likely to serve as a tool of repression than as a tool of religious freedom caused the language of the debate to shift to the more widely accepted and legitimated language of combating incitement to religious hatred.[33] The problem, however, lies in the malleable contours of that concept, and in any case it seems that the focus of attention has merely shifted from one contestable concept to another. Moreover, the question which continually gets lost is the fundamental one of whether we would do better to focus rather more on the idea of enhancing our understanding of the freedom of religion or belief for all, and focus rather less on the action to be taken against those who denigrate the beliefs of others. This latter element may be a legitimate *element* of the overall architecture of protection but it can hardly comprise that framework, nor provide an appropriate foundation for the articulation and development of a right to freedom of religion or belief. The reality of the situation is that most of the restrictions placed on the freedom of religion or belief, and as a result much of the hostility and

---

30 See A/HRC/Res. 16/18 (12 April 2011).
31 See the Statements made at the Ministerial Meeting on the Implementation of HRC Res. 16/18 in Istanbul on 15 July 2011 endorsing the Resolution by many leading figures, including the US Secretary of State, Hillary Clinton.
32 Thus both the Freedom of Expression advocates of Art. 19 and the OIC were supporters of Resolution 16/18. Yet in its 2009 'Camden Principles on Freedom of Expression', Principle 12, Art. 19 take the former, narrow, approach, whilst it has become increasingly clear that the OIC take the latter, expansive approach. See also UN Human Rights Committee, General Comment No. 34, Freedoms of Opinion and Expression (102nd session) (2011) UN Doc. CCPR/C/2CG/34, paras 50–52 concerning the relationship between the freedom of expression and incitement of hate crimes, which affirms that 'Articles 19 and 20 are compatible with and complement each other'. It is interesting that it was thought necessary to say so.
33 Indeed, at the end of 2011, in the wake of a follow-up meeting with the OIC to the Istanbul Meeting (n. 31), the US Secretary of State was widely accused in the media and online of supporting the criminalisation of criticism of Islam.

violence which believers face, are not the product of anti-religious sentiment within the populous at large but result from the negative stereotyping and antipathy of many state systems and structures to particular forms of religion or belief. Calling upon states to engage in the repression of those who denigrate religion is all very well, but holding states to account for their own failure to act in a fashion which respects and protects the rights of all believers would be a very much better place to start. This point will be returned to, in different ways, in the final two sections of this chapter.

3 Issues

In recent times there has been considerable focus on a number of issues in which there is perceived to be a straightforward 'clash' between the freedom of religion and belief and other rights within the human rights framework. In a work of this nature it is not appropriate to focus on the details of particular current controversies. It is, however, useful to look at them in order to see what they reveal about the nature of our understanding of religion as a right. To that end, this section will briefly introduce a number of 'headline' issues which have caused considerable debate and which remain ongoing sources of controversy. This will be followed by an outline of what might be regarded as 'baseline' issues which, whilst arguably more foundational to the experience of rights holders, do not seem to be able to gain such traction in the overall debate upon the subject as the headline issues. The final section will look at why this might be the case, and how it might be remedied.

3.1 The headline issues

3.1.1 . . . and expression

The interplay between the freedom of religion and belief and the freedom of expression is a matter of enduring contention. Long before the idea of human rights were ever conceived of, questions have been asked concerning the extent to which, and the manner in which, persons might speak or otherwise express their views concerning the beliefs of others. One might legitimately have thought that the recognition of both the freedom of religion and the freedom of expression as human rights might have had the effect of mitigating the extremes of debate, but it seems to have had the opposite effect. Ever since the Salman Rushdie affair there has been a tendency in some quarters to view religion as a potential 'gag' on expression, an idea reinforced by some of the responses to the infamous 'Danish Cartoons'. On the other hand, some religious believers see the freedom of expression as a vehicle for pedalling distressingly hurtful comments or attitudes. Indeed, it has come to seem an entirely uncontroversial proposition that whilst the exercise of the freedom of expression might legitimately embrace 'imparting "information" or "ideas" . . . that shock, offend or disturb the State or any sector of the population',[34] 'those who choose to exercise their freedom of religion . . . must tolerate and accept the denial by others of their religious belief and even the propagation by others of doctrines hostile to their faith.'[35]

34 *Handyside v UK*, Judgment of 7 December 1976, Series A, No. 24, para. 49.
35 *Otto-Preminger-Institut v Austria*, Judgment of 20 September 1994, Series A, No. 295-A, para. 47.

Thus put, it is not difficult to see why these are so often seen as 'rights in collision', attracting all the attention which usually attends such clashes of fundamentals. Moreover, it is not difficult to see why many of a religious persuasion consider that the demands of restraint seem to be more heavily placed upon them and their sensibilities. It is perhaps inevitable that matters concerning the freedom of expression will attract considerable publicity. What is not inevitable, but appears to be commonplace, is for these rights to be portrayed as being 'at odds' with each other. The European Court of Human Rights has stressed the extent to which both rights are foundational to the good of democratic societies:[36] yet rather than engage with each other on this basis when issues arise, the tendency is to seek to resolve them by attempting to assert the primacy of one over the other. This again makes for a perfect 'religion and . . .' question, with all the in-built propensity to controversy which that brings.

3.1.2 . . . and symbols

There can be little doubt that one of the most contentious issues to have been raised before the European Court of Human Rights in recent times has concerned the presence of religious clothing or symbols in the educational arena, with key cases dealing with the wearing of headscarves by students[37] and the presence of religious symbols in classrooms.[38] The Court's approach currently oscillates between focusing upon the potential impact which the presence of such clothing or religious symbols in state institutions might have upon perceptions of the impartiality of the state in matters of religion or belief in general, and focusing on the actual impact that the wearing or presence of such symbols actually has upon the rights of others. In other words, is it their symbolic significance or their practical impact which is at the heart of the matter? Put in such terms, it becomes clearer that the underlying issue runs even deeper again, and concerns the place of religion in the public life of the society concerned.

The most significant decision of the European Court on this question is without doubt *Lautsi v Italy*, in which the Grand Chamber unpicked one of its most serious errors of recent times. In a whole string of cases, to be touched on in the next section, the Court articulated the proposition that the state, when exercising its regulatory powers in respect of religious bodies, was to do so in a neutral and impartial fashion.[39] This entirely appropriate stance

---

36 It routinely says that 'freedom of expression constitutes one of the essential foundations of a democratic society, one of the basic conditions for its progress and for the development of everyone' (since *Handyside* (n. 34) and that 'freedom of thought, conscience and religion is one of the foundations of a "democratic society" within the meaning of the Convention' (*Kokkinakis v Greece*, Judgment of 25 May 1993, Series A, No. 260-A, para. 31).

37 The leading cases remain *Dahlab v Switzerland*, App. No. 42393/98, ECHR (Dec) 2001-V and *Leyla Sahin v Turkey* [GC], App. No. 44774/98, ECHR 2005-XI, which though not entirely *ad idem* have both been routinely applied by the Court in subsequent cases such as *Dogru v France*, No. 27058/05, 4 December 2008, and *Kervanci v France*, No. 31645/04, 4 December 2008 concerning France.

38 *Lausti v Italy*, App. No. 30814/06, Judgment of 3 November 2009; [GC], Judgment of 18 March 2011. For a series of short explorations of *Lausti* from a variety of perspectives see (2011) 6 *Religion and Human Rights* 203–85.

39 The leading case on this remains *Metropolitan Church of Bessarabia and Others v Moldova*, App. No. 45701/99, para. 133, ECHR 2001-XII. For an examination of this approach see M. Evans and P. Petkoff, 'A Separation of Convenience? The Concept of Neutrality in the Jurisprudence of the European Court of Human Rights' (2008) 36 *Religion, State and Society* 205.

became misunderstood to mean that the state was to 'be' neutral in matters concerning religion, and thus it was argued that the state ought not to be seen to lend credence to any particular religion by permitting it to be visible within it. Such reasoning leads to bans on members of the public wearing religious clothing in public buildings and is difficult to reconcile with the idea that individuals have the right to manifest their beliefs in public through observance. The Grand Chamber decision in *Lautsi v Italy* pulled the Court back from the brink of jurisprudential disaster by suggesting that the obligation upon states to be neutral and impartial does not necessarily require the public realm – in this case, a public school room – to be 'free' of religion.[40] It remains to be seen whether this now enables a proper proportion to return to the 'symbols' debate – but once again this illustrates the propensity for the issues concerning the relationship between 'religion and . . .' (in this case, in the final analysis, public life) to achieve prominence in public and in rights-based discourse.

3.2 The baseline issues

Some issues to do with the freedom of religion do not seem able to attract attention in the same way as do issues concerning films, books, clothes and symbols. Recent influential studies have pointed to a clear correlation between those countries in which there are significant governmental and social restrictions upon the freedom of religion and high levels of religious persecution and conflict.[41] As reflected in the title of the recent book by Grim and Finke, there is a price to pay for denying religious freedom.[42] If one looks at the subject matter of the case law of the European Court, one of the recurring issues concerns the denial of legal registration to many religious communities who thereby find themselves unable to own property or assert their rights as a community.[43] Others find their meetings disrupted and their members intimidated or arrested.[44] In other words, some of the most fundamental aspects of the freedom of religion are violated on a routine basis and the presence of international human rights law does not appear to be a particularly powerful counterfoil. Although there have now been many judgments by the ECHR on matters concerning registration of religious communities and the need to respect the internal autonomy and property of religious institutions, recent trends in legislation within numerous Council of Europe member states have been towards imposing further restrictions upon religious

---

40 This flows both from its reasoning in *Lausti* [GC] (n. 38) paras 60 and 69 and from the more general result, which was to see the presence of such symbols as falling within the margin of appreciation of the state.

41 See B. Grim, 'Religion, Law and Social Conflict in the 21st Century: Findings from Sociological Research' (2012) 1 *Oxford Journal of Law and Religion* 249.

42 B. Grim and R. Finke, *The Price of Freedom Denied: Religious Persecution and Conflict in the 21st Century* (New York, CUP, 2011).

43 Among many examples see, e.g. *Metropolitan Church of Bessarabia and Others v Moldova* (n. 39); *Moscow Branch of the Salvation Army v Russia*, App. No. 72881/01, ECHR 2006-XI; *Church of Scientology Moscow v Russia*, Sapp. No. 18147/02, 5 April 2007; *Religionsgemeinschaft der Zeugen Jehovas and Others v Austria*, App. No. 40825/98, 31 July 2008; *Kimlya and Others v Russia*, App. Nos. 76836/01 and 32782/03, ECHR 2009; *Lang v Austria*, App. No. 28648/03, 19 March 2009.

44 E.g. *97 Members of the Gldani Congregation of Jehovah's Witnesses and Others v Georgia*, App. No. 71156/01, ECHR 2007-V; *Öllinger v Austria*, No. 76900/01, ECHR 2006-IX; *Sergey Kuznetsov v Russia*, App. No. 10877/04, 23 October 2008; *Milanovic v Serbia*, App. No. 44614/07, 14 December 2010.

communities and religious believers rather than in lifting them.[45] What is striking is that all these violations – and very serious violations – are not 'about' the 'freedom of religion and . . .' anything. There is no juxtaposition or clash of rights. There may be multiple breaches – such as violations of the freedom of association, of expression, of family life, of torture or inhuman or degrading treatment or the right to life – but no 'clashes'. In any realistic scale of categorisation these are, in fact, just 'about' the freedom of religion or belief. Perhaps that is just not enough?

In the face of a rising tide of concern, the relative impotence of the machinery of international human rights protection to effectively engage with the problems revealed has resulted in increased pressure to address issues through political channels. There has been a notable increase in the interest shown to freedom of religion issues by the European Parliament and other organs of the EU,[46] and by the Parliamentary Council of Europe.[47] If some of the most fundamental problems concerning the enjoyment of the freedom of religion are not more energetically engaged with by the machinery of the international human rights networks, there is every likelihood that there may be a further politicisation of a relationship which is already highly – some might say dangerously – politicised.

3.3 A unifying role of respect?

Against this background, is there really a positive contribution which can be made by viewing the interrelationship between religion and human rights in a more holistic, mutually reflexive fashion as was suggested at the end of the opening section of this chapter? Certainly, a positive contribution is unlikely to flow from a continuation of the ultimately sterile debates concerning the primacy of one body of thinking, whether it be religion or human rights, over the other. Nor is it likely to come from seeking to identify a series of lowest common denominators on which both religious adherents and/or human rights advocates can agree. Indeed, why should there be such agreement? There is often little consensus between religious believers on many moral or ethical issues and, lest it be forgotten, often an equally disparate spread of opinions between human rights thinkers on such issues too: though human rights-thinking recognises 'absolute' rights – including the freedom of thought, conscience and

45 See, for example, the critical reaction to the new Hungarian Constitution which entered into force in January 2012, which, according to an editorial in *The Times* entitled 'Back to Autocracy', 'attempts to reimpose state regulation of religion by reducing the number of acknowledged faiths and sects from 300 to 14 while denying any official place in society for Muslim, Buddhist or Hindu congregations unless they have operated in Hungary for at least 20 years' (*The Times*, p. 2 Leader Column, 02.01. 2012).
46 See generally R. McCea, *Religion and the Public Order of the European Union* (Oxford, OUP, 2010).
47 See, for example, Parliamentary Assembly Recommendation 1987 (2011) on 'Combating all forms of discrimination based on religion' (adopted 25 November 2011), which evidences some dissatisfaction in the efficacy of the legal approaches, by asking the Committee of Ministers 'when supervising the execution of judgments of the European Court of Human Rights concerning freedom of religion, notably those concerning registration of religious communities and acts of violence based on religion, [to] strive to ensure their speedy execution' (para. 1.4).

religion itself – the contours and status of even these rights continues to give rise to debate,[48] and little is immutable.

It is not a question of choosing, negotiating or deciding upon the nature of the relationship and factoring this into the manner in which outcomes will be determined in relation to particular issues which arise. Understandings and approaches change within religious and within human rights thinking and so there is never going to be a fixed and stable answer to the question of the relationship between them. To seek to do so is to be aiming at an ever-moving target. Rather, one needs to step back and seek to better understand the key components of religion as a human right and then, bearing this in mind, seek out the principles by which its interaction with other rights are to be governed. This will not indicate what those outcomes will be, and will certainly not ensure a consensus for those outcomes which are decided upon, but should make it possible to find an approach to the protection of religion as a human right which coheres with human rights thinking in a fashion which transcends the 'either/or', or 'the religion and' questions which have become so dominant and so damaging.

This may not be as difficult as is seems. It remains instructive that in the first cases to be determined by the European Court of Human Rights concerning the interplay between religion and expression, it swiftly identified a value which is not mentioned in either Article 9 or in Article 10, but which it thought offered a lens through which to consider the question: this was the lens of mutual 'respect'. As the Court put it, 'a State may legitimately consider it necessary to take measures aimed at repressing certain forms of conduct, including the imparting of information and ideas, judged incompatible with the respect for the freedom of thought, conscience and religion of others.'[49] The key points emerging from the Court's approach to the intersection of the freedom of religion and the freedom of expression are that both rights are of value and should be enjoyed to the fullest extent possible without negatively impacting on the enjoyment of the rights of others. Mutual respect for the rights of others regarding what is said and how it is said might suggest that restraint would be welcome; but it is not for the state to be the instrument of restraint unless there is a pressing social need to do so. The value of this approach has recently been affirmed by the UN Human Rights Committee, in its latest General Comment No. 34 on the Freedom of Expression.[50]

There are lessons to be learnt from the approaches adopted by the European Court in this body of jurisprudence which are of relevance for other questions concerning the enjoyment of the freedom of religion or belief as a part of the canon of human rights law: does the subject matter of the contestation, and of the outcomes which the parties are seeking to achieve, evidence a mutuality of respect rather than an assertion of right? It should be made

---

48 See, for example, the debates in the mid–2000s concerning the absolute nature of the prohibition of torture, as exemplified by the contributions to collections of essays such as K. Greenberg, *The Torture Debate in America* (CUP, Cambridge, 2005); S. Levinson, *Torture: A Collection* (New York, OUP, 2004); J. Wisnewski and R. Emerick, *The Ethics of Torture* (London, Continuum, 2009); J. Wisnewski, *Understanding Torture (Contemporary Ethical Debates)* (Edinburgh, University of Edinburgh Press, 2010).

49 *Kokkinakis v Greece*, Judgment of 25 May 1993, Series A, No. 260-A, para. 48; *Otto-Preminger-Institut v Austria*, Judgment of 20 September 1994, Series A, No. 295-A, para. 47.

50 See UN Human Rights Committee, General Comment No. 34 (n. 32), para. 48: 'Prohibitions of displays of *lack of respect for* a religion or other belief system, including blasphemy laws, are incompatible with the Covenant' (emphasis added).

clear that respect, in this context, does not imply endorsement of, let alone agreement with, the beliefs in question. Indeed, it may well be that a respectful consideration will nevertheless result in the rejection of some viewpoints as being simply unworthy of respect within the human rights framework.[51] Nevertheless, a respect-based approach to rights has already emerged in the jurisprudence of the European Court of Human Rights, and may well be worth exploring further as a means of meeting the future challenge posed by religion and human rights.

4 Conclusion: advancing freedom of religion and human rights

It might be objected that positing so nebulous and malleable an idea as respect as a possible means of mediating a solution to the problem of religion and human rights is tantamount to abandoning the exercise altogether. This final section will attempt to show that this is not the case by suggesting that there are some very practical steps which might flow from the adoption of such an approach, and which could be of very real practical value in advancing the freedom of religion or belief.

4.1 Advancing freedom of religion or freedom of thought conscience and religion?

The opening section of the chapter argued that it was necessary to take religious rights seriously. This is a clear requirement of a respect-based approach to the freedom of religion. The opening section also argued that the freedom of religion was under pressure 'from within', this being the parallelism with non-religious patterns of thought and conscience. Without wishing in any way to suggest that such other patterns of thought are not to be taken seriously, it seems beyond dispute that one of the effects of this is that religious belief is not seen as being in any way different to any other form of belief. Yet for many believers this is simply not the case: their beliefs are not just important to them, but are self-defining. A human rights regime that does not recognise that religious beliefs may have a special quality to them in the eyes of believers is not starting from an optimal place when it comes to evidencing respect. A workable respect agenda might not take as its starting point the assertion that religious beliefs are no different from non-religious, or from anti-religious beliefs. It may be that there is something to be said for recognising that there is a need to respect the right to thought, to conscience and to religion, whilst also recognising that these are not all species of the same thing. The architecture of prevention outlined about does not preclude this – indeed, to the extent that it protects the manifestation of religion and belief, it endorses it. However, the tendency is to read it in the opposite way. Perhaps it ought not be.

---

51 See, for example, the decision of the Court in *Norwood v the United Kingdom* (Dec.), App. No. 2313/03, ECHR 2004-XI (in the context of Art. 10) and the judgment in *Mouvement Raelian Suisse v Switzerland*, App. No. 16354/06, para. 61, 13 January 2011 in which the Chamber of the Court went out of its way to hold open (though not decide) the question of whether Raelian beliefs were to be considered within the scope of under Art. 9 (though the grounds for its hesitation are kept opaque). The Grand Chamber, in its Judgment of 13 July 2012, paras 78–80 can also be read in a similar fashion, and it certainly did not disown the comments of the Chamber on this point.

4.2 Advancing by whom?

4.2.1 The role of the international community

The international community obviously has a critical role to play in furthering the freedom of religion. It always has done so – though this has often taken the form of aggressive support for one form of belief system at the expense of others, with all the misery of conflict, war, domination and oppression following in its wake. Addressing freedom of religion in terms of human rights rather than in terms of political influence is a hugely attractive alternative. Yet in recent times we have seen that the failure of the international community to take the freedom of religion seriously as a human right has fuelled the politicisation of religion in many quarters. That politicisation has increasingly been used as an argument for not developing a rights-based approach and even for challenging the legitimacy of that rights-based approach – the 'challenge from without', mentioned in the opening section. Once again, thinking about the freedom of religion from the perspective of mutual respect can play a role in depoliticising the debate by making it a less potent instrument of political contestation, reclaiming the possibility of its being re-engaged with within human rights communities in a more effective fashion.

4.2.2 The role of religious communities

One of the most under-exploited forces for achieving progress on freedom of religion seems – paradoxically – to be religious communities and religious leaders themselves. Whilst often drawing attention to violations of the rights of their own communities, it is a regrettable fact that religious communities are also the source, directly or indirectly, of a great many violations of the religious rights of others. Some unsympathetic voices point to this phenomenon as evidence of hypocrisy and as a reason to cast doubt on the worth of the freedom at all, suggesting that one is merely fostering a source of potential rights violators. The lack of respect shown by the followers of religion X to the followers of religion Y in country A is certainly a powerful counter-argument to the claim that the followers of religion Y should show respect to the followers of religion X in country B. The point is almost too embarrassingly simplistic to make, but a respect-based approach by religious communities and religious leaders, championing the religious rights of believers in faiths other than their own, would be a powerful endorsement of the rights of all.[52] Unequivocal endorsement of the respect to be shown to all religious believers, irrespective of their faiths, by religious leaders and religious communities would be another powerful implication of a respect-based approach to the freedom of religion as a human right.

4.2.3 The role of national actors

It is increasingly understood that international human rights need to be not only implemented but also enforced through national as well as international means. To that end, there has been increasing focus in recent years on the establishment of national human rights

---

52 For an exploration of such practice, and some tensions, see, for example, the various declarations considered by R. Amesbury, 'Inter-Religious Declarations of Human Rights: Grounding Rights or Constructing Religion', (2010) 5 *Religion and Human Rights* 43.

mechanisms and institutions, in addition to the traditional national actors of state and civil society. It also means that the dynamic of international human rights protection is now even more multidirectional, looking not only from the national to the international level, and vice versa, but also looking between tiers of national engagement. As regards freedom of religion, this has certain consequences. Elements of what might be the national human rights infrastructure have not always been entirely comfortable when engaging with religion and religious communities, and vice versa. In some countries the very idea of state institutions engaging with all – or engaging with any – religious organisations and faith communities is deeply problematic. Yet given the direction of travel in the protection of international human rights, these are challenges which need to be met. Once again, the idea of mutual respect may provide a helpful starting point for initiating engagements at a national level, which might otherwise be difficult due to the political, religious or ideological context. It ought to assist in providing a means and a space for dialogue which is less 'heavily charged' with implications than is so often considered to be the case.

4.3 The practical agenda

The last word should be that there is a pressing need for the freedom of religion to be reconsidered within the architecture of human rights, both conceptually and practically. Conceptually, it has been suggested that the idea of mutual respect might provide a helpful starting point, but there has to be a place and process within which to do so. The paucity of the normative framework surrounding religion as a human right and the global inaction to address this has already been noted, as has the drift towards politicisation which this has fostered. It may be that the time has come to return to the table in order to engage again with the freedom of religion in a way which is less politicised and more focused on securing a rights-based approach based on mutual respect. Such an approach might yield an outcome which could then benefit from the normative and structural support provided by the international human rights regime and form a recognised and respected component of it. If ever there was a key challenge for the coming years, this is one indeed.

Select bibliography

W. Cole Durham and B. Tahzib-Lie (eds), *Facilitating Freedom of Religion or Belief: A Deskbook* (Dordrecht, Martinus Nijhoff, 2004).

C. Evans, *Religious Freedom under the European Convention on Human Rights* (Oxford, OUP, 2001).

M. Evans, 'Advancing Freedom of Religion or Belief: Agendas for Change', (2012) 1 *Oxford Journal of Law and Religion* 5–14.

M. Evans, 'From Cartoons to Crucifixes' in E. Reed and M. Dumper (eds), *Civil Liberties, National Security and Prospects for Consensus: Legal, Philosophical and Religious Perspectives* (Cambridge, CUP, 2012), pp 83–113.

B. Grim and R. Finke, *The Price of Freedom Denied: Religious Persecution and Conflict in the 21st Century* (New York, CUP, 2011).

R. McCrea, *Religion and the Public Order of the European Union* (Oxford, OUP, 2010).

32

Counter-terrorism and human rights

Martin Scheinin

1 Situating the theme

1.1 'The long decade'

The atrocious terrorist attacks of 11 September 2001 and the wave of counter-terrorism measures that followed together constitute the worst backlash in human rights protection of the whole period since the breakthrough of the concept of human rights in the aftermath of Nazism and the Second World War.[1] During the 'long decade' after 9/11, states and the international community introduced measures ranging from the use of military force to discriminatory profiling, from torture and extrajudicial executions to massive retention of telecommunications data, and from creating new forms of emergency powers derogating from ordinary law to the closing of borders through stricter immigration controls. Some of these measures, particularly by authoritarian regimes, have been maliciously constructed to target political opponents, religious minorities or any form of dissent, under the slogan of countering terrorism. Many other steps taken, typically in Western democracies, have been panic reactions in the sense that every new act of terrorism has created a public demand that politicians must 'do something', and quite often this 'something' has been further restrictions upon human rights, without proper assessment of the efficiency, necessity and proportionality of the actual measure. As there has been a massive shift of economic resources, including public money, to counter-terrorism and other security infrastructure, an economic incentive has resulted for the emergence of a whole industry of new counter-terrorism technologies that have found a fluctuating but lucrative market.

---

1 For an assessment, see M. Scheinin, 'Human Rights and Counter-Terrorism: Lessons from a Long Decade', in D. Jenkins, A. Henriksen and A. Jacobsen (eds), *The Long Decade: How 9/11 Has Changed the Law* (OUP, 2012).

1.2 Human rights compliance in counter-terrorism strategy

Initially, counter-terrorism appeared to take its own course and simply ignore human rights issues and human rights voices. The Security Council of the United Nations declared the phenomenon of international terrorism as a threat to international peace and security, and imposed under Chapter VII of the UN Charter an extensive and mandatory counter-terrorism agenda upon states through Resolution 1373 (2001). A Counter-Terrorism Committee (CTC) was created to monitor states' compliance with the resolution, and human rights actors found themselves marginalised when the CTC did not want to hear them and when some states invoked Article 103 of the UN Charter as an explanation why their counter-terrorism obligations would trump their human rights commitments.

Gradually, human rights actors found their ways to get at least some attention from governments and UN-level counter-terrorism bodies. Some of the treaty bodies, most notably the UN Human Rights Committee acting under the International Covenant on Civil and Political Rights (ICCPR), developed a systematic practice of addressing and assessing states for their counter-terrorism measures.[2] In 2005 the UN Commission on Human Rights, soon to be replaced by the UN Human Rights Council, established the mandate of a Special Rapporteur on the promotion and protection of human rights and fundamental freedoms while countering terrorism.[3] More importantly, in September 2006 the UN General Assembly unanimously adopted a resolution that contained a Global Counter-Terrorism Strategy.[4] Measures to ensure respect for human rights for all and the rule of law form one of the four pillars of the Strategy and at the same time a component in all other pillars. The title of the fourth pillar identifies this principle as the 'fundamental basis' of the fight against terrorism. The Strategy recognises that it is necessary to address the long-term structural conditions conducive to the spread of terrorism, which include, inter alia, lack of rule of law and violations of human rights, ethnic, national and religious discrimination, political exclusion, socio-economic marginalisation and lack of good governance. The Strategy represents a clear affirmation by member states that effective counter-terrorism measures and the protection of human rights are not conflicting, but complementary and mutually reinforcing goals, and that human rights and the rule of law are the fundamental basis of their counter-terrorism strategies.

It may be that at least for some governments the adoption of the Strategy was more lip service than a genuine commitment to human rights. That said, the Strategy has served as the basis for counter-terrorism coordination at the international level, so that for instance the counter-terrorism committees of the Security Council[5] and their expert secretariats have come to much closer interaction with the human rights world.[6] Even if the track record of,

---

2 See Concluding Observations by the Human Rights Committee on periodic reports by governments since October 2001, available at http://www2.ohchr.org/english/bodies/hrc/sessions.htm. Also, see A. Seibert-Fohr, 'The Relevance of International Human Rights Standards for Prosecuting Terrorists', in C. Walter, S. Vöneky, V. Röben and F. Schorkopf (eds), *Terrorism as a Challenge for National and International Law: Security versus Liberty* (Springer, 2004) 139.

3 United Nations (UN) Commission on Human Rights, Resolution 2005/80 (1 April 2005). Currently the mandate of the Special Rapporteur is contained in: Human Rights Council, Resolution 15/15 (7 October 2010).

4 UN General Assembly (GA) Res. 60/288 (8 September 2006) UN Doc. A/RES/60/288.

5 The Counter-Terrorism Committee and the 1267/1989 Al Qaeda Sanctions Committee.

6 One forum for such interaction is the inter-agency 'Counter-Terrorism Implementation Task Force', see http://www.un.org/en/terrorism/ctitf/index.shtml.

say, the CTC, is not perfect in the field of human rights, there has been gradual recognition of the fact that politically motivated abusively broad national definitions of human rights are not effective in relation to real risks of terrorism.[7] It has also been recognised that insensitivity to human rights in counter-terrorism will have counter-productive consequences, both at the level of 'root causes' of terrorism (or conditions conducive to the spread of terrorism) as perpetuating exclusion and resentment, and at the level of 'triggering causes', that is the psychological factors that may push a bitter individual to make the inexcusable choice of resorting to acts of terrorism.

1.3 Best practice

Both Security Council Resolution 1624 (2005), which concerned terrorist screening and passenger security procedures, and the resolution establishing the mandate of the Special Rapporteur on human rights and counter-terrorism include the task of identifying elements of 'best practice' in countering terrorism. When there has been growing acceptance amongst counter-terrorism professionals that effective counter-terrorism measures and the protection of human rights are complementary to each other and mutually reinforcing, there has also been broader understanding for seeing human rights compliance not as an obstacle to countering terrorism but as a strategic choice for better counter-terrorism. As a consequence, governments and their counter-terrorism experts have become increasingly interested in human rights compliance in counter-terrorism not only as a legally binding constraint but also as a resource, as a form of best practice in counter-terrorism.[8]

In the final report as Special Rapporteur on human rights and counter-terrorism, this author formulated 10 areas of best practice, defined as existing or emerging practice of states and international organisations that is both effective in countering terrorism and complies with human rights or promotes their enjoyment.[9] The 10 selected areas of best practice include issues such as a model definition of terrorism, model definition of incitement to terrorism, and models for review and remedies provisions in counter-terrorism legislation.

2 Selected substantive issues

Particularly since 9/11, the impact of counter-terrorism measures upon the enjoyment of human rights has been broad and deep, so that it would not make sense to try to list the substantive issues that have arisen. The annual thematic reports to the Human Rights Council

---

7 For causes of terrorism, see for instance, A.P. Schmid, 'Root Causes of Terrorism: Some Conceptual Notes, a Set of Indicators, and a Model' (2005) (1) *Democracy and Security* 127–36.

8 Reference is made to the website of the Counter-Terrorism Committee of the Security Council which quotes a CTC human rights policy: 'CTC and CTED, under direction of the Committee, should incorporate human rights into their communications strategy, as appropriate, noting the importance of States ensuring that in taking counter-terrorism measures they do so consistent with their obligations under international law, in particular human rights law, refugee law and humanitarian law, as reflected in the relevant Security Council resolutions.' The website text then continues: 'The Committee and CTED now routinely take account of relevant human rights concerns in all their activities, including the preparation of preliminary implementation assessments (PIAs) relating to resolution 1373 (2001), country visits and other interactions with Member States.' http://www.un.org/en/sc/ctc/rights.html (last visited 11 May 2013).

9 Report of the UN Special Rapporteur on the promotion and protection of human rights and fundamental freedoms while countering terrorism (22 December 2010) UN Doc. A/HRC/16/51) para. 10.

and the General Assembly by the UN Special Rapporteur on human rights and counter-terrorism have sought to map and address a fairly wide range of those issues, moving from one topic to another.[10] Partly reflecting upon those reports and a parallel series of reports by the UN High Commissioner for Human Rights, the annual resolution by the General Assembly on human rights and counter-terrorism has gradually accumulated a listing of substantive human rights concerns. By December 2011, the list had grown to comprise 18 items represented by subparagraphs (a) to (r) under paragraph 6 of the resolution.[11]

Below, three substantive issues or areas are addressed by way of example. Other examples might include issues such as the impact of counter-terrorism measures upon economic, social and cultural rights,[12] or upon international refugee law,[13] as well as the right to a fair trial in terrorism cases,[14] or discriminatory terrorist profiling.[15]

2.1 Torture, secret detention, renditions, extrajudicial executions

A considerable share of the attention of international human rights bodies, activists and scholars has been devoted to what this author describes as 'the tip of the pyramid': gross violations of human rights committed in the name of countering terrorism, but nevertheless targeting a limited group of individuals. The post-9/11 human rights debate has focused on torture, arbitrary or secret detention, extrajudicial executions and extraordinary renditions.[16] All these are manifestly unlawful measures, also when taken under the justification of fighting against terrorism. Real terrorists, persons wrongly suspected of terrorism, innocent persons believed to have information about terrorists, and targets of politically or otherwise maliciously motivated abuse of a government's counter-terrorism powers have all been victims of these practices in the West and East, in the North and South. Nevertheless, in absolute numbers the group of affected individuals has been small in comparison to the wide range of all human rights infringements in the name of counter-terrorism. That quantitative

---

10 Among the Reports of the UN Special Rapporteur on the promotion and protection of human rights and fundamental freedoms while countering terrorism: UN Doc. A/61/267 (freedom of association and peaceful assembly); UN Doc. A/62/263 (refugee law and asylum); UN Doc. A/63/223 (right to a fair trial); UN Doc. A/64/211 (gender); UN Doc. A/HRC/6/17 (economic, social and cultural rights); UN Doc. A/HRC/10/3 (intelligence agencies); UN Doc. A/HRC/13/37 (right to privacy).

11 UN GA Res. 66/71 (19 December 2011) UN Doc. A/RES/66/171.

12 See UN Human Rights Council, 'Report of the UN Special Rapporteur on the promotion and protection of human rights and fundamental freedoms while countering terrorism' (2008) UN Doc. A/HRC/6/17.

13 See UN Human Rights Council, 'Report of the UN Special Rapporteur on the promotion and protection of human rights and fundamental freedoms while countering terrorism' (2007) UN Doc. A/62/263.

14 See UN GA, 'Report of the UN Special Rapporteur on the promotion and protection of human rights and fundamental freedoms while countering terrorism' (2008) UN Doc. A/63/223.

15 See, UN Human Rights Council, 'Report of the UN Special Rapporteur on the promotion and protection of human rights and fundamental freedoms while countering terrorism' (2007) UN Doc. A/HRC/4/26; and D. Moeckli, *Human Rights and Non-discrimination in the 'War on Terror'* (OUP, 2008).

16 E.g. F. de Londras, *Detention in the 'War on Terror': Can Human Rights Fight Back?* (CUP, 2011); J.G. Johnston, 'The Risk of Torture as a Basis for Refusing Extradition and the Use of Diplomatic Assurances to Protect against Torture after 9/11', (2011) 11 *Int'l Crim. L. Rev. 1*; P. Alston, 'The CIA and Targeted Killings Beyond Borders', (2011) 2 *Harv. Nat'l Sec. J.* 283.

comparison does not mean that the human rights community would have been wrong in focusing on these gross human rights violations. The number of victims was never the main criterion for human rights people feeling the urge to speak out and defend human rights.

The more significant problems have been twofold. Firstly, as the problem of the gross human rights violations mentioned above has been vast, many human rights actors have close to exhausted their limited capacity, to the effect that other dimensions of the total phenomenon of counter-terrorism measures impacting human rights have received too little attention, including interferences in the human rights of members of the general population or segments of it. Secondly, as the post-9/11 response to terrorism took place in an atmosphere characterised by fear, even panic, high media attention and high political attention, the focusing of many human rights actors on gross human rights violations of a limited group of individuals has been used to stigmatise these actors or the whole human rights movement as 'siding with the terrorists'. In times of fear and panic this has contributed to a vicious circle where the voice of the human rights community has been marginalised even where it has raised concerns related to everybody's right to privacy or other matters situated at the base of the 'pyramid', that is affecting us all. As a result, voices about 'striking a new balance' between security and human rights have carried further than they would otherwise merit.

After these caveats, attention needs to be drawn to some instances where human rights bodies and other actors dealing with human rights have made remarkable contributions when addressing 'the tip of the pyramid', that is gross human rights violations of a fairly limited group of people, committed in the name of countering terrorism.

Five years before 9/11, the European Court of Human Rights decided, in the case of *Chahal v the United Kingdom*, in clear and uncompromised terms that the European Convention on Human Rights (ECHR)[17] absolutely prohibits refoulement when there is a 'real risk' of a person being subjected to treatment contrary to Article 3 of the Convention if he is returned to his own country.[18] After 9/11 some governments have requested the European Court of Human Rights to reconsider its position on the absolute nature of the non-refoulement obligation, inter alia, by proposing a 'balancing' approach to replace it. The European Court of Human Rights confronted the challenge head-on in the case of *Saadi v Italy*, decided in February 2008.[19] In a Grand Chamber ruling the Court maintained its position on the absolute nature of ECHR Article 3 and went to some length in dismissing the offered alternative approach of balancing.[20] The Grand Chamber acknowledged the 'immense difficulties' countries face in modern times in protecting their communities from terrorist violence and

---

17 European Convention for the Protection of Human Rights and Fundamental Freedoms (ECHR) (adopted 4 November 1950, entered into force 3 September 1953) 213 UNTS 222.

18 *Chahal v the United Kingdom*, European Court of Human Rights App. No. 22414/93 (ECtHR, Grand Chamber Judgment of 15 November 1996), para. 107. See, also, para. 79: '. . . The Court is well aware of the immense difficulties faced by states in modern times in protecting their communities from terrorist violence. However, even in these circumstances, the Convention prohibits in absolute terms torture or inhuman or degrading treatment or punishment, irrespective of the victim's conduct'; and para. 80: 'The prohibition provided by Article 3 against ill-treatment is equally absolute in expulsion cases. Thus, whenever substantial grounds have been shown for believing that an individual would face a real risk of being subjected to treatment contrary to Article 3 if removed to another State, the responsibility of the Contracting State to safeguard him or her against such treatment is engaged in the event of expulsion.'

19 App. No. 37201/06 (ECtHR, Grand Chamber Judgment of 28 February 2008) (*Saadi*).

20 See also *Saadi* (n. 19) para. 139 where the Court dismisses that the standard of proof concerning the risk of torture could be affected by the dangerousness of the person.

emphasised that this must not call into question 'the absolute nature' of Article 3.[21] Thereafter the Court dismissed the balancing approach advocated by some governments:

> Accordingly, the Court cannot accept the argument of the United Kingdom Government, supported by the respondent Government, that a distinction must be drawn under Article 3 between treatment inflicted directly by a signatory state and treatment that might be inflicted by the authorities of another state, and that protection against this latter form of ill-treatment should be weighed against the interests of the community as a whole . . . Since protection against the treatment prohibited by Article 3 is absolute, that provision imposes an obligation not to extradite or expel any person who, in the receiving country, would run the real risk of being subjected to such treatment. As the Court has repeatedly held, there can be no derogation from that rule . . . It must therefore reaffirm the principle stated in the Chahal judgment . . . that it is not possible to weigh the risk of ill-treatment against the reasons put forward for the expulsion in order to determine whether the responsibility of a state is engaged under Article 3, even where such treatment is inflicted by another state. In that connection, the conduct of the person concerned, however undesirable or dangerous, cannot be taken into account . . .[22]

Where the European Court of Human Rights can be said to have bowed to pressure is when considering the role of diplomatic assurances in assessing whether a real risk of torture exists. In the case of *Othman (Abu Qatada) v the United Kingdom*, the Court's conclusion that the applicant's return by the United Kingdom to Jordan would not expose him to a real risk of ill-treatment was based on an extensive discussion on the relevance of assurances given by Jordan to the United Kingdom.[23]

For cases where UN human rights treaty bodies have maintained their integrity when confronted with the challenge of terrorism, reference can be made for instance to the UN Human Rights Committee communications of *Polay Campos v Peru*[24] and *Alzery v Sweden*.[25] The former is a pre-9/11 case as it relates to terrorism in Peru during the 1980s. The Committee was firm in applying the provisions of the ICCPR in their ordinary meaning and in line with the Committee's established jurisprudence. The latter case was closely related to the parallel case of *Agiza v Sweden* that was before the Committee Against Torture.[26] Both cases relate to the rendition by the US Central Intelligence Agency (CIA) of two Egyptian individuals from Sweden to Egypt, after Sweden had decided on their deportation without allowing for judicial review prior to their physical removal. In both cases, the Committee found multiple violations of the prohibition against torture and other forms of inhuman treatment.

---

21 Ibid. para. 137.
22 Ibid. para. 138.
23 *Othman (Abu Qatada) v the United Kingdom*, App. No. 8139/09 (ECtHR, Judgment of 17 January 2012), para. 186–205, opened by the line 'However, it not for this Court to rule upon the propriety of seeking assurances, or to assess the long term consequences of doing so; its only task is to examine whether the assurances obtained in a particular case are sufficient to remove any real risk of ill-treatment.'
24 *Polay Campos v Peru*, UN Human Rights Committee, Communication No. 577/1994 (1994) UN Doc. CCPR/C/61/D/577/1994.
25 *Alzery v Sweden*, UN Human Rights Committee, Communication No. 1416/2006 (2005) UN Doc. CCPR/C/88/D/1416/2005.
26 *Agiza v Sweden*, UN Committee Against Torture, Communication No. 233/2003 (2003) UN Doc. CAT/C/34/D/233/2003.

These cases are important also because they relate to the practices by George W. Bush's administration in the United States of secret detention and extraordinary renditions, which have been subject to much attention and reporting by human rights bodies and experts within international organisations. At the UN level, two Special Rapporteurs and two Working Groups belonging to the Special Procedures of the Human Rights Council produced a global Joint Study on secret detention.[27] Within the Council of Europe, both the Parliamentary Assembly and the Secretary General produced reports on the involvement of European countries in the practices in question.[28] Also the European Parliament produced an important report on US rendition practices in Europe.[29]

2.2 Privacy and data protection

The impact of counter-terrorism measures upon everybody's right to privacy was mentioned above as an example of measures at 'the base of the pyramid', that is as developments that during the post-9/11 'long decade' have impacted negatively on the enjoyment of the human rights of all. Although some of this impact may represent genuine trade-offs where societies have democratically decided to give away some of the privacy rights of their members in exchange for better security, there are nevertheless severe human rights problems here also. Firstly, not all interferences with the right to privacy have been permissible limitations on this human right. Instead, there have also been outright violations of privacy rights, including interception of confidential communications without judicial authorisation or proper oversight, breaches of lawyer–client or doctor–patient confidentiality, discriminatory data mining and profiling operations in breach of data protection principles, and the hasty introduction of privacy-intrusive new technologies driven by panic rather than a proper assessment of the effectiveness, efficiency, necessity and proportionality of the measure.[30] Secondly, although George Orwell wrote his dystopian novel *1984* more than half a century earlier, it was only after 9/11 that the width and depth of privacy-intrusive measures introduced in the name of countering terrorism has reached a magnitude that justifies speaking of the erosion of

27 UN Human Rights Council, Special Rapporteur on the promotion and protection of human rights and fundamental freedoms while countering terrorism, Special Rapporteur on torture and other cruel, inhuman or degrading treatment or punishment, Working Group on Arbitrary Detention and Working Group on Enforced and Involuntary Disappearances, 'Joint study on global practices in relation to secret detention in the context of countering terrorism' (20 May 2010) UN Doc. A/HRC/13/42).

28 D. Marty, 'Alleged secret detentions and unlawful inter-state transfers of detainees involving Council of Europe member states' (12 June 2006) Council of Europe, Parliamentary Assembly, Doc. 10957; D Marty, 'Secret detentions and illegal transfers of detainees involving Council of Europe member states: second report' (11 June 2007) Council of Europe, Parliamentary Assembly, Doc. 11302 rev.; 'Report by the Secretary General on the use of his powers under Article 52 of the European Convention on Human Rights' (28 February 2006) Doc. SG/Inf. (2006) 5 and Supplementary Report, Doc. SG/Inf. (2006) 13.

29 European Parliament, Temporary Committee on the alleged use of European countries by the CIA for the transportation and illegal detention of prisoners, 'Report on the alleged use of European countries by the CIA for the transportation and illegal detention of prisoners, 2006/2200(INI)' (30 January 2007) Doc. PE 382.246v02-00.

30 UN Human Rights Council, 'Report of the Special Rapporteur on the promotion and protection of human rights and fundamental freedoms while countering terrorism' (28 December 2009) UN Doc. A/HRC/13/37.

the right to privacy. This erosion has been greatly enhanced by the loose use of slogans such as 'I've got nothing to hide' or 'It is time to strike a new balance between privacy and security'.[31]

These considerations were among the reasons for the choice of the right to privacy as the theme for the 2010 report to the UN Human Rights Council by the Special Rapporteur on human rights and counter-terrorism.[32] That report includes a stocktaking of counter-terrorism measures that have had a negative impact upon the enjoyment of the right to privacy. It dismisses the populist slogan of 'striking a new balance' on the abstract level and calls for an analytically rigorous permissible limitations test for the step-by-step assessment of proposed interferences in the right. Methodologically, the proposed permissible limitations test builds upon three elements:

(i) Even if only some human rights are absolute in the sense that they do not allow for restrictions or derogation, every human right should be understood as including an essential core that is not subject to permissible limitations.

(ii) Even if the main international provision on the right to privacy, namely Article 17 of the ICCPR, textually prohibits only arbitrary or unlawful interferences or attacks on privacy, its proper interpretation as to what intrusions are permissible need not differ from the interpretation of those provisions that already textually include a full-fledged permissible limitations test, such as Articles 21 and 22 of the same Covenant. This view is supported by the existing interpretive practice of the UN Human Rights Committee.[33]

(iii) Drawing inspiration mainly from the permissible limitations test elaborated for freedom of movement in General Comment No. 27 of the UN Human Rights Committee, a proper assessment of the permissibility of restrictions upon privacy should include the following steps: (a) any restrictions must be provided by the law; (b) the essence of a human right is not subject to restrictions; (c) restrictions must be necessary in a democratic society; (d) any discretion exercised when implementing the restrictions must not be unfettered; (e) for a restriction to be permissible, it is not enough that it serves a legitimate aim; it must be necessary for reaching that legitimate aim; (f) restrictive measures must conform to the principle of proportionality; they must be appropriate to achieve their protective function; they must be the least intrusive instrument amongst those which might achieve the desired result; and they must be proportionate to the interest to be protected; and (g) any restrictions must be consistent with the other rights guaranteed in the Covenant.[34]

The proposed test for permissible limitations includes, as indicated in item (iii)(b), the idea of the right to privacy including an inviolable core. That may relate to a *forum internum* dimension of privacy, i.e. a right to the inviolability of one's own private thoughts. However, it is proposed here that the status of inviolable core extends also to some of the most intimate

31 On these discussions, see, D.J. Solove, ' "I've Got Nothing to Hide" and Other Misunderstandings of Privacy', (2007) 44 *San Diego Law Review* 745; GWU Law School Public Law Research Paper No. 289. Available at SSRN: http://ssrn.com/abstract=998565 (accessed on 23 February 2013).

32 UN Human Rights Council, 'Report of the Special Rapporteur on the promotion and protection of human rights and fundamental freedoms while countering terrorism' (28 December 2009) UN Doc. A/HRC/13/37, paras 14–19. See Art. 17(1) of the ICCPR and Art. 12 of the UDHR.

33 Ibid. para. 16.

34 Ibid. para. 17.

choices one makes when confiding in another person due to a special relationship of trust – for instance a sexual partner, a doctor or a lawyer. The last item, (iii)(g), in turn, reflects a holistic view on human rights which is of particular importance in the case of the right to privacy due to the capacity of right to privacy provisions serving as a 'general clause' for the progressive development of human rights to protect their background values such as human dignity and autonomy of the person.[35] Finally, the step-by-step design of the permissible limitations test and the formulation of the proportionality assessment as part of it – item (iii)(f) – is intended to dismiss an abstract and all-encompassing act of balancing by demonstrating the proper (limited) scope that 'balancing', or more appropriately proportionality, should have in assessing the permissibility of restrictions. As formulated in a subsequent Special Rapporteur's report: 'Law is the balance, not a weight to be measured.'[36]

2.3 Terrorist listings

Many countries and also international organisations including the United Nations have resorted to sanctions against known or suspected terrorists. This is done through so-called terrorist lists that may comprise both individuals and entities and result in various measures, such as the freezing of assets and prohibition of financial transactions with the listed individual or entity, or the prevention of any international travel by an individual. The rationale behind the terrorist lists lies in their preventive effect in relation to the financing of terrorism and also in the intention to put pressure on the persons involved, so that they would cease to be engaged with terrorism. Hence, the sanctions are said to be of administrative nature and of limited duration.[37] The introduction of and compliance with sanctions is a legal obligation of states, including under Security Council Resolution 1373 (2001).

As constructed and implemented, the terrorist listing regimes include many shortcomings that ultimately make them vulnerable to human rights-based criticism. The best-known case is the so-called 1267 sanctions regime, originally established through Security Council Resolution 1267 (1999) in respect of the Taleban leaders in Afghanistan as a measure limited in time and in space, but expanded through Security Council resolution 1390 into a global list of persons associated with Al-Qaeda or the Taleban. In 2011 the regime was split into separate lists for the Taleban (Security Council Resolution 1988) and Al-Qaeda (Resolution 1989) associates. As all these Security Council resolutions have been adopted under Chapter VII of the UN Charter, they establish binding legal obligations for all member states and are said to enjoy primacy in respect of other international obligations of the same states, by virtue of Article 103 of the UN Charter.[38]

35 Here, reference is made primarily to the evolution of the case law by the European Court of Human Rights under Art. 8 of the ECHR.

36 Report of the Special Rapporteur on the promotion and protection of human rights and fundamental freedoms while countering terrorism (22 December 2010) UN Doc. A/HRC/16/51 para. 12.

37 Third report of the Analytical Support and Sanctions Monitoring Team appointed pursuant to resolution 1526 (2004) concerning Al-Qaeda and the Taliban and associated individuals and entities (9 September 2005) UN Doc. S/2005/572, para. 41.

38 For a more detailed account and assessment, see, UN GA, 'Report of the Special Rapporteur on the promotion and protection of human rights and fundamental freedoms while countering terrorism' (6 August 2010) UN Doc. A/65/258; and L. Ginsborg and M. Scheinin, 'You Can't Always Get What You Want: The Kadi II Conundrum and the Security Council 1267 Terrorist Sanctions Regime' (2011) 8 *Essex Human Rights Review* 7.

Over the years, several piecemeal improvements have been made in the 1267 terrorist listing regime in response to the growing criticism particularly based on human rights. Nevertheless, after the major changes introduced through Resolution 1989, the system still includes several shortcomings, notably the following four: (a) the ultimate power to list and delist individuals or entities as terrorists rests with a diplomatic or political body, the Security Council, or its 1267 Committee composed of the same 15 states; (b) even if the Office of the Ombudsperson for this sanctions regime is now entitled to produce a report proposing delisting and such a proposal becomes by default the decision to delist, any member state of the Security Council is entitled to transfer the case to the full Security Council where its normal voting rules, including the right of veto for its five permanent members, will apply to any proposal to delist someone;[39] (c) despite calls for transparency and the submission of reasons for listing someone as a terrorist, the actual decisions may still be based on intelligence rather than evidence, and there is no requirement that the information in question is even shared in the form of documents with the other members of the Security Council; and (d) finally, even if the listings are said to be of preventive nature, they do not lapse automatically and can therefore stay in place for years – in many actual cases for more than a decade.[40]

In recent years, there have been several judicial challenges to the national implementation of the sanctions imposed by the Security Council through the inclusion of a person on its 1267 sanctions list. Here it suffices to refer to three cases where such disputes have been taken to regional courts or international bodies. While the courts or expert bodies in question did not possess the power directly to review the terrorist listing by the Security Council, they engaged in reviewing the conduct by the European Union or by individual states in the UN-level listing of the persons concerned, or in the implementation of sanctions imposed by the Security Council. In all three cases, the individuals concerned were ultimately taken off the 1267 terrorist list while the indirect review by the court or body in question was underway or after its conclusion.

2.3.1 The *Kadi* case[41]

Probably the best-known judicial challenge to terrorist listing by the Security Council is the case of Yassin Abdullah Kadi (or Qadi), an Egyptian-born Saudi Arabian businessman. After being listed by the 1267 Sanctions Committee, Mr Kadi contested the implementation of the sanctions by the EU. His case was heard twice by the EU Court of First Instance (renamed as the EU General Court) and twice on appeal by the European Court of Justice (ECJ). Mr Kadi was delisted on 5 October 2012, just before the oral hearing before the ECJ in the second round of appeal procedures.[42] Here, reference is made to the 3 September 2008 ruling by the EJC that annulled the EU-level listing of Mr Kadi but granted the EU Council a mercy

---

39 Security Council Resolution 1989 (17 June 2011) para. 23. The Office of the Ombudsperson was created by Security Council Resolution 1904 (17 December 2009). See http://www.un.org/en/sc/ombudsperson/index.shtml.

40 The most notorious case is that of Mr Kadi (discussed below), who was on the 1267 sanctions list from 17 October 2001 to 5 October 2012.

41 Joined Cases C-402/05 P and C-415/05 P *Yassin Abdullah Kadi and Al Barakaat International Foundation v Council of the European Union*, European Court of Justice, Grand Chamber Judgment of 3 September 2008 (the *Kadi* case).

42 Security Council, Press Release of 5 October 2012, available at: http://www.un.org/News/Press/docs//2012/sc10785.doc.htm, accessed on 7 March 2013.

period of three months to provide a proper legal basis for possibly retaining him on the list.[43] As the Council did relist him, the litigation continued, at least until Mr Kadi was finally delisted in October 2012 by the 1267 Sanctions Committee itself. The ECJ found a double violation of Mr Kadi's fundamental rights, namely the right to property[44] and the rights of the defence, in particular the right to be heard, and the right to effective judicial review of those rights.[45] The former finding was related to the freezing of Mr Kadi's assets by EU countries, and the latter to the inadequate nature of any remedies Mr Kadi might have at the EU level in respect of the implementation of the sanctions imposed by the UN Security Council.

2.3.2 Sayadi & Vinck v Belgium[46]

In 2002, Belgium informed the 1267 Sanctions Committee of the Security Council that the two individuals concerned, Mr Sayadi and Ms Vinck were, respectively, the director and secretary of Fondation Secours International, reportedly the European branch of the Global Relief Foundation, an American association that had one month earlier been put on the 1267 sanctions list. After two years of unsuccessful criminal investigations in Belgium, a Belgian court in early 2005 ordered the government to seek the delisting of these persons. While the Belgian government sought the delisting of the individuals at the UN level, it was unable to obtain the unanimous approval of its request within the 1267 Sanctions Committee, even during 2007–08 when Belgium was a member of the Security Council and for part of that time even Chair of the 1267 Sanctions Committee. Confronted with the case through an individual communication against Belgium, the UN Human Rights Committee attributed the negative human rights consequences of the listing to Belgium, as Belgium had initiated it. Paradoxically, Belgium's subsequent effort to get these persons delisted was taken by the Human Rights Committee as evidence of the listing being unfounded. Consequently, the Committee took the view that Belgium had violated ICCPR Articles 12 (freedom of movement) and 17 (privacy and family life, honour and reputation) in relation to the two authors. On 20 July 2009, Mr Sayadi and Ms Vinck were finally removed from the 1267 terrorist list.[47]

2.3.3 Nada v Switzerland[48]

The case concerned Mr Nada, an Egyptian and Italian dual national, and the role of Switzerland in implementing the sanctions emanating from the 1267 regime, to the effect that Mr Nada was constrained to live in the small Italian enclave of Campione, surrounded by Switzerland. The applicant was on the 1267 terrorist list from November 2001. In 2008

---

43 The *Kadi* case (n. 41).

44 Ibid. para. 370–71.

45 Ibid. 349–53.

46 Human Rights Committee, Communication No. 1472/2006, Final Views of 22 October 2008.

47 See http://www.un.org/sc/committees/1267/pdf/consolidatedlist.pdf (as of 20 July 2009). For a more extensive discussion on the case and its relationship with the *Kadi* case, see M. Scheinin, 'Is the ECJ Ruling in *Kadi* Incompatible with International Law?' (2009) 28 *Yearbook of European Law* 637.

48 App. No. 10593/08 (ECtHR, Grand Chamber Judgment of 12 September 2012).

Italy unsuccessfully sought his delisting at the Security Council level. In September 2009 Switzerland made a submission favorable to the applicant, and soon thereafter the 1267 Sanctions Committee agreed to delist him. The applicant nevertheless pursued his case against Switzerland in the European Court of Human Rights, which in September 2012 found violations of ECHR Articles 8 (right to respect for private and family life) and 13 (right to an effective remedy). In its view Switzerland, by constraining the applicant to live in the small enclave of Campione, had interfered with the way he enjoyed his private and family life, despite having some latitude in implementing the UN-imposed sanctions.[49] As the interference was disproportionate in relation to the legitimate aims of the prevention of crime and the protection of Switzerland's national security and public safety, Switzerland had violated Article 8.[50] It appears that for the assessment of the Court it was quite important that although the Swiss domestic investigations into the applicant's links to terrorism had come to a negative conclusion in 2005, it was only in 2009 that Switzerland informed the Security Council of this outcome.[51] For the overall assessment of the 1267 sanctions regime and its implementation by UN member states, it is perhaps even more important that the Court found a violation of Article 13 due to the inability of the applicant to have an effective remedy in Switzerland to invoke his Article 8 rights by demanding his removal from the Swiss national list implementing the UN-level listing.[52]

Both this author and his successor as Special Rapporteur on human rights and counter-terrorism have criticised the 1267 sanctions regime for not being in accordance with international human rights law. In a 2006 report to the General Assembly, the Special Rapporteur looked into the impact of terrorist listing regimes upon the freedom of association.[53] The report included a call for national judicial review over the implementation of UN-imposed sanctions, as long as the UN itself did not provide for proper or adequate international review.[54] In a subsequent 2010 report to the General Assembly, the last one by the first holder of the mandate, the Special Rapporteur offered a general assessment of compliance by the United Nations Organisation itself with human rights standards while countering terrorism.[55] According to the Special Rapporteur, the transformation of the 1267 sanctions regime into a permanent and global list of terrorists, resulting in mandatory sanctions pursuant to Chapter VII of the UN Charter, despite falling short of the fundamental principles of the right to fair trial, amounted to action *ultra vires*, exceeding the powers conferred on the Council under Chapter VII of the Charter.[56] In a 2012 report to the General Assembly, the new Special Rapporteur Ben Emmerson QC made an assessment of the sanctions regime after the strengthening of the role of the Ombudsperson pursuant to Security Council Resolution 1989 (2011), concluding that the Al-Qaeda sanctions regime continues to fall short of international minimum standards of due process, and recommending a number of further reforms.[57]

---

49 Ibid. para. 180.
50 Ibid. para. 198.
51 Ibid. paras 187–188.
52 Ibid. para. 213.
53 UN GA, 'Report of the Special Rapporteur on the promotion and protection of human rights and fundamental freedoms while countering terrorism' (16 August 2006) UN Doc. A/61/267.
54 Ibid. para. 39.
55 UN GA, 'Report of the Special Rapporteur on the promotion and protection of human rights and fundamental freedoms while countering terrorism' (6 August 2010) UN Doc. A/65/258.
56 Ibid. para. 57.
57 UN GA, 'Report of the Special Rapporteur on the promotion and protection of human rights and fundamental freedoms while countering terrorism' (26 September 2012) UN Doc. A/67/396 para. 59.

3 Challenges for the future

There are two important contemporary challenges that international human rights law needs to tackle in order to remain meaningful in the broader discourse about how the international community and individual states will respond to the threat of international terrorism. These challenges relate at the same time to the theoretical or methodological self-understanding of international human rights law, and to real practical questions about proper strategies against terrorism and the place of international human rights law within them.

3.1 Can human rights law cope with tough challenges?

Although the rhetoric of the George W. Bush administration about a 'global war on terror' have been proven to be just that – rhetoric – and are not present with the same populist appeal as in 2001–08, the much older discussion on the relationship between international human rights law and international humanitarian law (IHL) has not gone away. As such and as a matter of law, international human rights law has the answers: (a) IHL (the international law of armed conflict) is applicable only during international or non-international armed conflict and has no validity beyond that scope of application, i.e. in situations that do not qualify as an armed conflict.[58] And (b) during armed conflict – international or non-international – IHL will be applicable and will operate as *lex specialis* in relation to international human rights law, provided that the term *lex specialis* is understood not as superseding human rights or derogating from it but, rather, as informing the proper *interpretation* of international human rights law.[59]

That said, the question remains whether these answers are sufficient. Does international human rights law have the authority and legitimacy needed in tough times? As is well known, the Barack Obama administration in the United States has replaced the methods of detention, torture and interrogation with a huge expansion of targeted killings, mostly by drones, to combat the threat of terrorism. The response by international human rights law may be either to characterise these measures as extrajudicial executions and, by definition, as violations of the right to life, or to discuss whether and where the loss of life was a measure of legitimate targeting of a person engaged in hostilities as a part of an ongoing armed conflict. The former approach runs the risk of not being legitimate in the eyes of the informed public. The latter approach may require concessions, as to how an armed conflict, its geographical limits, its parties and its participants are defined. If the latter, more demanding but in the view of the current author correct, approach is chosen, one needs to resist the temptation to defer to experts of international humanitarian law. As one of their perfectly legitimate axioms is the protection of bystanders (civilians), they may be eager to extend the scope of armed conflict

---

58 See UN Human Rights Council, 'Report of the Special Rapporteur on extrajudicial, summary or arbitrary executions, Philip Alston' (28 May 2010) UN Doc. A/HRC/14/24/Add.6. See also K. Anderson, 'Targeted Killing and Drone Warfare: How We Came to Debate Whether There Is a "Legal Geography of War" ',(2011) *Future Challenges in National Security and Law*; Christopher Greenwood, 'Scope of Application of Humanitarian Law', in D. Fleck (ed.), *The Handbook of International Humanitarian Law* (OUP, 2008) 45.

59 See UN Human Rights Committee, General Comment No. 29, 'Article 4: states of Emergency' (2001) UN Doc. CCPR/C/21/Rev.1/Add.11; HRC, General Comment No. 31, 'Nature of the General Legal Obligation Imposed on States Parties to the Covenant' (2004) UN Doc. CCPR/C/21/Rev.1/Add.13.

in order to trigger that protection. For international human rights law, to resist that temptation will be equally important as securing the protection of the general population. Hence, it appears that also in the future it will be for international human rights law to contest the existence of an armed conflict or to remain critical as to what actors are considered to be involved as parties in an armed conflict.[60]

In order to be legitimate, such an answer needs to be coupled with the willingness of international human rights law to address many other tough questions. When counter-terrorism professionals acknowledge and accept that terrorism can most successfully be combated through methods that comply with human rights, human rights professionals must be ready to discuss what are those methods. For instance, permissible methods of interrogation, use of firearms in the context of suicide terrorism, and the proper scope of permissible limitations to human rights for concrete issues that arise in counter-terrorism, are all challenging questions that need to be addressed.

3.2 What does human rights law offer to victims of terrorism?

Another equally challenging question, which also boils down to issues of the legitimacy, rather than the juridical correctness, of the answer, is what human rights law can offer to victims of terrorism. Traditionally, some authoritarian regimes have referred to the rights of victims of terrorism in order to shy away from rightful criticism for the human rights violations the governments in question have committed in the name of countering what they label as terrorism. Sadly, on too many of such occasions it was evident that the regime cared neither of the human rights of the alleged terrorists nor of the human rights of their victims, but in fact reduced the victims to mere means for its own goals. The response by human rights groups and Western governments tended to be that as terrorists were non-state actors, they were not capable of committing human rights violations, even when their actions amounted to very serious crimes. Hence, human rights violations committed by terrorist groups could not be on the agenda of any human rights body and human rights actors should continue to focus on governments as human rights violators.

Today, the situation may be different. Globalisation has relativised the position of states as centres of power, through the emergence of equally powerful other actors, such as multinational corporations and international financial institutions. The liberalisation of trade and investment regimes has resulted in deregulation on the side of nation states and a situation where other public and private actors are capable of directly affecting the enjoyment of human rights across borders. As a consequence, there is a need for international human rights law evolving to also address other actors than the nation state as the single potential human rights violator. As a consequence, human rights in relation to actors other than states, including private actors, has become a legitimate topic for scholarship, advocacy and litigation.[61] This

---

60 For the criteria of being capable of being a party to an armed conflict, see, e.g., *Prosecutor v Ramush Haradinaj, Idriz Balaj and Lahi Brahimaj*, ICTY, Trial Chamber, Judgment, Case No. IT-04-84-T, 3 April 2008, para. 60. The current UN Special Rapporteur on human rights and counter-terrorism, Ben Emmerson, QC, has launched an inquiry in the issue of the use of drones and other forms of targeted killing for the purpose of counter-terrorism and counter-insurgency, see http://www.ohchr.org/Documents/Issues/Terrorism/SRCTBenEmmersonQC.24January12.pdf (accessed on 12 May 2013).

61 A. Clapham, *Human Rights Obligations of Non-State Actors* (OUP, 2011).

author has elsewhere stated that the issue of human rights obligations of private actors (the so-called third-party effect) is not a conceptual but a practical problem.[62] If there were a procedure in place for holding actors other than states to account for human rights abuses, the outcome of such proceedings would establish that the actor in question did violate human rights.[63]

The human rights of victims of terrorism are important and require more attention than traditionally given by human rights stakeholderss. As Special Rapporteur on human rights and counter-terrorism this author addressed the situation and rights of victims of terrorism, inter alia, during country visits and in mission reports on them,[64] as well as in a final report on best practice in countering terrorism.[65] The new Special Rapporteur Ben Emmerson QC has gone further than this, by addressing the human rights of victims as the main theme of his first set of annual reports and announcing, in his very first report to the General Assembly, his commitment to 'ensuring that proportionate attention is paid to the rights of direct and indirect victims of acts of terrorism'.[66] In a June 2012 report to the UN Human Rights Council, he identified terrorist acts of lethal violence as 'a grave violation of the human rights of the victim', and proposed the elaboration of a new international instrument on the human rights of victims of terrorism and the corresponding obligations on states.[67]

Select bibliography

Annual reports to the UN General Assembly and Human Rights Council by the Special Rapporteur on the promotion and protection of human rights and fundamental freedoms while countering terrorism. Available at: http://www.ohchr.org/EN/Issues/Terrorism/Pages/Annual.aspx.

International Commission of Jurists, 'Assessing Damage, Urging Action: Report of the Eminent Jurists Panel on Terrorism, Counter-Terrorism and Human Rights' (2009).

L. Doswald-Beck, *Human Rights in Times of Conflict and Terrorism* (OUP, 2011).

D. Jenkins, A. Henriksen and A. Jacobsen (eds), *The Long Decade: How 9/11 Has Changed the Law* (OUP, 2012).

62 M. Scheinin, 'Characteristics of Human Rights Norms', in C. Krause and M. Scheinin (eds), *International Protection of Human Rights: A Textbook,* 2nd edn (Åbo Akademi University Institute for Human Rights, 2012) 36.

63 For a proposal on creating such a procedure through an international treaty adopted by states but open also to other actors voluntarily accepting the binding jurisdiction of the proposed court, see J. Kozma, M. Nowak and M. Scheinin, *A World Court of Human Rights – Consolidated Statute and Commentary* (Vienna: Neuer Wissenschaftlicher Verlag, 2010).

64 See, for example the reports on missions to Turkey (E/CN.4/2006/98/Add.2), Israel and the occupied Palestinian territory (A/HRC/6/17/Add.4), Peru (A/HRC/16/51/Add.3) and Spain (A/HRC/10/3/Add.2).

65 UN Human Rights Council, 'Report of the Special Rapporteur on the promotion and protection of human rights and fundamental freedoms while countering terrorism' (22 December 2010) UN doc. A/HRC/16/51. See Practice 6 and accompanying explanations, paras 24–25.

66 UN GA, 'Report of the Special Rapporteur on the promotion and protection of human rights and fundamental freedoms while countering terrorism' (18 August 2011) UN Doc. A/66/310 para. 20.

67 UN Human Rights Council, 'Report of the Special Rapporteur on the promotion and protection of human rights and fundamental freedoms while countering terrorism' (4 June 2012) UN Doc. A/HRC/20/14 paras 64 and 66.

33

International development, global impoverishment, and human rights

Upendra Baxi

1 Towards a creative juxtaposition?

The juxtaposition of these three keywords – international development, global impoverishment, and human rights – enables some meaningful conversation, and global social action, concerning international development (now often also named as 'global governance'). In particular, the discourses concerning 'extreme poverty' (EP) and global poverty (GP) offers key linkages reconceptualising the 'tasks' of development and the 'ends 'of human rights'.

The three keywords offer many different conceptual, normative, and institutional histories. International development (ID) fosters changing conceptions of global 'development' (section 33.3 below) not all of which directly relate to global poverty or human rights norms and standards (hereafter HR); ID may not be grasped outside a variety of institutions and networks that it spawns, as students of international organisations and relations know well. The relationship between the 'technical' and 'political' elements offers different and changing contexts of international organisations: one may, for example, compare in this regard 'technical' ID arrangements such as the World Meteorological Organization with some specialised agencies of the UN system, for example, the WHO, FAO, ILO, UNESCO. ID systems that provide early warnings of 'natural' disasters – floods, earthquakes and tsunamis, and now global warming symptoms – have a bearing upon conditions of global poverty; yet, they do their tasks well only by virtue of their technical expertise. In contrast, the specialised agencies remain, poignantly, sites of contestation about their deference to HR, though not always in their quotidian operations. Where the 'technical' ends and the distinctively or specifically 'political' begins poses a difficult question, indeed![1]

It is at any rate clear that UN/HR discursivity, now more specifically reframed/reinforced by the internal UN agendum linking HR with the specific normative and policy engagements with problems of world poverty, poses several paradigmatic concerns. Foremost

---

1 See, for example, J. Braithwaite and P. Drahos, *Global Business Regulation* (Cambridge University Press, 2000). Despite its title, this work remains worth recalling as a safe guide navigating the passages between the 'technical' and the 'political' in ID.

amongst this, of course, is the 'technical element' providing estimates of 'extreme poverty' (EP) and 'global poverty' (GP) conditions: Section 33.2 tries to address this complexity. The concluding part of this chapter further speaks to some silences in EP/GP discourses such as the relative neglect of institutional frameworks of the ID humanitarian regimes of law and policy (for example, the laws regulating international conflicts, and the conditions of necessitous migrants addressed by the UNHCR) and some concerns regarding global reparative justice. In the main, this chapter addresses the place of contemporary human rights law formations in relation to world poverty, acutely informed of course by Thomas Pogge's insistence that the '*recent* design of global institutional order' carries major 'human rights deficits' entailing ways of privileging the 'feasibility of a more poverty-alleviating alternative design'.[2] What then may be included/excluded by the term 'global institutional order' cannot but remain contested. This, in turn, invites recourse to different narratives concerning two genres or thoughtways: we later attend thus to the philosophical/metaethical discourse concerning human rights as contrasted with the legal/juridical discourse.

Even so, I believe that a juxtaposition of these three keywords is 'creative' as directed to achieve orders of 'overlapping consensus'[3] about an ethically *decent* world ordering at least in the first half of the twenty-first century. We need travel no further than the anorexic discourse of Millenium Development Goals (MDGs) and Programmes of Action to understand the fact that the conditions of extreme poverty constitute a global scandal.

Surely, the 'scandal' consists in part in our choice of vocabulary/diction. While in what follows, I use the term 'poverty' in deference to common convention, my own choice of the keyword is 'impoverishment',[4] if only because this directs attention to deliberate acts of rational policy planning choices that create and sustain conditions of severe deprivation and conditions of sub-human existence for millions of people. More vividly put, an elementary global social fact is just this: vast swathes of humanity remain born and made 'poor' by some ID experiments at 'global development', and national policies and plans, which recurrently produce/reproduce the circuits of global poverty.

True, there are good grounds for caution in reading EP/GP discourses as marking a paradigm shift in ID politics[5] – even when there now exists a degree of hospitality accorded to the diction of 'impoverishment' and rethinking it via normative politics animated by the pertinence of the very idea of human rights, and even some of its core norms and standards.

Nevertheless, some crucial elements towards a normative paradigm shift need to be acknowledged. First, a widespread belief now exists suggesting that the elimination of salient conditions of EP remains entirely *feasible* in the present stage of world economic and social development. To take away this foundational belief (that is, justifiably held 'true' belief) is to render insensible any talk of any human rights–based approach to EP, and GP (the latter held

---

2 T. Pogge, 'Reply to Critics: Severe Poverty as a Violation of Negative Duties', (2005) 19(1) *Ethics & International Affairs* 55–83 at 55.

3 See J. Rawls, *Political Liberalism* (Columbia University Press, 1993).

4 U. Baxi, 'Introduction', in U. Baxi (ed.), *Law & Poverty: Selected Essays* (N.M. Tripathi, 1989). Thomas Pogge, while deploying the term 'global poverty', actually addresses contemporary conditions of global impoverishment.

5 T. Pogge, *Politics as Usual: What Lies Behind the Pro-Poor Rhetoric* (Polity, 2010). See, further, U. Baxi, 'A Report for All Seasons?: Small Notes on Reading in Larger Freedom', in C. Raj Kumar and D.K. Srivastava (eds), *Human Rights and Development: Law, Policy, and Governance* (LexisNexis, 2006); and P. Alston, 'Ships Passing in the Night: The Current State of the Human Rights and Development Debate Seen through the Lens of the Millennium Development Goals' (2005) 27(3) *Human Rights Quarterly* 755–829.

within the ID metaphorical regimes of its *reduction/alleviation*). Second, the logics, languages, and paralogics (rhetoric) of contemporary human rights, as well as wider enunciations of the 'principle of humanity',[6] remain relevant (more than ever before) to tasks at hand. Third, an emergent ID consensus concerning combating EP as an urgent human rights concern operates on a 'fast forward,' or accelerated, 'now-time' for global social action whereas GP/ID tasks operate on a 'slow-motion' history ID time. Fourth, there are cogent reasons to affirm and celebrate both HR and global justice informed concerns: I may do no better than to invite your attention to an emergent Academics Stand Against Global Poverty (ASAP) discourse.[7] Fifth, and by the same token, 'movement knowledges'[8] ought to be read as transforming our ways of reading EP/GP discourses in some new languages of global justice.[9]

At the outset, then, a word of apology is owed for my rather untidy address here of a mélange of concerns, replete with a flurry of acronyms!

2 'Rule by experts': changing approaches to impoverishment

The production of erudite knowledges about EP/GP cannot but remain an endeavour at 'objective'/'scientific' construction of the profiles of global/regional, and country/region-specific ID understandings of profiles and populaces of impoverishment. In some ways, these translate the narratives of specific embodiment/disembodiment of suffering, distress, and humiliation as presenting 'raw data' awaiting the advent of forever-nuanced criteria of definition, measurement, and identification. These cultures of 'scientism' inherent to the contemporary 'rule by experts' contrasts with cultures of aesthetic representation of human abuse and violation, especially as converting social bodies into pre-social ones.[10] Nor, rather surprisingly, does the 'scientific' discourse address forms of biopolitics and biopower: the ownership of new forms of life produced by GRN technologies (genetics robotics and nanotechnologies) and the extraordinary sovereignty now marshalled by agribusiness and agrochemical global corporations, undoubtedly variously to the causation and further aggravation of EP/GP conditions.[11]

Within the enclosure of disciplinary limits, the rule by experts still produces 'scientifically' established measures of EP/GP conditions, of considerable pertinence for theory, movement, and action. Well worth recalling at the outset is the fact that such scientific measures/methods are also cultural productions; in a recent analysis Frederica Misturelli and Claire Heffernan

---

6 See, T. Campbell, 'Poverty as a Violation of Human Rights: Inhumanity or Injustice' and A. Gewirth, 'Duties to Fulfill the Human Rights of the Poor', in T. Pogge (ed.) *Freedom from Poverty as a Human Right: Who Owes What to the Very Poor?* (UNESCO and OUP, 2005). This work will be cited hereafter as 'Pogge, 2005'.

7 See T. Pogge and L. Cabrera, 'Outreach Impact, Collaboration: Why Academics Should Stand Against Poverty' (2012) 26(2) *Ethics & International Affairs*, 163–82; and O. O'Neil, 'Global Poverty and the Limits of Academic Expertise' (2012) 26(2) *Ethics and International Affairs*, 183–89.

8 See L. Cox and C.F. Fominaya, 'Movement Knowledge: What Do We Know, How Do We Create Knowledge' (2009) 1(1) *Interface: A Journal For And About Social Movements* 1–20.

9 See, a germinal contribution by M. Kirk, 'Beyond Charity: Helping NGOs Lead a Transformative Discourse on Global Poverty and Social Justice' (2012) 26(2) *Ethics & International Affairs* 245–63.

10 U. Baxi, 'Towards an Aesthetic of Human Rights: Preliminary Reflections', a paper presented to the Institute of Law as Culture, Bonn, October 2011 (forthcoming in an Institute publication of selected papers, 2013).

11 See U. Baxi, *Human Rights in a Posthuman World: Critical Essays* (OUP, 2007) (hereafter referred to as a 'Baxi, *Posthuman*'); R. Brownsword, *Rights, Regulation, and Technological Revolution* (OUP, 2008); and K.S. Rajan, *Biocapital: The Constitution of Postgenomic Life* (Duke University Press, 2006).

extend methods of 'memetic' analysis to global poverty measurement and identification. They suggest how the three 'memes' (units of cultural information) – 'basic needs', 'deprivation', and 'multidimensionality' – coequally 'inform and compete with one another';[12] and further demonstrate that approaches to poverty also differ with governmental, donor, and NGO 'memes' because these offer different 'core' elements defining 'poverty' thus restricting or expanding, as the case may be, the assignations of HR responsibilities for combating 'poverty' conditions.[13] Perhaps, then memetic frameworks also help us understand reasons why expert 'definitions' of 'poverty' tend to avoid descriptors such 'oppressive poverty', 'pauperisation', 'immiseration', and even for the most part 'impoverishment.' 'Deprivation' is the nearest term that experts prefer to use, provided it remains measurable/quantifiable.

A relatively easy descriptor is 'basic material needs' (BMN); however, identification and measurement of BMN varies a great deal, as we know full well, in contexts of bright lines that define international poverty lines (IPL) at \$1, or now adjusted upwards to \$1.25 income per day. No matter how adjusted in terms of PPP (purchasing power parity), IPL remains a contentious category, indeed![14] The most favoured BMN approaches reinforce the meme of 'deprivation'.[15] Further, it is not always clear why the ILO insistence, as early as 1976, concerning the inclusion of 'essential services provided by and for the community at large, such as safe drinking water, sanitation, public transport, and health and educational facilities'[16] for a long while did not offer or form crucial ingredients for any BMN approach.

Memetic transformation now remains fully at view, and at stake, by the languages of the 'multidimensionality' of 'poverty' with any uni-linear or monolithic perspective (as further fully illustrated by some instruments of global social policy, such as the World Development Reports, the UNDP human rights indicators, or the MDGs talk and action). This transformation, in turn, disrupting some staid binaries between basic material and non-material needs owes a great deal to the pioneering work of Henry Shue,[17] and more recently the inaugural corpus of Martha Nussbaum and Amartya Sen, accentuating considerations of autonomy and agency via the ideas of 'capabilities' and 'flourishing'.[18] Indeed, the OHCHR report by Professors Paul Hunt, Manfred Nowak and Siddiq Osmani, in my view at least, put this new wisdom most eminently in the service of articulation of human right(s) against poverty (see section 33.4 onwards below).[19]

---

12 See their text: F. Misturelli and C. Heffernan 'The Shape of Change: A Memetic Analysis of the Definitions of Poverty from 1970s to 2000s' (2012) 24 (Supplement) *Journal of International Development* S3–S15 at S14–15.

13 Ibid., at S14.

14 See L. Chen and M. Ravallion, 'The Developing World is Poorer than Thought but No Less Successful in the Fight Against Poverty', (2008) World Bank Policy Research Working Paper 4703; P. Collier, *The Bottom Billion* (OUP, 2007); and recently A. Sumner, 'Global Poverty and the New Bottom Billion: What If Three-quarters of the World's Poor Live in Middle Income Countries?' (2010) Institute of Development Studies Working Paper 349.

15 See, Misturelli and Heffernan (n. 12) at S11, Table 5.

16 ILO, *Employment, Needs: A One- World Problem. Tripartite World Conference on Employment, Income Distribution and Social Progress, and the International Division of Labour* 32 (International Labour Office, 1976).

17 See C.R. Beitz and R.E. Goodin (eds), *Global Basic Rights* (OUP, 2011).

18 See, especially, S. Alkire, *Valuing Freedoms: Sen's Capability Approach and Poverty Reduction* (OUP, 2005); P. Vizard, *Poverty and Human Rights: Sen's 'Capability Perspective' Explored* (OUP, 2006).

19 OHCHR, *Human Rights and Poverty Reduction: A Conceptual Framework* (UN, 2004) (hereafter cited as the 'Hunt Report').

With all the internal disagreements concerning method to measure conditions of EP/GP, identification of the populations adversely affected (especially those slightly above the IPL), and appropriate policy/law product mix (such as the MDGs) that may optimally address EP forms, scientific discourse has had some extraordinary impacts on global knowledge/power formations.

For one thing, living in denial of EP/GP conditions is no longer a viable governance option – either globally or nationally; new forms of legitimation of power occur best via participation in ID experimentations at 'good governance' linking HR approaches to within nation and global forms of EP. In many ways, then, whether or not fully thus intended, this discourse contributes coequally to the 'politics of production' and the 'production of politics' concerning the place of HR in combating EP/GP.[20] Indeed, startling revelations and reiterations (of the absolute numbers of below-IPL peoples, and poignant percentiles about starvation, malnutrition, infant and child mortality rates, and rates of morbidity and mortality of adult populations, especially women and young girls)[21] replenish a common endowment of solidarity amongst social movement and human rights actors and communities cutting across the political geographies of the 'North' and the 'South'. New forms of production of politics *of* and *for* human rights[22] provide the normative wherewithal for acts of counter-power (even some insurgent practices of 'civil society' activisms) often launching 'moral' crusades against the political obscenity/global scandal of EP conditions. These events do not speak with any singular voice concerning measures of law, policy, and administration combating EP/GP; even so, movement knoweldges insist that human rights may not be taken seriously without taking equally seriously social and human suffering entailed in impoverishment.

A most remarkable development related to the growth of expert knowledges about impoverishment may best be described as the 'epistemic' turn: the last few decades have been marked by renovation in political philosophy, and in particular theories about global justice, human rights, and human and social development.

3 The idea of development

The idea of 'development' (understood as a directed measure of social transformation) has many histories.[23] This section deals with five distinct but related aspects that affect understandings of the place of HR in the contexts of EP/GP. First, the formative contexts of Eurocentric progress narratives leave behind images of 'development' as *justifiable predation*: 'development' has been primarily understood with the imagery of early forms of predatory globalisation bearing the imprimatur of the four 'Cs' – conquest, colonisation, commerce, and Christianity[24] – the birthmarks of the Westphalian international legal orderings and the

---

20 I redeploy somewhat this phrase regime of M. Burawoy, *The Politics of Production: Factory Regimes Under Capitalism and Socialism* (Routledge, 1985), at 254–56.

21 The citations of such poignant statistics has now become commonplace and remain variously appropriable by various consistencies such as the political establishment, ID bureaucracies UN-systems agents and human rights agencies, social movement actors, mass and social media, MDG communities, and public intellectuals.

22 See, for an elaboration of this distinction U. Baxi, *The Future of Human Rights*, 3rd edn (OUP, 2012) (hereafter cited as 'Baxi, *Future*').

23 See, Baxi, *Posthuman* (n. 11) ch. 3.

24 U. Baxi, 'The Renascent Access Notions: Globalization and Access to Justice', in A. Kadwani Dias and G. Honwana Welch (eds), *Justice for the Poor: Perspectives on Accelerating Access* (OUP, 2009).

rise of the specifically 'modern' conceptions of HR in this era thus justify a Divine Right to Empire, and of systematic relegation of the non-European others as a sub-human species.[25]

Second, anti-colonial/anti-imperialist movements of the twentieth century identified some causal pathways of understanding the Eurocentric idea of development as itself a form of radical evil responsible for widespread pauperisation and immiseration of the colonised subjects. I have in view here at least two salient texts: Sir Dadabhai Naroji's work entitled *Poverty and un-British Rule in India*[26] and Walter Rodney's text *How Europe Underdeveloped Africa*,[27] texts surely worth recalling in the contemporaneous EP/GP discourse.

Third, some larger forms of cultural critiques of the idea of 'development' remain necessary. Mohandas Gandhi, in the early decade of the twentieth century, in his monograph *Hind Swaraj*, narrated the idea of development inherent to 'Western' forms of industrial capitalism as *toxic*. In so doing, he fully anticipated the forms of eco-critique of the dominant paradigms of development and generated what many of us know today under the name of 'sustainable development'. Cultural resistance occurs in a different form with Ayatollah Khomeini's critique of 'Western' development as instancing so many forms of 'Westtoxification'.

Fourth, more circumspect critiques of 'development' differentiate this notion from that of the ideology of *developmentalism*[28] – the pursuit of economic growth as an end in itself regardless of human and social costs – or more feelingly expressed, the production of conditions of 'living death' for the masses of here and now – impoverished individuals and entire populations of the worst-off humans everywhere. The idea of development undergoes many revisitations. Starting with the Club of Rome Report on 'the limits to growth', the 1970s and 1980s reform the idea of development under rubrics such as 'growth with equity', 'sustainable development', 'Another Development' (presenting both the narratives of alternatives to development and of 'alternate development') and also as 'inclusive' and 'participatory' development, and now some talk about 'post-development'. Further, given the *genesis amnesia*, and even amidst our current infatuation with over sixty years of UDHR talk, we also need surely to recall the Charter of Philadelphia birthing the ILO; the 'spirit' of Philadelphia animated by its postulates remain:

(a) labour is not a commodity;
(b) freedom of expression and of association are essential to sustained progress;
(c) poverty anywhere constitutes a danger to prosperity everywhere;
(d) the war against want requires to be carried on with unrelenting vigour within each nation, and by continuous and concerted international effort in which the representatives of workers and employers, enjoying equal status with those of governments, join with them in free discussion and democratic decision with a view to the promotion of the common welfare.[29]

Fifth, it is striking that with the rise of neoliberal ideology, one hears of ID imageries in the languages of 'fair globalisation'; these, however, remain also fully consistent with 'disciplinary'

---

25 See Baxi, *Future* (n. 22) ch. 2, for the elaboration of contrast between 'modern' and 'contemporary' HR paradigms.
26 D. Naroji, *Poverty and un-British Rule in India* (London 1901, reprinted Commonwealth Publishers, 1988).
27 W. Rodney, *How Europe Underdeveloped Africa* (Bogle-L'Ouverture, 1972).
28 W. Easterly, 'The Ideology of Developmentalism', (Jul/Aug 2007) 161 *Foreign Policy* at 31.
29 A. Supiot, *The Spirit of Philadelphia: Social Justice vs. the Total Market* (Verso, 2012).

and 'regulatory' globalisation.[30] A very brief profiling of these two globalisations should perforce suffice here. Disciplinary globalisation refers to varied phenomena: the structural adjustment programmes imposed by international financial institutions; trade, aid and 'developmental' conditionalities; and in some cases regimes of economic sanctions, imposed under the UN Charter, or as more often is the case by some coalitions of willing states. Regulatory globalisation refers paradigmatically at a global level to the WTO, at supranational levels to the EU, and many regional arrangements, including the North American Free Trade Agreement (NAFTA), Association of South East Asian Nations (ASEAN), Asia Pacific Economic Community (APEC), and to some extent now the South Asian Association for Regional Cooperation (SAARC). Further, this form operates below the radar screen in many an unequal bilateral investment treaty and the regime of arbitration of international commercial and investment disputes.

In some senses, the dominant paradigm of 'free trade' and investment regimes thus articulated by these two forms involves some enormous trade-offs between extant HR norms and standards, contributing to the recession of the future of human rights on the one hand and manifestly contributes (as learned from the global financial crisis of 2008, and the subsequent eurozone crisis) to at least short-run aggravation of the conditions of EP and GP. I suggest elsewhere that thinking of HR in the imagery of the UDHR needs to take account of a paradigm shift towards a 'trade-related, market friendly HR paradigm'.[31] Even as I turn now to a consideration of HR in the global poverty discourse, it needs saying that this HR paradigm shift seems far from acutely problematic for the UN-system enunciations and endeavours.

4 Reading the place of 'human rights' in the UN EP/GP discourse

An immensely varied set of UN expert committee 'reports' and a plethora of UN resolutions ('reportage', hereafter) generates an illusionary effect about the elevated status and secure place for HR; yet, the reality is otherwise. Put charitably, one may name the reportage as HR work in progress; put realistically the HR elements/aspects constitute at best floating signifiers.

A prime reason for this state of affairs is that the authorship of the reportage is scattered among various UN 'beings' and 'entities'. The UN-system marks an ongoing relationship amongst its complex and multilayered internal bureaucracy presided over by the office of the Secretary-General, various Commissions, Specialised Agencies, and Offices, and guest artists such as expert consultants and increasingly Special Rapporteurs. The HR spheres are no exception, save perhaps that the reportage of the Human Rights Treaty Bodies commands a privileged normative space.

A 'census' of guest artists (that is of who they are, how they are selected, the constraints within which they work, and their aspirations/achievements) is certainly necessary; equally called for is a steady exclusion of dissident voices. However, this chapter is scarcely a site either

---

30 See S. Gill, *Power and Resistance in the New World Order* (Palgrave-Macmillan, 2003); D. Schneiderman, *Constitutionalizing Economic Globalization: Investment Rules and Democracy's Promise* (Cambridge University Press, 2008). See further, J.P. Sasse, *An Economic Analysis of Bilateral Investment Treaties* (Springer Fachmedien, 2011) at 177–98.

31 See Baxi, *Future* (n. 22) chs 8 and 9; and also U. Baxi, 'Epilogue: Changing Paradigms of Human Rights', in J. Eckert et al. (eds), *Law Against the State: Ethnographic Forays into Law's Transformations* (Cambridge University Press, 2012) at 266–85.

for mapping the trajectories of multitudinous authorship of the place of HR in this discourse or for offering even scope for some broad sociological remarks. What follows, *faute de mieux*, are some implicit stories about the overall impact.

4.1 Chronologies

Many narrative hazards stand posed by this reportage. Concepts and chronologies get mixed up in a variety of ways. We lack chronological narratives even of the reportage. For example, the 2012 Final Draft Report of Magdalena Sepúlveda, the UN Human Right Council's Special Rapporteur on Extreme Poverty,[32] is able only to annex a chronology of reportage events from 2000 onwards; this is perhaps understandable, given the advent of the MDG discourse.

The rituals of UN declaration of days and decades do not play any significant role in this Report; yet, these remain crucial for construction of UN-system temporalities (and the UN-calendar ordained lifetimes for its guest artists – the myriad distinguished rapporteurs and the galaxy of experts). Why was the International Day for the Eradication of Poverty – 17 October – proclaimed as early as 22 December 1992, followed by a swift declaration the same year proclaiming the International Year for the Eradication of Poverty? How may we understand the 17 December 2007 proclamation of the first UN Decade for the Eradication of Poverty (1997–2006)? And what may it mean to say that we all now live under a December 2008 declaration of the Second Decade (2008–17)? Even for those who regard all these UN performances as symbolic, the question concerning the contexts of symbolisation remain far from impertinent.

More is at stake. Today, no one reads or mentions the 1996 Despouy Report,[33] which incidentally is a most remarkably refreshing text going for the jugular, as it were! This apart, a selective but well-organised amnesia remains operative in UN reportage. It has no space for recall of an entire UN history urging dedication of a minimum of 1 per cent of the GDP of the industrialised nations as an international obligation culminating into the fully aborted 1974 UN Declaration on a New International Economic Order; and concerning the Right to a New Informational Order, this finds no mention even in reports submitted by leading academic experts. A certain logic of intra-UN censorship is thus fully at work even when the UN discourse now urges more sincere commitments by all towards human rights, to fundamental freedoms, rights to participation in governance, and the rule of law and democracy as perquisites for combating EP/GP.

In any event my ambition towards an adequate archival recall delayed the writing of this chapter; this must obviously now remain a task for another day![34] Instead, I now seek to offer elements of an understanding of ways in which the UN reportage seeks to outline acts of reading contemporary HR.

---

32 See, for the text of the report, Human Rights Council, 'Final draft of the guiding principles on extreme poverty and human rights, submitted by the Special Rapporteur on extreme poverty and human rights, Magdalena Sepúlveda Carmona' (18 July 2012) UN Doc. UN/A/HRC/21/39 (referred to hereafter as 'Sepúlveda Report'); see also, M. Sepúlveda and C. Nyst, *The Human Rights Approach to Social Protection* (Ministry for Foreign Affairs of Finland, 2012).

33 ECOSOC, 'Final report on Human Rights and Extreme Poverty, submitted by the Special Rapporteur, Mr Leandro Despouy' (28 June 1996) UN Doc E/CN.4/Sub.2/1996/13.

34 But see M. Solomon, *Global Responsibility for Human Rights, World Poverty, and the Development of International Law* (OUP, 2007).

4.2 Narrative styles

The reportage on EP/GP marks no departure whatsoever frrm the UN narrative styles. To take a most recent example, General Assembly 65/214 of 25 March 2011 has (at least by my count) seventeen perambulatory recitals, followed by twenty operative paragraphs! This is not uncommon by any means; in turn the Human Rights Council, the OHCHR, and Independent Experts (of all hues) have their own similar liturgy of recitals. In an earlier reflection, I was moved to name this as 'dense intertextuality' of UN narrative styles.[35] However, these remain fully at odds with any serious-minded effort at securing the place of HR in the UN impoverishment discourse. Clearly, the narrative styles:

(a) render incomprehensible what human rights may be said to owed to the globally impoverished persons and populations;
(b) dissipate the communicative energies, intensities, and urgency otherwise charactering summons for urgent global social action confronting addressal/redressal of EP/GP conditions;
(c) conflate some bright lines that need to be maintained always between acts of global social policy (such as the MDG) and the extant and well-developed HR treaty and customary law obligations;
(d) complicate, rather than demonstrably foster, communicative relationships between the UN–system 'guest artists' and the UN-bureaucrats;
(e) generate, overall, among, within, and beyond, HR communities, construed on the one hand as experts in international human rights law (IHRL) and on the other, HR movement knowledge producers, a veritable situation of anomie;
(f) create, thus further, on the one hand situations of human rights weariness (states of moral, even metaphysical, fatigue with the constant liturgies inherent to the UN narrative styles) and on the other states of HR wariness concerning HR based EP/GP talk amidst the continually reproduced 'worst-off' suffering humans and communities of the oppressed peoples.[36]

Any suggestions towards even some modest changes in this regard will, at the threshold, be met with the objection on two grounds: the frameworks of diplomacy govern communicative styles and narrative simplification for wider publics occurs variously within the UN system. Unfortunately, this chapter may not fully engage all of this, except via some incidental remarks that now follow.

4.3 Global impoverishment and the basic UDHR values

Understandably, taking the UDHR values as axiomatic, without entering the discourse concerning 'values' in general has little use for controversies such as whether values are no more than rationalisation of strategic interests, or 'constructs of domination', or for the 'universality'/cultural specificity scope of values. Rather, the reportage proceeds in a firm

---

35 U. Baxi, 'The Politics of Reading Human Rights', in S. Meckled-Garcia and B. Cali (eds), *The Legalization of Human Rights: Multidisciplinary Approaches* (Routledge, 2006) at 330–65; and Baxi, *Future* (n. 22) ch. 9.
36 See Baxi, *Future* (n. 22) ch. 3.

belief that values provide good enough guides for policy and action and further that the core values are best sourced in the UDHR. Thus, there is not a single resolution or a report which does not foreground the value of human dignity always inherently violated by EP/GP conditions. However, what we also encounter are dignity-plus articulations; that is reinforcement of dignity with other core UDHR values.

To take a recent example, the 2011 General Assembley Resolution above, paragraph 1, summates all practices of the UN reportage in affirming as well as declaring that 'extreme poverty and exclusion from society constitute a violation of human dignity'. This is accompanied by urging that:

> [P]eople living in poverty and vulnerable groups . . . [should] be empowered to organize themselves and to participate in all aspects of political, economic, social and cultural life, in particular the planning and implementation of policies that affect them, thus enabling them to become genuine partners in development.

While no one may doubt this desideratum, the question is whether the UDHR prescription (Article 27) goes as far as this formulation suggests (note that clause (2) in fact speaks of the protection of intellectual property rights as an aspect of fundamental freedoms and as rights). Further, the majestic Article 28 entitling everyone to 'a social and international order in which the rights and freedoms set forth in this Declaration can be fully realised' remains rather imaginatively overworked via the components of 'empowerment', ways of self-organisation of the impoverished and the vulnerable and generalised considerations of 'participipation' in all spheres of social life, and in policies and programmes affecting them so that at the end point they become 'partners in development'.

Although the perambulatory recital cites the UN Declaration on the Right to Development (UD-RTD) of 1986, the text of the Resolution ignores the different construction of dignity-plus imagery of 'participation'.[37] The UD-RTD remains more specific: participation has to be an 'active, free and meaningful' participative process that ensures 'fair distribution of income'.[38] This latter is only imaginable when models of development address the tasks of 'eradication of social injustices' by 'appropriate economic and social reforms'.[39] States, in particular, owe obligations to take steps to 'eliminate obstacles to development resulting from failure to observe civil and political rights as well as economic, social, and cultural rights', since human rights form a seamless web of 'interdependence and indivisibility'.[40] To say the least, the differences in the construction of dignity-plus cannot be more striking, especially when one further attends to the ongoing UN work on the 'development' of the 'right to development'.[41]

Taking one of the most carefully formulated HR and poverty reports (the Hunt Report), dignity-plus signifies concern with values such as 'capabilities' and 'freedoms': as the Report puts it: 'The reason why the conception of poverty is concerned with basic freedoms is that these are recognised as being fundamentally valuable for minimal human dignity.'[42]

37 UN Doc. A/RES/41/128 (4 December 1986).
38 Ibid., Art. 2(3).
39 Ibid., Art. 8.
40 Ibid., Art. 6(2).
41 See, for further elaboration, Baxi, *Posthuman* (n. 11) ch. 4.
42 (n. 19) at 9.

The qualifier 'minimal' in relation to dignity raises a cache of normative concerns; the notion of 'basic freedoms' raises anxieties about what may be named as basic or auxiliary freedoms; besides, it would be too much to say that the UDHR enunciation of dignity as a foundational value anticipated the emergence of a sophisticated genre of 'capability theory'; further many of its virtuoso exponents regard the idea of freedom(s) as going well beyond its possible deviations from the notion of dignity. The Hunt Report stands alone by its reflexivity concerning all this – a compliment not always extendable to the UN reportage that, as we note soon enough, remains all to willing to relate almost all HR norms and standards to EP/GP contexts.

The overall point of these observations is to suggest a future analytic of reading transformations of the value of dignity into dignity-plus. At least one semi-sociological remark may be permitted: the UN-system has its own orders of inter-agency 'basic needs' (at times known in the metaphor of 'turf wars') and this contributes to complex, and often contradictory, constructions of dignity-plus. We now turn to the complexities that arise when UDHR 'values' are sought to be related to HR against poverty.

4.4 Complexities of juridification: the legal and the juridical

The processes of 'juridificiation'[43] present many complexities and these aggravate as concerns the reproduction of the idea and values of human rights in the languages of IHRL.[44] In the context of this chapter, I wish to add a further complexity by suggesting a distinction between two elements: the 'legal' and the 'juridical' as forms of production of IHRL.

By 'juridical' I refer to *aspirational law formations*, as contrasted with the 'legal' – the distinctive *orderings of legally binding obligations*. The former is typified (to translocate Lon Fuller's distinctions) by a *morality of aspiration*; the latter remains preoccupied with *morality of duty*.[45] Put another way, aspirational law assumes forms of HR declarations, the UDHR furnishing a paradigmatic instance. There is no question that any postulation of human rights against poverty must initially remain an aspect of the law in the making. To complete this summary remark, I may further say that staid distinctions between 'soft' and 'hard' IHRL remain the least helpful (perhaps a richer distinction was offered by earlier generations of international lawpersons via the registers of *de lege feranda* and *lex lata*). In any event, an ethic of aspiration is already at work in endeavors to relate EP/GP conditions to the HR states and estates: I may do no better than to evoke a fecund statement in the Hunt Report: 'poverty reduction and human rights are not two projects, but two mutually reinforcing approaches to the same project'.[46]

This fully said, the question that needs serious engagement concerns the place of HR languages, logics, and paralogics in the UN-system reportage. First, this involves forms of

---

43 See L. Chr. Blichner and A. Molander, 'Mapping Juridification', (2008) 14(1) *European Law Journal* 36–54.

44 See J. Eckert, Z. Olzem Biner, B. Donahue and C. Strumpell, 'Introduction: Law's Travels, and Transformations', in Eckert et al. (eds) (n. 31) at 1–23; and J. Eckert, 'Rumours of Rights' in the same volume at 147–70; see, further, Baxi, *Future* (n. 22) ch. 7.

45 I discuss this aspect in relation to Amartya Sen's elements of a theory of human rights in Baxi, *Posthuman* (n. 11) ch. 2; and more recently in a contribution to C. Geraty and C. Douznas (eds.), *Cambridge Companion to Human Rights Law* (Cambridge, 2012) (specifically in the context of re-invention of human rights).

46 (n. 19) at 3.

politics of naming novel configurations of singular or multiple HRAP (human right against poverty). A threshold concern here is just this: does HRAP-naming describe EP/GP conditions as HR-violative or does it seek to prescribe a global impoverishment regime of new HR norms and standards? We see in section 33.5 ways in which some eminent philosophers (including HR theorists) approach this distinction.

Second, HRAP aspirational enunciations invite examination of sources of derivation; put another way HRAP-type enunciations may not afford to ignore the claims of validation from within the UN Charter's designation of authoritative sources of international law obligations. In the present state of knowledge, it hardly remains possible to suggest that these may be securely based on customary international law sources; if so, these must *somehow* rest primarily on international law human rights treaty obligations, constantly expanded via the General Comments of the UN human rights treaty bodies,[47] and now somewhat further supplemented, and at times rather fiercely, by a variety of Special Rapporteurs.[48]

Third, even aspirational HRAP enunciations may not remain entirely uninformed by some Hohfeldian grammars of rights. Are these to be regarded as claim-rights-rights/ interests enforceable at law or do they mark other jural relations such as privilege/no right, power/liability, or immunity/disability? The MDG discourse suggests a privilege/no right relationship: that is states are at liberty to meet the deadlines contemplated by the MDG goals (such as reduction by half of the absolute numbers of starving peoples) in a form in which no one's right may be said to be infringed were the schedules of action (or inaction) further revised. Or perhaps this new right expresses a power/liability relationship in which sovereign state actors and international organisations have the power to change the conditions of EP/GP, and the impoverished remain exposed to the liability thus created? Or, further is it the case that the new right addresses are immunity/disability type jural relations – that is, might HRAP really amount to *immunity* from globally caused EP conditions? It may, of course, be maintained that this sort of framework of analysis is inapt for aspirational law or international law generally; if so, one must ask a serious question: what alternate ways remain at hand for any serious-minded HRAP talk?

Fourth, the question of community of duty-bearers remains equally crucial; the Final Draft of the Guiding Principles on Extreme Poverty and Human Rights (the Sepúlveda Report), while speaking fully in Part VI (and elsewhere) to a myriad of IHRL duties of states, even in mixed voices of 'policy' and HR elements, errs rather egregiously in not addressing IHRL responsibilities of the agents and actors within the UN-system and related international organisations.[49] What, if any, fiduciary obligations may the various personifications of the 'international community' be said to owe to the globally impoverished?

Even as constraints of space prevent us addressing of this crucial aspect, we surely need to briefly note Part VII of the Sepúlveda Report, which speaks to us about a compound category of 'non-state actors, including business enterprises'.[50] These have 'at the very minimum, the

---

47 See as concerns all this, OHCHR, *Draft Guidelines: A Human Rights Approach to Poverty Reduction Strategies* (UN, 2002).
48 OHCHR, *A Technical Review* (2009) concerning these guidelines provides a register of enormous contestation!
49 HRC, Final draft of the guiding principles on extreme poverty and human rights, submitted by the Special Rapporteur on extreme poverty and human rights, Magdalena Sepúlveda Carmona (18 July 2012) UN Doc. A/HRC/21/39.
50 Ibid., paras 100, 101.

responsibility to respect human rights, which means to avoid causing or contributing to adverse human rights impacts through their activities, products or services, and to deal with such impacts when they occur.'[51] Yet this very language seems to address primarily the 'business enterprises', unless of course the phrase-regime referring to 'activities, products or services' were also to embrace these as provided by armed opposition groups!

Prescinding this, most disappointing remains the urging in paragraph 101 of the Report that:

> [B]usinesses should adopt a clear policy commitment to respect human rights, including those of persons living in poverty, and to undertake a human rights due diligence process to identify and assess any actual or potential impacts on human rights posed by the company's own activities and by business partners associated with those activities. They should prevent and mitigate the adverse effects of their actions on the rights of persons living in poverty, including by establishing or participating in operational-level grievance mechanisms for individuals or communities that face such impacts

There is no reference whatsoever here to the 2003 Norms on the Responsibilities of Transnational Corporations and Other Business Enterprises with Regard to Human Rights (the Norms) and allied entities – as if the UN-system discourses regarding this never even *happened*![52] It is true that the Special Representative of the Secretary General, John Ruggie, has not merely harshly critiqued the Norms but has proposed a framework that makes any talk of HR approaches to multinational corporations (MNCs) rather impertinent. The above cited paragraph, for the most part, reflects a similar message, except in its last sentence that directs attention to an ethical duty to develop some sorts of participatory corporate social responsibility (CSR) approaches that may somehow 'prevent and mitigate ... actual or potential impacts' of corporate governance. The return to voluntarism, to say the least, justifies an order of immunity and impunity for the worst violations of human rights by MNCs and their institutional affiliates and other normative cohorts.[53]

Fifth, and at least as regards what HRAP may embrace, the Sepúlveda Report seems to suggest that almost all extant IHRL norms and standards ought to extend to any conceptualisation of HRAP.[54] If so the question is *not* whether the catalogue is comprehensive but whether it is *fully so*! Put another way the Report's identification of 'persons living under poverty' remains incomplete without at least some reference to causes of impoverishment (and denial of minimal IHRL standards and norms), for example, to refugees and stateless persons, populaces impoverished by sanctions and military invasions in the name of humanitarian intervention and now increasingly under the regime of global politics of regime change, the MNCs caused mass disaster communities of violated human communities (as

---

51 Ibid.

52 See UN Doc. E/CN.4/Sub.2/2003/12/Rev.2 (2003); Baxi, *Future* (n. 22) ch. 9 and the literature therein canvassed.

53 See the Report of Permanent Peoples' Tribunal Concerning Human Rights Violations by Leading Agrochemcial and Agribuisness MNCs (Banaglore, India, 15 December 2011), see http://awake-andstilldreaming.wordpress.com/2011/12/15/permanent-peoples-tribunal-declares-agrochemical-tncs-guilty-of-human-rights-violations/ (accessed on 8 May 2013).

54 Part V of the Report specifically mentions a cluster of fourteen human rights, each in turn inviting further normative disaggregation!

with and since Bhopal,[55] and the near-future communities of those impoverished by climate change).

Finally (and without being exhaustive) the UN reportage presents a varied landscape. Most of its core recommendations while ostensibly addressing human rights norms and standards in effect turn out to be anodyne policy prescriptions. Policies remain notoriously contingent political productions, as every student of the MDG well knows. Policy regimes national and global, further provide charters of discretion, as students of economic, social and cultural rights also know well. Many 'development' polices (as students of the work of the World Commission on Dams, for example, well know) indulge in a specialism known as cost–benefit analysis which fails to acknowledge, let alone take seriously, HR-oriented ways of indentifying impoverishment as well as rule of law costs entailed in some horrendous develop-mental displacement costs causing, as well as aggravating, EP conditions. These are sought to be 'justified' via some inchoate approaches – the dominant *habitus* of cost/benefit analyses – not only 'justifying' why the impoverished here and now ought almost always to bear the costs of 'development' but also appealing to the prospects of their inter-generational 'well-being'! Even the Hunt Report in drawing precious distinctions[56]does not specifically address HR and IHRL type approaches to the critique of the cost–benefit framework of analysis.

5 Philosophical/metaethical discourse

We are transported into an entirely different realm with this discourse because it:

(a) considers human rights as moral rights, independently of the patterns of juridification;
(b) raises questions of explication of two key components: the idea of being and remaining 'human' and the idea of having rights;
(c) addresses the idea of being and remaining human in terms of dignity, freedom, agency, and security (vulnerability);
(d) places, thus, the idea of having, and exercising, human rights in the contexts of relation-ship between self, society, and community;
(e) raises further concerns about 'justification' of the idea of human rights, in turn even presupposing a human right to justification;
(f) in many ways proceeds to relate (in our times at least and since the magisterial corpus of John Rawls) the idea of human rights to imageries of 'justice' as an aspect of the basic structure of social institutions, especially the specifically political assemblage of the 'state' institutions;
(g) this in particular opening up spaces for different 're-mappings' of territories of human rights/justice symbiotic relationships, conceptualising justice not only as a 'metaphysical' but 'political' virtue.[57]

---

55 U. Baxi, 'Writing about Impunity and Environment: The "Silver Jubilee" of the Bhopal Catastrophe', (2010) 1(1) *Journal of Human Rights and the Environment* 23–44.

56 The 'three different ways in which human rights can be [made] relevant to poverty' are 'constitutive relevance, instrumental relevance and constraint-based relevance'; further directing our attention to 'instrumental relevance' – whether 'causative' and 'evaluative' – as at least addressing 'the ability of certain HR standards/clusters' that 'promote the cause of poverty reduction.' Hunt Report (n. 19) at 11.

57 Given space-constraints, and surely for intrisnic reasons as well, I may only refer here to the recent sterling work of R. Forst, *Contexts of Justice: Political Philosophy Beyond Liberalism and Communitarianism* (California University Press, 2002; John M. M. Farell, trans.)

All these territories of thought remain rather well known to the *cognoscenti*; this concluding section may now only summarily provide vignettes of the transformations concerning the place of HR in EP/GP discourse. The UN-system reportage thus far addressed scarcely acknowledges the UNESCO-fostered initiative 'Ethical and Human Rights Dimensions of Poverty: Towards a New Paradigm in the Fight Against Poverty', which marks some new points of departures led notably by Thomas Pogge and his critics.[58]

And, in the main, I rely primarily on an overview of his positions by Pogge in his reply to critics.[59] He appeals to 'the minimal human rights standard' which also furnishes an approach to global justice with which to grasp, and combat, 'the scandal of severe poverty persisting on a massive scale'.[60] The 'standard of human rights' as a standard of social justice as well is a first step towards the recognition of 'human rights deficit'. This standard is minimal in the sense that it does not refer to all the IHRL norms and standards; unlike most UN reportage, Pogge offers a 'thin' (non-maximal) view of human rights.[61] Primarily, he offers an institutional perspective – that is ways in which institutional arrangements and orderings may contribute to human harm or HR violations (without denying of course an interactional perspective where such harm or violations may occur by wrongful conduct). This approach asks us 'to be concerned about avoidably unfulfilled human rights not so far as they exist at all but only in so far as they are produced by coercive social institutions in whose imposition we are involved.'[62] This important shift helps clarify the basis of collective moral responsibility of all social agents:

> [A]ccording to which a human right to X gives you a moral claim against all others that they not harm you by cooperating without compensating protection and reform efforts, in imposing upon an institutional order under which you lack secure access to X as part of foreseeable and avoidable human rights deficit.[63]

EP conditions, clearly, epitomise the '*recent* design of institutional global order'; this design is unjust because it harms 'the global poor by *foreseeably* subjecting them to *avoidable* severe poverty'.[64] Human rights deficits may arise then only when the harms are foreseeable and 'reasonably avoidable' and when alternative design of the relevant international order would not produce comparable human rights deficits or other ills of comparable magnitude.[65] In this way, indicated by some, real world utopic thoughtways that speak to us about reasons why the 'affluent persons must *cooperate* by way of duties/obligations of avoiding "harm to others" by

58 See, for example, T. Pogge, *World Poverty and Human Rights: Cosmopolitan Responsibilities and Reforms* (Polity, 2002) (hereafter referred to as Pogge, *WPHR*); Pogge, 2005 (n. 6); Pogge and Cabrera (n. 7) and the literature therein referred; and A. Jaggar (ed.), *Thomas Pogge and His Critics* (Polity, 2010).

59 T. Pogge, 'Reply to Critics: Severe Poverty as a Violation of Negative Duties', (2005) 19(1) *Ethics & International Affairs* 55–83.

60 Ibid. at 57.

61 But see, Pogge, *WPHR* (n. 58) at 48–49, identification of the threshold condition for identifying violatons of basic needs oriented HR. These are 'physicial integrity, susbsitence supplies . . . feedom of movement and action, as well as basic education and economic participation', subject to a further listing.

62 Ibid. at 172.

63 Pogge (n. 59) at 67.

64 Ibid., 55 (emphasis added).

65 Ibid., 60.

making uncompensated contributions . . . imposing on them an institutional order that fore-seeably produces avoidable human rights deficits'.[66]

Space constraints do not allow elaboration of reasons why Pogge considers the present institutional order deficient in terms especially of the analytic of the three 'Ps' (as Alison Jaggar names these): protectionism, patents, and pharmaceuticals. Pogge offers some cogent evidence of how each of these components of the present international order causes, as well as contributes, to EP conditions as both entirely foreseeable and reasonably avoidable. How far recourse to this discourse (informed as well with some lively contestations of Pogge's perspectives) may have enriched the legal and juridical discourse is a question that needs to be seriously addressed in terms of juridification of HRAP.

In this context remains, particularly, Pogge's reiterated insistence that at the very least human rights create a negative duty:

> [N]ot to cooperate in the imposition of a coercive international order that avoidably leaves human rights unfulfilled without making reasonable efforts to aid its victims and to promote institutional reform.[67]

At least by this token, the UN reportage fails overall. If any reiteration is required, I may single out here its reticence – even on a normative threshold of HRAP enunciation – to address even the catastrophic HR violation aggravating massive human suffering (and EP/GP conditions) caused by MNCs and allied business enterprises/entities.

To say this is not to present Pogge's prescriptions as a panacea! Without addressing the rich contestations of his perspectives offered by his critics, I may only add at least three remarks by way of a 'dangerous supplement' (to evoke a phrase of Jacques Derrida). Pogge's construction of human rights deficits of the 'recent design' of international order needs, first, to include various orders of impositions of foreseeable and avoidable human harms and human rights violations of necessitous migrants, refuges, asylum-seekers, and internally displaced peoples.[68] Second, acts and feats of 'military humanism' – such as wars on 'terror' and of 'regime change' by coalitions of (almost forever) willing states – likewise invite reconstruction of human rights deficits. And, third, there remain concerns about global reparative justice for causation of EP/GP conditions by not-too-remote practices of militarised global governance in the early, middle, and late phases of the Cold War – here of course leaving aside some intractable but no less crucial range of concerns righting wrongs of past historic wrongs, such as colonial predation.

It is not clear why the UN-reportage may remain so fully orphaned by the available approaches; even when these may seem to illustrate the 'poverty of theory', this enterprise remains pertinent (to say the least) for any worthwhile enunciation seeking to ensure a safe harbour for HRAP-type enunciation. Future authors of any such enunciation may regard it wiser to stay on board with Pogge's offerings of orders of negative duties and obligations. Even so, considerations urged thus far, perhaps, may not remain ethically extravagant even in terms of fashioning an expanded agendum for an enterprise directed to 'real-world justice'?

---

66 Ibid., 61.
67 Ibid. at 170.
68 See M. Bebdict Dembour and T. Kelly (eds), *Are Human Rights for Migrants?: Critical Reflections on the Status of Irregular Migrants in Europe and the United States* (Routledge, 2011), and my Afterword in the same volume.

Select bibliography

U. Baxi, 'Writing about Impunity and Environment: The "Silver Jubilee" of the Bhopal Catastrophe', (2010) 1(1) *Journal of Human Rights and the Environment* 23–44.

U. Baxi, 'Reinventing Human Rights in an Ear of Hyperglobalisation: a Few Wayside Comments', in C. Gearty and C. Douzinas (eds), *The Cambridge Companion to Human Rights Law* (Cambridge University Press, 2013) 150–70.

R. Dworkin, *Justice for Hedgehogs* (Belknap Press, 2013).

M. Nussbaum, *Frontiers of Justice: Disability, Nationality, Species Membership (Tanner Lectures of Human Values* (Harvard University Press, 2007).

M. Nussbaum, *Women and Human Development: The Capabilities Approach (The Seeley Lectures)* (Cambridge University Press, 2001).

J. Rawls, *The Law of Peoples: With 'The Idea of Public Reason Revisited'* (Harvard University Press, 2001).

A. Sen, *The Idea of Justice* (Penguin, 2010).

34

Gender challenges for international human rights

Andrew Byrnes

1 Introduction

This chapter provides an overview of some of the major developments that gender analysis and activism has stimulated in international human rights law in the last four decades. Feminist activists, scholars and advocates have argued that the 'mainstream' human rights system is androcentric in substance and practice, and have challenged it to deliver on its promises to guarantee rights for all humans, to expand its coverage to gendered patterns of violations that have been neglected by it, and to re-examine the conceptual limitations which have led to those failures.

The chapter deals primarily with human rights violations inflicted on women which are explicitly based on their sex or which have a disproportionate sex-based impact; however, it also briefly discusses other violations with a gendered dimension. While sex-based classifications and gendered assumptions about the appropriate roles of women and men are deployed overwhelmingly to the disadvantage of women, they may also lead to a violation of the rights of men (and reinforce prevailing stereotypes and assumptions about women's capacities and roles to the detriment of women).[1]

1.1 Sex, gender, and the problems of binary classification and universal categories

This chapter employs the common distinction between 'sex' and 'gender':

> The term 'sex' . . . refers to biological differences between men and women. The term 'gender' refers to socially constructed identities, attributes and roles for women and men and society's social and cultural meaning for these biological differences resulting in

---

1 See D. Otto, 'International Human Rights Law: Towards Rethinking Sex/Gender Dualism and Asymmetry', in M. Davies and V. Munro (eds), *A Research Companion to Feminist Legal Theory* (Ashgate, 2013), available as Melbourne Legal Studies Research Paper No. 624, available at: http://ssrn.com/abstract=2178769, accessed on 18 February 2013.

hierarchical relationships between women and men and in the distribution of power and rights favouring men and disadvantaging women. This social positioning of women and men is affected by political, economic, cultural, social, religious, ideological and environmental factors and can be changed by culture, society and community.[2]

The sex/gender distinction, developed in the 1960s and 1970s, allowed the notion that women's biology was their destiny to be challenged, by distinguishing between biological sex and socially ascribed gender roles based on but not made inevitable by biological sex. However, some scholars argue that aspects of 'sex' are also culturally determined.[3] Other challenges to the binary male/female classification arise from 'the existence of chromosomal or genital variations [which mean] that a significant population does not fit neatly into pre-existing biological definitions of men and women',[4] so that a person's sex may be ambiguous (intersex). The relationship between sex and gender identity adds further complexity.[5]

1.2 Equality of women and men and international human rights

The UN Charter recognised the equality of men and women,[6] a position reaffirmed in the Universal Declaration of Human Rights,[7] and subsequently in the two International Covenants on Civil and Political Rights[8] and on Economic, Social and Cultural Rights.[9] This commitment was also given institutional form by the establishment of the UN Commission on the Status of Women (CSW), an intergovernmental body mandated to advance the position of women,[10] which adopted a number of treaties addressing common forms of discrimination against women, including their exclusion from political activities[11] and the loss of

---

2 UN Committee on the Elimination of Discrimination Against Women (CEDAW), General Recommendation No. 28, 'The Core Obligations of States Parties under Article 2 of the Convention' (2010) UN Doc. CEDAW/C/GC/28, para. 5. See also UN Committee on Economic, Social and Cultural Rights (CESCR), General Comment No. 16, 'The equal rights of men and women to the enjoyment of all economic, social and cultural rights (art. 3)' (34th session) (2005) UN DoE/C.12/2005/4, para. 14.

3 Otto (n. 1), and D. Rosenblum, 'Unsex CEDAW, or What's Wrong with Women's Rights' (2011) 20 *Columbia Journal of Gender and the Law* 1.

4 International Gay and Lesbian Human Rights Commission, 'Foreword: Dilemmas of Definition', in *Equal and Indivisible: Drafting Inclusive Shadow Reports for CEDAW* (IGLHRC, 2009) at 3.

5 See Gay and Lesbian Alliance Against Defamation (GLAAD), 'Transgender Glossary of Terms', *GLAAD Media Reference Guide*, 8th edn (2010), available at: http://www.glaad.org/reference/transgender, accessed on 18 February 2013.

6 See generally K. Tomaševski, *Women and Human Rights* (Zed Books, 1993); A.S. Fraser, 'Becoming Human: The Origins and Development of Women's Human Rights' (1999) 21 *Human Rights Quarterly* 853; B.E. Hernandez-Truyol, 'Human Rights Through a Gendered Lens: Emergence, Evolution, Revolution', in K.D. Askin and D.M. Koenig (eds), *Women and International Human Rights Law*, vol. 1 (Transnational Publishers, 1999) at 3.

7 UNGA Res. 217 (10 December 1948).

8 International Covenant on Civil and Political Rights (adopted 16 December 1966, entered into force 23 March 1976) 999 UNTS 171.

9 International Covenant on Economic, Social and Cultural Rights (adopted 16 December 1966, entered into force 3 January 1976) 993 UNTS 3.

10 L. Reanda, 'Human Rights and Women's Rights: The United Nations Approach' (1981) 3 *Human Rights Quarterly* 11.

11 Convention on the Political Rights of Women (adopted 20 December 1952, entered into force 7 July 1954)193 UNTS 135.

nationality on marriage to a foreign national.[12] These were followed by the UN Declaration on the Elimination of Discrimination against Women,[13] which affirmed the right to equality in relation to political rights, nationality, economic and social life, education, marriage and family life, and before and under the law, and subsequently developed into the 1979 Convention on the Elimination of All Forms of Discrimination against Women (CEDAW).[14] The broader context for these developments was the resurgence of the global feminist movement and a series of events organised under UN auspices, including International Women's Year in 1975 and the UN Decade for Women (1976–85), during which a number of important international conferences were held[15] that advanced agendas relating to women's human rights.[16] During this time feminist advocates and scholars increasingly turned their attention to the 'mainstream' human rights system,[17] exploring the extent to which it acknowledged and responded to violations of women's human rights and dignity.[18]

2 Critiques of the dominant human rights system[19]

Many different critiques have been launched against the international human rights system from gender perspectives,[20] especially in relation to violations of the rights of

---

12 Convention on the Nationality of Married Women (adopted 29 January 1957, entered into force 11 August 1958) 309 UNTS 65. See also conventions by adopted by UNESCO on the right to equality in education and by the International Labour Organization: Convention Concerning Equal Remuneration for Men and Women Workers for Work of Equal Value (adopted 29 June 1951, entered into force 23 May 1953) (ILO No. 100), 165 UNTS 303, and Convention Concerning Discrimination in Employment and Occupation (adopted 25 June 1958, entered into force 15 June 1960) (ILO No. 111), 362 UNTS 31.

13 UNGA Res. 2263 (XXII) (7 November 1967).

14 Convention on the Elimination of All Forms of Discrimination against Women (adopted 18 December 1980, entered into force 3 September 1981) 1249 UNTS 13.

15 Mexico (1975), Copenhagen (1980) and Nairobi (1985).

16 See, e.g. N. Reilly, *Women's Human Rights: Seeking Justice in a Globalizing Age* (Polity Press, 2009) at 46–68.

17 See, among other accounts, K. Engle, 'International Human Rights and Feminism: When Discourses Meet' (1992) 13 *Michigan Journal of International Law* 517; F.D. Gaer, 'And Never the Twain Shall Meet? The Struggle to Establish Women's Rights as International Human Rights', in C.E. Lockwood et al. (eds), *The International Human Rights of Women: Instruments of Change* (American Bar Association, 1998) at 4–89; Fraser (n. 6); K. Engle, 'International Human Rights and Feminisms: Where Discourses Keep Meeting', in D. Buss and A. Manji (eds), *International Law: Modern Feminist Approaches* (Hart, 2005) at 47–66.

18 See J. Kerr (ed.), *Ours by Right: Women's Rights as Human Rights* (Zed Books, 1993); R.J. Cook (ed.), *International Human Rights Law and Women's Human Rights* (University of Pennsylvania Press, 1994); J. Peters and A. Wolper (eds), *Women's Rights, Human Rights: International Feminist Perspectives* (Routledge, 1995); K.D. Askin and D.M. Koenig (eds), *Women and International Human Rights Law*, vols 1, 2 and 3 (Transnational Publishers (1999–2001); K. Knop (ed.), *Gender and Human Rights* (OUP, 2004); Buss and Manji (n. 17).

19 See generally D. Otto, 'Gender Issues and International Human Rights: An Overview', University of Melbourne Legal Studies Research Paper No. 606, available at: http://ssrn.com/abstract=2154770, accessed on 18 February 2013 and Introduction to D. Otto (ed.), *Gender Issues and Human Rights*, 3 vols (Edward Elgar 2012). See also D. Otto, 'Feminist Approaches', in T. Carty (ed.), *Oxford Bibliographies Online: International Law* (OUP, 2012).

20 See generally J. Neuwirth, 'Towards a Gender-Based Approach to Human Rights Violations' (1987) 9 *Whittier Law Review* 399; C. Bunch, 'Women's Rights as Human Rights: Toward a Re-Vision of Human Rights' (1990) 12 *Human Rights Quarterly* 486; H. Charlesworth, C. Chinkin and S. Wright, 'Feminist Approaches to International Law' (1991) 85 *American Journal of International*

women.[21] Some of those critiques question the very utility of rights discourse generally and also specifically for addressing the violations that women face.[22] Others question the conceptual foundations of the human rights system, arguing that it: is premised on an individualistic approach;[23] focuses on the fears of violations that (some) men are more likely to suffer;[24] in relation to gender has as its principal organising concepts equality and non-discrimination which tend to involve a comparison with men's entitlements, limit the opportunities to reflect the specificities of women's experiences and have little transformative potential; fails to recognise or respond to those violations that women suffer that can readily be seen to fall within well-established categories of rights violations; is overwhelmingly concerned with the public spheres of the state and the market,[25] leaving the private sphere of the family – where many violations of women's rights occur – largely unregulated;[26] privileges the heterosexual family as 'natural'; fails to recognise that many of the violations that women suffer are from non-state actors in the market, community and family; is culturally imperialistic or limited;[27] and gives undue preference to civil and political rights when a greater attention to economic and social rights would be much more helpful to women.[28] Other limitations

Law 613; A. Byrnes, 'Women, Feminism and International Human Rights Law – Methodological Myopia, Fundamental Flaws or Meaningful Marginalisation? Some Current Issues' (1992) 12 Australian Yearbook of International Law 205; H. Charlesworth and C. Chinkin, The Boundaries of International Law (Manchester University Press, 2000) at 201–49; R. Johnstone, 'Feminist Influences on the United Nations Human Rights Treaty Bodies' (2006) 28 Human Rights Quarterly 148 at 149–54.

21 See A. Edwards, Violence against Women under International Human Rights Law (CUP, 2011) at 36–87.
22 See, e.g. C. Smart, Feminism and the Power of Law (Routledge, 1989); E. Kingdom, What's Wrong with Rights? Problems for a Feminist Politics of Law (Edinburgh University Press, 1991).
23 See, e.g. K. Jackson, 'Justice for All? Human Nature and the Feminist Critique of Liberalism', in J.F. O'Barr (ed.), Women and a New Academy: Gender and Cultural Contexts (University of Wisconsin Press, 1989) at 122; A. Scales, 'The Emergence of Feminist Jurisprudence: An Essay' (1986) 95 Yale Law Journal 1373 at 1391; A. Rao, 'Right in the Home: Feminist Theoretical Perspectives On International Human Rights' (1993) 1 National Law School Journal, Feminism and Law, 63 at 72; J. Cobbiah, 'African Values and the Human Rights Debate: An African Perspective' (1987) 9 Human Rights Quarterly 309 at 312–20.
24 See, e.g. H. Charlesworth, 'Alienating Oscar? Feminist Analysis of International Law', in D.G. Dallmeyer (ed.), Reconceiving Reality: Women and International Law (American Society of International Law, 2004) at 1, 8.
25 C. Romany, 'Women as Aliens: A Feminist Critique of the Public/Private Distinction in International Human Rights Law' (1993) 6 Harvard Human Rights Journal 87.
26 See, e.g. R. Eisler, 'Human Rights: Toward an Integrated Theory for Action' (1987) 9 Human Rights Quarterly 287 at 288–96; Charlesworth, Chinkin and Wright (n. 20) 625–30; F.E. Olsen, 'International Law: Feminist Critiques of the Public/Private Distinction' in Dallmeyer (n. 24) 157; Rao (n. 23).
27 See R. Coomaraswamy, 'To Bellow Like a Cow: Women, Ethnicity and the Discourse of Rights' in Cook (n. 18) 39.
28 S. Wright, 'Economic Rights and Social Justice: A Feminist Analysis of Some International Human Rights Conventions' (1992) 12 Australian Yearbook of International Law 242; C. Chinkin and S. Wright, 'The Hunger Trap: Women, Food and Self-Determination' (1993) 14 Michigan Journal of International Law 262 at 312–15; H. Charlesworth and C. Chinkin, 'The Gender of Ius Cogens' (1993) 15 Human Rights Quarterly 63 at 69; United Nations Development Fund for Women, Report submitted by the United Nations Development Fund for Women (UNIFEM) to the World Conference on Human Rights, (1993) UN Doc. A/CONF.157/PC/61/Add.17, 9.

identified are the underrepresentation of women in the human rights system;[29] the persistent heteronormativity of the system; the enduring characterisation of women as victims or as in need of protection carried over from pre-UN Charter treaties;[30] and the relative weakness of sex-specific human rights institutions.[31] More recent critiques have also drawn attention to the assumptions of binary forms of sex/gender that underlie both the dominant and gender-specific instruments and institutions. Even where measures have been adopted to address violations of women's rights, there is further criticism of their limitations – for example, the problems involved in essentialising the category of woman and the attendant privileging of the perspectives of First World women (or some of them) while failing to reflect the multiple factors that interact to constitute violations around the world.[32]

This is a daunting – and incomplete – list of the critiques made both of the human rights system and its response to gender issues. Nonetheless, many concerned with women's human rights have considered that there is significant potential within the system to respond more effectively to violations of women's human rights and to articulate new understandings of what constitutes a human rights violation from gendered perspectives, and have engaged with it, advocating such changes.[33]

This has led to the elaboration of new substantive norms, the establishment of new mechanisms focusing on women-specific violations, more responsive case law and other jurisprudence, as well as many thematic and country reports which document and analyse gendered violations. The UN Declaration on the Elimination of Violence against Women,[34] the Inter-American Convention on the Prevention, Punishment, and Eradication of Violence against Women (Convention of Belém do Pará)[35] and the Protocol to the African Charter on Human and Peoples' Rights on the Rights of Women in Africa[36] are examples of this progress, while the inclusion of a specific article on women with disabilities in the Convention on the Rights of Persons with Disabilities[37] might also be mentioned. The strengthening of existing

29 See UN Annual meeting of the chairpersons of human rights bodies, 'Background and information on enhancing and strengthening the expertise and independence of treaty body members' (2012), UN Doc. HRI/MC/2012/2, at 2–7, Tables 1–11 and Edwards (n. 21) 92–108.

30 D. Otto, 'Disconcerting "Masculinities": Reinventing the Gendered Subject(s) of International Human Rights Law', in Buss and Manji (n. 17) 105.

31 See, e.g. Reanda (n. 10); F. Hosken, 'Toward a Definition of Women's Human Rights' (1981) 3 *Human Rights Quarterly* 1; M. Galey, 'International Enforcement of Women's Rights' (1984) 6 *Human Rights Quarterly* 463.

32 See, e.g., S. Tamale and J. Oloka-Onyango, " 'The Personal is Political", or Why Women's Rights are Indeed Human Rights: An African Perspective on International Feminism' (1995) 17 *Human Rights Quarterly* 691; R. Kapur, 'The Tragedy of Victimization Rhetoric: Resurrecting the "Native" Subject in International/Post-Colonial Feminist Legal Politics' (2002) 15 *Harvard Human Rights Journal* 1.

33 See generally Engle, 'International Human Rights and Feminisms: When Discourses Keep Meeting' (n. 17).

34 UNGA Res. 48/104 (20 December 1993).

35 Convention of Belém do Pará (adopted 9 June 1994, entered into force 9 June 1994) 1438 UNTS 63.

36 Protocol to the African Charter on Human and Peoples' Rights on the Rights of Women in Africa (adopted 11 July 2003, entered into force 25 November 2005) OAU Doc. CAB/LEG/66.6 (Maputo Protocol). See F. Banda, 'Blazing a Trail: The African Protocol on Women's Rights comes into force' (2006) 50(1) *Journal of African Law* 72; R. Murray, 'Women's Rights and the Organization of African Unity and the African Union: The Protocol on the Rights of Women in Africa', in Buss and Manji (n. 17) 253.

37 Convention on the Rights of Persons with Disabilities (adopted 13 December 2006, entered into force 3 May 2008) 2515 UNTS 3, Art. 6.

woman-specific mechanisms and the establishment of new ones are illustrated by the Optional Protocol to the CEDAW,[38] the UN Special Rapporteur on Violence against Women,[39] the UN Working Group on the Issue of Discrimination against Women in Law and Practice,[40] and parallels at regional levels.[41] At the UN level, calls for the integration of gender issues into the work of the treaty bodies and the special procedures of the then Commission on Human Rights (succeeded in 2006 by the Human Rights Council) has led to a significant, though uneven, expansion of documentation of women's violations and related analysis and policy recommendations since the 1990s.[42] Notable examples are the work done in relation to women and the rights to housing,[43] to health,[44] to be free from torture and cruel, inhuman or degrading treatment,[45] and in the context of ounter-terrorism.[46]

There have been significant advances in the development of jurisprudence that is more sensitive to gender issues in general and women's perspectives in particular. An example is the general comments and recommendations of a number of the UN human rights treaty bodies – gender issues have been explicitly (though unevenly) included in these documents, with the general comments of the Human Rights Committee (HRC)[47] and the Committee on Economic, Social and Cultural Rights (CESCR)[48] perhaps the most prominent examples apart from those of the CEDAW Committee.[49] In the concluding observations of various treaty bodies (the CESCR, HRC and the Committee against Torture,) women's perspectives and broader gender perspectives have been increasingly incorporated.[50] Similar developments have been in evidence in regional systems.[51]

38 Optional Protocol to the CEDAW (adopted 6 October 1999, entered into force 22 December 2000) 2131 UNTS 83.
39 Originally established by the UN Commission on Human Rights Res. 1994/45 (4 March 1994), and most recently renewed in 2011 by UNHRC Res. 16/7 (8 April 2011).
40 Established pursuant to UNHRC Res. 15/23 (1 October 2010).
41 See, e.g. the Office of the Rapporteur on the Rights of Women of the Inter-American Commission on Human Rights, established in 1994, and the Rapporteur on the Rights of Women of the African Commission on Human and Peoples' Rights.
42 See UN Human Rights Council, 'Thematic study of the Office of the United Nations High Commissioner for Human Rights on discrimination against women, in law and practice' (2010) UN Doc. A/HRC/15/40 (Thematic Study) at paras 29–36.
43 See the reports on the subject of the Special Rapporteur on housing (2000–2008), Miloon Kothari: UN Doc. E/CN.4/2003/55, UN Doc. E/CN.4/2005/43, and UN Doc. E/CN.4/2006/118.
44 See, e.g., 'Report of the Special Rapporteur on the right of everyone to the enjoyment of the highest attainable standard of physical and mental health, Paul Hunt', (2004) UN Doc. E/CN.4/2004/49.
45 See, e.g., 'Report of the Special Rapporteur on torture and other cruel, inhuman or degrading treatment or punishment, Manfred Nowak', (2008) UN Doc. A/HRC/7/3 (focusing on women and torture).
46 See 'Report of the Special Rapporteur on the promotion and protection of human rights and fundamental freedoms while countering terrorism, Martin Scheinin', (2009) UN Doc. A/64/211.
47 UN Human Rights Committee (HRC), General Comment No. 28, 'Equality of rights between men and women (art. 3)' (2000) UN Doc. CCPR/C/21/Rev.1/Add.10.
48 CESCR, General Comment No. 16 (n. 2).
49 See Johnstone (n. 20); F. van Leeuwen, *Women's Rights Are Human Rights: the Practice of the United Nations Human Rights Committee and the Committee on Economic, Social and Cultural Rights* (Intersentia, 2010), and Otto (n. 30).
50 See Thematic Study (n. 42) paras 37–51.
51 See, e.g., Inter-American Commission on Human Rights, 'Legal standards related to gender equality and women's rights in the Inter-American human rights system: development and application', (2011) OEA Ser.L/V/II.143 Doc.60.

At the same time, feminist engagement with the human rights system has been complex and at times troubled, reflecting a tension between the desire to address immediate problems using the tools currently available – whatever their limitations – and a coherent and persuasive theoretical approach.[52] Each advance produces reflection on its own inadequacies; and further challenges for the system and those engaging with it.

3 Concepts of equality and violations of rights

Violations of rights which have a gendered element may be analysed in a number of ways: as violations of independent rights guarantees, as violations of these guarantees in conjunction with the obligation not to discriminate on the ground of sex or gender, or as violations of freestanding guarantees of equality under or before the law or of equal protection of the law.

Various concepts of equality have been deployed in analysing claims of violations of women's human rights.[53] A formal equality approach, presuming that identical treatment is equality in the absence of some objective and reasonable justification, has been dominant, and important for attacking traditional stereotypes and historical exclusions. A substantive equality approach, which recognises biological or social differences between women and men (or subgroups of them), has permitted challenges to be made to practices that indirectly discriminate against women, discriminate by failing to take into account biological differences, and to social structures and patterns of conduct that adversely and disproportionately affect women. These approaches still largely take male experience(s) as given, with women's different experiences having to fit into male categories or to be a form of difference that should be considered on a par with the existing categories of violations.[54] Other concepts of equality have also been employed (including the concept of transformative equality, which seeks to fundamentally reorder androcentric social structures that disadvantage women).[55] Human rights bodies have generally been comfortable working with direct discrimination cases, less so with indirect discrimination;[56] although the treaties cover indirect or disparate impact discrimination explicitly or implicitly, there has been less extensive reasoned analysis of this form of discrimination, though recent years have seen more indirect discrimination cases and analysis.[57]

---

52 H. Charlesworth, 'Talking to Ourselves? Feminist Scholarship in International Law', in S. Kouvo and Z. Pearson (eds), *Feminist Perspectives on Contemporary International Law: between Resistance and Compliance?* (Hart, 2011) at 17, 19.

53 See A. Byrnes, 'Article 1', in M. Freeman, C. Chinkin and B. Rudolf (eds), *The UN Convention on the Elimination of All Forms of Discrimination against Women: A Commentary* (OUP, 2012) (*CEDAW Commentary*) at 51; and D. Shelton, 'Prohibited Discrimination in International Human Rights Law', in A. Constantinides and N. Zaikos (eds), *The Diversity of International Law* (Brill, 2009) at 259–92; O. Mjöll Arnardóttir, *Equality and Non-Discrimination under the European Convention on Human Rights* (Brill, 2003).

54 See Edwards (n. 21) 304–20.

55 See A. Byrnes, 'Article 2', in *CEDAW Commentary* (n. 53) at 71 and S. Fredman, 'Beyond the Dichotomy of Formal and Substantive Equality: Towards a New Definition of Equal Rights', in I. Boerefijn et al. (eds), *Temporary Special Measures: Accelerating de facto Equality of Women under Article 4(1) UN Convention on the Elimination of All Forms of Discrimination Against Women* (Intersentia, 2003) at 111.

56 See C. Tobler, *Limits and Potential of the Concept of Indirect Discrimination* (European Commission, 2008) at 11–15.

57 Ibid.

Human rights bodies have consistently upheld the right (and in some cases obligation) of states to undertake positive action or temporary special measures to respond to current patterns of exclusion of women or the effects of past discrimination.[58] This has been considered to be a means of achieving substantive equality, and some treaties explicitly clarify that such measures are not discriminatory.[59] The fields of employment, education and public and political life have been the principal areas in which such measures have been taken.[60]

This has thrown up some tensions between different legal regimes, especially between the EU and ECHR approaches,[61] and also the EU/EFTA and UN regimes.[62]

3.1 Formal equality, traditional attitudes and stereotypes

International human rights bodies have made significant progress, so far as formal sexual and gender equality is concerned. This approach, with its starting point of identical treatment for all unless differential treatment can be supported by an 'objective and reasonable justification', has provided the framework for the project of liberal inclusion of women, especially in the 'public sphere'. Often drawing on the language that rejects traditional attitudes and stereotypes about the capacities and choices of women and men, this approach affirms the entitlement of all to the same opportunities. Even though it is essentially based on a male model – women are entitled to access what men have – in practice, it has led to important gains.

Many sex-based laws and policies based on assumptions or stereotypes about the capacities and appropriate roles of women and men have been held by international bodies to violate guarantees of non-discrimination or substantive rights. Legal provisions which subordinate women to men within marriage or which are based on women's traditional roles and remove the choice of women as to whether or not they wish to assume such roles, have been found wanting in many cases. For example, in *Ato del Avellanal v Peru*[63] the UN Human Rights Committee found that the denial to married women of the right to represent matrimonial property before the courts was a violation of the guarantee of equality of women and men in Article 2 of the International Covenant on Civil and Political Rights (ICCPR). Similarly, in *Morales de Sierra v Guatemala*[64] the Inter-American Commission on Human Rights found various provisions of the Guatemalan Civil Code inconsistent with equality guarantees in the

---

58 See 'The concept and practice of affirmative action, Final report submitted by Mr. Marc Bossuyt, Special Rapporteur, in accordance with Sub-Commission resolution 1998/5', (2002) UN Doc. E/CN.4/Sub.2/2002/21, and D. Schick, L. Waddington and M. Bell (eds), *Cases, Materials and Text on National, Supranational and International Non-Discrimination Law* (Hart, 2007) at 757–869.

59 See HRC, General Comment No. 18, 'Non-discrimination' (37th session) (1989), para. 10; CEDAW, General Recommendation No. 25, 'Temporary special measures' (30th session) (2004); CESCR, General Comment No. 20, 'Non-discrimination in economic, social and cultural rights' (42nd session) (2009), UN Doc. E/C.12/GC/20, para. 9.

60 See, e.g., HRC, *Jacobs v Belgium*, (2004) UN Doc. CCPR/C/81/D/943/2000; HRC, General Comment No. 28 (n. 47), para 29.

61 S. van der Post, 'Positive Measures in Employment Law: Different Approaches under CEDAW and EU Gender Equality Legislation' (2011–12) *European Gender Equality Law Review* 21.

62 See *EFTA Surveillance Authority v Norway*, Court of the European Free Trade Association, Case E-1/02 (24 January 2003) and A. Byrnes, 'Article 23', in *CEDAW Commentary* (n. 53) 531, 532–33.

63 HRC, *Ato del Avellanal v Peru* (1988) UN Doc. Supp. No. 40 (A/44/40).

64 *Morales de Sierra v Guatemala*, IACHR, OEA/Ser.L/V/II.95 Doc. 7 rev. at 144 (1997).

American Convention on Human Rights[65] and the CEDAW. These included provisions that the husband had the right to administer marital property, stipulating the 'special right and obligation' of the wife to care for minor children and the home, that married women might work outside the home only if this did not prejudice her role as wife and mother, and that a husband might oppose such a course of action if certain conditions were made out. The Commission held that these provisions created a situation of *de jure* dependency of the wife, created lack of equilibrium in spousal authority within the marriage, applied stereotyped ideas about the roles of women and men which would perpetuate de facto discrimination against women in the family, and also that they impeded the ability of men to develop their roles within the marriage and the family. International human rights bodies have taken similar approaches in relation to differential treatment under immigration laws[66] and nationality laws.[67]

The principle of family unity and the dominant position of the male within the family has also been successfully challenged in cases relating to family names, in particular whether a married couple can be obliged to have one family name and, if so, what form it should take.[68] For example, in *Burghartz v Switzerland*,[69] the European Court of Human Rights held that it was unacceptable discrimination under the European Convention on Human Rights[70] to permit a wife to add her surname to her husband's name (chosen as the family name) but not to permit a husband to add his name to his wife's surname when her name was chosen as the family name.[71] A number of human rights bodies have also affirmed the right of each spouse to retain their own family name after marriage.[72]

Human rights bodies have also found discriminatory assumptions and stereotypes about women's participation in the paid labour force once they marry or have children. The UN Human Rights Committee has held that distinctions between (married) men and women based on the assumption that the woman would not be a principal earner, violated the equality guarantees of the ICCPR.[73] The European Court of Human Rights has found that acting on an assumption that women give up their jobs when their first child is born as the basis for

---

65 American Convention on Human Rights (adopted 22 November 1969, entered into force 18 July 1978) 1144 UNTS 12.

66 See, e.g., HRC, *Aumeeruddy-Cziffra v Mauritius* (1981) UN Doc. CCPR/C/12/D/35/1978 and *Abdulaziz, Cabales and Balkandali v United Kingdom*, App. Nos. 9214/80; 9473/81; 9474/81 (ECtHR, Judgment of 28 May 1985).

67 *Advisory Opinion on Proposed Amendments to the Naturalization Provisions of the Constitution of Costa Rica*, Advisory Opinion OC-4/84, IACtHR Series A No. 4 (19 January 1984). See International Law Association Committee on Feminism and International Law, *Final Report on Women's Equality and Nationality in International Law* (ILA, 2000).

68 See also HRC, General Comment No. 19, 'Protection of the family, the right to marriage and equality of the spouses (art. 23)' (39th session) (1990), para. 7.

69 *Burghartz v Switzerland*, App. No. 16213/90 (ECtHR, Judgment of 22 February 1994).

70 European Convention for the Protection of Human Rights and Fundamental Freedoms (adopted 4 November 1950, entered into force 3 September 1953) 213 UNTS 222.

71 See also HRC, *Müller and Engelhard v Namibia*, (2002) UN Doc. CCPR/C/74/D/919/2000, para. 6.8.

72 HRC, General Comment No. 28 (n. 47) para. 25; CEDAW, General Recommendation No. 21, 'Equality in marriage and family relations (13th session) (1994), para. 24; *Ünal Tekeli v Turkey*, App. No. 29865/96 (ECtHR, Judgment of 16 November 2004).

73 See the discussion in J. Möller and A. de Zayas, *The United Nations Human Rights Committee Case Law 1977–2008: A Handbook* (N.P. Engel, 2009) at 407–15.

withdrawing a disability pension involved impermissible sex-based discrimination in relation to the enjoyment of the right to a fair hearing (Article 6(1) in conjunction with Article 14 of the Convention).[74]

These cases, and decisions on other aspects of family life, have rejected the acceptability of laws that discriminate between women and men in their roles as spouses and legal subjects, affirming the right of women to equality in the form of identical treatment and their independent identity as a legal person.

The identification of discrimination in the form of stereotypes that are adverse to women's interests has a long history in case law and treaty provisions,[75] and has begun to be employed in new contexts.[76] An important example is *Vertido v Philippines*[77] in which the CEDAW Committee held that the use by a trial judge in a rape trial of stereotyped assumptions about women's responses to sexual assault violated Article 5(a), as well as other Articles of the CEDAW. The Committee has also found this analysis attractive in other cases as a separate or supporting basis for its finding of violations, holding in one case that a decision to postpone surgery for a pregnant woman 'was influenced by the stereotype that protection of the foetus should prevail over the health of the mother',[78] and found that a domestic court's refusal to grant a permanent protection order reflected 'stereotyped, preconceived and thus discriminatory notions of what constitutes domestic violence'.[79]

4 Making visible violations of women's human rights

4.1 The case of torture

A priority of women's human rights advocates has been to render violation of women's rights visible and to have their gravity recognised by having them characterised and condemned in terms of established 'mainstream' categories of violations. One of the classic examples given by feminist critics of androcentric myopia in international human rights is the scope of 'torture' under international law.[80] Critics have charged that many crimes of violence against women, especially crimes of sexual violence, inflict severe pain and suffering on women and are sex-specific, and thus fall within the definition of torture, but are rarely characterised as such.

---

74 *Schuler-Zgraggen v Switzerland*, App. No. 14518/89 (ECtHR, Judgment of 24 June 1993).
75 See, in particular, Art. 5(a) of the CEDAW, discussed in R. Holtmaat, 'Article 5', in *CEDAW Commentary* (n. 53) 141.
76 See generally J. Cook and S. Cusack, *Gender Stereotyping: Transnational Legal Perspectives* (University of Pennsylvania Press, 2010). Gender stereotypes cases are not limited to stereotypes applied to the disadvantage only of women. See, e.g., *Markin v Russia*, App. No. 30078/06 (ECtHR, Judgment of 22 March 2012), para. 143.
77 CEDAW, *Vertido v Philippines* (2010) UN Doc. CEDAW/C/46/D/18/2008. See S. Cusack and A.S.H. Timmer, 'Gender Stereotyping in Rape Cases: The CEDAW Committee's Decision in *Vertido v The Philippines*' (2011) 11 *Human Rights Law Review* 329.
78 CEDAW, *LC v Peru*, (2011) UN Doc. CEDAW/C/50/D/22/2009, para. 8.15.
79 CEDAW, *VK v Bulgaria*, (2011) UN Doc. CEDAW/C/49/D/20/2008, para. 9.12.
80 See, e.g., C.A. MacKinnon, 'On Torture: A Feminist Perspective on Human Rights', in K.E. Mahoney and P. Mahoney (eds), *Human Rights in the Twenty-first Century: A Global Challenge* (Martinus Nijhoff, 1993) at 21.

Furthermore, the definition of 'torture' in Article 1 of the UN Convention against Torture and Other Forms of Cruel, Inhuman or Degrading Treatment[81] – which requires some form of official involvement or acquiescence in an act and a purpose to be shown before an act amounts to 'torture' for the purposes of the treaty – has been much criticised. Critics have pointed to this as an illustration of how international law in general and human rights law in particular embodies a public/private distinction (here state versus non-state actors), with the result that the many forms of violence that women experience which meet the pain and suffering threshold, are not captured by the category of torture, because they are inflicted by non-state actors.[82] Strong advocacy around and increased awareness of this issue has produced significant developments, and there is now a considerable body of jurisprudence holding that rape and other forms of sexual violence amount to torture, or to cruel or inhuman or degrading treatment.[83]

The requirement of the involvement of a public official link has also come under challenge but has proved not to be as limiting as may once have been thought. The Committee against Torture has taken a broad view of what falls under the term 'acquiescence'.[84] Furthermore, while the concept of 'torture' under the Torture Convention may require a close nexus with a public official, it is not necessarily so limited under other treaties or under customary international law. For example, in international criminal/humanitarian law the war crime or crime against humanity of torture may be committed by a non-state actor without the need to show that there has been the involvement or acquiescence of a public official.[85] Under human rights treaties torture may arguably be committed by a non-state actor without any direct official involvement.[86] In short, feminist analysis and advocacy have meant that the established definitions have been read broadly so far as state acquiescence is concerned and have led to the recognition of a wider range of wrongs inflicted on women.[87]

4.2 Violence against women as a conceptual challenge for human rights law: the obligation of states in relation to non-state actors

In addition to characterising different forms of violence inflicted by or acquiesced to by state officials as torture or violations of other rights, women's human rights advocates have sought to conceptualise violence against women as a separately named violation of women's rights,

---

81 UN Convention against Torture and Other Forms of Cruel, Inhuman or Degrading Treatment (adopted 10 December 1984, entered into force 26 June 1987) 1465 UNTS 85.

82 See generally A. Byrnes, 'The Convention against Torture', in Askin and Koenig (n. 18), vol. 2 at 183, 189–94.

83 See L. Tojo, *Summaries of Jurisprudence/Gender-based Violence* (Center for Justice and International Law (CEJIL), 2010). Leading cases include *Aydin v Turkey*, App. No. 23178/94 (ECtHR, Judgment of 25 September 1997), *Mejía vs Perú,* IACHR, OEA/Ser.L/V/II.91, Doc. 7. rev, (1996). See also *Rosendo Cantú v Mexico*, IACtHR, Series C No. 216 (2010) (Preliminary Objections, Merits, Reparations, and Costs), Nowak (n. 45) para. 34 and generally Byrnes (n. 82) 191–94.

84 UN Committee Against Torture, General Comment No. 2, 'Implementation of Article 2 by States Parties' (39th session) (2007) UN Doc. CAT/C/GC/2/CRP. 1/Rev.4, para 18.

85 *Prosecutor v Kunarac et al.* (Trial Chamber Judgment) ICTY-96-23 and ICTY-96-23/1-A (22 February 2001), para. 497; (Appeals Chamber Judgment) (12 June 2002), paras 142–48.

86 HRC, General Comment No. 20, 'Prohibition of torture and cruel treatment or punishment (Art. 7) (44th session) (1992), para. 13. See also *González et al v Mexico (Cotton Field case)*, IACtHR, Series C No. 205 (2009) (Preliminary Objection, Merits, Preparations and Costs), Separate Concurring Opinion of Judge Cecilia Medina Quiroga, para. 17.

87 See generally Edwards (n. 21) 198–262.

as well as having it recognised as a form of discrimination against women.[88] This has led to the adoption of specific instruments which address the topic of violence against women and set out the obligations of states to prevent and punish it, including the Declaration on the Elimination of Violence against Women,[89] and the Convention of Belém do Pará.[90] While these proclaim a right to be free from violence, they also link the guarantee closely to established catalogues of human rights.

Another important dimension of the work around violence against women has been the development of international human rights law in relation to the acts of non-state actors. The last twenty years have seen a significant evolution of jurisprudence exploring how the acts of non-state actors can be brought within the traditional state-obligation framework of international law. While not confined to gendered violations, this area has been of particular prominence in that regard.[91]

These developments have arisen from the expansion of the scope of positive obligations on states under human rights treaties and the elaboration of the obligation of 'due diligence', the obligation of the state to take all appropriate or reasonable measures to prevent, punish and ensure reparation for violations of rights by non-state actors.[92] The due diligence obligation, with its origins in the classical law of state responsibility for injuries to aliens,[93] was given new life in the context of human rights law by the Inter-American Court of Human Rights in *Velásquez Rodriguez v Honduras*[94] in relation to responsibility of the state for disappearances carried out by non-state paramilitary groups. The Inter-American organs,[95] the European Court of Human Rights[96] and the CEDAW Committee[97] have all developed the doctrine in the context of violence against women, as has the UN Special Rapporteur on violence against women.[98]

---

88 See C. Chinkin, 'Violence Against Women', in *CEDAW Commentary* (n. 53) 442.

89 UNGA Res. 48/104 (20 December 1993).

90 Convention of Belém do Pará (n. 35). The Maputo Protocol (n. 36) also has a number of provisions relating to violence against women.

91 See D.Q. Thomas and M.E. Beasley, 'Domestic Violence as a Human Rights Issue', (1993) 15 *Human Rights Quarterly* 36, and R. Copelon, 'Recognizing the Egregious in the Everyday: Domestic Violence As Torture' (1994) 25 *Columbia Human Rights Law Review* 291.

92 See generally C. Benninger-Budel (ed.), *Due Diligence and its Application to Protect Women from Violence* (Martinus Nijhoff, 2008).

93 Byrnes (n. 55) 88–90.

94 *Velásquez Rodriguez v Honduras*, IACtHR, Series C No. 4 (1988).

95 See, e.g. *Cotton Field case* (n. 86) and *Maria da Penha Maia Fernandes v Brazil*, IACHR, OEA/Ser.L/V/II.111 Doc. 20 rev. at 704, (2001), para. 56. See generally K. Tiroch, 'Violence against Women by Private Actors: The Inter-American Court's Judgment in the Case of *Gonzalez et al ("Cotton Field") v. Mexico*' (2010) 14 *Max Planck Yearbook of United Nations Law* 371.

96 See, e.g., *Opuz v Turkey*, App. No. 33401/02 (ECtHR, Judgment of 9 June 2009), discussed in L. Hasselbacher, 'State Obligations Regarding Domestic Violence: The European Court of Human Rights, Due Diligence, and International Legal Minimums of Protection' (2010) 8(2) *Northwestern University Journal of International Human Rights* 190.

97 See, e.g., CEDAW, *AT v Hungary*, (2005) UN Doc. CEDAW/C/32/D/2/2003; CEDAW, *Goecke v Austria*, (2007) UN Doc. CEDAW/C/39/D/5/2005; CEDAW, *Yildirim v Austria*, (2007) UN Doc. CEDAW/C/39/D/6/2005; CEDAW, *Jallow v Bulgaria*, (2012) UN Doc. CEDAW/C/52/D/32/2011; *SVP v Bulgaria*, (2012) UN Doc. CEDAW/C/53/D/31/2011.

98 'The due diligence standard as a tool for the elimination of violence against women, Report of the Special Rapporteur on Violence against Women, its Causes and Consequences, Yakin Ertürk', UN Doc. E/CN.4/2006/61, paras 14–105. See also 'Preliminary report submitted by the Special Rapporteur on violence against women, its causes and consequences, Ms Radhika Coomaraswamy,

4.3 Sexual rights and reproductive rights

The categories of 'sexual rights' and 'reproductive rights' overlap, but are not identical.[99] Reproductive rights include the right of women to decide on whether to have children (and with whom), and the number and spacing of children, and the right to information about contraceptive options and to adequate health care. 'Sexual rights' include but go beyond this, encompassing rights to the free expression of and non-discrimination in relation to one's sexuality and gender identity, as an individual, in relation to one's personal relationships and as a member of a social and political community.

International human rights law has steadily expanded its protection of women's reproductive rights. Human rights bodies have applied a substantive equality analysis, in a context in which biological differences between women and men mean that a straightforward identical treatment model is not available. The major human rights treaties recognise that pregnancy and maternity are sex-specific conditions that require special (generally protective) responses. However, the right of women and men to found a family, guaranteed in the major human rights instruments, is essentially the right of a heterosexual couple to have children, free from state interference; the relevant guarantees do not explicitly recognise the woman's primary and independent role in such decisions.

However, international human rights bodies have built a solid body of practice that affirms the right of a woman to exercise control over her body and reproductive capacity and to be supported by the state in the choices she makes in that regard.[100] At times they have drawn on specific rights such as the right to respect for private life or family life, the right to life, and the right to health; on other occasions, a non-discrimination or equality analysis in conjunction with these rights has been invoked.[101]

For example, the right of a woman to decide whether or not to proceed with a pregnancy without the consent of a partner or the putative father has been affirmed,[102] as has the right

in accordance with Commission on Human Rights resolution 1994/45', (1994) UN Doc. E/CN.4/1995/42. See also Inter-American Commission on Human Rights, 'Access to Justice for Women Victims of Violence in the Americas', (20 January 2007) OEA/Ser.L/V//II. Doc. 68 at 11–19, paras 23–45. See generally B. Meyersfeld, *Domestic Violence and International Law* (Hart, 2010) at 42–52, 232–35; A. Byrnes and E. Bath, 'Violence against Women, the Obligation of Due Diligence, and the Optional Protocol to the Convention on the Elimination of All Forms of Discrimination against Women – Recent Developments' (2008) 8 *Human Rights Law Review* 517 at 524; J. Murdoch, 'Unfulfilled Expectations: the Optional Protocol to the Convention on the Elimination of All Forms of Discrimination against Women' (2010–11) *European Human Rights Law Review* 26 at 43–44.

99 See A.M. Miller, 'Sexual but Not Reproductive: Exploring the Junctions and Disjunctions of Sexual and Reproductive Rights' (2000) 4(2) *Health and Human Rights* 68; M.J. Roseman and A.M. Miller, 'Normalizing Sex and Its Discontents: Establishing Sexual Rights in International Law' (2011) 34 *Harvard Journal of Law and Gender* 313.

100 See, in particular, CEDAW, General Recommendation No. 21 (n. 72) paras 21–23; General Recommendation No. 24, 'Women and health (art. 12)' (20th session) (1999); CESCR, General Comment No. 14, 'The right to health (art. 12)' (22nd session) (2000) UN Doc. E/C.12/2000/4. See also Inter-American Commission on Human Rights, 'Access to maternal health services from a human rights perspective', (2010) OEA/Ser.L/V/II, Doc. 69; R. Cook, B.M. Dickens and M.F. Fathalla, *Reproductive Health and Human Rights. Integrating Medicine, Ethics, and Law* (OUP, 2004) at 148–215.

101 See also CEDAW, General Recommendation No. 24 (n. 100) and General Recommendation No. 21 (n. 72), paras 21–23; and CESCR, General Comment No. 14 (n. 100).

102 *Paton v United Kingdom*, European Commission of Human Rights, Application No. 8416/78, Judgment of 13 May 1980).

of access to information about family planning and contraception and to affordable contraceptives.[103] Forced sterilization, or sterilization without full and informed consent, has been held to violate a range of rights, including the right not to be subject to torture, to bodily integrity, to respect for private and family life, and to health (and information about health choices).[104]

International human rights law does not unequivocally guarantee a right to abortion on demand.[105] However, international human rights bodies have stressed the importance of women and girls having access to information about and access to contraceptive methods.[106] Where abortion is available in a state, there is an obligation on the state to have in place legal and administrative measures that will enable a prompt decision on a woman's eligibility and also timely access to the medical procedure.[107] Where abortion is banned, or available only on limited grounds, international human rights bodies have been critical of the criminalisation of women who seek abortions or who are subject to other disadvantages or penalties because they do this,[108] and have held incompatible with the right to freedom of expression (including the freedom to impart and receive information) restrictions on the dissemination of information about the availability of abortion abroad.[109]

5 Custom, religion and tradition

Assertions of women's human rights have frequently been met with rejection or qualified acceptance by reference to their purported inconsistency with customs, traditional practices, cultural norms or religious beliefs and practices.[110] Sometimes this rejection is a convenient trope designed to brush off challenges to established (male) authority; at other times it reflects a genuine concern about universalist human rights discourse and its claimed failure to understand and respect non-Western traditions. Within feminist scholarship there has also been hesitancy about the relationship between what are sometimes seen as Western human rights norms (or at least Western priorities) which do not take account of the fact that women's experiences can differ markedly, which may be seen as denying or devaluing important aspects of women's identity, or which lead to strategies that are likely to be ineffective in particular social contexts.

---

103 See also *Artavia Murillo et al (in vitro fertilization) v Costa Rica*, IACtHR, Series C No. 257 (2012) (Preliminary Objections, Merits, Reparations and Costs).

104 See, e.g., CEDAW, *Szijjarto v Hungary*, (2006) UN Doc. CEDAW/C/36/D/4/2004; *VC v Slovakia*, App. No. 18968/07 (ECtHR, Judgment of 8 November 2011).

105 C. Zampas and J.M. Gher, 'Abortion as a Human Right—International and Regional Standards' (2008) 8(2) *Human Rights Law Review* 249; C.G. Ngwena, 'Protocol to the African Charter on the Rights of Women: Implications for Access to Abortion at the Regional Level' (2010) 110 *International Journal of Gynecology and Obstetrics* 163. See also *A, B and C v Ireland*, App. No. 25579/05 (ECtHR, Judgment of 16 December 2010), para. 241.

106 See Inter-American Commission on Human Rights, 'Access to information on reproductive health from a human rights perspective', (2011) OEA Ser.L/V/II. Doc. 61.

107 *Tysiąc v Poland*, App. No. 5410/03 (ECtHR, Judgment of 20 March 2007); *A, B and C v Ireland* (n. 105) para. 267; HRC, *KL v Peru*, HRC (2005) UN Doc. CCPR/C/85/D/1153/2003; *LC v Peru* (n. 78).

108 See R.J. Cook and V. Undurraga, 'Article 12', in *CEDAW Commentary* (n. 53) 311 at 319–23.

109 *Open Door Counselling Ltd and Dublin Well Woman Centre v Ireland*, App. No. 14234/88; 14235/88 (ECtHR, Judgment of 29 October 1992).

110 See J. Connors, 'Article 28', in *CEDAW Commentary* (n. 53) 565.

Human rights bodies are certainly committed to a universalist ethic so far as women's fundamental human rights are concerned. The CEDAW Committee, for example, has firmly rejected any suggestion that appeals to culture, custom or customary law, tradition or religion justify a denial of women's equality in the context of the CEDAW.[111] Other human rights (treaty) bodies have taken similar positions, especially in relation to particular practices (such as FGM/FC,[112] son preference, early marriage and dowry, early pregnancy, nutritional taboos and practices related to child delivery).[113] While human rights bodies have recognised that the notion of 'the family' protected by human rights law is a flexible one,[114] they have also expressed the view that practices such as polygamy are inconsistent with women's equality.[115]

Some commentators have criticised human rights advocates and bodies for setting up an opposition between culture and women's human rights, portraying culture as static and inimical to the values represented by rights.[116] Yet human rights bodies (including those focused on women's human rights) have affirmed the importance of women's culture and religious beliefs to their sense of identity, recognised that cultures are dynamic, not frozen, and that progressive interpretations of cultures and religion are frequently available for those who wish to strive for human rights goals within particular cultural or religious contexts.[117] In the same way, the focus has been on *harmful* traditional practices[118] – those which palpably cause harm to women and girls and which reflect their relative disempowerment in their communities (even when some of those practices fall within the domain of and are carried out by other women). Frequently, the contention seems to arise not so much from disagreement over whether these practices are acceptable, but over questions of strategy and how to eliminate them most effectively within a given cultural context.

Such discussions give rise to challenges to traditional, often male-dominated interpreters and arbiters of the relevant traditions, customs and religions. Equally importantly, they raise complex issues of how one implements universal standards in local contexts, and also how one

---

111 See F. Raday, 'Culture, Religion and CEDAW's Article 5(a)', in H.B. Schöpp-Schilling and C. Flinterman (eds), *The Circle of Empowerment: Twenty-Five Years of the UN Committee on the Elimination of Discrimination against Women* (Feminist Press, 2007) at 68.

112 See 'Changing a Harmful Social Convention: Female Genital Mutilation/Cutting', *Innocenti Digest* 12 (2005).

113 See OHCHR, 'Fact Sheet No. 23, Harmful Traditional Practices Affecting the Health of Women and Children' (1995); B. Winter, D. Thompson and S. Jeffreys, 'The UN Approach to Harmful Traditional Practices' (2002) 4(1) *International Feminist Journal of Politics* 72; R.C. Carpenter, 'Some Other Conceptual Problems' (2004) 6(2) *International Feminist Journal of Politics* 308; B. Winter, D. Thompson and S. Jeffreys, 'Our Response to the "Reply" to our Article, "The UN Approach to Harmful Traditional Practices" ' (2004) 6(2) *International Feminist Journal of Politics* 314.

114 See, e.g., CEDAW, General Recommendation No. 21 (n. 72), para. 13.

115 Ibid. para. 14.

116 See, e.g., S. Engle Merry, 'Constructing a Global Law – Violence against Women and the Human Rights System' (2003) 28 *Law and Social Inquiry* 941, 946; S. Engle Merry, 'Human Rights Law and the Demonization of Culture (And Anthropology Along the Way)' (2003) 26(1) *PoLAR: Political and Legal Anthropology Review* 55.

117 See, e.g., M. Addo, 'Practice of United Nations Human Rights Treaty Bodies in the Reconciliation of Cultural Diversity with Universal Respect for Human Rights' (2010) 32 *Human Rights Quarterly* 601. Though it has justly been noted that culture tends to be identified as such predominantly when it is the non-Western other. See Holtmaat (n. 75) 150.

118 See Raday (n. 111).

balances competing rights, when in fact there is a conflict between two rights.[119] Human rights law provides only limited guidance for resolving direct conflicts between rights claims. The interaction between religious freedom and women's equality is frequently cited as a field where these issues arise acutely, though one should not overstate the inconsistencies or under-estimate the consistencies (in particular through internal interpretations that are consistent with women's equality). Nevertheless, there are circumstances in which claims based on religious beliefs come directly into conflict with claims based on equality. The answer as to which must bend may vary depending on how the question is asked. Human rights bodies have tended to come down in favour of women's rights to equality, especially where the right to participate in the political or public sphere is concerned,[120] or fundamental rights to bodily integrity are at issue.[121] The situation has been more complicated in relation to the wearing of religious garb (especially head or face coverings) by women who assert their right to do so as a matter of religious expression or personal choice. The meaning of such actions and their relationship to achieving the goal of equality may not be the same in every political and social context, and decisions which have upheld prohibitions on the wearing of such clothing in the pursuit of women's equality[122] have also been criticised for in some cases failing to understand the full complexity of a situation.[123]

6 Intersectionality

A major challenge for human rights law is the complex nature of discrimination, which is often the result of a number of factors, rather than a single individual or group characteristic. The complexity and variety of women's experiences has not only been reflected in discussions about intersectionality as a legal concept (sometimes also termed 'multiple discrimination'),[124] but also in the feminist and Third World critiques of some feminist analyses of women's oppression.[125] The anti-essentialist argument has been made that there is no unified category of 'women' that can be deployed in human rights discourse, but only many different groups of women whose experiences, needs and priorities vary significantly, so that discrimination on the basis of sex may not be the primary or even the most pressing concern for particular groups of women. Others have responded that, notwithstanding this, there is a universal dimension to discrimination based on sex (even if it takes different forms) and that as a

119 See in relation to the rights of the child and women's human rights: S. Goonesekere and R. de Silva-de Alwis, 'Women's and Children's Rights in a Human Rights Based Approach to Development', UNICEF Division of Policy and Planning Working Paper (2005) at ii; S. Goonesekere, 'Realizing Human Rights of Women and Children: Some Reflections on Law and Policy' (2001) 44(2) *Development* 15.

120 *Staatkundig Gereformeerde Partij v Netherlands*, App. No. 58369/10 (ECtHR, Judgment of 10 July 2012), paras 71 and 77.

121 See, e.g., *Pichon and Sajous v France*, App. No. 49853/99 (ECtHR, Judgment of 2 October 2001).

122 See, e.g., *Leyla Sahin v Turkey*, App. No. 44774/98 (ECtHR, Judgment of 29 June 2004).

123 See I. Radačić, 'Gender Equality Jurisprudence of the European Court of Human Rights' (2008) 19 *European Journal of International Law* 841 at 852–57; R. Rebouché, 'The Substance of Substantive Equality: Gender Equality and Turkey's Headscarf Debate' (2009) 24(5) *American University International Law Review* 711. See also M.D. Evans, *Manual on the Wearing of Religious Symbols in Public Areas* (Council of Europe, 2009) at 21.

124 J.E. Bond, 'International Intersectionality: A Theoretical and Pragmatic Exploration of Women's International Human Rights Violations', (2003) 52 *Emory Law Journal* 71.

125 See Otto, *Gender Issues and Human Rights* (n. 19) 13–15.

practical matter, use of the category of 'women' and sex discrimination analysis can be a useful response to practical needs.[126]

More conventionally, there has been increasing recognition of the variety of women's experiences and the need to reflect that discrimination is frequently against particular groups of women.[127] Some international human rights bodies have been slow to recognise this explicitly, sometimes finding discrimination on a single ground where it seems that a fuller account would have referred to other dimensions of the woman's life. However, by focusing on particular groups of women and the specific violations inflicted on them, many human rights bodies have long applied an intersectional approach implicitly. Nevertheless, the recognition of the intersection of different grounds of discrimination has been more frequently acknowledged explicitly in the last decade or so[128] and is likely to be an area in which more nuanced analysis develops.

7 Heteronormativity and the persistence of a binary approach to 'sex'

Discrimination on the basis of one's sexuality and gender identity is also fundamentally a gender issue. Assumptions about the appropriate forms of conduct and acceptable relationships between persons of the same or opposite biological sex underpin attitudes to and the treatment of persons who do not conform to the heterosexual norm. In relation to women in particular this may take various sex-specific forms of violations, ranging from 'corrective rape' to forced marriages, as well as failure to recognise personal relationships with members of the same sex.

Denials of rights based on sexual orientation and gender identity have been dealt with by the international human rights system for many years,[129] but have gained a more prominent place on the political agenda in recent years.[130] However, full equality in the enjoyment of rights without regard to sexual orientation or gender identity has not yet been attained.[131] The issues of sexual orientation and gender identity are distinct, though related, and also overlap with the categories of sexual rights and reproductive rights.

---

126 Charlesworth and Chinkin (n. 20) 52–56; B.E. Hernandez-Truyol, 'Unsex CEDAW? No! Super-Sex It!' (2011) 20 *Columbia Journal of Gender and Law* 195.

127 In relation to CEDAW, see Byrnes (n. 53) 68–70.

128 See UN Committee on the Elimination of Racial Discrimination, General Recommendation No. 25, 'Gender related dimensions of racial discrimination' (56th session) (2000).

129 See E. Heinze, *Sexual Orientation: A Human Right* (Martinus Nijhoff, 1995); P. Johnson, *Homosexuality and the European Court of Human Rights* (Routledge, 2012).

130 See generally 'Discriminatory laws and practices and acts of violence against individuals based on their sexual orientation and gender identity, Report of the United Nations High Commissioner for Human Rights', (2011) UN Doc. A/HRC/19/41. See also Council of Europe, *Discrimination on Grounds of Sexual Orientation and Gender Identity in Europe*, 2nd edn (Council of Europe, 2011); European Court of Human Rights Press Unit, 'Factsheet – Sexual Orientation Issues' (2012).

131 See, in particular, The Yogyakarta Principles – Principles on the application of international human rights law in relation to sexual orientation and gender identity (2007), available at: http://www.yogyakartaprinciples.org/principles_en.pdf, accessed on 18 February 2013. See also M. O'Flaherty and J. Fisher, 'Sexual Orientation, Gender Identity and International Human Rights Law: Contextualising the Yogyakarta Principles' (2008) 8 *Human Rights Law Review* 207 and 'Jurisprudential Annotations to the Yogyakarta Principles' (November 2007), available at: www.yogyakartaprinciples.org/yogyakarta-principles-jurisprudential-annotations.pdf, accessed on 18 February 2013.

The criminalisation of sexual conduct between consenting adults of the same sex (but not between couples of the opposite sex) has long been held to violate the right to respect for private life and/or the obligation not to discriminate.[132] Sexual orientation has been held to fall within guarantees against discrimination based on 'other status'[133] or 'sex'.[134] Human rights bodies have held that denying to same-sex partners a survivor's pension and other partner benefits that heterosexual de facto couples enjoy is discriminatory.[135] However, they have not been prepared to insist that same-sex couples be treated on a par with *de jure* married couples, if the state draws a distinction between the rights of *de jure* and de facto heterosexual couples.[136] The enjoyment of the right to family life without discrimination has also been guaranteed in cases in which persons have been discriminated against in the enjoyment of their parental rights because of their sexual orientation, in particular in cases where one parent subsequently lives in a same-sex relationship. However, cases where one or both members of a same-sex couple seek to adopt children but have been denied the right on the grounds of their sexuality, and have challenged the denial, have had mixed success.[137]

Despite the progress, there is still no full recognition of same-sex relationships on the same basis as heterosexual relationships. International bodies have been prepared to accept that such relationships form part of private and family life,[138] and that there should be no discrimination in relation to the enjoyment of certain rights. However, international human rights law has not yet affirmed the right of same-sex couples to marry. Marriage is still largely seen in human rights law as being based fundamentally on a heterosexual binary: while convergence in substance with the rights of de facto married couples has been required, there continues to be resistance to accepting that this extends to the right to formally marry. The guarantee of the right to marry contained in international instruments has been interpreted as extending only to heterosexual partners, and thus far attempts to invoke other equality guarantees in the treaties to ground a right to marry have been unsuccessful.[139]

The tenacity of the underlying binary assumption can be seen in cases involving the rights of transgender persons (transsexuals) and their partners in the context of marriage.[140] Strasbourg jurisprudence has held that states must recognise sex changes in certain circumstances as part of a person's right to respect for private life, so that identification documents

---

132 See, e.g., *Dudgeon v United Kingdom*, App. No. 7525/76 (ECtHR, Judgment of 22 October 1981) and HRC, *Toonen v Australia* (1994) UN Doc. CCPR/C/50/D/488/1992; European Court of Human Rights Press Unit, 'Factsheet – Homosexuality (criminal aspects) (2012). The Strasbourg Court has also found violations in the maintenance of different ages of consent for homosexual as opposed to heterosexual sexual relations.

133 See the review of the international and regional jurisprudence in *Atala v Chile*, IACtHR, Report No. 139/09, (2012), paras 83–93.

134 *Toonen v Australia* (n. 132).

135 See, eg, HRC, *Young v Australia*, 2003) UN Doc. CCPR/C/78/D/941/2000; HRC, *X v Colombia* (2007) UN Doc. CCPR/C/89/D/1361/2005. However, see *Serife Yiğit v Turkey*, App. No. 3976/05 (ECtHR, Judgment of 2 November 2010); *Korosidou v Greece*, App. No. 9957/08 (ECtHR, Judgment of 10 February 2011).

136 See, e.g. *Schalk and Kopf v Austria*, App. No. 30141/04 (ECtHR, Judgment of 24 June 2010), para. 108.

137 Compare *Atala v Chile* (n. 133) with the cases referred to in 'Factsheet – Sexual Orientation Issues' (n. 130).

138 See, e.g. *Schalk and Kopf v Austria* (n. 136).

139 HRC, *Joslin v New Zealand*, (2002), UN Doc. CCPR/C/75/D/902/1999. See Australian Human Rights Commission, *Position Paper on Marriage Equality* (2012).

140 See European Court of Human Rights Press Unit, 'Factsheet – Gender Identity Issues' (2012).

must reflect a person's change of sex.[141] A consequence has been the recognition of the right of a transgender person who has undergone a sex change process to marry a person of the opposite sex to the person's new sex. This acceptance still reinforces the male–female binary of the right to marry (although it subverts it from one perspective in so far as it challenges assumptions about the stability of biological sex categories), in that the right still operates on the notion of two different biological sexes as the critical element.[142]

This is made clear by cases in which one member of a male–female married couple undergoes a sex-change process. In such a case the Court has held that it is not a violation of the Convention to require that the couple divorce if the person who has undergone a sex change wishes his or her new sex to be recognised under law.[143] Once again, the heterosexual basis of the right to marry and a binary understanding of sex and gender identity is reinforced – and it is far from clear what place there is for an intersex person in this framework.

8 And yet despite all this . . .

Notwithstanding all the normative and institutional advances, the denial of women's human rights around the world continues to be widespread[144] – violence against women is ubiquitous and systematic, women are particularly exposed to poverty (as are many men), women are still underrepresented in political and public life in most countries, women's access to economic resources is still generally less than that of men, women tend to be concentrated in sex-segregated and vulnerable sectors of the economy, women continue to die as a result of childbirth in shocking and unconscionable numbers, the impact of economic crises has been particularly burdensome for women in many cases, transnational businesses have a very mixed track record in many industries (sometimes with the active encouragement of governments), and in some regions new or resurgent fundamentalisms challenge what gains have been made. The dominant international (economic) discourse – of economic rationalism and free trade – has presented challenges for women in economies around the world. Yet human rights seem to be largely excluded from that dominant discourse,[145] notwithstanding the acceptance of many of the same substantive goals – this is reflected in the relatively small impact that international human rights law has made on the world of international economic law and international trade law.

These represent not just technical challenges of exegesis and implementation, but of broader political and social struggles in which the values of human rights are pitted against other claims or justificatory frameworks, some of which perpetuate the power and influence of those who resist the claims of rights, others which reflect the belief that they provide the way to realise in substance the goals of human rights (even if the language and methodology

---

141 *Goodwin v the United Kingdom*, App. No. 28957/95 (ECtHR, Judgment of 11 July 2002).

142 See *Schalk and Kopf v Austria* (n. 136), concurring opinion of Judge Malinverni (joined by Judge Kovler), para. 2.

143 *Parry v United Kingdom*, App. No. 42971/05 (ECtHR, Judgment of 28 November 2006) and *R and F v United Kingdom*, App. No. 35748/05 (ECtHR, Judgment of 28 November 2006).

144 See, e.g. World Bank, 'Gender Equality and Development, World Development Report 2012' (2012) at 13–22.

145 See F. Beveridge, 'Feminist Perspectives in International Economic Law', in Buss and Manji (n. 17) at 173; G. Moon, 'Fair in Form, But Discriminatory in Operation—WTO Law's Discriminatory Effects on Human Rights in Developing Countries' (2011) 14(3) *Journal of International Economic Law* 553.

of human rights is not the best way to achieve them). Human rights is an important framework for defining goals and measuring progress, but a deeper commitment to justice and action is required to bring these rights to life for millions of women around the world. As Mahmoud Fathalla, a past president of the International Federation of Obstetricians and Gynecologists, put it in relation to the scandalous levels of maternal mortality around the world, 'Women are not dying of diseases we can't treat . . . They are dying because societies have yet to make the decision that their lives are worth saving.'[146] Persuading societies to make that decision and similar decisions in relation to other violations is a pressing task, and human rights are but one of the tools in that struggle.

Select bibliography

K.D. Askin, and D.M. Koenig (eds), *Women and International Human Rights Law*, 3 vols (Transnational Publishers, 1999).

F. Banda, *Women, Law and Human Rights: An African Perspective* (Hart, 2005).

R.J. Cook (ed.), *International Human Rights Law and Women's Human Rights* (University of Pennsylvania Press, 1994).

R. Emerton, et al., *International Women's Rights Cases* (Cavendish, 2005).

M. Freeman, C. Chinkin and B. Rudolf (eds), *The UN Convention on the Elimination of All Forms of Discrimination against Women: A Commentary* (OUP, 2012).

D. Otto, 'Feminist Approaches', in T. Carty (ed.), *Oxford Bibliographies Online: International Law* (OUP, 2012).

D. Otto, (ed.), *Gender Issues and Human Rights*, 3 vols (Edward Elgar Publishing, 2012).

146 Quoted in Amnesty International USA, 'Maternal Health is a Human Right', available at: www. amnestyusa.org/our-work/campaigns/demand-dignity/maternal-health-is-a-human-right, accessed on 18 February 2013.

35

The extraterritorial application of international human rights law on civil and political rights*

Ralph Wilde

1 Introduction

The policy and practice of any given state has an impact on the enjoyment of human rights not only on the part of people within that state's sovereign territory. Also, often there is a significant extraterritorial impact on people in the rest of the world. In the case of civil and political rights, relevant extraterritorial activity includes the conduct of warfare, occupation, other military action, anti-migration and anti-piracy initiatives at sea, sanctions regimes, extraordinary rendition, strikes by so-called 'drones' and the operation of extraterritorial detention and interrogation sites housing combatants and migrants, including refugees.

Domestic and international public policy concerned with the obligations of states towards the enjoyment of human rights by people outside their territories potentially has a legal dimension in international human rights treaty law.[1] However, in the field of civil and political rights, a frequent question is raised as to whether certain activities relevant here, notably those associated with the US eras of George W. Bush's 'War on Terror' and President Barack

* The work on this piece was funded by the Leverhulme Trust and the European Research Council.

1 For academic commentary on this topic, see, e.g. the sources listed at the end of this chapter, and Ralph Wilde, 'Legal "Black Hole"?: Extraterritorial State Action and International Treaty Law on Civil and Political Rights', (2005) 26 *MJIL* 739 (Wilde 2005); Ralph Wilde, 'Case Note, *R (Al-Skeini) v Secretary of State for Defence (The Redress Trust intervening)'*, (2008) 102(3) *AJIL* 628 (Wilde 2008); Ralph Wilde, 'From Trusteeship to Self-Determination and Back Again: the Role of the Hague Regulations in the Evolution of International Trusteeship, and the Framework of Rights and Duties of Occupying Powers', (2009) 31 *Loyola of Los Angeles International and Comparative Law Review* 75–132; Ralph Wilde, 'Compliance with Human Rights Norms Extraterritorially: "Human Rights Imperialism"?', in Laurence Boisson de Chazournes and Marcelo Kohen (eds), *International Law and the Quest for its Implementation* (Brill/Martinus Nijhoff, 2010); various authors, *Maastricht Principles on Extraterritorial Obligations of States in the area of Economic, Social and Cultural Rights*, adopted 28 September 2011 (Maastricht Principles); Fons Coomans and Rolf Künnemann, *Cases and Concepts on Extraterritorial Obligations in the Area of Economic, Social and Cultural Rights* (Intersentia, 2012) (Coomans and Künnemann); Malcolm Langford, Wouter Vandenhole, Martin Scheinin and Willem van Genugten (eds), *Global Justice, State Duties: The Extraterritorial Scope of Economic, Social and Cultural Rights in International Law* (CUP, 2013) (Langford, Vanderhole, Scheinin and van Genugten).

Obama's policy of a similar nature (e.g. 'drone' strikes, rendition and extraterritorial detention and interrogation), take place in a 'legal black hole', usually taken to denote the absence not necessarily of all law, but of those areas of law that would provide checks and balances to guard against human rights abuses.[2] Whether and to what extent international human rights law concerned with civil and political rights (which, it is claimed, provides such checks and balances) applies extraterritorially is indeed contested and uncertain. The case law and commentary is sparse and often highly situation-specific, and states take varying and mutually inconsistent positions on it, from the rejection of extraterritorial application per se by certain states (e.g. the USA), to the willingness of certain states (e.g. in Europe) to accept the constraints of human rights law abroad in particular circumstances.[3]

In this context, the present chapter addresses two fundamental interrelated questions. In the first place, does international human rights law on civil and political rights apply extraterritorially and, if so, on what basis and in which circumstances? In the second place, what is the significance of some of the underlying political ideas at stake – for example, the claim that a 'legal black hole' is problematic, and needs to be remedied – for the meaning and scope of the law on applicability?

The focus is on civil and political rights only, not also on economic, social and cultural rights.[4] The latter set of rights also raise important issues in the extraterritorial context, and states are bound by international legal rules covering both sets of rights.[5] However, the law on the extraterritorial application of civil and political rights has important differences in terms of treaty provisions,[6] enjoys a significant body of specific case law and other authoritative commentary,[7] and implicates special policy questions worthy of discrete evaluation, notably as concerns the relationship between the individual and the state[8] and the notion of a 'legal black hole'.[9]

The foregoing analysis evaluates relevant treaty provisions and how they have been interpreted by judicial and international expert-body decisions.[10] In particular, decisions (in their various forms) from the following bodies are reviewed: the International Court of Justice;[11]

---

2 See the discussion and sources cited in Wilde 2005 (n. 1). This issue is discussed further below, in section 35.5.

3 See Wilde 2005 (n. 1).

4 Due to space limitations, this chapter does not cover the extraterritorial application of non-refoulement obligations in refugee law and human rights law, or the obligations of international organisations.

5 On the extraterritorial application of economic, social and cultural rights, see e.g. Maastricht Principles; Coomans and Künnemann; Langford, Vanderhole, Scheinin and van Genugten, and sources cited therein (n. 1).

6 In particular, the use of the term 'jurisdiction' as the trigger for applicability; see below, section 35.2.1.

7 Notably the jurisprudence relating to the European Convention on Human Rights. See below, section 35.2.

8 See below section 35.5.2.

9 See below section 35.5.3.

10 For the treaty provisions, see the sources cited in nn. 17–20, 22–26, 31 below.

11 *Legal Consequences of the Construction of a Wall in the Occupied Palestinian Territories, Advisory Opinion,* 2004 ICJ 163 (9 July) (*Wall* Advisory Opinion); *Case Concerning Armed Activities on the Territory of the Congo (DRC v Uganda),* 2005 ICJ 116 (19 December), at paras 216–17 (*DRC v Uganda*); *Application of the International Convention on the Elimination of All Forms of Racial Discrimination (Georgia v Russian Federation)* Order Indicating Provisional Measures (*Georgia v Russia* Provisional Measures), 15 October 2008, available at: http://www.icj-cij.org/docket/files/140/14801.pdf, paras 109, 149.

the United Nations Human Rights Committee;[12] the European Commission and Court of Human Rights;[13] the Inter-American Commission on Human Rights;[14] the United Nations Committee Against Torture;[15] and the courts of England and Wales.[16]

2 Applicability provisions in human rights treaties

2.1 'Jurisdiction'

Some of the main international human rights treaties addressing civil and political rights, the International Covenant on Civil and Political Rights (ICCPR), the American Convention on Human Rights (ACHR) and the European Convention on Human Rights (ECHR) and their Protocols, the Convention against Torture (CAT), as well as the Convention on the Rights of the Child (CRC) (which also covers economic, social and cultural rights) do not conceive obligations simply in terms of the acts of states parties. Instead, responsibility is conceived in a particular context: the state's 'jurisdiction'. Under the ECHR and some of its

---

12 General Comment No. 31, UN Doc. CCPR/C/21/Rev.1/Add. 13 (26 May 2004) (HRC General Comment No. 31) para. 10; *Lilian Celiberti de Casariego v Uruguay*, Comm. No. 56/1979, UN Doc. CCPR/C/13/D/56/1979 (29 July 1981) *(Celiberti de Casariego)*, para. 10.3, *Lopez Burgos v Uruguay*, Communication No. R.12/52, Supp. No. 40, at 176, UN Doc. A/36/40 (1981) *(Lopez Burgos)*, para. 12.3; *Mabel Perreira Montero v Uruguay (Montero)*, Comm. No. 106/1981, UN Doc. CCPR/C/OP/2 at 136 (1990) (31 March 1983), para. 5.

13 *Gillow v United Kingdom*, App. No. 13/1984/85/132 (ECtHR, Judgment of 23 October 1986), *(Gillow)*, para. 62; *Bui Van Thanh v United Kingdom*, App. No. 16137/90 (ECtHR, Eur. Comm'n H.R., 12 March 1990) *(Bui Van Thanh)*; *WM. v Denmark*, App. No. 17392/90, 73 Eur. Comm'n H.R. Dec. & Rep. 193 (1992), 196 *(WM)*; *Loizidou v Turkey*, 310 ECtHR (ser. A) (1995) (Preliminary Objections) *(Loizidou* (Preliminary Objections)), para. 62; *Loizidou v Turkey*, 1996-VI, ECtHR, (ser. A) 2216, (GC) (Merits), *(Loizidou (Merits))*, paras 52–56; *Yonghong v Portugal*, App. No. 50887/99 (ECtHR, Judgment of 25 November 1999) *(Yonghong)*; *Öcalan v Turkey*, App. No. 46221/99 (ECtHR, Admissibility Decision, 14 December 2000) *(Öcalan* Admissibility Decision) and 2005-IV ECtHR (GC) *(Öcalan* GC); *Cyprus v Turkey*, 2001-IV ECtHR, 1 (GC), at para. 77 *(Cyprus v Turkey)*; *Issa and Others v Turkey*, ECtHR, Admissibility Decision of 30 May 2000 *(Issa* (Admissibility)) and 41 ECtHR 27 (2004) (Merits) *(Issa* (Merits)), para. 71; *Banković v Belgium*, 2001–XII ECtHR, 333 (GC), at para. 70–71 *(Banković)*; *Ilascu and Others v Moldova and Russia*, ECtHR, App. No. 48787/99 (Grand Chamber), Reports 2004-VII (8 July 2004) *(Ilascu)*; *Solomou v Turkey*, ECtHR, App. No. 36832/97, 24 June 2008, *(Solomou)*, Paras. 43–52; *Isaak v Turkey*, ECtHR, App. No. 44587/98, 28 Sept 2006, Admissibility, page 21 *(Isaak)*; *Andreou v Turkey*, ECtHR, App. No. 45653/99, Admissibility decision, 3 June 2008 *(Andreou* (Admissibility)), p. 11, and Merits, 27 October 2009, *(Andreou* (Merits)) para. 25; *Al-Saadoon and Mufdhi v United Kingdom*, App. No. 61498/08 (ECtHR, Chamber decision, 2 March 2010) *(Al-Saadoon)*; *Al-Skeini v United Kingdom*, App. No. 55721/07 (ECtHR, Judgment of 7 July 2011) *(Al-Skeini* (ECtHR)).

14 *Coard v US*, Case 10.951, Report No.109/99, OEA/Ser.L./V/II.85, doc. 9 rev. (1999), *(Coard)*, paras 37, 39, 41.

15 *Consideration of Reports Submitted by States Parties under Article 19 of the Convention, Conclusions and Recommendations: United States of America*, UN Doc. CAT/C/USA/CO/2 (25 July 2006), para. 15; General Comment No. 2: *Implementation of Article 2 by States Parties*, 23 November 2007, UN doc. CAT/C/GC/2 (24 January 2008), para. 16.

16 *R. v Immigration Officer at Prague Airport and another (Respondents) ex parte European Roma Rights Centre and others (Appellants)* [2004] UKHL 55, 9 December 2004 *(Roma Rights)*; *R. (on the application of Al-Skeini and others) v Secretary of state for Defence (The Redress Trust intervening)* [2007] UKHL 26; [2007] 3 WLR 33 *(Al-Skeini* (HL)); [2005] EWCA (Civ) 1609 (21 December 2005) *(Al-Skeini* (CA)); [2004] EWHC 2911 (Admin), 14 December 2004, *(Al-Skeini* (DC)).

Protocols and the ACHR, the state is obliged to 'secure' the rights contained in the treaty within its 'jurisdiction'.[17] Under the CAT, the state is obliged to take measures to prevent acts of torture 'in any territory under its jurisdiction'.[18] Under the CRC, states parties are obliged to 'respect and ensure' the rights in the treaty to 'each child within their jurisdiction'.[19] The ICCPR formulation is slightly different from the others in that applicability operates in relation to those 'within [the state's] territory and subject to its jurisdiction'.[20]

Thus a nexus to the state – termed 'jurisdiction' – has to be established before its obligations are in play (the significance of the separate reference to 'territory' in the ICCPR will be considered below[21]).

2.2 Colonial extension clauses

Several early human rights treaties, for example the ECHR (and some of its subsequent Protocols) and the 1948 Genocide Convention contain a 'colonial clause' allowing the states parties to make a declaration that the rights contained in the treaty will apply in 'territories for whose international relations it is responsible', a term referring to colonial and (UN) Trusteeship territories, now in the case of the former (there are no more Trusteeship territories) sometimes referred to using alternative euphemistic terminology such as 'dependencies' or 'overseas territories'.[22] Similarly, the 1926 Slavery Convention contains an 'opt–out' clause which allows states parties to declare that their acceptance of the Convention does not bind some of the territories placed under their jurisdiction,[23] whilst the 1956 Supplementary Slavery Convention, although providing that '[t]his Convention shall apply to all non self-governing, trust, colonial and other non-metropolitan territories for the international relations of which any State Party is responsible', requires states parties to specify to which territories the Convention applies.[24]

---

17 European Convention for the Protection of Human Rights and Fundamental Freedoms, 4 Nov., 1950, 213 UNTS 221 (ECHR), Art. 1; ECHR Protocol No. 1 (ECHR Protocol 1), Art. 4; ECHR Protocol No. 6 (ECHR Protocol 6), Art. 5; ECHR Protocol No. 13 (ECHR Protocol 13), Art. 4. American Convention on Human Rights, 22 November 1969, OAS Treaty Series No. 36, 1144 UNTS 123, O.A.S. Off. Rec. OEA/Ser. L/V/II.23, Doc. 21, Rev. 6 (22 November 1969) (ACHR), Art. 1.

18 Convention against Torture and Other Cruel, Inhuman or Degrading Treatment or Punishment, GA Res. 46, UN GAOR, 39th Sess., Supp. No. 51, UN Doc. A/39/51, 10 December 1984, 1465 UNTS 85 (CAT), Art. 2.

19 Convention on the Rights of the Child, GA Res. 44/25, Annex, 44 UN GAOR Supp. No. 49, UN Doc. A/44/49 (20 November 1989), 1577 UNTS 3 (CRC), Art. 2.1.

20 International Covenant on Civil and Political Rights, GA Res. 2200A/XXI, 16 December 1966, UN Doc. A/6316 (19 December 1966), 999 UNTS 171 (ICCPR), Art. 2.

21 See section 35.2.2.

22 ECHR, Art. 56 (formerly 63) (n. 17); ECHR Protocol No. 1, Art. 4 (n. 17); ECHR Protocol No. 6 (n. 17), Art. 5; ECHR Protocol No. 13 (n. 17), Art. 4; Convention on the Prevention and Punishment of the Crime of Genocide, New York, 9 December 1948, UNTS, vol. 78, p. 277 (Genocide Convention) Art. 25.

23 International Convention with the Object of Securing the Abolition of Slavery and the Slave Trade, Geneva, 25 September 1926, LNTS, vol. 60, p. 253, as amended by the Protocol Amending the Slavery Convention, approved by GA Res. 794 (VIII) of 23 October 1953, entered into force on 7 December 1953 (1926 Slavery Convention) Art. 9.

24 Convention on the Abolition of Slavery, the Slave Trade, and Institutions and Practices Similar to Slavery, Supplementary to the International Convention signed at Geneva on 25 September 1926, Geneva, 7 September 1956 (1956 Supplemental Slavery Convention), Art. 12(1).

The question of whether, in each case, a territorial unit covered by such clauses falls within, or outside, the sovereign territory of the states party to human rights treaties is beyond the scope of this chapter. In the case of territories in the former category, the clauses are concerned with the scope of application within a state's territory; in the case of territories in the latter category, they determine extraterritorial applicability. Similar colonial extension clauses were not included in later human rights treaties, including the ICCPR, the CRC and the CAT. Whether, for those other treaties that do have a colonial extension clause, the 'jurisdiction' test can trigger applicability in overseas territories as an alternative to the operation of the extension clause is addressed below.

2.3 No general applicability provision: American Declaration, African Charter, CEDAW and CERD

Certain other international human rights instruments do not contain a general provision, whether using the term 'jurisdiction' or something else equivalent, stipulating the scope of applicability of the obligations they contain: the 1948 (Inter-) American Declaration of the Rights and Duties of Man (not a treaty), the 1981 African Charter on Human and Peoples' Rights, the International Convention on the Elimination of All Forms of Racial Discrimination (ICERD or CERD), the International Convention on the Elimination of All Forms of Discrimination Against Women (CEDAW) and the Optional Protocol to the Convention on the Rights of the Child on the Involvement of Children in Armed Conflict of 2000.[25]

In the case of the CERD, a sub-set of obligations are conceived in the context of the state's 'jurisdiction'. The obligation concerning racial segregation and apartheid applies to parties with respect to 'territories under their jurisdiction'.[26] Similarly, the provision of remedies operates with respect to people in the state's 'jurisdiction', in terms of both the obligation borne by the state to provide such remedies itself, and the jurisdiction of the international Committee on the Elimination of Racial Discrimination, if it has been accepted, to hear complaints against parties.[27]

The Inter-American Commission on Human Rights has treated the American Declaration as if it does contain the 'jurisdiction' trigger, without an explanation for this assumption.[28] Similarly, the International Court of Justice appeared to treat the African Charter and the Optional Protocol to the Convention on the Rights of the Child on the Involvement of Children in Armed Conflict of 2000 as if they contained the 'jurisdiction' trigger, again without any explanation.[29]

---

25 American Declaration of the Rights and Duties of Man, adopted by the Ninth International Conference of American States, Bogotá, Colombia, 1948, OAS Res. XXX (1948) (American Declaration); African Charter on Human and Peoples' Rights (OAU Doc. CAB/LEG/67/3 rev. 5, 27 June 1981) (ACHPR); International Convention on the Elimination of All Forms of Discrimination Against Women, New York, 18 December 1979, UNTS, vol. 1249, p. 13 (CEDAW); International Convention on the Elimination of All Forms of Racial Discrimination (ICERD or CERD) Adopted by General Assembly Resolution 2106 (XX), 21 December 1965; Optional Protocol to the Convention on the Rights of the Child on the Involvement of Children in Armed Conflict of 2000 (CRC Optional Protocol).
26 CERD Art. 3 (n. 25).
27 CERD Arts 6 (domestic remedies), 14.1 (jurisdiction of the Committee) (n. 25).
28 *Coard*, para. 37 (n. 14).
29 *DRC v Uganda*, paras 216–17 (n. 11).

3 Extraterritorial meaning of the term 'jurisdiction' in human rights treaties

3.1 Relevance of the international law meaning of 'jurisdiction'

An area of international law also named 'jurisdiction' exists separately from international human rights law.[30] The international law concept of 'jurisdiction' is concerned with rules prescribing the particular circumstances where a state is legally permitted to exercise its legal authority – for example prescriptive, enforcement or adjudicative – over a particular situation, such as prosecuting its own nationals for crimes committed abroad.

In the *Banković* decision concerning the NATO bombing of Belgrade in 1999, the Grand Chamber of the European Court of Human Rights seemed to suggest that the meaning of 'jurisdiction' in the ECHR should somehow reflect the meaning of that term in public international law generally.[31] However, insofar as the Court intended make such a suggestion, it does not fit with how the Court and other authoritative bodies have approached the issue in other decisions, where extraterritorial jurisdiction has been defined as simply a factual test, without the additional normative consideration of whether or not the activity under consideration constitutes a lawful exercise of jurisdiction as a matter of general international law. For example, the Court held that Turkey's presence in Northern Cyprus constituted the exercise of jurisdiction for ECHR purposes because of the nature of control exercised, stressing that such jurisdiction could subsist on this basis regardless of the legality of the exercise of control.[32]

As for the ICCPR, the UN Human Rights Committee, in a passage that can be interpreted as alluding to the relevance of the legality of extraterritorial action to the question of whether such action is regulated by the Covenant, stated in General Comment No. 31 that the principle of making available the enjoyment of Covenant rights to all individuals regardless of nationality, 'applies to those within the power or effective control of the forces of a State Party acting outside its territory, regardless of the circumstances in which such power or effective control was obtained'.[33]

3.2 Whether or not 'jurisdiction' can have an extraterritorial meaning at all

The consistent jurisprudence and authoritative statements of the relevant international human rights review bodies and the International Court of Justice regarding the ECHR, the ACHR and the CAT has been to interpret the term 'jurisdiction' in these treaties as operating extraterritorially in certain circumstances.[34]

Although there is less authoritative commentary on the extraterritorial applicability of the CRC, the meaning of 'jurisdiction' in this treaty is arguably similar. The International Court of Justice appeared to assume so in affirming the applicability of this treaty to Israel's presence in the Palestinian territories in the *Wall* Advisory Opinion, and to Uganda in the Democratic Republic of the Congo (DRC) in the *DRC v Uganda* judgment.[35]

---

30 See, e.g., James Crawford, *Brownlie's Principles of Public International Law* (2012), ch. 21, and sources cited therein.
31 *Banković*, paras 59–61 (n. 13).
32 *Loizidou* (Preliminary Objections), para. 62; *Loizidou* (Merits), paras 52–56 (n. 13), See also *Cyprus v Turkey*, para. 77 (n. 13).
33 HRC General Comment No. 31, para. 10 (n. 12).
34 See the sources cited in nn. 10, 13–15 above.
35 *Wall* Advisory Opinion, para. 113 (n. 11); *DRC v Uganda*, paras 216–17 (n. 11).

The aforementioned treatment by the International Court of Justice of the applicability of the ACHPR and the Optional Protocol to the CRC, in terms of whether situations at issue constituted the exercise of 'jurisdiction' (despite that term not being used in these instruments), was a part of the Court's affirmation that these instruments were capable of extraterritorial application on this basis.[36] Similarly, the aforementioned treatment of the applicability of the (Inter-) American Declaration by the Inter-American Commission on Human Rights in terms of the exercise of 'jurisdiction' was in the context of extraterritorial activity, which it regarded as capable of constituting the exercise of jurisdiction and thereby falling under the scope of the obligations in the Declaration.[37]

As mentioned earlier, the ICCPR provision on scope of application addresses those 'within [the state's] territory and subject to its jurisdiction'.[38] By including the word 'territory' in addition to 'jurisdiction', it might be read to suggest that jurisdiction is limited to territory, thereby ruling out extraterritorial applicability. However, this position is difficult to sustain given the affirmation of extraterritorial applicability by the International Court of Justice and the UN Human Rights Committee.[39] An absolutist denial of extraterritorial applicability not only lacks support in, but also is rejected by, the jurisprudence and other authoritative interpretations on this issue. The key question has not been whether human rights law treaty obligations apply extraterritorially, but, rather, in what circumstances this occurs.

As will be explained, the term has been understood in the extraterritorial context as a connection between the state, on the one hand, and either the territory in which the relevant acts took place – referred to herein as a *spatial* or *territorial* connection – or the individual affected by them – referred to herein as a *personal, individual* or, because of the type of state action involved, *state-agent-authority* connection. Within these two categories, there is considerable uncertainty due to the sparse nature of case law and a variety of views taken by states, interpretative/enforcement bodies such as courts, and expert commentators.

3.3 Jurisdiction trigger (1): territorial control

3.3.1 General concept

Extraterritorial jurisdiction understood spatially conceives obligations as flowing from the fact of effective control over territory. This approach was articulated in decisions relating to the aforementioned *Cyprus v Turkey* case, the *Loizidou* case regarding the same situation, the aformentioned *Banković* and *Al-Skeini* cases, and the *Issa* case concerning Turkey in Iraq, all before the European Court of Human Rights (and also the courts of England and Wales as far as *Al-Skeini* is concerned). It is also adopted, to a certain extent, in the *Wall* Advisory Opinion and the *DRC v Uganda* judgment of the International Court of Justice.[40]

---

36 On the ACHPR and the CRC Optional Protocol (n. 25), see *DRC v Uganda*, paras 216–17 (n. 11).
37 *Coard*, para. 37 (n. 14).
38 ICCPR, Art. 2 (n. 20).
39 In the *Wall* Advisory Opinion (n. 11); and HRC General Comment No. 31 (n. 12).
40 *Cyprus v Turkey* (n. 13); *Loizidou* (Preliminary Objections) (Merits) (n. 13); *Banković* (n. 13); *Al-Skeini* (DC), (CA), (HL), (ECtHR) (nn. 13, 16); *Issa* (n. 13); *Wall* Advisory Opinion (n. 11); *DRC v Uganda* (n. 11).

3.3.2 Effective 'overall' control of a distinct entity/regime

In one of its judgments in the *Loizidou* case, the European Court of Human Rights empha-sised that Turkey exercised effective control operating 'overall'; in such circumstances, it was unnecessary to identify whether the exercise of control was detailed.[41] So if the state is in effective overall control of a territorial unit, everything within that unit falls within its 'juris-diction', even if at lesser levels powers are exercised by other actors (e.g. if particular activities are devolved to other states or local actors).[42] The exercise of this type of control also leads to a generalised obligation to secure the 'entire range of substantive rights' in the area in question.[43]

3.3.3 Can it be a sliding scale depending on the level of control?

In the *Banković* case, the applicants claimed that 'jurisdiction' under Article 1 of the ECHR could be said to exist on the basis of effective territorial control to the extent that such control was in fact exercised, and that, accordingly, in the words of the European Court of Human Rights, 'the extent of the positive obligation under Article 1 of the Convention to secure Convention rights would be proportionate to the level of control in fact exercised'.[44] This might be understood to suggest a 'sliding scale' or 'cause and effect' concept of jurisdiction based on territorial control: obligations apply insofar as control is exercised; their nature and scope is set in proportional relation to the level of control.[45]

The European Court of Human Rights rejected this argument; it held that the concept of jurisdiction could not be 'divided and tailored in accordance with the particular circum-stances of the extra-territorial act in question'.[46] However, in the later *Issa* decision of 2004, the Court, having concluded that Turkey did not exercise 'overall control' in the area of Northern Iraq in question, did not end its consideration of whether the Turkish presence constituted the exercise of 'jurisdiction'. Rather, it went on to consider 'whether at the rele-vant time Turkish troops conducted operations in the area where the killings took place'.[47] The assumption was that if the troops had been doing this, which the Court found on the facts they had not, jurisdiction would have subsisted. Unfortunately, the Court failed to indi-cate whether at this stage it was considering extraterritorial jurisdiction defined as territorial control (as opposed to the alternative definition based on control over individuals), but if it was, one might discern a more receptive attitude towards the broader cause-and-effect concept than in the earlier dictum in *Banković*.

This concept was picked up in the English Court of Appeal stage of the *Al-Skeini* case by Lord Justice Sedley, who considered the idea that applicability might depend not on 'enforce-ability as a whole' but 'whether it lay within the power of the occupying force to avoid or remedy the particular breach in issue'.[48] Although he acknowledged that this was blocked by

41 *Loizidou (Merits)*, para. 56 (n. 13).
42 See also *Cyprus v Turkey*, para. 77 (n. 13).
43 See also *Cyprus v Turkey*, para. 77, (n. 13); *Isaak,* p. 20 (n. 13); *Solomou,* p. 47 (n. 13).
44 *Banković*, para. 46 and 47 (n. 13).
45 See also *Banković*, para. 75 (n. 13).
46 *Banković*, paras 75–76 (n. 13).
47 *Issa*, para. 76 (n. 13).
48 *Al-Skeini* (CA), para. 198 (Lord Justice Sedley) (n. 16).

the *Banković* dictum, he rejected the underlying logic of the dictum and suggested that the European Court of Human Rights might sooner or later revisit it.[49] Indeed, there is possibly a further approach to jurisdiction defined spatially (considered in section 35.3.3.4 immediately below), and other approaches regarding the alternative trigger for jurisdiction as control over individuals (considered in section 35.3.4.3 below), which may offer greater opportunities for the kind of flexibility considered here.

3.3.4 Does it cover bombing/shooting?

In the *Banković* decision, the European Court of Human Rights rejected applicability of the ECHR in the context of the NATO bombing of a radio and TV station in Belgrade, holding that aerial bombardment did not constitute the exercise of territorial control so as meet the test for the territorial/spatial concept of extraterritorial jurisdiction.[50]

The *Andreou v Turkey* case concerned soldiers of the Turkish Republic of Northern Cyprus located on the TRNC side of the neutral UN buffer zone between the TRNC and the rest of Cyprus, who shot into the buffer zone and hit the applicant, Mrs Andreou, who had moved in this area. The European Court of Human Rights held that Mrs Andreou came within Turkey's extraterritorial jurisdiction because:

> even though the applicant sustained her injuries in territory over which Turkey exercised no control, the opening of fire on the crowd from close range, which was the direct and immediate cause of those injuries, was such that the applicant must be regarded as 'within [the] jurisdiction' of Turkey.[51]

As established in the aforementioned earlier decisions about Northern Cyprus, the TRNC side of the buffer zone from which the shots were fired constituted Turkish extraterritorial jurisdiction for the purposes of the ECHR on the basis of effective territorial control. The Court focused on the act performed in this space – 'the opening of fire' – as being the determinative act, rather than its effect, which took place outside Turkish extraterritorial jurisdiction, on the Greek side. The Court did not, then, consider whether shooting per se constituted an exercise of jurisdiction, since the territory from which the shot fired already constituted extraterritorial Turkish jurisdiction for a different reason.

This finding raises the possibility that a continuous act that starts in the state's jurisdiction, whether territorial or extraterritorial, will be covered by human rights law in its entirety, including if the end point is, as here, more generally extraterritorial jurisdiction. Revisiting *Banković*, it might be asked whether bombing which is initiated from the state's jurisdiction, for example missiles launched from state territory which land extraterritorially, or aircraft located outside the jurisdiction when the bombing mechanism is operated from within the jurisdiction (such as in the case of remotely operated aircraft, so-called 'drones') would be covered by human rights obligations.

---

49 Ibid. paras 201–02. The idea of dividing and tailoring was criticised at the House of Lords stage. See in particular *Al-Skeini* (HL) paras 79–80 (Lord Rodger) and 128–30 (Lord Brown) (n. 16).

50 *Banković*, paras 75–76 (n. 13).

51 *Andreou* (Merits), para. 25 (n. 13).

3.3.5 The looser test of effective authority/decisive influence from *Ilascu*

The *Ilascu* decision of the Grand Chamber of the European Court of Human Rights in 2004 concerned complaints of violations of the ECHR by the authorities of the Moldovan Republic of Transdniestria (MRT), an entity in the territory of Moldova which had declared its independence in 1992–93, with Russian support, and was not recognised as an independent state by other states. The applicants argued that Moldova was responsible because what they complained of took place in Moldovan territory, and Russia was responsible because it was supporting the breakaway MRT.[52]

As far as Russian responsibility was concerned, the Court held that:

> [the MRT] set up in 1991–92 with the support of the Russian Federation, vested with organs of power and its own administration, remains under the effective authority, or at the very least under the decisive influence, of the Russian Federation, and in any event that it survives by virtue of the military, economic, financial and political support given to it by the Russian Federation.[53]

In consequence, the acts complained of fell within the extraterritorial exercise of jurisdiction by Russia. The test of 'effective authority . . . or at the very least . . . decisive influence', or 'in any event' survival 'by virtue of . . . support' suggests a much wider definition of extraterritorial jurisdiction than the earlier decisions on this issue. It is broad enough to cover the behavior of a state within its own territory exclusively. Moreover, it suggests a test for causation that is very loose. Authorities in a range of places could meaningfully be described as surviving by virtue of the support from, and/or being subject to the decisive influence of, other states. It remains to be seen whether this broader test is picked up in future decisions.

3.4 Jurisdiction trigger (2): control over individuals

3.4.1 Introduction

The second main trigger for extraterritorial jurisdiction concerns control over individuals. This is referred to herein and in some of the relevant judicial decisions as a *personal, individual* or, because of the type of state action involved, *state-agent-authority* connection. This connection has been understood variously as *control* (like the spatial relationship discussed already), *power* or *authority*. This test has been held to be met, triggering the applicability of human rights obligations, in the context of extraterritorial abductions (the *Celiberti de Casariego* and *Lopez Burgos* decisions by the UN Human Rights Committee and the *Öcalan* decisions by the European Court of Human Rights),[54] lethal physical violence by public agents (the *Isaak* decision by the European Court of Human Rights),[55] detention of individuals (the *Coard* decision by the Inter-American Commission of Human Rights, the *Al-Skeini* and *Al-Saadoon* decisions of the English courts and the European Court of Human

---

52 *Ilascu*, paras 71–72 and 86–87 (n. 13).
53 *Ilascu*, para. 392 (n. 13).
54 *Celiberti de Casariego*, para. 10.3 (n. 12); *Lopez Burgos*, para. 12.3 (n. 12); *Öcalan* (GC), para. 91 (n. 13).
55 *Isaak*, 'Admissiblity', page 21 (n. 13).

Rights)[56] presence in an embassy (the *WM* decision of the European Commission of Human Rights)[57] and the issuance of a passport (the *Montero* decision by the UN Human Rights Committee).[58]

3.4.2 Narrower and broader notions of control over individuals

In the domestic proceedings in the *Al-Skeini* case concerning UK forces in Iraq, a distinction emerged between two different conceptions – narrow or broad – of the 'control over individuals' test. The narrow basis defines this trigger for jurisdiction extraterritorially as covering control exercised over individuals only in state-run facilities such as ships, embassies and, as affirmed in *Al-Skeini* in the English courts, detention facilities.[59] The broad basis, by contrast, defines this trigger as such control short of any state-run facility context, in any situation.

The distinction between these conceptions of the individual/state agent authority basis for extraterritorial 'jurisdiction' was moot in *Al-Skeini* because the relevant situation under evaluation in that case fell within the narrower test (it concerned the torture and killing of an individual held in a UK military base). The distinction is potentially relevant, however, to other situations.

None of the pre-*Al-Skeini* Strasbourg decisions concerned with the 'individual' heading of extraterritorial jurisdiction, even if sometimes covering situations taking place in state-run facilities, affirmed a requirement of such a location as being part of the test for applicability.[60] Nonetheless, in the English courts, the narrower version of the test – with the requirement – ultimately prevailed in the final decision at the House of Lords (as it was then).[61] When a different aspect of the case was brought before the European Court of Human Rights, the Court engaged in a general review of the law on extraterritorial jurisdiction, and in its observations on its previous case law on the 'individual' trigger, stated that it did not consider that jurisdiction arose in the decisions under evaluation:

> solely from the control exercised by the Contracting State over the buildings, aircraft or ship in which the individuals were held. What is decisive in such cases is the exercise of physical power and control over the person in question.[62]

This suggests that extraterritorial jurisdiction may not be understood to subsist simply because the state operates facilities abroad – there has to be 'physical power and control' exercised over individuals within those facilities in order for such treatment to be regulated by the Convention. What is left open is whether the exercise of such power outside state-run facilities would also be covered. Moreover, it is unclear what the caveat amounts to – what exactly would fall within, and outside, the boundaries of the test – in the context of state-run facilities, and how this approach is reconciled with the finding in the *WM* case, which concerned

---

56 *Coard*, para. 1–4, 37, 39 41 (n. 14); *Al-Skeini* (DC) (CA) (HL), *passim* (n. 16); *Al-Saadoon, passim* (n. 13).
57 *WM*, p. 196, section 'The Law', para. 1, (n. 13).
58 *Montero* para. 5 (n. 12).
59 *Al-Skeini* (DC) (CA) (HL) *passim* (n. 16); see also Wilde 2008 (n. 1).
60 See the relevant sources above n. 13.
61 *Al-Skeini* (HL), *passim* (n. 16).
62 *Al-Skeini* (ECtHR), para. 136 (n. 13).

the mere physical presence in an Embassy, without any reference to additional, more direct 'physical power and control'.[63]

Perhaps the Court had in mind a different consideration: that states should not ordinarily be made responsible for the human rights of all individuals within their foreign premises, simply by virtue of presence on such premises – there has to be a more direct connection to a rights violation, which is established through the requirement of physical power and control. Such a consideration is, however, about the substance of rights and obligations, not whether they should be applicable. Specifically, it seeks to secure negative rights concerned with non-interference exclusively, without also the broader provision of positive rights.

3.4.3 Being shot renders an individual within the jurisdiction?

A 2008 decision of the European Court of Human Rights appears to suggest that merely being subject to lethal armed force could be sufficient to fall within the extraterritorial jurisdiction of the state responsible for that action. At the same event in and around the UN buffer zone in between the TRNC and the rest of Cyprus which led to the aforementioned shooting of Mrs Andreou, another Greek Cypriot, Solomos Solomou, broke through the UN cordon from the Greek side into the UN buffer zone, crossed in to the TRNC side of the buffer zone, and climbed a flagpole, to protest at the Turkish occupation of the north.[64] He was hit by shots fired from the TRNC side of the buffer zone.[65] This might have been treated as taking place within Turkish jurisdiction on the basis of effective overall control of the TRNC. However, curiously the European Court of Human Rights focused on not the opening of fire, but the experience of being shot, treating this as an exercise of state agent control.[66] The emphasis was thus on control exercised over the individual, rather than on control exercised over the territory within which the individual and/or the soldiers are located. In the context of the case, the only direct nexus of control is being in receipt of a lethal bullet. Indeed, it is logical to conclude that a concept of effective control over individuals that has been found to encompass abduction (as mentioned, in the *Lopez Burgos* and *Celiberti de Casariego* decisions) would also cover lethal armed force (and, indeed, a contrary conclusion would be perverse).

The other decisions on bombing and shooting – *Banković* and *Andreou* – ultimately turned on whether the bombing and shooting in question took place in foreign-state-controlled territory, or themselves constituted the exercise of such territorial control by the states involved. The shift away from territory to the individual in *Solomou* suggests a new approach to the applicability of human rights law to such action, with potentially broad consequences. If it is possible to bring this action within the 'individual' heading of jurisdiction, whether or not the alternative 'territorial' basis for applicability is met is no longer exclusively determinative of applicability. Even if the 'sliding scale' or 'cause and effect' conception of jurisdiction as control over territory is supposedly ruled out by *Banković* (a conclusion which is, as mentioned, placed in question by *Issa*), a test of jurisdiction as control over individuals understood in this way would be sufficient to trigger human rights obligations.

63 *WM*, p. 196, Section 'The Law', para. 1 (n. 13).
64 *Solomou, passim*, esp. para. 48 (n. 13).
65 Ibid. at para. 12.
66 Ibid. at paras 49–51.

3.5 A new hybrid test from Al-Skeini?

The *Al-Skeini* decision of the European Court of Human Rights in 2011 introduces a treatment of extraterritorial jurisdiction that appears to combine both the 'territorial' and 'individual' triggers that had hitherto been treated separately. The decision concerned the shooting of individuals by UK soldiers in streets and houses where the soldiers were temporarily present, in the context of the broader UK military presence in Iraq. The Court placed emphasis on the fact that the United Kingdom:

> assumed in Iraq the exercise of some of the public powers normally to be exercised by a sovereign government. In particular, the United Kingdom assumed authority and responsibility for the maintenance of security in South East Iraq. In these exceptional circumstances, the Court considers that the United Kingdom, through its soldiers engaged in security operations in Basrah during the period in question, exercised authority and control over individuals killed in the course of such security operations, so as to establish a jurisdictional link between the deceased and the United Kingdom for the purposes of Article 1 of the Convention.[67]

This leaves open the question of whether killing outside the broader context of the territorially defined exercise of authority and responsibility would be sufficient to establish a jurisdictional link. There is no specific reference to such a broader role in *Solomou*; but an equivalent activity by Turkey in northern Cyprus had already been determined to exist, and to constitute the exercise of jurisdiction, in the earlier, canonical cases relating to that situation.

3.6 No trigger – what if no exercise of jurisdiction in own territory?

In the *Ilascu* case mentioned earlier, the Court was asked to determine both Russian and Moldovan responsibility for the acts of the MRT authorities. As far as Moldova was concerned, the issue was not extraterritorial applicability – the MRT was part of Moldovan territory, even if it was a breakaway republic – but whether the loss of control within that territory somehow altered the understanding of jurisdiction for the purposes of applying the Convention as far as Moldova was concerned.

This implicates a broader issue: should jurisdiction always be assumed to exist within a state's territory? How is this reconciled with notions of extraterritorial jurisdiction based on territorial control, which make the foreign state obliged to implement all the rights in the treaty in a generalised sense? Is the host state nonetheless also responsible for doing the same thing with respect to its obligations?

In *Ilascu*, the Grand Chamber of the European Court of Human Rights held that there was a 'presumption' that jurisdiction is exercised normally throughout state territory, but that:

> This presumption may be limited in exceptional circumstances, particularly where a state is prevented from exercising its authority in part of its territory. That may be as a result of military occupation by the armed forces of another state which effectively controls the territory concerned . . . acts of war or rebellion, or the acts of a foreign state supporting the installation of a separatist state within the territory of the state concerned.[68]

---

67 *Al-Skeini* (ECtHR), para. 149 (n. 13).
68 *Ilascu*, para. 312 (n. 13).

This suggests that in some instances a finding of the extraterritorial exercise of jurisdiction on the part of one state will necessarily denote (whether or not it is addressed) some sort of diminution in the liability for securing rights in the territorial jurisdiction for another state. The Grand Chamber also concluded that:

> even in the absence of effective control over the Transdniestrian region, Moldova still has a positive obligation under Article 1 of the Convention to take the diplomatic, economic, judicial or other measures that it is in its power to take and are in accordance with international law to secure to the applicants the rights guaranteed by the Convention.[69]

This is significant because it suggests a 'sliding scale' of territorial jurisdiction – the state must do what it can – which the Court in *Banković* had appeared to reject *extraterritorially* as far as the test based on territorial control was concerned. It might be speculated that this reflects a greater need to subject the state to obligations in its own territory and with respect to its own nationals (most of whom reside in that territory and few of whom reside extraterritorially). But such a need relates to what the obligations mean in substance rather than whether they apply. As with what was mentioned earlier regarding the dictum from *Al-Skeini* on the exercise of physical power and control over individuals in state-run facilities, the distinction between applicability and the meaning of substantive obligations (here, it seems, they should be limited to positive obligations) is blurred.

3.7 Does the 'jurisdiction' clause apply as an alternative basis for extraterritorial applicability for treaties with 'colonial' clauses?

It will be recalled that certain early human rights treaties, notably the ECHR and its Protocols, contain a 'colonial clause' through which states parties can declare that they will extend the rights in the treaties to their colonies. In many cases, states that had and/or still have such overseas territories exercised and/or exercise the degree of control over such territories and/or the people within them on an individual level so as to meet the 'jurisdiction' test for applicability contained in separate clauses of the ECHR and its Protocols. This raises the question as to whether these treaties would apply on 'jurisdictional' grounds even if a 'colonial clause' declaration has *not* been made.

This issue came before the European Court of Human Rights in two cases related to Macau and Hong Kong before the handovers to China, when these territories were subject to Portuguese and UK sovereignty. The European Court of Human Rights held that for overseas territories, the only way ECHR obligations can apply is through a 'colonial clause' declaration.[70]

This position on the exclusive determinacy of 'colonial clause' extension or non-extension as far as applicability is concerned creates the potential for a divergent situation under the ECHR and its Protocols when compared with the ICCPR, because of the different basis on which those treaties apply extraterritorially. Given the overlap in the rights covered as between the ECHR and its Protocols, on the one hand, and the ICCPR, on the other, a situation may arise where the nature of the state action in an overseas territory meets the jurisdictional test, and on the facts impacts on the enjoyment of a particular right common to both

---

69 *Ilascu*, paras 361–65 (n. 13).
70 *Bui Van Thanh*, pp. 4–5 (n. 13); *Yonghong*, p. 3 (n. 13). See also *Gillow*, para. 62 (n. 13).

sets of treaties, but only the obligation in the ICCPR applies because the state has not made an express extension of the relevant part of the ECHR or its Protocols.

4 Treaties with free-standing models of applicability: approaches from CEDAW and CERD

Earlier it was explained that in the case of some of the human rights instruments that have a conception of scope of application or responsibility not linked to the exercise of 'jurisdiction' (i.e. a 'free-standing' conception), the treaties have nonetheless been treated for the purposes of extraterritorial applicability as if they contained the 'jurisdiction' provision. This was the approach taken by the Inter-American Commission on Human Rights as far as the (Inter-) American Declaration on Human Rights was concerned, and the International Court of Justice as far as the ACHPR and the Optional Protocol to the CRC on the Involvement of Children in Armed Conflict of 2000 were concerned.

A second approach to the extraterritorial scope of treaties with a free-standing conception of applicability provisions is simpler. It was adopted by the UK House of Lords (as it was then) in the *Roma Rights* case of 2004 concerning the posting of UK immigration officials at Prague airport, a policy intended to prevent individuals from travelling to the United Kingdom who would then make a claim for refugee protection there.[71] The complainants argued that the officials applied the immigration regulations in a manner that discriminated against the Roma people, and therefore constituted unlawful racial discrimination. Lady Hale, in her conclusions on discrimination with which the majority agreed, seemed to assume that the prohibition of discrimination on grounds of race in CERD applied extraterritorially,[72] and Lord Steyn in the same decision held that the discriminatory nature of the UK immigration operation at Prague Airport involved a 'breach' of the United Kingdom's obligations under CERD.[73] Both judges appeared to assume applicability, without recourse to a particular factual doctrine such as the exercise of 'jurisdiction' which had to be met in order for the obligations to be in play.

The effect of the International Court of Justice's 1998 order for provisional measures in the *Georgia v Russia* case is to offer further support to this 'free-standing' approach to applicability. The Court held that the CERD provisions at issue 'appear to apply' extraterritorially because there is no express restriction on territorial application in relation to either the treaty generally or the provisions at issue in particular.[74] The Court's Order called upon 'Both Parties, within South Ossetia and Abkhazia and adjacent areas in Georgia' to take certain acts to comply with the Convention, a determination that assumed the extraterritorial application of CERD to Russian forces in Georgia.[75]

This decision offers a particular approach to understanding the extraterritorial application of treaties such as the CERD which have free-standing models of applicability not expressly qualified by jurisdiction: the absence of a restriction on applicability, whether of a general character, or specific to the particular obligations in the treaty at issue, should be taken to suggest that the provisions *should* apply. In other words, as far as the significance of

---

71 See Opinion of Lord Bingham, *Roma Rights* case, para. 4 (n. 16).
72 See Opinion of Lady Hale, *Roma Rights* case, paras 97–102 (n. 16).
73 Opinion of Lord Steyn, *Roma Rights* case, para. 44 (on CERD) and para. 46 (n. 16).
74 *Georgia v Russia* (Provisional Measures), para. 109 (n. 11).
75 Ibid. at para. 149.

treaty provisions is concerned, the enquiry on extraterritorial applicability depends on not establishing this in a positive sense, but, rather, establishing whether it has been ruled out negatively though restrictive provisions. Such an approach to treaties with free-standing provisions can be seen as offering a potential explanation for the approach adopted by the UK House of Lords in *Roma Rights,* and a general doctrine to be followed in relation to such treaties, as an alternative to the approach of reading a concept of 'jurisdiction' into them.

5 Broader normative ideas and their relevance to the legal framework

5.1 Introduction

As with any area of law, the question of whether and to what extent international human rights law on civil and political rights should and does apply extraterritoriality implicates broader political ideas. Considering these ideas has the potential to deepen understandings of the debates around the value and the meaning of the legal framework. The merit of such an approach is acute when, as is the case here, the very applicability of the law itself is in question. The following section addresses the relevance of two broader sets of normative ideas: first, those concerned with the political relationship between the individual and the state as it is understood in human rights law and, second, those associated with the notion of a 'legal black hole'.

5.2 The political relationship between the individual and the state

Political ideas about the relationship between the individual and the state place into question assumptions that underpin certain important general concepts of international human rights law, when the operation of these concepts is considered in the extraterritorial context. The ideas at issue concern the state's existential claim to legitimacy insofar as it exercises control over its citizens and the territory in which they live and over which the state enjoys sovereignty. Although international human rights law is ostensibly concerned not with the relationship between the state and its nationals exclusively (although some political rights in particular are), but, rather, the state and all individuals in its 'jurisdiction',[76] an assumption that jurisdiction is usually exercised in a state's territory, and that most individuals there are the state's own nationals, would seem to explain approaches to the substance of the law, referred to further below, which assume, reference and depend on the state's claim to legitimacy in the particular context of its own sovereign territory and nationals. How, then, should human rights be understood in the light of the profoundly different political basis on which a state acts extraterritorially – outside its sovereign territory, and in a context where most, if not all individuals affected by its acts, are non-nationals – where ideas of the legitimacy of its presence are understood very differently compared to ideas underpinning the political basis for its actions at 'home'? The significance of this general question is illustrated through the following three examples of different aspects of international human rights law.

---

76 On the non-nationality basis for human rights law, see, e.g., N. Rodley, 'Non-State Actors and Human Rights' in this volume.

5.2.1 Deference to the state, including the 'margin of appreciation'

In the first place, the substantive rules of international human rights law often incorporate a degree of deference to the state's own determination of local cultural and societal traditions when accommodation to these traditions is accepted as a legitimate limitation on human rights, such as in the 'margin of appreciation' doctrine particularly associated with the European Convention on Human Rights.[77] Such ideas necessarily assume and depend on political concepts about the particular link between the state and the people in its territory. How should such ideas be understood when the state acts abroad, and the political link between it and the people affected by its actions is of a different character?

5.2.2 Remedies

In the second place, the extraterritorial context raises distinct questions about the character of remedies for human rights violations.[78] The conventional wisdom in international human rights law is that there should be an effective 'domestic remedy' for such violations, and that the primary means through which the remedy is realised is through the state's legal system, with international human rights complaint mechanisms performing a subsidiary role to provide a remedy as a last resort (usually requiring the exhaustion of domestic remedies as an admissibility requirement).[79] The application of this requirement in the extraterritorial context implicates broader constitutional theories about the role of national courts in operating checks and balances against the executive.

Such theories emphasise the ideas of legitimacy that underpin the function of the courts in challenging the executive, rooted in part in the role they play as part of a constitutional system within the state, aimed ultimately at protecting that state and its people. They foreground the potential for tensions to arise when national courts are called up on to adjudicate conformity to human rights standards by the executive branch of their state when it is acting abroad, outside the overall polity and national population the courts and the executive form part of and serve. By the same token, they also draw attention to the tensions that exist with the idea of national courts of one state operating as a 'domestic remedy' in relation to a foreign state acting in the territorial space within which these courts operate. Ultimately, they place into question the primacy accorded to a domestic remedy, and the subsidiary status given to an international remedy, in the context of a violation of human rights law extraterritorially.

---

77 On the margin of appreciation, see, e.g., Eyal Benvenisti, 'Margin of Appreciation, Consensus, and Universal Standards', (1999) 31 *INT'L L. & POL.* 843, 844–45 and sources cited therein.

78 On such remedies generally, see e.g. Dinah Shelton, *Remedies in International Human Rights Law* (OUP, 2006) and sources cited therein.

79 On the legal obligation to provide a domestic remedy, see, e.g. ICCPR, Art. 2, para. 3(a), ECHR, Art. 13 (nn. 20 and 17 respectively). On the exhaustion of domestic remedies as an admissibility requirement for a case to be heard before an international complaints mechanism, see e.g. (First) Optional Protocol to the International Covenant on Civil and Political Rights, GA res. 2200A (XXI), 21 UN GAOR Supp. (No. 16) at 59, UN Doc. A/6316 (1966), 999 UNTS 302, opened for signature 16 Dec. 1966, entry into force 23 March 1976 (ICCPR Optional Protocol 1), Art. 2; ECHR, Art. 35, para. 1 (n. 17).

5.2.3 Emergencies/derogations in the extraterritorial context

In the third place, the political and legal mismatch between the identity of the state acting extraterritorially, and the identity of the people and territory in which it is acting, has important implications for normative concepts crafted to regulate the circumstances in which a state can and should be permitted take 'emergency' measures limiting rights when its survival is threatened. Certain international human rights treaties, such as the ICCPR and the ECHR, enshrine these concepts in 'derogation' provisions.[80]

There is a question as to whether or not the test for activating a derogation – the existence of a 'public emergency' (ICCPR) or 'war or other public emergency' (ECHR) which 'threatens' (ICCPR)/is 'threatening' (ECHR) the 'life of the nation' (both instruments) covers all forms of extraterritorial security threats in relation to which a derogation would be needed in order for necessary responsive action to be compatible with human rights law.[81] The question arises because of the reference to the 'life of the nation'. If that nation is defined as the foreign state acting extraterritorially (and the nationals it claims to act on behalf of), and not also the state/non-state territory in which it is acting, and the affected population, does the test only cover threats extraterritorially which can be linked back to the foreign state as their object/target? If so, would only war, occupation and other forms of military action relating to self-defence be covered, leaving outside the test other military action, for example that pursuant to Security Council authorisation under Chapter VII of the United Nations Charter outside of self-defence, including for reasons concerned with the protection of human rights, and even action that is defensive, but of another state/population, not the state taking the action?

There is a potentially highly important linkage here between the legitimacy of derogations, of limiting rights in emergency situations, on the one hand, and the legitimacy of intervention/foreign war, occupation and other forms of military action, on the other, the latter normative question being addressed by other areas of international law (e.g. the law on the use of force, United Nations law) rather than human rights law (although the law of self-determination is clearly relevant here). At the root of the derogations regime is an assumption of entitlement on the part of the state to take extreme measures limiting rights, because of ideas associated with the legitimacy of the cause: that the state needs to be able to ensure its continued survival, to maintain the state institutions that protect the rights of its people.[82] Equivalent ideas also underpin the international legal rules concerned with whether a state has the right to go to war in self-defence, unilaterally, without any multilateral approval.[83]

That said, international law and public policy now enshrines, to a certain extent, the cosmopolitan notion of 'community obligations' which seek to move the position of states away from an exclusive concern with their own survival and that of their people, to also being interested in the welfare of others extraterritorially.[84] If a state acts abroad ostensibly on this

---

80 See ICCPR (n. 20), Art. 4; ECHR (n. 17), Art. 15; ACHR (n. 17), Art. 27; Joan Fitzpatrick, *Human Rights in Crisis: The International System for Protecting Rights During States of Emergency* (University of Pennsylvania Press, 1994), and sources cited therein.

81 ICCPR, Art. 15.1 (n. 20); ECHR, Art. 4.1 (n. 17). On this issue, see also *Banković* (n. 13), paras 41, 62.

82 See Fitzpatrick (n. 80), *passim,* and sources cited therein.

83 See e.g. the discussion and sources cited in Christine Gray, *International Law and the Use of Force,* 3rd edn (OUP, 2008) (Gray).

84 See, e.g., Christian Tams, *Enforcing Obligations* Erga Omnes *in International Law* (CUP, 2010), and sources cited therein.

basis, for example to end gross violations of human rights, then a new ground for a legitimate 'threat' as far as it is concerned – to another nation, or people, not itself at all, or at least not exclusively – is necessarily in play. Similarly, if a state acts pursuant to a request for assistance from another state, then the object of the threat this action relates to is necessarily 'other' than it. For international law to allow action of this kind as a matter of the law on the use of force and/or UN law, on the one hand, but then assume its illegitimacy in the law of human rights as far as the derogations test is concerned, on the other, would be perverse.

That said, whether and in what circumstances international law allows the use of force extraterritorially outside the context self-defence is a relatively contested and complex matter when compared to self-defence.[85] Many argue that the default position in international law is a limit to self-defence, with extraterritorial military action for other purposes, including to protect human rights, only permissible if Security Council authorisation under Chapter VII of the UN Charter is forthcoming, and/or at the invitation of the state in whose territory the action is taken.[86] Here, then, the notion of the interest of 'others' – the 'international community', the state in whose territory the action is taken – is promoted, but requiring a form of sanction derived from those identified with this other interest – the Security Council in the case of the 'international community', the other state in the case of the invitation – in order for action pursuant to the interest to be lawful. It could be said, then, that a derogation regime which affirms a default position of permissible limitations only for wars of self-defence would be compatible with a somewhat equivalent presumption, in terms of legitimate grounds, in the law on the use of force.

The question then would be how this default position could or would be departed from in circumstances where military action for non–self-defence purposes was lawfully conducted as a matter of the law on the use of force – through UN Security Council Chapter VII authority and/or agreement by the host state. This issue lay behind the *Al-Jedda* case before the courts of England and Wales and the European Court of Human Rights, concerning the practice of security detention or internment by the UK military in Iraq.[87] The UK government had not entered a derogation to the ECHR relating to this or any other aspect of its military action in Iraq. It claimed that the Security Council had authorised it to conduct this practice as part of the broader mandate given to certain foreign forces in Iraq under Chapter VII of the UN Charter, and that the authorisation had the legal effect of modifying any inconsistent obligations under the ECHR. Put differently, it was claimed that there was in the manner of what might be called a 'constructive' or 'effective' derogation (having an effect like a derogation but not operating through the derogation regime) enabled by Security Council authority. It was suggested that this was possible through Article 103 of the United Nations Charter, which provides that:

> In the event of a conflict between the obligations of the Members of the United Nations under the present Charter and their obligations under any other international agreement, their obligations under the present Charter shall prevail.[88]

The idea was that the supposed authorisation of internment made by the Security Council in a resolution passed under Chapter VII of the UN Charter, enjoying normative status as a

---

85 See Gray (n. 83), and sources cited therein.
86 Ibid.
87 *Al-Jedda v The United Kingdom* App. No. 27021/08 (ECtHR, 7 July 2011) (*Al-Jedda*).
88 Charter of the United Nations, 24 October 1945, 1 UNTS XVI, Art. 103.

matter of UN law, constituted an 'obligation' under the Charter for Article 103 purposes, thereby trumping any conflicting obligations the UK had under the ECHR.[89]

The European Court of Human Rights sidestepped the question of whether the Security Council might be able to make determinations with this legal effect in human rights law (including whether this was based on a correct interpretation of Article 103), by focusing on a prior matter: there was a presumption that the Security Council would not intend to modify member states' human rights obligations, and this could not be rebutted when the supposed authority at issue was, as here, ambiguous.[90]

The case did not, therefore, resolve the broader question of whether the Security Council can and should have the role the UK claimed it performed in *Al-Jedda*, to perform an equivalent function in limiting human rights obligations in the context of extraterritorial security threats as derogation provisions play in the context of security threats in a state's own territory – proactive, ad hoc law-changing as a substitute for the operation of existing normative regulations.

One might begin to consider the answer to this question through a comparison in the different ways each normative regime would operate. The human rights regime operates as a regulatory framework grafted onto state behaviour, regardless, as addressed earlier, of whether or not the behaviour is itself pursuant to a legal entitlement more broadly in international law. It is, moreover, relational and context-specific in its application in any given case: is there an emergency, does it constitute a threat to the nation, is the restriction for a legitimate purpose, is it proportionate to that purpose and so on.[91] The Security Council authorisation regime, by contrast, is not regulatory and context-specific but authoritative and absolute in nature: the test is not whether or not the restriction is compatible with particular standards in the circumstances, but whether or not an entitlement to operate it has been granted by the Council. Is there something special about the extraterritorial context when compared to the territorial context that necessitates the operation of this different normative approach to the question of how restrictions on individual rights should be treated as a matter of law? More broadly, what are the relative merits of these two different legal strategies for legitimising restrictions on human rights?

It may be that the Security Council approach has only been considered because of a concern that the 'life of the nation' test in derogations law would be interpreted to cover only direct threats to the state acting extraterritorially. Accepting this view, the drastic step of seeking to argue that the Council could and did modify human rights obligations extraterritorially could be seen as the only means of ensuring restrictions which might, in principle, have been compatible with human rights law, *mutatis mutandis*, in the domestic context, but could not fit within the test extraterritorially because the test itself did not encompass extraterritorial situations. The law-making role asserted by the UN Security Council is deployed to remedy a defect in human rights treaty law: that the law on derogations cannot encompass extraterritorial situations.

It has to be asked how likely it is that courts and other authoritative interpretation bodies would define the 'life of the nation' test so as to render the derogations regime incapable of fair and effective operation extraterritorially, thereby placing into question the viability of the extraterritorial application of human rights law in general, even when, as addressed above, the latter issue has long been accepted and affirmed by them. Is there a serious prospect of such

---

89 See *Al-Jedda* (n. 87), *passim*.
90 *Al-Jedda* (n. 87), para. 102.
91 See the sources cited above n. 80.

bodies adopting an approach to interpreting human rights law that would render inoperable to military action abroad the special regime of limitations conceived for emergency situations? Given the generous latitude that has been given to states by courts in applying the derogations rules, addressed further below,[92] it seems more probable that the 'threat to the nation' in the derogations test would be interpreted so as to encompass security threats faced by states acting extraterritorially.

However, bearing in mind the foregoing analysis on the links between the legitimacy of extraterritorial military action itself (the law on the use of force issue) and the legitimacy of restrictions on human rights taken in response to extraterritorial security threats (the derogations law issue), it may be that a court or other interpretation body considering the question of whether there is a 'threat to the nation' for the purposes of the law of derogations might deem it necessary to go into the cognate question of the legitimacy of the military action itself. This might be especially the case for military action outside of self-defence where, as reviewed earlier, there is a general view that international law requires special authority, whether through the consent of the host state or authorisation by the UN Security Council.

It might be argued that the human rights law 'threat to the nation' only covers threats that the state has the legal right to respond to: that the permissibility of an extra opportunity to limit rights (beyond the standard opportunity provided by limitation clauses) presupposes a legitimate entitlement to respond to the 'emergency' that supposedly provides the underlying rationale for the extra opportunity in the first place.[93] Whereas with domestic security threats, such a right is, as reviewed earlier, assumed by a legal regime that accepts the state's monopoly on the use of violence and affirms its existential rationale to secure the kind of ordered society within which rights can be protected. For extraterritorial security threats, however, there is no such assumption outside of self-defence. A court might be persuaded to take the view that a state taking military action extraterritorially in order to respond to a non-self-defence threat would need to establish its legal entitlement to do so in order to be able to avail itself of the derogation provisions of human rights law.

Earlier, it was remarked that it would be perverse for one area of international law – the law on the use of force – to permit certain forms of extraterritorial military action, but then another area of international law – human rights law – to operate (in the derogations rules) as if such action lacked legitimacy. Equally, it might be said that it would be peculiar if military action that was illegal as a matter of the law on the use of force would be treated as legitimate when it came to the operation of human rights law, in the particular sense that the state taking the action, although actually lacking a lawful basis for doing so, would be granted extra privileges to restrict rights on the basis that it has a legitimate role in responding to a security threat.

The upshot of an approach that would graft the law on the use of force onto an aspect of the law of derogations would be that a state taking extraterritorial military action would only be able to avail itself of the operation of the derogations regime in international human rights law if the action at issue was lawful as a matter of the law on the use of force. This takes things back to the earlier discussion of the link with the concept of 'jurisdiction' in general public international law: the point that human rights law applies extraterritorially regardless of whether the state action at issue is or is not lawful as a matter of general international law. Here, it is not that human rights law would not apply if the state has no lawful right to be

---

92 See Fitzpatrick (n. 80), and sources cited therein.
93 On the rationale for derogations, see Fitzpatrick (n. 80), and sources cited therein.

acting extraterritorially; rather, the state would not be able to benefit from the extra ability to restrict rights provided by the derogations regime in particular. In other words, it is, as it were, the applicability of the derogations regime that would be contingent on the broader legality of the extraterritorial action at issue; the applicability of human rights law in a general sense would be unaffected by the wider question of legality.

This approach would create a significant new issue for those states that engage in military action extraterritorially and which are subject to the kind of judicial scrutiny of conformity to human rights law through national and international mechanisms that is of a more pronounced character when compared to the nature of such scrutiny when the application of the law on the use of force is concerned. Of course, for states seeking to avoid judicial scrutiny of the lawfulness of military action by courts applying human rights law, the alternative route to legal justification of Security Council authority – such as it is, actually, possible – can be seen as offering a way to restrict rights without having the 'threat to the life of the nation' test in derogations law considered. In one sense there is an irony in such an approach, in that a body with primary responsibility for issues of international peace and security, and so the international law rules on the use of force, can supposedly be deployed in an attempt to modify another area of international law – human rights law – in a manner that could ensure that other bodies that have a primary responsibility for the enforcement of that other area of international law – human rights courts – do not stray into the law on the use of force as part of their analysis. The UK lost in *Al-Jedda* on the narrow question of the lawfulness of security detentions/internment in Iraq. However, in its strategy of framing this question as being a matter of whether authority had been forthcoming from the UN Security Council, the UK avoided the risk of the considerably broader question of the legality of its military presence in Iraq being brought before the Court as part of a consideration of the law of derogations.

5.3 The 'legal black hole' – what is at stake?

As mentioned earlier, the issue of the extraterritorial application of human rights law has become foregrounded by the popular concern that certain extraterritorial arrangements – the most prominently invoked situation being the US detention and interrogation facilities in Guantánamo Bay – constitute 'legal black holes', and that this situation is problematic in a fashion that justifies an important, sometimes pre-eminent, position on the agenda of global human rights concerns. What are the merits of this portrayal of the question of whether international human rights law should apply extraterritorially?

The notion that the facility in Guantánamo Bay, and other forms of extraterritorial activities by foreign states, are legal vacuums is absurd: the states involved in them claim that the law plays a major role in constituting these arrangements. In Guantánamo, for example, most fundamentally international law provides, through treaties between Cuba and the US, the entitlement of the US to administer the area on which it operates the Naval Base housing the detainees.[94] In Iraq, the site of the Abu Ghraib abuses that also led to 'legal vacuum' concerns, and the actions of UK soldiers that led to the *Al-Skeini* and *Al-Jedda* decisions addressed above that form part of some of the canonical case law in this area, UN Security Council resolutions, and later agreements with the post-occupation Iraqi government, were invoked by the

---

94 Agreements Between the United States of America and Cuba: 16–23 February 1903, Art. I, UST No. 418, (available at http://avalon.law.yale.edu/20th_century/dip_cuba002.asp); 2 July 1903, UST No. 426 (available at http://avalon.law.yale.edu/20th_century/dip_cuba003.asp); 29 May 1934, UTS No. 866 (available at http://avalon.law.yale.edu/20th_century/dip_cuba001.asp).

foreign military powers in their claim to a lawful entitlement to engage in the invasion, occupation and post-occupation military presence in the state.[95]

As scholars such as Susan Marks point out, representing situations like Guantánamo as lacking law as a mode of criticism is problematic: the role of the law in potentially facilitating these situations is concealed.[96] In what in critical theory – specifically, ideology critique – is termed a 'strategy of inversion', such representations suggest that with the application of law these problematic situations will be brought to an end. The portrayal is descriptively inaccurate and normatively problematic, implying a political role for the law in relation to such situations different from that which it actually performs. By way of what is termed 'dissimulation' in critical theory, the law is presented in an inherently redemptive rather than normatively complex and ambivalent manner.

That said, despite the absolutist implication of terms like 'legal black hole,' as mentioned earlier such terms are mostly invoked to articulate a concern with the absence of not all law but a particular area of it: the full range of necessary legal standards that should apply whenever the state exercises control over territory and the individuals within it, including those standards governing the detention of individuals, and independent remedies for enforcing those standards. As a term of critique, the 'legal black hole' idea speaks to a fear that, when states move away from their own sovereign territories, they somehow also effect a partial or complete move away from the arena of necessary legal regulation as far as the treatment of individuals is concerned.

This constitutes one of the main arguments implicated in the question of whether human rights law should apply extraterritorially: the notion that a 'legal black hole' of this nature would otherwise prevail, that such a situation is undesirable, and so efforts – political, activist, judicial – to remedy such a situation are meritorious.

Indeed, some of the advocacy in this area comes close to suggesting that international human rights law is somehow the pre-eminent means of realising effective checks and balances against states; that all it would take to bring an end to certain objectionable practices is the application and enforcement of international human rights law. Here, then, is the general redemptionist idea earlier associated with all law applied to human rights law, which is invested with a transformatory capacity.

This is a difficult thesis to maintain, given the various devices that exist within human rights law permitting the state to limit rights, from the attenuated way rights themselves are defined, to reservations, restriction clauses, derogation provisions and the concept mentioned earlier of the 'margin of appreciation', through which the state's own view of what limitations on rights are necessary is deferred to.[97]

Even for non-derogable rules like the prohibition on torture and inhuman and degrading treatment there is debate about which practices fall within the scope of what is prohibited.[98] The rules concerning the application of human rights in emergency situations have been criticised for according too much latitude to states because of the generous interpretations of derogation provisions made by international review mechanisms, especially the ECHR

---

95 See Marc Weller, *Iraq and the Use of Force in International Law* (OUP, 2010); Stefan Talmon, *The Occupation of Iraq*, two volumes (Hart, forthcoming 2014), and the sources cited therein.

96 Susan Marks, 'State-Centrism, International Law, and the Anxieties of Influence' (2006) 19 *Leiden Journal of International Law* 339.

97 See above, nn. 77 and 80.

98 See Nigel S. Rodley with Matt Pollard, *The Treatment of Prisoners Under International Law*, 3rd edn (OUP, 2013), ch. 3, and sources cited therein.

Strasbourg machinery with its invocation of a broad 'margin of appreciation' involving deference to states' own decisions as to the existence of an 'emergency' situation and the necessity and proportionality of restrictions introduced to respond to this threat.[99] The challenge here is whether the inadequate nature of the test applied to state action renders this area of the law incapable of delivering what it promises, thereby serving ironically to legitimate infringements on individual rights without having actually placed the states involved under any meaningful constraints.

One cannot help wondering, then, whether the application of human rights law extraterritorially fully addresses the political objectives that lead those calling for it to make their arguments. For example, would international human rights law properly applied actually require the US to release or prosecute all the detainees in Guantánamo Bay, Bagram and other extraterritorial detention and interrogation centres, the policy that has been advocated by most mainstream opponents and an expert panel in its report to the United Nations Commission on Human Rights?[100] Not only does the call to 'release or prosecute' perhaps miss the point of many of the Guantánamo detentions; it is far from clear that some form of security detention would necessarily be impermissible in international human rights law.[101] Critics may thus be placing faith in a normative regime that even on its own terms may not speak fully to their agenda.

Alongside concerns relating to the substantive content of international human rights law are other worries relating to the value of this regime of law as an effective review mechanism, notably relating to enforcement. Whereas the European Court of Human Rights can hear complaints from individuals against all Council of Europe member states,[102] many of whom being engaged in extraterritorial activity, the UN Human Rights Committee's (somewhat) equivalent jurisdiction of issuing Views on individual communications making complaints about non-compliance with the ICCPR does not operate with respect to the United States nor to some other states acting extraterritorially.[103] And even when some form of scrutiny mechanism does operate, for example through the reporting procedure to the Human Rights Committee under the ICCPR,[104] the limited remit of some country-specific NGOs can mean that the crucial assistance role that NGOs play in the operation of human rights mechanisms can be relatively minimal when extraterritorial activity is under evaluation.

Beyond these and other limitations with the law, the nature of extraterritorial activities means that many of them take place in conditions of near total secrecy. Whatever the truth of the 'legal black hole' designations, it is certainly true that certain extraterritorial activities take place in circumstances where the opportunities for scrutiny by third parties are markedly constrained and sometimes entirely absent. In the light of these concerns, one should not be too sanguine as to the value of international human rights law to provide meaningful and effective review of extraterritorial state action.

---

99 See the citations above nn. 77 and 80, and the sources cited therein.
100 On the expert panel, see UN Commission on Human Rights, *Situation of Detainees at Guantánamo Bay – Report*, UN doc. E/CN.4/2006/120, 15 February 2006, obtainable from http://www. ohchr.org/english/bodies/chr/sessions/62/listdocs.htm, para. 95.
101 See, e.g. symposium edition Security Detention in (2009) 40(3) *Case Western Reserve Journal of International Law* 315, and sources cited therein.
102 See ECHR (n. 17), Art. 34.
103 Because the US has not ratified the Optional Protocol to the ICCPR allowing for this. See ICCPR Optional Protocol 1 (n. 79).
104 See ICCPR (n. 20), Art. 40.

That said, is there not a legitimate purpose to calling for the application of human rights law even without an exaggerated view of the difference it would make? Even allowing for concerns about the derogation test, for example, at a bare minimum the law here still provides an absolute prohibition on breaches of non-derogable rights such as the right to be free from torture.[105]

It is also significant that, as mentioned earlier, certain states seek to deny the applicability of human rights treaties: this would surely be unnecessary if such states considered the substantive content of these instruments and/or the associated modes of enforcement as placing them under no meaningful constraint.

It should be asked how helpful it is to seek to counter the essentialism that the application of human rights law would bring about a transformation in the fate of people subject to the extraterritorial actions of states with its opposite, that such application would be of no benefit whatsoever. Another option exists, of course, which is to be concerned with extraterritorial applicability as a modest initiative to serve certain policy objectives.

In assessing the merits of such a position, one must place the particular set of policy concerns at issue in a broader context, and consider the validity of focusing on them in the light of what is left outside the frame of analysis. The operation of extraterritorial detention facilities and the conduct of military actions in Afghanistan and Iraq form part of a broader process of the projection of power abroad by states and the complex interrelationship between the activities of powerful states and the welfare of individuals outside their territory.

One might ask what is at stake when what was even at the high point a situation involving only a few hundred men in Guantánamo seemed to occupy a more prominent position as a global human rights cause célèbre than, for example, the tens of millions of women, men and children infected with HIV in developing countries who lack access to affordable anti-retroviral drugs. This focus implicates the skewed agenda of much mainstream human rights policy, with its pattern of dominant and subaltern issues: the focus on civil and political rights more than economic, social and cultural rights (as reflected in this chapter); on the exceptional and the extreme more than the pervasive and everyday; on the male more than the female; on the public more than the private; and on particularly dramatic incidents more than broader, long-term structural problems.[106]

This skewed agenda takes things back to the earlier point about the ideological representation of international law. When one moves beyond the law's role in offering some safeguards, for example the right to a public enquiry established in *Al-Skeini*, one sees the law, for example, having initially been invoked as a bar preventing the production of affordable generic HIV anti-retroviral drugs through intellectual property rights.[107]

Not only, then, could it be said that the fetishisation of the arrangements in Guantánamo and other situations involving extreme violations of civil and political rights reinforce the

---

105 See the sources cited above n. 98. On the absolute nature of the prohibition on torture, see e.g. Nigel S. Rodley with Matt Pollard, *The Treatment of Prisoners Under International Law*, 3rd edn (OUP, 2013), ch. 2, and sources cited therein.

106 For an excellent review of many of the main critiques of international human rights law, see Frédéric Mégrét, 'Where Does the Critique of International Human Rights Law Stand? An Exploration in 18 Vignettes', in David Kennedy and José María Benyeto (eds), *New Approaches to International Law: Lessons from the European experience* (TMC Asser Press, 2012).

107 See, e.g., M. Westerhaus and A. Castro, 'How Do Intellectual Property Law and International Trade Agreements Affect Access to Antiretroviral Therapy?', (2006) 3(8) *PLoS Med*: e332, obtainable from http://www.plosmedicine.org/article/info%3Adoi%2F10.1371%2Fjournal.pmed.0030332.

unjustified dominance of certain political causes over others. Also, a greater focus on an area of public policy where to a certain extent the law may make a positive difference, albeit a marginal one, when compared to the level of focus on an issue where the law may be more squarely part of the problem, brings with it the risk, as in the aforementioned use of the term 'legal black hole', of fostering a misleading presentation of the role of law as necessarily redemptive.

Indeed, it would be an irony if the silence or active support of the law on many of the most important causes of human misery in today's world has led to a strategy to turn away from these causes to relatively minor human rights problems like the situation of a few hundred men in Guantánamo, because it is here that the law might make more of a positive difference; in other words, for a broader political agenda on human rights to be determined by what is realisable through the law. Another approach to this problem would of course be to step outside the worldview of the law and be freed of its limitations.

To a certain extent, though, this challenge relates to matters internal to the law, which can be addressed within it. The problem that issues concerned with the civil rights of a few hundred men in Guantánamo seemed to be given greater attention than the right to health of tens of millions of women, men and children infected with HIV could be countered by a greater focus on the extraterritorial applicability of those areas of human rights law concerned with economic, social and cultural rights.[108] Equally, the problem that international legal standards concerned with intellectual property were operating as an impediment to the production of affordable anti-retroviral drugs for people in the global south could be, and is being, countered by initiatives to change this area of international law.[109]

But an internal recalibration of priorities within a law-determined agenda still ultimately retains the limitations of such an agenda. There is no escape from a need to be more modest in the claims made about the value of the law, acknowledging its potential to make differences in certain discrete areas, but not holding it out to be more than it is worth, as somehow a substitute for the more complex and broad-ranging business of transforming the political culture both nationally and internationally in order to create greater transparency and accountability in relation to state actions overseas. A consideration of the applicability of international human rights law may ultimately be a valid response to the need for greater scrutiny of extraterritorial action, provided that as such it is understood to be but one relatively minor part of a much wider necessary initiative. Such broader political ideas are being generated and movements being built around them, but to rely on that and continue to focus on legal strategies is, in one sense, perverse: free-riding on work by others addressing ultimately more significant matters, in favour of work focusing on relatively marginal issues. Moreover, this does nothing to challenge, and indeed may worsen, the dominance within parts of the mainstream human rights policy agenda of issues peripheral to the lives of most people in the world.

6 Conclusion

Whether and to what extent states bear international legal obligations with respect to the civil and political rights of people outside their sovereign territories has been subject to piecemeal treatment by certain courts such as the International Court of Justice and European Court of

---

108 See the sources cited above, n. 5.
109 See the source cited above, n. 107.

Human Rights, and other interpretative bodies such as the UN Committee on Human Rights. This chapter has sought to identify and critically evaluate the significance of the general concepts potentially suggested in these key texts, as well as some of the broader political ideas which underpin the general topic and illuminate what is at stake when choices are made as to the legal approaches to it. Much remains unclear, and the scope for the normative regime to develop in the future, as new situations are addressed and the ideas in existing texts are revisited, challenged and built upon, is significant.

Select bibliography

Fons Coomans and Menno Kamminga (eds), *Extraterritorial Application of Human Rights Treaties* (Intersentia, 2004).

Karen da Costa, *The Extraterritorial Application of Selected Human Rights Treaties* (Brill, 2012).

Mark Gibney and Sigrun Skogly (eds), *Universal Human Rights and Extraterritorial Obligations* (University of Pennsylvania Press, 2010).

Michał Gondek, *The Reach of Human Rights in a Globalising World: Extraterritorial Application of Human Rights Treaties* (Intersentia, 2009).

Marko Milanovic, *Extraterritorial Application of Human Rights Treaties: Law, Principles, and Policy* (OUP, 2011).

36

Enforcement and remedies

Dinah Shelton

The enforcement of human rights is first and foremost the responsibility of each state, which is bound to comply in good faith with norms of customary international law and with the treaties in force to which the state is a party (*pacta sunt servanda*).[1] Indeed, the Vienna Declaration and Programme of Action affirmed that 'the promotion and protection of human rights and fundamental freedoms is the first responsibility of government.'[2] If a state fails, by an act or omission attributable to it, to comply with any international obligation, the law of state responsibility requires that such breach cease and generates a new legal duty to afford reparation for any harm caused by the violation.[3]

The law of state responsibility was developed in the context of reciprocal inter-state obligations, the breach of which generally produces an injured state or states to complain of the violation. Such a legal framework is not fully satisfactory when applied to human rights law, however, because another state rarely suffers direct injury due to a state's failure to observe human rights. This lack of reciprocity has led to descriptions of human rights obligations

---

1 Vienna Convention on the Law of Treaties, Art. 26 (1969) 1155 UNTS 331; Human Rights Committee, General Comment 31, 'The Nature of the General Legal Obligation Imposed on States Parties to the Covenant' (2004) UN Doc CCPR/C/21/Rev1/Add.13.
2 Vienna Declaration and Programme of Action (1993) UN Doc A/CONF.157/23 para. 1.
3 *Factory at Chorzów, Jurisdiction*, Judgment No. 8, 1927, P.C.I.J., Series A, No. 9, International Law Commission, Articles on State Responsibility, GA Res. 56/83 (12 December, 2001), Arts 1 and 28–31. The Inter-American Court of Human Rights (IACtHR) reiterated the basic rules of state responsibility in its first contentious case: 'the States Parties [have] the fundamental duty to respect and guarantee the rights recognized in the Convention. Any impairment of those rights which can be attributed under the rules of international law to the action or omission of any public authority constitutes an act imputable to the State, which assumes responsibility in the terms provided by the Convention.' The Court added: 'An illegal act which violates human rights and which is initially not directly imputable to a State (for example, because it is the act of a private person or because the person responsible has not been identified) can lead to international responsibility of the State, not because of the act itself, but because of the lack of due diligence to prevent the violation or to respond to it as required by the Convention.' *Velásquez Rodríguez v Honduras*, IACtHR, Ser. C No. 4, (1988) paras 164, 172.

as 'unilateral' in nature:[4] that is, obligations directed internally at protecting individuals and groups within the territory and subject to the jurisdiction of the state,[5] rather than being obligations performed for the benefit of other states. The doctrine of obligations *erga omnes*[6] serves in part to maintain the framework of state responsibility by establishing that at least some human rights duties are owed to the international community as a whole,[7] obviating the need for an injured state to complain of a violation. In fact, most human rights treaties include the possibility of inter-state complaints among their compliance mechanisms, although states rarely submit such complaints, as discussed later in this chapter.

The deficiencies of the traditional framework of state responsibility have necessitated the creation of international procedures and mechanisms to monitor and promote compliance with human rights obligations, enhance enforcement, and provide remedies to individuals and groups whose rights have been violated. Global and regional agreements have thus mandated the formation of independent monitoring bodies and increasingly granted them investigatory functions and jurisdiction to hear complaints[8] brought by non-state actors. Acceptance of such jurisdiction is often made optional for the states parties, however, and

---

4 See, e.g.: *Austria v Italy*, App. No. 788/60 (1961) 4 Eur YB 116 at 140; see also *The Effect of Reservations on the Entry into Force of the American Convention on Human Rights (Arts 74 and 75)*, IACtHR (Advisory Opinion OC-2/82) (24 September 1980) Ser. A No. 2, paras 29, 33. In this Advisory Opinion 'The Court . . . emphasize[s], that modern human rights treaties in general, and the American Convention in particular, are not multilateral treaties of the traditional type concluded to accomplish the reciprocal exchange of rights for the mutual benefit of the contracting States. Their object and purpose is the protection of the basic rights of individual human beings irrespective of their nationality, both against the State of their nationality and all other contracting States. In concluding these human rights treaties, the States can be deemed to submit themselves to a legal order within which they, for the common good, assume various obligations, not in relation to other States, but towards all individuals within their jurisdiction. [T]he Convention must be seen for what in reality it is: a multilateral legal instrument of framework enabling States to make binding unilateral commitments not to violate the human rights of individuals within their jurisdiction.'

5 The Covenant on Civil and Political Rights (ICCPR) (1966) 999 UNTS 171 and the American Convention on Human Rights (1969) 1144 UNTS 123 require states parties to 'respect' and 'ensure' the rights proclaimed in the respective treaties. In contrast, under the Covenant on Economic, Social, and Cultural Rights (ICESCR) (1966) 993 UNTS 3 each state party 'recognizes' the rights therein and 'undertakes to take steps, individually and through international assistance and cooperation, especially economic and technical, to the maximum of its available resources, with a view to achieving progressively the full realization of the rights . . . by all appropriate means, including particularly the adoption of legislative measures'. The European Convention on Human Rights (1950) 213 UNTS 221 obliges states parties to 'secure' the rights in the Convention and Protocols, while the African Charter on Human and Peoples Rights (1981) 21 ILM 58 calls on its parties to 'recognize' and 'give effect' to the rights it enshrines.

6 *Case concerning Barcelona Traction, Light and Power Company, Ltd (Belgium v Spain) (Second Phase)* [1970] International Court of Justice (ICJ) Rep at 3 *et seq.*

7 As described by the ICJ, obligations *erga omnes* are those owed to the international community as a whole and 'derive, for example, in contemporary international law, from the outlawing of acts of aggression, and of genocide, as also from the principles and rules concerning the basic rights of the human person, including protection from slavery and racial discrimination. Some of the corresponding rights of protection have entered into the body of general international law . . .; others are conferred by international instruments of a universal or quasi-universal character.' Ibid. para. 33.

8 Probably in an effort to avoid suggesting that the procedure invoked by individuals is a judicial one, many treaties avoid the word complaint and instead use softer terms like petition or communication.

supplements other international procedures to promote compliance, such as discussion and debates in political fora, review by expert bodies of periodic state reports, and investigation of particular countries or issues. Most of these procedures involve some degree of fact-finding and result in recommendations to improve compliance, but three regional systems add courts with jurisdiction to issue binding judgments and afford remedies to victims.

This chapter examines the variety of compliance-monitoring procedures, enforcement mechanisms, and remedies in international human rights law.[9] In evaluating the institutions and procedures, it is important to recall that they have been established by treaties to which states must consent[10] and which often may be subject to reservation and/or denunciation.[11] While human rights bodies in exercising their functions interpret the rights guaranteed, the obligations imposed, and their own express, inherent, and implied powers in a manner intended to make human rights fully effective, states parties retain authority to amend the treaties and 'reform' the institutions they have created.[12] In the exercise of their functions all human rights monitoring bodies lack true powers of enforcement and depend upon the political will of the states parties for their funding, personnel, and cooperation to maintain compliance review and implementation of the decisions taken. Support from civil society organisations and the media is particularly important in generating the requisite political will.

1 Diplomatic Initiatives

Initially, the only 'procedure' available at the United Nations (UN) to promote and protect human rights was political debate, that could potentially conclude with a resolution of criticism or condemnation.[13] From the first session of the General Assembly member states invoked the human rights clauses of the UN Charter, especially those concerning self-determination and non-discrimination.[14] Delegations have referred to the human rights

---

9 The chapter does not discuss bilateral political, economic, and other initiatives nor does it address in any detail UN Security Council sanctions or humanitarian intervention as means to enforce human rights law.

10 The desire for universal acceptance of the core human rights agreements regionally and globally is often insisted on by states parties to the treaties, but there is no mechanism whereby to impose an obligation on a state to adhere to a particular treaty. The strongest initiative at present is the Council of Europe's decision to condition membership in the organisation on acceptance of the European Convention on Human Rights, as discussed herein.

11 Among UN human rights treaties, only the ICCPR and the ICESCR and the Convention on the Elimination of All Forms of Discrimination against Women (CEDAW) (1979) 1249 UNTS 13 contain no provision permitting denunciation. At the regional level, denunciation is also expressly allowed by the European and American Conventions.

12 Reform is sometimes advocated with the intent of weakening institutions or procedures after they have produced decisions critical of particular governments. A good example can be found in the 2011 decision of the Southern Africa Development Community (SADC) to suspend the operations of the SADC Tribunal and re-examine the scope of the Tribunal's jurisdiction after the court delivered a judgment against Zimbabwe condemning various land seizures as discriminatory and in violation of the African Charter on Human and Peoples' Rights.

13 Institutional efforts in this early period were primarily focused on standard-setting and defining internationally guaranteed rights.

14 During the first session of the UN General Assembly (UNGA), Egypt, supported by Latin American states, introduced a resolution that passed unanimously to condemn racial and religious persecution. UNGA Res. 103(I) (19 November 1946) UN Doc. A/RES/1031 at 200. India then sought a resolution to condemn South Africa for its policies of racial discrimination, accusing the government of gross and systematic human rights violations in breach of the principles and purposes of the UN

obligations of members at each subsequent General Assembly session.[15] The introduction of human rights issues for discussion and debate almost invariably confronted objections from target states that any mention of their human rights situation violated the principle of state sovereignty as reflected in Article 2(7) of the UN Charter, which prohibits the organisation from intervening in matters exclusively within the domestic jurisdiction of member states. Such objections have become less frequent with general recognition that human rights are a legitimate matter of international concern under the United Nations Charter, but they have not entirely disappeared.[16]

In the former UN Commission on Human Rights as well as in the General Assembly, diplomatic protocol and widespread resistance to discussing human rights in any but the most general terms made it difficult in the early decades to adopt resolutions condemning human rights violations. While individual countries were occasionally criticised, not until 1967 did the Economic and Social Council welcome a decision of the Commission on Human Rights to place the question of violations on its annual agenda.[17] The same resolution empowered the Commission and its subsidiary body, where appropriate, to 'make a thorough study of situations which reveal a consistent pattern of violations of human rights'; and to report and make recommendations to the Economic and Social Council.[18] Direct criticism of countries became more prevalent under this agenda item. Although resolutions were only rarely expressed in strongly critical language, states sought vigorously to avoid being the subject of a Commission resolution. The often-heated debates led to allegations of selectivity and politicisation and, eventually, to the replacement of the Commission by the Human Rights Council (HRC).

Specific states and 'human rights situations that require . . . attention' remain on the agenda of the Human Rights Council, as well as the agendas of the General Assembly and Security Council, but the principles that guide the UN's programme of work, including, inter alia, universality, impartiality, non-selectiveness, constructive dialogue, and

---

Charter. The resolution passed with the required two-thirds majority. See UNGA Res. 44(I) (8 December 1946) UN Doc. A/64/Add.1 at 69. The issue of South Africa's racial policies remained on the agenda of the UN in every session until the end of apartheid. See, generally, P. Gordon Lauren, *The Evolution of International Human Rights: Visions Seen* (U Penn Press, 1998) 217; D. Shelton, 'International Human Rights Law: Principled, Double, or Absent Standards?' (2007) 25 *Journal of Law and Inequality* 467.

15 In addition, as standard-setting progressed, the obligations of member states pursuant to Arts 55 and 56 have been explicitly referred to in the preambles of nearly all UN human rights treaties. Occasionally, states have asserted the Charter's human rights obligations in litigation before the ICJ. In the *Hostages Case* [1980] ICJ 3, the United States asked the ICJ to condemn Iran's seizure of 52 US hostages as a violation of fundamental human rights recognised by the international community: 'The existence of such fundamental rights for all human beings, with the existence of a corresponding duty on the part of every State to respect and observe them, are now reflected, inter alia, in the Charter of the United Nations.' Case *Concerning United States Diplomatic and Consular Staff in Tehran, Memorial of the United States (US v Iran)* (Pleadings) [1980] ICJ at 182, citing Arts 1, 55, and 56 of the UN Charter.

16 Russia's veto on 5 February 2012 of a proposed UN Security Council resolution on Syria was justified in part on the claim that it interfered in Syria's internal affairs.

17 The item was entitled 'Question of the violation of human rights and fundamental freedoms, including policies of racial discrimination and segregation and of apartheid, in all countries, with particular reference to colonial and other dependent countries and territories', ESC Res. 1235 (XLII) (1967).

18 Ibid.

cooperation,[19] indicate a preference among a majority of members to avoid country-specific resolutions. The Human Rights Council's framework asks states 'to secure the broadest possible support' for country-specific resolutions, preferably at least fifteen members.[20] Not surprisingly, there have been fewer country-specific resolutions introduced or adopted since the demise of the former Commission.

In addition to the bodies previously mentioned, the UN Secretary-General carries out a number of human rights activities both directly and through the Office of the High Commissioner of Human Rights (OHCHR). The OHCHR provides services to the Human Rights Council, its special procedures, and the treaty-monitoring bodies. In recent years, the Office has expanded its activities to gather and disseminate information on human rights, and to provide technical and advisory services to member states. Additionally, the Office has expanded the number and resource of its field offices. The work of the field offices began as primarily promotional, although the 'field presences' increasingly have taken on the role of on-site monitoring.[21] Finally, the High Commissioner and other senior members of the UN Secretariat often make public statements on human rights situations and issues of concern, including apparent violations of rights.

2 Enforcing member state obligations

Regional human rights systems were created in part because their proponents recognised that compliance and enforcement mechanisms at the global level would not be strong. Those proposing the adoption of a European convention, for example, made clear their intent to have a system of collective enforcement and remedies, judicial as well as political.[22] One technique the Council of Europe and other regional organisations have utilised to enforce human rights obligations has been to condition membership and/or participation in the organisation on compliance with human rights.

Membership in the Council of Europe[23] requires European states to conform to the basic principles of the organisation – democratic governance, rule of law, and respect for human rights. Through the Parliamentary Assembly (PACE) the Council of Europe seeks specific commitments from applicants respecting human rights and monitors compliance with the commitments made. If the commitments are not forthcoming or the problems are deemed

19 HRC Res. 5/1, Sec. V.
20 Ibid. para. 112(d).
21 Descriptions of the many field presences may be found on the website of the Office of the High Commissioner for Human Rights (OHCHR), http://www.ohchr.org/EN/Countries/Pages/WorkInField.aspx, accessed on 18 March 2012.
22 The 1948 *Message to Europeans,* adopted by the Congress of Europe, expressed this intent: 'We desire a Charter of Human Rights guaranteeing liberty of thought, assembly and expression as well as the right to form a political opposition; We desire a Court of Justice with adequate sanctions for the implementation of this Charter.' Council of Europe, 'Reform of the Control System of the European Convention on Human Rights' (1992) Doc. No. H (92) 14, at 4 (quoting *Message to Europeans,* Congress of Europe May 8–10, 1948). A resolution adopted by the same Congress stated its conviction 'that in the interest of human values and human liberty, the (proposed) Assembly should make proposals for the establishment of a Court of Justice with adequate sanctions for the implementation of this Charter, and to this end any citizen of the associated countries shall have redress before the Court, at any time and with the least possible delay, of any violation of his rights as formulated in the Charter.' Ibid.
23 Statute of the Council of Europe, Arts 4, 5 and 6.

too serious, PACE may recommend that a state not be admitted. The Committee of Ministers may suspend or terminate membership for breach of these same basic principles. In fact, only one state has been denied entry[24] and one state withdrew from the organisation[25] rather than face expulsion for violating human rights obligations. Commentators have criticised the Council of Europe for not applying its principles more rigorously,[26] while others maintain that the ability to exercise pressure from within on member states justifies the absence of more frequent sanctions or withholding membership.[27]

The Organization of American States (OAS) has taken a somewhat different approach, maintaining state membership in order to insist on compliance with the state's legal obligations, while conditioning participation of the government on respect for democracy, human rights and the rule of law.[28] In 1992, the OAS adopted the Washington Protocol[29] to the OAS Charter[30] and became the first regional organisation to allow suspension of participation in the event that a state's democratically elected government is overthrown by force.[31] As in the

---

24 Belarus has been denied entry into the Council of Europe because the Parliamentary Assembly considers the government deficient in commitment to the core principles of human rights, democracy and the rule of law. The Council of Europe also expects observer states to respect these principles.

25 On 12 December 1969, the same day the Committee of Ministers was to meet to decide the Greek cases (*Denmark, Norway, Sweden and the Netherlands v Greece*, App. Nos 3321/23/67 and 3344/67, 24 January 1968, 11 *YB Eur Conv Hum Rts*) and vote on a motion submitted by the Parliamentary Assembly to suspend or expel the government from the Council of Europe due to its human rights violations, Greece denounced the Convention. It later returned, following the restoration of democratic governance.

26 P. Leuprecht, 'Innovations in the European System of Human Rights Protection: Is Enlargement Compatible with Reinforcement?' (1998) 8 *Transnational Law & Contemporary Problems* 313.

27 See, e.g., the debate in the Parliamentary Assembly over admission of Belarus, Council of Europe Doc 9543, Report of the Debate of 26 September 2002.

28 At the Tenth Inter-American Conference in 1954, Resolution XXVII, *Strengthening of the System for the Protection of Human Rights* declared that the strengthening of democracy and the promoting of its effective exercise require measures to ensure the full operation of democratic institutions, among them systems for the protection of the rights and freedoms of man through international or collective action. The Conference concluded that fundamental human rights can be achieved only under a system of representative democracy. Resolution XXX addressed the right to vote and to participate in government, paying tribute to those countries that had taken measures to extend the right of suffrage and eliminate discrimination, as well as lauding their efforts to broaden and strengthen institutions of representative democracy. The subsequent Declaration of Caracas expressed the conviction of the American states that 'one of the most effective means of strengthening their democratic institutions is to increase respect for the individual and social rights of man, without any discrimination.'

29 Protocol of Washington (1992) 1-E Rev, OEA/Ser.A/2 Add. 3.

30 Charter of the Organization of American States (OAS Charter) (1948) 119 UNTS 3.

31 Even earlier, the Fifth Meeting of Consultation of the Ministers of Foreign Affairs in 1959 adopted the Declaration of Santiago, Chile, which affirms that effective exercise of representative democracy is the best vehicle for the promotion of social and political progress. Fifth Meeting of Consultation of Ministers of Foreign Affairs, *Final Act* (1959) Doc. No. OEA/Ser.C/II.5, at 4–6. The resolution made it explicit that 'the existence of antidemocratic regimes constitutes a violation of the principles on which the Organization of American States is founded, and a danger to united and peaceful relationships in the hemisphere.' Ibid. This resolution was invoked in 1962 to suspend the government of Cuba from participation. In 2009, the OAS General Assembly rescinded its 1962 resolution excluding Cuba from participating in the OAS, deciding that 'the participation of the Republic of Cuba in the OAS will be the result of a process of dialogue initiated at the request of the Government of Cuba, and in accordance with the practices, purposes, and principles of the OAS.' Res. AG/RES 2438 (XXXIX-O/09), 9 June 2009.

case of the Council of Europe, the OAS has been criticised for failing to take enforcement actions more frequently.

The Organisation for Security and Cooperation in Europe (OSCE) has engaged in linking benefits and obligations since its origin, using the metaphor of 'baskets' of commitments in the Helsinki Final Act.[32] To benefit from of one basket of commitments, participating states had to comply with the commitments contained in the other baskets. This issue linkage has been particularly successful in promoting compliance with human rights commitments. Participating states periodically convene intergovernmental conferences to undertake a thorough review of the implementation of the provisions of the Final Act. The meetings help focus public attention on the failure of certain states to live up to their human rights commitments.[33]

3 Independent monitoring bodies

Although each state is primarily responsible for ensuring the exercise of human rights, not all do so and there remains a critical need for international supervision and monitoring. Most human rights treaties foresee the creation of independent committees of experts to monitor compliance, although the monitoring functions are often stated in a general manner.[34] States writing such treaties have been notably reluctant, however, to include measures that amount to enforcement, such as allowing binding judgments to be taken or sanctions imposed for non-compliance. Nonetheless, some of the treaty-monitoring mechanisms have been strengthened through the adoption of additional protocols, such as those adopted to supplement the International Convention Against Torture and Other Cruel, Inhuman or Degrading Treatment or Punishment[35] and the CEDAW.[36]

---

32 The Helsinki Final Act consisted of four chapters, or so-called baskets. Basket I, entitled 'Questions Relating to Security in Europe,' consists of two sections ('Principles Guiding Relations Between Participating States' and 'Confidence-Building Measures and Certain Aspects of Security and Disarmament'). Basket II deals with 'Cooperation in the Field of Economics, of Science and Technology and of the Environment.' The subject of Basket III is 'Cooperation in Humanitarian and Other Fields.' Basket IV, the final chapter, spelled out the so-called follow-up process.

33 The European Court of Human Rights has relied on OSCE documents in several cases. See *Russian Conservative Party of Entrepreneurs & Others v Russia*, 2007-I ECtHR 1, in which the European Court of Human Rights quoted from the OSCE Final Report on parliamentary elections in the Russian Federation, using it in part to hold that the elections 'acclaimed as competitive and pluralistic by international observers' did not unduly restrict the individual applicant's right to take part in free elections. Ibid. para. 80. The Court also referred to OSCE findings in *Chapman v United Kingdom*, 2001-I ECtHR 41, concerning the situation of Roma and Sinti minorities in Europe generally and the UK specifically; and in *Sukhovetskyy v Ukraine*, 2006-VI ECtHR 193, holding that there was no violation in requiring electoral candidates to pay a financial deposit.

34 The Committee on the Elimination of Discrimination against Women (CEDAW Committee), for example, was established 'for the purpose of considering the progress made in the implementation of the . . . Convention'. CEDAW (n. 11) Art. 17, para. 1; the Committee on the Rights of the Child has the function 'of examining the progress made by states parties in achieving the realization of the obligations undertaken' in the United Nations Convention on the Rights of the Child, Art. 43, para. 1 (1989) 1577 UNTS 3.

35 Optional Protocol to the Convention against Torture and Other Cruel, Inhuman, or Degrading Treatment or Punishment (2002) 2375 UNTS 237.

36 Optional Protocol to the Convention on the Elimination of Discrimination against Women (1999) 2131 UNTS 83. See n. 11.

The texts establishing regional human rights bodies describe in very general terms their functions. The European Court of Human Rights is 'to ensure the observance of the engagements undertaken by the High Contracting Parties in the Convention and the Protocols thereto[.]'[37] In practice, the European Court is a typical judicial body that hears and decides complaints filed by victims alleging violations of their human rights. The Court also has limited advisory jurisdiction. The Inter-American Court of Human Rights and African Court for Human and Peoples' Rights are similar.

The European Court is the only full-time human rights body at the regional level. The other courts and commissions must rely on their secretariats for maintaining the system between sessions. Such an arrangement risks creating the impression – or even the reality – that the secretariats are the primary bodies responsible for deciding cases and fulfilling the mandates of the bodies.

In contrast to the limited but powerful role of the courts, the regional commissions have a wide variety of functions, generally grouped under the headings of promotion and protection of human rights. In the American system, the Inter-American Commission of Human Rights (IACHR) has 'competence with respect to matters relating to the fulfilment of the commitments made by the States Parties' to the American Convention,[38] as well as jurisdiction to monitor the observance of human rights by all OAS member states.[39] The Protocol of San Salvador and other OAS human rights treaties have extended the Commission's mandate to monitor compliance with the human rights obligations of their states parties. The Commission has summed up its promotional and protective functions as follows. The IACHR has the principal function of promoting the observance and the defence of human rights. In carrying out its mandate, the Commission:

(a) Receives, analyses and investigates individual petitions which allege human rights violations, pursuant to Articles 44 to 51 of the Convention . . . .

(b) Observes the general human rights situation in the member states and publishes special reports regarding the situation in a specific state, when it considers it appropriate.

(c) Carries out on-site visits to countries to engage in more in-depth analysis of the general situation and/or to investigate a specific situation. These visits usually result in the preparation of a report regarding the human rights situation observed, which is published and sent to the General Assembly.

(d) Stimulates public consciousness regarding human rights in the Americas. To that end, carries out and publishes studies on specific subjects, such as: measures to be taken to ensure greater independence of the judiciary; the activities of irregular armed groups; the human rights situation of minors and women, and; the human rights of indigenous peoples.

(e) Organizes and carries out conferences, seminars and meetings with representatives of Governments, academic institutions, non-governmental groups, [etc. . . .] in order to disseminate information and to increase knowledge regarding issues relating to the Inter-American human rights system.

---

37 European Convention on Human Rights (n. 5) Art. 19.
38 American Convention on Human Rights (n. 5) Art. 33.
39 OAS Charter (n. 30) Art. 106; Statute of the Inter-American Commission on Human Rights, Art. 1 (1992) OASTS Res. 447 (IX-0/79), OEA/Ser.P/IX.0.2/80.

(f) Recommends to the member states of the OAS the adoption of measures which would contribute to human rights protection.

(g) Requests states to adopt specific 'precautionary measures' to avoid serious and irreparable harm to human rights in urgent cases. The Commission may also request that the Court order 'provisional measures' in urgent cases which involve danger to persons, even where a case has not yet been submitted to the Court.

(h) Submits cases to the Inter-American Court and appears before the Court in the litigation of cases.

(i) Requests advisory opinions from the Inter-American Court regarding questions of interpretation of the American Convention.[40]

The African Commission for Human and Peoples' Rights has promotional and protective functions. Its promotional mandate includes the power to undertake studies, convene conferences and workshops, initiate publication programmes, disseminate information and collaborate with national and local institutions concerned with human and peoples' rights. As part of this promotional effort, the Commission may 'give its views or make recommendation to Governments'.[41] The Commission may thus bring to the attention of individual governments problem areas revealed by its studies as well as by its review of states' implementation reports. It has adopted a system of 'country rapporteurs' and undertakes visits to individual countries. The Commission also has appointed special or 'thematic' rapporteurs for summary and extra-judicial executions, prisons and conditions of detention, and the rights of women.[42]

The African Commission has a type of advisory jurisdiction that allows it to 'interpret all the provisions of the present Charter' when so requested by a state party, an institution of the African Union (AU) or an African organisation recognised by the AU.[43] The Commission is also empowered 'to formulate and lay down, principles and rules aimed at solving legal problems relating to human and peoples' rights and fundamental freedoms upon which African Governments may base their legislations'.[44] The Commission thus may further develop regional human rights standards by preparing draft legislation and proposing legal solutions to disputes. In fulfilling these interpretive and promotional functions, as well as in its petition procedures, the Commission may draw upon the full range of international law on human and peoples' rights. Article 60 lists as sources of 'inspiration': the UN and AU Charters, the Universal Declaration of Human Rights, African instruments on human and peoples' rights and 'other instruments adopted by the United Nations and by African countries in the field of human and peoples' rights as well as the provisions of various instruments

---

40 *Annual Report of the Inter-American Commission on Human Rights*, OEA/Ser.L/V/II, Doc. 51, corr. 1, 30 December 2009, at 7.

41 African Charter on Human and Peoples' Rights, Art. 45(1)(a), (1981) OAU Doc. CAB/LEG/67/3 rev. 5, 21 I.L.M. 58.

42 See F. Viljoen, 'State Reporting under the African Charter on Human and Peoples' Rights: A Boost from the South' (2000) 44 *J. Afr. L.* 110; J. Harrington, 'Special Rapporteurs of the African Commission on Human and Peoples' Rights' (2001) *1 Afr. Hum. Rts J.* 247.

43 The African Charter on Human and Peoples Rights mentions the Organisation of African Unity (OAU) in several of its provisions. The OAU was replaced by the African Union (AU) in 2002 and assumed all of its functions in respect to the African Commission and the African Charter on Human and Peoples' Rights. For consistency, this chapter will refer throughout to the AU rather than the OAU.

44 African Charter on Human and Peoples' Rights (n. 41) Art. 45(1)(b).

adopted within the Specialised Agencies of the United Nations of which the parties to the present Charter are members'. Article 61 adds that the Commission may take into consideration, 'as subsidiary measures to determine the principles of law', various other human rights agreements to which the member states of the AU are parties, together with 'African practices consistent with international norms on human and peoples' rights, customs generally accepted as law, general principles of law recognised by African states as well as legal precedents and doctrine'. This broad mandate permits the African Commission to identify and apply the law most favourable to the rights of individuals and groups in Africa.

The critical aspect of all treaty bodies is that they are composed of independent experts who serve in their individual capacity. While they are nominated by the states parties, they are obligated not to take instructions from their government, but to maintain their autonomy and independence. The quality of the individuals who serve is a significant factor in the success or not of the activities of the body to promote compliance with states' human rights obligations.

4 Periodic state reporting

The only mandatory compliance procedure for all UN member states and parties to the core UN human rights treaties is an obligation to file periodic state reports. States undoubtedly view reporting as the least intrusive and most non-confrontational device to promote compliance. Well before the adoption of UN and regional human rights treaties, the International Labour Organization had established a procedure of state reporting to monitor compliance with its treaties and recommendations, a system still in effect.[45]

States parties to UN human rights treaties must submit reports periodically on steps they have taken to implement the provisions of the relevant treaty. The treaties say little about how each respective treaty body is to handle the state reports. Nearly all call for 'consideration', 'study', or 'examination' of reports and allow for the adoption of 'general comments' or 'suggestions and general recommendations'. Nearly all of the treaties expressly allow the relevant committee to request additional information from states parties and the states parties to make observations on a treaty body's comments, recommendations, or suggestions. Beyond these few indications, the treaties are silent as to reporting procedures. The fact that treaty bodies are generally given authority to draft their own rules of procedure has facilitated the development of relatively robust reporting systems, although all of them are in a state of crisis due to the sheer number of reports and the limited time and resources available to consider them.[46]

45 The organisation still requires that member states report not only on ratified but also on unratified conventions and indicate the obstacles to ratification. The ILO independent Committee of Experts meets annually to examine reports and may follow up with 'Direct Requests' to governments and to organisations of workers and employers in the state concerned. If the Committee discovers serious or persistent problems, it may make 'Observations' to the government, which are published in the Committee's annual report to the Conference. In addition, the ILO has complaints procedures, but they are not open to individuals. See L. Swepston, 'The International Labour Organization', in H. Hannum (ed.), *Guide to International Human Rights Practice,* 4th edn (Univ. U. Penn. Press, 2004).

46 See Report of the Secretary General on measures taken to implement resolution 9/8 and obstacles to its implementation, including recommendations for further improving the effectiveness of, harmonising and reforming the treaty body system (2011) UN Doc. A/HRC/19/28, ('No matter what suggestions for enhanced efficiency will derive from the treaty body strengthening process, they will not detract from the treaty bodies' critical need for enhanced resources.' Ibid. para. 20.)

Among the positive measures that enhance reporting procedures are the guidelines on reporting and prepared lists of issues and questions for state parties that each treaty body has issued. Although not provided for in the treaties, all human rights treaty bodies have also adopted the practice introduced by the Committee on the Elimination of Racial Discrimination in 1972 of considering states parties' reports in public in the presence of representatives from the reporting state.[47] Treaty bodies also now follow the practice established by Committee on Economic, Social and Cultural Rights (CESCR) in 1990 of formulating 'concluding observations' following the consideration of the reports of states parties. These observations indicate the positive aspects and principal subjects of concern, including difficulties that have hampered the implementation of the treaty, making suggestions and recommendations to the state party. Several treaty bodies have also adopted formal procedures to monitor implementation of concluding observations and usually request states parties to provide information on compliance with the recommendations that have been made.

On the negative side, all reporting systems are confronted with the problem of absent or delayed reports. The High Commissioner for Human Rights reported at the end of 2011 that only one third of states parties comply in a timely manner with their reporting obligations. Treaty bodies have initiated various practices designed to encourage timely reporting, including listing the states parties whose reports are overdue and sending them reminders about their reporting obligation. Perhaps most effectively, nearly all committees have adopted the practice, pioneered by CERD in 1991, of proceeding with examination of implementation of the relevant treaty by the state party if it fails to submit a report. Equally problematic, the system is not capable of coping with all of the reports, should states fully comply with their reporting duties. Treaty bodies simply lack the time and resources to make an in-depth analysis of all the issues and all the reports. By March of 2012, for example, 281 reports were pending consideration by the treaty bodies.[48]

Despite these problems, when the Human Rights Council was created in 2006, the General Assembly adopted the reporting procedure, asking the Council to '[u]ndertake a universal periodic review [UPR] based on objective and reliable information, of the fulfil-ment of each state of its human rights obligations and commitments in a manner which ensure universality of coverage and equal treatment with respect to all states'.[49] The UPR is essentially a process of peer review based on the standards the UN Charter, the Universal Declaration of Human Rights, and the treaties to which the state under review is a party. The Council also considers information from relevant sources within the UN system and from other stakeholders including NGOs and national human rights institutions. It then engages in

---

47 Treaty bodies nonetheless may consider reports in the absence of a delegation if one fails to appear.
48 Report of the United Nations High Commissioner for Human Rights on the strengthening of the human rights treaty bodies pursuant to Assembly resolution 66/254, UN Doc. A/66/860, p. 23. The situation is no better at the regional level, which has added to the reporting burden on states. The reporting obligation appears in the European Social Charter (Arts 21, 22), European Charter for Regional or Minority Languages (Art. 15), the European Convention on Human Rights and Biomedicine (Art. 30), the Protocol to the American Convention on Economic, Social and Cultural Rights (Art. 19), the American Convention on Persons with Disabilities (Art. VI), the Arab Charter on Human Rights (Art. 48), and the African Charter on Human and Peoples Rights (Art. 62). The African Commission on Human and Peoples' Rights reported that as of the end of 2010, only 9 of 53 states parties had filed all their reports. Almost one-quarter of the states had never submitted a report.
49 UNGA Res. 60/251 (3 April 2006) para. 5(e). See F.D. Gaer, 'A Voice Not an Echo: Universal Periodic Review and the UN Treaty Body System', (2007) 7 *Hum. Rts L. Rev.* 109.

an 'interactive dialogue' with representatives of the state under review. Based on all of the information gathered, the Council adopts a report after some discussion and makes recommendations to the reporting state.[50] While it is perhaps premature to evaluate the procedure, the limited amount of time and information that is available to the Council suggests a procedure that is unlikely to be effective. Moreover, the fact that the Council is composed of member state delegations and not independent experts risks politicisation of the process.

5 General comments

The supervisory organs of all the major human rights bodies issue General Comments or 'General Recommendations'.[51] The Human Rights Committee began the practice in the 1980s, and all of the bodies have gradually expanded the scope of these texts beyond technical or reporting issues, to comment on the nature of the obligations of states parties and the substantive meaning of various articles. Strictly speaking General Comments are not a monitoring or compliance measure, but they assist in determining a state's obligations and thereby may facilitate implementation and enforcement.

6 Inter-state complaints

International law envisages the possibility that one state may initiate proceedings against another state to settle a legal dispute, assuming that both states accept the jurisdiction of an appropriate judicial or arbitral tribunal. Many human rights treaties provide for inter-state complaints whenever one state alleges that another is acting in breach of the relevant treaty. Among the major UN treaties, only CERD makes this procedure mandatory. Under all of the other treaties, states must separately accept the inter-state complaints procedure when or after ratifying the treaty. The regional systems are split on the mandatory nature of inter-state complaints. Inter-state complaints may be filed of right in the European and African systems but are optional in the American system.

To date, no inter-state complaint has been filed under any of the UN procedures. The European system has received about a dozen complaints involving politically charged cases such as divided Cyprus,[52] Northern Ireland,[53] the military coup in Greece in 1967,[54] and the conflict between Georgia and Russia.[55] Two inter-state cases have been filed in the Inter-American system, the first of which was declared inadmissible.[56] The

---

50 See generally, P. Sen, *Universal Periodic Review of Human Rights: Toward Best Practices* (Commonwealth Secretariat, 2009).

51 More than 100 general comments or recommendations have been adopted by the treaty bodies, a current list of which may be found at http://www2.ohchr.org/english/bodies/treaty/comments. htm, accessed on 28 March 2012.

52 *Cyprus v Turkey*, App. No. 25781/94, 2001-IV (ECtHR, Judgment of 10 May 2001).

53 *Ireland v The United Kingdom*, App. No. 5310/71 (ECtHR, Judgment of 18 January 1978).

54 *Denmark, Norway, Sweden, Netherlands v Greece*, App. Nos 3321/67, 3322/67, 3323/67 and 3344/67, 1969 YB Eur Conv on Hum Rts 1 (ECHR).

55 *Georgia v Russia*, App. No. 13255/07 (ECtHR, Admissibility decision of 3 July 2009). This is the case of the alleged harassment of Georgian migrants in Russia.

56 *Nicaragua v Costa Rica*, IACHR, Report No 11/07, Interstate Case 01/06, Admissibility decision of 8 March 2007; *Ecuador v Colombia*, IACHR, Interstate Case PI-2, Admissibility decision of 21 October 2010.

Democratic Republic of the Congo submitted the first complaints to the African Commission on Human and Peoples Rights (as well as to the International Court of Justice) over incursions into its territory by Rwanda, Burundi, and Uganda).[57] At the same time, more matters related to human rights are being submitted with increasing frequency to the International Court of Justice.[58] Such cases may originate in larger disputes between the states parties, and may be deemed an unfriendly act or lead to responsive accusations against the initiating, state. These concerns, plus the cost and time involved in litigation, explain why states rarely bring such cases. Nonetheless, inter-state litigation can still serve to enforce the human rights obligations of the responding state, whatever the motivation for bringing the action.

7 Individual communications or complaints

The right of individual petition has long been considered the key to effective enforcement of international human rights law, but (perhaps because of this?) petition procedures at the global level are almost entirely optional with the states parties. All such procedures are considered subsidiary to domestic enforcement and the emphasis remains on adequate and effective local remedies, which must be provided by the state and utilised by victims. The Inter-American Court has explained the rationale for the exhaustion requirement:

> The rule of prior exhaustion of domestic remedies allows the state to resolve the problem under its internal law before being confronted with an international proceeding. This is particularly true in the international jurisdiction of human rights, because the latter reinforces or complements the domestic jurisdiction.[59]

The mere fact that a domestic remedy does not produce a result favourable to the petitioner does not in and of itself demonstrate the inexistence or exhaustion of all effective domestic remedies.

The right of petition was slow in coming to the United Nations. Despite the fact that the UN received thousands of complaints from individuals alleging human rights violations for over a decade after 1945, no UN organ would consider such petitions (except in the context of trust and non-self-governing territories). In 1959 the UN Commission on Human Rights was finally authorised to review summaries of communications about human rights

---

57 *Democratic Republic of Congo v Burundi, Rwanda, and Uganda*, ACHPR, Communication 227/99, Report on the Merits of May 2003.

58 See, e.g., *Case Concerning Application of the Convention on the Prevention and Punishment of the Crime of Genocide (Bosnia and Herzegovina v Serbia and Montenegro)* (Judgment) [2007] ICJ; *Case Concerning Aerial Herbicide Spraying (Ecuador v Colombia)* (Application filed on 31 March 2008) ICJ, available at: http://www.icj-cij.org/docket/index.php?p1=3&p2=1&code=ecol&case=138&k=ee, accessed on 27 March 2012; *Application of the International Convention on the Elimination of All Forms of Racial Discrimination (Georgia v Russian Federation)* (Application filed on 15 August 2008) ICJ; *Jurisdictional Immunities of the State (Germany v Italy)* (Application filed on 23 December 2008) ICJ, this application regards whether Italy breached international law by allowing cases of forced labour to be brought against Germany despite claims of sovereign immunity; *Questions Relating to the Obligation to Prosecute or Extradite (Belgium v Senegal)* (Application filed on 19 February 2009) ICJ, this application regards whether Senegal has breached an international obligation either to prosecute or extradite the former President of Chad, Hissène Habré.

59 *Velásquez Rodríguez v Honduras* (n. 3) paras 61–62.

violations, but even then the prevailing view was that the Commission had no power to take any action in regard to any complaint concerning human rights.[60]

In 1970, the Economic and Social Council adopted Resolution 1503 (XLVIII) (1970), which authorised the Commission and Sub-Commission to examine, in closed sessions, communications from individuals and other sources concerning 'situations which appear to reveal a consistent pattern of gross and reliably attested violations of human rights'. When the Human Rights Council replaced the Commission in 2006, Resolution 1503 provided the foundation for the Council to continue having a confidential complaint procedure.

Today individuals and groups have a number of avenues within the United Nations system to lodge complaints about human rights violations. In addition to the 1503 legacy, six of the UN treaty bodies (Committee against Torture (CAT), CEDAW Committee,[61] CERD, Committee on Migrant Workers (CMW), Committee on the Rights of Persons with Disabilities (CRPD) and the Human Rights Committee[62]) are entitled to consider individual communications where states parties have accepted this procedure. A protocol to extend the right of petition to the ICESCR[63] entered into force 5 May 2013. Unlike the UN, regional systems make the complaint procedure mandatory. Specialised agencies also have petition or complaint procedures. UNESCO, for example, established a non-judicial procedure in 1978, which allows a victim or anyone with reliable knowledge about a human rights violation concerned with education, science, or culture to submit a petition to UNESCO.[64]

Unlike the global system, regional systems require states to accept the right of individuals or groups to bring petitions alleging violation of the rights guaranteed by the regional instruments. In Europe alone, over 800 million individuals have the right to bring complaints to the European Court of Human Rights. The result of the expansion of the Council of Europe has been a rising case-load that threatens the future of the system. On 1 January 2013, approximately 126,850 applications were pending. The interplay between complaints and compliance is evident in the system, where repetitious complaints are a large problem, as is non-compliance with prior judgments. Of the cases pending in 2013, over one-third of them concern just two states: Russia (21.6%) and Turkey (13.2%).

Other regional systems are similarly burdened with a rising case-load linked to non-compliance and with a lack of staff and other resources to respond to the problems. The African Commission had a single attorney on a short-term contract at the end of 2010. The Inter-American Commission, a part-time body of seven members, has a case-load of approximately 1,600 complaints a year, which it must process while also undertaking promotional activities.

8 UN special procedures and regional rapporteurs

The former UN Commission on Human Rights over several decades developed its system of UN 'special procedures': independent experts appointed to work individually or in working

---

60 See ESC Res. 728F (XXVIII) (1959).

61 See above n. 34.

62 The CESCR, upon the entry into force of the Optional Protocol to the ICESCR, and the Committee on Enforced Disappearances, once operational, will also be empowered to consider individual complaints.

63 See above n. 5.

64 UNESCO Decision 3.3, 104 UNESCO Executive Board, UNESCO Doc. 104 X/Decision (1978). See S.P. Marks, 'The UN Educational, Scientific, and Cultural Organization', in H. Hannum (ed.), *Guide to International Human Rights Practice,* 4th edn (U. Penn. Press, 2004).

groups to examine human rights situations in particular countries or in connection with certain issues or themes. The first such mandate was the working group on enforced disappearances, created in 1980 at the initiative of NGOs and the UN Secretariat, who believed that this was the only politically feasible way to address gross violations of human rights then taking place in Argentina and Chile.

When the Human Rights Council replaced the Commission, it was instructed to 'review and, where necessary, improve and rationalize'[65] all of the special procedures; in fact, all of the thematic procedures were continued and few new ones were created, while some country-specific mandates were discontinued without formal debate.[66]

The mandates of the special procedures vary (beyond the differences in the assigned countries or themes), in accordance with the specific resolutions of the Council reauthorising or establishing them. Nonetheless, there are some common features in the mandates and the corresponding work methods, especially since the Human Rights Council adopted a Code of Conduct in 2006, establishing rules that govern all procedures;[67] the Council also adopted a uniform method and set of criteria for selection of mandate holders.[68]

Thematic special procedures investigate the situation of human rights in all parts of the world, irrespective of whether a particular government is a party to human rights treaties. Indeed, most of the Human Rights Council resolutions establishing or reauthorising thematic mandates do not specify the human rights instruments, be they declarations or treaties, that are to be utilised in the work of the mandate.

Mandate holders are expected to take the measures necessary to monitor and respond quickly to allegations of human rights violations, either globally or in a specific country or territory, and to report on their activities. Yet, the rate of responses by governments to communications from the special procedures on specific cases of alleged human rights abuse has been discouraging. In 2009, mandate holders sent a total of 689 communications (excluding cases dealt with by the Working Group on Enforced or Involuntary Disappearances), and less than one-third of them (32 per cent) received responses from governments.[69]

---

65 UNGA Res. 60/251 (n. 49) para. 6.
66 As of mid-2012, there were country rapporteurs for Myanmar (mandate established 1992), Palestinian Occupied Territories (1993), Somalia (1993), Haiti (1995), Burundi (2004), Democratic People's Republic of Korea (2004), and Sudan (2005). Additionally, there were 32 thematic experts or working groups established to examine enforced or involuntary disappearances (established 1980); extrajudicial, summary, or arbitrary executions (1982); torture (1985); freedom of religion (1986); the sale of children and child prostitution and pornography (1990); arbitrary detention (1991); racism and xenophobia (1993); freedom of opinion and expression (1993); the independence of the judiciary (1994); violence against women (1994); toxic and dangerous products and wastes (1995); children and armed conflict (1997); poverty (1998); right to education (1998); migrants (1999); human rights defenders (2000); economic reform policies and foreign debt (2000); right to housing (2000); right to food (2000); indigenous peoples (2001); physical and mental health (2002); people of African descent (2002); internally displaced persons (2004); human trafficking (2004); mercenaries (2005); minorities (2005); international solidarity (2005); protection of human rights while countering terrorism (2005); transnational corporations (2005); contemporary forms of slavery (2007); the right to water (2008); cultural rights (2009); and discrimination against women (2010).
67 HRC resolution 5/1 (18 June 2007) paras 54–64.
68 Institution-building of the United Nations Human Rights Council, HRC Res. 5/1 (18 June 2007) Annex.
69 OHCHR, *United Nations Special Procedures: Facts and Figures* 7 (2009).

The Inter-American and African Commissions also utilise the procedure of designating thematic rapporteurs. In the Inter-American system, all but one of the rapporteurships – the exception being freedom of expression – concern vulnerable groups (women, children, afro-descendants, indigenous peoples, human rights defenders, migrant workers, and detainees). The African system focuses more on specific rights or areas of concern. It is the first to appoint a rapporteur on extractive industries and human rights.

9 Early warning and urgent action procedures

From 1993, CERD has developed procedures relating to early warning measures and urgent action, the former directed at preventing existing problems in states parties from escalating into new conflict or preventing a resumption of conflict, and the latter to respond to problems requiring immediate attention to prevent or limit the scale or number of serious violations of the Convention.[70] Since that time other treaty bodies have followed with similar initiatives.[71] In addition to the urgent action procedures, which can be general in nature, nearly all human rights bodies have developed a system of precautionary or provisional measures to request states to take action to avoid an imminent threat of serious and irreparable injury to individuals or groups.[72] More recent human rights treaties have expressly provided for such measures, while the ability to issue precautionary measures has been implied by other treaty bodies as necessary to ensure the effectiveness of complaints procedures. Moreover, most human rights bodies hold that compliance with such measures is required to ensure the proper administration of complaints procedures.

10 Remedies

Human rights litigation and complaint procedures may serve various purposes. A first aim is largely forward-looking, to uphold the international rule of law and bring state laws and practices into conformity with human rights norms. Human rights bodies regularly express their concern with this aspect of the cases before them. In recent years, the Inter-American Commission has emphasised non-repetition of violations in its pleadings before the Inter-American Court. The second aim of complaints procedures should be to afford redress to the petitioners. To a large extent, this aim requires assessing the consequences of the violation in order to erase those consequences or to compensate the victims if the harm cannot be eliminated. Redress also aims to uphold the rule of law, but it is foremost concerned with placing the victims as closely as possible to the position they would have enjoyed had the violation not occurred. A third aim, closely related to the first two, is to identify and express condemnation of the violations and the violators. While punishment is not the goal of human rights litigation, the language used by tribunals in

---

70 Report of the Committee on the Elimination of Racial Discrimination (15 September 1993) A/48/18, Annex III.
71 Four treaty bodies – the Committee against Torture, the Committee on the Elimination of Discrimination against Women, the Committee on the Rights of Persons with Disabilities and the Committee on Enforced Disappearances (once established) – may initiate confidential inquiries if they receive reliable information containing well-founded indications of serious, grave or system-atic violations of their respective conventions in a state party.
72 See generally Eva Rieter, *Preventing Irreparable Harm: Provisional Measures in International Human Rights Adjudication* (Intersentia, 2010).

their judgments may serve to express condemnation or outrage in the face of particularly serious violations.[73]

As with many other issues in human rights law, remedies are only partly and often vaguely addressed in the basic instruments of regional human rights bodies. Regional courts are granted remedial powers by express provisions in their respective treaties, but no equivalent provisions exist for the commissions or for UN bodies. The ICJ has held that the power to afford reparations is implicit in jurisdiction to hear a case, as a necessary concomitant to deciding disputes.[74] This power extends to all aspects of reparations, as the ICJ has stated:

> If the Court should limit itself to saying that there is a duty to pay compensation without deciding what amount of compensation is due, the dispute would not be finally decided. An important part of it would remain unsettled[.] It would not give full effect to the Resolutions but would leave open the possibility of a further dispute.[75]

Other courts engaged in dispute settlement and compliance have also assumed that they may award reparations and make related orders.

The remedial powers of international tribunals vary according to the express provisions of the relevant treaties, but the jurisprudence is similar and was the basis for the rules codified in the UN Basic Principles on reparation.[76] International law has long expressed a preference for restitution as a remedy, where this is possible.[77] Some human rights violations, for example wrongful detention, allow for restitution of the right violated by freeing the person detained. Others rights, like life, cannot be restored once lost and thus require a difficult assessment of the monetary value of the right lost, as a substitute for restitution. Regional tribunals have struggled with the question of assessing compensatory damages as well as the scope of their powers to remedy violations through non-monetary means, often under the heading of satisfaction.[78]

The term 'satisfaction' as used in arbitral treaties and in the European Convention draws upon international practice in regard to state responsibility for injury to aliens. In this body of law, satisfaction could require punishment of the guilty and assurances as to future conduct, monetary awards, or declaration of the wrong, especially when coupled with an apology from the offending state.[79] Many such non-monetary remedies afforded under the heading of satisfaction in inter-state proceedings are now applied in the human rights context, especially apologies, guarantees of non-repetition, and/or punishment of wrongdoers.[80]

---

73 See generally, D. Shelton, *Remedies in International Human Rights Law,* 2nd edn (OUP, 2005).

74 'In general, jurisdiction to determine the merits of a dispute entails jurisdiction to determine reparation.' *Military and Paramilitary Activities in and Against Nicaragua (Nicaragua v US)* [1986] ICJ 14, para. 283.

75 *Corfu Channel Case (Albania v UK)* [1949] ICJ 4, 26.

76 *Basic Principles and Guidelines on the Right to a Remedy and Reparation for Victims of Gross Violations of International Human Rights Law and Serious Violations of International Humanitarian Law* (2005) UN Doc. E/CN.4/2005/59.

77 See *Chorzów Factory Case*, n. 3.

78 See Shelton n. 73.

79 Ibid. ch. 3; James Crawford, *The International Law Commission's Articles on State Responsibility: Introduction, Text and Commentaries* (Cambridge University Press, 2002).

80 See, e.g. *Loayza Tamayo Case (Reparations),* 42 Inter-AmCtHR (ser. C)(1999).

The Human Rights Committee, in General Comment 31,[81] summarised the duties of states parties to afford accessible and effective remedies and to cease ongoing violations. The Committee noted that a failure by a state party to investigate allegations of violations could in and of itself give rise to a separate breach of the Covenant.

In terms of reparations, the obligation to provide an effective remedy is seen as central to the efficacy of domestic enforcement. This is interpreted to mean that the Covenant generally entails appropriate compensation, but may also involve restitution, rehabilitation, and measures of satisfaction, such as public apologies, public memorials, guarantees of non-repetition, and changes in relevant laws and practices, as well as bringing to justice the perpetrators of human rights violations. A failure to investigate, as well as a failure to bring to justice perpetrators of violations recognised as criminal under either domestic or international law, may give rise to a separate breach of the Covenant.

At the regional level, Article 41 of the European Convention denies the European Court the power to annul member state laws or decisions that are in conflict with the Convention, a power no international court has been granted. The Court's consistent view has been that this provision also serves to deny it the power to direct the state itself to cure the underlying problem. With a rising case-load and repetitive cases resulting from state failure to comply with its obligations, the Committee of Ministers suggested the Court should take a broader approach to remedying violations and indicate the measures the state should take, a practice that is slowly emerging.

The American Convention grants the Inter-American Court the ability to order compensation and other remedial measures. The African Court has perhaps the broadest remedial powers, being given the authority to 'order any appropriate measures' to remedy a violation found. As of 2013, the Court had not decided the merits of any case, so the scope and application of this power remains to be seen.

The Inter-American and African Commissions, lacking express provisions on remedies, have generally recommended in general terms the appropriate action to be taken by a state found to have violated human rights. Neither commission has quantified compensation in any case. In other cases, the African Commission has recommended specific remedial measures that appear close to injunctive orders.[82]

In general, human rights bodies appear generally to be attending more to the issue of reparations. The conclusion of the UN's two-decade-long process of drafting Guidelines and Principles on reparations has likely assisted in this evolution, by providing a consensus view of the states on what is required, but the rising case-load of human rights tribunals is also a spur to developing better remedies for violations, ones that will avoid repetitive cases.

11 For the future

Manfred Nowak has expressed well some of the concerns of those who work on or with human rights bodies about their present effectiveness and future viability:

---

81 Human Rights Committee, General Comment 31, Nature of the General Legal Obligation on States Parties to the Covenant, UN Doc. CCPR/C/21/Rev.1/Add.13.
82 For Commission decisions calling for cessation of the breach and restoration of the liberty of wrongfully held detainees, see: *Constitutional Rights Project v Nigeria,* Communication No. 60/91 (1996), Communication No. 87/93 (1996) and *Center for Free Speech v Nigeria*, Communication 206/97, 13th Annual Activity Report of the African Commission 1999–2000 (calling for the release of detainees). On the African Commission's practice generally, see G.J. Naldi, 'Reparations in the Practice of the African Commission on Human and Peoples' Rights' (2001) 14 *Leiden J. Int'l L.* 681.

[T]he proliferation of UN human rights treaties with different but overlapping reporting obligations and with separate treaty monitoring bodies working on an unpaid, voluntary and part-time basis, together with a trend towards universal ratification of these treaties, has led to an unmanageable and deeply frustrating situation for all involved. Governments complain about the high number of reports they are obliged to draft periodically, and which often are examined many years after their submission, and the expert bodies complain about the lack of discipline among governments and the limited time they are given to examine the numerous reports . . . [O]nly a major structural reform can help to solve the on-going crisis.[83]

Nowak's comments can be extended to the complaints procedures and other compliance mechanisms discussed herein. All human rights bodies, global and regional, are faced with expanding mandates and limited resources. The UN Office of the High Commissioner for Human Rights functions because of outside contributions; only 20 per cent of its funding comes from the regular UN budget.[84] This is replicated in regional institutions: some 55 per cent of the funding for the Inter-American Commission on Human Rights comes from governments and other entities outside the OAS, which contributes only 5 per cent of its budget to human rights.[85] The lack of political will to create effective compliance bodies and procedures is evident not only in the limited funding afforded, but also in sporadic attention given to compliance with recommendations, decisions, and judgments of human rights bodies. States sometimes seek to cut back on the functions of human rights bodies or, in rare instances, have denounced human rights treaties.

While there are many causes for concern, the overall picture remains positive. The growth of regional human rights systems in new regions brings additional institutional mechanisms and support for human rights where it has been lacking or marginal. The affirmation of universal norms in this process is also a cause for celebration. Finally, the support of many states and governments for global and regional mechanisms to assist the states in fulfilling their primary obligations to promote and protect human rights is very real. It will probably always be a struggle to maintain progress and avoid backsliding, but there can be little doubt that international human rights law and institutions have brought improvement to the lives of millions of persons throughout the world.

Select bibliography

P. Alston and J. Crawford, *The Future of UN Human Rights Treaty Monitoring* (OUP, 2000).

M. Kamminga, *Interstate Accountability for Violations of Human Rights* (U. Penn. Press, 1992).

B.G. Ramcharan, 'State Responsibility for Violations of Human Rights Treaties', in B. Cheng and E. Brown (eds), *Contemporary Problems of International Law: Essays in Honour of Georg Schwarzenberger on His Eightieth Birthday* (Stevens & Sons Ltd, 1988).

D. Shelton, *Remedies in International Human Rights Law*, 2nd edn (OUP, 2006).

---

83 M. Nowak, *U.N. Covenant on Civil and Political Rights: CCPR Commentary*, 2nd edn (Kehl am Rhein, 2005) 712–53 at 718–19.

84 OHCHR, Annual Report 2011.

85 IACHR, Annual Report 2012.

37

Victims' participation and reparations in international criminal proceedings

Megan Hirst

The establishment of the International Criminal Court (ICC) marked the beginning of a new era for those victims[1] of massive crimes whose cases reach an international criminal forum. They could now seek reparations directly from a person convicted of these crimes. In addition, they could present their 'views and concerns' in international judicial proceedings.

However, a debate has emerged as to whether these developments constitute an advance for the human rights of victims, or an erosion of the fair trial rights of accused persons. Supporters see victim participation and reparations as remedying deficiencies identified in previous international criminal mechanisms,[2] and as a move towards the attainment of 'human rights'.[3] However, they often do not explain how it is that victim engagements in an international trial realises human rights, or they do so by reference to untested assumptions regarding the likely outcomes of these mechanisms. There is thus a need for improved analysis,

---

1 In this chapter the term 'victim' refers to persons who have suffered harm as a result of a crime. This is the core concept in the definitions used by those international tribunals which permit victim participation and/or reparations, and is based on Art. 8 of the Basic Principles and Guidelines on the Right to a Remedy and Reparation for Victims of Gross Violations of International Human Rights Law and Serious Violations of International Humanitarian Law (Basic Principles and Guidelines), UNGA Res. 60/147 (16 December 2005). See also ICC, Rules of Procedure and Evidence (RPE), ICC-ASP/1/3 (Part II-A) (2002), Rule 85; Special Tribunal for Lebanon, Rules of Procedure and Evidence (RPE), STL/BD/2009/01/Rev.4 (2009), Rule 2; Extraordinary Chambers of the Courts of Cambodia Internal Rules (ECCC Internal Rules) (2011), Glossary.
2 S. SáCouto and K. Cleary, 'Victims' Participation in the Investigations of the International Criminal Court' (2008) 17 *Transnational Law and Contemporary Problems* 73–106, at 79–82; C. Jorda and J. de Hemptinne, 'The Status and Role of the Victim', in A. Cassese, P. Gaeta and J. Jones (eds), *The Rome Statute of the International Criminal Court: A Commentary* (Vol. II) (OUP, 2002), 1390–91.
3 G. Bitti and G. González Rivas, 'The Reparations Provisions for Victims Under the Rome Statute of the International Criminal Court', in Permanent Court of Arbitration (ed.), *Redressing Injustices Through Mass Claims Processes: Innovative Responses to Unique Challenges* (OUP, 2006), 320; S. Karstedt, 'From Absence to Presence, From Silence to Voice: Victims in International and Transitional Justice Since the Nuremberg Trials' (2010) 17 *International Review of Victimology* 9–30.

both theoretical and empirical: how (if at all) do victim participation and reparations in international criminal proceedings[4] represent the attainment of human rights? What are the outcomes in practice when victims access international criminal proceedings via these mechanisms? This chapter seeks to contribute some ideas on the first of these questions.

Opponents of victim engagements in international trials have argued that these mechanisms risk undermining fair trial guarantees and the rights of accused persons: especially the presumption of innocence, the principle of equality of arms and the right to an expeditious trial.

The present chapter will argue that neither of these opposing perspectives captures the complete picture. On the one hand, in positioning victim participation and reparations in international criminal proceedings as a human rights issue, we should see these possibilities not only in terms of remedial rights, but also as manifestations of procedural or due process rights. Additionally, it is argued that when considering their potential *adverse* impacts we should think not only of their (arguably limited) impact on the fair trial rights of the accused, but also of the impact on the rights and interests of *other victims*.

1 History and content of victim participation and reparations in international criminal proceedings

1.1 History of victims' role in international criminal proceedings

The foundational international criminal mechanisms established following the Second World War afforded no appreciable role to victims. They utilised a largely common law procedural model and involved prosecutions reliant almost entirely on documentary evidence. Victims played a minimal role as witnesses, had no status as participants in their own right, and were unable to request reparations in the criminal proceedings.[5]

The ad hoc International Criminal Tribunals for the former Yugoslavia ('ICTY') and Rwanda ('ICTR') did not significantly depart from this approach in theoretical terms. However, the nature of the crimes before them and the evidence available meant that in many cases victims became involved as prosecution witnesses. Eventually these Tribunals were criticised regarding the role they afforded to victims. It has been said that victim communities in the former Yugoslavia and Rwanda were unaware, felt no affinity with or were actively distrusting of the work of the Tribunals.[6] Those victims who became witnesses are described as having been 'extraneous' to the proceedings, or a mere instrument of the Prosecution.[7] These criticisms are best understood in the context of movements within some national

---

4 There is a need for the same analysis concerning victim participation in domestic proceedings: I. Edwards, 'An Ambiguous Participant: The Crime Victim and Criminal Justice Decision-Making' (2004) 44 *British Journal of Criminology* 967–82 at 972.

5 E. Stover, *The Witnesses: War Crimes and the Promise of Justice in The Hague* (University of Pennsylvania Press, 2005), 17–21; Y. Danieli, 'Reappraising the Nuremberg Trials and Their Legacy: The Role of Victims in International Law' (2006) 27 *Cardozo Law Review* 1633–49; S. Karstedt, 'From Absence to Presence, From Silence to Voice: Victims in International and Transitional Justice Since the Nuremberg Trials' (2010) 17 *International Review of Victimology* 9–30.

6 Stover (n. 5) 144–45; SáCouto and Cleary (n. 2) at 81–82.

7 Jorda and de Hemptinne (n. 2), 1390–91. Regarding the experience for victims of testifying before the ICTY see M-B. Dembour and E. Haslam, 'Silencing Hearings? Victim-Witnesses at War Crimes Trials' (2004) 15 *European Journal of International Law* 151–77.

justice systems which promoted victims' rights in criminal proceedings.[8] These victims' rights movements achieved the creation of non-binding international instruments which set standards for the human rights of victims, including victims of international crimes. The two most significant of these were:

(a) the Declaration of Basic Principles of Justice for Victims of Crime and Abuse of Power ('Declaration of Basic Principles'), which included provisions relating to restitution, compensation and assistance, but also for victims' 'access to justice and fair treatment' encompassing the principle of 'allowing the views and concerns of victims to be represented and considered at appropriate stages of the proceedings where their personal interests are affected, without prejudice to the accused . . .';[9]
(b) the Basic Principles and Guidelines on the Right to a Remedy and Reparation for Victims of Gross Violations of International Human Rights Law and Serious Violations of International Humanitarian Law[10] ('Basic Principles and Guidelines').

European and African institutions also enacted instruments concerning compensation and standing rights for victims of crime.[11] Meanwhile, common law jurisdictions have increasingly established procedural mechanisms to enable forms of victim participation in criminal proceedings.[12]

It was against this backdrop that negotiations for the creation of the ICC were finalised. Ultimately ICC granted various new roles to victims, of which the two most important were:

(a) the possibility for the Court to order that a person convicted by it pay reparations to victims,[13] and the creation of an independent Trust Fund for Victims to manage and/or contribute other resources to reparations awards;[14]
(b) the possibility for victims, under certain conditions, to express their 'views and concerns' in proceedings before the Court[15] (based closely on Article 6(b) of the Declaration of Basic Principles).

---

8 J. Doak, *Victims' Rights, Human Rights and Criminal Justice: Reconceiving the Role of Third Parties* (Hart, 2008), 7–19.
9 Declaration of Basic Principles of Justice for Victims of Crime and Abuse of Power, UNGA Res. 40/34 (29 November 1985), Annex, Art. 6(b).
10 Basic Principles and Guidelines (n. 1). These developments also coincided with the publication of the Updated Set of Principles for the protection and promotion of human rights through action to combat impunity (Updated Set of Principles), UN Doc. E/CN.4/2005/102/Add.1 (8 February 2005), Annex.
11 Council of Europe, European Convention on the Compensation of Victims of Violent Crimes (1983) ETS No. 116; Council of Europe, Recommendation No. R (85) 11 of the Committee of Ministers to Member States on the Position of the victim in the Framework of Criminal Law and Procedure (28 June 1985); European Union, Council Framework Decision of 15 March 2001 on the standing of victims in criminal proceedings, OJEC L82/1; European Union, Council Directive 2004/80/EC of 29 April 2004 relating to compensation to crime victims, OJEU L261/15; African Commission on Human and Peoples' Rights, Principles and Guidelines on the Right to a Fair Trial and Legal Assistance in Africa, DOC/OS(XXX)247, Part P.
12 J.C. Ochoa, *The Rights of Victims in Criminal Justice Proceedings for Serious Human Rights Violations* (Brill, 2013) at 137–42; M.E.I. Brienen and E.H. Hoegen, *Victims of Crime in 22 European Criminal Justice Systems* (WLP, 2010).
13 Rome Statute, Art. 75.
14 Ibid., Art. 79; ICC, Regulations of the Trust Fund for Victims, ICC-ASP/4/Res.3 (2005).
15 Ibid., Art. 68(3).

These developments have since been replicated in other international tribunals.[16] Victims may express their 'views and concerns' before the Special Tribunal for Lebanon ('STL')[17] and may participate and seek reparations as 'civil parties' before the Extraordinary Chambers in the Courts of Cambodia ('ECCC').[18]

1.2 Reparations in international criminal proceedings

The concept of reparations is not novel in international law. It has long been recognised that 'any breach of an engagement involves an obligation to make reparation'.[19] However, this classical statement of principle concerned state liability to make reparation to another state. Of more recent origin is its extension to encompass an individual's entitlement to reparations from a state, for human rights violations or violations of international humanitarian law.[20] This entitlement to reparation has been developed through the jurisprudence of human rights treaty bodies, and codified as part of the Basic Principles and Guidelines.[21]

Indeed, the Basic Principles and Guidelines not only codify obligations concerning reparations paid to individual victims by a state. They additionally provide that 'In cases where a person, a legal person, or other entity is found liable for reparation to a victim, such party should provide reparation to the victim or compensate the state if the state has already provided reparation to the victim.'[22] Despite this, until recently no international mechanism existed for determining the liability of *individuals* to provide such reparations. It is in this respect that the ICC provided an innovation concerning reparations – by establishing an international forum in which victims of an international wrong could be awarded reparations to be paid by an individual found to be criminally responsible for that wrong. To date, only the ECCC has followed this lead.[23]

At the ICC a Chamber may award reparations – including restitution, compensation or rehabilitation – against a convicted person.[24] Reparations may be paid through the Trust Fund for Victims,[25] an independent institution established by the Rome Statute,[26] which

---

16 Cf. the Special Court for Sierra Leone, which does not have provisions of this kind in relation to victims. The Special Panels for Serious Crimes in East Timor initially granted victims special standing rights and the possibility of being awarded compensation under UNTAET Regulation No.2000/30 on Transitional Rules of Criminal Procedure, especially ss. 12, 25, 49. However, those rules were never used. They were replaced by new domestic legislation on criminal procedure which has regulated trials before the Special Panels since 1 January 2006, and which does not contain equivalent provisions relating to victims: Decree Law No. 13/2005 Approving the Criminal Procedure Code.

17 Statute of the Special Tribunal of Lebanon, Art. 17.

18 ECCC Internal Rules, rr. 23–23 *quinquies*.

19 *Case Concerning the Factory at Chorzów (Germany v Poland)* (Claim for indemnity) (Merits), PCIJ Rep. Series A Nos 17, 28, para. 73.

20 For example: *Legal Consequences of the Construction of a Wall in the Occupied Palestinian Territory* (Advisory Opinion) [2004] ICJ Rep. 2004 (I), paras 152–153.

21 Basic Principles and Guidelines (n. 1), Art. 15–23.

22 Ibid., Art. 15.

23 A power to make orders for compensation against convicted persons was initially granted to the Special Panels for Serious Crimes in East Timor, but never used. See n. 16 above.

24 Rome Statute, Art. 75(2).

25 Ibid.

26 Ibid, Art. 79.

may also contribute resources to a reparations award from voluntary donations collected by it.[27] The Trust Fund for Victims also maintains a second mandate,[28] according to which it disburses donations collected for the benefit of victims in situations where the ICC is operating, whether or not they are victims of a crime which is the subject of a case before the ICC.[29] This second mandate has been implemented in Uganda and the Democratic Republic of Congo, by funding organisations undertaking projects for the benefit of victims.[30]

The first ICC decision on reparations, in the case of *The Prosecutor v Thomas Lubanga Dyilo*[31] (although suspended pending its appeal at the time of writing[32]) demonstrated that, in practice, reparations procedures following a conviction may not differ substantially from the work undertaken by the Trust Fund for Victims under its second mandate. After establishing principles relevant to reparations in the case, including that they shall be collective in nature, Trial Chamber I substantially delegated decision making regarding the scope, nature and beneficiaries of reparations to the Trust Fund for Victims, with monitoring and supervision to be performed by a newly constituted Chamber.

At the ECCC, the possibilities available for reparations are more limited. Only 'collective and moral reparations' may be ordered and these may not take the form of monetary compensation.[33] No mechanism analogous to the ICC Trust Fund for Victims exists at the ECCC. As at the ICC, reparations may only be awarded against a convicted person.[34] On this basis, limited symbolic reparations were provided as part of the first judgment of the ECCC in the *Case of KAING Guek Eav alias Duch*, namely: (a) the naming of civil parties in the judgment along with a recognition that they had suffered harm as a result of the crimes for which the accused was convicted;[35] and (b) the publication of compiled statements of apology made by the accused during the trial.[36] Numerous other requests for reparations were rejected, including on the basis that they would have involved an award

---

27 Regulations of the Trust Fund for Victims, reg. 56.
28 At the ICC, assistance provided under the 'second mandate' is not referred to as 'reparations', the latter term being reserved for measures judicially ordered against a convicted person under Art. 75 of the Rome Statute.
29 Regulations of the Trust Fund for Victims, reg. 48.
30 ICC, 'Trust Fund For Victims, Reviewing Rehabilitation Assistance and Preparing for Delivering Reparations: Programme Progress Report', (Summer 2011), 9–14, http://www.trustfundforvictims.org/sites/default/files/imce/TFV%20Programme%20Report%20Summer%202011.pdf, accessed 28 September 2012.
31 *The Prosecutor v Thomas Lubanga Dyilo* ('*Lubanga Case*') (Decision establishing the principles and procedures to be applied to reparations) ICC-01/04–01/06–2904 (7 August 2012).
32 *Lubanga Case* (Decision on the admissibility of the appeals against Trial Chamber I's 'Decision establishing the principles and procedures to be applied to reparations' and on the further conduct of the proceedings) ICC-01/04-01/06-2953 (14 December 2012).
33 ECCC Internal Rules, r. 23 *quinquies* (1).
34 *Case of KAING Guek Eav Alias Duch* (Judgment) Case File 001/18–07–2007/ECCC/TC (26 July 2010), paras 661–663; *Case of KAING Guek Eav Alias Duch* (Appeal Judgment) Case File 001/18–07–2007/ECCC/SC (3 February 2012), para. 643. Ultimately the two measures granted did not involve orders against the accused but rather measures to be taken by the ECCC itself, although the Chamber noted that 'strictly speaking' reparations are 'limited to measures ordered against the Accused': *Case of KAING Guek Eav Alias Duch* (Judgment), para. 667.
35 *Duch* (Judgment), ibid., paras 667, 682.
36 Ibid., paras 668, 683.

against a person other than the convicted accused[37] or a material (non-symbolic) award,[38] because they were insufficiently certain or ascertainable,[39] or as a result of the indigence of the accused.[40]

Other international or internationalised criminal institutions have referred in their legal texts to reparations mechanisms. The ICTY, ICTR, STL and the Special Court for Sierra Leone ('SCSL') provide for the transmission of judgments convicting a person to national authorities in order that victims may seek compensation through domestic mechanisms.[41] The regulations establishing the Special Panels for Serious Crimes ('SPSC') in East Timor enabled the creation of a trust fund for the benefit of victims of crimes within the SPSC's jurisdiction,[42] although such a fund was never created.[43] However, none of these institutions themselves involved a mechanism for determining the liability of an individual to pay reparations to victims.

1.3 Victim participation and civil party involvement

The other new role for victims in international criminal proceedings is the provision of limited standing for them to be heard in such proceedings. To date this has been realised in some form at the ICC, STL and ECCC.[44] This development is conceptually rooted in civil law traditions which provide a role for victims as 'civil parties'[45] and is also linked to victims' rights movements which have seen the expansion of victims' roles in common law systems. However, the standing provided to victims before these tribunals is (like other aspects of their procedural law) *sui generis*.

Before the ECCC, victims can participate as civil parties in a system based loosely on the French concept of *parties civiles*. Civil parties can exercise various modalities of participation which are stated to be for the purpose of supporting the prosecution and seeking collective and moral reparations.[46]

In contrast, before the ICC and the STL victim participation is not linked to reparation and nor are victims' limited to interventions in support of the prosecution. Rather, victims are able to express their 'views and concerns' in proceedings which affect their

---

37 Ibid., para. 671.
38 Ibid., paras 670, 674.
39 Ibid., paras 665, 673.
40 Ibid., paras 664, 666, 672; *Case of KAING Guek Eav Alias Duch* (Appeal Judgment) (n. 34), paras 668, 692, 703.
41 ICTY Rules of Procedure and Evidence, r. 106; ICTR Rules of Procedure and Evidence, r. 106; SCSL Rules of Procedure and Evidence, r. 105; Statute of the STL, Art. 25 (the Statute of the STL additionally provides that the Tribunal may, in its decisions, identify victims of the crimes for which a person is convicted: Art. 25(1)).
42 UNTAET Reg. 2000/15 On the Establishment of Panels with Exclusive Jurisdiction over Serious Criminal Offences, section 25.
43 International Center for Transitional Justice, 'Unfulfilled Expectations: Victims' perceptions of justice and reparations in Timor-Leste,' (February 2010), 7 http://www.ictj.org/sites/default/files/ICTJ-TimorLeste-Unfulfilled-Expectations-2010-English.pdf, accessed 28 September 2012.
44 Victims were granted the possibility of participation before the Special Panels for Serious Crimes in East Timor, but this was never implemented in practice. See n. 16 above.
45 For an overview of some civil law approaches to victim participation see: J. Doak, 'Victims' Rights in Criminal Trials: Prospects for Participation' (2005) 32 *Journal of Law and Society* 294–316 at 308–14.
46 ECCC Internal Rules, r. 23.

interests, so long as such participation is not inconsistent with the rights of the defence. Victim participants are grouped together and share a legal representative appointed and paid for by the Court.[47] The legal representative may then be granted opportunities to make opening and closing statements, lead evidence, question witnesses, make oral and written submissions, and participate in appeals.[48] A small number of victims have also been able to speak in person in the proceedings.[49] Any such interventions are made as a matter of judicial discretion (taking into account the victims' interests and the rights of the accused[50]) not as a right, since victims do not have the status of party and in this respect must be distinguished from *parties civiles*.

In both the ECCC and ICC/STL systems, victims must first apply to be granted recognition and thereby standing.[51] While the substantive and evidentiary requirements of these procedures are different before each body, they share a general requirement to demonstrate by written application that the person meets the definition of victim (broadly: a person who has suffered harm as a result of the crime(s) in question[52]). These applications are then in some instances the subject of observations from the prosecution and defence before being determined by a judge or chamber.[53]

47 ICC RPE, r. 90; *The Prosecutor v Germain Katanga and Mathieu Ngudjolo Chui (Katanga and Ngudjolo Case)* (Order on the organisation of common legal representation of victims) ICC-01/04–01/07–1328 (22 July 2009); *The Prosecutor v Jean-Pierre Bemba Gombo (Bemba Case)* (Fifth Decision on Victims' Issues Concerning Common Legal Representation of Victims) ICC-01/05–01/08–322 (16 December 2008); *Bemba Case* (Decision on common legal representation for victims for the purpose of trial) ICC-01/05–01/08–1005 (10 November 2010); *The Prosecutor v William Samoei Ruto, Henry Kiprono Kosgey and Joshua Arap Sang (Ruto Case)* (Decision on Victims' Participation at the Confirmation of Charges Hearing and in the Related Proceedings) ICC-01/09–01/11–249 (5 August 2011), paras 63–82; *The Prosecutor v Francis Kirimi Muthaura, Uhuru Muigai Kenyatta and Mohammed Hussein Ali (Kenyatta Case)* (Decision on Victims' Participation at the Confirmation of Charges Hearing and in the Related Proceedings) ICC-01/09–02/11–267 (26 August 2011), paras 77–96; *The Prosecutor v Laurent Gbagbo* (Decision on Victims' Participation and Victims' Common Legal Representation at the Confirmation of Charges Hearing and in the Related Proceedings) ICC-02/11–01/11–138 (4 June 2012), paras 35–45; STL Rules RPE, r. 86(D); *The Prosecutor v Ayyash et al* (Decision on Victims' Participation in The Proceedings) STL-11–01/PT/PTJ (8 May 2012), paras 108–112; ECCC Internal Rules, rule 23(3) and rule 23*ter*.
48 STL RPE, rule 87(B); *Lubanga Case* (Trial Chamber I) (Decision on victims' participation) ICC-01/04–01/06–1119 (18 January 2008), paras 101–122; *Katanga and Ngudjolo Case* (Decision on the Modalities of Victim Participation) ICC-01/04–01/07–1788-tENG (22 January 2010), para. 93; *Katanga and Ngudjolo Case* (Directions for the conduct of the proceedings and testimony in accordance with rule 140) ICC-01/04–01/07–1665-Corr (1 December 2009).
49 *Lubanga Case* (Decision on the request by victims a/0225/06, a/0229/06 and a/0270/07 to express their views and concerns in person and to present evidence during the trial) ICC-01/04–01/06–2032-Anx (26 June 2009); *Katanga and Ngudjolo Case*, Decision authorising the appearance of Victims a/0381/09, a/0018/09, a/0191/08, and pan/0363/09 acting on behalf of a/0363/09) ICC-01/04–01/07–2517-tENG (9 November 2010); *Bemba Case* (Decision on the supplemented applications by the legal representatives of victims to present evidence and the views and concerns of victims) ICC-01/05–01/08–2138 (22 February 2012).
50 Rome Statute Art. 68(3); STL Statute Art. 17; STL RPE r. 87(B).
51 Except in the *Ruto Case* and the *Kenyatta Case*, following decisions by Trial Chamber V which removed this requirement in those cases, and ordered that victims' legal representatives in those cases represent *all* persons harmed by the crimes charged: *Ruto Case* (Decision on victims' representation and participation) ICC-01/09–01/11–460 (3 October 2012); *Kenyatta Case* (Decision on victims' representation and participation) ICC-01/09–02/11–498 (3 October 2012).
52 ICC RPE, r. 85(a); STL RPE, r. 2; ECCC Internal Rules, glossary.
53 ICC RPE, r. 89(1); STL RPE, r. 86(C); ECCC Internal Rules, r. 23*bis*.

2 Victim participation and reparations: an implementation of victims' human rights?

The advent of victim participation and reparations in international criminal proceedings is often positioned as a victory for victims' human rights. However, this is usually done without legal precision regarding the nature of the link between human rights and the involvement of victims in international criminal proceedings.

2.1 The right to a remedy and the obligation to investigate

Scholars and jurists who have considered how victim participation and reparations can be understood as an implementation of human rights most frequently link them to the right to a remedy.[54] The right to a remedy of a person who suffers harm due to serious human rights violations is well established.[55] It is usually discussed as encompassing three overlapping and interrelated aspects: access to justice, reparations and truth.[56]

The right to a remedy is closely linked to an obligation on states to effectively investigate (and if appropriate prosecute and punish) serious criminal acts. Significantly, human rights bodies have held that this obligation to investigate can arise even where a crime is committed by non-state actors.[57] It has been treated as having two possible sources: (a) the state's 'procedural obligation' to ensure the protection of the 'most fundamental'[58] human rights: notably the right to life,[59] to freedom from torture and ill-treatment,[60] and freedom from

54 *Katanga and Ngudjolo Case* (Decision on the Set of Procedural Rights Attached to Procedural Status of Victim at the Pre-Trial Stage of the Case) ICC-01/04–01/07–474 (13 May 2008), paras 31–44; *Case of Ieng Sary* (Directions on Unrepresented Civil Parties' Right to Address the Pre-Trial Chamber in Person) (Pre-Trial Chamber) Case File 002/19–09–2007-ECCC/OCIJ (PTC03) (29 August 2008), para. 5; B. McGonigle Leyh, *Procedural Justice? Victim Participation in International Criminal Proceedings* (Intersentia, 2011), 339–41; R. Aldana-Pindell, 'In Vindication of Justiciable Victims' Rights to Truth and Justice for State-Sponsored Crimes' (2002) 35 *Vanderbilt Journal of Transnational Law* 1399–501.

55 Universal Declaration of Human Rights, Art. 8; International Covenant on Civil and Political Rights, Art. 2(3); United Nations Convention against Torture, Art. 14.

56 Basic Principles and Guidelines (n. 1) Art. 11; Updated Set of Principles (n. 10). See also M.C. Bassiouni, 'International Recognition of Victims' Rights' (2006) 6 *Human Rights Law Review* 203–80, 260–76.

57 Human Rights Committee, General Comment No. 31 (26 May 2004), para. 8; Committee Against Torture, General Coment No. 2 (24 January 2008), para. 18; International Convention for the Protection of All Persons from Enforced Disappearance, Art. 3; *Velasquez-Rodriguez case*, IACtHR, Series A No. 4 (1988) (Judgment), para. 172; *Menson and Others v UK*, App. No. 47916/99, Decision on Admissibility (ECtHR, 6 May 2003).

58 *Jordan v The United Kingdom*, App. No. 24746/94 (ECtHR, Judgment of 4 August 2001), paras 102–103; *Kelly and Others v The United Kingdom*, App. No. 30054/96 (ECtHR, Judgment of 4 May 2001), paras 91–92; *Shanaghan v The United Kingdom*, App. No. 37715/97 (ECtHR, Judgment of 4 May 2001), paras 85–86; see also *McCann and Others v The United Kingdom*, App. No. 18984/91 (ECtHR, Judgment of 27 September 1995), para. 147.

59 Ibid.

60 *Assenov v Bulgaria*, App. No. 24760/94 (ECtHR, Judgment of 28 October 1998), paras 101–106.

slavery;[61] and (b) the right of victims to a remedy, at least in relation to conduct by state agents.[62]

2.2 Participation and reparations as embodiment of the right to a remedy?

At first glance, it appears simple to position victim engagement in international criminal proceedings within this human rights framework.

The provision of reparations within international criminal proceedings can certainly constitute a remedy as envisaged by the Basic Principles and Guidelines and the human rights jurisprudence. This is most evident in respect of crimes committed by state officials: where private actors are concerned, the Basic Principles and Guidelines require that reparations be paid,[63] but probably surpass customary international law in this regard.

Of course reparations following an international trial will rarely constitute a complete remedy. This may be because only one of multiple perpetrators of the violation is tried and convicted, or because the form of reparations provided is more limited than that which is needed to address the harm suffered. Despite this, the possibility for victims to receive reparations from a person convicted at international trial can be conceived of as an implementation of the right to a remedy.

Positioning victim participation within the framework of the right to a remedy poses a greater conceptual challenge. Some commentators implicitly suggest that participation can itself constitute a form of reparations, by bringing about therapeutic benefits or other beneficial outcomes for the victim.[64] However, the existence of a connection between participation and such outcomes are yet to be demonstrated, and indeed it appears plausible that in some instances participation in proceedings may lead to adverse psychological consequences for victims.[65] The only study to date on victim views following participation in an international criminal trial revealed generally positive attitudes, a mixture of other outcomes and no reports of a 'catharsis or healing effect.'[66]

Another possibility is suggested by the jurisprudence of human rights bodies when considering the role of victims in domestic accountability mechanisms. These almost universally

---

61 *Rantsev v Cyprus and Russia*, App. No. 25965/04 (ECtHR, Judgment of 7 January 2010), para. 287.

62 Universal Declaration of Human Rights, Art. 8; ICCPR, Art. 2(3); American Convention on Human Rights, Art. 29; European Convention for the Protection of Human Rights and Fundamental Freedoms, Art. 13; African Charter on Human and Peoples' Rights, Art. 7; *Aksoy v Turkey*, App. No. 21987/93 (ECtHR, Judgment of 18 December 1996), paras 95–100; *Mentes v Turkey*, App. No. 23186/94 (ECtHR, Judgment of 18 November 1997), paras 89–92; *Bautista de Arellana v Colombia*, HRC, Communication No. 563/1993 (1995) UN Doc. CCPR/C/55/D/563, para. 8.6.

63 Art. 15.

64 For example see Bitti and González Rivas (n. 3) 320.

65 J. Doak, 'The Therapeutic Dimension of Transitional Justice: Emotional Repair and Victim Satisfaction in International Trials and Truth Commissions' (2011) 11 *International Criminal Law Review* 263–98; H.M. Weinstein, 'The Myth of Closure, the Illusion of Reconciliation: Final Thoughts on Five Years as Co-Editor-in-Chief' (2011) 5 *International Journal of Transitional Justice* 1–10; A.P. Jorge-Birol, 'Victims' Participation in the Criminal Justice System and its Impact on Peace-Building', in W. Benedek, C. Daase, V. Dimitrijević and P. van Duyne, *Transnational Terrorism, Organized Crime and Peace-Building* (Palgrave Macmillan, 2010).

66 P.P. Pham, P. Vinck, M. Balthazard, J. Strasser and C. Om, 'Victim Participation and the Trial of Duch at the Extraordinary Chambers in the Courts of Cambodia' (2011) 3 *Journal of Human Rights Practice* 264–87 at 284.

link victims' participation in proceedings to the obligation to conduct an effective investigation into serious human rights violations. The European Court of Human Rights (ECtHR) has in some cases found violations of this obligation when minimum procedures enabling victim participation in domestic proceedings were not implemented. In the Court's reasoning, two conceptual approaches can be distinguished, reflecting the legal bases mentioned above as sources of the obligation to investigate.

First, the ECtHR has identified a 'procedural obligation' requiring an investigation where a fundamental right is violated. This is a part of a state's obligation under Article 1 of the Convention to 'secure' fundamental rights.[67] It requires an 'effective investigation' which is 'capable of leading to the identification and punishment of those responsible'.[68] This is said, in turn, to require that 'in all cases, the next of kin of the victim must be involved in the procedure to the extent necessary to safeguard his legitimate interests'.[69] Thus, the Court has found a violation of the procedural obligation where the victim's family was:

- given inadequate information regarding a decision not to prosecute;[70]
- denied advance access to witness statements to be relied on during an inquest;[71]
- not advised of the inquest date and thus unable to participate;[72]
- not advised of the procedure for requesting legal assistance to obtain remedies;[73]
- unable to access the case file or papers in an administrative investigation;[74]
- not notified of a judicial determination upholding a decision not to initiate criminal proceedings, thereby rendering them unable to appeal;[75]
- limited in its participation in an inquiry to attendance at those parts in which they were themselves giving evidence, and without being able to put questions to witnesses;[76]
- made to wait until the publication of the final report of an inquiry to learn of the evidence that had been presented.[77]

As this list demonstrates, the extent of victim engagement required according to the ECtHR's case law is limited, and mostly concerns the adequate provision of information. Moreover, the ECtHR has not gone so far as to indicate a minimum level of victim engagement that is always required in criminal proceedings. Rather, the 'procedural obligation' to conduct an

---

67 *Rantsev v Cyprus and Russia* (n. 61), para. 231; *Oğur v Turkey*, App. No. 21594/93 (ECtHR, Judgment of 20 May 1999), para. 88.

68 *Oğur v Turkey* (n. 67) para. 88; *Paul and Audrey Edwards v The United Kingdom*, App. No. 46477/99 (ECtHR, Judgment of 14 March 2002), para. 71.

69 *Rantsev v Cyprus and Russia* (n. 61) para. 232; *Jordan v The United Kingdom* (n. 58) para. 109; *McKerr v The United Kingdom*, App. No. 28883/95 (ECtHR, Judgment of 4 May 2001), para. 115; *Kelly and Others v The United Kingdom* (n. 58) para. 98; *Shanaghan v The United Kingdom* (n. 58) para. 92; *Paul and Audrey Edwards v UK* (n. 68) para. 73.

70 *Jordan v The United Kingdom* (n. 58) paras 123–124, 142; *Kelly and Others v The United Kingdom* (n. 58) paras 117–118, 136; *Shanaghan v The United Kingdom* (n. 58) paras 107–108, 122.

71 *Jordan v The United Kingdom* (n. 58) paras 133–134, 142; *Kelly and Others v The United Kingdom* (n. 58) paras 127–128, 136; *Shanaghan v The United Kingdom* (n. 58) paras 116–117, 122.

72 *Rantsev v Cyprus and Russia* (n. 61) para. 238.

73 Ibid, para. 239.

74 *Oğur v Turkey* (n. 67) para. 92.

75 Ibid.

76 *Paul and Audrey Edwards v UK* (n. 68) para. 84.

77 Ibid.

'effective investigation' varies case by case. Since victim participation in this context is not an end in itself, but rather a means by which to ensure the efficacy of investigations, it seems that, where other safeguards are in place, victim participation may not be required.

The second approach taken by the ECtHR to victim participation as an implementation of human rights relies on the obligation to provide a remedy for violations. In a small number of cases the Court considered that a failure to effectively investigate a killing not only constituted a violation of the procedural obligation discussed above, but also a violation of Article 13 of the European Convention which requires that a person who suffers a violation under the Convention shall have an effective remedy before a national authority. The Court stated that this requires 'in addition to the payment of compensation where appropriate, a thorough and effective investigation capable of leading to the identification and punishment of those responsible *and including effective access for the relatives to the investigatory procedure*'[78] (emphasis added). An instance in which a victim's family was not informed about a criminal trial or provided with an opportunity to participate therein was held by the Court to constitute a violation of Article 13, though the Court did not clearly identify which failures were determinative of this finding.[79] However, despite stating that the requirements of Article 13 are 'broader than a Contracting State's procedural obligation . . . to conduct an effective investigation',[80] the different content of the obligation has not been detailed by the Court. Moreover, in most cases where the Court has found a violation of the procedural obligation, it has then declined to consider issues arising under Article 13.[81]

Case law from the Inter-American Court of Human Rights (IACtHR) demonstrates a difference of emphasis, but an otherwise similar approach. The IACtHR has tended to rely on Articles 8 and 25 of the American Convention, which respectively provide for fair trial rights and an effective remedy. In cases concerning the right to life and forcible disappearances the Court applies these two obligations together, and interprets them as requiring an effective investigation.[82] Concerning the role of victims in such an investigation the Court has stated that pursuant to Article 8, victims or their next of kin 'should have substantial possibilities of being heard and acting in the respective proceedings, both in order to clarify the facts and punish those responsible, and to seek due reparation.'[83]

The IACtHR has also at times adopted an approach similar to that of the ECtHR in respect of the 'procedural obligation' arising out of fundamental rights. Thus, the IACtHR has held that 'the general obligation to ensure the human rights embodied in the Convention, contained in Article 1(1) thereof, entails the obligation to investigate cases of violations of the

---

78 *Kaya v Turkey*, App. No. 22729/93 (ECtHR, Judgment of 19 February 1998), para. 107; *Gül v Turkey*, App. No. 22676/93 (ECtHR, Judgment of 14 December 2000), para. 100.

79 *Gül v Turkey* (n. 78) paras 98–102.

80 *Kaya v Turkey* (n. 78) para. 107; see also *Gül v Turkey* (n. 78) para. 102.

81 *Jordan v The United Kingdom* (n. 58) paras 156–165; *Kelly and Others v The United Kingdom* (n. 58) paras 150–159; *Shanaghan v The United Kingdom* (n. 58) paras 131–140; *McKerr v The United Kingdom* (n. 69) paras 167–176.

82 *Goiburú v Paraguay*, IACtHR, Series C No. 153 (2006) (Judgment), para. 117; see also *Barrios Altos v Peru*, IACtHR, Series C No. 75 (2001) (Judgment), paras 42–43.

83 *Case of the 'Street Children' (Villagran Morales et al.) v Guatemala*, IACtHR, Series C No. 32 (1999) (Judgment), para. 227; see also *Goiburú v Paraguay* (n. 82) para. 117: 'During the investigation and judicial proceedings, the victims or their next of kin must have ample opportunity to take part and be heard, both in the elucidation of the facts and the punishment of those responsible, and in the quest for fair compensation, in accordance with domestic law and the American Convention.'

substantive right that must be protected and safeguarded'.[84] States must 'prevent, investigate and punish any violation of the right recognised by the Convention'[85] at least in respect of 'extrajudicial executions, forced disappearances and other grave human rights violations'.[86] Although the implications of this obligation for the participation of victims have not been detailed, the IACtHR has referred to a duty to 'investigate and punish those responsible and, also, inform the next of kin about the whereabouts of the disappeared and, if applicable, compensate them'.[87]

In addition, the IACtHR has gone further than its European counterpart in finding that the rights to a fair trial and an effective remedy also entail that victims know the truth about the events.[88] However, it has not elucidated what this entitlement may mean for victims' role in investigations and other criminal procedures.

Other human rights bodies, while requiring the investigation of serious human rights violations,[89] have not identified if and to what extent this may require victim involvement in an investigation or prosecution.[90]

2.3 Limitations of a remedy-based approach to victim participation as a human right

Recognition by human rights bodies of some entitlements for victims to participate in criminal proceedings has rightly been viewed by victims' advocates as an advance. However, limitations are apparent in the approach taken by these bodies, which treats victim participation as linked to a state's obligation to effectively investigate.

First, the content of states' obligations in this regard is to undertake an *effective* investigation: that is, an investigation sufficient to identify the perpetrators and reveal the facts concerning the violation. Deriving a requirement of victim participation therefrom thus assumes that there is a correlation between the involvement of victims and the efficacy of an investigation.

However, an investigation or criminal proceeding does not *require* victim participation in order to be effective. Rigorous and successful investigations and prosecutions are routinely carried out without substantial victim participation (for example, in some common law jurisdictions) and it is difficult to envisage a judicial finding of a violation of the obligation to investigate in such instances. It is clearly possible for victims to benefit from an effective investigation – which brings perpetrators to justice and reveals the truth about events – without having themselves participated in it.

Nor has it been shown that victim participation in fact tends to lead to a more effective investigation or prosecution, or to more reliable determinations of fact. Empirical research in

---

84 *Goiburú v Paraguay* (n. 82) para. 88; see also *Bamaca-Velásquez v Guatemala*, IACtHR, (2000) (Judgment), paras 210–211.

85 *Velasquez Rodriguez case* (n. 57) paras 166, 174.

86 *Goiburú v Paraguay* (n. 82) para. 88.

87 Ibid., 89.

88 *Bámaca-Velásquez v Guatemala* (n. 84) para. 201; *Barrios Altos v Peru* (n. 82) paras 47–48; *Castillo Páez v Peru*, IACtHR, Series C No. 43 (1997) (Judgment), para. 90.

89 For example: *Celis Laureano v Peru*, HRC, Communication No. 540/1993 (1996) UN Doc. CCPR/C/56/D/540/1993, paras 8.3 and 10.

90 Cf. Committee on the Elimination of Racial Discrimination, General Comment No. XXXI, paras 17 and 19(a) which mandate a role for victims in judicial proceedings, although without clarifying the legal basis of such a requirement.

this field is only just beginning. Some results from the domestic context show that victim engagement has minimal impact on outcomes in criminal proceedings.[91] No evidence exists to demonstrate that victim participation enhances the outcomes of investigations or prosecutions, objectively seen. Certainly, numerous commentators critical of victim participation have postulated the converse – namely that victim involvement detracts from the efficacy of a trial. Even the commonly stated premise that including victims' views and concerns assists a court in reaching a finding based on the truth is surely open to question, since there is no basis to presume that victim evidence is inherently more credible than that from other sources.[92] Some forms of part of victim participation clearly have little or no impact on the investigation. Many participating victims will be content to benefit from information and explanations by their legal representative without actively expressing a view in the proceedings. This form of passive participation has no bearing on the effectiveness of the investigation or prosecution undertaken, but remains a meaningful form of participation for some victims.

Second, those who treat victim participation as part of an entitlement to an effective investigation or prosecution ultimately share the 'instrumentalist' approach for which the ad hoc tribunals have been criticised. Thus victim participation is not seen as an implementation of the rights of participating victims' themselves, but as a means for facilitating outcomes in terms of investigations or prosecutions.

Treating victim participation as valuable because of its contribution to the efficacy of an investigation or trial has practical consequences. This can be seen in some decisions of the ICC, which link victims' participation to the 'broader purpose of assisting the bench in its pursuit of the truth',[93] and therefore permit participation (notably the questioning of witnesses, the leading of evidence and the appearance in person at trial) only where it is shown likely to assist the Chamber in finding the truth.[94] On this approach, victims are provided with an opportunity based on their knowledge and credibility, rather than because of their status as a person who suffered harm through the crimes charged. They are excluded from participation if deemed unable to contribute sufficiently to truth-seeking by virtue, for example, of their ignorance concerning the matters in contest, or because their credibility is in doubt, or because the Court already has sufficient evidence on the facts which are within the victims'

---

91 E. Erez and P. Tontodonato, 'The Effect of Victim Participation in Sentencing on Sentencing Outcome' (1990) 28 *Criminology* 451–74.
92 Indeed in the *Lubanga* judgment, the ICC's Trial Chamber I rejected as not credible the evidence given by the three participating victims who had been permitted to appear in person: *Lubanga Case* (n. 49) paras 485–502.
93 *Lubanga Case* (Decision on the Manner of Questioning Witnesses by the Legal Representatives of Victims) ICC-01/04–01/06–2172 (16 September 2009), para. 27, citing the ICC Appeals Chamber: *Lubanga Case* (Judgment on the appeals of The Prosecutor and The Defence against Trial Chamber I's Decision on Victims' Participation of 18 January 2008) ICC-01/04–01/06–1432 (11 July 2008); see also *Lubanga Case* (n. 48) paras 108, 133; *Katanga and Ngudjolo Case* (n. 48), paras 20, 47, 82; *Katanga and Ngudjolo Case* (Decision on Modalities of Victim Participation at Trial) (n. 48), paras 65, 75, 81, 91, 96.
94 *Katanga and Ngudjolo Case* (Directions for the conduct of the proceedings and testimony in accordance with rule 140) (n. 48) para. 30; *Bemba Case* (n. 49), paras 23–24. But cf. the dissent of Judge Steiner, who referred to the approach of the majority as '[a] utilitarian approach toward the role of victims before the Court': *Bemba Case* (Partly Dissenting Opinion of Judge Sylvia Steiner on the Decision on the supplemented applications by the legal representatives of victims to present evidence and the views and concerns of victims) ICC-01/05–01/08–2138, ICC-01/05–01/08–2140 (23 Febraury 2012), paras 11, 14.

knowledge. It is by reference to this logic that some who argue for the restriction of victim participation see such participation as justifiable only where it contributes to specified outcomes in the criminal justice process.[95]

As argued below, such an approach does not reflect the real nature and purpose of victim participation, which seeks to make standing contingent not on usefulness, but on the 'personal interests' of victims in the proceedings.

2.4 Victim participation as procedural right

An alternate categorisation of victims' participation in international criminal tribunals is possible. This sees it as a realisation of a procedural fair trial right afforded to persons whose victimhood is linked to a case before an international tribunal. The possibility for a victim to express 'views and concerns' in international criminal proceedings thus represents a form of natural justice, providing victims with an opportunity to be heard.

Indeed, moves to increase victim engagement in domestic criminal proceedings largely reflect victims' concerns about *process* rather than *outcome*. That is – they address victims' desires to have their voice heard in criminal trials, rather than to bring about a particular result in those trials.[96] Likewise the rules enabling international victim participation provide for procedural entitlements (opportunities to be heard) rather than seeking to guarantee a particular outcome (such as an effective prosecution). The phrasing of the ICC and STL texts reflect this objective. They allow victim views to be heard based not on their usefulness to the trial, but based on whether 'the personal interests of the victims are affected', a formulation evocative of the natural justice principle *audi alteram partem*, according to which a person is entitled to be heard before a decision is taken which affects his or her rights or interests. It is precisely because they have suffered harm from the crime, and thereby have a 'personal interest' in the proceedings, that victims are given special standing rights. It is this personal interest, and not the victim's level of knowledge or credibility that is the touchstone for his or her participation.

However, despite the guarantee for all persons of a 'fair and public hearing' in the determination of their rights and obligations,[97] human rights bodies have not gone so far as to interpret requiring a fair hearing for victims in criminal cases. The ECtHR has applied a strict approach. To date it has found that a criminal trial only involves a determination of a victim's rights or obligations where it can result in a binding determination of a specific civil right: either a right to compensation or the protection of a reputation.[98] It has refused to apply the fair hearing requirement to inquest proceedings[99] or where victims' interest in a

---

95 C. Stahn, H. Olasolo and K. Gibson, 'Participation of Victims in Pre-Trial Proceedings of the ICC' (2006) 4 *Journal of International Criminal Justice* 219–38, at 221 and 238; M. Jouet, 'Reconciling the Conflicting Rights of Victims and Defendants at the International Criminal Court' 26 *Saint Louis University Public Law Review* 249–308, at 296–300.

96 Erez and Tontodonato (n. 91), 542 and the studies cited therein.

97 ICCPR, Art. 14; ECHR, Art. 6; IACHR, Art. 8.

98 *Perez v France*, App. No. 47287/99 (ECtHR, Judgment of 12 February 2004), paras 57–72. See also the discussion in A. Mezykowska, 'Does the Victim of a Crime Have the Right to a Fair Trial?' (2011) 31 *Polish Yearbook of International Law* 285–313, at 292–99. Although the Court sought to simplify and clarify its previous case law on this issue in the *Perez* case, the approach in that decision gives rise to its own difficulties and apparent inconsistencies: S. Treschel, *Human Rights in Criminal Proceedings* (OUP, 2005), 40–42.

99 *Rantsev v Cyprus and Russia*, (n. 61) para. 331.

trial were limited to accessing confidential case materials and clarifying the circumstances surrounding their family members' deaths.[100] Where victims have argued a violation of their fair trial rights by an inability to adequately participate in investigations, the Court has instead referred to the 'procedural obligation' to investigate[101] or the obligation to provide a remedy.[102]

In contrast, the IACtHR has relied on Article 8 of the American Convention – which guarantees a fair hearing – in many cases involving complaints about inadequate procedures for investigation and prosecution of human rights violations. However, it has treated Article 8 and Article 25 (the right to a remedy) as equivalent, and essentially as requiring effective procedures, rather than as stipulating a particular role for victims.[103] Thus the IACtHR does not treat the hearing of victims in a criminal trial as required for a fair hearing under Article 8.

It is true that these human rights bodies have oversight over domestic justice systems with a range of procedural approaches and dealing also with minor crimes, in which victims' interests might be considered to be less than in those of more serious crimes. This may explain why no *requirement* for victim participation can be found in their jurisprudence. However, it is unfortunate that where human rights bodies *have* found that states violated human rights by denying victims access to criminal investigations or hearings, they viewed it as a failure of the investigation's effectiveness, not as a failure to provide victims with a fair hearing.

Despite the fact that human rights bodies have not yet done so, it is possible to conceive of victim participation in criminal proceedings as a form of fair hearing right (at least where the gravest crimes are concerned). However, on a strict approach – such as that adopted by the ECtHR – the significance of the crime and its harm in a victim's life is not itself enough to justify a right to be heard in proceedings to determine a person's responsibility for the crime. Rather it is necessary to identify a *legal right* held by victims which is determined by a criminal trial, thereby engaging the victims' right to a fair hearing.

Where, as at the ICC, reparations may follow from the conviction of an accused person, it is arguable that this creates an entitlement for victims to be heard – in order to protect their interests in obtaining reparations through a conviction.[104] While victims are entitled to reparations under international law, it is not clear whether international criminal tribunals will view this as a 'right' arising or enforceable within their proceedings, given, for example, the discretionary language used in Article 75 of the Rome Statute and rule 23 *quinquies* of the ECCC Internal Rules. However, it is arguable that a tribunal's conviction, in respect of specified crimes, creates a legal right for the victims of those crimes to reparations from the convicted person, regardless of the options available for the enforcement of that right. Conversely, the fact that an acquittal would preclude the possibility of reparations may be a sufficient basis for considering that the case involves a determination of the victims' civil rights.

However, since many victims participate in international trials for reasons unrelated to reparations, it would be preferable to identify an alternative basis which reflects more

100 *Janowiec and Others v Russia*, App. Nos 55508/07 and 29520/09, Decision on Admissibiltiy (ECtHR, Judgment of 5 July 2011), para. 118.
101 *Rantsev v Cyprus and Russia*, (n. 61), para. 331; *Paul and Audrey Edwards v UK* (n. 68) para. 90.
102 *Aksoy v Turkey* (n. 62) para. 94; *Mentes v Turkey* (n. 62) para. 88.
103 See especially *Case of the 'Street Children ' (Villagran-Morales et al.) v Guatemala* (n. 83) paras 230 et seq.
104 *Perez v France* (n. 98) paras 57–72.

genuinely the interest sought to be protected by the voicing of views and concerns. Several theoretical possibilities can be proposed, although none of them meets the threshold set to date by the ECtHR.

Victims' right to an effective investigation in respect of the crimes suffered (discussed above) may serve as a basis for their entitlement to a fair hearing in trials concerning those crimes. This approach differs from that critiqued above in that it does not propose that victims are entitled to participate in so far as this contributes to an effective investigation. Rather, victims are entitled to be kept informed about proceedings in order to observe whether the investigation and prosecution are undertaken satisfactorily, and are able to make interventions where they believe this is not the case. Such an approach reflects that a key justification for victim participation in international trials is to ensure the effectiveness of prosecutions by maintaining their accountability (to the victims).

Likewise, if victims have a right to have the truth about crimes made known publicly,[105] it is arguable that they should be entitled to a hearing during judicial proceedings which will make factual findings regarding the crime(s), in order that their version of the truth can be taken into account in establishing the public record.

Finally, throughout proceedings in an international criminal case, numerous interlocutory decisions are made, at least some of which have the potential to have an impact on the rights of victims. For examples, decisions concerning confidentiality of information or the imposition of protective measures may have a bearing on victims' personal security, privacy or dignity or on their access to information concerning themselves. In such instances natural justice should require that victims have the possibility of being heard.

Although an approach along these lines is yet to be recognised by human rights bodies, this is an evolving area of law. Given trends in common law jurisdictions toward victim involvement,[106] and the inclusion of victim participation requirements in various soft law instruments[107] and at least one widely ratified international convention, it is possible that customary law will eventually extend to include a fair trial right for victims to be heard in criminal cases. It is to be hoped that such a right will be understood as part of a fair trial right.

3 Victim participation and reparations as a challenge to human rights

A discussion of the human rights implications of victim participation and reparations in international criminal proceedings would not be complete without considering whether these phenomena may undermine human rights. Those who oppose victim involvement in

---

105 Some human rights bodies have ordered that society must be made aware of the truth concerning atrocities; however, the 'holder' of such a right has not been precisely identified: see *Case of Bámaca-Velásquez v. Guatemala*, IACtHR, Series C No. 90 (2002) (Reparations and Costs) paras 76–77; *Case of Myrna Mack Chang v Guatemala*, IACtHR, Series C No. 101 (2003) (Merits, Reparations and Costs), paras 274–275; *The 'Srebrenica Cases'*, Human Rights Chamber for Bosnia and Herzegovina (2003) (Admissibility and Merits), para. 212.

106 Declaration of Basic Principles of Justice for Victims of Crime and Abuse of Power (n. 9), Art. 6; Updated Set of Principles (n. 10), Principle 19; Principles on the Effective Investigation and Documentation of Torture and Other Cruel, Inhuman or Degrading Treatment or Punishment, UNGA Res. 9842 (4 December 2000), Art. 4.

107 Protocol to Prevent, Suppress and Punish Trafficking in Persons, especially Women and Children (2000), Art. 6(2).

international criminal proceedings usually argue these mechanisms risk eroding defence rights. Such arguments are analysed below. A further and less commonly considered question is then posed, namely whether victim engagements in international criminal procedures constitute a challenge to the human rights of other victims.

3.1 Rights of the defence

Numerous critics of victims' active engagement in international criminal proceedings have argued that it interferes with the rights of the accused.[108] However, an analysis of the impacts of victim participation on the defence's fair trial rights reveals that this issue is not clear-cut.[109] Similar concerns have been raised in relation to domestic proceedings (for example in the context of common law systems which have allowed victim impact statements and similar measures).[110] Despite this, no decision from a human rights court or treaty body has found the rights of an accused person to have been infringed through the participation of victims or by the awarding of reparations in a domestic criminal trial. It may be that this question has simply not yet been argued. In any event, the system of victim participation and reparations implemented in international criminal tribunals and the context of the crimes involved are distinct enough that they arguably give rise to different or greater concerns, and these therefore warrant consideration. The arguments most commonly made[111] as to how victim participation and reparations may interfere with defence rights, are the following.

3.1.1 Presumption of innocence

The right of an accused person to be presumed innocent is well established in human rights law[112] as well as in the texts of the international tribunals.[113] Some have argued that systems of victim participation, such as those adopted at the ICC, ECCC and STL, violate this presumption insofar as they involve, prior to judgment, a judicial decision recognising persons as having suffered harm due to the crimes charged.[114] It is argued that this pre-empts the judicial determination of matters which fall on the prosecution to establish beyond reasonable doubt.[115]

---

108 See for example: M. Rauschenbach and D. Scalia, 'Victims and International Criminal Justice: a Vexed Question?' (2008) 90 *International Review of the Red Cross*, 441–59, at 449–50.

109 In the domestic context, some commentators have also pointed out that the tendency to talk of victims' participation and defence rights as being in natural opposition is an oversimplification: see Edwards (n. 4).

110 Erez and Tontodonato (n. 91) 453–54; Doak (n. 45) 297–98.

111 For a comprehensive discussion see McGonigle Leyh (n. 54), 346–57.

112 ICCPR, Art. 14(2); ECHR, Art. 6(2); IACHR Art. 8(2); African Charter on Human and Peoples' Rights, Art. 7(1).

113 Rome Statute Art. 66(1); ICTY Statute Art. 21(3); ICTR Statute Art. 20(3); STL Statute Art. 16(3)(a); SCSL Statute Art. 17(3); ECCC Internal Rules, r. 21(1)(d).

114 Stahn et al. (n. 95), 223–24; E. Baumgartner, 'Aspects of Victim Participation in the Proceedings of the International Criminal Court' (2008) 90 *International Review of the Red Cross* 409–40 at 421; S. Zappalà, 'The Rights of Victims *v.* the Rights of the Accused' (2010) 8 *Journal of International Criminal Justice* 137–64, 146–47.

115 Jouet (n. 95) 271–74.

This concern is misplaced. Judicial decisions to accept participating victims (at the ICC or STL) or civil parties (at the ECCC) involve a standard of proof (prima facie)[116] which is lower than that for a finding of guilt, and are able to be reconsidered or overturned later in the proceedings. Indeed both the ICC and the ECCC have ultimately rejected victim or civil party status to persons who were at first accepted using the lower standard of proof.[117] The use of a lower standard to determine some matters which will ultimately be decided at judgment using the 'beyond reasonable doubt' standard is not unusual. For example, by the time of a trial at the ICC, a Pre-Trial Chamber has necessarily already confirmed the charges by finding that there are 'substantial grounds to believe' that the person charged committed each of the crimes charged.[118] This finding on the lower standard does not compromise the presumption of innocence. In the same way, the presumption is not undermined by factual findings made on a prima facie standard in respect of victims' applications for participation.

3.1.2 Equality of arms

A second argument often made as to how victim participation might erode defence rights concerns the principle of equality of arms, a key aspect of defence fair trial rights[119] applied before the international criminal tribunals.[120] Most commonly, the claim is made that victim participation infringes this principle because it generates a second accuser (a 'prosecutor bis'[121]) who can lead more evidence and raise further allegations which must be countered by the defence, while potentially relieving parts of the prosecution's burden of proof.[122]

However, the contention that involving an additional participant in proceedings can disrupt the 'delicate balance' existing between the parties[123] misrepresents the principle of equality of arms. The balance between the parties in international criminal proceedings is not achieved quantitatively, but by the use of procedural mechanisms. The balance is not affected by the number of accused (and therefore defence teams) involved in a single case, nor by reference to the number of staff working in the prosecution. Nor is the balance said to be disturbed when the prosecution runs more alternative arguments in its case. For

---

116 STL RPE, r. 86(B)(i), *The Prosecutor v Ayyash et al.* (n. 47), paras 2–3, 61–62; *Case of KAING Guek Eav Alias Duch* (Judgment) (n. 34) para. 636; *Situation in Darfur, Sudan* (Corrigendum to Decision on the Applications for Participation in the Proceedings of Applicants a/0011/06 to a/0015/06, a/0021/07, a/0023/07 to a/0033/07 and a/0035/07 to a/0038/07) ICC-02/05–111-Corr (14 December 2007) para. 5.

117 *Lubanga Case* (Judgment pursuant to Article 74 of the Statute), ICC-01/04–01/06–2842 (14 March 2012), para. 502; *Case of KAING Guek Eav Alias Duch* (Judgment), (n. 34), paras 647, 648.

118 Rome Statute, Art. 61(7).

119 *Bulut v Austria*, App. No. 17358/90 (ECtHR, Judgment of 22 February 1996); *Frank Robinson v Jamaica*, HRC, Communication No. 223/1987 (1989) UN Doc. CCPR/C/35/D/223/1987.

120 For example: *The Prosecutor v Duško Tadić* (Appeals Judgment) ICTY-94–1-A (15 July 1999), paras 44–52.

121 C. Van den Wyngaert, 'Victims Before International Criminal Courts: Some Views and Concerns of an ICC Trial Judge', Lecture, Luxembourg, 21 November 2011, 10–11.

122 SáCouto and Cleary (n. 2), 85; Doak (n. 45) 298; M.E. Wojcik, 'False Hope: The Rights of Victims Before International Criminal Tribunals' (2010) 28 *L'Observateur des Nations Unies* 1–31 at 16; Zappalà, (n. 114) 150; C.H. Chung, 'Victims' Participation at the International Criminal Court: Are Concessions of the Court Clouding the Promise?' (2008) 6 *Northwestern Journal of International Human Rights* 459–545 at 519.

123 Doak (n. 45) 298.

the same reasons an additional participant does not interfere with the equality of arms so long as appropriate procedural mechanisms are in place – for example requirements that any evidence to be led by participating victims is disclosed in sufficient time.[124] In fact, procedural controls on victim participation go well beyond than this, since judges may prevent or limit any proposed instance of participation on the basis that it is contrary to the rights of the defence.[125]

In addition, concerns about prejudice to the equality of arms are premised on a flawed conception of how participating victims stand vis-à-vis the parties, at least before the ICC and STL. In contrast to the ECCC, where civil parties are intended to support the prosecution,[126] at the ICC and STL victims may challenge the prosecution's approach to the case. Indeed, victim participation in these institutions is intended in part to establish prosecutorial accountability and it is by no means certain that victims will support the prosecution's positions. Whether by design or inadvertence, victim participation may be more of a threat to the prosecution (or to the coherence of prosecution strategy) than it is to the defence.[127] It is therefore not surprising that in practice it has frequently been the prosecutor, and not the defence,[128] who objects to the role of victims at the international level or seeks to limit their presence.[129]

Finally, experience to date shows that victims will usually not lead large amounts of evidence or introduce many substantial new arguments in a case. In the first three cases at the ICC victims' legal representatives led minimal amounts of evidence. In comparison to the size and complexity of the prosecution cases in these trials, responding to such small amounts of additional material are not likely to create a significant impact for the defence.

3.1.3 Expeditiousness of proceedings

The most frequently expressed concern about victims' participation and reparations is that these procedures result in delays which infringe on the defence's right to an expeditious trial.[130] This was key among the reasons why the ICTY and ICTR judges recommended against expanding victims' rights before those tribunals.[131]

---

124 As required by the STL RPE, r. 112 and case law of the ICC: *Katanga and Ngudjolo Case* (Judgment on the Appeal of Mr Katanga Against the Decision of Trial Chamber II of 22 January 2010 Entitled 'Decision on the Modalities of Victim Participation at Trial') ICC-01/04–01/07–2288 (16 July 2010), paras 42–55.

125 As expressly provided by the Rome Statute Art. 68(3) and the Statute of the STL Art. 17.

126 ECCC Internal Rules, r. 23

127 Jorda and de Hemptinne (n. 2) 1412.

128 Indeed where the defence does not dispute that the crime alleged occurred, but only the accused's responsibility for it, the defence may express some sympathy for the situation of the victims.

129 Although its April 2010 Policy Paper represented a significant softening of the ICC Prosecutor's position on victim participation, it nonetheless argued for limitations to their participation – including that they should not be entitled to access confidential material: ICC Office of the Prosecutor (OTP), 'Policy Paper on Victims' Participation', (April 2010), 21.

130 Jorda and de Hemptinne (n. 2) 1412; Jouet (n. 95) 278; McGonigle Leyh (n. 54), 352–53; SáCouto and Cleary (n. 2) 83–85; Stahn et al (n. 95) 223; Zappalà, (n. 114) 143.

131 'Victims' compensation and participation', Appendix to Letter dated 12 October from the President of the International Tribunal for the Former Yugoslavia addressed to the Secretary General, S/2000/1063 (Annex), 3 November 2000, paras 33–36; Letter dated 9 November 2000 from the President of the International Criminal Tribunal for Rwanda addressed to the Secretary-General (Letter from the President of the ICTR), S/2000/1198 (Annex), 15 December 2000.

There are three ways in which victim participation and reparations may slow proceedings. These are manageable to varying extents and have different levels of potential impact on the rights of the accused.

- First, the process by which victims apply for and are accepted as participants can consume significant time and resources where the victim universe in a case is sizeable. The Registry must first receive, assess, process, redact and report on applications before providing them to the Chamber and/or the parties, requiring substantial time and resources.[132] The opportunity, where applicable, for parties to provide observations on applications, which are then considered by the judges, is a further source of delay.
- Once victims are granted status to participate, steps taken by their legal representatives contribute to the length of proceedings. During hearings the making of oral submissions, questioning of witness or the leading of evidence requires time. Where victims' legal representatives file written submissions this mean more time spent by the parties in responses, as well as more material to be considered by judges.
- Third, matters relating to reparations can draw out the trial itself if judges permit evidence relevant to reparations to be heard,[133] or can mean an additional period of reparations proceedings following judgment.

Experience to date is illuminating regarding the first two kinds of delay. It is true that where a case involves numerous victims, the application process for participation can cause delays and absorb resources which might have been devoted to other tasks.[134] However, this is arguably the result of the specific procedural approach employed for determining victim applications, which can be altered to increase efficiency.[135] For example, the ICC's procedure requiring parties' observations on victims applications[136] is time and resource-intensive and arguably adds minimal value to judicial decisions at this stage owing to the heavy redaction of the applications received by the parties.[137] In contrast, the STL has adopted a more efficient

---

132 As attested by a number of ICC Registry reports: see for example *The Prosecutor v Callixte Mbarushimana* (Proposal on victim participation in the confirmation hearing) ICC-01/04–01/10–213 (6 June 2011) paras 5–6; *Ruto Case* (Request for instructions on the processing of victims' applications) ICC-01/09–01/11–144 (24 June 2011); *Kenyatta Case* (Request for instructions on the processing of victims' applications) ICC-01/09–02/11–134 (24 June 2011); see also McGonigle Leyh (n. 54) 350–52.

133 ICC Regulations of the Court, reg. 56.

134 See for example submissions made to this effect by the defence in the *Bemba Case*, including: *Bemba Case* (Defence Application for Appropriate Decisions by Trial Chamber III Prior to the Commencement of the Trial Scheduled for 22 November 2010, ICC-01/05–01/08–987-tENG (1 November 2010), paras 11 and 13; *Bemba Case* (Defence Response to the Third Transmission of Victims' Applications for Participation in the Proceedings) ICC-01/05–01/08–945 (11 October 2010) paras 6–12; *Bemba Case* (Observations de la Défense sur les 206 demandes de participation transmises le 9 septembre 2011) ICC-01/05–01/08–1810, (3 October 2011) paras 3–9; *Bemba Case* (Observations de la Défense sur la «Onzième transmission aux parties et aux représentants légaux des versions expurgées des demandes de participation à la procédure») ICC-01/05–01/08–1754 (16 September 2011) paras 3–9.

135 As identified by the ICC Office of the Prosecutor: 'Bureaucratic or resource-related arguments (i.e. numbers of victims) require practical solutions: they do not constitute an obstacle to participation *per se*.' ICC OTP, 'Policy Paper on Victims' Participation' (n. 129), 1.

136 ICC RPE, r. 89(1).

137 Van den Wyngaert (n. 121) 6.

system, which allows the parties to comment only on legal issues identified by the Pre-Trial Judge.[138] In two cases at the ICC, the requirement to apply in writing for participation has been removed altogether.[139]

Regarding the second potential source of delay, it is notable that the system before the ICC and STL involves a built-in control mechanism. Participating victims in these institutions do not enjoy an automatic entitlement to make interventions in the proceedings, but must seek authorisation to do so. Participation is only authorised to the extent that it is consistent with the rights of the accused, including the right to a timely trial. To date, significant delays have not resulted, as attested by the Presiding Judge in the *Lubanga Case*, who said that 'the involvement of victims has not greatly added to the length of the case'.[140]

Finally, in respect of reparations, it is difficult at this stage to draw significant conclusions. Proceedings in the *Duch* case at the ECCC involved minimal evidence and submissions in relation to reparations, and this seems likely to be case where reparations of a purely symbolic nature are awarded. Trial proceedings to date at the ICC have not involved significant use of evidence relating to reparations. And while separate reparations proceedings have not yet been held in any case, it is doubtful whether they could be said to impact on defence rights since they may only arise following a conviction, and thus do not delay proceedings leading to judgment.

Therefore, while the rights of an accused to an expeditious trial may certainly be affected by victim participation and reparations proceedings, this need not be the case. Careful design of procedural rules and adequate judicial oversight can together ensure that any delays are kept within acceptable limits.

3.2 Rights and interests of other victims

Less attention has been given to whether the rights and interests of other victims might be adversely affected where some victims participate in or seek reparations before an international criminal tribunal. Many commentators apparently assume that engaging victims is inherently conducive to outcomes which are considered beneficial to broader victim communities: reconciliation, truth-finding and the accountability of perpetrators.[141] However, such a correlation has not been established. Indeed, negative outcomes for other victims are possible if procedures for victim participation and reparations are not carefully and appropriately tailored.

---

138 STL RPE, r. 86(C)(i), *The Prosecutor v Ayyash et al.* (Decision on Defence Motion of 17 February 2012 for an Order to the Victims' Participation Unit to Refile its Submission *Inter Partes* and Inviting Submissions on Legal Issues Related to Applications for the Status of Victim Participating in the Proceedings) STL-11–01/PT/PTJ (5 April 2012).

139 *Ruto Case* (n. 51); *Kenyatta Case* (n. 51).

140 A. Fulford, 'The Reflections of a Trial Judge', Speech to the Assembly of States Parties, The Hague, 6 December 2010, para. 20.

141 Stahn et al. (n. 95), 221; Jorda and de Hemptinne (n. 2), 1397–98; Jouet (n. 95), 257–58; Aldana-Pindell (n. 54), 1457–58; Bitti and González Rivas (n. 3) 320.

First, the possible (though avoidable) impacts discussed above concerning the expeditious disposal of proceedings also affect victims, who have an interest in,[142] and a right to,[143] the prompt completion of trials.

Second, as explained above, victim participation can in some instances prove detrimental to the prosecution case. While it should not be assumed that all victims seek a conviction (for example some may consider that persons other than the accused are responsible for the crime), studies predictably suggest that this is a common interest among victim communities.[144] However, although acquittals may not be desirable for victims, they do not amount to an infringement of victims' right to a remedy, which only requires an effective investigation (and, where possible, prosecution) rather than guaranteeing a particular outcome.[145] Where managed appropriately through judicial oversight, is doubtful that victim participation could render a prosecution 'ineffective' in this sense.

Third, the highly selective nature of international prosecutions means that rights secured to victims through these processes will benefit relatively few victims. In most contexts where mass atrocities have occurred, the great majority of crimes will not be prosecuted before an international tribunal.[146] Some have questioned the implementation of victim participation and/or reparations adherence to the principle that victims should have equal access to justice.[147]

Regarding victims' participation, the extent to which this is a concern depends on the nature and purpose of such participation. If participation is viewed as a remedy – something to which all victims are equally entitled – it is indeed problematic for only some to participate. However, if, as argued above, participation embodies a procedural fair trial right, arising not by virtue of a violation having occurred, but from the initiation of legal proceedings, the problem of equal treatment is reduced. In this case the main challenge is to ensure that all victims who are linked to the proceedings instituted are provided with an equal opportunity to participate. It is true that to date even this goal has proved elusive, owing largely to resource limitations, logistical challenges in effectively and safely engaging with victim communities, and cumbersome procedural mechanisms. However, these are not problems fundamental to victim participation per se, but rather arise from limitations in the current means used to effect such participation.

---

142 In a 2010 report, the ICC Registry stated that of 396 victims' representations made concerning the opening of an investigation in Kenya, 252 (63.6%) included a comment regarding the need for speedy trials: ICC, 'Situation in the Republic of Kenya: Public Redacted Version of Corrigendum to the Report on Victims' Representations', ICC-01/09–17-Corr-Red (29 March 2010), paras 118–119; see also more generally SáCouto and Cleary, (n. 2) 84.

143 *The Prosecutor v Norman, Kallon and Gbao* (Decision on the Applications for a Stay of Proceedings and Denial of Right to Appeal) SCSL-2003–08-PT, SCSL-2003–07-PT, SCSL-2003–09-PT (4 November 2003), paras 8, 11.

144 See for example the surveys conducted by the Human Rights Center at the University of Berkeley in several ICC situation countries, available at: www.law.berkeley.edu/hrc.htm, accessed 28 September 2012.

145 *Velasquez-Rodriguez* case (n. 57) para. 177.

146 The STL currently has one case on its docket, the ECCC four, and even the ICC has implemented a prosecutorial strategy which focuses on a small number of apparently symbolic cases in each situation coming before it – the maximum to date in one situation being five. The ICC Office of the Prosecutor has itself identified this difficulty: ICC OTP, 'Policy Paper on Victims' Participation' (n. 129), 8.

147 Aldana-Pindell (n. 54) 1451–57; Van den Wyngaert (n. 121) 13–14; Baumgartner (n. 114) 438.

Regarding reparations, unequal treatment is a clearer cause for concern. As set out above, all victims of gross human rights violations are entitled to reparations. However, in the great majority of cases no mechanism exists for the provision of such reparations, and they are not realised in practice. Where a small number of criminal cases provide an avenue for accessing reparations to some victims, a question of fairness clearly arises in respect of the numerous other victims who are not able to benefit from this mechanism. As the ICTY Rules Committee explained when rejecting the idea of a reparations mandate to that tribunal:

> Whatever method of funding of compensation is undertaken, it must be acknowledged that it will be unfair in certain respects, in that many victims of the crimes in the former Yugoslavia will not be eligible for such awards. Many will be victims of crimes of individuals who are either not indicted by the Tribunal or who have been indicted but who are not apprehended ... For these reasons, consideration should be given to a more comprehensive method of awarding compensation.[148]

The problem of unequal treatment is exacerbated because many of the criteria according to which a case is selected for prosecution (for example the seniority of suspects or the sufficiency of evidence available) are not criteria according to which one victim's claim for reparations would usually be distinguished from another in a situation of mass violations. Thus the availability of reparations for one group of victims while others obtain none is likely to appear arbitrary to those involved. At the ICC, such problems might in theory be alleviated where other forms of victim assistance are provided through the TFV's second mandate. However, in practice a shortage of funds and the long period of time required for establishing such programmes limit these possibilities.

Because of such difficulties some have argued that reparations and other remedies for victims would be better realised through mechanisms other than international trials, for example truth or compensation commissions.[149] It is certainly true that such mechanisms have some advantages over international criminal trials. However, equally each mechanism also brings its own drawbacks. There are therefore benefits to relying on a combination of mechanisms, while recognising the inherent limitations involved in each.[150]

Where shortcomings in criminal trials (and victim engagements therein) are identified there is a need to identify whether, or to what extent, these are inherent in the mechanism itself as opposed to being attributable to procedures which are flawed or improperly implemented and which can therefore be improved.

Even where limitations are inherent in the mechanism itself, this need not be a reason for setting it aside altogether. The conclusion that a mechanism cannot itself provide a complete and adequate response must be distinguished from a conclusion that the mechanism is actually causing harm. In the latter instance a cause exists to abandon the mechanism. In the former case, it is more appropriate to implement additional and complementary approaches, taking into account the nature and context of the violations and the victims.

This chapter has argued that victim participation at international tribunals arises not as part of a remedy, but rather as a question of natural justice by virtue of the fact that a trial is

---

148 Victims' Compensation and participation, (n. 131), para. 41. See also the Letter from the President of the ICTR (n. 131) paras 9, 13–14.
149 See Van den Wyngaert (n. 121) 16–17; Rauschenbach and Scalia (n. 108) 456–59.
150 Doak (n. 65).

to be held concerning the international crime which caused harm to the victim. Thus the appropriate question is not how all victims may become involved in international criminal proceedings, but rather how those victims affected by a trial can be granted an effective hearing which does not prejudice the rights of the accused and is not harmful to the rights, interests and well-being of other victims.

Regarding reparations, it is recognised that victims have a right to receive reparations from an individual whose culpability for the harm suffered by the victims has been established. And from this it follows that where a conviction is reached in a criminal trial, the provision of reparations should be facilitated as best as possible. Where this can be done through the international criminal tribunal itself in a way which minimises harm to victims, this should be done. In this respect it is necessary for international tribunals to develop jurisprudence and principles which will enable them to take appropriate decisions to ensure not only the fairness of proceedings for the accused, but also the minimisation of harm for victims to maximise complementary interplay with other mechanisms.

Select bibliography

A. de Brouwer and M. Keikkila, 'Victim Issues: Participation, Protection, Reparation, and Assistance', in Göran Sluiter, Håkan Friman, Suzannah Linton, Sergey Vasiliev and Salvatore Zappalà (eds) *International Criminal Procedure: Principles and Rules* (OUP, 2013).

C. McCarthy, *Reparations and Victim Support in the International Criminal Court* (Cambridge University Press, 2012).

B. McGonigle Leyh, *Procedural Justice? Victim Participation in International Criminal Proceedings* (Intersentia, 2011).

A. Seibert-Fohr, *Prosecuting Serious Human Rights Violations* (Oxford University Press, 2009).

38

Continuing evolution of the United Nations treaty bodies system

Nadia Bernaz

1 Introduction

During its first meeting in June 1947, the drafting committee in charge of working on a bill of rights decided that the task warranted work on two separate documents. One would be a manifesto, a non-binding declaration accessible to laypersons, specifically non-lawyers. The other would be a binding international treaty, building on the rights recognised in the declaration.[1] Thus, shortly after the adoption of the Universal Declaration of Human Rights (UDHR) in December 1948,[2] the Commission on Human Rights resumed its drafting work.[3] In 1966, after more than fifteen years of debates on the texts both within the Commission and the Third Committee of the General Assembly, the UN General Assembly adopted the twin International Covenants on Civil and Political Rights[4] and Economic, Social and Cultural Rights[5] (hereinafter ICCPR and ICESCR). Together with the UDHR, these treaties form the International Bill of Rights. They are commonly said to represent the minimum rights guaranteed to all human beings. One year earlier, in 1965, the UN General Assembly adopted the International Convention on the Elimination of All Forms of Racial Discrimination (hereinafter Convention on the Elimination of Racial Discrimination or CERD).[6] Against this firm background, the United Nations has subsequently encouraged the

---

1 UN Commission on Human Rights, Drafting Committee (1st session) (1947) UN Doc. E/CN 4/AC 1/SR 6, 7.
2 Universal Declaration of Human Rights, UNGA Res. 217A (III) (10 December 1948) UN Doc. A/810, 71.
3 Yearbook of the United Nations (1948–1949), 538.
4 International Covenant on Civil and Political Rights (1966) 999 UNTS 171.
5 International Covenant on Economic, Social and Cultural Rights (1966) 993 UNTS 3.
6 International Convention on the Elimination of All Forms of Racial Discrimination (1965) 660 UNTS 195.

protection of more vulnerable groups (women,[7] children,[8] migrant workers[9] and persons with disabilities[10]) and specific rights (the right not to be subjected to torture[11] or to enforced disappearance[12]) through the adoption of six distinct UN treaties between 1979 and 2006. Although these treaties do not set up identical procedures, they share a number of key features. For example each of them has a body of experts monitoring their application – the treaty body – and all of them share a common secretariat,[13] as well as comparable working methods. Thus, the treaties and their respective monitoring bodies have been described as forming a system,[14] a term discussed in the next section of this chapter.

The treaties have been adopted successively, with no apparent coherent plan. States parties to many of these treaties are bound by multiple reporting requirements, sometimes on similar if not identical issues. Over the years, the Office of the High Commissioner for Human Rights has encouraged reforms so as to rationalise the procedures followed by each body, at least in the treatment of state reports. New routes for further reforms have also been explored in a considerable amount of academic literature and during high level consultations, essentially on procedural matters.[15] It is also commonly asserted that, ideally, reform plans should have as a primary objective the evolution of the treaty bodies towards the enhanced protection of rights within domestic systems, as was usefully recalled in various recently adopted documents.[16]

In this context, the primary aim of the chapter is to trace the continuing procedural evolution of the treaty bodies, while also assessing the effectiveness both of the structures in place and the proposed reforms in promoting and protecting human rights. Section 38.2 of the chapter briefly presents the treaty bodies system. Section 38.3 identifies the main procedural challenges faced by the treaty bodies and reviews the reforms that have already been undertaken to address them. Finally, section 38.4 brings the reform debate up to date and looks at the prospects for further change.

7 Convention on the Elimination of All Forms of Discrimination against Women (1979) 1249 UNTS 13 (CEDAW).
8 Convention on the Rights of the Child (1989) 1577 UNTS 3 (CRC).
9 International Convention on the Protection of the Rights of All Migrant Workers and Members of their Families (1990) 2220 UNTS 3 (CPRMW).
10 Convention on the Rights of Persons with Disabilities (2006) 2515 UNTS 3 (CRPD).
11 Convention against Torture and Other Cruel, Inhuman or Degrading Treatment or Punishment (1984) 1465 UNTS 85 (Convention against Torture or CAT).
12 International Convention for the Protection of All Persons from Enforced Disappearance (2006) UN Doc A/61/488 (CPPED).
13 Until 31 December 2007, CEDAW was serviced by the Division for the Advancement of Women in New York. Since January 2008, it has been serviced by the Office of the High Commissioner for Human Rights, just like the other bodies.
14 Dublin Statement on the Process of Strengthening of the United Nations Human Rights Treaty Body System (2009), para 3, available at: http://www2.ohchr.org/english/bodies/HRTD/docs/DublinStatement.pdf, accessed on 15 December 2011. Hereinafter Dublin Statement.
15 See for example (2007) 7(1) *Human Rights Law Review*. Details on the consultations in n. 50 of this chapter.
16 Dublin Statement (n. 14), para. 7. Seoul Statement on Strengthening the UN Human Rights Treaty Body System (2011), para. 1(a), available at: http://www2.ohchr.org/english/bodies/HRTD/docs/SeoulStatement.pdf, accessed on 17 January 2012. Hereinafter Seoul Statement. Pretoria Statement on the Strengthening and Reform of the UN Human Rights Treaty Body System (2011), para. 2.2, available at: http://www2.ohchr.org/english/bodies/HRTD/hrtd_process.htm, accessed on 17 January 2012. Hereinafter Pretoria Statement.

2 The treaty bodies: presentation of the system

Of the nine treaties mentioned in the introduction, the latest to have entered into force is the International Convention for the Protection of All Persons from Enforced Disappearance (CPPED), in December 2010. Each Convention has a dedicated treaty body. The Committee on Enforced Disappearance, the most recently created, held its first session in November 2011. In addition, over sixty states party to the Convention against Torture have also ratified an Optional Protocol which creates a Subcommittee on Prevention of Torture and Other Cruel, Inhuman or Degrading Treatment or Punishment of the Committee against Torture (hereinafter Subcommittee on Prevention of Torture).[17] This body's main function is to carry out regular visits to states that have ratified the Optional Protocol. In a way, it is a tenth treaty body, though its limited and rather unusual functions make it different from the other bodies.

The treaty bodies, including the Subcommittee on Prevention of Torture, use five mechanisms to monitor the implementation of the treaties. First, they all receive regular reports from states. These reports are the final product of self-assessment exercises undertaken by states on the measures they have taken to implement the treaty, their practice in relation to the rights protected and the remaining challenges impeding the full application of the treaty. It is the only mechanism provided for in all treaties, without opt-out possibilities for states, and perhaps the greatest support for the theory that the treaty bodies actually form a coherent system. Thomas Buergenthal suggests that the reason why this mechanism has enjoyed wide state support is as follows:

> [W]hile states have tended to believe that inter-state and individual petition systems would threaten their freedom of action, reporting systems have on the whole not been seen by them as involving much of a risk in that regard . . . It should be emphasized, however, that the assumption that the reporting requirement is 'harmless' is not necessarily valid . . . In fact, experience suggests that there is nothing inherently weaker about a reporting system when compared with other measures of implementation.[18]

Indeed, the treaty bodies' examination of the state reports is usually non-consensual and while the language used in concluding observations tends to be more diplomatic than peremptory, one cannot say that states' sensitivities are particularly spared. The treaty bodies publicly expose serious human rights violations on the part of states. For example, in the latest concluding observations regarding the United Kingdom, the Human Rights Committee declared that:

> The state party should conduct prompt and independent investigations into all allegations concerning suspicious deaths, torture or cruel, inhuman or degrading treatment or punishment inflicted by its personnel (including commanders), in detention facilities in Afghanistan and Iraq.[19]

17 Optional Protocol to the Convention against Torture and other Cruel, Inhuman or Degrading Treatment or Punishment (2002) 2375 UNTS 237.
18 T. Buergenthal, 'The U.N. Human Rights Committee' (2001) 5 *Max Planck Yearbook of United Nations Law* 341 at 347.
19 UN Human Rights Committee, 'Concluding Observations' United Kingdom of Great Britain and Northern Ireland (2008) UN Doc. CCPR/C/GBR/CO/6, para. 14.

Such international scrutiny, also known as 'naming and shaming', concerns all the mechanisms used by the treaty bodies, and not only reporting. It is at best unpleasant for states and can be clearly damaging for their interests, hence providing some form of incentive for change at the domestic level.[20] Despite some advantages, this monitoring mechanism is not without its problems. Indeed, as states are under an obligation to submit reports for each UN human rights treaty they are a party to, reporting raises a number of challenges from delays in submissions to the poor quality of reports.[21]

Second, six bodies may receive inter-state communications whereby a state party refers violations in another state party to the body in charge of monitoring the treaty.[22] This possibility is optional with certain treaty bodies and is provided for in the treaties. States must choose to opt in in order for communications against them to be admissible and for them to be allowed to submit a communication against another state. Before other bodies, this possibility is provided for in a separate optional protocol that states choose to ratify or not.[23] Finally, the Convention on the Elimination of Racial Discrimination provides for an inter-state complaint mechanism by default and grants the Committee on the Elimination of Racial Discrimination competence to receive and examine these communications.

Despite being provided for in relation to seven treaties, inter-state communications have never been used before any of the treaty bodies. Speaking about inter-state complaint mechanisms before all human rights bodies and courts, and not only before the UN treaty bodies, one author explained the rarity of utilisation of this mechanism by the fact that 'the implementation of the inter-state complaint procedure is often perceived to be politically motivated, and potentially too damaging and threatening to a state's interests'.[24] In other words, states generally pursue their own agenda first and addressing human rights violations in another state rarely fits into their foreign policy choices. The same author further pointed out that the inter-state complaint procedure is only one tool that states can use when they have concerns about human rights in another state. Diplomatic tools, or more radical ones such as the adoption of 'domestic legislation restricting financial assistance or trade with the state concerned',[25] are perceived to be more effective and less confrontational and are usually favoured.

Third, eight bodies may receive individual communications directly from victims or their relatives. For all eight bodies, this is an optional mechanism and states must have agreed separately, either by making a declaration or by ratifying an optional protocol. An optional protocol to the Convention on the Rights of the Child, opened for signature in 2012 and not yet entered into force, will provide for this possibility as well. This mechanism is what allows

---

20 For a thorough analysis of naming and shaming, see E. Domínguez Redondo, 'International Human Rights Enforcement: Is There Life beyond Naming and Shaming?' *New Zealand Law Review* (2012, Part IV).

21 See section 38.3 below.

22 These are the bodies in charge of monitoring the following treaties: CERD, ICESCR, ICCPR, CAT, CPRMW, CPPED. The Committee on the Rights of the Child will be able to receive inter-state communications but the optional protocol to the Convention that opens this possibility has not entered into force yet: Optional Protocol to the Convention on the Rights of the Child on a communications procedure (2011) UN Doc. A/HRC/RES/17/18.

23 See table below for more detail.

24 S. Leckie, 'The Inter-State Complaint Procedure in International Human Rights Law: Hopeful Prospects or Wishful Thinking?' (1988) 10(2) *Human Rights Quarterly* 249 at 250.

25 Ibid. at 252.

the treaty bodies to be described as quasi-jurisdictional bodies. Upon receiving communications and after having ruled on their admissibility, the bodies must initially attempt to get the petitioner and the state to reach some sort of agreement. These conciliatory functions are clearly non-jurisdictional in nature. However, if no agreement is reached, the bodies engage in a legal assessment of the claims made and determine whether provisions of the treaties have been violated or not. In doing so, they act like a court of human rights would, except that their decisions are not binding.[26]

Fourth, certain treaty bodies may carry out inquiries where there is suspicion of grave and systematic violations of the treaty they monitor by a state party. This mechanism is provided for in two treaties – the Convention against Torture and the Convention on Enforced Disappearance – and in four optional protocols, including the protocol to the Convention on the Rights of the Child, which has not yet entered into force. For three of these protocols, CEDAW,[27] the Convention on the Rights of Persons with Disabilities[28] and the protocol to the Convention on the Rights of the Child, this is only one mechanism among others that the protocol sets up, and states may ratify the protocols while opting out of this particular mechanism. By contrast, the Optional Protocol to the International Covenant on Economic Social and Cultural Rights, which is not yet in force, also provides for this mechanism among others but states need to specifically opt in to the system so as to allow the Committee to carry out inquiries in the future.[29]

Finally, the Subcommittee on Prevention of Torture is the only body which may carry out visits in the states party to the Optional Protocol to the Convention against Torture. The Protocol gives the Subcommittee unrestricted access to places of detention[30] and it should be given the opportunity to interview detainees privately.[31] In December 2011, the Subcommittee had published twelve reports on twelve different countries.

These mechanisms and the respective attributions of the treaty bodies are summarised in the table overleaf.

---

26 See discussion on the non-binding nature of the treaty bodies' decisions in section 38.4 below.
27 Optional Protocol to the Convention on the Elimination of All Forms of Discrimination against Women, Art. 8, (1999) 2131 UNTS 83.
28 Optional Protocol to the Convention on the Rights of Persons with Disabilities, Art. 6, (2006) UN Doc. A/61/611.
29 Optional Protocol to the International Covenant on Economic, Social and Cultural Rights, Art. 11, (2008) UN Doc A/63/435.
30 Optional Protocol (n. 17) Art. 12(a).
31 Ibid. Art. 14(1)(d).

	State reports	Inter-state communications	Individual communications	Inquiries	Visits
CERD	✓	✓	✓ (optional)	✗	✗
ICESCR	✓	✓ (OP)	✓ (OP)	✓ (OP – states must opt in)	✗
ICCPR	✓	✓ (optional)	✓ (OP)	✗	✗
CEDAW	✓	✗	✓ (OP)	✓ (OP – states can opt out)	✗
CAT	✓	✓ (optional)	✓ (optional)	✓	✓ (carried out by SPT, created by OP)
CRC	✓	✓ (OP)	✓ (OP)	✓ (OP – states can opt out))	✗
CPRMW	✓	✓ (optional)	✓ (optional)	✗	✗
CRPD	✓	✗	✓ (OP)	✓ (OP P states can opt out)	✗
CPPED	✓	✓ (optional)	✓ (optional)	✓	✗

OP: Optional Protocol

SPT: Subcommittee on Prevention of Torture

The similarities between the bodies' functions and monitoring tools raise the question as to whether the treaty bodies and the mechanisms they use form a system. The reasons why the diverse UN human rights procedures are not considered to form a system are in great part due to the lack of interconnectedness between the intergovernmental and treaty-based procedures.[32] However, merely examining the treaty bodies, and their numerous similarities in terms of structure, working methods and monitoring mechanisms used, makes it difficult not to view them as a whole, at least to some extent. This impression is further reinforced by the fact that since 1991 states may submit a single core document containing background information of relevance to all treaty bodies, in lieu of including this information as the first part of each report they submit.[33] Moreover, states have been regularly encouraged to follow the same instructions in relation to the form and the content of their reports to all treaty bodies.[34]

The sum of procedures used and common practices both adopted and encouraged by the treaty bodies leads to the conclusion that the treaty bodies form a system. However, they could certainly be more integrated, and some have even suggested the creation of a single body to replace the nine current treaty bodies, so as to simplify the system and make it more efficient. This is one of the many proposals of reform put forward in recent years, which

32 N. Bernaz, 'Reforming the UN Human Rights Protection Procedures: a Legal Perspective on the Establishment of the Universal Periodic Review Mechanism', in K. Boyle (ed.), *New Institutions for Human Rights Protection* (OUP, 2009), 75.

33 UN Secretary General, 'Preparation of the Initial Parts of States Party Reports ('Core Documents') under the Various International Human Rights Instruments' (1992) UN Doc. HRI/CORE/1. See section 38.3.

34 UN Secretary General, 'Compilation of Guidelines on the Form and Content of Reports to be Submitted by States Parties to the International Human Rights Treaties' (2009) UN Doc. HRI/GEN/2/Rev. 6. See also section 38.3.

section 38.4 briefly covers. Before getting into this, the next section presents the main procedural challenges the treaty bodies face and the reforms already undertaken to address them.

3 Main challenges and past reforms

The challenges currently facing the treaty bodies are various in nature. First and probably foremost, the system is under-resourced. In March 2011, in her opening statement to the Human Rights Council for the Introduction of her annual report, the UN High Commissioner for Human Rights pointed out that 'the treaty body system is now almost double the size it was in 2004 ... Regrettably, the growth of its funding resources has not kept apace.'[35] On this occasion, she also announced that different consultation processes were underway to reflect on plans to strengthen the system. Yet, she warned, 'we all need to acknowledge that, in and of themselves, streamlining and strengthening cannot displace the need to find and allocate additional resources to match the growth of the system'.[36] More resources are needed, a position supported by a large number of treaty bodies' experts.[37]

The second main challenge concerns the system's effectiveness and, in particular, the difficulties around the follow-up to the bodies' decisions. All treaty bodies have developed the habit of requesting information from states parties about the implementation of the previous concluding observations. Only a few of them have set up a specific and more elaborate follow-up procedure, involving a rapporteur or a coordinator to follow up.[38]

Finally, and this is the challenge that has attracted the most discussions, the reporting system has become increasingly complex over the years. Arguably, the complexity does not stem from the obligations themselves, which are relatively straightforward, compared to other treaties for example in the field of trade law, but rather from the fact that there is overlap between the regimes. There are now nine UN human rights treaties placing reporting obligations on states parties. Many states who are parties to several of these treaties are struggling to keep apace and are late in submitting their reports, when they submit them at all. It is commonly asserted that 'late reporting and outright failure to submit reports to treaty monitoring bodies have been persistent characteristics of the system'.[39] Clearly, this is not the treaty bodies system's primary responsibility, but that of states. It falls on states to write their reports on time so as to abide by their obligations. That said, the reality is that there tends to be significant overlap between the various reports, and that submitting so many similar reports can be viewed as a waste of time and resources. Leaving aside the Convention on the Elimination of Racial Discrimination, all of the other treaties were adopted after the twin

35 Statement by Navanethem Pillay, United Nations High Commissioner for Human Rights at the Introduction of the Annual Report Geneva (3 March 2011), available at http://www.ohchr.org/EN/NewsEvents/Pages/DisplayNews.aspx?NewsID=10794&LangID=E, accessed on 15 December 2011.

36 Ibid.

37 Dublin Statement (n. 14) para. 23. Marrakesh Statement on Strengthening the Relationship between NHRIs and the Human Rights Treaty Bodies System (2010), para. 19, available at: http://www2.ohchr.org/english/bodies/HRTD/docs/MarrakeshStatement_en.pdf, accessed on 17 January 2012. Hereinafter Marrakesh Statement.

38 Report on the Working Methods of the Human Rights Treaty Bodies Relating to the State Party Reporting Process (2010) UN Doc. HRI/ICM/2010/2, paras 75–82.

39 M. O'Flaherty and C. O'Brien, 'Reform of UN Human Rights Treaty Monitoring Bodies: A Critique of the Concept Paper on the High Commissioner's Proposal for a Unified Standing Treaty Body' (2007) 7 *Human Rights Law Review* 141 at 142.

Covenants. Apart from the Covenants themselves, the other treaties, including CERD, are meant either to further certain rights or to provide special protection for more vulnerable groups. The scope of the Covenants is extremely wide and, arguably, the other UN human rights treaties do not grant additional rights as such but, rather, go into more detail on rights already protected by the Covenants. In other words, the ground covered by the other treaties is similar to that covered by the Covenants. In this context, the significant overlaps between state reports, or at least between the reports to the Human Rights Committee and the Committee on Economic, Social and Cultural Rights on the one hand, and the reports to all the other treaty bodies on the other, are not surprising. This may simply be a consequence of the way in which the system was built.

In order to address the complexity issue and save the resources of the treaty bodies and states, dialogue among treaty bodies has been encouraged so as to foster the development of common procedures. Two distinct types of meetings have been taking place: the meetings of the chairpersons of the treaty bodies and inter-committee meetings. The first meeting of the chairpersons of the treaty bodies was held in 1983 and since 1995 they have been organised annually.[40] Inter-committee meetings include the chairpersons and two additional members from each of the committees. The first one was held in Geneva in 2002.[41] These regular meetings have been critical in the adoption of harmonised reporting guidelines for states and common working methods among all the treaty bodies,[42] although a lot remains to be done in both areas.[43]

Among the changes introduced is the practice of requesting a core document from states party to at least one of the treaties. The core document is meant to contain basic information about the state which is unlikely to change dramatically from one report to another. This includes the demographic, economic, social and cultural characteristics of the state, constitutional, political and legal structure of the state, information on its acceptance of international human rights norms, including which human rights treaties it has ratified, and whether it has made reservations or has derogated from certain provisions. States should also provide information about the legal framework for the protection of human rights at the national level, the framework within which human rights are promoted at the national level, the reporting process at the national level and, finally, information on non-discrimination and equality and effective remedies.[44] This core document should form the first part of all the reports submitted by the state. The objective is twofold: having states provide information which can prove crucial for the treaty bodies in their examining of the reports and saving time and resources of states, which do not have to constantly repeat the same information. The common core document is simply meant to be updated if necessary.

---

40 Information on meetings of the chairpersons and Inter-Committee Meetings available at: http://www2.ohchr.org/english/bodies/icm-mc/index.htm, accessed on 17 January 2012.
41 Ibid.
42 Report on the Working Methods of the Human Rights Treaty Bodies Relating to the State Party Reporting Process (2010) UN Doc HRI/ICM/2010/2.
43 International Seminar of Experts on the Reforms of the United Nations Human Rights Treaty Body System, 'The Poznan Statement on the Reforms of the United Nations Human Rights Treaty Body System' (28–29 September 2010), para. 16, available at: http://www2.ohchr.org/english/bodies/HRTD/docs/PoznanStatement.pdf, accessed on 17 January 2012. Hereinafter Poznan Statement.
44 Compilation of Guidelines (n. 34) paras 31–59.

A more drastic way to deal with the complexity challenge would be to introduce significant changes in state obligations by requiring a single report from them, irrespective of how many treaties they have ratified. This report, in turn, would be examined by a single treaty body. This radical reform plan was put forward in 2006 in a 'concept paper' by the then UN High Commissioner for Human Rights.[45] It prompted much discussion and new initiatives and coincided with perhaps equally radical reform plans, such as the creation of a World Court of Human Rights.

4 Current reform plans and prospects for further change

The rationale for the High Commissioner for Human Rights' single treaty body was as follows:

> The proposal of a unified standing treaty body is based on the premise that, unless the international human rights treaty system functions and is perceived as a unified, single entity responsible for monitoring the implementation of all international human rights obligations, with a single, accessible entry point for rights-holders, the lack of visibility, authority and access which affects the current system will persist. The proposal is also based on the recognition that, as currently constituted, the system is approaching the limits of its performance, and that, while steps can be taken to improve its functioning in the short and medium term, more fundamental, structural change will be required in order to guarantee its effectiveness in the long term.[46]

In short, this proposal was aimed both at clarifying the current system and at rendering it less costly. The concept paper reform plan, however, attracted very little support – or even hostility – from states and other stakeholders.[47] The consensus among treaty bodies members seems to be that 'reform that may require the amendment of treaties should be embarked upon only if the goals sought to be achieved cannot be attained by any other means and those goals are such as to justify the protracted and sometimes unpredictable process of amendment'.[48]

In the end, the idea of a profound overhaul was abandoned and more gradual reform plans encouraged by the UN High Commissioner for Human Rights, Navi Pillay. In September 2009, in her statement to the Human Rights Council, Pillay called on 'states parties to human rights treaties and other stakeholders to initiate a process of reflection on how to streamline and strengthen the treaty body system'.[49] In this context, a number of meetings with various stakeholders have taken place, each resulting in a final statement or report,

---

45 Concept Paper on the High Commissioner's Proposal for a Unified Standing Treaty Body, UN Doc. HRI/MC/2006/CRP 1 (2006).

46 Ibid. para. 27.

47 Dublin Statement (n. 14) para. 4. However, some stakeholders still support the idea of a unified body, at least to deal with communications. See Report of the Expert Meeting on Petitions, following consultations in Geneva (2011), 4, available at http://www2.ohchr.org/english/bodies/HRTD/hrtd_process.htm, accessed on 17 January 2012. Hereinafter Geneva Report.

48 Dublin Statement (n. 14) para. 16. See also: F. Hampson, 'An Overview of the Reform of the UN Human Rights Machinery' (2007) 7(1) *Human Rights Law Review* 7 at 12–13.

49 UN Human Rights Council, Statement of Navanethem Pillay, UN High Commissioner for Human Rights (12th session) (14 September 2009), available at: http://www2.ohchr.org/english/bodies/HRTD/docs/StatementHC12thSessionHRC.pdf, accessed on 17 January 2012.

comprising their positions, recommendations and proposals for reform.[50] The reforms proposed do not merely concern the bodies per se, but also the interactions between the bodies and other stakeholders indirectly involved in their work, such as non-governmental organisations (NGOs) and national human rights institutions. The proposals aim to achieve two main goals: making the system more effective and bringing it closer to the rights holders.

4.1 Making the system more effective

A number of proposals aim to make the system more effective in three main ways: improving the quality of state reports, enhancing working methods and developing reliable follow-up mechanisms.

4.1.1 Improving state reports

Following the meeting of National Human Rights Institutions in Marrakesh in June 2010, one of the changes suggested was to streamline the reporting system so as to reduce the volume of documentation treaty bodies have to deal with. As stated in the Marrakesh statement:

> [A]ll treaty bodies' documentation, including states parties' reports, should be strictly limited to the recommended number of pages, in accordance with the harmonized reporting guidelines adopted by the Inter-Committee Meeting and Chair Persons Meeting.[51]

Moreover, state parties should 'submit and regularly update the common core document and treaty specific reports' and 'new and innovative working methods and procedures, such as the lists of issues prior to reporting [should] be further explored with a view to better focus the debate on the key strategic priorities in States Parties under review as established by the treaty bodies'.[52]

---

50 Dublin Statement (n. 14); Marrakesh Statement (n. 37); Poznan Statement (n. 43); Seoul Statement (n. 16); Report of the Informal Technical Consultation with States Parties in Sion (2011), available at http://www2.ohchr.org/english/bodies/HRTD/hrtd_process.htm, accessed on 17 January 2012; Pretoria Statement (n. 16); Implementation of UN Treaty Body Concluding Observations: The Role of National and Regional Mechanisms in Europe (Bristol 2011), available at http://www2.ohchr.org/english/bodies/HRTD/docs/Summary_Proceedings_Bristol_Sept2011_24.10.2011.pdf, accessed on 17 January 2012; Report of the Lucerne Academic Consultation on Strengthening the United Nations Treaty Body System (Lucerne 2011), available at http://www2.ohchr.org/english/bodies/HRTD/hrtd_process.htm, accessed on 17 January 2012. Hereinafter Lucerne Report; Geneva Report (n. 47); Strengthening the United Nations Human Rights Treaty Body System Dublin II Meeting Outcome Document (Dublin 2011), available at: http://www2.ohchr.org/english/bodies/HRTD/docs/DublinII_Outcome_Document.pdf, accessed on 17 January 2012; and The Universal Periodic Review Process and the Treaty Bodies: Constructive Cooperation or Deepening Division? (Maastricht 2011), http://www2.ohchr.org/english/bodies/HRTD/hrtd_process.htm, accessed on 17 January 2012.
51 Marrakesh Statement (n. 37) para. 16(a).
52 Ibid. para. 16(b).

4.1.2 Enhancing working methods

First, during the Civil Society Consultation on Treaty Body Strengthening held in Seoul in April 2011, the participants suggested that 'the master calendar of deadlines related to Treaty Body sessions currently being developed by the OHCHR should include information on all steps in the reporting process at least two years in advance of the consideration of a State Party's report by a Treaty Body'.[53] This proposal aims at allowing NGOs to better prepare for the reporting process. Having a clearer idea about deadlines would make it easier for them to draft their own shadow reports and to actively and perhaps more successfully push for a greater involvement of civil society in the drafting of state reports.

Second, during the Academic Consultation on Strengthening the United Nations Treaty Body System held in Lucerne in October 2011, participants reiterated the idea of creating chambers, or sub-committees, within all treaty bodies. This idea had been put forward by the High Commissioner for Human Rights in her proposal for a unified treaty body.[54] In Lucerne, however, the introduction of chambers was discussed in relation to all treaty bodies, not as a single one. As stated in the final report of this meeting:

> The participants also discussed the possibility of working in smaller sub-committees or chambers as at least two committees have done, in order to deal with more reports at each session. This was seen as an option which could also be considered at present by the treaty bodies which do not currently operate in chambers. If the chambers were to be composed of 3 or 5 members with specific language groups in mind, the costs of translation might be reduced, though other conference servicing costs might increase.[55]

Finally, the area where the greatest changes were proposed concerns increased cooperation and coordination between treaty bodies and harmonisation of their working methods. As stated by the participants to the International Seminar held in Poznan in September 2010, 'the system needs to move from a "light" to an "advanced" coordination and harmonization mode'.[56] This can be achieved 'through increasing use of cross-references to the work of other treaty bodies [to] avoid inconsistencies',[57] 'increased development of general comments and where appropriate joint general comment to reinforce the indivisibility and interdependence of all human rights'[58] and the harmonisation of remedies.[59] Moreover, the participants recommended the recognition of 'the role of Treaty bodies' members during inter-sessional periods . . . in order to facilitate . . . coordination of common activities and representation'.[60] To enhance the circulation of information among treaty body members and from one body to the other, the creation of a secure intranet connection was proposed.[61]

---

53 Seoul Statement (n. 16) para. 3(b)v.
54 Concept Paper on the High Commissioner's Proposal for a Unified Standing Treaty Body (n. 45) paras 41–45.
55 Lucerne Report (n. 50) 6.
56 Poznan Statement (n. 43) para. 16.
57 Marrakesh Statement (n. 37) para. 16(c).
58 Ibid. para. 17.
59 Geneva Report (n. 47) 3.
60 Poznan Statement (n. 43) para. 17.
61 Ibid. para. 18.

Another aspect of harmonisation concerns the relationship between the treaty bodies system and the other UN human rights procedures such as the Universal Periodic Review (UPR)[62] and special procedures.[63] A better circulation of information and greater cross referencing among all these mechanisms was encouraged by participants to the consultation process.[64]

4.1.3 Developing reliable follow-up mechanisms

The participants to the Consultation on treaty body strengthening with UN entities and specialised agencies, held in Geneva in November 2011, discussed the issue of follow-up mechanisms at length and made a series of interesting proposals, entailing various degrees of harmonisation among the treaty bodies, from common practices across the board to a mere compilation of best practices that treaty bodies could pick and choose from.[65] Among other ideas that the participants put forward was that of 'holding meetings on implementation of recommendations between the Rapporteur(s) on Follow-Up and members of delegations coming to Geneva or New York for the consideration of the state reports'.[66] Yet another idea was the development of 'concerted actions among the . . . [treaties bodies], such as joint appeals for implementation of recommendations, common press releases etc.'[67] Participants were also concerned with ensuring consistency with the other UN procedures and suggested that the procedures of the Human Rights Council play a great role in the follow-up of the treaty bodies' work, 'in particular by always including information on non-implementation of recommendations in the UPR compilation documents and in the materials prepared by the Council's Special Rapporteurs/working groups for their country visits.'[68]

A recurrent problem in relation to follow-up is the fact that for treaty bodies to engage in it effectively amounts to adding an arguably entirely different task to their already busy schedules. Moreover, there are doubts as to the bodies' capacity and perhaps legitimacy to carry out follow-up tasks themselves. As Françoise Hampson pointed out, 'without its own police force or bailiffs, an international judicial or quasi-judicial system needs the support of a political body if effect is to be given to its pronouncements.'[69] With this in mind, 'one expert . . . proposed to have a Special Rapporteur on Follow-Up of the Human Rights Council, who should have regular contacts with appointed focal points on follow-up in each Committee'.[70] However, this idea was labelled 'too ambitious at this stage'.[71]

---

62 UN General Assembly, Universal Periodic Review Annex, 'Exploring Complementarity between Treaty Monitoring Bodies and the Universal Periodic Review Process' (2009) UN Doc. A/HRC/12/G/1. See also, Bernaz (n. 32) 87–91.

63 N. Rodley, 'United Nations Human Rights Treaty Bodies and Special Procedures of the Commission on Human Rights – Complementarity or Competition?' (2003) 25(4) *Human Rights Quarterly* 882.

64 See for example in relation to follow-up, Geneva Report (n. 47) 2.

65 Ibid.

66 Ibid.

67 Ibid.

68 Ibid.

69 Hampson (n. 48) at 12.

70 Geneva Report (n. 47) 2.

71 Ibid. 3.

4.2 Bringing the system closer to the rights holders

The lack of knowledge about the treaty bodies among the general public remains a critical problem for the system as a whole. Outside a limited group of human rights professionals, there is little awareness about the bodies which, perhaps, do not play the protective role they were designed to play.[72] Two streams of reforms have been proposed to address this issue, and are briefly discussed below.

4.2.1 Itinerant bodies and use of new technologies

The first stream of reform proposals aims at enhancing the visibility of the treaty bodies by bringing them out of the UN buildings, physically or at least through the use of new technologies. In relation to the former option, two groups of participants to the consultation process have suggested that the treaty bodies should hold meetings outside Geneva and New York, so as to widen awareness about the treaty bodies system.[73] In effect, this would amount to making the treaty bodies itinerant, at least to some extent. While the logistics around this practice would pose its own challenges, there is arguably a lot to gain by embracing it. This would attract attention from local or regional media, and generally enhance the circulation of information about the bodies in question.

An easier, less costly though not uncontroversial[74] way to enhance awareness about the treaty bodies would be to webcast treaty bodies public meetings, as is being done for the UN Human Rights Council's Universal Periodic Review exercise.[75] The participants to the Seoul consultation further advocated in favour of the generalisation of video conferencing, so that 'NGOs not physically present at the NGO briefings or pre-sessional working group meetings have an opportunity to provide oral briefings to the Treaty Bodies'.[76]

The participants to the Pretoria consultation proposed that information about the treaty bodies be disseminated not only on the United Nations website, but more widely 'including through national, regional and international media, and through social networks',[77] so as to address the issue of 'inadequate public understanding of the significant and important work of the treaty bodies'.[78] They even made arguably more innovative proposals:

> OHCHR should be more proactive in reaching out to and engaging NGOs in the treaty body process. To this end, we recommend that OHCHR: a) develop a comprehensive up-to-date list of NGOs; b) further enhance civil society communications including through regular, accessible email updates and newsletters; and c) enhance the use of social media such as Facebook and Twitter to engage civil society in the work of treaty bodies.[79]

72 M. Nowak, 'The Need for a World Court of Human Rights' (2007) 7(1) *Human Rights Law Review* 251 at 253–54.
73 Marrakesh Statement (n. 37) para. 18; Poznan Statement (n. 43) para. 22.
74 E. Domínguez Redondo, 'The Universal Periodic Review of the UN Human Rights Council: An Assessment of the First Session' (2008) 7(3) *Chinese Journal of International Law* 721 at 733 fn. 34.
75 Poznan Statement (n. 43) para. 23.
76 Seoul Statement (n. 16) para. 3(b)(vi).
77 Pretoria Statement (n. 16) para. 3.1.
78 Ibid. para. 3.
79 Ibid. para. 3.2.

4.2.2 Mainstreaming the decisions and the issue of their binding effect

Finally, the second stream of proposals aims to develop the use of the treaty bodies' case law and expertise in domestic proceedings, so as to mainstream their work and make it more relevant to a wider audience. In this context, two proposals stand out. First, there is the idea championed by Manfred Nowak of creating a World Court of Human Rights to monitor the treaties.[80] A World Court would certainly attract more attention than the current human rights treaty bodies, making the UN treaties more visible. However, the hurdles to pass prior to the establishment of such a court would be considerable. As a result, this proposal does not seem to have prompted enthusiastic reactions from states and has not been discussed during the latest consultation process.

Second, participants to the Lucerne consultation discussed the possibility of setting up procedures so as to develop links with domestic judicial systems. With this in mind:

> [O]ne suggestion made was that of a national court applying to a treaty body for advice in a matter of substance which could then guide the court (under a procedure analogous to article 267 of the Treaty on the Functioning of the European Union under which national courts may refer a question to the European Court of Justice for a preliminary ruling). This could take the form of an 'interpretative comment' on the particular issue, addressing the substance of a particular aspect of a right rather than the situation of the victim.[81]

Though not without merits, as it 'could make the opinions of the treaty bodies more relevant and applicable',[82] the participants feared that this procedure might 'lead to delays in national judicial processes'.[83] Additionally, it could 'be seen as a request to pre-judge a case which might later come before the treaty body in question as an individual complaint, and would in any case probably require amendment of a number of treaties'.[84]

Another issue would be to establish whether the decisions taken by the treaty bodies following this procedure would be binding. At the moment, the decisions of the treaty bodies – case law or concluding observations following the presentation of state reports – are non-binding, which is often presented as one of the major flaws of the system.[85] Both the creation of a World Court of Human Rights and the creation of a system linking domestic courts to the treaty bodies through the possibility to make preliminary rulings would require change in this area. A Court would necessarily have to make binding decisions. Otherwise, the word 'court' would be an overstatement.[86] Similarly, a system of preliminary rulings could be seen as a waste of time if the domestic courts were not under the obligation to abide by it.

Leaving these proposals to the side, it could be argued that the fact that the decisions of the treaty bodies are not binding constitutes an obstacle to the development of public awareness of the treaty bodies system. Indeed, for non specialists it surely is difficult to grasp the relevance of a system based on soft law. The current system, however, has numerous advantages. The decision to create human rights bodies and not courts, thus institutions without the

---

80 Nowak (n. 72).
81 Lucerne Report (n. 50) 10.
82 Ibid. 10
83 Ibid.
84 Ibid.
85 Nowak (n. 72) 252.
86 Ibid. 254.

power to make binding decisions, was taken early on during the negotiations for the two 1966 Covenants.[87] It must have appeared to the drafters that if such power was to be granted, a considerably smaller number of states would ratify the treaties. A glance at the current situation of the regional human rights mechanisms confirms this assumption. Leaving the European Court of Human Rights to the side, only a small number of American and African states have accepted the optional jurisdiction of the Inter-American and the African Courts of Human Rights respectively. By contrast, all states party to the American or African regional human rights treaties have accepted that bodies which cannot adopt binding decisions should be able to play an active part in the monitoring of the treaties. Hence, had the UN treaty bodies been granted the power to adopt binding decisions, there would most probably have been fewer ratifications.

The debate is not new between the pragmatists who think that human rights treaties should be ratified by the largest number of states possible, and the idealists who think that the integrity of the treaties and the mechanisms they set up should be guaranteed at all costs, even if this means attracting fewer states parties.[88] Along with the pragmatic side, it is argued here that the non-binding nature of their decisions allows the treaty bodies to engage with as many states as possible, which is a positive aspect of the system.

It could be said that other mechanisms, such as the Universal Periodic Review, allow for engagement with a large number of states, in fact all UN member states, on human rights issues. In this context, since there is already a non-binding and relatively soft mechanism, the UPR, it could make sense to support the possibility for the treaty bodies to adopt binding decisions, albeit in relation to a limited number of states. This argument brings about two series of comments. First, the treaties were adopted before the UPR, and it is probably too late to establish this division of labour between the two mechanisms whereby the UPR would adopt non-binding decisions, while the treaty bodies would adopt binding ones. Indeed, this would imply amending all the UN human rights treaties, a largely unrealistic task. Second, despite some similarities, there is a major difference between the treaty bodies assessing state reports and the Human Rights Council conducting the UPR. While they all look at states' human rights records, the UPR exercise is conducted by peer states. By contrast, the treaty bodies are independent and look at situations as human rights professionals. Therefore, the treaty bodies provide real added value compared to the Human Rights Council conducting the UPR.[89]

In short, the treaty bodies cannot adopt binding decisions, but this very fact has probably encouraged wide ratification of the treaties and provided for numerous opportunities to have independent professionals question states on their human rights records. In this context, the non-binding nature of the treaty bodies decisions is unlikely to be called into question. The treaty bodies system must find other ways to bring itself closer to the rights holders.

---

87 Interestingly, the Australian Delegation proposed the establishment of an International Human Rights Court as early as 1947. See UN Commission on Human Rights, Drafting Committee on an International Bill of Human Rights (1st session) (1947) UN Doc. E/CN 4/21. The idea was abandoned due to lack of support. See L. Kutner, 'Proposals for a United Nations Writ of Habeas Corpus and an International Court of Human Rights' (1954) 28 *Tulane Law Review* 417 at 426.

88 This debate is similar to the one on reservations to human rights treaties. See, for example, W. Schabas, 'Reservations to Human Rights Treaties: Time for Innovation and Reform' (1994) 32 *Canadian Yearbook of International Law* 39 at 40–41.

89 In turn, the UPR provides added value compared to treaty bodies' work. See Domínguez Redondo (n. 74).

5 Conclusion

Since the very beginning of their work, the treaty bodies have adopted dozens of decisions in specific cases (jurisprudence), hundreds of concluding observations in relation to state reports, as well as corresponding follow-up documents. They have adopted over one hundred general comments or general recommendations on how certain rights protected in the treaties have evolved and should be interpreted, and on more procedural matters such as reservations. They have also carried out country visits and adopted various other documents. Clearly, the complaint procedures set up by the treaties are used, albeit against a limited number of willing states, and while the delay in state reporting is a recurrent problem, a significant number of reports have been submitted to and assessed by the treaty bodies.

These figures show that the treaty bodies have enthusiastically engaged in the practical work of interpreting the law in given situations and of assessing how individual states comply with human rights obligations deriving from the treaties they have ratified. The concluding observations, the jurisprudence in specific cases, the general comments and general recommendations, to name just the main types of documents, all further the standard-setting role played by the treaties themselves. Through their detailed interpretative work, the treaty bodies contribute to the introduction of more precision in international human rights law, far beyond the looser, idealist approach to be found in the Universal Declaration of Human Rights. In their jurisprudence, they have used legalistic language, furthering human rights law, not only promoting vague principles.

The treaty bodies' interpretations have clarified and considerably widened the provisions, hence providing guidance for future state practice. The decisions and various documents adopted form a body of soft law which can help lawyers or NGOs frame human rights claims introduced outside the bodies themselves: before domestic courts or outside the court rooms, in advocacy work. This, in turn, can strengthen the protection and promotion of human rights. More generally, all these documents make for an invaluable source of information on state practice for human rights defenders, lawyers and academics around the world. On this note, the fact that the members of the treaty bodies enjoy a large degree of independence obviously is an essential and positive aspect of the system.

In sum, furthering and clarifying international human rights standards is probably the area where the contribution of the treaty bodies has been the greatest, and this despite the numerous challenges the bodies have been facing, which are outlined in this chapter. As seen, this contribution is relatively easy to assess, though with a limited degree of precision. By contrast, it is more difficult to evaluate the precise direct contribution of the treaty bodies in the protection of human rights, as opposed to their contribution through standard setting.

Assessing precisely the role of the treaty bodies in the direct protection of human rights would imply looking at the number of lives saved, the number of human rights violations remedied and, potentially, the number of human rights violations prevented thanks to the intervention of the treaty bodies in their concluding observations or decisions on specific cases. Unfortunately, these figures do not exist. Therefore, the contribution cannot be evaluated in quantitative terms. Yet, it does exist.

NGOs and human rights defenders have repeatedly mentioned that, in many cases, bringing a situation to the attention of the treaty bodies, or for that matter to the attention of any international human rights mechanism, or simply threatening to do so, can end ongoing violations and prevent further ones. This is a clear positive contribution to the protection of human rights, which is all the more remarkable because none of the documents adopted by the treaty bodies are binding, as discussed above.

Victims of human rights abuses, however, demand and deserve more. The history of the treaty bodies system shows a continuing evolution towards more protection against such abuses, through the addition of specialised treaties and procedural reforms. Yet, none of the current reform plans, even the most ambitious, can be expected to completely bypass the inherent limitations of the system. It would be wholly unrealistic to expect the bodies to remedy or even merely expose all human rights violations occurring around the globe, especially since they are only one of the UN human rights procedures. That said, things can always be improved. In this context, the chapter has focused on the various reforms, introduced or simply discussed, aimed at allowing the bodies to continue playing a key, though limited, role in the protection and promotion of human rights.

Select bibliography

N. Bernaz, 'Reforming the UN Human Rights Protection Procedures: a Legal Perspective on the Establishment of the Universal Periodic Review Mechanism', in K. Boyle (ed.), *New Institutions for Human Rights Protection* (OUP, 2009), 75–92.

T. Buergenthal, 'The U.N. Human Rights Committee' (2001) 5 *Max Planck Yearbook of United Nations Law* 341.

E. Domínguez Redondo, 'International Human Rights Enforcement: Is There Life beyond Naming and Shaming?' *New Zealand Law Review* (2012, Part IV).

F. Hampson, 'An Overview of the Reform of the UN Human Rights Machinery' (2007) 7(1) *Human Rights Law Review* 7.

S. Leckie, 'The Inter-State Complaint Procedure in International Human Rights Law: Hopeful Prospects or Wishful Thinking?' (1988) 10(2) *Human Rights Quarterly* 249.

M. Nowak, 'The Need for a World Court of Human Rights' (2007) 7(1) *Human Rights Law Review* 251.

M. O'Flaherty and C. O'Brien, 'Reform of UN Human Rights Treaty Monitoring Bodies: A Critique of the Concept Paper on the High Commissioner's Proposal for a Unified Standing Treaty Body' (2007) 7 *Human Rights Law Review* 141.

N. Rodley, 'United Nations Human Rights Treaty Bodies and Special Procedures of the Commission on Human Rights – Complementarity or Competition?' (2003) 25(4) *Human Rights Quarterly* 882.

39

The future of the United Nations Special Procedures

Ted Piccone

1 Introduction

The relatively long and lively history of the UN Special Procedures system of independent experts appointed to monitor human rights around the world, along with new data assessing the impact on the ground, points to a future that is mainly hopeful, provided experts and advocates remain vigilant against threats to undermine their independence. The purpose of this chapter, building upon two years of research assessing the Special Procedures mechanism at the national level, is to briefly explain the main contours of the system and the key factors that shape its effectiveness, and to recommend steps for strengthening and more deeply integrating it within the broader UN system.

2 Who and what are the Special Procedures?

The term 'Special Procedures' refers to the special rapporteurs, special representatives, independent experts and working groups mandated by the UN's political bodies to monitor and report on human rights violations and recommend ways to promote and protect human rights.[1] The UN member states created these mechanisms over 40 years ago to serve as independent eyes and ears evaluating the application of international human rights norms to concrete situations. The Special Procedures carry out this function by: undertaking fact-finding missions to countries of concern; issuing communications to governments, including urgent appeals and requests for corrective action; calling public attention to specific violations; elaborating on human rights norms; and providing periodic reports to the Human Rights Council (HRC) and General Assembly of the United Nations.

The mechanisms operate as critical nodes in a larger UN system composed of treaty bodies, political resolutions, the High Commissioner for Human Rights, technical assistance,

---

1 Under criteria established by the Human Rights Council in 2007, these experts are selected based on their expertise, experience in the field of human rights, independence, impartiality, personal integrity and objectivity. Human Rights Council Resolution 5/1, Section II.A (18 June 2007).

and field offices, connecting to each part in different and unique ways. They serve as the main entry point into the broader UN system for victims and human rights defenders from every corner of the world, offering a practical forum for the promotion and protection of human rights. By most accounts, they have played a critical role in shaping the content of international human rights norms, shedding light on how states comply with such norms, and advancing measures to improve respect for them. They are considered by many to be, in the words of then UN Secretary-General Kofi Annan, 'the crown jewel of the system'.[2]

Despite their well-deserved place in the international human rights architecture, the contribution of Special Procedures to the implementation of international human rights standards at the national level has been little understood. In addition, their role, considered by some states as overly intrusive or confrontational, has sparked intense debate at the HRC even after member states completed the five-year review of the Council in 2010–11.

2.1 A snapshot of Special Procedures today

Since the initial appointment by the UN Commission on Human Rights of an Ad Hoc Working Group to inquire into the situation of human rights in southern Africa in 1967, the Special Procedures mechanisms have grown to become one of the UN system's most important instruments for promotion of universal human rights norms at the national and international level. When the Commission on Human Rights was replaced by the HRC in 2006, states decided to keep the Special Procedures mechanisms largely intact. The HRC has since created several new Special Procedures mandates, a further reaffirmation of their utility as tools for the promotion and protection of human rights. Mandates are established to monitor and report on thematic issues – such as freedom of expression, prohibition on torture or the right to adequate housing – as well as group rights and country-specific situations.

As of January 2013, 36 thematic mandates are in operation, an increase of 71 per cent since 2000. However, only 12 country-specific mandates are in operation, a decline of almost 15 per cent over the same period.[3] This shift reflects two important trends. First, it reflects the creation of new mandates dealing with economic, social and cultural rights of particular concern to developing countries. Second, it demonstrates the successful efforts by some states, particularly those with bad human rights records, to avoid the 'naming and shaming' tactics associated with country-specific mandates in favour of thematic mandates and the peer review and technical assistance aspects of the new mechanism known as the Universal Periodic Review ('UPR'). This latter trend was tempered in March 2011 when the new HRC established its first country-specific mandate, a special rapporteur to address the human rights situation in the Islamic Republic of Iran. This country-specific mandate was followed by the establishment of rapporteurs for Côte d'Ivoire and Syria in 2011, and Belarus

---

2 'The Special Procedures are the crown jewel of the system. They, together with the High Commissioner and her staff, provide the independent expertise and judgment which is essential to effective human rights protection. They must not be politicized, or subjected to governmental control.' UN. Secretary-General Kofi Annan, Speech at the Time Warner Center, New York (8 December 2006), available at: http://www.pfcmc.com/News/ossg/sg/stories/statments_full.asp?statID=39.

3 A list of current mandate holders is available at: http://www2.ohchr.org/english/bodies/chr/special/index.htm. The OHCHR Annual Report (2000) 147 refers to 35 mandates, of which 21 were thematic and 14 were country/territory-specific. The report is available at: http://www.ohchr.org/Documents/AboutUs/annualreport2000.pdf.

and Eritrea in 2012. These are positive signals that the HRC is willing to use independent experts to address new country-specific issues.

The experts appointed by the HRC to serve as Special Procedures are independent of governments, serve in their personal capacities and carry out their mandates on a voluntary basis. Under new reforms adopted in 2006, they may serve no more than six years in total (thematic mandate holders typically serve two terms of three years and country-specific mandate holders typically serve for one-year renewable terms). Their authority is derived from their professional qualifications to address specific human rights situations objectively, as well as from the political mandate they receive from the HRC. Governments rely on the experts to gather facts, identify problems and make recommendations, but systematic follow-up to the findings is, at present, negligible. One of the experts' greatest assets is a sense of passion and commitment to the cause of human rights which, when combined with subject matter expertise, political skills and good judgement, represents a dynamic force for cata-lysing attention and action to the protection of human rights.

The main points of reference for Special Procedures when examining a state's human rights record range broadly from the general provisions of the Universal Declaration of Human Rights and other internationally recognised human rights standards to the specific terms of the mandates received from the HRC. They may rely on particular instruments of 'hard' treaty law as well as on relevant declarations, resolutions and guiding principles consti-tuting 'soft law'. In this regard, they have several important advantages over treaty bodies: they are not restricted to the text of any one convention; they may examine any UN member state, not just those states that have become party to a particular treaty; they may make *in situ* visits to any country in the world (assuming the government concerned grants permission); and they may receive and act upon individual complaints without prior exhaustion of domestic remedies. This combination of features gives them a uniquely flexible and independent role to play in a system otherwise dominated by states. They operate, in the words of one commen-tator, in the space between universal norms and local realities, allowing the experts to elabo-rate and interpret international standards grounded in concrete situations, 'to define rights in real time'.[4]

When it comes to state cooperation with Special Procedures, it should be noted that no specific treaty instrument binds states to cooperate with them or to comply with the Special Procedures' recommendations. The HRC has, however, urged 'all states to cooperate with, and assist, the special procedures in the performance of their tasks, and to provide all informa-tion in a timely manner, as well as respond to communications . . . without undue delay'.[5] The Special Procedures, similar to the HRC and UPR, are considered Charter-based mecha-nisms, which adds a further element of legitimacy to the call for compliance. Furthermore, upon creating the HRC, the General Assembly decided that states elected to the new body 'shall fully cooperate with the Council'.[6] These provisions offer some leverage for the Special Procedures to insist on state cooperation, but in reality they rely mainly on political pressure and moral suasion to influence state behaviour.

4 J.I. Naples-Mitchell, 'Perspectives of UN special rapporteurs on their role: inherent tensions and unique contributions to human rights' (February 2011) 15(2) *The International Journal of Human Rights* 232–48.
5 Human Rights Council Resolution A/HRC/RES/5/2 (18 June 2007) operative para. 1. See also Human Rights Council Resolution A/HRC/RES/11/11 (18 June 2009) preamble.
6 Human Rights Council Resolution A/RES/60/251 (3 April 2006) para. 9.

2.2 Recent developments and continued challenges

In recent years there have been two significant opportunities to further institutionalise Special Procedures and to address several systemic problems that continue to challenge them. Both the founding of the HRC in 2006 and its mandated five-year review in 2011 opened the door to assess, and thereby potentially remedy, several challenges, including: the uncoordinated proliferation of mandates that has resulted in some overlap, duplication and dilution; issues regarding working methods and state cooperation; and levels of resources and support from UN and non-UN actors. In the end, however, these junctures provided little more than a forum to rehash persistent challenges and as a consequence resulted in few decisions and little reform.

When the UN General Assembly established the HRC in 2006, it called upon the newly founded body to 'review, and where necessary, improve and rationalise all mandates, mechanisms, functions, and responsibilities of the Commission on Human Rights in order to maintain a system of Special Procedures'.[7] Since the Special Procedures had proliferated in an uncoordinated manner, there was plenty of room for review and consolidation. As part of its Institution Building ('IB') negotiations, the HRC undertook a process of 'review, rationalization, and improvement ['RRI'] of mandates' that would 'focus on the relevance, scope, and contents of the mandates'.[8] Despite lofty goals to review all mandates, the status quo was largely preserved in the end. State sponsors of particular mandates were unwilling to give up or consolidate their pet issues. Only the mandates on Cuba and Belarus were terminated, in a last-minute political deal not germane to the RRI process.

The IB process also provided the space for the introduction of a Code of Conduct for Special Procedures.[9] Some antagonistic member states had long been demanding that the Special Procedures improve their working methods and objected to the independence of the Special Procedures. Sponsored by the Africa Group, the Code of Conduct was adopted as part of the IB package, and now serves as a basis to regulate and supervise the mandate holders. However, it contains no procedure for handling specific allegations. Instead, complaints tend to get aired during interactive dialogues with Special Procedures or in other venues. Some experts consider the Code of Conduct a useful step towards greater professionalisation of Special Procedures, while others (including some rapporteurs) say it has had a chilling effect on their ability – and that of the Office of the High Commissioner for Human Rights (OHCHR) staff – to speak out clearly against violations.[10]

The five-year review of the HRC in 2011 provided another opportunity to address some of the shortcomings of the system, but instead was used by hostile member states to organise attempts to rein in mandate holders and regulate their behaviour. Supportive states and civil society were largely left playing defence, trying to ensure preservation of the independence of rapporteurs.

Perhaps the most dangerous proposal during the five-year review was one put forth by Algeria and Egypt that would have posed a serious threat to the independence of the system.

---

7 Ibid. para. 6.
8 HRC Resolution 5/1 (18 June 2007) paras 54–64.
9 HRC Resolution 5/2 (18 June 2007), annex.
10 Interview with former mandate holder (30 June 2009) and confidential response from UN staff to project questionnaire. For an in-depth discussion, see Philip Alston, 'Hobbling the Monitors: Should U.N. Human Rights Monitors be Accountable?' Summer 2011 *Harvard International Law Journal* 52(2) .

The proposal was to establish a legal committee to evaluate state complaints of special rapporteurs' non-compliance with the Code.[11] In the end the effort was defeated, largely thanks to a counter-effort led by France proposing the establishment of a Code of Conduct for member states.[12] Similar to attacks on the working methods of Justice Dieye, the first UN special rapporteur on human rights in 1978, this is yet another example of an enduring effort to limit the independence of these experts.

Another proposal defeated during the 2011 review called for increased transparency of funds allocated to Special Procedures and the termination of earmarked funds so that all voluntary contributions made to the system would be equitably allocated.[13] Led by the Nonaligned Movement ('NAM'), Organisation of Islamic Cooperation ('OIC') and Africa Group, this attempt was initiated under the assumption that mandates centred on economic, social and cultural rights received less funding than those focused on civil and political rights. This initiative disintegrated when the OHCHR noted during consultations around the 2011 review that mandates concerning economic, social and cultural rights had actually received more funding from the 2008–10 earmarked voluntary contributions.[14]

In the end no major changes to the system of Special Procedures – or the HRC more broadly – were implemented as part of the 2011 review. Minor but important improvements were achieved regarding the role of National Human Rights Institutions ('NHRIs') vis-à-vis the Council and Special Procedures.[15] The 2011 Review also enacted changes to the process for appointing rapporteurs.[16] Though relatively minor, these reforms did help increase the

---

11 Republic of Algeria, Submission to the First Intergovernmental Working Group on the Review of Work and Functioning of the Human Rights Council (29 October 2010), available on HRC extranet. The submission proposes the 'establishment, in the context of the review on the basis of equitable geographic distribution of a Human Rights Council Legal Committee on compliance with the Code of Conduct'.

12 France, Draft Code of Conduct for States in their relationships with Special Procedures (8 December 2010), available on HRC extranet.

13 Arabic Republic of Egypt on behalf of the Non Aligned Movement, Submission to the First Intergovernmental Working Group on the Review of Work and Functioning of the Human Rights Council (24 September 2010), available on HRC extranet. The submission proposes that 'there shall be an exclusive reliance on UN regular budget funding and a ban on any fundraising by, or voluntary contribution to, individual mandate holders. Any voluntary contributions should be made to OHCHR in the form of non-earmarked resources, and OHCHR should allocate them equally to all mandate holders, and all contributions should be subject to public disclosure.'

14 During the HRC 2011 review, the OHCHR submitted a paper on resource structure for Special Procedures, available on the HRC extranet. It states that 'contributions earmarked for specific mandates over the period 2008–2010 have been directed mainly at economic, social and cultural rights mandates, with $2,079,944 (53.7% of the total earmarked contributions) being provided for these mandates; contributions of $1,048,933 (27%) have been directed to civil and political rights mandates and $747,180 (19.3%) have been directed to mandates supported by the Groups in Focus Section.'

15 First, NHRIs that are in full compliance with the Paris Principles, known as A-status, can now speak during the interactive dialogues during Council sessions, following the representative of the government under discussion. Second, NHRIs are now authorised to nominate Special Procedures candidates. Review of the work and functioning of the Human Rights Council, UN Doc, A/HRC/RES/16/21 (12 April 2011) Part II, paras 28, 22.

16 Candidates must now submit a motivational letter as part of the nominations process. The OHCHR will maintain separate lists for each public candidacy, and if the President of the Council decides to deviate from the recommendation of the consultative group in the appointments process, he or she must justify this decision. Human Rights Council, UN Doc., A/HRC/RES/16/21 (12 April 2011) Part II, paras 28, 22.

transparency of the appointments process and expanded the role for external UN stakeholders in the dialogue and appointments processes.

3 Key factors that shape the effectiveness of Special Procedures

The UN's independent experts on human rights have played a valuable and, in some cases, decisive role in drawing attention to chronic and emerging human rights issues and in catalysing improvements in respect for human rights on the ground, including direct support to victims. At the same time, state cooperation with the Special Procedures is highly uneven and generally disappointing, with some notable exceptions. Cooperation by states ranges from regularly accepting country visits by multiple independent experts and high response rates to their communications, to virtually zero recognition or dialogue with the rapporteurs. This failure by member states to fulfil their responsibilities to cooperate with the Special Procedures and address the recommendations they make is the main obstacle hampering their ability to fulfil the mandates given to them by states.

The Special Procedures are also hindered by a host of other challenges, including inadequate training and resources, insufficient understanding of the local context for their work, and the lack of a systematic process for following up their recommendations. Despite these obstacles, the Special Procedures mechanism represents one of the most effective tools of the international human rights system and deserves further strengthening and support. A variety of factors help to determine state responsiveness to Special Procedures' scrutiny of their human rights performance. The main factors are identified and described below.

The credibility of the United Nations in the country concerned, as the premier global body to develop and uphold universal norms and foster international cooperation. The moral power of the UN's 'blue stationery', the international backing it conveys, and the public attention a UN expert commands often yield significant pressure to generate positive state action.

The timing of a visit as it relates to a country's political and human rights situation. Countries in transition, moving away from conflict or authoritarian rule and toward a more open, peaceful and democratic society, tend to offer more opportunities for external influence than countries locked in civil conflict or burdened by a closed system. In intensely polarised situations, opposing sides at the national level will seek to manipulate a rapporteur's visit and the subsequent report to their own advantage, hindering impact. This is not to say, however, that efforts to engage closed regimes or conflict situations should be dropped as a UN expert often offers the only avenue for human rights issues to be examined and publicly aired.

The quality and specificity of the Special Procedures' research, analysis and recommendations and the level of preparation before a visit. On the one hand, it is strongly felt by key governmental and non-governmental actors that a well-grounded report with solid evidence, strong legal arguments and concrete recommendations is one of the most important elements for achieving progress.[17] On the other hand, general, aspirational recommendations have little impact and make follow-up difficult. In some cases, factual mistakes or statements by rapporteurs perceived as unduly harsh or unbalanced were used by states and others to attack and

---

17 Human Rights Council, Manual on the Special Procedures of the Human Rights Council, para. 98, states that Special Procedures recommendations should be SMART: specific, measurable, attainable, realistic and time-bound. 15th Annual Meeting, Draft Revised manual (June 2008), available at http://www2.ohchr.org/english/bodies/chr/special/annual_meetings/docs/manual-SpecialProceduresDraft0608.pdf.

undermine not only their work but that of other UN actors as well. The language, tone and style a rapporteur uses matters almost as much as the content of what he or she has to say in reporting. Positive words acknowledging progress where it exists can go a long way toward helping government officials accept the more critical findings of a rapporteur's report. Indeed, one senior government official explained that a report that failed to present the government's side of the story was 'thrown into the trash'.[18]

The willingness of the relevant government to cooperate with the Special Procedures' visit. For example, a well-placed, sympathetic official or leading parliamentarian can often make a difference in facilitating the Special Procedure's work and implementation of recommendations. The willingness and ability of the government to organise inter-ministerial coordination mechanisms to address concerns raised by the rapporteurs is another important factor. Conversely, obstruction and interference by government agents can frustrate or neutralise the work of Special Procedures. Some government officials have unrealistic expectations and imagine that the expert's mission is to endorse state policy rather than serve as an objective critic and shut down cooperation in the wake of a negative report.

The ability of local and international NGOs and victims' groups to communicate their grievances in a timely and effective manner and to engage in follow-up advocacy. In many cases, the principal reason any follow-up action was taken by governments was due to a persistent NGO adopting the Special Procedures' recommendations as a platform for a long-term advocacy campaign. In Northern Ireland, for example, a coalition led by British Irish Rights Watch worked closely with the Special Rapporteur on the Independence of Judges and Lawyers (Mr Param Cumaraswamy) to prepare his visit and to follow up his recommendations. After six years of determined advocacy, all but one of his recommendations had been implemented by the relevant government authorities. On the other hand, special rapporteurs must be vigilant and aware of the risk of being manipulated by non-governmental groups who seek to use their visits as part of a propaganda campaign to allege human rights abuses against the government without substantiation.

The level of freedom of the media to report on Special Procedures' activities. In most countries, a visit by a senior UN expert generates widespread attention which is greatly enhanced by a robust and well-briefed media corps. On the other hand, the rapporteur's ready access to the media can complicate a mission, prompting strong government criticism. In a seminal dispute and case eventually decided in 1999, the International Court of Justice rejected a $112 million claim for defamation, filed by the Malaysian Government against Param Cumaraswamy, the Special Rapporteur for Independence of Judges and Lawyers. The ICJ ruled that UN special rapporteurs must be regarded as 'experts on mission' and accorded certain privileges and immunities, such as immunity from defamation proceedings, when acting in their official capacity.[19] Other more recent examples include the critical US response to statements made by the special representative for Internally Displaced Persons regarding its actions after Hurricane Katrina; Spain's denunciation of the Special Rapporteur on the promotion and protection of human rights while countering terrorism regarding comments made on his visit

18 From an informal interview conducted by the author.
19 Difference Relating to Immunity From Legal Process of a Special Rapporteur of the Commission on Human Rights, Advisory Opinion, ICJ Reports 1999, available at: http://www.icj-cij.org/docket/files/100/7619.pdf. ICJ press release available at: http://www.icj-cij.org/docket/index.php?pr=154&code=numa&p1=3&p2=1&p3=6&case=100&k=9.

to the Basque country; and Brazil's public attack on the Special Rapporteur on the Right to Food in response to his comments regarding genocide.[20]

The capacity of and attention paid by the UN country team and other relevant UN agencies such as the UN High Commissioner for Refugees (UNHCR) and the UN Development Programme (UNDP). The potential contribution of these actors to the success of a country visit is great but in practice has varied. The UN presence ranges in size and capacity from a small country office with only a few staff capable of providing assistance before, during or after the Special Procedures' visit, to a major field presence with dozens of in-country staff well-positioned to help organise the visit, provide advice to the rapporteurs on key elements, and incorporate their findings and recommendations in the work plan following the visit. Some country teams prefer to remain at arm's length from the rapporteurs due to the sensitive topics they raise. Others admit that while the rapporteurs can be critical and say things that are tough to hear, what they say needs to be said and their reports can help bring about reform and technical assistance.

4 Steps to strengthen Special Procedures

As Sir Nigel Rodley notes: 'The more the system acts like a system, the stronger it will be. It should not, and does not, depend on the wit and wisdom of a single special rapporteur.'[21] The lessons learned from four decades of human rights monitoring by the UN's independent experts offer something for everyone concerned with promoting greater respect for universal human rights standards around the world. Strengthening the Special Procedures system, however, will remain a contentious affair, as most states are naturally inclined to avoid the bitter pill of internationally sanctioned independent scrutiny of their human rights records. The 100 per cent participation rate in the new UPR process, by contrast, demonstrates that most states willingly engage in scrutiny when it is led and controlled by them as both jury and judge.[22] This observation only reinforces the importance of protecting the independence of the Special Procedures mechanism, a key feature which endows it with a higher degree of credibility and impact.

An examination of the Special Procedures' experience thus far reveals a number of issues in need of redress by the international community. The appointments process, resources, working methods, state cooperation, training, and coordination with other UN bodies and agencies are all areas requiring attention. At the top of the list is institutionalising follow-up and implementation of the recommendations. These issues are each addressed below through a series of recommendations, large and small, that aim to build from current good practices to achieve a new level of seriousness, credibility and success for the Special Procedures. As

---

20 For more on Spain's response, see Report of the Working Group on the Universal Periodic Review, Spain Addendum, A/HRC/15/6/Add.1 (13 September 2010); for more on Brazil's response, see *New York Times*, 'Brazil Accuses a U.N. Human Rights Envoy of Bias,' 19 March 2002: A.3., http://www.nytimes.com/2002/03/19/world/brazil-accuses-a-un-human-rights-envoy-of-bias.html.

21 Sir Nigel Rodley, 'The Role of Special Rapporteurs workshop', University of Leeds (24 June 2010). A summary of the workshop proceedings is available at http://www.law.leeds.ac.uk/assets/files/research/cfig/special-rapporteurs-workshop-report.pdf.

22 Although Israel was not present for its own review in January 2013, a deferral was secured until the 17th Working Group session in October 2013. Israel is expected to engage in the process at that time. See UPR Info, 'Human Rights Council President Met with Ambassador of Israel' (21 March 2013), http://www.upr-info.org/+Human-Rights-Council-President-met+.html.

UN Member states look ahead to a future review of the HRC in 2018 or beyond[23] there will be ample time to consider these suggestions. There is no need, however, to wait that long. The urgency of human rights crises in real time will only increase the demand for the kind of services the Special Procedures uniquely provide. With ongoing reflection and some political will and leadership, the goal of strengthening these catalysts for rights is achievable.

4.1 Follow-up procedures

Given the significant investment of resources devoted to the Special Procedures' country visits, and the important contribution they can make toward advancing human rights at the national level, the lack of any systematic mechanism to follow up such visits is glaring, and an embarrassment to the UN human rights system. The UPR process offers at least one avenue to put the recommendations made by the Special Procedures back on the table, but the schedule of reviews – only once every four and half years – is entirely insufficient for proper follow-up. Requiring mid-term status reports on UPR implementation, a practice already begun by several states, would keep implementation of Special Procedures recommendations on the agenda. Similarly, treaty bodies can do more to consult and build upon the relevant special rapporteur recommendations. We know from experience that impact is greatest where some combination of actors – states, OHCHR field offices, other elements of the UN system, Special Procedures, national human rights institutions and civil society – remain focused on addressing the problems raised and the recommendations offered in the country visit report. These stakeholders, individually and collectively, can take a number of actions:

a. One year after a country visit the rapporteur should write to the state concerned to raise relevant issues regarding the recommendations. The rapporteur should also request the state to submit a progress report within three months of the rapporteur's follow-up query.
b. Outgoing rapporteurs and their staff should be required to brief incoming Special Procedures on the status of pending and recent visits and communications as well as concrete ideas for potential follow-up.
c. Special Procedures and their staff should prioritise follow-up visits to selected states within a two- to three-year period of the previous visit.
d. States should create focal points of action in relevant ministries and organise inter-ministerial working groups to address all recommendations from UN human rights actors, including establishment of a work plan, a clear division of responsibilities and provision of, or requests for, technical assistance, as necessary.
e. The UN Country Team, OHCHR staff in the field, UNHCR personnel and other relevant actors should facilitate follow-up activities, incorporate the Special Procedures' recommendations into their work plans and regularly report back directly to the High Commissioner for Human Rights and the relevant special rapporteur on progress toward fulfilling recommendations.
f. NHRIs, ombudspersons and parliamentary bodies can also play important roles as more independent facilitators and advocates for follow-up. Special Procedures should engage

---

23 UN General Assembly, 'Review of the Human Rights Council' (20 July 2011) A/RES/65/281. The UN General Assembly, when adopting the outcome of the five-year review, decided that its status as a subsidiary body of the General Assembly should be reviewed in 'no sooner than ten years and no later than fifteen years'.

them throughout their country-level work to ensure better understanding of local context and to facilitate monitoring, follow-up and implementation.

g. National and international human rights and humanitarian NGOs and other civil society actors should work together to follow up on a special rapporteur's mission by monitoring state compliance with recommendations, carrying out advocacy campaigns to press for reforms and keeping Special Procedures regularly informed of problems and progress.

4.2 Resources

The human rights portfolio of the United Nations is chronically underfunded, operating on a shoestring budget of $193 million, which represents less than 3 per cent of the UN regular budget. Within this budget window, support to Special Procedures is approximately $13 million, or less than 7 per cent.[24] To do their job effectively, rapporteurs are left with no choice but to seek additional support from outside the UN system, a step that raises some concerns regarding transparency and equity. To redress this dramatic shortfall, expand financial flexibility and reduce inequities, member states in partnership with OHCHR should:

a. increase funding so that each mandate holder is able to visit at least three countries each year, and has at least two full-time professional OHCHR staff dedicated to their mandate.
b. raise funding and staff support for country-specific rapporteurs to the same level as thematic mandates.
c. continue to reduce earmarking of contributions to specific mandates and increase voluntary contributions to the general account for Special Procedures as a way to rebalance the distribution of resources across all mandates.
d. adjust allocation of resources in such a way that guarantees a minimum floor of funding for each mandate, including country-specific mandates, while providing additional resources for mandates that are particularly time and labour-intensive based on established criteria such as volume of communications received, follow-up activities and the emergency nature of violations.
e. create a dedicated fund where Special Procedures can apply for added resources for special projects such as elaborating standards, conducting trainings and organising workshops in the field.
f. open a new trust fund account for Special Procedures as an additional option for public and private donors that seek to contribute to the pool of funds available to all mandates. Individual mandate holders should still be free to fundraise independently.
g. expand OHCHR staff devoted to press relations, website design and social media to increase their outreach to targeted audiences, raise awareness of the human rights situation in different countries, and bolster the important public education role Special Procedures play at the national and international levels.

Mandate holders should receive an annual research honorarium or stipend, to compensate them for mandate-related research expenses incurred in the course of preparing country visits, thematic and country reports and follow-up communications with stakeholders. Such

24 OHCHR Annual Report on Activities and Results, Management and Funding, Financial Statements, 2010, pp. 88–95. Available at: http://www2.ohchr.org/english/ohchrreport2010/web_version/ohchr_report2010_web/index.html#/home.

funds could be spent at the discretion of the expert to support research staff in their home institutions, organise and attend thematic seminars, create digital platforms for outreach or undertake follow-up activities at the national or regional level.

Other UN agencies that work on issues related to particular mandates should expend resources to support the work of the special rapporteurs through direct financial support to their mandates, assignment of specialised staff, in-country assistance and funding for follow-up activities. The mandate for internally displaced persons is a model in this regard.

Mandate holders able to raise additional resources outside the UN budget for the effective fulfilment of their mandate should find ways to share such financial information more widely. OHCHR should appoint a staff person dedicated to helping mandate holders who request assistance to raise funds from external donors. An annual report from rapporteurs to OHCHR posted on its website identifying specific donors and donation levels, along with a statement disavowing any influence on the content of their work, would reduce suspicions of improper influence and comport with standard good practices of transparency.

4.3 Country visits and communications

While there are several positive examples of progress regarding the implementation of international human rights norms as a direct result of the work of the Special Procedures, the mechanism is severely challenged by member states' failure to fulfil their responsibilities to cooperate with the HRC and its mechanisms. An enduring resistance to, or rejection of, perceived intervention in internal affairs, expressed mainly by states seeking to avoid scrutiny, remains a major obstacle. In other cases, a lack of diplomatic resources allocated to reporting and follow-up is a problem.

To address the unfulfilled commitment states have to cooperate with the UN's mechanisms, and in particular with the Special Procedures, the following measures should be taken:

a. All states should cooperate with the HRC by issuing standing invitations for country visits by all Special Procedures, responding promptly (within three months) to requests for such visits, agreeing to the dates of a visit within one year of a request, accepting the standard terms of reference for such visits (including freedom of mobility) and cooperating fully during visits.

b. OHCHR should maintain a public list of countries that fail to implement standing invitations that have been issued in accordance with the above criteria and remove those states that reject or do not effectively honour their standing invitation commitments from the list.[25]

c. Likewise, member states should fulfil their responsibilities to respond to all Special Procedures communications in a timely and complete manner. Responses should set forth steps taken to address violations or provide explanations for failing to do so. In the case of urgent appeals, states should respond substantively to the allegation within 30 days. For other allegations, states should respond substantively within 60 days.

25 Human Rights Watch has suggested distinguishing between usage of the terms 'effective' and 'ineffective' standing invitations rather than grouping together all states that have issued standing invitations. For a standing invitation to be considered effective, the government making the invitation should respond to requests for visits by special procedures within six months and should actually schedule the visit within two years. For full explanation and text see: Human Rights Watch, *Curing the Selectivity Syndrome: The 2011 Review of the Human Rights Council,* June 2010, p. 18.

d. Similarly, Special Procedures and OHCHR should confirm receipt of information from victims and defenders in the field and of any subsequent communication with governments regarding their case. Victims and defenders should also be given an opportunity to comment on states' responses to official communications.

e. The HRC Secretariat should regularly publish data on each state's record of responding to Special Procedures communications and reports, the quality of the state's response (as a few rapporteurs do now) and more details on the status of requests to visit.

f. States should use a government's record of cooperation with the HRCs mechanisms, including its responsiveness to Special Procedures communications and requests for country visits, as criteria for election and re-election of any candidate for membership on the Council. This would give meaning to the General Assembly's directive that all HRC members 'shall fully cooperate with the Council'. Any candidate running for a seat on the Council should demonstrate their qualifications by implementing the above guidelines as a matter of policy and practice. Civil society should use these criteria to lobby for and against certain candidates to the HRC.

States with positive records of cooperation with the HRC's mechanisms should be priority candidates for technical assistance and other resources from the UN system and donors to help them address specific human rights concerns. Similarly, states with a record of persistent lack of cooperation should be brought to the attention of the full HRC for further discussion. Such lack of cooperation should be critically considered when states elect members to a seat on the HRC, as well as during their UPR review.

When selecting which states to visit, Special Procedures, with the assistance of OHCHR, should consider how to maximise the effectiveness of their visit based on five key factors: (a) the timing of the visit as it relates to a country's political and human rights situation; (b) the independent media; (c) the willingness of the host government to cooperate with the rapporteur; (d) active civil society participation; and (e) contributions by the UN country team. The last two factors are particularly important for effective follow-up to the visit and implementation of recommendations. Thinking earlier about points of leverage that could help effect change, including through bilateral relationships valuable to the host country, is another important factor.

It is critical that mandate holders make proper preparations for their visit by contacting a wide range of stakeholders in the country concerned well in advance of their visit. A questionnaire sent before the visit to key actors would help illuminate the most pressing issues, identify the most relevant parties for direct interviews, and educate the mandate holder on the political context. Thorough preparation, along with a robust and diverse agenda of meetings in the country concerned, will allow rapporteurs to make the most of their preliminary report to the media, a key window of opportunity for impact. Special Procedures, along with OHCHR, have a special obligation to take all necessary precautions to protect cooperating witnesses and victims from retributions.

After a period of more intensive fact-checking, rapporteurs should endeavour to complete their final report in a timely fashion and keep relevant stakeholders informed and engaged through wide dissemination of the report in the country of concern. Employing balanced language that cites progress where it exists and offers constructive criticism for failings has served most rapporteurs well. Recommendations for action should be specific, measurable, attainable, realistic and time-bound ('SMART').

States should agree to improve the quality of the interactive dialogue with Special Procedures, including by allotting more time to each individual mandate holder for presentation of his or her report, holding a separate dialogue on each country mission report, and ensuring the NHRIs (certified at the A-level) of the relevant country have adequate time to speak subsequently to the country concerned.

The HRC Secretariat should continuously update its new public database on communications and ensure it is searchable by country and mandate, so that all information regarding communications and state responses can be easily found. This is particularly important to victims, who are rarely informed of the status of the complaints they submit to the Special Procedures. In addition, the Special Procedures' annual report to the HRC should include the status of that year's new communications and outstanding ones, as the Working Group on Enforced and Involuntary Disappearances does. Similarly, any individual alleging a human rights violation should automatically receive a reply from the relevant rapporteur(s) or their staff acknowledging receipt and indicating what the process for consideration entails.

Publications of Special Procedures communications, reports and government responses should be available in the main languages of the country concerned.

4.4 Appointments

The selection process for Special Procedures, while much improved under the 2006 institution-building package, still suffers from a lack of transparency, politicisation and apparent back-room deals in which experts do not always appear well matched to their mandates. The June 2010 episode in which states such as Algeria and India demanded their candidates receive certain mandates and the President of the HRC modified his final list of nominees per demands from the Africa Group and Organisation of Islamic Cooperation further degraded a process that should emphasise expertise, independence and objectivity as the main criteria for selection.

The HRC and the OHCHR should improve the selection process by reaching out early and often to a wide network of relevant stakeholders, advertising vacancies publicly, setting clear deadlines for applications and providing further information about each individual candidate to help states and civil society assess qualifications, experience and suitability for particular mandates. These issues were somewhat addressed during the HRC's five-year review – candidates must now submit a short motivational statement and shortlisted candidates must be interviewed, for example – but merit further attention to ensure that the strongest candidates are considered.[26] Civil society has a special role to play in identifying qualified candidates with a proven track record of expertise in promoting and defending human rights and should more proactively recruit, nominate and support top candidates.

Qualified candidates with a diverse life experience, including practical knowledge of human rights, politics, communications and diplomacy, should be actively recruited.

4.5 Training

The inadequacy of proper training and orientation is a glaring problem but one that is relatively easy to fix. To support further professionalisation and greater effectiveness of the Special Procedures, it is essential that the Special Procedures receive additional training and guidance before carrying out their duties. This should include specialised instruction from experienced

26 Human Rights Council, 'Review of the work and functioning of the Human Rights Council' (12 April 2011) A/HRC/Res/16/21, Section II, para. 22.

mandate holders who have invaluable experience handling politically sensitive missions. A panel of former mandate holders could be charged by the Coordination Committee of Special Procedures, which is comprised of current mandate holders, to prepare written materials on the history and lessons learnt of their work with a focus on the diplomatic, political, fund-raising and communication skills needed to maximise effectiveness on the ground. Specialised training on proper methods of fact-finding in the human rights field would also be useful and should be based on prior UN guidelines for fact-finding missions.[27] The skills training should be provided within two months of a mandate holder's appointment.

4.6 Working methods and code of conduct

Both member states and Special Procedures have responsibilities toward each other and the broader UN human rights system for it to work effectively on behalf of victims. These responsibilities include a faithful adherence by member states to the Code of Conduct, including every state's duty to fully cooperate with the Special Procedures, respect their independence and provide all information requested in a timely manner. States should furthermore refrain from using the Code of Conduct to block scrutiny of their human rights records or to harass and intimidate the mandate holders and should criticise such attacks when they occur.

Mandate holders must uphold the professional standards set forth in the Code of Conduct and the Manual of Procedures on their own merit but also to prevent further attacks on their independence. More frequent meetings of their Coordination Committee along with regular consultations with the High Commissioner (or his or her Deputy) and with member states would help build trust.

If a state wishes to allege a violation of the Code of Conduct, it should follow the Internal Advisory Procedure to Review Practices and Working Methods adopted in June 2008 by the Coordination Committee.[28] The Coordination Committee should, in turn, be more transparent with the President of the HRC and with states on steps taken to address concerns regarding an individual expert's behaviour on mission. In this way, all parties involved will have more confidence in the Special Procedures' own rules for self-regulating their activities.

The President of the HRC should also be more proactive in explicitly recognising the legal and professional standing of the Coordination Committee and support regular consultations between the Committee and member states. The President should also take the initiative to redirect Council discussion of a special rapporteur's conduct to the Coordination Committee as early as possible. The High Commissioner's Office or a small group of former mandate holders appointed by the Coordination Committee could also be involved as observers to the Committee's deliberations.

Proposals to create a formal 'ethics committee' or panel of jurists to handle complaints of Special Procedures' behaviour should continue to be rejected as a costly diversion. It would

---

27 The UN's general standards for fact-finding missions can be found in the Declaration on Fact-finding by the UN in the Field of the Maintenance of International Peace and Security, UN Doc. A/RES/46/59, Annex (1992).

28 Coordination Committee of Special Procedures, 'Internal Advisory Procedure to Review Practices and Working Methods,' (25 June 2008), available at http://www2.ohchr.org/english/bodies/chr/special/annual_meetings/docs/InternalAdvisoryProcedure.doc.

unreasonably occupy the Special Procedures' limited time in a series of potentially harassing, frivolous and politicised complaint procedures and would undermine rather than strengthen the Special Procedures as a body of professional, independent UN experts.

4.7 Relations with the Human Rights Council and OHCHR

The Special Procedures are creatures of the HRC, yet too often are politicised, marginalised or depicted as an unreliable source of information by states. To some degree, given the sensitive nature of their work, this type of defensive posturing is inevitable. But more could be done to improve communications between the collective body of special rapporteurs and member states as a way to build trust and improve cooperation. Other steps that could be taken to make good use of the Special Procedures' expertise include: (a) giving rapporteurs an opportunity to comment on pending resolutions that affect their mandates; (b) inviting relevant mandate holders to present statements at the HRC's special sessions; (c) and finding ways for the special rapporteurs to serve as an early warning function to call the HRC's attention to burgeoning human rights crises.

The evident tensions between the Special Procedures and OHCHR staff are a function of the conflicts inherent in a bureaucracy directly responsible to the High Commissioner and the Secretary-General yet also charged with servicing the Special Procedures and other mechanisms created by member states. Recent High Commissioners and their staff have tended to avoid conflict with member states by ignoring or abandoning the Special Procedures in times of need (e.g. in the face of unwarranted attacks by states) or micromanaging their work to prevent such attacks. There is no easy solution to this problem, but it would certainly help if the High Commissioner herself did more to defend the work of the Special Procedures and instructed her staff to do likewise. She should also find a way to improve internal communications and coordination among different branches of OHCHR, including with the field offices, to improve support not only to the Special Procedures but to the treaty bodies as well.

OHCHR could also do more to accommodate the unique challenges facing the Special Procedures. For example, it should revise its staffing system so that an incoming rapporteur gets the benefit of the incumbent professional staff member for that mandate for at least six months but preferably a year. Rapporteurs' views on the quality of OHCHR staff support should be given weight in rotation and promotion decisions. New OHCHR staff should get more intensive training in how to support the mandate holders. Support for communications outreach and media training should be expanded given the importance of media attention to a mandate holder's effectiveness. OHCHR should seek a more flexible arrangement for translation and interpretation services so that local interpreters may be hired, often at a fraction of the cost.

OHCHR should also facilitate further discussion and proposals around the rationalisation of mandates. This remains unfinished business from the 2011 review when efforts to rationalise mandates devolved into an overly politicised struggle aimed at reducing the sheer number of mandates and curbing mandate holders' independence. Without guidelines to regulate the establishment of new mandates, they continue to proliferate in an uncoordinated manner, straining already scarce resources and fostering confusion and unhealthy competition. Before the HRC creates new mandates, OHCHR – in coordination with the Coordinating Committee of Special Procedures – should explain to the Council how the proposed mechanism relates to existing mandates and identify areas of overlap. Any effort to rationalise mandates must include input from OHCHR, Special Procedures themselves, and civil society organisations.

4.8 Relations with UPR, treaty bodies and other UN human rights and humanitarian actors

The Special Procedures operate within a larger international system for promoting and protecting human rights. Much more could be done to integrate them further into this framework to maximise effectiveness of their mandates. The UPR mechanism offers a valuable opportunity for integrating the work of Special Procedures. The UPR process should continue to incorporate Special Procedures' findings and recommendations in both the input and outcome reports, while distinguishing them clearly from the recommendations issued by member states during the UPR review session. Similarly, Special Procedures should invoke and follow up on relevant UPR recommendations in their reporting.

Where they exist, country-specific mandate holders should be called upon at all stages of the relevant country review as subject matter experts. Thematic mandate holders could also be asked to participate in reviews of countries they have recently visited. Special Procedures' recommendations should continue to be refined to ensure actionable steps are identified for the UPR review. Special rapporteur visits to states could be timed to take place within a year of a country's upcoming review to maximise attention to resulting recommendations.

Treaty bodies should adopt the practice followed by the Human Rights Committee of the ICCPR of regularly consulting all relevant Special Procedure reports for states under review and raising their recommendations in the course of the review. Special Procedures should do likewise.

The Secretary-General should require UN Country Teams to incorporate Special Procedures' recommendations into their annual work plans and to appoint a focal point in each country team responsible for follow-up monitoring and reporting on state actions to address such recommendations. A similar effort should be addressed toward mainstreaming Special Procedures' recommendations into activities of UN peacekeeping missions, building on new rules requiring directors of UN peacekeeping operations in the field to report on human rights issues to the High Commissioner.

OHCHR should spearhead coordination with specialised UN voluntary funds to connect Special Procedures' recommendations to funding priorities. This is beginning to happen in an ad hoc way. For example, the Voluntary Trust Fund on Contemporary Forms of Slavery has cooperated with the special rapporteur on the same subject on four project grants to grass-roots Haitian NGOs to combat child labour and provide assistance to child domestic workers and their families.[29] Similarly, the UN Voluntary Funds for Victims of Torture, for Indigenous Populations, and for Violence against Women could be tapped for resources to help states implement Special Procedures' recommendations in those areas.

With the creation of a new Assistant Secretary-General for Human Rights in New York, the time is ripe to connect the Special Procedures more directly to key UN bodies at UN headquarters, particularly the Security Council and the Third (Human Rights) Committee. The Assistant Secretary-General should have as a top priority the mission of mainstreaming the work of the Special Procedures into the activities of relevant UN actors in New York, including briefings before the Security Council in special cases, and working closely with key departments such as the Department of Peacekeeping Operations (DPKO). He must also be the focal point for ensuring that the UN's Fifth Committee on budgetary resources allocates additional resources to support the Special Procedures.

29 OHCHR Report: Activities and Results (2009) 177.

5 Conclusion

While the Special Procedures effectively monitor violations and, under certain circumstances, catalyse change at the national level, there remains much room for further strengthening and institutionalisation of this key UN mechanism. A multitude of actors – the HRC, OHCHR, member states, the mandate holders and their staffs – must cooperate and coordinate to achieve these goals. By more diligently preparing for country visits, prioritising follow-up visits and remaining in close communication with states regarding their recommendations, Special Procedures can shore up their efficacy and increase their impact on the ground. Increasing funding will ensure adequate resources for the independent experts and their staff so OHCHR can more effectively support their mandates. Finally, states must recognise their own responsibilities within the system and cooperate with this and other mechanisms. Civil society, the media and national human rights institutions also have vital roles to play in shaping and amplifying the impact of the Special Procedures' work. Ultimately, all actors have a responsibility to act in a spirit of partnership on behalf of the victims of rights violations to acknowledge past violations and work together to prevent future violations.

Select bibliography

E. Domínguez, *Los Procedimientos Públicos Especiales De La Comisión De Derechos Humanos De Naciones Unidas* (Tirant lo Blanch, 2005).

J. Gutter, *Thematic Procedures of the United Nations Commission on Human Rights and International Law: In Search of a Sense of Community* (Intersentia, 2006).

P. Hunt, 'The UN Special Rapporteur on the Right to Health: Key Objectives, Themes, and Interventions' (2003) 7(1) *Health and Human Rights* 1–27.

L. Miko, *Challenges Facing the System of Special Procedures of the United Nations Commission on Human Rights* (Abo Akademi University Institute for Human Rights, 2001).

I. Nifosi, *The UN Special Procedures in the Field of Human Rights* (Intersentia, 2005).

T. Piccone, *Catalysts for Rights: The Unique Contribution of the UN's Independent Experts on Human Rights* (Brookings Institution, 2010).

P.S. Pinheiro, 'Musings of a UN Special Rapporteur on Human Rights' (2003) 9(1) *Global Governance* 7–14.

B.G. Ramcharan, *The Protection Roles of UN Human Rights Special Procedures* (Martinus Nijhoff Publishers, 2008).

M. Schmidt, 'Follow-up Activities by UN Human Rights Treaty Bodies and Special Procedures Mechanisms of the Human Rights Council – Recent Developments', in G. Alfredsson, J. Grimheden, B.G. Ramcharan and A. de Zayas (eds), *International Human Rights Monitoring Mechanisms: Essays in Honour of Jakob Th. Möller,* 2nd edn (Martinus Nijhoff Publishers, 2009).

L.S. Sunga, 'What Effect If Any Will the UN Human Rights Council Have on Special Procedures?', in G. Alfredsson, J. Grimheden, B.G. Ramcharan and A. de Zayas (eds), *International Human Rights Monitoring Mechanisms: Essays in Honour of Jakob Th. Möller,* 2nd edn (Martinus Nijhoff Publishers, 2009).

T. Van Boven, 'Urgent Appeals on Behalf of Torture Victims', in J. Cohen-Jonathan (ed.), *Libertés, justice, tolérance: mélanges en hommage au doyen Gérard Cohen-Jonathan* (Bruylant, 2004).

40

The role and future of the Human Rights Council

Allehone M. Abebe

1 Transitioning from the UN Commission on Human Rights

The UN Human Rights Council was established by General Assembly Resolution 251/60 on 19 June 2006, replacing the former Commission on Human Rights (the Commission), an institution that had been widely criticised by governments, the UN, academics and civil society organisations alike. The Commission, established in 1946 as a subsidiary body of the UN Economic and Social Council (ECOSOC), was the central inter-governmental platform within the United Nations to take action on emerging human rights situations. It was criticised for its 'selective and political' approaches to human rights situations where developing countries were subjected to the Commission's severe scrutiny and criticism. Others also challenged the effectiveness of the Commission's response to human rights situations in various countries. The membership of states with questionable human rights records was often cited as one of the Commission's significant weaknesses – an example of how the Commission was used by states as a means of shielding themselves from human rights scrutiny and criticism. The fact that the Commission was not created as a principal organ of the United Nations (or a subsidiary body of the General Assembly, for that matter) was also identified as an institutional weakness which denied the Commission the opportunity to bring human rights concerns to principal organs of the United Nations. These criticisms were reinforced by the report of the Secretary-General's High-Level Panel, which noted that 'the Commission's capacity to perform these tasks has been undermined by eroding credibility and professionalism'.[1]

The Commission had its own achievements, too. It was, for instance, successful in establishing and managing numerous thematic and country-specific mandate holders, and also in supporting the involvement of non-governmental organisations (NGOs) in its work. It served as a successful convenor for significant standard-setting initiatives which resulted in the development of key human rights instruments. It shed light on human rights violations in

---

1 Report of the Secretary-General's High-Level Panel on Threats, Challenges and Change, 'A more secure world: Our shared responsibility' (2004) UN Doc. A/59/565, para. 283.

countries which were under colonial administration or apartheid rule, such as South Africa.[2] During the most difficult period of Cold War rivalry, it maintained important institutional mechanisms which played key roles in highlighting human rights concerns in many parts of the world. Throughout the decades of its existence, the Commission debated human rights problems in a number of countries, adopted numerous resolutions and established procedures and mechanisms to implement myriad human rights activities.[3] The Commission's failings, however, were hard to ignore.

The UN, under the leadership of the former Secretary-General, Kofi Annan, sought to remedy the aforementioned gaps by placing human rights as one of the key pillars of the reform of the United Nations, and by initiating a process of transforming the Commission which, in his view, lacked 'credibility and professionalism'.[4] In *Larger Freedom*, he specifically called for a 'smaller standing Human Rights Council' whose members would be elected directly by the General Assembly and which would abide by the highest human rights standards.[5] According to the Secretary General, a Council would be able to 'accord human rights a more authoritative position, corresponding to the primacy of human rights in the Charter of the United Nations'.[6] At the 2005 World Summit, heads of state and government endorsed the proposal of the Secretary-General and created a Human Rights Council which would be responsible for (a) 'promoting universal respect for the protection of all human rights and fundamental freedoms for all'; (b) addressing 'situations of violations of human rights . . . and make recommendations thereon'; (c) promoting 'effective coordination and the mainstreaming of human rights within the United Nations system'.[7] They also mandated the president of the General Assembly to conduct negotiations 'with the aim of establishing the mandate, modalities, functions, size, composition, membership, working methods and procedures of the Council'.[8]

2 The establishment of the Human Rights Council

The General Assembly led a series of discussions among member states, with civil society organisations and other actors, and adopted a landmark resolution in 2006 by which the Human Rights Council was formally established.[9] Resolution 60/251, the constitutive document for the Council, was a result of lengthy and at times heated negotiations which touched on topics ranging from the membership of the Council to the Council's mandates and responsibilities, the Council's status within the UN system, the role and responsibilities of Special Procedures and the question of how to institute a peer review mechanism to monitor states' human rights record. The Resolution stipulated that the Council should:[10] (a) support universal application of human rights including through the Universal Periodic Review process; (b) 'promote human rights education and learning as well as advisory services,

2 Chatham House, 'The UN Human Rights Council: A Five Year Assessment' (Meeting Summary, 16 November 2011) 3, available at http://www.chathamhouse.org/publications/papers/view/180011.
3 Ibid. 3.
4 Report of the Secretary-General, 'In larger freedom: towards development, security and human rights for all' (2005) UN Doc. A/59/2005, para. 182.
5 Ibid. para. 183.
6 Ibid. para. 183.
7 2005 World Summit Outcome, GA Res. 60/1 (24 October 2005) paras 158–59.
8 Ibid. para. 160.
9 GA Res. 60/251 (3 April 2006).
10 Ibid. para. 5.

technical assistance and capacity building'; (c) provide a 'forum for dialogue on thematic' human rights issues; (d) provide recommendations on developments of human rights standards to the General Assembly; (e) respond to human rights emergencies and crisis; and (f) promote international cooperation among governments, regional organisations, national human rights institutions and civil society organisations.

Resolution 60/251 reaffirmed all relevant international human rights instruments and recognised 'the work undertaken by the Commission on Human Rights and the need to preserve and build on its achievements and to redress its shortcomings'. It designated the Council as a subsidiary organ of the General Assembly, constituting 47 member states whose membership is distributed based on equitable geographical representation. Accordingly, the membership of states is geographically designated as follows: 13 African states, 6 Eastern European states; 8 Latin American and Caribbean states; and 7 Western European and other states. Members serve on the Council for a period of three years and may not be eligible for immediate election after two consecutive terms. As a subsidiary body of the General Assembly, the Council was to have improved access to this highest organ of the United Nations, with the Council's decisions enjoying enhanced authority and legitimacy. The Council may also report both to the plenary of the General Assembly and its Third (Human Rights) Committee.

Largely as a result of the intense debate over membership during the last years of the Commission, negotiations over the new Council were overwhelmed by a particular concern on the composition of the Council.[11] With the aim of improving the membership of the Council, Resolution 60/251 incorporated a number of innovations such as reduction of the number of the members of the Council (47 from the Commission's 53), election of members on an individual basis, a requirement of a majority vote for an election to the Council, a requirement of 'pledges' by candidates, and procedures for a suspension of membership where appropriate. While members of the Council were 'elected directly and individually' by a majority of members of the Council, the Resolution allocated seats to geographical representations in order to maintain 'equitable geographic distribution'.[12]

With respect to pledges, the Resolution provided elements which states should consider while voting for candidates to the Council. Accordingly, it stipulates that member states shall take into account the contribution of candidates to the promotion and protection of human rights and their voluntary pledges and commitments made thereto. Provisions on pledges were welcome tools in securing some commitments from states which seek membership of the Council. No formal procedure has been agreed upon for reviewing and monitoring the implementation of these pledges. Nevertheless, it was incorporated in the Resolution that members of the Council shall have their human rights record 'reviewed under the universal periodic review mechanism during their term of membership'.[13] It is also provided that the General Assembly 'may suspend the rights of membership in the Council of a member of the Council that commits gross and systematic violations of human rights'.[14]

In an acknowledgement of the weaknesses of the decisions of the former Commission, Resolution 60/251 urged the Council to be 'action oriented'. The Council also works as a

---

11 P. Alston, 'Reconceiving the UN Human Rights Regime: Challenges Confronting the New Human Rights Council' (CHRJ Working Paper No. 4, 2006) 6.
12 GA Res. 61/251 (n. 9) paras 7 and 14.
13 Ibid. para. 9.
14 Ibid. para. 8.

standing body which meets as required in its special sessions in addition to its three key regular sessions each year. Based in Geneva, Switzerland, the Council holds three regular sessions 'for a total duration of no less than ten weeks' spread throughout the year.[15] A peer review mechanism called the Universal Periodic Review (UPR) was established to review the human rights records of all states. The Resolution also maintained the existing relationship between the former Commission and the Office of the High Commissioner for Human Rights (OHCHR) as defined by General Assembly Resolution 48/141 of 20 December 1993 – a position that remains one of the most contentious issues between those who want to see the Council exercise an oversight role over OCHCR, and others who argue that giving the Council such an authority will undermine OHCHR's independence. With respect to important human rights stakeholders such as national human rights institutions and civil society organisations, it was provided that the Council would maintain this relationship based on ECOSOC Resolution 1996/31. The Council also maintained the confidential complaint procedure referred to as the 1503 procedure, taking its name from the resolution that established it in 1970. With respect to the status of the Council more broadly, it was decided that the General Assembly will review the status of the Council within five years. The main element of the review by the General Assembly was the question of whether the Council should remain a subsidiary body of the Assembly or whether its status should be upgraded to that of one of the principal organs of the United Nations. Following a series of negotiations, the General Assembly decided to maintain the status of the Council as a subsidiary organ of the General Assembly, but to review the matter at an appropriate moment in the future.[16]

While the aforementioned innovations and changes were required to respond to some of the specific criticisms levelled against the Human Rights Commission, it is important to underscore the general environment in which the reform process took place. The establishment of the Council came at a time when the world was experiencing multifaceted global challenges: a post-9/11 world where states' anti-terrorism measures posed risks to individual rights and freedoms; the complex nature of armed conflicts in which the role of non-state actors became more challenging to regulate; increasing awareness of the role and responsibility of private entities in human rights was apparent; a sharp conflicting relationship between the freedoms of religion, expression and speech came to the fore; the rights of individuals who had been consistently ignored by states, such as the lesbian, gay, bisexual and transgender (LGBT) community, became increasingly recognised; and the world became increasingly wary of the serious threat from the effects of climate change. The period also saw the important and powerful role that emerging states such as Brazil, China, India, Mexico and South Africa could play in international organisations. In the realm of human rights and rule of law, the roles and the evolving responsibilities of the International Criminal Court (ICC) and major developments in international criminal law, the multifaceted challenges of the UN human rights treaty body system, the role of regional mechanisms, the involvement of the UN Security Council including in the protection of civilian discourse, the participation of other organisations such as the World Health Organization (WHO), the World Trade Organization (WTO) and the International Labour Organization (ILO) in the human rights sphere have become apparent. The UN humanitarian reform process has also led a more proactive role by protection-mandated agencies such as the UN High Commissioner for Refugees (UNHCR) and the UN Children's Fund (UNICEF) in promoting protection in

15 Ibid. para. 10.
16 GA Res. 65/281 para. 3.

humanitarian settings.[17] While key proposals to reform UN human rights mechanisms including through the establishment of a human rights court with a global jurisdiction[18] and the transformation of treaty bodies[19] were already widely known, the reform process which led to the birth of the Council was preoccupied with much narrower and largely procedural concerns.

3 Institutional building: change and continuity

Despite the initial scope of the Secretary-General's reform agenda, the ambit of the reform of the Human Rights Council agreed in 2005 was considerably limited by the strictures of Resolution 60/251, which resulted from diverse expectations and disagreements among key stakeholders on what should be considered as key pillars of the new Council.[20] Notably, Resolution 251/60 also requested the Council to determine the institutional mechanisms and procedures required to implement its new mandate. It specifically requested the Council to 'assume, review and, where necessary, improve and rationalize all mandates, mechanisms, functions and responsibilities of the Commission on Human Rights'.[21]

The 'Institution-building Package', as the outcome of the negotiations which was adopted by consensus on 18 June 2007, defines some of the key institutional aspects of the new organ and its working methods and procedures.[22] These include the UPR, the Council's agenda and programme of work, Special Procedures, the advisory committee and the complaints procedure. The Council's formal sessions, together with the series of other meetings including that of the UPR and the various working groups, have made the calendar of the Council extremely heavy. This has created an immense workload and responsibility on member states, while its impact on determining views of a state to consider membership of the Council cannot be undermined.

3.1 The Council's agenda and working methods/procedures

The new arrangement allowed both member states and other stakeholders including observers to discuss both thematic issues and country-specific situations. The fact that the agenda maintained a specific item on the 'human rights situation in Palestine and other occupied Arab territories' (Item 7), for some, maintained the former Commission's practice of selectivity and politicisation. Similar to the situation in the case of the Commission, states assume the responsibility of putting the situation on the agenda of the Council, even though other actors such as NGOs and Special Procedures may have a limited role.

---

17 For a wide-ranging discussion of the impact of the United Nations Humanitarian Reform since 2005, see 'Humanitarian Reform: fulfilling its promise?' (2007) 29 *Forced Migration Review*.

18 M. Nowak, 'The Need for a World Court of Human Rights' (2007) 7(1) *Human Rights Law Review* 251–59.

19 M. Bowman, 'Towards a Unified Standing Treaty Body for Monitoring Compliance with UN Human Rights Conventions? Legal Mechanisms for Treaty Reform' (2007) 7(1) *Human Rights Law Review* 225–49. See also Office of the High Commissioner for Human Rights, *The Treaty Body Strengthening Process*, available at: http://www2.ohchr.org/english/bodies/HRTD/, accessed on 28 September 2012.

20 Alston (n. 11) 1.

21 GA Res. 60/251 (n. 9) para. 6.

22 Institution-building of the United Nations Human Rights Council, HRC Res. 5/1 (18 June 2007) Annex.

With respect to the organisation of an ordinary session of the Council, it was agreed that the Council would meet regularly and that it would hold three ordinary sessions per year for no less than 10 weeks in total. In addition, the Council can hold special sessions based on the support of one third of its membership. In practice, the special sessions were relatively easier to organise and have become important tools for addressing human rights emergencies such as in Syria, Libya and Palestine. The Council also maintained the Commission's rule of procedures in relying on informal consultations and negotiations to draft and develop resolutions. For its formal sessions, the Council applies the rules of procedure of the General Assembly. The introduction of seminars and panels on various topics has been an important source of innovation by the Council.

3.2 Evaluation of states' human rights record through the Universal Periodic Review

The establishment of the Universal Periodic Review (UPR) is one of the most important innovations of the Council. Drawing from peer-review mechanisms used both by the international and regional mechanisms, the UPR was primarily intended to respond to the often cited criticism of 'double-standard, selectivity and politicisation' of the former Commission. Its objectives include: (a) improving 'human rights situations on the ground', (b) assessing 'positive developments and challenges' countries are facing in fulfilling their human rights obligations, (c) sharing best practices, (d) promoting technical cooperation and international cooperation.[23] The review is based on key human rights instruments. With an eye on engagement of the Council in countries involving armed conflicts, it was stated that 'the review shall take into account applicable international humanitarian law'.[24] The process is based on a national report which is expected to be developed through a consultative process involving key government institutions, national human rights institutions, NGOs and civil society at the national level. In addition to the national report, the review process will also rely on two additional documents: (a) a compilation of inputs from treaty bodies and human rights mechanisms; and (b) a summary of inputs from other stakeholders, such as national human rights institutions, NGOs and civil society, in the UPR.

Members of the Council are expected to be reviewed during the period of their membership, as a signal of their commitment to human rights and readiness to be vetted. The review is undertaken by a Working Group of the Council comprising all its members. It was agreed that the Council's Working Group will hold three annual sessions in which observers may also participate. A group of three state delegations, the Troika, drawn from the Council's membership, has the task 'to facilitate each review, including the preparation of the report of the Working Group'.[25] During the negotiation of the 'Institution-building Package', the proposal on direct participation of NGOs and individual experts in the process was fiercely resisted by some states. They were only allowed to attend the review in the Working Group and make general observations during the adoption of the report of the Working Group by the Council's plenary. The outcome of the UPR includes a summary of the proceedings, recommendations which the state under review has accepted or rejected and voluntary

23 Ibid
24 Ibid. para. 1(2).
25 Ibid. para. 18(d).

commitments made by the state. No formal agreement was reached with respect to a specific follow-up mechanism to monitor the implementation of the recommendations. It was, however, agreed that the subsequent review would focus on the implementation of the preceding outcome.

The relationship between the UPR and other human rights mechanisms, states' engagement and capacity, follow-up and monitoring, and the participation of other stakeholders were issues raised during the negotiations over the 'Institution-building Text or Package'. In order to address these concerns, 'the Institution-building Package' stipulated that the UPR should 'complement and not duplicate other human rights mechanisms, thus representing an added value'.[26] With respect to the challenges associated with states' capacity to engage in the review process, a general principle was incorporated in 'the Institution-building text' which underlined the need to implement the UPR review in a manner that would 'not be overly burdensome to the concerned state or the agenda of the Council'.[27] Based on strong lobbying and a push by developing countries, states also agreed to establish a 'Universal Periodic Review Voluntary Trust Fund', aimed at supporting the participation of developing countries, particularly the Least Developed Countries.[28] For the purposes of follow-up of the UPR recommendations, 'the Institution-building Package' inter alia provided that 'the international community will assist in implementing the recommendations and conclusions'.[29]

3.3 Maintaining and strengthening Special Procedures

The Council maintained the key roles and functions of both country-specific and thematic Special Procedures. The term 'Special Procedures' refers to Special Rapporteurs, Independent Experts and Working Groups. As of April 2013, there were 36 thematic and 13 country-specific mandates. They are supported by OHCHR. Overall, the Special Procedures are considered one of the key pillars of the international human rights system within the Human Rights Council. Their reports and interactive dialogues with member states and other stakeholders during the sessions of the Council were instrumental in highlighting human rights concerns in many parts of the world. They have also become instrumental in providing advisory services, technical assistance and capacity-building.

The institution-building effort by the Council focused on the appointment of mandate holders, the code of conduct, the review of future of country-specific mandates and the 'rationalisation and improvement' of mandates. The 'Institution-building Package' attempted to identify technical and objective criteria for selecting Special Procedures with the aim of ensuring the professionalisation of their selection and the monitoring of their activities. A new Consultative Group was established from member states which will oversee the selection procedure and the adoption of a public roster to be maintained by the OHCHR.[30] A

---

26 Ibid. para. 3(f).
27 Ibid. para. 3(h).
28 It is notable that this decision was reflected in a footnote in the text. The Council adopted Resolution 6/7 (28 September 2007) establishing the UPR Fund and later agreed on terms of reference for the operationalisation of the fund.
29 HRC Res. 5/1, Annex (n. 22) para. 36.
30 Information regarding the Consultative Group and the selection procedure of mandate holder is available at: http://www.ohchr.org/EN/HRBodies/SP/Pages/Nominations.aspx, accessed on 3 June 2013.

five-member Consultative Group with one state from each regional group will prepare a shortlist, which the President of the Council will then use to pick a consensus candidate. This process has been criticised for encouraging a selection process that highlights the influence of political consideration and bargaining instead of individual merits and competence of the individual concerned. Accordingly, a new procedure of vetting the competence and capacity of individual candidates has been introduced. The procedure draws candidates from nominations and public roster maintained by OHCHR. Mandate holders remain as a voluntary role performed by highly qualified individuals. The Special Procedure mechanism is significantly under-resourced.

As expected, the establishment of country-specific mandate holders has drawn the fiercest criticism from states which continue to resist the establishment of country-specific rapporteurs, citing the UPR as a proper, universal channel for a review of the human rights situation in a country. This led to the termination of of Special Procedures mandates on Cuba and Belarus (though that for Belarus has since been re-established).[31] Despite the evidence of continuing deterioration of human rights situations in Congo, the Council decided, largely as a result of the pressure from the African Group,[32] to abolish the Independent Expert on Congo in 2008. The African Group also vigorously lobbied for the termination of the Special Rapporteur on Sudan. Though unsuccessful, the resolution renewing the mandate was watered down. Compared to its position regarding country-specific mandates, member states have shown greater resourcefulness in establishing thematic mandates. A number of new thematic Special Procedures have been established in the areas of freedom of assembly, cultural rights, the promotion of equitable and democratic order, the responsibility of transitional cooperation and business enterprises, slavery, socio-economic rights such as safe drinking water and sanitation, and discrimination against women in law and practice.

A code of conduct, originally proposed by the African Group, has been negotiated and adopted as a part of the Annex of the Institution-Building Text. While the accountability framework applicable in the context of conduct of Special Procedures is relevant, ensuring its enforcement and the question of what kind of oversight mechanism should be responsible for such a task has been controversial. Special Rapporteurs themselves support self-regulation, whereas some member states and commentators support the establishment of an independent review mechanism.[33] Recent calls by groups of states within the Council calling for a scrupulous application of the Code of Conduct lays bare ongoing initiatives to put pressure on the Special Procedures.[34]

While the reports of the Special Rapporteurs have been instrumental in highlighting human rights challenges in different contexts, there remains an overlap between the investigative role of mandate holders and the role of commissions of inquiry. Joint statements, joint-country visits and collaboration with regional human rights mechanisms are areas where further development and improvement can be expected. Increasingly, Special Procedures are

---

31 HRC Res. 20/13 (2012).
32 Regional and political groupings including the African Group, the Arab Group, the Organisation of Islamic Conference, the Western European and other Groups, serve as informal forum of coordination and negotiation.
33 P. Alston, 'Hobbling the Monitors: Should U.N. Human Rights Monitors be Accountable?' (2011) 28(2) *Harvard International Law Journal* 563–648.
34 International Service on Human Rights, 'Human Rights Council' (2012) 3 *Human Rights Monitor Quarterly* 1–5 at 1, fn. 5.

developing a practice of issuing joint statements and undertaking joint studies. Unlike the growth in the number of Special Procedures, the resources and support available has unfortunately not increased.

3.4 The Advisory Committee, the complaint mechanism and subsidiary bodies

The Advisory Committee has been established to play the role of a 'think tank' with the responsibility of advising the Council on thematic issues.[35] It replaced the former Sub-Commission on the Promotion and Protection Human Rights. The authority and mandate of the Committee is limited to undertaking studies and providing recommendations based on a request by the Council. Unlike the case of Special Procedures, its members are elected directly by the Council. Since it become operational, the Committee has helped the Council to draw upon a number of key standards, conducted studies and presented to the Council for approval several research proposals. The Committee's work in preparing draft declarations on human rights education and training, leprosy-related discrimination and the right of peoples to peace are major achievements. It has also conducted studies on a wide range of topics including missing persons, international cooperation in the area of human rights, terrorist hostage taking and the right to food. With regard to new areas of research, the Committee submitted for the Council's consideration and approval proposals on a range of topics including access to justice and corruption, the role of local government in human rights, human rights in humanitarian actions, a model law on equal opportunity and non-discrimination, and globalisation and youth. While the Committee has been instrumental in influencing a number of key standard-setting exercises, including the elaboration of a draft declaration on human rights education and training and a draft declaration of the right of peoples to peace, it does not enjoy the competence to take independent initiatives and as such can only act upon the initiative of the Council.

The Council maintained a complaint procedure as an important pillar of its mechanisms in order to 'address consistent patterns of gross and reliably attested violations of all human rights and all fundamental freedoms'.[36] It established two working groups with distinct responsibilities and composition. The Working Group on Communications consists of five states that are members of the Human Rights Council's Advisory Committee. Its main responsibility involves deciding on the admissibility of communications and transmitting those which 'appear to reveal a consistent pattern of gross and reliably attested violations of human rights and fundamental freedoms'[37] to the Council's Working Group on Situations. The latter is appointed from representatives of member states of the Council, who will serve in their individual capacities. The Council also established subsidiary bodies, including the Social Forum, Forum on Minority Issues and the Expert Mechanism on the rights of indigenous peoples. Nevertheless, the specific guidelines on the operationalisation of these mechanisms were left outside of the framework of the 'Institution-building Package'.

35 HRC Res. 5/1, Annex (n. 22) paras 65–84. Information regarding the functioning and achievements of the Committee is available at: http://www.ohchr.org/EN/HRBodies/HRC/AdvisoryCommittee/Pages/AboutAC.aspx, accessed on 3 June 2013.
36 HRC Res. 5/1, Annex (n. 22) para. 85. For a balanced review of the 1503 Procedure under the Commission, see H. Tolley, 'The Concealed Crack in the Citadel: The UN Commission on Human Rights' Response to Confidential Communications' (1984) 6(4) *Human Rights Quarterly* 420–62.
37 HRC Res. 5/1, Annex (n. 22) para. 95.

4 Achievements of the Council

The Council's meetings have become more regular, transparent and timely. It has also responded to some of the urgent human rights situations, including by holding special sessions. At the time of writing, the Council has already held 19 special sessions which often led to the adoption of key resolutions. The majority of these special sessions highlighted human rights concerns in individual countries. The Council has served as an effective platform to discuss contemporary thematic issues, including topics such as human rights and counter-terrorism, natural disasters and climate change, impacts of economic crises on human rights, and the human rights of lesbian, gay, bisexual and transgender (LGBT) persons. In its historic decision during its 17th regular session, the Council restated the universality of human rights; expressed grave concern at acts of violence and discrimination against persons on the basis of their sexual orientation and gender identity, instructed the OHCHR to document discriminatory laws and practices and acts of violence and requested the Council to convene a panel discussion.[38] This decision was considered by the Human Rights Council as 'a first bold step into a territory previously considered off-limits'.[39] Both OHCHR's report and the finding of the panel underscored the need to take several positive measures at the national level.[40] With respect to the particular role of the Human Rights Council, it was recommended that the Council should regularly monitor discrimination and violence based on grounds of sexual orientation and gender identity, and that the Council takes measures to ensure the mainstreaming of such a task within the mandate of the Special Rapporteurs.[41]

But the Council's first few years were difficult. Even during its first year where much of the time was spent on procedural issues of building its mechanisms, the Council held four special sessions. These initial special sessions focused on human rights developments concerning Israel, fuelling a legitimate concern that the Council has unfairly singled out Israel. Concerning Sri Lanka, the Council adopted a decision which was very much muted in its response to what many considered were serious human rights and humanitarian developments on the ground.[42] In March 2012, the Council was able to adopt, by a narrow majority, a resolution in which it expressed its concern about the genuineness of the government-led reconciliation and called on the government to take credible actions in implementing the report of Sri Lankan Lessons Learnt and Reconciliation Commission, and present it with a Comprehensive Action Plan.[43]

The Council's special sessions have also gradually focused on a wide range of human rights issues in a number of states, including Côte d'Ivoire, Eritrea, Syria, North Korea and Libya.

---

38 Human Rights, Sexual Orientation and Gender Identity, HRC Res. 17/19 (14 July 2011).
39 Human Rights Watch, 'Landmark UN Vote on Sexual Orientation' *Human Rights Watch* (Geneva, 17 June 2011).
40 Report of the United Nations High Commissioner for Human Rights, 'Discriminatory laws and practices and acts of violence against individuals based on their sexual orientation and gender identity' (2011) UN Doc. A/HRC/19/41, 24–25.
41 See the Summary of the HRC panel on sexual orientation and gender identity (7 March 2012), available at: http://www.ohchr.org/EN/Issues/Discrimination/Pages/PanelsexualOrientation. aspx, accessed on 29 September 2012.
42 HRC Res. S-11/1 (27 May 2009). See Human Rights Watch, 'Sri Lanka: UN Rights Council Fails Victims' *Human Rights Watch* (Geneva, 27 May 2009) available at: http://www.hrw.org/ news/2009/05/27/sri-lanka-un-rights-council-fails-victims, accessed on 13 June 2012.HRC Res. 22/13 (2013).
43 HRC Res. 19/2 (3 April 2012).

The relative ease with which the Council managed to organise special sessions was made possible by the fact that out of the 47 members, the support of only 16 member states is needed to request a special session. In organising these special sessions and achieving a consensus or a majority decision, the key role of emerging democracies, such as Mexico, India and Brazil, was quite important. These special sessions regularly led to the adoption of resolutions. Through these special sessions, the Council was able to create awareness about key human rights emergencies, condemned violations, established fact-finding missions to investigate violations, mandated the OHCHR to monitor further developments and requested other institutions to pay full attention to these human rights concerns. The response to the 'Arab spring' represented one of the high points for the Human Rights Council where it held a number of special sessions, established inquiry commissions in response to situations in Libya and Syria, and established a country-specific mandate holder on Syria and recommended the consideration of the situation in Libya to the General Assembly for the suspension of its membership in the Council.[44] The confirmation of suspension by the General Assembly in 2011 marked the first time a member state of the Council (or even the Commission) had been suspended for its human rights record.[45]

This stirred a review process covering all members of the United Nations, and established several commissions of inquiry to undertake in-depth studies on current situations of grave human rights violations. Despite the absence of formal voting rights during the adoption of the Council's resolutions, observer states continue to play an instrumental role, including by sponsoring resolutions. The practice that the Council's procedure encourages the adoption of decisions by consensus increases the participation of observer states and other stakeholders, including NGOs who would otherwise not be able to participate in the Council's formal decision-making processes.

4.1 Standard-setting and development of international human rights law

As was the case with its predecessor and in line with its mandate to 'make recommendations to the General Assembly for the . . . development of international law in the field of human rights',[46] the Council has taken a proactive role in the development of international normative standards. It has initiated the development of a number of key international standards while finalising important human rights standards which were initiated by the Commission. These included the International Convention on Enforced Disappearances,[47] the Additional Protocol to the Convention on the Rights of the Child[48] and the Additional Protocol to the International Covenant on Economic, Social and Cultural Rights.[49] The Council also adopted various soft law instruments, such as the UN Declaration on the Rights of Indigenous Peoples[50] and the UN Declaration on Human Rights Education and Training.[51] Following in the footsteps of

44 HRC Res. S-15/1 (3 March 2011).
45 GA Res. 1970/2011 (26 February 2011). In an equally notable resolution, the GA adopted Res. A/66/L.9 (15 November 2011) reinstating Libya's membership in the Council.
46 GA Res. 60/251 (n. 9) para. 5(c).
47 HRC Res. 1/1 (29 June 2006).
48 HRC Res. 17/18 (14 July 2011).
49 HRC Res. 8/2 (18 June 2008).
50 HRC Res. 2006/2 (29 June 2006).
51 HRC Res. 16/1 (8 April 2011).

the widely recognised UN Guiding Principles on Internal Displacement,[52] the Council, through its Special Procedures, developed similar soft laws on topics ranging from business and human rights[53] to development-based evictions and displacement.[54]

There are also ongoing discussions in the area of the right to development, complementarity standards in the fight against racism, and the role of non-state military actors where progress has not been achieved due to a lack of consensus among member states on these issues. Notable normative developments were also achieved as the Council's adopted key resolutions expanding the application of international human rights standards in access to medicine, sexual orientation, environment and climate change, natural disasters, protection of journalists during armed conflicts, freedom of peaceful assembly, human rights and the internet, and the protection of human rights under counter-terrorism measures. It held annual sessions on the integration of gender in the work of the Human Rights Council and has encouraged OHCHR to examine protection of human rights in the context of armed conflict.

4.2 Ensuring a universal human rights assessment of states through the UPR

The UPR has emerged as one of the most important tools for scrutinising human rights situations based on a constructive and balanced approach. Both in engagement with the Council and in the process put together at the national level for the preparation of state reports to the UPR, many states have given a higher political profile to the UPR. While countries with problematic human rights records often lobbied and mobilised 'friendly' states to make favourable statements during the review process, the process allowed the opportunity for key relevant human rights issues to be raised and discussed.[55] As was seen during the review of Haiti and Somalia, the review has been conducted in a manner that took into account the challenges states under review face such as limited institutional capacity and the existing political and security situation in the country which may limit broader consultation of the national consultation to develop the UPR outcome. The UPR process has also allowed the opportunity to monitor the implementation of the recommendations of treaty bodies. The

---

52 UN High Commissioner for Refugees, 'Guiding Principles on Internal Displacement' (1998) UN Doc. E/CN.4/1998/53/Add.2. For the impact of the Guiding Principles on similar initiatives in the Human Rights Council, see A. Abebe, 'Special Rapporteurs as Law Makers: The Developments and Evaluation of the normative framework for protecting and assisting internally displaced persons' (2011) 15(2) *International Journal of Human Rights* 286–96.

53 The Guiding Principles on Business and Human Rights were developed by the respective Special Representative of the Secretary-General. See Report of the Special Representative of the Secretary-General on the issue of human rights and transnational corporations and other business enterprises, 'Guiding Principles on Business and Human Rights: Implementing the United Nations "Protect, Respect and Remedy" Framework' (2011) UN Doc. A/HRC/17/31, Annex.

54 Basic Principles and Guidelines on Development-Based Eviction and Displacement, Annex to the Report of the Special Rapporteur on adequate housing as a component of the rights to an adequate standard of living (2007) UN Doc. A/HRC/4/18.

55 For a review of the UPR process, see A. Abebe, 'Of Shaming and Bargaining: African States and the Universal Periodic Review of the United Nations Human Rights Council' (2006) 9(1) *Human Rights Law Review* 22–25; See also E. MacMahon, 'Herding Cats and Sheep: Assessing State and Regional Behavior in the Universal Periodic Review Mechanism of the United Nations Human Rights Council' (July 2010) available at http://www.upr-info.org/IMG/pdf/McMahon_Herding_Cats_and_Sheeps_July_2010.pdf, accessed on 2 May 2012; see also F. Gaer, 'A Voice not an Echo: Universal Periodic Review and the United Treaty Body System' (2007) 7(1) *Human Rights Law Review* 109–39.

UPR has been widely praised for creating a universal forum for a fair and balanced assessment of human rights situations in specific countries. Every member state has already gone through the first cycle of the review process.[56] The level of seniority of delegation participating in the Geneva-based process is often testament to how seriously many states have taken the process. The process is also often considered as a constructive peer-evaluation and has also been cast as immune from politicisation, finger-pointing and unfair criticism. Though not provided for, numerous states have reported back to the Human Rights Council on measures that they have taken to implement UPR recommendations. By allowing contributions from the treaty bodies, the UPR has created new opportunities for alignment and compatibility between the Human Rights Council and treaty bodies. At the national level, states are also encouraged to promote a participatory process in preparing the national report. The UPR has also triggered a proliferation of national human rights action plans. This, however, does not mean that the process has been immune to shortcomings. Issues of insufficient participation for NGOs in the review process, the implementation of recommendations and the duration of the review process were considered as possible areas for further improvements. Some have also pointed out the lack of capacity, particularly in developing countries which do not have diplomatic representations in Geneva, to meaningfully participate in the process including as active members of the reviewing Troika.[57]

4.3 Responding to human rights emergencies

The Council's regular sessions have been used to highlight human rights situations within states. This has been done, for example, when the Council examines human rights concerns brought to its attention by various stakeholders. The reports of the Special Procedures are another important tool that is often used to highlight urgent human rights situations. The same can be said about the role of the UPR. The most targeted mechanism of addressing human rights emergencies in a specific country, however, remains the special sessions which result in 'action-oriented' resolutions. In a notable shift from the practice of the Commission, the Council focuses more on monitoring and follow-up.[58] Despite the initial fear that the Council would be less inclined and able to establish country-specific mandates, key sponsors were able to muster broad support for the establishment of country-specific mandates on Côte d'Ivoire, Eritrea, Belarus, Iran and Syria.

Despite consistent pressure and criticisms from numerous quarters, the High Commissioner for Human Rights, Ms Navi Pillay, has been an excellent and courageous advocate for a proactive role by the Council. The debate on the review of the Council saw interest on the part of some states to bring the Office of the High Commissioner for Human Rights within the purview of the Council's scrutiny. OHCHR, as well as NGOs, Western governments and reform-minded states often resisted such moves.

56 Israel suspended its relations with the Human Rights Council (HRC) in a letter published on 14 May 2012. It did not submit a national report due in October 2012, which triggered the Human Rights Council to call on Israel to resume its cooperation with the Council including its UPR mechanism and rescheduled its UPR in 2013, at the 17th Working Group session (21 October–1 November 2013).
57 Abebe, (n. 55) 25.
58 R. Brett, 'Neither Mountain nor Molehill: UN Human Rights Council: One Year On' (QUNO, 2007) 4–5.

The Council established a number of international commissions of inquiry to undertake studies of human rights situations particularly in conflict situations, triggering both a promise and challenging areas for the Council in the development of international humanitarian law.[59] In Côte d'Ivoire, Libya, Syria, Tunisia and OPT/Israel, the Council appointed fact-finding and inquiry bodies to study human rights situations and present it with recommendations. The experience of the Council with these bodies has posed major questions including on how the Council should be related to the Security Council and to the International Criminal Court. Though challenged by a few states, the Council generally embraced its role in the promotion and protection of international humanitarian law.[60] The review of states' human rights performance in the UPR has also relied on international humanitarian law.

5 The Council's weaknesses and a second chance at a reform

Despite some of its achievements, the implementation period has shown that the Council indeed suffered from important weaknesses.[61] The Council's response to human rights violations and developments in certain countries, such as Sri Lanka and Bahrain, were severely criticised.[62] States and civil society organisations consider the Council's attention on Israel as biased. The US cited this as one of the reasons for its disengagement with the Council in 2008. The Government of Israel has also officially and publicly stated that it no longer co-operates with the Council, citing its 'biased' approach.[63] Other challenges include: (a) the lack of sufficient space for NGOs, including during the exercise of the Universal Periodic Review, and in the handling of complaints in the individual complaint mechanism; (b) the influence of 'block politics' and regional alignment; (c) lack of resources for the implementation of the Council's decisions; (d) the politicisation of the work of the OHCHR; (e) the under-utilisation and ineffectiveness of the confidential and individual complaint procedure that replaced the former system; (f) the Council's tendency to respond to human rights situations which are in the public eye. The Council is a political organ in which the role of states is central. An oversight role on the human rights records of states by a political organ will remain a significant challenge despite well-intended reform measures. With respect to the individual complaint mechanism, commentators found the current system seriously flawed and that either it should be fundamentally changed or 'disestablished'.[64]

The new membership arrangement under which the African and Asian states assume 26 seats out of 47 members of the Council has created a new dynamic in power relationships in decision making in which an African–Asian alignment could easily block major decisions. Prior to the membership of the United States in the Council, EU states often struggled to get majority votes for some draft decisions which did not resonate with delegations from the African, OIC and some countries in the Asian region. As the United States assumed direct

---

59 See P. Alston, J. Morgan-Foster and W. Abresch, 'The Competence of the UN Human Rights Council and its Special Procedures in Relation to Armed Conflicts: Extrajudicial Executions in the "War on Terror" ' (2009) 19(1) *European Journal of International Law* 183–29.

60 HRC Res. 9/9 (21 September 2008).

61 B.G. Ramcharan, *The Human Rights Council* (Routledge, 2011).

62 Human Rights Watch, 'The UN Landmark Vote' (n. 39).

63 BBC, 'Israel ends contact with UN Human Rights Council' *BBC News* (Geneva, 26 March 2012) available at: http://www.bbc.co.uk/news/world-middle-east-17510668, accessed on 29 September 2012.

64 Chatham House (n. 2) 9.

participation and leadership following its membership, the Western Group was galvanised and used its allies to make headway in some important decisions. These included quite significant decisions on appointment of country-specific rapporteurs, such as the ones on Iran and Belarus, and on thematic decisions on topics ranging from LGBT issues to freedom of assembly.

In order to address some of these shortcomings, identify good practices and implement the request in Resolution 251/60 to undertake a review of its work, the Council established an open-ended intergovernmental working group.[65] A number of key formal and informal consultations were held to undertake the necessary consultations and negotiations.[66] The various stakeholders had different expectations and promoted different priorities for the reform process. Whilst there was a rhetorical 'consensus' on the scope of the review, some wanted a much broader and more ambitious review process, whereas others chose a rather 'minimalist' approach.

States and NGOs underscored the need to stay within the framework of the 'Institution-building Package', and not to renegotiate the instrument. The substantive issues covered by the review process included topics such as the UPR, the Special Procedures, the Advisory Committee, complaint procedure, agenda, framework for the programme of work and method of work and rules of procedure. Following months of consultations and negotiations, the Council adopted by a consensus an outcome document on 25 March 2011.[67] This review resulted in a few innovations. With respect to special procedures, the right of national human rights institutions to submit candidates has been affirmed and the Consultative Group has been mandated to interview shortlisted candidates for the position of mandate holders. With respect to the UPR, the review focused on a number of specific and practical issues, such as the focus of the second cycle of the UPR, the order of review of countries and the question of how to ensure that both member and observer states of the Council which wish to directly participate in the review can do so.[68] The Council also established the office of the President of the Council with expanded secretariat. While no specific mandate has been created for the President, this will most likely be a future area of a reform.

In addition to the review conducted by the Council itself, the General Assembly also led a review process which specifically looked at the status of the Council – an issue that was debated and discussed by a consultation and negotiation mechanism established by the General Assembly in New York. Other issues covered by the review of the General Assembly include reporting and a period for a future review of the Council. Failing to agree on major reform proposals, including on enhancing the status of the Council into 'a principal organ' of the United Nations, the General Assembly adopted by a majority decision agreeing to institutionalised existing ad hoc arrangements of the Council's reporting to both the General

---

65 HRC Res. 16/21 (12 April 2011).
66 See Outcome of the Retreat of Algiers, 20–21 February 2010; Reflection Group on the Strengthening of the Human Rights Council, First Meeting 29–30 October 2009, Mexico City; Second Meeting of the Reflection Group on the strengthening of the Human Rights Council, 25–26 January 2010, Paris; Summary Report of the Open-Ended Seminar on the Review of the Human Rights Council, Montreux, 20 April 2010. These documents are available at http://www.ohchr.org/EN/HRBodies/HRC/Pages/InformalInitiatives.aspx, accessed on 29 September 2012.
67 HRC Res. 16/21 (n. 65).
68 Annex to HRC Res. 5/1 (n. 44) notes that '[t]he universal periodic review is an evolving process; the Council, after the conclusion of the first review cycle, may review the modalities and the periodicity of this mechanism, based on best practices and lessons learned'.

Assembly's plenary and its Third Committee; deciding that the annual report of the Council will cover the period from 1 October to 30 September; and aligning the Council's cycle with the calendar year instead of starting in June each year.[69] Citing UN General Assembly's failure to address the question of the status of the Council, the lack of competitive elections of members and review of the implementation of pledges made by states, observers criticised the review as being 'bureaucratic'.[70]

6 The Council's future role

Though the HRC's performance in the last six years has been largely positive, its future will be shaped by the ability of its members, observer states and all stakeholders to maintain the reform momentum and prove the Council's relevance in responding to contemporary and urgent human rights challenges. Its role and position as a 'gate keeper' of human rights is under increasing scrutiny as other institutions both at the international and regional levels are playing proactive roles in the promotion and protection of human rights. Indeed, the Council's relationship with the Security Council, the General Assembly, the International Criminal Court, international commissions of inquiry and regional human rights mechanisms deserves closer attention. So far, the series of reforms of the Council has focused on the relationship between the Council and the General Assembly. The holding of the Council's special sessions and the various steps taken by the Council's mandate holders to scrutinise human rights situations in several countries has increasingly been used to respond to emergency human rights situations. The UPR Working Group and other institutional mechanisms hold a series of meetings throughout the year, offering an opportunity for the protection and promotion of human rights. For states with a small and weak diplomatic representation in Geneva, the participation in these mechanisms is quite a cumbersome process. The provision of technical assistance in this regard by the Council and OHCHR leaves more to be desired.

The Council's new standards on membership have not completely deterred states with problematic human rights records from becoming members. The fact that membership of states has been allocated on regional and geographical basis has not helped. Though members are required to show the highest standards of compliance with human rights standards, implementing this in practice has not been easy. The role of the Council in suspending Libya from being a member, following the uprising in the country and violations of human rights by authorities, has been considered as a positive development. The participation of post-Arab Spring governments, particularly Libya and Tunisia, in the Council, however, reaffirms that the greatest assurance for human rights comes from greater democratisation and openness at the country level.

Regional and political groupings, that is the African Group, the Organisation of Islamic Conference (OIC), the Group of Latin American and Caribbean Countries (GRULAC) and the Western European and Others Groups (WEOG), are influential forums for coordination. The Human Rights Council is a political organ where states often work through regional alliances or blocs. The fact that developing countries have assumed a more assertive and prominent role in the Council than in the case of the former Commission meant that proposals espoused by the Western Group have to be seriously negotiated. Certain initiatives proposed

---

69 GA Res. 65/281.
70 International Service for Human Rights, 'Review of the Council: General Assembly Status Review Another Lost Opportunity' (2011) 3 *Human Rights Monitor Quarterly* 7–9 at 7.

by groupings of states with large numbers of members have been successfully adopted. This has happened, for example, in the case of a proposal by the Organisation of the Islamic Conference (OIC) to ensure that the mandate of the Special Rapporteur on Freedom of Expression also includes abuses of freedom of expression amounting to 'racial and religious intolerance'. On many occasions, proposals by Western countries were either abandoned or had to be significantly watered down in order to obtain the support of the wider membership. States, however, have made some efforts towards building inter-regional relationships which has resulted in the initiation and adoption of a number of key decisions by cross-regional groupings. Consensus has been reached on a range of particularly divisive thematic issues such as sexual orientation, and freedom of expression and religion. The establishment of mandate holders through these informal cross-regional forums has also been of relevance.

A number of special sessions were held and condemnatory resolutions have been adopted on Israel, fuelling the often cited criticism that the Council disproportionately focuses on Israel. The role of 'reform-minded' emerging states, such as Brazil, Mexico, India and South Africa, also served as an important facilitator for building of consensus and taking some bold initiatives forward.

The Council's more targeted intervention in country situations will continue to face resistance by states. States may also be tempted to use the UPR as a pretext to resist country-specific mandates. While the Council's recent engagements in human rights situations in Belarus, Eritrea, Syria and Iran have led to the establishment of country-specific mandates, there has been a consistent resistance by states to country-specific mandates. In light of such general sentiment, the Council's decision to hold several special sessions on Israel and its maintenance of a permanent agenda item on human rights situations associated with issues in Palestine and other occupied territories has been subjected to criticism.

As already stated above, the limited role of NGOs is one of the areas where the Council finds itself out of step with the important role these actors play in the promotion and protection of human rights. There are some specific areas of particular concern. First, the participation of NGOs during the consideration of reports by the Working Group in the UPR process has been quite limited. Attempts to extend the role of NGOs in this exercise failed due largely to the objections by states which do not want to see an increased role for NGOs. Although NGOs actively participate in the various working groups of the Council, they do not enjoy a formal membership and direct participation in negotiations of outcome documents, including resolutions. NGOs also often expressed frustration that the Council does not allow a greater role for NGOs to influence its debate or for the handling of the individual complaints the Council examines. The participation of NGOs which are not based in Geneva has also been raised.[71] In a world where information technologies and communication mechanisms have quickly been changing the way in which institutions are doing business, the Council should take a more progressive step in allowing communities of human rights activists and NGOs to effectively participate in its work.

The Council's relationship with a changing role of the Office of the High Commission for Human Rights has been a quite delicate institutional problem. OHCHR continues to undertake important and impressive work in supporting the Human Rights Council, often under

---

71 T. Rathgeber, 'Reviewing the UN Human Rights Council: Perspectives from Civil Society' (Friedrich Ebert Stiftung, November 2010) 5.

budgetary and other resource constraints. Providing full and effective secretarial services to the numerous activities of the Council is indeed a great burden.

Supporting the increasing number of fact-finding missions has been an important challenge, often forcing the OHCHR to divert its limited resources from equally important activities. Initiatives to address this particular challenge including through the setting up of the 'contingency budgetary facility did not find wide-support; and the recent review of the Council by the General Assembly on the subject matter was inconclusive'.[72] The Council also relies on the OHCHR with regard to the preparation of almost all of its thematic and country-specific reports. Moreover, the Office supports the mandates of Special Procedures. The call for formal reporting by OHCHR to the Council and the push by some members to regulate the staffing of the OHCHR, however, pose serious challenges to its effectiveness and independence. During several sessions, Cuba together with a number of key developing countries sponsored resolutions which called for an enhanced supervisory role of the Council in overseeing the activities and staffing of the OHCHR.[73]

Select bibliography

A. Abebe, 'Of Shaming and Bargaining: African States and the Universal Periodic Review of the United Nations Human Rights Council' (2006) 9(1) *Human Rights Law Review* 22–25.

P. Alston, 'Hobbling the Monitors: Should U.N. Human Rights Monitors be Accountable?' (2011) 28(2) *Harvard International Law Journal* 563–648.

P. Alston, 'Reconceiving the UN Human Rights Regime: Challenges Confronting the New Human Rights Council' (CHRJ Working Paper No. 4, 2006).

R. Brett, 'Neither Mountain nor Molehill: UN Human Rights Council: One Year On' (QUNO, 2007).

Chatham House, 'The UN Human Rights Council: A Five Year Assessment' (Meeting Summary, 16 November 2011).

International Service on Human Rights, 'Review of the Council: General Assembly Status review another lost opportunity' (2011) 3 *Human Rights Monitor Quarterly* 7–9.

M. Nowak, 'The Need for a World Court of Human Rights' (2007) 7(1) *Human Rights Law Review* 251–59.

B.G. Ramcharan, *The Human Rights Council* (Routledge, 2011).

T. Rathgeber, 'Reviewing the UN Human Rights Council: Perspectives from Civil Society' (Friedrich Ebert Stiftung, November 2010).

---

72 International Service for Human Rights, 'Review of the Council' (n. 70) 9.
73 HRC Res. 19/12 (22 March 2012).

41

Transitional justice

Juan E. Méndez and Catherine Cone

'Transitional justice' suggests the idea of justice in motion. By definition, transitional justice suggests a type of justice that plays a leading, albeit transient, role in shaping a transition from atrocities to the rule of law through a specifically tailored set of tools. The reality, however, is that a transition period can span as much as a few decades.[1] The reason for the often-lengthy transition lies in the backdrop of any transitional justice process – the particular society's attempt to come to terms with large-scale past abuses in order to ensure accountability, serve justice and achieve true reconciliation.[2] Based on our preferred definition of 'transition', the process is never complete until it reaches those fundamental objectives. However, even when set against this backdrop, the transitional justice stage is not always so clearly defined because it is not always limited to post-conflict situations. Increasingly, transitional justice is implemented in contexts where there is no clean break from conflict, 'no defining moment of transition, no sense of a rupture with the past offering a new leaf or fresh start for the society'.[3] Consequently, transitional justice is better understood as a range of mechanisms that can be implemented within a framework that includes both judicial and non-judicial mechanisms, such as prosecutions, reparations, truth-seeking and institutional reform.[4]

To best achieve the ends of transitional justice, the mechanisms underlying the process have resulted in binding norms in international human rights law and international humanitarian law that are at times directly treaty-based – for example the Geneva Conventions of 1949, the Genocide Convention, the Convention Against Torture and the recent UN

---

1 N. Roht-Arriaza, 'Transitional Justice and Peace Agreements' (2005) International Council on Human Rights Policy Working Paper, http://www.ichrp.org/files/papers/63/128_-_Transitional_Justice_and_Peace_Agreements_Roht-Arriaza__Naomi__2005.pdf, accessed on 18 February 2012.
2 UN Secretary-General, 'Rule of Law Tools for Post-Conflict States: The Rule of Law and Transitional Justice in Conflict and Post-Conflict Societies' (2004) UN Doc. S/2004/616 (UN Secretary-General Transitional Justice Report) para. 8.
3 A. Lyons, 'Introduction: For a Just Transition in Colombia', in A. Lyons (ed.), *Contested Transitions: Dilemmas of Transitional Justice in Colombia and Comparative Experience* (International Center for Transitional Justice [ICTY] 2011) 15. The UN Secretary-General Transitional Justice Report emphasises how transitional justice is applicable both in conflict and post-conflict settings.
4 UN Secretary-General Transitional Justice Report, (n. 2) para. 8.

Convention on Forced Disappearances. Otherwise, these principles have been distilled by regional courts, treaty bodies and authoritative special procedures of the United Nations from general international human rights law and the law of armed conflict, specifically from the duty to ensure and the right to a remedy. These resulting binding norms include four distinct obligations that are applicable to war crimes and crimes against humanity: (1) to investigate and disclose the truth of these atrocities; (2) to justice, that is to investigate, prosecute and punish those responsible, whether state agents or members of organised groups, who have committed war crimes or crimes against humanity; (3) to offer reparations to victims; and (4) to reform institutions that have been the vehicle of these atrocities, and other measures to ensure non-repetition. It is with those obligations in mind that we turn to the underlying normative framework grounding transitional justice.

1 Normative framework underlying transitional justice

The normative framework underlying transitional justice begins with the 1948 Universal Declaration of Human Rights where states affirmed that recognising inherent dignity and equal and inalienable rights serves as the foundation for freedom, justice and peace.[5] Following the Declaration, the International Covenant on Civil and Political Rights (ICCPR) required states to uphold the rule of law, even when faced with exigent circumstances, and to provide standardised and equal treatment in the administration of justice.[6] The ICCPR's derogation clause also provides an exception under which a state may take measures allowing it to partially forgo its obligations in a 'public emergency', but the Article provides no derogation from the state's obligation to uphold certain rights, an emergency notwithstanding.[7] Additionally, the 'Basic Principles and Guidelines on the Right to a Remedy and Reparation for Victims of Gross Violations of International Human Rights Law and Serious Violations of International Humanitarian Law' set forth the right to a remedy and reparations for victims of gross human rights violations and international crimes and serves as a foundation for international human rights law, further grounding the transitional justice framework.[8] Applying

---

5 Universal Declaration of Human Rights, preamble, (1948) UNGA Res. 217 A(III).
6 ICCPR, Arts 2, 4 and 26, (1966) 999 UNTS 171. These Articles provide for equality before the law through fair and public hearings, the presumption of innocence and certain minimum procedural guarantees. Art. 2 of the ICCPR obliges states to take the necessary steps to give effect to the rights set forth by ensuring an effective remedy for violations and by providing for determination of claims by competent judicial, administrative or legislative authorities as well as enforcement of these remedies when granted. Art. 26 recognises all persons as equal before the law and entitles them to equal protection of the law without discrimination.
7 ICCPR Art. 4, paras 1–2, Arts 6, 7, 8, 11, 15, 16 and 18. These precepts declare certain rights to be non-derogable thus mandating the state's compliance, including, among others: life, freedom from torture and cruel, inhuman or degrading treatment, slavery, liberty of movement, and freedom of expression.
8 See Basic Principles and Guidelines on the Right to a Remedy and Reparation for Victims of Gross Violations of International Human Rights Law and Serious Violations of International Humanitarian Law, UNGA Res. 60/147, (21 March 2006) UN Doc. A/Res. 60/147 (2006 Basic Principles and Guidelines); 1985 Declaration of Basic Principles of Justice for Victims of Crime and Abuse of Power, UNGA Res. 40/34, (29 November 1985) UN Doc. A/Res. 40/34 (1985 Basic Principles of Justice); Responsibility of States for Internationally Wrongful Acts, UNGA Res. 56/83 (28 January 2002) UN Doc. A/Res. 56/83. These documents mandate that any state that committed internationally wrongful acts provides effective recourse to victims including providing guarantees of non-repetition and reparations. See also, A. Cassese, *International Law,* 2nd edn (Oxford University Press, 2005) 393–94.

the combined logic of non-derogable rights and state obligations, international law thus provides, *a fortiori*, that these rights and duties cannot be derogated *ex post facto* via amnesties or de facto impunity. The notion that there is no derogation from certain rights and obligations serves as the legal backbone for accountability efforts. Lastly, the rule of law cannot be sufficiently underscored in reinforcing the underlying international human rights framework because '[f]or a legal system to ensure justice and the protection of the rule of law to all, it must incorporate these fundamental norms and standards'.[9]

Transitional justice is premised on an expansive view of international human rights law that accounts for more than just existing international human rights treaties and related principles. Consequently, evolving standards derived from soft law as well as appropriate interpretations of hard law also constitute the relevant international legal context relating to transitional justice. However, soft law can play an equally significant role despite its non-binding nature because soft law can become binding law once the principles embodied in that soft law are reflected in customary international law.[10] Additionally, great value can be extracted from international case law interpreting the rights and obligations provided for in treaties and customary international law. Rights and remedies for victims and the corresponding state obligations gain their meaning and are only fully effectuated once acted upon by courts that have the power to interpret these rights and obligations.[11] In turn, the international bodies' decisions requiring states to investigate and bring to justice perpetrators in cases of serious violations of physical integrity are interpretations of a common general provision found in international human rights law instruments obliging states parties to respect or secure the rights embodied in the instrument.[12]

Legacies of widespread or systematic violations of fundamental human rights trigger affirmative obligations on the part of the territorial state in the aftermath of international crimes such as torture, war crimes and crimes against humanity.[13] Current international law has now codified that in these cases, the state is accordingly required to provide: justice, truth, reparations, and institutional reform as a guarantee of non-repetition in efforts to address and redress such gross violations.[14] To be valid, justice in this context must entail criminal prosecution of all those responsible, including high and low level offenders; maintaining legitimacy by conducting prosecutions within the standards of fair trial and due process; overcoming legal and de facto obstacles; and living up to the obligation to extradite or prosecute.[15] Similarly, truth-telling efforts should be implemented through an organised and systematic process, especially where violations have been surrounded by secrecy or denial. Expert

9 See UN Secretary-General Transitional Justice Report (n. 2) para. 9, fn. 7.

10 Ibid.

11 See Cassese (n. 8) 183. Cassese posits how the decisions of judicial bodies interpreting treaties, although secondary law, carry great weight because they interpret treaties that are primary or 'hard law'. See also, M.C. Bassiouni, 'International Recognition of Victims' Rights' (2006) 16(2) *Hum. Rts. L. Rev.* 211–27 at 226.

12 Bassiouni (n. 11) at 226.

13 See J.E. Méndez, 'Accountability for Past Abuses' (1997) 19(2) *Hum. Rts. Q.* 255 at 259–62. In this document, Méndez discusses the four main state obligations as an emerging norm at the time, e.g. 1997; Bassiouni (n. 11). See also, below nn. 22–23 and accompanying text.

14 Méndez, ibid.

15 See below nn. 22–23 and accompanying text. See also, J. Zalaquett, 'Confronting Human Rights Violations Committed by Former Governments: Applicable Principles and Political Constraints' (1990) *13 Hamline L. Rev.* 623–60 at 630, 643.

Priscilla Hayner together with the UN Secretary-General established a set of core principles that truth-telling efforts should meet: (1) be implemented as the product of a national choice based on a broad consultative process; (2) accompany other transitional justice mechanisms as part of a comprehensive transitional justice strategy; (3) respond to unique, country-specific needs; (4) count on genuine political will and operational independence; and (5) rely on international support.[16]

In regard to reparations, there is little guidance on *quantum* or mode of reparation, but at a minimum, state programmes are required to universally cover victims and provide for simple, accessible procedures. Therefore, an administrative scheme is preferable to judicial determinations.[17] Lastly, as relates to institutional reform, efforts should embody an assertion of civilian, democratic supervision of state institutions through which violations were committed (police, armed forces, prosecutors, and courts in some cases). Moreover, the state should emphasise vetting officials to disqualify those who have abused their power and provide for mechanisms of control and supervision ('horizontal accountability') and human rights education.[18]

In assessing the current transitional justice landscape, it is imperative that states recognise that their obligations do not comprise a menu of duties from which to choose what is most appropriate, but instead represent an affirmative responsibility to pursue, in good faith and to the best of the state's abilities, each of the four obligations. However, obligations are understood and evaluated in terms of means, not of results. Therefore, a state satisfies these norms of international law as long as it does all that is within its power to achieve justice, reveal the truth, offer reparations and conduct institutional reform.[19]

2 Mechanisms of transitional justice

Transitional justice was able to take root in providing remedies for victims only when societies and states confronting legacies of mass atrocities took it upon themselves to address large-scale or systematic human rights violations and international crimes. The political will and

---

16 UN Secretary-General, 'Rule of Law Tools for Post-Conflict States: Truth Commissions' (2006) UN Doc. HR/PUB/06/1 (UN Secretary-General Truth Commissions Report) at 5–6, available at: http://www.unhcr.org/cgi-bin/texis/vtx/refworld/rwmain?page=search&docid=46cebc3d2 &skip=0&query=RULE%20OF%20LAW%20TOOLS%20FOR%20POST-CONFLICT%20 STATES, accessed on 24 February 2012.

17 See below nn. 45–46 and accompanying text.

18 See below, section 41.2.4, Institutional Reform, and nn. 49–50, 52 and accompanying text.

19 To be effective, any transitional justice programme will necessarily have to take into account gender when implementing all of the transitional justice tools. The United Nations Secretary General (UN SG), for example, specifically advocates for taking a gender-sensitive perspective into account. Specifically, the UN SG advocates for incorporating gender in justice efforts by seeking to particularly empower women; in truth-telling, by being responsive to gender-specific crimes; in reparations, by including and taking into account women in the design and enacting of reparations programmes; and in vetting, by accounting for women in the composition of newly organised or newly reformed institutions. See UN Secretary-General Transitional Justice Report, (n. 2) paras 35, 36, 46, 51; OHCHR, 'Rule of Law Tools for Post-Conflict States: Reparations Programmes' (2008) UN Doc. HR/PUB/08/1 (OHCHR Reparations Report) at 36, available at: http://www. ohchr.org/Documents/Publications/ReparationsProgrammes.pdf, accessed on 26 February 2012; OHCHR, 'Rule of Law Tools for Post-Conflict States, Vetting: an operational framework' (2006) UN Doc. HR/PUB/06/5 (OHCHR Vetting Framework) at 26–27, available at: http://www. ohchr.org/Documents/Publications/RuleoflawVettingen.pdf, accessed on 26 February 2012.

accompanying societal demand for accountability began in Latin America following the fall of authoritarian regimes. It led to a seismic shift in national processes reckoning with legacies of abuse.

2.1 Justice

The most significant component in the accountability spectrum to emerge was that of prosecutions. In setting out a series of best practices in the field of prosecutorial initiatives, which form an integral part of transitional justice, the United Nations suggests that any prosecutorial initiative, whether domestic or internationally assisted, 'should be underpinned by a *clear political commitment* to accountability that understands the complex goals involved'.[20] Tied to the clear political commitment required for a successful prosecutorial initiative is the desire to combat impunity. It is internationally recognised that investigations and prosecutions serve to end impunity for human rights violations because they indicate the state's willingness not only to meet its obligations under international law but also to tow a firm line prohibiting and preventing future violations.[21] As such, seriously undertaken investigations and prosecutions can serve as powerful prevention tools impeding any perpetrator's ability to repeat cycles of abuse. The duty to pursue accountability derives from various international human rights instruments including the ICCPR, European Convention on Human Rights (ECHR), and the American Convention on Human Rights (ACHR). The ICCPR requires that in instances where an individual's fundamental rights (meaning those rights set forth in the ICCPR such as the right to life, security and liberty of person, to be free from torture and ill-treatment, and so on) are violated, the state is required to ensure the individual an effective remedy before a competent authority and provide enforcement of that remedy once granted.[22] The ECHR and ACHR, as interpreted by respective competent judicial bodies, similarly provide that states are compelled to prosecute and punish in cases of serious human rights violations and commissions of international crimes, even if the crimes occurred during a time of peace

20 OHCHR, 'Rule of Law Tools for Post-Conflict States: Prosecutorial Initiatives' (2006) UN Doc. HR/PUB/06/4 (OHCHR Prosecutorial Initiatives Report) at 2, available at: http://www.ohchr. org/Documents/Publications/RuleoflawProsecutions.en.pdf, accessed on 24 February 2012 (emphasis added). A clear political commitment is chief among the five guiding considerations for any prosecutorial initiative, thus the vital role political will plays in successful accountability efforts within transitional justice is emphasised.

21 ECOSOC, 'Set of Principles for the protection and promotion of human rights through action to combat impunity' (1997) UN Doc. E/CN.4Sub.2/1997/20/Rev.1, annex II; updated, see E/CN.4/2005/102/Add.1 These principles emphasise that 'impunity arises from a failure by states to meet their obligations to investigate violations; to take appropriate measures in respect of the perpetrators, particularly in the area of justice, by ensuring that those suspected of criminal responsibility are prosecuted, tried and duly punished; to provide victims with effective remedies and to ensure that they receive reparation for the injuries suffered; to ensure the inalienable right to know the truth about violations; and to take other necessary steps to prevent a recurrence of violations.'

22 ICCPR (n. 6) Art. 2, para. 3. See also, HRC, General Comment 31, 'The Nature of the General Legal Obligation Imposed on State Parties to the Covenant', (2004) UN Doc. CCPR/C/21/ Rev.1/Add. 13, para. 8. In this General Comment, the HRC explains how states violate their duties under the ICCPR by permitting or failing 'to take appropriate measures or to exercise due diligence to prevent, punish, investigate or redress the harm' to the wronged individual.

because those crimes amount to crimes against humanity.[23] Moreover, prosecutions must reach executors as well as all those who participated, gave orders and ensured impunity. International jurisprudence recognises the reality that international crimes involve both direct and indirect participation. For this reason, international crimes can be tried under various legal theories including command responsibility and *autoría mediata* (literally: mediated authorship, i.e., committing the act through others in an apparatus of power or through a joint criminal enterprise).[24] More than just trying all those responsible, justice efforts also need to overcome legal and de facto obstacles.[25]

Accountability as a general practice plays an integral role in a state's ability to successfully and comprehensively deal with past abuses. First, it broadly conveys a disapproval of violations and support for human rights values, including democratic participation.[26] As the UN Human Rights Committee (HRC) declared in its report on prosecutorial initiatives, prosecutions 'convey to citizens a *disapproval of violations* and *support for certain democratic values*. A strong expression of formal disapproval by state institutions committed to human rights and democratic values can help to persuade citizens as well as institutions of the centrality of those values.'[27] Second, accountability for gross violations serves as a deterrent.[28] Third, when domestic systems lead accountability measures in the very place where the abuses occurred, the prosecutions become a reassertion of the rule of law and of the integrity of judicial institutions.[29]

---

23 See *Almonacid-Arellano v Chile*, IACtHR (ser. C) No. 154 (26 September 2006) (Merits, Reparations, and Costs Judgment) para. 114; *Barrios Altos v Peru*, IACtHR (ser. C) No. 75 (2001) (Merits, Reparation, and Costs Judgment): in *Barrios Altos v Peru* the IACtHR found that the state of Peru had failed to prosecute and punish extrajudicial killings at Barrios Altos as required under the ACHR, consequently denying victims access to justice; *Velasquez-Rodriguez v Honduras*, IACtHR (ser. C) No. 4 (1988) (Merits Judgment): in *Velasquez-Rodriguez v Honduras* the IACtHR explains that states must prevent, investigate, and punish any violation of the rights recognised by the Convention; *Kolk and Kislyiy v Estonia*, App. Nos. 23052/04, 24018/04 (ECtHR, 2006): in *Kolk and Kislyiy v Estonia* the ECtHR holds that prosecution and punishment of crimes against humanity adheres to the ECHR's Art. 7(2) because even though the crimes were committed during a time of peace, the acts, at the time committed, were already criminal and prohibited by general principles of law recognised by civilised nations. See also, Bassiouni (n. 11) at 226–27. Bassiouni emphasises how the Court's finding in *Velasquez-Rodriguez* requires the state to take reasonable steps needed to carry out a serious investigation of violations committed and to identify those responsible as well as impose the appropriate punishment such that the investigations are conducted in a serious manner and not as a mere formality.
24 See *Prosecutor v Limaj* (Trial Judgment) ICTY-IT-03–66–T (30 November 2005) para. 515: in *Prosecutor v Limaj* the ICTY discusses the command responsibility theory; *Casos Barrios Altos, La Cantuta y Sótanos del SIE* (Alberto Fujimori) (Judgment 13.j) paras 723–724, 726.
25 See *Gomes Lund v Brazil*, IACtHR (ser. C) No. 219, 45 (24 November 2010) (Merits, Reparations, and Costs Judgment) paras 147–77; *Almonacid-Arellano v Chile* (n. 23) paras 105–114; *Barrios Altos v Peru* (n. 23) para. 5.
26 See P. de Greiff, 'Deliberative Democracy and Punishment' (2002) 5 *Buff. Crim. L. Rev.* 373–403 at 374. In this article de Greiff argues that the process of law-making, particularly through its formulation of 'coercively enforceable' rules, provides a space for deliberative democratic participation in the punishment process.
27 See OHCHR Prosecutorial Initiatives Report (n. 20) at 4.
28 Rome Statute of the International Criminal Court (ICC), Preamble (17 July 1998) 2187 UNTS 3 (Rome Statute): the Rome Statute declares that state parties enacted the Rome Statute to contribute to the prevention of international crimes which is achieved through investigations and prosecutions; the Convention on the Prevention and Punishment of the Crime of Genocide Arts 1, 4, 5, 6 (9 December 1948) 78 UNTS 277 (Genocide Convention).
29 See OHCHR Prosecutorial Initiatives Report (n. 20) at 3–4.

Not only do domestic prosecutions restore the rule of law, they also help build confidence in the legal and judicial systems – assuming the system has sufficient capacity to proceed with prosecutions.[30] In cases where the state is unable to prosecute international crimes or grave human rights violations due to a lack of capacity or lack of political will, the International Criminal Court (ICC) can step in to try the perpetrators of these crimes through the principle of complementarity.[31] Or, the international community by way of individual country courts can also step in and try serious international crimes by asserting universal jurisdiction.[32] Both international and mixed tribunals (which incorporate both international and domestic features) have been instrumental in this regard. To be credible, however, accountability measures, whether domestic or international, must adhere to international standards of due process.[33] Given the significance of due process measures, some of these measures also apply to reparations, truth-telling and institutional reform efforts.

2.2 Truth-telling

In addition to prosecutions, truth-telling is another instrumental component in the transitional justice framework. The right to truth figured prominently in the emerging body of law on victims' rights, particularly in the UN General Assembly's 1985 Basic Principles of Justice and the 2006 Basic Principles and Guidelines.[34] Besides these international instruments, international and regional courts interpreted the right to truth as requiring states to establish the facts and context for victims (or victims' family members) of human rights violations in cases of enforced disappearances, extrajudicial killings or other grave atrocities.[35] International scholars have noted that the truth is especially important to surviving human rights victims for several reasons: '(1) the truth alleviates the suffering of the surviving victims; (2) [it] vindicates the memory or status of the direct victim of the violation; (3) [it] encourages the state to confront its dark past; and (4) . . . [thereby], to seek reform.'[36]

In Peru, for example, truth-telling efforts were particularly successful because the proceedings were conducted through public hearings where victims had a chance to be heard. Moreover, Peru comprehensively covered and investigated violations committed by state actors as well as insurgents.[37] In contrast, in Argentina, where a protracted debate continues

---

30 Ibid.
31 Rome Statute (n. 28) Arts 1, 17. These Articles state that the Court asserts sole jurisdiction over the most serious crimes only when the state is unwilling or unable to prosecute and investigate the crimes.
32 See Restatement (Third) of Foreign Relations (2011) para. 404.
33 ICCPR (n. 6) Art. 14. This Article provides for a fair and public hearing, presumption of innocence, right to appeal, and protection against double jeopardy, to name a few guarantees.
34 See 1985 Basic Principles of Justice (n. 8); 2006 Basic Principles and Guidelines (n. 8) paras 11, 22 and 24.
35 See *Gomes Lund* (n. 25) para. 108; *Manuel Cepeda Vargas v Colombia*, IACtHR (ser. C) No. 213 (26 May 2010) (Merits, Reparations, and Costs Judgment) paras 117–19. These decisions explain that the duty to investigate extrajudicial executions implies determining patterns of collaborative action and all individuals who participated together with corresponding responsibilities. See also, *Barrios Altos* (n. 23) para. 5. This case explains how the state of Peru's failure to prosecute and punish extrajudicial killings at Barrios Altos consequently denied victims access to the right to truth.
36 See R. Aldana-Pindell, 'In Vindication of Justiciable Victims' Rights to Truth and Justice for State-Sponsored Crimes' (2002) 35 *Vand. J. Transnat'l L.* 1399–501 at 1401.
37 See generally, G. Ninaquispe and K. Ninaquispe, 'The Role of Civil Society in Demanding and Promoting Justice', in L. Magarrell and L. Filippini (eds), *The Legacy of Truth, Criminal Justice in the Peruvian Transition* (International Center for Transitional Justice, 2006) 39 at 42–43.

over whether prosecutions and truth-telling should also focus on insurgents, expert Fabricio Guariglia indicates that, unlike Peru, Argentina presents a different case, which adequately focused its transitional justice efforts on state actors rather than insurgents, because: (1) no international crime of terrorism existed at the time of the commission of the acts (nor is it clear that it even exists today given terrorism's emerging status as a possible international crime); (2) even if the crimes committed by insurgents could be tried as war crimes, the actors were not sufficiently organised nor their acts of sufficient intensity to meet the definition of war crimes; and (3) any acts committed by Argentina's insurgents similarly fail to meet the elements of crimes against humanity because the acts were not specifically targeted at civilian populations nor part of a widespread or systematic policy implemented by the insurgency.[38]

In determining overall best practices, truth commissions should consider a number of lessons that have emerged after years of truth-telling experiences. First, in cases of armed conflict, truth commissions should confront both sides (state and non-state actors to the extent that both sides may have committed violations of the laws of war). Second, commissions should name names in order to tell the whole truth, particularly where no other opportunity exists to determine individual responsibility for violations. However, if naming names can interfere with judicial functions, truth commissions should instead transmit the allegations about individual perpetrators to the appropriate prosecutorial or judicial authorities. Third, states have some leeway in selecting the members of the truth commission given that state practices have varied in this regard. So long as the commission is not headed by actors confronted by conflicts of interest (e.g. employing perpetrators or supporters of one side of the conflict on a truth commission), states should explore commission leadership that makes the most sense in that particular state's circumstances.[39]

States should consider not just best practices but also a number of concerns that arise in the area of truth-telling. For example, because current practices trend toward truth and

---

38 F. Guariglia, '*Crímenes internacionales y actores no estatales, El caso argentino*', in *Centro de Estudios Legales y Sociales* (CELS), and International Center for Transitional Justice (ICTJ), in *Hacer Justicia: Nuevos debates sobre el juzgamiento de crímenes de lesa humanidad en Argentina* (*Siglo XXI Editores* 2011) 143 at 146–64. International crimes (and more specifically war crimes or crimes against humanity) are prosecuted in disregard of statutes of limitations, amnesties or pardons because, with respect to them, the state is obligated to investigate, prosecute and punish perpetrators. In contrast, offences committed by armed groups that are not part of an organised effort to achieve power, or that are not part of a generalised attack on the civilian population, are offences under domestic law and statutes of limitation, amnesties and pardons are fully applicable to them. In the case of Peru, the Commission on Truth and Reconciliation and Peruvian courts found and demonstrated that the Shining Path guerrilla unmistakably targeted civilians in the highlands and in the jungles of Peru. In addition, it must be said with respect to Argentina that any evidence that could be used to convict surviving members of the armed groups of the 1970s is mostly unavailable because the military dictatorship tried to kill all of them (and many others who were not armed) and made no effort to gather evidence.

39 For example, some states have elected to appoint bi-partisan commissions comprised of broad representation by the state's political forces, e.g. US Armed Services Committee inquiry into torture violations in Iraq and Afghanistan. In other instances, states opt for non-partisan leadership by individuals known for their integrity and who by definition would not be tainted by the armed conflict. In Honduras in the 1990s, rather than implement a traditional truth commission, the state chose to have the Ombudsman lead its truth investigations. The Ombudsman's office is now credited with producing a significant and thorough report that is equally as good as that of a truth commission. In this regard see L. Valladares and S.C. Peacock, *In Search of Hidden Truths – An Interim Report on Declassification by the National Commissioner for Human Rights in Honduras* (1998), available at: http://www.gwu.edu/~nsarchiv/latin_america/honduras/hidden_truths/hidden.htm, accessed on 26 February 2012.

reconciliation commissions, there is a concern that states will pursue reconciliation efforts to the exclusion of justice and accountability. However, international law requires states to guarantee victims' rights to investigate violations without delay and to do so in a serious, impartial and effective manner.[40] Implicit in the victim's right to demand investigation is his or her right to participate in the perpetrator's trial. To ensure effective victim participation – often a poorly executed component in some truth-seeking efforts – a victim should appear as a private accuser, or be given the ability to offer evidence with due regard to the rights of the defendant.[41] In sum, truth-telling initiatives, when properly implemented, can complement the accountability piece which will necessarily be limited. There will always be perpetrators who escape justice due to lack of evidence or insufficiency of prosecutorial resources. Moreover, since prosecutions will likely not be able to investigate and try all offenders, or will choose to go after those bearing the highest responsibility for the crimes, truth-seeking initiatives have a better chance of covering the wider universe of human rights violations. In such instances, truth-telling complements the 'justice' aspect of accountability rather than substituting for it.

2.3 Reparations

Just as states are obligated to take appropriate measures to prevent and investigate violations, prosecute those responsible for violations and provide justice to victims, states are similarly required to provide 'adequate, effective and prompt reparation for harm suffered' following gross violations of international human rights law or serious violations of international humanitarian law.[42] Reparations play a vital role in any transitional justice approach because they are the transitional justice component that focuses most directly and explicitly on the victims' situation.[43] Reparations seek 'to provide some repair for rights that have been trampled, for harms suffered, for indignities endured. Crucially, care should be taken that reparations are not framed as a hand-out. Rather, a reparations programme should uphold the status of victims as bearers of rights, and convey the sense that it is on this basis that they are owed reparations.'[44] The right to reparation includes, in some combination and as appropriate: restitution, compensation, rehabilitation, satisfaction and guarantees of non-repetition.[45]

40 *Gomes Lund* (n. 25) para. 108. See also, *Manuel Cepeda Vargas* (n. 35) paras 117–119.
41 See International Crisis Group, *Correcting Course: Victims and the Justice and Peace Law in Colombia*, available at: http://www.crisisgroup.org/~/media/Files/latin-america/colombia/recting_course____ victims_and_the_justice_and_peace_law_in_colombia.pdf, accessed on 20 October 2011.
42 2006 Basic Principles and Guidelines (n. 8) para. 11(b).
43 ICTJ, *Reparations in Theory and Practice,* at 2 (2007) (ICTJ Reparations Report), available at: http:// ictj.org/sites/default/files/ICTJ-Global-Reparations-Practice-2007-English.pdf, accessed on 26 February 2012.
44 Ibid.
45 2006 Basic Principles and Guidelines (n. 8) paras 18–23. In this document restitution is defined as the state's attempt to restore the victim to his or her original situation before the violation occurred and can include, as appropriate: 'restoration of liberty, enjoyment of human rights, identity, family life and citizenship, return to one's place of residence, restoration of employment and return of property'. The state is also required to provide compensation for any 'economically assessable damage', as appropriate and proportional to the gravity of the violation and circumstances. Compensation can take into account: physical or mental harm; lost opportunities, including employment, education and social benefits; material damages and loss of earnings, including loss of earning potential; moral damage; costs required for legal or expert assistance, medicine and medical services, and psychological and social services. Rehabilitation is intended to cover medical and

Other transitional justice mechanisms like truth-telling, accountability measures, ceasing of ongoing violations and non-repetition measures, are intended to accompany reparation in order to reassure victims that reparation is not an empty promise or a temporary stopgap measure.[46]

Reparation is not just about state action but also about victim participation. Victim participation in assessing harm done and determining adequate reparations ensures a transitional justice process that itself seeks to remedy the social exclusion of those who have experienced violations. In Peru, for example, where many of the victims resided in highland areas typically overlooked by Peruvians of predominantly urban and affluent parts, victims demanded individual as well as collective reparations as a way to assert their status as individual citizens of equal value.[47] In addition to allowing for victim participation, reparations can also acknowledge recognition of responsibility for abuses committed that both complement other initiatives of transitional justice and generally carry more direct impact in victims' lives.

2.4 Institutional reform

The remaining vital component of the transitional justice framework is institutional reform. Deep institutional reform, particularly of the security and judicial sectors, is often needed 'to advance prospects for rule of law in the future, but . . . also [to] take into account the involvement of state institutions, officials or armed forces in serious past human-rights abuses'.[48] Institutional reform requires significant overhauling of an entire system with various components: vetting of abusers, education of institutional employees and establishing external controls over the institutions.[49] Vetting refers to the processes undertaken to assess an

psychological care as well as legal and social services while satisfaction and guarantees of non-repetition are more expansive. See also, OHCHR Prosecutorial Initiatives Report (n. 20) at 14. This report describes how satisfaction is a broad category of measures ranging from a cessation of violations, to truth-seeking, the search for the disappeared, the recovery and reburial of remains, public apologies, judicial and administrative sanctions, commemoration and memorialisation, and human rights training. Guarantees of non-repetition include institutional reforms, strengthening judicial independence, protecting human rights workers, human rights training, fostering international human rights standards and psychological and social services.

46 ICTJ Reparations Report (n. 43) at 1. See also P. de Greiff, 'Introduction. Repairing the Past: Compensation for victims of Human Rights Violations' in P. de Greiff (ed.), *The Handbook of Reparations* (Oxford University Press, 2006) 1 at 6–13. De Greiff suggests that in assessing a particular reparation programme's achievements and identifying its potential gaps, one begins by evaluating the programme's scope, completeness, comprehensiveness, complexity, integrity/coherence, finality and munificence.

47 ICTJ Reparations Report (n. 43) at 5. The Report notes how victims in Peru insisted on collective reparation as 'a way to overcome the amorphous group identity that made it easier for urban elites to be indifferent to their fate during long years of repression'.

48 Priscilla Hayner, *Negotiating Justice: Guidance for Mediators* (ICTJ 2009) at 11, available at: http://ictj.org/sites/default/files/HDCenter-Global-Negotiating-Justice-2009-English.pdf, accessed on 26 February 2012.

49 See also, OHCHR Vetting Framework (n. 19) at 3. This report notes other institutional reform measures, including: 'the creation of oversight, complaint and disciplinary procedures; the reform or establishment of legal frameworks; the development or revision of ethical guidelines and codes of conduct; changing symbols that are associated with abusive practices; and the provision of adequate salaries, equipment and infrastructure'.

individual's integrity as a means of determining his or her suitability for public employment.[50] 'Integrity' is defined as 'a person's adherence to relevant standards of human rights and professional conduct, including her or his financial propriety'.[51] Therefore, within transitional justice frameworks, vetting processes are designed to screen public employees or candidates for public employment to determine if their prior conduct – most importantly their respect for human rights standards – merits their exclusion from public institutions.[52] Education also plays an integral role in inculcating a greater respect and understanding of international human rights norms while external controls provide a valuable check on state institutions, the armed forces and even the judiciary. Some types of external controls can even include citizen oversight by establishing reporting mechanisms that citizens can avail themselves of in cases of abuse.

Perhaps the greatest contribution offered by institutional reform is its role in furthering prevention of future violations. A state's institutional reform efforts aimed at building fair and efficient institutions play a critical role in averting future abuses because their purpose is to improve or create (where none may have previously existed) accountability in positions and organisations of authority. Where these entities may have previously enjoyed unchecked power to violate international human rights and humanitarian law, institutional reform allows this no longer. However, effective and sustainable institutional reform is a complex and challenging task that requires a country-specific or case-by-case approach to determine the appropriate and precise content and scope of reform measures needed, as dictated by the specific state's circumstances.[53]

3 Implementing state-specific transitional justice frameworks – in conflict and otherwise

As reiterated in the realm of institutional reform, transitional justice is not intended to be implemented through a singular universal model. That being said, the principles of transitional justice – truth, justice, reparations and institutional reform – are universal and understood as broad goals to be achieved in a process that will necessarily be country-specific and culturally relevant to each community. In planning mission mandates and developing assistance programmes for countries emerging from conflict, the United Nations advises its agencies to consider the particular rule of law and justice needs of the particular host country.[54] When the emphasis is on using foreign experts and implementing foreign models and foreign-conceived transitional justice solutions, as opposed to building local sustainable capacity and improving upon the state's existing experience and expertise, transitional justice efforts often

---

50 R. Duthie, 'Introduction', in A. Meyer-Rieckh and P. de Greiff (eds), *Justice as Prevention, Vetting Public Employees in Transitional Societies* (Social Science Research Council, 2007) 17 at 17.

51 ICTJ, 'Vetting Public Employees in Post Conflict Settings', in *Justice as Prevention, Vetting Public Employees in Transitional Societies* (n. 50) 547 at 548.

52 Duthie (n. 50) at 17.

53 OHCHR Vetting Framework (n. 19) at 4.

54 UN Secretary-General Transitional Justice Report (n. 2) para. 14. This Report notes how individual country needs should be assessed, based on factors such as 'the nature of the underlying conflict, the will of the parties, any history of widespread abuse, the identification of vulnerable groups, such as minorities and displaced persons, the situation and role of women, the situation of children, rule of law implications of peace agreements and the condition and nature of the country's legal system, traditions and institutions.'

tend to fail more than they succeed.[55] Therefore, each society has an obligation to design a locally tailored transitional justice framework.

Perhaps one of the greatest challenges in developing an appropriate and effective locally designed transitional justice framework exists when a country seeks to implement transitional justice mechanisms during a conflict. States that have applied transitional justice in ongoing conflict settings recognise that doing so inherently creates tension. In Colombia, where an internal conflict has spanned five decades, transitional justice mechanisms and rhetoric have been appropriated by analogy.[56] Unlike predecessor comparative transitional justice experiments, in Colombia there is no defining transition *from* the conflict. The government contends that transitional justice is a wholly appropriate framework because the definitive dismantling of the paramilitaries from 2002 to 2006 provided the key point of 'transition'.[57] Perhaps the greatest 'design flaw' in the Colombian approach is the state's unwillingness to transform or address any role it may have played in dirty warfare.[58] Moreover, the state can successfully continue to avoid discussing its responsibility and assuage demands for reform by highlighting how the fragile partial peace achieved must be maintained even if at a high cost – partial attainment of justice in investigating and prosecuting perpetrators and only partial truth and reparations for victims.[59] However, the judiciary and civil society sectors have successfully embraced transitional justice to 'confront the legacy of past abuses by state actors and to provoke a transformation of current political and military bodies and structures'.[60]

Facing similar challenges to its Colombian counterpart, the Special Tribunal for Lebanon (STL) met with great resistance when it was implemented during the ongoing conflict in 2007. Specifically, the Tribunal's legitimacy was challenged by a few factors: '(1) Lebanon's historical context, including its 15-year war followed by selective impunity; (2) the highly selective nature of the jurisdiction of the STL; and (3) the political context and fears that the STL itself [would] act as an instrument for foreign powers.'[61] Moreover, Lebanon established the STL amid severe internal and regional political crises.[62] From its onset, opinions were deeply divided over the STL's desirability and legitimacy.[63] One of the greatest concerns focused on 'whether the Tribunal [could] function as an independent judicial institution in

---

55 See ibid. paras 15–16, indicating how the most successful transitional justice experiences greatly derive their success from the quantity and quality of local public and victim consultation carried out.

56 Lyons (n. 3) at 16.

57 Ibid. at 18–19. Lyons notes how Colombia's transitional justice framework is weak because it largely leaves out both the state and leftist guerrilla groups from the equation – the latter groups have achieved some individual demobilisations but no real negotiated peace.

58 Ibid, at 19.

59 Ibid.

60 Ibid. at 20. Lyons highlights that the Constitutional Court and Criminal Cassation Chamber of the Supreme Court of Justice challenged the transitional justice framework, known as the Justice and Peace Law, as originally enacted, by inserting significant modifications and seeking to bring the Justice and Peace process in line with international and domestic standards of justice and victims' rights. Civil society actors have made great strides through documentation efforts and other unofficial truth-seeking and memory construction.

61 M. Wierda, et al., 'Early Reflections on Local Perceptions, Legitimacy and Legacy of the Special Tribunal for Lebanon' (2007) 5 *J. Int'l Crim. Just.* 1065 at 1065.

62 ICTJ, *Handbook on the Special Tribunal for Lebanon* (ICTY, 2008) (ICTJ STL Handbook) at 16, available at: http://ictj.org/sites/default/files/ICTJ-Lebanon-STL-Handbook-2008-English.pdf, accessed on 26 February 2012.

63 Ibid.

these circumstances'.[64] Though these kinds of concerns are somewhat routine in the international and hybrid tribunal context, questions regarding the Tribunal's independence took on special importance when applied to the STL's ability to progress and function *because of* the country's delicate situation.[65]

In anticipation of these legitimate concerns, the STL enacted a number of safeguards through its statute to ensure the STL's independence.[66] The critical safeguards aimed at ensuring the STL's independence, transparency and greater state cooperation included: (1) its location in the Hague, that is, removed from the area of conflict; (2) its mixed national and international composition; (3) the continued funding for the STL provided through Resolution 1757 to ensure its sustainability should the state not pay its share of funding; (4) the requirement that judges and prosecutors be independent when performing their functions, for example, by not accepting or seeking instructions from the government or any other source; and (5) the obligation that staff act with impartiality and independence, monitored by corresponding rules of discipline which if violated could lead to dismissal.[67] The Lebanon example consequently illustrates how, in spite of the challenges of implementing transitional justice mechanisms during conflict, transitional justice measures can be tailored to address the particularly problematic setting in which they are implemented.

In addition to the specific concerns raised in the Colombia and Lebanon contexts, a set of general problems tend to recur whenever transitional justice is applied in conflict settings, particularly as relates to the prosecutions (or justice) component. The first step in any justice effort involves documenting crimes to a sufficient standard.[68] However, in conflict settings, actors rarely engage in the kind of documentation that goes beyond reporting violations to gathering the kinds of evidence useful to a subsequent criminal procedure because many of the crimes involved are system crimes which necessarily involve detailed analysis of the particular practices and structure of military and paramilitary organisations.[69] This kind of analysis, as well as the equally crucial assessments of local context and dynamics of violence and testimony, of 'insiders', are difficult to obtain and by default would tend to continue changing as the conflict continues.[70] That is to say, evidence relating to system crimes cannot be useful unless gathered after a conflict has ended because it is then that investigators can form the most comprehensive picture possible of what kinds of patterns, systems and institutions were in place to facilitate the commission of international crimes.

Nonetheless, groups that are working on the ground may still contribute to evidence-gathering efforts in the midst of conflict in the following ways: (1) identifying and establishing links and maintaining contact with potential witnesses; (2) retrieving and preserving documentary evidence; (3) taking statements from victims and witnesses; (4) documenting statements by perpetrators that may reflect their intent; and (5) conflict mapping.[71] Also,

---

64 Ibid.
65 Ibid.
66 Ibid. at 17.
67 Ibid.
68 T. Unger and M. Wierda, 'Pursuing Justice in Ongoing Conflict: A Discussion of Current Practice', in K. Ambos et al. (eds), *Building a Future on Peace and Justice, Studies on Transitional Justice, Peace and Development* (Springer-Verlag, 2009) 263 at 292–93.
69 Ibid. at 293.
70 See ibid.
71 Ibid. at 239–94. The authors explain that conflict mapping is a technique that provides a quantitative analysis identifying trends and patterns of abuse. These documents can serve as a lead for further criminal investigations.

investigations during a conflict are often underlined by a sense of urgency because evidence can be lost, destroyed or weakened with the passage of time.[72] Despite all of the difficulties in application, countries can succeed in implementing the transitional justice framework by utilising models that are tailored to the country's specific circumstances and sensitive to the particular culture's needs. However, even when applying transitional justice in conflict settings, sensitivity to a host country's needs does not translate to a blank cheque for evading the state's obligations to provide justice, truth, reparations or institutional reform, all of which are to be pursued in good faith.[73]

4 Transitional justice as part of conflict resolution: applying transitional justice where peace negotiations are possible

Efforts to bring a conflict to an end almost inevitably bring out a painful dilemma between the pursuit of peace and the legitimate interests of the victims of atrocities to see justice done. There is no question that the threat of prosecution would be a disincentive for leaders of insurgent forces to agree to lay down their arms. They will always demand amnesty as a condition, and often even as a condition for sitting down and talking about peace. An amnesty for insurgents for the sake of peace conversely provides an excuse for the government to perpetuate impunity for the crimes committed by state agents. In a way, the 'peace and justice dilemma' (the authors refuse to call it 'peace versus justice') is a re-enactment of earlier arguments against justice in transitions to democracy. In the 1980s in Latin America it was often argued that truth-telling and investigation and prosecution of crimes would imperil fragile democracies and prompt the military to return from the barracks and reinstate dictatorships. General Augusto Pinochet famously said, in the early years of Chile's return to democracy, that 'democracy is all well and good, but if you touch only one of my men that is the end of the rule of law'. Fortunately, in Chile and elsewhere democratic forces refused to be blackmailed and, despite fits and starts and occasional backtracking, there has been no retreat from the process of dealing with the past.

Asking people to choose between democracy and justice was nothing but blackmail. Still, many genuinely democratic actors argued that the dilemma was real and, therefore, it was preferable to pursue truth-telling and reparations but not prosecutions, because the criminal justice process was equated with revenge and therefore contrary to national reconciliation, and particularly because it carried with it the threat of a return to the dictatorial past. As a result, some observers expressed a preference for truth-telling and also for a formal renunciation of prosecutions.[74] This preference for 'truth and reconciliation' over prosecutions has often been identified with the South African transition. While it is true that the Truth and Reconciliation Commission implemented a scheme that exchanged amnesty for the beneficiary's contribution to the truth of human rights violations, it is highly misleading to identify

---

72 Ibid. at 294. The authors suggest that, to avoid the risk of lost or weakened evidence, states implement mechanisms that ensure the effective protection of evidential sites or documents and protocols governing the chain of custody. See also, section 41.4 text beginning with 'Similarly, justice contributes to crime prevention . . .'.

73 See also below section 41.4 text beginning with 'Here is where the transitional justice mechanisms can serve . . .'.

74 Zalaquett (n. 15) at 623–60; C. Krauthammer, 'Truth, Not Trials', *The Washington Post* (9 September 1994) at A27.

the South African experiment with a total renunciation of prosecutions. In fact, amnesty ('indemnity') in that scheme was predicated on full and truthful confessions. Most of the requests for amnesty were refused because they were not related to the criteria set forth in the law. Most potential beneficiaries of amnesty did not even bother to request it so they were technically still subject to prosecution. Finally, a few prosecutions did take place of those who did not apply and sentences continue to be served by those whose applications failed. Today, no one proposes that truth and reparations should be the only objectives to be pursued in dealing with legacies of gross and consistent human rights violations.

It is not surprising, then, that justice is seen as an obstacle to peace as it was earlier seen as an obstacle to the stability of democracy. The dilemma between democracy and justice was a false dilemma, but the same cannot be said about the dilemma between peace and justice, at least while the conflict is ongoing. Undoubtedly, a promise to investigate and prosecute atrocities and a flat refusal to consider amnesty is hardly a way to persuade rebels to give up their arms, if their signature in a peace process will also mean that they will be marched off to jail. But the fact that the dilemma is real does not mean that in ongoing conflict peace trumps justice under all circumstances. The legitimate demands for justice from the victims have to be accommodated in the peace process; if they are ignored, the peace thus obtained may not be sustainable in the long term, as it leaves open wounds in the fabric of society. Just as important, it is fundamentally unfair to ask the victims of the conflict to also bear the burdens of an unjust peace in the form of impunity and denial of their rights. Here, too, the insistence on amnesty as a condition for peace is also blackmail. In this case it is aggravated because the parties to the conflict are essentially saying that if they do not get impunity, they will continue to fight and worse: that they will continue to commit atrocities against the civilian population. The international community cannot accept these conditions and that is why the United Nations has adopted and reaffirmed the policy that its mediators will not accept peace deals that violate international law.[75]

Peace and justice are not in conflict with each other and should not be seen as mutually exclusive. They are two equally important values to be realised in policy and agreements and in their execution, by ways in which justice and peace are made to reinforce each other. The problem is not so much in conceiving them as mutually reinforcing but to find specific ways, adapted to context and circumstances, by which they become effective in reinforcing each other. Insistence on justice should not lead to the conclusion that there is nothing that can be offered to the parties to the conflict in terms of reconciliation.

Amnesties that do not generate impunity for war crimes and crimes against humanity are not prohibited by international law; rather, at least in the case of internal armed conflict, amnesty is actually required by international law.[76] At the end of a conflict not of an international character, the parties shall endeavour to give each other the most broad and generous amnesty possible.[77] It is clear, however, that the amnesty contemplated in the laws of war covers the criminal offence in domestic law of rising up in arms against the state, called 'rebellion', 'sedition' or 'treason' in different domestic jurisdictions. It also covers other offences incidental to the conflict, like attacks on legitimate military targets, even if death results. Relatively minor offences committed by government forces are also subject

---

75 UN Guidelines for Mediators (1999), revised and reaffirmed (2005); Rule of Law and Transitional Justice in Conflict and Post-Conflict Situations (2004), reaffirmed (2011).
76 Additional Protocol II to the Geneva Conventions (1977) 16 ILM 1442, Art. 6.5.
77 Ibid.

to amnesties that are not incompatible with international law. What emphatically these amnesties are not meant to cover are war crimes committed by agents of either party to the conflict, such as indiscriminate attacks on civilians, torture, outrages against the personal dignity of prisoners and killing adversaries who are *hors de combat* because they are wounded or have surrendered. It follows, therefore, that in the course of peace talks a broad amnesty to those who have participated in the conflict can and actually should be offered to those who have not committed war crimes. In addition, as a matter of current practice, international tribunals do not prosecute alleged perpetrators of war crimes or crimes against humanity who were under eighteen at the time they committed such offences.[78] For conflicts that feature child recruitment, an amnesty can and should be offered to juveniles; in fact, they should be treated as victims of an international crime and encouraged to return to their homes.

These examples show that the international standard that demands justice for mass atrocities does not prohibit amnesties that have a potential broad scope and that, for that reason, constitute a useful tool in the hands of peacemakers and mediators. What is definitely not in that toolkit is an amnesty for those bearing the greatest responsibility of war crimes and crimes against humanity. Undoubtedly, this limits the options of what can be offered to the leaders of the parties to the conflict in exchange for peace. On the positive side, narrower options force the parties and mediators to look for solutions that have a better chance of achieving a lasting peace, precisely because such solutions will strive to balance the community's interest in peace with the victims' legitimate demands for justice.

Here is where the transitional justice mechanisms can serve a very useful purpose. Prosecutions, at least for those bearing the highest responsibility for serious abuse, should not be ruled out completely, but it is clear that most atrocities will not be in fact investigated and prosecuted and that the expectations of justice of many victims will not be satisfied. Especially in those conflicts where international tribunals are called to intervene, prosecutions will be limited to a handful of defendants. Under the principle of complementarity, the territorial state should assume the responsibility of prosecuting other cases in domestic courts, as long as they are independent, impartial and capable of affording fair trials. This condition will in most cases be difficult to satisfy, though states should be encouraged to build up such capacity and be assisted in that endeavour. Even in the most optimistic scenario, however, there is little chance that every atrocity committed in the course of the conflict will be adequately investigated and prosecuted. Since the universe of such episodes will always be quite large, it must be anticipated that most victims will see their aspirations for justice dashed if the expectation is that each case will be dealt with through the criminal justice system.

Therefore, prosecutions of major perpetrators by international courts should be accompanied by some domestic prosecutions of equally serious cases, and all other cases should be treated under comprehensive, holistic mechanisms that afford the victims access and participation. An appropriate combination of truth-telling, reparations and institutional reform can offer the victims a sense that their plight is understood and vindicated. The best practices of transitional justice can be adapted to post-conflict situations or under circumstances where they are surrounded by guarantees of transparency, consultation with and participation by all relevant stakeholders, especially the victims and their communities.

The execution of transitional justice mechanisms in the most effective way naturally will require a context of peace already achieved. But the peace agreement can include a roadmap and a timeline for the various transitional justice processes, as well as a sequence in which they

---

78 Rome Statute (n. 28) Art. 26.

will be executed. In fact, the discussion itself of future transitional justice mechanisms can build confidence among the parties to the peace talks and other stakeholders. Sequencing can allow for the necessary capacity building so that the different processes can be executed most effectively. This may be especially necessary for domestic prosecutions if the conflict has rendered the country with a judiciary that does not meet minimum standards of independence, impartiality or efficiency. Reparations need to cover as many of the offended victims as possible and that requires a rigorous census that can only come after a detailed examination of all the events throughout the conflict period. Institutional reform is necessarily sequenced as well, as it will require a vetting process that itself depends on adequate information about the same events.

Domestic prosecutions will probably work better if they are instituted after a truth-telling process that describes the general picture and establishes institutional and chain-of-command responsibilities. If international tribunals are involved, sequencing presents a special challenge, because the international court or its prosecutor must preserve their autonomy from non-judicial organs or actors, and it would be problematic to subject their jurisdiction to time constraints or to preliminary steps or events that can condition the exercise of jurisdiction. Nevertheless, sequencing of international prosecutions will have to be analysed on a case-by-case basis. With that caveat, however, sequencing as here described can render a useful service to the peace process as it allows the building of blocks by which peace establishes itself and solidifies. Peace is never achieved only by the signing of a document; it has to be nurtured and steered through obstacles over a time continuum. The more detailed the plotting of its different stages, the more likely that the varying stages will be executed fairly and successfully and to the satisfaction of all stakeholders. At the same time, the process is more likely to be supported if all interested parties can assess objectively whether it is moving forward, and can take action to remove obstacles if it is not.

Most of the transitional justice mechanisms will necessarily take place after the peace agreement has been signed. But under certain circumstances it may also be possible to conceive of certain aspects to be agreed upon and implemented while the conflict is still going on, in which case they can be conceived of as confidence-building measures. For example, in the peace talks to end the war in El Salvador in the early 1990s, UN mediators succeeded in getting the parties to agree to respect human rights and the laws of war even before a ceasefire, and to accept international supervision of those commitments. The deployment of international civilian observers allowed for the beginning of some effort to document violations and to encourage victims to come forward with their plights. Local authorities were encouraged by international observers to live up to their obligations to protect civilians and prevent abuses. All of this had an immediate and direct effect in drastic reduction of abuses committed by both sides, and contributed to confidence building that facilitated the peace process and led to a successful conclusion of a definitive – and lasting – peace in that country. Additionally, in Uganda, the ICC's intervention empowered the civilian population to participate in peace negotiations, while in Darfur, the act of holding discussions for the various ethnic communities on grazing rights and water rights was in itself valuable. The fact that displaced communities spoke up for themselves signified a watershed moment for these communities, even if the Sudanese government did not take reconciliation efforts seriously.

Nevertheless, in most cases it will be necessary to silence the guns before any attempt to deal with the legacy of violations is made. Victims and civil society organisations will be justified in objecting to amnesties and impunity as pre-conditions for initiating talks. On the other hand, they should not object to a ceasefire even if at that time there are no assurances that there will be an effective reckoning with the past. Even a fragile and uncertain lull in the fighting is more conducive to dealing with that past than the context of raging armed conflict. The opportunity to object to blanket amnesties and to insist on accountability will come during the peace talks or even later: trials in the Southern Cone of Latin America prove that the legitimate demands for justice never go away and will eventually overcome unlawful amnesties and other obstacles.[79]

In addressing the often painful debate of how best to pursue justice and peace, the key lies in acknowledging that no lasting peace can be secured where justice is sacrificed and that justice, though inviolable, must be pursued in a manner that minimises further harm to the society in conflict.

5 Conclusion: the future of transitional justice

Justice is a human value that justifies itself. Societies ought to pursue justice for victims of abuse, first and foremost out of a sense of fairness and respect for human dignity. In other words, we do not need additional reasons to support the idea that societies have an obligation to offer just satisfaction to those who have been wronged. We do hope that justice contributes to peace, to the building of more decent societies, to the citizens' trust in institutions and to prevention of future crimes. But even if those lofty goals were not immediately realised, an effort to give victims their due would be amply justified.

Justice should not be pursued only for its utilitarian value but also for the achievement of other, equally worthy objectives. If justice were only a means to obtain a lasting peace, in some instances strong arguments could be made to subordinate the rights and aspirations of innocent victims to the need to silence the guns. We must recognise that at times justice and peace collide with each other. But we have also demonstrated that it is possible – indeed, necessary – to find ways in which peace and justice can support and nurture each other and that the end result is likely to be more conducive to lasting peace. There are many ways (and many historic examples) in which justice can be made to foster peace.

Similarly, justice contributes to crime prevention even if the empirical evidence of the relationship is not always available. When it comes to mass atrocities, the empirical link is even harder to prove, but it is nevertheless clear that the international community has repeatedly decided that war crimes and crimes against humanity must be punished as a way to deter similar events in the future. Elsewhere we have explored the conditions under which justice contributes to prevention.[80] Among other requirements, it is clear that justice helps prevent mass atrocities only if it accompanies other initiatives of a political, diplomatic, military and humanitarian nature. Moreover, justice – and more specifically, employing the collective

---

79 *Prosecutor v Furundzija* (Judgment) ICTY-IT-95–17/1-T (10 December 1998) para. 155; *Barrios Altos* (n. 23) paras 39–41; *Kallon and Kamara,* Special Court for Sierra Leone Decision on Challenge to Jurisdiction: Lomé Accord Amnesty (13 March 2004). See also, OHCHR, 'Rule of Law and Amnesties' (2009) UN Doc. HR/PUB/09/1, available at: http://www.ohchr.org/Documents/Publications/Amnesties_en.pdf, accessed on 26 February 2012.

80 J.E. Mendez, *Justice and Prevention* (August 2010) (presented to the Kampala Review Conference of the Assembly of State Parties of the ICC, June 2010) (on file with author).

cadre of transitional justice mechanisms – serves as a powerful preventative shield from impunity by making resumption of violations less likely.[81]

Justice helps build more decent societies because it upholds the rule of law and because it establishes that no victim is too powerless or vulnerable to be denied the benefits of full citizenship. Also, justice is essential because it signifies that a decent society does not countenance unfair privileges for the powerful. In the process, it builds the citizens' trust in institutions that in the long run will be the only guarantee of fairness to all. A body of evidence already exists that societies that confront the legacies of an authoritarian past perform better in terms of human rights than those that try to bury the past on account of a false 'reconciliation'.[82]

Perhaps the best way to argue in favour of justice for mass atrocities is that its opposite, impunity, can certainly – and self-evidently – conspire against peace, against prevention, against the rule of law and against the credibility of democratic institutions. Impunity invites violent retribution and it invites repetition by the same or other perpetrators. The spectacle of impunity for major crimes undermines the citizens' trust in institutions, especially the judiciary. It also generates distrust and distance between society and law enforcement, national security and defence agencies of the state. In contrast, prosecution of perpetrators confers legitimacy on the judiciary and allows the citizenry to distinguish between the permanent institutions of the state (like security and law enforcement sectors) and those who have abused their power through them. In cases where the violations have had a distinct ethnic, racial or religious dimension, restoring justice serves to eliminate long-term animosities between communities, so that the injustices of the present are not blamed on descendants of the criminals in generations to come.

In mass atrocities, a major problem remains in that the sheer number of episodes, of victims and of perpetrators will make it impossible to provide justice to every victim. International criminal justice is premised on the need to prosecute only those 'bearing the highest responsibility' for the atrocities.[83] Even in the best of circumstances – where domestic courts take on their own responsibility to investigate, prosecute and punish – there will always be a number of crimes that go unpunished for a variety of reasons: loss of evidence over time, limited judicial and prosecutorial infrastructure, manipulation of procedures by defendants, and ever-present political pressures over all actors and stakeholders. In that regard, transitional justice mechanisms offer a better way to ensure accountability and to expand the reach of justice to most, if not all, victims.

---

81 Ibid. In the Balkans, refusing to lift ICTY arrest warrants against Karadzic and Mladic 'not only did not impede the Dayton talks: it actually made it possible to reach an agreement to end the wars in the Former Yugoslavia'. When justice is sacrificed, it is often to disastrous effect, leading to a recurrence of violence – ironically the very thing perpetrators claim will not happen if they are assured that justice is bypassed to their benefit. For example, the 1999 Lomé Peace Agreement on the conflict in Sierra Leone included a blanket amnesty to appease the perpetrators of atrocious crimes, yet within months of signing the peace accord fighting resumed in a more extreme and violent fashion. Conversely, in Côte d'Ivoire, evidence shows that legal advisors to the government heeded warnings by then Special Advisor on the Prevention of Genocide, Juan Méndez, to refrain from further hate speech rather than subject Côte d'Ivoire to the ICC's jurisdiction. Hate speech initiated by armed militias subsided shortly thereafter, thus confirming the value in using justice – or the spectre of it – as a legitimate prevention tool.

82 See Kathryn Sikkink, *The Justice Cascade* (Norton, 2011).

83 ICC, *Paper on some policy issues before the Office of the Prosecutor*, at 3, available at: http://www.icc-cpi. int/NR/rdonlyres/1FA7C4C6-DE5F-42B7-8B25-60AA962ED8B6/143594/030905_Policy_ Paper.pdf, accessed on 5 February 2012.

A truth-seeking and truth-telling exercise adapted to the culture and circumstances offers victims a meaningful voice and ensures respect in their dignity as human beings. It also recognises their plight and signifies that they are no longer considered second-class citizens. The same can be said of a well-designed and executed programme of reparations that attempts to compensate victims for their suffering in material and non-material ways that do not insult their dignity as victims. Apologies and moral reparations should always be a part of the programme, as should cultural and societal efforts to memorialise the tragedy of repression and to remember the victims. Institutional reform and vetting of members of security forces and other bodies also restore confidence even when individual determination of guilt or innocence in a criminal trial is not possible, as long as a measure of due process is preserved.

All of these processes represent a holistic, comprehensive approach to justice and one that aspires to the largest degree of universality. That is why it is more likely to satisfy the aspirations of all victims and to contribute most effectively to peace, to prevention, to the rule of law and to stability of democracy, than a singular emphasis on prosecutions. Nevertheless, transitional justice mechanisms achieve those goals only if they are not conceived as poor alternatives to justice, or as 'justice lite'. Therefore, they only work when and if they include criminal prosecutions at the heart of the process, even if those prosecutions are reasonably and transparently limited in scope. Truth, reparations, memory and institutional reform, and where necessary a measure of concrete reconciliation between communities, will not only complement the effort to bring criminal investigations, prosecutions and effective punishment of the most culpable: they will also expand and universalise their effect so that all stakeholders can see that justice is being served.

Select bibliography

1985 Declaration of Basic Principles of Justice for Victims of Crime and Abuse of Power, UNGA Res. 40/34, (29 November 1985) UN Doc. A/Re.s 40/34.

Basic Principles and Guidelines on the Right to a Remedy and Reparation for Victims of Gross Violations of International Human Rights Law and Serious Violations of International Humanitarian Law, UNGA Res. 60/147, (21 March 2006) UN Doc. A/Res. 60/147.

M. Cherif Bassiouni, 'International Recognition of Victims' Rights' (2006) 16(2) *Hum. Rts. L. Rev.* 211–27.

P. de Greiff (ed.), *The Handbook of Reparations* (Oxford University Press, 2006).

P. Hayner, *Unspeakable Truths: Confronting State Terror and Atrocity* (Routledge, 2001).

J.E. Méndez, 'Accountability for Past Abuses', 19 *Hum. Rts. Q.* 255, 259–62 (1997).

A. Meyer-Rieckh and P. de Greiff (eds), *Justice as Prevention, Vetting Public Employees in Transitional Societies* (Social Science Research Council, 2007).

OHCHR, 'Rule of Law Tools for Post-Conflict States: Reparations Programmes' (2008) UN Doc. HR/PUB/08/1 (OHCHR Reparations Report), available at: http://www.ohchr.org/Documents/Publications/ReparationsProgrammes.pdf, accessed on 26 February 2012.

N. Roht-Arriaza and J. Mariezcurrena (eds), *Transitional Justice in the 21st Century: Beyond Truth versus Justice* (Cambridge University Press, 2006).

R. Teitel, *Transitional Justice* (Oxford University Press, 2000).

UN Secretary-General, 'Rule of Law Tools for Post-Conflict States: The Rule of Law and Transitional Justice in Conflict and Post-Conflict Societies' (2004) UN Doc. S/2004/616 (UN Secretary-General Transitional Justice Report).

Index